You get:

• an entire book on the Web, continually updated by authors to reflect the latest trends in Financial Reporting.

• quizzes, learning strategies, answers to selected solutions, links to real companies' annual reports, and more.

• exclusive access to a chat room where you can ask David Spiceland and Jim Sepe questions.

• video and audio to illustrate more complex features.

• a convenient means of distance learning.

Registering is easy!

Just visit our Web site:
http://mhhe.com/spiceland
Be sure to have your special password ready.

Your Student Password: **spiceland**

Your Student User Name: **accounting**

Instructors! Don't forget our

Expanded Instructor Web Page!

• free access to instructors for the entire term of adoption.

• includes all features available on expanded student page.

• contains additional teaching strategies, solutions, classroom activities, and more.

To register, please contact your Irwin/McGraw-Hill representative or visit our Web site: http://mhhe.com/spiceland.

Irwin/McGraw-Hill
A Division of The **McGraw·Hill** Companies

INTERMEDIATE
ACCOUNTING

INTERMEDIATE
ACCOUNTING

J. David Spiceland
University of Memphis

James F. Sepe
Santa Clara University

Irwin
McGraw-Hill

Boston, Massachusetts   Burr Ridge, Illinois   Dubuque, Iowa
Madison, Wisconsin   New York, New York   San Francisco, California   St. Louis, Missouri

McGraw-Hill

A Division of The McGraw·Hill Companies

INTERMEDIATE ACCOUNTING

This book is printed on acid-free paper.

1 2 3 4 5 6 7 8 9 0 QPK/QPK 9 0 9 8 7

ISBN 0-256-22677-6

Publisher: *Jeffrey J. Shelstad*
Editoral coordinator: *Martin Quinn*
Executive editor: *Stephen M. Patterson*
Project manager: *Lynne Basler*
Produciton supervisor: *Karen Thigpen*
Senior designer: *Laurie J. Entringer*
Compositor: *GAC/Shepard Poorman*
Typeface: *10/12 Times Roman*
Printer: *R. R. Donnelley & Sons Company*

Library of Congress Cataloging-in-Publication Data
Spiceland, J. David
    Intermediate accounting / J. David Spiceland, James F. Sepe.
      p.   cm.
    Includes index.
    ISBN 0–256–22677–6 (alk. paper)
     1. Accounting.   I. Sepe, James F.   II. Title.
HF5635.S7838   1998
657'.044 — dc21   97–28329

PREFACE

Decision-Making Perspective

The role of financial reporting is to communicate information that supports business decision making. Without understanding how decision makers use accounting information, it is difficult for accounting students to fully understand financial reporting issues or, more importantly, to critically evaluate reporting alternatives.

This text frames the financial reporting function of accounting in the context of the decision-support role it serves. What motivates managers' selection of financing alternatives? How do creditors use information about accounts receivable and inventory to evaluate a company's effectiveness in managing its assets? Which information is most useful to investors when assessing a firm's profitability? Why do managers choose a particular accounting method over an allowable alternative? This perspective is responsive to the recommendations of the Accounting Education Change Commission (AECC) and the education section of the American Accounting Association which identify the need for accounting curricula to emphasize professional judgment and critical thinking skills.

We provide the decision-making perspective in a variety of ways:

a. Topics are presented in the context of the economic and political environment in which firms and standard-setters operate.
b. Most chapters include one or more sections entitled "Decision Makers' Perspective" which offer insights into how the information discussed in the chapters affect decisions made by investors, creditors, managers, and others.
c. Chapters 4 and 5 provide overviews of how decision makers use financial information to assess profitability and risk.
d. Each chapter includes multiple cases in the assignment material that require students to critically evaluate information from financial reports in order to make decisions.
e. Each chapter opens with a brief Financial Reporting Case that poses interesting questions about topics in the upcoming chapter. The questions are answered at the end of the chapter and marginal notations throughout the chapter point out locations where each question is addressed.

Flexibility of Course Focus

A major feature of this text is its unique array of assignment materials. Flexibility is the key here. Instructors can adapt the focus of their courses through their choice of assignment materials. Assignment materials include the traditional options of discussion questions, exercises, problems, and cases. However, tradition stops there. To develop students' critical thinking skills, case materials are significantly expanded. Each chapter includes several categories of cases, including:

Group Interaction Cases.   Encourage students to work in groups to achieve resolution of various accounting issues and practice oral communication skills.

Writing Cases.   Provide the opportunity to not only apply critical thinking skills but also to persuade by means of typical business communication media.

Internet Cases.   Require students to draw upon resources available on the Internet to address issues discussed in the chapter.

Critical Thought Cases.   Require students to critically analyze issues in order to apply concepts learned to situations not explicitly considered in the text.

Discussion Cases.   Request discussions of conceptual issues raised in the chapter.

Financial Analysis Cases.   Direct students to gather, assemble, and analyze information from financial reports for the purpose of making business and investment decisions.

Ethics Cases.   Encourage consideration of ethical issues as they pertain to accounting decisions including the ramifications of those decisions on various stakeholders in the outcome.

Trueblood Cases.   Identifies Robert M. Trueblood cases widely available from the Deloitte & Touche Foundation that are appropriate for use with each chapter. Short descriptions are provided and suggestions are offered for opportunities for class discussion, group projects, and writing assignments.

International Cases.   Focus on differences and similarities between U.S. standards and practices and those of other countries.

Integrating Cases.   Relate topics from two or more chapters.

Research Cases.   Require the student to seek out additional information such as official standards, annual reports, or library resources to make a decision.

Real-World Cases.   Provocative situations that relate chapter material to actual business situations and require decisions pertaining to the situations illustrated or described.

Consistent Quality of Assignment Materials

To assure consistent quality of assignment materials, every question, exercise, problem, and case is personally developed, solved, and tested by the principal authors (with the exception of selected CPA exam problems included to provide an entrance exam perspective). None has been developed by graduate students or research assistants. The intent is to maintain quality, uniformity, and consistency with chapter coverage. Significantly, too, solutions go beyond merely providing answers, but also provide detailed supporting calculations, annotations, and concept descriptions where appropriate.

> "SS has provided an interesting, relevant and even entertaining approach to the intermediate accounting course. The writing style of the entire text is pleasant, informative and easy to read. Without question, the SS style, however measured, is superior to all others."
> **–Dennis H. Hudson**
> Associate Professor
> The University of Tulsa

Conversational Writing Style

A key focus of our preparation of this text was to foster a friendly dialogue between the text and each individual student. Specifically, we wanted to actively avoid the encyclopedic presentation that seems to have evolved in some textbooks in response to the increasing volume of accounting material. The tone of our presentation is intentionally conversational—creating the impression of *speaking with* the student, as opposed to *teaching to* the student. This approach creates a clear, readable presentation that is better able to involve, inform, and motivate the students.

Conceptual Emphasis

A stated objective of most intermediate accounting textbooks is to achieve an appropriate balance between procedures and theory. We share this objective, but do not feel that there necessarily is a tradeoff between the "why" and the "how." Instead, we believe that a true understanding of **how** a particular procedure is applied demands a clear understanding of **why** it is applied. Without a thorough comprehension of the basis for its application, students merely memorize the mechanics of a procedure. Students have a learned tendency to memorize. Traditional presentation often does little to dissuade that tendency.

Not only does memorization fail to achieve the desired objective of an intermediate accounting course, but it also is an inefficient method of study. We stress continually the why as the basis for the how, not solely to teach students the theoretical structure of accounting, but also to enhance their understanding of accounting procedures. We try to avoid *"method" ology*. That is, avoid showing how something is done without explaining why. We also try never to miss an opportunity to remind students how an issue is similar to related issues.

How often are we told by students that they "knew" the material covered on the test, but were unable to provide the correct answer to specific questions? When probed, they usually will agree that what they "knew" were mechanical procedures as presented in the text, but did not understand **why** those procedures applied. Accordingly, when the format of the questions was varied on an exam, they were unable to apply the appropriate procedures. Continually focusing on the **why**, *in concert with* the **how**, is our commitment.

Organizational Efficiency

We have made significant improvements in our organization (a) by relying more heavily on appendices and multi-part chapters, (b) by reorganizing chapters into a more logical sequence, and (c) by more efficient intra-chapter organization. These are not merely space-saving changes, but also enhance the text's ability to teach.

We combine related topics and sequence chapters with common characteristics in close proximity with one another (a) to achieve efficiency of presentation and more importantly (b) to enhance learning. Topics often are made to seem more complex than they are by creating the illusion (or not dispelling it) that essentially similar topics are distinct issues (e.g., separate and sometimes dissimilar treatment of notes, bonds, and leases). Much less space is needed and learning is enhanced when "common threads" among topics are emphasized and the topics are presented in as similar a fashion as possible.

These improvements are described below.

CONTENTS

Section One: The Role of Accounting as an Information System

> 1   Environment and Theoretical Structure of Financial Accounting

The coverage of the financial accounting environment and the theoretical structure of financial accounting are combined into one chapter (Chapter 1).

Traditionally, early chapters of an intermediate text are overly verbose, tending to lull students into a false sense of serenity. Most students enter intermediate accounting replete with anticipation and expecting to be challenged. A concise, well-written **single** chapter, combining the discussion of the accounting environment with the development of the conceptual basis of financial accounting, will immediately channel the students' excitement into the consideration of thought-provoking issues. By capturing the students' interest at the outset of the course, it can be better maintained during the course.

> 2   Review of the Accounting Process
> 3   Income Statement and Statement of Cash Flows
> 4   Income Measurement

The discussion of income measurement (Chapter 4) is presented in the chapter immediately following the review of the income statement (Chapter 3).

Sequencing the discussion of income measurement following the overview of the income statement seems so natural, we wonder why more books have not done it. How can a student really understand the importance and the limitations of the income statement without a thorough understanding of the revenue recognition principles upon which it is based? We also introduce profitability analysis in this chapter to support the "Decision-Makers' Perspective" provided throughout the book.

A secondary benefit is that this placement "beefs up" the early part of the book. By the nature of their review role, the first five chapters of most intermediate books are less challenging than later chapters. This tends to cause students to lose their initial excitement and interest. By encountering more challenging topics earlier in the course, students will become more involved and their enthusiasm can be maintained.

5   Balance Sheet and Financial Disclosures
6   Time Value of Money Concepts

Section Two: Economic Resources

Tangible and intangible operational assets are presented in a single chapter (Chapter 10). Similarly, utilization (including depreciation, amortization, and depletion) and disposition issues related to both tangible and intangible issues are presented together in a single chapter (Chapter 11).

7   Cash and Receivables
8   Inventories – Measurement
9   Inventories – Additional Issues
10 Operational Assets – Acquisition

Combining the coverage of tangible and intangible operational assets into one chapter (Chapter 10) is a logical improvement. Property, plant and equipment, natural resources, and intangible assets share so many common characteristics that separate chapters necessarily duplicate a great deal of discussion. The combination of these topics is consistent with our theme of avoiding redundancy and duplicity. We also avoid the artificial significance often attributed to relatively unimportant aspects of intangible assets, seemingly for the sole purpose of justifying an entire chapter devoted to intangible assets. Because of similarities in the combined material, the single chapter approach is considerably more concise than two chapters. Two short chapters being replaced by a single chapter of equal combined length would not be an improvement.

11 Operational Assets – Utilization and Disposition

Section Three: Financial Instruments

Chapters dealing with various financial instruments are presented together in sequence. (Chapter 12, "Investments" through Chapter 19, "Shareholders' Equity").

All liabilities are presented in logical sequence (Chapters 13-18).

The multi-year, continuing FASB project on financial instruments highlights the importance and commonality of these topics. Grouping the chapters that describe financial instruments underscores their shared characteristics.

12 Investments
13 Current Liabilities and Contingencies

Some intermediate accounting textbooks discuss long-term liabilities, such as notes and bonds, in one chapter and discuss tax allocation, leases, and pensions considerably later. Each of these topics involves liabilities, and any theoretical discussion should consider their shared characteristics. Thus, their coverage in sequence seems intuitive. Accounting for lease liabilities is most similar to that of bonds and long-term notes. Consequently, discussing leases immediately following long-term liabilities is pedagogically efficient.

The sequential placement of these chapters is consistent with our objective of presenting the material in a more efficient order. Students benefit from seeing that we account for debt essentially the same way, regardless of whether it's packaged as notes, bonds, capital leases, or another form of liability. In fact, to emphasize the point, we use the same numerical situation from chapter to chapter to illustrate bonds, notes, and leases. Scattering such similar topics among several chapters as many texts do, encourages students to view these as disconnected accounting issues when, actually, accounting for debt is but a single issue with several related variations.

A single "Employee Benefit Plans" chapter (Chapter 18) brings together the several types of benefits employees receive, including postretirement benefit plans other than pensions and stock-based benefit plans.

14 Bonds and Long-Term Notes
15 Leases
16 Accounting for Income Taxes
17 Pensions
18 Other Employee Benefit Plans

The benefits of this organization are similar to those of grouping liabilities together; students readily see that accounting objectives for similar items are the same. In this case, students see that the accounting objective of every employee benefit (from salary to postretirement benefits to stock-based compensation plans) is the same: *To report compensation expense in the period(s) the compensation is earned.*

Other texts scatter these closely related topics among several chapters, for instance, stock compensation benefits in one chapter (as "dilutive securities" perhaps), health care benefits in another chapter, postretirement benefits in still another chapter, and vacation benefits and postemployment benefits in yet another chapter. Students understandably interpret these scattered topics as being several unrelated topics, in fact, unrelated to the other topics in the chapters in which they appear. No wonder students come away interpreting a handful of basic accounting issues as being dozens of separate accounting issues. This chapter is one more example of how students benefit from our consistent presentation of related topics in cohesive groups, highlighting their similarities, avoiding redundancy and duplicity, and making learning and teaching easier.

Consistently, as we move from pensions in the previous chapter to other postretirement benefits in the first part of this chapter, we continue the same example situation of Jessica Farrow, an employee of Global Communications, but shift the focus from her pension benefits to her postretirement health care benefits. Students benefit from unavoidably seeing the similarities and inherent differences between the two types of benefits and how accountants deal with them.

Postretirement benefit plans other than pensions and stock-based benefit plans are two emerging issues that share similarities in that they each deal with accounting for employee benefits. They are dissimilar in that one (other postretirement benefits) represents a liability and the other (stock-based compensation) primarily creates shareholders' equity, but a liability in some instances. These simultaneous similarities and dissimilarities offer an attractive opportunity for a transition chapter, an interface between the several liability chapters (13-17) and shareholders' equity (19). Combined, the sequence of Chapters 13-19 represents the right-hand side of a balance sheet—equities. The transition chapter emphasizes the shared characteristics of these topics in addition to their differences.

19   Shareholders' Equity

> The presentation of topics related to paid-in capital and retained earnings is incorporated into one shareholders' equity chapter (Chapter 19).

Incorporating the coverage of the accounting for paid-in capital and retained earnings links related topics in a single chapter. This is made possible without an unduly long chapter by de-emphasizing some traditional, but relatively less important shareholders' equity topics. For example, we omit coverage of "appropriated" retained earnings in favor of a brief description of the much more common "restriction" of retained earnings. We also present stock options, covered in some texts in the retained earnings chapter, in our Employee Benefit Plans chapter.

Section Four: Additional Financial Reporting Issues

20   Earnings Per Share
21   Accounting Changes and Error Corrections
22   Statement of Cash Flows Revisited

Focus on Realism.   Real-world examples are routinely and extensively employed to enhance the presentation in three ways (1) to add realism to a discussion, (2) to illustrate a concept, or (3) to serve as the foundation for a Concept Review, a problem, or a case. (Most chapters include one or more "Real World Cases.") Also, references to (and occasional excerpts from) popular press coverage and academic research are included to add realism and plausibility. These are not included merely for the sake of having done so—only when they clearly enhance the presentation.

Case Implementation Manual.   Most accounting instructors are not trained specifically to teach ethics, international accounting, group interaction techniques, Internet techniques, and writing. To assist instructors desiring to add one or more of these dimensions to their courses, we offer a Case Implementation Manual designed to provide instructional support in teaching cases in these areas. The manual is prepared in concert with our Board of Advisors that includes recognized experts in each of these fields. They offer their expertise in providing background material necessary to give students the perspective they need to derive maximum benefit from these cases and suggest how instructors can incorporate these cases to their best advantage. The Solutions Manual, also, includes detailed solutions to every case.

"Concept Review" Exercises.   We include *within* each chapter one or more "Concept Review" exercise with solutions. Students are able to reinforce their understanding of the chapter material and practice applying the concepts and procedures learned in the chapter prior to attempting their homework assignment. When chapters explain more than one distinct major topic, a concept review exercise immediately follows the discussion of each topic.

Incremental Illustrations.   Efficiency often is sacrificed when a situation is created to explain an issue and then later in the same chapter a **new** situation is presented to explain a *related* issue. Students easily can get distracted by the new situation without seeing the relationship between the two issues.

a.   We use "incremental illustrations" in which the situation is held constant while incremental information is added. The pensions, earnings per share, and cash flow chapters offer good examples—one situation for the entire chapter.

b.   The three "Concept Reviews" in the shareholders' equity chapter are three sequential years for a single company.

c.   Many of the exercises and problems are variations of other exercises and problems with new information added. The assignments can be assigned individually to illustrate particular accounting issues. When assigned in combination, students easily see the impact of differences in factual situations.

With each of these variations of our incremental illustration approach, students benefit from the satisfying feeling of having learned all the nuances, rather than wondering how each of these separate situations tie together. Complex issues are more likely to "seem simple."

Additional Considerations.   To maintain an appropriate level of rigor and comprehensiveness of topic coverage without sacrificing clarity of explanation or adding unnecessary verbiage, we incorporate passages within the text entitled "Additional Considerations." These are "on the spot" considerations of important, but incidental or infrequent aspects of the primary topics to which they relate. Their parenthetical nature is highlighted visually by distinctive enclosures in lightly shaded boxes of consistent, and distinctive appearance.

Often, a concept or procedure that is applicable to a "typical" situation would require modification under more unusual circumstances. Omitting a discussion of the more unusual circumstances frequently is inappropriate. However, intermingling that discussion with the primary text presentation, as some texts do, tends to cloud the central issue. Similarly, presenting the more difficult or unusual aspects of topics in separate sections at the end of a chapter, as some texts do, requires students to reorient their thoughts to the earlier situations now being expanded upon. On the other hand, presenting Additional Considerations as adjuncts to central issues **at the point of departure,** as we do, enhances the students' depth of comprehension without sacrificing their basic understanding.

Instructors can assign or not assign additional considerations as they wish to achieve their chosen course focus.

Additional Consideration

The method just described is referred to as the "book value method," since the new shares are recorded at the book value of the bonds being redeemed. It is by far the most popular method in practice. Another acceptable approach, the "market value method," records the new shares at the market value of the shares themselves or of the bonds, whichever is more determinable. Because the market value most likely will differ from the book value of the bonds, a gain or loss on conversion will result. Assume for illustration that the market value of HTL's stock is $30 per share at the time of the conversion:

	($ in millions)	
Convertible bonds payable (1/2 the account balance)	50	
Premium on bonds payable (1/2 the account balance)	1	
Loss on conversion of bonds (plug)	9	
Common stock ([50,000 bonds x 40 shares] × $1 par)		2
Paid-in capital – excess of par ([50,000 × 40 shares] x $29)		58

Ethical Dilemmas are incorporated within the narrative. The intent is to raise the students' consciousness on accounting issues with ethical ramifications and to provide a source of classroom discussion.

Marginal comments are used to provide emphasis or an alternate perspective.

Marginal Comments.   These plentiful notations highlight key points or provide additional insight.

Global Perspectives.   These are integrated within the discussion to emphasize that our economy does not operate in isolation and that accounting principles differ from country to country.

ACKNOWLEDGMENTS

We would like to thank the many people who made important contributions to the successful completion of this textbook project. Without their help and support we could not have achieved our goal. First of all, we recognize and thank the following outstanding faculty reviewers. These individuals provided significant inputs to the final version of the text.

Charlene Abendroth, California State University—Hayward

Barbara J. Askren, Loyola University of Chicago

Janice Bell, California State University—Northridge

Larry Bergin, Winona State University

Kurt H. Buerger, Angelo State University

Charles Carslaw, University of Nevada—Reno

C. Douglas Cloud, Pepperdine University

Richard J. Fahringer, Southern Connecticut State University (Ret.)

Larry E. Farmer, Middle Tennessee State University

Richard Fern, Eastern Kentucky University

Gary Freeman, University of Colorado—Colorado Springs

Patrick Heaston, Drake University

Gordon Hosch, University of New Orleans

Dennis H. Hudson, University of Tulsa

Scott I. Jerris, West Virginia University

Susan C. Kattelus, Eastern Michigan University

Dennis Knutson, University of Wisconsin—Eau Claire

Barry L. Lewis, University of Colorado

Heidemarie Lundblad, California State University—Northridge

Susan A. Lynn, University of Baltimore

Edward Maloof, University of Texas—San Antonio

Ronald Mano, Weber State University

Dale E. Marxen, Mankato State University

David C. May, Wayne State University

Dennis Murray, University of Colorado—Denver

Priscilla O'Clock, Xavier University

Elsa V. Parsegian, Youngstown State University

William Pasewark, University of Houston

Ralph Peck, Utah State University

Edward G. Philips, University of New Mexico (Emeritus)

Karl B. Putnam, University of Texas—El Paso

Robert G. Rambo, University of New Orleans

John T. Rigsby, Mississippi State University

Theresa P. Rollins, Villanova University

Marc Rubin, Miami University—Ohio

Maribeth Schlictman, University of Southern Carolina

James Schmutte, Ball State University

Douglas Sharp, Wichita State University

Dan Smith, University of Georgia

Thomas L. Stober, University of Notre Dame

Kenneth E. Stone, Central Missouri State University

Donald L. Tang, Portland State University (Ret.)

Paula B. Thomas, Middle Tennessee State University

C. Torben Thompsen, California State University—Fresno

Kathryn Verreault, University of Massachusetts—Lowell

Ralph E. Welton, Clemson University

James S. Worthington, Auburn University

Jerry R. Yares, University of West Florida

Mary Yates, Central Missouri State University

Joni J. Young, University of New Mexico

An important part of the development process involved class testing earlier drafts of the text. We wish to thank the following faculty and universities for helping us with this critical phase of the project: Orapin Duangploy, University of Houston—Downtown; Elizabeth Grace, San Jose State University; Margaret Shelton, University of Houston—Downtown; Robert Shepherd, San Jose State University; and Philip Siegel, Monmouth University. We would particularly like to acknowledge faculty at our own universities who class-tested a number of versions of the text. Their patience and contributions were invaluable. These individuals are: George Kelly, Lynn Pringle, Bill O'Brien, and Neal Ushman at Santa Clara University, and Larry DuCharme, Jim Lukawitz, and George Minmier at the University of Memphis.

In addition, we are indebted to the rest of the project team for developing supplements to the text. These include the test bank authors, Guy Owings, Pittsburg State University, and Russell Hardin, Pittsburg State University; case implementation manual authors, Dr. Maurice L. Hirsch, Jr., Southern Illinois University, James A. Schweikart, Ph.D., C.P.A., University of Richmond, Dr. Mary E. Harston, St. Mary's University, Timothy J. Louwers, University of Houston, and William R. Pasewark, Ph.D., C.P.A., University of Houston; power point slides authors, Jon A. Booker, Charles W. Caldwell, Susan C. Galbreath, and Richard S. Rand, Jr., all of Tennessee Technological University; and spreadsheet template author, Jack E. Terry, ComSource Associates.

Also, Barbara Schnathorst, University of Colorado, made significant contributions to the accuracy of the text and solutions manual. She read the entire text, solved all numerical examples and concept review exercises, and solved all the end-of-chapter material. We also thank Daniel J. Kwiat, C.P.A., for his help with the solutions manual.

We are most grateful for the talented assistance and support from the many people at Irwin/McGraw Hill. We would particularly like to thank Jeff Shelstad our sponsoring editor, now accounting and finance publisher, for overseeing the project and providing insightful support throughout; development editor Martin Quinn for his ingenuity and tireless efforts in pulling it together; project manager Lynne Basler for managing the editorial process; copyeditor Margaret Haywood for a terrific job in polishing the text; Heather Woods, Marketing Manager, Melissa Caughlin, Marketing Coordinator, Laurie Entringer our designer; Randy Gawlik for his help with our website; Lee Ann Bezazian for her support and encouragement; and Glenn Turner and his Burston House staff for providing important feedback and for managing a final round of reviews. At critical stages of the project, members of McGraw-Hill's management team, in particular Mike Junior and John Black, were there to offer direction and help with important decisions.

We are especially indebted to Greg Patterson for championing the project from the very beginning, for his creative talents, and for so believing in the project that, in addition to his usual responsibilities with McGraw-Hill, assumed the additional role of National Marketing Manager for this textbook.

Our thanks also goes to Federal Express Corporation for allowing us to use its 1996 Annual Report in the appendix to Chapter 1 and throughout the text. We also acknowledge permission from the AICPA to adapt material from the Uniform CPA Examination and Dow Jones & Co., Inc., for permission to excerpt material from *The Wall Street Journal*.

Finally, a special remembrance to Vera Sepe, Jim's mother, who passed away during the writing of the text.

Jim Sepe
David Spiceland

CONTENTS IN BRIEF

SECTION 1

THE ROLE OF ACCOUNTING AS AN INFORMATION SYSTEM

1   Environment and Theoretical Structure of Financial Accounting
2   Review of the Accounting Process
3   The Income Statement and Statement of Cash Flows
4   Income Measurement and Profitability Analysis
5   The Balance Sheet and Financial Disclosures
6   Time Value of Money Concepts

SECTION 2

ECONOMIC RESOURCES

7   Cash and Receivables
8   Inventories: Measurement
9   Inventories: Additional Issues
10   Operational Assets: Acquisition
11   Operational Assets: Utilization and Disposition

SECTION 3

FINANCIAL INSTRUMENTS

12   Investments
13   Current Liabilities and Contingencies
14   Bonds and Long-Term Notes
15   Leases
16   Accounting for Income Taxes
17   Pensions
18   Employee Benefit Plans
19   Shareholders' Equity

SECTION 4

ADDITIONAL FINANCIAL REPORTING ISSUES

20   Earnings Per Share
21   Accounting Changes and Error Corrections
22   The Statement of Cash Flows Revisited

Index

CONTENTS

SECTION 1

THE ROLE OF ACCOUNTING AS AN INFORMATION SYSTEM   1

CHAPTER

1   Environment and Theoretical Structure of Financial Accounting   2

PART A: FINANCIAL ACCOUNTING ENVIRONMENT   4

THE ECONOMIC ENVIRONMENT AND FINANCIAL REPORTING   5
  The Investment-Credit Decision—A Cash Flow
    Perspective   6
  Cash Versus Accrual Accounting   7
THE DEVELOPMENT OF FINANCIAL ACCOUNTING AND REPORTING
    STANDARDS   8
  Historical Perspective and Standards   9
  The Establishment of Accounting Standards—A Political
    Process   11
  Our Global Marketplace   14
  The Role of the Auditor   14

PART B: THE CONCEPTUAL FRAMEWORK   15

OBJECTIVES OF FINANCIAL REPORTING   16
QUALITATIVE CHARACTERISTICS OF ACCOUNTING INFORMATION
    17
  Primary Qualitative Characteristics   17
  Secondary Qualitative Characteristics   19
PRACTICAL BOUNDARIES (CONSTRAINTS) TO ACHIEVING DESIRED
    QUALITATIVE CHARACTERISTICS   19
  Cost Effectiveness   19
  Materiality   20
  Conservatism   20
ELEMENTS OF FINANCIAL STATEMENTS   21
RECOGNITION AND MEASUREMENT CONCEPTS   23
  Recognition   23
  Measurement   23
  Underlying Assumptions   24
  Accounting Principles   25

ETHICS IN ACCOUNTING   27
  Ethics and Professionalism   27
  Analytical Model for Ethical Decisions   28
APPENDIX: FEDERAL EXPRESS CORPORATION FINANCIAL
    STATEMENTS   30
QUESTIONS FOR REVIEW OF KEY TOPICS   45
EXERCISES   45
CASES   49

CHAPTER

2   Review of the Accounting Process   54

THE BASIC MODEL   56
  The Accounting Equation   56
  Account Relationships   58
THE ACCOUNTING PROCESSING CYCLE   59
CONCEPT REVIEW EXERCISE: JOURNAL ENTRIES FOR EXTERNAL
    TRANSACTIONS   67
ADJUSTING ENTRIES   69
  Prepayments   70
  Accruals   72
  Estimates   74
CONCEPT REVIEW EXERCISE: ADJUSTING ENTRIES   76
PREPARING THE FINANCIAL STATEMENTS   77
  The Income Statement   77
  The Balance Sheet   78
  The Statement of Cash Flows   79
  The Statement of Shareholders' Equity   80
THE CLOSING PROCESS   80
CONCEPT REVIEW EXERCISE: FINANCIAL STATEMENT
    PREPARATION AND CLOSING   82
CONVERSION FROM CASH BASIS TO ACCRUAL BASIS   83
APPENDIX 2A: USE OF A SPREADSHEET   85
APPENDIX 2B: REVERSING ENTRIES   87
APPENDIX 2C: SUBSIDIARY LEDGERS AND SPECIAL
    JOURNALS   88

QUESTIONS FOR REVIEW OF KEY TOPICS   90

EXERCISES   91

PROBLEMS   96

C H A P T E R

3

The Income Statement and Statement of Cash Flows   102

PART A: THE INCOME STATEMENT   104

INCOME FROM CONTINUING OPERATIONS   104
   Revenues, Expenses, Gains, and Losses   104
   Income Tax Expense   105
   Operating versus Nonoperating Activities   105
   Income Statement Formats   106
SEPARATELY REPORTED ITEMS   107
   Intraperiod Income Tax Allocation   108
   Discontinued Operations   109
   Extraordinary Items   113
   Cumulative Effect of a Change in Accounting Principle   116
CORRECTION OF ACCOUNTING ERRORS   120
   Prior Period Adjustment   120
EARNING PER SHARE DISCLOSURES   120
CONCEPT REVIEW EXERCISE: INCOME STATEMENT
     PRESENTATION   121
COMPREHENSIVE INCOME   122

PART B: THE STATEMENT OF CASH FLOWS   124

USEFULNESS OF THE STATEMENT OF CASH FLOWS   124
CLASSIFYING CASH FLOWS   124
   Operating Activities   124
   Investing Activities   125
   Financing Activities   126
   Noncash Investing and Financing Activities   126
CONCEPT REVIEW EXERCISE: STATEMENT OF CASH FLOWS   126

QUESTIONS FOR REVIEW OF KEY TOPICS   128

EXERCISES   129

PROBLEMS   134

CASES   137

C H A P T E R

4

Income Measurement and Profitability Analysis   142

PART A: REVENUE RECOGNITION   144

REVENUE RECOGNITION AT POINT OF DELIVERY   144
REVENUE RECOGNITION BEFORE DELIVERY   145
   Long-Term Contracts   145
   A Comparison of The Two Methods—
     Income Recognition   148
CONCEPT REVIEW EXERCISE: LONG-TERM CONSTRUCTION
     CONTRACTS   154
   Service Sales   155
REVENUE RECOGNITION AFTER DELIVERY   156
   Installment Sales   156
   Real Estate Sales   160

CONCEPT REVIEW EXERCISE: INSTALLMENT SALES   160
   Right of Return   161
FRANCHISE SALES   162
   Initial Franchise Fee   163
   Continuing Franchise Fees   163

PART B: PROFITABILITY ANALYSIS   164

USING FINANCIAL STATEMENT INFORMATION   164
   Activity Ratios   165
   Profitability Ratios   166
PROFITABILITY ANALYSIS—AN ILLUSTRATION   168

APPENDIX 4: INTERIM REPORTING   170

REPORT REVENUES AND EXPENSES   171
REPORTING UNUSUAL ITEMS   171
EARNINGS PER SHARE   171

QUESTIONS FOR REVIEW OF KEY TOPICS   172

EXERCISES   173

PROBLEMS   178

CASES   182

C H A P T E R

5

The Balance Sheet and Financial Disclosures   188

PART A: THE BALANCE SHEET   191

USEFULNESS AND LIMITATIONS   191
CLASSIFICATIONS   192
   Assets   193
   Liabilities   196
   Shareholders' Equity   198
CONCEPT REVIEW EXERCISE: BALANCE SHEET CLASSIFICATION
   198

PART B: FINANCIAL DISCLOSURES   200

DISCLOSURE NOTES   200
   Summary of Significant Accounting Policies   200
   Subsequent Events   201
   Noteworthy Events and Transactions   201
MANAGEMENT DISCUSSION AND ANALYSIS   203
MANAGEMENT'S RESPONSIBILITIES   203
AUDITORS' REPORT   203
COMPENSATION OF DIRECTORS AND TOP EXECUTIVES   205

PART C: RISK ANALYSIS   207

   Liquidity Ratios   207
   Financing Ratios   208

APPENDIX 5: REPORTING DISAGGREGATED
    INFORMATION   212

QUESTIONS FOR REVIEW OF KEY TOPICS   214

EXERCISES   215

PROBLEMS   220

CASES   224

C H A P T E R

6 | Time Value of Money Concepts 234

PART A: BASIC CONCEPTS 236

TIME VALUE OF MONEY 236
  Simple versus Compound Interest 236
VALUING A SINGLE CASH FLOW AMOUNT 237
  Future of a Single Amount 237
  Present Value of a Single Amount 238
  Solving for Other Values When FV and PV Are Known 239
CONCEPT REVIEW EXERCISE: VALUING A SINGLE CASH FLOW
    AMOUNT 241
PREVIEW OF ACCOUNTING APPLICATIONS OF PRESENT VALUE
    TECHNIQUES—SINGLE CASH AMOUNT 242

PART B: BASIC ANNUITIES 243

FUTURE VALUE OF AN ANNUITY 244
  Future Value of an Ordinary Annuity 244
  Future Value of an Annuity Due 244
PRESENT VALUE OF AN ANNUITY 245
  Present Value of an Ordinary Annuity 245
  Present Value of an Annuity Due 246
  Present Value of a Deferred Annuity 247
SOLVING FOR UNKNOWN VALUES IN PRESENT VALUE SITUATIONS
    249
CONCEPT REVIEW EXERCISE: ANNUITIES 251
PREVIEW OF ACCOUNTING APPLICATION OF PRESENT VALUE
    TECHNIQUES—ANNUITIES 252
  Valuation of Long-Term Leases 252
  Valuation of Pension Obligations 253
SUMMARY OF TIME VALUE OF MONEY CONCEPTS 254

APPENDIX 6: PRESENT AND FUTURE VALUE TABLES 256

QUESTIONS FOR REVIEW OF KEY TOPICS 262

EXERCISES 262

PROBLEMS 265

CASES 268

SECTION 2

ECONOMIC RESOURCES 271

C H A P T E R

7 | Cash and Receivables 272

PART A: CASH AND RECEIVABLES 274

INTERNAL CONTROL OF CASH 274
  Internal Control Procedures—Cash Receipts 275
  Internal Control Procedures—Cash Disbursements 275
BANK RECONCILIATION 275
PETTY CASH 277
RESTRICTED CASH AND COMPENSATING BALANCES 278

PART B: CURRENT RECEIVABLES 279

ACCOUNTS RECEIVABLE 279
  Initial Valuation of Accounts Receivable 279
  Subsequent Valuation of Accounts Receivable 281

CONCEPT REVIEW EXERCISE: UNCOLLECTIBLE ACCOUNTS
    RECEIVABLE 287
NOTES RECEIVABLE 288
  Interest-Bearing Notes 288
  Noninterest-Bearing Notes 289
  Subsequent Valuation of Notes Receivable 290
FINANCING WITH RECEIVABLES 291
  Assigning of Accounts Receivable 291
  Transfer of Receivables 293
CONCEPT REVIEW EXERCISE: FINANCING WITH RECEIVABLES
    297

DECISION MAKERS' PERSPECTIVE 298

QUESTIONS FOR REVIEW OF KEY TOPICS 301

EXERCISES 301

PROBLEMS 307

CASES 310

C H A P T E R

8 | Inventories: Measurement 314

PART A: RECORDING AND MEASURING INVENTORY 316

TYPES OF INVENTORY 316
  Merchandising Inventories 316
  Manufacturing Inventories 316
PERPETUAL INVENTORY SYSTEM 317
PERIODIC INVENTORY SYSTEM 318
A COMPARISON OF THE PERPETUAL AND PERIODIC INVENTORY
    SYSTEMS 319
WHAT IS INCLUDED IN INVENTORY? 320
  Physical Quantities Included in Inventory 320
EXPENDITURES INCLUDED IN INVENTORY 321
INVENTORY COST FLOW ASSUMPTIONS 323
  Specific Identification 324
  Average Cost 325
  First-In, First-Out (FIFO) 326
  Last-In, First-Out (LIFO) 327
  Comparison of Cost Flow Methods 329
  Decision Makers' Perspective—Factors Influencing Method
    Choice 330
CONCEPT REVIEW EXERCISE: INVENTORY COST FLOW
    METHODS 333
  Decision Makers' Perspective—Financial Analysis 335

PART B: METHODS OF SIMPLIFYING LIFO 337

LIFO INVENTORY POOLS 337
  Dollar-Value LIFO 338
  Advantages of DVL 338
  Cost Indexes 338
  The DVL Inventory Estimation Technique 339
CONCEPT REVIEW EXERCISE: DOLLAR-VALUE LIFO 339

QUESTIONS FOR REVIEW OF KEY TOPICS 341

EXERCISES 342

PROBLEMS 347

CASES 351

C H A P T E R

9

Inventories: Additional Issues 356

PART A: REPORTING—LOWER OF COST OR MARKET 358

Determining Market Value 358
Applying Lower of Cost or Market 360
Adjusting Cost to Market 361
CONCEPT REVIEW EXERCISE: LOWER-OF-COST-OR-MARKET 362

PART B: INVENTORY ESTIMATION TECHNIQUES 363

THE GROSS PROFIT METHOD 363
A Word of Caution 364
THE RETAIL INVENTORY METHOD 365
Retail Terminology 366
Cost Flow Methods 367
Other Issues Pertaining to the Retail Method 369
CONCEPT REVIEW EXERCISE: RETAIL INVENTORY METHOD 370

PART C: DOLLAR-VALUE LIFO RETAIL 371

CONCEPT REVIEW EXERCISE: DOLLAR-VALUE LIFO RETAIL
METHOD 373

PART D: CHANGE IN INVENTORY METHOD AND INVENTORY
ERRORS 374

CHANGE IN ACCOUNTING PRINCIPLE 374
Changes Not Involving LIFO 374
Change to the LIFO Method 375
Change from the LIFO Method 376
INVENTORY ERRORS 376
When the Inventory Error Is Discovered the Following Year
378
When the Inventory Error Is Discovered Subsequent to the
Following Year 378
APPENDIX 9: PURCHASE COMMITMENTS 379
QUESTIONS FOR REVIEW OF KEY TOPICS 381
EXERCISES 382
PROBLEMS 388
CASES 393

C H A P T E R

10

Operational Assets: Acquisition 398

PART A: VALUATION AT ACQUISITION 400

TYPES OF OPERATIONAL ASSETS 400
COSTS TO BE CAPITALIZED 401
Property, Plant, and Equipment 401
Intangible Assets 404
LUMP-SUM PURCHASES 407
NONCASH ACQUISITIONS 408
Deferred Payments 408
Issuance of Equity Securities 410
Donated Assets 410
Acquisition By Exchange 411
CONCEPT REVIEW EXERCISE: NONMONETARY EXCHANGES 415
DECISION MAKERS' PERSPECTIVE 416

PART B: SELF-CONSTRUCTED ASSETS AND RESEARCH AND
DEVELOPMENT 417

SELF-CONSTRUCTED ASSETS 417
Overhead Allocation 418
Interest Capitalization 418
Research and Development (R&D) 422
APPENDIX 10: OIL AND GAS ACCOUNTING 427
QUESTIONS FOR REVIEW OF KEY TOPICS 428
EXERCISES 429
PROBLEMS 434
CASES 438

C H A P T E R

11

Operational Assets: Utilization and Disposition 444

PART A: DEPRECIATION, DEPLETION, AND AMORTIZATION
446

COST ALLOCATION—AN OVERVIEW 446
MEASURING COST ALLOCATION 447
Service Life 447
Allocation Base 447
Allocation Method 448
DEPRECIATION OF OPERATIONAL ASSETS 448
Time-Based Depreciation Methods 448
Activity-Based Depreciation Methods 450
DECISION MAKERS' PERSPECTIVE—SELECTING A DEPRECIATION
METHOD 451
CONCEPT REVIEW EXERCISE: DEPRECIATION METHODS 452
GROUP AND COMPOSITE DEPRECIATION METHODS 453
DEPLETION OF NATURAL RESOURCES 454
AMORTIZATION OF INTANGIBLE ASSETS 456

PART B: ADDITIONAL ISSUES 457

PARTIAL PERIODS 457
CHANGES IN ESTIMATES 459
CHANGE IN DEPRECIATION METHOD 460
ERROR CORRECTION 461
COMPARISON WITH MACRS (TAX DEPRECIATION) 462
IMPAIRMENT OF VALUE 462

PART C: SUBSEQUENT EXPENDITURES AND
DISPOSITION 464

EXPENDITURES SUBSEQUENT TO ACQUISITION 465
Repairs and Maintenance 465
Additions 465
Improvements 466
Rearrangements 466
Costs of Defending Intangible Rights 467
DISPOSITION OF OPERATIONAL ASSETS 467

APPENDIX 11: RETIREMENT AND REPLACEMENT METHODS OF
DEPRECIATION 469

QUESTIONS FOR REVIEW OF KEY TOPICS 470
EXERCISES 470
PROBLEMS 476
CASES 480

SECTION 3

FINANCIAL INSTRUMENTS   485

C H A P T E R

12   Investments   486

PART A: ACCOUNTING FOR INVESTMENT SECURITIES   488

WHEN AN INVESTMENT SECURITY IS ACQUIRED TO BE HELD TO MATURITY   489
  When the Fair Value Isn't Readily Determinable   490
WHEN AN INVESTMENT IS TO BE HELD FOR AN UNSPECIFIED PERIOD OF TIME   490
  When Investment Securities Are Classified as Available for Sale   492
  When Investment Securities Are Classified as Trading Securities   494
  Transfers Between Reporting Categories   495
CONCEPT REVIEW EXERCISE: VARIOUS INVESTMENT SECURITIES   495
FINANCIAL STATEMENT PRESENTATION AND DISCLOSURE   497

PART B: THE EQUITY METHOD   498

HOW THE EQUITY METHOD RELATES TO CONSOLIDATED FINANCIAL STATEMENTS   498
WHAT IS SIGNIFICANT INFLUENCE?   499
  A Single Entity Concept   500
FURTHER ADJUSTMENTS   500
REPORTING THE INVESTMENT   502
  What If Conditions Change   503
IF AN EQUITY METHOD INVESTMENT IS SOLD   504
CONCEPT REVIEW: THE EQUITY METHOD   504
JOINT VENTURES   506
DECISION-MAKERS' PERSPECTIVE   506

APPENDIX 12A: INVESTMENTS IN DERIVATIVES   508

APPENDIX 12B: OTHER INVESTMENTS (SPECIAL PURPOSE FUNDS, INVESTMENTS IN LIFE INSURANCE POLICIES)   512

APPENDIX 12C: IMPAIRMENT OF AN INVESTMENT IN A RECEIVABLE DUE TO A TROUBLED DEBT RESTRUCTURING   513

QUESTIONS FOR REVIEW OF KEY TOPICS   514

EXERCISES   516

PROBLEMS   521

CASES   523

C H A P T E R

13   Current Liabilities and Contingencies   528

PART A: CURRENT LIABILITIES   530

CHARACTERISTICS OF LIABILITIES   530
WHAT IS A CURRENT LIABILITY?   531
OPEN ACCOUNTS AND NOTES   531
  Accounts Payable and Trade Notes Payable   531

  Short-Term Notes Payable   532
  Commercial Paper   535
ACCRUED LIABILITIES   535
  Accrued Interest Payable   535
  Salaries, Commissions and Bonuses   535
LIABILITIES FROM ADVANCE COLLECTIONS   536
  Deposits and Advances from Customers   536
  Collections for Third Parties   537
A CLOSER LOOK AT THE CURRENT AND NONCURRENT CLASSIFICATION   538
  Current Maturities of Long-Term Debt   538
  Obligations Callable by the Creditor   538
  When Short-Term Obligations Are Expected to Be Refinanced   538
CONCEPT REVIEW EXERCISE: CURRENT LIABILITIES   539

PART B: CONTINGENCIES   540

LOSS CONTINGENCIES   541
  Product Warranties and Guarantees   542
  Premiums   544
  Litigation Claims   545
  Subsequent Events   546
  Unasserted Claims and Assessments   547
GAIN CONTINGENCIES   547
CONCEPT REVIEW EXERCISE: CONTINGENCIES   548
  Decision-Makers' Perspective   549

APPENDIX 13: PAYROLL-RELATED LIABILITIES   551

QUESTIONS FOR REVIEW OF KEY TOPICS   553

EXERCISES   553

PROBLEMS   558

CASES   562

C H A P T E R

14   Bonds and Long-Term Notes   570

PART A: BONDS AND NOTES   572

THE NATURE OF LONG-TERM DEBT   572
BONDS   572
  The Bond Indenture   573
  Recording Bonds at Issuance   574
  Determining Interest–Effective Interest Method   576
  The Straight-Line Method–A Practical Expediency   579
CONCEPT REVIEW EXERCISE: ISSUING BONDS AND RECORDING INTEREST   581
  Debt Issue Costs   582
VARIATIONS IN DEBT INSTRUMENTS   583
  Zero-Coupon Bonds   583
  Convertible Bonds   584
  Bonds with Detachable Warrants   586
LONG-TERM NOTES   587
  Note Issued for Cash   587
  Note Exchanges for Assets Or Services   588
  Installment Notes   590
CONCEPT REVIEW EXERCISE: NOTE WITH AN UNREALISTIC INTEREST RATE   591

PART B: RETIREMENT, RESTRUCTURING, AND DISCLOSURE OF DEBT 592

RETIREMENT OF DEBT 592
Retirement on the Maturity Date 592
Early Extinguishment 592
CONCEPT REVIEW EXERCISE: ISSUANCE AND EARLY RETIREMENT OF DEBT 593
TROUBLED DEBT RESTRUCTURING 594
Debt Is Settled 594
Debt Is Continued, but with Modified Terms 595
FINANCIAL STATEMENT DISCLOSURES 598
Risk Disclosures 598
Decision-Makers' Perspective 598
QUESTIONS FOR REVIEW OF KEY TOPICS 602
EXERCISES 602
PROBLEMS 607
CASES 612

C H A P T E R

15 Leases 618

PART A: ACCOUNTING BY THE LESSOR AND LESSEE 620

ADVANTAGES OF LEASING: A DECISION-MAKERS' PERSPECTIVE 620
CAPITAL LEASES AND INSTALLMENT NOTES COMPARED 621
LEASE CLASSIFICATION 622
Classification Criteria 623
Additional Lessor Conditions 624
OPERATING LEASES 625
Advance Payments 626
Leasehold Improvements 627
NONOPERATING LEASES—LESSEE AND LESSOR 627
Depreciation 629
Accrued Interest 630
CONCEPT REVIEW EXERCISE: DIRECT FINANCING LEASE 631
SALES-TYPE LEASES 632

PART B: OTHER LEASE ACCOUNTING ISSUES 634

RESIDUAL VALUE 634
Who Gets the Residual Value? 634
When the Residual Value Is Guaranteed 635
When the Residual Value Is Not Guaranteed 637
BARGAIN PURCHASE OPTIONS 639
When a BPO Is Exercisable Before the End of the Lease Term 641
EXECUTORY COSTS 641
DISCOUNT RATE 642
When the Lessee's Incremental Borrowing Rate Is Less than the Lessor's Implicit Rate 643
When the Lessor's Implicit Rate Is Unknown 643
LESSOR'S INITIAL DIRECT COSTS 644
CONTINGENT RENTALS 644
A BRIEF SUMMARY 645
CONCEPT REVIEW EXERCISE: VARIOUS LEASE ACCOUNTING ISSUES 646
SALE-LEASEBACK ARRANGEMENTS 648
Capital Leases 648
Operating Leases 650
Losses on Sale-Leasebacks 650

REAL ESTATE LEASES 650
Leases of Land Only 650
Leases of Land and Building 651
Leases of Only Part of a Building 651
LEVERAGED LEASES 651
LEASE DISCLOSURES 651
A DECISION MAKER'S PERSPECTIVE: FINANCIAL STATEMENT IMPACT 652
Balance Sheet and Income Statement 653
Statement of Cash Flow Impact 654
QUESTIONS FOR REVIEW OF KEY TOPICS 655
EXERCISES 655
PROBLEMS 662
CASES 669

C H A P T E R

16 Accounting for Income Taxes 674

PART A: DEFERRED TAX ASSETS AND DEFERRED TAX LIABILITIES 676

CONCEPTUAL UNDERPINNING 676
TEMPORARY DIFFERENCES 677
DEFERRED TAX LIABILITIES 677
The FASB's Balance Sheet Approach 678
Types of Temporary Differences 679
DEFERRED TAX ASSETS 682
VALUATION ALLOWANCE 685
NONTEMPORARY DIFFERENCES 687
CONCEPT REVIEW EXERCISE: TEMPORARY AND PERMANENT DIFFERENCES 688

PART B: OTHER TAX ACCOUNTING ISSUES 689

TAX RATE CONSIDERATIONS 689
When Enacted Tax Rates Differ 690
Changes in Tax Laws Or Rates 690
MULTIPLE TEMPORARY DIFFERENCES 692
OPERATING LOSSES 694
Operating Loss Carryforward 694
Operating Loss Carryback 695
FINANCIAL STATEMENT PRESENTATION 696
Balance Sheet Classification 696
Disclosure Notes 697
TAX EFFECTS OF ACCOUNTING CHANGES AND ERROR CORRECTION 698
Change in an Accounting Principle 698
CORRECTION OF AN ERROR 699
INTRAPERIOD TAX ALLOCATION 700
CONCEPTUAL CONCERNS 701
DECISION-MAKER'S PERSPECTIVE 702
CONCEPT REVIEW EXERCISE: MULTIPLE DIFFERENCES AND OPERATING LOSS 703

APPENDIX 16: INVESTMENT REVENUE FROM EQUITY METHOD INVESTEES 706

QUESTIONS FOR REVIEW OF KEY TOPICS 706
EXERCISES 707
PROBLEMS 715
CASES 720

CHAPTER

17 | Pensions 726

PART A: THE NATURE OF PENSION PLANS   728

DEFINED CONTRIBUTION PENSION PLANS   729
DEFINED BENEFIT PENSION PLANS   730
PENSION EXPENS—AN OVERVIEW   731

PART B: THE PENSION OBLIGATION AND PLAN ASSETS   732

THE PENSION OBLIGATION   732
  Accumulated Benefit Obligation   732
  Vested Benefit Obligation   733
  Projected Benefit Obligation   733
  Illustration Expanded to Consider the Entire Employee
    Pool   737
PENSION PLAN ASSETS   738

PART C: DETERMINING PENSION EXPENSE   739

THE RELATIONSHIP BETWEEN PENSION EXPENSE AND CHANGES IN
    THE PBO AND PLAN ASSETS   739
  Components of Pension Expense   741
INCOME SMOOTHING   744
RECORDING THE PERIODIC EXPENSE AND PERIODIC FUNDING   745

PART D: REPORTING ISSUES   746

PUTTING THE PIECES TOGETHER   746
RECONCILIATION OF FUNDED STATUS WITH THE AMOUNT
    RECOGNIZED IN THE BALANCE SHEET   747
MINIMUM LIABILITY   748
  Measurement   748
  Offsetting   748
  Additional Liability   749
TRANSITION COST   751
PENSION DISCLOSURES—A COMPROMISE   752
  Decision-Makers' Perspective   752
SETTLEMENT OR CURTAILMENT OF PENSION PLANS   754
CONCEPT REVIEW EXERCISE: PENSION PLANS   754

QUESTIONS FOR REVIEW OF KEY TOPICS   756

EXERCISES   757

PROBLEMS   763

CASES   767

CHAPTER

18 | Employee Benefit Plans 772

PART A: POSTRETIREMENT BENEFITS OTHER THAN
    PENSIONS   774

WHAT IS A POSTRETIREMENT BENEFIT PLAN?   775
  The Substantive Plan   775
  Postretirement Health Benefits and Pension Benefits
    Compared   775
  Determining the Net Cost of Benefits   776
POSTRETIREMENT BENEFIT OBLIGATION   776
  Measuring the Obligation   777

Attribution   777
Postretirement Benefit Expense   777
Recording the Expense   778
Components of the Expense   779
Determining the Expense   782
A Comprehensive Illustration   783
Disclosures   784
CONCEPT REVIEW: OTHER POSTRETIREMENT BENEFITS   785

PART B: PRERETIREMENT COMPENSATION PLANS   787

STOCK-BASED COMPENSATION PLANS   787
  Stock Award Plans   787
  Stock Option Plans   788
  Stock Appreciation Rights   795
  Broad-Based (Noncompensatory) Plans   798
VARIOUS BONUS PLANS   799
  Annual Bonuses   799
  Performance Share Plans and Long-Term Cash Bonuses   799
OTHER EMPLOYEE COMPENSATION   800
  Stock Purchase Plans   800
  Vacations, Sick Days, and Other Paid Future Absences   800
  Postemployment Benefits   802
  Employee Stock Ownership Plans (ESOPS)   802
CONCEPT REVIEW: PRERETIREMENT COMPENSATION PLANS   803

APPENDIX 18A: RETIREE HEALTH CARE BENEFIT
    OBLIGATIONS AND EXPENSE—A COMPREHENSIVE
    ILLUSTRATION   806

APPENDIX 18B: OPTION-PRICING THEORY   807

QUESTIONS FOR REVIEW OF KEY TOPICS   809

EXERCISES   809

PROBLEMS   815

CASES   818

CHAPTER

19 | Shareholders' Equity 824

PART A: THE NATURE OF SHAREHOLDERS' EQUITY   826

FINANCIAL REPORTING OVERVIEW   826
THE CORPORATE ORGANIZATION   828
  Limited Liability   829
  Ease of Raising Capital   829
  Disadvantages   830
  Types of Corporations   830
  Hybrid Organizations   830
  The Model Business Corporation Act   831

PART B: PAID-IN CAPITAL   831

FUNDAMENTAL SHARE RIGHTS   831
DISTINGUISHING CLASSES OF SHARES   832
  Typical Rights of Preferred Shares   832
THE CONCEPT OF PAR VALUE   833
ACCOUNTING FOR THE ISSUANCE OF SHARES   834
  Shares Sold for Cash   834
  Shares Sold on Credit   834
  Shares Sold for Noncash Consideration   835
  More than One Security Sold for a Single Price   836

Share Issue Costs 836
CONCEPT REVIEW EXERCISE: EXPANSION OF CORPORATE
    CAPITAL 837
REACQUIRED SHARES 838
    Decision-Makers' Perspective 838
    Shares Formally Retired 839
    Shares Viewed as Treasury Stock 839
    Accounting for Shares Reacquired 840
    Treasury Stock 840
    Resale of Shares 842
CONCEPT REVIEW EXERCISE: TREASURY STOCK 843

PART C: RETAINED EARNINGS 844
CHARACTERISTICS OF RETAINED EARNINGS 844
DIVIDENDS 844
    Liquidating Dividend 844
    Retained Earning Restrictions 845
    Cash Dividends 845
    Property Dividends 846
STOCK DIVIDENDS AND SPLITS 846
    Stock Dividends 846
    Stock Splits 848
    Stock Splits Effected in the Form of Stock Dividends
        (Large Stock Dividends) 848
DECISION-MAKERS' PERSPECTIVE 849
CONCEPT REVIEW EXERCISE: CHANGES IN RETAINED EARNINGS
    851

APPENDIX 19A: QUASI REORGANIZATIONS 854
QUESTIONS FOR REVIEW OF KEY TOPICS 855
EXERCISES 856
PROBLEMS 862
CASES 867

SECTION 4

ADDITIONAL FINANCIAL REPORTING ISSUES 873

C H A P T E R

20 | Earnings Per Share 874

PART A: SIMPLE CAPITAL STRUCTURE 876
ISSUANCE OF NEW SHARES 877
STOCK DIVIDENDS AND STOCK SPLITS 877
REACQUIRED SHARES 878
EARNINGS AVAILABLE TO COMMON SHAREHOLDERS 879

PART B: COMPLEX CAPITAL STRUCTURE 880
POTENTIALLY DILUTIVE SECURITIES 880
OPTIONS, RIGHTS AND WARRANTS 880
CONVERTIBLE SECURITIES 882
    Convertible Bonds 882
    Convertible Preferred Stock 884
ANTIDILUTIVE SECURITIES 885
    Options, Warrants, Rights 885
    Convertible Securities 886

Order of Entry for Multiple Convertible Securities 887
CONCEPT REVIEW EXERCISE: BASIC AND DILUTED EPS 888

PART C: ADDITIONAL EPS ISSUES 889
CONTINGENTLY ISSUABLE SHARES 889
SUMMARY OF THE EFFECT OF POTENTIALLY DILUTIVE SECURITIES
    EARNINGS PER SHARE 890
ACTUAL CONVERSIONS 890
OPTIONS OR WARRANTS OUTSTANDING FOR ONLY PART OF THE
    PERIOD 892
FINANCIAL STATEMENT PRESENTATION OF EARNINGS PER SHARE
    DATA 892
DECISION-MAKERS' PERSPECTIVE 893
CONCEPT REVIEW EXERCISE: ADDITIONAL EPS ISSUES 894
QUESTIONS FOR REVIEW OF KEY TOPICS 896
EXERCISES 897
PROBLEMS 900
CASES 904

C H A P T E R

21 | Accounting Changes and Error Corrections 910

PART A: ACCOUNTING CHANGES 912
CHANGE IN ACCOUNTING PRINCIPLE 913
    Motivation for Accounting Choices: Decision-Makers'
        Perspective 914
    The Current Approach: Most Changes in Accounting
        Principle 914
    The Retroactive Approach: Certain Specified Changes in
        Accounting Principle 918
    The Prospective Approach: Certain Specified Changes in
        Accounting Principle 920
CHANGE IN ACCOUNTING ESTIMATE 921
CHANGE IN REPORTING ENTITY 922
ERROR CORRECTION 923
CONCEPT REVIEW EXERCISE: ACCOUNTING CHANGES 924

PART B: CORRECTION OF ACCOUNTING ERRORS 925
PRIOR PERIOD ADJUSTMENTS 926
ERROR CORRECTION ILLUSTRATED 927
    Error Discovered in the Same Reporting Period That It
        Occurred 927
    Error Affecting Previous Financial Statements, But Not Net
        Income 927
    Error Affecting a Prior Year's Net Income 927
CONCEPT REVIEW EXERCISE: CORRECTION OF ERRORS 931
QUESTIONS FOR REVIEW OF KEY TOPICS 933
EXERCISES 934
PROBLEMS 939
CASES 946

C H A P T E R

22 The Statement of Cash Flows
    Revisited 950

DECISION-MAKERS' PERSPECTIVE: USEFULNESS OF CASH FLOW
    INFORMATION 952
CASH INFLOWS AND OUTFLOWS 952
ROLE OF THE STATEMENT OF CASH FLOWS 953
EVOLUTION OF THE STATEMENT OF CASH FLOWS 954
    Cash and Cash Equivalents 955
    Primary Elements of the Statement of Cash Flows 956
PREPARATION OF THE STATEMENT OF CASH FLOWS 960
    Preparing a Spreadsheet 961
    Income Statement Accounts 964
    Balance Sheet Accounts 971
CONCEPT REVIEW EXERCISE: COMPREHENSIVE REVIEW 976
ALTERNATIVE PRESENTATION OF CASH FLOWS FROM OPERATING
    ACTIVITIES—INDIRECT METHOD 979
DECISION-MAKERS' PERSPECTIVE: CASH FLOW RATIOS 981

APPENDIX 22A: SPREADSHEET FOR THE INDIRECT METHOD
    984

APPENDIX 22B: THE T-ACCOUNT METHOD OF PREPARING THE
    STATEMENT OF CASH FLOWS 988

QUESTIONS FOR REVIEW OF KEY TOPICS 989

EXERCISES 990

PROBLEMS 997

CASES 1008

INDEX 1013

1

THE ROLE OF ACCOUNTING AS AN INFORMATION SYSTEM

ENVIRONMENT AND THEORETICAL STRUCTURE OF FINANCIAL ACCOUNTING

OVERVIEW

The primary function of financial accounting is to provide relevant financial information to users external to the business enterprise. The focus of financial accounting is on the information needs of investors and creditors. These users make critical resource allocation decisions that affect the nation's economy. The primary means of conveying financial information to investors, creditors, and other external users is through financial statements and related notes.

In this chapter you explore some important topics that will serve as a foundation for a more detailed study of financial statements, the way the elements of these statements are measured, and the concepts underlying these measurements and related disclosures.

LEARNING OBJECTIVES   After studying this chapter, you should be able to:

1. Describe the function and primary focus of financial accounting.
2. Explain the difference between cash and accrual accounting.
3. Define generally accepted accounting principles (GAAP) and discuss the historical development of accounting standards.
4. Explain why the establishment of accounting standards is characterized as a political process.
5. Explain the purpose of the FASB's conceptual framework.
6. Identify the objectives of financial reporting, the qualitative characteristics of accounting information, and the elements of financial statements.
7. Describe the four basic assumptions underlying GAAP.
8. Describe the four broad accounting principles that guide accounting practice.

MISGUIDED MARKETING MAJOR

During a class break in your investments class, a marketing major tells the following story to you and some friends:

The chief financial officer of a large company is interviewing three candidates for the top accounting position with his firm. He asks each the same question:

CFO:	What is two plus two?
First candidate:	Four.
CFO:	What is two plus two?
Second candidate:	Four.
CFO:	What is two plus two?
Third candidate:	What would you like it to be?
CFO:	You're hired.

After you take some good-natured ribbing from the nonaccounting majors, your friend says, "Seriously, though, there must be ways the accounting profession prevents that kind of behavior. Aren't there some laws, or rules, or something? Are they based on some sort of theory, or are they just arbitrary?"

QUESTIONS

1. What should you tell your friend about the presence of accounting standards in the United States? Who has the authority for standard setting? Who has the responsibility?
2. What is the economic and political environment in which standard setting occurs?
3. What is the relationship among management, auditors, investors, and creditors that tends to preclude the "What would you like it to be?" attitude?
4. In general, what is the conceptual framework that underlies accounting principles?

A FINANCIAL ACCOUNTING ENVIRONMENT

Have you ever received a C grade on a paper and thought you deserved better? In 1965 Fred Smith did. His term paper for an economics class proposed a revolutionary air freight delivery method that revolved around a "hub and spokes" system. The hub would be located in a middle-America location (Memphis was eventually chosen) with spokes radiating out to cities across the country. A package from Los Angeles, destined for New York, would be flown in on the Los Angeles spoke in a few hours to the hub location in Memphis. There it would be sorted and routed out on the return flight of the plane that had just brought in shipments from New York, arriving before dawn. Los Angeles to New York overnight!

> "The concept is interesting and well formed, but in order to earn better than a 'C,' the idea must be feasible." — quote from a Yale University professor in response to Federal Express founder Fred Smith's paper proposing reliable overnight delivery service.

Fred Smith had so much confidence in his idea that in 1971 he created a company called Federal Express. On April 17, 1973, when operations officially began, the company served 25 cities and delivered 186 packages. The company struggled at first, and it wasn't until three years later that it reported its first profit of $3.6 million. Two decades later, Federal Express Corporation's annual profit exceeded $300 million and annual revenue topped $10 billion. Average package volume reached approximately 2.5 million daily worldwide.[1]

Many factors contributed to the success of Federal Express. The company's founder was visionary in terms of his package delivery system. The hub and spokes concept is now used throughout the air freight industry. A key factor contributing to the growth and success of Federal Express was its access to external capital (resources). At various times in the company's brief history, the ability to raise external capital from investors and creditors was critical to its phenomenal growth. For example, several bank loans provided financing in the early years, and in 1978, an initial public offering of the company's stock provided over $17 million in equity financing.

Investors and creditors use many different kinds of information before supplying capital to business enterprises like Federal Express. The information is used to assess the future risk and return of their potential investments in the enterprise.[2] For example, information about the enterprise's products and its management is of vital importance to this assessment. In addition, various kinds of financial information are extremely important to investors and creditors.

Financial accounting is concerned with providing relevant financial information to various external users. The chart in Graphic 1–1 illustrates a number of financial information supplier groups as well as several external user groups. Of these groups, the primary focus of financial accounting is on the financial information provided by *profit-oriented companies to their present and potential investors and creditors*. The reason for this focus is discussed in a later section of this chapter. External users, often referred to as *financial intermediaries,* include financial analysts, stockbrokers, mutual fund managers, and credit rating organizations. These users provide advice to investors and creditors and/or make investment-credit decisions on their behalf.

On the other hand, **managerial accounting** deals with the concepts and methods used to provide information to an organization's *internal* users, that is, its managers. You study managerial accounting elsewhere in your curriculum.

The primary means of conveying financial information to investors, creditors, and other external users is through financial statements and related disclosure notes. The financial statements most frequently provided are (1) the balance sheet or statement of financial position, (2) the income statement or statement of operations, (3) the statement of cash flows, and (4) the statement of shareholders' equity. As you progress through this text, you will review and expand your knowledge of the information in these financial statements, the way the elements in these statements are measured, and the concepts underlying these measurements and

Federal Express

| Investors and creditors use information to assess the future risk and return of their potential investments.

| **Learning objective 1**
Describe the function and primary focus of financial accounting.

| The primary focus of **financial accounting** is on the information needs of investors and creditors.

| Financial statements convey financial information to external users.

---

[1]Vance Trimble, *Overnight Success* (New York: Crown Publishers, Inc., 1993).

[2]Risk refers to the variability of possible outcomes from an investment, and return is the amount received over and above the investment and usually is expressed as a percentage.

GRAPHIC   1–1

Financial Information Supplier Groups and External User Groups

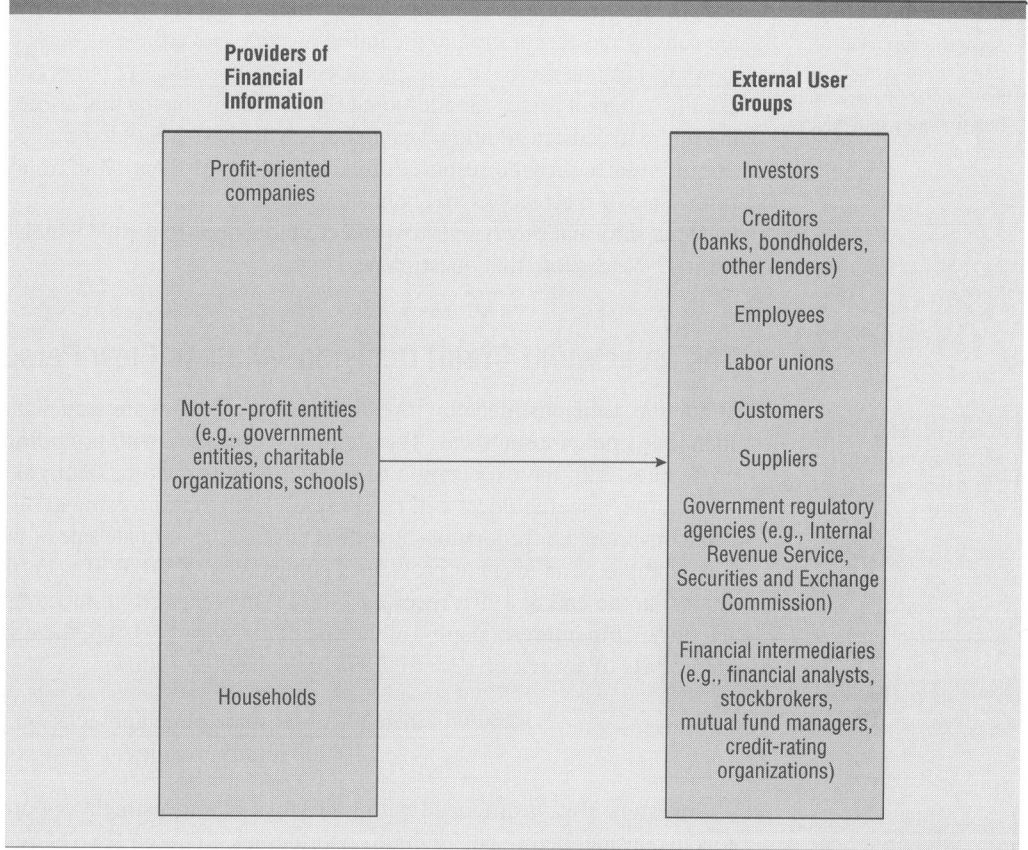

related disclosures. We use the term *financial reporting* to refer to the process of providing this information to external users.

The appendix to this chapter contains recent financial statements, including related disclosure notes, for Federal Express Corporation. We occasionally refer to the Federal Express financial statements in this chapter and others to illustrate certain points. You also can refer to these statements as new topics are introduced in later chapters.

Federal Express Corporation

The Economic Environment and Financial Reporting

In the United States, we have a highly developed free-enterprise economy with the majority of productive resources privately owned rather than government owned. It's important in this type of system that a mechanism exist to allocate the scarce resources of our society, both natural resources and labor, in an efficient manner. Resources should be allocated to private enterprises that will use them best to provide goods and services desired by society and not to enterprises that will waste them. The mechanisms that foster this efficient allocation of resources are the **capital markets**. We can think of the capital markets simply as a composite of all investors and creditors.

> The **capital markets** provide a mechanism to help our economy allocate resources efficiently.

> **Corporations** acquire capital from investors in exchange for ownership interest and from creditors by borrowing.

The dominant form of business organization in the United States, in terms of the ownership of productive resources, is the **corporation**.[3] The corporate form makes it easier for an enterprise to acquire resources through the capital markets. Investors provide resources to a corporation in exchange for evidence of ownership interest, that is, shares of stock. Creditors such as banks lend resources to the corporation. Also, creditors can lend the corporation resources through the medium of bonds. Stocks and bonds usually are traded on organized security markets such as the New York Stock Exchange and the American Stock Exchange. The advantages and disadvantages of the corporate form are discussed at greater length in Chapter 19.

The transfers of these stocks and bonds among individuals and institutions are referred to as **secondary market** transactions. Corporations receive no new resources from secondary market trans-

---

[3]Although corporations control the majority of resources in the United States, sole proprietorships and partnerships actually outnumber corporations.

Secondary market transactions provide for the transfer of stocks and bonds among individuals and institutions.

actions. New resources are provided in *primary* market transactions in which the shares or bonds are sold by the corporation to the initial owners. Nevertheless, secondary market transactions are extremely important to the efficient allocation of resources in our economy. These transactions help establish market prices for additional shares and for bonds that corporations may wish to issue in the future to acquire additional capital. Also, many shareholders and bondholders might be unwilling to initially provide resources to corporations if there were no available mechanism for the future sale of their stocks and bonds to others.

What information do investors and creditors need to decide which companies will be provided capital? We explore that question next.

The Investment-Credit Decision—A Cash Flow Perspective

Investors and creditors both are interested in earning a fair return on the resources provided.

While the decisions made by investors and by creditors are somewhat different, they are similar in at least one important way. They both are concerned with providing resources, usually cash, to companies with the expectation of receiving more cash in return at some time in the future. A corporation's shareholders will receive cash from their investment through periodic dividend distributions from the corporation, as well as through the ultimate sale of the ownership shares of stock. For example, if an investor provides a company with $10,000 cash (that is, purchases ownership shares) at the end of 1997, receives $400 in dividends from the company during 1998, and sells the ownership interest (shares) at the end of 1998 for $10,600, the investment would have generated a **rate of return** of 10% for 1998, calculated as follows:

$$\frac{\$400 \text{ dividends} + \$600 \text{ share price appreciation}}{\$10,000 \text{ initial investment}} = 10\%$$

The expected **rate of return** and uncertainty, or risk, of that return are key variables in the investment decision.

Investors always are faced with more than one investment opportunity. There are many factors to consider before one of these opportunities is chosen. Two extremely important variables are the *expected rate of return* from each investment option, and the *uncertainty,* or *risk,* of that expected return. For example, consider the following two investment options:

1. Invest $10,000 in a savings account insured by the U.S. government that will generate a 5% rate of return.
2. Invest $10,000 in a profit-oriented company.

While the rate of return from option 1 is known with virtual certainty, the return from option 2 is uncertain. The amount and timing of the cash to be received in the future from option 2 are unknown. Investors require information about the company that will help them estimate the unknown return.

A company will be able to provide a return to investors and creditors only if it can generate a profit from selling its products or services.

In the long run, a company will be able to provide investors with a return only if it can generate a profit. That is, it must be able to use the resources provided by investors and creditors to generate cash receipts from selling a product or service that exceed the cash disbursements necessary to provide that product or service. If this excess can be generated, the marketplace is implicitly saying that society's resources have been efficiently allocated. The marketplace is assigning a value to the product or service that exceeds the value assigned to the resources used to produce that product or service.

In summary, the primary objective of financial accounting is to provide investors and creditors with information that will help them make investment and credit decisions. More specifically, the information should help investors and creditors evaluate the *amounts*, *timing*, and *uncertainty* of the enterprise's future cash receipts and disbursements. The better this information is, the more efficient will be investor and creditor resource allocation decisions. Financial accounting, in providing key elements of the information set used by capital market participants, plays a vital societal role in the resource allocation process. The importance of this role to society explains why the primary focus of financial accounting is on the information needs of investors and creditors.

The objective of financial accounting is to provide investors and creditors with useful information for decision making.

The Financial Accounting Standards Board, the current private sector body responsible for setting accounting standards in the United States, has published a conceptual framework for financial reporting (discussed later in this chapter). The first concept statement of the framework describes the specific objectives of external financial reporting. These objectives affirm the importance of the cash flow information needs of investors and creditors.

ILLUSTRATION   1–1

Cash Basis Accounting

	Year 1	Year 2	Year 3	Total
Sales (on credit)	$100,000	$100,000	$100,000	$300,000
Net Operating Cash Flows:				
Cash receipts from customers	$ 50,000	$125,000	$125,000	$300,000
Cash disbursements:				
Prepayment of three years' rent	(60,000)	–0–	–0–	(60,000)
Salaries to employees	(50,000)	(50,000)	(50,000)	(150,000)
Utilities	(5,000)	(15,000)	(10,000)	(30,000)
Net cash flow	$ (65,000)	$ 60,000	$ 65,000	$ 60,000

Throughout this text, you will be reminded of this cash flow perspective. For example, Chapter 3 describes certain events that are reported separately on the income statement due to the fact that these historical events have implications for future cash flows that are different from the normal operating activities. Separation of these events from normal operating activities provides financial statement users with information to more easily predict an enterprise's future cash flows.

Cash Versus Accrual Accounting

Learning objective 2
Explain the difference between cash and accrual accounting.

Even though predicting future cash flows is the primary objective, the model best able to achieve that objective is the **accrual accounting** model. A competing model is **cash basis accounting**. Each model produces a periodic measure of performance that could be used by investors and creditors for predicting future cash flows.

Net operating cash flow is the difference between cash receipts and cash disbursements from providing goods and services.

Cash Basis Accounting.   Cash basis accounting produces a measure called **net operating cash flow**. This measure is the difference between cash receipts and cash disbursements during a reporting period from transactions related to providing goods and services to customers.

Net operating cash flow is very easy to understand and all information required to measure it is factual. Also, it certainly relates to a variable of critical interest to investors and creditors. What could be better in helping to predict future cash flows from selling products and services than current cash flows from these activities? Remember, a company will be able to provide a return to investors and creditors only if it can use the capital provided to generate a positive net operating cash flow. However, there is a major drawback to using the current period's operating cash flow to predict future operating cash flows. Over the life of the company, net operating cash flow definitely is the variable of concern. However, over short periods of time, *operating cash flows may not be indicative of the company's long-run cash-generating ability* (that is, its ability to generate positive net operating cash flows in the future).

To demonstrate this, consider the following example. In Illustration 1–1 net operating cash flows are determined for the Carter Company during its first three years of operations.

Over the three-year period, Carter generated a positive net operating cash flow of $60,000. At the end of this three-year period, Carter has no outstanding debts. Because total sales and cash receipts over the three-year period were each $300,000, nothing is owed to Carter by customers. Also, at the beginning of the first year, Carter prepaid $60,000 for three years' rent on the facilities. There are no uncompleted transactions at the end of the three-year period. In that sense, we can view this three-year period as a micro version of the entire life of a company.

The company incurred utility costs of $10,000 per year over the period. However, during the first year only $5,000 actually was paid, with the remainder being paid the second year. Employee salary costs of $50,000 were paid in full each year.

Over short periods of time, operating cash flow may not be an accurate predictor of future operating cash flows.

Is net operating cash flow for year 1 (negative $65,000) an accurate indicator of future cash-generating ability?[4] Obviously, it is not a good predictor of the positive net cash flows that occur in the next two years. Is the three-year pattern of net operating cash flows indicative of the company's year-by-year performance? No. But, if we measure the same activities by the accrual

---

[4]A negative cash flow is possible only if invested capital (i.e., owners contributed cash to the company in exchange for ownership interest) is sufficient to cover the cash deficiency. Otherwise, the company would have to either raise additional external funds or go bankrupt.

ILLUSTRATION   1–2

Accrual Accounting

The accrual accounting model provides a measure of periodic performance called net income, the difference between revenues and expenses.

	Carter Company Income Statements			
	Year 1	**Year 2**	**Year 3**	**Total**
Revenues	$100,000	$100,000	$100,000	$300,000
Expenses				
Rent	20,000	20,000	20,000	60,000
Salaries	50,000	50,000	50,000	150,000
Utilities	10,000	10,000	10,000	30,000
Total expenses	80,000	80,000	80,000	240,000
Net Income	$ 20,000	$ 20,000	$ 20,000	$ 60,000

accounting model, we get a more accurate prediction of future operating cash flows and a more reasonable portrayal of the balanced operating performance of the company over the three years.

Accrual Accounting.   The accrual accounting model measures the entity's accomplishments and resource sacrifices during the period, regardless of when cash is received or paid. The accrual accounting model's measure of periodic accomplishments is called *revenues*, and the periodic measure of resource sacrifices is called *expenses*. The difference between revenues and expenses is *net income*.[5]

Net income is the difference between **revenues** and **expenses**.

How would we measure revenues and expenses in this very simplistic situation? Illustration 1–2 offers a possible solution.

Net income of $20,000 for year 1 appears to be a reasonable predictor of the company's cash-generating ability as total net operating cash flow for the three-year period is a positive $60,000. Also, compare the three-year pattern of net operating cash flows in Illustration 1–1 to the three-year pattern of net income in Illustration 1–2. The net income pattern is more representative of the steady operating performance over the three-year period.[6]

Net income is considered a better indicator of future operating cash flows than is current net operating cash flows.

While this example is somewhat simplistic, it allows us to see the motivation for using the accrual accounting model. Accrual income attempts to measure the accomplishments and sacrifices that occurred during the year, which may not correspond to cash inflows and outflows.

Does this mean that information about cash flows from operating activities is not useful? No. Indeed, when combined with information about cash flows from investing and financing activities, this information provides valuable input into decisions made by investors and creditors. In fact, collectively, this cash flow information constitutes the statement of cash flows—one of the basic financial statements.[7]

The Development of Financial Accounting and Reporting Standards

Accrual accounting is the financial reporting model used by the majority of profit-oriented companies and by many not-for-profit companies. The fact that companies use the same model is important to financial statement users. Investors and creditors use financial information to make their resource allocation decisions. It's critical that they be able to *compare* financial information among companies. To facilitate these comparisons, financial accounting employs a body of standards known as **Generally Accepted Accounting Principles**, often abbreviated as **GAAP** (and pronounced *gap*). GAAP are a dynamic set of both broad and specific guidelines that companies should follow when measuring and reporting the information in their financial statements and related notes. The more important broad principles or standards are discussed in a subsequent section of this chapter and revisited throughout the text in the context of accounting applications for which they provide conceptual support.[8] More specific standards, such as how to measure and report a lease transaction, receive more focused attention in subsequent chapters.

Learning objective 3
Define generally accepted accounting principles (GAAP) and discuss the historical development of accounting standards.

OPENING CASE

Question 1

---

[5]Net income also includes gains and losses, which are discussed later in the chapter.

[6]Empirical evidence that accrual accounting provides a better measure of short-term performance than cash flows is provided by Patricia DeChow, "Accounting Earnings and Cash Flows as Measures of Firm Performance: The Role of Accrual Accounting," *Journal of Accounting and Economics* 18 (1994), pp. 3-42.

[7]The statement of cash flows is discussed in detail in Chapters 3 and 22.

[8]The terms *standards* and *principles* sometimes are used interchangeably.

Historical Perspective and Standards

Pressures on the accounting profession to establish uniform accounting standards began to surface after the stock market crash of 1929. Some feel that a contributing factor to the stock market crash and the subsequent depression was inflated prices of corporation ownership shares caused by misleading financial statement information.

The 1933 Securities Act and the 1934 Securities Exchange Act were designed to restore investor confidence. The 1933 act sets forth accounting and disclosure requirements for initial offerings of securities (stocks and bonds). The 1934 act applies to secondary market transactions and mandates reporting requirements for companies whose securities are publicly traded on either organized stock exchanges or in over-the-counter markets.[9] The 1934 act also created the **Securities and Exchange Commission (SEC)**.

> The **Securities and Exchange Commission (SEC)** was created by Congress with the 1934 Securities Exchange Act.

In the 1934 act, *Congress gave the SEC both the power and responsibility for setting accounting and reporting standards for companies whose securities are publicly traded.* However, the SEC, a government appointed body, always has delegated the responsibility for setting accounting standards to the private sector. It is important to understand that the SEC delegated only the responsibility, not the authority, to set standards. The power still lies with the SEC. If the SEC does not agree with a particular standard promulgated by the private sector, it can, as in the past, force a change in the standard.

> The **SEC** has the authority to set accounting standards for companies, but always has delegated the responsibility to the accounting profession.

The SEC does issue its own accounting standards in the form of *Financial Reporting Releases (FRRs)*, which regulate what must be reported by companies to the SEC itself. These standards usually agree with those previously issued by the private sector.

Early Standard Setting.   The first private sector body to assume the task of setting accounting standards was the **Committee on Accounting Procedure (CAP)**. The CAP was a committee of the **American Institute of Accountants (AIA)**. The AIA, which was renamed the **American Institute of Certified Public Accountants (AICPA)** in 1957, is the national organization of professional public accountants. From 1938 to 1959, the CAP issued 51 *Accounting Research Bulletins (ARBs)* which dealt with specific accounting and reporting problems. No theoretical framework for financial accounting was established. This approach of dealing with individual issues without a framework led to stern criticism of the accounting profession.

> The **Committee on Accounting Procedure (CAP)** was the first private sector standard-setting body.

In 1959 the **Accounting Principles Board (APB)** replaced the CAP. Members of the APB also belonged to the AICPA. The APB operated from 1959 through 1973 and issued 31 *Accounting Principles Board Opinions (APBOs),* various *Interpretations*, and four *Statements*. The *Opinions* also dealt with specific accounting and reporting problems. Many *ARBs* and *APBOs* have not been superseded and still represent authoritative GAAP.

> The **Accounting Principles Board (APB)** followed the CAP.

The APB's main effort to establish a theoretical framework for financial accounting and reporting was *APB Statement No. 4*, "Basic Concepts and Accounting Principles Underlying Financial Statements of Business Enterprises." Unfortunately, the effort was not successful.

The APB was composed of members of the accounting profession and was supported by their professional organization. Members participated in the activities of the board on a voluntary, part-time basis. The APB was criticized by industry and government for its inability to establish an underlying framework for financial accounting and reporting and for its inability to act quickly enough to keep up with financial reporting issues as they developed. Perhaps the most important flaw of the APB was it perceived lack of independence. Composed almost entirely of public accountants, the board was subject to the criticism that the clients of the represented public accounting firms were exerting self-interested pressure on the board and influencing their decisions. Other interest groups were underrepresented in the standard-setting process.

Current Standard Setting.   Criticism of the APB led to the creation in 1973 of the **Financial Accounting Standards Board (FASB)** and its supporting structure. The FASB differs from its predecessor in many ways. There are seven, full-time members of the FASB, compared to 18–21 part-time members of the APB. While all of the APB members belonged to the AICPA, FASB members represent various constituencies concerned with accounting standards. Members have

> The **FASB** currently sets accounting standards.

---

[9]Reporting requirements for SEC registrants include Form 10-K, the annual report form, and Form 10-Q, the report that must be filed for the first three quarters of each fiscal year.

included representatives from the accounting profession, profit-oriented companies, accounting educators, and government. The APB was supported financially by the AICPA, while the FASB is supported by its parent organization, the **Financial Accounting Foundation (FAF)**. The FAF's principal charge is to raise funds to support the activities of the FASB.[10] The FASB is, therefore, an independent, private sector body whose members represent a broad constituency of interest groups.[11]

In 1984, the FASB's **Emerging Issues Task Force (EITF)** was formed. The EITF membership includes 15 individuals from public accounting and private industry, along with a representative from the FASB and an SEC observer. The membership of the task force is designed to include individuals who are in a position to be aware of emerging financial reporting issues. The task force considers these emerging issues and attempts to reach a consensus on how to account for them. If consensus can be reached, generally no FASB action is required. The task force disseminates its ruling in the form of *EITF Issues.* These pronouncements are considered part of generally accepted accounting principles.

If a consensus can't be reached, FASB involvement may be necessary. The EITF plays an important role in the standard-setting process by identifying potential problem areas and then acting as a filter for the FASB. This speeds up the standard-setting process and allows the FASB to focus on important issues.

One of the FASB's most important activities has been the formulation of a **conceptual framework**. The conceptual framework project, discussed in more depth later in this chapter, deals with theoretical and conceptual issues and provides an underlying structure for current and future accounting and reporting standards. The FASB has issued six *Statements of Financial Accounting Concepts (SFACs)* to describe its conceptual framework. The board also has issued over 120 specific accounting standards, called *Statements of Financial Accounting Standards (SFASs),* as well as numerous FASB *Interpretations* and *Technical Bulletins.*

Graphic 1–2 summarizes this discussion on accounting standards. The top of the graphic shows the hierarchy of standard-setting authority. Congress gave the SEC the responsibility and authority to set accounting standards, specifically for companies whose securities are publicly traded. The SEC has delegated the task to various private sector bodies (currently the FASB) while retaining its legislated authority.

The bottom of the graphic summarizes the various sources of GAAP. Generally accepted accounting principles include the authoritative pronouncements of the SEC, CAP, APB, and FASB. Some specific accounting transactions are not covered by an authoritative pronouncement issued by one of these bodies. In these cases, accountants look to other sources, such as various bulletins and industry guides published by the AICPA as well as publications of accounting educators. These publications also are included as sources of GAAP.[12]

> The **Emerging Issues Task Force (EITF)** identifies financial reporting issues and attempts to resolve them without involving the FASB.

> In addition to issuing specific accounting standards, the FASB has formulated a **conceptual framework** to provide an underlying theoretical and conceptual structure for accounting standards.

Additional Consideration

Accounting standards and the standard-setting process discussed above relate to standards governing the measurement and reporting of information for profit-oriented organizations. In 1984, the **Government Accounting Standards Board (GASB)** was created to develop accounting standards for governmental units such as states and cities. The GASB operates under the oversight of the Financial Accounting Foundation and the Governmental Accounting Standards Advisory Council.

---

[10]The FAF's primary sources of funding are contributions and the sales of the FASB's publications. The FAF is governed by trustees, the majority of whom are appointed from the membership of six founding organizations. These organizations represent important constituencies involved with the financial reporting process. For example, one of the founding organizations is the Association of Investment Management and Research (formerly known as the Financial Analysts Federation) which represents financial information *users,* and another is the Financial Executives Institute which represents financial information *preparers.* The FAF also raises funds to support the activities of the Government Accounting Standards Board (GASB).

[11]The FASB organization also includes the **Financial Accounting Standards Advisory Council** (FASAC). The major responsibility of the FASAC is to advise the FASB on the priorities of its projects, including the suitability of new projects that might be added to its agenda.

[12]The FASB's concept statements do not constitute GAAP but provide a structure for evaluating current standards and for issuing new standards.

Accounting Standard Setting

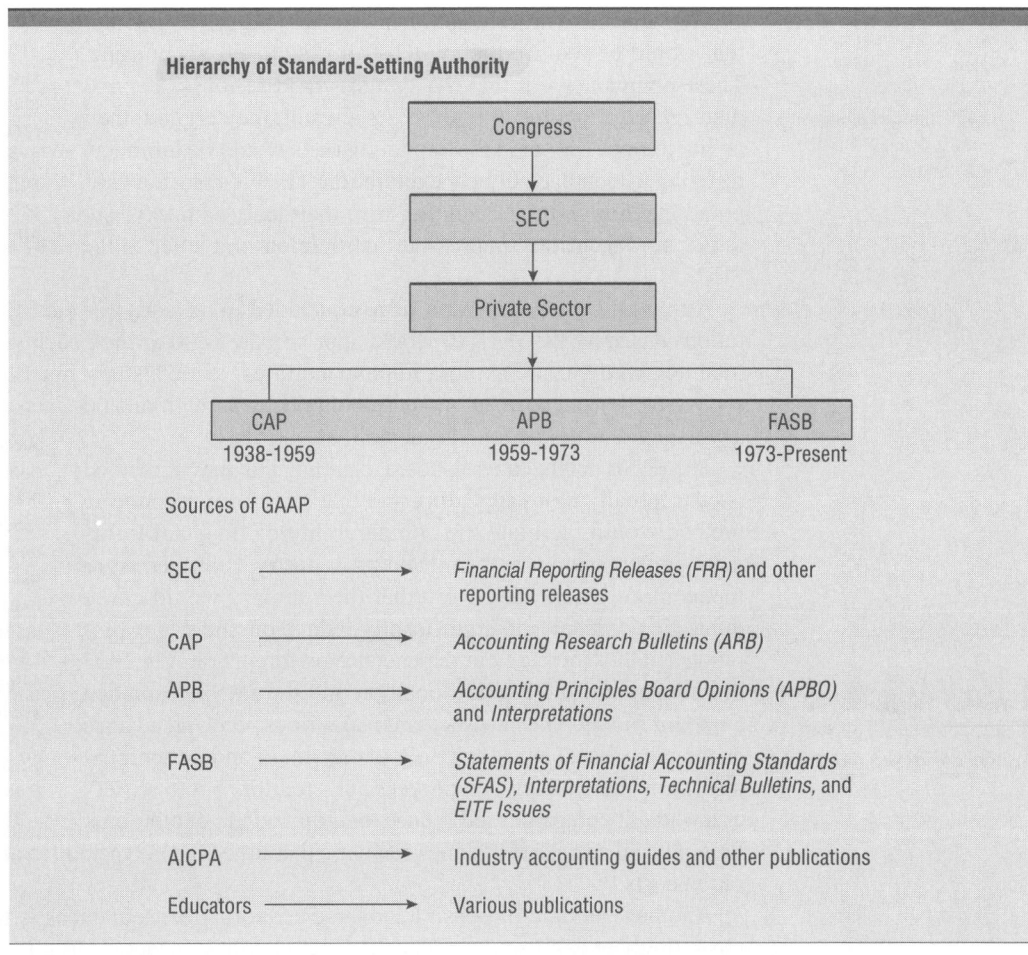

The Establishment of Accounting Standards—A Political Process

Learning objective 4
Explain why the establishment of accounting standards is characterized as a political process.

OPENING CASE

Question 2

The FASB must consider potential economic consequences of a change in an accounting standard or the introduction of a new standard.

The setting of accounting and reporting standards often has been characterized as a *political process*. Standards, particularly changes in standards, can have significant differential effects on companies, investors and creditors, and other interest groups. A change in an accounting standard or the introduction of a new standard can result in a substantial redistribution of wealth within our economy.

The role of the FASB in setting accounting standards is a complex one. Sound accounting principles can provide significant guidance in determining the appropriate method to measure and report an economic transaction. However, the FASB must gauge the potential economic consequences of a change in a standard to the various interest groups as well as to society as a whole. One obvious desired consequence is that the new standard will provide a better set of information to external users and thus improve the resource allocation process.

Possible *adverse* economic consequences may not be so obvious. For example, in 1977 the FASB issued *SFAS 19*. This standard required that all oil and gas exploration companies use the same accounting method for oil and gas exploration costs. The method, called the *successful efforts (SE) method*, requires that exploration costs that do *not* result in the discovery of oil or gas (sometimes referred to as *dry holes*) be included as expenses in the period the expenditures are made.

Prior to *SFAS 19*, many companies used an alternative method, called the *full-cost (FC) method*. The FC method permits costs incurred in searching for oil and gas within a large geographical area to be capitalized as assets and expensed in the future as oil and gas are removed from that area. FC accounting allows a company to spread out over a number of reporting periods the expense related to the cost of exploring, even for dry holes. The rationale for the FC method is that incurring the exploration costs related to dry holes was necessary to finding the successful wells. The exact location of oil and gas can't be pinpointed, so numerous wells must be drilled in order to locate the gusher.

SFAS 19 met with criticism from the oil and gas companies that would be required to switch from FC to SE accounting. These companies felt that the switch would seriously depress their reported income over time. As a result, they argued, their ability to raise capital in the capital markets would be inhibited, resulting in a cutback of new exploration. The First Boston Corporation, an investment banking firm that deals with the issuing of new securities, expressed that opinion in a letter to the SEC.

FIRST BOSTON In our opinion, the change to the successful efforts method in financial reporting will reduce the ability of small exploration companies to attract sufficient capital to proceed with expanded exploration for domestic oil.[13]

Arthur D. Little, a research firm, concluded in its study for the SEC that reductions in exploration caused by the *SFAS 19* would approximate $600 million each year, or about 8% of the then total annual domestic exploration expenditures. Little's study noted the serious implications of such reductions in terms of increased imports of foreign oil and a worsening of the nation's trade deficit.

The FASB defended its standard, claiming that the SE method is conceptually more appealing and that a uniform accounting method would facilitate the comparability of financial information of companies in the oil and gas industry. However, arguments more compelling were that the standard would cause domestic companies to significantly reduce oil and gas exploration and thus increase our dependence on foreign oil. The SEC did not support the FASB's position and the FASB rescinded *Standard No. 19*. The new standard had serious *potential* adverse economic consequences not only to certain oil and gas companies, their shareholders, employees and creditors but to society as a whole if companies did reduce their oil and gas exploration.

ARTHUR D. LITTLE A reduced domestic drilling effort of this magnitude will have important repercussions on oil imports. Based on an average finding cost of $3.50 per barrel, a $600 million reduction in exploration/drilling effort would mean a reduction in new reserve additions of 170 million barrels. If valued at today's import price of $14 per barrel, the adverse impact on balance of payments would total $2.4 billion over the life of the reserves.[14]

Presently, oil and gas companies can use either the SE or FC method to account for oil and gas exploration costs.

Another example of possible adverse economic consequences is the issue of accounting for postretirement employee health care benefits. Many corporations guarantee to pay the health care and life insurance costs of their employees after retirement. Traditionally, these companies accounted for these benefits as expenses in the period in which they made payments to or on behalf of retired employees. In 1989, the FASB proposed that these costs be accounted for by recognizing expenses over the period of employment rather than after retirement.

Companies feared that the new standard would seriously depress their annual income, and as a result, they would be forced to reduce their health care costs for retirees to soften the effect of the new standard. A survey of 992 large companies found that during the two years following the adoption of the new standard, 79% of the companies surveyed changed their retiree medical plans. Of those, 78% increased retirees' share of costs and 1% eliminated all coverage.[15] As a specific example, American Telephone and Telegraph Co. in 1989 negotiated with its union to pay health care benefits to retirees only up to a maximum fixed amount, as opposed to unlimited medical benefits offered by many companies. Of course, AT&T's decision to limit retiree medical benefits may have been purely a business decision unrelated to the new reporting requirements.[16] This issue is covered in depth in Chapter 18.

Carl Landegger, chairman of The Black Clawson Company, expressed his fear of the new accounting standard in open hearings before the FASB in 1989. The FASB reacted to these fears by modifying their originally proposed accounting treatment to ease possible adverse economic

[13]Letter from Paul L. Miller, president, The First Boston Corporation, to the SEC, October 13, 1977.

[14]Statement of Richard F. Messing, vice president, Arthur D. Little, Inc., delivered at Department of Energy hearings, Washington, D.C., February 21, 1978.

[15]Rod Coddington, "USA Snapshots," Hewitt Associates Survey of 992 Large Employers, *USA Today* (November 8, 1991).

[16]A change in an accounting standard does not directly affect the cash flow of a company. For example, changing from the cash to the accrual method of accounting for postretirement health care benefits does not *directly* change the amounts and timing of the cash payments the company has to make to retirees. However, real cash flow effects could result for a number of reasons. As a result of the change in a standard, (1) a company could alter the way it operates, (2) income tax payments could change, or (3) the new standard could cause the violation of a debt agreement thus increasing financing costs.

consequences to current and future retirees covered by these postretirement health care plans. The resulting standard, *SFAS 106*, "Employers' Accounting for Postretirement Benefits Other Than Pensions," was issued in 1990.

CARL LANDEGGER **If this becomes GAAP [generally accepted accounting principles], it will cause pain. It will cause evil. People will literally lose their health care benefits.**[17]

A more recent example of the effect of economic consequences on standard setting is the highly controversial debate surrounding accounting for executive stock options. Key executives often are given the option to buy shares in the future at a preset price as an integral part of their total compensation package. The accounting objective for any form of compensation is to report compensation expense during the period of service for which the compensation is given. At issue is the amount of compensation to be recognized as expense for stock options.

Historically, options have been measured at their intrinsic value, which is the simple difference between the market price of the shares and the option price at which they can be acquired. For instance, an option that permits an employee to buy $60 stock for $42 has an intrinsic value of $18. The problem is that plans in which the exercise price equals the market value of the underlying stock at the date of grant (which describes most plans) have no intrinsic value and thus result in zero compensation when measured this way, even though the fair value of the options can be quite substantial. To the FASB and many others, it seems counterintuitive to not record any compensation expense for arrangements that routinely provide a large part of the total compensation of executives.

Public pressure sometimes prevails over conceptual merit in the standard-setting arena.

The FASB issued an exposure draft of a new standard in 1993 that would have required companies to measure options at their *fair values* at the time they are granted and to expense that amount over the appropriate service period. After lengthy debate, the FASB bowed to public pressure and consented to encourage, rather than require, that the fair value of options be recognized as expense. This debate is discussed at greater length in Chapter 18.

The FASB undertakes a series of information-gathering steps before issuing a substantive accounting standard.

The FASB's dilemma is to balance accounting considerations and political considerations resulting from perceived possible adverse economic consequences. To help solve this dilemma, the board undertakes a series of elaborate information-gathering steps before issuing a substantive accounting standard involving alternative accounting treatments for an economic transaction. These steps include open hearings, deliberations, and requests for written comments from interested parties. For example, 467 comment letters were received on the 1989 proposal concerning accounting for postretirement employee health care benefits. Graphic 1-3 outlines the FASB's standard-setting process.

These steps are the FASB's attempt to acquire consensus as to the preferred method of accounting, as well as to anticipate adverse economic consequences. The board's process is similar to that of an elected political representative, a U.S. congresswoman for example, trying to determine consensus among her constituency before voting on a bill on the floor of the House of Representatives. For this reason, accounting standard setting is a political process.

GRAPHIC 1–3

The FASB's Standard-Setting Process

STEP	EXPLANATION
1. Identification of problem.	A measurement or reporting issue is identified by the Emerging Issues Task Force and placed on the FASB's agenda.
2. Research and analysis.	The FASB's technical staff investigates the issue.
3. *Discussion memorandum (DM).*	The DM, a detailed analysis of the problem along with alternative solutions, is prepared and disseminated to interested parties.
4. Public response.	Public hearings are held to discuss the issue and letters of response are sent to the FASB which then analyzes this feedback.
5. *Exposure draft (ED).*	A preliminary draft of a proposed statement, called an exposure draft, is issued. The ED details the proposed treatment for the problem.
6. Public response.	Written responses to the ED are accepted and analyzed. The ED is revised, if necessary, depending on the board's analysis.
7. A *Statement* is issued.	An *SFAS* is issued if five of the seven FASB members support the revised ED.

[17]Carl Landegger, reprinted in *Accounting Today* (October 23, 1989), p. 1.

Our Global Marketplace

Advances in communication and transportation systems continue to expand the marketplace in which companies operate. The world economy is more integrated than ever, and many of the larger U.S. corporations are truly multinational in nature. These multinational corporations have their home in the United States but operate and perhaps raise capital in other countries. For example, Coca-Cola, IBM, Colgate-Palmolive, Gillette, and many other companies generate more than 50 percent of their revenue from foreign sales. It is not uncommon for even relatively small companies to transact business in many different countries.

Of course, many foreign corporations operate in the United States as well. In fact, companies such as CBS Records, Firestone Tire & Rubber, and Tropicana Products are owned by companies that reside in other countries. The financial marketplace also has taken on a global dimension, with many companies crossing geographic boundaries to raise capital. For example, more than 500 companies have their securities listed on at least one stock exchange outside their home country. This expanded marketplace requires that company management understand the laws, customs, regulations, *and* accounting and reporting standards of many different countries.

Toward International Accounting Standards.   Most industrialized countries have organizations responsible for determining accounting and reporting standards. In some countries, the United Kingdom for instance, the responsible organization is a private sector body similar to the FASB in the United States. In other countries, such as Germany, the organization is a governmental body.

Accounting standards prescribed by these various groups are not the same. Standards differ from country to country for many reasons, including different legal systems, levels of inflation, degrees of sophistication and use of capital markets, and political and economic ties with other countries. These differences can cause problems for multinational corporations. A company doing business in more than one country may find it difficult to comply with more than one set of accounting standards if there are important differences among the sets. It has been argued that different national accounting standards impair the ability of companies to raise capital in international markets.

In response to this problem, the **International Accounting Standards Committee (IASC)** was formed in 1973 to develop worldwide accounting standards. The objective of the IASC is to harmonize the world's accounting standards and eliminate those differences that cannot be explained by legitimate environmental variables. The IASC has issued over 30 *International Accounting Standards.* Compliance with these standards is voluntary because the IASC has no authority to enforce them. However, the IASC is gaining support around the globe as more and more countries begin to comply with its pronouncements.[18]

In the United States, the move toward harmonization of accounting standards recently took a major step forward with the cooperation of the FASB and the IASC on the earnings per share (EPS) issue. In 1994, the FASB and the IASC began working on projects leading toward the issuance of new standards for the computation of EPS. The intent of the FASB's project was to issue an EPS standard that would be compatible with the new international standard and, at the same time, simplify U.S. GAAP. Chapter 20 describes this new standard. The two organizations worked together to achieve compatibility.

Global Perspectives, designated by the symbol ◁▷ , are included throughout the text to emphasize that our economy does not operate in isolation and to introduce you to some of the differences and similarities in accounting and reporting practices around the world. In addition, your instructor may assign end-of-chapter international cases to further explore these differences and similarities.

The Role of the Auditor

It is the responsibility of management to apply accounting standards when communicating with investors and creditors through financial statements. Another group, **auditors,** serves as an independent intermediary to help ensure that management has in fact appropriately applied GAAP in preparing the company's financial statements. Auditors examine (audit) financial statements to

---

[18]Gerhard G. Mueller, Helen Gernon, and Gary Meek, *Accounting: An International Perspective* (Homewood, IL: Irwin, 1991).

express a professional, independent opinion. The opinion reflects the auditors' assessment of the statements' "fairness," which is determined by the extent to which they are prepared in compliance with GAAP.

Federal Express Corporation

The report of the independent auditors for Federal Express Corporation's financial statements is in the appendix. The first two paragraphs explain the scope of the audit, and the third states the auditors' opinion. After conducting its audit, the accounting firm Arthur Andersen LLP stated that "In our opinion, the financial statements referred to above present fairly,. . ., in conformity with generally accepted accounting principles." This is known as a *clean opinion*. If there had been any material departures from GAAP or other problems that caused the auditors to question the fairness of the statements, the report would have been modified to inform readers.

| Auditors offer credibility to financial statements.

The auditor adds credibility to the financial statements, increasing the confidence of capital market participants who rely on the information. Auditors, therefore, play an important role in the resource allocation process.

| **Certified Public Accountants (CPAs)** are licensed by states to provide audit services.

In most states, only individuals licensed as **Certified Public Accountants (CPAs)** in the state can represent that the financial statements have been audited in accordance with generally accepted auditing standards. Requirements to be licensed as a CPA vary from state to state, but all states specify education, testing, and experience requirements. The testing requirement is to pass the Uniform CPA Examination. The AICPA sets auditing standards and writes and administers the Uniform CPA Examination.

PART

B The Conceptual Framework

OPENING CASE

Question 4

The increasing complexity of our business world creates growing pressure on the FASB to delicately balance the many constituents of the accounting standard-setting process. The task of the FASB is made less complex if there exists a set of cohesive objectives and fundamental concepts on which financial accounting and reporting can be based. One of the important agenda items for the FASB after coming into existence in 1973 was the establishment of these objectives and concepts. After a number of years, the board's efforts resulted in the **conceptual framework**, which has been described as

| **Learning objective 5**
Explain the purpose of the FASB's conceptual framework.

a constitution, a coherent system of interrelated objectives and fundamentals that can lead to consistent standards and that prescribe the nature, function, and limits of financial accounting and reporting. The fundamentals are the underlying concepts of accounting, concepts that guide the selection of events to be accounted for, the measurement of those events, and the means of summarizing and communicating them to interested parties.[19]

| The conceptual framework does not prescribe GAAP. It provides an underlying foundation for accounting standards.

The FASB has disseminated this framework through six *Statements of Financial Accounting Concepts. SFAC 4* deals with the objectives of financial reporting for nonprofit organizations and *SFAC 3* was superseded by *SFAC 6*. The remaining four statements are discussed below. It is important to realize that the conceptual framework provides structure and direction to financial accounting and reporting and does not directly prescribe GAAP.

> FASB **The Concepts Statements will guide the Board in developing accounting standards by providing the Board with a common foundation and basic reasoning on which to consider merits of alternatives.**[20]

The financial statements and their elements are most informative when they possess specific qualitative characteristics, subject to the constraints of materiality, cost effectiveness, and conservatism. Proper recognition and measurement of financial information rely on several assumptions and principles that underlie the financial reporting process.

The remainder of this chapter is devoted to discussions of each of the five components of the conceptual framework that bear on financial statements as depicted in Graphic 1–4, beginning with the objectives of financial reporting.

---

[19]"Conceptual Framework for Financial Accounting and Reporting: Elements of Financial Statements and Their Measurement," *Discussion Memorandum* (Stamford, Conn.: FASB, 1976), p. 2.

[20]Introduction to "Objectives of Financial Reporting by Nonbusiness Organizations," *Statement of Financial Accounting Concepts No. 4* (Stamford, Conn.: FASB, 1980).

GRAPHIC   1–4

The Conceptual Framework

*Important graphic

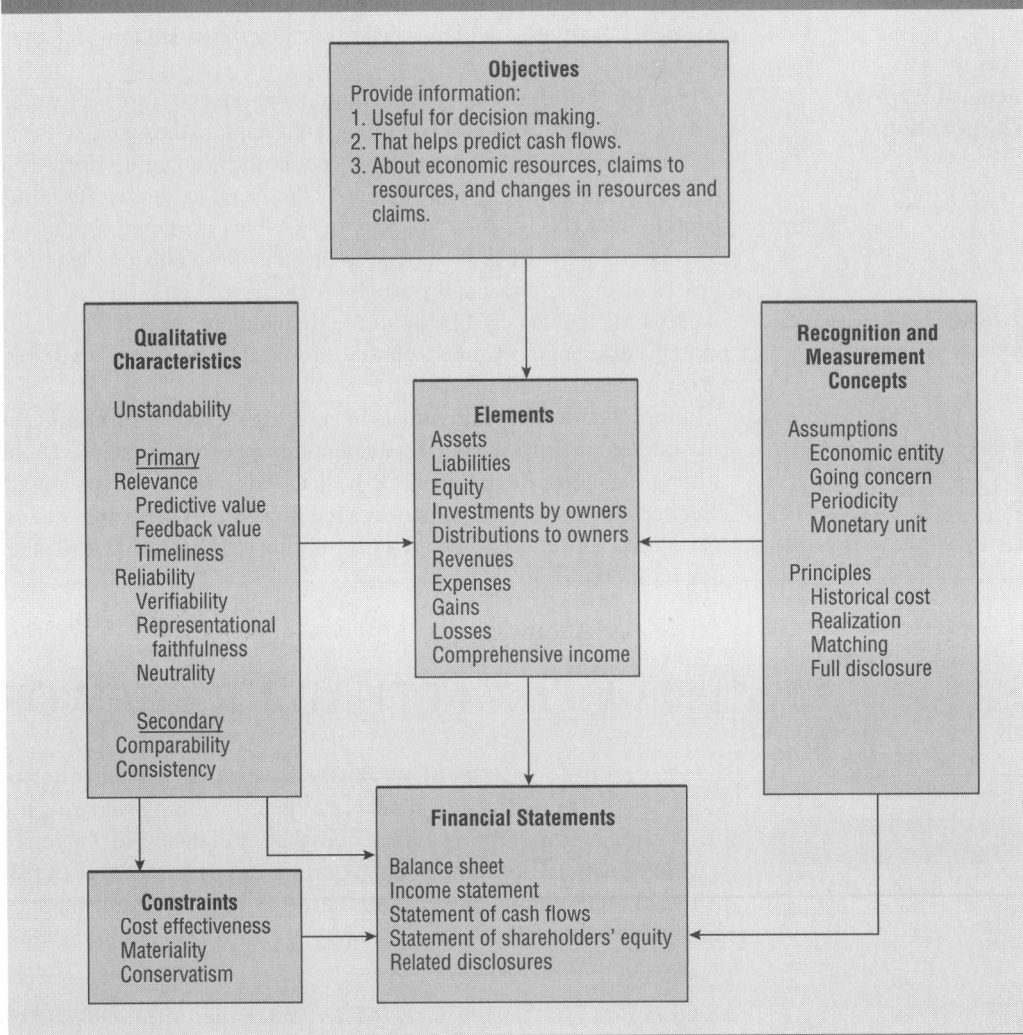

Objectives of Financial Reporting

Learning objective 6
Identify the objectives of financial reporting.

SFAC 1 establishes the objectives of financial reporting.

SFAC 1 affirms that investors and creditors are the primary external users of financial information.

In specifying the overriding objectives of financial reporting, the board considered the economic, legal, political, and social environment in the United States. The objectives would be quite different in a socialist economy where the majority of productive resources are government owned.

Implicit in the objectives is an overall societal goal of serving the public interest by providing

evenhanded financial and other information that, together with information from other sources, facilitates efficient functioning of capital markets and otherwise assists in promoting efficient capital allocation of scarce resources in the economy.[21]

The importance to our economy of providing capital market participants with information was discussed previously, as were the specific cash flow information needs of investors and creditors. *SFAC 1* articulates this importance and investor and creditor needs through three basic financial reporting objectives listed in Graphic 1–5.

The first objective specifies a focus on investors and creditors. In addition to the importance of investors and creditors as key users, information to meet their needs is likely to have general utility to other groups of external users who are interested in essentially the same financial aspects of a business as are investors and creditors.

The second objective refers to the specific cash flow information needs of investors and creditors. The third objective emphasizes the need for information about economic resources and

---

[21]Introduction to "Objectives Of Financial Reporting for Business Enterprises," *Statement of Financial Accounting Concepts No. 1* (Stamford, Conn.: FASB, 1978).

GRAPHIC   1 – 5

Financial Reporting Objectives

The primary objective of financial reporting is to provide useful information for decision making.

1. Financial reporting should provide information that is useful to present and potential investors and creditors and other users in making rational investment, credit, and similar decisions.

   The information should be comprehensible to those who have a reasonable understanding of business and economic activities and are willing to study the information with reasonable diligence.

2. Financial reporting should provide information to help present and potential investors and creditors and other users to assess the amounts, timing, and uncertainty of prospective cash receipts.

   Since investors' and creditors' cash flows are related to enterprise cash flows, financial reporting should provide information to help assess the amounts, timing, and uncertainty of prospective net cash inflows to the related enterprise.

3. Financial reporting should provide information about the economic resources of an enterprise; the claims to those resources (obligations); and the effects of transactions, events, and circumstances that cause changes in resources and claims to those resources.

   These are sources, direct or indirect, of future cash inflows and cash outflows.

claims to those resources. This information would include not only the amount of resources and claims at a particular point in time but also changes in resources and claims that occur over periods of time. This information is key to predicting future cash flows.

Qualitative Characteristics of Accounting Information

To satisfy the stated objectives, information should possess certain characteristics. The purpose of *SFAC 2* is to outline the desired qualitative characteristics of accounting information.

Learning objective 6 Identify the qualitative characteristics of accounting information.

Graphic 1–6 indicates these qualitative characteristics, presented in the form of a hierarchy of their perceived importance. Notice that the main focus, as stated in the first concept statement is on **decision usefulness**—the ability to be useful in decision making. **Understandability** means that users must understand the information within the context of the decision being made. This is a user-specific quality because users will differ in their ability to comprehend any set of information. The first stated financial reporting objective of *SFAC 1* is to provide comprehensible information to those who have a reasonable understanding of business and economic activities and are willing to study the information.

To be useful, information must make a difference in the decision process.

Primary Qualitative Characteristics

To be decision useful, accounting information should be **relevant** and **reliable**.

The primary decision-specific qualities that make accounting information useful are **relevance** and **reliability**. Both are critical. No matter how reliable, if information is not relevant to the decision at hand, it is useless. Conversely, relevant information is of little value if it cannot be relied on. Let's look closer at each of these two characteristics, including the components that make those qualities desirable. We also consider two secondary qualities—comparability and consistency.

Relevant information usually possesses both **predictive value** and **feedback value**.

Relevance.   To be relevant, information must possess **predictive value** and/or **feedback value**. Generally, useful information will possess both qualities. For example, if net income and its components confirm investor expectations about future cash-generating ability, then net income has feedback value for investors. This confirmation can also be useful in predicting future cash-generating ability as expectations are revised.

Information is **timely** if it is available to users before a decision is made.

Timeliness also is an important component of relevance. Information is timely when it is available to users early enough to allow its use in the decision process. The need for timely information requires that companies provide information to external users on a periodic basis.

Characteristics of reliable information are **verifiability**, **representational faithfulness**, and **neutrality**.

Reliability.   **Reliability** is the extent to which information is *verifiable, representationally faithful*, and *neutral*. **Verifiability** implies a consensus among different measurers. For example, the historical cost of a piece of land to be reported on the balance sheet of a company is usually highly verifiable. The cost can be traced to an exchange transaction, the purchase of the land. However, the market value of that land is much more difficult to verify. Appraisers could differ in their assessment of market value. The term *objectivity* often is linked to verifiability. The historical cost of the land is objective but the land's market value is subjective, influenced by the measurer's

GRAPHIC   1–6

**Hierarchy of Desirable
Characteristics of Accounting
Information**

Qualitative Characteristics

Understandability

Decision Usefulness

User-specific
Quality

Overriding
Objective

Relevance   Reliability

Primary
Qualities

Components

Predictive
Value   Feedback
Value   Timeliness   Verifiability   Neutrality   Representational
Faithfulness

Comparability   Consistency

Secondary
Qualities

Cost Effectiveness Constraint
(benefits exceed costs)

Materiality Constraint
(recognition threshold)

Constraints

**Representational
faithfulness** means
agreement between a
measure and a real-world
phenomenon that the
measure is supposed to
represent.

past experience and prejudices. A measurement that is subjective is difficult to verify, which makes it more difficult for users to rely on.

Representational faithfulness exists when there is agreement between a measure or description and the phenomenon it purports to represent. For example, assume that the term *inventory* on a balance sheet of a retail company is understood by external users to represent items that are intended for sale in the ordinary course of business. If inventory includes, say, machines used to produce inventory, then it lacks representational faithfulness.

Several years ago, accountants used the term *reserve for doubtful accounts* to describe anticipated bad debts related to accounts receivable. For many, the term *reserve* means that a sum of money has been set aside for future bad debts. Because this was not the case, this term lacked representational faithfulness. The description "reserve . . ." now has been changed to "allowance for uncollectible accounts" or "allowance for doubtful accounts." In Federal Express Corporation's financial statements, the balance sheet in the appendix reports *Receivables, less allowance for doubtful accounts of $30,809,000 and $31,173,000* at the end of 1996 and 1995, respectively.

**Federal Express
Corporation**

Accounting standards
should not favor any
particular groups or
companies nor influence
behavior in any specific
way.

Reliability assumes the information being relied on is neutral with respect to parties potentially affected. In that regard, **neutrality** is highly related to the establishment of accounting standards. You learned earlier that changes in accounting standards can lead to adverse economic consequences to certain companies, their investors and creditors, and other interest groups. Accounting standards should be established with overall societal goals and specific objectives in mind and should try not to favor particular groups or companies.

The FASB faces a difficult task in balancing neutrality and the consideration of economic consequences. A new accounting standard may favor one group of companies over others, but the FASB must convince the financial community that this was a consequence of the standard and not an objective used to set the standard. Donald Kirk, one of the members of the first group to serve on the FASB, stressed the importance of neutrality in the standard-setting process.

A trade-off often is required
between various degrees of
relevance and reliability.

The qualities of relevance and reliability often clash. For example, a net income forecast provided by the management of a company may possess a high degree of relevance to investors and creditors trying to predict future cash flows. However, a forecast necessarily contains subjectivity in the estimation of future events. GAAP presently do not require companies to provide forecasts of any financial variables.

DONALD KIRK **If financial reporting is to be credible, there must be public confidence that the standard-setting system is credible, that selection of board members is based on merit and not the influence of special interests, and that standards are developed neutrally with the objective of relevant and reliable information, not purposeful manipulation.**[22]

---

[22]Donald J. Kirk, chairman of the FASB, quoted in *Status Report,* December 23, 1986.

Secondary Qualitative Characteristics

Graphic 1–6 identifies two secondary qualitative characteristics important to decision usefulness—comparability and consistency. **Comparability** is the ability to help users see similarities and differences among events and conditions. We already have discussed the importance of the ability of investors and creditors to compare information across companies to make their resource allocation decisions. Closely related to comparability is the notion that **consistency** of accounting practices over time permits valid comparisons between different periods. The predictive and feedback value of information is enhanced if users can compare the performance of a company over time.[23]

> Accounting information should be **comparable** across different companies and over different time periods.

Practical Boundaries (Constraints) To Achieving Desired Qualitative Characteristics

Most of us learn early in life that we can't get everything we desire. The latest electronic gadget may have all the qualitative characteristics that current technology can provide, but limited resources may lead us to purchase a fully functional model with fewer bells and whistles. **Cost effectiveness** also constrains the accounting choices we make. Specifically, it's important that the benefits of endowing accounting information with all the qualitative characteristics we've discussed exceed the costs of doing so.

A related constraint on the type of information we provide is the concept of **materiality**. For an additional $20 you can add the latest enhancement to that electronic gadget you're considering. However, despite the higher specs, if you feel it will provide no discernible improvement in the performance of the product as you will use it, why pay the extra $20? In an accounting context, if a more costly way of providing information is not expected to have a material effect on decisions made by those using the information, the less costly method may be acceptable.

Cost effectiveness and materiality impart practical constraints on each of the qualitative characteristics of accounting information. Both suggest that a certain accounting treatment might be different from that dictated solely by consideration of desired qualities of information.

Cost Effectiveness

> The costs of providing accounting information include any possible adverse economic consequences of accounting standards.

The costs of providing accounting information include those of gathering, processing, and disseminating information. There also are costs to users when interpreting information. In addition, costs include possible adverse economic consequences of implementing accounting standards. These costs in particular are difficult, if not impossible, to quantify.

An example of this is the standard that requires companies operating in more than one operating segment to disclose certain disaggregated financial information.[24] In addition to information gathering, processing, and dissemination costs, many companies feel that this reporting requirement imposes what could be called *competitive disadvantage costs*. These companies do not want their competitors to have the disaggregated data.

> Information is *cost effective* only if the perceived benefit of increased *decision usefulness* exceeds the anticipated costs of providing that information.

The perceived benefit from this or any accounting standard is increased *decision usefulness* of the information provided, which improves the resource allocation process. It is inherently impossible to quantify this benefit. The elaborate information-gathering process undertaken by the FASB in setting accounting standards is an attempt to assess both costs and benefits of a proposed accounting standard, even if in a subjective, nonquantifiable manner.

In the case of reporting disaggregated information, the FASB decided that the perceived benefits of disclosing this information exceeded the costs of providing it. As previously discussed, the FASB was influenced by the SEC to rescind *SFAS 19*, thus allowing companies to continue to use either the full-cost or the successful efforts method. The perceived costs to society of requiring successful efforts accounting for oil and gas exploration costs exceeded the perceived benefits, even though successful efforts accounting was considered to be conceptually more appealing.

---

[23]Companies occasionally do change their accounting practices which makes it difficult for users to make comparisons among different reporting periods. Chapter 3 and Chapter 21 describe the disclosures that a company makes in this situation to restore consistency among periods.

[24]In January 1996, the FASB issued an exposure draft entitled "Reporting Disaggregated Information about a Business Enterprise." At the time this text was published, a new standard had not yet been issued. The contents of the exposure draft are described in an appendix to Chapter 5. The new standard replaces *SFAS 14,* "Financial Reporting for Segments of a Business Enterprise."

Materiality

Materiality is another pervasive constraint. Information is material if it can have an effect on a decision made by users. One consequence of considering materiality is that GAAP need not be followed if an item is immaterial. For example, GAAP requires that receivables be measured at their net realizable value. If bad debts are anticipated, they should be estimated and subtracted from the face amount of receivables for balance sheet measurement. This is called the *allowance method* of accounting for bad debts. However, if the amount of anticipated bad debts is not considered to be large enough to affect decisions made by users, the *direct write-off method* of accounting for bad debts can be used even though it is not a generally accepted technique. This method does not require estimation of bad debts for existing receivables.

> Information is **material** if it has an effect on decisions.

The threshold for materiality will depend principally on the *relative* dollar amount of the transaction. For example, $10,000 in total anticipated bad debts for a multibillion dollar company like Federal Express would not be considered material. The method used to account for these anticipated bad debts will not affect the decisions made by Federal Express Corporation's financial statement users. This same $10,000 amount, however, could easily be material for a neighborhood pizza parlor. The FASB has been reluctant to establish any quantitative materiality guidelines. The threshold for materiality has been left to the subjective judgment of the company preparing the financial statements and its auditors.

> Professional judgment determines what amount is material in each situation.

Materiality is concerned not only with the dollar amount of an item but with the nature of the item as well. For example, an activity such as the illegal payment of $10,000 to an official of a foreign government to secure a valuable contract, would probably be considered material even if the amount is small relative to the size of the company.

Conservatism

Conservatism is a frequently cited characteristic of accounting information. It is not, however, a desired qualitative characteristic but a practical justification for some accounting choices. In that sense, conservatism serves as a third constraint on the achievement of various qualitative characteristics.[25]

> **Conservatism** is a justification for some accounting practices, *not* a desired qualitative characteristic of accounting information.

The need for conservatism often is discussed in conjunction with the estimates required to comply with GAAP. For example, assume that a company estimated that its anticipated bad debts on existing receivables could be any number between $20,000 and $30,000, with the most likely amount being $25,000, and that these amounts are material. A conservative estimate would be $30,000, thus showing the lowest amount (of a range of possible values) on the balance sheet for net receivables and the highest expense so the lowest net income on the income statement.

However, financial accounting information users could just as easily be misled by a conservative estimate as by an optimistic one. If $25,000 is the best estimate of anticipated bad debts, then that is the number that should be used. Conservatism is *not* a desirable characteristic nor is it an accounting principle. Nevertheless, there seem to be some accounting practices, such as the lower-of-cost-or-market method for measuring inventory (Chapter 9), that appear to be generated by a desire to be conservative. However, these practices are motivated by other accounting principles such as the realization principle as discussed later in this chapter. They also are influenced by practical realities of our legal system. Investors and creditors who lose money from stock purchases or loans are less likely to sue when bad news is exaggerated and good news is underestimated. While recognizing the role that conservatism plays in how information is reported, we also need to emphasize that it is not a desired characteristic from a qualitative standpoint. Instead, conservatism is a practical constraint on the extent to which other qualitative characteristics are instilled in accounting information.

Now that we've discussed the qualities that the elements of financial statements should possess, let's look more closely at the elements themselves.

---

[25]The FASB's hierarchy of qualitative characteristics does not specifically identify conservatism as a constraint. Most theorists include conservatism as one of the underlying accounting principles that guide accounting practice. Our classification recognizes its very real role in accounting choices as well as the practical motivation for those choices.

Elements of Financial Statements

SFAC 6 defines 10 elements of financial statements. These elements are "the building blocks with which financial statements are constructed—the classes of items that financial statements comprise."[26] They focus directly on items related to measuring performance and to reporting financial position. The definitions of these elements operationalize the resources, claims, and changes identified in the third objective of financial reporting in *SFAC 1*.[27] The *accrual accounting* model actually is embodied in the element definitions. The FASB recognized that accrual accounting produces information that is more successful in predicting future cash flows than is cash flow accounting.

| The 10 elements of
financial statements defined
in *SFAC 6* describe
financial position and
periodic performance.

The 10 elements are: (1) assets, (2) liabilities, (3) equity, (4) investments by owners, (5) distributions to owners, (6) revenues, (7) expenses, (8) gains, (9) losses, and (10) comprehensive income.

You probably already know in general terms what most of these elements mean. But as you will see when they are discussed, it is helpful to have a deeper understanding of their meaning. You may recognize the first three elements—assets, liabilities, and equity—as those that portray the financial position of an enterprise.

Assets are probable future economic benefits obtained or controlled by a particular entity as a result of past transactions or events.

| Assets represent probable
future economic benefits
controlled by the enterprise.

A key characteristic of this definition is that an asset represents *probable* future economic benefits. A receivable is an asset only if it is probable that future benefits will result, that cash will be collected. The *controlled by* aspect of the definition also is important. The employees of a company certainly represent future economic benefits to a company. However, they are not owned or controlled by the company and do not qualify as assets.

Liabilities are probable future sacrifices of economic benefits arising from present obligations of a particular entity to transfer assets or provide services to other entities in the future as a result of past transactions.

| Liabilities represent
obligations to other entities.

Most liabilities require the future payment of cash, the amount and timing of which are specified by a legally enforceable contract. Actually, though, a liability need not be payable in cash. Instead, it may require the company to transfer other assets or to provide services. For example, a warranty liability is created for the seller when a product is sold and the seller guarantees to fix or replace the product if it proves defective and it is probable that a material amount of product sold will, in fact, prove defective. A liability also need not be represented by a written agreement, nor be legally enforceable. For example, a company might choose to pay a terminated employee's salary for a period of time after termination even though not legally required to do so. The commitment creates a liability at the date of termination.

Equity or net assets, called **shareholders' equity** or **stockholders' equity** for a corporation, is the residual interest in the assets of an entity that remains after deducting liabilities.

| Equity is a residual
amount, the owners'
interest in assets after
subtracting liabilities.

Assets and liabilities are measured directly; equity is not. Equity is simply a residual amount. The accounting equation illustrates financial position.

$$\underbrace{\text{Assets} - \text{Liabilities}}_{\textit{Net Assets}} = \text{Equity}$$

For a corporation, equity arises primarily from two sources: (1) amounts *invested* by shareholders in the corporation and (2) amounts *earned* by the corporation on behalf of its shareholders. These two sources are reported as (1) **paid-in capital** and (2) **retained earnings**. We discuss this classification of shareholders' equity in more depth in Chapter 19.

---

[26]"Elements of Financial Statements," *Statement of Financial Accounting Concepts No. 6* (Stamford, Conn.: FASB 1985), par. 5.
[27]Graphic 1–5.

The next two elements defined in *SFAC 6* deal with changes in equity from owner transactions.

Investments by owners are increases in equity resulting from transfers of resources (usually cash), to a company in exchange for ownership interest.

A corporation's issuance of ownership shares of stock in exchange for cash represents an investment by owners.

> **Investments by owners** and **distributions to owners** are transactions describing any owner contribution to and withdrawal from the company.

Distributions to owners are decreases in equity resulting from transfers *to* owners.

A cash dividend paid by a corporation to its shareholders is the most common distribution to owners.

Revenues, gains, expenses, and losses describe changes in equity due to operating transactions.

Revenues are inflows or other enhancements of assets or settlements of liabilities from delivering or producing goods, rendering services, or other activities that constitute the entity's ongoing major, or central, operations.

> **Revenues** are gross inflows resulting from providing goods or services to customers.

A key characteristic is that revenues are inflows. The enterprise is acquiring something in exchange for providing goods and services to customers. Also, providing these goods and services represents a major operation of the enterprise.

On the other hand, if selling the item is not part of the central operations of the business but instead is only an incidental result of those operations, the inflow of assets would produce a gain rather than a revenue.

Gains are increases in equity from peripheral, or incidental, transactions of an entity.

> **Gains** result from selling assets *used* in the business for an amount greater than the asset's book value.

If Federal Express sold a piece of machinery used to deliver packages for an amount greater than its book value (original cost less depreciation recorded up to the date of sale), a gain would result. Gains are net inflows, the difference between the amount received and book value. Revenues are gross inflows, measured as the amount received or to be received for the goods or services without regard to the cost of providing the goods or services.

Expenses are outflows or other using up of assets or incurrences of liabilities during a period from delivering or producing goods, rendering services, or other activities that constitute the entity's ongoing major, or central, operations.

> **Expenses** are gross outflows incurred in generating revenue.

A key characteristic is that expenses represent outflows of resources incurred in the process of generating revenues.

> **Losses** are net outflows from selling assets *used* in the business for an amount less than the asset's book value.

Losses represent decreases in equity arising from peripheral, or incidental, transactions of the entity.

If Federal Express sold that piece of machinery used to deliver packages for *less* than its book value, a loss would result. So, losses are the opposite of gains—they are net *outflows* rather than net inflows. They differ from expenses by being net rather than gross outflows and by being peripheral, or incidental, transactions rather than major, or central, operations. Revenues plus gains less expenses and losses for a period equals **net income** or **net loss**, the so-called bottom line of the income statement.[28]

You should note that the definitions of these nine elements are in basic agreement with those used in practice. But, *SFAC 6* also introduced a new term, the 10th element, called *comprehensive income.*

---

[28]Some companies use the term *net earnings* instead of net income. If earnings are negative, the term used is *net loss*.

> **Comprehensive income** is the change in equity of an entity during a period from nonowner transactions. It includes all changes in equity during a period except investments by owners and distributions to owners.

Comprehensive income often does not equal net income.

Under present GAAP, net income as reported on the income statement often doesn't equal comprehensive income. The difference is the treatment of certain changes in assets and liabilities *not* included in the determination of net income for the period in which they are recognized but instead reported directly as separate components of shareholders' equity on the balance sheet. For example, in your study of investments in Chapter 12, you will learn that for certain types of investments valued at fair values on the balance sheet, the changes in those values are not included in net income but rather in a separate component of shareholders' equity. Comprehensive income is discussed in Chapter 3.

Federal Express Corporation

The income statements of Federal Express are in the appendix. The company's net income for the most recent fiscal year was $307,777,000.

Recognition and Measurement Concepts

Now that the various elements of financial statements have been identified, we discuss when they should be recognized (recorded) and how they should be measured. *SFAC 5* addresses these issues. **Recognition** refers to the process of admitting information into the basic financial statements. **Measurement** is the process of associating numerical amounts to the elements. For example, a revenue was previously defined as an inflow of assets from selling a good or providing a service. But, *when* should the revenue event be recorded, and at *what* amount?

Recognition

According to *SFAC 5*, an item should be recognized in the basic financial statements when it meets the following four criteria, subject to a cost effectiveness constraint and materiality threshold:

Recognition criteria

1. *Definition*   The item meets the definition of an element of financial statements.
2. *Measurability* The item has a relevant attribute measurable with sufficient reliability.
3. *Relevance*   The information about it is capable of making a difference in user decisions.
4. *Reliability*   The information is representationally faithful, verifiable, and neutral.[29]

These obviously are very general guidelines. The concept statement does not address *specific* recognition issues.

Measurement

The question of measurement involves two choices: (1) the choice of a unit of measurement, and (2) the choice of an attribute to be measured. *SFAC 5* essentially confirmed existing practice in both of these areas. The monetary unit or measurement scale used in financial statements is nominal units of money without any adjustment for changes in purchasing power. In addition, the board acknowledged that different attributes such as historical cost, net realizable value, and present value of future cash flows are presently used to measure different financial statement elements, and that they expected that practice to continue. For example, property, plant, and equipment are measured at historical cost; accounts receivable is measured at its net realizable value; and most long-term liabilities, such as bonds, are measured at the present value of future cash payments.

Answers to the recognition and measurement questions are imbedded in generally accepted accounting principles. *SFAC 5* confirmed some of the more important of these principles used in present practice. GAAP consist of broad principles and specific standards. The accrual accounting model is an example of a broad principle. Before addressing additional key broad principles, we look at some important assumptions that underlie those fundamental principles.

---

[29]"Recognition and Measurement in Financial Statements," *Statement of Financial Accounting Concepts No. 5* (Stamford, Conn.: FASB 1984), par. 63.

Underlying Assumptions

The four basic assumptions underlying GAAP are (1) the economic entity assumption, (2) the going concern assumption, (3) the periodicity assumption, and (4) the monetary unit assumption.

Economic Entity Assumption. An essential assumption is that all economic events can be identified with a particular economic entity. Investors desire information about an economic entity that corresponds to their ownership interest. For example, if you were considering buying some ownership stock in Federal Express, you would want information on the various operating units that constitute Federal Express. You would need information not only about their United States operations but also about their European and other international operations. Also, you would not want the information about Federal Express combined with that of United Parcel Service (UPS), another air freight company. These would be two separate *economic entities*. The financial information for the various companies (subsidiaries) in which Federal Express owns a controlling interest (greater than 50% ownership of voting stock) should be combined with that of Federal Express (the parent). The parent and its subsidiaries are separate *legal* entities but one *accounting* entity.

Another key aspect of this assumption is the distinction between the economic activities of owners and those of the company. For example, the economic activities of a sole proprietorship, Uncle Jim's Restaurant, should be separated from the activities of its owner, Uncle Jim. Uncle Jim's personal residence, for instance, is not an asset of the business.

Going Concern Assumption. Another necessary assumption is that, in the absence of information to the contrary, it is anticipated that a business entity will continue to operate indefinitely. Accountants realize that the **going concern assumption** does not always hold since there certainly are many

business failures. However, companies are begun with the hope of a long life, and many achieve that goal.

This assumption is critical to many broad and specific accounting principles. For example, the assumption provides justification for measuring many assets based on their historical costs. If it were known that an enterprise was going to cease operations in the near future, assets and liabilities would not be measured at their historical costs but at their current liquidation values. Similarly, depreciation of a building over an estimated life of 40 years presumes the business will operate that long.

Periodicity Assumption. The **periodicity assumption** relates to the qualitative characteristic of *timeliness*. External users need *periodic* information to make decisions. This need for periodic information requires that the economic life of an enterprise (presumed to be indefinite) be divided into artificial time periods for financial reporting. Corporations whose securities are publicly traded are required to provide financial information to the SEC on a quarterly and annual basis. Financial statements often are prepared on a monthly basis for banks and others that might need more timely information.

The annual time period (the fiscal year) used to report to external users for many companies is the calendar year. However, other companies have chosen a **fiscal year** that does not correspond to the calendar year. The accounting profession and the Securities and Exchange Commission advocate that companies adopt a fiscal year that corresponds to their natural business year. A natural business year is the 12-month period that ends when the business activities of a company reach their lowest point in the annual cycle. Many retailers, Wal-Mart for example, have adopted a fiscal year ending on January 31. Business activity in January generally is quite slow following the very busy Christmas period. We can see from the Federal Express financial statements that

the company's fiscal year ends on May 31. The Campbell Soup Company's fiscal year ends in July; Clorox's in June; Kmart's in January.

Monetary Unit Assumption. Recall that to *measure* financial statement elements, a unit or scale of measurement must be chosen. Information would be difficult to use if, for example, assets were listed as "three machines, two trucks, and a building." A common denominator is needed to measure all elements. The dollar in the United States is the most appropriate common denominator to express information about financial statement elements and changes in those elements.

One problem is that this monetary unit concept assumes that the monetary unit is stable over time. That is, the value of the dollar, in terms of its ability to purchase certain goods and services, is constant over time. This obviously does not strictly hold. The U.S. economy has experienced periods of rapidly changing prices. To the extent that prices are unstable, and those machines, trucks and building were purchased at different times, the monetary unit used to measure them is not the same. The effect of changing prices on financial information generally is discussed elsewhere in your accounting curriculum, often in an advanced accounting course.

Accounting Principles

Learning objective 8
Describe the four broad accounting principles that guide accounting practice.

Four key broad accounting principles guide accounting practice: (1) the historical cost principle, (2) the realization principle (also known as the revenue recognition principle), (3) the matching principle, and (4) the full-disclosure principle. These principles deal with the critical issues of recognition and measurement. The accrual accounting model is embodied in each of the principles.

The **historical cost principle** states that asset and liability measurements should be based on the amount given or received in the exchange transaction.

Historical Cost Principle.   The FASB recognized in *SFAC 5* that elements in financial statements currently are measured by different attributes. In general, however, GAAP measure assets and liabilities based on their *original transaction value*, that is, their **historical costs**. For an asset, this is the fair value of what is given in exchange (usually cash) for the asset at its initial acquisition. For liabilities, it is the current cash equivalent received in exchange for assuming the liability. For example, if a company borrowed $1 million cash and signed an interest-bearing note promising to repay the cash in the future, the liability would be valued at $1 million, the cash received in exchange.[30]

Historical cost measurement provides important cash flow information and also is highly verifiable.

Why base measurement on historical costs? After all, the current value of a company's manufacturing plant might seem more meaningful than its original cost. First, historical cost provides important cash flow information as it represents the cash or cash equivalent paid for an asset or received in exchange for the assumption of a liability. Second, because historical cost valuation is the result of an exchange transaction between two independent parties, the agreed on exchange value is objective and highly *verifiable*. Alternatives such as measuring an asset at its current market value involve *estimating* a selling price. An example given earlier in the chapter concerned the valuation of a parcel of land. Appraisers could easily differ in their assessment of current market value.

A departure from historical cost valuation sometimes is appropriate.

There are occasions where a departure from measuring an asset based on its historical cost is warranted. Some assets, for instance, are measured at their *net realizable value*. For example, if customers purchased goods or services on account for $10,000, the asset, accounts receivable, would initially be valued at $10,000, the original transaction value. Subsequently, if $2,000 in bad debts were anticipated, net receivables should be valued at $8,000, the net realizable value. Departures from historical cost measurement such as this provide more appropriate information in terms of the overall objective of providing information to aid in the prediction of future cash flows.

Revenue should be recognized when the earnings process is virtually complete and collection is reasonably assured.

Realization Principle.   Determining accounting income by the accrual accounting model is a challenging task. When to recognize revenue is critical to this determination. Revenues are inflows of assets resulting from providing a product or service to a customer. At what point is this event recognized by an increase in assets? The **realization principle** requires that two criteria be satisfied before revenue can be recognized:

1.   The earnings process is judged to be complete or virtually complete.
2.   There is reasonable certainty as to the collectibility of the asset to be received (usually cash).

Both revenue recognition criteria usually are met at the **point-of-sale**.

These criteria help ensure that a revenue event is not recorded until an enterprise has performed all or most of its earnings activities for a financially capable buyer. The primary earnings activity that triggers the recognition of revenue is known as the *critical event*. The critical event for many businesses occurs at the **point-of-sale**. This usually takes place when the goods or services sold to the buyer are *delivered* (i.e., title is transferred).

The *timing* of revenue recognition is a key element of earnings measurement. An income statement should report the results of all operating activities for the time period specified in the financial statements. A one-year income statement should report the company's accomplishments only for that one-year period. Revenue recognition criteria help ensure that a proper cut-off is made each reporting period and that exactly one year's activity is reported in that income statement. Not

---

[30]This current cash equivalent for many liabilities also will equal the present value of future cash payments. This is illustrated in a subsequent chapter.

adhering to revenue recognition criteria could result in overstating revenue and hence net income in one reporting period and, consequently, understating revenue and net income in a subsequent period. Notice that revenue recognition criteria allow for the implementation of the accrual accounting model. Revenue should be recognized in the period it is earned, *not necessarily in the period in which cash is received*.

Some revenue-producing activities call for revenue recognition at a time other than the point-of-sale. For example, revenue recognition could take place *during* the earnings process, such as with long-term construction contracts. This and other important exceptions to point-of-sale revenue recognition are discussed in Chapter 4. That chapter also describes in more detail the concept of an earnings process and how it relates to performance measurement.

Matching Principle.   When are expenses recognized? The **matching principle** states that expenses are recognized in the same period as the related revenues. There is a cause-and-effect relationship between revenue and expense recognition implicit in this definition. In a given period, revenue is recognized according to the realization principle. The matching principle then requires that all expenses incurred in generating that same revenue also be recognized. The net result is a measure—net income—that matches current period accomplishments and sacrifices. This accrual-based measure provides a good indicator of future cash-generating ability.

Although the concept is straightforward, its implementation can be difficult. The difficulty arises in trying to identify cause-and-effect relationships. Many expenses are not incurred *directly* because of a revenue event. Instead, the expense is incurred to generate the revenue, but the association is indirect.

The matching principle is implemented by one of four different approaches, depending on the nature of the specific expense. Only the first approach involves an actual cause-and-effect relationship between revenue and expense. In the other three approaches, the relationship is indirect.

An expense can be recognized:

1.   Based on an exact cause-and-effect relationship between a revenue and expense event.
2.   By associating an expense with the revenues recognized in a specific time period.
3.   By a systematic and rational allocation to specific time periods.
4.   In the period incurred, without regard to related revenues.

The first approach is appropriate for *cost of goods sold*. There is a definite cause-and-effect relationship between Dell Computer's revenue from the sale of personal computers and the costs to produce those computers. Commissions paid to salespersons for obtaining revenues also is an example of an expense recognized based on this approach.

Unfortunately, for most expenses there is no obvious cause-and-effect relationship between a revenue and expense event. In other words, the revenue event does not directly *cause* expenses to be incurred. Many expenses, however, can be related to periods of time during which revenue is earned. For example, the monthly salary paid to an office worker is not directly related to any specific revenue event. The employee provides services during the month. The asset used to pay the employee, cash, provides benefits to the company only for that one month and *indirectly* relates to the revenue recognized in that same period.

Some costs are incurred to acquire assets that provide benefits to the company for more than one reporting period. Refer again to the Carter Company example in Illustration 1–1 on page 7. At the beginning of year 1, $60,000 in rent was paid covering a three-year period. This asset, prepaid rent, helps generate revenues for more than one reporting period. In that example, we chose to "systematically and rationally" allocate rent expense equally to each of the three one-year periods rather than to charge the expense to year 1.

The fourth approach to expense recognition is called for in situations when costs are incurred but it is impossible to determine in which period or periods, if any, revenues will occur. For example, consider the cost of advertising. Advertising expenditures are made with the presumption that incurring that expense will generate incremental revenues. Let's say Federal Express spends $1 million for a series of television commercials. It's difficult to determine when, how much, or even whether additional revenues occur as a result of that particular series of ads. Because of this difficulty, advertising expenditures are recognized as expense in the period incurred, with no attempt made to match them with revenues.

> Any information useful to decision makers should be provided in the financial statements, subject to the cost effectiveness constraint.

The Full-Disclosure Principle.   Remember, the purpose of accounting is to provide information that is useful to decision makers. So, naturally, if there is accounting information not included in the primary financial statements that would benefit users, that information should be provided too. The **full-disclosure principle** means that the financial reports should include any information that could affect the decisions made by external users. Of course, the benefits of that information, as noted earlier, must exceed the costs of providing the information. Supplemental information is disclosed in a variety of ways, including:

1. **Parenthetical comments** or **modifying comments** placed on the face of the financial statements.
2. **Disclosure notes** conveying additional insights about company operations, accounting principles, contractual agreements, and pending litigation.
3. **Supplemental financial statements** that report more detailed information than is shown in the primary financial statements.

Federal Express Corporation

We find examples of these disclosures in the Federal Express financial statements in the appendix. A parenthetical or modifying comment is provided in the common stockholders' investment section of the balance sheet with disclosure of the number of shares of stock authorized, issued, and outstanding. The statements include several notes as well as a supplemental statement disclosing information about the company's quarterly operating results. We discuss and illustrate disclosure requirements as they relate to specific financial statement elements in later chapters as those elements are discussed.

Graphic 1–7 provides a summary of the accounting assumptions and principles that guide the recognition and measurement of accounting information.

GRAPHIC   1–7

Summary of Recognition and Measurement Concepts

Assumptions	Description
Economic entity	All economic events can be identified with a particular economic entity.
Going concern	In the absence of information to the contrary, it is anticipated that a business entity will continue to operate indefinitely.
Periodicity	The life of a company can be divided into artificial time periods to provide timely information to external users.
Monetary unit	In the United States, financial statement elements should be measured in terms of the U.S. dollar.
Principles	
Historical cost	Asset and liability measurements should be based on the amount given or received in an exchange transaction.
Realization	Revenue should be recognized only after the earnings process is virtually complete and there is reasonable certainty of collecting the asset to be received from the customer.
Matching	Expenses should be recognized in the same reporting period as the related revenues.
Full disclosure	Any information that could change the decisions made by external users should be provided in the financial statements, subject to the cost effectiveness constraint.

Ethics in Accounting

> **Ethics** deals with the ability to distinguish right from wrong.

Ethics is a term that refers to a code or moral system that provides criteria for evaluating right and wrong. Ethical dilemmas are situations where an individual or group is faced with a decision that tests this code. Many of these dilemmas are simple to recognize and resolve. For example, have you ever been tempted to call your professor and ask for an extension on the due date of an assignment by claiming a fictitious illness? Temptation like this will test your personal ethics.

Accountants, like others operating in the business world, are faced with many ethical dilemmas, some of which are complex and difficult to resolve. For instance, the capital markets' focus on periodic profits may tempt a company's management to bend or even break accounting rules to inflate reported net income. In these situations, technical competence is not enough to resolve the dilemma.

Ethics and Professionalism

One of the elements that many believe distinguishes a profession from other occupations is the acceptance by its members of a responsibility for the interests of those it serves. A high standard of ethical behavior is expected of those engaged in a profession. These standards often are articulated in a code of ethics. For example, law and medicine are professions that have their own codes of professional ethics. These codes provide guidance and rules to members in the performance of their professional responsibilities.

Public accounting has achieved widespread recognition as a profession. The AICPA, the national organization of certified professional public accountants, has its own Code of Professional Conduct which prescribes the ethical conduct members should strive to achieve. Similarly, the **Institute of Management Accountants (IMA)**—the primary national organization of accountants working in industry and government—has its own code of ethics, as does the **Institute of Internal Auditors**—the national organization of accountants providing internal auditing services for their own organizations.

Analytical Model for Ethical Decisions

Ethical codes are informative and helpful. However, the motivation to behave ethically must come from within oneself and not just from the fear of penalties for violating professional codes. Presented below is a sequence of steps that provide a framework for analyzing ethical issues. These steps can help you apply your own sense of right and wrong to ethical dilemmas:[31]

Step 1. Determine the facts of the situation. This involves determining the who, what, where, when, and how.

Step 2. Identify the ethical issue and the stakeholders. Stakeholders may include shareholders, creditors, management, employees, and the community.

Step 3. Identify the values related to the situation. For example, in some situations confidentiality may be an important value that may conflict with the right to know.

Step 4. Specify the alternative courses of action.

Step 5. Evaluate the courses of action specified in step 4 in terms of their consistency with the values identified in step 3. This step may or may not lead to a suggested course of action.

Step 6. Identify the consequences of each possible course of action. If step 5 does not provide a course of action, assess the consequences of each possible course of action for all of the stakeholders involved.

Step 7. Make your decision and take any indicated action.

Ethical dilemmas, designated by the symbol , are presented throughout the text. These dilemmas are designed to raise your consciousness on accounting issues with ethical ramifications. The analytical steps outlined above provide a framework with which to evaluate these situations. In addition, your instructor may assign end-of-chapter ethics cases for further discussion and application.

ETHICAL DILEMMA

You have recently been employed by a large retail chain that sells sporting goods. One of your tasks is to help prepare periodic financial statements for external distribution. The chain's largest creditor, National Savings & Loan, requires quarterly financial statements, and you are currently working on the statements for the three-month period ending June 30, 1997.

During the months of May and June, the company spent $1,200,000 on a large radio and TV advertising campaign. The $1,200,000 included the costs of producing the commercials as well as the radio and TV time purchased to run the commercials. All of the costs were charged to advertising expense. The company's chief financial officer (CFO) has asked you to prepare a June 30 adjusting entry to remove the costs from advertising expense and to set up an asset called *prepaid advertising* that will be expensed in July. The CFO explained that "This advertising campaign has produced significant sales in May and June and I think it will continue to bring in customers through the month of July. By recording the ad costs as an asset, we can match the cost of the advertising with the additional July sales. Besides, if we expense the advertising in May and June, we will show an operating loss on our income statement for the quarter. The bank requires that we continue to show quarterly profits in order to maintain our loan in good standing."

[31]Adapted from Harold Q. Langenderfer and Joanne W. Rockness, "Integrating Ethics into the Accounting Curriculum: Issues, Problems, and Solutions," *Issues in Accounting Education* (Spring 1989). These steps are consistent with those provided by the American Accounting Association's Advisory Committee on Professionalism and Ethics in their publication *Ethics in the Accounting Curriculum: Cases and Readings, 1990.*

Solution to Financial Reporting Case (at the opening of the chapter)

1. What should you tell your friend about the presence of accounting standards in the United States? Who has the authority for standard setting? Who has the responsibility?

In the United States we have a set of standards known as generally accepted accounting principles. GAAP are a dynamic set of both broad and specific guidelines that companies should follow when measuring and reporting the information in their financial statements and related notes. The Securities and Exchange Commission has the authority to set accounting standards for companies but always has delegated the responsibility to the accounting profession. At present, the Financial Accounting Standards Board is the private sector body responsible for standard setting.

2. What is the economic and political environment in which standard setting occurs?

The setting of accounting and reporting standards often has been characterized as a *political process*. Standards, particularly changes in standards, can have significant differential effects on companies, investors and creditors, and other interest groups. A change in an accounting standard or the introduction of a new standard can result in a substantial redistribution of wealth within our economy. The FASB must consider potential economic consequences of a change in an accounting standard or the introduction of a new standard.

3. What is the relationship among management, auditors, investors, and creditors that tends to preclude the "What would you like it to be?" attitude?

It is the responsibility of management to apply accounting standards when communicating with investors and creditors through financial statements. Auditors serve as independent intermediaries to help ensure that the management-prepared statements are presented fairly in accordance with GAAP. In providing this assurance, the auditor precludes the "What would you like it to be?" attitude.

4. In general, what is the conceptual framework that underlies accounting principles?

The conceptual framework is a coherent system of interrelated objectives and fundamentals that can lead to consistent standards and that prescribe the nature, function, and limits of financial accounting and reporting. The fundamentals are the underlying concepts of accounting, concepts that guide the selection of events to be accounted for, the measurement of those events, and the means of summarizing and communicating them to interested parties.

▌ The Bottom Line

1.   Financial accounting is concerned with providing relevant financial information to various external users. However, the primary focus is on the financial information provided by profit-oriented companies to their present and potential investors and creditors.

2.   Cash basis accounting provides a measure of periodic performance called net operating cash flow, which is the difference between cash receipts and cash disbursements from transactions related to providing goods and services to customers. Accrual accounting provides a measure of performance called net income, which is the difference between revenues and expenses. Periodic net income is considered a better indicator of future operating cash flows than is current net operating cash flows.

3.   Generally accepted accounting principles (GAAP) comprise a dynamic set of both broad and specific guidelines that companies follow when measuring and reporting the information in their financial statements and related notes. The Securities and Exchange Commission (SEC) has both the authority and responsibility to set accounting standards. However, the SEC has always delegated the responsibility to a private sector body, at this time the Financial Accounting Standards Board (FASB).

4.   Accounting standards can have significant differential effects on companies, investors, creditors, and other interest groups. For this reason, the setting of accounting standards often has been characterized as a political process.

5.   The FASB's conceptual framework is a set of cohesive objectives and fundamental concepts on which financial accounting and reporting is based.

6.   The objectives of financial reporting are concerned with providing information to help investors and creditors predict future cash flows. The primary decision-specific qualities that make accounting information useful are relevance and reliability. To be relevant, information must possess predictive value and/or feedback value and must be provided in a timely manner. The characteristics of reliable information are verifiability, representational faithfulness, and neutrality. The 10 elements of financial statements are assets, liabilities, equity, investments by owners, distributions to owners, revenues, expenses, gains, losses, and comprehensive income.

7.   The four basic assumptions underlying GAAP are (1) the economic entity assumption, (2) the going concern assumption, (3) the periodicity assumption, and (4) the monetary unit assumption.

8.   The four broad accounting principles that guide accounting practice are (1) the historical cost principle, (2) the realization principle, (3) the matching principle, and (4) the full-disclosure principle.

FEDERAL EXPRESS CORPORATION
FINANCIAL STATEMENTS

Consolidated Statements of Income			Federal Express Corporation and Subsidiaries
Years ended May 31			
In thousands, except Earnings Per Share	1996	1995	1994
➡ **Revenues**	$10,273,619	$9,392,073	$8,479,456
Operating Expenses:			
Salaries and employee benefits (Notes 8 and 9)	4,619,990	4,425,202	4,104,800
Rentals and landing fees (Note 4)	959,055	818,599	703,028
Depreciation and amortization	719,609	652,287	599,357
Fuel	578,614	502,417	472,786
Maintenance and repairs	617,657	544,170	464,557
Other	2,154,870	1,858,254	1,604,296
	9,649,795	8,800,929	7,948,824
➡ **Operating Income**	623,824	591,144	530,632
Other Income (Expense):			
Interest, net (Note 1)	(95,599)	(114,687)	(142,392)
Other, net (Note 14)	11,734	45,627	(9,778)
	(83,865)	(69,060)	(152,170)
Income before Income Taxes	539,959	522,084	378,462
Provision for Income Taxes (Note 7)	232,182	224,496	174,092
➡ **Net Income**	$ 307,777	$ 297,588	$ 204,370
➡ **Earnings Per Share** (Note 6)	$ 5.39	$ 5.27	$ 3.65
➡ **Average Shares Outstanding** (Note 6)	57,138	56,494	56,012
The accompanying Notes to Consolidated Financial Statements are an integral part of these statements.			

Consolidated Balance Sheets

May 31

In thousands	1996	1995
→ **Assets**		
Current Assets:		
Cash and cash equivalents	$ 93,419	$ 357,548
Receivables, less allowance for doubtful accounts of $30,809 and $31,173	1,271,599	1,130,254
Spare parts, supplies and fuel	222,110	193,251
Deferred income taxes (Note 7)	92,606	115,801
Prepaid expenses and other	48,527	72,228
Total current assets	1,728,261	1,869,082
Property and Equipment, at Cost (Notes 1, 3, 4 and 12):		
Flight equipment	3,372,647	3,006,693
Package handling and ground support equipment	2,148,509	1,841,108
Computer and electronic equipment	1,439,883	1,224,050
Other	1,717,478	1,625,860
	8,678,517	7,697,711
Less accumulated depreciation and amortization	4,561,916	3,982,467
Net property and equipment	4,116,601	3,715,244
Other Assets:		
Goodwill (Note 1)	380,748	397,272
Equipment deposits and other assets (Note 12)	473,361	451,774
Total other assets	854,109	849,046
	$6,698,971	$6,433,372

The accompanying Notes to Consolidated Financial Statements are an integral part of these balance sheets.

Federal Express Corporation and Subsidiaries

	1996	1995
→ **Liabilities and Stockholders' Investment**		
Current Liabilities:		
Current portion of long-term debt (Note 3)	$ 8,009	$ 255,448
Accounts payable	705,532	618,621
Accrued expenses (Note 2)	904,856	904,466
Total current liabilities	1,618,397	1,778,535
Long-Term Debt, Less Current Portion (Note 3)	1,325,277	1,324,711
Deferred Income Taxes (Note 7)	64,034	55,956
Other Liabilities (Note 1)	1,115,124	1,028,601
Commitments and Contingencies (Notes 4, 12 and 13)		
Common Stockholders' Investment (Note 6):		
Common Stock, $.10 par value; 200,000 shares authorized;		
56,885 and 56,174 shares issued	5,689	5,617
Additional paid-in capital	815,137	775,255
Retained earnings	1,766,578	1,466,427
	2,587,404	2,247,299
Less treasury stock and deferred compensation	11,265	1,730
Total common stockholders' investment	2,576,139	2,245,569
	$6,698,971	$6,433,372

Consolidated Statements of Cash Flows   Federal Express Corporation and Subsidiaries

Years ended May 31

In thousands	1996	1995	1994
➡ Operating Activities			
Net income	$ 307,777	$ 297,588	$ 204,370
Adjustments to reconcile net income to cash			
provided by operating activities:			
Depreciation and amortization	719,609	652,287	599,357
Provision for uncollectible accounts	38,963	36,334	45,763
Provision for deferred income taxes and other	26,489	25,976	3,810
Gain from disposals of property and equipment	(5,397)	(39,997)	(11,897)
Changes in assets and liabilities, net of effects			
from dispositions of businesses:			
Increase in receivables	(191,334)	(167,319)	(173,902)
Increase in other current assets	(41,992)	(24,101)	(7,826)
Increase in accounts payable, accrued			
expenses and other liabilities	100,515	258,373	110,508
Other, net	(8,050)	(8,424)	(2,905)
Cash provided by operating activities	946,580	1,030,717	767,278
➡ Investing Activities			
Purchases of property and equipment, including deposits			
on aircraft of $68,202, $113,073 and $112,138	(1,412,242)	(1,060,761)	(1,087,708)
Proceeds from dispositions of property and equipment:			
Sale-leaseback transactions	176,500	—	581,400
Reimbursements of A300 deposits	143,859	138,203	38,794
Other dispositions	26,504	59,523	46,148
Other, net	77,208	87,925	27,843
Cash used in investing activities	(988,171)	(775,110)	(393,523)
➡ Financing Activities			
Proceeds from debt issuances	17,298	45,460	10,777
Principal payments on debt	(264,004)	(349,523)	(198,243)
Proceeds from stock issuances	36,566	13,081	53,759
Other, net	(12,398)	—	(2,581)
Cash used in financing activities	(222,538)	(290,982)	(136,288)
➡ Cash and Cash Equivalents			
Increase (decrease) during the year	(264,129)	(35,375)	237,467
Balance at beginning of year	357,548	392,923	155,456
Balance at end of year	$ 93,419	$ 357,548	$ 392,923

The accompanying Notes to Consolidated Financial Statements are an integral part of these statements.

Consolidated Statements of Changes in Common Stockholders' Investment				Federal Express Corporation and Subsidiaries	

In thousands, except shares	Common Stock	Additional Paid-in Capital	Retained Earnings	Treasury Stock	Deferred Compensation
➡ **Balance at May 31, 1993**	$5,474	$699,385	$ 969,515	$ (36)	$ (2,957)
Purchase of treasury stock	—	—	—	(185)	—
Forfeiture of restricted stock	—	—	—	(1,224)	—
Issuance of common and treasury stock under employee incentive plans (1,153,248 shares)	115	59,844	—	670	(8)
Amortization of deferred compensation	—	—	—	—	1,467
Foreign currency translation adjustment	—	—	(11,725)	—	—
Net income	—	—	204,370	—	—
➡ **Balance at May 31, 1994**	5,589	759,229	1,162,160	(775)	(1,498)
Forfeiture of restricted stock	—	—	—	(231)	—
Issuance of common stock under employee incentive plans (288,724 shares)	28	16,026	—	—	—
Amortization of deferred compensation	—	—	—	—	774
Foreign currency translation adjustment	—	—	6,679	—	—
Net income	—	—	297,588	—	—
➡ **Balance at May 31, 1995**	5,617	775,255	1,466,427	(1,006)	(724)
Purchase of treasury stock	—	—	—	(12,398)	—
Forfeiture of restricted stock	—	—	—	(1,068)	1,130
Issuance of common and treasury stock under employee incentive plans (886,195 shares)	72	39,882	—	14,472	(13,898)
Amortization of deferred compensation	—	—	—	—	2,227
Foreign currency translation adjustment	—	—	(7,626)	—	—
Net income	—	—	307,777	—	—
➡ **Balance at May 31, 1996**	$5,689	$815,137	$1,766,578	$ —	$(11,265)

The accompanying Notes to Consolidated Financial Statements are an integral part of these statements.

Notes to Consolidated Financial Statements

➡ **Note 1: Summary of Significant Accounting Policies**

Principles of consolidation. The consolidated financial statements include the accounts of Federal Express Corporation and its wholly-owned subsidiaries (the "Company"). All significant intercompany accounts and transactions have been eliminated.

Property and equipment. Expenditures for major additions, improvements, flight equipment modifications, and certain overhaul costs are capitalized. Maintenance and repairs are charged to expense as incurred, except for B747 airframe and engine overhaul maintenance which is accrued and charged to expense on the basis of hours flown. The cost and accumulated depreciation of property and equipment disposed of are removed from the related accounts, and any gain or loss is reflected in the results of operations.

For financial reporting purposes, depreciation and amortization of property and equipment is provided on a straight-line basis over the asset's service life or related lease term as follows:

Flight equipment	7 to 20 years
Package handling and ground support equipment	5 to 30 years
Computer and electronic equipment	3 to 10 years
Other	2 to 30 years

Aircraft airframes and engines are assigned residual values ranging from 10% to 20% of asset cost. All other property and equipment have no assigned residual values. Vehicles, which are included in package handling and ground support equipment, are depreciated on a straight-line basis over 5 to 10 years.

For income tax purposes, depreciation is generally computed using accelerated methods.

Deferred gains. Gains on the sale and leaseback of aircraft and other property and equipment are deferred and amortized over the life of the lease as a reduction of rent expense. Included in other liabilities at May 31, 1996 and 1995, were deferred gains of $337,118,000 and $293,000,000, respectively.

Deferred lease obligations. While certain of the Company's aircraft and facility leases contain fluctuating or escalating payments, the related rent expense is recorded on a straight-line basis over the lease term. Included in other liabilities at May 31, 1996 and 1995, were $260,977,000 and $216,683,000, respectively, representing the cumulative difference between rent expense and rent payments.

Self-insurance reserves. The Company is self-insured up to certain levels for workers' compensation, employee health care and vehicle liabilities. Reserves are based on the actuarially estimated cost of claims. Included in other liabilities at May 31, 1996 and 1995, were $278,000,000 and $294,000,000, respectively, representing self-insurance reserves for the Company's workers' compensation and vehicle liabilities.

Capitalized interest. Interest on funds used to finance the acquisition and modification of aircraft and construction of certain facilities up to the date the asset is placed in service is capitalized and included in the cost of the asset. Capitalized interest was $39,254,000, $27,381,000 and $29,738,000 for 1996, 1995 and 1994, respectively.

Advertising. Advertising costs are generally expensed as incurred and are included in other operating expenses. Advertising expenses were $138,408,000, $147,288,000 and $122,002,000 in 1996, 1995 and 1994, respectively.

Cash equivalents. Cash equivalents are cash in excess of current operating requirements invested in short-term, interest-bearing instruments with maturities of three months or less at the date of purchase and are stated at cost, which approximates market value. Interest income was $9,850,000 in 1996, $16,236,000 in 1995 and $9,778,000 in 1994.

Spare parts, supplies and fuel. Spare parts, supplies and fuel are stated principally at standard cost (approximates actual cost on a first-in, first-out basis) which is not in excess of current replacement cost.

Goodwill. Goodwill is the excess of the purchase price over the fair value of net assets of businesses acquired. It is amortized on a straight-line basis over periods ranging up to 40 years. Accumulated amortization was $114,606,000 and $100,527,000 at May 31, 1996 and 1995, respectively.

Foreign currency translation. Translation gains and losses of the Company's foreign operations that use local currencies as the functional currency are accumulated and reported as a separate component of common stockholders' investment. Transaction gains and losses that arise from exchange rate fluctuations on transactions denominated in a currency other than the local functional currency are included in the results of operations.

Income taxes. Deferred income taxes are provided for the tax effect of temporary differences between the tax basis of assets and liabilities and their reported amounts in the financial statements. The Company uses the liability method to account for income taxes, which requires deferred taxes to be recorded at the statutory rate expected to be in effect when the taxes are paid.

   The Company has not provided for U.S. federal income taxes on its foreign subsidiaries' earnings deemed to be permanently reinvested. Quantification of the deferred tax liability, if any, associated with permanently reinvested earnings is not practicable.

Revenue recognition. Revenue is generally recognized upon delivery of shipments. For shipments in transit, revenue is recorded based on the percentage of service completed.

Earnings per share. Earnings per share is computed based on the weighted average number of common and common equivalent shares outstanding during the period. Common equivalent shares are the shares of common stock that would be issued upon the exercise of all dilutive outstanding stock options, less the assumed repurchase of treasury shares. Earnings per share assuming full dilution is substantially the same as earnings per share as stated and, accordingly, is not shown separately.

Recent pronouncements. During 1997, the Company will adopt the provisions of two Statements of Financial Accounting Standards ("SFAS") recently issued by the Financial Accounting Standards Board. SFAS 121, "Accounting for the Impairment of Long-Lived Assets and for Long-Lived Assets to Be Disposed Of," requires that long-lived assets and certain identifiable intangibles be reviewed periodically for impairment. The Company does not expect the adoption of SFAS 121 to have a material effect on its financial statements.

   SFAS 123, "Accounting for Stock-Based Compensation," defines a fair-value based method of measuring and recording compensation costs for employee stock compensation programs. This new standard, however, permits companies to follow the intrinsic-value based method presently required by Accounting Principles Board Opinion No. 25, as long as they also provide pro forma footnote disclosure of the effect that the fair-value based method would have had on net income and earnings per share had that method been adopted. Management intends to adopt the pro forma disclosure alternative beginning in 1997.

Reclassifications. Certain amounts for 1995 and 1994 have been reclassified to conform to the 1996 presentation.

Use of estimates. The preparation of the consolidated financial statements in conformity with generally accepted accounting principles requires management to make estimates and assumptions that affect the reported amounts of assets and liabilities and disclosure of contingent assets and liabilities at the date of the financial statements and the reported amounts of revenues and expenses during the reporting period. Actual results could differ from those estimates.

Notes to Consolidated Financial Statements

➜ Note 2: Accrued Expenses

May 31

In thousands	1996	1995
Compensated absences	$211,499	$192,785
Insurance	194,209	176,806
Taxes other than income taxes	153,905	137,037
Employee benefits	111,912	127,870
Salaries	78,384	100,024
Aircraft overhaul	59,343	53,540
Other	95,604	116,404
	$904,856	$904,466

➜ Note 3: Long-Term Debt

May 31

In thousands	1996	1995
Unsecured notes payable, interest rates of 6.25% to 10.57%, due through 2013	$ 934,181	$1,187,413
Unsecured sinking fund debentures, interest rate of 9.63%, due through 2020	98,392	98,323
Capital lease obligations and tax exempt bonds, due through 2017, interest rates of 6.75% to 8.30%	255,100	255,100
Less bond reserves	11,096	11,096
	244,004	244,004
Other debt, interest rates of 9.68% to 9.98%	56,709	50,419
	1,333,286	1,580,159
Less current portion	8,009	255,448
	$1,325,277	$1,324,711

The Company has a revolving credit agreement with domestic and foreign banks that provides for a commitment of $1,000,000,000 through May 31, 2000, all of which was available at May 31, 1996. Interest rates on borrowings under this agreement are generally determined by maturities selected and prevailing market conditions. The agreement contains certain covenants and restrictions, none of which are expected to significantly affect operations or the ability to pay dividends. As of May 31, 1996, approximately $957,000,000 was available for the payment of dividends. Commercial paper borrowings are backed by unused commitments under the revolving credit agreement and reduce the amount available under the agreement.

Tax exempt bonds were issued by the Memphis-Shelby County Airport Authority ("MSCAA") and the City of Indianapolis. A lease agreement with the MSCAA and a loan agreement with the City of Indianapolis covering the facilities and equipment financed with the bond proceeds obligate the Company to pay rentals and loan payments, respectively, equal to principal and interest due on the bonds.

Scheduled annual principal maturities of long-term debt for the five years subsequent to May 31, 1996, are as follows: $8,000,000 in 1997; $126,700,000 in 1998; $265,500,000 in 1999; $14,900,000 in 2000; and $11,300,000 in 2001.

The Company's long-term debt, exclusive of capital leases, had carrying values of $1,130,000,000 and $1,390,000,000 at May 31, 1996 and 1995, respectively, compared with fair values of approximately $1,245,000,000 and $1,470,000,000 at those dates. The estimated fair values were determined based on quoted market prices or on the current rates offered for debt with similar terms and maturities.

Federal Express Corporation and Subsidiaries

→ **Note 4: Lease Commitments**

The Company utilizes certain aircraft, land, facilities and equipment under capital and operating leases which expire at various dates through 2024. In addition, supplemental aircraft are leased under agreements which generally provide for cancellation upon 30 days' notice.

Property and equipment recorded under capital leases at May 31 was as follows:

In thousands	1996	1995
Package handling and ground support equipment	$346,479	$378,438
Facilities	133,435	133,435
Computer and electronic equipment and other	7,143	7,175
	487,057	519,048
Less accumulated amortization	329,678	347,738
	$157,379	$171,310

Rent expense under operating leases for the years ended May 31 was as follows:

In thousands	1996	1995	1994
Minimum rentals	$820,896	$707,182	$621,174
Contingent rentals	61,164	43,005	21,540
	$882,060	$750,187	$642,714

Contingent rentals are based on mileage under supplemental aircraft leases.

A summary of future minimum lease payments under capital leases and non-cancelable operating leases (principally aircraft and facilities) with an initial or remaining term in excess of one year at May 31, 1996, follows:

In thousands	Capital Leases	Operating Leases
1997	$ 15,561	$ 724,161
1998	15,561	732,675
1999	15,561	715,247
2000	15,561	671,798
2001	15,561	638,510
Thereafter	356,085	7,634,161
	$433,890	$11,116,552

At May 31, 1996, the present value of future minimum lease payments for capital lease obligations was $199,004,000.

→ **Note 5: Preferred Stock**

The Certificate of Incorporation authorizes the Board of Directors, at its discretion, to issue up to 4,000,000 shares of Series Preferred Stock. The stock is issuable in series which may vary as to certain rights and preferences and has no par value. As of May 31, 1996, none of these shares had been issued.

Notes to Consolidated Financial Statements

→ **Note 6: Common Stockholders' Investment**

Under the provisions of the Company's stock incentive plans, options may be granted to certain key employees (and, under the 1993 plan, to directors who are not employees of the Company) to purchase common stock of the Company at a price not less than its fair market value at the date of grant. The following summarizes information for the past three years with respect to those plans:

	Number of Shares Under Option	Option Price Per Share
Outstanding at May 31, 1993	3,147,043	$30.56–$70.19
Granted	982,750	54.31– 70.81
Exercised	(1,142,249)	30.56– 70.19
Canceled	(111,758)	34.31– 62.94
Outstanding at May 31, 1994	2,875,786	$30.56–$70.81
Granted	671,800	56.13– 75.88
Exercised	(288,724)	30.56– 62.94
Canceled	(89,997)	30.56– 75.88
Outstanding at May 31, 1995	3,168,865	$30.56–$75.88
Granted	909,000	59.13– 82.31
Exercised	(710,945)	30.56– 75.88
Canceled	(167,640)	34.50– 82.31
Outstanding at May 31, 1996	3,199,280	$30.56–$82.31
Exercisable at May 31, 1996	1,226,400	$30.56–$75.88

At May 31, 1996, 942,731 shares were available for future grants under the above-mentioned stock incentive plans.

Under the terms of the Company's restricted stock plans, shares of the Company's common stock may be awarded to key employees. Restrictions on the shares expire over a period of one to ten years from the date of award. The value of shares awarded under these plans is recorded as a reduction of common stockholders' investment and is being amortized to compensation expense as restrictions on such shares expire. Shares awarded under the plans totaled 175,250 in 1996 and 11,000 in 1994. No shares were awarded in 1995. During 1996, 1995 and 1994, 14,500, 3,750 and 18,438 shares, respectively, were forfeited. At May 31, 1996, 128,938 shares were available for future awards.

At May 31, 1996, there were 4,270,949 shares of common stock reserved for issuance under the above-mentioned plans.

In 1988, the Board of Directors authorized the purchase of up to approximately 5,300,000 shares of the Company's common stock on the open market. As of May 31, 1996, a total of 2,911,305 shares at an average cost of $43.85 per share had been purchased and reissued under the above-mentioned plans.

Federal Express Corporation and Subsidiaries

➡ **Note 7: Income Taxes**

The components of the provision for income taxes for the years ended May 31 were as follows:

In thousands	1996	1995	1994
Current provision:			
Federal	$142,512	$137,041	$131,724
Foreign	37,759	29,787	16,387
State	18,007	23,405	26,862
	198,278	190,233	174,973
Deferred provision (credit):			
Federal	27,962	24,058	2,263
Foreign	2,351	9,072	2,524
State	3,591	1,133	(5,668)
	33,904	34,263	(881)
	$232,182	$224,496	$174,092

The Company's operations included the following income (loss) with respect to entities in foreign locations for the years ended May 31:

In thousands	1996	1995	1994
Entities with pre-tax income	$ 153,000	$ 149,000	$ 127,000
Entities with pre-tax losses	(228,000)	(173,000)	(210,000)
	$ (75,000)	$ (24,000)	$ (83,000)

Income (losses) from entities which are structured as foreign subsidiaries are not included in the U.S. consolidated income tax return. Approximately $60,000,000, $29,000,000 and $14,000,000 of net foreign subsidiary income were not taxable for federal income tax purposes in 1996, 1995 and 1994, respectively. Income taxes have been provided for foreign operations based upon the various tax laws and rates of the countries in which the Company's operations are conducted. There is no direct relationship between the Company's overall foreign income tax provision and foreign pre-tax book income due to the different methods of taxation used by countries throughout the world.

A reconciliation of the statutory federal income tax rate to the Company's effective income tax rate for the years ended May 31 follows:

	1996	1995	1994
Statutory U.S. income tax rate	35.0%	35.0%	35.0%
Increase resulting from:			
Goodwill amortization	0.9	1.0	1.3
Foreign operations	1.7	0.9	3.5
State income taxes, net of federal benefit	2.6	3.1	3.6
Other, net	2.8	3.0	2.6
	43.0%	43.0%	46.0%

Notes to Consolidated Financial Statements

The significant components of deferred tax assets and liabilities as of May 31 were as follows:

In thousands	1996		1995	
	Deferred Tax Assets	Deferred Tax Liabilities	Deferred Tax Assets	Deferred Tax Liabilities
Depreciation	$ —	$324,221	$ —	$303,088
Deferred gains on sales of assets	81,370	—	67,912	—
Employee benefits	45,137	—	69,563	—
Self-insurance reserves	165,020	—	165,197	—
Other	151,355	90,089	137,063	76,802
	$442,882	$414,310	$439,735	$379,890

➡ **Note 8: Pension and Profit Sharing Plans**

The Company sponsors pension plans covering substantially all employees. The largest plan covers U.S. domestic employees age 21 and over, with at least one year of service, and provides benefits based on final average earnings and years of service. Plan funding is actuarially determined, subject to certain tax law limitations.

International defined benefit plans provide benefits primarily based on final earnings and years of service and are funded in accordance with local laws and income tax regulations.

The following table sets forth the funded status of the plans as of May 31:

In thousands	1996	1995
Plan assets at fair value	$2,725,896	$2,093,422
Actuarial present value of the projected benefit obligation for service rendered to date	2,571,086	1,972,009
Plan assets in excess of projected benefit obligation	154,810	121,413
Unrecognized net gains from past experience different from that assumed and effects of changes in assumptions	(74,425)	(123,929)
Prior service cost not yet recognized in net periodic cost	(7,398)	(6,449)
Unrecognized transition amount	3,239	3,679
Pension asset (liability)	$ 76,226	$ (5,286)
Accumulated benefit obligation	$1,626,877	$1,203,126
Vested benefit obligation	$1,538,267	$1,140,545

| | | Federal Express Corporation and Subsidiaries | |

Net periodic pension cost for the years ended May 31 included the following components:

In thousands	1996	1995	1994
Service cost — benefits earned during the period	$ 184,305	$ 182,617	$176,861
Interest cost on projected benefit obligation	165,635	143,408	127,959
Actual return on plan assets	(463,819)	(192,939)	(82,019)
Net amortization and deferral	256,968	19,333	(64,727)
	$ 143,089	$ 152,419	$158,074

The weighted-average discount rate and rate of increase in future compensation levels used in determining the actuarial present value of the projected benefit obligation were 8.0% and 5.5%, respectively, in 1996, 8.6% and 6.0%, respectively, in 1995 and 8.1% and 6.0%, respectively, in 1994. The expected long-term rate of return on assets was 9.5% in 1996, 1995 and 1994. Plan assets consist primarily of marketable equity securities and fixed income instruments.

The Company also has a profit sharing plan, which covers substantially all U.S. domestic employees age 21 and over, with at least one year of service with the Company as of the contribution date, as defined in the plan. The plan provides for discretionary contributions by the Company which are determined annually by the Board of Directors. Profit sharing expense was $54,000,000 in 1996, $52,200,000 in 1995 and $36,800,000 in 1994.

→ **Note 9: Postretirement Benefit Plans**

The Company offers medical and dental coverage to all eligible U.S. domestic retirees and their eligible dependents. Vision coverage is provided for retirees only. Substantially all of the Company's U.S. domestic employees become eligible for these benefits at age 55 and older, if they have permanent, continuous service with the Company of at least 10 years after attainment of age 45 if hired prior to January 1, 1988, or at least 20 years after attainment of age 35, if hired on or after January 1, 1988. Life insurance benefits are provided to retirees of the former Tiger International, Inc. who retired prior to acquisition.

The following table sets forth accrued postretirement benefit cost as of May 31:

In thousands	1996	1995
Accumulated postretirement benefit obligation:		
Retirees	$ 39,539	$ 35,816
Fully eligible active employees	31,472	24,400
Other active employees, not fully eligible	80,001	60,769
	151,012	120,985
Unrecognized net gain	15,402	25,421
	$166,414	$146,406

Net postretirement benefit cost for the years ended May 31 was as follows:

In thousands	1996	1995	1994
Service cost	$12,085	$12,870	$12,392
Interest cost	11,275	10,617	10,174
Amortization of accumulated gains	(780)	—	—
	$22,580	$23,487	$22,566

Notes to Consolidated Financial Statements

Future medical benefit costs were estimated to increase at an annual rate of 10.5% during 1997, decreasing to an annual growth rate of 5.5% in 2007 and thereafter. Future dental benefit costs were estimated to increase at an annual rate of 8.5% during 1997, decreasing to an annual growth rate of 5.5% in 2009 and thereafter. The Company's cost is capped at 150% of 1993 employer cost and, therefore, will not be subject to medical and dental trends after the capped cost is attained, projected to be in 1999. Primarily because of the cap on the Company's cost, a 1% increase in these annual trend rates would not have a significant impact on the accumulated postretirement benefit obligation at May 31, 1996, or 1996 benefit expense. The weighted average discount rates used in estimating the accumulated postretirement obligation were 7.4% and 8.6% at May 31, 1996 and 1995, respectively. The Company pays claims as incurred.

➜ **Note 10: Business Segment Information**

The Company is in a single line of business — the worldwide transportation and distribution of documents, packages and freight. For reporting purposes, operations are classified into two geographic areas, U.S. domestic and international. Shipments which either originate in or are destined to locations outside the U.S. are categorized as international.

A summary of selected financial information for U.S. domestic and international operations for the years ended May 31 follows:

In thousands	U.S. Domestic	International	Total Worldwide
Revenues:			
1996	$7,466,311	$2,807,308	$10,273,619
1995	6,839,418	2,552,655	9,392,073
1994	6,199,940	2,279,516	8,479,456
Operating Income (Loss):			
1996	$ 542,168	$ 81,656	$ 623,824
1995	465,527	125,617	591,144
1994	559,629	(28,997)	530,632
Identifiable Assets:			
1996	$5,449,353	$1,249,618	$ 6,698,971
1995	5,321,811	1,111,561	6,433,372
1994	4,883,644	1,108,854	5,992,498

Identifiable assets used jointly in U.S. domestic and international operations (principally aircraft) have been allocated based on estimated usage. International revenues related to services originating in the U.S. totaled $1,316,100,000, $1,201,100,000 and $1,020,000,000 for the years ended May 31, 1996, 1995 and 1994, respectively.

➜ **Note 11: Supplemental Cash Flow Information**

Cash paid for interest expense and income taxes for the years ended May 31 was as follows:

In thousands	1996	1995	1994
Interest (net of capitalized interest)	$108,052	$138,833	$158,149
Income taxes	204,487	185,964	167,209

In March 1995, the Company issued three series of loan certificates totaling $50,300,000 in exchange for a leased B747 aircraft.

Federal Express Corporation and Subsidiaries

→ **Note 12: Commitments and Contingencies**

The Company's annual purchase commitments under various contracts as of May 31, 1996, were as follows:

In thousands	Aircraft	Aircraft-Related[1]	Other[2]	Total
1997	$482,800	$185,000	$194,400	$862,200
1998	478,600	64,200	37,800	580,600
1999	240,800	18,500	15,600	274,900
2000	124,200	9,900	—	134,100

[1]Primarily aircraft modifications, rotables, spare parts and engines.

[2]Facilities, vehicles, computer and other equipment.

At May 31, 1996, the Company was committed to purchase nine Airbus A300, 12 Airbus A310 and ten MD11 aircraft to be delivered through 2000. Deposits and progress payments of $199,880,000 had been made toward these purchases. In April 1996, the Company canceled its options to purchase up to 36 additional Airbus A300s for delivery beginning in 1999. The Company may be required to purchase seven additional MD11 aircraft for delivery beginning no later than 2000 under a put option agreement.

The Company has entered into contracts which are designed to limit its exposure to fluctuations in jet fuel prices. Under these contracts, the Company makes (or receives) payments based on the difference between a specified lower (or upper) limit and the market price of jet fuel, as determined by an index of spot market prices representing various geographic regions. The difference is recorded as an increase or decrease in fuel expense. At May 31, 1996, the Company had contracts with various financial institutions covering a total notional volume of 365,300,000 gallons (approximately 54% of the Company's annual jet fuel consumption), with some contracts extending through May 1997. At May 31, 1995, the Company had similar contracts covering a total notional volume of 97,400,000 gallons (approximately 16% of the Company's annual jet fuel consumption), with some contracts extending through August 1996. During 1996, the Company received $1,977,000 under jet fuel contracts. Based on current market prices, the fair value of outstanding contracts at May 31, 1996 and 1995, was approximately $1,370,000 and $141,000, respectively.

→ **Note 13: Legal Proceedings**

On May 14, 1996, a class-action suit was filed by customers of the Company in the United States District Court for the District of Minnesota. The complaint generally alleges that the Company breached its contract with the plaintiffs in transporting packages shipped by them by continuing to collect a 6.25% federal excise tax on the transportation of property shipped by air after the tax expired on December 31, 1995. The plaintiffs assert that the benefit to the Company is believed to be in excess of $30,000,000. The plaintiffs seek certification as a class action, damages, an injunction to enjoin the Company from continuing to collect the excise tax referred to above, and an award of attorneys' fees and costs. Other customers of the Company filed two separate lawsuits, one in California state court during April 1996 and one in Minnesota state court during June 1996, containing substantially similar allegations and requests for relief.

During June 1996, the Company reached an agreement with the plaintiffs in all three lawsuits to consolidate the three lawsuits in the United States District Court for the District of Minnesota. The plaintiffs are in the process of filing the necessary motions to accomplish this consolidation.

The Company intends to vigorously defend itself in these cases. No amount has been reserved for these contingencies.

The Company is subject to other legal proceedings and claims which arise in the ordinary course of its business. In the opinion of management, the aggregate liability, if any, with respect to these other actions will not materially adversely affect the financial position or results of operations of the Company.

Notes to Consolidated Financial Statements

→ **Note 14: Unusual Events**

The Company received $7,800,000 and $9,700,000 in 1996 and 1995, respectively, from the bankruptcy estate of a firm engaged by the Company in 1990 to remit payments of employee withholding taxes. These amounts are a partial recovery of a $32,000,000 loss incurred by the Company in 1991 that resulted from the firm's failure to remit certain tax payments to appropriate authorities. The Company has received a total of $17,900,000 from the bankruptcy estate of the firm. All major issues pertaining to the bankruptcy have been resolved, and any additional amounts the Company may receive are expected to be insignificant.

In 1995, the Company sold two dedicated warehousing and contract distribution companies in the United Kingdom. A gain of $35,700,000 was recorded from the sale.

→ **Note 15: Summary of Quarterly Operating Results (Unaudited)**

In thousands, except earnings per share	First Quarter	Second Quarter	Third Quarter	Fourth Quarter
1996				
Revenues	$2,453,394	$2,547,012	$2,535,470	$2,737,743
Operating income	149,230	170,905	77,943	225,746
Income before income taxes	129,886	154,952	52,637	202,484
Net income	75,334	89,871	27,156	115,416
Earnings per share	$ 1.33	$ 1.57	$ .47	$ 2.01
Average shares outstanding	56,688	57,260	57,258	57,346
1995				
Revenues	$2,231,127	$2,358,765	$2,332,594	$2,469,587
Operating income	142,985	176,376	97,672	174,111
Income before income taxes	107,267	151,120	110,714	152,983
Net income	61,142	86,139	63,107	87,200
Earnings per share	$ 1.08	$ 1.53	$ 1.12	$ 1.54
Average shares outstanding	56,614	56,385	56,374	56,601

Report of Independent Public Accountants   Federal Express Corporation and Subsidiaries

To the Stockholders of Federal Express Corporation:

We have audited the accompanying consolidated balance sheets of Federal Express Corporation (a Delaware corporation) and subsidiaries as of May 31, 1996 and 1995, and the related consolidated statements of income, common stockholders' investment and cash flows for each of the three years in the period ended May 31, 1996. These financial statements are the responsibility of the Company's management. Our responsibility is to express an opinion on these financial statements based on our audits.

We conducted our audits in accordance with generally accepted auditing standards. Those standards require that we plan and perform the audit to obtain reasonable assurance about whether the financial statements are free of material misstatement. An audit includes examining, on a test basis, evidence supporting the amounts and disclosures in the financial statements. An audit also includes assessing the accounting principles used and significant estimates made by management, as well as evaluating the overall financial statement presentation. We believe that our audits provide a reasonable basis for our opinion.

In our opinion, the financial statements referred to above present fairly, in all material respects, the financial position of Federal Express Corporation and subsidiaries as of May 31, 1996 and 1995, and the results of their operations and their cash flows for each of the three years in the period ended May 31, 1996, in conformity with generally accepted accounting principles.

Arthur Andersen LLP

Memphis, Tennessee
July 1, 1996

Questions for Review of Key Topics

Question	1–1	What is the function and primary focus of financial accounting?
Question	1–2	What is meant by the phrase *efficient allocation of resources*? What mechanism fosters the efficient allocation of resources in the United States?
Question	1–3	Identify two important variables to be considered when making an investment decision.
Question	1–4	What must a company do in the long run to be able to provide a return to investors and creditors?
Question	1–5	What is the primary objective of financial accounting?
Question	1–6	Define net operating cash flows. Briefly explain why periodic net operating cash flows may not be a good indicator of future operating cash flows.
Question	1–7	What is meant by GAAP? Why is it important that all companies follow GAAP in reporting to external users?
Question	1–8	Explain the roles of the SEC and the FASB in the setting of accounting standards.
Question	1–9	Explain the role of the auditor in the financial reporting process.
Question	1–10	Explain what is meant by *adverse economic consequences* of new accounting standards or changes in standards.
Question	1–11	Why does the FASB undertake a series of elaborate information-gathering steps before issuing a substantive accounting standard?
Question	1–12	What is the purpose of the FASB's conceptual framework project?
Question	1–13	Discuss the terms *relevance* and *reliability* as they relate to financial accounting information.
Question	1–14	What are the components of relevant information? What are the components of reliable information?
Question	1–15	Explain what is meant by: The benefits of accounting information must exceed the costs.
Question	1–16	What is meant by the term *materiality* in financial reporting?
Question	1–17	Briefly define the financial accounting elements: (1) assets, (2) liabilities, (3) equity, (4) investments by owners, (5) distributions to owners, (6) revenues, (7) expenses, (8) gains, (9) losses, and (10) comprehensive income.
Question	1–18	What are the four basic assumptions underlying GAAP?
Question	1–19	What is the going concern assumption?
Question	1–20	Explain the periodicity assumption.
Question	1–21	What are the four key broad accounting principles that guide accounting practice?
Question	1–22	What are two important reasons to base the valuation of assets and liabilities on their historical cost?
Question	1–23	Describe the two criteria that must be satisfied before revenue can be recognized.
Question	1–24	What are the four different approaches to implementing the matching principle? Give an example of an expense that is recognized under each approach.
Question	1–25	In addition to the financial statement elements arrayed in the basic financial statements, what are some other ways to disclose financial information to external users?

Execises

Exercise 1–1
Accrual accounting

Listed below are several transactions that took place during the first two years of operations for the law firm of Pete, Pete, and Roy.

	Year 1	Year 2
Amounts billed to customers for services rendered	$170,000	$220,000
Cash collected from customers	160,000	190,000
Cash disbursements:		
Purchase of insurance policy...............................	60,000	- 0 -
Salaries paid to employees for services rendered during the year	90,000	100,000
Utilities	30,000	40,000

In addition, you learn that the company incurred utility costs of $35,000 in year one, that there were no liabilities at the end of year two, no anticipated bad debts on receivables, and that the insurance policy covers a three-year period.

Required:
1. Calculate the net operating cash flow for years 1 and 2.
2. Prepare an income statement for each year similar to Illustration 1–2 on page 8 according to the accrual accounting model.
3. Determine the amount of receivables from customers that the company would show on its year 1 and year 2 balance sheets prepared according to the accrual accounting model.

Exercise 1–2
Sources of GAAP

Different organizations historically and currently have issued various pronouncements that constitute the body of generally accepted accounting principles. Presented below are some of these organizations as well as various authoritative pronouncements. Match each organization with the one or more pronouncement(s) with which it is associated.

Organization	Pronouncements
1. Accounting Principles Board	a. *Statements of Financial Accounting Concepts*
2. Financial Accounting Standards Board	b. *Financial Reporting Releases*
3. Securities and Exchange Commission	c. *Accounting Research Bulletins*
4. Committee on Accounting Procedure	d. *Statements of Financial Accounting Standards*
5. AICPA	e. *APBOs*
	f. *Industry Accounting Guides*
	g. *Technical Bulletins*

Exercise 1–3
Participants in establishing GAAP

Three groups that participate in the process of establishing GAAP are users, preparers, and auditors. These groups are represented by various organizations. For each organization listed below, indicate which of these groups it primarily represents.

1. Securities and Exchange Commission
2. Financial Executives Institute
3. American Institute of Certified Public Accountants
4. Institute of Management Accountants
5. Association of Investment Management and Research

Exercise 1–4
Financial statement elements

For each of the items listed below, identify the appropriate financial statement element or elements.

1. Obligation to transfer cash or other resources as a result of a past transaction.
2. Dividends paid by a corporation to its shareholders.
3. Inflow of an asset from providing a good or service.
4. The financial position of a company.
5. Increase in equity during a period from nonowner transactions.
6. Increase in equity from peripheral or incidental transaction.
7. Sale of an asset used in the operations of a business for less than the asset's book value.
8. The owners' residual interest in the assets of a company.
9. An item owned by the company representing probable future benefits.
10. Revenues plus gains less expenses and losses.
11. An owner's contribution of cash to a corporation in exchange for ownership shares of stock.
12. Outflow of an asset related to the production of revenue.

Exercise 1–5
Concepts; terminology; conceptual framework

for exam study Cantey [handwritten note]

Listed below are several terms and phrases associated with the FASB's conceptual framework. Pair each item from List A (by letter) with the item from List B that is most appropriately associated with it.

List A	List B
_____ 1. Predictive value	a. Decreases in equity resulting from transfers to owners.
_____ 2. Relevance	b. Requires consideration of the costs and value of information.
_____ 3. Timeliness	c. Important for making interfirm comparisons.
_____ 4. Distribution to owners	d. Applying the same accounting practices over time.
_____ 5. Feedback value	e. Along with relevance, a primary decision-specific quality.
_____ 6. Reliability	f. Agreement between a measure and the phenomenon it purports to represent.
_____ 7. Gain	g. Information is available prior to the decision.
_____ 8. Representational faithfulness	h. Pertinent to the decision at hand.
_____ 9. Comprehensive income	i. Implies consensus among different measurers.
_____10. Materiality	j. Information confirms expectations.
_____11. Comparability	k. The change in equity from nonowner transactions.
_____12. Neutrality	l. The process of admitting information into financial statements.
_____13. Recognition	m. Accounting information should not favor a particular group.
_____14. Consistency	n. Results if an asset is sold for more than its book value.
_____15. Cost effectiveness	o. Information is useful in predicting the future.
_____16. Verifiability	p. Concerns the relative size of an item and its effect on decisions.

Exercise 1–6
Multiple choice; conceptual framework

The following questions dealing with the FASB's conceptual framework are adapted from questions that appeared on recent CPA examinations. Determine the response that best completes the statements or questions.

1. According to the FASB conceptual framework, which of the following situations violates the concept of reliability?
   a. Data on segments having the same expected risk and growth rates are reported to analysts estimating future profits.
   b. Financial statements are issued nine months late.
   c. Management reports to stockholders regularly refer to new projects undertaken, but the financial statements never report project results.
   d. Financial statements include property with a carrying amount increased to management's estimate of market value.

2. According to *Statements of Financial Accounting Concepts,* neutrality is an ingredient of

	Reliability	Relevance
a.	Yes	Yes
b.	Yes	No
c.	No	Yes
d.	No	No

3. According to the FASB conceptual framework, predictive value is an ingredient of

	Relevance	Reliability
a.	No	No
b.	Yes	Yes
c.	No	Yes
d.	Yes	No

4. According to the FASB conceptual framework, earnings
   a. Are the same as comprehensive income.
   b. Exclude certain gains and losses that are included in comprehensive income.
   c. Include certain gains and losses that are excluded from comprehensive income.
   d. Include certain losses that are excluded from comprehensive income.

5. According to the FASB conceptual framework, which of the following relates to both relevance and reliability?

	Consistency	Verifiability
a.	Yes	Yes
b.	Yes	No
c.	No	Yes
d.	No	No

Exercise 1-7
Basic assumptions, principles, and constraints

Listed below are several terms and phrases associated with basic assumptions, underlying principles, and constraints. Pair each item from List A (by letter) with the item from List B that is most appropriately associated with it.

List A	List B
_____ 1. Matching principle	a. The enterprise is separate from its owners and other entities.
_____ 2. Periodicity	b. A common denominator is the dollar.
_____ 3. Historical cost principle	c. The entity will continue indefinitely.
_____ 4. Materiality	d. Record expenses in the period the related revenue is recognized.
_____ 5. Realization principle	e. The original transaction value upon acquisition.
_____ 6. Going concern assumption	f. All information that could affect decisions should be reported.
_____ 7. Monetary unit assumption	g. The life of an enterprise can be divided into artificial time periods.
_____ 8. Economic entity assumption	h. Criteria usually satisfied at point of sale.
_____ 9. Full-disclosure principle	i. Concerns the relative size of an item and its effect on decisions.

Exercise 1–8
Basic assumptions and principles

Listed below are several statements that relate to financial accounting and reporting. Identify the basic assumption, broad accounting principle, or pervasive constraint that applies to each statement.

1. Jim Marley is the sole owner of Marley's Appliances. Jim borrowed $100,000 to buy a new home to be used as his personal residence. This liability was not recorded in the records of Marley's Appliances.
2. Apple Computer, Inc., distributes an annual report to its shareholders.
3. Hewlett-Packard Corporation depreciates machinery and equipment over their useful lives.

4. The Crosby Company lists land on its balance sheet at $120,000, its original purchase price, even though the land has a current market value of $200,000.
5. The Honeywell Corporation records revenue when products are delivered to customers, even though the cash has not yet been received.
6. Liquidation values are not normally reported in financial statements even though many companies do go out of business.
7. IBM Corporation, a multibillion dollar company, purchased some small tools at a cost of $800. Even though the tools will be used for a number of years, the company recorded the purchase as an expense.

Exercise 1–9
Basic assumptions and principles

Identify the basic assumption or broad accounting principle that was violated in each of the following situations.

1. The Pastel Paint Company purchased land two years ago at a price of $250,000. Because the value of the land has appreciated to $400,000, the company has valued the land at $400,000 on its most recent balance sheet.
2. The Atwell Corporation has not prepared financial statements for external users for over three years.
3. The Klingon Company sells farm machinery. Revenue from a large order of machinery from a new buyer was recorded the day the order was received.
4. Don Smith is the sole owner of a company called Hardware City. The company recently paid a $150 utility bill for Smith's personal residence and recorded a $150 expense.
5. The Golden Book Company purchased a large printing machine for $1,000,000 (a material amount) and recorded the purchase as an expense.
6. The Ace Appliance Company is involved in a major lawsuit involving injuries sustained by some of its employees in the manufacturing plant. The company is being sued for $2,000,000, a material amount, and is not insured. The suit was not disclosed in the most recent financial statements because no settlement had been reached.

Exercise 1–10
Basic assumptions and principles

For each of the following situations, indicate whether you agree or disagree with the financial reporting practice employed and state the basic assumption, pervasive constraint, or accounting principle that is applied (if you agree) or violated (if you disagree).

1. The Wagner Corporation adjusted the valuation of all assets and liabilities to reflect changes in the purchasing power of the dollar.
2. The Spooner Oil Company changed its method of accounting for oil and gas exploration costs from successful efforts to full cost. No mention of the change was included in the financial statements. The change had a material effect on Spooner's financial statements.
3. The Cypress Manufacturing Company purchased machinery having a five-year life. The cost of the machinery is being expensed over the life of the machinery.
4. The Rudeen Corporation purchased equipment for $180,000 at a liquidation sale of a competitor. Because the equipment was worth $230,000, Rudeen valued the equipment on its subsequent balance sheet at $230,000.
5. The Davis Bicycle Company received a large order for the sale of 1,000 bicycles at $100 each. The customer paid Davis the entire amount of $100,000 on March 15. However, Davis did not record any revenue until April 17, the date the bicycles were delivered to the customer.
6. The Gigantic Corporation purchased two small calculators at a cost of $32.00. The cost of the calculators was expensed even though they had a three-year estimated useful life.
7. The Esquire Company provides financial statements to external users every three years.

Exercise 1–11
Basic assumptions, principles, and constraints

Listed below are the basic assumptions, underlying principles, and constraints discussed in this chapter.

a. Economic entity assumption
b. Going concern assumption
c. Periodicity assumption
d. Monetary unit assumption
e. Historical cost principle
f. Realization principle

g. Matching principle
h. Full-disclosure principle
i. Cost effectiveness
j. Materiality
k. Conservatism

Identify by letter the assumption, principle, or constraint that relates to each statement or phrase below.

____ 1. Revenue is recognized only after certain criteria are satisfied.
____ 2. Information that could affect decision making should be reported.
____ 3. Cause-and-effect relationship between revenues and expenses.
____ 4. The basis for measurement of many assets and liabilities.

____ 5. Relates to the qualitative characteristic of timeliness.

____ 6. All economic events can be identified with a particular entity.

____ 7. The benefits of providing accounting information should exceed the cost of doing so.

____ 8. A consequence is that GAAP need not be followed in all situations.

____ 9. A practical justification for some accounting choices.

____ 10. Assumes the entity will continue indefinitely.

____ 11. Inflation causes a violation of this assumption.

Exercise 1–12
Multiple choice; concept statements, basic assumptions, principles

Determine the response that best completes the following statements or questions.

1. The primary objective of financial reporting is to provide information
   a. about a firm's economic resources and obligations.
   b. useful in predicting future cash flows.
   c. concerning the changes in financial position resulting from the income-producing efforts of the entity.
   d. about a firm's financing and investing activities.

2. *Statements of Financial Accounting Concepts* issued by the FASB
   a. represent GAAP.
   b. have been superseded by *SFAS*s.
   c. are subject to approval of the SEC.
   d. identify the conceptual framework within which accounting standards are developed.

3. In general, revenue is recognized as earned when the earning process is virtually complete and
   a. the sales price has been collected.
   b. a purchase order has been received.
   c. there is reasonable certainty as to the collectibility of the asset to be received.
   d. a contract has been signed.

4. In depreciating the cost of an asset, accountants are most concerned with
   a. conservatism.
   b. the realization principle.
   c. full disclosure.
   d. the matching principle.

5. The primary objective of the matching principle is to
   a. provide full disclosure.
   b. record expenses in the period that related revenues are recognized.
   c. provide timely information to decision makers.
   d. promote comparability between financial statements of different periods.

6. The separate entity assumption states that, in the absence of contrary evidence, all entities will survive indefinitely.
   a. True.
   b. False

Cases

Critical Thought Case 1–1
The development of accounting standards

In 1934, Congress created the Securities and Exchange Commission (SEC) and gave the commission both the power and responsibility for setting accounting and reporting standards in the United States.

Required:
1. Explain the relationship between the SEC and the various private sector standard-setting bodies that have, over time, been delegated the responsibility to set accounting standards.
2. Can you think of any reasons why the SEC has delegated this responsibility rather than set standards directly?

Internet Case 1–2
Accessing SEC information through the Internet

Internet access to the worldwide web has provided a wealth of information accessible with our personal computers. Many chapters in this text contain an "Internet Case" that requires you to access the web to research an accounting issue. The purpose of this case is to introduce you to the Internet home page of the Securities and Exchange Commission (SEC) and its EDGAR database.

Required:

1. Access the SEC home page on the Internet. You can use a web browser or anonymous FTP. The web address is http://www.sec.gov/. To use anonymous FTP, use your File Transfer Protocol software to connect to sec.gov and log in as user "anonymous" with a password of your electronic mail address.
2. Choose the subaddress "About the SEC" and answer the following questions:
   a. What are the two basic objectives of the 1933 Securities Act?
   b. The Securities Act Amendments of 1964 extended disclosure and reporting provisions of the 1934 Securities Exchange Act to include equity securities in the over-the-counter market. What is the "size test" for determining which over-the-counter companies must file registration forms with the SEC?
3. Return to the SEC home page and access EDGAR. Describe the contents of the database.

Research Case 1–3
Accounting standards in China

Economic reforms in the People's Republic of China are moving that nation toward a market-driven economy. China's accounting practices must also change to accommodate the needs of potential investors. In an article entitled "Accounting Standards in the People's Republic of China: Responding to Economic Reforms," Professors Winkle, Huss, and Xi-Zhu discuss the need for revisions in Chinese accounting standards.

Required:

1. In your library or from some other source, locate the indicated article in *Accounting Horizons*, September 1994.
2. Briefly describe recent efforts to revise China's accounting standards.
3. What are some of the current differences between U.S. and Chinese accounting standards listed in the article?
4. In the authors' commentary, what do they identify as an important impediment to growth in China?

Group Interaction Case 1–4
Relevance and reliability

Some theorists contend that companies that create pollution should report the social cost of that pollution on income statements. They argue that such companies are indirectly subsidized as the cost of pollution is borne by society while only production costs (and perhaps minimal pollution fines) are shown on the income statement. Thus, the product sells for less than would be necessary if all costs were included.

Assume that the FASB is considering a standard to include the social costs of pollution on the income statement. The process would require considering both relevance and reliability of the information produced by the new standard. Your instructor will divide the class into from two to six groups depending on the size of the class. The mission of your group is to explain how the concepts of relevance and reliability relate to this issue.

Required:

Each group member should consider the question independently and draft a tentative answer prior to the class session for which the case is assigned.

In class, each group will meet for 10 to 15 minutes in different areas of the classroom. During that meeting, group members will take turns sharing their suggestions for the purpose of arriving at a single group treatment.

After the allotted time, a spokesperson for each group (selected during the group meetings) will share the group's solution with the class. The goal of the class is to incorporate the views of each group into a consensus answer to the question.

Writing Case 1–5
Accounting standard setting

One of your friends is a financial analyst for a major stock brokerage firm. Recently she indicated to you that she had read an article in a weekly business magazine that alluded to the political process of establishing accounting standards. She had always assumed that accounting standards were established by determining the approach that conceptually best reflected the economics of a transaction.

Required:

Write a one to two page article for a business journal explaining what is meant by the political process for establishing accounting standards. Be sure to include in your article a discussion of the need for the FASB to balance accounting considerations and economic consequences.

International Case 1–6
The move toward internationalization of accounting standards

The International Accounting Standards Committee (IASC) was founded in 1973 to develop worldwide accounting standards. A recent article entitled "*Wake-Up Call to American Business: International Accounting Standards Are on the Way*" addresses the prospects for a single set of global accounting standards.

Required:

1. In your library or from some other source, locate the indicated article in the *Journal of Accountancy*, July 1993.
2. According to the authors, what is the attitude of the American business community toward international accounting standards?

3. What is the SEC's position on the acceptability of international accounting standards?
4. What is the IOSCO, and what is its role in the development of international accounting standards?
5. What is the authors' conclusion on the possibility of international acceptance of pronouncements issued by the IASC?

Ethics Case 1–7
The auditors' responsibility

It is the responsibility of management to apply accounting standards when communicating with investors and creditors through financial statements. Another group, auditors, serves as an independent intermediary to help ensure that management has in fact appropriately applied GAAP in preparing the company's financial statements. Auditors examine (audit) financial statements to express a professional, independent opinion. The opinion reflects the auditors' assessment of the statements' fairness, which is determined by the extent to which they are prepared in compliance with GAAP.

Some feel that it is impossible for an auditor to give an independent opinion on a company's financial statements because the auditors' fees for performing the audit are paid by the company. In addition to the audit fee, quite often the auditor performs other services for the company such as preparing the company's income tax returns.

Required:
How might an auditor's ethics be challenged while performing an audit?

Discussion Case 1–8
Qualitative characteristics

Generally accepted accounting principles do not require companies to disclose forecasts of any financial variables to external users. A friend, who is a finance major, is puzzled by this and asks you to explain why such relevant information is not provided to investors and creditors to help them predict future cash flows.

Required:
Explain to your friend why this information is not provided to investors and creditors.

Critical Thought Case 1–9
GAAP, comparability, and the role of the auditor

Mary McQuire is trying to decide how to invest her money. A friend recommended that she buy the stock of one of two corporations and suggested that she should compare the financial statements of the two companies before making a decision.

Required:
1. Do you agree that Mary will be able to compare the financial statements of the two companies?
2. What role does the auditor play in ensuring comparability of financial statements between companies?

Critical Thought Case 1–10
Cost effectiveness

Statement of Financial Accounting Concepts No. 2, "Qualitative Characteristics of Accounting Information," includes a discussion of the pervasive constraint **cost effectiveness**. Assume that the FASB is considering revising an important accounting standard.

Required:
1. What is the desired benefit from revising an accounting standard?
2. What are some of the possible costs that could result from a revision of an accounting standard?
3. What does the FASB do in order to assess possible benefits and costs of a proposed revision of an accounting standard?

Discussion Case 1–11
The realization principle

A new client, the Wolf Company, asks your advice concerning the point in time that the company should recognize revenue from the rental of its office buildings. Renters usually pay rent on a quarterly basis at the beginning of the quarter. The owners contend that the critical event that motivates revenue recognition should be the date the cash is received from renters. After all, the money is in hand and is very seldom returned.

Required:
1. Describe the two criteria that must be satisfied before revenue can be recognized.
2. Do you agree or disagree with the position of the owners of Wolf Company? Support your answer.

Discussion Case 1–12
The matching principle

Revenues measure the accomplishments of a company during the period. Expenses are then matched with revenues to produce a periodic measure of performance called *net income*.

Required:
1. Explain what is meant by the phrase *matched with revenues*.
2. Describe the four approaches used to implement the matching principle and label them 1 through 4.
3. For each of the following, identify which matching approach should be used to recognize the cost as expense.
   a. The cost of producing a product.
   b. The cost of advertising.

   c. The cost of monthly rent on the office building.
   d. The salary of an office employee.
   e. Depreciation on an office building.

Real World Case 1–13
Elements; disclosures;
Hewlett-Packard Company

Selected financial statements from the 1995 annual report of Hewlett-Packard Company follow. Use these statements to answer the following questions:

1. The company's fiscal year ends on what date?
2. What amounts did Hewlett-Packard report for the following items for 1995:
    a. Total net revenues
    b. Total costs and expenses
    c. Net income (earnings)
    d. Total assets
    e. Total shareholders' equity
3. How many shares of common stock did the company have authorized, issued, and outstanding at the end of 1995?
4. Why do you think Hewlett-Packard reports more than one year of data in its financial statements?

Hewlett-Packard Company and Subsidiaries

Consolidated Balance Sheet

October 31
In millions except par value and number of shares

	1995	1994
Assets		
Current assets:		
Cash and cash equivalents	$ 1,973	$ 1,357
Short-term investments	643	1,121
Accounts and notes receivable	6,735	5,028
Inventories:		
Finished goods	3,368	2,466
Purchased parts and fabricated assemblies	2,645	1,807
Other current assets	875	730
Total current assets	16,239	12,509
Property, plant and equipment:		
Land	485	508
Buildings and leasehold improvements	3,810	3,472
Machinery and equipment	4,452	3,958
	8,747	7,938
Accumulated depreciation	(4,036)	(3,610)
	4,711	4,328
Long-term investments and other assets	3,477	2,730
Total assets	$24,427	$19,567
Liabilities and shareholders' equity		
Current liabilities:		
Notes payable and short-term borrowings	$ 3,214	$ 2,469
Accounts payable	2,422	1,466
Employee compensation and benefits	1,568	1,256
Taxes on earnings	1,494	1,245
Deferred revenues	782	598
Other accrued liabilities	1,464	1,196
Total current liabilities	10,944	8,230
Long-term debt	663	547
Other liabilities	981	864
Shareholders' equity:		
Preferred stock, $1 par value		
(authorized: 300,000,000 shares; issued: none)	—	—
Common stock and capital in excess of $1 par value		
(authorized: 1,200,000,000 shares; issued and outstanding:		
509,955,000 in 1995 and 509,654,000 in 1994)	871	1,033
Retained earnings	10,968	8,893
Total shareholders' equity	11,839	9,926
Total liabilities and shareholders' equity	$24,427	$19,567

Consolidated Statement of Earnings

For the years ended October 31
In millions except par value and number of shares

	1995	1994
Net revenue:		
Equipment	$27,125	$21,380
Services	4,394	3,611
	31,519	24,991
Costs and expenses:		
Cost of equipment sold	17,069	13,012
Cost of services	2,945	2,478
Research and development	2,302	2,027
Selling, general and administrative	5,635	4,925
	27,951	22,442
Earnings from operations	3,568	2,549
Interest income and other, net	270	29
Interest expense	206	155
Earnings before taxes	3,632	2,423
Provision for taxes	1,199	824
Net earnings	$ 2,433	$ 1,599
Net earnings per share	$ 4.63	$ 3.07

2

CHAPTER

REVIEW OF THE ACCOUNTING PROCESS

OVERVIEW

Chapter 1 explained that the primary means of conveying financial information to investors, creditors, and other external users is through financial statements and related notes. The purpose of this chapter is to review the fundamental accounting process used to produce the financial statements. This review establishes a framework for the study of the concepts covered in intermediate accounting.

Actual accounting systems differ significantly from company to company. This chapter focuses on the many features that tend to be common to any accounting system.

LEARNING OBJECTIVES   After studying this chapter, you should be able to:

1. Analyze routine economic events—transactions—and record their effects on a company's financial position using the accounting equation format.
2. Record transactions using the general journal format.
3. Post the effects of journal entries to T-accounts and prepare an unadjusted trial balance.
4. Identify and describe the different types of adjusting journal entries.
5. Record adjusting journal entries in general journal format and prepare an adjusted trial balance.
6. Describe the four basic financial statements.
7. Explain the closing process.

ENGINEERING PROFITS

By the time you finish this chapter, you should be able to respond appropriately to the questions posed in this case. Compare your response to the solution provided at the end of the chapter.

After graduating from college last year, two of your engineering-major friends started an internet consulting practice. They began operations on July 1 and felt they did quite well during their first year. Now they would like to borrow $20,000 from a local bank to buy new computing equipment and office furniture. To support their loan application, the friends presented the bank with the following income statement for their first year of operations ending June 30:

Consulting revenue		$96,000
Operating expenses:		
Salaries	$32,000	
Rent	9,000	
Supplies	4,800	
Utilities	3,000	
Advertising	1,200	(50,000)
Net income		$46,000

The bank officer noticed that there was no depreciation expense on the income statement and has asked your friends to revise the statement after making year-end adjustments. After agreeing to help, you discover the following information:

a. The friends paid $80,000 for equipment when they began operations. They think the equipment will be useful for five years.

b. They pay $500 a month to rent office space. In January, they paid a full year's rent in advance. This is included in the $9,000 rent expense.

c. Included in consulting revenue is $13,000 they received from a customer in June as a deposit for work to be performed in August.

QUESTIONS

1. What purpose do adjusting entries serve?
2. What year-end adjustments are needed to revise the income statement? Did your friends do as well their first year as they thought?

A solid foundation is vital to a sound understanding of intermediate accounting. So, we review the fundamental accounting process here to serve as a framework for the new concepts you will learn in this course.

Chapter 1 introduced the theoretical structure of financial accounting and the environment within which it operates. The primary function of financial accounting—to provide relevant financial information to external users—is accomplished by periodically disseminating financial statements and related notes. This chapter reviews the *process* used to identify, analyze, record, summarize, and then report the economic events affecting a company's financial position.

The accounting systems that businesses actually use differ significantly from company to company. Larger companies generally use more complex systems than smaller companies. The types of economic events affecting companies also cause differences in systems. This chapter focuses on the many features that tend to be common to all accounting systems.

It is important to understand that this chapter and its appendixes are not intended to describe the actual accounting systems but, instead, to provide an overview of the basic model that underlies all accounting systems. In most business enterprises, the sheer volume of data that must be processed precludes a manual accounting system. Fortunately, the computer provides a solution. Electronic data processing is fast, accurate, and affordable.

Many large and medium-sized companies own or rent their own mainframe computers and employ company-specific data processing systems. Smaller companies can take advantage of computer technology with relatively inexpensive micro- and minicomputers and generalized data processing software packages such as Quicken and Peachtree Accounting Software.

The Basic Model

Economic events cause changes in the financial position of the company.

External events involve an exchange between the company and another entity.

Internal events do not involve an exchange transaction but do affect the company's financial position.

The first objective of any accounting system is to identify the **economic events** that can be expressed in financial terms by the system.[1] An economic event is any event that *directly* affects the financial position of the company. Recall from Chapter 1 that financial position comprises assets, liabilities, and owners' equity. Broad and specific accounting principles determine which events should be recorded, when the events should be recorded, and the dollar amount at which they should be measured.

Economic events can be classified as either external events or internal events. **External events** involve an exchange between the company and a separate economic entity. Examples are purchasing merchandise inventory for cash, borrowing cash from a bank, and paying salaries to employees. In each instance, the company receives something (merchandise, cash, and services) in exchange for something else (cash, assumption of a liability, and cash).

On the other hand, **internal events** directly affect the financial position of the company but don't involve an exchange transaction with another entity. Examples are the depreciation of machinery and the use of supplies. As we will see later in the chapter, these events must be recorded to properly reflect a company's financial position and results of operations in accordance with the accrual accounting model.

The Accounting Equation

Learning objective 1
Analyze routine economic events—transactions—and record their effects on a company's financial position using the accounting equation format.

Each event, or **transaction,** has a dual effect on the accounting equation.

The **accounting equation** underlies the process used to capture the effect of economic events.

$$\text{Assets} = \text{Liabilities} + \text{Owners' Equity}$$

The elements of the equation were defined in Chapter 1.

This general expression portrays the equality between the total economic resources of an entity (its assets) — shown on the left side of the equation — and the total claims to those resources (liabilities and equity) — shown on the right side. In other words, the resources of an enterprise are provided by either creditors or owners.

The equation also implies that each economic event affecting this equation will have a dual effect because resources always must equal claims to those resources. For illustration, consider the events (we refer to these throughout the text as **transactions**) in Illustration 2–1.

---

[1]There are many economic events that affect a company *indirectly* and are not recorded. For example, when the Federal Reserve changes its discount rate, it is an important economic event that can affect the company in many ways, but it is not recorded by the company.

Each transaction is analyzed to determine its effect on the equation and on the specific financial position elements.

ILLUSTRATION   2–1

Transaction Analysis

1. **An attorney invested $50,000 to open a law office.**

An investment by the owner causes both assets and owners' equity to increase.

Assets	=	Liabilities	+	Owners' Equity
+$50,000 (cash)				+$50,000 (investment by owner)

2. **$40,000 was borrowed from a bank and a note payable was signed.**

This transaction causes assets and liabilities to increase. A bank loan increases cash and creates an obligation to repay it.

Assets	=	Liabilities	+	Owners' Equity
+$40,000 (cash)		+$40,000 (note payable)		

3. **Supplies costing $3,000 were purchased on account.**

Buying supplies on credit also increases both assets and liabilities.

Assets	=	Liabilities	+	Owners' Equity
+$3,000 (supplies)		+$3,000 (accounts payable)		

4. **Services were performed on account for $10,000.**

Transactions 4, 5, and 6 are revenue and expense transactions. Revenues and expenses (and gains and losses) are events that cause owners' equity to change. Revenues and gains describe inflows of assets, causing owners' equity to increase. Expenses and losses describe outflows of assets (or increases in liabilities), causing owners' equity to decrease.

Assets	=	Liabilities	+	Owners' Equity
+$10,000 (receivables)				+$10,000 (revenue)

5. **Salaries of $5,000 were paid to employees.**

Assets	=	Liabilities	+	Owners' Equity
–$5,000 (cash)				–$5,000 (expense)

6. **$500 of supplies were used.**

Assets	=	Liabilities	+	Owners' Equity
–$500 (supplies)				–$500 (expense)

7. **$1,000 was paid on account to the supplies vendor.**

This transaction causes assets and liabilities to decrease.

Assets	=	Liabilities	+	Owners' Equity
–$1,000 (cash)		–$1,000 (accounts payable)		

The accounting equation can be expanded to include a column for each type of asset and liability and for each type of change in owners' equity.

 Owners' equity for a corporation, called *shareholders' equity*, is classified by source as either **paid-in capital** or **retained earnings.**

As discussed in Chapter 1, owners of a corporation are its shareholders, so owners' equity for a corporation is referred to as shareholders' equity. Shareholders' equity for a corporation arises primarily from two sources: (1) amounts *invested* by shareholders in the corporation and (2) amounts *earned* by the corporation (on behalf of its shareholders). These are reported as (1) **paid-in capital** and (2) **retained earnings.** Retained earnings equals net income less distributions to shareholders (primarily dividends) from the inception of the corporation. Graphic 2–1 shows the basic accounting equation for a corporation with shareholders' equity expanded to highlight its composition. We use the corporate format throughout the remainder of the chapter.

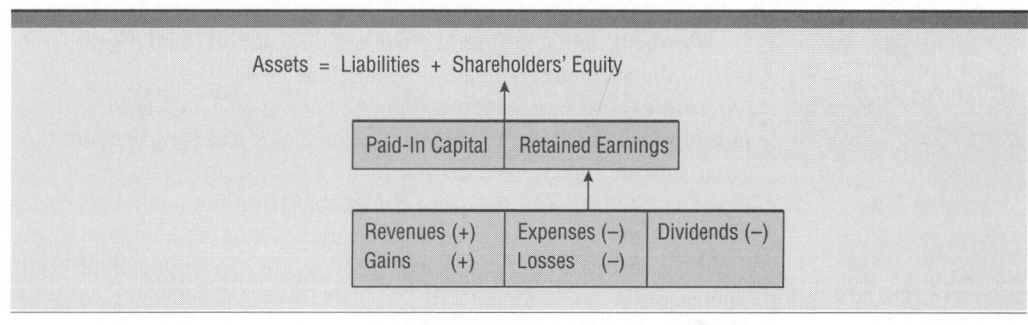

Account Relationships

All transactions could be recorded in columnar fashion as increases or decreases to elements of the accounting equation. However, even for a very small company with few transactions, this would become cumbersome. So, most companies use a process called the **double-entry system.** The term *double-entry* refers to the dual effect that each transaction has on the accounting equation.

Elements of the accounting equation are represented by **accounts** which are contained in a **general ledger.** Increases and decreases in each element of a company's financial position are recorded in these accounts. A separate account is maintained for individual assets and liabilities, retained earnings, and paid-in capital. Also, to accumulate information needed for the income statement, we use separate accounts to keep track of the changes in retained earnings caused by revenues, expenses, gains, and losses. The number of accounts depends on the complexity of the company's operations.

An account includes the account title, an account number to aid the processing task, and columns or fields for increases, decreases, the cumulative balance, and the date. For instructional purposes we use **T-accounts** instead of formal ledger accounts. A T-account has space at the top for the account title and two sides for recording increases and decreases.

Account Title

For centuries, accountants have effectively used a system of **debits** and **credits** to increase and decrease account balances in the ledger. Debits merely represent the *left* side of the account and credits the *right* side, as shown below.

Account Title

| debit side | credit side |

Whether a debit or a credit represents an increase or a decrease depends on the type of account. Accounts on the left side of the accounting equation (assets) are *increased* (+) by *debit* entries and *decreased* (-) by *credit* entries. Accounts on the right side of the accounting equation (liabilities and shareholders' equity) are *increased* (+) by *credit* entries and *decreased* (-) by *debit* entries. This arbitrary, but effective, procedure ensures that for each transaction the net impact on the left sides of accounts always equals the net impact on the right sides of accounts.

For example, consider the bank loan in our earlier illustration. An asset, cash, increased by $40,000. Increases in assets are *debits*. Liabilities also increased by $40,000. Increases in liabilities are *credits*.

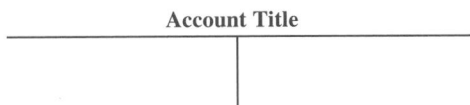

| **Assets** | **=** | **Liabilities + Owners' Equity** |

Cash		Note Payable
debit	credit	debit	credit
40,000			40,000
+			+

The debits equal the credits in every transaction (dual effect), so both before and after a transaction the accounting equation is in balance.

Prior exposure to the terms debit and credit probably comes from your experience with a bank account. For example, when a bank debits your checking account for service charges, it decreases your account balance. When you make a deposit, the bank credits your account, increasing your account balance. You must remember that from the bank's perspective, your bank account balance is a liability—it represents the amount that the bank owes you. Therefore, when the bank debits your account, it is decreasing its liability. When the bank credits your account, its liability increases.

GRAPHIC   2 – 2

Accounting Equation, Debits and Credits, Increases and Decreases

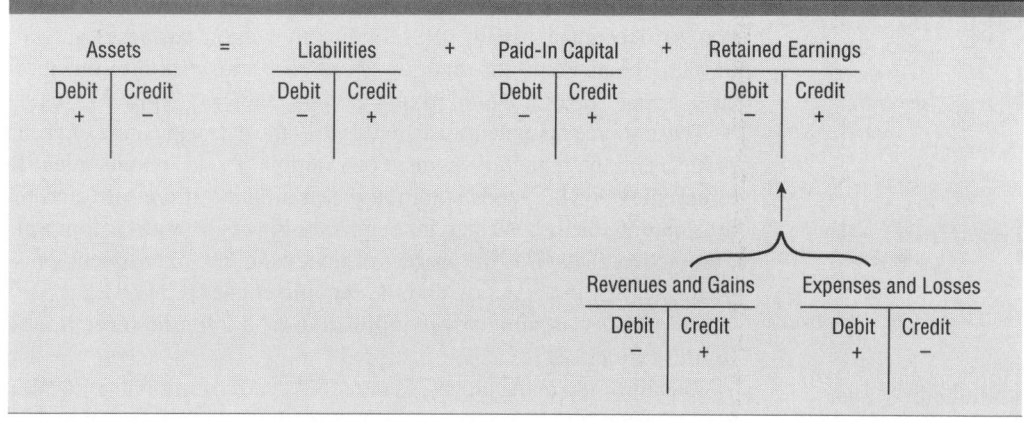

Graphic 2–2 illustrates the relationship among the accounting equation, debits and credits, and the increases and decreases in financial position elements.

Notice that increases and decreases in retained earnings are recorded *indirectly*. For example, an expense represents a decrease in retained earnings, which requires a debit. That debit, however, is recorded in an appropriate expense account rather than in retained earnings itself. This allows the company to maintain a separate record of expenses incurred during an accounting period. The debit to retained earnings for the expense is recorded in a closing entry (reviewed later) at the end of the period, only after the expense total is reflected on the income statement. Similarly, an increase in retained earnings due to a revenue is recorded indirectly with a credit to a revenue account, which is later reflected as a credit to retained earnings.

The general ledger accounts serve as control accounts. Subsidiary accounts associated with a particular general ledger control account are maintained in separate subsidiary ledgers. For example, a subsidiary ledger for accounts receivable contains individual account receivable accounts for each of the company's credit customers. Subsidiary ledgers are discussed in more detail in Appendix 2C.

Permanent accounts represent the basic financial position elements of the accounting equation.

Temporary accounts keep track of the changes in the retained earnings component of shareholders' equity.

Each general ledger account can be classified as either *permanent* or *temporary*. **Permanent accounts** represent assets, liabilities, and shareholders' equity at a point in time. **Temporary accounts** represent changes in the retained earnings component of shareholders' equity for a corporation caused by revenue, expense, gain, and loss transactions. It would be cumbersome to record each revenue/expense, gain/loss transaction directly into the retained earnings account. The different types of events affecting retained earnings should be kept separate to facilitate the preparation of the financial statements. The balances in these temporary accounts are periodically, usually once a year, closed or zeroed out, and the net effect is recorded in the permanent retained earnings account. The temporary accounts need to be zeroed out to measure income on an annual basis. This closing process is discussed in a later section of this chapter.

The Accounting Processing Cycle

Now that we've reviewed the basics of the double-entry system, let's look closer at the process used to identify, analyze, record, and summarize transactions and prepare financial statements. This section deals only with *external transactions,* those that involve an exchange transaction with another entity. Internal transactions are discussed in a later section.

The 10 steps in the accounting processing cycle are:

1. Obtain information about external transactions from **source documents.**
2. **Transaction analysis.**
3. Record the transaction in a **journal.**
4. **Post** from the journal to the general ledger accounts.
5. Prepare an **unadjusted trial balance.**
6. Record **adjusting entries** and post to the general ledger accounts.
7. Prepare an **adjusted trial balance.**
8. Prepare **financial statements.**
9. **Close** the temporary accounts to retained earnings (at year-end only).
10. Prepare a **post-closing trial balance** (at year-end only).

We now discuss these in order.

Step 1: Obtain information about transactions from **source documents.**

The first step in the process is to *identify* external transactions affecting the accounting equation. An accountant usually does not directly witness business transactions. A mechanism is needed to relay the essential information about each transaction to the accountant. **Source documents** such as sales invoices, bills from suppliers, and cash register tapes serve this need.

These source documents usually identify the date and nature of each transaction, the participating parties, and the monetary terms. For example, a sales invoice identifies the date of sale, the customer, the specific goods sold, the dollar amount of the sale, and the payment terms. With this information, the second step in the processing cycle, **transaction analysis,** can be accomplished. Transaction analysis is the process of reviewing the source documents to determine the dual effect on the accounting equation and the specific elements involved.

Step 2: **Transaction analysis.**

This process is summarized in Illustration 2–2 for the seven transactions described previously in Illustration 2–1.

The third step in the process is to record the transaction in a **journal.** Journals provide a chronological record of all economic events affecting a firm. Each journal entry is expressed in terms of equal debits and credits to accounts affected by the transaction being recorded. Debits and credits represent increases or decreases to specific accounts, depending on the type of account, as explained earlier. For example, for credit sales, a debit to accounts receivable and a credit to sales revenue is recorded in a sales journal.

Step 3: Record the transaction in a **journal.**

A sales journal is an example of a **special journal** used to record a repetitive type of transaction. Appendix 2C discusses the use of special journals in more depth. In this chapter and throughout the text, we use the **general journal** format to record all transactions.

Any type of transaction can be recorded in a general journal. It has a place for the date of the transaction, a place for account titles, account numbers, and supporting explanations, a place for debit entries, and a place for credit entries. A simplified journal entry is used throughout the text that lists the account titles to be debited and credited and the dollar amounts. A common convention is to list the debited accounts first, indent the credited accounts, and use the first of two columns for the debit amounts and the second column for the credit amounts. For example, the **journal entry** for the bank loan in Illustration 2–1, which requires a debit to cash and a credit to note payable, is recorded as follows:

Learning objective 2
Record transactions using the general journal format.

To record the borrowing of cash and the signing of a note payable.

Cash	40,000	
Note payable		40,000

Step 4 is to periodically transfer or *post* the debit and credit information from the journal to individual ledger accounts. Recall that a ledger is simply a collection of all of the company's various accounts. Each account provides a summary of the effects of all events and transactions on that individual account. This process is called **posting.** Posting involves transferring debits and credits recorded in individual journal entries to the specific accounts affected. As discussed earlier in the chapter, most accounting systems today are computerized, with the journal and ledger kept on magnetic tape or disk. For these systems, the journal input information is automatically and instantly posted to the ledger accounts.

Step 4: **Post** from the journal to the general ledger accounts.

These first four steps in the processing cycle are illustrated using the external transactions in Illustration 2–3 which occurred during the month of July 1997, the first month of operations for the Dress Right Clothing Corporation. The company operates a retail store that sells men's and women's clothing. Dress Right is organized as a corporation so owners' equity is classified by source as either paid-in capital or retained earnings.

The local bank requires that Dress Right furnish financial statements on a monthly basis. The transactions listed in the illustration are used to demonstrate the accounting processing cycle for the month of July, 1997.

For each transaction, a source document provides the necessary information to complete steps two and three in the processing cycle, transaction analysis and recording the appropriate journal entry. Each transaction listed in Illustration 2–3 is analyzed below, preceded by the necessary journal entry.

To record the issuance of capital stock.

July 1

Cash	60,000	
Capital stock		60,000

ILLUSTRATION   2 – 2
Transaction Analysis, the Accounting Equation, and Debits and Credits

Transaction	Transaction Analysis	Accounting Equation Assets = Liabilities + Owners' Equity	Account Entry
1. An attorney invested $50,000 to open a law office.	Assets (cash) and owners' equity each increased by $50,000. *Cumulative balances*	+50,000 = +50,000 50,000 = 50,000	**Cash** 50,000 ┃ **Owners' Equity** ┃ 50,000
2. $40,000 was borrowed from a bank and a note payable was signed.	Assets (cash) and liabilities (note payable) each increased by $40,000 *Cumulative balances*	+40,000 +40,000 90,000 = 40,000 + 50,000	**Cash** 50,000 ┃ 40,000 ┃ **Note Payable** ┃ 40,000
3. Supplies costing $3,000 were purchased on account.	Assets (supplies) and liabilities (accounts payable) each increased by $3,000 *Cumulative balances*	+3,000 +3,000 93,000 = 43,000 + 50,000	**Supplies** 3,000 ┃ **Accounts Payable** ┃ 3,000
4. Services were performed on account for $10,000.	Assets (accounts receivable) and owners' equity (revenue) each increased by $10,000. *Cumulative balances*	+10,000 +10,000 103,000 = 43,000 + 60,000	**Accounts Receivable** 10,000 ┃ **Owners' Equity (Revenue)** ┃ 10,000
5. Salaries of $5,000 were paid to employees.	Assets (cash) decreased and owners' equity decreased (salaries expense increased) by $5,000. *Cumulative balances*	−5,000 −5,000 98,000 = 43,000 + 55,000	**Cash** 40,000 ┃ 5,000 50,000 ┃ **Owners' Equity (Salaries Expense)** 5,000 ┃
6. $500 of supplies were used.	Assets (supplies) decreased and owners' equity decreased (supplies expense increased) by $500. *Cumulative balances*	−500 −500 97,500 = 43,000 + 54,500	**Supplies** 3,000 ┃ 500 **Owners' Equity (Supplies Expense)** 500 ┃
7. $1,000 was paid on account to the supplies vendor.	Assets (cash) and liabilities (accounts payable) each decreased by $1,000. *Cumulative balances*	−1,000 −1,000 96,500 = 42,000 + 54,500	**Cash** 40,000 ┃ 5,000 50,000 ┃ 1,000 **Accounts Payable** 1,000 ┃ 3,000

ILLUSTRATION   2–3

External Transactions for July 1997

July	1	Two individuals each invested $30,000 in the corporation. 3,000 shares of capital stock were issued to each investor.
	1	Borrowed $40,000 from a local bank and signed a note payable requiring payment of principal and 10% interest in six months.
	1	Paid $24,000 in advance for one year's rent on the store building.
	1	Purchased furniture and fixtures from Acme Furniture for $12,000 cash.
	3	Purchased $60,000 of clothing inventory on account from the Birdwell Wholesale Clothing Company.
	6	Purchased $2,000 of supplies for cash.
	4–31	Sold merchandise costing $20,000 for $35,000 cash.
	9	Sold clothing on account to St. Jude's School for Girls for $3,500. The clothing cost $2,000.
	16	Subleased a portion of the building to a jewelry store. Received $1,000 in advance for the first two months' rent beginning on July 16.
	20	Paid Birdwell Wholesale Clothing $25,000 on account.
	20	Paid salaries to employees for the first half of the month, $5,000.
	25	Received $1,500 on account from St. Jude's.

This first transaction is an investment by owners that increases an asset, cash, and also increases shareholders' equity. Increases in assets are recorded as debits and increases in shareholders' equity are recorded as credits. We use the paid-in capital account called capital stock because stock was issued in exchange for cash paid in.[2]

To record the borrowing of cash and the signing of a note payable.

July 1

Cash	40,000	
Note payable		40,000

This transaction causes increases in both cash and the liability, note payable. Increases in assets are debits and increases in liabilities are credits. The note requires payment of $40,000 in principal and $2,000 ($40,000 × 10% × 6/12) in interest in six months. However, at this point we are concerned only with the external transaction that occurs when the cash is borrowed and the note payable signed. Later we discuss how the interest is recorded.

To record the payment of one year's rent in advance.

July 1

Prepaid rent	24,000	
Cash		24,000

This transaction decreased cash (a credit) and increased an asset called prepaid rent, which is debited. Dress Right acquired the right to use the building for one full year. This is an asset because it represents a future benefit to the company. As we will see later, this asset expires over the one-year rental period.

To record the purchase of furniture and fixtures.

July 1

Furniture and fixtures	12,000	
Cash		12,000

This transaction increases one asset, furniture and fixtures, and decreases another, cash.

To record the purchase of merchandise inventory.

July 3

Inventory	60,000	
Accounts payable		60,000

---

[2]The different types of capital stock are discussed in Chapter 19.

This purchase of merchandise on account is recorded by a debit to inventory, an asset, and a credit to accounts payable, a liability. Increases in assets are debits, and increases in liabilities are credits.

The Dress Right Clothing Company uses the *perpetual inventory system* to keep track of its merchandise inventory. This system requires that the cost of merchandise purchased be recorded in inventory, an asset account. When inventory is sold, the inventory account is decreased by the cost of the item sold. Chapters 8 and 9 cover the topic of inventory in depth.

To record the purchase of supplies.

July 6		
Supplies	2,000	
Cash		2,000

The acquisition of supplies is recorded as a debit to the asset account supplies (an increase) and a credit to the asset cash (a decrease). Supplies are recorded as an asset because they represent future benefits.

To record the month's cash sales and the cost of those sales.

July 4–31		
Cash	35,000	
Sales revenue		35,000
Cost of goods sold (expense)	20,000	
Inventory		20,000

During the month of July, cash sales to customers totaled $35,000. The company's assets (cash) increase by this amount as does shareholders' equity. This increase in equity is recorded by a credit to the temporary account sales revenue.

At the same time, an asset, inventory, decreases and retained earnings decreases. Recall that expenses are outflows or using up of assets from providing goods and services. Dress Right incurred an expense equal to the cost of the inventory sold. The temporary account cost of goods sold increases. However, this increase in an expense represents a *decrease* in shareholders' equity—retained earnings—and accordingly the account is debited. Both of these transactions are *summary* transactions. Each sale made during the month requires a separate and similar entry.

To record a credit sale and the cost of that sale.

July 9		
Accounts receivable	3,500	
Sales revenue		3,500
Cost of goods sold	2,000	
Inventory		2,000

This transaction is similar to the cash sale above. The only difference is that the asset acquired in exchange for merchandise is accounts receivable rather than cash.

To record the receipt of rent in advance.

July 16		
Cash	1,000	
Unearned rent revenue (liability)		1,000

Cash increases by $1,000 so the cash account is debited. At this point, Dress Right does not recognize revenue even though cash has been received. Recall that the first criteria required for revenue recognition as stated in the realization principle is that the "earnings process is judged to be complete or virtually complete." Dress Right does not earn the revenue until it has provided the jewelry store with the use of facilities; that is, the revenue is earned as the rental period expires. On receipt of the cash, a liability called *unearned rent revenue* increases and is credited. This liability represents Dress Right's obligation to provide the use of facilities to the jewelry store.

Additional Consideration

Periodic Inventory System

The principal alternative to the perpetual inventory system is the periodic system. This system requires that the cost of merchandise purchased be recorded in a temporary account called *purchases*. When inventory is sold, the inventory account is not decreased and cost of goods sold is not recorded. Cost of goods sold for a period is determined and the inventory account is adjusted only at the end of a reporting period.

For example, the purchase of $60,000 of merchandise on account by Dress Right Clothing is recorded as follows:

Purchases	60,000	
Accounts payable		60,000

No cost of goods sold entry is recorded when sales are made in the periodic system.

At the end of July, the amount of ending inventory is determined (either by means of a physical count of goods on hand or by estimation) to be $38,000 and cost of goods sold for the month is determined as follows:

Beginning inventory	-0-
Plus: Purchases	60,000
Less: Ending inventory	(38,000)
Cost of goods sold	22,000

The following journal entry records cost of goods sold for the period and adjusts the inventory account to the actual amount on hand (in this case from zero to $38,000):

Cost of goods sold	22,000	
Inventory	38,000	
Purchases		60,000

Inventory is discussed in depth in Chapters 8 and 9.

To record the payment of accounts payable.

July 20

Accounts payable	25,000	
Cash		25,000

This transaction decreases both an asset (cash) and a liability (accounts payable). Decreases in assets are credits, and decreases in liabilities are debits.

To record the payment of salaries for the first half of the month.

July 20

Salaries expense	5,000	
Cash		5,000

Employees were paid for services rendered during the first half of the month. The cash expenditure did not create an asset since no future benefits result. Cash decreases and is credited; shareholders' equity decreases and is debited. The debit is recorded in the temporary account salaries expense.

To record receipt of cash on account.

July 25

Cash	1,500	
Accounts receivable		1,500

This transaction is an exchange of one asset, accounts receivable, for another asset, cash.

General Journal   Page 1

Date	Account Title and Explanation	Post Ref.	Debit	Credit
1997				
July 1	Cash	100	60,000	
	Capital stock	300		60,000
	To record the issuance of capital stock.			
1	Cash	100	40,000	
	Note payable	220		40,000
	To record the borrowing of cash and the signing of a note payable.			
1	Prepaid rent	130	24,000	
	Cash	100		24,000
	To record the payment of one year's rent in advance.			
1	Furniture and fixtures	150	12,000	
	Cash	100		12,000
	To record the purchase of furniture and fixtures.			
3	Inventory	140	60,000	
	Accounts payable	210		60,000
	To record the purchase of merchandise inventory.			
6	Supplies	125	2,000	
	Cash	100		2,000
	To record the purchase of supplies.			
4–31	Cash	100	35,000	
	Sales revenue	400		35,000
	To record cash sales for the month.			
4–31	Cost of goods sold	500	20,000	
	Inventory	140		20,000
	To record the cost of cash sales.			
9	Accounts receivable	110	3,500	
	Sales revenue	400		3,500
	To record credit sale.			
9	Cost of goods sold	500	2,000	
	Inventory	140		2,000
	To record the cost of a credit sale.			
16	Cash	100	1,000	
	Unearned rent revenue	230		1,000
	To record the receipt of rent in advance.			
20	Accounts payable	210	25,000	
	Cash	100		25,000
	To record the payment of accounts payable.			
20	Salaries expense	510	5,000	
	Cash	100		5,000
	To record the payment of salaries for the first half of the month.			
25	Cash	100	1,500	
	Accounts receivable	110		1,500
	To record the receipt of cash on account.			

Illustration 2–4 summarizes each of the transactions just illustrated as they would appear in a general journal. In addition to the date, account titles, debit and credit columns, the journal also has a column titled Post Ref. (Posting Reference). This usually is a number assigned to the general ledger account that is being debited or credited. For purposes of this illustration, all asset accounts have been assigned numbers in the 100s, all liabilities are 200s, permanent shareholders' equity accounts are 300s, revenues are 400s, and expenses are 500s.

The ledger accounts also contain a posting reference, usually the page number of the journal in which the journal entry was recorded. This allows for easy cross-referencing between the journal and the ledger. Page 1 is used for Illustration 2–4.

Learning objective 3
Post the effects of journal entries to T-accounts and prepare an unadjusted trial balance.

Step 4 in the processing cycle is to transfer the debit/credit information from the journal to the general ledger accounts. Illustration 2–5 contains the ledger accounts (in T-account form) for Dress Right *after* all of the general journal transactions have been posted. The reference GJ1 next to each of the posted amounts indicates that the source of the entry is page one of the general journal.

ILLUSTRATION   2-5

General Ledger Accounts

Balance Sheet Accounts

Cash				100
July 1 GJ1	60,000	24,000	July 1 GJ1	
1 GJ1	40,000	12,000	1 GJ1	
4-31 GJ1	35,000	2,000	6 GJ1	
16 GJ1	1,000	25,000	20 GJ1	
25 GJ1	1,500	5,000	20 GJ1	
July 31 Bal.	**69,500**			

Prepaid Rent		130
July 1 GJ1	24,000	
July 31 Bal.	**24,000**	

Accounts Receivable				110
July 9 GJ1	3,500	1,500	July 25 GJ1	
July 31 Bal.	**2,000**			

Inventory				140
July 3 GJ1	60,000	20,000	July 4-31	
		2,000	9 GJ1	
July 31 Bal.	**38,000**			

Supplies		125
July 6 GJ1	2,000	
July 31 Bal.	**2,000**	

Furniture and Fixtures		150
July 1 GJ1	12,000	
July 31 Bal.	**12,000**	

Accounts Payable				210
July 20 GJ1	25,000	60,000	July 3 GJ1	
		35,000	**July 31 Bal.**	

Note Payable			220
	40,000	July	1 GJ1
	40,000	**July 31 Bal.**	

Unearned Rent Revenue			230
	1,000	July 16 GJ1	
	1,000	**July 31 Bal.**	

Capital Stock			300
	60,000	July	1 GJ1
	60,000	**July 31 Bal.**	

Retained Earnings		310

Income Statement Accounts

Sales Revenue			400
	35,000	July	4-31
	3,500		9 GJ1
	38,500	**July 31 Bal.**	

Cost of Goods Sold			500
July 4-31 GJ1	20,000		
July 9 GJ1	2,000		
July 31 Bal.	**22,000**		

Salaries Expense		510
July 20 GJ1	5,000	
July 31 Bal.	**5,000**	

Step 5: Prepare an **unadjusted trial balance**.

Before financial statements are prepared and before adjusting entries are recorded (internal transactions) at the end of an accounting period, an **unadjusted trial balance** usually is prepared—step 5. A trial balance is simply a list of the general ledger accounts and their balances at a particular date. Its purpose is to check for completeness and to prove that the sum of the accounts with debit balances equals the sum of the accounts with credit balances, that is, the accounting equation is in balance. The fact that the debits and credits are equal does not necessarily mean that the

ILLUSTRATION   2–6

Unadjusted Trial Balance

At any time, the total of all debit balances should equal the total of all credit balances.

Dress Right Clothing Corporation
Unadjusted Trial Balance
July 31, 1997

Account Title	Debits	Credits
Cash	69,500	
Accounts receivable	2,000	
Supplies	2,000	
Prepaid rent	24,000	
Inventory	38,000	
Furniture and fixtures	12,000	
Accounts payable		35,000
Note payable		40,000
Unearned rent revenue - *liability acct.*		1,000
Capital stock		60,000
Retained earnings		- 0 -
Sales revenue		38,500
Cost of goods sold	22,000	
Salaries expense	5,000	
Totals	174,500	174,500

equal balances are correct. The trial balance could contain offsetting errors. As we will see later in the chapter, this trial balance also facilitates the preparation of adjusting entries.

The unadjusted trial balance at July 31, 1997, for the Dress Right Clothing Corporation appears in Illustration 2–6. Notice that the balance in the retained earnings account is zero. That is because this is the company's first year of operations. The increases and decreases in retained earnings for July are recorded indirectly in revenue and expense accounts. Before the start of the next year, these increases and decreases are transferred to the retained earnings account.

CONCEPT REVIEW EXERCISE   JOURNAL ENTRIES FOR EXTERNAL TRANSACTIONS

The Wyndham Wholesale Company began operations on August 1, 1997. The following transactions took place during the month of August.

try to do this for 9/15 class

    a. Owners invested $50,000 cash in the corporation in exchange for 5,000 shares of capital stock.

    b. Equipment is purchased for $20,000 cash.

    c. On the first day of August, $6,000 rent on a building is paid for the months of August and September.

    d. Merchandise inventory costing $38,000 is purchased on account. The company uses the perpetual inventory system.

    e. $30,000 is borrowed from a local bank, and a note payable is signed.

    f. Credit sales for the month are $40,000. The cost of merchandise sold is $22,000.

    g. $15,000 is collected on account from customers.

    h. $20,000 is paid on account to suppliers of merchandise.

    i. Salaries of $7,000 are paid to employees for August.

    j. A bill for $2,000 is received from the local utility company for the month of August.

    k. $20,000 cash was loaned to another company, evidenced by a note receivable.

    l. The corporation paid its shareholders a cash dividend of $1,000.

Required:
1. Prepare a journal entry for each transaction.
2. Prepare an unadjusted trial balance as of August 31, 1997.

CONCEPT REVIEW EXERCISE   SOLUTION

1. Prepare a journal entry for each transaction.
    a. The issuance of capital stock for cash increases both cash and shareholders' equity (capital stock).

| Cash | 50,000 | |
| Capital stock | | 50,000 |

b. The purchase of equipment increases equipment and decreases cash.

| Equipment | 20,000 | |
| Cash | | 20,000 |

c. The payment of rent in advance increases prepaid rent and decreases cash.

| Prepaid rent | 6,000 | |
| Cash | | 6,000 |

d. The purchase of merchandise on account increases both inventory and accounts payable.

| Inventory | 38,000 | |
| Accounts payable | | 38,000 |

e. Borrowing cash and signing a note increases both cash and note payable.

| Cash | 30,000 | |
| Note payable | | 30,000 |

f. The sale of merchandise on account increases both accounts receivable and sales revenue. Also, cost of goods sold increases and inventory decreases.

| Accounts receivable | 40,000 | |
| Sales revenue | | 40,000 |

| Cost of goods sold | 22,000 | |
| Inventory | | 22,000 |

g. The collection of cash on account increases cash and decreases accounts receivable.

| Cash | 15,000 | |
| Accounts receivable | | 15,000 |

h. The payment of suppliers on account decreases both accounts payable and cash.

| Accounts payable | 20,000 | |
| Cash | | 20,000 |

i. The payment of salaries for the period increases salaries expense (decreases retained earnings) and decreases cash.

| Salaries expense | 7,000 | |
| Cash | | 7,000 |

j. The receipt of a bill for services rendered increases both an expense (utilities expense) and accounts payable.

Utilities expense	2,000	
Accounts payable		2,000

k. The lending of cash to another entity and the signing of a note increases note receivable and decreases cash.

Note receivable	20,000	
Cash		20,000

l. Cash dividends paid to shareholders reduce both retained earnings and cash.

Retained earnings[3]	1,000	
Cash		1,000

2. Prepare an unadjusted trial balance as of August 31, 1997.

Account Title	Debits	Credits
Cash	21,000	
Accounts receivable	25,000	
Prepaid rent	6,000	
Inventory	16,000	
Note receivable	20,000	
Equipment	20,000	
Accounts payable		20,000
Note payable		30,000
Capital stock		50,000
Retained earnings	1,000	
Sales revenue		40,000
Cost of goods sold	22,000	
Salaries expense	7,000	
Utilities expense	2,000	
Totals	140,000	140,000

Adjusting Entries

Step 6 in the processing cycle is to record in the general journal and post to the ledger accounts the effect of *internal events* on the accounting equation. These transactions do not involve an exchange transaction with another entity and, therefore, are not initiated by a source document. They are recorded at the end of any period when financial statements must be prepared. These transactions are commonly referred to as **adjusting entries.**

Even when all transactions and events are analyzed, corrected, journalized, and posted to appropriate ledger accounts, some account balances will require updating. Adjusting entries are required to implement the *accrual accounting model.* More specifically, these entries are required to satisfy the *realization principle* and the *matching principle.* Adjusting entries help ensure that all revenues earned in a period are recognized in that period, regardless of when the cash payment is received. Also, they enable a company to recognize all expenses incurred during a period, regardless of when cash payment is made. As a result, a period's income statement provides a more complete measure of a company's operating performance and a better measure for predicting future operating cash flows. The balance sheet also provides a more complete assessment of assets and liabilities as sources of future cash receipts and disbursements. You might think of adjusting entries as a method of bringing the company's financial information up to date before preparing the financial statements.

Adjusting entries are necessary for three situations:

[3]An alternative is to debit a temporary account—dividends—which is closed to retained earnings at the end of the fiscal year along with the other temporary accounts.

1. **Prepayments,** sometimes referred to as *deferrals.*
2. **Accruals.**
3. **Estimates.**

Prepayments

> Prepayments are transactions in which the cash flow *precedes* expense or revenue recognition.

Prepayments occur when the cash flow *precedes* either expense or revenue recognition. For example, a company may buy supplies in one period but *use* them in a later period. The cash outflow creates an asset (supplies) which then must be expensed in a future period as the asset is used up. Similarly, a company may receive cash from a customer in one period but provide the customer with a good or service in a future period. For instance, magazine publishers usually receive cash in advance for magazine subscriptions. The cash inflow creates a liability (unearned revenue) which is recognized as revenue in a future period when it is earned.

> Prepaid expenses represent assets recorded when a cash disbursement creates benefits beyond the current reporting period.

Prepaid Expenses. **Prepaid expenses** are the costs of assets acquired in one period and expensed in a future period. Whenever cash is paid, and it is not to (1) satisfy a liability or (2) pay a dividend or return capital to owners, it must be determined whether or not the payment creates future benefits or whether the payment benefits only the current period. The purchase of machinery, equipment, or supplies or the payment of rent in advance are examples of payments that create future benefits and should be recorded as assets. The benefits provided by these assets expire in future periods and their cost is expensed in future periods as related revenues are recognized.

> The adjusting entry required for a prepaid expense is a *debit to an expense* and a *credit to an asset.*

To illustrate this concept, assume that a company paid a radio station $2,000 in July for advertising. If that $2,000 were for advertising provided by the radio station during the month of July, the entire $2,000 would be expensed in the same period as the cash disbursement. If, however, the $2,000 was a payment for advertising to be provided in a future period, say the month of August, then the cash disbursement creates an asset called *prepaid advertising*. An adjusting entry is required at the end of August to increase advertising expense (decrease shareholders' equity) and to decrease the asset prepaid advertising by $2,000. The adjusting entry for a prepaid expense is, therefore, a *debit to an expense* and a *credit to an asset.*

The unadjusted trial balance can provide a starting point for determining which adjusting entries are required for a period, particularly for prepayments. Review the July 31, 1997, unadjusted trial balance for the Dress Right Clothing Corporation in Illustration 2–6 on page 67 and try to anticipate the required adjusting entries for prepaid expenses.

> **Learning objective 5**
> Record adjusting journal entries in general journal format.

The first asset that requires adjustment is supplies, $2,000 of which were purchased during July. This transaction created an asset as the supplies will be used in future periods. The company could either track the supplies used or simply count the supplies at the end of the period and determine the dollar amount of supplies remaining. Assume that Dress Right determines that at the end of July, $1,200 of supplies remain. The following adjusting journal entry is required.

> To record the cost of supplies used during the month of July.

July 31		
Supplies expense	800	
Supplies		800

Supplies

Beg. bal.	0		
	2,000	800	
Bal.	1,200		

After this entry is recorded and posted to the ledger accounts, the supplies (asset) account is reduced to a $1,200 debit balance, and the supplies expense account will have a $800 debit balance.

The next prepaid expense requiring adjustment is rent. Recall that at the beginning of July, the company paid $24,000 to its landlord representing one year's rent in advance. As it is reasonable to assume that the rent services provided each period are equal, the monthly rent is $2,000. At the end of July 1997, one month's prepaid rent has expired and must be recognized as expense.

> To record the cost of expired rent for the month of July.

July 31		
Rent expense ($24,000 ÷ 12)	2,000	
Prepaid rent		2,000

After this entry is recorded and posted to the ledger accounts, the prepaid rent account will have a debit balance of $22,000, representing 11 remaining months at $2,000 a month, and the rent expense account will have a $2,000 debit balance.

The final prepayment involves the asset represented by furniture and fixtures that was purchased for $12,000. This asset has a long life but nevertheless will expire over time. For the previous two adjusting entries, it was fairly straightforward to determine the amount of the asset that expired during the period.

However, it is difficult, if not impossible, to determine how much of the benefits from using the furniture and fixtures expired during any particular period. Recall from Chapter 1 that one approach to implementing the matching principle is to "recognize an expense by a systematic and rational allocation to specific time periods."

Assume that the furniture and fixtures have a useful life of five years or 60 months and will be worthless at the end of that period, and that we choose to allocate the cost equally over the period of use. The amount of monthly expense, called *depreciation expense,* is $200 ($12,000 ÷ 60 months = $200), and the following adjusting entry is recorded.

To record depreciation of furniture and fixtures for the month of July.	**July 31**	
	Depreciation expense	200
	Accumulated depreciation - furniture and fixtures	200

The entry reduces an asset, furniture and fixtures, by $200. However, the asset account is not reduced directly. Instead, the credit is to an account called *accumulated depreciation.* This is a valuation account, or a contra account, to furniture and fixtures. The purpose of the contra account is to keep the original cost of the asset intact while reducing it indirectly. On the balance sheet, furniture and fixtures is reported net of accumulated depreciation. This topic is covered in depth in Chapter 11.

After this entry is recorded and posted to the ledger accounts, the accumulated depreciation account will have a credit balance of $200 and the depreciation expense account will have a $200 debit balance.

Unearned Revenues.   **Unearned revenues** are created when a company receives cash from a customer in one period for goods or services that are to be provided in a future period. The cash receipt, an external transaction, is recorded as a debit to cash and a credit to a liability. This liability reflects the company's obligation to provide goods or services in the future.

> **Unearned revenues** represent liabilities recorded when cash is received from customers in advance of providing a good or service.

To illustrate an unearned revenue transaction, assume that during the month of June a magazine publisher received $24 in cash for a 24-month subscription to a monthly magazine. The subscription begins in July. On receipt of the cash, the publisher records a liability, unearned subscription revenue, of $24. Subsequently, revenue of $1 is earned as each monthly magazine is published and mailed to the customer. An adjusting entry is required each month to increase shareholders' equity (revenue) to recognize the $1 in revenue earned and to decrease the liability. The adjusting entry for unearned revenues, therefore, is a *debit to a liability,* in this case unearned subscription revenue, and a *credit to revenue.*

> The adjusting entry required when unearned revenues are earned is a *debit to a liability* and a *credit to revenue.*

Once again, the unadjusted trial balance provides information concerning unearned revenues. For Dress Right Clothing Corporation, the only unearned revenue on the trial balance is unearned rent revenue. Recall that the company subleased a portion of its building to a jewelry store for $500 per month. On July 16, the jewelry store paid Dress Right $1,000 in advance for the first two months' rent. The transaction was recorded as a debit to cash and a credit to unearned rent revenue.

At the end of July, how much of the $1,000 has been earned? Approximately one-half of one month's rent has been earned, or $250, requiring the following adjusting journal entry.

To record the amount of unearned rent revenue earned during July.	**July 31**	
	Unearned rent revenue	250
	Rent revenue	250

After this entry is recorded and posted to the ledger accounts, the unearned rent revenue account is reduced to a credit balance of $750 for the remaining one and one-half months' rent, and the rent revenue account will have a $250 credit balance.

Alternative Approach to Record Prepayments. The same end result can be achieved for prepayments by recording the external transaction directly into an expense or revenue account. In fact, many companies prefer this approach. For simplicity, bookkeeping instructions may require all cash payments for expenses to be debited to the appropriate expense account and all cash receipts for revenues to be credited to the appropriate revenue account. The adjusting entry then records the *unexpired* prepaid expense (asset) or unearned revenue (liability) as of the end of the period.

For example, on July 1, 1997, Dress Right paid $24,000 in cash for one year's rent on its building. The entry included a debit to prepaid rent. The company could have debited rent expense instead.

Alternative approach:
July 1

Rent expense	24,000	
Cash		24,000

The adjusting entry then records the amount of prepaid rent as of the end of July, $22,000, and reduces rent expense to $2,000, the cost of rent for the month of July:

Alternative approach:
July 31

Prepaid rent	22,000	
Rent expense		22,000

The net effect of handling the transactions in this manner is the same as the previous treatment. Either way, the prepaid rent account will have a debit balance at the end of July of $22,000, and the rent expense account will have a debit balance of $2,000. What's important is that an adjusting entry is recorded to ensure the appropriate amounts are reflected in both the expense and asset before *financial statements are to be prepared.*

Accruals

Accruals occur when the cash flow comes *after* either expense or revenue recognition. For example, a company often uses the services of another entity in one period and pays for them in a subsequent period. An expense must be recognized in the period incurred and an accrued liability recorded. Also, goods and services often are provided to customers on credit. In such instances, a revenue is recognized in the period earned and an asset, a receivable, is recorded.

Many accruals involve external transactions that automatically are recorded from a source document. For example, a sales invoice for a credit sale provides all the information necessary to record the debit to accounts receivable and the credit to sales revenue. However, there are some accruals that involve internal transactions and thus require adjusting entries. Because accruals involve recognition of expense or revenue before cash flow, the unadjusted trial balance will not be as helpful in identifying required adjusting entries as with prepayments.

Accrued Liabilities. For **accrued liabilities,** we are concerned with expenses incurred but not yet paid. Dress Right Clothing Corporation requires two adjusting entries for accrued liabilities at July 31, 1997.

The first entry is for employee salaries for the second half of July. Recall that on July 20 the company paid employees $5,000 for salaries for the first half of the month. Salaries for the second half of July will probably be paid in early August. Nevertheless, the company incurred an expense in July for services provided to it by its employees. Also, there exists an obligation at the end of July to pay the salaries earned by employees. An adjusting entry is required to increase salaries expense (decrease shareholders' equity) and to increase liabilities for the salaries payable. The adjusting entry for an accrued liability always includes a *debit to an expense,* and a *credit to a liability.* Assuming that salaries for the second half of July are $5,500, the following adjusting entry is recorded.

To record accrued salaries at the end of July.

July 31

Salaries expense 5,500
     Salaries payable 5,500

After this entry is recorded and posted to the general ledger, the salaries expense account will have a debit balance of $10,500 ($5,000 + 5,500), and the salaries payable account will have a credit balance of $5,500.

The unadjusted trial balance does provide information about the second required accrued liability entry. On the trial balance we can see a balance in the note payable account of $40,000. The company borrowed this amount on July 1, 1997. The entire $40,000 is payable in six months, along with 10% interest. Whenever the trial balance reveals interest-bearing debt, and interest is not paid on the last day of the period, an adjusting entry is required for the amount of interest that has built-up (accrued) since the last payment date. In this case, we calculate interest as follows:

$$\text{Principal} \times \text{Interest rate} \times \text{Time} = \text{Interest}$$
$$\$40,000 \times 10\% \times {}^1/_{12} = \$333 \text{ (rounded)}$$

Interest rates always are stated as the annual rate. Therefore, the above calculation uses this annual rate multiplied by the principal amount multiplied by the amount of time outstanding, in this case one month or one-twelfth of a year.

To accrue interest expense for July on note payable.

July 31

Interest expense 333
     Interest payable 333

After this entry is recorded and posted to the ledger accounts, the interest expense account will have a debit balance $333, and the interest payable account will have a credit balance of $333.[4]

Accrued Receivables.   **Accrued receivables** involve the recognition of revenue earned before cash is received. An example of an internal accrued revenue event is the recognition of interest earned on a loan to another entity. For example, assume that Dress Right loaned another corporation $30,000 at the beginning of August, evidenced by a note receivable. Terms of the note call for the payment of principal, $30,000, and interest at 8% in three months. An external transaction records the cash disbursement—a debit to note receivable and a credit to cash of $30,000.

> **Accrued receivables** involve situations when the revenue is earned in a period prior to the cash receipt.

What adjusting entry would be required at the end of August? Dress Right needs to record the interest revenue earned but not yet received and the corresponding receivable. Interest receivable increases and interest revenue (shareholders' equity) also increases. The adjusting entry for accrued receivables always includes a *debit to an asset,* a receivable, and a *credit to revenue.* In this case, at the end of August Dress Right recognizes $200 in interest revenue ($30,000 × 8% × $^1/_{12}$) and makes the following adjusting entry.

> The adjusting entry required to record an accrued revenue is a *debit to an asset,* a receivable, and a *credit to revenue.*

To accrue interest revenue earned in August on note receivable.

August 31

Interest receivable 200
     Interest revenue 200

There are no accrued revenue adjusting entries required for Dress Right at the end of July.

The required adjusting entries for prepayments and accruals are recapped in Graphic 2–3. Each case involves recognizing an expense or revenue in a period that differs from the period in which cash was paid or received. These entries are necessary to properly measure operating performance and financial position according to the accrual accounting model.

---

[4]Dress Right Clothing is a corporation. Corporations are income-tax-paying entities. Income taxes—federal, state and local—are assessed on an annual basis and payments are made throughout the year. An additional adjusting entry would be required for Dress Right to accrue the amount of estimated income taxes payable that are applicable to the month of July. Accounting for income taxes is introduced in Chapter 3 and covered in depth in Chapter 16.

GRAPHIC   2 – 3
Adjusting Entries

	Adjusting Entries			
	Expenses		**Revenues**	
Prepayments (initially recorded as assets or liabilities)	*Debit* *Credit*	Expense Asset	*Debit* *Credit*	Liability Revenue
Prepayments (initially recorded as expenses or revenues)	*Debit* *Credit*	Asset Expense	*Debit* *Credit*	Revenue Liability
Accruals	*Debit* *Credit*	Expense Liability	*Debit* *Credit*	Asset Revenue

Estimates

Accountants often must make estimates in order to comply with the accrual accounting model.

A third classification of adjusting entries is **estimates.** Accountants often must make estimates of future events to comply with the accrual accounting model. For example, the calculation of depreciation expense requires an estimate of expected useful life of the asset being depreciated as well as its expected residual value. We discussed the adjusting entry for depreciation expense in the context of its being a prepayment, but it also could be thought of as an estimate.

One situation involving an estimate that does not fit neatly into either the prepayment or accrual classification is **bad debt expense.** Chapter 1 introduced briefly the allowance method of accounting for bad debts. This method requires an estimate of the amount of accounts receivable that will ultimately prove to be uncollectible. This estimate is required to properly match the bad debt expense with the revenue it helps generate as well as reflect the collectible portion of the receivable on the balance sheet.

The July 31, 1997, unadjusted trial balance for Dress Right shows a balance in accounts receivable of $2,000. Assume that the company's management felt that of this amount, only $1,500 would ultimately be collected. An adjusting entry is required to decrease accounts receivable and increase bad debt expense (decrease shareholders' equity) by $500. The adjusting entry is:

To record bad debt expense for July.

July 31		
Bad debt expense	500	
Allowance for uncollectible accounts		500

Notice that the accounts receivable account is not reduced directly. A contra account, called *allowance for uncollectible accounts,* is credited. After this entry is recorded and posted to the ledger accounts, bad debt expense will have a debit balance of $500 and the allowance for uncollectible accounts account will have a credit balance of $500.[5]

The contra account is used to keep intact in the accounts receivable account the total amount of receivables that are still outstanding. The allowance account will always have a credit balance equal to estimated bad debts on existing accounts receivable. Only when the account is actually written off as uncollectible would accounts receivable be reduced. At this point, the $500 is just an estimate. On the balance sheet, accounts receivable is shown net of the allowance account, in this case $1,500. Chapter 7 addresses the topics of accounts receivable and bad debts in more depth.

Illustration 2–7 recaps the July 31, 1997, adjusting entries for Dress Right Clothing Corporation as they would appear in a general journal.

Learning objective 5
Prepare an adjusted trial balance.

After the adjusting entries are posted to the general ledger accounts, the next step — *step 7 —* in the processing cycle is to prepare an **adjusted trial balance.** The term adjusted refers to the fact that adjusting entries have now been posted to the accounts. Illustration 2–8 shows the July 31, 1997, adjusted trial balance for Dress Right Clothing Corporation.

---

[5]If the allowance for uncollectible accounts had a credit balance before the adjusting entry, say $150, then the adjusting entry would have required only a $350 debit to bad debt expense and credit to the allowance account.

ILLUSTRATION   2–7

The General Journal —
Adjusting Entries

DRESS RIGHT CLOTHING CORPORATION

General Journal   Page 2

Date	Account Title and Explanation	Post Ref.	Debit	Credit
1997				
July 31	Supplies expense	520	800	
	Supplies	125		800
	To record the cost of supplies used during the month of July.			
31	Rent expense	530	2,000	
	Prepaid rent	130		2,000
	To record the cost of expired rent for the month of July.			
31	Depreciation expense	540	200	
	Accumulated depreciation— furniture and fixtures	155		200
	To record depreciation for furniture and fixtures for the month of July.			
31	Unearned rent revenue	230	250	
	Rent revenue	410		250
	To record the amount of unearned rent revenue earned during July.			
31	Salaries expense	510	5,500	
	Salaries payable	230		5,500
	To record accrued salaries at the end of July.			
31	Interest expense	550	333	
	Interest payable	240		333
	To accrue interest expense for July on notes payable.			
31	Bad debt expense	560	500	
	Allowance for uncollectible accounts	115		500
	To record bad debt expense for July.			

ILLUSTRATION   2–8

Adjusted Trial Balance

DRESS RIGHT CLOTHING CORPORATION
Adjusted Trial Balance
July 31, 1997

Step 7: Prepare an
**adjusted trial
balance.**

Account Title	Debits	Credits
Cash	69,500	
Accounts receivable	2,000	
Allowance for uncollectible accounts		500
Supplies	1,200	
Prepaid rent	22,000	
Inventory	38,000	
Furniture and fixtures	12,000	
Accumulated depreciation—furniture and fixtures		200
Accounts payable		35,000
Note payable		40,000
Unearned rent revenue		750
Salaries payable		5,500
Interest payable		333
Capital stock		60,000
Retained earnings		- 0 -
Sales revenue		38,500
Rent revenue		250
Cost of goods sold	22,000	
Salaries expense	10,500	
Supplies expense	800	
Rent expense	2,000	
Depreciation expense	200	
Interest expense	333	
Bad debt expense	500	
Totals	181,033	181,033

CONCEPT REVIEW EXERCISE   ADJUSTING ENTRIES

The Wyndham Wholesale Company needs to prepare financial statements at the end of August 1997 for presentation to its bank. An unadjusted trial balance as of August 31, 1997, was presented in a previous concept review exercise on page 69.

The following information also is available:
a. The company anticipates that of the $25,000 in accounts receivable from customers, $2,500 will *not* be collected.
b. The note payable requires the entire $30,000 in principal plus interest at 10% to be paid on July 31, 1998. The date of the loan is August 1, 1997.
c. Depreciation on the equipment for the month of August is $500.
d. The note receivable is dated August 16, 1997. The note requires the entire $20,000 in principal plus interest at 12% to be repaid in 120 days (The loan was outstanding 15 days during August).
e. The prepaid rent of $6,000 represents rent for the months of August and September.

Required:
1. Prepare any necessary adjusting entries at August 31, 1997.
2. Prepare an adjusted trial balance as of August 31, 1997.
3. What is the effect on income (overstated or understated) if the adjusting entries are not made?

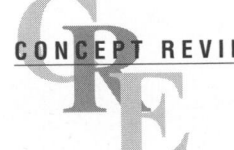

CONCEPT REVIEW EXERCISE   SOLUTION

1. Prepare any necessary adjusting entries at August 31, 1997.
   a. An adjusting entry is required to adjust allowance for uncollectible accounts to $2,500. Because there is no balance in the allowance account before adjustment, the adjusting entry must record a bad debt expense of $2,500.

Bad debt expense	2,500	
Allowance for uncollectible accounts		2,500

   b. An adjusting entry is required to accrue the interest expense on the note payable for the month of August. Accrued interest is calculated as follows:

$$\$30,000 \times 10\% \times 1/12 = \$250$$

Interest expense	250	
Interest payable		250

   c. Depreciation expense on the equipment must be recorded.

Depreciation expense	500	
Accumulated depreciation-equipment		500

   d. An adjusting entry is required for the 15 days of accrued interest revenue earned on the note receivable. Accrued interest is calculated as follows:

$$\$20,000 \times 12\% \times 15/360 = \$100$$

Interest receivable	100	
Interest revenue		100

e. An adjusting entry is required to recognize the amount of prepaid rent expense that expired during August.

Rent expense	3,000	
Prepaid rent		3,000

2. Prepare an adjusted trial balance as of August 31, 1997.

Account Title	Debits	Credits
Cash	21,000	
Accounts receivable	25,000	
Allowance for uncollectible accounts		2,500
Prepaid rent	3,000	
Inventory	16,000	
Interest receivable	100	
Note receivable	20,000	
Equipment	20,000	
Accumulated depreciation—equipment		500
Accounts payable		20,000
Interest payable		250
Note payable		30,000
Capital stock		50,000
Retained earnings	1,000	
Sales revenue		40,000
Interest revenue		100
Cost of goods sold	22,000	
Salaries expense	7,000	
Utilities expense	2,000	
Bad debt expense	2,500	
Interest expense	250	
Depreciation expense	500	
Rent expense	3,000	
Totals	143,350	143,350

3. What is the effect on income (overstated or understated), if the adjusting entries are not made?

Adjusting entry	Income Overstated (understated)
Uncollectible accounts	$2,500
Interest expense	250
Depreciation expense	500
Interest revenue	(100)
Rent expense	3,000
Net effect, income overstated by	$6,150

We now turn our attention to the preparation of financial statements.

Preparing the Financial Statements

The purpose of each of the steps in the processing cycle to this point is to provide information for step 8—preparation of the **financial statements.** The adjusted trial balance contains the necessary information. After all, the financial statements are the primary means of communicating financial information to external parties.

Learning objective 6
Describe the four basic financial statements.

Step 8: Preparation of **financial statements.**

The **income statement** is a change statement.

The Income Statement

The purpose of the **income statement** is to summarize the operating activities of the company during a particular period of time. It is a change statement in that it reports the changes in shareholders' equity (retained earnings) that occurred during the period as a result of operating transactions (revenues, expenses, gains, and losses). Illustration 2–9 shows the income statement for Dress Right Clothing Corporation for the month of July 1997.

The income statement indicates a profit for the month of July of $2,417. During the month, the company was able to increase its net assets (equity) from activities related to selling its product. Chapter 3 discusses the format and content of the income statement in more depth.

leave people format

DRESS RIGHT CLOTHING CORPORATION
Income Statement
For the Month of July 1997

Sales revenue		$38,500
Cost of goods sold		22,000
Gross profit		16,500
Rent revenue		250
		16,750
Other expenses:		
Salaries expense	$10,500	
Supplies expense	800	
Rent expense	2,000	
Depreciation expense	200	
Interest expense	333	
Bad debt expense	500	
Total other expenses		14,333
Net income		$ 2,417

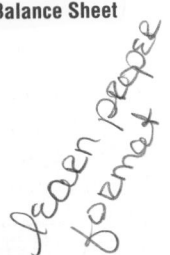

leave people format

DRESS RIGHT CLOTHING CORPORATION
Balance Sheet
at July 31, 1997
Assets

Current assets:		
Cash		$ 69,500
Accounts receivable	$ 2,000	
Less: Allowance for uncollectible accounts	500	1,500
Supplies		1,200
Inventory		38,000
Prepaid rent		22,000
Total current assets		132,200
Property and equipment:		
Furniture and fixtures	12,000	
Less: Accumulated depreciation	200	11,800
Total assets		$144,000

Liabilities and Shareholders' Equity

Current liabilities:		
Accounts payable		$ 35,000
Salaries payable		5,500
Unearned rent revenue		750
Interest payable		333
Note payable		40,000
Total current liabilities		81,583
Shareholders' equity:		
Capital stock, 6,000 shares issued and outstanding	$ 60,000	
Retained earnings	2,417*	
Total shareholders' equity		62,417
Total liabilities and shareholders' equity		$144,000

*Beginning retained earnings + net income − dividends = Ending retained earnings
     0   + $2,417 −   0   = $2,417

The Balance Sheet

The balance sheet is a position statement that presents an organized list of assets, liabilities, and equity at a particular point in time.

The purpose of the **balance sheet,** which often is called the **statement of financial position,** is to present the financial position of the company on a particular date. Unlike the income statement, which is a change statement reporting events that occurred *during a period of time,* the balance sheet is a statement that presents an organized list of assets, liabilities, and shareholders' equity *at a point in time.* Illustration 2–10 shows the balance sheet for Dress Right Clothing at July 31, 1997.

Illustration 2–10 illustrates a classified balance sheet. Assets and liabilities are grouped according to common characteristics. For example, most balance sheets contain the classifications of

current assets and **current liabilities.** Current assets are those assets that are cash, will be converted into cash, or will be used up within one year or the operating cycle, whichever is longer. Current liabilities are those liabilities that will be satisfied within one year or the operating cycle, whichever is longer. In most cases, the operating cycle is shorter than one year. The concept of an operating cycle along with a more detailed discussion of the balance sheet is contained in Chapter 5.

Examples of assets not classified as current include property and equipment and long-term receivables and investments. The only noncurrent asset that Dress Right has at July 31, 1997, is furniture and fixtures, which is classified under the property and equipment category.

All liabilities not classified as current are listed as noncurrent or long-term. All of Dress Right's liabilities at July 31, 1997, are current as they will be satisfied, paid off, within the next 12 months. If, for example, the note payable were due to be paid off in two years, the note payable is classified as a long-term liability below current liabilities.

Shareholders' equity lists the paid-in capital portion of equity—capital stock—and retained earnings. The income statement summarizes the revenue, expense, gain, and loss transactions that increased retained earnings. The net effect of these transactions, net income of $2,417, is classified as retained earnings. These temporary accounts are not yet actually transferred, or closed, to the permanent retained earnings account in the general ledger but are summarized as retained earnings for financial reporting. The closing process is discussed later in this chapter.

The Statement of Cash Flows

Similar to the income statement, the **statement of cash flows** also is a change statement, disclosing the events that caused cash to change during the period. The statement classifies all transactions affecting cash into one of three categories: (1) **operating activities,** (2) **investing activities,** and (3) **financing activities.** Operating activities are inflows and outflows of cash related to the transactions entering into the determination of net income. Investing activities involve the acquisition and sale of (1) long-term assets used in the business and (2) nonoperating investment assets. Financing activities involve cash inflows and outflows from transactions with creditors and owners.

The statement of cash flows for Dress Right for the month of July 1997 is shown in Illustration 2–11. As this is the first period of operations for Dress Right, the cash balance at the beginning of the period is zero. The net increase in cash of $69,500, therefore, equals the ending balance of cash disclosed on the balance sheet. The statement of cash flows is discussed in Chapters 3 and 22.

ILLUSTRATION   2–11

Statement of Cash Flows

DRESS RIGHT CLOTHING CORPORATION
Statement of Cash Flows
For the Month of July 1997

Cash flows from operating activities:		
Cash inflows:		
From customers	$ 36,500	
From rent	1,000	
Cash outflows:		
For rent	(24,000)	
For supplies	(2,000)	
To suppliers of merchandise	(25,000)	
To employees	(5,000)	
Net cash used by operating activities		$(18,500)
Cash flows from investing activities:		
Purchase of furniture and fixtures		(12,000)
Cash flows from financing activities:		
Issue of capital stock	$ 60,000	
Increase in notes payable	40,000	
Net cash provided by financing activities		100,000
Net increase in cash		$ 69,500

The Statement of Shareholders' Equity

The **statement of shareholders' equity** discloses the sources of changes in the permanent shareholders' equity accounts.

The final statement, the **statement of shareholders' equity,** also is a change statement. It discloses the sources of the changes in the various permanent shareholders' equity accounts that occurred during the period. Illustration 2–12 shows the statement of shareholders' equity for Dress Right for the month of July 1997.[6]

The individual operating transactions causing retained earnings to change are summarized on the income statement. Therefore, this statement only shows the net effect of these transactions on retained earnings, in this case an increase of $2,417. If the company had paid dividends to its shareholders during July, this would have reduced retained earnings.

ILLUSTRATION   2–12

Statement of Shareholders' Equity

DRESS RIGHT CLOTHING CORPORATION
Statement of Shareholders' Equity
For the Month of July 1997

	Capital Stock	Retained Earnings	Total Shareholders' Equity
Balance at July 1, 1997	- 0 -	- 0 -	- 0 -
Issue of capital stock	$60,000		$60,000
Net income for July, 1997		$2,417	$ 2,417
Balance at July 31, 1997	$60,000	$2,417	$62,417

The Closing Process

At the end of any interim reporting period the accounting processing cycle is now complete. An interim reporting period is any period when financial statements are produced other than at the end of the fiscal year. However, at the end of the fiscal year two final steps are necessary, closing the temporary accounts—step 9—and preparing a post-closing trial balance—step 10.

Step 9: **Close** the temporary accounts to retained earnings (at year-end only).

Learning objective 7
Explain the closing process.

The **closing process** serves a *dual purpose*: (1) the temporary accounts (revenues and expenses) are reduced to *zero balances,* ready to measure activity in the upcoming accounting period, and (2) these temporary account balances are *closed (transferred) to retained earnings* to reflect the changes that have occurred in that account during the period. Often, an intermediate step is to close revenues and expenses to **income summary**; then income summary is closed to retained earnings. The use of the income summary account is just a bookkeeping convenience that provides a check that all temporary accounts have been properly closed (that is, the balance equals net income or loss).

To illustrate the closing process, assume that the fiscal year-end for Dress Right Clothing Corporation is July 31. Using the adjusted trial balance in Illustration 2–8, we can prepare the following general journal entries.

To close the revenue accounts to income summary.

July 31		
Sales revenue	38,500	
Rent revenue	250	
Income summary		38,750

The first closing entry transfers the revenue account balances to income summary. Because revenue accounts have credit balances, they are debited to bring them to zero. After this entry is posted to the accounts, both revenue accounts have a zero balance.

---

[6]Some companies choose to disclose the changes in the retained earnings component of shareholders' equity in a separate statement or in a combined statement of income and retained earnings.

To close the expense
accounts to income summary.

July 31

Income summary	36,333	
Cost of goods sold		22,000
Salaries expense		10,500
Supplies expense		800
Rent expense		2,000
Depreciation expense		200
Interest expense		333
Bad debt expense		500

The second closing entry transfers the expense account balances to income summary. As expense accounts have debit balances, they are credited to bring them to zero. After this entry is posted to the accounts, the expense accounts have a zero balance and the income summary account has a credit balance equal to net income for the period, in this case $2,417.

Income Summary

Expenses	36,333	38,750	Revenues
		2,417	Net

To close the income summary
account to retained earnings.

July 31

Income summary	2,417	
Retained earnings		2,417

After this entry is posted to the accounts, the temporary accounts have zero balances and retained earnings has increased by the amount of the net income. It is important to remember that the temporary accounts are closed only at year-end and not at the end of any interim period. Closing the temporary accounts during the year would make it difficult to prepare the annual income statement.

Step 10: Prepare a **post-closing trial balance** (at year-end only).

After the closing entries are posted to the ledger accounts, a **post-closing trial balance** is prepared. The purpose of this trial balance is to verify that the closing entries were prepared and posted correctly and that the accounts are now ready for next year's transactions. Illustration 2–13 shows the post-closing trial balance for Dress Right at July 31, 1997, assuming a July 31 fiscal year-end.

ILLUSTRATION   2–13

Post-Closing Trial Balance

DRESS RIGHT CLOTHING CORPORATION
Post-Closing Trial Balance
July 31, 1997

Account Title	Debits	Credits
Cash	69,500	
Accounts receivable	2,000	
Allowance for uncollectible accounts		500
Supplies	1,200	
Prepaid rent	22,000	
Inventory	38,000	
Furniture and fixtures	12,000	
Accumulated depreciation—furniture and fixtures		200
Accounts payable		35,000
Note payable		40,000
Unearned rent revenue		750
Salaries payable		5,500
Interest payable		333
Capital stock		60,000
Retained earnings		2,417
Totals	144,700	144,700

CONCEPT REVIEW EXERCISE   FINANCIAL STATEMENT PREPARATION AND CLOSING

Refer to the August 31, 1997, adjusted trial balance of the Wyndham Wholesale Company presented in a previous concept review exercise on page 77.

Required:
1. Prepare an income statement and a statement of shareholders' equity for the month ended August 31, 1997, and a classified balance sheet as of August 31, 1997.
2. Assume that August 31 is the company's fiscal year-end. Prepare the necessary closing entries and a post-closing trial balance.

CONCEPT REVIEW EXERCISE   SOLUTION

1. Prepare an income statement and a statement of shareholders' equity for the month ended August 31, 1997, and a classified balance sheet as of August 31, 1997.

WYNDHAM WHOLESALE COMPANY
Income Statement
For the Month of August 1997

Sales revenue		$40,000
Cost of goods sold		22,000
Gross profit		18,000
Interest revenue		100
		18,100
Other expenses:		
Salaries expense	$7,000	
Utilities expense	2,000	
Bad debt expense	2,500	
Interest expense	250	
Depreciation expense	500	
Rent expense	3,000	
Total other expenses		15,250
Net income		$ 2,850

WYNDHAM WHOLESALE COMPANY
Statement of Shareholders' Equity
For the Month of August 1997

	Capital Stock	Retained Earnings	Total Shareholders' Equity
Balance at July 1, 1997	- 0 -	- 0 -	- 0 -
Issue of capital stock	$50,000		$50,000
Net income for August 1997		$2,850	2,850
Less: Dividends		(1,000)	(1,000)
Balance at July 31, 1997	$50,000	$1,850	$51,850

WYNDHAM WHOLESALE COMPANY
Balance Sheet
At August 31, 1997

Assets

Current assets:		
Cash		$ 21,000
Accounts receivable	$ 25,000	
Less: Allowance for uncollectible accounts	2,500	22,500
Inventory		16,000
Interest receivable		100
Note receivable		20,000
Prepaid rent expense		3,000
Total current assets		82,600
Property and equipment:		
Equipment	20,000	
Less: Accumulated depreciation	500	19,500
Total assets		$102,100

Liabilities and Shareholders' Equity

Current liabilities:
Accounts payable		$ 20,000
Interest payable		250
Note payable		30,000
Total current liabilities		50,250

Shareholders' equity:
Capital stock, 5,000 shares issued and outstanding	$ 50,000	
Retained earnings	1,850	
Total shareholders' equity		51,850
Total liabilities and shareholders' equity		$102,100

2. Assume that August 31 is the company's fiscal year-end. Prepare the necessary closing entries and a post-closing trial balance.

To close the revenue accounts to income summary.

August 31		
Sales revenue	40,000	
Interest revenue	100	
Income summary		40,100

To close the expense accounts to income summary.

August 31		
Income summary	37,250	
Cost of goods sold		22,000
Salaries expense		7,000
Utilities expense		2,000
Bad debt expense		2,500
Interest expense		250
Depreciation expense		500
Rent expense		3,000

To close the income summary account to retained earnings.

August 31		
Income summary	2,850	
Retained earnings		2,850

Post-Closing Trial Balance

Account Title	Debits	Credits
Cash	21,000	
Accounts receivable	25,000	
Allowance for uncollectible accounts		2,500
Prepaid rent	3,000	
Inventory	16,000	
Interest receivable	100	
Note receivable	20,000	
Equipment	20,000	
Accumulated depreciation—equipment		500
Accounts payable		20,000
Interest payable		250
Note payable		30,000
Capital stock		50,000
Retained earnings		1,850
Totals	105,100	105,100

Conversion from Cash Basis to Accrual Basis

In Chapter 1, we discussed and illustrated the differences between cash and accrual accounting. Adjusting entries, for the most part, are conversions from cash to accrual. Prepayments and accruals occur when cash flow precedes or follows expense or revenue recognition.

Accountants sometimes are called on to convert cash basis financial statements to accrual basis financial statements, particularly for small businesses. You now have all of the tools needed to make this conversion. For example, if the amount of cash paid for insurance during the fiscal year is $20,000 and you determine that there was $5,000 in prepaid insurance at the beginning of the year and $3,000 at the end of the year, then you can determine *insurance expense* for the year. Prepaid insurance decreased by $2,000 during the year, then insurance expense must be $22,000 ($20,000 in cash paid *plus* the decrease in prepaid insurance). You can visualize as follows:

	Prepaid Insurance
Balance, beginning of year	$ 5,000
Plus: Cash paid	20,000
Less: Insurance expense	?
Balance, end of year	$ 3,000

Insurance expense of $22,000 completes the explanation of the change in the balance of prepaid insurance. Prepaid insurance of $3,000 is reported as an asset on an accrual basis balance sheet.

Illustration 2–14 provides an example of a conversion from cash basis net income to accrual basis net income.

ILLUSTRATION   2–14

Cash to Accrual

The Krinard Cleaning Services Company maintains its records on the cash basis, with one exception. The company recognizes equipment as an asset and records depreciation expense. During 1997, Krinard collected $165,000 from customers, paid $92,000 in operating expenses, and recorded $10,000 in depreciation expense, resulting in net income of $63,000. The owner has asked you to convert this $63,000 in net income to full accrual net income by considering the following information about accounts receivable, prepaid expenses, and accrued liabilities:

	January 1, 1997	December 31, 1997
Accounts receivable	$16,000	$25,000
Prepaid expenses	7,000	4,000
Accrued liabilities (for operating expenses)	2,100	1,400

Accrual net income is $69,700, determined as follows:

Cash basis net income	$63,000
Add: Increase in accounts receivable	9,000
Deduct: Decrease in prepaid expenses	(3,000)
Add: Decrease in accrued liabilities	700
Accrual basis net income	$69,700

When converting from cash to accrual income, we add (deduct) increases (decreases) in assets. For example, an increase in accounts receivable means that the company earned more revenue than cash collected, requiring the addition to cash basis income. Also, we add (deduct) decreases (increases) in accrued liabilities. For example, a decrease in interest payable means that the company incurred less interest expense than the cash interest paid, requiring the addition to cash basis income.

Solution to Financial Reporting Case (at the opening of the chapter)

1. What purpose do adjusting entries serve?

Adjusting entries help ensure that only revenues actually earned in a period are recognized in that period, regardless of when cash is received. In this instance, for example, $13,000 cash has been received for services that haven't yet been performed. Also, adjusting entries enable a company to recognize all expenses incurred during a period, regardless of when cash is paid. Without depreciation, the friends' cost of using the equipment is not taken into account. Conversely, without adjustment, the cost of rent is overstated by $3,000 paid in advance for part of next year's rent.

With adjustments, we get an accrual income statement that provides a more complete measure of a company's operating performance and a better measure for predicting future operating cash flows. Similarly, the balance sheet provides a more complete assessment of assets and liabilities as sources of future cash receipts and disbursements.

2. What year-end adjustments are needed to revise the income statement? Did your friends do as well their first year as they thought?

Three year-end adjusting entries are needed:

1. Depreciation expense ($80,000 ÷ 5 years)	16,000	
Accumulated depreciation—equipment		16,000
2. Prepaid rent ($500 × 6 months [July—Dec.])	3,000	
Rent expense		3,000
3. Consulting revenue	13,000	
Unearned consulting revenue		13,000

No, your friends did not fare as well as their cash based statement would have indicated. With appropriate adjustments, their net income is actually only $20,000:

Consulting revenue ($96,000 – 13,000)		$83,000
Operating expenses:		
Salaries	$32,000	
Rent ($9,000 – 3,000)	6,000	
Supplies	4,800	
Utilities	3,000	
Advertising	1,200	
Depreciation	16,000	63,000
Net income		$20,000

The Bottom Line

1. The accounting equation underlies the process used to capture the effect of economic events. The equation (Assets = Liabilities + Owners' Equity) implies an equality between the total economic resources of an entity (its assets) and the total claims to those resources (liabilities and equity). It also implies that each economic event affecting this equation will have a dual effect because resources always must equal claims to those resources.

2. After determining the dual effect of external events on the accounting equation, the transaction is recorded in a journal. A journal is a chronological list of transactions in debit/credit form.

3. The next step in the processing cycle is to periodically transfer, or *post,* the debit and credit information from the journal to individual general ledger accounts. A general ledger is simply a collection of all of the company's various accounts. Each account provides a summary of the effects of all events and transactions on that individual account. This process is called *posting.* An unadjusted trial balance is then prepared.

4. The next step in the processing cycle is to record in the general journal and post to the ledger accounts the effect of *internal events* on the accounting equation. These transactions do not involve an exchange transaction with another entity. They are recorded at the end of any period when financial statements must be prepared for external use. These transactions are commonly referred to as *adjusting entries.* After these entries are posted to the general ledger accounts, an adjusted trial balance is prepared.

5. Adjusting entries can be classified into three types: (1) prepayments, (2) accruals, and (3) estimates. Prepayments are transactions in which the cash flow *precedes* expense or revenue recognition. Accruals involve transactions where the cash outflow or inflow takes place in a period *subsequent* to expense or revenue recognition. Estimates for items such as future bad debts on receivables often are required to comply with the accrual accounting model.

6. The adjusted trial balance is used to prepare the financial statements. The four basic financial statements are: (1) the income statement, (2) the balance sheet, (3) the statement of cash flows, and (4) the statement of shareholders' equity. The purpose of the income statement is to summarize the operating activities of the company that occurred during a particular period of time. The balance sheet presents the financial position of the company on a particular date. The statement of cash flows discloses the events that caused cash to change during the reporting period. The statement of shareholders' equity discloses the sources of the changes in the various permanent shareholders' equity accounts that occurred during the period.

7. At the end of the fiscal year, a final step in the accounting processing cycle, closing, is required. The closing process serves a *dual purpose*: (1) the temporary accounts (revenues and expenses) are reduced to *zero balances,* ready to measure activity in the upcoming accounting period, and (2) these temporary account balances are *closed (transferred) to retained earnings* to reflect the changes that have occurred in that account during the period. Often, an intermediate step is to close revenues and expenses to *income summary;* then *income summary* is closed to *retained earnings.*

APPENDIX

2A

USE OF A SPREADSHEET

A **spreadsheet** can be used as a tool to facilitate the preparation of adjusting and closing entries and the financial statements.

A **spreadsheet** often is used to organize the accounting information needed to prepare adjusting and closing entries and the financial statements. It is an informal tool only and is not part of the accounting system. There are many different ways to design and use spreadsheets. We will illustrate a representative method using the financial information for the Dress Right Clothing Corporation presented in the chapter. Computerized programs such as Lotus 1-2-3 and Excel facilitate the use of spreadsheets.

ILLUSTRATION 2A-1

Spreadsheet, Dress Right Clothing Corporation, July, 1997

	Unadjusted Trial Balance		Adjusting Entries		Adjusted Trial Balance		Income Statement		Balance Sheet	
Account Title	Dr.	Cr.	Dr.	Cr.	Dr.	Cr.	Dr.	Cr.	Dr.	Cr.
Cash	69,500				69,500				69,500	
Accounts receivable	2,000				2,000				2,000	
Allowance for uncollectible accounts		0		(7) 500		500				500
Supplies	2,000			(1) 800	1,200				1,200	
Prepaid rent	24,000			(2) 2,000	22,000				22,000	
Inventory	38,000				38,000				38,000	
Furniture & fixtures	12,000				12,000				12,000	
Accumulated depreciation-furniture & fixtures		0		(3) 200		200				200
Accounts payable		35,000				35,000				35,000
Note payable		40,000				40,000				40,000
Unearned rent revenue		1,000	(4) 250			750				750
Salaries payable		0		(5) 5,500		5,500				5,500
Interest payable		0		(6) 333		333				333
Capital stock		60,000				60,000				60,000
Retained earnings		0								
Sales revenue		38,500				38,500		38,500		
Rent revenue		0		(4) 250		250		250		
Cost of goods sold	22,000				22,000		22,000			
Salaries expense	5,000		(5) 5,500		10,500		10,500			
Supplies expense	0		(1) 800		800		800			
Rent expense	0		(2) 2,000		2,000		2,000			
Depreciation expense	0		(3) 200		200		200			
Interest expense	0		(6) 333		333		333			
Bad debt expense	0		(7) 500		500		500			
Totals	174,500	174,500	9,583	9,583	181,033	181,033				
Net income							2,417			2,417
Totals							38,750	38,750	144,700	144,700

Illustration 2A–1 presents the completed spreadsheet. The spreadsheet is utilized after and instead of step 5 in the processing cycle, preparation of an unadjusted trial balance.

Step 1. The account titles as they appear in the general ledger are entered in column 1 and the balances of these accounts are copied onto columns 2 and 3, entitled Unadjusted Trial Balance. The accounts are copied in the same order as they appear in the general ledger, which usually is assets, liabilities, shareholders' equity permanent accounts, revenues, and expenses. The debit and credit columns are totaled to make sure that they balance. This procedure is repeated for each set of columns in the spreadsheet to check for accuracy.

> The first step is to enter account titles in column 1 and the unadjusted account balances in columns 2 and 3.

Step 2. The end-of-period adjusting entries are determined and entered directly on the spreadsheet in columns 4 and 5, entitled Adjusting Entries. The adjusting entries for Dress Right Clothing Corporation were discussed in detail in the chapter and exhibited in general journal form in Illustration 2–7 on page 76. You should refer back to this illustration and trace each of the entries to the spreadsheet. For spreadsheet purposes, the entries have been numbered from (1) to (7) for easy referencing.

> The second step is to determine end-of-period adjusting entries and enter them in columns 4 and 5.

For example, entry (1) records the cost of supplies used during the month of July with a debit to supplies expense and a credit to supplies for $800. A (1) is placed next to the $800 in the debit column in the supplies expense row as well as next to the $800 in the credit column in the supplies row. This allows us to more easily reconstruct the entry for general journal purposes and locate errors if the debit and credit columns do not balance.

Step 3. The effects of the adjusting entries are added to or deducted from the account balances listed in the Unadjusted Trial Balance columns and copied across to columns 6 and 7, entitled Adjusted Trial Balance. For example, supplies had an unadjusted balance of $2,000. Adjusting entry (1) credited this account by $800, reducing the balance to $1,200.

> Step 3 adds or deducts the effects of the adjusting entries on the account balance.

Step 4. The balances in the temporary retained earnings accounts, revenues and expenses, are transferred to columns 8 and 9, entitled Income Statement. The difference between the total debits and credits in these columns is equal to net income or net loss. In this case, because credits and revenues exceed debits and expenses, a net income of $2,417 results. To balance the debits and credits in this set of columns, a $2,417 debit entry is made in the line labeled Net income.

> The fourth step is to transfer the temporary retained earnings account balances to columns 8 and 9.

Step 5. The balances in the permanent accounts are transferred to columns 10 and 11, entitled Balance Sheet. To keep the debits and credits equal in the spreadsheet, a $2,417 credit must be recorded to offset the $2,417 debit recorded in step 4 and labeled as net income. This credit represents the fact that when the temporary accounts are closed out to retained earnings, a $2,417 credit to retained earnings will result. The credit in column 11, therefore, represents the increase in retained earnings for the period, that is, net income.

> The fifth step is to transfer the balances in the permanent accounts to columns 10 and 11.

After the spreadsheet is completed, the financial statements can be prepared directly from columns 8-11. The financial statements for Dress Right Clothing Corporation are shown in Illustrations 2–9 through 2–12. The accountant must remember to then record the adjusting entries in the general journal and post them to the general ledger accounts. An adjusted trial balance should then be prepared which should be identical to the one in the spreadsheet. At fiscal year-end, the income statement columns can then be used to prepare closing entries.

APPENDIX

2B

REVERSING ENTRIES

Accountants sometimes use **reversing entries** at the beginning of a reporting period. These optional entries remove the effects of some of the adjusting entries made at the end of the previous reporting period for the sole purpose of simplifying journal entries made during the new period. If the accountant does use reversing entries, these entries are recorded in the general journal and posted to the general ledger accounts on the first day of the new period.

Reversing entries are used most often with accruals. For example, the following adjusting entry for accrued salaries was recorded at the end of July 1997 for the Dress Right Clothing Corporation in the chapter:

> To record accrued salaries at the end of July.

July 31		
Salaries expense	5,500	
Salaries payable		5,500

If reversing entries are not used, when the salaries actually are paid in August, the accountant needs to remember to debit salaries payable and not salaries expense.

The account balances before and after salary payment can be seen below with the use of T-accounts.

Salaries Expense		Salaries Payable	
Bal. July 31 10,500			5,500 Bal. July 31
	(Cash Payment) 5,500		
			-0- Balance

If the accountant for Dress Right employs reversing entries, the following entry is made on August 1, 1997:

To reverse accrued salaries expense recorded at the end of July.

August 1
Salaries payable   5,500
    Salaries expense   5,500

This entry reduces the salaries payable account to zero and reduces the salary expense account by $5,500. When salaries actually are paid in August, the debit is to salaries expense, thus increasing the account by $5,500.

Salaries Expense		Salaries Payable	
Bal. July 31 10,500			5,500 Bal. July 31
	5,500 (Reversing entry) 5,500		
(Cash payment) 5,500			
Balance 10.500			-0- Balance

We can see that balances in the accounts after cash payment is made are identical. The use of reversing entries for accruals, which is optional, simply allows cash payments or cash receipts to be entered directly into the temporary expense or revenue accounts without regard to the accruals made at the end of the previous period.

APPENDIX

2C

must read

SUBSIDIARY LEDGERS AND SPECIAL JOURNALS

Subsidiary Ledgers

The general ledger contains what are referred to as *control accounts*. In addition to the general ledger, a **subsidiary ledger** contains a group of subsidiary accounts associated with a particular general ledger control account. For example, there will be a subsidiary ledger for accounts receivable that keeps track of the increases and decreases in the account receivable balance for each of the company's customers purchasing goods or services on credit. After all of the postings are made from the appropriate journals, the balance in the accounts receivable control account should equal the sum of the balances in the accounts receivable subsidiary ledger accounts. Subsidiary ledgers also are used for accounts payable, plant and equipment, investments, and other accounts.

Accounting systems employ a **subsidiary ledger** which contains a group of subsidiary accounts associated with particular general ledger control accounts.

Special Journals

An actual accounting system employs many different types of journals. The purpose of each journal is to record, in chronological order, the dual effect of a transaction in debit/credit form. The chapter used the general journal format to record each transaction. However, even for small companies with relatively few transactions, the general journal is used to record only a few types of transactions.[7]

The majority of transactions are recorded in **special journals.** These journals capture the dual effect of *repetitive* types of transactions. For example, cash receipts are recorded in a **cash receipts journal,** cash disbursements in a **cash disbursements journal,** credit sales in a **sales journal,** and the purchase of merchandise on account in a **purchases journal.**

For most external transactions, **special journals** are used to capture the dual effect of the transaction in debit/credit form.

---

[7]For example, end-of-period adjusting entries would be recorded in the general journal.

Special journals simplify the recording process in the following ways:

1. Journalizing the effects of a particular transaction is made more efficient through the use of specifically designed formats.
2. Individual transactions are not posted to the general ledger accounts but are accumulated in the special journals and a summary posting is made on a periodic basis.
3. The responsibility for recording journal entries for the repetitive types of transactions is placed on individuals who have specialized training in handling them.

The concepts of subsidiary ledgers and special journals are illustrated using the *sales journal* and the *cash receipts journal*.

Sales Journal

All credit sales are recorded in the **sales journal.**

The purpose of the **sales journal** is to record all credit sales. Every entry in the sales journal has exactly the same effect on the accounts; the sales revenue account is credited and the accounts receivable control account is debited. Therefore, there is only one column needed to record the debit/credit effect of these transactions. Other columns are needed to capture information for updating the accounts receivable subsidiary ledger. Illustration 2C–1 presents the sales journal for Dress Right Clothing Corporation for the month of August 1997.

ILLUSTRATION 2C–1

Sales Journal, Dress Right Clothing Corporation, August 1997

				Page 1
Date	Accounts Receivable Subsidiary Account No.	Customer Name	Sales Invoice No.	Cr. Sales Revenue (400) Dr. Accounts Receivable (110)
1997				
August 5	801	Leland High School	10-221	1,500
August 9	812	Mr. John Smith	10-222	200
August 18	813	Greystone School	10-223	825
August 22	803	Ms. Barbara Jones	10-224	120
August 29	805	Hart Middle School	10-225	650
				3,295

During the month of August, the company made five credit sales, totaling $3,295. This amount is posted as a debit to the accounts receivable control account, account number 110, and a credit to the sales revenue account, account number 400. The T-accounts for accounts receivable and sales revenue appear below. The reference SJ1 refers to page one of the sales journal.

General Ledger

Accounts Receivable	110		Sales Revenue	400
July 31 Balance 2,000				
Aug. 31 SJ1 3,295			3,295 Aug. 31 SJ1	

In a computerized accounting system, as each transaction is recorded in the sales journal, the subsidiary ledger accounts for the customer involved will automatically be updated. For example, the first credit sale of the month is to Leland High School for $1,500. The sales invoice number for this sale is 10-221 and the customer's subsidiary account number is 801. As this transaction is entered, the subsidiary account 801 for Leland High School is debited for $1,500.

Accounts Receivable Subsidiary Ledger

Leland High School	801
August 5 SJ1 1,500	

As cash is collected from this customer, the cash receipts journal records the transaction with a credit to the accounts receivable control account and a debit to cash. At the same time, the accounts receivable subsidiary ledger account number 801 also is credited. After the postings are made from the special journals, the balance in the accounts receivable control account should equal the sum of the balances in the accounts receivable subsidiary ledger accounts.

Cash Receipts Journal, Dress Right Clothing Corporation, August 1997

Page 1

Date	Explanation or Account Name	Dr. Cash (100)	Cr. Accounts Receivable (110)	Cr. Sales Revenue (400)	Cr. Other	Other Accounts
1997						
Aug. 7	Cash sale	500		500		
Aug. 11	Borrowed cash	10,000			10,000	Note payable (220)
Aug. 17	Leland High School	750	750			
Aug. 20	Cash sale	300		300		
Aug. 25	Mr. John Smith	200	200			
		11,750	950	800	10,000	

Cash Receipts Journal

The purpose of the **cash receipts journal** is to record all cash receipts, regardless of the source. Every transaction recorded in this journal produces a debit entry to the cash account with the credit to various other accounts. Illustration 2C–2 shows a cash receipts journal using transactions of the Dress Right Clothing Corporation for the month of August 1997.

> All cash receipts are recorded in the **cash receipts journal.**

Because every transaction results in a debit to the cash account, No. 100, a column is provided for that account. At the end of August, an $11,750 debit is posted to the general ledger cash account with the source labeled CR1, cash receipts journal, page 1.

Because cash and credit sales are common, separate columns are provided for these accounts. At the end of August, a $950 credit is posted to the accounts receivable general ledger account, No. 110, and a $800 credit is posted to the sales revenue account, No. 400. Two additional credit columns are provided for uncommon cash receipt transactions, one for the credit amount and one for the account being credited. We can see that in August, Dress Right borrowed $10,000 requiring a credit to the note payable account, No. 220.

In addition to the postings to the general ledger control accounts, each time an entry is recorded in the accounts receivable column, a credit is posted to the accounts receivable subsidiary ledger account for the customer making the payment. For example, on August 17, Leland High School paid $750 on account. The subsidiary ledger account for Leland High School is credited for $750.

Accounts Receivable Subsidiary Ledger

Leland High School			801
August 5 SJ1	1,500		
		750	August 17 CR1

Questions for Review of Key Topics

Question	2–1	Explain the difference between external events and internal events. Give an example of each type of event.
Question	2–2	Each economic event or transaction will have a dual effect on financial position. Explain what is meant by this dual effect.
Question	2–3	What is the purpose of a journal? What is the purpose of a general ledger?
Question	2–4	Explain the difference between permanent accounts and temporary accounts. Why does an accounting system include both types of accounts?
Question	2–5	Describe how debits and credits affect assets, liabilities, and permanent owners' equity accounts.
Question	2–6	Describe how debits and credits affect temporary owners' equity accounts.
Question	2–7	What is the first step in the accounting processing cycle? What role do source documents fulfill in this step?
Question	2–8	Describe what is meant by transaction analysis.
Question	2–9	Describe what is meant by posting, the fourth step in the processing cycle.
Question	2–10	Describe the events that correspond to the following two journal entries:

1. Inventory   20,000
       Accounts payable   20,000
2. Accounts receivable   30,000
       Sales revenue   30,000

   Cost of goods sold   18,000
       Inventory   18,000

Question	2–11	What is an unadjusted trial balance? An adjusted trial balance?
Question	2–12	Define adjusting entries and discuss their purpose.
Question	2–13	Define closing entries and their purpose.
Question	2–14	Define prepaid expenses and provide at least two examples.
Question	2–15	Unearned revenues represent liabilities recorded when cash is received from customers in advance of providing a good or service. What adjusting journal entry is required at the end of a period to recognize the amount of unearned revenues that were earned during the period?
Question	2–16	Define accrued liabilities. What adjusting journal entry is required to record accrued liabilities?
Question	2–17	Describe the purpose of each of the four primary financial statements.
Question 2–18 [based on Appendix 2A]		What is the purpose of a spreadsheet? In an 11-column spreadsheet similar to Illustration 2A–1, what would be the result of incorrectly transferring the balance in a liability account to column 9, the credit column under income statement?
Question 2–19 [based on Appendix 2B]		Define reversing entries and discuss their purpose.
Question 2–20 [based on Appendix 2C]		What is the purpose of special journals? In what ways do they simplify the recording process?
Question 2–21 [based on Appendix 2C]		Explain the difference between the general ledger and a subsidiary ledger.

Exercises

Exercise 2–1
Transaction analysis

The following transactions occurred during March 1997 for the Wainwright Corporation. The company owns and operates a wholesale warehouse.

1. Issued 20,000 shares of capital stock in exchange for $200,000 in cash.
2. Purchased equipment at a cost of $40,000. $10,000 cash was paid and a note payable was signed for the balance owed.
3. Purchased inventory on account at a cost of $90,000. The company uses the perpetual inventory system.
4. Credit sales for the month totaled $120,000. The cost of the goods sold was $70,000.
5. Paid $5,000 in rent on the warehouse building for the month of March.
6. Paid $6,000 to an insurance company for fire and liability insurance for a one-year period beginning April 1, 1997.
7. Paid $60,000 on account for the merchandise purchased in 3.
8. Collected $55,000 from customers on account.
9. Recorded depreciation expense of $1,000 for the month on the equipment.

Required:
Analyze each transaction and show the effect of each on the accounting equation for a corporation.
Example:

	Assets	= Liabilities +	Paid-In Capital +	Retained Earnings
1.	+200,000(cash)		+ 200,000(capital stock)	

Exercise 2–2
Journal entries

Prepare journal entries to record each of the transactions listed in Exercise 2–1.

Exercise 2–3
T-accounts and trial balance

Post the journal entries prepared in Exercise 2–2 to T-accounts. Assume that the opening balances in each of the accounts is zero. Prepare a trial balance from the ending account balances.

Exercise 2–4
Journal entries

The following transactions occurred during the month of June 1997 for the Stridewell Corporation. The company owns and operates a retail shoe store.

1. Issued 100,000 shares of capital stock in exchange for $500,000 cash.
2. Purchased furniture and fixtures at a cost of $100,000. $40,000 was paid and a note payable was signed for the balance owed.
3. Purchased inventory on account at a cost of $200,000. The company uses the perpetual inventory system.
4. Credit sales for the month totaled $180,000. The cost of the goods sold was $90,000.

5. Paid $6,000 in rent on the store building for the month of June.
6. Paid $3,000 to an insurance company for fire and liability insurance for a one-year period beginning June 1, 1997.
7. Paid $120,000 on account for the merchandise purchased in 3.
8. Collected $55,000 from customers on account.
9. Paid shareholders a cash dividend of $5,000.
10. Recorded depreciation expense of $2,000 for the month on the furniture and fixtures.
11. Recorded the amount of prepaid insurance that expired for the month.

Required:
Prepare journal entries to record each of the transactions listed above.

Exercise 2–5
The accounting processing cycle

Listed below are several terms and phrases associated with the accounting processing cycle. Pair each item from List A (by letter) with the item from List B that is most appropriately associated with it.

List A	List B
____ 1. Source documents	a. Records the dual effect of a transaction in debit/credit form.
____ 2. Transaction analysis	b. Internal events recorded at the end of a reporting period.
____ 3. Journal	c. Primary means of disseminating information to external decision makers.
____ 4. Posting	d. To zero out the temporary owners' equity accounts.
____ 5. Unadjusted trial balance	e. Determine the dual effect on the accounting equation.
____ 6. Adjusting entries	f. List of accounts and their balances before recording adjusting entries.
____ 7. Adjusted trial balance	g. List of accounts and their balances after recording closing entries.
____ 8. Financial statements	h. List of accounts and their balances after recording adjusting entries.
____ 9. Closing entries	i. A means of organizing information; not part of the formal accounting system.
____ 10. Post-closing trial balance	j. Transferring balances from the journal to the ledger.
____ 11. Spreadsheet	k. Used to identify and process external transactions.

Exercise 2–6
Debits and credits

Indicate whether a debit will increase (I) or decrease (D) each of the following accounts:

Increase (I) or Decrease (D)	Account
1. _____	Inventory
2. _____	Depreciation expense
3 _____	Accounts payable
4. _____	Prepaid rent
5. _____	Sales revenue
6. _____	Capital stock
7. _____	Wages payable
8. _____	Cost of goods sold
9. _____	Utility expense
10. _____	Equipment
11. _____	Accounts receivable
12. _____	Allowance for uncollectible accounts
13. _____	Bad debt expense
14. _____	Interest expense
15. _____	Interest revenue
16. _____	Gain on sale of equipment

Exercise 2–7
Transaction analysis; debits and credits

Some of the ledger accounts for the Sanderson Hardware Company are numbered and listed below. For each of the October 1997 transactions numbered 1 through 12 below, indicate by account number which accounts should be debited and credited. The company uses the perpetual inventory system. Assume that appropriate adjusting entries were made at the end of September.

(1) Accounts payable	(2) Equipment	(3) Inventory
(4) Accounts receivable	(5) Cash	(6) Supplies
(7) Supplies expense	(8) Prepaid rent	(9) Sales revenue
(10) Retained earnings	(11) Note payable	(12) Capital stock
(13) Unearned revenue	(14) Rent expense	(15) Wages payable
(16) Cost of goods sold	(17) Wage expense	(18) Interest expense

	Account(s) Debited	Account(s) Credited
Example: Purchased inventory for cash	3	5

1. Paid a cash dividend.
2. Paid rent for the next three months.
3. Sold goods to customers on account.
4. Purchased inventory on account.
5. Purchased supplies for cash.
6. Paid employees wages for September.
7. Issued capital stock in exchange for cash.
8. Collected cash from customers for goods sold in 3.
9. Borrowed cash from a bank and signed a note.
10. At the end of October, recorded the amount of supplies that had been used during the month.
11. Received cash for advance payment from customer.
12. Accrued employee wages for October.

Exercise 2–8
Adjusting entries

Prepare the necessary adjusting entries at December 31, 1997, for the Falwell Company for each of the following situations. Assume that no financial statements were prepared during the year and no adjusting entries were recorded.

1. A three-year fire insurance policy was purchased on July 1, 1997, for $6,000. The company debited insurance expense for the entire amount.
2. Depreciation on equipment totaled $15,000 for the year.
3. The company determined that accounts receivable in the amount of $6,500 will probably not be collected. The allowance for uncollectible accounts account has a credit balance of $2,000 before any adjustment.
4. Employee salaries of $18,000 for the month of December will be paid in early January 1998.
5. On November 1, 1997, the company borrowed $100,000 from a bank. The note requires principal and interest at 12% to be paid on April 30, 1998.
6. On December 1, 1997, the company received $3,000 in cash from another company that is renting office space in Falwell's building. The payment, representing rent for December and January, was credited to unearned rent revenue.

Exercise 2–9
Adjusting entries

Prepare the necessary adjusting entries at December 31, 1997, for the Microchip Company for each of the following situations. Assume that no financial statements were prepared during the year and no adjusting entries were recorded.

1. On October 1, 1997, Microchip lent $60,000 to another company. A note was signed with principal and 10% interest to be paid on September 30, 1998.
2. On November 1, 1997, the company paid its landlord $6,000 representing rent for the months of November through January. Prepaid rent was debited.
3. On August 1, 1997, collected $12,000 in advance rent from another company that is renting a portion of Microchip's factory. The $12,000 represents one year's rent and the entire amount was credited to rent revenue.
4. Depreciation on machinery is $4,500 for the year.
5. Vacation pay for the year that had been earned by employees but not paid to them or recorded is $7,000.
6. Microchip began the year with $2,000 in its asset supplies account. During the year, $6,500 in supplies were purchased and debited to supplies. At year-end, supplies costing $3,250 remain on hand.

Exercise 2–10
Financial statements and closing entries

The December 31, 1997, adjusted trial balance for the Blueboy Cheese Corporation is presented below.

Account Title	Debits	Credits
Cash	21,000	
Accounts receivable	300,000	
Allowance for uncollectible accounts		20,000
Prepaid rent	10,000	
Inventory	50,000	
Equipment	600,000	
Accumulated depreciation—equipment		250,000
Accounts payable		40,000
Note payable (due in six months)		60,000

Account Title	Debits	Credits
Salaries payable		8,000
Interest payable		2,000
Capital stock		400,000
Retained earnings		100,000
Sales revenue		800,000
Cost of goods sold	480,000	
Salaries expense	120,000	
Rent expense	30,000	
Depreciation expense	60,000	
Interest expense	4,000	
Bad debt expense	5,000	
Totals	1,680,000	1,680,000

Required:

1. Prepare an income statement for the year ended December 31, 1997, and a classified balance sheet as of December 31, 1997.
2. Prepare the necessary closing entries at December 31, 1997.

Exercise 2–11
Closing entries

The American Chip Corporation's fiscal year-end is December 31. The following is a partial adjusted trial balance as of December 31, 1997.

Account Title	Debits	Credits
Retained earnings		80,000
Sales revenue		650,000
Interest revenue		3,000
Cost of goods sold	320,000	
Salaries expense	100,000	
Rent expense	15,000	
Depreciation expense	20,000	
Interest expense	5,000	
Insurance expense	6,000	

Required:

Prepare the necessary closing entries at December 31, 1997.

Exercise 2–12
Cash versus accrual
accounting; adjusting entries

The Righter Shoe Store Company prepares monthly financial statements for its bank. The November 30 and December 31, 1997, balance sheets contained the following account information:

	Nov. 30		Dec. 31	
	Dr.	Cr.	Dr.	Cr.
Supplies	1,000		3,000	
Prepaid insurance	6,000		4,250	
Wages payable		10,000		15,000
Unearned rent revenue		2,000		1,000

The following information also is known:
a. The December income statement revealed $2,000 in supplies expense.
b. No insurance payments were made in December.
c. $10,000 was paid to employees during December for wages.
d. On November 1, 1997, a tenant paid Righter $3,000 in advance rent for the period November through January. Unearned rent revenue was credited.

Required:

1. What was the cost of supplies purchased during December?
2. What was the adjusting entry recorded at the end of December for prepaid insurance?
3. What was the adjusting entry recorded at the end of December for accrued wages?
4. What was the amount of rent revenue earned in December? What adjusting entry was recorded at the end of December for unearned rent?

Exercise 2–13
External transactions and
adjusting entries

The following transactions occurred during 1997 for the Beehive Honey Corporation:

February 1	Borrowed $12,000 from a bank and signed a note. Principal and interest at 10% will be paid on January 31, 1998.
April 1	Paid $3,600 to an insurance company for a two–year fire insurance policy.
July 17	Purchased supplies costing $2,800 on account. The company records supplies purchased in an asset account. At the December 31, 1997, year-end, supplies costing $1,250 remained on hand.
November 1	A customer borrowed $6,000 and signed a note requiring the customer to pay principal and 8% interest on April 30, 1998.

Required:

1. Record each transaction in general journal form. Omit explanations.
2. Prepare any necessary adjusting entries at the December 31, 1997, year-end. No adjusting entries were made during the year for any item.

Exercise 2–14
Accrual accounting income determination

During the course of your examination of the financial statements of the Hales Corporation for the year ended December 31, 1997, you discover the following:

a. An insurance policy covering three years was purchased on January 1, 1997, for $3,000. The entire amount was debited to insurance expense and no adjusting entry was made for this item.
b. During 1997, the company received a $1,000 cash advance from a customer for merchandise to be manufactured and shipped in 1998. The $1,000 was credited to sales revenue. No entry was made for the cost of the merchandise.
c. There were no supplies listed on the balance sheet under assets. However, you discover that supplies costing $750 were on hand at December 31.
d. Hales borrowed $20,000 from a local bank on October 1, 1997. Principal and interest at 12% will be paid on September 30, 1998. No accrual was made for interest.
e. Net income reported on the 1997 income statement is $30,000 before reflecting any of the above items.

Required:

Determine the proper amount of net income for 1997.

Exercise 2–15
[based on Appendix 2A]
Spreadsheet

The December 31, 1997, unadjusted trial balance for the Wolkstein Drug Company is presented below. December 31 is the company's fiscal year-end.

Account Title	Debits	Credits
Cash	20,000	
Accounts receivable	35,000	
Allowance for uncollectible accounts		2,000
Prepaid rent	5,000	
Inventory	50,000	
Equipment	100,000	
Accumulated depreciation — equipment		30,000
Accounts payable		23,000
Wages payable		- 0 -
Capital stock		100,000
Retained earnings		29,000
Sales revenue		323,000
Cost of goods sold	180,000	
Wage expense	71,000	
Rent expense	30,000	
Depreciation expense	- 0 -	
Utility expense	12,000	
Bad debt expense	4,000	
Totals	507,000	507,000

The following year-end adjusting entries are required:

a. Depreciation expense for the year on the equipment is $10,000.
b. The company has determined that the allowance for uncollectible accounts should be $5,000.
c. Accrued wages payable at year-end are $4,000.

Required:

1. Prepare and complete a spreadsheet similar to Illustration 2A–1.
2. Prepare an income statement for 1997 and a balance sheet as of December 31, 1997.

Exercise 2–16
[based on Appendix 2B]
Reversing entries

The employees of Xitrex, Inc., are paid each Friday. The company's fiscal year-end is June 30, which falls on a Wednesday for the current year. Wages are earned evenly throughout the five-day workweek, and $10,000 will be paid on Friday, July 2.

Required:

1. Prepare an adjusting entry to record the accrued wages as of June 30, a reversing entry on July 1, and an entry to record the payment of wages on July 2.
2. Prepare journal entries to record the accrued wages as of June 30 and the payment of wages on July 2 assuming a reversing entry is not made.

Exercise 2–17
[based on Appendix 2C]
Special journals

The White Company's accounting system consists of a general journal (GJ), a cash receipts journal (CR), a cash disbursements journal (CD), a sales journal (SJ) and a purchases journal (PJ). For each of the following, indicate which journal should be used to record the transaction.

Transaction	Journal
1. Purchased merchandise on account.	_____
2. Collected an account receivable.	_____
3. Borrowed $20,000 and signed a note.	_____
4. Recorded depreciation expense.	_____
5. Purchased equipment for cash.	_____
6. Sold merchandise for cash (the sale only, not the cost of the merchandise).	_____
7. Sold merchandise on credit (the sale only, not the cost of the merchandise).	_____
8. Recorded accrued wages payable.	_____
9. Paid employee wages.	_____
10. Sold equipment for cash.	_____
11. Sold equipment on credit.	_____
12. Paid a cash dividend to shareholders.	_____
13. Issued capital stock in exchange for cash.	_____
14. Paid accounts payable.	_____

Problems

Problem 2–1
Accounting cycle through unadjusted trial balance

The Halogen Laminated Products Company began business on January 1, 1997. During January, the following transactions occurred:

Jan. 1 Issued capital stock in exchange for $100,000 cash.

2 Purchased inventory on account for $35,000 (the perpetual inventory system is used).

4 Paid an insurance company $2,400 for a one-year insurance policy.

10 Sold merchandise on account for $12,000. The cost of the merchandise was $7,000.

15 Borrowed $30,000 from a local bank and signed a note. Principal and interest at 10% is to be repaid in six months.

20 Paid employees $6,000 wages for the first half of the month.

22 Sold merchandise for $10,000 cash. The cost of the merchandise was $6,000.

24 Paid $15,000 to suppliers for the merchandise purchased on January 2.

26 Collected $6,000 on account from customers.

28 Paid $1,000 to the local utility company for January gas and electricity.

30 Paid $4,000 rent for the building. $2,000 was for January rent, and $2,000 for February rent.

Required:

1. Prepare general journal entries to record each transaction. Omit explanations.
2. Post the entries to T-accounts.
3. Prepare an unadjusted trial balance as of January 30, 1997.

Problem 2–2
Accounting cycle through unadjusted trial balance

The following is the post-closing trial balance for the Whitlow Manufacturing Corporation as of December 31, 1996:

Account Title	Debits	Credits
Cash	5,000	
Accounts receivable	2,000	
Inventory	5,000	
Equipment	11,000	
Accumulated depreciation — equipment		3,500
Accounts payable		3,000
Capital stock		10,000
Retained earnings		6,500
Sales revenue		- 0 -
Cost of goods sold	- 0 -	
Wage expense	- 0 -	
Rent expense	- 0 -	
Advertising expense	- 0 -	
Totals	23,000	23,000

The following transactions occurred during January, 1997:

Jan. 1 Sold merchandise for cash, $3,500. The cost of the merchandise was $2,000. The company uses the perpetual inventory system.

2 Purchased equipment on account for $5,500 from the Strong Company.

4   Received a $150 bill from the local newspaper for an advertisement that appeared in the paper on January 2.

8   Sold merchandise on account for $5,000. The cost of the merchandise was $2,800.

10   Purchased merchandise on account for $9,500.

13   Purchased equipment for cash, $800.

16   Paid the entire amount due to the Strong Company.

18   Received $4,000 from customers on account.

20   Paid $800 to the owner of the building for January's rent.

30   Paid employees $3,000 for salaries for the month of January.

31   Paid a cash dividend of $1,000 to shareholders.

Required:

1   Set up T-accounts and enter the beginning balances as of January 1, 1997.

2.   Prepare general journal entries to record each transaction. Omit explanations.

3.   Post the entries to T-accounts.

4.   Prepare an unadjusted trial balance as of January 31, 1997.

Problem 2–3
Adjusting entries

The Pastina Company manufactures and sells various types of pasta to grocery chains as private label brands. The company's fiscal year-end is December 31. The unadjusted trial balance as of December 31, 1997, appears below.

Account Title	Debits	Credits
Cash	30,000	
Accounts receivable	40,000	
Allowance for uncollectible accounts		3,000
Prepaid rent	2,000	
Prepaid insurance	- 0 -	
Supplies	1,500	
Inventory	60,000	
Note receivable	20,000	
Interest receivable	- 0 -	
Equipment	80,000	
Accumulated depreciation — equipment		30,000
Accounts payable		28,000
Wages payable		- 0 -
Note payable		50,000
Interest payable		- 0 -
Unearned revenue		- 0 -
Capital stock		60,000
Retained earnings		24,500
Sales revenue		148,000
Interest revenue		- 0 -
Cost of goods sold	70,000	
Wage expense	18,900	
Rent expense	11,000	
Depreciation expense	- 0 -	
Interest expense	- 0 -	
Supplies expense	1,100	
Insurance expense	6,000	
Bad debt expense	3,000	
Totals	343,500	343,500

Information necessary to prepare the year-end adjusting entries appears below.

1.   Depreciation on the equipment for the year is $10,000.

2.   The company estimates that of the $40,000 in accounts receivable outstanding at year-end, $5,500 probably will not be collected.

3.   Employee wages are paid twice a month, on the 22nd for wages earned from the 1st through the 15th, and on the 7th of the following month for wages earned from the 16th through the end of the month. Wages earned from December 16 through December 31, 1997, were $1,500.

4.   On October 1, 1997, Pastina borrowed $50,000 from a local bank and signed a note. The note requires interest to be paid annually on September 30 at 12%. The principal is due in 10 years.

5.   On March 1, 1997, the company lent a supplier $20,000 and a note was signed requiring principal and interest at 8% to be paid on February 28, 1998.

6.   On April 1, 1997, the company paid an insurance company $6,000 for a two-year fire insurance policy. The entire $6,000 was debited to insurance expense.

7. $800 of supplies remained on hand at December 31, 1997.

8.   A customer paid Pastina $2,000 in December for 1,500 pounds of spaghetti to be manufactured and delivered in January 1998. Pastina credited sales revenue.

9. On December 1, 1997, $2,000 rent was paid to the owner of the building. The payment represented rent for December and January 1998, at $1,000 per month.

Required:

Prepare the necessary December 31, 1997, adjusting journal entries.

Problem 2–4
Accounting cycle; adjusting entries through post-closing trial balance

Refer to Problem 2–3 and complete the following steps:

1. Enter the unadjusted balances from the trial balance into T-accounts.
2. Post the adjusting entries prepared in Problem 2–3 to the accounts.
3. Prepare an adjusted trial balance.
4. Prepare an income statement and a statement of shareholders' equity for the year ended December 31, 1997, and a classified balance sheet as of December 31, 1997. Assume that no capital stock was issued during the year and that $4,000 in cash dividends were paid to shareholders during the year.
5. Prepare closing entries and post to the accounts.
6. Prepare a post-closing trial balance.

Problem 2–5
Adjusting entries

The Howarth Company's fiscal year-end is December 31. Below are the unadjusted and adjusted trial balances for December 31, 1997.

	Unadjusted		Adjusted	
Account Title	**Debits**	**Credits**	**Debits**	**Credits**
Cash	50,000		50,000	
Accounts receivable	35,000		35,000	
Allowance for uncollectible accounts		2,000		3,500
Prepaid rent	2,000		1,200	
Supplies	1,500		800	
Inventory	60,000		60,000	
Note receivable	30,000		30,000	
Interest receivable	- 0 -		1,500	
Equipment	45,000		45,000	
Accumulated depreciation — equipment		15,000		20,000
Accounts payable		32,000		32,000
Wages payable		- 0 -		6,200
Note payable		50,000		50,000
Interest payable		- 0 -		2,500
Unearned rent revenue		- 0 -		2,000
Capital stock		46,000		46,000
Retained earnings		20,000		20,000
Sales revenue		244,000		244,000
Rent revenue		6,000		4,000
Interest revenue		- 0 -		1,500
Cost of goods sold	126,000		126,000	
Wage expense	45,000		51,200	
Rent expense	11,000		11,800	
Depreciation expense	- 0 -		5,000	
Supplies expense	1,100		1,800	
Interest expense	5,400		7,900	
Bad debt expense	3,000		4,500	
Totals	415,000	415,000	431,700	431,700

Required:

Prepare the adjusting journal entries that were made at December 31, 1997.

Problem 2–6
Accounting cycle

The general ledger of the Karlin Company, a consulting company, at January 1, 1997, contained the following account balances:

	Debits	Credits
Cash	30,000	
Accounts receivable	15,000	
Allowance for uncollectible accounts		500
Equipment	20,000	
Accumulated depreciation		6,000
Salaries payable		9,000
Capital stock		40,000
Retained earnings		9,500
Total	65,000	65,000

The following is a summary of the transactions for the year:
a. Sales of services, $100,000, of which $30,000 was on credit.
b. Collected on accounts receivable, $27,300.

c.   Issued shares of capital stock in exchange for $10,000 in cash.
d.   Paid salaries, $50,000 (of which $9,000 was for salaries payable).
e.   Paid operating expenses, $24,000 (use an account called operating expenses).
f.   Purchased equipment for $15,000 in cash.
g   Paid $2,500 in cash dividends to shareholders.

Required:

1.   Set up the necessary T-accounts and enter the beginning balances from the trial balance.
2.   Prepare a general journal entry for each of the summary transactions listed above.
3.   Post the journal entries to the accounts.
4.   Prepare an unadjusted trial balance.
5.   Prepare and post adjusting journal entries. Accrued salaries at year-end amounted to $1,000. Depreciation for the year on the equipment is $2,000. The allowance for uncollectible accounts is estimated to be $1,500.
6.   Prepare an adjusted trial balance.
7.   Prepare an income statement for 1997 and a balance sheet as of December 31, 1997.
8.   Prepare and post closing entries.
9.   Prepare a post-closing trial balance.

Problem 2–7
Adjusting entries and income effects

The information necessary for preparing the 1997 year-end adjusting entries for Vito's Pizza Parlor appears below. Vito's fiscal year-end is December 31.

a.   On July 1, 1997, purchased $10,000 of IBM Corporation bonds at face value. The bonds pay interest twice a year on January 1 and July 1. The annual interest rate is 12%.
b.   Vito's depreciable equipment has a cost of $30,000, a five-year life, and no salvage value. The equipment was purchased in 1995. The straight-line depreciation method is used.
c.   On November 1, 1997, the bar area was leased to Jack Donaldson for one year. Vito's received $6,000 representing the first six months' rent and credited unearned rent revenue.
d.   On April 1, 1997, the company paid $2,400 for a two-year fire and liability insurance policy and debited insurance expense.
e.   On October 1, 1997, the company borrowed $20,000 from a local bank and signed a note. Principal and interest at 12% will be paid on September 30, 1998.
f.   At year-end there is a $1,800 debit balance in the supplies (asset) account. Only $700 of supplies remain on hand.

Required:

1.   Prepare the necessary adjusting journal entries at December 31, 1997.
2.   Determine the amount by which net income would be misstated if Vito's failed to make these adjusting entries. (Ignore income tax expense.)

Problem 2–8
Adjusting entries

The Excalibur Corporation manufactures and sells video games for personal computers. The unadjusted trial balance as of December 31, 1997, appears below. December 31 is the company's fiscal year-end. The company uses the perpetual inventory system.

Account Title	Debits	Credits
Cash	23,300	
Accounts receivable	32,500	
Allowance for uncollectible accounts		100
Supplies	- 0 -	
Prepaid rent	- 0 -	
Inventory	65,000	
Equipment	75,000	
Accumulated depreciation—equipment		10,000
Accounts payable		26,000
Wages payable		3,000
Note payable		30,000
Capital stock		80,000
Retained earnings		16,050
Sales revenue		180,000
Cost of goods sold	95,000	
Interest expense	- 0 -	
Wage expense	32,350	
Rent expense	14,000	
Supplies expense	2,000	
Utility expense	6,000	
Bad debt expense	- 0 -	
Totals	345,150	345,150

Information necessary to prepare the year-end adjusting entries appears below.

1. The equipment was purchased in 1995 and is being depreciated using the straight-line method over an eight-year useful life with no salvage value.
2. Accrued wages at year-end should be $4,500.
3. The company estimates that 2% of all year-end accounts receivable will probably not be collected.
4. The company borrowed $30,000 on September 1, 1997. The principal is due to be repaid in 10 years. Interest is payable twice a year on each August 31 and February 28 at an annual rate of 10%.
5. The company debits supplies expense when supplies are purchased. Supplies on hand at year-end cost $500.
6. Prepaid rent at year-end should be $1,000.

Required:

Prepare the necessary December 31, 1997, adjusting entries.

Problem 2–9
Cash versus accrual accounting

Selected balance sheet information for the Wolf Company at November 30, and December 31, 1997, is presented below. The company uses the perpetual inventory system.

	Nov. 30		Dec. 31	
	Dr.	Cr.	Dr.	Cr.
Accounts receivable	10,000		3,000	
Prepaid insurance	5,000		7,500	
Inventory	7,000		6,000	
Accounts payable		12,000		15,000
Wages payable		5,000		3,000

The following cash flow information also is available:

a. Cash collected from credit customers—$80,000.
b. Cash paid for insurance—$5,000.
c. Cash paid to suppliers of inventory—$60,000 (the entire accounts payable amounts relate to inventory purchases).
d. Cash paid to employees for wages—$10,000.

Required:

1. Determine the following for the month of December:
   a. Sales revenue
   b. Cost of goods sold
   c. Insurance expense
   d. Wage expense
2. Assuming that all sales to customers are made on credit, prepare a summary journal entry to record the month's sales and cost of those sales.

Problem 2–10
Accounting cycle; unadjusted trial balance through closing

The unadjusted trial balance as of December 31, 1997, for the Bagley Consulting Company appears below. December 31 is the company's fiscal year-end.

Account Title	Debits	Credits
Cash	8,000	
Accounts receivable	9,000	
Allowance for uncollectible accounts		50
Prepaid insurance	3,000	
Land	200,000	
Buildings	50,000	
Accumulated depreciation—buildings		20,000
Equipment	100,000	
Accumulated depreciation—equipment		40,000
Accounts payable		35,000
Salaries payable		- 0 -
Unearned rent revenue		- 0 -
Capital stock		200,000
Retained earnings		56,450
Sales revenue		90,000
Interest revenue		3,000
Rent revenue		7,500
Salaries expense	37,000	
Bad debt expense	- 0 -	
Depreciation expense	- 0 -	
Insurance expense	- 0 -	
Utility expense	30,000	
Maintenance expense	15,000	
Totals	452,000	452,000

Required:

1. Enter the account balances in T-accounts.
2. From the trial balance and information given, prepare adjusting entries and post to the accounts.
   a. The buildings have an estimated useful life of 50 years with no salvage value. The company uses the straight-line depreciation method.
   b. The equipment is depreciated at 10 percent of original cost per year.
   c. Prepaid insurance expired during the year, $1,500.
   d. It is estimated that 10% of the accounts receivable balance will be uncollectible.
   e. Accrued salaries at year-end, $1,500.
   f. Unearned rent revenue at year-end should be $1,200.
3. Prepare an adjusted trial balance.
4. Prepare closing entries.
5. Prepare a post-closing trial balance.

Problem 2–11
Accrual accounting; financial statements

The McGuire Corporation began operations in 1997. The company purchases computer equipment from manufacturers and then sells to retail stores. During 1997, the bookkeeper used a check register to record all cash receipts and cash disbursements. No other journals were used. The following is a recap of the cash receipts and disbursements made during the year.

Cash receipts:	
Sale of capital stock	$ 50,000
Collections from customers	320,000
Borrowed from local bank on April 1, note signed requiring principal and interest at 12% to be paid on March 31, 1998	40,000
Total cash receipts	$410,000
Cash disbursements:	
Purchase of merchandise	$220,000
Payment of salaries	80,000
Purchase of equipment	30,000
Payment of rent on building	14,000
Miscellaneous expenses	10,000
Total cash disbursements	$354,000

You are called in to prepare financial statements at December 31, 1997. The following additional information was provided to you:

1. Customers owed the company $22,000 at year-end. Of this amount, it was anticipated that $3,000 would probably not be collected. There were no actual bad debt write-offs in 1997.
2. At year-end, $30,000 was still due to suppliers of merchandise purchased on credit.
3. At year-end, merchandise inventory costing $50,000 still remained on hand.
4. Salaries owed to employees at year-end amounted to $5,000.
5. On December 1, $3,000 in rent was paid to the owner of the building used by McGuire. This represented rent for the months of December through February.
6. The equipment, which has a 10-year life and no salvage value, was purchased on January 1, 1997. Straight-line depreciation is used.

Required:
Prepare an income statement for 1997 and a balance sheet as of December 31, 1997.

Problem 2–12
[based on Appendix 2A]
Spreadsheet

Using the information from Problem 2–8, prepare and complete a spreadsheet similar to Illustration 2A–1. Use the information in the spreadsheet to prepare an income statement and a statement of shareholders' equity for 1997 and a balance sheet as of December 31, 1997. Cash dividends paid to shareholders during the year amounted to $6,000. Also prepare the necessary closing entries assuming that adjusting entries have been correctly posted to the accounts.

THE INCOME STATEMENT AND STATEMENT OF CASH FLOWS

OVERVIEW

The purpose of the income statement is to summarize the profit-generating activities that occurred during a particular reporting period. The purpose of the statement of cash flows is to provide information about the cash receipts and cash disbursements of an enterprise that occurred during the period.

This chapter has a twofold purpose: (1) to consider important issues dealing with income statement content, presentation, and disclosure, and (2) to provide an *overview* of the statement of cash flows, which is covered in depth in Chapter 22.

LEARNING OBJECTIVES   After studying this chapter, you should be able to:

1. Explain the importance of income from continuing operations and describe its components.
2. Explain the reason for applying intraperiod tax allocation to certain income statement components.
3. Define what is meant by discontinued operations and describe the appropriate income statement presentation for these transactions.
4. Define extraordinary items and describe the appropriate income statement presentation for these transactions.
5. Describe and illustrate the measurement and reporting requirements for the cumulative effect of a change in accounting principle.
6. Explain the accounting treatment of changes in estimates.
7. Briefly describe the accounting treatment for the correction of errors.
8. Define earnings per share (EPS) and explain required disclosures of EPS for certain income statement components.
9. Describe the purpose of the statement of cash flows.
10. Identify and describe the various classifications of cash flows presented on the statement of cash flows.

ELI LILLY

By the time you finish this chapter, you should be able to respond appropriately to the questions posed in this case. Compare your response to the solution provided at the end of the chapter.

Your friend, Becky Morgan, just received 200 shares of stock of Eli Lilly & Company as a gift from her grandfather. Along with a warm letter and the shares came the most recent financial statements of the company. Becky knows that you are an accounting major and pleads with you to explain some items on the company's income statement. "I remember studying the income statement in my introductory accounting course," says Becky, "but I am still confused. What is this item *discontinued operations*? And how about *restructuring costs*? These don't sound good. Are these something I should worry about?" You agree to help her out after taking a look at the company's income statements.

ELI LILLY & COMPANY
(Dollars in millions)

Year ended December 31		1995		1994
Net sales		$6,763.8		$5,711.6
Cost of sales	$1,885.7		$1,679.7	
Research and development	1,042.3		897.1	
Marketing and administrative	1,854.0		1,398.3	
Restructuring costs	-		66.0	
Interest expense	286.3		103.8	
Other income—net	(70.1)		(131.9)	
		4,998.2		4,013.0
Income from continuing operations before income taxes		1,765.6		1,698.6
Income taxes		459.0		513.5
Income from continuing operations		1,306.6		1,185.1
Discontinued operations, net of tax		984.3		101.0
Net income		$2,290.9		$1,286.1

QUESTIONS

1. In addition to discontinued operations, what other events sometimes are reported separately on the income statement that you might tell Becky about? Why are these items reported separately?
2. Explain to Becky what is meant by a discontinued operation and describe to her how one is reported on an income statement.
3. How would you explain restructuring costs to Becky? Are they necessarily a negative?

In Chapter 1 we discussed the critical role of financial accounting information in allocating resources within our economy. Ideally, resources should be allocated to private enterprises that will (1) provide the goods and services our society desires, and (2) at the same time provide a fair rate of return to those who supply the resources. A company will be able to achieve these goals only if it can use the resources society provides to generate revenues from selling products and services that exceed the expenses necessary to provide those products and services (that is, generate a profit).

> The **income statement** displays a company's operating performance, that is, its net profit or loss, during the reporting period.

The purpose of the **income statement**, sometimes called the **statement of operations** or **statement of earnings**, is to summarize the profit-generating activities that occurred during a particular reporting period. Many investors and creditors perceive it as the statement most useful for predicting future profitability (future cash generating ability).

The purpose of the **statement of cash flows** is to provide information about the cash receipts and cash disbursements of an enterprise that occurred during a period. In describing cash flows, the statement provides valuable information about the operating, investing, and financing activities that occurred during the period.

> The income statement and statement of cash flows report changes that occurred during a particular reporting period.

Both the income statement and statement of cash flows are change statements. The income statement reports the changes in shareholders' equity (retained earnings) that occurred during the reporting period as a result of operating transactions (revenues, expenses, gains, and losses). The statement of cash flows also is a change statement, disclosing the events that caused cash to change during the period. Unlike these two change statements, the balance sheet is a position statement that provides an organized list of assets, liabilities, and shareholders' equity *at a point in time*. The balance sheet is discussed in Chapter 5.

This chapter is divided into two parts. The first part describes the content and presentation of the income statement and related disclosure issues. The second part provides an overview of the statement of cash flows.

A THE INCOME STATEMENT

> In addition to net income, the components of the income statement and their presentation also are important to financial statement users.

Financial analysts are concerned with more than just the bottom line of the income statement—net income. The specific components of net income also can be helpful in an assessment of future cash flows. Relatedly, the format used to report these components can convey information to users about their relative size and the relationships among them. And sometimes critical characteristics of components of income can only be related by supplemental disclosures. This part of the chapter provides a detailed discussion of the various components of the income statement, alternative presentation formats, and associated disclosures.

Income From Continuing Operations

Learning objective 1
Explain the importance of income from continuing operations and describe its components.

The need to provide information to help predict future cash flows places considerable importance on GAAP for describing the amount of income from the entity's continuing operations. Clearly, it is the operating transactions that probably will continue into the future that are the best predictors of future cash flows. The components of **income from continuing operations** are revenues, expenses (including income taxes), gains, and losses.

Revenues, Expenses, Gains, and Losses

> **Income from continuing operations** includes the **revenues, expenses, gains,** and **losses** that will probably continue in future periods.

Revenues are inflows of resources resulting from providing goods or services to customers. For merchandising companies like Wal-Mart, the *main* source of revenue is sales revenue derived from selling merchandise. Service firms such as Federal Express and State Farm Insurance generate revenue by providing services.

Expenses are outflows of resources incurred in generating revenue. They represent the *costs* of providing goods and services. The *matching principle* is a key player in the way we measure expenses. We attempt to establish a causal relationship between revenues and expenses. If causality can be determined, expenses are reported in the same period that the revenue is recognized. If a causal relationship cannot be established, the expense is either related to a particular period, allocated over several periods, or expensed as incurred.

Gains and losses are increases or decreases in equity from peripheral or incidental transactions of an entity. In general, these gains and losses are those changes in equity that do not result directly from operating activities (for example, the sale of products or services) but nonetheless are related to them. For example, gains and losses from the routine sale of equipment, buildings, or other operating assets and from the sale of investment assets normally would be included in income from continuing operations. Later in the chapter we discuss certain gains and losses that are excluded from continuing operations.

Income Tax Expense

Income taxes represent a major expense to a corporation, and accordingly, income tax expense is given special treatment on the income statement. Income taxes are levied on taxpayers in proportion to the amount of taxable income that is reported to taxing authorities. Like individuals, corporations are income-tax-paying entities.[1] Because of the importance and size of **income tax expense** (sometimes called *provision for income taxes*), it always is disclosed as a separate expense on corporate income statements.

Federal, state, and sometimes local taxes are assessed annually and usually are determined by applying a designated percentage, the tax rate, to **taxable income**. Taxable income comprises revenues, expenses, gains, and losses as measured according to the regulations of the appropriate taxing authority.

Many of the components of taxable income and income reported on the income statement coincide. But sometimes tax rules and GAAP differ with respect to when and even whether a particular revenue or expense is included in income. When tax rules and GAAP differ regarding the timing of revenue or expense recognition, the actual payment of taxes may occur in a period different from when income tax expense is reported on the income statement. A common example is when a corporation takes advantage of tax laws by legally deducting more depreciation in the early years of an asset's life on its federal income tax return than it reports on its income statement. The amount of tax actually paid in the early years is less than the amount that is found by applying the tax rate to the reported GAAP income before taxes. We discuss this and other issues related to accounting for income taxes in Chapter 16. At this point, consider income tax expense to be simply a percentage of income before taxes.

Operating Versus Nonoperating Activities

Many corporate income statements distinguish between **operating activities** and **nonoperating activities** within continuing operations. Operating activities include revenues and expenses directly related to the principal revenue-generating activities of the company. For example, operating activities for a manufacturing company include sales revenues from the sale of products and all expenses related to this activity. Income from investments, gains and losses from the sale of operating assets, interest revenue, and interest expense are reported as arising from nonoperating activities.[2] A financial institution like a bank considers interest revenue and interest expense operating activities because they relate to the principal revenue-generating activities for that type of business.

Graphic 3–1 presents the 1996, 1995, and 1994 income statements for Federal Express Corporation. Notice that Federal Express distinguishes between operating and nonoperating activities. Nonoperating revenues, expenses, gains and losses, and income tax expense (called provision for income taxes) are added or subtracted from operating income to arrive at net income. As Federal Express has no separately reported items, *income from continuing operations equals net income*.[3]

Income tax expense is shown as a separate expense on the income statement.

While the actual measurement of income tax expense can be complex, at this point we can consider income tax expense to be a simple percentage of income before taxes.

A distinction often is made between **operating** and **nonoperating** activities.

---

[1]Partnerships are not tax-paying entities. Their taxable income or loss is included in the taxable income of the individual partners.

[2]Even though these activities are nonoperating, they are still included in income from continuing operations because they are expected to continue in future periods.

[3]In a later section we discuss three items that are reported separately from continuing operations—discontinued operations, extraordinary items, and cumulative effect of a change in accounting principle.

GRAPHIC   3–1

Income Statements—Federal
Express Corporation

**Federal Express
Corporation**

Income Statements (in thousands, except earnings per share)	Year Ended May 31		
	1996	**1995**	**1994**
Revenues	$10,273,619	$9,392,073	$8,479,456
Operating expenses:			
Salaries and employee benefits	4,619,990	4,425,202	4,104,800
Rentals and landing fees	959,055	818,599	703,028
Depreciation and amortization	719,609	652,287	599,357
Fuel	578,614	502,417	472,786
Maintenance and repairs	617,657	544,170	464,557
Other	2,154,870	1,858,254	1,604,296
	9,649,795	8,800,929	7,948,824
Operating income	623,824	591,144	530,632
Other income (expense):			
Interest, net	(95,599)	(114,687)	(142,392)
Other, net	11,734	45,627	(9,778)
	(83,865)	(69,060)	(152,170)
Income before income taxes	539,959	522,084	378,462
Provision for income taxes	232,182	224,496	174,092
Net income	$ 307,777	$ 297,588	$ 204,370
Earnings per share	$ 5.39	$ 5.27	$ 3.65

Now let's consider the formats used to report the components of income.

Income Statement Formats

No specific standards dictate how income from continuing operations must be displayed, so companies have considerable latitude in how they present the components of income from continuing operations. This flexibility has resulted in a considerable variety of income statement presentations. However, we can identify two general approaches, the single-step and the multiple-step formats, that might be considered the two extremes, with the income statements of most companies falling somewhere in between.

The **single-step** format first lists all the revenues and gains included in income from continuing operations. Then, expenses and losses are grouped, subtotaled, and subtracted—in a single step—from revenues and gains to derive income from continuing operations. Operating and nonoperating activities are not separately classified. Illustration 3–1 shows an example of a single-step income statement for a hypothetical manufacturing company, Maxwell Gear Corporation.

> A **single-step** income statement format groups all revenues and gains together and all expenses and losses together.

ILLUSTRATION   3–1

Single-Step Income
Statement

MAXWELL GEAR CORPORATION
Income Statement
For the Year Ended December 31, 1997

Revenues and gains:		
Sales		$573,522
Interest and dividends		26,400
Gain on sale of operating assets		5,500
Total revenues and gains		605,422
Expenses and losses:		
Cost of goods sold	$302,371	
Office salaries	47,341	
Depreciation	24,888	
Miscellaneous	16,300	
Interest	6,200	
Loss on sale of investments	8,322	
Income taxes	80,000	
Total expenses and losses		485,422
Net income		$120,000

ILLUSTRATION   3–2

Multiple-Step Income Statement

↑ most used format

MAXWELL GEAR CORPORATION
Income Statement
For the Year Ended December 31, 1997

Sales revenue		$573,522
Cost of goods sold		302,371
Gross profit		271,151
Operating expenses:		
Office salaries	$47,341	
Depreciation	24,888	
Miscellaneous	16,300	
Total operating expenses		88,529
Operating income		182,622
Other income (expense):		
Interest and dividend revenue	26,400	
Gain on sale of operating assets	5,500	
Interest expense	(6,200)	
Loss on sale of investments	(8,322)	
Total other income, net		17,378
Income before income taxes		200,000
Income tax expense		80,000
Net income		$120,000

A **multiple-step** income statement format includes a number of intermediate subtotals before arriving at income from continuing operations.

The **multiple-step** format reports a series of intermediate subtotals such as gross profit, operating income, and income before taxes. The Federal Express income statements in Graphic 3–1 are a variation of the multiple-step format. Illustration 3–2 presents a multiple-step income statement for the Maxwell Gear Corporation.

An advantage of the single-step format is its simplicity. Revenues and expenses are not classified or prioritized. A primary advantage of the multiple-step format is that it separately reports operating and nonoperating transactions. This information could be useful in analyzing trends. The classification of expenses by function also provides information. For example, reporting gross profit for merchandising companies highlights the important relationship between sales revenue and cost of goods sold. It is important to note that this issue is one of presentation. The bottom line, net income, is the same regardless of the format used. A recent survey of income statements of 600 large public companies indicates that the multiple-step format is used twice as often as the single-step format.[4]

Although a company has considerable flexibility in reporting income from continuing operations, the presentation order of certain other income statement items is mandated. We address these separately reported items next.

Separately Reported Items

The predictive ability of an income statement is significantly enhanced if normal and recurrent transactions are separated from unusual and nonrecurrent items. The income statement is a historical report, summarizing the most recent operating activities of a company. The information in the statement is useful if it can help users predict the future. Toward this end, users should be made aware of events reported on the income statement that are not likely to occur again in the foreseeable future.

OPENING CASE

Question 1

GAAP requires that certain transactions be reported separately on the income statement, below income from continuing operations.

There are three types of events that, if they have a material effect[5] on the income statement, require separate reporting and disclosure: (1) discontinued operations, (2) extraordinary items, and (3) the cumulative effect of a change in accounting principle.[6] In fact, these are the only three events that are allowed to be reported below continuing operations. As previously discussed, although a company has considerable flexibility in reporting income from *continuing operations*, the presentation order of these three is mandated as follows:

---

[4]*Accounting Trends and Techniques—1995* (New York: AICPA, 1995), p. 315.

[5]The concept of materiality was discussed in Chapter 1.

[6]"Reporting Results of Operations," *Opinions of the Accounting Principles Board No. 30* (New York: AICPA, 1973).

Income from continuing operations	$xxx
Discontinued operations (net of $xx in taxes)	xx
Extraordinary items (net of $xx in taxes)	xx
Cumulative effect of a change in accounting principle (net of $xx in taxes)	xx
Net income	$xxx

The objective is to separately report all of the income effects of these items. Therefore, their income tax effects also are included in the separate presentation rather than as part of the amount reported as income tax expense. The process of associating income tax effects with the income statement components that create those effects is referred to as *intraperiod tax allocation*. We address this process before defining the separately reported items more precisely.

Intraperiod Income Tax Allocation

Learning objective 2
Explain the reason for applying intraperiod tax allocation to certain income statement components.

Intraperiod tax allocation associates (allocates) income tax expense (or income tax benefit if there is a loss) with each component of income that causes it.[7] For example, assume a company experienced an extraordinary gain during the year.[8] The amount of income tax expense deducted from income from continuing operations is the amount of income tax expense that the company would have incurred *if there were no extraordinary gain*. The effect on income taxes caused by the extraordinary item is deducted from the extraordinary gain itself on the income statement. Illustration 3–3 demonstrates this concept.

ILLUSTRATION   3–3

Intraperiod Tax Allocation

The Maxwell Gear Corporation had income from continuing operations of $200,000 before income tax expense and an extraordinary gain of $60,000 in 1997. The income tax rate is 40% on all items of income or loss. Therefore, the company's total income tax expense is $104,000 (40% × $260,000).

How should the company allocate the tax expense between income from continuing operations and the extraordinary gain? A partial income statement, beginning with income from continuing operations before income tax expense, *ignoring* intraperiod tax allocation, is shown in Illustrations 3–3a.

ILLUSTRATION   3–3a

Income statement presented *incorrectly*—no intraperiod tax allocation (extraordinary gain)

Income from continuing operations before income taxes	$200,000
Income tax expense	(104,000)
Income before extraordinary gain	96,000
Extraordinary gain (gross)	60,000
Net income	$156,000

The deficiency of this presentation is that the apparent contribution to net income of (a) income before the extraordinary gain (that is, income from continuing operations) and (b) the extraordinary gain, is misleading. If the extraordinary gain had not occurred, income tax expense would not have been $104,000 but rather $80,000 (40% × $200,000). Similarly, the net benefit of the extraordinary gain is not $60,000, but rather $36,000 ($60,000 minus 40% × $60,000). The total tax expense of $104,000 must be *allocated*, $80,000 to continuing operations and $24,000 (40% × $60,000) to the extraordinary gain. The appropriate income statement presentation appears in Illustration 3–3b.

ILLUSTRATION   3–3b

Income statement— intraperiod tax allocation (extraordinary gain)

Income from continuing operations before income taxes	$200,000
Income tax expense	(80,000)
Income before extraordinary gain	120,000
Extraordinary gain (net of $24,000 tax expense)	36,000
Net income	$156,000

---

[7]*Intraperiod* tax allocation concerns the association of income tax with income statement components. *Interperiod* tax allocation, covered in Chapter 16, addresses the problem created when taxable income does not equal income before taxes as determined by GAAP because of differences in the timing of revenue or expense recognition.

[8]The criteria for classifying gains and losses as extraordinary are discussed in a later section of this chapter.

Net income is $156,000 either way. Intraperiod tax allocation is not an issue of measurement but an issue of presentation. The $120,000 income before extraordinary gain properly reflects income from continuing operations *including* the appropriate tax effects. Also, notice that income tax expense represents taxes that relate to the total of all of the revenue, expense, gain, and loss items included in continuing operations. Each of the items following continuing operations (discontinued operations, extraordinary items, and cumulative effect of a change in accounting principle) are presented *net of their tax effect*. No items included in the computation of income from continuing operations are reported net of tax.

In the illustration, the extraordinary gain caused additional income tax expense to be incurred. What if the company had experienced an extraordinary loss of $60,000 instead of an extraordinary gain? In that case, rather than creating additional tax, the loss actually decreases tax due to its reducing taxable income by $60,000. The company's total income tax expense would be $56,000 [40% × ($200,000 – 60,000)].

The extraordinary loss *decreased* the amount of tax the company otherwise would have had to pay by $24,000. This is commonly referred to as a *tax benefit*. A partial income statement, beginning with income from continuing operations before income tax expense, *ignoring* intraperiod tax allocation is shown in Illustration 3–3c.

ILLUSTRATION   3–3c

**Income statement presented
incorrectly—no intraperiod
tax allocation (extraordinary
loss)**

Income from continuing operations before income taxes	$200,000
Income tax expense	(56,000)
Income before extraordinary loss	144,000
Extraordinary loss	(60,000)
Net income	$ 84,000

Once again, income before the extraordinary loss (i.e., income from continuing operations) is misleading. If the extraordinary loss had not occurred, income tax expense would not have been $56,000 but rather $80,000 (40% × $200,000). The total tax expense of $56,000 must be *allocated,* $80,000 tax expense to continuing operations and $24,000 tax benefit to the extraordinary loss. The appropriate income statement presentation appears in Illustration 3–3d.

Income from continuing operations before income taxes	$200,000
Income tax expense	(80,000)
Income before extraordinary loss	120,000
Extraordinary loss (net of $24,000 tax benefit)	(36,000)
Net income	$ 84,000

ILLUSTRATION   3–3d

**Income statement—
intraperiod tax allocation
(extraordinary loss)**

Now that we have seen how to report items net of their related tax effects, let's look closer at all three items reported net of tax below income from continuing operations: discontinued operations, extraordinary items, and changes in accounting principle.

Discontinued Operations

The Clorox Company is engaged in the production and marketing of nondurable consumer products. Prior to 1995, the company's lines of business included bottled water and frozen foods. These were large segments of business for Clorox, accounting for approximately 10% of total company sales in 1993. However, early in 1994, Clorox decided to discontinue these lines of business and sold the related operating assets.[9] This is an example of a **discontinued operation.**

If a company disposes of a manufacturing division and has no other division engaged in producing the same product line, we classify the transaction as a discontinued operation. On the other hand, if the same company disposes of its West Coast shoe manufacturing division but continues to manufacture shoes at its East Coast division, this would not constitute a discontinued operation. The company is still manufacturing and selling shoes. Normal expansion and contraction is not a discontinued operation. For example, the opening or closing of one store in a chain is not a discontinued operation nor is the addition or discontinuance of one product in a product line.

[9]The primary reason companies discontinue operations usually is that the line of business is no longer profitable.

Suppose that same shoe manufacturer also owned and operated a chain of retail stores. If the company decided to dispose of all the assets of the retail stores but continued to manufacture and sell shoes to other retailers, the disposal of the retail stores qualifies as a discontinued operation. A major class of customer would no longer be served directly, and the assets and operations of the company's retail business can be clearly distinguished from the manufacturing activity.

Disposal in Same Year as Measurement Date.   By definition, the income or loss stream from an identifiable discontinued operation no longer will continue. If Clorox did not separately report the results of the discontinuance of its bottled water and frozen foods businesses, its 1994 and 1993 comparative income statements (in condensed form) would have appeared as in Illustration 3–4a.

ILLUSTRATION   3–4a

Income Statements Presented Incorrectly *without* Separate Reporting of Discontinued Operation

THE CLOROX COMPANY
Income Statements
Years Ended June 30

| | ($ in thousands) | |
	1994	1993
Net sales	$1,855,649	$1,807,462
Costs and expenses	1,505,796	1,533,714
Income before income taxes	349,853	273,748
Income tax expense	137,796	106,697
Net income	$ 212,057	$ 167,051

The company generated net income of $212,057,000 and $167,051,000 in 1994 and 1993, respectively. However, an analyst concerned with Clorox's future profitability is more interested in the 1994 and 1993 results after separating the effects of the discontinued bottled water and frozen foods businesses from the results of operations that will continue. This information might have a significant impact on the analyst's assessment of future profitability.

The actual income statements (in condensed form) are presented in Illustration 3–4b. A portion of the disclosure note that appeared in the company's annual report is shown also, providing more detailed information about the effects of the discontinued operation.

ILLUSTRATION   3–4b

Income Statements with Separate Reporting of Discontinued Operation

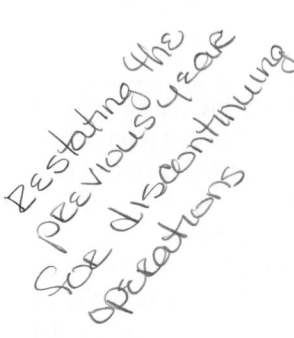

THE CLOROX COMPANY
Income Statements
Years Ended June 30

| | ($ in thousands) | |
	1994	1993
Net sales	$1,836,949	$1,634,171
Costs and expenses	1,530,316	1,358,986
Income before income taxes	306,633	275,185
Income tax expense	126,640	107,267
Income from continuing operations	179,993	167,918
Income (loss) from discontinued operations*	32,064	(867)
Net income	$ 212,057	$ 167,051

*The tax effects of the components can be shown on the statement or, as Clorox did, in a disclosure note.

The following information also was disclosed in a note:

Results of discontinued operations are classified separately on the income statements and include the following ($ in thousands):

	1994	1993
Net sales	$18,700	$173,291
Income from operations before income taxes	1,043	(1,437)
Income tax (expense) benefit	(409)	570
Income (loss) from operations	634	(867)
Gain on sale of businesses	42,177	—
Income taxes	10,747	—
Net gain on sale of businesses	31,430	—
Net Income (loss) from discontinued operations	$32,064	$ (867)

The net-of-tax income effects of a discontinued operation must be disclosed separately on the income statement, below income from continuing operations.

Compare the two income statements for their ability to predict future profitability. The income statements in Illustration 3–4b separate the net-of-tax income effects of the discontinued operation. The revenues, expenses, gains, losses, and income tax related to the discontinued operation have been removed from continuing operations and disclosed separately. Even though the operation was discontinued in 1994, it is important for comparative purposes to separate out the effects for any prior years presented (1993). This allows an apples-for-apples comparison of income from *continuing* operations.

A key in the assessment of profitability is the 7% increase in income from *continuing operations* from $167,918,000 in 1993 to $179,993,000 in 1994. This is a significantly different picture from the one presented in Illustration 3–4a which shows an increase in *net income* of 27%.

Notice in the disclosure note that the 1994 income effect of the discontinued operations, $32,064,000 in net income, comprises two components:

The income effect of discontinued operations is divided into two components: **income (loss) from operations** and **gain (loss) on disposal**.

1. Income from operations—$634,000
2. Gain on sale (disposal)—$31,430,000

Companies often report the two components, along with their tax effects, directly on the income statement. For Clorox, the applicable portion of its income statement would appear as follows ($ in thousands):

	1994	1993
Income from continuing operations	$179,993	$167,918
Discontinued operations:		
Income (loss) from operations (net of $409 taxes in 1994 and a tax benefit of $570 in 1993)	$ 634	$ (867)
Gain on disposal (net of $10,747 taxes)	31,430	—
Net income (loss) from discontinued operations	32,064	(867)
Net income	$212,057	$167,051

Income (loss) from operations is net income from the beginning of the year to the date the company adopts a formal plan to dispose of the segment.

The first component, **income (loss) from operations**, represents the net-of-tax effects of the revenues, expenses, gains, and losses of the discontinued operations from the beginning of the fiscal year through the measurement date. The **measurement date** is the date the company adopts a formal plan to dispose of the business segment.

The second component, **gain (loss) on disposal** actually comprises two separate amounts:

The **gain (loss) on disposal** includes (a) the net-of-tax income (loss) during the phaseout period plus (b) the net-of-tax effects of the sale of the assets of the segment.

1. Income (loss) from operations (revenues, expenses, gains, and losses, net of income taxes), from the measurement date to the actual **disposal date** (closing date). This period is known as the *phaseout period*.
2. The actual gain or loss (net of income taxes) on the sale of the segment's assets. An estimate of the gain or loss is necessary if disposal occurs after the end of the fiscal year.[10]

Revenues, expenses, gains, and losses from the measurement date to the disposal date are included in the gain (loss) on disposal because they are considered to be related to the actual disposal. In other words, they are phaseout benefits or costs of the process of liquidating the assets of the segment. Included in these costs are such items as employee relocation costs and severance pay.

The time-line in Graphic 3–2 depicts the division of net income (loss) from discontinued operations into the two components.

GRAPHIC   3 – 2

Discontinued operations (disposal in same year as measurement date)

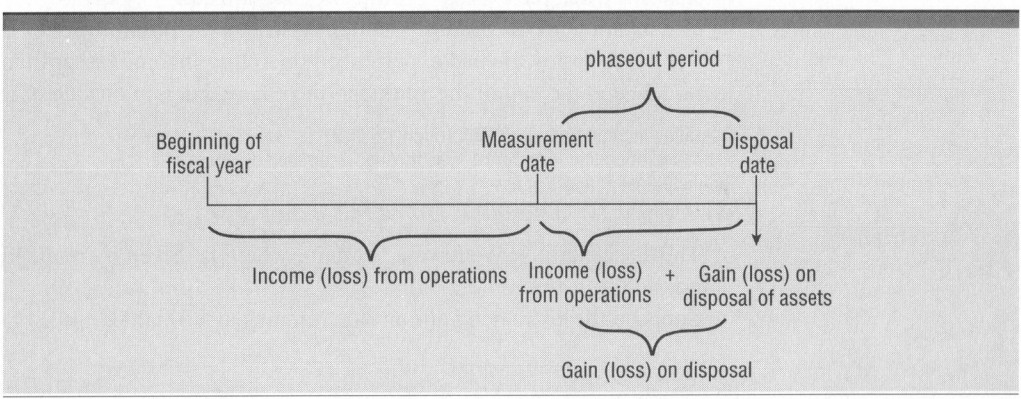

[10]If the disposal date is after the end of the fiscal year in which the measurement date occurs, the period in which this second component is reported will depend on whether it is a net gain or a net loss. We address this situation in the next section.

In the year prior to disposal, there is, of course, only the income (loss) from operations component of discontinued operations. This amount, an $867,000 1993 loss for Clorox, represents the revenues, expenses, gains, and losses, net of tax, for the entire year of 1993.

Disposal in the Year After the Measurement Date.   The previous section addressed the situation in which the *measurement date* occurs in the same fiscal year as the *disposal date*. But what if the disposal date occurs in a fiscal year subsequent to the year of the measurement date (the date a formal plan of disposal is set).

Graphic 3–3 illustrates the situation assuming a fiscal year-end of December 31.

GRAPHIC   3 – 3

Discontinued operations (disposal in year subsequent to measurement date)

Recall that the second income effect component of discontinued operations, the **gain (loss) on disposal**, is actually a composite of income or loss, net of taxes, during the phaseout period and the gain or loss, net of income taxes, on the sale of assets. If actual disposal occurs after the end of the fiscal year, the income (loss) includes the realized (actual) operating income (loss) from the measurement date to the end of the fiscal year as well as the estimated operating income (loss) from the end of the year to the anticipated disposal date. This amount is then combined with the gain or loss on the sale of the segment's assets, which also must be estimated, to determine total gain (loss) on disposal. *The period in which this is reported depends on whether it is a net gain (realized plus estimated) or a net loss (realized plus estimated).*

> When the disposal date occurs after the year of the measurement date, the period in which the gain (loss) on disposal is reported depends on whether it is a net gain or net loss.

If the realized and estimated components result in an overall loss, the loss is reported in the same year as the measurement date. If an overall gain results, the reporting of the gain is more complex. An estimated gain can be reported in the measurement year only to the extent of realized losses.

Let's look at three possible overall gain scenarios, designating realized income or loss from the measurement date to the end of the fiscal year as R, the combined estimated component (estimated operating income or loss from the end of the fiscal year to the disposal date plus the estimated gain or loss on disposal) as E, and + to indicate gain (income) and – to indicate loss.

Scenario 1: R+ and E–. In this case, realized operating income exceeds estimated losses. The overall net gain is reported in the measurement year.

Scenario 2: R+ and E+. As both components are gains (income), only the realized operating income is recognized in the measurement year. The estimated component is recognized in the year of disposal, when it is realized.

Scenario 3: R– and E+. Because there is a realized operating loss, the estimated gain (income) can be recognized in the measurement year but only to the extent of the realized loss. Therefore, no amount of gain or loss is reported in the measurement year. The net gain is reported in the year of disposal when the excess (E minus R) is realized.[11]

The example in Illustration 3–5 demonstrates the possibilities.

Suppose Worldwide had experienced operating income rather than loss between the measurement date and the end of the year, and the estimated gain on sale of assets had been $40,000:

Operating income from 9/30/97 through 12/31/97	$ 60,000
Estimated operating loss from 1/1/98 through estimated disposal date	(80,000)
Estimated gain on sale of assets	40,000
Net before-tax gain on disposal	$ 20,000

This is scenario 1. We have a net gain, which is driven by realized income. The $20,000 gain is reported in 1997.

Suppose the estimated gain on sale remains at $100,000:

[11]"Reporting Results of Operations," *Opinions of the Accounting Principles Board No. 30* (New York: AICPA, 1973), par. 15.

ILLUSTRATION   3–5

Discontinued Operations (Disposal in Year Subsequent to Measurement Date)

On September 30, 1997, the Worldwide Communications Corporation adopted a formal plan to discontinue its cellular phone business. The book value of the assets identified with the segment was $1,000,000. The closing date of the sale of the assets was anticipated to be March 31, 1998, after the 1997 financial statements have been issued. A before-tax operating loss of $60,000 was incurred from September 30 through December 31, 1997, the end of the company's fiscal year. In addition, the company estimated an operating loss, including phaseout costs, of $80,000 from January 1, 1998, through the estimated disposal date. Also, it was anticipated that the assets of the segment would be sold for $1,100,000.

The *gain (loss) on disposal* includes three elements:

Operating loss from 9/30/97 through 12/31/97	$(60,000)
Estimated operating loss from 1/1/98 through estimated disposal date	(80,000)
Estimated gain on sale of assets	100,000
Net before-tax loss on disposal	$(40,000)

The three elements are depicted in the time diagram below.

Because the net of the three items is a loss, the $40,000 loss is reported, net-of-tax, on the 1997 income statement. If the actual loss differed from this estimated loss and the difference was material, it would be reported as a gain or loss from discontinued operations on the 1998 income statement. As discussed later in this chapter, a change in an estimate is reflected in the financial statements of the year of the change.

Operating income from 9/30/97 through 12/31/97	$ 60,000
Estimated operating loss from 1/1/98 through estimated disposal date	(80,000)
Estimated gain on sale of assets	100,000
Net before-tax gain on disposal	$ 80,000

This is scenario 2, with R $60,000 and E $20,000, both positive. Only the realized income of $60,000 is recognized in 1997. The remaining gain is recognized in 1998 when realized.

Let's change the situation again to include a realized operating loss:

Operating loss from 9/30/97 through 12/31/97	$ (60,000)
Estimated operating income from 1/1/98 through estimated disposal date	80,000
Estimated gain on sale of assets	100,000
Net before-tax gain on disposal	$120,000

This is scenario 3. No gain (loss) on disposal is reported in 1997. The entire gain is recognized in 1998 when realized.[12]

Extraordinary Items

Learning objective 4
Define extraordinary items and describe the appropriate income statement presentation for these transactions.

Occasionally, an unusual event may occur that materially affects the current year's income but is unlikely to occur again in the foreseeable future. If such an item is allowed to simply alter net income without pointing out its extraordinary nature, investors and creditors may be misled into basing predictions of future income on current income that includes the nonrecurring event. For that reason, **extraordinary items** are "red flagged" on an income statement by being reported separately, net of tax, and appropriately labeled. Extraordinary items are events and transactions that are both:

1. Unusual in nature.
2. Infrequent in occurrence.[13]

---

[12]For a thorough discussion of reporting discontinued operations, see Allison Collins, "Discontinued Operations: Expanded Coverage for Intermediate Accounting," *Accounting Educators' Journal* (Spring 1995).

[13]"Reporting Results of Operations," *Opinions of the Accounting Principles Board No. 30* (New York: AICPA, 1973), par. 20.

Extraordinary items are material gains and losses that are both *unusual* in nature and *infrequent* in occurrence.

These criteria must be considered in light of the environment in which the entity operates. There obviously is a considerable degree of subjectivity involved in the determination. The concepts of unusual and infrequent require judgment. In making these judgments, an accountant should keep in mind the overall objective of the income statement. The key question is how the event relates to a firm's future profitability. If it is judged that the event, because of its unusual nature and infrequency of occurrence, *is not likely to occur again,* separate reporting is warranted.

Companies often experience *unexpected* events that are not considered extraordinary items. The loss of a major customer or the death of the company president are unexpected events that likely will affect a company's future but are both normal risks of operating a business that could recur in the future. Other gains and losses from unexpected events that are *not* considered extraordinary include the effects of a strike, including those against competitors and major suppliers, and the adjustment of accruals on long-term contracts.[14]

Determining whether an item is unusual and infrequent should consider the environment in which the company operates.

A key point in the definition of an extraordinary item is that determining whether an event satisfies both criteria depends on the environment in which the firm operates. The environment includes factors such as the type of products or services sold and the geographical location of the firm's operations. What is extraordinary for one firm may not be extraordinary for another firm. For example, a loss caused by a hurricane in Florida may not be judged to be extraordinary. However, hurricane damage in New York may indeed be unusual and infrequent.

Companies occasionally must recall a product due to a defect discovered after the product has been produced and sold. For example, in the auto industry new car models occasionally are recalled for mechanical adjustments. These adjustments can cause significant losses. Because product recall losses in the auto industry do occasionally occur and are not unusual for that industry, they are not judged to be extraordinary. In contrast, though, consider the disclosure note from Johnson and Johnson's 1982 financial statements shown in Graphic 3–4 that describes a widely publicized extraordinary recall.

GRAPHIC   3–4

Extraordinary loss disclosure—Johnson & Johnson

Notes: Extraordinary Charge

As a result of the criminal tampering with TYLENOL Extra-Strength Capsules in the Chicago area during the third quarter of 1982, the Company withdrew all TYLENOL capsule products from the market. The withdrawal costs, including disposal, handling, couponing, and other associated costs, resulted in an extraordinary after-tax charge of $50 million.

This product recall event resulted in a new package design for the product (in fact for the entire industry) reducing the likelihood that similar losses would occur in the future, and the loss was considered to be an extraordinary item.

Logic and reasoning must be applied to the determination of whether or not an event is extraordinary. Keep in mind that the income statement should be a guide to predicting the future. If it is extremely unlikely that a material gain or loss will occur again in the future, the usefulness of the income statement in predicting the future is enhanced if the income effects of that gain or loss are reported separately.

Extraordinary gains and losses are presented, net of tax, on the income statement below discontinued operations.

As shown previously in the table on page 108, the net-of-tax effects of extraordinary gains and losses are presented on the income statement below discontinued operations. In addition, a disclosure note is necessary to describe the nature of the event and the tax effects, if they are not indicated on the face of the income statement.

Material gains and losses from the early extinguishment (retirement) of debt always are reported as extraordinary items.

There is one major exception to identifying extraordinary items as those being unusual and infrequent. When debt is extinguished (retired) prior to its scheduled maturity date, any material gain or loss must always be reported as an extraordinary item whether or not the usual criteria are met.[15] This treatment is not consistent with the objective of separately classifying only those items that are not likely to occur again in the foreseeable future. This exception, specifically required by the FASB, is discussed in greater detail in Chapter 14.

---

[14]Ibid., par. 23.

[15]A gain or loss would result if the book value of the debt was different from the amount paid to liquidate the debt.

A material gain or loss that is either unusual or infrequent should be reported as a separate component of continuing operations.

OPENING CASE

Question 3

Unusual or Infrequent Items.   If an event is material and is either unusual or infrequent—but not both—it should be *included in continuing operations* but reported as a separate income statement component. An example might be a material loss caused by obsolescence of inventory. This is not an unusual event but may be infrequent for some companies. Rather than include this loss with other gains and losses or with other expenses, a separate line item on the income statement should report the loss. Unlike extraordinary items, the loss is not reported separately from continuing operations and is not reported net of tax.

Restructuring costs.   An increasingly common example of an unusual or infrequent item is **restructuring costs**. These costs generally relate to asset write-downs or facility closings. They do not constitute discontinued operations nor extraordinary items so they must be included as a component of income from continuing operations. In 1995, Fieldcrest Cannon, Inc., reported restructuring costs (restructuring charges) of $20.5 million as part of its operating costs. Graphic 3–5 shows the pertinent portion of its 1995 and 1994 income statements.

GRAPHIC   3 – 5

Fieldcrest Cannon, Inc., income statements—restructuring costs

FIELDCREST CANNON, INC.
Income Statements

	($ in thousands)	
	1995	**1994**
Net sales	$1,095,193	$1,063,731
Cost of sales	966,642	898,437
Selling, general and administrative	108,194	94,756
Restructuring charges	20,469	—
Operating income (loss)	$ (112)	$ 70,538

The disclosure note shown in Graphic 3–6 describes the charge.

GRAPHIC   3 – 6

Disclosure of restructuring costs—Fieldcrest Cannon, Inc.

Note 2. Restructuring Charges

During 1995 the Company reorganized its New York operations and relocated sales, marketing and design personnel to Kannapolis, N.C. In conjunction with the reorganization, the Company offered a voluntary early retirement program to its salaried employees. In December 1995 the Company announced the closing of two yarn mills and agreed to sell a warehouse. As a result of these actions the Company incurred restructuring charges of $20.5 million in 1995. The restructuring charges include approximately $15.6 million primarily for severance and termination benefits for 54 employees, the voluntary early retirement program which was accepted by 87 employees and lease costs in connection with the New York reorganization and $4.4 million for the write-down of yarn equipment and $.5 million for termination benefits associated with closing the yarn mills. These charges increased the 1995 loss by $12.1 million, or $1.37 per share.

Notice that a portion of the restructuring costs was related to the closing of two yarn mills, an event that was not announced until December 1995. This indicates that at least some of the actual restructuring activities probably had not yet taken place, but the costs (and a related liability or asset reduction) were accrued when the action was approved. What if the estimates turn out to be incorrect?

The income statements for Apple Computer, Inc., reported the following amounts in 1994 and 1993 as part of operating expenses ($ in thousands):

	1994	1993
Restructuring costs	$(126,855)	$320,856

Why the *negative* expense in 1994? A review of the disclosure note that accompanied Apple's financial statements reveals that in 1993 the company recorded restructuring costs that included estimated employee-related expenses and estimated facilities, equipment, and other expenses associated with the consolidation of operations and the relocation and termination of certain operations and employees. In 1994, Apple lowered its estimate of the total costs associated with the restructuring and recorded an adjustment that increased income. As we discuss later in this chapter, when an estimate is changed in a reporting period after the period the estimate was made, the company should record the effect of the change in the current period rather than restate prior years' financial statements to correct the estimate.

The appearance of restructuring costs on corporate income statements has increased significantly in the 1980s and 1990s. Many U.S. companies have reacted to increased competition by streamlining their operations. The popular term heard often is *downsizing*. Mr. Robert Willens, an accounting analyst at Lehman Brothers, a large brokerage firm, attributes the increase in corporate restructurings to increased foreign competition.

> ROBERT WILLENS-LEHMAN BROTHERS **The competitive pressures that exist in an increasingly global marketplace have led to more and more restructurings.[16]**

The SEC became concerned about the frequency with which companies were accruing restructuring costs in the period management adopted the restructuring plan. One of their chief concerns was that some companies were improperly accruing costs in an effort to manipulate income.[17] For example, employee relocation costs incurred in conjunction with a restructuring may produce future benefits to the company through greater operating efficiency. If so, accrual prior to any action may result in premature expense recognition of these costs.

The FASB's Emerging Issues Task Force responded to the SEC's concern with *EITF Issue No. 94-3*, "Liability Recognition for Costs to Exit an Activity (including Certain Costs Incurred in a Restructuring)." The *Issue* discusses the various types of costs related to restructurings and establishes criteria that limit which costs can be accrued in the period management approves a restructuring plan. In general, costs that have no future economic benefit that are incurred as a result of a commitment by a company's management to execute a restructuring plan should be accrued at the commitment date. A commitment date occurs when a number of specified conditions are met. The *Issue* also increases the disclosure requirements for certain types of restructuring costs.

Cumulative Effect of a Change in Accounting Principle

Learning objective 5
Describe and illustrate the measurement and reporting requirements for the cumulative effect of a change in accounting principle.

The third item reported separately after income from continuing operations is the **cumulative effect of a change in accounting principle**. A change in accounting principle refers to a change from one acceptable accounting method to another. There are many situations in which there are alternative treatments for similar transactions. Common examples of these situations include the choice among FIFO, LIFO, and average cost for the measurement of inventory and between straight-line and other depreciation methods for plant and equipment.

Occasionally, a company will change from one generally accepted treatment to another. When these changes in accounting principles occur, information lacks consistency, hampering the ability of external users to compare financial information over reporting periods. If, for example, depreciation expense is measured in one reporting period using an accelerated depreciation method and the straight-line method in a subsequent period, depreciation expense and hence net income for the two periods are not comparable. Difficulties created by inconsistency and lack of comparability are alleviated somewhat by the way we report accounting changes.

The general accounting treatment for a change in accounting principle is to show the cumulative effect of the change on the income statement below extraordinary items.

The general method of accounting for this type of change requires that its effects be reflected in the statements in the year the change is made rather than by retroactively restating prior years' comparative financial statements as if the new accounting principle had been in use. The cumulative effect of a change in accounting principle should be reflected in the financial statements of the change year.[18] Previous financial statements included for comparative purposes should be presented as previously reported.

The cumulative effect of a change in accounting principle is the cumulative effect on the income of previous years from having used the previous method rather than the new method. Stated dif-

---

[16]Robert Willens, quote appears in *The Wall Street Journal*, November 2, 1994, p. C2.

[17]There are those who contend that companies intentionally manipulate reported income. The manipulation is not always intended to produce higher income but to achieve a smooth pattern of income over time to appear less risky or volatile. For example, accelerated recognition and overestimation of restructuring costs is a technique that companies could use to understate income in an otherwise good year and then use the "banked" income in the following year in case income declines. Manipulating income and income smoothing are discussed in an Additional Consideration later in the chapter.

[18]"Accounting Changes," *Opinions of the Accounting Principles Board No. 20* (New York: AICPA, 1971).

ferently, it's the difference between the balance in retained earnings at the beginning of the period of the change and what that balance would have been if the new method had been applied all along.[19]

Illustration 3–6 provides an example.

ILLUSTRATION   3–6

Change in Accounting Principle

The Maxwell Gear Corporation uses the double-declining balance (DDB) depreciation method for most of its equipment. In 1997, the company switched from the DDB method to straight-line depreciation for a large group of equipment purchased at the beginning of 1995. This equipment was purchased at a cost of $50 million. The machinery has an expected useful life of five years and no estimated salvage value.

Cumulative effect of the change:

	($ in millions)	
	DDB	**Straight-Line**
1995 depreciation	$20 ($50 × 40%)	$10 ($50 ÷ 5)
1996 depreciation	12 ([$50 − 20] × 40%)	10 ($50 ÷ 5)
Accumulated depreciation and 1995–96 reduction in income	$32	$20

difference
$12

The cumulative income effect is reported—net of the tax effect of the change—on the income statement as a separate item of income, between extraordinary items and net income, as shown here:

Reported as a separate component of income:

	($ in millions)	
	1997	**1996**
Income before extraordinary item and accounting change	$xxx	$xxx
Extraordinary gain (loss), net of tax	xx	xx
Cumulative effect of accounting change (net of $3.6 tax)	8.4	
Net income	$xxx	$xxx

The cumulative after-tax effect on prior years' income is a separate item of income between extraordinary items and net income.

Reporting the income effect net of tax is consistent with the way we report the other two separately reported income statement items: extraordinary gains and losses and discontinued operations.

The before-tax cumulative effect of the change in Maxwell Gear's depreciation method is $12 million. If Maxwell Gear's tax rate is 30%, the cumulative tax effect of the depreciation change is $3.6 million ($12 million × 30%). This is because, under straight-line depreciation, the reduction of income for depreciation is $12 million less, causing tax expense to be higher by that amount times the tax rate. The higher tax expense partially offsets the lower depreciation expense when determining the net, after-tax, cumulative effect of the change.

Of course, the asset side of the balance sheet also is adjusted for the depreciation change. In our illustration, accumulated depreciation is reduced by $12 million.

If the switch had been from straight-line to DDB depreciation rather than from DDB to straight-line, the effects would have been reversed. The cumulative effect of the change would have been a negative component of net income. That is, income (and therefore retained earnings) would have been $8.4 million less ($12 million – $3.6 million) in prior years if DDB depreciation had been used rather than straight-line.

To assist interyear comparisons, additional disclosure is required for various pro forma (as if) amounts for each period presented. Specifically, income statements should include pro forma restatement of (a) income before extraordinary items, (b) net income, and (c) earnings per share. In other words, these specific items, calculated as if the new method had been in effect in those prior years, are reported as supplemental information. In addition, a disclosure note is required that describes the change, the justification for the change, and the effect of the change on the current period's income.[20]

Graphic 3–7 describes an accounting change made by Ralston Purina Company mandated by *SFAS 106*.[21]

---

[19]There are a few specific changes in accounting principles that are treated differently by actually restating prior years' financial statements. These exceptions are discussed in Chapter 21.

[20]Pro forma and other disclosures are discussed and illustrated in Chapter 21.

[21]*SFAS 106* permits companies to choose between immediate recognition of the cumulative effect of the accounting change—Ralston Purina's choice—or to defer recognition over future periods. Chapter 18 describes these options.

GRAPHIC   3–7

Disclosure of change in accounting principle— Ralston Purina Company

Postretirement Benefits Other Than Pensions (in part)

(dollars in millions)

Effective October 1, 1992, the Company adopted SFAS 106. This standard requires that the estimated cost of postretirement benefits other than pensions be accrued over the period such benefits are earned. The Company elected to recognize the cumulative effect of this accounting change in 1993. As a result, the RPG Group recorded a non-cash charge of $204.2 ($130.7 after income taxes) which represents the excess of the accumulated postretirement benefit obligation over accruals recorded prior to the adoption of SFAS 106.

Because of their unique nature, some changes in accounting principle are more appropriately accounted for *retroactively* than by the usual approach described above. For these exceptions to the general manner of treating a change in accounting principle, prior years' financial statements are *restated* to reflect the use of the new accounting method. Chapter 21 provides more detailed coverage of the measurement and disclosure requirements for a change in accounting principle.

Accounting changes fall into one of three categories: (1) a change in an accounting principle, (2) a change in estimate, or (3) a change in reporting entity. We just discussed changes in accounting principles. A brief overview of each of the other two changes is provided here. Chapter 21 covers accounting changes in detail.

Learning objective 6
Explain the accounting treatment of changes in estimates.

A **change in accounting estimate** is reflected in the financial statements of the current period and future periods.

Change in Accounting Estimate.   Estimates are a necessary aspect of accounting. Some common accounting estimates are the estimation of the amount of future bad debts on existing accounts receivable, the estimation of the useful life and salvage value of a depreciable asset, and the estimation of future warranty expenses.

Because estimates require the prediction of future events, it's not unusual for them to turn out wrong. When an estimate is revised as new information comes to light, accounting for the change in estimate is quite straightforward. We do not restate prior years' financial statements to reflect the new estimate; nor do we include the cumulative effect of the change in current income. Instead, we merely incorporate the new estimate in any related accounting determinations from there on.[22]

Consider the example in Illustration 3–7.

ILLUSTRATION   3–7

Change in Accounting Estimate

The Maxwell Gear Corporation purchased machinery in 1994 for $2 million. The useful life of the machinery was estimated to be 10 years with no salvage value. The straight-line depreciation method was used in 1994 through 1996, with a full year of depreciation taken in 1994. In 1997, the company revised the useful life of the machinery to eight years.

Neither depreciation expense nor accumulated depreciation reported in prior years is restated. No account balances are adjusted. The cumulative effect of the estimate change is not included in current income. Rather, in 1997 and later years, the adjusting entry to record depreciation expense simply will reflect the new useful life. In 1997, the entry is:

Depreciation expense (below)	280,000	
Accumulated depreciation		280,000

	$2,000,000	Cost
$200,000		Old annual depreciation ($2,000,000 ÷ 10 years)
× 3 years	600,000	Depreciation to date (1994–1996)
	1,400,000	Book value as of 1/1/97
	÷ 5	Estimated remaining life (8 years – 3 years)
	$ 280,000	New annual depreciation

If the after-tax income effect of the change in estimate is material, the effect on net income and earnings per share must be disclosed in a note, along with the justification for the change. In

---

[22]If the original estimate was based on erroneous information or calculations or was not made in good faith, the revision of that estimate constitutes the correction of an error.

this example, assuming a 40% tax rate, the after-tax effect of the change is a decrease in income of $48,000 [$80,000 ($280,000 revised depreciation – $200,000 old depreciation) multiplied by 60% (1-40% tax rate)].

The Owens-Corning Fiberglass Corporation disclosed a change in the useful lives of some of its depreciable assets as shown in Graphic 3–8.

GRAPHIC   3 – 8

**Change in estimate—
Owens-Corning Fiberglass
Corporation**

Note 6: Depreciation of Plant and Equipment

During 1993, the Company completed a review of its fixed asset lives. The Company determined that as a result of actions taken to increase its preventive maintenance and programs initiated with its equipment suppliers to increase the quality of their products, actual lives for certain asset categories were generally longer than the useful lives for depreciation purposes. Therefore, the Company extended the estimated useful lives of certain categories of plant and equipment, effective April 1, 1993. The effect of this change in estimate reduced depreciation expense for the year ended December 31, 1993 by $14 million and increased income before cumulative effect of accounting change by $ 8 million ($.19 per share).

Change in Reporting Entity.   A third type of change—the **change in reporting entity**—involves the preparation of financial statements for an accounting entity other than the entity that existed in the previous period.[23] For example, if Company A acquired Company B during 1997, consolidated financial statements are generally required that combine the statements of the two companies as if they were a single reporting entity. The combined financial statements for A and B for 1997 would not be comparable to the financial statements of the separate companies for 1996.[24]

A **change in reporting
entity** requires that
financial statements of prior
periods be *retroactively
restated.*

A change in reporting entity is reported by restating all previous period's financial statements presented for comparative purposes as if the new reporting entity existed in those periods. In other words, in our example, the financial statements are presented as if A and B had been combined in prior years. In addition, in the first set of financial statements issued after the change, a disclosure note is required that describes the nature of the change, the reason it occurred, and the effect of the change on net income, income before extraordinary items, and related per share amounts for all periods presented.

Additional Consideration

Manipulating income and income smoothing

   An often debated contention is that, within GAAP, managers have the power, to a limited degree, to manipulate reported company income. And the manipulation is not always in the direction of higher income. One author states that "Most executives prefer to report earnings that follow a smooth, regular, upward path. They hate to report declines, but they also want to avoid increases that vary wildly from year to year; it's better to have two years of 15% earnings increases than a 30% gain one year and none the next. As a result, some companies 'bank' earnings by understating them in particularly good years and use the banked profits to polish results in bad years."[25]

   How can managers manipulate income? We have just discussed one way, changing an accounting method. However, this method is transparent, in that the effects on income of switching from one accounting method to another must be disclosed. Income also can be manipulated by means of the many estimates required to measure income according to the accrual accounting model. Estimates of bad debts, inventory obsolescence, and future warranty costs are just a few of the estimates commonly made. A company and its auditors may have different opinions about the level of these estimates but can usually agree on an acceptable range. Income can be managed within this range.

   A third category of income manipulations relates to the timing of revenue and expense recognition. For example, research and development expenditures could be delayed to the following year in order to boost this year's income. (Refer back to the Ethical Dilemma in Chapter 1 on page 28 for an example of a situation involving the timing of expense recognition.)

---

[23]Chapter 21 discusses the different types of situations that result in a change in accounting entity.

[24]The issuance of *SFAS 94,* "Consolidation of All Majority-Owned Subsidiaries," resulted in hundreds of reporting entities being altered to include previously unconsolidated finance subsidiaries.

[25]Ford S. Worthy, "Manipulating Profits: How It's Done," *Fortune,* June 25, 1984, p. 50.

Correction of Accounting Errors

Errors occur when transactions are either recorded incorrectly or not recorded at all. We briefly discuss the correction of errors here as an overview and in later chapters in the context of the effect of errors on specific chapter topics. In addition, Chapter 21 provides comprehensive coverage of the correction of errors.

Learning objective 7
Briefly describe the accounting treatment for the correction of errors.

Accountants employ various control mechanisms to ensure that transactions are accounted for correctly. In spite of this, errors occur. When errors do occur, they can affect any one or several of the financial statement elements on any of the financial statements a company prepares. In fact, many kinds of errors simultaneously affect more than one financial statement. When errors are discovered, they should be corrected.

Most errors are discovered in the same year that they are made. These errors are simply corrected by a journal entry. If an error is discovered in a year subsequent to the year the error is made, accounting treatment depends on whether or not the error is material with respect to its effect on the financial statements. In practice, the vast majority of errors are not material and are, therefore, simply corrected in the year discovered.

Prior Period Adjustments

Material errors discovered after the year the error is made are rare. The correction of these errors is considered to be a **prior period adjustment**.[26] A prior period adjustment refers to an addition to or reduction in the beginning retained earnings balance in a statement of shareholders' equity (or statement of retained earnings if that's presented instead).

When it's discovered that the ending balance of retained earnings in the period prior to the discovery of an error was incorrect as a result of that error, the balance is corrected. However, simply reporting a corrected amount might cause misunderstanding for someone familiar with the previously reported amount. Explicitly reporting a prior period adjustment on the statement of shareholders' equity (or statement of retained earnings) avoids this confusion.

In addition to reporting the prior period adjustment to retained earnings, previous years' financial statements that are incorrect as a result of the error are retroactively restated to reflect the correction. Also, a disclosure note communicates the impact of the error on income.

EPS = NI − preferred dividends ÷ # of common shares

Earnings Per Share Disclosures

Financial statement users often use summary indicators, called ratios, to more efficiently make comparisons among different companies and over time for the same company. Besides highlighting important relationships among financial statement variables, ratios also accommodate differences in company size.

Learning objective 8
Define earnings per share (EPS) and explain required disclosures of EPS for certain income statement components.

One of the most widely used ratios is **earnings per share (EPS)**, which shows the amount of income earned by a company expressed on a per share basis. In its simplest form, it is computed by dividing net income for the period by the weighted average number of common shares outstanding for the period. The ratio's computation can become complex if the company has potentially dilutive items outstanding. That is, the company may have certain securities outstanding that are convertible into common shares or stock options that could create additional common shares if the options were exercised. These items could cause EPS to decrease (become diluted). Because of the complexity of the calculations and the importance of EPS to investors, we devote an entire chapter (Chapter 20) to this topic. At this point, we focus on the basic calculation and financial statement presentation of EPS.

Earnings per share (EPS) is the amount of income achieved during a period for each share of common stock outstanding.

All corporations whose common stock is publicly traded must report EPS on the face of the income statement. In Graphic 3–1 on page 106, Federal Express disclosed earnings per share of $5.39 for 1996, computed by dividing net income of $307,777,000 by average common shares outstanding of 57,138,000.

All corporations whose common stock is publicly traded must disclose EPS.

The EPS for income from continuing operations, and for each item below continuing operations, must be disclosed.

When the income statement includes one or more of the separately reported items below income from continuing operations, EPS data must also be reported separately for income from continuing operations and net income. Per share amounts for discontinued operations, extraordinary items, and the cumulative effect of a change in accounting principle would be disclosed on the face of the income statement. The Promus Companies, a major casino entertainment

---

[26]"Prior Period Adjustments," *Statement of Financial Accounting Standards No. 16* (Stamford, Conn.: FASB, 1977).

Federal Express Corporation

(Harrah's) and hotel business (Embassy Suites), reported discontinued operations (the hotel business) and a change in accounting principle in 1994 and discontinued operations and an extraordinary item in 1993, and accordingly reported corresponding per share amounts as shown in Graphic 3–9. The graphic provides an example of a comprehensive income statement.

GRAPHIC   3–9

EPS disclosures—Promus Companies

PROMUS COMPANIES Consolidated Statements of Income (In Part) Fiscal Year Ended December 31		
(in thousands, except per share amounts)	**1994**	**1993**
Revenues	$1,339,406	$1,020,645
Operating expenses and corporate expenses	1,070,219	810,612
Operating income	269,187	210,033
Interest expense	(78,322)	(73,080)
Provision for settlement of litigation and related costs	(53,449)	(400)
Other income, including interest income	1,867	2,462
Income before income taxes and minority interest	139,283	139,015
Provision for income taxes	(75,391)	(59,394)
Minority interests*	(13,908)	(4,754)
Income from continuing operations	49,984	74,867
Earnings from discontinued hotel operations, net of tax provisions of $26,798, and $13,869†	36,319	16,926
Income before extraordinary items and cumulative effect of change in accounting principle	86,303	91,793
Extraordinary item, net of tax benefit of $3,415	—	(5,447)
Cumulative effect of change in accounting principle, net of tax benefit of $4,317	(7,932)	—
Net income	$ 78,371	$ 86,346
Earnings (loss) per share		
Continuing operations	$ 0.49	$ 0.73
Discontinued operations, net	0.35	0.16
Extraordinary items, net	—	(0.05)
Cumulative effect of change in accounting principle, net	(0.08)	—
Net income (loss)	$ 0.76	$ 0.84

*Minority interests arise when a subsidiary that is not 100% owned is consolidated. This topic is addressed in Advanced Accounting courses.
†The hotel business was spun-off from the casino business and two separate corporations formed. Accordingly, there is no gain or loss from disposal of the hotel business and only income from operations for the discontinued hotel operations is reported.

CONCEPT REVIEW EXERCISE   INCOME STATEMENT PRESENTATION

The Samuelson Construction Company builds office buildings. They also own and operate a chain of motels throughout the Southwest. On September 30, 1997, the company decided to sell the entire motel business for $40 million. The sale was completed on December 15, 1997. 1997 income statement information is provided below for the two segments of the company.

($ in millions)	Construction Business	Motel Business
Sales revenue	$ 450.0	$ 200.0
Operating expenses	(226.0)	(210.0)
Other income (loss)*	16.0	(30.0)
Income (loss) before income taxes	240.0	(40.0)
Income tax expense (benefit†	96.0	(16.0)
Net income (loss)	$ 144.0	$ (24.0)

*For the motel business, the entire amount represents the loss on sale of assets of the business. Book value of assets is $70 million, sold for $40 million.
†A 40% tax rate applies to all items of income or loss.

The sales revenue and operating expenses of the motel business occurred as follows:

	($ in millions)	
	Jan. 1–Sept. 30	October 1–Dec. 15
Sales revenue	$150.0	$50.0
Operating expenses	145.0	65.0

In addition to the revenues and expenses of the construction and motel businesses, the following material events also occurred during the year:

1. Samuelson experienced a before-tax gain of $20 million from the retirement of long-term debt three years prior to the debt's scheduled maturity.
2. The company changed its method of depreciation from the double-declining–balance method to the straight-line method. Depreciation expense for 1997 has been correctly computed using the straight-line method. Cumulative prior years' depreciation expense would have been $5 million lower had the straight-line method been employed in prior years.

Required:
Prepare a 1997 income statement for the Samuelson Construction Company including EPS disclosures. 10 million shares of common stock were outstanding throughout 1997.

CONCEPT REVIEW EXERCISE   SOLUTION

SAMUELSON CONSTRUCTION COMPANY
Income Statement
For the Year Ended December 31, 1997

		($ in millions)
Sales revenue		$450.0
Operating expenses		226.0
Operating income		224.0
Other income		16.0
Income from continuing operations before income taxes		240.0
Income tax expense		96.0
Income from continuing operations		144.0
Discontinued operations:		
Income from operations (net of $2.0 tax expense)	3.0*	
Loss on disposal (net of $18.0 tax benefit)	(27.0)†	(24.0)
Income before extraordinary item and accounting change		120.0
Extraordinary gain from the early extinguishment of debt (net of $8.0 tax expense)		12.0
Cumulative effect of a change in accounting principle (net of $2.0 tax expense)		3.0
Net income		$135.0
Earnings per share:		
Income from continuing operations		$14.40
Discontinued operations		(2.40)
Extraordinary gain		1.20
Cumulative effect of a change in accounting principle		.30
Net income		$13.50

*The 3.0 million figure is determined by taking the operating income of the motel business from the beginning of the year through the measurement date of $5.0 million [$150 − 145 = $5] and subtracting the tax effect of $2.0 million [40% × $5.0].
†The $27.0 million loss is determined by adding the operating loss from the measurement date to the disposal date of $15.0 million [$50 − 65 = $(15)], to the loss on disposal of $30.0 million = $45.0 million pre-tax loss on disposal, and then subtracting the $18.0 million tax benefit [40% × $45].

Comprehensive Income
One unsettled income issue is whether or not certain transactions affecting equity should be included in the determination of periodic income and included on the income statement. The FASB's *Concept Statement 6* defines the term **comprehensive income** as the change in equity from nonowner transactions. The calculation of net income, however, excludes certain transactions that otherwise would be included in comprehensive income. These few transactions are discussed in other parts of the text. For example, in Chapter 12 you will learn that certain investments are reported on the balance sheet at their fair values, but the net unrealized holding gains and losses resulting from changes in fair values are *not* included in net income. Instead, they are reported as separate components of shareholders' equity, outside of income.

Comprehensive income is the total nonowner change in equity for a reporting period.

The Income Statement

There are significant differences from country to country in the presentation and content of the income statement as well as in the accounting methods used to measure income statement amounts. Many of the measurement differences are highlighted in the specific chapters that deal with the specific issues. For example, differences in inventory measurement methods, differences in the treatment of goodwill, and the method used to value and depreciate property and equipment are but three of several areas where global practices differ widely.

There also are many differences in the presentation and content of the income statement. Here are just a few examples:

1. The title of the statement. For example, in the United Kingdom (U.K.) it is called the Group Profit and Loss Account.
2. Revenue terminology. In a number of countries (for example, the U.K. and Denmark), sales revenue is referred to as turnover.
3. The treatment of extraordinary gains and losses. In some countries, such as The Netherlands, certain extraordinary gains and losses are not included in the income statement but are shown as direct adjustments to shareholders' equity. In other countries, such as the U.K., extraordinary gains and losses are shown on the income statement at their gross amounts, not net-of-tax. In Korea, accounting principles specify certain transactions that must be reported as extraordinary. These transactions include casualty losses, gains and losses on the disposition of fixed assets, and gains and losses on the disposition of investments.
4. The treatment of a change in accounting principle. For example, in Australia, a change in accounting principle is treated as an adjustment to retained earnings. No cumulative effect is shown on the income statement.

The Financial Accounting Standards Board recently proposed a new standard that requires companies to report both net income and comprehensive income and reconcile the differences between the two.[27] Be sure to realize that net income is actually a part of comprehensive income, along with **other comprehensive income** items—the transactions previously reported as separate components of shareholders' equity. The reconciliation simply extends net income to include other comprehensive items, reported net of tax, as shown in Illustration 3–8.

ILLUSTRATION   3–8

Comprehensive Income

	($ in millions)	
Net income		$135
Other comprehensive income:		
Foreign currency translation adjustments, net of tax*	$16	
Unrealized gains (losses) on investment securities, net of tax†	22	
Unrealized pension cost, net of tax‡	(3)	35
Comprehensive income		$170

*Gains or losses from changes in foreign currency exchange rates. The amount could be an addition to or reduction in shareholders' equity. (This item is discussed elsewhere in your accounting curriculum.)
†Changes in the market value of some investments produce unrealized gains (losses) that increase (reduce) shareholders' equity (described in Chapter 12).
‡Reporting a pension liability sometimes requires a reduction in shareholders' equity (described in Chapter 17).

> Reporting comprehensive income can be accomplished with either one or two financial statements.

The presentation shown in Illustration 3–8 can be included as an extension to the income statement, in a statement of changes in equity, or reported (exactly the same way) as a separate statement of comprehensive income. The latter statement begins with net income followed by other comprehensive income to arrive at comprehensive income. In either case, the components of other comprehensive income could be displayed net of tax, or alternatively, before tax with one amount shown for the aggregate income tax expense or benefit.[28]

---

[27]"Reporting Comprehensive Income," *Proposed Statement of Financial Accounting Standards* (Norwalk, Conn.: FASB, 1996).
[28]The proposed standard does not require the reporting of comprehensive income per share.

The retained earnings component of shareholders' equity includes only the net income portion of comprehensive income. The total of other comprehensive income for a period is transferred to a separate component of shareholders' equity at the end of a reporting period.

Net income and comprehensive income are identical for an enterprise that has no other comprehensive income items. Throughout this chapter, we assumed no differences between the two income numbers so we could concentrate on the measurement and reporting of net income in an income statement. Components of other comprehensive income are described elsewhere.

Now that we have discussed the presentation and content of the income statement, we turn our attention to the statement of cash flows.

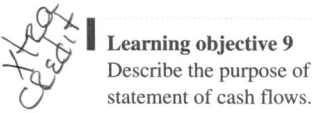

PART B   THE STATEMENT OF CASH FLOWS

Learning objective 9
Describe the purpose of the statement of cash flows.

In addition to the income statement and the balance sheet, **a statement of cash flows (SCF)** is an essential component within the set of basic financial statements.[29] Specifically, when a balance sheet and an income statement are presented, a statement of cash flows is required for each income statement period. The purpose of the SCF is to provide information about the cash receipts and cash disbursements of an enterprise that occurred during a period. Similar to the income statement, it is a *change* statement, summarizing the transactions that caused cash to change during a reporting period. The term *cash* refers to *cash plus cash equivalents*. Cash equivalents, discussed in Chapter 5, include highly liquid (easily converted to cash) investments such as treasury bills and certificates of deposit. Chapter 22 is devoted exclusively to the SCF. A brief overview is provided here.

A **statement of cash flows** is presented for each period for which results of operations are provided.

Usefulness of the Statement of Cash Flows

We discussed the difference between cash and accrual accounting in Chapter 1. It was pointed out and illustrated that over short periods of time, operating cash flows may not be indicative of the company's long-run cash-generating ability, and that accrual-based net income provides a more accurate prediction of future operating cash flows. Nevertheless, information about cash flows from operating activities, when combined with information about cash flows from other activities, can provide information helpful in assessing future profitability, liquidity, and long-term solvency. After all, a company must pay its debts with cash, not with income.

Of particular importance is the amount of cash generated from operating activities. In the long run, a company must be able to generate positive cash flow from activities related to selling its product or service. These activities must provide the necessary cash to pay debts, provide dividends to shareholders, and provide for future growth.

Classifying Cash Flows

A list of cash flows is more meaningful to investors and creditors if they can determine the type of transaction that gave rise to each cash flow. Toward this end, the statement of cash flows classifies all transactions affecting cash into one of three categories: (1) operating activities, (2) investing activities, and (3) financing activities.

Learning objective 10
Identify and describe the various classifications of cash flows presented on the statement of cash flows.

Operating Activities

The inflows and outflows of cash that result from activities reported on the income statement are classified as cash flows from **operating activities**. In other words, this classification of cash flows includes the elements of net income reported on a cash basis rather than an accrual basis.[30]

Operating activities are inflows and outflows of cash related to the transactions entering into the determination of net operating income.

---

[29]"Statement of Cash Flows," *Statement of Financial Accounting Standards No. 95* (Stamford, Conn.: FASB, 1987).

[30]Cash inflows related to gains and losses from the sale of assets shown on the income statement are reported as investing activities in the SCF.

Cash inflows include cash received from:

1. Customers from the sale of goods or services.
2. Interest and dividends from investments.

These amounts may differ from sales and investment income reported on the income statement. For example, sales revenue measured on the accrual basis reflects revenue earned during the period, not necessarily the cash actually collected. Revenue will not equal cash collected from customers if receivables from customers changed during the period.

Cash outflows include cash paid for:

1. The purchase of inventory.
2. Salaries, wages, and other operating expenses.
3. Interest on debt.
4. Income taxes.

Likewise, these amounts may differ from the corresponding accrual expenses reported on the income statement. Expenses are reported when incurred, not necessarily when cash is actually paid for those expenses. Also, some revenues and expenses, like depreciation expense don't affect cash at all and aren't reported on the statement of cash flows.

The difference between the inflows and outflows is called *net cash flows from operating activities*. This is equivalent to net income if the income statement had been prepared on a cash basis rather than an accrual basis.

By the **direct method**, the cash effect of each operating activity is reported directly on the SCF.	**Direct and Indirect Methods of Reporting.** Two generally accepted formats can be used to report operating activities, the direct method and the indirect method. Under the **direct method,** the cash effect of each operating activity is reported directly on the statement. For example, *cash received from customers* is reported as the cash effect of sales activities. Income statement transactions that have no cash flow effect, such as depreciation, are simply not reported.

※ The **indirect method**, on the other hand, arrives at net cash flow from operating activities indirectly by starting with reported net income and working backwards to convert that amount to a cash basis. For example, depreciation expense would be added back to net income because this expense reduces net income but does not entail a cash disbursement. Also, adjustments are necessary for changes in certain current assets and liabilities. For instance, if accounts receivable increased during the period, credit sales revenue exceeded cash collected from customers. This increase in accounts receivable must be deducted from net income to arrive at cash flow from operating activities. Both methods produce the same net cash flows from operating activities; they are merely alternative approaches to reporting the cash flows. The FASB, in *SFAS 95*, stated its preference for the direct method. However, either method is acceptable and both are used in practice.

By the **indirect method**, cash flows from operating activities is derived indirectly by starting with reported net income and adding and subtracting items to convert that amount to a cash basis.

Method usually used ↗

The choice of presentation method for cash flow from operating activities has no effect on how investing activities and financing activities are reported. We now look at how cash flows are classified into those two categories.

Investing Activities

Cash flows from **investing activities** include inflows and outflows of cash related to the acquisition and disposition of long-term assets used in the operations of the business (such as property,

Investing activities involve the acquisition and sale of (1) long-term assets used in the business and (2) nonoperating investment assets.

plant, and equipment) and investment assets (except those classified as cash equivalents). The purchase and sale of inventories are not considered investing activities. Inventories are purchased for the purpose of being sold as part of the company's operations, so their purchase and sale are included with operating activities rather than investing activities.

Cash outflows from investing activities include cash paid for:

1. The purchase of long-term assets used in the business.
2. The purchase of investment securities like stocks and bonds of other entities (other than those classified as cash equivalents).
3. Loans to other entities.

Later, when the assets are disposed of, cash inflow from the sale of the assets (or collection of loans and notes) also is reported as cash flows from investing activities. As a result, cash inflows from these transactions are considered investing activities:

1. The sale of long-term assets used in the business.
2. The sale of investment securities (other than cash equivalents).
3. The collection of a nontrade receivable (excluding the collection of interest, which is an operating activity).

Net cash flows from investing activities represents the difference between the inflows and outflows.

Financing Activities

Financing activities involve cash inflows and outflows from transactions with creditors (excluding trade creditors) and owners.

Financing activities relate to the external financing of the company. Cash inflows occur when cash is borrowed from creditors or invested by owners. Cash outflows occur when cash is paid back to creditors or distributed to owners. The payment of interest to a creditor, however, is classified as an operating activity.

Cash inflows include cash received from:

1. Owners when shares are sold to them.
2. Creditors when cash is borrowed through notes, loans, mortgages, and bonds.

Cash outflows include cash paid to:

1. Owners in the form of dividends or other distributions.
2. Owners for the reacquisition of shares previously sold.
3. Creditors as repayment of the principal amounts of debt (excluding trade payables that relate to operating activities).

Net cash flows from financing activities is the difference between the inflows and outflows.

Noncash Investing and Financing Activities

Significant investing and financing transactions not involving cash also are reported in the SCF.

As we just discussed, the statement of cash flows provides useful information about the investing and financing activities in which a company is engaged. Even though these primarily result in cash inflows and cash outflows, there may be significant investing and financing activities occurring during the period that do not involve cash flows at all. In order to provide complete information about these activities, the SCF shows any significant *noncash* investing and financing activities (that is, noncash exchanges). An example is the acquisition of equipment (an investing activity) by issuing either a long-term note payable or equity securities (a financing activity). These noncash activities are reported either in a separate schedule or in a note.

An illustration of a statement of cash flows is provided in the following concept review exercise.

CONCEPT REVIEW EXERCISE   STATEMENT OF CASH FLOWS

The following are summary transactions that occurred during 1997 for the Lashlee Parts Company:

Cash received from:	
Customers	$660,000
Interest on note receivable	12,000
Sale of investments	20,000
Proceeds from note payable	100,000
Sale of equipment	40,000
Issuance of common stock	200,000
Cash paid for:	
Purchase of investments	100,000
Interest on note payable	18,000
Purchase of equipment	120,000
Operating expenses	440,000
Principal on note payable	150,000
Payment of dividends to shareholders	30,000

The balance of cash and cash equivalents is $130,000 at the *beginning* of 1997 and $304,000 at the *end* of 1997.

Required:
Prepare a statement of cash flows for 1997 for the Lashlee Parts Company. Use the direct method for reporting operating activities.

CONCEPT REVIEW EXERCISE   SOLUTION

LASHLEE PARTS COMPANY
Statement of Cash Flows
For the Year Ended December 31, 1997

Cash flows from operating activities:		
Collections from customers	$ 660,000	
Interest on note receivable	12,000	
Interest on note payable	(18,000)	
Payment of operating expenses	(440,000)	
Net cash inflows from operating activities		$ 214,000
Cash flows from investing activities:		
Purchase of investments	(100,000)	
Sale of investments	20,000	
Purchase of equipment	(120,000)	
Sale of equipment	40,000	
Net cash outflows from investing activities		(160,000)
Cash flows from financing activities:		
Proceeds from note payable	100,000	
Payment of note payable	(150,000)	
Issuance of common stock	200,000	
Payment of dividends	(30,000)	
Net cash inflows from financing activities		120,000
Net increase in cash		174,000
Cash and cash equivalents, January 1		130,000
Cash and cash equivalents, December 31		$ 304,000

Solution to Financial Reporting Case (at the opening of the chapter)

1. In addition to discontinued operations, what other events sometimes are reported separately on the income statement that you might tell Becky about? Why are these items reported separately?

2. Explain to Becky what is meant by a discontinued operation and describe to her how one is reported on an income statement.

In addition to discontinued operations, extraordinary items and the cumulative effect of changes in accounting principles also are reported separately on the income statement when they are present. The predictive ability of an income statement is significantly enhanced if normal and recurrent transactions are separated from unusual and nonrecurrent items. The income statement is a historical report, summarizing the most recent operating activities of a company. The information in the statement is useful if it can help users predict the future. Toward this end, users should be made aware of events reported on the income statement that are not likely to occur again in the foreseeable future.

A discontinued operation occurs when a company closes a segment of its business. This can be either a separate line of business or separate class of customer. The net-of-tax effect of discontinued operations is separately reported below income from continuing operations. These effects are divided into two components: (1) income or loss from operations of the discontinued segment and (2) gain or loss on disposal of the discontinued segment's assets.

3. How would you explain restructuring costs to Becky? Are they necessarily a negative?

Restructuring costs include employee severance and termination benefits plus other costs associated with the shutdown or relocation of facilities or downsizing of operations. These costs are an example of an unusual or infrequent item that does not constitute discontinued operations nor extraordinary items so they must be included as a component of income from continuing operations. It's not necessarily bad. In fact, the objective is to make operations more efficient. The costs are incurred now in hopes of better earnings later.

The Bottom Line

1. The primary need of investors and creditors is information that is useful in predicting future cash flows. The transactions from continuing operations are important to any assessment of future cash flows. The components of income from continuing operations are revenues, expenses (including income taxes), gains, and losses.

2. Intraperiod tax allocation associates tax expense (or tax benefit) with continuing operations and with any item reported below continuing operations.

3. A discontinued operation refers to the disposal or other closing of a segment of the business, defined as either a separate line of business or class of customer. The net-of-tax effect of discontinued operations is separately reported below income from continuing operations.

4. Extraordinary items are material gains and losses that are both unusual in nature and infrequent in occurrence. The net-of-tax effects of extraordinary items are presented on the income statement below discontinued operations, if any.

5. The general accounting treatment for a change in accounting principle is to show the net-of-tax cumulative effect of the change on the income statement of the year of the change below extraordinary items. In addition, disclosure reports various pro forma (as if) amounts for each period presented and also describes the change, the justification for the change, and the effect of the change on the current period's income.

6. A change in accounting estimate is treated currently and prospectively, rather than by restating prior years' financial statements to correct the estimate, or by including the cumulative effect of the change in current income. In other words, the new estimate merely is used from that point on.

7. Most errors are corrected simply with a correcting entry. However, material errors discovered in a year subsequent to the year the error was made are considered prior period adjustments. The correction of the error is accounted for by restating prior years' financial statements, causing an adjustment to beginning of period retained earnings.

8. Earnings per share (EPS) is the amount of income achieved during a period expressed per share of common stock outstanding. The EPS must be disclosed for income from continuing operations and for each item below continuing operations.

9. When a company provides a set of financial statements that reports both financial position and results of operations, a statement of cash flows is reported for each period for which results of operations are provided. The purpose of the statement is to provide information about the cash receipts and cash disbursements that occurred during the period.

10. To enhance the usefulness of the information, the statement of cash flows classifies all transactions affecting cash into one of three categories: (1) operating activities, (2) investing activities, or (3) financing activities.

Questions for Review of Key Topics

Question	3–1	The income statement is a change statement. Explain what is meant by this.
Question	3–2	What transactions are included in income from continuing operations? Briefly explain why it is important to segregate income from continuing operations from other transactions affecting net income.
Question	3–3	Distinguish between operating and nonoperating activities.
Question	3–4	Briefly explain the difference between the single-step and multiple-step income statement formats.
Question	3–5	Define intraperiod tax allocation. Why is the process necessary?
Question	3–6	Define what is meant by a segment of a business in the context of reporting the results of discontinued operations. How are discontinued operations reported on the income statement?
Question	3–7	Explain what is meant by the measurement date and the disposal date as they relate to reporting discontinued operations.

Question	3–8	Define extraordinary items. What transaction, related to debt, always must be reported as an extraordinary item?
Question	3–9	How should extraordinary gains and losses be reported on the income statement?
Question	3–10	Describe the income statement presentation for a material gain or loss that meets only one of the two criteria required for extraordinary items.
Question	3–11	What is meant by a change in accounting principle? Describe the income statement presentation for a change in accounting principle.
Question	3–12	Define earnings per share (EPS). For which income statement items must EPS be disclosed?
Question	3–13	Accountants very often are required to make estimates, and very often those estimates prove incorrect. In what period(s) is the effect of a change in accounting estimate reported?
Question	3–14	The correction of a material error discovered in a year subsequent to the year the error was made is considered a prior period adjustment. Briefly describe the accounting treatment for prior period adjustments.
Question	3–15	Describe the purpose of the statement of cash flows.
Question	3–16	Identify and briefly describe the three categories of cash flows reported on the statement of cash flows.
Question	3–17	Explain what is meant by noncash investing and financing activities pertaining to the statement of cash flows. Give an example of one of these activities.
Question	3–18	Distinguish between the direct method and the indirect method for reporting the results of operating activities on the statement of cash flows.

Exercises

Exercise 3–1
Income statement format;
single step and multiple step

The following is a partial trial balance for the Green Star Corporation as of December 31, 1997:

Account Title	Debits	Credits
Sales revenue		1,200,000
Interest revenue		30,000
Gain on sale of equipment		50,000
Cost of goods sold	720,000	
Salaries expense	110,000	
Depreciation expense	50,000	
Interest expense	40,000	
Rent expense	25,000	
Income tax expense	100,000	

100,000 shares of common stock were outstanding throughout 1997.

Required:
1. Prepare a single-step income statement for 1997, including EPS disclosure.
2. Prepare a multiple-step income statement for 1997, including EPS disclosure.

Exercise 3–2
Income statement format;
single step and multiple step

The following is a partial trial balance for General Lighting Corporation as of December 31, 1997:

Account Title	Debits	Credits
Sales revenue		2,350,000
Rental revenue		80,000
Loss on sale of equipment	22,500	
Loss from flood damage (event is both unusual and infrequent)	120,000	
Cost of goods sold	1,200,300	
Loss from write-down of inventory due to obsolescence	200,000	
Salaries expense	300,000	
Depreciation expense	100,000	
Interest expense	90,000	
Rent expense	50,000	

300,000 shares of common stock were outstanding throughout 1997. Income tax expense has not yet been accrued. The income tax rate is 40%.

Required:
1. Prepare a single-step income statement for 1997, including EPS disclosure.
2. Prepare a multiple-step income statement for 1997, including EPS disclosure.

Exercise 3–3
Multiple-step income
statement

Coffey Corporation's trial balance for the year ended December 31, 1997, included the following income statement accounts:

Account Title	Debits	Credits
Sales revenue		1,600,000
Gain on early debt extinguishment		100,000
Cost of goods sold	960,000	
Adjustment due to accounting change in depreciation method	80,000	
Selling expenses	235,000	
Administrative expenses	150,000	
Interest expense	25,000	

The trial balance does not include the accrual for income taxes. Coffey's income tax rate is 30%. 100,000 shares of common stock were outstanding throughout 1997.

Required:
Prepare a multiple-step income statement for 1997, including appropriate EPS disclosure.

(AICPA adapted)

Exercise 3–4
Income statement
presentation; intraperiod
tax allocation

The following income statement was prepared by the accountant of the Axel Corporation:

AXEL CORPORATION
Income Statement
For the Year Ended December 31, 1997

Revenues and gains:		
Sales		$592,000
Interest and dividends		32,000
Gains from early extinguishment of debt		86,000
Total revenues and gains		710,000
Expenses and losses:		
Cost of goods sold	$295,000	
Selling expenses	67,000	
Administrative expenses	87,000	
Interest	26,000	
Restructuring costs	55,000	
Income taxes	72,000	
Total expenses and losses		602,000
Net Income		$108,000
Earnings per share		$1.08

Required:
Prepare a multiple-step income statement for 1997 applying generally accepted accounting principles. The income tax rate is 40%.

Exercise 3–5
Discontinued operations

The Chance Company had two operating divisions, one manufacturing farm equipment and the other office supplies. The farm equipment segment had been unprofitable, and on September 1, 1997, the company adopted a plan to sell the assets of the division. The actual sale was effected on December 15, 1997, at a price of $600,000. The book value of the division's assets was $1,000,000, resulting in a before-tax loss of $400,000 on the sale.

The division incurred before-tax operating losses of $100,000 from the beginning of the year to August 31 and $30,000 from September 1 through December 15. The income tax rate is 40%. Chance's after-tax income from its continuing operations is $350,000.

Required:
Prepare an income statement for 1997 beginning with income from continuing operations. Include appropriate EPS disclosures assuming that 100,000 shares of common stock were outstanding throughout the year.

Exercise 3–6
Income statement
presentation

The Esquire Comic Book Company had income before tax of $1,000,000 in 1997 *before* considering the following material items:

1. The company switched from the sum-of-the-years'-digits method to the straight-line method of depreciation for all of its equipment. The change caused an increase in before-tax income of $50,000 for 1997. The before-tax cumulative effect of the change on prior years' income was a $120,000 increase.
2. Esquire sold one of its operating divisions, which qualified as a segment according to APBO 30. The before-tax loss on disposal, including operating losses from the measurement date to the disposal date, was $350,000. The before-tax operating losses from the beginning of the year through the measurement date were $100,000.
3. The company incurred restructuring costs of $70,000 during the year.

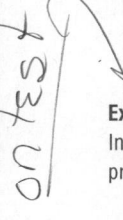
[handwritten margin notes: on test; part of operations; cumulative change; only break out previous years & cumulative change; part of operations]

Required:

Prepare a 1997 income statement for Esquire beginning with income from continuing operations. Assume an income tax rate of 40%. Ignore EPS disclosures.

Exercise 3–7
Discontinued operations; disposal subsequent to year of measurement date

Kandon Enterprises, Inc. has two operating divisions, one manufactures machinery and the other breeds and sells horses. The horse division has been unprofitable, and on November 15, 1997, Kandon adopted a formal plan to sell the division. The sale was completed on April 30, 1998.

On November 15, 1997, the book value of the assets of the horse division was $250,000. The before-tax operating loss of the division from January 1, the beginning of the fiscal year, through November 14, 1997, was $100,000. The operating loss from November 15 through December 31 was $40,000. Also, the company estimated that the loss from operating the division from January 1, 1998, until the disposal date would approximate $60,000. The selling price of the division's assets was estimated to be $200,000. The company's effective tax rate is 40%. The after-tax income from continuing operations for 1997 is $400,000.

Required:

1. Prepare a partial income statement for 1997 beginning with income from continuing operations. Ignore EPS disclosures.
2. Repeat requirement 1 assuming that the estimated sales price of the horse division's assets was $400,000, instead of $200,000.

Exercise 3–8
Accounting change

The Canliss Milling Company purchased machinery on January 2, 1995, for $800,000. A five-year life was estimated and no salvage value was anticipated. Canliss decided to use the straight-line depreciation method and recorded $160,000 in depreciation in 1995 and 1996. Early in 1997, the company revised the *total* estimated life of the machinery to eight years.

Required:

1. What type of accounting change is this?
2. Briefly describe the accounting treatment for this change.
3. Determine depreciation for 1997.

Exercise 3–9
Accounting change

[This is a variation of the previous exercise]

The Canliss Milling Company purchased machinery on January 2, 1995, for $800,000. A five-year life was estimated and no salvage value was anticipated. Canliss decided to use the straight-line depreciation method and recorded $160,000 in depreciation in 1995 and 1996. Early in 1997, the company changed its depreciation method to the double-declining-balance (DDB) method. DDB depreciation for 1995, 1996, and 1997 is $320,000, $192,000, and $115,200, respectively.

Required:

1. What type of accounting change is this?
2. What would appear on the 1997 income statement related to this change? Assume an income tax rate of 40%. Ignore EPS disclosures.

Exercise 3–10
Earnings per share

The Esposito Import Company had 1 million shares of common stock outstanding during 1997. Its income statement reported the following items: income from continuing operations, $5 million; loss from discontinued operations, $1.6 million; extraordinary gain, $2.2 million; cumulative effect of a change in accounting principle, $700,000. All of these amounts are net of tax.

Required:

Prepare the 1997 EPS presentation for the Esposito Import Company.

Exercise 3–11
Multiple choice; income statement presentation

The following questions dealing with income statement presentation are adapted from questions that appeared in recent CPA examinations. Determine the response that best completes the statements or questions.

1. In Baer Food Co.'s 1997 single-step income statement, the section titled Revenues consisted of the following:

Net sales revenue		$187,000
Results from discontinued operations:		
Loss from operations of segment (net of $1,200 tax effect)	$(2,400)	
Gain on disposal of segment (net of $7,200 tax effect)	14,400	12,000
Interest revenue		10,200
Gain on sale of equipment		4,700
Cumulative change in 1995 and 1996 income due to change in depreciation method (net of $750 tax effect)		1,500
Total revenues		$215,400

In the revenues section of the 1997 income statement, Baer Food should have reported total revenues of:
a. $216,300
b. $215,400
c. $203,700
d. $201,900

2. A transaction that is unusual but *not* infrequent should be reported separately as a(an)
   a. Extraordinary item, net of applicable income taxes.
   b. Extraordinary item, but *not* net of applicable income taxes.
   c. Component of income from continuing operations, net of applicable income taxes.
   d. Component of income from continuing operations, but *not* net of applicable income taxes.

3. On September 30, 1997, a commitment was made to dispose of a business segment in early 1998. The segment operating loss for the period October 1 to December 31, 1997, should be included in the 1997 income statement as part of
   a. Loss on disposal of the discontinued segment.
   b. Operating loss of the discontinued segment.
   c. Income or loss from continuing operations.
   d. Extraordinary gains or losses.

4. The cumulative effect of changing to a new accounting principle on the amount of retained earnings at the beginning of the period in which the change is made should be included in net income of:

	Future Periods	Period of Change
a.	No	No
b.	Yes	No
c.	Yes	Yes
d.	No	Yes

5. On October 1, 1997, Host Co. approved a plan to dispose of a segment of its business. Host expected that the sale would occur on April 1, 1998, at an estimated gain of $350,000. The segment had actual and estimated operating losses as follows:

1/1/97 to 9/30/97	$(300,000)
10/1/97 to 12/31/97	(200,000)
1/1/98 to 3/31/98	(400,000)

   In its 1997 income statement, what should Host report as a loss on disposal of the segment before income taxes?
   a. $200,000
   b. $250,000
   c. $500,000
   d. $600,000

6. Earnings per share data should be reported on the face of the income statement for:

	Income before Extraordinary Items	Cumulative Effect of a Change in Accounting Principle
a.	Yes	Yes
b.	Yes	No
c.	No	No
d.	No	Yes

Exercise 3–12

Statement of cash flows; classifications

The statement of cash flows classifies all cash inflows and outflows into one of the three categories shown below and lettered from a through c. In addition, certain transactions that do not involve cash are reported on the statement as noncash investing and financing activities, labeled d.
   a. Operating activities
   b. Investing activities
   c. Financing activities
   d. Noncash investing and financing activities

Required:

For each of the following transactions, use the letters above to indicate the appropriate classification category.

1. _____ Purchase of equipment for cash.
2. _____ Payment of employee salaries.
3. _____ Collection of cash from customers.
4. _____ Cash proceeds from a note payable.
5. _____ Purchase of common stock of another corporation for cash.

6. _____ Issuance of common stock for cash.
7. _____ Sale of machinery for cash.
8. _____ Payment of interest on note payable.
9. _____ Issuance of bonds payable in exchange for land and building.
10. _____ Payment of cash dividends to shareholders.
11. _____ Payment of principal on note payable.

Exercise 3–13
Statement of cash flows preparation

The following summary transactions occurred during 1997 for Bluebonnet Bakers:

Cash received from:

Customers	$380,000
Interest on note receivable	6,000
Principal on note receivable	50,000
Sale of investments	30,000
Proceeds from note payable	100,000

Cash paid for:

Purchase of inventory	160,000
Interest on note payable	5,000
Purchase of equipment	85,000
Salaries to employees	90,000
Principal on note payable	25,000
Payment of dividends to shareholders	20,000

The balance of cash and cash equivalents at the beginning of 1997 was $17,000.

Required:

Prepare a statement of cash flows for 1997 for Bluebonnet Bakers. Use the direct method for reporting operating activities.

Exercise 3–14
Statement of cash flows directly from transactions

The following transactions occurred during March 1997 for the Wainwright Corporation. The company owns and operates a wholesale warehouse. [These are the same transactions analyzed in Exercise 2–1, when we determined their effect on elements of the accounting equation.]
1. Issued 20,000 shares of capital stock in exchange for $200,000 in cash.
2. Purchased equipment at a cost of $40,000. $10,000 cash was paid and a note payable was signed for the balance owed.
3. Purchased inventory on account at a cost of $90,000. The company uses the perpetual inventory system.
4. Credit sales for the month totaled $120,000. The cost of the goods sold was $70,000.
5. Paid $5,000 in rent on the warehouse building for the month of March.
6. Paid $6,000 to an insurance company for fire and liability insurance for a one-year period beginning April 1, 1997.
7. Paid $60,000 on account for the merchandise purchased in 3.
8. Collected $55,000 from customers on account.
9. Recorded depreciation expense of $1,000 for the month on the equipment.

Required:

1. Analyze each transaction and classify each as a financing, investing and/or operating activity (a transaction can represent more than one type of activity). In doing so, also indicate the cash effect of each, if any. If there is no cash effect, simply place a check mark (✔) in the appropriate column(s).
   Example:

Financing	Investing	Operating
1. $200,000		

2. Prepare a statement of cash flows. Assume the cash balance at the beginning of the month was $40,000.

Exercise 3–15
Multiple choice; statement of cash flows

The following questions dealing with the statement of cash flows are adapted from questions that appeared in recent CPA examinations. Determine the response that best completes the statements or questions.
1. The primary purpose of a statement of cash flows is to provide relevant information about
   a. Differences between net income and associated cash receipts and disbursements.
   b. An enterprise's ability to generate future positive net cash flows.
   c. The cash receipts and cash disbursements of an enterprise during a period.
   d. An enterprise's ability to meet cash operating needs.
2. In a statement of cash flows, proceeds from issuing equity instruments should be classified as cash inflows from
   a. Lending activities.
   b. Operating activities.

    c. Investing activities.

    d. Financing activities.

3. In a statement of cash flows, payments to acquire debt instruments of other entities (other than cash equivalents) should be classified as cash outflows for

    a. Operating activities.

    b. Investing activities.

    c. Financing activities.

    d. Lending activities.

Exercise 3–16
Concepts; terminology

Listed below are several terms and phrases associated with income statement presentation and the statement of cash flows. Pair each item from List A (by letter) with the item from List B that is most appropriately associated with it.

List A	List B
_____ 1. Intraperiod tax allocation	a. Unusual, infrequent, and material gains and losses.
_____ 2. Measurement date	b. Starts with net income and works backwards to convert to cash.
_____ 3. Disposal date	c. Reports the cash effects of each operating activity directly on the statement.
_____ 4. Operating activities (income statement)	d. Correction of a material error of a prior period.
_____ 5. Extraordinary items	e. Related to the external financing of the company.
_____ 6. Segment (according to *APBO 30*)	f. Associates tax with income statement item.
_____ 7. Gain/loss from early extinguishment of debt.	g. Plan to dispose of segment adopted.
_____ 8. Earnings per share	h. Related to the transactions entering into the determination of net income.
_____ 9. Prior period adjustment	i. Related to the acquisition and disposition of long-term assets.
_____ 10. Financing activities	j. Required disclosure for publicly traded corporation.
_____ 11. Operating activities (SCF)	k. Always reported as extraordinary item, if material.
_____ 12. Investing activities	l. Directly related to principal revenue-generating activities.
_____ 13. Direct method	m. Separate line of business or class of customer.
_____ 14. Indirect method	n. Closing date of sale of segment.

Problems

Problem 3–1
Multiple-step income statement

The Whalen Company's records show the following account balances at December 31, 1997:

Sales	$15,000,000
Cost of goods sold	9,000,000
General and administrative expenses	1,000,000
Selling expenses	500,000
Interest expense	700,000

Income tax expense has not yet been determined. The following events also occurred during 1997:

1. ✓$300,000 in restructuring costs were incurred in connection with plant closings.

2. The company operates a factory in South America. During the year, the foreign government took over (expropriated) the factory and paid Whalen $1,000,000, which was one-fourth of the book value of the assets involved.

3. ✓ Inventory costing $400,000 was written off as obsolete. Material losses of this type were incurred twice in the last 10 years.

4. It was discovered that depreciation expense for 1996 was understated by $50,000 due to a mathematical error.

5. ✓ The depreciation method used for the office building was changed from the double-declining-balance to the straight-line method. The cumulative effect of the change on prior years' income is an increase of $60,000. Depreciation expense for 1997, included in general and administrative expenses, has been correctly computed using the straight-line method.

Required:
Prepare a multiple-step income statement for 1997. Assume an income tax rate of 40%. Ignore EPS disclosures.

Problem 3–2
Comparative income
statements; multiple-step
format

Selected information about income statement accounts for the Reed Company are presented below (the company's fiscal year ends on December 31):

	1997	1996
Sales	$4,000,000	$3,500,000
Cost of goods sold	2,500,000	2,000,000
Administrative expenses	800,000	675,000
Selling expenses	360,000	312,000

Several events occurred during 1997 that have *not* yet been reflected in the above accounts:

1. On July 1, the company adopted a plan to discontinue a major line of business. The assets of the segment were sold on September 30 for $50,000 less than their book value. Results of operations for the segment were as follows:

	7/1/97– 9/30/97	1/1/97– 6/30/97
Sales	$100,000	$300,000
Cost of goods sold	90,000	270,000
Operating income before taxes	$ 10,000	$ 30,000

2. A fire caused $50,000 in uninsured damages to the main office building. The fire was considered to be an infrequent but not unusual event.
3. Interest revenue in the amount of $150,000 was earned.
4. $5 million face value of bonds payable were repurchased (paid off) prior to maturity, resulting in a loss of $100,000.
5. Inventory that had cost $40,000 had become obsolete because a competitor introduced a better product. The inventory was sold as scrap for $5,000.
6. Interest expense on bonds payable was $200,000.

Required:

Prepare a multiple-step income statement for the Reed Company for 1997, showing 1996 information in comparative format, including income taxes computed at 40% and EPS disclosures assuming 300,000 shares of common stock. The *1996* sales and cost of goods sold figures *include* $500,000 in sales and $390,000 in cost of goods sold that pertain to the discontinued operation. Assume there were no other income or expense items in 1996 related to the discontinued operation.

Problem 3–3
Discontinued operations

The following condensed income statement of Mabel Corporation is presented for the two years ended December 31, 1997 and 1996:

	1997	1996
Sales	$10,000,000	$9,600,000
Cost of goods sold	6,200,000	6,000,000
Gross profit	3,800,000	3,600,000
Operating expenses	2,200,000	2,400,000
Operating income	1,600,000	1,200,000
Gain on sale of division	900,000	
	2,500,000	1,200,000
Income tax expense	1,250,000	600,000
Net income	$ 1,250,000	$ 600,000

On April 1, 1997, Mabel entered into an agreement to sell for $3,200,000 the assets and product line of one of its separate lines of business. The sale was consummated on December 31, 1997, and resulted in a gain on disposition of $900,000 (before taxes). The division's contribution to Mabel's reported income before taxes for each year was as follows:

| 1997 | $640,000 loss |
| 1996 | $500,000 loss |

These losses were incurred ratably throughout the year. (that is, in equal amounts each quarter). Assume an income tax rate of 50%.

Required:

1. Define what constitutes an operation or segment of a company according to *APBO 30*.
2. Recast the comparative income statements according to generally accepted accounting principles. Begin the statement with a recalculated income from continuing operations before income taxes. Ignore EPS disclosures.

(AICPA adapted)

Problem 3–4
Discontinued operations;
disposal subsequent to year
of measurement date

The Brady Corporation reported income from continuing operations (after tax) of $800,000 for its fiscal year ended December 31, 1997. Brady is discontinuing a major line of business. The plan to discontinue was adopted on July 1, 1997. The segment generated a before-tax operating loss of $70,000 for the period January 1 through June 30, 1997. The company anticipated a disposal date of April 15, 1998. The following are several situations, numbered 1 through 8, involving differing phaseout period operating results and gain/loss on disposal of the segment's assets.

Situation	Operating Income (Loss) from July 1 through December 31	Estimated Operating Income (Loss) from January 1, 1998 through Disposal	Estimated Gain (Loss) on Sale of Assets
1	$(100,000)	$ (50,000)	$ 80,000
2	(100,000)	(200,000)	(300,000)
3	100,000	200,000	(400,000)
4	(300,000)	(200,000)	600,000
5	300,000	100,000	200,000
6	400,000	(100,000)	(200,000)
7	300,000	(200,000)	250,000
8	300,000	(250,000)	275,000

Required:
For each of the situations, determine the appropriate gain (loss) on disposal of the segment that should be recognized in 1997 and 1998.

Problem 3–5
Income statement presentation

For the year ending December 31, 1997, Micron Corporation had income from continuing operations before taxes of $1,200,000 before considering the following transactions and events. All of the items described below are before taxes and the amounts should be considered material:

1. During 1997, Micron decided to call in an outstanding issue of bonds. As a result, the firm recognized a gain on the early extinguishment of bonds of $400,000.
2. In November of 1997, Micron sold its Waffle House restaurant chain which qualified as a separate line of business. The company had adopted a plan to sell the chain in May of 1997. The operating income of the chain from January 1, 1997, through May 1997 was $100,000. The operating income from May until November was $50,000 and the loss on sale of the chain's assets was $300,000.
3. In 1997, Micron sold one of its six factories for $1,200,000. At the time of the sale, the factory had a carrying value of $1,100,000.
4. In 1995, Micron's accountant omitted the annual adjustment for patent amortization expense of $120,000. The error was not discovered until December, 1997.

Required:
1. Prepare Micron's income statement, beginning with income from continuing operations before taxes, for the year ended December 31, 1997. Assume an income tax rate of 30%. Ignore EPS disclosures.
2. Briefly explain the motivation for segregating certain income statement events from income from continuing operations.

Problem 3–6
Statement of cash flows

The Diversified Portfolio Corporation provides investment advice to customers. A condensed income statement for the year ended December 31, 1997 appears below:

Service revenue	$900,000
Operating expenses	700,000
Income before income taxes	200,000
Income tax expense	80,000
Net income	$120,000

The following balance sheet information also is available:

	12/31/97	12/31/96
Cash	$275,000	$ 70,000
Accounts receivable	120,000	100,000
Accounts payable (operating expenses)	70,000	60,000
Income taxes payable	10,000	15,000

In addition, the following transactions took place during the year:
1. Common stock was issued for $100,000 in cash.
2. Long-term investments were sold for $50,000 in cash. The original cost of the investments also was $50,000.
3. $80,000 in cash dividends was paid to shareholders.
4. The company has no outstanding debt, other than those payables listed above.
5. Operating expenses include $30,000 in depreciation expense.

Required:

Prepare a statement of cash flows for 1997 for the Diversified Portfolio Corporation. Use the direct method for reporting operating activities.

Problem 3–7
Income statement
presentation; unusual items

The preliminary 1997 income statement of Alexian Systems, Inc., is presented below:

ALEXIAN SYSTEMS, INC.
Income Statement
For the Year ended December 31, 1997

($ in millions, except earnings per share)	
Revenues and gains:	
Net sales	$ 425
Interest	3
Other income	126
Total revenues and gains	554
Expenses:	
Cost of goods sold	270
Selling and administrative	154
Income taxes	52
Total expenses	476
Net Income	$ 78
Earnings per share	$3.90

Additional facts:
1. Selling and administrative expenses include $26 million in restructuring costs.
2. Included in other income is an extraordinary gain of $120 million. The remaining $6 million is from the gain on sale of operating assets.
3. Cost of goods sold was increased by $5 million to correct an error in the calculation of 1996's ending inventory. The amount is material.

Required:

For each of the three additional facts listed above, discuss the appropriate presentation of the item described. Do not prepare a revised statement.

Problem 3–8
Income statement
presentation; unusual items

This is a variation of the previous problem focusing on income statement presentation.

Required:

Refer to the information presented in Problem 3–7. Prepare a revised income statement for 1997 reflecting the additional facts. Use a multiple-step format. Assume that an income tax rate of 40% applies to all income statement items, and that 20 million shares of common stock were outstanding throughout the year.

Problem 3–9
Comprehensive income
statement

The Rembrandt Paint Company had the following income statement items for the year ended December 31, 1997 ($ in thousands):

Net sales	$18,000	Cost of goods sold	$10,500
Interest income	200	Selling and administrative	
Interest expense	350	expenses	2,500
Extraordinary gain	3,000	Restructuring costs	800

In addition, during the year the company completed the disposal of its plastics business and incurred a loss from operations of $1.6 million and a gain on disposal of the segment's assets of $2 million. Also, early in the year Rembrandt switched its method of computing depreciation. The cumulative effect of the change is $(600,000). 500,000 shares of common stock were outstanding throughout 1997. Income tax expense has not yet been accrued. The income tax rate is 30% on all items of income (loss).

Required:

Prepare a multiple-step income statement for 1997, including EPS disclosure.

Cases

Discussion Case 3–1
Income statement
presentation

Hillside Company had a loss during the year ended December 31, 1997, that is properly reported as an extraordinary item.

On July 1, 1997, Hillside committed itself to a formal plan for sale of a business segment. A loss is expected from the proposed sale. Segment operating losses were incurred continuously throughout 1997 and were expected to continue until final disposition in 1998.

Required:

1   How should Hillside report the extraordinary items in its income statement? Why?
2.   How should Hillside report the effect of discontinued operations in its 1997 income statement?
     Do not discuss earnings per share requirements.

(AICPA adapted)

Group Interaction Case 3–2
Income statement
presentation of gain

McMinville Corporation manufactures paper products. In 1993, the company purchased several large tracts of timber for $22 million with the intention of harvesting the timber rather than buying this critical raw material from outside suppliers. However, in 1997, McMinville abandoned the idea and all of the timber tracts were sold for $31 million. Net income for 1997, before considering this event, is $17.5 million and the company's effective tax rate is 30%.

The focus of this case is the income statement presentation of the gain on the sale of the timber tracts. Your instructor will divide the class into from two to six groups depending on the size of the class. The mission of your group is to reach consensus on the appropriate income statement presentation of the gain.

Required:

Each group member should deliberate the situation independently and draft a tentative argument prior to the class session for which the case is assigned.

In class, each group will meet for 10 to 15 minutes in different areas of the classroom. During that meeting, group members will take turns sharing their suggestions for the purpose of arriving at a single group treatment.

After the allotted time, a spokesperson for each group (selected during the group meetings) will share the group's solution with the class. The goal of the class is to incorporate the views of each group into a consensus approach to the situation.

Writing Case 3–3
Income statement
presentation

Carter Hawley Hale Stores (CHHS), Inc. is one of the largest department store retailers in the United States. At the end of fiscal 1989, the company operated 113 stores in the sunbelt regions of the country. The company's divisions included The Broadway, with 43 stores in Southern California and eleven stores in the southwest, and Emporium, with 22 stores in the greater San Francisco Bay Area. The company's fiscal year ends on the Saturday closest to July 31.

On October 17, 1989, a 7.1 Richter scale earthquake caused significant amounts of monetary damage to the San Francisco Bay Area. This was the largest earthquake to hit the Bay Area since the quake of 1906 destroyed much of San Francisco. California is lined with many active earthquake faults. Hundreds of small earthquakes occur each year throughout the state.

The Emporium division of CHHS suffered extensive damage as a result of the October 17 earthquake. Twelve of the twenty-two stores were closed for varying periods of time, with the Oakland store hardest hit. In total, uninsured damage was $27.5 million ($16.5 million after tax benefits).

For the fiscal year ending August 4, 1990, CHHS reported an after-tax loss of $9.47 million *before* considering the earthquake loss. Total revenues for the year were $2.857 billion.

Required:

Assume that you are the CHHS controller. The chief financial officer of CHHS has asked you to prepare a short report (1–2 pages) in memo form giving your recommendation as to the proper reporting of the earthquake damage costs on the income statement for the year ending August 4, 1990. Explain why your recommendation is appropriate. Be sure to include in your report any references to authoritative pronouncements that support your recommendation.

Real World Case 3–4
Income statement
presentation

The following headline appeared in the October 9, 1994, edition of *The Wall Street Journal*:

Kmart plans to close 100 stores, slash management ranks by 10% and lay off some 5,350 workers, continuing the retailer's effort to shore up its struggling discount stores.

The article further stated that the store closings will affect about 5% of the company's discount stores. No cost estimates for the store closings were provided.

Required:

How should Kmart report the cost of the store closings in its 1994 income statement?

Ethics Case 3–5
Restructuring costs

After a decade of consistent income growth in the 1980s, the Cranor Corporation's profits have declined steadily. The company's financial statements reported the following net income figures for the past four years:

	1996	1995	1994	1993
Net income ($ in millions)	$18.3	$21.8	$26.3	$30.5

In response to declining profits, in June 1997 company management approved a restructuring plan that would streamline the company's operations. A number of facilities would be closed and approximately 30% of the company's employees would be terminated or relocated. Management estimates that the restructuring will be complete by the end of 1998.

The company controller, Jim Dietz, estimated that restructuring costs will total $11.5 million (before taxes), of which only one-third will be incurred during 1997. Jim has suggested the following to the chief executive officer:

If we accrue the entire $11.5 million restructuring costs, 1997 net income will be approximately $9 million. I think my estimate of $11.5 million is accurate, but I suggest that we accrue restructuring costs of $14.5 million in 1997. Since income is going to be way down this year anyway, we might as well accrue the extra $3 million in costs just in case my estimate is too low. If the extra $3 million in costs do not materialize, then 1998 income will benefit. In fact, with the extra $3 million income in 1998, along with the effects of the restructuring beginning to take effect, profits could be up to as much as $21.5 million. The stock market will really appreciate an increase in income for a change, particularly an increase that brings us back up to an income figure comparable to the one we reported two years ago.

Required:

Discuss the ethical dilemma faced by Jim Dietz and the company's chief executive officer.

Critical Thought Case 3–6
Income statement presentation

Each of the following situations occurred during 1997 for one of your audit clients:
1. The write-off of inventory due to obsolescence.
2. Discovery that depreciation expenses were omitted by accident from 1996's income statement.
3. The useful lives of all machinery were changed from eight to five years.
4. The depreciation method used for all equipment was changed from the declining-balance to the straight-line method.
5. Ten million dollars face value of bonds payable were repurchased (paid off) prior to maturity resulting in a material loss of $500,000. The company involved has retired debt prior to maturity three times in the last 10 years.
6. Restructuring costs were incurred.
7. The Stridewell Company, a manufacturer of shoes, sold all of its retail outlets. It will continue to manufacture and sell its shoes to other retailers. A loss was incurred in the disposition of the retail stores.

Required:
1. For each situation, identify the appropriate reporting treatment from the list below (consider each event to be material):
   a. As an extraordinary item.
   b. As an unusual or infrequent gain or loss.
   c. As a prior period adjustment.
   d. As a change in accounting principle.
   e. As a discontinued operation.
   f. As a change in accounting estimate.
2. Indicate whether each situation would be included on the income statement in continuing operations (CO) or below continuing operations (BC), or if it would appear as an adjustment to retained earnings (RE). Use the format shown below to answer requirements 1 and 2.

Situation	Treatment (a–f)	Financial Statement Presentation (CO, BC, or RE)
1.		
2.		
3.		
4.		
5.		
6.		
7.		

Discussion Case 3–7
Income statement presentation

The following events occurred during 1997 for various audit clients of your firm. Consider each event to be independent and the effect of each event to be material.
1. A manufacturing company recognized a loss on the sale of equipment used in its manufacturing operations.
2. An automobile manufacturer sold all of the assets related to its financing segment. The segment provided the financing for the majority of the autos sold by the company.

3. A company changed its depreciation method from the double-declining-balance method to the straight-line method.
4. The Sonjay Corporation paid off one of its long-term bond issues before the scheduled maturity debt and recognized a gain. This was the third time in the last 10 years that the company had incurred gains on the early retirement of debt.
5. Due to obsolescence, a company engaged in the manufacture of high-technology products incurred a loss on the write-down of inventory.
6. One of your clients discovered that 1996's depreciation expense was overstated. The error occurred because of a miscalculation of depreciation for the office building.
7. A cosmetics company decided to discontinue the manufacture of a line of women's lipstick. Other cosmetic lines will be continued. A loss was incurred on the sale of assets related to the lipstick product line.

Required:
Discuss the 1997 financial statement presentation of each of the above events. Do not consider earnings per share disclosures.

International Case 3–8
Comparison of income statement presentation in the U.K. and the United States.

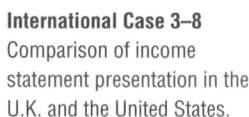

Cadbury Schweppes is a major global manufacturer of beverages and confectionery located in Great Britain whose products are sold in over 170 countries. Presented below is a recent company income statement:

CADBURY SCHWEPPES
Group Profit and Loss Account
For the 52 Weeks Ended 1 January 1994

(in thousands of pounds, except earnings per ordinary share)	Continuing Operations	Acquisitions	1993	1992
Turnover	3,655.7	69.1	3,724.8	3,372.4
Cost of sales	(1,935.0)	(39.4)	(1,974.4)	(1,793.8)
Gross profit	1,720.7	29.7	1,750.4	1,578.6
Distribution costs, including marketing	(948.1)	(16.8)	(964.9)	(903.1)
Administration expenses	(323.5)	(7.8)	(331.3)	(288.2)
Other operating income/(charges)	(19.8)	1.6	(18.2)	(16.6)
Trading profit	429.3	6.7	436.0	370.7
Share of profits of associated undertakings	13.4	—	13.4	13.9
Operating profit	442.7	6.7	449.4	384.6
Profit on sale of investment			11.9	—
Loss re properties			(1.5)	(1.3)
Profit on ordinary activities before interest			459.8	383.3
Net interest			(43.5)	(50.6)
Profit on ordinary activities before taxation			416.3	332.7
Tax on profit on ordinary activities			(129.1)	(94.2)
Profit on ordinary activities after taxation			287.2	238.5
Minority interests			(44.2)	(35.7)
Preference dividends			(6.2)	(7.2)
Profit for the financial year			236.8	195.6
Dividends to ordinary shareholders			(116.4)	(98.0)
Profit retained for the financial year			120.4	97.6
Earnings per ordinary share of 25p			30.59p	26.41p

Required:
Describe the differences between income statement presentation in the United Kingdom with that of the United States.

Critical Thought Case 3–9
Management incentives for change

It has been suggested that not all accounting choices are made by management in the best interest of fair and consistent financial reporting.

Required:
What motivations can you think of for management's choice of accounting methods?

Research Case 3–10
Changes in accounting principles

When a company changes an accounting principle, justification for the change is required in a disclosure note. Quite often, the stated justification is that the new accounting method is a more appropriate way to measure the related economic transaction. However, there are those that feel management makes accounting changes in order to manipulate earnings. Professors Pincus and Wasley in "The Incidence of Accounting Changes and Characteristics of Firms Making Accounting Changes," investigate accounting changes and possible motivations for making them.

Required:

1. In your library or from some other source, locate the indicated article in *Accounting Horizons,* June 1994.
2. What is the most frequent type of voluntary accounting change?
3. What inferences do the authors make about the use of voluntary accounting changes to manipulate earnings and what conclusion do they reach?

Trueblood Accounting Case 3–11
Extraordinary item

This Robert M. Trueblood case is recommended for use with this chapter. The case provides an excellent opportunity for class discussion, group projects, and writing assignments. The case, along with Professor's Discussion Material, can be obtained from the Deloitte & Touche Foundation.

Case 93–9: *Short Circuited Land*

This case is designed to explore the treatment of losses as either ordinary or extraordinary. Special attention is focused on the criteria for whether a loss qualifies as an extraordinary loss or whether a loss would be considered ordinary or in other words, an operating loss.

Financial Analysis Case 3–12
Income statement information

Refer to the income statements of Federal Express Corporation in the Appendix to Chapter 1.

Required:

1. What was the percentage increase or decrease in the company's net income from 1995 to 1996? From 1994 to 1995?
2. Using 1996 data, what is the company's approximate income tax rate?
3. Show how Federal Express arrived at earnings per share of $5.27 in 1995.
4. Using 1996 data, what is the percentage of net income relative to revenue dollars?

Internet Case 3–13
Income statement information

EDGAR, the Electronic Data Gathering, Analysis, and Retrieval system, performs automated collection, validation, indexing, and forwarding of submissions by companies and others who are required by law to file forms with the U.S. Securities and Exchange Commission (SEC). All publicly traded domestic companies use EDGAR to make the majority of their filings. (Some foreign companies file voluntarily). Form 10-K or 10-KSB, which include the annual report, is required to be filed on EDGAR. The SEC makes this information available on the Internet.

Required:

1. Access EDGAR on the Internet. You can use a web browser or anonymous FTP. The web address is http://www.sec.gov/. To use anonymous FTP, use your File Transfer Protocol software to connect to sec.gov and log in as user "anonymous" with a password of your electronic mail address.
2. Search for a public company with which you are familiar. Access the most recent 10-K filing. Search or scroll to find the financial statements and related notes.
3. Answer the following questions related to the company's income statement:
    a. Does the company use the single-step or multiple-step format, or a variation?
    b. Does the income statement contain any separately reported items in any year presented (discontinued operation, extraordinary item, cumulative effect of a change in accounting principle)? If it does, describe the event that caused the item. (Hint: there should be a related disclosure note.)
    c. Describe the trend in net income over the years presented.
4. Repeat requirements 2 and 3 for two additional companies.

INCOME MEASUREMENT AND PROFITABILITY ANALYSIS

OVERVIEW

Key to income measurement is the timing of revenue and expense recognition. The matching principle states that expenses are recognized in the period in which the related revenues are recognized. When revenue is recognized, therefore, is critical to income measurement. The focus of this chapter is revenue recognition. The chapter also introduces financial statement analysis — transforming financial information into forms more useful for analysis.

LEARNING OBJECTIVES   After studying this chapter, you should be able to:

1. List the two criteria that must be satisfied before revenue can be recognized and explain why these criteria usually are satisfied at the point of product delivery.
2. Distinguish between the percentage-of-completion and completed contract methods of recognizing revenue for long-term contracts.
3. Describe the installment sales and cost recovery methods of recognizing revenue for certain installment sales and explain the conditions under which these methods might be used.
4. Discuss the implications for revenue recognition of allowing customers the right of return.
5. Discuss the revenue recognition issues involving franchise sales.
6. Describe the techniques used by financial analysts to transform financial information into forms more useful for analysis.
7. Identify and calculate the common ratios used to assess profitability.

You Don't Have To Be a Rocket Scientist

By the time you finish this chapter, you should be able to respond appropriately to the questions posed in this case. Compare your response to the solution provided at the end of the chapter.

"Good news! I got the job," he said, closing the door behind him.

Your brother, an aerospace engineer, goes on to explain that he's accepted a position at McDonnell Douglas Corporation, the world's leading producer of military aircraft and one of the largest NASA and U.S. defense contractors. He will supervise a long-term government contract beginning Tuesday.

"I got the salary I was asking for too," he continued. "Ms. Watson also said I'll be getting a bonus tied to the gross profit on the project. It didn't hit me until I left her office, though, that this project will take two and a half years to complete. I hope I don't have to wait that long to get my bonus." Pointing to a page where he's circled part of a disclosure note, your brother hands you McDonnell Douglas's annual report. "I can't believe they wait that long to record income on all these multiyear projects. You're the accountant in the family; is that what this note is telling us?"

Revenue Recognition (in part)

Revenues and earnings on fixed-price government contracts are generally recognized on the percentage-of-completion method of accounting as costs are incurred . . . .

QUESTIONS

1. Does your brother have to wait two and a half years to get his bonus? Explain.
2. How are gross profits recognized using the percentage-of-completion method?
3. Are there other situations in which revenue is recognized at times other than when a product is delivered?

A REVENUE RECOGNITION

In Chapter 3 we discussed the *nature of income* and its presentation on the income statement. In this chapter we turn our attention to the *measurement* of periodic accounting income. Of primary interest here is the timing of revenue recognition. This is an important issue not only in its own right but also because the matching principle states that expenses should be recognized in the period in which the related revenues are recognized.

> Revenue recognition criteria help ensure that an income statement reflects the actual accomplishments of a company for the period.

Why is the timing of revenue recognition so important? An income statement should report the results of operations only for the time period specified in the report. That is, a one-year income statement should report the company's accomplishments and sacrifices (revenues and expenses) only for that one-year period.[1] Revenue recognition criteria help ensure that a proper cutoff is made each period and that no more than one year's activity is reported on the income statement. Revenues reflect positive inflows from activities, activities that generate cash flows. By comparing these activity levels period to period, a user can better assess future activities and thus future cash flows.

Relatedly, recognizing revenue presumes that an asset has been received or will be received in exchange for the goods or services sold. Not adhering to revenue recognition criteria could mean overstating income in one reporting period and understating income in a subsequent period if the asset to be received is never collected or must be returned to the buyer.

> **Learning objective 1**
> List the two criteria that must be satisfied before revenue can be recognized and explain why these criteria usually are satisfied at the point of product delivery.

The **realization principle** requires that two criteria be satisfied before revenue can be recognized:

1. The earnings process is judged to be complete or virtually complete, *(the earnings process refers to the activity or activities performed by the company to generate revenue).*
2. There is reasonable certainty as to the collectibility of the asset to be received (usually cash).

The actual point in time when these criteria are satisfied depends on the type of product or service provided, the terms of the sales agreement, and the financial condition of the buyer. We now discuss situations when it's appropriate to recognize revenue (a) at the point of delivery, (b) before delivery, and (c) after delivery. We also discuss the various accounting methods commonly used to recognize revenues in these situations.

Revenue Recognition at Point of Delivery

Consider the timing of revenue recognition for a typical manufacturing company that sells its products on credit. Usually the buyer is given a length of time, say 30 days, to pay for the goods after they have been delivered. Graphic 4–1 shows several alternative points in time during the earnings process that could be considered the critical event for revenue recognition. It should be pointed out that revenue actually is earned *throughout* the earnings process. The critical event is the point in time when the realization principle is satisfied.[2]

> While revenue often is earned during a period of time, revenue usually is recognized at one specific point in time when both revenue recognition criteria are satisfied.

The product delivery date occurs when legal title to the goods passes from seller to buyer. This occurs either on the date the product is shipped from the seller's facility or when the goods actually are received by the buyer, depending on the terms of the sales agreement. If the goods are shipped *f.o.b. (free on board) shipping point*, then legal title to the goods changes hands at the point of shipment when the seller delivers the goods to the common carrier (for example, a trucking company) and the purchaser is responsible for shipping costs and transit insurance. On the other hand, if the goods are shipped *f.o.b. destination*, the seller is responsible for shipping and legal title does not pass until the goods arrive at the customer's location.[3]

> The point of delivery refers to the date legal title to the product passes from seller to buyer.

Let's consider the date production ends. At that point, it might be said that the earnings process is virtually complete. After all, the majority of the costs that must be expended to generate revenue

---

[1]In addition to reporting on an annual basis, companies often provide information quarterly and, on occasion, monthly. This information, referred to as *interim financial statements,* pertains to any financial report covering a period of less than one year. The key accounting issues related to the presentation of interim statements are discussed in Appendix 4.

[2]For services, revenue often is recognized over a period of time rather than at one particular point. Examples are rent revenue and interest revenue. Some complications that can arise with recognition of service revenues are addressed in a subsequent section of this chapter.

[3]We discuss this aspect of title transfer in Chapter 7.

GRAPHIC   4–1

Earnings process for a typical manufacturing company

| Materials purchased | Production begins | Production in process | Production ends | Product delivered | Cash is collected |

have been incurred. The product has been produced and the remaining tasks are to sell the product and collect the cash.

However, at this point there usually exists significant uncertainty as to the collectibility of the asset to be received. We don't know if the product will be sold, nor the selling price or the buyer if eventually sold. Because of these uncertainties, revenue recognition usually is delayed until the point of product delivery. At that point we know the product has been sold, the price, and the buyer. The only remaining uncertainty involves the ultimate cash collection, which usually can be accounted for by estimating and recording allowances for possible return of the product and for uncollectibility of the cash, that is, bad debts. Both of these estimates are discussed in Chapter 7.

In addition, at the point of delivery, legal title to the goods is transferred. A critical element of the contract between buyer and seller—product delivery—is now fulfilled and the earnings process normally is virtually complete.

There are some revenue-producing activities, however, that call for revenue recognition at a time other than the point of delivery. We now turn to the more common of these activities.

ETHICAL DILEMMA

The Precision Parts Corporation manufactures automobile parts. The company has reported a profit every year since the company's inception in 1974. Management prides itself on this accomplishment and believes one important contributing factor is the company's incentive plan that rewards top management a bonus equal to a percentage of operating income *if the operating income goal for the year is achieved.* However, 1997 has been a tough year, and prospects for attaining the income goal for the year are bleak.

Tony Smith, the company's chief financial officer, has determined a way to increase December sales by an amount sufficient to boost operating income over the goal for the year and earn bonuses for all top management. A reputable customer ordered $120,000 of parts to be shipped on January 15, 1998. Tony told the rest of top management "I know we can get that order ready by December 31 even though it will require some production line overtime. We can then just leave the order on the loading dock until shipment. I see nothing wrong with recognizing the sale in 1997, since the parts will have been manufactured and we do have a firm order from a reputable customer." The company's normal procedure is to ship goods f.o.b. destination and to recognize sales revenue when the parts are received by the customer.

Revenue Recognition Before Delivery

Long-Term Contracts

Learning objective 2
Distinguish between the percentage-of-completion and completed contract methods of recognizing revenue for long-term contracts.

Sometimes when the earnings process occurs over long periods of time, it's not practical to recognize revenue at the delivery point. Long-term projects in the construction industry highlight the timing problem. At issue is when revenue and related expenses should be recognized on long-term projects encompassing more than a single accounting time period. Examples would be construction contracts for such things as an office building, a bridge, or a nuclear power plant.

The general revenue recognition criteria suggest that revenue should be recognized when a construction project is finished (that is, when the earnings process is virtually complete). In the construction industry this is known as the **completed contract method** of revenue recognition. The problem with this method is that all revenues, expenses, and resulting income from the project are recognized in the period in which the project is completed; no revenues or expenses are reported on the income statements of earlier reporting periods in which much of the work may have been performed. Net income should provide a measure of periodic accomplishment to help predict future accomplishments. Clearly, income statements prepared using the completed contract method do not fairly report each period's accomplishments when a construction project

OPENING CASE

Question 1

The **completed contract method** is equivalent to recognizing revenue at point of delivery, that is, when the construction project is complete.

The **percentage-of-completion method** allocates a fair share of a project's revenues and expenses to each reporting period during construction.

spans more than one reporting period. Much of the earnings process is far removed from the point of delivery.

The **percentage-of-completion method** of revenue recognition for long-term construction and other projects is designed to help address this problem. This method allocates a fair share of the project's expected revenues and expenses to each period in which the earnings process occurs, that is, the construction period. Although the contract usually specifies total revenues, the project's expenses are not known until completion. Consequently, it is necessary for a company to estimate the project's future costs at the end of each reporting period to estimate total gross profit to be earned on the project.

Illustration 4–1 provides information to compare accounting for long-term contracts using the completed contract and percentage-of-completion methods.

ILLUSTRATION   4–1

Completed Contract and Percentage-of-Completion Methods Compared

At the beginning of 1997, the Harding Construction Company received a contract to build an office building for $5 million. The project is estimated to take three years to complete. According to the contract, Harding will bill the buyer in installments over the construction period according to a prearranged schedule. Information related to the contract is as follows:

	1997	1998	1999
Construction costs incurred during the year	$1,500,000	$1,000,000	$1,600,000
Construction costs incurred in prior years	– 0 –	1,500,000	2,500,000
Cumulative construction costs	1,500,000	2,500,000	4,100,000
Estimated costs to complete at end of year	2,250,000	1,500,000	– 0 –
Total estimated and actual construction costs	$3,750,000	$4,000,000	$4,100,000
Billings made during the year	$1,200,000	$2,000,000	$1,800,000
Cash collections during year	1,000,000	1,400,000	2,600,000

Construction costs include the labor, materials, and overhead costs directly related to the construction of the building. Notice how the total of estimated and actual construction costs changes from period to period. Cost revisions are typical in long-term contracts where costs are estimated over long periods of time.

The completed contract method records all costs of construction in an asset (inventory) account called **construction in progress**; no income is recognized until project completion.

The completed contract method does not properly portray a company's performance over the construction period.

Completed Contract Method.   With the completed contract method, all costs of construction are recorded in an asset account called **construction in progress.** This account is equivalent to the asset work-in-process inventory in a manufacturing company. *No revenues or expenses related to this project are recognized in 1997 and 1998.* Construction in progress will show a balance of $1,500,000 and $2,500,000 at the end of 1997 and 1998, respectively, and $4,100,000 when the project is completed in 1999. This asset is then "sold" and revenue of $5,000,000 and cost of construction (similar to cost of goods sold) of $4,100,000 (gross profit of $900,000) are recognized in 1999.

Does this solution capture the reality of the situation? To the contrary, it seems to suggest that the construction company was idle or unproductive for two years and then produced a sizable profit the third year. For this reason, the percentage-of-completion method is preferable, and the completed contract method should be used only "when lack of dependable estimates or inherent hazards cause forecasts to be doubtful . . ."[4]

OPENING CASE

Question 2

Percentage-of-Completion Method.   The percentage-of-completion method recognizes a portion of the estimated gross profit each period based on progress to date. Progress to date depends on three factors:

1.   The costs incurred to date.
2.   The most recent estimate of the project's total cost.
3.   The most recent gross profit estimate.

[4]"Long-Term Construction-Type Contracts," *Accounting Research Bulletin No. 45* (New York: AICPA 1955).

Let's first focus on the calculation of periodic gross profit for each of the three years of construction. We then address the gross profit components—revenue and cost of construction. Progress to date usually is assumed to be the *proportion of the project's cost incurred to date divided by total estimated costs*. This fraction, the estimated percentage of completion, is assumed to be a measure of progress. It should be mentioned that this measure is based on costs and could differ significantly from an estimate of physical progress made by an engineer or architect. This method, often referred to as the *cost-to-cost method* of estimating a percentage of completion, is more readily verifiable than an estimate made by an engineer or an architect. Even so, it too is subject to manipulation. For example, cost incurrence could be accelerated to increase the estimate of percent complete.

The objective of determining a percentage of completion is to measure activity or project accomplishment to date. If the cost-to-cost approach does not properly parallel this accomplishment, then another method should be used. For example, the construction of a road might encounter a particularly difficult section of terrain requiring abnormal costs to be incurred without much progress being made on the road. In such a case, the cost-to-cost method might not adequately reflect how much of the project has actually been completed.

Illustration 4–1a shows the calculation of gross profit for each of the years for our Harding Construction Company example.

> Progress to date can be estimated as the proportion of the project's cost incurred to date divided by total estimated costs, or by relying on an engineer's or architect's estimate.

ILLUSTRATION   4–1a

Percentage-of-Completion Method—Allocation of Gross Profit to Each Period

	1997	1998	1999
Contract price	$5,000,000	$5,000,000	$5,000,000
Actual costs to date	1,500,000	2,500,000	4,100,000
Estimated costs to complete	2,250,000	1,500,000	- 0 -
Total project cost	3,750,000	4,000,000	4,100,000
Total gross profit (estimated for 1997 and 1998, actual in 1999)—Contract price minus total costs	$1,250,000	$1,000,000	$ 900,000
Percentage-of-completion—actual costs to date	$1,500,000	$2,500,000	(project is
divided by the estimated total project cost	$3,750,000	$4,000,000	complete)
	= 40%	= 62.5%	100%
Total project gross profit	$1,250,000	$1,000,000	$ 900,000
Multiplied by the estimated % of completion	40 %	62.5 %	100 %
Gross profit earned to date	$ 500,000	$ 625,000	$ 900,000
Less gross profit recognized in previous periods	–0–	(500,000)	(625,000)
Gross profit recognized currently	$ 500,000	$ 125,000	$ 275,000

At the end of each period, the revised project gross profit estimate is multiplied by the revised estimate of the percentage of completion. The result is the estimated gross profit earned from inception to date. The current period's gross profit is calculated by subtracting from this amount the gross profit recognized in previous periods.

Obviously, income statements are more informative if the sales revenue and cost components of gross profit are reported rather than the net figure alone. So, the income statement for each year will report the appropriate revenue and cost of construction amounts. For example, in 1997 the gross profit of $500,000 consists of revenue of $2,000,000 (40% multiplied by the $5,000,000 contract price) and $1,500,000 in cost of construction. In subsequent periods, revenue is calculated by multiplying the percentage of completion by the contract price and then subtracting revenue recognized in prior periods. The cost of construction is the difference between revenue and gross profit. In most cases, cost of construction also equals the construction costs incurred during the period.[5] The table in Illustration 4–1b shows the revenue and cost of construction recognized in each of the three years of our example.

---

[5]Cost of construction does not equal the construction costs incurred during the year when a loss is projected on the entire project. This case is illustrated later in the chapter.

ILLUSTRATION   4–1b

Percentage-of-Completion
Method—Allocation of
Revenue and Cost of
Construction to Each Period

1997

Revenue recognized ($5,000,000 × 40%)	$2,000,000
Cost of construction	1,500,000
Gross profit	$ 500,000

1998

Revenue recognized to date ($5,000,000 × 62.5%)	$3,125,000	
Less: Revenue recognized in 1997	(2,000,000)	
Revenue recognized		$1,125,000
Cost of construction		1,000,000
Gross profit		$ 125,000

1999

Revenue recognized to date ($5,000,000 × 100%)	$5,000,000	
Less: Revenue recognized in 1997 and 1998	(3,125,000)	
Revenue recognized		$1,875,000
Cost of construction		1,600,000
Gross profit		$ 275,000

A Comparison of the Two Methods – Income Recognition

A period-by-period comparison of the gross profit patterns produced by each method of revenue recognition is presented below:

	Percentage-of-Completion	Completed Contract
Gross profit recognized:		
1997	$500,000	–0–
1998	125,000	–0–
1999	275,000	$900,000
Total gross profit	$900,000	$900,000

Although both methods yield identical gross profit of $900,000 for the entire three-year period, the timing differs. The completed contract method defers all gross profit to 1999, when the project is completed. Obviously, the percentage-of-completion method provides a better measure of the company's economic activity and progress over the three-year period. That's why the percentage-of-completion method is preferred, and, as mentioned above, the completed contract method should be used only in situations where the company is unable to make dependable estimates of future costs necessary to apply the percentage-of-completion method.[6]

Our discussion to this point has concentrated on income recognition. Notice that *the amount billed and the cash actually received have no effect on income recognition*. We now turn our attention to the balance sheet effect of accounting for long-term construction contracts.

> The percentage-of-completion method provides a more realistic measure of a project's periodic profitability.

Balance Sheet Effects Compared.   Summary journal entries for *both* the percentage-of-completion and completed contract methods are shown in Illustration 4–1c for construction costs, billings, and cash receipts.

ILLUSTRATION   4–1c

Journal Entries—Costs,
Billings, and Receipts

	1997		1998		1999	
Construction in progress	1,500,000		1,000,000		1,600,000	
Cash, materials, etc.		1,500,000		1,000,000		1,600,000
To record construction costs.						
Accounts receivable	1,200,000		2,000,000		1,800,000	
Billings on construction contract		1,200,000		2,000,000		1,800,000
To record progress billings.						
Cash	1,000,000		1,400,000		2,600,000	
Accounts receivable		1,000,000		1,400,000		2,600,000
To record cash collections.						

---

[6]For income tax purposes, the completed contract method may be used for home construction contracts and certain other real estate construction contracts. All other contracts must use the percentage-of-completion method.

Notice that periodic billings are credited to **billings on construction contract.** This account is a valuation (contra) account to the asset construction in progress. At the end of each period, the balances in these two accounts are compared. If the net amount is a debit, it is reported on the balance sheet as an asset. Conversely, if the net amount is a credit, it is reported as a liability.[7]

> **Billings on construction contract** are subtracted from construction in progress to determine balance sheet presentation.

A debit balance essentially represents an unbilled receivable. The construction company is incurring construction costs (and recognizing gross profit using the percentage-of-completion method) for which it will be paid by the buyer. If the construction company bills the buyer an amount exactly equal to these costs (and profits recognized) then the accounts receivable balance properly reflects the claims of the construction company. If, however, the amount billed is less than the costs incurred (plus profits recognized) the difference represents the remaining claim to cash.

On the other hand, if the amount billed exceeds the costs incurred (plus profits recognized), then the overbilled accounts receivable overstate the amount of the claim to cash earned to that date and must be reported as a liability. This is similar to the situation when a customer pays for a product or service in advance. The advance is properly shown as a liability representing the obligation to provide the good or service in the future.

Accounting under each of the methods is precisely the same to this point. But, as explained earlier, gross profit (revenue less cost of construction) is recognized differently by the two approaches. The entries shown in Illustration 4–1d are the additional journal entries required using the percentage-of-completion method to recognize periodic revenue and cost of construction and to close the construction contract accounts (construction in progress and billings on construction contracts) and for the completed contract method at the end of the project to recognize revenue and cost of construction and to close the construction contract accounts.

ILLUSTRATION   4–1d

Journal Entries—Profit Recognition and Closing

	1997	1998	1999
PERCENTAGE-OF-COMPLETION:			
Construction in progress (gross profit)	500,000	125,000	275,000
Cost of construction	1,500,000	1,000,000	1,600,000
Revenue from long-term contracts	2,000,000	1,125,000	1,875,000
To record gross profit.			
Billings on construction contract			5,000,000
Construction in progress			5,000,000
To close accounts.			
COMPLETED CONTRACT:			
Construction in progress (gross profit)			900,000
Cost of construction			4,100,000
Revenue from long-term contracts			5,000,000
To record gross profit.			
Billings on construction contract			5,000,000
Construction in progress			5,000,000
To close accounts.			

> Under the completed contract method, profit is recognized only at the completion of the project.

Why debit construction in progress for the amount of gross profit recognized? In the typical manufacturing situation, inventory prior to sale is stated at cost. The difference between the historical cost of the inventory and its sales price (the gross profit) is not recognized until product delivery. In other words, assets are not increased until the inventory is sold.

The percentage-of-completion method departs from historical cost and recognizes a portion of the markup between the cost and the selling price of inventory prior to delivery. In our illustration, at the end of 1997 the total estimated cost is $3,750,000 and the estimated markup to sales price is $1,250,000. The inventory is increased by $500,000 which represents 40% of this total markup. The completed contract method recognizes the actual markup when the project is completed.

---

[7]If the company is engaged in more than one long-term contract, all contracts for which construction in progress exceeds billings are grouped together and all contracts for which billings exceed construction in progress also are grouped. This would result in the presentation of both an asset and a liability on the balance sheet.

The construction in progress account and the billings on construction contracts account before closing entries are illustrated below for both methods using T-accounts:

Percentage-of-completion

Construction in Progress

1997 construction costs	1,500,000
1997 gross profit	500,000
1998 construction costs	1,000,000
1998 gross profit	125,000
1999 construction costs	1,600,000
1999 gross profit	275,000
Balance, before closing	5,000,000

Completed contract

Construction in Progress

1997 construction costs	1,500,000
1998 construction costs	1,000,000
1999 construction costs	1,600,000
1999 gross profit	900,000
Balance, before closing	5,000,000

> Construction in progress includes periodic profit by the percentage-of-completion method.

> Billings are the same by either method.

Billings on Construction Contract

1,200,000	1997 billings
2,000,000	1998 billings
1,800,000	1999 billings
5,000,000	Balance, before closin

Billings on Construction Contract

1,200,000	1997 billings
2,000,000	1998 billings
1,800,000	1999 billings
5,000,000	Balance, before closin

The balance sheet presentation for the construction-related accounts by both methods is shown in Illustration 4–1e.

ILLUSTRATION   4–1e

Percentage-of- Completion Method—Allocation of Revenue and Cost of Construction to Each Period

Balance Sheet (end of year)		1997	1998	1999
Percentage-of-completion:				
Current assets:				
Accounts receivable		$200,000	$800,000	
Construction in progress	$2,000,000			
Less: Billings	(1,200,000)			
Costs and profit in excess of billings		800,000		
Current liabilities:				
Billings ($3,200,000) in excess of costs and profits ($3,125,000)			75,000	
Completed contract:				
Current assets:				
Accounts receivable		$200,000	$800,000	
Construction in progress	$1,500,000			
Less: Billings	(1,200,000)			
Costs in excess of billings		300,000		
Current liabilities:				
Billings ($3,200,000) in excess of costs ($2,500,000)			700,000	

GLOBAL PERSPECTIVE

There are significant differences among countries in the method used to recognize profit on long-term contracts. Practices in many countries, such as the U.K., Denmark, Norway, Belgium, Brazil, and Japan are similar to the U.S. The percentage-of-completion method is preferred and the completed contract method can be used only in unusual situations. In Germany, the completed contract method is used in almost all cases and recognizing gross profit prior to contract completion is rare. In the Netherlands, the percentage-of-completion method can only be used when a separate identifiable portion of the work in progress is finished and payment has been made. In Switzerland, companies can use either method.

> Disclosure of the method used to account for long-term contracts will appear in the summary of significant accounting policies.

The first disclosure note to any set of financial statements usually is a summary of significant accounting policies. This note discloses the method the company uses to account for its long-term contracts. As an example of this, Graphic 4–2 shows the disclosure note that appeared in a recent annual report of The American Ship Building Company.

GRAPHIC   4–2

Disclosure of revenue recognition policy for construction contracts— The American Ship Building Company

Notes: Accounting for Construction Contract

Revenues, costs, and profits applicable to construction and conversion contracts are included in the consolidated statements of operations using the labor percentage of completion accounting method. Contract losses are recognized in full in the year the losses are identified. The completed contract method was used for income tax reporting in the years this method was allowed.

The performance of contracts may extend over several years and, in the interim periods, estimates of total contract costs and profits are used for reporting the results of the Company's operations. Revisions in the estimates required by subsequent performance and final contract settlements are included as adjustments to the results of operations in the periods such revisions and settlements occur.

Long-Term Contract Losses.   The Harding Construction Company example above involves a situation in which a profit was realized on the construction contract. Unfortunately, losses sometimes occur on long-term contracts.

Periodic loss occurs for profitable project.   At times, a loss must be recognized in at least one period over the life of the project even though the project as a whole is profitable. We determine the loss in precisely the same way we determined the profit in profitable years. For example, assume the same $5 million contract for Harding Construction Company described in Illustration 4–1 but with the following cost information:

	1997	1998	1999
Construction costs incurred during the year	$1,500,000	$1,260,000	$1,840,000
Construction costs incurred in prior years	–0–	1,500,000	2,760,000
Cumulative construction costs	1,500,000	2,760,000	4,600,000
Estimated costs to complete at end of year	2,250,000	1,840,000	–0–
Total estimated and actual construction costs	$3,750,000	$4,600,000	$4,600,000

At the end of 1997, gross profit of $500,000 (revenue of $2,000,000 less cost of construction of $1,500,000) is recognized as previously determined.

At the end of 1998, the company still forecasts a profit of $400,000 ($5,000,000 – $4,600,000) on the project and, at that time, the project is estimated to be 60% complete ($2,760,000 ÷ $4,600,000). Applying this percentage to the anticipated gross profit of $400,000 results in a gross profit *to date* of $240,000. But remember, a gross profit of $500,000 was recognized in 1997.

This situation is treated as a *change in accounting estimate* because it resulted from a change in the estimation of costs to complete at the end of 1997. Costs to complete—$4,600,000—were much higher than the end of 1997 estimate of $3,750,000. Recall from our discussion of changes in accounting estimates in Chapter 3 that we don't go back and restate the prior year's gross profit. Instead, the 1998 income statement would report *a loss of $260,000* ($500,000 – 240,000). The loss consists of revenue of $1,000,000 ($5,000,000 × 60% = $3,000,000 less 1997 revenue of $2,000,000) less cost of construction of $1,260,000 (cost incurred in 1998). The following journal entry records the loss:

Recognized losses on long-term contracts reduce the construction in progress account.

1998

Cost of construction	1,260,000	
Revenue from long-term contracts		1,000,000
Construction in progress (loss)		260,000

The 1999 income statement would report a gross profit of $160,000 determined as follows:

Project gross profit	$400,000
Less: Gross profit recognized in prior periods ($500,000 – 260,000)	(240,000)
1999 gross profit	$160,000

The 1999 gross profit comprises $2,000,000 in revenue ($5,000,000 less revenue of $3,000,000 recognized in 1997 and 1998) and $1,840,000 in cost of construction (cost incurred in 1999).

Of course, by the completed contract method, no profit or loss is recorded in 1997 or 1998. Instead, a $400,000 gross profit (revenue of $5,000,000 and cost of construction of $4,600,000) is recognized in 1999.

Loss is projected on the entire project.   A more conservative approach is indicated when a loss actually is projected on the entire contract. Again consider the Harding Construction Company example but with the following cost information:

	1997	1998	1999
Construction costs incurred during the year	$1,500,000	$1,260,000	$2,440,000
Construction costs incurred in prior years	–0–	1,500,000	2,760,000
Cumulative construction costs	1,500,000	2,760,000	5,200,000
Estimated costs to complete at end of year	2,250,000	2,340,000	–0–
Total estimated and actual construction costs	$3,750,000	$5,100,000	$5,200,000

> An estimated loss on a long-term contract is fully recognized in the first period the loss is anticipated, regardless of the revenue recognition method used.

At the end of 1998, revised costs indicate a loss of $100,000 for the entire project ($5,000,000 – $5,100,000). In this situation, the *total* anticipated loss must be recognized in 1998 for both the percentage-of-completion method and the completed contract method. As a gross profit of $500,000 was recognized in 1997 using the percentage-of-completion method, *a $600,000 loss is recognized in 1998*. Once again, this situation is treated as a change in accounting estimate with no restatement of 1997 income. If the completed contract method is used, because no gross profit is recognized in 1997, the $100,000 loss for the project is recognized in 1998.

If the loss is not recognized in 1998, construction in progress would be valued at an amount greater than the company expects to realize from the contract. The construction in progress account is reduced to $2,660,000 ($2,760,000 in costs to date less $100,000 loss recognized to date). This amount combined with the estimated costs to complete of $2,340,000, equals the realizable contract price of $5,000,000. Recognizing losses on long-term projects in the period the losses become known is equivalent to measuring inventory at the lower of cost or market.

Comparison of Periodic Gross Profit (Loss), Loss on Entire Contract.   The pattern of gross profit (loss) over the contract period for the two methods is summarized in the following table. Notice that an unanticipated increase in costs of $100,000 causes a further loss of $100,000 to be recognized in 1999.

	Percentage-of-Completion	Completed Contract
Gross profit (loss) recognized:		
1997	$ 500,000	–0–
1998	(600,000)	$(100,000)
1999	(100,000)	(100,000)
Total project loss	$(200,000)	$(200,000)

The table in Illustration 4–1f shows the revenue and cost of construction recognized in each of the three years using the percentage-of-completion method.

Revenue is recognized in the usual way by multiplying a percentage of completion by the total contract price. In situations where a loss is expected on the entire project, cost of construction for the period will no longer be equal to cost incurred during the period. The easiest way to compute cost of construction is to add the amount of the recognized loss to the amount of revenue recognized. For example, in 1998 revenue recognized of $706,000 is added to the loss of $600,000 to arrive at the cost of construction of $1,306,000.[8]

---

[8]The cost of construction also can be determnined as follows:

Loss to date (100% recognized)		$ 100,000
Add:		
Remaining total project cost, not including the loss ($5,100,000 – 100,000)	$5,000,000	
Multiplied by the percentage of completion	× .5412	2,706,000
Total		2,806,000
Less: Cost of construction recognized in 1997		(1,500,000)
Cost of construction recognized in 1998		$1,306,000

ILLUSTRATION   4-1f

Percentage-of-Completion Method: Allocation of Revenue and Cost of Construction to Each Period—Loss on Entire Project

1997		
Revenue recognized ($5,000,000 × 40%)		$2,000,000
Costs of construction		1,500,000
Gross profit		$ 500,000
1998		
Revenue recognized to date ($5,000,000 × 54.12%*)	$2,706,000	
Less: Revenue recognized in 1997	(2,000,000)	
Revenue recognized		$ 706,000
Cost of construction†		1,306,000
Loss		$ (600,000)
1999		
Revenue recognized to date ($5,000,000 × 100%)	$5,000,000	
Less: Revenue recognized in 1997 and 1998	(2,706,000)	
Revenue recognized		$2,294,000
Cost of construction†		2,394,000
Loss		$ (100,000)

*$2,760,000 ÷ $5,100,000 = 54.12%
†The difference between revenue and loss

The journal entries to record the losses in 1998 and 1999 are as follows:

Recognized losses on long-term contracts reduce the construction in progress account.

1998		
Cost of construction	1,306,000	
Revenue from long-term contracts		706,000
Construction in progress (loss)		600,000
1999		
Cost of construction	2,394,000	
Revenue from long-term contracts		2,294,000
Construction in progress (loss)		100,000

Using the completed contract method, no revenue or cost of construction are recognized until the contract is complete. In 1998, a loss on long-term contracts (an income statement account) of $100,000 is recognized. In 1999, the income statement will report revenue of $5,000,000 and cost of construction of $5,100,000, thus reporting the additional loss of $100,000. The journal entries to record the losses in 1998 and 1999 are as follows:

1998		
Loss on long-term contracts	100,000	
Construction in progress (loss)		100,000
1999		
Cost of construction	5,100,000	
Revenue from long-term contracts		5,000,000
Construction in progress (loss)		100,000

You can see from this that use of the percentage-of-completion method in this case produces a large overstatement of income in 1997 and a large understatement in 1998 caused by a change in the estimation of future costs. Recall that if a company feels that it is unable to make dependable forecasts of future costs, the completed contract method should be used.

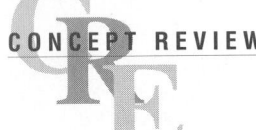

CONCEPT REVIEW EXERCISE   LONG-TERM CONSTRUCTION CONTRACTS

During 1997, the Samuelson Construction Company began construction of an office building for the City of Gernon. The contract price is $8,000,000 and the building will take approximately 18 months to complete. Completion is scheduled for early in 1999. The company's fiscal year ends on December 31.

The following is a year-by-year recap of construction costs incurred and the estimated costs to complete the project as of the end of each year. Progress billings and cash collections also are indicated.

	1997	1998	1999
Construction costs incurred during the year	$1,500,000	$4,500,000	$1,550,000
Construction costs incurred in prior years	–0–	1,500,000	6,000,000
Cumulative construction costs	1,500,000	6,000,000	7,550,000
Estimated costs to complete at end of year	4,500,000	1,500,000	–0–
Total estimated and actual construction costs	$6,000,000	$7,500,000	$7,550,000
Billings made during the year	$1,400,000	$5,200,000	$1,400,000
Cash collections during year	1,000,000	4,000,000	3,000,000

Required:
1. Determine the amount of gross profit or loss to be recognized in each of the three years applying both the percentage-of-completion and completed contract methods.
2. Prepare the necessary summary journal entries for each of the three years to account for construction costs incurred, recognized revenue and cost of construction, contract billings, and cash collections and to close the construction accounts in 1999 using the percentage-of-completion method only.
3. Prepare a partial balance sheet for 1997 and 1998 to include all construction-related accounts using the percentage-of-completion method.

CONCEPT REVIEW EXERCISE   SOLUTION

1. Determine the amount of gross profit or loss to be recognized in each of the three years applying both the percentage-of-completion and completed contract methods.

Percentage-of-completion Method

	1997	1998	1999
Contract price	$8,000,000	$8,000,000	$8,000,000
Less: costs to complete	6,000,000	7,500,000	7,550,000
Total estimated gross profit to date	2,000,000	500,000	450,000
Multiplied by % of completion*	25%	80%	100%
Gross profit recognized to date	500,000	400,000	450,000
Less gross profit recognized in prior years	–0–	(500,000)	(400,000)
Gross profit (loss) recognized	$ 500,000	$ (100,000)	$ 50,000

* Estimates of percentage-of-completion:

1997	1998	1999
$\dfrac{1,500,000}{6,000,000} = 25\%$	$\dfrac{6,000,000}{7,500,000} = 80\%$	Project complete

Completed Contract Method

	1997	1998	1999
Gross profit recognized	–0–	–0–	$450,000

2. Prepare the necessary summary journal entries for each of the three years to account for construction costs incurred, recognized revenue and cost of construction, contract billings, and cash collections and to close the construction accounts in 1999 using the percentage-of-completion method only.

	1997	1998	1999
Construction in progress	1,500,000	4,500,000	1,550,000
Cash, materials, etc.	1,500,000	4,500,000	1,550,000
To record construction costs.			
Construction in progress			
(gross profit)	500,000		50,000
Cost of construction	1,500,000		1,550,000
Revenue from long-term			
contracts (below)	2,000,000		1,600,000
To record gross profit.			
Cost of construction		4,500,000	
Revenue from long-term			
contracts (below)		4,400,000	
Construction in progress (loss)		100,000	
To record loss.			
Accounts receivable	1,400,000	5,200,000	1,400,000
Billings on construction contract	1,400,000	5,200,000	1,400,000
To record progress billings.			
Cash	1,000,000	4,000,000	3,000,000
Accounts receivable	1,000,000	4,000,000	3,000,000
To record cash collections.			
Billings on construction contract			8,000,000
Construction in progress			8,000,000
To close accounts.			

Revenue recognized:
1997: $8,000,000 × 25% = $2,000,000

1998: $8,000,000 × 80% = $6,400,000
  Less: Revenue recognized in 1997 (2,000,000)
  Revenue recognized in 1998 $4,400,000

1999: $8,000,000 × 100% = $8,000,000
  Less: Revenue recognized in 1997 and 1998 (6,400,000)
  Revenue recognized in 1999 $1,600,000

3. Prepare a partial balance sheet for 1997 and 1998 to include all construction related accounts using the percentage-of-completion method.

Balance Sheet (end of year)

		1997	1998
Current assets:			
Accounts receivable		$400,000	$1,600,000
Construction in progress	$2,000,000		
Less: Billings	(1,400,000)		
Costs and profit in excess of billings		600,000	
Current liabilities:			
Billings ($6,600,000) in excess of costs and			
profits ($6,400,000)			200,000

Service Sales

Many of the largest companies in the world earn revenue by providing services to their customers. These activities provide another situation when revenue is earned over a period of time. The timing of revenue and related expense recognition for services varies depending on the nature and timing of the service(s) being provided.

Completed Performance Method.   Some service transactions require the seller to perform several different activities spread out over different reporting periods. However, if there is one final activity that is deemed critical to the earnings process, all revenue and costs are deferred until this final activity has been performed. For example, a moving company will pack, load, transport, and deliver household goods for a fixed fee. Although packing, loading, and transporting all are important to the earning process, delivery is the culminating event of the process. So, the entire fee is recognized as revenue after the goods have been delivered. This procedure is known as the **completed performance method.** Federal Express employs this method. The company's summary of significant accounting policies disclosure note indicates that "Revenue is generally recognized upon delivery of shipments."

> If there is one final service that is critical to the earnings process, revenues and costs are deferred and recognized after this service has been performed.

Federal Express Corporation

Proportional Performance Method.   In other cases, the **proportional performance method** is more appropriate. This method is analogous to the percentage-of-completion method for long-term contracts. It recognizes revenue based on the proportional performance of each activity when the activities extend beyond one accounting period. For example, suppose a country club charges a two-year membership fee of $2,400, which allows the member to have complete use of its facilities. The fee should be recognized as revenue proportionally over the two-year period. In this case, it would seem logical to recognize $100 in revenue each month over the two-year period (that is, straight-line method) because services performed likely are similar over the period.

Specific Performance Method.   On the other hand, if service activities performed are not identical from one accounting period to the next, any systematic and rational method that reasonably relates revenue recognition to performance could be used. Typical of such situations is when service revenue is earned upon performing a single activity. For example, a doctor earns service revenue on completion of surgery. This method is called the **specific performance method.**

When recognizing revenue in each of these situations, consideration should be given to a possible refund of fees collected and to potential uncollectibility of accounts receivable. Estimates of refunds or bad debts may be appropriate.

Graphic 4–3 shows the revenue recognition policies for the various services provided by AT&T Corp.

GRAPHIC   4–3

Disclosure of revenue recognition policies— AT&T Corp.

Revenue Recognition (in part):

Revenue from	Basis of Recognition
Telecommunications Services	Minutes of traffic processed and contracted fees
Rentals and Other Services	Proportionately over contract period or as services are performed
Financial Services and Leasing	Over the life of the finance receivables using the effective interest method, or straight-line method over the life of the operating lease

---

Revenue from telecommunication services are recognized using the specific performance method based on minutes of traffic processed. Rental and other service revenue are recognized using the proportional performance method. Financial services and leasing are two activities addressed in subsequent chapters.

Revenue Recognition After Delivery

OPENING CASE

Question 3

> At times, revenue recognition is delayed beyond the point of delivery due to a high degree of uncertainty related to ultimate cash collection.

Some revenue-producing activities call for revenue recognition after the product has been delivered. These situations involve significant uncertainty as to the collectibility of the cash to be received, caused either by the possibility of the product being returned or, with credit sales, the possibility of bad debts. Usually, these remaining uncertainties can be accounted for by estimating and recording allowances for anticipated returns and bad debts, thus allowing revenue and related expenses to be recognized at point of delivery. But occasionally, an abnormal degree of uncertainty causes point of delivery revenue recognition not to be appropriate. Revenue recognition after delivery sometimes is appropriate for installment sales and when a right of return exists. We now look at these situations.

Installment Sales

Customers sometimes are allowed to pay for purchases in installments over a long period of time. Many large retail stores such as Sears and J.C. Penney sell certain products on an installment plan. Uncertainty about collection of a receivable normally increases with the length of time allowed for payment. Should revenue and related expenses from these sales be recognized at point of delivery (sale of the product), or should recognition be delayed?

In most situations, the increased uncertainty concerning the collection of cash from installment sales can be accommodated satisfactorily by estimating uncollectible amounts. If, however, the installment sale creates a situation where there is significant uncertainty concerning cash collection making it impossible to make a reasonable assessment of future bad debts, revenue and expense recognition should be delayed. Two accounting methods, the **installment sales method** and the **cost recovery method,** are available to handle such situations. The use of these methods is contrary to the objective of recognizing revenue in the period the activity takes place. We emphasize that these methods should be used only in situations involving exceptional uncertainty.[9]

As an example of exceptional uncertainty, consider J.W. Mays, Inc. Mays sold all of its right, title, and interest in a certain lease, covering property located in Glen Oaks, New York. Total consideration was $6,000,000 of which $5,000,000 was paid in the year of sale with a deferred payment of $1,000,000 evidenced by a promissory note due in five years. Graphic 4–4 shows the company's disclosure note explaining their treatment of the sale.

Learning objective 3
Describe the installment sales and cost recovery methods of recognizing revenue for certain installment sales and explain the conditions under which these methods might be used.

GRAPHIC 4–4

Disclosure of use of installment method— J.W. Mays, Inc.

3. Note Receivable—Glen Oaks Leasehold (in part):

Based upon information made available to the Company, the purchaser entered into a new venture which is subject to all the risks inherent in the establishment of a new business enterprise. The principles in this new venture have had limited operating experience in a retail operation of this magnitude. The likelihood of the success of this retail operation should be considered in light of the problems, expenses, complications, delays and potential competition which are encountered in connection with the development of this type of business venture. Accordingly, the Company has elected to report the gain on the sale under the installment method in accordance with Accounting Principles Board Opinion No. 10, and to defer the unrealized gain of $861,436 on the $1,000,000 note until the note is paid.

The **installment sales method** recognizes gross profit by applying the gross profit percentage on the sale to the amount of cash actually received.

Installment Sales Method.   To deal with the uncertainty of collection, the **installment sales method** recognizes revenue and costs only when cash payments are received. Each payment is assumed to be composed of two components: (1) a partial recovery of the cost of the item sold and (2) a gross profit component. These components are determined by the gross profit percentage applicable to the sale. For example, if the gross profit percentage (gross profit ÷ sales price) is 40%, then 60% of each dollar collected represents cost recovery and the remaining 40% is gross profit. Consider the example in Illustration 4–2.

ILLUSTRATION 4–2

Installment sales method

On November 1, 1997, the Belmont Corporation, a real estate developer, sold a tract of land for $800,000. The sales agreement requires the customer to make four equal annual payments of $200,000 plus interest on each November 1, beginning November 1, 1997. The land cost $560,000 to develop. The company's fiscal year ends on December 31.

The gross profit of $240,000 represents 30% of the sales price ($240,000 ÷ $800,000). The collection of cash and the recognition of gross profit under the installment method are summarized below. We ignore the collection of interest charges and the recognition of interest revenue to concentrate on the collection of the $800,000 sales price and the recognition of gross profit on the sale.

Gross profit recognition, installment sales method

Date	Cash Collected	Cost Recovery (70%)	Gross Profit (30%)
Nov. 1, 1997	$200,000	$140,000	$ 60,000
Nov. 1, 1998	200,000	140,000	60,000
Nov. 1, 1999	200,000	140,000	60,000
Nov. 1, 2000	200,000	140,000	60,000
Totals	$800,000	$560,000	$240,000

---

[9]For example, these methods are occasionally used in real estate sales involving significant dollar amounts and long payment periods. Real estate sales are discussed briefly later in this chapter.

This illustrates that the gross profit recognized in a period will be equal to the gross profit percentage multiplied by the period's cash collection. The following journal entries are recorded (interest charges ignored):

Inventory is credited for the portion of the receivable that represents the cost of the land sold. The difference is deferred gross profit.

Contra acct (handwritten annotation)

Nov. 1, 1997		
Installment receivables	800,000	
Inventory		560,000
Deferred gross profit		240,000
To record installment sale.		

This first entry records the installment receivable and the reduction of inventory. The difference between the $800,000 selling price and the $560,000 cost of sales represents the gross profit on the sale of $240,000. As it will be recognized only as collections are made, it is recorded in an account called *deferred gross profit*. This is a valuation (contra) account to the installment receivable. It will be reduced to zero as the payments are received.[10]

When payments are received, gross profit is recognized, calculated by applying the gross profit percentage to the cash collected (30% × $200,000).

Nov. 1, 1997		
Cash	200,000	
Installment receivables		200,000
To record cash collection from installment sale.		
Deferred gross profit	60,000	
Realized gross profit (REVENUE)		60,000
To recognize gross profit from installment sale.		

The second set of entries records the collection of the first installment and recognizes the gross profit component of the payment, $60,000. Journal entries to record the remaining three payments are identical.

At the end of 1997, the balance sheet would report the following:

Installment receivables	$600,000
Less: Deferred gross profit	(180,000)
Installment receivables (net)	$420,000

The net amount of the receivable represents the portion of the remaining payments that represents cost recovery (70% × $600,000). The installment receivables are classified as current assets if they will be collected within one year (or within the company's operating cycle, if longer); otherwise, they are classified as noncurrent assets.

The income statement for 1997 would report a gross profit from installment sales of $60,000. Sales and cost of goods sold usually are not reported on the income statement, just the resulting gross profit. But if installment sales are significant, the 1997 income statement in this illustration would report sales of $200,000 and cost of goods sold of $140,000.

---

[10]Accountants sometimes record installment sales in the following manner:

Installment sales receivable	800,000	
Installment sales		800,000
To record installment sales.		
Cost of installment sales	560,000	
Inventory		560,000
To record the cost of installment sales.		

Then at the end of the period, the following adjusting/closing entry is recorded:

Installment sales	800,000	
Cost of installment sales		560,000
Deferred gross profit on installment sales		240,000

The text entries concentrate on the effect of the transactions and avoid this unnecessary procedural complexity.

Additional Consideration

The problem of accounting for bad debts is discussed in significant depth in Chapter 7. However, bad debts related to receivables on sales accounted for using the installment method create a unique problem. Assume that in the example described in Illustration 4–2, the Belmont Corporation collected the first payment but the customer was unable to make the remaining payments. Typically, the seller would repossess the item sold and the following journal entry is made:

Repossessed inventory	420,000	
Deferred gross profit	180,000	
Installment receivable		600,000

This entry removes the receivable and the remaining deferred gross profit and records the repossessed land in an inventory account. The entry assumes that the land's current fair value is equal to the net receivable of $420,000. If the land's fair value at the date of repossession is less than $420,000, a loss on repossession is recorded (debited).

Cost Recovery Method.   In situations where there is an extremely high degree of uncertainty regarding the ultimate cash collection on an installment sale, an even more conservative approach, the **cost recovery method** can be used. This method defers all gross profit recognition until the cost of the item sold has been recovered. The gross profit recognition pattern applying the cost recovery method to the Belmont Corporation situation used in Illustration 4–2 to demonstrate the installment sales method is shown below.

> The **cost recovery method** defers all gross profit recognition until cash equal to the cost of the item sold has been received.

> Cost recovery method

Date	Cash Collected	Cost Recovery	Gross Profit
Nov. 1, 1997	$200,000	$200,000	$ –0–
Nov. 1, 1998	200,000	200,000	–0–
Nov. 1, 1999	200,000	160,000	40,000
Nov. 1, 2000	200,000	– 0 –	200,000
Totals	$800,000	$560,000	$240,000

The journal entries using this method are similar to those by the installment sales method except that $40,000 in gross profit is recognized in 1999 and $200,000 in 2000.

> The cost recovery journal entry is identical to the installment sales method.

Nov. 1, 1997

Installment receivables	800,000	
Inventory		560,000
Deferred gross profit		240,000

To record installment sale.

Nov. 1, 1997, 1998, 1999 and 2000

Cash	200,000	
Installment receivables		200,000

To record cash collection from installment.

Nov. 1, 1997 and 1998

No entry for gross profit.

> When payments are received, gross profit is recognized only after cost has been fully recovered.

Nov. 1, 1999

Deferred gross profit	40,000	
Realized gross profit		40,000

To recognize gross profit from installment sale.

Nov. 1, 2000

Deferred gross profit	200,000	
Realized gross profit		200,000

To recognize gross profit from installment sale.

Real Estate Sales

Real estate sales include the sales of lots to builders and the sales of homes, buildings, and parcels of land to builders. Such sales often are made on an installment basis with relatively small down payments and long payment periods, perhaps 25 years or more. These payment characteristics, combined with the general speculative nature of many of these transactions, translates into significant uncertainty concerning the collectibility of the installment receivable. Furthermore, these transactions often require the seller to perform significant services *after* the sale has been made, such as managing the property.

These problems mean the realization principle criteria may not be satisfied at the date of sale, so revenue (and cost) recognition may need to be postponed. If significant after-sale services are required of the seller, cash collections should be recorded as unearned revenue and all costs (e.g., cost of the real estate sold and selling costs) deferred until the revenue recognition criteria are met.

Even if the seller is not obliged to perform significant activities after the sale, the question of collectibility still remains. If the seller is unable to make a reliable estimate of uncollectible amounts, the installment sales or cost recovery methods may be appropriate for revenue and profit recognition. *SFAS 66* establishes standards for recognition of profit on real estate sales transactions.[11]

SFAS 66 also addresses **retail land sales.** These are sales, on a volume basis, of lots that constitute subdivisions of large tracts of land. The characteristics of these sales are similar to those of real estate sales. Depending on the specific circumstances, profit should be recognized either at the point of delivery (the full accrual method), by the percentage-of-completion method or by the installment sales method.

GLOBAL PERSPECTIVE

Many countries follow the U.S. practice of recognizing revenue on installment sales at date of sale, unless the installment sale creates a situation where there is significant uncertainty concerning cash collection, in which case revenue and expense recognition are delayed.

There are, however, some countries where accounting procedures do not differentiate between installment and other credit sales. Italy, Spain, Norway, the Netherlands, France, and Belgium are examples of countries that fall into this category.

CONCEPT REVIEW EXERCISE   INSTALLMENT SALES

Boatwright Implements, Inc., manufactures and sells farm machinery. For most of its sales, revenue and cost of sales are recognized at the delivery date. In 1997, it sold three large pieces of machinery to a new customer for $100,000. The cost of the machinery was $60,000. Payment will be made in five annual installments of $20,000 each, with the first payment due in 1997. Boatwright usually does not allow its customers to pay in installments. Due to the unusual nature of the payment terms and the uncertainty of collection of the installment payments, Boatwright is considering alternative methods of recognizing profit on this sale.

Required:
Ignoring interest charges, prepare a table showing the gross profit to be recognized from 1997 through 2001 on the sale using the following three methods:

1. Point of delivery revenue recognition.
2. The installment sales method.
3. The cost recovery method.

---

[11]"Accounting for Sales of Real Estate," *Statement of Financial Accounting Standards No. 66* (Stamford, Conn.: FASB, 1982).

	Point of delivery	Installment Sales Method (40% × cash collection)	Cost Recovery Method
1997	$40,000	$ 8,000	$ –0–
1998	- 0 -	8,000	–0–
1999	- 0 -	8,000	–0–
2000	- 0 -	8,000	20,000
2001	– 0 –	8,000	20,000
Totals	$40,000	$40,000	$40,000

Right of Return

Learning objective 4
Discuss the implications for revenue recognition of allowing customers the right of return.

Retailers usually give their customers the right to return merchandise if they are not satisfied. In most situations, even though the right to return merchandise exists, revenues and expenses can be appropriately recognized at point of delivery. Based on past experience, a company usually can estimate the returns that will result for a given volume of sales. These estimates are used to reduce both sales and cost of goods sold in anticipation of returns. The purpose of these estimates is to avoid overstating gross profit in the period of sale and understating gross profit in the period of return. The specific accounting treatment for sales returns is illustrated in Chapter 7 in conjunction with discussing the valuation of accounts receivable.

When the **right of return** exists, revenue cannot be recognized at point of delivery unless the seller is able to make reliable estimates of future returns.

Because the return of merchandise can retroactively negate the benefits of having made a sale, the seller must be able to make reliable estimates of future returns before revenue is recognized in situations when the **right of return** exists.[12] The most critical of these criteria is that the seller must be able to make reliable estimates of future returns. In certain situations, these criteria are not satisfied at the point of delivery of the product. For example, manufacturers of semiconductors like Intel Corporation and Motorola Corporation usually sell their products through independent distributor companies. Economic factors, competition among manufacturers, and rapid obsolescence of the product motivate these manufacturers to grant the distributors the right of return if they are unable to sell the semiconductors. So, revenue recognition often is deferred beyond the delivery point to the date the products actually are sold by the distributor to an end user.

As an example, the disclosure note shown in Graphic 4–5 appeared in a recent annual report of Intel Corporation.

GRAPHIC 4–5

Disclosure of revenue recognition policy—Intel Corporation

> *Notes : Revenue Recognition*
>
> Certain of Intel's sales are made to distributors under agreements allowing right of return and price protection on merchandise unsold by the distributors. Because of rapid technological obsolescence and frequent sales price reductions in the industry, Intel defers recognition of such sales until the merchandise is sold by the distributors.

For Intel, the event critical to revenue recognition is *not* the delivery of the product to the buyer but the ultimate sale of the product by the buyer (the distributor company) to an end user.

Anytime a company recognizes revenue at a point other than the point of delivery, the revenue recognition method used is disclosed in the summary of significant accounting policies. Intel's disclosure note is an example. Graphic 4–6, a disclosure note from a recent financial statement of Amdahl Corporation, a manufacturer of mainframe computers, provides another example.

GRAPHIC 4–6

Disclosure of revenue recognition policy—Amdahl Corporation

> *Notes: Revenue Recognition (in part)*
>
> Revenue from equipment sales are generally recognized when equipment has been shipped, installed, and financing arrangements have been completed.

---

[12]Other, less critical, criteria are listed in *SFAS 48.* "Revenue Recognition When Right of Return Exists," *Statement of Financial Accounting Standards No. 48* (Stamford, Conn.: FASB, 1981).

As the note indicates, revenue is delayed beyond the point of product delivery. Amdahl waits until the product has been properly installed and financing has been arranged by the buyer. Why does Amdahl delay revenue recognition? Until the product has been installed and financing arranged, there is a high degree of uncertainty concerning the possibility the product might be returned.

Franchise Sales

Learning objective 5
Discuss the revenue recognition issues involving franchise sales.

The use of franchise arrangements has become increasingly popular in the United States over the past 30 years. Many retail outlets for fast food, restaurants, motels, and auto rental agencies are operated as franchises. In the franchise arrangements, the **franchisor,** for example McDonald's Corporation, grants to the **franchisee,** quite often an individual, the right to sell the franchisor's products and use its name for a specified period of time. The restaurant where you purchased your last BIG MAC was probably owned and operated by an individual under a franchise agreement, not by McDonald's Corporation.

The fees to be paid by the franchisee to the franchisor usually comprise (1) the *initial franchise fee* and (2) *continuing franchise fees.* The services to be performed by the franchisor in exchange for the initial franchise fee, in addition to the right to use its name and sell its products, might include assistance in finding a location, constructing the facilities, and training employees. The initial franchise fee usually is a fixed amount, but it may be payable in installments.

The continuing franchise fees are paid to the franchisor for continuing rights as well as for advertising and promotion and other services provided over the life of the franchise agreement. These fees sometimes are a fixed annual or monthly amount, a percentage of the volume of business done by the franchise, or a combination of both.

The continuing franchise fees usually do not present any accounting difficulty and are recognized by the franchisor as revenue in the periods they are received, which correspond to the periods the services are performed by the franchisor. The challenging revenue recognition issue pertains to the initial franchise fee. In the early 1960s and 1970s, many franchisors recognized the entire initial franchise fee as revenue in the period in which the contract was signed. In many cases, there were significant services to be performed and the fee was collectible in installments over an extended period of time creating uncertainty as to cash collection.

Specific guidelines for revenue recognition of the initial franchise fee are provided by *SFAS 45.* A key to these conditions is the concept of *substantial performance.* It requires that substantially all of the initial services of the franchisor required by the franchise agreement have been performed before the initial franchise fee can be recognized as revenue. The term *substantial* requires professional judgment on the part of the accountant. In situations when the initial franchise fee is collectible in installments, even after substantial performance has occurred, the installment sales or cost recovery methods should be used for profit recognition, if a reasonable estimate of uncollectibility cannot be made.

Consider the example in Illustration 4–3.

> *SFAS 45* requires that the franchisor has substantially performed the services promised in the franchise agreement and that the collectibility of the initial franchise fee is reasonably assured before the fee can be recognized as revenue.

> FASB   **Franchise fee revenue from an individual franchise sale ordinarily shall be recognized, with an appropriate provision for estimated uncollectible amounts, when all material services or conditions relating to the sale have been substantially performed or satisfied by the franchisor.**[13]

ILLUSTRATION   4–3

Franchise sales

On March 31, 1997, the Red Hot Chicken Wing Corporation entered into a franchise agreement with Thomas Keller. In exchange for an initial franchise fee of $50,000, Red Hot will provide initial services to include the selection of a location, construction of the building, training of employees, and consulting services over several years. $10,000 is payable on March 31, 1997, with the remaining $40,000 payable in annual installments which include interest at an appropriate rate. In addition, the franchisee will pay continuing franchise fees of $1,000 per month for advertising and promotion provided by Red Hot, beginning immediately after the franchise begins operations. Thomas Keller opened his Red Hot franchise for business on September 30, 1997.

---

[13]"Accounting for Franchise Fee Revenue," *Statement of Financial Accounting Standards No. 45* (Stamford, Conn.: FASB, 1981).

Initial Franchise Fee

Assuming that the initial services to be performed by Red Hot subsequent to the contract signing are substantial but that collectibility of the installment receivable is reasonably certain, the following journal entry is recorded:

Revenue from initial franchise services is deferred until the services are rendered.

March 31, 1997		
Cash	10,000	
Note receivable	40,000	
Unearned franchise fee revenue		50,000
To record franchise agreement and down payment.		

The unearned franchise fee revenue would then be recognized when the initial services have been performed. This could occur in increments, or at one point in time, depending on the circumstances.[14] For example, in our illustration, if substantial performance was deemed to have occurred when the franchise began operations, the following entry would be recorded:

Sept. 30, 1997		
Unearned franchise fee revenue	50,000	
Franchise fee revenue		50,000
To recognize franchise fee revenue.		

If collectibility of the installment receivable is uncertain and there is no basis for estimating uncollectible amounts, the initial entry would record a credit to deferred franchise fee revenue which is then recognized as being earned using either the installment sales or cost recovery methods.

Continuing Franchise Fees

Continuing franchise fee revenue is recognized on a monthly basis as follows:

Cash (or accounts receivable)	1,000	
Service revenue		1,000
To recognize continuing franchise fee revenue.		

Expenses incurred by the franchisor in providing these continuing franchise services should be recognized in the same periods as the service revenue.

There are other situations where revenue recognition requires a more refined policy than simply recognizing revenue at the point of delivery. The FASB has issued detailed industry-specific revenue recognition standards for such industries as insurance, record and music, cable television, and motion picture.[15] These industry standards are beyond the scope of this text. However, in each case, the objective is the same: to recognize revenue in a manner consistent with the realization principle.

---

[14]Franchise agreements sometimes require that any payments made to the franchisor be refunded if the franchise fails to open. If this condition is present, it would be an important factor in deciding whether to recognize any revenue before the franchise begins operations.

[15]"Accounting and Reporting by Insurance Enterprises," *Statement of Financial Accounting Standards No. 60* (Stamford, Conn.: FASB, 1982), "Financial Reporting in the Record and Music Industry," *Statement of Financial Accounting Standards No. 50* (Stamford, Conn.: FASB, 1981), "Financial Reporting by Cable Television Companies," *Statement of Financial Accounting Standards No. 51* (Stamford, Conn.: FASB, 1981), "Financial Reporting by Producers and Distributors of Motion Picture Films," *Statement of Financial Accounting Standards No. 53* (Stamford, Conn.: FASB, 1981),

---

Additional Consideration

In certain circumstances, revenue is recognized at the completion of the production process (before delivery). This approach generally is used by companies that deal in precious metals, and ". . . agricultural, mineral, and other products, units of which are interchangeable and have an immediate marketability at quoted prices . . ."[16] This is called the *production basis* of recognizing revenue and is accomplished by writing inventory up from cost to market value.

Recall that in a typical manufacturing situation, revenue is not recognized at the completion of the production process due to significant uncertainty as to the collectibility of the asset to be received. We don't know if the product will be sold, nor the selling price, nor the buyer if eventually sold. These uncertainties are not significant when there is immediate marketability at quoted market prices for products like precious metals.

In cases when the production basis of recognizing revenue is used, full disclosure of the fact is required.

---

not responsible for this part 2 (p164-169)

PART **B** PROFITABILITY ANALYSIS

Using Financial Statement Information

I Learning objective 6
Describe the techniques used by financial analysts to transform financial information into forms more useful for analysis.

I Comparative financial statements allow financial statement users to compare year-to-year financial position, results of operations, and cash flows.

I No accounting numbers are meaningful in and of themselves.

You recall that the overriding objective of financial reporting is providing information that investors and creditors can use to make decisions. Nevertheless, it's sometimes easy to lose sight of that objective while dealing with the intricacies that specific concepts and procedures can involve. Here we provide an overview of financial statement analysis and then demonstrate the use of ratios, a popular financial analysis technique, to analyze profitability.

Investors, creditors, and others use information provided in corporate financial reports to make decisions. Although the financial reports focus primarily on the past performance and the present financial condition of the reporting company, information users are most interested in the outlook for the future. Trying to gain a glimpse of the future from past and present data entails using various tools and techniques to formulate predictions. This is the goal of financial statement analysis.

Financial statements are not presented in isolation. Every financial statement issued is accompanied by the corresponding financial statement of the preceding year, and often the previous two years. These are called **comparative financial statements**. They enable investors, creditors, and other users to compare year-to-year financial position, results of operations, and cash flows. These comparative data help an analyst detect and predict trends. Because operations often expand and contract in a cyclical fashion, analysis of any one year's data may not provide an accurate picture of a company.

Some analysts enhance their comparison by expressing each item as a percentage of that same item in the financial statements of another year (base amount) in order to more easily see year-to-year changes. This is referred to as **horizontal analysis**. Similarly, **vertical analysis** involves expressing each item in the financial statements as a percentage of an appropriate corresponding total, or base amount, but within the same year. For example, cash, inventory, and other assets can be restated as a percent of total assets; net income and each expense can be restated as a percent of revenues.

Regardless of the specific technique used, the essential point is that accounting numbers are virtually meaningless in isolation. Their value derives from comparison with other numbers. The most common way of comparing accounting numbers to evaluate the performance and risk of a firm is **ratio analysis**.

We use ratios every day. Batting averages indicate how well our favorite baseball players are performing. We evaluate basketball players by field goal percentage and rebounds per game. Speedometers measure the speed of our cars in terms of miles per hour. We compare grocery costs on the basis of price per pound or ounce. In each of these cases, the ratio is more meaningful than a single number by itself. Do 45 hits indicate satisfactory performance? It depends on the num-

---

[16]"Restatement and Revision of Accounting Research Bulletins," *Accounting Research Bulletin No. 43* (New York: AICPA 1953), Chapter 4, par. 16.

ber of at-bats. Is $2 a good price for cheese? It depends on how many ounces the $2 buys. Ratios make these measurements meaningful.

Evaluating information in ratio form allows analysts to control for size differences over time and among firms.

Likewise, we can use ratios to help evaluate a firm's performance and financial position. Is net income of $4 million a cause for shareholders to celebrate? Probably not if shareholders' equity is $10 billion. But if shareholders' equity is $10 million, that's a 40% return on equity! Although ratios provide more meaningful information than absolute numbers alone, the ratios are most useful when analyzed relative to some standard of comparison. That standard of comparison may be previous performance of the same company, the performance of a competitor company, or an industry average for the particular ratio.

Accountants should be conversant with ratio analysis for at least three reasons. First, when preparing financial statements, accountants should be familiar with the ways users will use the information provided to make better decisions concerning what and how to report. Second, when accountants participate in company decisions concerning operating and financing alternatives, they may find ratio analysis helpful in evaluating available choices. Third, during the planning stages of an audit, independent auditors often use ratio analysis to identify potential audit problems and determine the specific audit procedures that should be performed.

We introduce ratios related to profitability analysis in this chapter and ratios related to risk analysis in Chapter 5. You will also employ ratios in Decision Makers' Perspective sections of many of the chapters in this text. Financial analysis cases that benefit from ratio analysis are included in many of these chapters as well.

Activity Ratios

Learning objective 7
Identify and calculate the common ratios used to assess profitability.

Activity ratios measure a company's efficiency in managing its assets.

One key to profitability is how well a company manages and utilizes its assets. Some ratios are designed to evaluate a company's effectiveness in managing assets. Of particular interest is the activity, or turnover ratios, of certain assets; that is, the frequency with which those assets are replaced. The greater the number of times an asset turns over—the higher the ratio—the less cash a company must devote to that asset, and the more cash it can commit to other purposes. In other words, if these turnover ratios increase, fewer assets are required to maintain a given level of activity (revenue). Activity ratios do not measure profitability directly. However, they are important factors affecting profitability.

Although, in concept, the activity or turnover can be measured for any asset, activity ratios are most frequently calculated for accounts receivable, inventory, and total assets. These ratios are calculated as follows:

$$\text{Receivables turnover ratio} = \frac{\text{Net sales}}{\text{Average accounts receivable (net)}}$$

$$\text{Inventory turnover ratio} = \frac{\text{Cost of goods sold}}{\text{Average Inventory}}$$

$$\text{Asset turnover ratio} = \frac{\text{Net sales}}{\text{Average total assets}}$$

Receivables Turnover.   The **receivables turnover ratio** is calculated by dividing a period's net credit sales by the average net accounts receivable. Because income statements seldom distinguish between cash sales and credit sales, this ratio usually is computed using total net sales as the numerator. The denominator, average accounts receivable, is determined by adding beginning and ending net accounts receivable (gross accounts receivable less allowance for uncollectible accounts) and dividing by two.

The **receivables turnover ratio** offers an indication of how quickly a company is able to collect its accounts receivable.

The receivables turnover ratio provides an indication of a company's efficiency in collecting receivables. The ratio shows the number of times during a period that the average accounts receivable balance is collected. The higher the ratio, the shorter the average time between credit sales and cash collection.

The **average collection period** indicates the average age of accounts receivables.

A convenient extension of this ratio is the **average collection period**. This measure is computed simply by dividing 365 days by the receivables turnover ratio. The result is an approximation of the number of days the average accounts receivable balance is outstanding.

$$\text{Average collection period} = \frac{365}{\text{Receivables turnover ratio}}$$

Monitoring the receivables turnover ratio (and average collection period) over time can provide useful information about a company's future prospects. For example, a decline in the receivables turnover ratio (an increase in the average collection period) could be an indication of customer dissatisfaction with the company's products. Another possible explanation is that the company has changed its credit policy and is granting extended credit terms in order to maintain customers. Ratio analysis does not explain what might be wrong. It does provide information that highlights areas for further investigation.

Inventory Turnover.   An important activity measure for a merchandising company (a retail, wholesale, or manufacturing company) is the **inventory turnover ratio**. The ratio shows the number of times the average inventory balance is sold during a reporting period. It indicates how quickly inventory is sold. The more frequently a business is able to sell, or turn over, its inventory, the lower its investment in inventory must be for a given level of sales. The ratio is computed by dividing the period's cost of goods sold by the average inventory balance. The denominator, average inventory, is determined by adding beginning and ending inventory and dividing by two.[17]

> The **inventory turnover ratio** measures a company's efficiency in managing its investment in inventory.

A relatively high ratio, say compared to a competitor, usually is desirable. A high ratio indicates comparative strength, perhaps caused by a company's superior sales force, the existence of highly popular products, or maybe a successful advertising campaign. However, it might also be caused by a relatively low inventory level, which could mean stockouts and lost sales in the future. As with any ratio, care must be taken in evaluating this ratio.

On the other hand, a relatively low ratio, or a decrease in the ratio over time, usually is perceived to be unfavorable. Too much capital may be tied up in inventory. A relatively low ratio may result from overstocking, the presence of obsolete items, or poor marketing and sales efforts.

Similar to the receivables turnover, we can divide the inventory turnover ratio into 365 days to compute the **average days in inventory**. This measure indicates the number of days it normally takes to sell inventory.

$$\text{Average days in inventory} = \frac{365}{\text{Inventory turnover ratio}}$$

Asset Turnover.   A broad measure of asset efficiency is the **asset turnover ratio**. The ratio is computed by dividing a company's net sales or revenues by the average total assets available for use during a period. The denominator, average assets, is determined by adding beginning and ending total assets and dividing by two. The asset turnover ratio provides an indication of how efficiently a company utilizes all of its assets to generate revenue.

> The **asset turnover ratio** measures a company's efficiency using assets to generate revenue.

Industry standards are particularly important when evaluating asset turnover. Some industries are characterized by low turnover but typically make up for it with higher profit margins. Others have low profit margins but compensate with high turnover. Grocery stores typically have relatively low profit margins but relatively high asset turnover. In comparison, a manufacturer of specialized equipment will have a higher profit margin but a lower asset turnover ratio. But again, this ratio is best evaluated in conjunction with profit margin on sales. We do this in the next section.

Profitability Ratios

> **Learning objective 7** Identify and calculate the common ratios used to assess profitability.

A fundamental element of an analyst's task is to develop an understanding of a firm's profitability. Profitability ratios attempt to measure a company's ability to earn an adequate return relative to sales or resources devoted to operations. Resources devoted to operations can be defined as total assets or only those assets provided by owners, depending on the evaluation objective.

Three common profitability measures are (1) the profit margin on sales, (2) the return on assets, and (3) the return on shareholders' equity. These ratios are calculated as follows:

---

[17]Notice the consistency in the measure used for the numerator and denominator of the two turnover ratios. For the receivables turnover ratio, both numerator and denominator are based on sales dollars, whereas they are both based on cost for the inventory turnover ratio.

$$\text{Profit margin on sales} \quad = \quad \frac{\text{Net income}}{\text{Net sales}}$$

$$\text{Return on assets} \quad = \quad \frac{\text{Net income}}{\text{Average total assets}}$$

$$\text{Return on shareholders' equity} = \frac{\text{Net income}}{\text{Average shareholders' equity}}$$

> Profitability ratios assist in evaluating various aspects of a company's profit-making activities.

Profit Margin on Sales.   The **profit margin on sales** is simply net income divided by net sales. The ratio measures an important dimension of a company's profitability. It indicates the portion of each dollar of revenue that is available to cover expenses. It offers a measure of the company's ability to withstand either higher expenses or lower revenues.

> The **profit margin on sales** measures the amount of net income achieved per sales dollar.

As we discussed in the previous section, what is considered to be a desirable profit margin is highly sensitive to the nature of the business activity. For instance, you would expect a specialty shop to have a higher profit margin than, say, Wal-Mart. A low profit margin can be compensated for by a high asset turnover rate, and vice versa.

Return on Assets.   The **return on assets (ROA)** indicates a company's overall profitability. The ratio expresses income as a percentage of the average total assets available to generate that income. Because total assets are partially financed with debt and partially by equity funds, this is an inclusive way of measuring earning power that ignores specific sources of financing.

Recall from our previous discussion that a company's return on assets is related to both profit margin and asset turnover. Specifically, profitability can be achieved by either a high profit margin, high turnover, or a combination of the two.[18] In fact, the return on assets can actually be calculated by multiplying the profit margin ratio by the asset turnover ratio.

$$\text{Return on assets} = \text{Profit margin on sales} \times \text{Asset turnover}$$
$$= \frac{\text{Net income}}{\text{Net sales}} \times \frac{\text{Net sales}}{\text{Average total assets}}$$

The decomposition of return on assets illustrates why some companies with relatively small profit margins can be very profitable if they have high asset turnover. Alternatively, companies with relatively low asset turnover ratios can be profitable if they are able to sustain large profit margins.

Additional Consideration

The return on assets ratio often is computed as follows:

$$\text{Return on assets} = \frac{\text{Net income} + \text{interest expense (1–tax rate)}}{\text{Average total assets}}$$

The reason for adding back interest expense (net of tax) is that interest represents a return to suppliers of debt capital and should not be deducted in the computation of net income when computing the return on total assets. In other words, the numerator is the total amount of income available to both debt and equity capital.

Return on Shareholders' Equity.   One measure of profitability is the ability of management to generate net income from the resources owners provide. Sometimes viewed by shareholders as the key criterion of profitability, the ratio is obtained by dividing net income by average shareholders' equity.

> The **return on shareholders' equity** measures the return to suppliers of equity capital.

When the **return on shareholders' equity** is greater than the return on assets, management is using assets funded by debt to increase the income available for shareholders. This concept, known as *leverage*, is discussed in Chapter 5.

---

[18]This notion is sometimes referred to as Du Pont analysis because the Du Pont Company was a pioneer in emphasizing this relationship.

Additional Consideration

Sometimes when this ratio is calculated, shareholders' equity is viewed more narrowly to include only common shareholders. In that case, preferred stock is excluded from the denominator, and preferred dividends are deducted from net income in the numerator. The resulting rate of return on common shareholders' equity focuses on profits generated on resources provided by common shareholders.

Profitability Analysis—An Illustration

To illustrate the computation of the activity and profitability ratios, we analyze two well-known companies, Johnson & Johnson and Merck & Co., Inc. Johnson & Johnson (J & J) is the world's largest and most comprehensive manufacturer of health care products serving the consumer, pharmaceutical, and professional markets. Merck is the world's largest pharmaceutical company. The operations of these two companies are similar in terms of their involvement in pharmaceutical and other health care products. Illustration 4–4a presents selected financial statement information for the two companies.

ILLUSTRATION 4–4A

Selected Financial Information for Johnson & Johnson and Merck & Co., Inc.

	($ in millions)			
	J & J		**Merck**	
Balance Sheet	**1995**	**1994**	**1995**	**1994**
Accounts receivable (net)	$ 2,903	$ 2,601	$ 2,496	$ 2,352
Inventories	2,276	2,161	1,873	1,661
Total assets	17,873	15,668	23,832	21,857
Total liabilities	8,828	8,546	9,810	9,509
Total shareholders' equity	9,045	7,122	14,022	12,348
Two-year averages:				
Accounts receivable (net)	$ 2,752.0		$ 2,424.0	
Inventories	2,218.5		1,767.0	
Total assets	16,770.5		22,844.5	
Total shareholders' equity	8,083.5		13,185.0	
Income Statement	**1995**		**1995**	
Net sales	$18,842		$16,681	
Cost of goods sold	6,235		7,456	
Net income	2,403		3,335	

On the surface, it appears that Merck was slightly more profitable than J & J. Merck's 1995 net income is $3.335 billion compared to $2.403 billion for J & J. But that's not the whole story. Even though both are very large companies, Merck is larger than J & J in terms of total assets. Illustration 4–4b presents a comparison of the various activity and profitability ratios for 1995.

ILLUSTRATION 4–4B

Activity and Profitability Ratios—Johnson & Johnson (J & J) and Merck and Co., Inc.

		J & J		**Merck**	
Activity Ratios:					
Receivables turnover	=	$\frac{18,842}{2,752}$	= 6.85	$\frac{16,681}{2,424}$	= 6.88
Average collection period	=	$\frac{365}{6.85}$	= 53 days	$\frac{365}{6.88}$	= 53 days
Inventory turnover	=	$\frac{6,235}{2,218.5}$	= 2.81	$\frac{7,456}{1,767}$	= 4.22
Average days in inventory	=	$\frac{365}{2.81}$	= 130 days	$\frac{365}{4.22}$	= 86 days
Asset turnover	=	$\frac{18,842}{16,770.5}$	= 1.124	$\frac{16,681}{22,844.5}$	= .730
Profitability Ratios:					
Profit margin on sales	=	$\frac{2,403}{18,842}$	= .1275	$\frac{3,335}{16,681}$	= .1999
Return on assets	=	$\frac{2,403}{16,770.5}$	= .1433	$\frac{3,335}{22,844.5}$	= .1460
Return on shareholders' equity	=	$\frac{2,403}{8,083.5}$	= .2973	$\frac{3,335}{13,185}$	= .2529

Merck's inventory turnover ratio is higher than J & J's. A possible cause is the different mix of products sold by the two companies. J & J is more diversified than Merck in terms of its product lines and markets that it serves.

Merck's profit margin on sales also is significantly higher than J & J's. This again could be explained by the fact that Merck is primarily a pharmaceutical company, while J & J is more diversified. High profit margins are typical in the drug industry.

The returns on assets for the two companies are almost identical. As shown below, Merck's slower asset turnover is compensated for by its significantly higher profit margin on sales.

	Profit margin	$\times$	Asset turnover	$=$	Return on assets
J & J	.1275	$\times$	1.124	$=$	14.33%
Merck	.1999	$\times$	.730	$=$	14.60%

Both companies produced a higher return on shareholders' equity than return on assets. This means that they were both able to use assets funded by debt to increase the income available for shareholders. This is an example of favorable financial leverage to which we referred earlier.

The essential point of our discussion here is that raw accounting numbers alone mean little to decision makers. The numbers gain value when viewed in relation to other numbers. Similarly, the financial ratios formed by those relationships provide even greater perspective when compared with similar ratios of other companies, or relatedly, with averages for several companies in the same industry. Accounting information is useful in making decisions. Financial analysis that includes comparisons of financial ratios enhances the value of that information.

Solution to Financial Reporting Case (at the opening of the chapter)

1. Does your brother have to wait two and a half years to get his bonus? Explain.

No. The *general* revenue recognition criteria would suggest that revenue and costs should be recognized when a project is finished. The difficulty this would create is that all revenues, expenses, and resulting profit from the project are recognized when the project is completed; no revenues or expenses would be reported on the income statements of earlier reporting periods in which much of the work may have been performed. The percentage-of-completion method of revenue recognition for long-term projects addresses this problem. A fair share of the project's profit is allocated to each period in which the earnings process occurs. This is two and a half years in this instance.

2. How are gross profits recognized using the percentage-of-completion method?

The percentage-of-completion method recognizes part of the estimated gross profit each period. The amount recognized is based on progress to date which is estimated as the fraction of the project's cost incurred to date divided by total estimated costs. The estimated percentage of completion is multiplied by the revised project gross profit estimate. This yields the estimated gross profit earned from the beginning of the project. The gross profit recognized is calculated by subtracting from this amount the gross profit recognized in previous periods.

3. Are there other situations in which revenue is recognized at times other than when a product is delivered?

Yes, revenue recognition sometimes is delayed until after the product is delivered. These situations involve either the possibility of product returns or bad debts. In most cases, product returns and bad debts are estimated and revenues are recognized when a product is delivered. However, in situations involving an abnormal degree of uncertainty about cash collection caused by potential returns or bad debts, revenue recognition *after* delivery sometimes is appropriate.

The Bottom Line

1. The realization principle states that revenue should be recognized only after (1) the earnings process is virtually complete and (2) there is reasonable certainty of collecting the asset to be received from the customer. These criteria usually are satisfied at the point of product delivery. At that point, the majority of the productive activities have taken place and any remaining uncertainty concerning asset collection can be accounted for by estimating possible returns and bad debts.

2. The completed contract method recognizes revenues and costs on long-term construction contracts when the construction project is complete. The preferable method for recognizing revenues and costs for long-term construction contracts is the percentage-of-completion method, which assigns a fair share of the project's revenues and costs to each reporting period during construction.

3. The installment sales method recognizes gross profit in collection periods by applying the gross profit percentage on the sale to the amount of cash actually received. The cost recovery method defers all gross profit recognition until cash has been received equal to the cost of the item sold. These methods of recognizing revenue should only be used in situations where there is an unusually high degree of uncertainty regarding the ultimate cash collection on an installment sale.

4. In most situations, even though the right to return merchandise exists, revenues and expenses can be appropriately recognized at point of delivery. Based on past experience, a company usually can estimate the returns that will result for a given volume of sales. These estimates reduce both sales and cost of goods sold in anticipation of returns. Revenue cannot be recognized at the point of delivery unless the seller is able to make reliable estimates of future returns. Otherwise, revenue recognition is deferred beyond the delivery point.

5. The use of franchise arrangements has become increasingly popular. The fees to be paid by the franchisee to the franchisor usually are composed of: (1) the initial franchise fee and (2) continuing franchise fees. *SFAS 45* requires that the franchisor has substantially performed the services promised in the franchise agreement and that the collectibility of the initial franchise fee is reasonably assured before the fee can be recognized as revenue. The continuing franchise fees are recognized by the franchisor as revenue in the periods they are received, which correspond to the periods the services are performed by the franchisor.

6. Financial analysts use various techniques to transform financial information into forms more useful for analysis. Horizontal analysis and vertical analysis provide a useful way of analyzing year-to-year changes. Ratio analysis allows analysts to control for size differences over time and among firms while investigating important relationships among financial variables.

7. Activity and profitability ratios provide information about a company's profitability. Activity ratios include the receivables turnover ratio, the inventory turnover ratio, and the asset turnover ratio. Profitability ratios include the profit margin on sales, the return on assets, and the return on shareholders' equity.

Responsible for this → ✓

APPENDIX

4

INTERIM REPORTING

Interim reports are issued for periods of less than a year, typically as quarterly financial statements.

Financial statements covering periods of less than a year are called *interim reports.* Companies registered with the SEC, which include most public companies, must submit quarterly reports.[19] Though there is no requirement to do so, most also mail quarterly reports to their shareholders and typically include abbreviated, unaudited interim reports as supplemental information within their annual reports. For instance, Graphic 4A–1 shows the quarterly information disclosed in the 1995 annual report of Hershey Foods Corporation.

Interim reporting serves to enhance the timeliness of financial information.

For accounting information to be useful to decision makers, it must be available on a timely basis. One of the objectives of interim reporting is to enhance the timeliness of financial information. In addition, quarterly reports provide investors and creditors with additional insight on the seasonality of business operations that might otherwise get lost in annual reports.

The fundamental debate regarding interim reporting centers on the choice between the *discrete* and *integral part* approaches.

However, the downside to the benefits is the relative unreliability of interim reporting. With a shorter reporting period, questions associated with estimation and allocation are magnified. For example, certain expenses often benefit an entire year's operations and yet are incurred primarily within a single interim period. Similarly, should smaller companies use lower tax rates in the earlier quarters and higher rates in later quarters as higher tax brackets are reached? Another result of shorter reporting periods is the intensified effect of major events such as discontinued operations or extraordinary items. A second quarter casualty loss, for instance, that would reduce annual profits by 10% might reduce second quarter profits by 40% or more. Is it more realistic to allocate such a loss over the entire year? These and similar questions tend to hinge on the way we view an interim

---

[19]Quarterly reports are filed with the SEC on form 10-Q. Annual reports to the SEC are on form 10-K.

GRAPHIC   4A-1

Interim Data in Annual Report—Hershey Foods Corporation

Note 18: Quarterly Data (Unaudited)
Summary quarterly results were as follows:
(in thousands of dollars except per share amounts)

Year 1995	First	Second	Third	Fourth
Net sales	$867,446	$722,269	$981,101	$1,119,851
Gross profit	364,085	298,506	408,658	493,144
Net income	60,633	33,323	82,127	105,836[a]
Net income per share[b]	.70	.38	1.02	1.37

Year 1994	First	Second	Third	Fourth
Net sales	$883,890	$675,983	$966,511	$1,079,887
Gross profit	357,162	272,883	404,543	474,127
Net income	53,016	25,325	81,063	24,815[c]
Net income per share	.61	.29	.93	.29

[a]Net income for the fourth quarter and year 1995 included an after-tax credit of $2.0 million associated with adjustments to accrued restructuring reserves. Net income per share was similarly impacted.
[b]Quarterly income per share amounts for 1995 do not total to annual amounts due to the changes in weighted average shares outstanding during the year.
[c]Net income for the fourth quarter and year 1994 included an after-tax restructuring charge of $80.2 million. Net income per share was similarly impacted.

period in relation to the fiscal year. More specifically, should each interim period be viewed as a *discrete* reporting period or as an *integral part* of the annual period?

Reporting Revenues and Expenses

> With only a few exceptions, the same accounting principles applicable to annual reporting are used for interim reporting.

Existing practice and current reporting requirements for interim reporting generally follow the viewpoint that interim reports are an integral part of annual statements, although the discrete approach is applied to some items. Most revenues and expenses are recognized using the same accounting principles applicable to annual reporting. Some modifications are necessary to help cause interim statements to relate better to annual statements. This is most evident in the way costs and expenses are recognized. Most are recognized in interim periods as incurred. But when an expenditure clearly benefits more than just the period in which it is incurred, the expense should be allocated among the periods benefited on an allocation basis consistent with the company's annual allocation procedures. For example, annual repair expenses, property tax expense, and advertising expenses incurred in the first quarter that clearly benefit later quarters are assigned to each quarter through the use of accruals and deferrals. Costs and expenses subject to year-end adjustments, such as depreciation and bad debt expense, are estimated and allocated to interim periods in a systematic way. Similarly, income tax expense at each interim date should be based on estimates of the effective tax rate for the whole year. This would mean, for example, that if the estimated effective rate has changed since the previous interim period(s), the tax expense that period would be determined as the new rate times the cumulative pretax income to date, less the total tax expense reported in previous interim periods.

Reporting Unusual Items

> Discontinued operations and extraordinary items are reported entirely within the interim period in which they occur.

On the other hand, major events such as discontinued operations or extraordinary items should be reported separately in the interim period in which they occur. That is, these amounts should not be allocated among individual quarters within the fiscal year. The same is true for items that are unusual or infrequent but not both. Notice that treatment of these items is more consistent with the discrete view than the integral part view.

Earnings Per Share

> Quarterly EPS calculations follow the same procedures as annual calculations.

A second item that is treated in a manner consistent with the discrete view is earnings per share. EPS calculations for interim reports follow the same procedures as annual calculations that you will study in Chapter 20. The calculations are based on conditions actually existing during the particular interim period rather than on conditions estimated to exist at the end of the fiscal year.

Reporting Accounting Changes

The cumulative effect of changes in accounting principle are reflected in the first interim period.

Recall from Chapter 3 that when most accounting changes are adopted, the cumulative effect of the change on retained earnings must be determined and reported in earnings of the change period. For interim reporting, the cumulative effect should be reported in the *first* interim period of the fiscal year in which the change is made, even if the change actually is made in a later interim period. So, it is the cumulative effect on the income of previous years from using the new method rather than the previous method *as of the beginning of that fiscal year.*[20] Also, if the change occurs in an interim period other than the first, financial statement information for prechange interim periods are restated to reflect the new accounting method when those prior statements are presented again.[21]

Minimum Disclosures

Complete financial statements are not required for interim period reporting, but certain minimum disclosures are required as follows:[22]

- Sales, income taxes, extraordinary items, cumulative effect of accounting principle changes, and net income.
- Earnings per share.
- Seasonal revenues, costs, and expenses.
- Significant changes in estimates for income taxes.
- Discontinued operations, extraordinary items, and unusual or infrequent items.
- Contingencies.
- Changes in accounting principles or estimates.
- Significant changes in financial position.

When fourth quarter results are not separately reported, material fourth quarter events, including year-end adjustments, should be reported in disclosure notes to annual statements.

Questions for Review of Key Topics

Question 4–1 What are the criteria that must be satisfied before revenue can be recognized?

Question 4–2 Explain why, in most cases, revenue is recognized when the product is delivered rather than at the time the productive activity is completed.

Question 4–3 Distinguish between the percentage-of-completion and completed contract methods of accounting for long-term construction contracts with respect to income recognition. Under what circumstances should the completed contract method be used?

Question 4–4 Periodic billings to the customer are recorded as *billings on construction contract*. How is this account reported on the balance sheet?

Question 4–5 When is an estimated loss on a long-term construction contract recognized using the percentage-of-completion method? The completed contract method?

Question 4–6 Revenue recognition for most installment sales occurs at the point of product delivery. Under what circumstances would revenue recognition for installment sales be delayed beyond the delivery date?

Question 4–7 Distinguish between the installment sales method and the cost recovery method of accounting for certain installment sales.

Question 4–8 How is deferred gross profit resulting from the use of the installment sales method reported on the balance sheet?

Question 4–9 Briefly describe the guidelines provided by *SFAS 45* for the recognition of revenue by a franchisor for the initial franchise fee.

Question 4–10 Identify the three alternative methods used to recognize service revenue.

[20]Stated differently, the cumulative effect is the difference between the balance in retained earnings at the beginning of the period of the change and what that balance would have been if the new method had been applied all along.

[21]"Reporting Accounting Changes in Interim Financial Statements," *Statement of Financial Accounting Standards No. 3* (Stamford, Conn.: FASB, 1974), par. 9-10.

[22]"Interim Financial Reporting," *Accounting Principles Board Opinion No. 28* (New York: AICPA, 1973).

Question	4–11	Although ratios provide more meaningful information than absolute numbers alone, they are most useful when compared to some standard. What are some common standards of comparison for ratio analysis?
Question	4–12	Show the calculation of the following activity ratios: (1) the receivables turnover ratio, (2) the inventory turnover ratio, and (3) the asset turnover ratio. What information about a company do these ratios offer?
Question	4–13	Show the calculation of the following profitability ratios: (1) the profit margin on sales, (2) the return on assets, and (3) the return on shareholders' equity. What information about a company do these ratios offer?
Question 4–14 [based on Appendix 4]		Interim reports are issued for periods of less than a year, typically as quarterly financial statements. Should these interim periods be viewed as separate periods or integral parts of the annual period?

Exercises

Exercise 4–1
Construction accounting; percentage-of-completion and completed contract methods

The Gagliano Construction Company contracted to build an office building for $2,000,000. Construction began in 1997 and was completed in 1998. Data relating to the contract are summarized below:

	1997	1998
Costs incurred during the year	$ 300,000	$1,575,000
Estimated costs to complete as of 12/31	1,200,000	—
Billings during the year	360,000	1,640,000
Cash collections during the year	250,000	1,750,000

[handwritten: GP= 500,000 Total cost=1,500,000   GP= 125,000 Total cost=1,875,000]

Required:
1. Compute the amount of gross profit or loss to be recognized in 1997 and 1998 using the percentage-of-completion method.
2. Compute the amount of gross profit or loss to be recognized in 1997 and 1998 using the completed contract method.
3. Prepare a partial balance sheet to show how the information related to this contract would be presented at the end of 1997 using the percentage-of completion method.
4. Prepare a partial balance sheet to show how the information related to this contract would be presented at the end of 1997 using the completed contract method.

Exercise 4–2
Percentage-of-completion method; loss projected on entire project

On February 1, 1997, Arrow Construction Company entered into a three-year construction contract to build a bridge for a price of $8,000,000. During 1997, costs of $2,000,000 were incurred with estimated costs of $4,000,000 yet to be incurred. Billings of $2,500,000 were sent and cash collected was $2,250,000.

In 1998, costs incurred were $2,500,000 with remaining costs estimated to be $3,600,000. 1998 billings were $2,750,000 and $2,475,000 cash was collected. The project was completed in 1999 after additional costs of $3,800,000 were incurred. The company's fiscal year-end is December 31. Arrow uses the percentage-of-completion method.

Required:
1. Calculate the amount of gross profit or loss to be recognized in each of the three years.
2. Prepare journal entries for 1997 and 1998 to record the transactions described (credit various accounts for construction costs incurred).
3. Prepare a partial balance sheet to show the presentation of the project as of December 31, 1997 and 1998.

Exercise 4–3
Completed contract method; loss projected on entire project

[This is a variation of the previous exercise focusing on the completed contract method.]

On February 1, 1997, Arrow Construction Company entered into a three-year construction contract to build a bridge for a price of $8,000,000. During 1997, costs of $2,000,000 were incurred with estimated costs of $4,000,000 yet to be incurred. Billings of $2,500,000 were sent and cash collected was $2,250,000.

In 1998, costs incurred were $2,500,000 with remaining costs estimated to be $3,600,000. 1998 billings were $2,750,000 and $2,475,000 cash was collected. The project was completed in 1999 after additional costs of $3,800,000 were incurred. The company's fiscal year-end is December 31. Arrow uses the *completed contract* method.

Required:
1. Calculate the amount of gross profit or loss to be recognized in each of the three years.
2. Prepare journal entries for 1997 and 1998 to record the transactions described (credit various accounts for construction costs incurred).
3. Prepare a partial balance sheet to show the presentation of the project as of December 31, 1997 and 1998.

Exercise 4–4

Income (loss) recognition; percentage-of-completion and completed contract methods compared

The Brady Construction Company contracted to build an apartment complex for a price of $5,000,000. Construction began in 1997 and was completed in 1999. The following are a number of independent situations, lettered A through F, involving differing costs for the project. All costs are stated in thousands of dollars.

	Costs Incurred during Year			Estimated Costs to Complete - as of the End of the Year		
Situation	1997	1998	1999	1997	1998	1999
1	1,500	2,100	900	3,000	900	—
2	1,500	900	2,400	3,000	2,400	—
3	1,500	2,100	1,600	3,000	1,500	—
4	500	3,000	1,000	3,500	875	—
5	500	3,000	1,300	3,500	1,500	—
6	500	3,000	1,800	4,600	1,700	—

Required:

Copy and complete the following table.

	Gross Profit (Loss) Recognized					
	Percentage-of-Completion			Completed Contract		
Situation	1997	1998	1999	1997	1998	1999
1						
2						
3						
4						
5						
6						

Exercise 4–5

Percentage-of-completion method; solve for unknowns

In 1997, Long Construction Corporation began construction work under a three-year contract. The contract price is $1,600,000. Long uses the percentage-of-completion method for financial reporting purposes. The financial statement presentation relating to this contract at December 31, 1997, is as follows:

Balance Sheet

Accounts receivable (from construction progress billings)		$30,000
Construction in progress	$100,000	
Less: Billings on construction contract	(94,000)	
Cost of uncompleted contracts in excess of billings		6,000

Income Statement

Income (before tax) on the contract recognized in 1997	$20,000

Required:

1. What was the cost of construction actually incurred in 1997?
2. How much cash was collected in 1997 on this contract?
3. What was the estimated cost to complete as of the end of 1997?
4. What was the estimated percentage of completion used to calculate income in 1997?

(AICPA adapted)

Exercise 4–6

Installment sales method

The Charter Corporation, which began business in 1997, appropriately uses the installment sales method of accounting for its installment sales. The following data were obtained for sales made during 1997 and 1998:

	1997	1998
Installment sales	$360,000	$350,000
Cost of installment sales	216,000	245,000
Cash collections on installment sales during:		
1997	150,000	100,000
1998	—	120,000

Required:

1. How much gross profit should be recognized in 1997 and 1998 from installment sales?
2. What should be the balance in the deferred gross profit account at the end of 1997 and 1998?

Exercise 4–7

Installment sales method; journal entries

[This is a variation of the previous exercise focusing on journal entries.]

The Charter Corporation, which began business in 1997, appropriately uses the installment sales method of accounting for its installment sales. The following data were obtained for sales made during 1997 and 1998:

[handwritten: On exam]

	1997	1998
Installment sales	$360,000	$350,000
Cost of installment sales	216,000	245,000
Cash collections on installment sales during:		
1997	150,000	100,000
1998	—	120,000

[handwritten annotations: GP=40% $360,000 > $144,000 ; GP=30% 1998 $350,000 > 105,000]

Required:
Prepare summary journal entries for 1997 and 1998 to account for the installment sales and cash collections. The company uses the perpetual inventory system.

Exercise 4–8
Installment sales; alternative recognition methods

On July 1, 1997, the Foster Company sold inventory to the Slate Corporation for $300,000. Terms of the sale called for a down payment of $75,000 and three annual installments of $75,000 due on each July 1, beginning July 1, 1998. Each installment also will include interest on the unpaid balance applying an appropriate interest rate. The inventory cost Foster $120,000. The company uses the perpetual inventory system.

Required:
1. Compute the amount of gross profit to be recognized from the installment sale in 1997, 1998, 1999, and 2000 using point of delivery revenue recognition. Ignore interest charges.
2. Repeat requirement 1 applying the installment sales method.
3. Repeat requirement 1 applying the cost recovery method.

Exercise 4–9
Journal entries; point of delivery, installment sales, and cost recovery methods

[This is a variation of the previous exercise focusing on journal entries.]
On July 1, 1997, the Foster Company sold inventory to the Slate Corporation for $300,000. Terms of the sale called for a down payment of $75,000 and three annual installments of $75,000 due on each July 1, beginning July 1, 1998. Each installment also will include interest on the unpaid balance applying an appropriate interest rate. The inventory cost Foster $120,000. The company uses the perpetual inventory system.

Required:
1. Prepare the necessary journal entries for 1997 and 1998 using point of delivery revenue recognition. Ignore interest charges.
2. Repeat requirement 1 applying the installment sales method.
3. Repeat requirement 1 applying the cost recovery method.

Exercise 4–10
Installment sales and cost recovery methods; solve for unknowns

The Wolf Computer Company began operations in 1997. The company allows customers to pay in installments for many of its products. Installment sales for 1997 were $1,000,000. If revenue is recognized at the point of delivery, $600,000 in gross profit would be recognized in 1997. If the company instead uses the cost recovery method, $100,000 in gross profit would be recognized in 1997.

Required:
1. What was the amount of cash collected on installment sales in 1997?
2. What amount of gross profit would be recognized if the company uses the installment sales method?

Exercise 4–11
Real estate sales; gain recognition

On April 1, 1997, the Apex Corporation sold a parcel of undeveloped land to the Applegate Construction Company for $2,400,000. The book value of the land on Apex's books was $600,000. Terms of the sale required a down payment of $120,000 and 19 annual payments of $120,000 plus interest at an appropriate interest rate due on each April 1 beginning in 1998. Apex has no significant obligations to perform services after the sale.

Required:
1. Prepare the necessary journal entries for Apex to record the sale, receipt of the down payment, and receipt of the first installment assuming that Apex is able to make a reliable estimate of possible uncollectible amounts (that is, point of delivery profit recognition is used). Ignore interest charges.
2. Repeat requirement 1 assuming that Apex cannot make a reliable estimate of possible uncollectible amounts and decides to use the installment sales method for profit recognition.

Exercise 4–12
Franchise sales; revenue recognition

[handwritten: On exam]

On October 1, 1997, the Submarine Sandwich Company entered into a franchise agreement with an individual. In exchange for an initial franchise fee of $200,000, Submarine will provide initial services to the franchisee to include assistance in design and construction of the building, help in training employees, help in obtaining financing, and management advice over the first five years of the 10-year franchise agreement.

10% of the initial franchise fee is payable on October 1, 1997, with the remaining $180,000 payable in nine equal annual installments beginning on October 1, 1998. These installments will include interest at an appropriate rate. The franchise opened for business on January 15, 1998.

Required:

Assume that the initial services to be performed by Submarine Sandwich subsequent to October 1, 1997, are substantial and that collectibility of the installment receivable is reasonably certain. Substantial performance of the initial services is deemed to have occurred when the franchise opened. Prepare the necessary journal entries for the following dates (ignoring interest charges):

1. October 1, 1997
2. January 15, 1998

Exercise 4–13
Multiple choice; revenue recognition

The following questions dealing with revenue recognition are adapted from questions that appeared on recent CPA examinations. Determine the response that best completes the statements or questions.

1. Drew Co. produces expensive equipment for sale on installment contracts. When there is doubt about eventual collectibility, the income recognition method *least* likely to overstate income is
   a. At the time the equipment is completed.
   b. The installment method.
   c. The cost recovery method.
   d. At the time of delivery.

2. Hill Company began operations on January 1, 1997, and appropriately uses the installment method of accounting. Data available for 1997 are as follows:

Installment accounts receivable	$500,000
Installment sales	900,000
Cost of goods sold, as a percentage of sales	60%

   Using the installment method, Hill's realized gross profit for 1997 would be
   a. $360,000
   b. $240,000
   c. $200,000
   d. $160,000

   Questions 3 and 4 are based on the following data pertaining to Pell Co.'s construction jobs, which commenced during 1997:

	Project 1	Project 2
Contract price	$420,000	$300,000
Costs incurred during 1997	240,000	280,000
Estimated costs to complete	120,000	40,000
Billed to customers during 1997	150,000	270,000
Received from customers during 1997	90,000	250,000

3. If Pell used the completed contract method, what amount of gross profit (loss) would Pell report in its 1997 income statement?
   a. $(20,000)
   b. $0
   c. $340,000
   d. $420,000

4. If Pell used the percentage-of-completion method, what amount of gross profit (loss) would Pell report in its 1997 income statement?
   a. $(20,000)
   b. $20,000
   c. $22,500
   d. $40,000

Exercise 4–14
Concepts; terminology

Listed below are several terms and phrases associated with revenue recognition and profitability analysis. Pair each item from List A (by letter) with the item from List B that is most appropriately associated with it.

List A	List B
____ 1. Inventory turnover	a. Net income divided by net sales.
____ 2. Return on assets	b. Defers recognition until cash collected equals cost.
____ 3. Return on shareholders' equity	c. Defers recognition until project is complete.
____ 4. Profit margin on sales	d. Net income divided by assets.
____ 5. Cost recovery method	e. Contra account to construction in progress.
____ 6. Percentage-of-completion method	f. Net income divided by shareholders' equity.
____ 7. Completed contract method	g. Cost of goods sold divided by inventory.
____ 8. Asset turnover	h. Recognition is in proportion to work completed.
____ 9. Receivables turnover	i. Recognition is in proportion to cash received.

_____ 10. Right of return
_____ 11. Billings on construction contract
_____ 12. Installment sales method

j. Net sales divided by assets.
k. Net sales divided by accounts receivable.
l. Could cause the deferral of revenue recognition beyond delivery point.

Exercise 4–15
Inventory turnover; calculation and evaluation

The following is a portion of the condensed income statement for Rowan, Inc., a manufacturer of plastic containers:

Net sales		$2,460,000
Less: Cost of goods sold:		
Inventory, January 1	$ 630,000	
Net purchases	1,800,000	
Inventory, December 31	(690,000)	1,740,000
Gross profit		$ 720,000

Required:
1. Determine Rowan's inventory turnover.
2. What information does this ratio provide?

Exercise 4–16
Evaluating efficiency of asset management

The 1997 income statement of Anderson Medical Supply Company reported net sales of $8 million, cost of goods sold of $4.8 million, and net income of $800,000. The following table shows the company's comparative balance sheets for 1997 and 1996:

	($ in 000s)	
	1997	1996
Assets:		
Cash	$ 300	$ 380
Accounts receivable	700	500
Inventory	900	700
Property, plant, and equipment (net)	2,400	2,120
Total assets	$4,300	$3,700
Liabilities and Shareholders' Equity:		
Current liabilities	$ 960	$ 830
Bonds payable	1,200	1,200
Paid-in capital	1,000	1,000
Retained earnings	1,140	670
Total liabilities and shareholders equity	$4,300	$3,700

Some industry averages for Anderson's line of business are:

Inventory turnover	5 times
Average collection period	25 days
Asset turnover	1.8 times

Required:
Assess Anderson's asset management relative to its industry.

Exercise 4–17
Profitability ratios

The following condensed information was reported by Peabody Toys, Inc., for 1997 and 1996:

	($ in 000s)	
	1997	1996
Income statement information:		
Net sales	$5,400	$4,200
Net income	150	124
Balance sheet information:		
Current assets	800	750
Property, plant, and equipment (net)	1,100	950
Total assets	$1,900	$1,700
Current liabilities	$ 600	$ 450
Long-term liabilities	750	750
Paid-in capital	400	400
Retained earnings	150	100
Liabilities and shareholders' equity	$1,900	$1,700

Required:
1. Determine the following ratios for 1997:
   a. Profit margin on sales
   b. Return on assets

c. Return on shareholders' equity
2. Determine the amount of dividends paid to shareholders during 1997.

Exercise 4–18
[based on Appendix 4]
Interim financial statements;
income tax expense

Joplin Laminating Corporation reported income before income taxes during the first three quarters and management's estimates of the annual effective tax rate at the end of each quarter as shown below:

	Quarter		
	First	**Second**	**Third**
Income before income taxes	$50,000	$40,000	$100,000
Estimated annual effective tax rate	34%	30%	36%

Required:
Determine the income tax expense to be reported on the income statement in each of the three quarterly reports.

Exercise 4–19
[based on Appendix 4]
Interim reporting; recognizing
expenses

Security-Rand Corporation determines executive incentive compensation at the end of its fiscal year. At the end of the first quarter, management estimated that the amount will be $300 million. Depreciation expense for the year is expected to be $60 million. Also during the quarter, the company realized a gain of $23 million from selling two of its manufacturing plants.

Required:
What amounts for these items should be reported in the first quarter's income statement?

Exercise 4–20
[based on Appendix 4]
Interim financial statements;
reporting expenses

Shields Company is preparing its interim report for the second quarter ending June 30. The following payments were made during the first two quarters:

Expenditure	Date	Amount
Annual advertising	January	$800,000
Property tax for the fiscal year	February	350,000
Annual equipment repairs	March	260,000
Extraordinary casualty loss	April	185,000
Research and development	May	96,000

Required:
For each expenditure indicate the amount that would be reported in the quarterly income statements for the periods ending March 31, June 30, September 30, and December 31.

Problems

Problem 4–1
Income statement
presentation; installment sales
method (Chapters 3 and 4)

The Reagan Corporation computed income from continuing operations before income taxes of $4,200,000 for 1997. The following material items have not yet been considered in the computation of income:

1. The company sold equipment and recognized a gain of $50,000. The equipment had been used in the manufacturing process and was replaced by new equipment.
2. In December, the company received a settlement of $1,000,000 for a lawsuit it had filed based on antitrust violations of a competitor. The settlement was considered to be an unusual and infrequent event.
3. Inventory costing $400,000 was written off as obsolete. Material losses of this type were incurred twice in the last eight years.
4. On October 31, 1997, the company decided to stop selling its product to consumers. It will continue to sell the product but only to wholesalers. Retail operations prior to October 31 resulted in a loss of $100,000. The sale of assets of the retail business was completed on December 20, 1997, at a loss of $60,000. Retail operations from October 31 through December 20 resulted in no income or loss.
5. It was discovered that depreciation expense on the office building of $50,000 per year was not recorded in either 1996 or 1997.

In addition, you learn that *included* in revenues is $400,000 from installment sales made during the year. The cost of these sales is $240,000. At year-end, $100,000 in cash had been collected on the related installment receivables. Because of considerable uncertainty regarding the collectibility of receivables from these sales, the company's accountant should have used the installment sales method to recognize revenue and gross profit on these sales.

Also, the company's income tax rate is 40% and there were 1 million shares of common stock outstanding throughout the year.

Required:

Prepare an income statement for 1997 beginning with income from continuing operations before income taxes. Include appropriate EPS disclosures.

Problem 4–2
Percentage-of-completion method

In 1997, the Westgate Construction Company entered into a contract to construct a road for Santa Clara County for $10,000,000. The road was completed in 1999. Information related to the contract is as follows:

	1997	1998	1999
Costs incurred during the year	$2,400,000	$3,600,000	$2,200,000
Estimated costs to complete as of year-end	5,600,000	2,000,000	—
Billings during the year	2,000,000	4,000,000	4,000,000
Cash collections during the year	1,800,000	3,600,000	4,600,000

[handwritten: Total cost = 8,000,000   8,000,000   8,200,000]

Westgate uses the percentage-of-completion method of accounting for long-term construction contracts.

[handwritten: GP = 2,000,000   2,000,000   1,800,000]

Required:

1. Calculate the amount of gross profit to be recognized in each of the three years.
2. Prepare all necessary journal entries for each of the years (credit various accounts for construction costs incurred).
3. Prepare a partial balance sheet for 1997 and 1998 showing any items related to the contract.
4. Calculate the amount of gross profit to be recognized in each of the three years assuming the following costs incurred and costs to complete information:

[handwritten: see pg. 150]

	1997	1998	1999
Costs incurred during the year	$2,400,000	$3,800,000	$3,200,000
Estimated costs to complete as of year-end	5,600,000	3,100,000	—

5. Calculate the amount of gross profit to be recognized in each of the three years assuming the following costs incurred and costs to complete information:

	1997	1998	1999
Costs incurred during the year	$2,400,000	$3,800,000	$3,900,000
Estimated costs to complete as of year-end	5,600,000	4,100,000	—

Problem 4–3
Completed contract method

[This is a variation of the previous problem modified to focus on the completed contract method.]

Required:

Complete the requirements of Problem 4–2 assuming that Westgate Construction uses the completed contract method.

Problem 4–4
Construction accounting; loss projected on entire project

Curtiss Construction Company, Inc., entered into a fixed-price contract with Axelrod Associates on July 1, 1997, to construct a four-story office building. At that time, Curtiss estimated that it would take between two and three years to complete the project. The total contract price for construction of the building is $4,000,000. Curtiss appropriately accounts for this contract under the completed contract method in its financial statements. The building was completed on December 31, 1999. Estimated percentage of completion, *accumulated* contract costs incurred, estimated costs to complete the contract, and *accumulated* billings to Axelrod under the contract were as follows:

	At 12-31-97	At 12-31-98	At 12-31-99
Percentage of completion	10%	60%	100%
Costs incurred to date	$ 350,000	$2,500,000	$4,250,000
Estimated costs to complete	3,150,000	1,700,000	—
Billings to Axelrod	720,000	2,170,000	3,600,000

Required:

1. Prepare schedules to compute gross profit or loss to be recognized as a result of this contract for each of the three years.
2. Assuming Curtiss uses the percentage-of-completion method of accounting for long-term construction contracts, compute gross profit or loss to be recognized in each of the three years.
3. Assuming the percentage-of-completion method, compute the amount to be shown on the balance sheet at the end of 1997 and 1998 as either cost in excess of billings or billings in excess of costs

(AICPA adapted)

Problem 4–5
Installment sales and cost recovery methods

The Ajax Company appropriately accounts for certain sales using the installment sales method. The perpetual inventory system is used. Information related to installment sales for 1997 and 1998 is as follows:

[handwritten left margin: go thru all the entries done in class like done on the board]

	1997	1998
Sales	$300,000	$400,000
Cost of sales	180,000	280,000
Customer collections on:		
1997 sales	120,000	100,000
1998 sales		150,000

Required:

1. Calculate the amount of gross profit that would be recognized each year from installment sales.
2. Prepare all necessary journal entries for each year.
3. Repeat requirements 1 and 2 assuming that Ajax uses the cost recovery method to account for its installment sales.

Problem 4–6

Installment sales; alternative recognition methods

On August 31, 1997, the Silva Company sold merchandise to the Bendix Corporation for $500,000. Terms of the sale called for a down payment of $100,000 and four annual installments of $100,000 due on each August 31, beginning August 31, 1998. Each installment also will include interest on the unpaid balance applying an appropriate interest rate. The book value of the merchandise on Silva's books on the date of sale was $300,000. The perpetual inventory system is used. The company's fiscal year end is December 31.

Required:

1. Prepare a table showing the amount of gross profit to be recognized in each of the five years of the installment sale applying each of the following methods:
   a. Point of delivery revenue recognition.
   b. Installment sales method.
   c. Cost recovery method.
2. Prepare journal entries for each of the five years applying the three revenue recognition methods listed in requirement 1. Ignore interest charges.
3. Prepare a partial balance sheet as of the end of 1997 and 1998 listing the items related to the installment sale applying each of the three methods listed in requirement 1.

Problem 4–7

Franchise sales

The Olive Branch Restaurant Corporation sells franchises throughout the western states. On January 30, 1997, the company entered into the following franchise agreement with Jim and Tammy Masters:

1. The initial franchise fee is $1.2 million. $200,000 is payable immediately and the remainder is due in 10, $100,000 installments plus 10% interest on the unpaid balance each January 30, beginning January 30, 1998. The 10% interest rate is an appropriate market rate.
2. In addition to allowing the franchisee to use the franchise name for the 10-year term of the agreement, in exchange for the initial fee Olive Branch agrees to assist the franchisee in selecting a location, obtaining financing, designing and constructing the restaurant building, and training employees.
3. All of the initial down payment of $200,000 is to be refunded by Olive Branch and the remaining obligation canceled if, for any reason, the franchisee fails to open the franchise.
4. In addition to the initial franchise fee, the franchisee is required to pay a monthly fee of 3% of franchise sales for advertising, promotion, menu planning, and other continuing services to be provided by Olive Branch over the life of the agreement. This fee is payable on the 10th of the following month.

Substantial performance of the initial services provided by Olive Branch, which are significant, is deemed to have occurred when the franchise opened on September 1, 1997. Franchise sales for the month of September 1997, were $40,000.

Required:

1. Assuming that collectibility of the installment receivable is reasonably certain, prepare the necessary journal entries for Olive Branch on the following dates (ignore interest charges on the installment receivable and the costs of providing franchise services):
   a. January 30, 1997
   b. September 1, 1997
   c. September 30, 1997
   d. January 30, 1998
2. Assume that significant uncertainty exists as to the collection of the installment receivable and that Olive Branch elects to recognize initial franchise fee revenue using the installment method. Prepare the necessary journal entries for the dates listed in requirement 1 (ignore interest charges on the installment receivable and the costs of providing franchise services).

Problem 4–8
Calculating activity and
profitability ratios

Financial statements for Askew Industries for 1997 are shown below:

1997 Income Statement

	($ in 000s)
Sales	$ 9,000
Cost of goods sold	(6,300)
Gross profit	2,700
Operating expenses	(2,000)
Interest expense	(200)
Tax expense	(200)
Net income	$ 300

Comparative Balance Sheets

	December 31	
	1997	1996
Assets:		
Cash	$ 600	$ 500
Accounts receivable	600	400
Inventory	800	600
Property, plant, and equipment (net)	2,000	2,100
	$4,000	$3,600
Liabilities and Shareholders' Equity:		
Current liabilities	$1,100	$ 850
Bonds payable	1,400	1,400
Paid-in capital	600	600
Retained earnings	900	750
	$4,000	$3,600

Required:

Calculate the following ratios for 1997.
1. Inventory turnover ratio
2. Average days in inventory
3. Receivables turnover ratio
4. Average collection period
5. Asset turnover ratio
6. Profit margin on sales
7. Return on assets
8. Return on shareholders' equity

Problem 4–9
Use of ratios to compare two
companies in the same
industry

Presented below are condensed financial statements adapted from those of two actual companies competing in the pharmaceutical industry—Eli Lilly and Company and Merck & Co. ($ in millions, except per share amounts.)

Required:

Evaluate and compare the two companies by responding to the following questions.

Note: Because two-year comparative statements are not provided, you should use year-end balances in place of average balances as appropriate.

1. Which of the two companies appears more efficient in collecting its accounts receivable and managing its inventory?
2. Which of the two firms had greater earnings relative to resources available?
3. Have the two companies achieved their respective rates of return on assets with similar combinations of profit margin and turnover?
4. From the perspective of a common shareholder, which of the two firms provided a greater rate of return?

Balance Sheets

	Eli Lilly	Merck
Assets:		
Cash	$ 539.6	$ 829.4
Short-term investments	447.5	712.9
Accounts receivable (net)	950.1	2,094.3
Inventories	1,103.0	1,641.7
Other current assets	656.9	456.3
Current assets	3,697.1	5,734.6
Property, plant, and equipment (net)	4,200.2	4,894.6
Intangibles and other assets	1,726.3	9,298.3
Total assets	$9,623.6	$19,927.5

Liabilities and Shareholders' Equity:

Accounts payable	$ 329.6	$ 2,378.3
Short-term notes	524.8	1,736.0
Other current liabilities	2,073.6	1,781.4
Current liabilities	2,928.0	5,895.7
Long-term debt	835.2	1,120.8
Other long-term liabilities	1,291.6	2,889.3
Total liabilities	5,054.8	9,905.8
Common stock (par and additional paid-in capital)	477.6	4,576.5
Retained earnings	4,094.6	9,393.2
Less: treasury stock	(3.4)	(3,948.0)
Total shareholders' equity	4,568.8	10,021.7
Total liabilities and shareholders' equity	$9,623.6	$19,927.5

Income Statements

Net sales	$6,452.4	$10,498.2
Cost of goods sold	(1,959.0)	(2,497.6)
Gross profit	4,493.4	8,000.6
Operating expenses	(3,840.8)	(4,861.7)
Other income (expense) - net	49.3	(36.2)
Income before taxes	701.9	3,102.7
Tax expense	(210.8)	(936.5)
Net income	$ 491.1	$ 2,166.2
Net income per share	$ 1.67	$ 1.87

Problem 4–10
[based on Appendix 4]
Interim financial reporting

Branson Electronics Company is a small, publicly traded company preparing its first quarter interim report to be mailed to shareholders. The following information for the quarter has been compiled:

Revenues		$180,000
Cost of goods sold		35,000
Operating expenses:		
Fixed	$59,000	
Variable	48,000	117,000

Fixed operating expenses include payments of $50,000 to an advertising firm to promote the firm through various media throughout the year. The income tax rate for the firm's level of operations in the first quarter is 30%, but management estimates the effective rate for the entire year will be 36%.

Required:
Prepare the income statement to be included in Branson's first quarter interim report.

Cases

Discussion Case 4–1
Revenue recognition

Revenue earned by a business enterprise is recognized for accounting purposes at different times, according to the circumstances. In some situations, revenue is recognized approximately as it is earned in the economic sense. In other situations revenue is recognized at point of delivery.

Required:
1. Explain and justify why revenue often is recognized as earned at point of delivery.
2. Explain in what situations it would be useful to recognize revenue as the productive activity takes place.
3. At what times, other than those included in (1) and (2) above, may it be appropriate to recognize revenue?

Critical Thought Case 4–2
Revenue recognition; trade-ins

The Apex Computer Company manufactures and sells large, mainframe computers. The computers range in price from $1 to $3 million and gross profit averages 40% of sales price. The company has a liberal trade-in policy. Customers are allowed to trade in their computers for a new generation machine anytime within three years of sale. The trade-in allowance granted will vary depending on the number of years between original sale and trade-in. However, in all cases, the allowance is expected to be approximately 20% higher than the prevailing market price of the computer.

As an example, in 1997 a customer who purchased a computer in 1995 for $2 million (the computer cost Apex $1,200,000 to manufacture) decided to trade it in for a new computer. The sales price of the new computer was $2.5 million and a trade-in allowance of $600,000 was granted on the old machine. As a result of the trade-in allowance, the customer had to pay only $1.9 million ($2.5 million less $600,000) for the new computer. The old computer taken back by Apex had a resale value of $480,000. The new computer cost

$1.5 million to manufacture. The company accounted for the trade-in by recognizing revenue of $2,380,000 ($1.9 million received in cash + $480,000 value of old computer).

Required:

Does the company's revenue recognition policy for trade-ins seem appropriate? If not, describe the problem created by the liberal trade-in policy.

Group Interaction Case 4–3
Revenue recognition

Jerry's Ice Cream Parlor is considering a marketing plan to increase sales of ice cream cones. The plan will give customers a free ice cream cone if they buy 10 ice cream cones at regular prices. Customers will be issued a card that will be punched each time an ice cream cone is purchased. After 10 punches, the card can be turned in for a free cone.

Jerry Donovan, the company's owner, is not sure how the new plan will affect accounting procedures. He realizes that the company will be incurring costs each time a free ice cream cone is awarded, but there will be no corresponding revenue or cash inflow.

The focus of this case is the matching of revenues and expenses related to the free ice cream cones that will be awarded if the new plan is adopted. Your instructor will divide the class into from two to six groups depending on the size of the class. The mission of your group is to reach consensus on the appropriate accounting treatment for the new plan.

Required:

1. Each group member should deliberate the situation independently and draft a tentative argument prior to the class session for which the case is assigned.
2. In class, each group will meet for 10–15 minutes in different areas of the classroom. During that meeting, group members will take turns sharing their suggestions for the purpose of arriving at a single group treatment.
3. After the allotted time, a spokesperson for each group (selected during the group meetings) will share the group's solution with the class. The goal of the class is to incorporate the views of each group into a consensus approach to the situation.

Research Case 4–4
Revenue recognition

A recent article in *Business Week* entitled "Numbers Game at Bausch & Lomb?" questions the company's method of recognizing revenue resulting from a 1993 change in sales strategy. The article considers the possibility that the company ". . . may have used dubious methods to inflate yearend sales."

Required:

1. In your library or from some other source, locate the indicated article in *Business Week,* December 19, 1994.
2. Describe the change in sales strategy in question and the revenue recognition controversy it created.
3. What alternative method might Bausch & Lomb have used to recognize revenue from the controversial sales?

Ethics Case 4–5
Revenue recognition

The Horizon Corporation manufactures personal computers. The company began operations in 1990 and reported profits for the years 1992 through 1995. Due primarily to increased competition and price slashing in the industry, 1996's income statement reported a loss of $20 million. Just before the end of the 1997 fiscal year, a memo from the company's chief financial officer to Jim Fielding, the company controller, included the following comments:

If we don't do something about the large amount of unsold computers already manufactured, our auditors will require us to write them off. The resulting loss for 1997 will cause a violation of our debt covenants and force the company into bankruptcy. I suggest that you ship half of our inventory to J.B. Sales, Inc., in Oklahoma City. I know the company's president and he will accept the merchandise and acknowledge the shipment as a purchase. We can record the sale in 1997 which will boost profits to an acceptable level. Then J.B. Sales will simply return the merchandise in 1998 after the financial statements have been issued.

Required:

Discuss the ethical dilemma faced by Jim Fielding.

Discussion Case 4–6
Accounting for long-term construction contracts

At December 31, 1997, Roko Co. has two fixed price construction contracts in progress. Both contracts have monthly billings supported by certified surveys of work completed. The contracts are:

The Ski Park contract, begun in 1996, is 80% complete, is progressing according to bid estimates, and is expected to be profitable.

The Nassu Village contract, a project to construct 100 condominium units, was begun in 1997. Thirty-five units have been completed. Work on the remaining units is delayed by conflicting recommendations on how to overcome unexpected subsoil problems. While the total cost of the project is uncertain, a loss is not anticipated.

Required:
1. Identify the alternatives available to account for long-term construction contracts and specify the criteria used to determine which method is applicable to a given contract.
2. Identify the appropriate accounting method for each of Roko's two contracts and describe each contract's effect on income for 1997.
3. Indicate how the accounts related to the Ski Park contract should be reported on the balance sheet at December 31, 1997.

(AICPA adapted)

Discussion Case 4–7
Revenue recognition; long-term construction contracts

Two accounting students were discussing the alternative methods of accounting for long-term construction contracts. The discussion focused on which method was most like the typical revenue recognition method of recognizing revenue at point of product delivery. Bill argued that the completed contract method was preferable because it was analogous to recognizing revenue at the point of delivery. John disagreed and supported the percentage-of-completion method, stating that it was analogous to accruing revenue during the earnings process, that is, as the work was performed.

Required:
Discuss the arguments made by both students. Which argument do you support? Why?

Writing Case 4–8
Percentage-of-completion and completed contract methods

Willingham Construction is in the business of building high-priced, custom, single-family homes. The company, headquartered in Anaheim, California, operates throughout the Southern California area. The construction period for the average home built by Willingham is six months, although some homes have taken as long as nine months.

You have just been hired by Willingham as the assistant controller and one of your first tasks is to evaluate the company's revenue recognition policy. The company presently uses the completed contract method for all of its projects and management is now considering a switch to the percentage-of-completion method.

Required:
Write a 1 to 2 page memo to Virginia Reynolds, company controller, describing the differences between the percentage-of-completion and completed contract methods. Be sure to include references to GAAP as they pertain to the choice of method. Do not address the differential effects on income taxes nor the effect on the financial statements of switching between methods.

International Case 4–9
Comparison of revenue recognition in Sweden and the United States

Electrolux, headquartered in Sweden, is the European leader in food-service equipment and the second largest producer in the world. The revenue recognition disclosure, included in a recent financial statement, is reproduced below.

Other accounting and valuation principles (in part)

Revenue recognition

Sales of products and services are recorded as of the date of shipment. Sales include the sales value less VAT (Value-Added Tax), individual sales taxes, returns and trade discounts.

In most cases, sales of projects are not reported as operating income until the project has been fully invoiced. In certain exceptional cases referring to particularly large projects extending over several accounting years, revenue is recognized while the project is in progress, on condition that revenue can be computed for the part of the project that has been completed and that this contributes to a more accurate timing of Group income and expense.

Required:
On the basis of the information the disclosures provide, compare revenue recognition in Sweden with that in the United States.

Discussion Case 4–10
Revenue recognition; installment sale

On October 1, 1997, the Marshall Company sold a large piece of machinery to the Hammond Construction Company for $80,000. The cost of the machine was $40,000. Hammond made a down payment of $10,000 and agreed to pay the remaining balance in seven equal monthly installments of $10,000, plus interest at 12% on the unpaid balance, beginning November 1.

Required:
1. Identify three alternative methods for recognizing revenue and costs for the situation described and compute the amount of gross profit that would be recognized in 1997 using each method.

2.   Discuss the circumstances under which each of the three methods would be used.

Real World Case 4–11
Revenue recognition; right of return

The revenue recognition disclosure note for Advanced Micro Devices, Inc. appears below.

1. Accounting Policies (in part)

Deferred Income on Shipments to Distributors.

A portion of sales is made to distributors under terms allowing certain rights of return and price protection on unsold merchandise held by the distributors. These agreements can be canceled by either party upon written notice, at which time the company generally repurchases unsold inventory. Accordingly, recognition of sales to distributors and related gross profits are deferred until the merchandise is resold by the distributors.

The note indicates that Advanced Micro Devices defers the recognition of revenue on certain sales until the merchandise is sold by distributors.

Required:
Discuss the rationale for using this method.

The following Robert M. Trueblood cases are recommended for use with this chapter. The cases provide an excellent opportunity for class discussion, group projects, and writing assignments. The cases, along with Professor's Discussion Material, can be obtained from the Deloitte & Touche Foundation.

Trueblood Accounting Case 4–12
Revenue recognition for software license fees

Case 89-4: *Beau Guest - When Should Revenue Check In?*

This case explores alternative accounting policies for the recognition of software license fees. It provides the opportunity for the student to not only use judgment but also to do some basic research, by comparing the situation in the case with other FASB pronouncements.

Trueblood Accounting Case 4–13
Revenue recognition for the sales of future revenues

Case 93-5: *Sale of Future Revenues*

This case explores the criteria in the accounting literature for (1) classifying the sale of future revenues as income or debt and (2) the timing of revenue recognition.

Trueblood Accounting Case 4–14
Revenue recognition for extended warranty arrangements

Case 94–1: *Accounting for Extended Warranty Arrangements*

This case provides the students with an opportunity to learn the accounting considerations related to extended warranty arrangements when such arrangements are marketed by others and the obligation is assumed by entities other than the seller of the product. The critical question involves the timing of revenue recognition from the sale of extended warranties.

Trueblood Accounting Case 4–15
Revenue recognition for the purchase of life insurance policies

Case 96-7: *Hope for the Terminally Ill*

This case addresses the timing of revenue and expense recognition related to the purchase of life insurance policies from terminally ill individuals.

Internet Case 4–16
Revenue recognition; franchise sales

EDGAR, the Electronic Data Gathering, Analysis, and Retrieval system, performs automated collection, validation, indexing, and forwarding of submissions by companies and others who are required by law to file forms with the U.S. Securities and Exchange Commission (SEC). All publicly traded domestic companies use EDGAR to make the majority of their filings. (Some foreign companies file voluntarily.) Form 10-K or 10-KSB, which include the annual report, is required to be filed on EDGAR. The SEC makes this information available on the Internet.

Required:
1.   Access EDGAR on the Internet. You can use a web browser or anonymous FTP. The web address is http://www.sec.gov/. To use anonymous FTP, use your File Transfer Protocol software to connect to sec.gov and log in as user "anonymous" with a password of your electronic mail address.
2.   Search for Ben & Jerry's Homemade, Inc. Access the most recent 10-K filing. Search or scroll to find the financial statements and related notes.
3.   Answer the following questions related to the company's revenue recognition policies:
     a.   When does the company recognize franchise fee revenue for individual stores?
     b.   When does the company recognize franchise fee revenue relating to area franchise agreements?
4.   Repeat requirements 2 and 3 for two additional companies that you suspect also earn revenues through the sale of franchise rights. Compare their revenue recognition policies with the policies of Ben & Jerry's.

Financial Analysis Case 4–17
Evaluating profitability and
asset management; obtain
and compare annual reports
from companies in the same
industry

Performance and profitability of a company often are evaluated using the financial information provided by a firm's annual report in comparison with other firms in the same industry. Ratios are useful in this assessment.

Required:
Obtain annual reports from two corporations in the same primary industry. Using techniques you learned in this chapter and any analysis you consider useful, respond to the following questions:

1. How do earnings trends compare in terms of both the direction and stability of income?
2. Which of the two firms had greater earnings relative to resources available?
3. How efficiently are current assets managed?
4. Has each of the companies achieved its respective rate of return on assets with similar combinations of profit margin and turnover?
5. Are there differences in accounting methods that should be taken into account when making comparisons?

Note: You can obtain copies of annual reports from friends who are shareholders, the investor relations department of the corporations, from a friendly stockbroker, or from EDGAR (Electronic Data Gathering Retrieval) on the Internet (http://www.sec.gov).

Financial Analysis Case 4–18
Revenue recognition;
profitability analysis

**Federal Express
Corporation**

Refer to the financial statements and related disclosure notes of Federal Express Corporation in the appendix to Chapter 1.

Required:
1. What method does the company use to recognize revenue?
2. What percentage of total 1996 revenues was generated by international operations? (Hint: see Note 10.)
3. Compute the following ratios for 1996:
   a. Receivables turnover ratio
   b. Profit margin on sales
   c. Return on assets
   d. Return on shareholders' equity

5

THE BALANCE SHEET AND FINANCIAL DISCLOSURES

OVERVIEW

Chapter 3 stressed the importance of the income statement in helping investors and creditors predict future cash flows and provided an overview of the important information disclosed on the statement of cash flows. The balance sheet, along with accompanying disclosures, also provides relevant information to investors and creditors. This information is useful not only in helping to predict future cash flows but also in the related assessments of liquidity and long-term solvency.

The purpose of this chapter is to provide an overview of the balance sheet and financial disclosures. Using this information in decision making is discussed as well.

LEARNING OBJECTIVES   After studying this chapter, you should be able to:

1. Describe the purpose of the balance sheet and understand its usefulness and limitations.
2. Distinguish among current and noncurrent assets and liabilities.
3. Identify and describe the various balance sheet asset classifications.
4. Identify and describe the two balance sheet liability classifications.
5. Explain the purpose of financial statement disclosures.
6. Explain the purpose of the management discussion and analysis disclosure.
7. Explain the purpose of an audit and describe the content of the audit report.
8. Identify and calculate the common liquidity and financing ratios used to assess risk.

WHAT'S IT WORTH?

"I can't believe it. Why don't you accountants prepare financial statements that are relevant?" Your friend Jerry is a finance major and is constantly badgering you about what he perceives to be a lack of relevance of financial statements prepared according to generally accepted accounting principles. "For example, take a look at this balance sheet for Silicon Graphics that I just downloaded off the Internet. Silicon Graphics is the company in California that produces all those cool special effects for movies like Jurassic Park. Anyway, the stockholders' equity of the company according to the 1996 balance sheet is $1,675,318,000. But if you multiply the number of outstanding shares by the most recent stock price per share, the company's market value is more than twice that amount. I thought financial statements were supposed to help investors and creditors value a company." You decide to look at the company's balance sheet (at the top of the next page) and try to set Jerry straight.

QUESTIONS

1. Respond to Jerry's criticism that stockholders' equity does not represent the market value of the company. What information does the balance sheet provide?
2. The usefulness of the balance sheet is enhanced by classifying assets and liabilities according to common characteristics. What are the classifications used on Silicon Graphics' balance sheet and what elements do those categories include?

SILICON GRAPHICS, INC.
Balance Sheets

(Dollars in thousands)

As of June 30	1996	1995
Assets		
Current assets:		
Cash and cash equivalents	$ 257,080	$ 307,875
Short-term marketable securities	38,316	208,904
Accounts receivable, net of allowance for doubtful accounts of $23,767 and $13,645	978,874	627,738
Inventories	520,045	245,267
Prepaid expenses and other	301,940	73,579
Total current assets	2,096,255	1,462,553
Other marketable investments	161,541	264,043
Property and equipment, net	464,879	254,446
Other assets	435,571	225,577
Total assets	$3,158,246	$2,206,619
Liabilities and Stockholders' Equity		
Current liabilities:		
Short-term borrowings	$ 136,718	$ —
Accounts payable	261,120	165,152
Accrued compensation	103,996	75,483
Income taxes payable	59,827	62,567
Other current liabilities	261,040	134,562
Deferred revenues	273,549	122,748
Current portion of long-term debt	5,188	12,670
Total current liabilities	1,101,438	573,182
Long-term debt and other	381,490	287,267
Stockholders' equity:		
Preferred stock, $.001 par value, issuable in series, 2,000,000 shares authorized; shares issued and outstanding: 16,998	16,998	16,998
Common stock, $.001 par value, 500,000,000 shares authorized; shares issued: 172,410,082 in 1996; 160,478,815 in 1995	173	161
Additional paid-in capital	1,172,787	903,139
Retained earnings	461,311	385,915
Treasury stock, at cost: 35,614 shares in 1996	(867)	—
Accumulated translation adjustment and other	24,916	39,957
Total stockholders' equity	1,675,318	1,346,170
Total liabilities and stockholders' equity	$3,158,246	$2,206,619

The income statement and the statement of cash flows provide important information to investors and creditors. The balance sheet, along with accompanying disclosures, also provides a wealth of information to external decision makers. The information provided is useful not only in the prediction of future cash flows but also in the related assessments of liquidity and long-term solvency.

This chapter continues our discussion of the financial statements by providing an overview of the balance sheet and the financial disclosures that accompany the financial statements. The first part of the chapter describes the usefulness and limitations of the balance sheet and illustrates the content of the statement. The second part illustrates financial statement disclosures presented to external users in addition to the basic financial statements. In the third part we discuss how this information can be used by decision makers to assess business risk. That discussion introduces some common financial ratios used to assess liquidity and long-term solvency.

PART

A

Learning objective 1
Describe the purpose of the balance sheet and understand its usefulness and limitations.

THE BALANCE SHEET

The purpose of the **balance sheet**, sometimes called the **statement of financial position**, is to report a company's financial position as of a particular date. Unlike the income statement, which is a change statement reporting events that occurred *during a period of time*, the balance sheet presents an organized array of assets, liabilities, and shareholders' equity *at a point in time*. It is a freeze frame or snapshot of financial position at the end of a particular day marking the end of an accounting period.

Usefulness and Limitations

Carter Hawley Hale Stores (CHHS), Inc., was one of the largest department store retailers in the United States. In 1991, the company operated over 100 stores in the sunbelt regions of the country. The company's divisions included The Broadway and Emporium. During the 1980s, the company struggled financially and in February of 1991 declared bankruptcy. CHHS's February 2, 1991, quarterly balance sheet, filed with the SEC and made publicly available, disclosed the information in Graphic 5–1.

GRAPHIC   5–1

Quarterly balance sheet—
Carter Hawley Hale
Stores, Inc.

Balance Sheet (condensed)
As of February 2, 1991

Assets:	($ in thousands)
Current assets	$1,154,064
Property and equipment, net	511,690
Other assets	89,667
Total assets	$1,755,421
Liabilities:	
Current liabilities	$ 175,982
Long-term liabilities	1,852,066
Total liabilities	2,028,048
Shareholders' equity:	(272,627)
Total liabilities and shareholders' equity	$1,755,421

The negative shareholders' equity includes negative retained earnings of nearly $1 billion resulting from operating losses incurred over a number of years.

By the summer of 1991, the company's stock price had dropped to $1 per share from a 1989 high of $8. In June 1991, the following (condensed) balance sheet information was reported to the bankruptcy court:

	($ in thousands)
Property	$1,596,312
Debts	1,112,989
Excess of property over debts	$ 483,323

Has the financial position changed this dramatically from February to June? No. Differences in reporting requirements by the SEC and the bankruptcy court cause the apparent discrepancy. First, the property (assets) disclosed to the bankruptcy court does not include accounts receivable and debts do not include the related liabilities for which the receivables had been pledged as collateral. This accounts for the smaller asset and debt figures as compared to those disclosed in the February statement provided to the SEC.

But the striking difference is that the *negative equity* of $272,627,000 disclosed in the SEC report becomes a *positive equity* (excess of assets over liabilities) of $483,323,000 in the information disclosed to the bankruptcy court. This positive equity, divided by the number of common shares outstanding, results in a per share value of nearly $16. Why the discrepancy? The answer relates to the valuation of property. On the balance sheet submitted to the SEC, these assets are valued based on their original cost. However, the bankruptcy court requires assets to be reported at market value.[1] The market value of CHHS's property, which includes some valuable land in locations like San Francisco, was significantly higher than its original cost.

This example illustrates an important limitation of the balance sheet. *The balance sheet does not portray the market value of the entity* as a going concern, nor, as in the CHHS example, its liquidation value. Many assets are measured at their historical costs rather than their market values. Relatedly, many company resources including its trained employees, its experienced management team, and its reputation are not recorded as assets at all. For both of these reasons, the assets of a company minus its liabilities as shown on the balance sheet usually will not directly measure the company's market value. But that doesn't mean the balance sheet is without value. An important feature of the statement is that it describes the assets a company has available for generating future cash flows.

Another way the statement's content is informative is in combination with income statement items. For example, the relation between net income and assets provides a measure of return that is useful in predicting future profitability. In fact, many of the amounts reported on either of the two statements are more informative when viewed relative to an amount from the other statement.[2]

The balance sheet also provides important information about liquidity and long-term solvency. **Liquidity** refers to the period of time before an asset is converted to cash or until a liability is paid. This information is useful in assessing a company's ability to pay its *current* obligations. **Long-term solvency** refers to the riskiness of a company with regard to the amount of liabilities in its capital structure. Other things being equal, the risk to an investor or creditor increases as the percentage of liabilities, relative to equity, increases.

Solvency also provides information about *financial flexibility*—the ability of a company to alter cash flows in order to take advantage of unexpected investment opportunities and needs. For example, the higher the percentage of a company's liabilities to its equity, the more difficult it typically will be to borrow additional funds either to take advantage of a promising investment opportunity or to meet obligations. In general, the lower the financial flexibility, the higher the risk is that the enterprise will fail. In a subsequent section of this chapter, we introduce some common ratios used to assess liquidity and long-term solvency.

In summary, even though the balance sheet does not *directly measure* the market value of the entity, it provides valuable information that can be used to help *judge* market value.

Classifications

The usefulness of the balance sheet is enhanced when assets and liabilities are grouped according to common characteristics. *The broad distinction made on the balance sheet is the current versus noncurrent classification of both assets and liabilities.* The remainder of Part A provides an overview of the balance sheet. We discuss each of the three primary elements of the balance sheet (assets, liabilities, and shareholders' equity) in the order they are reported on the statement as well as the classifications typically made within the elements. The balance sheet elements were defined in Chapter 1 as follows:

Balance Sheet Elements

Assets are probable future economic benefits obtained or controlled by a particular entity as a result of past transactions or events.

Liabilities are probable future sacrifices of economic benefits arising from present obligations of a particular entity to transfer assets or provide services to other entities in the future as a result of past transactions.

Equity or net assets, called **shareholders' equity** or **stockholders' equity** for a corporation, is the residual interest in the assets of an entity that remains after deducting liabilities.

---

[1]The bankruptcy court requires market value information in order to assess, among other things, the ability of the company to pay its creditors if assets were liquidated.

[2]We explored some of these relationships in Chapter 4.

GRAPHIC   5–2

Classification of elements within a balance sheet

Assets:
Current assets
Investments and funds
Property, plant, and equipment
Intangible assets
Other assets

Liabilities:
Current liabilities
Long-term liabilities

Shareholders' Equity:
Paid-in capital
Retained earnings

Graphic 5–2 lists the balance sheet elements along with their subclassifications.

We intentionally avoid detailed discussion of the question of valuation in order to focus on an overview of the balance sheet. In later chapters we look closer at the nature and valuation of the specific assets and liabilities.

Assets

Learning objective 2
Distinguish among current and noncurrent assets and liabilities.

Current assets include cash and all other assets expected to become cash or be consumed within one year or the **operating cycle**, whichever is longer.

Individual current assets are listed according to their liquidity.

Current Assets.   Current assets include cash and several other assets that are reasonably expected to be converted to cash or consumed within the coming year, or within the normal operating cycle of the business if that's longer than one year. The **operating cycle** for a typical manufacturing company refers to the period of time necessary to convert cash to raw materials, raw materials to a finished product, the finished product to receivables, and then finally receivables back to cash. This concept is illustrated in Graphic 5–3.

In some businesses, such as shipbuilding or distilleries, the operating cycle extends far beyond one year. For example, if it takes two years to build an oil-carrying supertanker, then the ship-builder will classify as current those assets that will be converted to cash or consumed within two years. But for most businesses the operating cycle will be shorter than one year. In these situations the one-year convention is used to classify both assets and liabilities. Where a company has no clearly defined operating cycle, the one-year convention is used.

Graphic 5–4 presents the current asset section of Federal Express Corporation's 1996 and 1995 balance sheets that also appears in the appendix to Chapter 1. In keeping with common practice, the individual current assets are listed in the order of their liquidity (nearness to cash).

GRAPHIC   5–3

Operating cycle of a typical manufacturing company

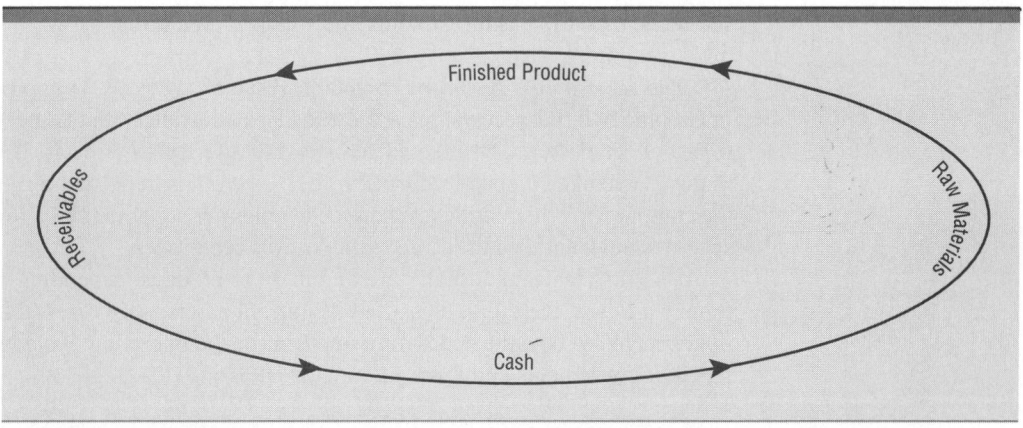

GRAPHIC   5-4

Current assets—Federal
Express Corporation

Federal Express
Corporation

| (In thousands) | May 31 | |
	1996	1995
Assets		
Current assets:		
Cash and cash equivalents	$ 93,419	$ 357,548
Receivables less allowance for doubtful		
accounts of $30,809 and $31,173	1,271,599	1,130,254
Spare parts, supplies and fuel	222,110	193,251
Deferred income taxes	92,606	115,801
Prepaid expenses and other	48,527	72,228
Total current assets	1,728,261	1,869,082

Learning objective 3
Identify and describe the
various balance sheet asset
classifications.

Cash and cash equivalents.   The most liquid asset, cash, is listed first. Cash includes cash on hand and in banks that is available for use in the operations of the business and such items as bank drafts, cashier's checks, and money orders. **Cash equivalents** frequently include certain negotiable items such as certificates of deposit, money market funds, and U.S. treasury bills. These are highly liquid investments that can be quickly converted into cash. Most companies draw a distinction between investments classified as cash equivalents and the next category of current assets, short-term investments, according to the scheduled maturity of the investment. It is common practice to classify investments that have a maturity date of three months or less from the date of purchase as cash equivalents. Federal Express Corporation's policy follows this practice and is disclosed in the summary of significant accounting policies disclosure note. The portion of the note from the company's 1996 financial statements is shown in Graphic 5–5.

GRAPHIC   5-5

Disclosure of cash
equivalents—Federal
Express Corporation

Federal Express
Corporation

Summary of Significant Accounting Policies (in part)

Cash Equivalents. Cash equivalents are cash in excess of current operating requirements invested in short-term, interest-bearing instruments with maturities of three months or less at the date of purchase and are stated at cost, which approximates market value.

Cash that is restricted for a special purpose and not available for current operations should not be classified as a current asset. For example, if cash is being accumulated to repay a debt due in five years, the cash is classified as investments and funds, a noncurrent asset.[3]

Short-term investments.   Liquid investments not classified as cash equivalents are reported as **short-term investments**, sometimes called temporary investments or short-term marketable securities. Investments in stock and debt securities of other corporations are included as short-term investments *if* the company intends to sell those securities within the next 12 months or operating cycle, whichever is longer. If, for example, a company owns 1,000 shares of IBM Corporation stock and intends to hold those shares for several years, the stock is a long-term investment and should be classified as investments and funds, a noncurrent asset.

Investments are classified
as current if management
intends to liquidate the
investment in the near term.

Accounts receivable.   **Accounts receivable** result from the sale of goods or services on credit. Notice in Graphic 5–4 that receivables are valued less allowance, that is, net of the amount not expected to be collected. Accounts receivable often are referred to as *trade receivables* because they arise in the course of a company's normal trade. *Nontrade receivables* result from loans or advances by the company to other entities. When receivables are supported by a formal agreement or note that specifies payment terms they are called **notes receivable**.

Accounts receivable usually are due in 30 to 60 days, depending on the terms offered to customers and are, therefore, classified as current assets. Any receivable, regardless of the source, not expected to be collected within one year or the operating cycle, whichever is longer, is classified as investments and funds, a noncurrent asset.

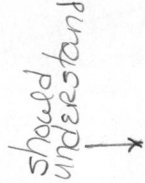
should understand →

---

[3]If the debt is due in the next year and classified as a current liability, then the cash also would be classified as current.

Inventories consist of assets that a retail or wholesale company acquires for resale or goods that manufacturers produce for sale.

Inventories.   **Inventories** include goods awaiting sale (finished goods), goods in the course of production (work in process) and goods to be consumed directly or indirectly in production (raw materials). Inventory for a wholesale or retail company consists only of finished goods, but the inventory of a manufacturer will include all three types of goods. Occasionally, a manufacturing company will report all three types of inventory directly on the balance sheet. More often, only the total amount of inventories is shown on the balance sheet and the balances of each type are shown in a disclosure note. For example, the note shown in Graphic 5–6 appears in the 1995 financial statements of IBM Corporation.

GRAPHIC   5–6

Inventories Disclosure—
IBM Corporation

D Inventories
(dollars in millions)

	At December 31,	
	1995	**1994**
Finished goods	$1,241	$1,442
Work in process	4,990	4,636
Raw materials	92	256
	$6,323	$6,334

Federal Express Corporation

Inventories are reported as current assets because they normally are sold within the operating cycle. Federal Express Corporation earns revenue by providing services to its customers rather than by selling goods. That is why there are no merchandise inventories listed on the company's balance sheet. Instead, the company shows an inventory of "spare parts, supplies and fuel." These assets will be *used* during the coming year in the process of earning service revenues.

Prepaid expenses are classified as current assets if the benefits purchased in advance will be consumed in the next year or operating cycle, whichever is longer.

Prepaid expenses.   Recall from Chapter 2 that a **prepaid expense** represents an asset recorded when an expense is paid in advance, creating benefits beyond the current period. Examples are prepaid rent and prepaid insurance. Even though these assets are not converted to cash they would involve an outlay of cash if not prepaid.

Whether a prepaid expense is current or noncurrent depends on when its benefits will be realized. For example, if rent on an office building were prepaid for one year, then the entire prepayment is classified as a current asset. However, if rent were prepaid for a period extending beyond the coming year, a portion of the prepayment is classified as an other asset, a noncurrent asset.[4] Federal Express Corporation combines prepaid expenses with other current assets on its balance sheet. Presumably, the "other" current asset category includes assets—such as short-term investments and nontrade receivables—that, because of lack of their relative magnitude, did not warrant separate disclosure.

Federal Express Corporation

Federal Express lists one other current asset on its balance sheet, "Deferred income taxes." This asset is discussed in Chapter 16.

When assets are expected to provide economic benefits beyond the next year, or operating cycle, they are reported as *noncurrent assets.* Typical classifications of noncurrent assets are (1) long-term investments and funds, (2) property, plant, and equipment, and (3) intangible assets.

Investments and funds are nonoperating assets not used directly in operations.

Investments and Funds.   Most companies occasionally acquire assets that are not used directly in the operations of the business. These "nonoperating" assets include investments in equity and debt securities of other corporations, land held for speculation, noncurrent receivables, and cash set aside for special purposes (such as for future plant expansion). These assets are classified as noncurrent because management does not intend to convert the assets into cash in the next year (or the operating cycle if that's longer).

Tangible, long-lived assets used in the operations of the business are classified as **property, plant, and equipment**.

Property, Plant, and Equipment.   Virtually all companies own assets classified as **property, plant, and equipment.** The common characteristics these assets share are that they are *tangible, long-lived and used in the operations of the business.* Property, plant, and equipment, along with intangible assets, often are referred to as **operational assets.** They usually are the primary revenue-generating assets of the business.

---

[4]Companies often include prepayments for benefits extending beyond one year as current assets when the amounts are not material.

Property, plant, and equipment includes land, buildings, equipment, machinery, and furniture, as well as natural resources, such as mineral mines, timber tracts, and oil wells. These various assets usually are reported as a single amount on the balance sheet, with details provided in a note. They are reported at original cost less accumulated depreciation (or depletion for natural resources) to date. Land often is listed as a separate item in this classification because it has an unlimited useful life and thus is not depreciated.

Intangible Assets.   Some assets used in the operations of a business have no physical substance. These are appropriately called **intangible assets**. Generally, these represent the ownership of an exclusive right to something such as a product, a process, or a name. This right can be a valuable resource in generating future revenues. Patents, copyrights, and franchises are examples. They are reported on the balance sheet net of accumulated amortization. Some companies include intangible assets as part of property, plant, and equipment, while others report them either in a separate intangible asset classification or as other noncurrent assets.

> **Intangible assets** generally represent exclusive rights that the company can use to generate future revenues.

Quite often, much of the value of intangibles is not reported on the balance sheet. For example, it would not be unusual for the historical cost of a patent to be significantly lower than its market value. As we discuss in a subsequent chapter, for internally developed intangibles, the costs that are included as part of historical cost are limited. Specifically, none of the research and development costs incurred in developing the intangible are included in cost.

Other Assets.   Balance sheets often include a catch-all classification of noncurrent assets called **other assets**. This classification includes long-term prepaid expenses, called *deferred charges*, and any noncurrent asset not falling in one of the other classifications. For instance, if a company's noncurrent investments are not material in amount, they might be reported in the other asset classification rather than in a separate investments and funds category.

Graphic 5–7 reproduces the noncurrent asset section of Federal Express Corporation's 1996 and 1995 balance sheets.

GRAPHIC   5–7

Property, plant, and equipment and other assets—Federal Express Corporation

Federal Express Corporation

(In thousands)	May 31	
	1996	1995
Assets		
Property and equipment, at cost:		
Flight equipment	3,372,647	3,006,693
Package handling and ground support equipment	2,148,509	1,841,108
Computer and electronic equipment	1,439,883	1,224,050
Other	1,717,478	1,625,860
	8,678,517	7,697,711
Less: accumulated depreciation and amortization	4,561,916	3,982,467
Net property and equipment	4,116,601	3,715,244
Other assets:		
Goodwill	380,748	397,272
Equipment deposits and other assets	473,361	451,774
Total other assets	854,109	849,046

Quite often, a company will present only the net amount of property, plant, and equipment on the balance sheet and provide details in a disclosure note.

For Federal Express, all other noncurrent assets are reported as other assets. This includes the intangible asset goodwill, equipment deposits, and other noncurrent assets.

We've seen how assets are grouped into current and noncurrent categories and that noncurrent assets always are subclassified further. Let's now turn our attention to liabilities. These, too, are separated into current and noncurrent (long-term) categories.

Liabilities

> **Learning objective 4**
> Identify and describe the two balance sheet liability classifications.

Liabilities represent the amounts owed to other entities. The information value of reporting these amounts is enhanced by classifying them as current liabilities and long-term liabilities. Graphic 5–8 shows the liability section of Federal Express Corporation's 1996 and 1995 balance sheets.

GRAPHIC   5 – 8

Liabilities—Federal Express
Corporation

Federal Express
Corporation

| (In thousands) | May 31 | |
	1996	1995
Liabilities		
Current liabilities:		
Current portion of long-term debt	$ 8,009	$ 255,448
Accounts payable	705,532	618,621
Accrued expenses	904,856	904,466
Total current liabilities	1,618,397	1,778,535
Long-term debt, less current portion	1,325,277	1,324,711
Deferred Income taxes	64,034	55,956
Other liabilities	1,115,124	1,028,601

> Current liabilities are expected to be satisfied within one year or the operating cycle, whichever is longer.

Current Liabilities.   Current liabilities are those obligations that are expected to be satisfied through the use of current assets or the creation of other current liabilities. So, this classification includes all liabilities that are expected to be paid within one year or the operating cycle, whichever is longer. An exception is a liability that management intends to refinance on a long-term basis. For example, if management intends to refinance a six-month note payable by substituting a two-year note payable and has the ability to do so, then the liability would not be classified as current even though it's due within the coming year. This exception is discussed in more detail in Chapter 13.

> Current liabilities usually include **accounts** and **notes payable, accrued liabilities,** and the **current maturities of long-term debt**.

The most common current liabilities are accounts payable, notes payable (short-term borrowings), accrued liabilities, and the currently maturing portion of long-term debt. **Accounts payable** are obligations to suppliers of merchandise or of services purchased on *open account*, with payment usually due in 30 to 60 days. **Notes payable** are written promises to pay cash at some future date (I.O.U.s). Unlike accounts payable, notes usually require the payment of explicit interest in addition to the original obligation amount. Notes maturing in the next year or operating cycle, whichever is longer, will be classified as current liabilities.

Accrued liabilities represent obligations created when expenses have been incurred but won't be paid until a subsequent reporting period. Examples are accrued salaries payable, accrued interest payable, and accrued taxes payable. Federal Express Corporation reported accrued liabilities (accrued expenses) of $904,856,000 at the end of 1996. In the disclosure note, shown in Graphic 5–9, the company provided the details.

GRAPHIC   5 – 9

Accrued expenses
disclosure—Federal Express
Corporation

Federal Express
Corporation

Note 2: Accrued expenses

| (In thousands) | May 31 | |
	1996	1995
Compensated absences	$211,499	$192,785
Insurance	194,209	176,806
Taxes other than income taxes	153,905	137,037
Employee benefits	111,912	127,870
Salaries	78,384	100,024
Aircraft overhaul	59,343	53,540
Other	95,604	116,404
	$904,856	$904,466

> Current liabilities include the **current maturities of long-term debt.**

Long-term notes, loans, mortgages, and bonds payable usually are reclassified and reported as current liabilities as they become payable within the next year (or operating cycle if that's longer).[5] Likewise, when long-term debt is payable in installments, the installment payable currently is reported as a current liability. For example, a $1,000,000 note payable requiring $100,000 in principal payments to be made in each of the next 10 years is classified as a $100,000 current liability—**current maturities of long-term debt**—and a $900,000 long-term liability.

Chapter 13 provides a more detailed analysis of current liabilities.

---

[5]Payment can be with current assets or the creation of other current liabilities.

Long-Term Liabilities.   Long-term liabilities are obligations that will *not* be satisfied in the next year or operating cycle, whichever is longer. They do not require the use of current assets or the creation of current liabilities for payment. Examples are long-term notes, bonds, pension obligations, and lease obligations.

But simply classifying a liability as long-term doesn't provide complete information to external users. For instance, long-term could mean anything from 2 to 20, 30, or 40 years. Payment terms, interest rates, and other details needed to assess the impact of these obligations on future cash flows and long-term solvency are reported in a disclosure note.

At the end of its 1996 fiscal year, Federal Express Corporation reported long-term debt, deferred income taxes, and other liabilities. A disclosure note indicated that long-term debt consisted of notes payable, bonds payable, and capital lease obligations. Each of these liabilities, as well as deferred income taxes, are discussed in later chapters. The long-term liability category called *other liabilities* relates primarily to deferred gains on certain lease transactions. This topic also is addressed in a later chapter.

> Noncurrent, or long-term liabilities, usually are those payable beyond the current year.

Shareholders' Equity

Recall from our discussions in Chapters 1 and 2 that owners' equity is simply a residual amount derived by subtracting liabilities from assets. For that reason, it's also sometimes called net assets. Also recall that owners of a corporation are its shareholders, so owners' equity for a corporation is referred to as shareholders' equity or stockholders' equity. Shareholders' equity for a corporation arises primarily from two sources: (1) amounts *invested* by shareholders in the corporation, and (2) amounts *earned* by the corporation (on behalf of its shareholders). These are reported as (1) **paid-in capital** and (2) **retained earnings**. Retained earnings represents the accumulated net income earned from the inception of the corporation and not (yet) paid to shareholders as dividends.

Graphic 5–10 presents the shareholders' equity section of Federal Express Corporation's 1996 and 1995 balance sheets. The company calls this section *common stockholders' investment*.

> Shareholders' equity is composed of **paid-in capital** (invested capital) and **retained earnings** (earned capital).

GRAPHIC   5–10

Stockholders' equity—
Federal Express Corporation

**Federal Express
Corporation**

	May 31	
(In thousands)	**1996**	**1995**
Common Stockholders' Investment:		
Common stock, $.10 par value; 200,000 shares authorized;		
56,885 and 56,174 shares issued	5,689	5,617
Additional paid-in capital	815,137	775,255
Retained earnings	1,766,578	1,466,427
	2,587,404	2,247,299
Less: treasury stock and deferred compensation	11,265	1,730
Total common shareholders' investment	2,576,139	2,245,569

From the inception of the corporation through May 31, 1996, Federal Express has accumulated net income, less dividends, of $1,766,578,000, which is reported as retained earnings. The company's paid-in capital is represented by common stock and additional paid-in capital, which collectively represent cash invested by shareholders in exchange for ownership interests.

Besides paid-in capital and retained earnings, shareholders' equity also may include a variety of other equity components. For example, Federal Express lists treasury stock and deferred compensation. We discuss these other equity components in later chapters.

CONCEPT REVIEW EXERCISE   BALANCE SHEET CLASSIFICATION

The following is a post-closing trial balance for the Sepia Paint Corporation at December 31, 1997, the end of the company's fiscal year:

Account Title	Debits	Credits
Cash	80,000	
Accounts receivable	200,000	
Allowance for uncollectible accounts		20,000

Balance Sheet

A global perspective in Chapter 3 pointed out that there are significant differences from country to country in the accounting methods used to measure income statement amounts. This, of course, pertains to the balance sheet as well. For example, differences in inventory measurement methods affect the calculation of cost of goods sold as well as the inventory balance reported on the balance sheet. Many of these measurement differences are highlighted in the specific chapters that deal with the specific issues.

In terms of balance sheet presentation, the classification of assets and liabilities into current and noncurrent categories is prevalent globally. However, significant differences do exist, particularly with respect to terminology. In the U.K., the term *stocks* refers to inventory. A U.S. investor would interpret stocks to mean investments in equity securities of other companies. In the United States, shareholders' equity is composed of paid-in capital and retained earnings. In many other countries, shareholders' equity is divided into capital and reserves. For example, in Germany, equity is divided into share capital, capital reserves, and revenue reserves. In India, liabilities whose existence is certain but whose value must be estimated, are called *provisions* and are listed separately.

Balance sheet presentation differences also exist. For example, a typical U.K. balance sheet begins with noncurrent assets, called *fixed assets.* Current assets are listed next and current liabilities are subtracted to arrive at net current assets, which is added to fixed assets. Long-term debt is then subtracted from this subtotal to arrive at net assets. The net asset total agrees with shareholders' interest, which is reported last.

Account Title	Debits	Credits
Inventories	300,000	
Prepaid expenses	30,000	
Note receivable (due in one month)	60,000	
Investments	50,000	
Land	120,000	
Buildings	550,000	
Machinery	500,000	
Accumulated depreciation—buildings and machinery		450,000
Patent (net of amortization)	50,000	
Accounts payable		170,000
Salaries payable		40,000
Interest payable		10,000
Note payable		100,000
Bonds payable (due in ten years)		500,000
Capital stock		400,000
Retained earnings		250,000
Totals	1,940,000	1,940,000

The $50,000 balance in the investment account consists of marketable equity securities of other corporations. The company's intention is to hold the securities for at least three years. The $100,000 note payable is an installment loan. $10,000 of the principal, plus interest, is due on each July 1 for the next 10 years.

Required:

Prepare a classified balance sheet for the Sepia Paint Corporation at December 31, 1997.

CONCEPT REVIEW EXERCISE   SOLUTION

Sepia Paint Corporation
Balance Sheet
At December 31, 1997

Assets

Current assets		
Cash		$ 80,000
Accounts receivable	$ 200,000	
Less: Allowance for uncollectible accounts	(20,000)	180,000
Note receivable		60,000
Inventories		300,000
Prepaid expenses		30,000
Total current assets		650,000

Investments		50,000
Property, plant, and equipment		
Land	120,000	
Buildings	550,000	
Machinery	500,000	
	1,170,000	
Less: Accumulated depreciation	(450,000)	
Net property, plant, and equipment		720,000
Intangibles		
Patent		50,000
Total assets		$1,470,000

Liabilities and Shareholders' Equity

Current liabilities		
Accounts payable		$ 170,000
Salaries payable		40,000
Interest payable		10,000
Current maturities of long-term debt		10,000
Total current liabilities		230,000
Long-term liabilities		
Note payable	$ 90,000	
Bonds payable	500,000	
Total long-term liabilities		590,000
Shareholders' equity		
Capital stock	400,000	
Retained earnings	250,000	
Total shareholders' equity		650,000
Total liabilities and shareholders' equity		$1,470,000

The usefulness of the balance sheet, as well as the other financial statements, is significantly enhanced by financial statement disclosures. We now turn our attention to these disclosures.

B FINANCIAL DISCLOSURES

Learning objective 5
Explain the purpose of financial statement disclosures.

Financial statements are included in the annual report a company mails to its shareholders. They are, though, only part of the information provided. Critical to understanding the financial statements and to evaluating the firm's performance and financial health are disclosure notes and other information included in the annual report.

Disclosure Notes

Disclosure notes typically span several pages and explain or elaborate on the data presented in the financial statements themselves. Throughout this text you will encounter examples of items that usually are disclosed this way. For instance, the market values of financial instruments and "off-balance-sheet" risk associated with financial instruments must be disclosed. Information providing details of pension plans, leases, debt, and assets also is disclosed in the notes. Disclosures must include certain specific notes such as a summary of significant accounting policies, descriptions of subsequent events, and related third-party transactions, but many notes are fashioned to suit the disclosure needs of the particular reporting enterprise. Actually, any explanation that contributes to investors' and creditors' understanding of the results of operations, financial position, or cash flows of the company should be included. Some common disclosures are made by some companies in the form of notes, while other companies disclose the same information as separate schedules or in other formats within the annual report. The specific format of disclosure is not important, only that the information is, in fact, disclosed.

The full-disclosure principle requires that financial statements provide all material, relevant information concerning the reporting entity.

Summary of Significant Accounting Policies

The **summary of significant accounting policies** conveys valuable information about the company's choices from among various alternative accounting methods.

There are many areas where management chooses from among equally acceptable alternative accounting methods. For example, management chooses whether to use accelerated or straight-line depreciation, whether to use FIFO, LIFO, or average cost to measure inventories, and whether the completed contract or percentage-of-completion method best reflects the performance of construction operations. It also defines which securities it considers to be cash equivalents and its

GRAPHIC   5–11

Summary of significant accounting policies—Ralston Purina Company

Summary of Significant Accounting Policies (in part)

The Company's significant accounting policies, which conform to generally accepted accounting principles and are applied on a consistent basis among years, except as indicated, are described below:

Principles of Consolidation—The consolidated financial statements include the accounts of the Company and its majority-owned subsidiaries. All significant intercompany transactions are eliminated. Investments in affiliated companies, 20% through 50%-owned, are carried at equity.

Minority interests in earnings of consolidated subsidiaries and the Company's share of the net earnings of unconsolidated companies carried at equity are included in selling, general and administrative expenses.

Financial Instruments—The Company enters into interest rate swap and cap agreements in the management of interest rate exposure. The differential to be paid or received is normally accrued as interest rates change and is recognized over the life of the agreements. In addition, in order to hedge foreign currency exposures on firm commitments, the Company regularly enters into forward foreign currency contracts. Gains and losses resulting from these instruments are recognized in the same period as the underlying hedged transaction.

Cash Equivalents for purposes of the statement of cash flows are considered to be all highly liquid investments with a maturity of three months or less when purchased. Cash flow from hedging transactions are classified in the same category as the cash flow from the item being hedged.

Inventories are valued generally at the lower of average cost or market.

Depreciation is generally provided on the straight-line basis by charges to costs or expenses at rates based on the estimated useful lives of the properties. Estimated useful lives range from 3 to 25 years for machinery and equipment and 10 to 50 years for buildings.

Intangible Assets, which are included in Investments and other Assets, represent the excess of cost over tangible assets of acquired businesses and are amortized over estimated periods of related benefit ranging from 5 to 40 years.

> The summary of significant accounting policies tells the analyst which choices were made in preparing the financial statements.

policies regarding the timing of recognizing revenues. Typically, the first disclosure note consists of a summary of significant accounting policies that discloses the choices the company makes.[6] Graphic 5–11 shows you a typical summary note from a recent annual report of the Ralston Purina Company.

Studying this note is an essential step in analyzing financial statements. Obviously, knowing which methods were used to derive certain accounting numbers is critical to assessing the adequacy of those amounts.

Subsequent Events

> A **subsequent event** is a significant development that takes place after the company's fiscal year-end but before the financial statements are issued.

When an event that has a material effect on the company's financial position occurs after the fiscal year-end but before the financial statements actually are issued, the event is disclosed in a **subsequent event** disclosure note. Examples are an issuance of debt or equity securities, a business combination, discontinued operations, an event that sheds light on the outcome of a loss contingency, and an event having a significant effect on operations. Graphic 5–12 illustrates the required disclosure by showing a note of the IBM Corporation, included with the company's December 31, 1995 financial statements, announcing a significant merger agreement.

Noteworthy Events and Transactions

Some transactions and events occur only occasionally, but when they do occur are potentially important to evaluating a company's financial statements. In this category are errors and irregularities, illegal acts, and related-party transactions.

---

[6]"Disclosure of Accounting Policies," *Accounting Principles Board Opinion No. 22* (New York: AICPA, 1972).

Subsequent events—IBM

Z Subsequent Events

On January 31, 1996, the company announced it had entered into a definitive merger agreement under which the company will commence a cash tender offer for Tivoli Systems Inc. at $47.50 per share. Tivoli, based in Austin, Texas, is a leading provider of systems management software and services that help customers reduce the cost and complexity of managing distributed client/server networks of personal computers and workstations.

The net cash cost of the transaction to the company is expected to be $743 million, including the purchase of Tivoli's outstanding shares, the vesting of a portion of the employee stock options, fees and expenses, less Tivoli's current cash.

When the merger is completed, it will result in a one-time charge to the company's earnings. The charge primarily involves expensing, as called for by accounting requirements, of amounts assigned to research and development of Tivoli software that has not reached technological feasibility. The charge will be taken in the quarter in which the merger is completed. The specific amount of the charge cannot be determined at this time based on currently available information.

Somewhat related to errors are **irregularities**, the difference being that errors are unintentional while irregularities are *intentional* distortions of financial statements.[7] Obviously, management fraud might cause a user to approach financial analysis from an entirely different and more cautious viewpoint.

Closely related to irregularities are **illegal acts** such as bribes, kickbacks, illegal contributions to political candidates, and other violations of the law. Accounting for illegal practices has been influenced by the Foreign Corrupt Practices Act passed by Congress in 1977. The Act is intended to discourage illegal business practices through tighter controls and also encourage better disclosure of those practices when encountered. Disclosures should consider the materiality of the impact of illegal acts on amounts disclosed in the financial statements.[8]

Sometimes a company will engage in transactions with owners, management, families of owners or management, affiliated companies, and other parties that can significantly influence or be influenced by the company. The economic substance of these transactions may differ from their legal form. Borrowing or lending money at an interest rate that differs significantly from the market interest rate is an example of a transaction that could result from a related-party involvement. Financial statement users are particularly interested in more details about these transactions to assess the effect of any differences between economic substance and legal form.

> The economic substance of **related-party transactions** should be disclosed, including dollar amounts involved.

When **related-party transactions** occur, disclosure is required of the nature of the relationship, a description of the transaction, and any dollar amounts involved.[9] Graphic 5–13 shows a disclosure note from a recent annual report of Tyson Foods. The note describes the company's relationships with the senior chairman of the board of directors and certain officers and directors.

Related-party transactions disclosure—Tyson Foods

Note 8 Transactions with Related Parties

The Company has operating leases for farms, equipment and other facilities with the Senior Chairman of the Board of Directors of the Company and certain members of his family, as well as a trust controlled by him, for rentals of $7.0 million in 1995, $6.8 million in 1994 and $6.4 million in 1993. Other facilities, including a cold storage distribution facility, are also leased from the Company's profit sharing plan and other officers and directors for rentals totaling $7.1 million in 1995, $6.7 million in 1994 and $6.2 million in 1993.

Certain officers and directors are engaged in poultry and swine growout operations with the Company whereby these individuals purchase animals, feed, housing and other items to raise the animals to market weight. The total value of these transactions amounted to $11.2 million in 1995, $11.4 million in 1994 and $11.3 million in 1993.

---

[7]"The Auditor's Responsibility to Detect and Report Errors and Irregularities," *Statement on Auditing Standards No. 53* (New York: AICPA, 1988).

[8]"Illegal Acts By Clients," *Statement on Auditing Standards No. 54* (New York: AICPA, 1988).

[9]"Related Party Disclosures," *Statement on Auditing Standards No. 57* (New York: AICPA, 1982).

Disclosures of irregularities, illegal acts, and related-party transactions can be quite sensitive. Although auditors must be considerate of the privacy of the parties involved, that consideration cannot be subordinate to users' needs for full disclosure.

We've discussed only a few of the disclosure notes most frequently included in annual reports. Other common disclosures include details concerning earnings per share calculations, income taxes, property and equipment, contingencies, long-term debt, leases, pensions, stock options, changes in accounting methods, fair values of financial instruments, and exposure to market risk and credit risk. We discuss and illustrate these in later chapters in the context of related financial statement elements.

> Disclosure notes for some financial statement elements are required. Others are provided when required by specific situations in the interest of full disclosure.

Management Discussion and Analysis

Learning objective 6
Explain the purpose of the management discussion and analysis disclosure.

Each annual report includes a fairly lengthy discussion and analysis provided by the company's management. In this section, management provides its views on significant events, trends, and uncertainties pertaining to the company's (a) operations, (b) liquidity, and (c) capital resources. Although the **management discussion and analysis (MDA)** section may embody management's biased perspective, it can offer an informed insight that might not be available elsewhere. Graphic 5–14 contains part of the liquidity and capital resources portion of the Walt Disney Company's MDA that followed a five-page discussion of operations in its 1995 annual report.

GRAPHIC   5-14

Management discussion and analysis—Walt Disney Company

> The management discussion and analysis provides a biased but informed perspective of a company's (a) operations, (b) liquidity, and (c) capital resources.

Management Discussion and Analysis of Financial Condition and Results of Operations

(In part: Liquidity and capital resources only)

The Company generates significant cash from operations and has substantial borrowing capacity to meet its operating and discretionary cash requirements.

Cash provided by operations increased 25% or $702.8 million to $3.51 billion in 1995, primarily due to increased operating income in each business segment.

Net borrowings (the Company's borrowings less cash and liquid investments) decreased $327 million to $1.4 billion. The decrease was primarily due to payments of existing debt and an increase in cash and liquid investments, partially offset by the issuance of $400 million of senior participating notes in the second quarter and $300 million of senior, unsecured debt obligations in the first quarter.

In 1995, the Company invested $1.89 billion to develop and produce film television properties and $896.5 million to design and develop new theme park attractions and resort properties, including Disney's Animal Kingdom, Disney Cruise Lines, the Blizzard Beach Water Park, Disney's BoardWalk and the town of Celebration.

The Company's financial condition remains strong. The Company believes that its cash, other liquid assets, and operating cash flows, access to equity capital markets and borrowing capacity taken together provide more than adequate resources to fund ongoing operating requirements and future capital expenditures related to the expansion of existing businesses and development of new projects.

Management's Responsibilities

Auditors examine financial statements and the internal control procedures designed to support the content of those statements. Their role is to attest to the fairness of the financial statements based on that examination. However, management prepares and is responsible for the financial statements and other information in the annual report. To enhance the awareness of the users of financial statements concerning the relative roles of management and the auditor, annual reports include a management's responsibilities section that asserts the responsibility of management for the information contained in the annual report as well as an assessment of the company's internal control procedures. Wording of this section is fairly standard. A typical disclosure is provided in Graphic 5–15.

Auditors' Report

Learning objective 7
Explain the purpose of an audit and describe the content of the audit report.

One step in financial analysis should be an examination of the **auditors' report**. This is the report issued by the CPAs who audit the financial statements and informs users of their audit findings. Every audit report looks similar to the one prepared by Deloitte & Touche LLP for the financial statements of Microsoft Corporation, as shown in Graphic 5–16.

GRAPHIC   5–15

Management's responsibilities—Hershey Foods Corporation

The management's responsibilities section avows the responsibility of management for the company's financial statements and internal control system.

Responsibility for Financial Statements

Hershey Foods Corporation is responsible for the financial statements and other financial information contained in this report. The Corporation believes that the financial statements have been prepared in conformity with generally accepted accounting principles appropriate under the circumstances to reflect in all material respects the substance of applicable events and transactions. In preparing the financial statements, it is necessary that management make informed estimates and judgments. The other financial information in this annual report is consistent with the financial statements.

The Corporation maintains a system of internal accounting controls designed to provide reasonable assurance that financial records are reliable for purposes of preparing financial statements and that assets are properly accounted for and safeguarded. The concept of reasonable assurance is based on the recognition that the cost of the system must be related to the benefits to be derived. The Corporation believes its system provides an appropriate balance in this regard. The Corporation maintains an Internal Audit Department which reviews the adequacy and tests the application of internal accounting controls.

The financial statements have been audited by Arthur Andersen LLP, independent public accountants, whose appointment was ratified by stockholder vote at the stockholders' meeting held on April 24, 1995. Their report expresses an opinion that the Corporation's financial statements are fairly stated in conformity with generally accepted accounting principles, and they have indicated to us that their examination was performed in accordance with generally accepted auditing standards which are designed to obtain reasonable assurance about whether the financial statements are free of material misstatement.

The Audit Committee of the Board of Directors of the Corporation, consisting solely of outside directors, meets regularly with the independent public accountants, internal auditors and management to discuss, among other things, the audit scopes and results. Arthur Andersen LLP and the internal auditors both have full and free access to the Audit Committee, with and without the presence of management.

GRAPHIC   5–16

Auditors' report—Microsoft Corporation

The **auditors' report** provides the analyst with an independent and professional opinion about the fairness of the representations in the financial statements.

Report of Independent Auditors

To the Board of Directors and Shareholders of Microsoft Corporation:

We have audited the accompanying consolidated balance sheets of Microsoft Corporation and subsidiaries as of June 30, 1995 and 1996, and the related statements of income, cash flows, and stockholders' equity for each of the three years ended June 30, 1996, appearing on pages 14, 15, 20, 21, 24 through 28, and 31. These financial statements are the responsibility of the Company's management. Our responsibility is to express an opinion on these financial statements based on our audits.

We conducted our audits in accordance with generally accepted auditing standards. Those standards require that we plan and perform the audit to obtain reasonable assurance about whether the financial statements are free of material misstatement. An audit includes examining, on a test basis, evidence supporting the amounts and disclosures in the financial statements. An audit also includes assessing the accounting principles used and significant estimates made by management, as well as evaluating the overall financial statement presentation. We believe that our audits provide a reasonable basis for our opinion.

In our opinion, such financial statements present fairly, in all material respects, the financial position of Microsoft Corporation and subsidiaries at June 30, 1995 and 1996, and the results of their operations and their cash flows for each of the three years ended June 30, 1996, in conformity with accounting principles generally accepted in the United States and International Accounting Standards.

Seattle, Washington
July 22, 1996

Deloitte & Touche LLP

The reason for the similarities is that auditors' reports must be in exact compliance with the specifications of the AICPA.[10] In most cases, including the report for Microsoft, the auditors will be satisfied that the financial statements "present fairly" the financial position, results of operations, and cash flows and are "in conformity with generally accepted accounting principles." These situations prompt an **unqualified opinion**. Sometimes circumstances cause the auditors' report to include an explanatory paragraph in addition to the standard wording, even though the report is unqualified. Most notably, these include:

a. *Lack of consistency* due to a change in accounting principle such that comparability is affected even though the auditor concurs with the desirability of the change.

b. *Uncertainty* as to the ultimate resolution of a contingency for which a loss is material in amount but not necessarily probable or probable but not estimable.

c. *Emphasis* of a matter concerning the financial statements that does not affect the existence of an unqualified opinion but relates to a significant event such as a related-party transaction.

Some audits result in the need to issue other than an unqualified opinion, in which case the auditor will issue a (an):

> The auditors' report calls attention to problems that might exist in the financial statements.

a. **Qualified opinion**   This contains an exception to the standard unqualified opinion but not of sufficient seriousness to invalidate the financial statements as a whole. Examples of exceptions are (a) nonconformity with generally accepted accounting principles, (b) inadequate disclosures, and (c) a limitation or restriction of the scope of the examination.

b. **Adverse opinion**   This is necessary when the exceptions are so serious that a qualified opinion is not justified. Adverse opinions are rare because auditors usually are able to persuade management to rectify problems to avoid this undesirable report.

c. **Disclaimer**   An auditor will disclaim an opinion if insufficient information has been gathered to express an opinion.

> The auditor should assess the firm's ability to continue as a going concern.

During the course of each audit, the auditor is required to evaluate the company's ability to continue as a going concern for a reasonable time. If the auditor determines there is significant doubt, an explanation of the potential problem must be included in the auditors' report.[11]

Obviously, the auditors' report is most informative when any of these deviations from the standard unqualified opinion are present. These departures from the norm should raise a red flag to a financial analyst and prompt additional search for information.

The auditors' report of Celgene Corporation, exhibited in Graphic 5–17, included a fourth paragraph after the standard first three paragraphs.

GRAPHIC   5–17

**Going concern paragraph—
Celgene Corporation**

The accompanying financial statements for 1994 have been prepared assuming that the Company will continue as a going concern. As discussed in note 1 to the financial statements, the Company's recurring losses from operations and limited capital resources raise substantial doubt about its ability to continue as a going concern. Management's plans as to this matter are also described in note 1. The financial statements do not include any adjustments that might result from the outcome of this uncertainty.

Compensation of Directors and Top Executives

In the early 1990s, the compensation large U.S. corporations pay their top executives became an issue of considerable public debate and controversy. Shareholders, employees, politicians, and the public in general began to question the huge pay packages received by company officials at the same time that more and more rank and file employees were being laid off as a result of company cutbacks. Contributing to the debate was the realization that the compensation gap between executives and lower level employees was

---

[10]"Reports on Audited Financial Statements," *Statement on Auditing Standards No. 58* (New York: AICPA, 1988).

[11]"The Auditor's Consideration of an Entity's Ability to Continue as a Going Concern," *Statement on Auditing Standards No. 59* (New York: AICPA, 1988).

A summary compensation table that outlines how much directors and top executives are paid and what retirement benefits they will receive.

A table of options granted that reports information about options given to individually identified executives in the most recent year, including:
- The number of options and dates granted.
- The percent of total options given to each top executive.
- The exercise price and expiration date of options.
- The company's estimate of the options' values.

A table of options holdings that reports information about all options currently held by individually identified executives, including:
- The number of options each executive owns and their value.
- The number of shares acquired in the most recent year by exercising options.
- The amount of profit realized from exercising options.

much wider than in Japan and most other industrial countries. During this time, it also became apparent that discovering exactly how much compensation corporations paid their top people was nearly impossible.

Part of the problem stemmed from the fact that disclosures of these amounts were meager; but a large part of the problem was that a substantial portion of executive pay often is in the form of stock options. Executive stock options give their holders the right to buy stock at a specified price, usually equal to the market price when the options are granted. When stock prices rise, executives can exercise their options and realize a profit. In some cases, options have made executive compensation seem extremely high. Stock options are discussed in depth in Chapter 18.

To help shareholders and others sort out the content of executive pay packages and better understand the commitments of the company in this regard, recent SEC requirements now provide for more disclosures on compensation to directors and executives, and in particular, concerning stock options. The **proxy statement** which must be sent each year to all shareholders, usually in the same mailing with the annual report, previously served primarily to invite shareholders to the meeting to elect board members and to vote on issues before the shareholders or to vote using an enclosed proxy card. Beginning with 1992 financial statements, the proxy statement assumed a larger role. Graphic 5–18 lists the information that the statement now also reports.

The **proxy statement**, which is sent each year to all shareholders, contains disclosures on compensation to directors and executives.

GLOBAL PERSPECTIVE

Disclosure Practices around The World

Most countries require specific disclosures by companies operating within their borders. Many of these disclosures are similar. However, the amount and types of required and voluntary disclosures differ from country to country. For example, in Israel, companies whose securities are publicly traded are required to disclose any receivable that exceeds five percent of total current assets. In Mexico, a disclosure reports the separate identification of long-term liabilities into the following categories: suppliers. affiliates, income tax, employees' profit sharing, and bank loans.

Several supplemental disclosures are uniquely European. These include information about shares and shareholders, certain employee disclosures, and environmental disclosures. An example of an environmental disclosure would be a discussion of safety measures adopted by the company in their manufacturing plants. In France, many enterprises are required to publish an annual social balance sheet. This report covers matters such as employment, training, health and safety conditions, employee benefits, and environmental issues. In general, European companies consider the full-disclosure concept to include a much broader set of information than do U.S. companies.

— read, but not covering in class

PART **C**

RISK ANALYSIS

Investors and creditors use financial information to assess the future risk and return of their investments in business enterprises. The balance sheet provides information useful to this assessment. A key element of risk analysis is investigating a company's ability to pay its obligations when they come due. This type of risk often is referred to as **default risk**. Another aspect of risk is **operational risk** which relates more to how adept a company is at withstanding various events and circumstances that might impair its ability to earn profits. Obviously, these two types of risk are not completely independent of one another. Inability to earn profits certainly increases a company's chances of defaulting on its obligations. Conversely, regardless of a company's long-run prospects for generating profits, if it can't meet its obligations, the company's operations are at risk.

Assessing risk necessarily involves consideration of a variety of economywide risk factors such as inflation, interest rates, and the general business climate. Industrywide influences including competition, labor conditions, and technological forces also affect a company's risk profile. Still other risk factors are specific to the company itself. Financial ratios often are used in risk analysis to investigate a company's **liquidity** and **long-term solvency**. As we discuss some of the more common ratios in the following paragraphs, keep in mind the inherent relationship between risk and return and thus between our profitability analysis in the previous chapter and our risk analysis in this chapter.

Liquidity Ratios

Learning objective 8
Identify and calculate the common liquidity and financing ratios used to assess risk.

Liquidity refers to the readiness of assets to be converted to cash. By comparing a company's liquid assets with its short-term obligations, we can obtain a general idea of the firm's ability to pay its short-term debts as they come due. Usually, current assets are thought of as the most liquid of a company's assets. Obviously, though, some are more liquid than others, so it's important also to evaluate the specific makeup of current assets. Two common measures of liquidity are (1) the current ratio, and (2) the acid-test ratio (or quick ratio) calculated as follows:

$$\text{Current ratio} = \frac{\text{Current assets}}{\text{Current liabilities}}$$

$$\frac{\text{Acid-test ratio}}{\text{(or quick ratio)}} = \frac{\text{Quick assets}}{\text{Current liabilities}}$$

Current Ratio. Implicit in the definition of a current liability is the relationship between current assets and current liabilities. The difference between current assets and current liabilities is called **working capital**. By comparing a company's obligations that will shortly become due with the company's cash and other assets that, by definition, are expected to shortly be converted to cash, the ratio offers some indication as to ability to pay those debts. Although used in a variety of decisions, it is particularly useful to those considering whether to extend short-term credit. The **current ratio** is computed by dividing current assets by current liabilities. A current ratio of 2 indicates that the company has twice as many current assets available as current liabilities.

> **Working capital**, the difference between current assets and current liabilities, is a popular measure of a company's ability to satisfy its short-term obligations.

Federal Express Corporation

Federal Express Corporation's working capital (in thousands) at the end of its 1996 fiscal year is $109,864 consisting of current assets of $1,728,261 (Graphic 5–4) minus current liabilities of $1,618,397 (Graphic 5–8). The current ratio can be computed as follows:

$$\text{Current ratio} = \frac{\$1,728,261}{\$1,618,397} = 1.07$$

> **Working capital** may not present an accurate or complete picture of a company's liquidity.

Care should be taken, however, in assessing liquidity based solely on working capital. Liabilities usually are paid with cash, not other components of working capital. A company could have difficulty paying its liabilities even with a current ratio significantly greater than 1.0. For example, if a significant portion of current assets consisted of inventories, and inventories usually aren't converted to cash for several months, there could be a problem in paying accounts payable due in 30 days. On the other hand, a current ratio of less than 1.0 doesn't necessarily mean the company will have difficulty meeting its current obligations. A line of credit, for instance, which the company can use to borrow funds, provides financial flexibility. Federal Express Corporation's 1996 annual report discloses a $1 billion credit line for example, "to finance temporary operating cash requirements." That also must be considered in assessing liquidity.

> The **acid-test ratio** provides a more stringent indication of a company's ability to pay its current obligations.

Federal Express Corporation

Acid-test Ratio (or Quick Ratio).   Some analysts like to modify the current ratio to consider only current assets that are readily available to pay short-term debts. One such variation in common use is the **acid-test ratio**. This ratio excludes inventories and prepaid items from current assets before dividing by current liabilities. By eliminating current assets less readily convertible into cash, the acid-test ratio provides a more rigorous indication of liquidity than does the current ratio.

Federal Express Corporation's quick assets at the end of its 1996 fiscal year (in thousands) total $1,365,018 ($93,419 + 1,271,599). The acid-test ratio can be computed as follows:

$$\text{Acid-test ratio} = \frac{\$1,365,018}{\$1,618,397} = .84$$

Are these liquidity ratios adequate? It's difficult to say without some point of comparison. As indicated previously, common standards for such comparisons are industry averages for similar ratios or ratios of the same company in prior years. Suppose Federal Express Corporation's ratios were less than the industry average. Would that be an indication that liquidity is a problem for Federal Express? Not necessarily, but it certainly would raise a red flag that calls for caution in analyzing other areas. Remember, each ratio is but one piece of the entire puzzle. For instance, as stated previously, profitability is perhaps the best indication of liquidity in the long run. We discussed ratios that measure profitability in the previous chapter.

> Liquidity ratios should be assessed in the context of both profitability and efficiency of managing assets.

Also, recall the discussion of receivables turnover and inventory turnover in Chapter 4. Management may be very efficient in managing current assets so that, for example, receivables are collected faster than normal or inventory is sold faster than normal, making those assets more liquid than they otherwise would be. Higher turnover ratios, say compared to a competitor, generally indicate a more liquid position for a given level of the current ratio.

Financing Ratios

> **Learning objective 8**
> Identify and calculate the common liquidity and financing ratios used to assess risk.

Investors and creditors, particularly long-term creditors, are vitally interested in a company's long-term solvency and stability. Financing ratios provide some indication of the riskiness of a company with regard to its ability to pay its long-term debts. Two common financing ratios are (1) the debt to equity ratio and (2) the times interest earned ratio. These ratios are calculated as follows:

$$\text{Debt to equity ratio} = \frac{\text{Total liabilities}}{\text{Shareholders' equity}}$$

$$\text{Times interest earned ratio} = \frac{\text{Net income + interest expense + taxes}}{\text{Interest expense}}$$

Debt to Equity Ratio.   The **debt to equity ratio** compares resources provided by creditors with resources provided by owners. It is calculated by dividing total liabilities (current and noncurrent) by total shareholders' equity (including retained earnings).[12]

> The **debt to equity ratio** indicates the extent of reliance on creditors, rather than owners, in providing resources.

The ratio provides a measure of creditors' protection in the event of insolvency. Other things being equal, the higher the ratio, the higher the risk. The higher the ratio, the greater the creditor claims on assets, so the higher the likelihood an individual creditor would not be paid in full if the company is unable to meet its obligations. Relatedly, a high ratio indicates not only more fixed interest obligations but probably a higher *rate* of interest as well because lenders tend to charge higher rates as the level of debt increases.

> **Federal Express Corporation**

Federal Express Corporation's total liabilities (in thousands) are $4,122,832 (current liabilities, $1,618,397 + long-term debt, $1,325,277 + deferred income taxes, $64,034 + other liabilities, $1,115,124 — Graphic 5–8), and shareholders' equity totals $2,576,139 (Graphic 5–10). The debt to equity ratio can be computed as follows:

$$\text{Debt to equity ratio} = \frac{\$4,122,832}{\$2,576,139} = 1.6$$

As with all ratios, the debt to equity ratio is more meaningful if compared to some standard such as an industry average or a competitor. For example, the 1995 debt to equity ratio for United Parcel Service of America (UPS), a major competitor, is 1.45—slightly lower than Federal Express Corporation's ratio. On the other hand, the ratio for Microsoft Corporation is only .35, indicating that Microsoft has significantly less debt in its capital structure than does Federal Express. Does this mean Microsoft's default risk is less than that of Federal Express? Other things equal—yes. Is that good? Not necessarily. As discussed in the next section, it may be that debt is being underutilized by Microsoft. More debt might increase the potential for return, but the price would be higher risk. This is a fundamental tradeoff faced by virtually all firms when trying to settle on the optimal capital structure.

> The **debt to equity ratio** indicates the extent of trading on the equity, or financial leverage.

Relationship between risk and profitability.   The proportion of debt in the capital structure also is of interest to shareholders. After all, shareholders receive no return on their investments until after all creditor claims are paid. Therefore, the higher the debt to equity ratio, the higher the risk to shareholders. On the other hand, shareholders have a seemingly discrepant desire for a high ratio in order to make use of leverage. By earning a return on borrowed funds that exceeds the cost of borrowing the funds, a company can provide its shareholders with a total return higher than it could achieve by employing equity funds alone. This is referred to as favorable **financial leverage**.

For illustration, consider a newly formed corporation attempting to determine the appropriate mix of debt and equity. The initial capitalization goal is $50 million. The capitalization mix alternatives have been narrowed to two: (1) $10 million in debt and $40 million in equity and (2) $30 million in debt and $20 million in equity.

Also assume that regardless of the capitalization mix chosen, the corporation will be able to generate a 16% annual return, *before payment of interest and income taxes*, on the $50 million in assets acquired. In other words, income before interest and taxes will be $8 million (16% × $50 million). If the interest rate on debt is 8% and the income tax rate is 40%, comparative net income for the first year of operations for the two capitalization alternatives can be calculated as follows:

	Alternative 1	Alternative 2
Income before interest and taxes	$8,000,000	$8,000,000
Less: Interest expense	(800,000)[a]	(2,400,000)[b]
Income before taxes	7,200,000	5,600,000
Less: Income tax expense (40%)	(2,880,000)	(2,240,000)
Net income	$4,320,000	$3,360,000

[a] 8% × $10,000,000
[b] 8% × $30,000,000

---

[12] A commonly used variation of the debt to equity ratio is found by dividing total liabilities by *total assets* (or total equities), rather than by shareholders' equity only. Of course, in this configuration the ratio measures precisely the same attribute of the firm's capital structure, but can be interpreted as the percentage of a company's total assets provided by funds from creditors, rather than by owners.

Choose alternative 1? Probably not. Although alternative 1 provides a higher net income, the return on the shareholders' investment is higher for alternative 2. Here's why.

<table>
<tr><td></td><td>Alternative 1</td><td>Alternative 2</td></tr>
<tr><td>Return on shareholders' equity[13] =</td><td>$\dfrac{\$4,320,000}{\$40,000,000}$</td><td>$\dfrac{\$3,360,000}{\$20,000,000}$</td></tr>
<tr><td>=</td><td>10.8%</td><td>16.8%</td></tr>
</table>

> **Favorable financial leverage** means earning a return on borrowed funds that exceeds the cost of borrowing the funds.

Alternative 2 generated a higher return for each dollar invested by shareholders. This is because the company leveraged its $20 million equity investment with additional debt. Because the cost of the additional debt (8%) is less than the return on assets invested (16%), the return to shareholders is higher. This is the essence of favorable financial leverage.

Be aware, though, leverage is not always favorable; the cost of borrowing the funds might exceed the returns they provide. If the return on assets turned out to be less than expected, the additional debt could result in a lower return on equity for alternative 2. If, for example, the return on assets invested (before interest and tax) had been 6%, rather than 16%, alternative 1 would have provided the better return on equity:

	Alternative 1	Alternative 2
Income before interest and taxes	$3,000,000	$3,000,000
Less: Interest expense	(800,000)[a]	(2,400,000)[b]
Income before taxes	2,200,000	600,000
Less: Income tax expense (40%)	(880,000)	(240,000)
Net income	$1,320,000	$ 360,000

a 8% x $10,000,000
b 8% x $30,000,000

<table>
<tr><td></td><td>Alternative 1</td><td>Alternative 2</td></tr>
<tr><td>Return on shareholders' equity[14] =</td><td>$\dfrac{\$1,320,000}{\$40,000,000}$</td><td>$\dfrac{\$360,000}{\$20,000,000}$</td></tr>
<tr><td>=</td><td>3.3%</td><td>1.8%</td></tr>
</table>

So, shareholders typically are faced with a tradeoff between the risk that high debt denotes and the potential for a higher return from having the higher debt. In any event, the debt to equity ratio offers a basis for making the choice.

Times Interest Earned Ratio. Another way to gauge the ability of a company to satisfy its fixed debt obligations is by comparing interest charges with the income available to pay those charges. The **times interest earned ratio** is designed to do this. It is calculated by dividing income before subtracting either interest expense or taxes by interest expense.

> The **times interest earned ratio** indicates the margin of safety provided to creditors.

Bondholders, noteholders, and other creditors can measure the margin of safety they are accorded by a company's earnings. If income is many times greater than interest expense, creditors' interests are more protected than if income just barely covers this expense. For this purpose, income should be the amount available to pay interest which is income before subtracting either interest or taxes, calculated by adding back to net income the interest and taxes that were deducted.

As an example, Federal Express Corporation's 1996 financial statements report the following items:

---

[13]If return is calculated on *average* shareholders' equity, we're technically assuming that all income is paid to shareholders in cash dividends so that beginning, ending, and average shareholders' equity are the same. On the other hand, if we assume *no* dividends are paid, rates of return would be:

<table>
<tr><td></td><td>Alternative 1</td><td>Alternative 2</td></tr>
<tr><td>Return on shareholders' equity =</td><td>$\dfrac{\$4,320,000}{[\$44,320,000 + 40,000,000]/2}$</td><td>$\dfrac{\$3,360,000}{[\$20,000,000 + \$23,360,000]/2}$</td></tr>
<tr><td>=</td><td>10.25%</td><td>15.50%</td></tr>
</table>

In any case our conclusions are the same.

[14]If we assume *no* dividends are paid, rates of return would be:

<table>
<tr><td></td><td>Alternative 1</td><td>Alternative 2</td></tr>
<tr><td>Return on shareholders' equity =</td><td>$\dfrac{\$1,320,000}{[\$41,320,000 + 40,000,000]/2}$</td><td>$\dfrac{\$360,000}{[\$20,000,000 + \$20,360,000]/2}$</td></tr>
<tr><td>=</td><td>3.25%</td><td>1.78%</td></tr>
</table>

Again, our conclusions are the same.

	(In thousands)
Net income	$307,777
Interest expense*	95,599
Income taxes	232,182
Income before interest and taxes	$635,558

*This amount actually is interest expense net of interest income. No separate disclosure of the components is provided in the financial statements.

The times interest earned ratio can be computed as follows:

$$\text{Times interest earned ratio} = \frac{\$635,558}{\$95,599} = 6.6 \text{ times}$$

The ratio of 6.6 times indicates a considerable margin of safety for creditors. Income could decrease many times and the company would still be able to meet its interest payment obligations.[15] In comparison, UPS's times interest earned ratio for 1995 is 56 times. UPS has less interest-bearing debt in its capital structure than does Federal Express and it earned higher income.

Especially when viewed alongside the debt-equity ratio, the coverage ratio seems to indicate a comfortable safety cushion for creditors. It also indicates a degree of financial mobility if the company were to decide to raise new debt funds to "trade on the equity" and attempt to increase the return to shareholders through favorable financial leverage.

Solution to Financial Reporting Case (at the opening of the chapter)

1. Respond to Jerry's criticism that stockholders' equity does not represent the market value of the company. What information does the balance sheet provide?

Jerry is correct. The financial statements are supposed to help investors and creditors value a company. However, the balance sheet is not intended to portray the market value of the entity. The assets of a company minus its liabilities as shown on the balance sheet (shareholders' equity) usually will not equal the company's market value for several reasons. For example, many assets are measured at their historical costs rather than their market values. Also, many company resources including its trained employees, its experienced management team, and its reputation are not recorded as assets at all. The balance sheet must be used in conjunction with other financial statements, disclosure notes, and other publicly available information.

The balance sheet does, however, provide valuable information that can be used by investors and creditors to help determine market value. After all, it is the balance sheet that describes the assets a company has available for generating future cash flows. The balance sheet also provides important information about liquidity and long-term solvency.

2. The usefulness of the balance sheet is enhanced by classifying assets and liabilities according to common characteristics. What are the classifications used on Silicon Graphics' balance sheet and what elements do those categories include?

Silicon Graphics' balance sheet contains the following asset and liability classifications:
Assets:

1. **Current assets** include cash and several other assets that are reasonably expected to be converted to cash or consumed within the coming year, or within the normal operating cycle of the business if that's longer than one year.
2. **Other marketable investments** represent investments in debt and equity securities of other corporations that management does not intend to convert into cash in the next year or operating cycle if that's longer.
3. **Property and equipment** are the tangible long-lived assets used in the operations of the business. This category includes land, buildings, equipment, machinery, and furniture, as well as natural resources.
4. **Other assets** is a catch-all classification of noncurrent assets and could include long-term prepaid expenses and any noncurrent asset not included in one of the other categories.

Liabilities:

1. **Current liabilities** are those obligations that are expected to be satisfied through the use of current assets or the creation of other current liabilities. Usually, this means liabilities that are expected to be paid within one year or the operating cycle, whichever is longer.
2. **Long-term debt and other** are obligations that will not be paid next year. Possibly included are long-term notes, bonds, leases, and pension obligations.

[15]Of course, interest is paid with cash not with "income." The times interest earned ratio often is calculated by using cash flow from operations before subtracting either interest payments or tax payments as the numerator and interest payments as the denominator.

The Bottom Line

1. The balance sheet, also known as the statement of financial position, is a position statement that presents an organized array of assets, liabilities, and shareholders' equity at a particular point in time. The statement does not portray the market value of the entity. However, the information in the statement can be useful in assessing market value, as well as in providing important information about liquidity and long-term solvency.

2. Current assets include cash and other assets that are reasonably expected to be converted to cash or consumed during one year, or within the normal operating cycle of the business if the operating cycle is longer than one year. All other assets are classified as various types of noncurrent assets. Current liabilities are those obligations that are expected to be satisfied through the use of current assets or the creation of other current liabilities. All other liabilities are classified as long term.

3. In addition to cash and cash equivalents, current assets include short-term investments, accounts receivable, inventories, and prepaid expenses. Other asset classifications include investments and funds, property, plant, and equipment, intangible assets, and other assets.

4. Current liabilities include notes and accounts payable, accrued liabilities, and the current maturities of long-term debt. Long-term liabilities include long-term notes, loans, mortgages, bonds, pension and lease obligations, as well as deferred income taxes.

5. Financial disclosures are used to convey additional information about the account balances in the basic financial statements as well as to provide supplemental information. This information is disclosed parenthetically in the basic financial statements or in notes or supplemental financial statements.

6. Annual financial statements will include management's discussion and analysis of key aspects of the company's business. The purpose of this disclosure is to provide external parties with management's insight into certain transactions, events, and circumstances that affect the enterprise, including their financial impact.

7. The purpose of an audit is to provide a professional, independent opinion as to whether or not the financial statements are prepared in conformity with GAAP. The audit report contains three paragraphs; the first two deal with the scope of the audit and the third paragraph states the auditors' opinion.

8. The balance sheet provides information that can be useful in assessing risk. A key element of risk analysis is investigating a company's ability to pay its obligations when they come due. Liquidity ratios and financing ratios provide information about a company's ability to pay its obligations.

APPENDIX

5

Responsible for this section

REPORTING DISAGGREGATED INFORMATION

Many companies operate in several business segments as a strategy to achieve growth and to reduce operating risk through diversification.

Financial analysis of diversified companies is especially difficult. Consider, for example, a company that operates in several distinct business segments including computer peripherals, home health care systems, textiles, and consumer food products. The results of these distinctly different activities will be aggregated into a single set of financial statements, making difficult an informed projection of future performance. It may well be that the five-year outlook differs greatly among the areas of the economy represented by the different segments. To make matters worse for an analyst, the integrated financial statements do not reveal the relative investments in each of the business segments nor the success the company has had within each area. Given the fact that so many companies these days have chosen to balance their operating risks through diversification, aggregated financial statements pose a widespread problem for analysts, lending and credit officers, and other financial forecasters.

Reporting by Operating Segment
To address the problem, the accounting profession requires companies engaged in more than one significant line of business to provide supplementary information concerning individual operating segments. The supplemental disaggregated data does not include complete financial statements for each reportable segment, only certain specified items.

Segment reporting facilitates the financial statement analysis of diversified companies.

Prior to 1997, *SFAS 14,* "Financial Reporting for Segments of a Business Enterprise," provided the specific reporting requirements for segment reporting.[16] *SFAS 14* applied the industry approach in determining reportable segments. The standard was the subject of much criticism because it allowed for inconsistent definitions of the term *industry* demonstrated by companies applying the standard. This inconsistency reduced the relevance and comparability of segment disclosures.

In January 1996, the Financial Accounting Standards Board issued an exposure draft entitled "Reporting Disaggregated Information about a Business Enterprise." At the time this text was published, a new standard based on this exposure draft replacing *SFAS 14* had not yet been issued. This appendix is based on the exposure draft.

What Is a Reportable Operating Segment?

The new standard employs a management approach in determining which segments of a company are reportable. Segment reporting is aligned with internal management reporting. Reportable segments are determined based on a company's internal financial reporting system which is the system that generates information for the financial statements in the company's annual report.

More formally, the following characteristics define an **operating segment:**[17]

An operating segment is a component of an enterprise:

- That engages in business activities from which it earns revenues and incurs expenses (including revenues and expenses relating to transactions with other components of the same enterprise).
- Whose operating results are regularly reviewed by the enterprise's chief operating decision maker to assess the performance of the individual segment and make decisions about resources to be allocated to the segment.
- For which discrete financial information is available that is generated by or based on the internal financial reporting system.

The FASB hopes that this new approach provides insights into the risk and opportunities management sees in the various areas of company operations. Also, reporting information produced for internal purposes should reduce the incremental cost to companies of providing the data. In addition, the board added quantitative thresholds to the definition of an operating segment to limit the number of reportable segments. Only segments of certain size (10% or more of total company revenues, assets, or net income) must be disclosed. However, a company must account for at least 75% of consolidated revenue through segment disclosures.

What Amounts Are Reported by an Operating Segment?

For areas determined to be reportable operating segments, the following disclosures are required:

a. General information about the operating segment.
b. Segment profit or loss as well as revenues and expenses included in segment profit or loss.
c. Segment assets, segment liabilities, and expenditures for additions to segment assets.[18]

In addition, an enterprise must provide a reconciliation of the total of the operating segments' profits or losses to the enterprise's income before income taxes, extraordinary items, discontinued operations, and the cumulative effect of changes in accounting principles, along with a reconciliation of the total operating segments' revenues to the enterprise's total revenues. A similar reconciliation is required for assets and liabilities.

---

[16]"Financial Reporting for Segments of a Business Enterprise," *Statement of Financial Accounting Standards No. 14* (Stamford, Conn.: FASB, 1976).
[17]"Reporting Disaggregated Information about a Business Enterprise," *Proposed Statement of Financial Accounting Standards* (Norwalk, Conn.: FASB, 1996), par. 11.
[18]Ibid.

Reporting by Geographic Area

In today's global economy it is sometimes difficult to distinguish domestic and foreign companies. Most large U.S. firms conduct significant operations in other countries in addition to having substantial export sales from this country. Differing political and economic environments from country to country means risks and associated rewards sometimes vary greatly among the various operations of a single company. For instance, manufacturing facilities in a South American country embroiled in political unrest pose different risks from having a plant in Vermont, or even Canada. Without disaggregated financial information, these differences cause problems for analysts.

> For operating segments not based on geography, information must be reported for the enterprise's country of domicile and in each other country from which the operating segment derives revenues and holds assets.

However, some enterprise's activities are not organized on the basis of differences in geographic areas of operations. For each operating segment that has not been determined based on geography, the enterprise must report revenues from external customers, long-lived segment assets, and expenditures during the period for long-lived segment assets (1) in the enterprise's country of domicile and (2) in each other country from which the operating segment derives revenues and holds assets.

Information about Major Customers

Some companies in the defense industry derive substantial portions of their revenues from contracts with the Defense Department. When cutbacks occur in national defense or in specific defense systems, the impact on a company's operations can be considerable. Obviously, financial analysts are extremely interested in information concerning the extent to which a company's prosperity depends on one or more major customers such as in the situation described here. For this reason, if 10% or more of the revenues of an enterprise is derived from transactions with a single customer, the enterprise must disclose that fact, the total amount of revenues from each such customer, and the identity of the operating segment or segments earning the revenues. The identity of the major customer need not be disclosed.

> Revenues from major customers must be disclosed.

GLOBAL PERSPECTIVE

There is more international uniformity regarding disaggregated disclosures than with many other accounting issues. More than 30 countries adopted *International Accounting Standard No. 14,* "Reporting Financial Information by Segment," issued in 1981 by the International Accounting Standards Committee. Under this standard, companies report revenues, operating profit or loss, and identifiable assets for both industry segments and geographic segments.

Recently, the FASB worked closely with the Accounting Standards Board of Canada and the International Accounting Standards Board (IASC) to develop similar new standards in this area.

Questions for Review of Key Topics

Question	5–1	Describe the purpose of the balance sheet.
Question	5–2	Explain why the balance sheet does not portray the market value of the entity.
Question	5–3	Define current assets and list the typical asset categories included in this classification.
Question	5–4	Define current liabilities and list the typical liability categories included in this classification.
Question	5–5	Describe what is meant by an operating cycle for a typical manufacturing company.
Question	5–6	Explain the difference(s) between investments in equity securities classified as current assets versus those classified as noncurrent assets.
Question	5–7	Describe the common characteristics of assets classified as property, plant, and equipment and identify some assets included in this classification.
Question	5–8	Distinguish between property, plant, and equipment and intangible assets.
Question	5–9	Explain how each of the following liabilities would be classified on the balance sheet: — A note payable of $100,000 due in five years. — A note payable of $100,000 payable in annual installments of $20,000 each, with the first installment due next year.
Question	5–10	Define the terms paid-in-capital and retained earnings.
Question	5–11	Disclosure notes are an integral part of the information provided in financial statements. In what ways are the notes critical to understanding the financial statements and to evaluating the firm's performance and financial health?

Question	5–12	A summary of the company's significant accounting policies is a required disclosure. Why is this disclosure important to external financial statement users?
Question	5–13	Define a subsequent event.
Question	5–14	Every annual report includes an extensive discussion and analysis provided by the company's management. Specifically, which aspects of the company must this discussion address? Isn't management's perspective too biased to be of use to investors and creditors?
Question	5–15	The auditors' report provides the analyst with an independent and professional opinion about the fairness of the representations in the financial statements. What are the four main types of opinion an auditor might issue? Describe each.
Question	5–16	What is a proxy statement? What information does it provide?
Question	5–17	Define the terms working capital, current ratio, and acid-test ratio (or quick ratio).
Question	5–18	Show the calculation of the following financing ratios: (1) the debt to equity ratio, and (2) the times interest earned ratio.
Question	5–19 [based on Appendix 5]	Segment reporting facilitates the financial statement analysis of diversified companies. What determines whether an operating segment is a reportable segment for this purpose?
Question	5–20 [based on Appendix 5]	For segment reporting purposes, what amounts are reported by each operating segment?

Exercises

Exercise 5–1
Balance sheet; missing elements

The following December 31, 1997, fiscal year-end account balance information is available for the Stonebridge Corporation:

Cash and cash equivalents	$ 5,000
Accounts receivable (net)	20,000
Inventories	60,000
Property, plant, and equipment (net)	120,000
Accounts payable	44,000
Wages payable	15,000
Paid-in-capital	100,000

The only asset not listed is short-term investments. The only liabilities not listed are a $30,000 note payable due in two years and related accrued interest of $1,000 due in four months. The current ratio at year-end is 1.5:1.

Required:
Determine the following at December 31, 1997:
1. Total current assets
2. Short-term investments
3. Retained earnings

Exercise 5–2
Balance sheet classification

The following are the typical classifications used in a balance sheet:
a. Current assets
b. Investments and funds
c. Property, plant, and equipment
d. Intangible assets
e. Other assets

f. Current liabilities
g. Long-term liabilities
h. Paid-in-capital
i. Retained earnings

Required:
For each of the following balance sheet items, use the letters above to indicate the appropriate classification category. If the item is a contra account (valuation account), place a minus sign before the chosen letter.

1. _____ Equipment
2. _____ Accounts payable
3. _____ Allowance for uncollectible accounts
4. _____ Land, held for investment
5. _____ Note payable, due in 5 years
6. _____ Unearned rent revenue
7. _____ Note payable, due in 6 months
8. _____ Income less dividends, accumulated
9. _____ Investment in XYZ Corp., long-term

10. _____ Inventories
11. _____ Patent
12. _____ Land, in use
13. _____ Accrued liabilities
14. _____ Prepaid rent
15. _____ Common stock
16. _____ Building, in use
17. _____ Cash
18. _____ Taxes payable

Exercise 5–3

Balance sheet classification

The following are the typical classifications used in a balance sheet:
a.   Current assets
b.   Investments and funds
c.   Property, plant, and equipment
d.   Intangible assets
e.   Other assets
f.   Current liabilities
g.   Long-term liabilities
h.   Paid-in capital
i.   Retained earnings

Required:

For each of the following 1997 balance sheet items, use the letters above to indicate the appropriate classification category. If the item is a contra account (valuation account), place a minus sign before the chosen letter.

1. _____ Accrued interest payable
2. _____ Franchise
3. _____ Accumulated depreciation
4. _____ Prepaid insurance, for 1999
5. _____ Bonds payable, due in 10 years
6. _____ Current maturities of long-term debt
7. _____ Note payable, due in 3 months
8. _____ Long-term receivables
9. _____ Bond sinking fund, will be used to retire bonds in 10 years

10. _____ Supplies
11. _____ Machinery
12. _____ Land, in use
13. _____ Unearned revenue
14. _____ Copyrights
15. _____ Preferred stock
16. _____ Land, held for speculation
17. _____ Cash equivalents
18. _____ Wages payable

Exercise 5–4

Balance sheet preparation

The following is a December 31, 1997, post-closing trial balance for the Jackson Corporation.

Account Title	Debits	Credits
Cash	30,000	
Accounts receivable	34,000	
Inventories	75,000	
Prepaid rent	6,000	
Marketable securities (short term)	10,000	
Machinery	145,000	
Accumulated depreciation—machinery		11,000
Patent (net of amortization)	83,000	
Accounts payable		8,000
Wages payable		4,000
Taxes payable		32,000
Bonds payable (due in 10 years)		200,000
Common stock		100,000
Retained earnings		28,000
Totals	383,000	383,000

Required:

Prepare a classified balance sheet for Jackson Corporation at December 31, 1997.

Exercise 5–5

Balance sheet preparation

The following is a December 31, 1997, post-closing trial balance for the Valley Pump Corporation.

Account Title	Debits	Credits
Cash	25,000	
Accounts receivable	62,000	
Inventories	81,000	
Interest payable		5,000
Marketable securities	38,000	
Land	120,000	
Buildings	300,000	
Accumulated depreciation—buildings		100,000
Equipment	75,000	
Accumulated depreciation—equipment		25,000
Copyright (net of amortization)	12,000	
Prepaid expenses	32,000	
Accounts payable		85,000
Notes payable		250,000
Allowance for uncollectible accounts		5,000
Common stock		200,000
Retained earnings		75,000
Totals	745,000	745,000

Additional information:
1.   The $120,000 balance in the land account consists of $100,000 for the cost of land where the plant and office buildings are located. The remaining $20,000 represents the cost of land being held for speculation.

2. The $38,000 in the marketable securities account represents an investment in the common stock of another corporation. Valley intends to sell one-half of the stock within the next year.
3. The notes payable account consists of a $100,000 note due in six months and a $150,000 note due in three annual installments of $50,000 each, with the first payment due in August of 1998.

Required:
Prepare a classified balance sheet for the Valley Pump Corporation at December 31, 1997.

Exercise 5–6
Balance sheet preparation; errors

The following balance sheet for the Los Gatos Corporation was prepared by a recently hired accountant. In reviewing the statement you notice several errors.

LOS GATOS CORPORATION
Balance Sheet
At December 31, 1997

Assets

Cash	$ 40,000
Accounts receivable	80,000
Inventories	65,000
Machinery (net)	120,000
Franchise (net)	20,000
Total assets	$325,000

Liabilities and Shareholders' Equity

Accounts payable	$ 60,000
Allowance for uncollectible accounts	5,000
Note payable	55,000
Bonds payable	100,000
Shareholders' equity	105,000
Total liabilities and shareholders' equity	$325,000

Additional information:
1. Cash includes a $20,000 bond sinking fund to be used for repayment of the bonds payable in 2001.
2. The cost of the machinery is $190,000.
3. Accounts receivable includes a $20,000 note receivable from a customer due in 2000.
4. The note payable includes accrued interest of $5,000. Principal and interest are both due on February 1, 1998.
5. The company began operations in 1995. Income less dividends since inception of the company totals $35,000.
6. 50,000 shares of no par common stock were issued in 1995. 100,000 shares are authorized.

Required:
Prepare a corrected, classified balance sheet.

Exercise 5–7
Balance sheet; current versus noncurrent classification

The Cone Corporation is in the process of preparing its December 31, 1997, balance sheet. There are some questions as to the proper classification of the following items:
a. $50,000 in cash set aside in a savings account to pay bonds payable. The bonds mature in 2001.
b. Prepaid rent of $24,000, covering the period January 1, 1998, through December 31, 1999.
c. Note payable of $200,000. The note is payable in annual installments of $20,000 each, with the first installment payable on March 1, 1998.
d. Accrued interest payable of $12,000 related to the note payable.
e. Investment in marketable securities of other corporations, $60,000. Cone intends to sell one-half of the securities in 1998.

Required:
Prepare a partial classified balance sheet to show how each of the above items should be reported.

Exercise 5–8
Financial disclosures

The following are typical disclosures that would appear in the notes accompanying financial statements. For each of the items listed, indicate where the disclosure would likely appear—either in (A) the significant accounting policies note or (B) a separate note.

1.	Inventory costing method	A
2.	Information on related party transactions	____
3.	Composition of property, plant, and equipment	____
4.	Depreciation method	____
5.	Subsequent event information	____
6.	Basis of revenue recognition on long-term contracts	____
7.	Important merger occurring after year-end	____
8.	Composition of receivables	____

Exercise 5–9
Multiple choice; financial disclosures

The following questions dealing with disclosures are adapted from questions that appeared on recent CPA examinations. Determine the response that best completes the statements or questions.

1. What is the purpose of information presented in notes to the financial statements?
    a. To provide disclosure required by generally accepted accounting principles.
    b. To correct improper presentation in the financial statements.
    c. To provide recognition of amounts not included in the totals of the financial statements.
    d. To present management's responses to auditor comments.

2. Which of the following information should be disclosed in the summary of significant accounting policies?
    a. Refinancing of debt subsequent to the balance sheet date.
    b. Guarantees of indebtedness of others.
    c. Criteria for determining which investments are treated as cash equivalents.
    d. Adequacy of pension plan assets relative to vested benefits.

3. Which of the following facts concerning fixed assets should be included in the summary of significant accounting policies?

	Depreciation method	Composition
a.	No	Yes
b.	Yes	Yes
c.	Yes	No
d.	No	No

Exercise 5–10
Concepts; terminology

Listed below are several terms and phrases associated with the balance sheet and financial disclosures. Pair each item from List A (by letter) with the item from List B that is most appropriately associated with it.

List A	List B
_____ 1. Balance sheet	a. Will be satisfied through the use of current assets.
_____ 2. Liquidity	b. Items expected to be converted to cash or consumed within one year or the operating cycle.
_____ 3. Current assets	c. The statements are presented fairly in conformity with GAAP.
_____ 4. Operating cycle	
_____ 5. Current liabilities	d. An organized array of assets, liabilities and equity.
_____ 6. Cash equivalent	e. Important to a user in comparing financial information across companies.
_____ 7. Intangible asset	
_____ 8. Working capital	f. Scope limitation or a departure from GAAP.
_____ 9. Accrued liabilities	g. Recorded when an expense is incurred but not yet paid.
_____ 10. Summary of significant accounting	
_____ 11. Subsequent events	h. Relates to the amount of time before an asset is converted to cash or a liability is paid.
_____ 12. Unqualified opinion	i. Occurs after the fiscal year-end but before the statements are issued.
_____ 13. Qualified opinion	j. Cash to cash.
	k. One-month certificate of deposit.
	l. Current assets minus current liabilities.
	m. Lacks physical existence.

Exercise 5–11
Calculating ratios

The 1997 balance sheet for Hallbrook Industries, Inc. is shown below.

HALLBROOK INDUSTRIES, INC.
Balance Sheet
December 31, 1997

	($ in 000s)
Assets:	
Cash	$ 100
Short-term investments	150
Accounts receivable	200
Inventories	400
Property, plant, and equipment (net)	1,000
Total assets	$1,850
Liabilities and Shareholders' Equity:	
Current liabilities	$ 400
Long-term liabilities	350
Paid-in capital	700
Retained earnings	400
Total liabilities and shareholders' equity	$1,850

The company's 1997 income statement reported the following amounts ($ in thousands):

Net sales	$4,600
Interest expense	20
Income tax expense	100
Net income	160

Required:

Determine the following ratios for 1997:

1. Current ratio
2. Acid-test ratio
3. Debt to equity ratio
4. Times interest earned ratio

Exercise 5–12

Calculating ratios; solve for unknowns

The current asset section of the Excalibur Tire Company's balance sheet consists of cash, marketable securities, accounts receivable, and inventories. The December 31, 1997, balance sheet revealed the following:

Inventories	$ 420,000
Total assets	2,800,000
Current ratio	2.25
Acid-test ratio	1.2
Debt to equity ratio	1.8

Required:

Determine the following 1997 balance sheet items:

1. Current assets
2. Shareholders' equity
3. Noncurrent assets
4. Long-term liabilities

Exercise 5–13

Effect of management decisions on ratios

Most decisions made by management impact the ratios analysts use to evaluate performance. Indicate (by letter) whether each of the actions listed below will immediately increase (I), decrease (D), or have no effect (N) on the ratios shown. Assume each ratio is less than 1.0 before the action is taken.

Action	Current Ratio	Acid-Test Ratio	Debt to Equity Ratio
1. Issuance of long-term bonds	____	____	____
2. Issuance of short-term notes	____	____	____
3. Payment of accounts payable	____	____	____
4. Purchase of inventory on account	____	____	____
5. Purchase of inventory for cash	____	____	____
6. Purchase of equipment with a 4-year note	____	____	____
7. Retirement of bonds	____	____	____
8. Sale of common stock	____	____	____
9. Write-off of obsolete inventory	____	____	____
10. Purchase of short-term investment for cash	____	____	____
11. Decision to refinance on a long-term basis some currently maturing debt	____	____	____

Exercise 5–14

Multiple choice; ratio analysis

The following questions dealing with ratio analysis are adapted from questions that appeared on recent CPA examinations. Determine the response that best completes the statements or questions.

1. At December 30, 1997, Vida Co. had cash of $200,000, a current ratio of 1.5:1 and a quick ratio of .5:1. On December 31, 1997, all cash was used to reduce accounts payable. How did these cash payments affect the ratios?

	Current Ratio	Quick Ratio
a.	Increased	Decreased
b.	Increased	No Effect
c.	Decreased	Increased
d.	Decreased	No Effect

2. In analyzing a company's financial statements, which financial statement would a potential investor primarily use to assess the company's liquidity and financial flexibility?
   a. Balance sheet.
   b. Income statement.
   c. Statement of retained earnings.
   d. Statement of cash flows.

Problems

Presented below is a list of balance sheet accounts presented in alphabetical order.

Problem 5–1

Balance sheet preparation

Accounts payable
Accounts receivable
Accumulated depreciation—buildings
Accumulated depreciation—equipment
Allowance for uncollectible accounts
Bond sinking fund
Bonds payable (due in 10 years)
Buildings
Cash
Common stock
Copyright
Equipment
Interest receivable (due in three months)

Inventories
Land (in use)
Long-term investments
Notes payable (due in 6 months)
Notes receivable (due in 2 years)
Patent
Preferred stock
Prepaid expenses
Rent payable (current)
Retained earnings
Short-term investments
Taxes payable
Wages payable

Required:

Prepare a classified balance sheet ignoring monetary amounts.

Problem 5–2

Balance sheet preparation;
missing elements

The data listed below are taken from a recent balance sheet of Amdahl Corporation. Some amounts, indicated by question marks, have been intentionally omitted.

	($ in thousands)
Cash and cash equivalents	$ 239,186
Short-term investments	353,700
Accounts receivable (net of allowance)	504,944
Inventories	?
Prepaid expenses (current)	83,259
Total current assets	1,594,927
Long-term receivables	110,800
Property and equipment (net)	?
Total assets	?
Notes payable and short-term debt	31,116
Accounts payable	?
Accrued liabilities	421,772
Other current liabilities	181,604
Total current liabilities	693,564
Long-term debt and deferred taxes	?
Total liabilities	956,140
Shareholders' equity	1,370,627

Required:

1. Determine the missing amounts.
2. Prepare Amdahl's classified balance sheet.

Problem 5–3

Balance sheet preparation

The following is a December 31, 1997, post-closing trial balance for Almway Corporation.

Account Title	Debits	Credits
Cash	45,000	
Investments	110,000	
Accounts receivable	60,000	
Inventories	200,000	
Prepaid insurance	9,000	
Land	90,000	
Buildings	420,000	
Accumulated depreciation—buildings		100,000
Equipment	110,000	
Accumulated depreciation—equipment		60,000
Patents (net of amortization)	10,000	
Accounts payable		75,000
Notes payable		130,000
Interest payable		20,000
Bonds payable		240,000
Common stock		300,000
Retained earnings		129,000
Totals	1,054,000	1,054,000

Additional information:

1. The investment account includes an investment in common stock of another corporation of $30,000 which management intends to hold for at least three years.

2. The land account includes land which cost $25,000 that the company has not used and is currently listed for sale.

3. The cash account includes $15,000 set aside in a fund to pay bonds payable that mature in 2000 and $23,000 set aside in a three-month certificate of deposit.

4. The notes payable account consists of the following:
   a. a $30,000 note due in six months.
   b. a $50,000 note due in six years.
   c. a $50,000 note due in five annual installments of $10,000 each, with the next installment due February 15, 1998.

5. The $60,000 balance in accounts receivable is net of an allowance for uncollectible accounts of $8,000.

6. The common stock account represents 100,000 shares of no par value common stock issued and outstanding. The corporation has 500,000 shares authorized.

Required:
Prepare a classified balance sheet for the Almway Corporation at December 31, 1997.

Problem 5–4
Balance sheet preparation; construction accounting

The following is a June 30, 1997, post-closing trial balance for Excell Construction Company.

Account Title	Debits	Credits
Cash	83,000	
Short-term investments	65,000	
Accounts receivable	180,000	
Construction in progress	300,000	
Prepaid expenses	32,000	
Land	75,000	
Buildings	320,000	
Accumulated depreciation—buildings		160,000
Equipment	265,000	
Accumulated depreciation—equipment		120,000
Accounts payable		173,000
Accrued expenses		45,000
Notes payable		100,000
Billings on construction contract		215,000
Mortgage payable		250,000
Common stock		100,000
Retained earnings		157,000
Totals	1,320,000	1,320,000

Additional information:

1. The company is in the business of constructing office buildings. The construction in progress account represents the costs incurred to date in constructing an office building for a customer under a long-term contract. The building will be completed early in 1998. The company uses the completed contract method to recognize gross profit on its projects.

2. The short-term investments account includes $18,000 in U.S. treasury bills purchased in May. The bills mature in July.

3. The accounts receivable account consists of the following:
   a. Amounts owed by customers $125,000
   b. Allowance for uncollectible accounts—trade customers   (15,000)
   c. Nontrade note receivable (due in three years)   65,000
   d. Interest receivable on note (due in four months)   5,000
      Total $180,000

4. The notes payable account consists of two notes of $50,000 each. One note is due on September 30, 1997, and the other is due on November 30, 1998.

5. The mortgage payable is payable in *semiannual* installments of $5,000 each plus interest. The next payment is due on October 31, 1997. Interest has been properly accrued and is included in accrued expenses.

6. Five hundred thousand shares of no par common stock are authorized, of which 200,000 shares have been issued and are outstanding.

7. The land account includes $50,000 representing the cost of the land on which the company's office building resides. The remaining $25,000 is the cost of land on which the company is constructing the office building for sale.

Required:
Prepare a classified balance sheet for the Excell Construction Company at June 30, 1997.

Problem 5–5

Balance sheet preparation; errors

The following balance sheet for the Hubbard Corporation was prepared by the company:

HUBBARD CORPORATION
Balance Sheet
At December 31, 1997

Assets

Buildings	$ 750,000
Land	250,000
Cash	60,000
Accounts receivable (net)	120,000
Inventories	240,000
Machinery	280,000
Patent (net)	100,000
Investment in marketable equity securities	60,000
Total assets	$1,860,000

Liabilities and Shareholders' Equity

Accounts payable	$ 215,000
Accumulated depreciation	255,000
Notes payable	500,000
Appreciation of inventories	80,000
Common stock, authorized and issued 100,000 shares of no par stock	430,000
Retained earnings	380,000
Total liabilities and shareholders' equity	$1,860,000

Additional information:

1. The buildings, land, and machinery are all stated at cost except for a parcel of land that the company is holding for future sale. The land originally cost $50,000 but, due to a significant increase in market value, is listed at $120,000. The increase in the land account was credited to retained earnings.
2. Marketable equity securities consist of stocks of other corporations and are recorded at cost, $20,000 of which will be sold in the coming year. The remainder will be held indefinitely.
3. Notes payable are all long-term. However, a $100,000 note requires an installment payment of $25,000 due in the coming year.
4. Inventories are recorded at current resale value. The original cost of the inventories is $160,000.

Required:

Prepare a corrected classified balance sheet for the Hubbard Corporation at December 31, 1997.

Problem 5–6

Balance sheet preparation

Presented below is the balance sheet for HHD, Inc., at December 31, 1997.

Current assets	$ 600,000	Current liabilities	$ 400,000
Investments	500,000	Long-term liabilities	1,100,000
Property, plant, and equipment	2,000,000	Shareholders' equity	1,800,000
Intangible assets	200,000		
Total assets	$3,300,000	Total liabilities and shareholders' equity	$3,300,000

The captions shown in the summarized statement above include the following:

a. Current assets: cash, $150,000; accounts receivable, $200,000; inventories, $225,000; and prepaid insurance, $25,000.
b. Investments: investments in common stock, short term, $90,000, and long term, $160,000; and bond sinking fund, $250,000.
c. Property, plant, and equipment: buildings, $1,500,000 less accumulated depreciation, $600,000; equipment, $500,000 less accumulated depreciation, $200,000; and land, $800,000.
d. Intangible assets: patent, $110,000; and copyright, $90,000.
e. Current liabilities: accounts payable, $100,000; notes payable, short term, $150,000, and long term, $90,000; and taxes payable, $60,000.
f. Long-term liabilities: bonds payable due 2002.
g. Shareholders' equity: preferred stock, $450,000; common stock, $1,000,000; retained earnings, $350,000.

Required:

Prepare a corrected classified balance sheet for HHD, Inc., at December 31, 1997.

Problem 5–7

Income statement and balance sheet preparation

The Melody Lane Music Company was started by John Ross early in 1997. Initial capital was acquired by issuing shares of common stock to various investors and by obtaining a bank loan. The company operates a retail store that sells records, tapes, and compact discs. Business was so good during the first year of operations that

John is considering opening a second store on the other side of town. The funds necessary for expansion will come from a new bank loan. In order to approve the loan, the bank requires financial statements.

John asks for your help in preparing the necessary statements and presents you with the following information for the year ending December 31, 1997:

a. Cash receipts consisted of the following:

From customers	$360,000
From issue of common stock	100,000
From bank loan	100,000

b. Cash disbursements were as follows:

Purchase of inventory	$300,000
Rent	15,000
Salaries	30,000
Utilities	5,000
Insurance	3,000
Purchase of equipment and furniture	40,000

c. The bank loan was made on March 31, 1997. A note was signed requiring payment of interest and principal on March 31, 1998. The interest rate is 12%.

d. The equipment and furniture were purchased on January 3, 1997, and have an estimated useful life of 10 years with no anticipated salvage value. Depreciation per year is $4,000.

e. Inventories on hand at the end of the year cost $100,000.

f. Amounts owed at December 31, 1997, were as follows:

To suppliers of inventory	$20,000
To the utility company	1,000

g. Rent on the store building is $1,000 per month. On December 1, 1997, four months' rent was paid in advance.

h. Assume that the company is not subject to federal, state, or local income tax.

Required:

1. Prepare a single-step, accrual-based income statement for the year ending December 31, 1997.
2. Prepare a balance sheet at December 31, 1997.

Problem 5–8
Creating a balance sheet from ratios; Chapters 4 and 5

The Cadux Candy Company's income statement for the year ended December 31, 1997, reported interest expense of $2 million and income tax expense of $12 million. Current assets listed on its balance sheet include cash, accounts receivable, and inventories. Property, plant, and equipment is the company's only noncurrent asset. Financial ratios for 1997 are listed below. Profitability and turnover ratios with balance sheet items in the denominator were calculated using year-end balances rather than averages.

Debt to equity ratio	1.0
Current ratio	2.0
Acid-test ratio	1.0
Times interest earned ratio	17 times
Return on assets	10%
Return on shareholders' equity	20%
Profit margin on sales	5%
Gross profit margin (gross profit divided by net sales)	40%
Inventory turnover	8 times
Receivables turnover	20 times

Required:
Prepare a December 31, 1997, balance sheet for the Cadux Candy Company.

Problem 5–9
Compare two companies in the same industry

Presented below are condensed financial statements adapted from those of two actual companies competing as the primary players in a specialty area of the food manufacturing and distribution industry. ($ in millions, except per share amounts.)

Balance Sheets

	Metropolitan	Republic
Assets:		
Cash	$ 179.3	$ 37.1
Accounts receivable (net)	422.7	325.0
Short-term investments		4.7
Inventories	466.4	635.2
Prepaid expenses and other current assets	134.6	476.7
Current assets	1,203.0	1,478.7
Property, plant, and equipment (net)	2,608.2	2,064.6
Intangibles and other assets	210.3	464.7
Total assets	$ 4,021.5	$ 4,008.0

	Metropolitan	Republic
Liabilities and Shareholders' Equity:		
Accounts payable	$ 467.9	$ 691.2
Short-term notes	227.1	557.4
Accruals and other current liabilities	585.2	538.5
Current liabilities	1,280.2	1,787.1
Long-term debt	535.6	542.3
Deferred tax liability	384.6	610.7
Other long-term liabilities	104.0	95.1
Total liabilities	2,304.4	3,035.2
Common stock (par and additional paid-in capital)	144.9	335.0
Retained earnings	2,476.9	1,601.9
Less: treasury stock	(904.7)	(964.1)
Total liabilities and shareholders' equity	$4,021.5	$4,008.0

Income Statements		
Net sales	$ 5,698.0	$ 7,768.2
Cost of goods sold	(2,909.0)	(4,481.7)
Gross profit	2,789.0	3,286.5
Operating expenses	(1,743.7)	(2,539.2)
Interest expense	(56.8)	(46.6)
Income before taxes	988.5	700.7
Tax expense	(394.7)	(276.1)
Net income	$ 593.8	$ 424.6
Net income per share	$2.40	$6.50

Required:

Evaluate and compare the two companies by responding to the following questions.

Note: Because comparative statements are not provided you should use year-end balances in place of average balances as appropriate.

1. Which of the two firms had greater earnings relative to resources available?
2. Have the two companies achieved their respective rates of return on assets with similar combinations of profit margin and turnover?
3. From the perspective of a common shareholder, which of the two firms provided a greater rate of return?
4. Which company is most highly leveraged and which has made most effective use of financial leverage?
5. Of the two companies, which appears riskier in terms of its ability to pay short-term obligations?
6. How efficiently are current assets managed?
7. From the perspective of a creditor, which company offers the most comfortable margin of safety in terms of its ability to pay fixed interest charges?

Cases

Discussion Case 5–1
Current versus noncurrent classification

A first-year accounting student is confused by a statement made in a recent class. Her instructor stated that the assets listed on the balance sheet of the IBM Corporation include computers that are classified as current assets as well as computers that are classified as noncurrent assets. In addition, the instructor stated that investments in marketable securities of other corporations could be classified on the balance sheet as either current or noncurrent assets.

Required:

Explain to the student the distinction between current and noncurrent assets pertaining to the IBM computers and the investments in marketable securities.

Discussion Case 5–2
Current versus noncurrent classification

1. Discuss the factors that determine whether an asset or liability should be classified as current or noncurrent on a balance sheet.
2. Identify six items that under different circumstances could be classified as either current or noncurrent. Indicate the factors that would determine the correct classification.

Discussion Case 5–3
Operating cycle

1. Define the concept of an operating cycle as applied in the preparation of a balance sheet.
2. Identify three types of businesses with an operating cycle shorter than one year and three types of businesses with cycles longer than one year.

Group Interaction Case 5–4
Inventory or property, plant, and equipment

The Red Hen Company produces, processes, and sells fresh eggs. The company is in the process of preparing financial statements at the end of its first year of operations and has asked for your help in determining the appropriate treatment of the cost of its egg-laying flock. The estimated life of a laying hen is approximately two years, after which they are sold to soup companies.

The controller considers the company's operating cycle to be two years and wants to present the cost of the egg-producing flock as inventory in the current asset section of the balance sheet. He feels that the hens are "goods awaiting sale." The chief financial officer does not agree with this treatment. He thinks that the cost of the flock should be classified as property, plant, and equipment because the hens are used in the production of product—the eggs.

   The focus of this case is the balance sheet presentation of the cost of the egg-producing flock. Your instructor will divide the class into from two to six groups depending on the size of the class. The mission of your group is to reach consensus on the appropriate presentation.

Required:
1.   Each group member should deliberate the situation independently and draft a tentative argument prior to the class session for which the case is assigned.
2.   In class, each group will meet for 10 to 15 minutes in different areas of the classroom. During that meeting, group members will take turns sharing their suggestions for the purpose of arriving at a single group treatment.
3.   After the allotted time, a spokesperson for each group (selected during the group meetings) will share the group's solution with the class. The goal of the class is to incorporate the views of each group into a consensus approach to the situation.

Critical Thought Case 5–5
Balance sheet; errors

   You recently joined the internal auditing department of Marcus Clothing Corporation. As one of your first assignments, you are examining a balance sheet prepared by a staff accountant.

MARCUS CLOTHING CORPORATION
Balance Sheet
at December 31, 1997

Assets

Current assets:		
Cash		$ 137,000
Accounts receivable , net		80,000
Note receivable		53,000
Inventories		240,000
Investments		66,000
Total current assets		576,000
Other assets:		
Land	$200,000	
Equipment, net	320,000	
Prepaid expenses	27,000	
Patent	22,000	
Total other assets		569,000
Total assets		$1,145,000

Liabilities and Shareholders' Equity

Current liabilities:		
Accounts payable		$ 125,000
Salaries payable		32,000
Total current liabilities		157,000
Long-term liabilities:		
Note payable	$100,000	
Bonds payable	300,000	
Interest payable	20,000	
Total long-term liabilities		420,000
Shareholders' equity:		
Common stock	500,000	
Retained earnings	68,000	
Total shareholders' equity		568,000
Total liabilities and shareholders' equity		$1,145,000

   In the course of your examination you uncover the following information pertaining to the balance sheet:
1.   The company rents its facilities. The land that appears on the statement is being held for future sale.
2.   The note receivable is due in 1999. The balance of $53,000 includes $3,000 of accrued interest. The next interest payment is due in July 1998.
3.   The note payable is due in installments of $20,000 per year. Interest on both the notes and bonds is payable annually.
4.   The company's investments consist of marketable equity securities of other corporations. Management does not intend to liquidate any investments in the coming year.

Required:

Identify and explain the deficiencies in the statement prepared by the company's accountant. Include in your answer items that require additional disclosure, either on the face of the statement or in a note.

Integrating Case 5–6
Balance sheet and income statement

The Rice Corporation is negotiating a loan for expansion purposes and the bank requires financial statements. Before closing the accounting records for the year ended December 31, 1997, Rice's controller prepared the following financial statements:

RICE CORPORATION
Balance Sheet
At December 31, 1997

Assets

	($ in 000s)
Cash	$ 275
Marketable securities	78
Accounts receivable	487
Inventories	425
Allowance for uncollectible accounts	(50)
Property and equipment, net	160
Total assets	$1,375

Liabilities and Shareholders' Equity

	($ in 000s)
Accounts payable and accrued liabilities	$ 420
Notes payable	200
Common stock	260
Retained earnings	495
Total liabilities and shareholders' equity	$1,375

RICE CORPORATION
Income Statement
For the Year Ended December 31, 1997

		($ in 000s)
Net sales		$1,580
Expenses:		
Cost of goods sold	$755	
Selling and administrative	385	
Miscellaneous	129	
Income taxes	100	
Total expenses		1,369
Net income		$ 211

Additional information:
1. The company's common stock is traded on an organized stock exchange.
2. The investment portfolio consists of short-term investments valued at $57,000. The remaining investments will not be sold until the year 2000.
3. Miscellaneous expense represents the before-tax loss from damages caused by an earthquake. The event is considered to be both unusual and infrequent.
4. Notes payable consist of two notes:
   Note 1: $80,000 face value dated September 30, 1997.
   Principal and interest at 10% are due on September 30, 1998.
   Note 2: $120,000 face value dated April 30, 1997. Principal is due in two equal installments of $60,000 plus interest on the unpaid balance. The two payments are scheduled for April 30, 1998, and April 30, 1999.
   Interest on both loans has been correctly accrued and is included in accrued liabilities on the balance sheet and selling and administrative expenses on the income statement.
5. Selling and administrative expenses include a $90,000 charge incurred by the company in restructuring some of its operations. The amount of the charge is material.

Required:

Identify and explain the deficiencies in the presentation of the statements prepared by the company's controller. Do not prepare corrected statements. Include in your answer a list of items that require additional disclosure, either on the face of the statement or in a note.

Critical Thought Case 5–7
Financial disclosures

You recently joined the auditing staff of Best, Best, and Krug, CPAs. You have been assigned to the audit of Clearview, Inc., and have been asked by the audit senior to examine the balance sheet prepared by Clearview's accountant.

CLEARVIEW, INC.
Balance Sheet
At December 31, 1997

Assets

		($ in millions)
Current assets:		
Cash		$ 10.5
Accounts receivable		112.1
Inventories		220.6
Prepaid expenses		5.5
Total current assets		348.7
Investments		22.0
Property, plant, and equipment, net		486.9
Total assets		$857.6

Liabilities and Shareholders' Equity

Current liabilities:		
Accounts payable		$ 83.5
Accrued taxes and interest		25.5
Current maturities of long-term debt		20.0
Total current liabilities		129.0
Long-term liabilities:		420.0
Total liabilities		549.0
Shareholders' equity:		
Common stock	$100.0	
Retained earnings	208.6	
Total shareholders' equity		308.6
Total liabilities and shareholders' equity		$857.6

Required:

Identify the items on the statement that most likely would require further disclosure either on the face of the statement or in a note. Further identify those items that would require disclosure in the significant accounting policies note.

Real World Case 5–8
Balance sheet and significant accounting policies disclosure

The balance sheet and disclosure of significant accounting policies taken from the 1995 annual report of International Business Machines Corporation (IBM) appear below. Use this information to answer the following questions:

1. What are the asset classifications contained in IBM's balance sheet?
2. What amounts did IBM report for the following items for 1995:
   a. Total assets
   b. Current assets
   c. Current liabilities
   d. Total shareholders' equity
   e. Retained earnings
   f. Inventories
3. What is the par value of IBM's common stock? How many shares of common stock are authorized and issued at the end of 1995?
4. Compute IBM's current ratio for 1995.
5. Identify the following items:
   a. The company's inventory valuation method.
   b. The company's depreciation method.
   c. The definition of cash equivalents.
   d. The method used to amortize goodwill.

CONSOLIDATED STATEMENT OF FINANCIAL POSITION
INTERNATIONAL BUSINESS MACHINES CORPORATION AND SUBSIDIARY COMPANIES

(Dollars in millions) At December 31:	Notes	1995	1994
Assets			
Current assets:			
Cash		$ 1,746	$ 1,240
Cash equivalents		5,513	6,682
Marketable securities	X	442	2,632
Notes and accounts receivable—trade, net of allowances		16,450	14,018
Sales-type leases receivable		5,961	6,351
Other accounts receivable		991	1,164
Inventories	D	6,323	6,334

(Dollars in millions)

At December 31:	Notes	1995	1994
Prepaid expenses and other current assets		3,265	2,917
Total current assets		40,691	41,338
Plant, rental machines and other property	E	43,981	44,820
Less: Accumulated depreciation		27,402	28,156
Plant, rental machines and other property—net		16,579	16,664
Software, less accumulated amortization (1995—$11,276; 1994, $10,793)		2,419	2,963
Investments and sundry assets	F	20,603	20,126
Total assets		$80,292	$81,091
Liabilities and Stockholders' Equity			
Current liabilities:			
Taxes	H	$ 2,634	$ 1,771
Short-term debt	G	11,569	9,570
Accounts payable		4,511	3,778
Compensation and benefits		2,914	2,702
Deferred income		3,469	3,475
Other accrued expenses and liabilities		6,551	7,930
Total current liabilities		31,648	29,226
Long-term debt	G	10,060	12,548
Other liabilities	M	14,354	14,023
Deferred income taxes	H	1,807	1,881
Total liabilities		57,869	57,678
Contingencies	N		
Stockholders' equity:			
Preferred stock, par value $.01 per share— shares authorized: 150,000,000 shares issued: 1995—2,610,711; 1994—11,145,000	S	253	1,081
Common stock, par value $1.25 per share— shares authorized: 750,000,000 shares issued: 1995—548,199,013; 1994—588,180,244	S	7,488	7,342
Retained earnings		11,630	12,352
Translation adjustments		3,036	2,672
Treasury stock, at cost (shares: 1995—424,583; 1994—469,500)		(41)	(34)
Net unrealized gain on marketable securities		57	—
Total stockholders' equity		22,423	23,413
Total liabilities and stockholders' equity		$80,292	$81,091

NOTES TO CONSOLIDATED FINANCIAL STATEMENTS
INTERNATIONAL BUSINESS MACHINES CORPORATION AND SUBSIDIARY COMPANIES

A} Significant accounting policies (in part)

Revenue

Revenue from hardware sales or sales-type leases is recognized when the product is shipped. Revenue from one-time-charge licensed software is recognized when the program is shipped with an appropriate deferral for post-contract customer support. This deferral is earned over the support period. Revenue from monthly software licenses is recognized as license fees accrue; from maintenance and services over the contractual period, or as the services are performed; from rentals and operating leases, monthly as the fees accrue; and from financing at level rates of return over the term of the lease or receivable. Revenue is reduced for estimated customer returns and allowances.

Cash Equivalents

All highly liquid investments with a maturity of three months or less at date of purchase are considered to be cash equivalents.

Inventories

Raw materials, work in process, and finished goods are stated at the lower of average cost or market.

Depreciation

Plant, rental machines and other property are carried at cost, and depreciated over their estimated useful lives using the straight-line method.

Goodwill

Goodwill is charged to earnings on a straight-line basis over the periods estimated to be benefited, currently not exceeding five years.

Critical Thought Case 5–9
Post fiscal year-end events

The fiscal year-end for the Northwest Distribution Corporation is December 31. The company's 1997 financial statements were issued on March 15, 1998. The following events occurred between December 31, 1997, and March 15, 1998:

1. On January 22, 1998, the company negotiated a major merger with Blandon Industries. The merger will be completed by the middle of 1998.
2. On February 3, 1998, Northwest negotiated a $10 million long-term note with the Credit Bank of Ohio. The amount of the note is material.

3. On February 25, 1998, a flood destroyed one of the company's manufacturing plants causing $600,000 of uninsured damage.

Required:
Determine the appropriate treatment of each of these events in the 1997 financial statements of Northwest Distribution Corporation.

Research Case 5–10
Disclosure of debt covenants

Classifying a liability as short or long term provides useful cash flow information to financial statement users. Additional cash flow information is contained in a disclosure note that provides information about the payment terms, interest rates, collateral, and scheduled maturity amounts of long-term debt. Quite often, debt agreements contain certain constraints placed by the lender on the borrower in order to protect the lender's investment. Many of these constraints, called *debt covenants*, are based on accounting information. Professors Press and Weintrop in "Financial Statement Disclosure of Accounting-Based Debt Covenants," investigate the adequacy of debt covenant disclosures in financial statements.

Required:
1. In your library or from some other source, locate the indicated article in *Accounting Horizons*, March 1991.
2. Describe the two types of accounting-based debt covenants—affirmative covenants and negative covenants—discussed by the authors.
3. What is the authors' conclusion about the adequacy of disclosure of accounting-based covenants in financial statements?

International Case 5–11
Comparison of audit reports in the U.K. and the United States

British Airways PLc is the largest international passenger airline in the world. The following is the Report of the Auditors accompanying the company's 1995 financial statements:

Report of the Auditors to the Members of British Airways PLc
We have audited the accounts on Pages 16 to 47, which have been prepared under the historical cost convention as modified by the revaluation of certain fixed assets and on the basis of the accounting policies set out on Pages 20 to 22.

Respective responsibilities of Directors and auditors
As described above, the Company's Directors are responsible for the preparation of the accounts. It is our responsibility to form an independent opinion, based on our audit, on those accounts and to report our opinion to you.

Basis of opinion
We conducted our audit in accordance with Auditing Standards issued by the Auditing Practices Board. An audit includes an assessment of the amounts and disclosures in the accounts. It also includes an assessment of the significant estimates and judgments made by the Directors in the preparation of the accounts and of whether the accounting policies are appropriate to the Group's circumstances, consistently applied and adequately disclosed.

We planned and performed our audit so as to obtain all the information and explanations which we considered necessary in order to provide us with sufficient evidence to give reasonable assurance that the accounts are free from material misstatement, whether caused by fraud or other irregularity or error. In forming our opinion we also evaluated the overall adequacy of the presentation of information in the accounts.

Opinion
In our opinion the accounts give a true and fair view of the state of affairs of the Company and of the Group at 31 March 1995 and of the profit of the Group for the year then ended and have been properly prepared in accordance with the Companies Act of 1985.

Ernst & Young
Chartered Accountants
Registered Auditor
London
22 May 1995

Required:
Compare the auditors' report in the United Kingdom with that of the United States.

Internet Case 5–12
Disclosures; proxy statement

EDGAR, the Electronic Data Gathering, Analysis, and Retrieval system, performs automated collection, validation, indexing, and forwarding of submissions by companies and others who are required by law to file forms with the SEC. All publicly traded domestic companies use EDGAR to make the majority of their filings. (Some foreign companies file voluntarily.) Form 10-K or 10-KSB, which include the annual report, is required to be filed on EDGAR. The SEC makes this information available on the Internet.

Required:

1. Access EDGAR on the Internet. You can use a web browser or anonymous FTP. The web address is http://www.sec.gov/. To use anonymous FTP, use your File Transfer Protocol software to connect to sec.gov and log in as user "anonymous" with a password of your electronic mail address.
2. Search for Tandem Computers, Inc. Access the 10-K filing for the fiscal year ended September 30, 1995. Search or scroll to find the disclosure notes and audit report.
3. Answer the following questions:
    a. Describe the two subsequent events disclosed by the company.
    b. Which firm is the company's auditor? What type of opinion did the auditor render? Does the audit report contain any explanatory paragraphs?
4. Search for Wendys International. Access the most recent proxy statement filed with the SEC (the proxy statement designation is Def 14A) and answer the following questions:
    a. What is the principal position of Dave Thomas?
    b. What was the annual compensation paid to Mr. Thomas?
    c. Mr. Thomas's compensation includes payments for services rendered as principal spokesman in the Company's television and radio commercials. At what rate was Mr. Thomas paid for these services?

Critical Thought Case 5–13
Debt versus equity

A common problem facing any business entity is the debt versus equity decision. When funds are required to obtain assets, should debt or equity financing be used? This decision also is faced when a company is initially formed. What will be the mix of debt versus equity in the initial capital structure? The characteristics of debt are very different from those of equity as are the financial implications of using one method of financing as opposed to the other.

Cherokee Plastics Corporation is formed by a group of investors to manufacture household plastic products. Their initial capitalization goal is $50,000,000. That is, the incorporators have decided to raise $50,000,000 to acquire the initial operating assets of the company. They have narrowed down the financing mix alternatives to two:

1. All equity financing.
2. $20,000,000 in debt financing and $30,000,000 in equity financing.

No matter which financing alternative is chosen, the corporation expects to be able to generate a 10% annual return, before payment of interest and income taxes, on the $50,000,000 in assets acquired. The interest rate on debt would be 8%. The effective income tax rate will be approximately 50%.

Alternative 2 will require specified interest and principal payments to be made to the creditors at specific dates. The interest portion of these payments (interest expense) will reduce the taxable income of the corporation and hence the amount of income tax the corporation will pay. The all-equity alternative requires no specified payments to be made to suppliers of capital. The corporation is not legally liable to make distributions to its owners. If the board of directors does decide to make a distribution, it is not an expense of the corporation and does not reduce taxable income and hence the taxes the corporation pays.

Required:

1. Prepare abbreviated income statements that compare first year profitability for each of the two alternatives.
2. Which alternative would be expected to achieve the highest first-year profits? Why?
3. Which alternative would provide the highest rate of return on shareholders' equity? Why?
4. What other related implications of the decision should be considered?

Critical Thought Case 5–14
Relationships among ratios

You are a part-time financial advisor. A client is considering an investment in common stock of a waste recycling firm. One motivation is a rumor the client heard that the company made huge investments in a new fuel creation process. Unable to confirm the rumor, your client asks you to determine whether the firm's assets had recently increased significantly.

Because the firm is small, information is sparse. Last quarter's interim report showed total assets of $324 million, approximately the same as last year's annual report. The only information more current than that is a press release last week in which the company's management reported "record net income for the year of $21 million, representing a 14.0% return on shareholders' equity. Performance was enhanced by the Company's judicious use of financial leverage on a debt/equity ratio of 2 to 1."

Required:

Use the information available to provide your client with an opinion as to whether the waste recycling firm invested in the new fuel creation process during the last quarter of the year.

Critical Thought Case 5–15
Using ratios to test
reasonableness of data

You are a new staff accountant with a large regional CPA firm participating in your first audit. You recall from your auditing class that CPAs often use ratios to test the reasonableness of accounting numbers provided by the client. Because ratios reflect the relationships among various account balances, if it is assumed that prior relationships still hold, prior years' ratios can be used to estimate what current balances should approximate. However, you never actually performed this kind of analysis until now. The CPA in charge of the audit of Covington Pike Corporation brings you the list of ratios shown below and tells you these reflect the relationships maintained by Covington Pike in recent years.

Profit margin on sales = 5%
Return on assets = 7.5%
Gross profit margin = 40%
Inventory turnover ratio = 6 times
Receivables turnover ratio = 25
Acid-test ratio = .9
Current ratio = 2 to 1
Return on shareholders' equity = 10%
Debt to equity ratio = 1/3
Times interest earned ratio = 12 times

Jotted in the margins are the following notes:

- Net income $15,000.
- Only one short-term note ($5,000); all other current liabilities are trade accounts.
- Property, plant, and equipment are the only noncurrent assets.
- Bonds payable are the only noncurrent liabilities.
- The effective interest rate on short-term notes and bonds is 8%.
- No investment securities.
- Cash balance totals $15,000.

Required:
You are requested to approximate the current year's balances in the form of a balance sheet and income statement, to the extent the information allows. Accompany those financial statements with the calculations you use to estimate each amount reported.

Real World Case 5–16
Obtain and critically evaluate
an actual annual report

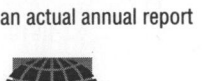

Financial reports are the primary means by which corporations report their performance and financial condition. Financial statements are one component of the annual report mailed to their shareholders and to interested others.

Required:
Obtain an annual report from a corporation with which you are familiar. Using techniques you learned in this chapter and any analysis you consider useful, respond to the following questions:
1. Do the firm's auditors provide a clean opinion on the financial statements?
2. Has the company made changes in any accounting methods it uses?
3. Have there been any subsequent events, errors and irregularities, illegal acts, or related-party transactions that have a material effect on the company's financial position?
4. What are two trends in the company's operations or capital resources that management considers significant to the company's future?
5. Is the company engaged in more than one significant line of business? If so, compare the relative profitability of the different segments.
6. How stable are the company's operations?
7. Has the company's situation deteriorated or improved with respect to liquidity, solvency, asset management, and profitability?
   Note: You can obtain a copy of an annual report from a local company, from a friend who is a shareholder, from the investor relations department of the corporation, from a friendly stockbroker, or from EDGAR (Electronic Data Gathering Retrieval) on the Internet (http://www.sec.gov).

Financial Analysis Case 5–17
Obtain and compare annual
reports from companies in the
same industry

Insight concerning the performance and financial condition of a company often comes from evaluating its financial data in comparison with other firms in the same industry.

Required:
Obtain annual reports from three corporations in the same primary industry. Using techniques you learned in this chapter and Chapter 4 and any analysis you consider useful, respond to the following questions:
1. Are there differences in accounting methods that should be taken into account when making comparisons?
2. How do earnings trends compare in terms of both the direction and stability of income?

3. Which of the three firms had greater earnings relative to resources available?
4. Has each of the companies achieved its respective rate of return on assets with similar combinations of profit margin and turnover?
5. Which corporation has made most effective use of financial leverage?
6. Of the three firms, which seems riskiest in terms of its ability to pay short-term obligations? Long-term obligations?
7. What factors might account for differences among price-earnings ratios for the companies' stock?

Note: You can obtain copies of annual reports from friends who are shareholders, from the investor relations department of the corporations, from a friendly stockbroker, or from EDGAR (Electronic Data Gathering Retrieval) on the Internet (http://www.sec.gov).

Financial Analysis Case 5–18
Balance sheet information

Federal Express Corporation

Refer to the financial statements and related disclosure notes of Federal Express Corporation in the appendix to Chapter 1.

Required:
1. What categories does the company use to classify its assets? Its liabilities?
2. What purpose do the disclosure notes serve?

Discussion Case 5–19
[based on Appendix 5]
Segment reporting concepts

Levens Co. operates in several distinct business segments. The company does not have any reportable foreign operations or major customers.

Required:
1. What is the purpose of operating segment disclosures?
2. Define an operating segment.
3. List the amounts to be reported by operating segment.

Ethics Case 5–20
[based on Appendix 5]
Segment reporting

You are in your third year as an accountant with McCarver-Lynn Industries, a multidivisional company involved in the manufacturing, marketing, and sales of surgical prosthetic devices. After the fiscal year-end, you are working with the controller of the firm to prepare supplemental business segment disclosures. Yesterday you presented her with the following summary information:

($ in millions)	Domestic	Union of South Africa	Egypt	France	Denmark	Total
Revenues	$ 845	$222	$265	$343	$311	$1,986
Capital expenditures	145	76	88	21	42	372
Assets	1,005	301	290	38	285	1,919

Upon returning to your office after lunch, you find the following memo:

Nice work. Let's combine the data this way

($ in millions)	Domestic	Africa	Europe	Total
Revenues	$ 845	$487	$654	$1,986
Capital expenditures	145	164	63	372
Assets	1,005	591	323	1,919

Some of our shareholders might react unfavorably to our recent focus on South African operations.

Required:
Do you perceive an ethical dilemma? What would be the likely impact of following the controller's suggestions? Who would benefit? Who would be injured?

TIME VALUE OF MONEY CONCEPTS

OVERVIEW

Time value of money concepts, specifically future value and present value, are essential in a variety of accounting situations. These concepts and the related computational procedures are the subjects of this chapter. Present values and future values of *single amounts* and present values and future values of *annuities* (series of equal periodic payments) are described separately but shown to be interrelated.

LEARNING OBJECTIVES   After studying this chapter, you should be able to:

1. Explain the difference between simple and compound interest.
2. Compute the future value of a single amount.
3. Compute the present value of a single amount.
4. Solve for either the interest rate or the number of compounding periods when present value and future value of a single amount are known.
5. Explain the difference between an ordinary annuity and an annuity due situation.
6. Compute the future value of both an ordinary annuity and an annuity due.
7. Compute the present value of an ordinary annuity, an annuity due, and a deferred annuity.
8. Solve for unknown values in annuity situations involving present value.
9. Briefly describe how the concept of the time value of money is incorporated into the valuation of long-term leases and pension obligations.

JOHN SMILEY'S SETTLEMENT[1]

On a rainy afternoon two years ago, John Smiley left work early to attend a family birthday party. Eleven minutes later, a careening truck slammed into his station wagon on the freeway causing John to spend two months in a coma. Now he can't hold a job or make everyday decisions and is in need of constant care. Last week, the 40-year old Smiley won an out-of-court settlement from the truck driver's company. He was given payment for all medical costs and attorney fees, plus a lump-sum settlement of $2,330,716. At the time of the accident, John was president of his family's business and earned approximately $200,000 per year. He had anticipated working 25 more years before retirement.

John's sister, an acquaintance of yours from college, has asked you to explain to her how the attorneys came up with the settlement amount. "They said it was based on his lost future income and a 7% rate of some kind," she explained. "But it was all 'legal-speak' to me."

QUESTIONS

1. How was the amount of the lump-sum settlement determined? Create a calculation that John's sister can look at.
2. What are some of the accounting applications that also take into account the time value of money?

[1]This case is adapted from an actual situation. Names are changed.

A BASIC CONCEPTS

Time Value of Money

The key to solving the problem described above is an understanding of the concept commonly referred to as the **time value of money**. This concept means that money invested today will grow to a larger dollar amount in the future. For example, $100 invested in a savings account at your local bank yielding 6% annually will grow to $106 in one year. The difference between the $100 invested now—the present value of the investment—and its $106 future value represents the time value of money.

The **time value of money** means that money can be invested today to earn interest and grow to a larger dollar amount in the future.

This concept has nothing to do with the worth or buying power of those dollars. Prices in our economy can change. If the inflation rate were higher than 6%, then the $106 you would have in the savings account actually would be worth less than the $100 you had a year earlier. The time value of money concept concerns only the growth in the dollar amounts of money.

The concepts you will learn in this chapter are useful in solving many business problems such as the determination of the accident settlement award presented at the beginning of the chapter. As we will see later in this and subsequent chapters, the concepts also are essential in valuing several assets and liabilities for financial reporting purposes.

Interest is the amount of money paid or received in excess of the amount borrowed or lent.

Interest is the rent paid for the use of money for some period of time. In dollar terms, it is the amount of money paid or received in excess of the amount of money borrowed or lent. If you lent the bank $100 today and received $106 a year from now, your interest earned would be $6. Interest also can be expressed as a rate at which money will grow. In this case, that rate is 6%. It is this interest that gives money its time value.

Simple versus Compound Interest

Learning objective 1
Explain the difference between simple and compound interest.

Simple interest is computed by multiplying an initial investment times both the applicable interest rate and the period of time for which the money is used. For example, simple interest earned each year on a $1,000 investment paying 10% is $100 ($1,000 × 10%).

Compound interest
includes interest not only on the initial investment but also on the accumulated interest in previous periods.

Compound interest results in increasingly larger interest amounts for each period of the investment. The reason is that interest is now being earned not only on the initial investment amount but also on the accumulated interest earned in previous periods.

For example, Cindy Crawford invested $1,000 in a savings account paying 10% interest *compounded* annually. How much interest will she earn each year, and what will be her investment balance after three years?

Date	Interest (Interest rate × Outstanding balance = Interest)	Balance
Initial deposit		$1,000
End of year 1	10% × $1,000 = $100	$1,100
End of year 2	10% × $1,100 = $110	$1,210
End of year 3	10% × $1,210 = $121	$1,331

With compound interest at 10% annually, the $1,000 investment would grow to $1,331 at the end of the three-year period. Of course, if Cindy withdrew the interest earned each year, she would earn only $100 in interest each year, that is, the amount of simple interest. If the investment period had been 20 years, 20 individual calculations would be needed. However, calculators, computer programs, and compound interest tables make these calculations much easier.

Interest rates are typically stated as annual rates.

Most banks compound interest more frequently than once a year. Daily compounding is common for savings accounts. More rapid compounding has the effect of increasing the actual rate, which is called the **effective rate**, at which money grows per year. It should be noted that interest is typically stated as an annual rate regardless of the length of the compounding period involved.

Now assume Cindy invested $1,000 in a savings account paying 10% interest *compounded* twice a year. There are two six-month periods paying interest at 5% (one-half of the annual rate). How much interest will she earn the first year, and what will be her investment balance at the end of the year?

Date	Interest (Interest rate × Outstanding balance = Interest)	Balance
Initial deposit		$1,000.00
After six months	5% × $1,000 = $50.00	$1,050.00
End of year 1	5% × $1,050 = $52.50	$1,102.50

The **effective yield** is the rate at which money actually will grow during a full year.

The $1,000 would grow by $102.50, the interest earned, to $1,102.50, $2.50 more than if interest were compounded only once a year. The effective annual interest rate, often referred to as the annual *yield*, is 10.25% ($102.50 ÷ $1,000).

Valuing a Single Cash Flow Amount

Learning objective 2
Compute the future value of a single amount.

Future Value of a Single Amount

In the first Cindy example, in which $1,000 was invested for three years at 10% compounded annually, the $1,331 is referred to as the **future value (FV)**. A time diagram is a useful way to visualize this relationship, with 0 indicating the date of the initial investment.

Future value of a single amount

$n = 3$, $i = 10\%$

The future value after one year can be calculated as $1,000 × 1.10 (1.00 + .10) = $1,100. After three years, the future value is $1,000 × 1.10 × 1.10 × 1.10 = $1,331. In fact, the future value of any invested amount can be determined as follows:

$$FV = I (1 + i)^n$$

The **future value** of a single amount is the amount of money that a dollar will grow to at some point in the future.

where: FV = Future value of the invested amount
    I = Amount invested at the beginning of the period
    i = Interest rate
    n = Number of compounding periods

The future value also can be determined by using Table 6A–1, Future Value of $1, in Appendix 6 on page 256. The table contains the future value of $1 invested for various periods of time, n, and at various rates, i.

With this table, it's easy to determine the future value of any invested amount simply by multiplying it by the table value at the *intersection* of the column for the desired rate and the row for the number of compounding periods. Graphic 6–1 contains an excerpt from Table 6A–1.

The table shows various values of $(1 + i)^n$ for different combinations of i and n. From the table you can find the future value factor for three periods at 10% to be 1.331. This means that $1

GRAPHIC   6–1

Future value of $1, (excerpt from Table 6–A1, Appendix 6)

Periods (*n*)	Interest Rates (*i*)					
	7%	8%	9%	10%	11%	12%
1	1.07000	1.08000	1.09000	1.10000	1.11000	1.12000
2	1.14490	1.16640	1.18810	1.21000	1.23210	1.25440
3	1.22504	1.25971	1.29503	1.33100	1.36763	1.40493
4	1.31080	1.36049	1.41158	1.46410	1.51807	1.57352
5	1.40255	1.46933	1.53862	1.61051	1.68506	1.76234
6	1.50073	1.58687	1.67710	1.77156	1.87041	1.97382
7	1.60578	1.71382	1.82804	1.94872	2.07616	2.21068
8	1.71819	1.85093	1.99256	2.14359	2.30454	2.47596

invested at 10% compounded annually will grow to approximately $1.33 in three years. So, the future value of $1,000 invested for three years at 10% is $1,331:

$$FV = I \times FV \text{ factor}$$
$$FV = \$1,000 \times 1.331^* = \$1,331$$

*Future value of $1: $n=3$, $i=10\%$

The future value function in financial calculators or in computer spreadsheet programs calculates future values in the same way. Determining future values (and present values) electronically avoids the need for tables such as those in the chapter appendix. It's important to remember that the n in the future value formula refers to the number of compounding periods, not necessarily the number of years. For example, suppose you wanted to know the future value *two* years from today of $1,000 invested at 12% with *quarterly* compounding. The number of periods is therefore eight and the compounding rate is 3% (12% annual rate divided by four, the number of quarters in a year). The future value factor from Table 6A–1 is 1.26677, so the future value is $1,266.77 ($1,000 × 1.26677).[2]

Present Value of a Single Amount

The example used to illustrate future value reveals that $1,000 invested today is equivalent to $1,100 received after one year, $1,210 after two years, or $1,331 after three years, assuming 10% interest compounded annually. Thus, the $1,000 investment (I) is the **present value (PV)** of the single sum of $1,331 to be received at the end of three years. It is also the present value of $1,210 to be received in two years and $1,100 in one year.

Remember that the future value of a present amount is the present amount *times* $(1 + i)^n$. Logically, then, that computation can be reversed to find the *present value* of a future amount to be the future amount *divided by* $(1 + i)^n$. We substitute PV for I (invested amount) in the future value formula above.

$$FV = PV (1 + i)^n$$
$$PV = \frac{FV}{(1 + i)^n}$$

In our example,

$$PV = \frac{\$1,331}{(1 + .10)^3} = \frac{\$1,331}{1.331} = \$1,000$$

Of course, dividing by $(1 + i)^n$ is the same as multiplying by its reciprocal, $1/(1 + i)^n$.

$$PV = \$1,331 \times \frac{1}{(1 + .10)^3} = \$1,331 \times .75131 = \$1,000$$

As with future value, these computations are simplified by using calculators, computer programs, or present value tables. Table 6A–2, Present Value of $1, on page 256 in Appendix 6 provides the solutions of $1/(1 + i)^n$ for various interest rates (i) and compounding periods (n). These amounts represent the present value of $1 to be received at the *end* of the different periods. The table can be used to find the present value of any single amount to be received in the future by *multiplying* that amount by the value in the table that lies at the *intersection* of the column for the appropriate rate and the row for the number of compounding periods.[3] Graphic 6–2 contains an excerpt from Table 6A–2.

---

[2]When interest is compounded more frequently than once a year, the effective annual interest rate, or yield, can be determined using the following equation:

$$\text{Yield} = (1 + \frac{1}{p})^p - 1$$

with i being the annual interest rate and p the number of compounding periods per year. In this example, the annual yield would be 12.55%, calculated as follows:

$$\text{Yield} = (1 + \frac{.12}{4})^4 - 1 = 1.1255 - 1 = .1255$$

Determining the yield is useful when comparing returns on investment instruments with different compounding period length.

[3]The factors in Table 6A–2 are the reciprocals of those in Table 6A–1. For example, the future value factor for 10%, three periods is 1.331, while the present value factor is .75131. $1 ÷ 1.331 = $.75131, and $1 ÷ .75131 = $1.331.

GRAPHIC   6 – 2

Present value of $1 ,
(excerpt from Table 6-2,
Appendix 6)

Periods (n)	Interest Rates (i)					
	7%	8%	9%	10%	11%	12%
1	.93458	.92593	.91743	.90909	.90090	.89286
2	.87344	.85734	.84168	.82645	.81162	.79719
3	.81630	.79383	.77218	.75131	.73119	.71178
4	.76290	.73503	.70843	.68301	.65873	.63552
5	.71299	.68058	.64993	.62092	.59345	.56743
6	.66634	.63017	.59627	.56447	.53464	.50663
7	.62275	.58349	.54703	.51316	.48166	.45235
8	.58201	.54027	.50187	.46651	.43393	.40388

Notice that the farther into the future the $1 is to be received, the less valuable it is now. This is the essence of the concept of the time value of money. Given a choice between $1,000 now and $1,000 three years from now, you would choose to have the money now. If you have it now, you could put it to use. But the choice between $740 now and $1,000 three years from now would depend on your time value of money. If your time value of money is 10%, you would be indifferent between having $751.31 now [$1,000 × .75131(PV of $1, $i = 10\%$, and $n = 3$)] and $1,000 three years from now, but would choose the $1,000 future amount over $740 now because $740 invested at 10% for three years would grow to only $984.94 [$740 × 1.331 (FV of $1, $i = 10\%$, $n = 3$)]. On the other hand, if your time value of money is 11% or higher, you would prefer the $740 now. Presumably, you would invest the $740 now and have it grow to $1,012.05 ($740 × 1.36763) in three years.

In our earlier example, $1,000 now is equivalent to $1,331 in three years, assuming the time value of money is 10%. Graphically, the relation between the present value and the future value can be viewed this way:

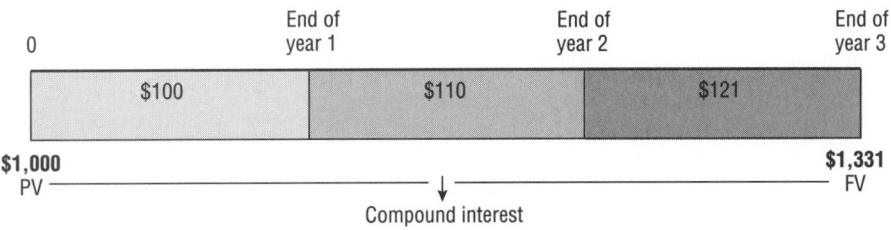

The calculation of future value requires the addition of interest, while the calculation of present value requires the removal of interest.

While the calculation of future value of a single sum invested today requires the *inclusion* of compound interest, present value problems require the *removal* of compound interest. The process of computing present value *removes* the $331 of interest earned over the three-year period from the future value of $1,331, just as the process of computing future value *adds* $331 of interest to the present value of $1,000 to arrive at the future value of $1,331.

Solving for Other Values When FV and PV Are Known

Learning objective 4
Solve for either the interest rate or the number of compounding periods when present value and future value of a single amount are known.

There are four variables in the process of adjusting single cash flow amounts for the time value of money: the present value (PV), the future value (FV), the number of compounding periods (n), and the interest rate (i). If you know any three of these, the fourth can be determined.

Determining the Unknown Interest Rate

ILLUSTRATION   6 – 1

Determining i when PV, FV,
and n are known

Suppose a friend asks to borrow $500 today and promises to repay you $605 two years from now. What is the annual interest rate you would be agreeing to?

The following time diagram illustrates the situation:

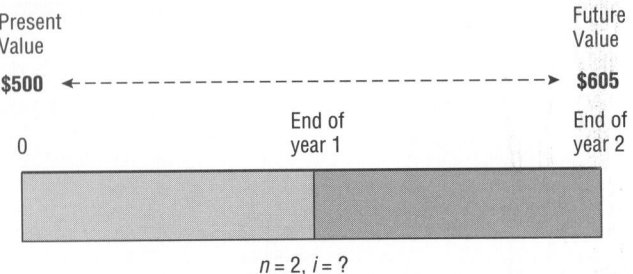

The interest rate is the discount rate that will provide a present value of $500 when discounting $605 to be received in two years:

> The unknown variable is the interest rate

$$\$500 \text{ (present value)} = \$605 \text{ (future value)} \times \textbf{?*}$$
*Present value of $1: $n=2$, $i=?$

Rearranging algebraically, we find that the present value table factor is

$$\$500 \text{ (present value)} \div \$605 \text{ (future value)} = .82645*$$
*Present value of $1: $n=2$, $i=?$

When you consult the present value table, Table 6A–2, you search row two ($n=2$) for this value and find it in the 10% column. So the effective interest rate is 10%. Notice that the computed factor value exactly equals the table factor value.[4]

Determining the Unknown Number of Periods

ILLUSTRATION   6–2

Determining *n* when PV, FV, and *i* are known

You want to invest $10,000 today to accumulate $16,000 for graduate school. If you can invest at an interest rate of 10% compounded annually, how many years will it take to accumulate the required amount?

The following time diagram illustrates the situation:

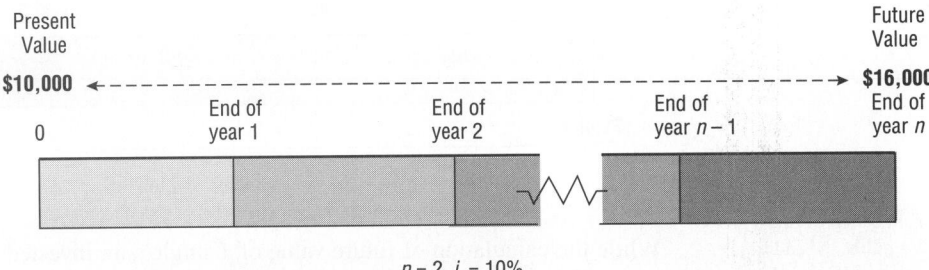

The number of years is the value of n that will provide a present value of $10,000 when discounting $16,000 at a rate of 10%:

> The unknown variable is the number of periods

$$\$10,000 \text{ (present value)} = \$16,000 \text{ (future value)} \times \textbf{?*}$$
*Present value of $1: $n=?$, $i=10\%$

Rearranging algebraically, we find that the present value table factor is

$$\$10,000 \text{ (present value)} \div \$16,000 \text{ (future value)} = .625*$$
*Present value of $1: $n=?$, $i=10\%$

When you consult the present value table, Table 6A-2, you search the 10% column ($i=10\%$) for this value and find .62092 in row five. So it would take approximately five years to accumulate $16,000 in the situation described.

---

[4]If the calculated factor lies between two table factors, interpolation is useful in finding the unknown value. For example, if the future value in our example is $600, instead of $605, the calculated PV factor is .83333 ($500 ÷ $600). This factor lies between the 9% factor of .84168 and the 10% factor of .82645. The total difference between these factors is .01523 (.84168 − .82645). The difference between the calculated factor of .83333 and the 9% factor of .82645 is .00688. This is 45% of the difference between the 9% and 10% factors:

$$\frac{.00688}{.01523} = .45$$

Therefore, the interpolated interest rate is 9.45% (9 + .45).

Additional Consideration

Solving for the unknown factor in either of these examples could just as easily be done using the future value tables. The number of years is the value of *n* that will provide a present value of $10,000 when discounting $16,000 at a discount rate of 10%:

$16,000 (future value) = $10,000 (present value)x ?*
*Future value of $1: *n*=?, *i*=10%

Rearranging algebraically, the future value table factor is

$16,000 (future value) ÷ $10,000 (present value) = 1.6*
*Future value of $1: *n*=?, *i*=10%

When you consult the future value table, Table 6A-1, you search the 10% column (*i*=10%) for this value and find 1.61051 in row five. So it would take approximately five years to accumulate $16,000 in the situation described.

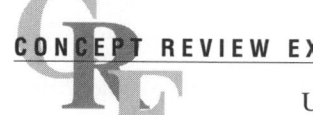

CONCEPT REVIEW EXERCISE   VALUING A SINGLE CASH FLOW AMOUNT

Using the appropriate table in Appendix 6, answer each of the following independent questions.

1. What is the future value of $5,000 at the end of six periods at 8% compound interest?
2. What is the present value of $8,000 to be received eight periods from today assuming a compound interest rate of 12%?
3. What is the present value of $10,000 to be received two *years* from today assuming an annual interest rate of 24% and *monthly* compounding?
4. If an investment of $2,000 grew to $2,520 in three periods, what is the interest rate at which the investment grew? Solve using both present and future value tables.
5. Approximately how many years would it take for an investment of $5,250 to accumulate to $15,000, assuming interest is compounded at 10% annually? Solve using both present and future value tables.

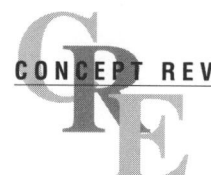

CONCEPT REVIEW EXERCISE   SOLUTION

1. FV = $5,000 (1.58687*)   = $7,934
    *Future value of $1: *n*=6, *i*=8% (from Table 6A–1)

2. PV = $8,000 (.40388*)   = $3,231
    *Present value of $1: *n*=8, *i*=12% (from Table 6A–2)

3. PV = $10,000 (.62172*)   = $6,217
    *Present value of $1: *n*=24, *i*=2% (from Table 6A–2)

4. Using present value table,

    $$\frac{\$2,000}{\$2,520} = .7937*$$

    *Present value of $1: *n*=3, *i*=? (from Table 6A–2, *i* = approximately **8%**)

    Using future value table,

    $$\frac{\$2,520}{\$2,000} = 1.260*$$

    *Future value of $1: *n*=3, *i*=? (from Table 6A–1, *i* = approximately **8%**)

5. Using present value table,

    $$\frac{\$5,250}{\$15,000} = .35*$$

    *Present value of $1: *n*=?, *i*=10% (from Table 6A–2, *n* = approximately **11 years**)

    Using future value table,

    $$\frac{\$15,000}{\$5,250} = 2.857*$$

    *Future value of $1: *n*=?, *i*=10% (from Table 6A–1, *n* = approximately **11 years**)

Preview of Accounting Applications of Present Value Techniques—Single Cash Amount

Monetary assets and **monetary liabilities** are valued at the present value of future cash flows.

Many assets and most liabilities are monetary in nature. **Monetary assets** include money and claims to receive money, the amount of which is fixed or determinable. Examples include cash and most receivables. **Monetary liabilities** are obligations to pay amounts of cash, the amount of which is fixed or determinable. Most liabilities are monetary. For example, if you borrow money from a bank and sign a note payable, the amount of cash to be repaid to the bank is fixed. Monetary receivables and payables are valued based on the fixed amount of cash to be received or paid in the future with proper reflection of the time value of money. In other words, most receivables and payables are valued at the present value of future cash flows, reflecting an appropriate time value of money.[5]

The example in Illustration 6–3 demonstrates this concept.

ILLUSTRATION   6–3

Valuing a note: one payment, explicit interest

Explicit Interest

The Stridewell Wholesale Shoe Company manufactures athletic shoes for sale to retailers. The company recently sold a large order of shoes to Harmon Sporting Goods for $50,000. Stridewell agreed to accept a note in payment for the shoes requiring payment of $50,000 in one year plus interest at 10%.

How should Stridewell value the note receivable and corresponding sales revenue earned? How should Harmon value the note payable and corresponding inventory purchased? As long as the interest rate explicitly stated in the agreement properly reflects the time value of money, the answer is $50,000, the face value of the note. It's important to realize that this amount also equals the present value of future cash flows at 10%. Future cash flows equal $55,000, $50,000 in note principal plus $5,000 in interest ($50,000 × 10%). Using a time diagram:

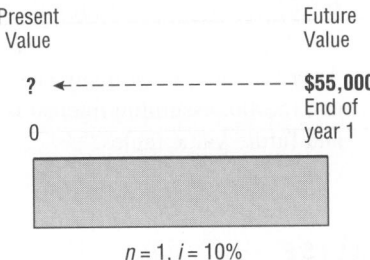

In equation form, we can solve for present value as follows:

$55,000 (future value) × .90909* = $50,000 (present value)

*Present value of $1: $n=1$, $i=10\%$

By calculating the present value of $55,000 to be received in one year, the interest of $5,000 is removed from the future value, resulting in a proper note receivable/sales revenue value of $50,000 for Stridewell and a $50,000 note payable/inventory value for Harmon.

While most notes, loans, and mortgages explicitly state an interest rate that will properly reflect the time value of money, there can be exceptions. Consider the example in Illustration 6–4.

ILLUSTRATION   6–4

Valuing a note: one payment, no explicit interest

No Explicit Interest

The Stridewell Wholesale Shoe Company recently sold a large order of shoes to the Harmon Sporting Goods. Terms of the sale require Harmon to sign a noninterest-bearing note of $60,500 with payment due in two years.

---

[5]"Interest on Receivables and Payables," *Accounting Principles Board Opinion No. 21* (New York: AICPA, 1971).

How should Stridewell and Harmon value the note receivable/payable and corresponding sales revenue/inventory? Even though the agreement states a noninterest-bearing note, the $60,500 does, in fact, include interest for the two-year period of the loan. We need to remove the interest portion of the $60,500 to determine the portion that represents the sales price of the shoes. We do this by computing the present value. The following time diagram illustrates the situation assuming that a rate of 10% reflects the appropriate interest rate for a loan of this type:

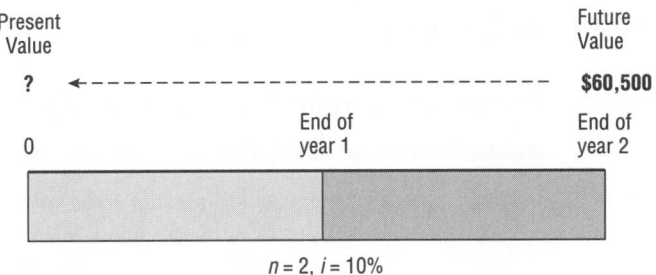

Again, using the present value of $1 table,

$$\$60,500 \text{ (future value)} \times .82645^* = \$50,000 \text{ (present value)}$$
*Present value of $1: n=2, i=10%

Both the note receivable for Stridewell and the note payable for Harmon initially will be valued at $50,000. The difference ($60,500 - 50,000) represents interest revenue/expense to be recognized over the life of the note. The appropriate journal entries are illustrated in later chapters.

B BASIC ANNUITIES

The previous examples involved the receipt or payment of a single future amount. Financial instruments frequently involve multiple receipts or payments of cash. If the same amount is to be received or paid each period, the cash flows are referred to as an **annuity**. A common annuity encountered in practice is a loan on which periodic interest is paid in equal amounts. For example, bonds typically pay interest semiannually in an amount determined by multiplying a stated rate by a fixed principal amount. Some loans and most leases are paid in equal installments during a specified period of time.

An agreement that creates an annuity can produce either an **ordinary annuity** or an **annuity due** (sometimes referred to as an annuity in advance) situation. The first cash flow of an ordinary annuity is made one compounding period *after* the date on which the agreement begins. The final cash flow takes place on the *last* day covered by the agreement. For example, an installment note payable dated December 31, 1997, might require the debtor to make three equal annual payments, with the first payment due on December 31, 1998, and the last one on December 31, 2000. The following time diagram illustrates an ordinary annuity:

Learning objective 5
Explain the difference between an ordinary annuity and an annuity due situation.

In an **ordinary annuity** cash flows occur at the *end* of each period.

Ordinary annuity

In an **annuity due** cash flows occur at the *beginning* of each period.

The first payment of an annuity due is made on the *first* day of the agreement, and the last payment is made one period *before* the end of the agreement. For example, a three-year lease of a building that begins on December 31, 1997, and ends on December 31, 2000, may require the first year's lease payment in advance on December 31, 1997. The third and last payment would take place on December 31, 1999, the beginning of the third year of the lease. The following time diagram illustrates this situation:

Annuity due

12/31/97	12/31/98	12/31/99	12/31/00
	1st payment	2nd payment	3rd payment

Future Value of an Annuity

Future Value of an Ordinary Annuity

ILLUSTRATION   6–5

Future value of an ordinary annuity

Sally Rogers wants to accumulate a sum of money to pay for graduate school. Rather than investing a single amount today that will grow to a future value, she decides to invest $10,000 a year over the next three years in a savings account paying 10% interest compounded annually. She decides to make the first payment to the bank one year from today.

The following time diagram illustrates this ordinary annuity situation. Time 0 is the start of the first period.

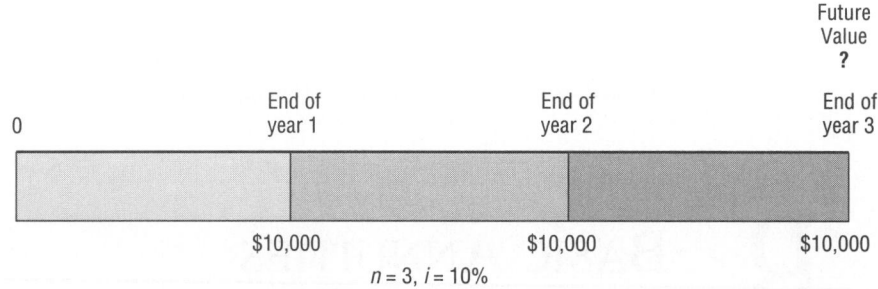

Future Value
?

0	End of year 1	End of year 2	End of year 3
	$10,000	$10,000	$10,000

$n = 3, i = 10\%$

Using the FV of $1 factors from Table 6A–1, we can calculate the future value of this annuity by calculating the future value of each of the individual payments as follows:

	Payment		FV of $1 $i = 10\%$		Future Value (at the end of year 3)	n
First payment	$10,000	×	1.21	=	$12,100	2
Second payment	10,000	×	1.10	=	11,000	1
Third payment	10,000	×	1.00	=	10,000	0
Total			3.31		$33,100	

> In the future value of an ordinary annuity, the last cash payment will not earn any interest.

From the time diagram, we can see that the first payment has two compounding periods to earn interest. The factor used, 1.21, is the FV of $1 invested for two periods at 10%. The second payment has one compounding period and the last payment does not earn any interest because it is invested on the last day of the three-year annuity period. Therefore, the factor used is 1.00.

> **Learning objective 6**
> Compute the future value of both an ordinary annuity and an annuity due.

This illustration shows that it's possible to calculate the future value of the annuity by separately calculating the FV of each payment and then adding these amounts together. Fortunately, that's not necessary. Table 6–A3, Future Value of an Ordinary Annuity, of Appendix 6 on page 258 simplifies the computation by summing the individual FV of $1 factors for various factors of n and i. For instance, the future value of $1 at the end of each of three periods invested at 10% is shown in Table 6–3 to be $3.31. We can simply multiply this factor by $10,000 to derive the FV of our ordinary annuity (FVA):

$$\text{FVA} = \$10,000 \text{ (annuity amount)} \times 3.31^* = \$33,100$$

*Future value of an ordinary annuity of $1: n=3, i=10%

Future Value of an Annuity Due

Let's modify the previous illustration to create an annuity due in Illustration 6–6.

ILLUSTRATION   6–6

Future value of an annuity due

Sally Rogers wants to accumulate a sum of money to pay for graduate school. Rather than investing a single amount today that will grow to a future value, she decides to invest $10,000 a year over the next three years in a savings account paying 10% interest compounded annually. She decides to make the first payment to the bank immediately. How much will Sally have available in her account at the end of three years?

The following time diagram depicts the situation. Again, note that 0 is the start of the first period.

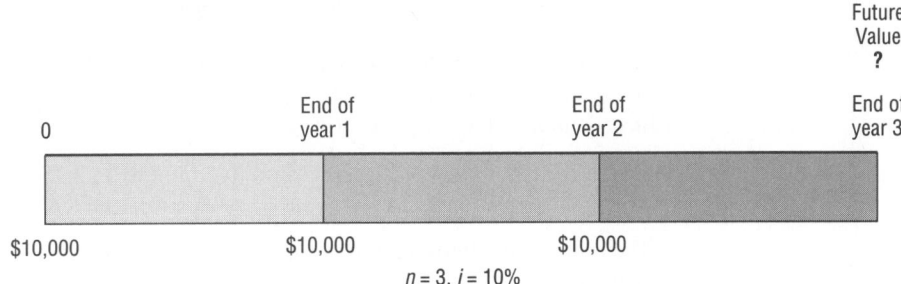

The future value can be found by separately calculating the FV of each of the three payments and then summing those individual future values:

In the future value of an annuity due, the last cash payment will earn interest.

	Payment		FV of $1 $i = 10\%$		Future Value (at the end of year 3)	n
First payment	$10,000	×	1.331	=	$13,310	3
Second payment	10,000	×	1.210	=	12,100	2
Third payment	10,000	×	1.100	=	11,000	1
Total			3.641		$36,410	

And, again, this same future value can be found by using the future value of an annuity due (FVAD) factor from Table 6A–5, Future Value of an Annuity Due, in Appendix 6 on page 260, as follows:

$$\text{FVAD} = \$10,000 \text{ (annuity amount)} \times 3.641^* = \$36,410$$

*Future value of an annuity due of $1: $n=3$, $i=10\%$

Of course, if *unequal* amounts are invested each year, we can't solve the problem by using the annuity tables. The future value of each payment would have to be calculated separately.

Present Value of an Annuity

Present Value of an Ordinary Annuity

Learning objective 7
Compute the present value of an ordinary annuity, an annuity due, and a deferred annuity.

OPENING CASE

Question 1

You will learn in later chapters that liabilities and receivables, with the exception of certain trade receivables and payables, are reported in financial statements at their present values. Most of these financial instruments specify equal periodic interest payments or installment payments. As a result, the most common accounting applications of the time value of money involve determining present value of annuities. As in the future value applications we discussed above, an annuity can be either an ordinary annuity or an annuity due. Let's look at an ordinary annuity first.

In the illustration on page 244, we determined that Sally Rogers could accumulate $33,100 for graduate school by investing $10,000 at the end of each of three years at 10%. The $33,100 is the future value of the ordinary annuity described. Another alternative is to invest one single amount at the beginning of the three-year period. This single amount will equal the present value

ILLUSTRATION   6–7

Present value of an ordinary annuity

Sally Rogers wants to accumulate a sum of money to pay for graduate school. She wants to invest a single amount today in a savings account earning 10% interest compounded annually that is equivalent to investing $10,000 at the end of each of the next three years.

at the beginning of the three-year period of the $33,100 future value. It will also equal the present value of the $10,000 three-year annuity.

The present value can be found by separately calculating the PV of each of the three payments and then summing those individual present values:

	Payment	PV of $1 $i = 10\%$		Present Value (at the beginning of year 1)	n
First payment	$10,000	× .90909	=	$ 9,091	1
Second payment	10,000	× .82645	=	8,264	2
Third payment	10,000	× .75131	=	7,513	3
Total		2.48685		$24,868	

A more efficient method of calculating present value is to use Table 6A–4, Present Value of an Ordinary Annuity, in Appendix 6 on page 258. Using Table 6A–4, we calculate the PV of the ordinary annuity (PVA) as follows:

$$PVA = \$10,000 \text{ (annuity amount)} \times 2.48685* = \$24,868$$

*Present value of an ordinary annuity of $1: $n=3$, $i=10\%$

The relationship between the present value and the future value of the annuity can be depicted graphically as follows:

Relationship between present value and future value—Ordinary Annuity

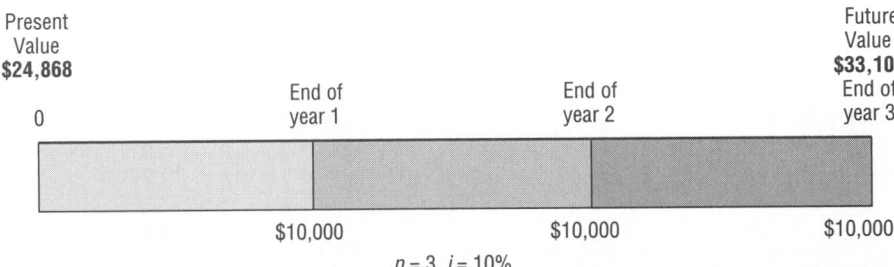

This can be interpreted in several ways:

1. $10,000 invested at 10% at the end of each of the next three years will accumulate to $33,100 at the end of the third year.
2. $24,868 invested at 10% now will grow to $33,100 after three years.
3. Someone whose time value of money is 10% would be willing to pay $24,868 now to receive $10,000 at the end of each of the next three years.
4. If your time value of money is 10%, you should be indifferent with respect to paying/receiving (a) $24,868 now, (b) $33,100 three years from now, or (c) $10,000 at the end of each of the next three years.

Additional Consideration

We also can verify that these are the present value and future value of the same annuity by calculating the present value of a single cash amount of $33,100 three years hence:

$$PV = \$33,100 \text{ (future value)} \times .75131* = \$24,868$$

*Present value of $1: $n = 3$, $i = 10\%$

Present Value of an Annuity Due

ILLUSTRATION   6–8

Present value of an annuity ue

In the previous illustration, suppose that the three equal payments of $10,000 are to be made at the *beginning* of each of the three years. Recall from the illustration on page 245 that the future value of this annuity is $36,410. What is the present value?

The following time diagram depicts this situation:

Present value of an annuity due

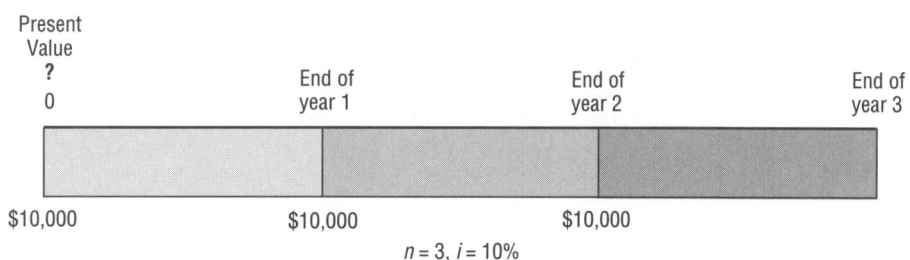

Once again, using individual PV factors of $1 from Table 6A–2, the PV of the annuity due can be calculated as follows:

	Payment		PV of $1 $i = 10\%$		Present Value (at the beginning of year 1)	n
First payment	$10,000	×	1.00000	=	$10,000	0
Second payment	10,000	×	.90909	=	9,091	1
Third payment	10,000	×	.82645	=	8,264	2
Total			2.73554		$27,355	

In the present value of an annuity due, no interest needs to be removed from the first cash payment.

The first payment does not contain any interest since it is made on the first day of the three-year annuity period. Therefore, the factor used is 1.00. The second payment has one compounding period and the factor used of .90909 is the PV factor of $1 for one period and 10%, and we need to remove two compounding periods of interest from the third payment. The factor used of .82645 is the PV factor of $1 for two periods and 10%.

The relationship between the present value and the future value of the annuity can be depicted graphically as follows:

Relationship between Present Value and Future Value—Annuity Due

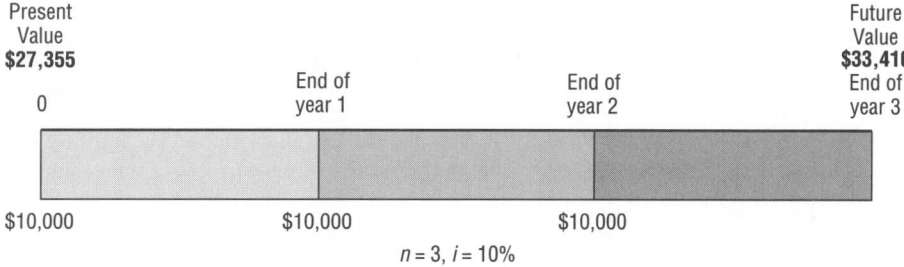

Using Table 6A–6, Present Value of an Annuity Due, in Appendix 6 on page 260, we can more efficiently calculate the PV of the annuity due (PVAD):

$$PVAD = \$10,000 \text{ (annuity amount)} \times 2.73554^* = \$27,355$$

*Present value of an annuity due of $1: $n=3$, $i=10\%$

To better understand the relationship between Tables 6A–4 and 6A–6, notice that the PVAD factor for three periods, 10%, from Table 6A–6 is 2.73554. This is simply the PVA factor for two periods, 10%, of 1.73554, plus 1.0. The addition of 1.0 reflects the fact that the first payment does not require the removal of any interest.

Present Value of a Deferred Annuity

A **deferred annuity** exists when the first cash flow occurs more than one period after the date the agreement begins.

Accounting valuations often involve the present value of annuities in which the first cash flow is expected to occur more than one time period after the date of the agreement. As the inception of the annuity is deferred beyond a single period, this type of annuity is referred to as a **deferred annuity**.[6]

---

[6]The future value of a deferred annuity is the same as the future amount of an annuity not deferred. That is because there are no interest compounding periods prior to the beginning of the annuity period.

ILLUSTRATION   6-9

Deferred annuity

At January 1, 1997, you are considering acquiring an investment that will provide three equal payments of $10,000 each to be received at the end of three consecutive years. However, the first payment is not expected until *December 31, 1999*. The time value of money is 10%. How much would you be willing to pay for this investment?

The following time diagram depicts this situation:

| Cash flows for a deferred annuity

The present value of the annuity can be calculated by summing the present values of the three individual cash flows, each discounted to today's PV:

	Payment		PV of $1 $i = 10\%$		Present Value	n
First payment	$10,000	×	.75131	=	$ 7,513	3
Second payment	10,000	×	.68301	=	6,830	4
Third payment	10,000	×	.62092	=	6,209	5
					$20,552	

A more efficient way of calculating the present value of a deferred annuity involves a two-step process:

1. Calculate the PV of the annuity as of the beginning of the annuity period.
2. Discount the single amount calculated in (1) to its present value *as of today*.

In this case, we compute the present value of the annuity as of December 31, 1998, by multiplying the annuity amount by the three-period ordinary annuity factor:

$$\text{PVA} = \$10,000 \text{ (annuity amount)} \times 2.48685^* = \$24,868$$

*Present value of an ordinary annuity of $1: $n=3$, $i=10\%$

This is the present value as of December 31, 1998. This single amount is then reduced to present value as of January 1, 1997, by making the following calculation:

$$\text{PV} = \$24,868 \text{ (future amount)} \times .82656^* = \$20,552$$

*Present value of $1: $n=2$, $i=10\%$

The following time diagram illustrates this two-step process:

| Present value of a deferred annuity—two-step process

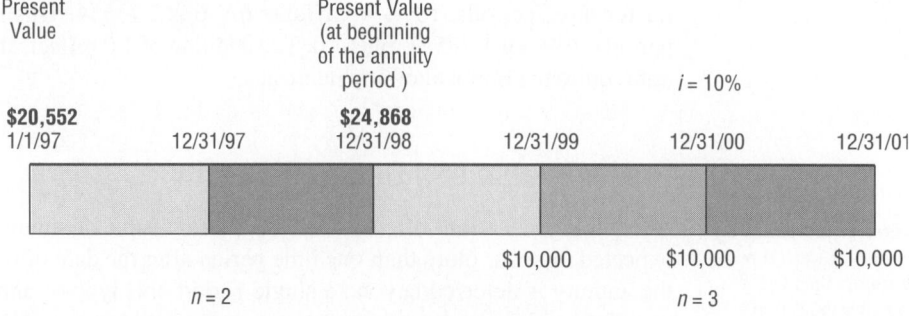

If you recall the concepts you learned in this chapter, you might think of other ways the present value of a deferred annuity can be determined. Among them:

1. Calculate the PV of an annuity due rather than an ordinary annuity and then discount that amount three periods rather than two: $10,000 × 2.73554 × .75131 = $20,552.

2. From Table 6A–4, subtract the two-period PVA factor (1.73554) from the five-period PVA factor (3.79079) and multiply the difference (2.05525) by $10,000 to get $20,552.

Solving for Unknown Values in Present Value Situations

In present value problems involving annuities, there are four variables: (1) present value of an ordinary annuity (PVA) or present value of an annuity due (PVAD), (2) the amount of each annuity payment, (3) the number of periods, *n*, and (4) the interest rate, *i*. If you know any three of these, the fourth can be determined.

ILLUSTRATION   6-10

Determining the annuity amount when other variables are known

Learning objective 8
Solve for unknown values in annuity situations involving present value.

Determining the unknown annuity amount—ordinary annuity

Assume that you borrow $700 from a friend and intend to repay the amount in four equal annual installments beginning one year from today. Your friend wishes to be reimbursed for the time value of money at an 8% annual rate. What is the required annual payment that must be made (the annuity amount), to repay the loan in four years?

The following time diagram illustrates the situation:

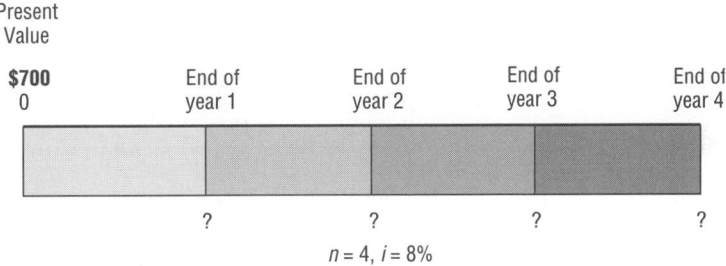

The required payment is the annuity amount that will provide a present value of $700 when discounting that amount at a discount rate of 8%:

The unknown variable is the annuity amount

$$\$700 \text{ (present value)} = 3.31213^* \times \text{annuity amount}$$

Rearranging algebraically, we find that the annuity amount is

$$\$700 \text{ (present value)} \div 3.31213^* = \$211.34 \text{ (annuity amount)}$$
*Present value of an ordinary annuity of $1: *n*=4, *i*=8%

You would have to make four annual payments of $211.34 to repay the loan. Total payments of $845.36 (4 × $211.34) would include $145.36 in interest ($845.36 – 700.00).

ILLUSTRATION   6-11

Determining *n* when other variables are known

Assume that you borrow $700 from a friend and intend to repay the amount in equal installments of $100 per year over a period of years. The payments will be made at the end of each year beginning one year from now. Your friend wishes to be reimbursed for the time value of money at a 7% annual rate. How many years would it take before you repaid the loan?

Once again, this is an ordinary annuity situation because the first payment takes place one year from now. The following time diagram illustrates the situation:

Determining the unknown number of periods—ordinary annuity

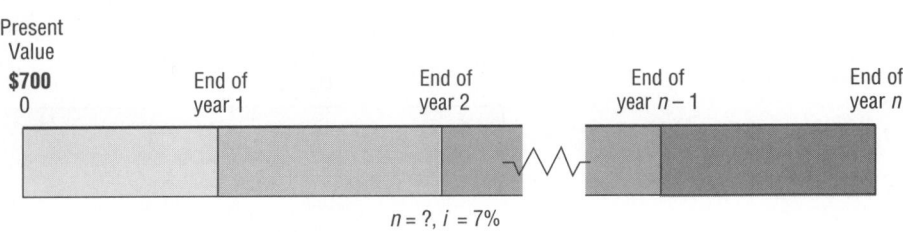

The number of years is the value of *n* that will provide a present value of $700 when discounting $100 at a discount rate of 7%:

$$\$700 \text{ (present value)} = \$100 \text{ (annuity amount)} \times \text{?*}$$
*Present value of an ordinary annuity of $1: n=?, i=7%

Rearranging algebraically, we find that the PVA table factor is:

$$\$700 \text{ (present value)} \div \$100 \text{ (annuity amount)} = 7.0*$$
*Present value of an ordinary annuity of $1: n=?, i=7%

When you consult the PVA table, Table 6A–4, you search the 7% column (i=7%) for this value and find 7.02358 in row 10. So it would take approximately 10 years to repay the loan in the situation described.

ILLUSTRATION   6–12

**Determining *i* when other
variables are known**

Suppose that a friend asked to borrow $331 today (present value) and promised to repay you $100 (the annuity amount) at the end of each of the next four years. What is the annual interest rate implicit in this agreement?

First of all, we are dealing with an ordinary annuity situation as the payments are at the end of each period. The following time diagram illustrates the situation:

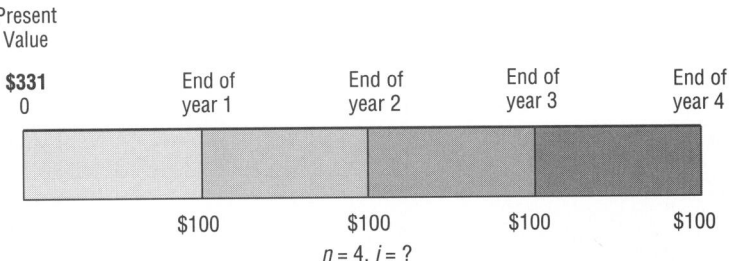

The interest rate is the discount rate that will provide a present value of $331 when discounting the $100 four-year ordinary annuity:

$$\$331 \text{ (present value)} = \$100 \text{ (annuity amount)} \times \text{?*}$$
*Present value of an ordinary annuity of $1: n=4, i=?

Rearranging algebraically, we find that the PVA table factor is:

$$\$331 \text{ (present value)} \div \$100 \text{ (annuity amount)} = 3.31*$$
*Present value of an ordinary annuity of $1: n=4, i=?

When you consult the PVA table, Table 6A–4, you search row four (n = 4) for this value and find it in the 8% column. So the effective interest rate is 8%.

ILLUSTRATION   6–13

**Determining *i* when other
variables are known—
unequal cash flows**

Suppose that you borrowed $400 from a friend and promised to repay the loan by making three annual payments of $100 at the end of each of the next three years plus a final payment of $200 at the end of year four. What is the interest rate implicit in this agreement?

The following time diagram illustrates the situation:

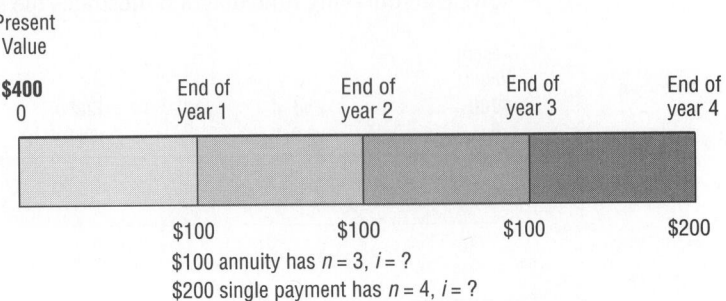

The interest rate is the discount rate that will provide a present value of $400 when discounting the $100 three-year ordinary annuity plus the $200 to be received in four years:

The unknown variable is the interest rate

$400 (present value) = $100 (annuity amount) × ?* + $200 (single payment) × ?†

*Present value of an ordinary annuity of $1: $n=3$, $i=?$
†Present value of $1: $n=4$, $i=?$

This equation involves two unknowns and is not as easily solved as the two previous examples. One way to solve the problem is to trial-and-error the answer. For example, if we assumed i to be 9%, the total PV of the payments would be calculated as follows:

$$PV = \$100 (2.53129^*) + \$200 (.70843†) = \$395$$

*Present value of an ordinary annuity of $1: $n = 3$, $i = 9\%$
†Present value of $1: $n = 4$, $i = 9\%$

Because the present value computed is less than the $400 borrowed, using 9% removes too much interest. Recalculating PV with $i = 8\%$ results in a PV of $405. This indicates that the interest rate implicit in the agreement is between 8% and 9%.

CONCEPT REVIEW EXERCISE   ANNUITIES

Using the appropriate table in Appendix 6, answer each of the following independent questions.

1. What is the future value of an annuity of $2,000 invested at the *end* of each of the next six periods at 8% interest?
2. What is the future value of an annuity of $2,000 invested at the *beginning* of each of the next six periods at 8% interest?
3. What is the present value of an annuity of $6,000 to be received at the *end* of each of the next eight periods assuming an interest rate of 10%?
4. What is the present value of an annuity of $6,000 to be received at the *beginning* of each of the next eight periods assuming an interest rate of 10%?
5. Jane bought a $3,000 audio system and agreed to pay for the purchase in 10 equal annual installments of $408 beginning one year from today. What is the interest rate implicit in this agreement?
6. Jane bought a $3,000 audio system and agreed to pay for the purchase in 10 equal annual installments beginning one year from today. The interest rate is 12%. What is the annual installment that must be made?
7. Jane bought a $3,000 audio system and agreed to pay for the purchase by making nine equal annual installments beginning one year from today plus a lump-sum payment of $1,000 at the end of 10 periods. The interest rate is 10%. What is the required annual installment?
8. Jane bought an audio system and agreed to pay for the purchase by making four equal annual installments of $800 beginning one year from today plus a lump-sum payment of $1,000 at the end of five years. The interest rate is 12%. What was the cost of the audio system? (Hint: What is the present value of the cash payments?)
9. Jane bought an audio system and agreed to pay for the purchase by making five equal annual installments of $1,100 beginning four years from today. The interest rate is 12%. What was the cost of the audio system? (Hint: What is the present value of the cash payments?)

CONCEPT REVIEW EXERCISE   SOLUTION

1. FVA = $2,000 (7.3359*) = $14,672
   *Future value of an ordinary annuity of $1: $n = 6$, $i = 8\%$ (from Table 6A–3)

2. FVAD = $2,000 (7.9228*) = $15,846
   *Future value of an annuity due of $1: $n = 6$, $i = 8\%$ (from Table 6A–5)

3. PVA = $6,000 (5.33493*) = $32,010
   *Present value of ordinary annuity of $1: $n = 8$, $i = 10\%$ (from Table 6A–4)

4. PVAD = $6,000 (5.86842*) = $35,211
   *Present value of an annuity due of $1: $n = 8$, $i = 10\%$ (from Table 6A–6)

5. $\dfrac{\$3,000}{\$408} = 7.35^*$

   *Present value of an ordinary annuity of $1: $n = 10$, $i = ?$ (from Table 6A-4, $i = $ approximately **6%**)

6.   Each annuity payment = $\dfrac{\$3,000}{5.65022^{*}}$ = $531

   *Present value of an ordinary annuity of $1: $n = 10$, $i = 12\%$ (from Table 6A–4)

7.   Each annuity payment = $\dfrac{\$3,000 - [\text{PV of }\$1,000\ (n=10,\ i=10\%)]}{5.75902^{*}}$

   Each annuity payment = $\dfrac{\$3,000 - (\$1,000 \times .38554\dagger)}{5.75902^{*}}$

   Each annuity payment = $\dfrac{\$2,614}{5.75902^{*}}$ = $454

   *Present value of an ordinary annuity of $1: $n = 9$, $i = 10\%$ (from Table 6A–4)
   †Present value of $1: $n = 10$, $i = 10\%$ (from Table 6A–2)

8.   PV = $800 (3.03735*) + $1,000 (.56743†) = $2,997
   *Present value of an ordinary annuity of $1: $n = 4$, $i = 12\%$ (from Table 6A–4)
   †Present value of $1: $n = 5$, $i = 12\%$ (from Table 6A-2)

9.   PVA = $1,100 (3.60478*) = $3,965
   *Present value of an ordinary annuity of $1: $n = 5$, $i = 12\%$ (from Table 6A–4)

This is the present value three years from today (the beginning of the five-year annuity). This single amount is then reduced to present value as of today by making the following calculation:

PV = $3,965 (.71178†) = $2,822
†Present value of $1: $n = 3$, $i = 12\%$ (from Table 6A–2)

Preview of Accounting Applications of Present Value Techniques—Annuities

The time value of money has many applications in accounting. Most of these applications involve the concept of present value. Because financial instruments typically spec-

Learning objective 9
Briefly describe how the concept of the time value of money is incorporated into the valuation of long-term leases and pension obligations.

ify equal periodic payments, these applications quite often involve annuity situations. For example, let's consider one accounting situation using an annuity due (long-term leases) and one using a deferred annuity (pension obligations).

Valuation of Long-Term Leases

OPENING CASE

Question 2

Companies frequently acquire the use of assets by leasing rather than purchasing them. Leases usually require the payment of fixed amounts at regular intervals over the life of the lease. You will learn in Chapter 15 that certain long-term, noncancelable leases are treated in a manner similar to an installment sale by the lessor and an installment purchase by the lessee. In other words, the lessor records a receivable and the lessee records a liability for the several installment payments. For the lessee, this requires that the leased asset and corresponding lease liability be valued at the present value of the lease payments. Consider the following example.

ILLUSTRATION   6–14

Valuing a long-term lease liability

On January 1, 1997, the Stridewell Wholesale Shoe Company signed a 25-year noncancelable lease agreement for an office building. Terms of the lease call for Stridewell to make annual lease payments of $10,000 at the *beginning* of each year, with the first payment due on January 1, 1997. Assuming that an interest rate of 10% properly reflects the time value of money in this situation, how should Stridewell value the asset acquired and the corresponding lease liability if it is to be treated in a manner similar to an installment purchase?

Certain long-term leases require the recording of an asset and corresponding liability at the present value of future lease payments.

Once again, by computing the present value of the lease payments, we remove the portion of the payments that represents interest, leaving the portion that represents payment for the asset itself. Because the first payment is due immediately, as is common for leases, this is an annuity due situation. In equation form:

$$\text{PVAD} = \$10,000 \text{ (annuity amount)} \times 9.98474^* = \$99,847$$

*Present value of an annuity due of $1: $n = 25$, $i = 10\%$

Stridewell initially will value the leased asset and corresponding lease liability at $99,847.

Journal entry at the inception of a lease

| Leased office building .... | 99,847 | |
| Lease payable .... | | 99,847 |

The difference between this amount and total future cash payments of $250,000 ($10,000 × 25) represents the interest that is implicit in this agreement. That difference is recorded as interest over the lease.

Valuation of Pension Obligations

Pension plans are important compensation vehicles used by most U.S. companies. These plans are essentially forms of deferred compensation as the pension benefits are paid to employees after they retire. You will learn in Chapter 17 that some pension plans create obligations during employees' service periods that must be paid during their retirement periods. These obligations are funded during the employment period. This means companies contribute cash to pension funds annually with the intention of accumulating sufficient funds to pay employees the retirement benefits they have earned. The amounts contributed are determined using estimates of retirement benefits. The actual amounts paid to employees during retirement depend on many factors including future compensation levels and length of life. Consider Illustration 6–15.

ILLUSTRATION   6 – 15

Valuing a pension obligation

On January 1, 1997, the Stridewell Wholesale Shoe Company hired Sammy Sossa. Sammy is expected to work for 25 years before retirement on December 31, 2021. Annual retirement payments will be paid at the end of each year during his retirement period, expected to be 20 years. The first payment will be on December 31, 2022. During 1997 Sammy earned an annual retirement benefit estimated to be $2,000 per year. The company plans to contribute cash to a pension fund that will accumulate to an amount sufficient to pay Sammy this benefit. Assuming that Stridewell anticipates earning 6% on all funds invested in the pension plan, how much would the company have to contribute at the end of 1997 to pay for pension benefits earned in 1997?

To determine the required contribution, we calculate the present value on December 31, 1997, of the deferred annuity of $2,000 that begins on December 31, 2022, and is expected to end on December 31, 2041.

The following time diagram depicts this situation:

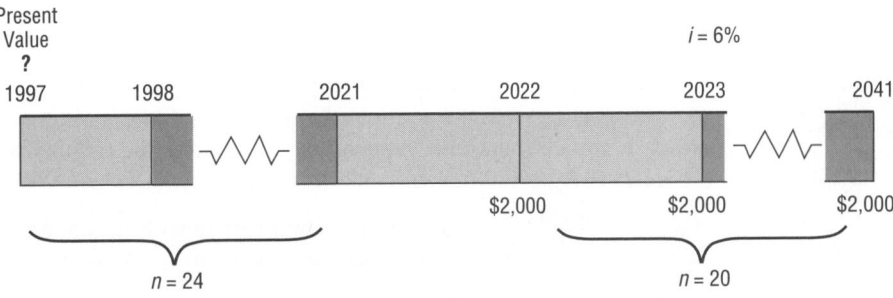

We can calculate the present value of the annuity using a two-step process. The first step computes the present value of the annuity as of December 31, 2021, by multiplying the annuity amount by the 20-period ordinary annuity factor:

$$\text{PVA} = \$2,000 \text{ (annuity amount)} \times 11.46992^* = \$22,940$$

*Present value of an ordinary annuity of $1: $n=20$, $i=6\%$

This is the present value as of December 31, 2021. This single amount is then reduced to present value as of December 31, 1997, by a second calculation:

$$PV = \$22{,}940 \text{ (future amount)} \times .24698^* = \$5{,}666$$

*Present value of $1: $n=24$, $i=6\%$

Stridewell would have to contribute $5,666 at the end of 1997 to fund the estimated pension benefits earned by its employee in 1997. Viewed in reverse, $5,666 invested now at 6% will accumulate a fund balance of $22,940 at December 31, 2021. If the fund balance remains invested at 6%, $2,000 can be withdrawn each year for 20 years before the fund is depleted.

Among the other situations you'll encounter using present value techniques are valuing bonds (Chapter 14), notes (Chapters 10 and 14), and postretirement benefits (Chapter 18).

Summary of Time Value of Money Concepts

Graphic 6–3 summarizes the time value of money concepts discussed in this chapter.

GRAPHIC 6–3

Summary of time value of money concepts

Concept	Summary	Formula	Table
Future value (FV) of $1	The amount of money that a dollar will grow to at some point in the future.	$FV = \$1(1+i)^n$	6A–1
Present value (PV) of $1	The amount of money today that is equivalent to a given amount to be received or paid in the future.	$PV = \dfrac{\$1}{(1+i)^n}$	6A–2
Future value of an ordinary annuity (FVA) of $1	The future value of a series of equal-sized cash flows with the first payment taking place at the end of the first compounding period.	$FVA = \dfrac{(1+i)^n - 1}{i}$	6A–3
Present value of an ordinary annuity (PVA) of $1	The present value of a series of equal-sized cash flows with the first payment taking place at the end of the first compounding period.	$PVA = \dfrac{1 - \dfrac{1}{(1+i)^n}}{i}$	6A–4
Future value of an annuity due (FVAD) of $1	The future value of a series of equal-sized cash flows with the first payment taking place at the beginning of the annuity period.	$FVAD = \left[\dfrac{(1+i)^n - 1}{i}\right] \times (1+i)$	6A–5
Present value of an annuity due (PVAD) of $1	The present value of a series of equal-sized cash flows with the first payment taking place at the beginning of the annuity period.	$PVAD = \left[\dfrac{1 - \dfrac{1}{(1+i)^n}}{i}\right] \times (1+i)$	6A–6

Solution to Financial Reporting Case (at the opening of the chapter)

1. How was the amount of the lump-sum settlement determined? Create a calculation that John's sister can look at.

The settlement was determined by calculating the present value of lost future income ($200,000 per year)[7] discounted at a rate that is expected to approximate the time value of money. In this case, the discount rate, i, apparently is 7% and the number of periods, n, is 25 (the number of years to John's retirement). John's settlement was calculated as follows:

$$\$200{,}000 \text{ (annuity amount)} \times 11.65358^* = \$2{,}330{,}716$$

*Present value of an ordinary annuity of $1: $n = 25$, $i = 7\%$ (from Table 6A–4)

2. What are some of the accounting applications that also take into account the time value of money?

Accounting applications that use annuity techniques include the valuation of long-term notes receivable and various long-term liabilities that include bonds, notes, leases, pension obligations, and postretirement benefits other than pensions. We study these in detail in later chapters.

---

[7]In the actual case, John's present salary was increased by 3% per year to reflect future salary increases.

The Bottom Line

1. A dollar today is worth more than a dollar to be received in the future. The difference between the present value of cash flows and their future value represents the time value of money. Interest is the rent paid for the use of money over time.

2. The future value of a single amount is the amount of money that a dollar will grow to at some point in the future. It is computed by *multiplying* the single amount by $(1+i)^n$, where i is the interest rate and n the number of compounding periods. The Future Value of $1 table allows for the calculation of future value for any single amount by providing the factors for various combinations of i and n.

3. The present value of a single amount is the amount of money today that is equivalent to a given amount to be received or paid in the future. It is computed by *dividing* the future amount by $(1+i)^n$. The Present Value of $1 table simplifies the calculation of the present value of any future amount.

4. There are four variables in the process of adjusting single cash flow amounts for the time value of money: present value (PV), future value (FV), i and n. If you know any three of these, the fourth can be computed easily.

5. An annuity is a series of equal-sized cash flows occurring over equal intervals of time. An ordinary annuity exists when the cash flows occur at the end of each period. An annuity due exists when the cash flows occur at the beginning of each period.

6. The future value of an ordinary annuity (FVA) is the future value of a series of equal-sized cash flows with the first payment taking place at the end of the first compounding period. The last payment will not earn any interest since it is made at the end of the annuity period. The future value of an annuity due (FVAD) is the future value of a series of equal-sized cash flows with the first payment taking place at the beginning of the annuity period (the beginning of the first compounding period).

7. The present value of an ordinary annuity (PVA) is the present value of a series of equal-sized cash flows with the first payment taking place at the end of the first compounding period. The present value of an annuity due (PVAD) is the present value of a series of equal-sized cash flows with the first payment taking place at the beginning of the annuity period. The present value of a deferred annuity is the present value of a series of equal-sized cash flows with the first payment taking place more than one time period after the date of the agreement.

8. In present value problems involving annuities, there are four variables: PVA or PVAD, the annuity amount, the number of compounding periods (n) and the interest rate (i). If you know any three of these, you can determine the fourth.

9. Most accounting applications of the time value of money involve the present values of annuities. Certain long-term leases require the lessee to compute the present value of future lease payments to value the leased asset and corresponding lease obligation. And pension plans require the payment of deferred annuities to retirees.

APPENDIX

6 PRESENT AND FUTURE VALUE TABLES

This table shows the future value of $1 at various interest rate (i) and time periods (n). It is used to calculate the future value of any single amount.

TABLE   6A–1

Future value of $1
$$FV = \$1(1 + i)^n$$

n\i	1.0%	1.5%	2.0%	2.5%	3.0%	3.5%	4.0%	4.5%
1	1.01000	1.01500	1.02000	1.02500	1.03000	1.03500	1.04000	1.04500
2	1.02010	1.03022	1.04040	1.05063	1.06090	1.07123	1.08160	1.09203
3	1.03030	1.04568	1.06121	1.07689	1.09273	1.10872	1.12486	1.14117
4	1.04060	1.06136	1.08243	1.10381	1.12551	1.14752	1.16986	1.19252
5	1.05101	1.07728	1.10408	1.13141	1.15927	1.18769	1.21665	1.24618
6	1.06152	1.09344	1.12616	1.15969	1.19405	1.22926	1.26532	1.30226
7	1.07214	1.10984	1.14869	1.18869	1.22987	1.27228	1.31593	1.36086
8	1.08285	1.12649	1.17166	1.21840	1.26677	1.31681	1.36857	1.42210
9	1.09369	1.14339	1.19509	1.24886	1.30477	1.36290	1.42331	1.48610
10	1.10462	1.16054	1.21899	1.28008	1.34392	1.41060	1.48024	1.55297
11	1.11567	1.17795	1.24337	1.31209	1.38423	1.45997	1.53945	1.62285
12	1.12683	1.19562	1.26824	1.34489	1.42576	1.51107	1.60103	1.69588
13	1.13809	1.21355	1.29361	1.37851	1.46853	1.56396	1.66507	1.77220
14	1.14947	1.23176	1.31948	1.41297	1.51259	1.61869	1.73168	1.85194
15	1.16097	1.25023	1.34587	1.44830	1.55797	1.67535	1.80094	1.93528
16	1.17258	1.26899	1.37279	1.48451	1.60471	1.73399	1.87298	2.02237
17	1.18430	1.28802	1.40024	1.52162	1.65285	1.79468	1.94790	2.11338
18	1.19615	1.30734	1.42825	1.55966	1.70243	1.85749	2.02582	2.20848
19	1.20811	1.32695	1.45681	1.59865	1.75351	1.92250	2.10685	2.30786
20	1.22019	1.34686	1.48595	1.63862	1.80611	1.98979	2.19112	2.41171
21	1.23239	1.36706	1.51567	1.67958	1.86029	2.05943	2.27877	2.52024
25	1.28243	1.45095	1.64061	1.85394	2.09378	2.36324	2.66584	3.00543
30	1.34785	1.56308	1.81136	2.09757	2.42726	2.80679	3.24340	3.74532
40	1.48886	1.81402	2.20804	2.68506	3.26204	3.95926	4.80102	5.81636

This table shows the present value of $1 at various interest rate (i) and time periods (n). It is used to calculate the present value of any single amount.

TABLE   6A–2

Present value of $1
$$PV = \frac{\$1}{(1 + i)^n}$$

n\i	1.0%	1.5%	2.0%	2.5%	3.0%	3.5%	4.0%	4.5%
1	0.99010	0.98522	0.98039	0.97561	0.97087	0.96618	0.96154	0.95694
2	0.98030	0.97066	0.96117	0.95181	0.94260	0.93351	0.92456	0.91573
3	0.97059	0.95632	0.94232	0.92860	0.91514	0.90194	0.88900	0.87630
4	0.96098	0.94218	0.92385	0.90595	0.88849	0.87144	0.85480	0.83856
5	0.95147	0.92826	0.90573	0.88385	0.86261	0.84197	0.82193	0.80245
6	0.94205	0.91454	0.88797	0.86230	0.83748	0.81350	0.79031	0.76790
7	0.93272	0.90103	0.87056	0.84127	0.81309	0.78599	0.75992	0.73483
8	0.92348	0.88771	0.85349	0.82075	0.78941	0.75941	0.73069	0.70319
9	0.91434	0.87459	0.83676	0.80073	0.76642	0.73373	0.70259	0.67290
10	0.90529	0.86167	0.82035	0.78120	0.74409	0.70892	0.67556	0.64393
11	0.89632	0.84893	0.80426	0.76214	0.72242	0.68495	0.64958	0.61620
12	0.88745	0.83639	0.78849	0.74356	0.70138	0.66178	0.62460	0.58966
13	0.87866	0.82403	0.77303	0.72542	0.68095	0.63940	0.60057	0.56427
14	0.86996	0.81185	0.75788	0.70773	0.66112	0.61778	0.57748	0.53997
15	0.86135	0.79985	0.74301	0.69047	0.64186	0.59689	0.55526	0.51672
16	0.85282	0.78803	0.72845	0.67362	0.62317	0.57671	0.53391	0.49447
17	0.84438	0.77639	0.71416	0.65720	0.60502	0.55720	0.51337	0.47318
18	0.83602	0.76491	0.70016	0.64117	0.58739	0.53836	0.49363	0.45280
19	0.82774	0.75361	0.68643	0.62553	0.57029	0.52016	0.47464	0.43330
20	0.81954	0.74247	0.67297	0.61027	0.55368	0.50257	0.45639	0.41464
21	0.81143	0.73150	0.65978	0.59539	0.53755	0.48557	0.43883	0.39679
24	0.78757	0.69954	0.62172	0.55288	0.49193	0.43796	0.39012	0.34770
25	0.77977	0.68921	0.60953	0.53939	0.47761	0.42315	0.37512	0.33273
28	0.75684	0.65910	0.57437	0.50088	0.43708	0.38165	0.33348	0.29157
29	0.74934	0.64936	0.56311	0.48866	0.42435	0.36875	0.32065	0.27902
30	0.74192	0.63976	0.55207	0.47674	0.41199	0.35628	0.30832	0.26700
31	0.73458	0.63031	0.54125	0.46511	0.39999	0.34423	0.29646	0.25550
40	0.67165	0.55126	0.45289	0.37243	0.30656	0.25257	0.20829	0.17193

5.0%	5.5%	6.0%	7.0%	8.0%	9.0%	10.0%	11.0%	12.0%	20.0%
1.05000	1.05500	0.06000	1.07000	1.08000	1.09000	1.10000	1.11000	1.12000	1.20000
1.10250	1.11303	1.12360	1.14490	1.16640	1.18810	1.21000	1.23210	1.25440	1.44000
1.15763	1.17424	1.19102	1.22504	1.25971	1.29503	1.33100	1.36763	1.40493	1.72800
1.21551	1.23882	1.26248	1.31080	1.36049	1.41158	1.46410	1.51807	1.57352	2.07360
1.27628	1.30696	1.33823	1.40255	1.46933	1.53862	1.61051	1.68506	1.76234	2.48832
1.34010	1.37884	1.41852	1.50073	1.58687	1.67710	1.77156	1.87041	1.97382	2.98598
1.40710	1.45468	1.50363	1.60578	1.71382	1.82804	1.94872	2.07616	2.21068	3.58318
1.47746	1.53469	1.59385	1.71819	1.85093	1.99256	2.14359	2.30454	2.47596	4.29982
1.55133	1.61909	1.68948	1.83846	1.99900	2.17189	2.35795	2.55804	2.77308	5.15978
1.62889	1.70814	1.79085	1.96715	2.15892	2.36736	2.59374	2.83942	3.10585	6.19174
1.71034	1.80209	1.89830	2.10485	2.33164	2.58043	2.85312	3.15176	3.47855	7.43008
1.79586	1.90121	2.01220	2.25219	2.51817	2.81266	3.13843	3.49845	3.89598	8.91610
1.88565	2.00577	2.13293	2.40985	2.71962	3.06580	3.45227	3.88328	4.36349	10.69932
1.97993	2.11609	2.26090	2.57853	2.93719	3.34173	3.79750	4.31044	4.88711	12.83918
2.07893	2.23248	2.39656	2.75903	3.17217	3.64248	4.17725	4.78459	5.47357	15.40702
2.18287	2.35526	2.54035	2.95216	3.42594	3.97031	4.59497	5.31089	6.13039	18.48843
2.29202	2.48480	2.69277	3.15882	3.70002	4.32763	5.05447	5.89509	6.86604	22.18611
2.40662	2.62147	2.85434	3.37993	3.99602	4.71712	5.55992	6.54355	7.68997	26.62333
2.52695	2.76565	3.02560	3.61653	4.31570	5.14166	6.11591	7.26334	8.61276	31.94800
2.65330	2.91776	3.20714	3.86968	4.66096	5.60441	6.72750	8.06231	9.64629	38.33760
2.78596	3.07823	3.39956	4.14056	5.03383	6.10881	7.40025	8.94917	10.80385	46.00512
3.38635	3.81339	4.29187	5.42743	6.84848	8.62308	10.83471	13.58546	17.00006	95.39622
4.32194	4.98395	5.74349	7.61226	10.06266	13.26768	17.44940	22.89230	29.95992	237.37631
7.03999	8.51331	10.28572	14.97446	21.72452	31.40942	45.25926	65.00087	93.05097	1469.7716

5.0%	5.5%	6.0%	7.0%	8.0%	9.0%	10.0%	11.0%	12.0%	20.0%
0.95238	0.94787	0.94340	0.93458	0.92593	0.91743	0.90909	0.90090	0.89286	0.83333
0.90703	0.89845	0.89000	0.87344	0.85734	0.84168	0.82645	0.81162	0.79719	0.69444
0.86384	0.85161	0.83962	0.81630	0.79383	0.77218	0.75131	0.73119	0.71178	0.57870
0.82270	0.80722	0.79209	0.76290	0.73503	0.70843	0.68301	0.65873	0.63552	0.48225
0.78353	0.76513	0.74726	0.71299	0.68058	0.64993	0.62092	0.59345	0.56743	0.40188
0.74622	0.72525	0.70496	0.66634	0.63017	0.59627	0.56447	0.53464	0.50663	0.33490
0.71068	0.68744	0.66506	0.62275	0.58349	0.54703	0.51316	0.48166	0.45235	0.27908
0.67684	0.65160	0.62741	0.58201	0.54027	0.50187	0.46651	0.43393	0.40388	0.23257
0.64461	0.61763	0.59190	0.54393	0.50025	0.46043	0.42410	0.39092	0.36061	0.19381
0.61391	0.58543 ✓	0.55839	0.50835	0.46319	0.42241	0.38554	0.35218	0.32197	0.16151
0.58468	0.55491	0.52679	0.47509	0.42888	0.38753	0.35049	0.31728	0.28748	0.13459
0.55684	0.52598	0.49697	0.44401	0.39711	0.35553	0.31863	0.28584	0.25668	0.11216
0.53032	0.49856	0.46884	0.41496	0.36770	0.32618	0.28966	0.25751	0.22917	0.08346
0.50507	0.47257	0.44230	0.38782	0.34046	0.29925	0.26333	0.23199	0.20462	0.07789
0.48102	0.44793	0.41727	0.36245	0.31524	0.27454	0.23939	0.20900	0.18270	0.06491
0.45811	0.42458	0.39365	0.33873	0.29189	0.25187	0.21763	0.18829	0.16312	0.05409
0.43630	0.40245	0.37136	0.31657	0.27027	0.23107	0.19784	0.16963	0.14564	0.04507
0.41552	0.38147	0.35034	0.29586	0.25025	0.21199	0.17986	0.15282	0.13004	0.03756
0.39573	0.36158	0.33051	0.27651	0.23171	0.19449	0.16351	0.13768	0.11611	0.03130
0.37689	0.34273	0.31180	0.25842	0.21455	0.17843	0.14864	0.12403	0.10367	0.02608
0.35894	0.32486	0.29416	0.24151	0.19866	0.16370	0.13513	0.11174	0.09256	0.02174
0.31007	0.27666	0.24698	0.19715	0.15770	0.12640	0.10153	0.08170	0.06588	0.01258
0.29530	0.26223	0.23300	0.18425	0.14602	0.11597	0.09230	0.07361	0.05882	0.01048
0.25509	0.22332	0.19563	0.15040	0.11591	0.08955	0.06934	0.05382	0.04187	0.00607
0.24295	0.21168	0.18456	0.14056	0.10733	0.08215	0.06304	0.04849	0.03738	0.00506
0.23138	0.20064	0.17411	0.13137	0.09938	0.07537	0.05731	0.04368	0.03338	0.00421
0.22036	0.19018	0.16425	0.12277	0.09202	0.06915	0.05210	0.03935	0.02980	0.00351
0.14205	0.11746	0.09722	0.06678	0.04603	0.03184	0.02209	0.01538	0.01075	0.00068

This table shows the future value of an ordinary annuity of $1 at various interest rates (*i*) and time periods (*n*). It is used to calculate the future value of any series of equal payments made at the *end* of each compounding period.

TABLE   6A–3

Future value of an ordinary annuity of $1

$$FVA = \frac{(1 + i)^n - 1}{i}$$

n \ i	1.0%	1.5%	2.0%	2.5%	3.0%	3.5%	4.0%	4.5%
1	1.0000	1.0000	1.0000	1.0000	1.0000	1.0000	1.0000	1.0000
2	2.0100	2.0150	2.0200	2.0250	2.0300	2.0350	2.0400	2.0450
3	3.0301	3.0452	3.0604	3.0756	3.0909	3.1062	3.1216	3.1370
4	4.0604	4.0909	4.1216	4.1525	4.1836	4.2149	4.2465	4.2782
5	5.1010	5.1523	5.2040	5.2563	5.3091	5.3625	5.4163	5.4707
6	6.1520	6.2296	6.3081	6.3877	6.4684	6.5502	6.6330	6.7169
7	7.2135	7.3230	7.4343	7.5474	7.6625	7.7794	7.8983	8.0192
8	8.2857	8.4328	8.5830	8.7361	8.8923	9.0517	9.2142	9.3800
9	9.3685	9.5593	9.7546	9.9545	10.1591	10.3685	10.5828	10.8021
10	10.4622	10.7027	10.9497	11.2034	11.4639	11.7314	12.0061	12.2882
11	11.5668	11.8633	12.1687	12.4835	12.8078	13.1420	13.4864	13.8412
12	12.6825	13.0412	13.4121	13.7956	14.1920	14.6020	15.0258	15.4640
13	13.8093	14.2368	14.6803	15.1404	15.6178	16.1130	16.6268	17.1599
14	14.9474	15.4504	15.9739	16.5190	17.0863	17.6770	18.2919	18.9321
15	16.0969	16.6821	17.2934	17.9319	18.5989	19.2957	20.0236	20.7841
16	17.2578	17.9324	18.6393	19.3802	20.1569	20.9710	21.8245	22.7193
17	18.4304	19.2014	20.0121	20.8647	21.7616	22.7050	23.6975	24.7417
18	19.6147	20.4894	21.4123	22.3863	23.4144	24.4997	25.6454	26.8551
19	20.8109	21.7967	22.8406	23.9460	25.1169	26.3572	27.6712	29.0636
20	22.0190	23.1237	24.2974	25.5447	26.8704	28.2797	29.7781	31.3714
21	23.2392	24.4705	25.7833	27.1833	28.6765	30.2695	31.9692	33.7831
30	34.7849	37.5387	40.5681	43.9027	47.5754	51.6227	56.0849	61.0071
40	48.8864	54.2679	60.4020	67.4026	75.4013	84.5503	95.0255	107.0303

This table shows the present value of an ordinary annuity of $1 at various interest rates (*i*) and time periods (*n*). It is used to calculate the present value of any series of equal payments made at the *end* of each compounding period.

TABLE   6A–4

Present value of an ordinary annuity of $1

$$PVA = \frac{1 - \frac{1}{(1 + i)^n}}{i}$$

n \ i	1.0%	1.5%	2.0%	2.5%	3.0%	3.5%	4.0%	4.5%
1	0.99010	0.96522	0.98039	0.97561	0.97087	0.96618	0.96154	0.95694
2	1.97040	1.95588	1.94156	1.92742	1.91347	1.89969	1.88609	1.87267
3	2.94099	2.91220	2.88388	2.85602	2.82861	2.80164	2.77509	2.74896
4	3.90197	3.85438	3.80773	3.76197	3.71710	3.67308	3.62990	3.58753
5	4.85343	4.78264	4.71346	4.64583	4.57971	4.51505	4.45182	4.38998
6	5.79548	5.69719	5.60143	5.50813	5.41719	5.32855	5.24214	5.15787
7	6.72819	6.59821	6.47199	6.34939	6.23028	6.11454	6.00205	5.89270
8	7.65168	7.48593	7.32548	7.17014	7.01969	6.87396	6.73274	6.59589
9	8.56602	8.36052	8.16224	7.97087	7.78611	7.60769	7.43533	7.26879
10	9.47130	9.22218	8.98259	8.75206	8.53020	8.31661	8.11090	7.91272
11	10.36763	10.07112	9.78685	9.51421	9.25262	9.00155	8.76048	8.52892
12	11.25508	10.90751	10.57534	10.25776	9.95400	9.66333	9.38507	9.11858
13	12.13374	11.73153	11.34937	10.98319	10.63496	10.30274	9.98565	9.68285
14	13.00370	12.54338	12.10625	11.69091	11.29607	10.92052	10.56312	10.22283
15	13.86505	13.34323	12.84926	12.38138	11.93794	11.51741	11.11839	10.73955
16	14.71787	14.13126	13.57771	13.05500	12.56110	12.09412	11.65230	11.23402
17	15.56225	14.90765	14.29187	13.71220	13.16612	12.65132	12.16567	11.70719
18	16.39827	15.67256	14.99203	14.35336	13.75351	13.18968	12.65930	12.15999
19	17.22601	16.42617	15.67846	14.97889	14.32380	13.70984	13.13394	12.59329
20	18.04555	17.16864	16.35143	15.58916	14.87747	14.21240	13.59033	13.00794
21	18.85698	17.90014	17.01121	16.18455	15.41502	14.69797	14.02916	13.40472
25	22.02316	20.71961	19.52346	18.42438	17.41315	16.48151	15.62208	14.82821
30	25.80771	24.01584	22.39646	20.93029	19.60044	18.39205	17.29203	16.28889
40	32.83469	29.91585	27.35548	25.10278	23.11477	21.35507	19.79277	18.40158

5.0%	5.5%	6.0%	7.0%	8.0%	9.0%	10.0%	11.0%	12.0%	20.0%
1.0000	1.0000	1.0000	1.0000	1.0000	1.0000	1.0000	1.0000	1.0000	1.0000
2.0500	2.0550	2.0600	2.0700	2.0800	2.0900	2.1000	2.1100	2.1200	2.2000
3.1525	3.1680	3.1836	3.2149	3.2464	3.2781	3.3100	3.3421	3.3744	3.6400
4.3101	4.3423	4.3746	4.4399	4.5061	4.5731	4.6410	4.7097	4.7793	5.3680
5.5256	5.5811	5.6371	5.7507	5.8666	5.9847	6.1051	6.2278	6.3528	7.4416
6.8019	6.8881	6.9753	7.1533	7.3359	7.5233	7.7156	7.9129	8.1152	9.9299
8.1420	8.2669	8.3938	8.6540	8.9228	9.2004	9.4872	9.7833	10.0890	12.9159
9.5491	9.7216	9.8975	10.2598	10.6366	11.0285	11.4359	11.8594	12.2997	16.4991
11.0266	11.2563	11.4913	11.9780	12.4876	13.0210	13.5795	14.1640	14.7757	20.7989
12.5779	12.8754	13.1808	13.8164	14.4866	15.1929	15.9374	16.7220	17.5487	25.9587
14.2068	14.5835	14.9716	15.7836	16.6455	17.5603	18.5312	19.5614	20.6546	32.1504
15.9171	16.3856	16.8699	17.8885	18.9771	20.1407	21.3843	22.7132	24.1331	39.5805
17.7130	18.2868	18.8821	20.1406	21.4953	22.9534	24.5227	26.2116	28.0291	48.4966
19.5986	20.2926	21.0151	22.5505	24.2149	26.0192	27.9750	30.0949	32.3926	59.1959
21.5786	22.4087	23.2760	25.1290	27.1521	29.3609	31.7725	34.4054	37.2797	72.0351
23.6575	24.6411	25.6725	27.8881	30.3243	33.0034	35.9497	39.1899	42.7533	87.4421
25.8404	26.9964	28.2129	30.8402	33.7502	36.9737	40.5447	44.5008	48.8837	105.9306
28.1324	29.4812	30.9057	33.9990	37.4502	41.3013	45.5992	50.3959	55.7497	128.1167
30.5390	32.1027	33.7600	37.3790	41.4463	46.0185	51.1591	56.9395	63.4397	154.7400
33.0660	34.8683	36.7856	40.9955	45.7620	51.1601	57.2750	64.2028	72.0524	186.6880
35.7193	37.7861	39.9927	44.8652	50.4229	56.7645	64.0025	72.2651	81.6987	225.0256
65.4388	72.4355	79.0582	94.4608	113.2832	136.3075	164.4940	199.0209	241.3327	1181.8816
120.7998	136.6056	154.7620	199.6351	259.0585	337.8824	442.5926	581.8261	767.0914	7343.8578

5.0%	5.5%	6.0%	7.0%	8.0%	9.0%	10.0%	11.0%	12.0%	20.0%
0.95238	0.94787	0.94340	0.93458	0.92583	0.91743	0.90909	0.90090	0.89286	0.83333
1.85941	1.84632	1.83338	1.80802	1.78326	1.75911	1.73554	1.71252	1.69005	1.52778
2.72325	2.69793	2.67301	2.62432	2.57710	2.53129	2.48685	2.44371	2.40183	2.10648
3.54595	3.50515	3.46511	3.38721	3.31213	3.23972	3.16987	3.10245	3.03735	2.58873
4.32948	4.27028	4.21236	4.10020	3.99271	3.88965	3.79079	3.69590	3.60478	2.99061
5.07569	4.99553	4.91732	4.76654	4.62288	4.48592	4.35526	4.23054	4.11141	3.32551
5.78637	5.68297	5.58238	5.38929	5.20637	5.03295	4.86842	4.71220	4.56376	3.60459
6.46321	6.33457	6.20979	5.97130	5.74664	5.53482	5.33493	5.14612	4.96764	3.83716
7.10782	6.95220	6.80169	6.51523	6.24689	5.99525	5.75902	5.53705	5.32825	4.03097
7.72173	7.53763	7.36009	7.02358	6.71008	6.41766	6.14457	5.88923	5.65022	4.19247
8.30641	8.09254	7.88687	7.49867	7.13896	6.80519	6.49506	6.20652	5.93770	4.32706
8.86325	8.61852	8.38384	7.94269	7.53608	7.16073	6.81369	6.49236	6.19437	4.43922
9.39357	9.11708	8.85268	8.35765	7.90378	7.48690	7.10336	6.74987	6.42355	4.53268
9.89864	9.58965	9.29498	8.74547	8.24424	7.78615	7.36669	6.98187	6.62817	4.61057
10.37966	10.03758	9.71225	9.10791	8.55948	8.06069	7.60608	7.19087	6.81086	4.67547
10.83777	10.46216	10.10590	9.44665	8.85137	8.31256	7.82371	7.37916	6.97399	4.72956
11.27407	10.86461	10.47726	9.76322	9.12164	8.54363	8.02155	7.54879	7.11963	4.77463
11.68959	11.24607	10.82760	10.05909	9.37189	8.75563	8.20141	7.70162	7.24967	4.81219
12.08532	11.60765	11.15812	10.33560	9.60360	8.95011	8.36492	7.83929	7.36578	4.84350
12.46221	11.95038	11.46992	10.59401	9.81815	9.12855	8.51356	7.96333	7.46944	4.86958
12.82115	12.27524	11.76408	10.83553	10.01680	9.29224	8.64869	8.07507	7.56200	4.89132
14.09394	13.41393	12.78336	11.65358	10.67478	9.82258	9.07704	8.42174	7.84314	4.94759
15.37245	14.53375	13.76483	12.40904	11.25778	10.27365	9.42691	8.69379	8.05518	4.97894
17.15909	16.04612	15.04630	13.33171	11.92461	10.75736	9.77905	8.95105	8.24378	4.99660

This table shows the future value of an annuity due of $1 at various interest rates (i) and time periods (n). It is used to calculate the future value of any series of equal payments made at the *beginning* of each ompounding period.

TABLE   6 A – 5

Future value of an annuity due of $1

$$FVAD = \left[\frac{(1+i)^n - 1}{i}\right] \times (1+i)$$

n \ i	1.0%	1.5%	2.0%	2.5%	3.0%	3.5%	4.0%	4.5%
1	1.0100	1.0150	1.0200	1.0250	1.0300	1.0350	1.0400	1.0450
2	2.0301	2.0452	2.0604	2.0756	2.0909	2.1062	2.1216	2.1370
3	3.0604	3.0909	3.1216	3.1525	3.1836	3.2149	3.2465	3.2782
4	4.1010	4.1523	4.2040	4.2563	4.3091	4.3625	4.4163	4.4707
5	5.1520	5.2296	5.3081	5.3877	5.4684	5.5502	5.6330	5.7169
6	6.2135	6.3230	6.4343	6.5474	6.6625	6.7794	6.8983	7.0192
7	7.2857	7.4328	7.5830	7.7361	7.8923	8.0517	8.2142	8.3800
8	8.3685	8.5593	8.7546	8.9545	9.1591	9.3685	9.5828	9.8021
9	9.4622	9.7027	9.9497	10.2034	10.4639	10.7314	11.0061	11.2882
10	10.5668	10.8633	11.1687	11.4835	11.8078	12.1420	12.4864	12.8412
11	11.6825	12.0412	12.4121	12.7956	13.1920	13.6020	14.0258	14.4640
12	12.8093	13.2368	13.6803	14.1404	14.6178	15.1130	15.6268	16.1599
13	13.9474	14.4504	14.9739	15.5190	16.0863	16.6770	17.2919	17.9321
14	15.0969	15.6821	16.2934	16.9319	17.5989	18.2957	19.0236	19.7841
15	16.2579	16.9324	17.6393	18.3802	19.1569	19.9710	20.8245	21.7193
16	17.4304	18.2014	19.0121	19.8647	20.7616	21.7050	22.6975	23.7417
17	18.6147	19.4894	20.4123	21.3863	22.4144	23.4997	24.6454	25.8551
18	19.8109	20.7967	21.8406	22.9460	24.1169	25.3572	26.6712	28.0636
19	21.0190	22.1237	23.2974	24.5447	25.8704	27.2797	28.7781	30.3714
20	22.2392	23.4705	24.7833	26.1833	27.6765	29.2695	30.9692	32.7831
21	23.4716	24.8376	26.2990	27.8629	29.5368	31.3289	33.2480	35.3034
25	28.5256	30.5140	32.6709	35.0117	37.5530	40.3131	43.3117	46.5706
30	35.1327	38.1018	41.3794	45.0003	49.0027	53.4295	58.3283	63.7524
40	49.3752	55.0819	61.6100	69.0876	77.6633	87.5095	98.8265	111.8467

This table shows the present value of an ordinary annuity of $1 at various interest rates (*i*) and time periods (*n*). It is used to calculate the present value of any series of equal payments made at the *beginning* of each compounding period.

TABLE   6 A – 6

Ppresent value of an annuity due of $1

$$PVAD = $$

$$\left[\frac{1 - \frac{1}{(1+i)^n}}{i}\right] \times (1+i)$$

n \ i	1.0%	1.5%	2.0%	2.5%	3.0%	3.5%	4.0%	4.5%
1	1.00000	1.00000	1.00000	1.00000	1.00000	1.00000	1.00000	1.00000
2	1.99010	1.96522	1.98039	1.97561	1.97087	1.96618	1.86154	1.95694
3	2.97040	2.95588	2.94156	2.92742	2.91347	2.89969	2.88609	2.87267
4	3.94099	3.91220	3.88388	3.85602	3.82861	3.80164	3.77509	3.74896
5	4.90197	4.85438	4.80773	4.76197	4.71710	4.67308	4.62990	4.58753
6	5.85343	5.78264	5.71346	5.64583	5.57971	5.51505	5.45182	5.38998
7	6.79548	6.69719	6.60143	6;.50813	6.41719	6.32855	6.24214	6.15787
8	7.72819	7.59821	7.47199	7.34939	7.23028	7.11454	7.00205	6.89270
9	8.65168	8.48593	8.32548	8.17014	8.01969	7.87396	7.73274	7.59589
10	9.56602	9.36052	9.16224	8.97087	8.78611	8.60769	8.43533	8.26879
11	10.47130	10.22218	9.98259	9.75206	9.53020	9.31661	9.11090	8.91272
12	11.36763	11.07112	10.78685	10.51421	10.25262	10.00155	9.76048	9.52892
13	12.25508	11.90751	11.57534	11.25776	10.95400	10.6633	10.38507	10.11858
14	13.13374	12.73153	12.34837	11.98318	11.63496	11.30274	10.98565	10.68285
15	14.00370	13.54338	13.10625	12.69091	12.29607	11.92052	11.56312	11.22283
16	14.86505	14.34323	13.84926	13.38138	12.93794	12.51741	12.11839	11.73955
17	15.71787	15.13126	14.57771	14.05500	13.56110	13.09412	12.65230	12.23402
18	16.56225	15.90765	15.29187	14.71220	14.16612	13.65132	13.16567	12.70719
19	17.39827	16.67256	15.99203	15.35336	14.75351	14.18968	13.65930	13.15999
20	18.22601	17.42617	16.67846	15.97889	15.32380	14.70984	14.13394	13.59329
21	19.04555	18.16864	17.35143	16.58916	15.87747	15.21240	14.59033	14.00794
25	22.24339	21.03041	19.91393	18.88499	17.93554	17.05837	16.24696	15.49548
30	26.06579	24.37608	22.84438	21.45355	20.18845	19.03577	17.98371	17.02189
40	33.16303	30.36458	27.90259	25.73034	23.80822	22.10250	20.58448	19.22966

5.0%	5.5%	6.0%	7.0%	8.0%	9.0%	10.0%	11.0%	12.0%	20.0%
1.0500	1.0550	1.0600	1.0700	1.0800	1.0900	1.1000	1.1100	1.1200	1.2000
2.1525	2.1680	2.1836	2.2149	2.2464	2.2781	2.3100	2.3421	2.3744	2.6400
3.3101	3.3423	3.3746	3.4399	3.5061	3.5731	3.6410	3.7097	3.7793	4.3680
4.5256	4.5811	4.6371	4.7507	4.8666	4.9847	5.1051	5.2278	5.3528	6.4415
5.8019	5.8881	5.9753	6.1533	6.3359	6.5233	6.7156	6.9129	7.1152	8.9299
7.1420	7.2669	7.3938	7.6540	7.9228	8.2004	8.4872	8.7833	9.0890	11.9159
8.5491	8.7216	8.8975	9.2598	9.6366	10.0285	10.4359	10.8594	11.2997	15.4991
10.0265	10.2563	10.4913	10.9780	11.4876	12.0210	12.5795	13.1640	13.7757	19.7989
11.5779	11.8754	12.1808	12.8164	13.4866	14.1929	14.9374	15.7220	16.5487	24.9587
13.2068	13.5835	13.9716	14.7836	15.6455	16.5603	17.5312	18.5614	19.6546	31.1504
14.9171	15.3856	15.8699	16.8885	17.9771	19.1407	20.3843	21.7132	23.1331	38.5805
16.7130	17.2868	17.8821	19.1406	20.4953	21.9534	23.5227	25.2116	27.0291	47.4966
18.5986	19.2926	20.0151	21.5505	23.2149	25.0192	26.9750	29.0949	31.3926	58.1959
20.5786	21.4087	22.2760	24.1290	26.1521	28.3609	30.7725	33.4054	36.2797	71.0351
22.6575	23.6411	24.6725	26.8881	29.3243	32.0034	34.9497	38.1899	41.7533	86.4421
24.8404	25.9964	27.2129	29.8402	32.7502	35.9737	39.5447	43.5008	47.8837	104.9306
27.1324	28.4812	29.9057	32.9990	36.4502	40.3013	44.5992	49.3959	54.7497	127.1167
29.5390	31.1027	32.7600	36.3790	40.4463	45.0185	50.1591	55.9395	62.4397	153.7400
32.0660	33.8683	35.7856	39.9955	44.7620	50.1601	56.2750	63.2028	71.0524	185.6880
34.7193	36.7861	38.9927	43.8652	49.4229	55.7645	63.0025	71.2651	80.6987	224.0256
37.5052	39.8643	42.3923	48.0057	54.4568	61.8733	70.4027	80.2143	91.5026	270.0307
50.1135	53.9660	58.1564	67.6765	78.9544	92.3240	108.1818	126.9988	149.3339	566.3773
69.7608	76.4194	83.8017	101.0730	122.3459	148.5752	180.9434	220.9132	270.2926	1418.2579
126.8398	144.1189	164.0477	213.6096	279.7810	368.2919	486.8518	645.8269	859.1424	8812.6294

5.0%	5.5%	6.0%	7.0%	8.0%	9.0%	10.0%	11.0%	12.0%	20.0%
1.00000	1.00000	1.00000	1.00000	1.00000	1.00000	1.00000	1.00000	1.00000	1.00000
1.95238	1.94787	1.94340	1.93458	1.92593	1.91743	1.90909	1.90090	1.89286	1.83333
2.85941	2.84632	2.83339	2.80802	2.78326	2.75911	2.73554	2.71252	2.69005	2.52778
3.72325	3.69793	3.67301	3.62432	3.57710	3.53129	3.48685	3.44371	3.40183	3.10648
4.54595	4.50515	4.46511	4.38721	4.31213	4.23972	4.16987	4.10245	4.03735	3.58873
5.32948	5.27028	5.21236	5.10020	4.99271	4.88965	4.79079	4.69590	4.60478	3.99061
6.07569	5.99553	5.91732	5.76654	5.62288	5.48592	5.35526	5.23054	5.11141	5.32551
6.78637	6.68297	6.58238	6.38929	6.20637	6.03295	5.86842	5.71220	5.56376	4.60459
7.46321	7.33457	7.20979	6.97130	6.74664	6.53482	6.33493	6.14612	5.96764	4.83716
8.10782	7.95220	7.80169	7.51523	7.24689	6.99525	6.75902	6.53705	6.32825	5.03097
8.72173	8.53763	8.36009	8.02358	7.71008	7.41766	7.14457	6.88923	6.65022	5.19247
9.30641	9.09254	8.88687	8.49867	8.13896	7.80519	7.49506	7.20652	6.93770	5.32706
9.86325	9.61852	9.38384	8.94269	8.53608	8.16073	7.81369	7.49236	7.19437	5.43922
10.39357	10.11708	9.85268	9.35765	8.90378	8.48690	8.10336	7.74987	7.42355	5.53268
10.89864	10.58965	10.29498	9.74547	9.24424	8.78615	8.36669	7.98187	7.62817	5.61057
11.37966	11.03758	10.71225	10.10791	9.55948	9.06069	8.60608	8.19087	7.81086	5.67547
11.83777	11.46216	11.10590	10.44665	9.85137	9.31256	8.82371	8.37916	7.97399	5.72592
12.27407	11.86461	11.47726	10.76322	10.12164	9.54363	9.02155	8.54879	8.11963	5.77463
12.68959	12.24607	11.82760	11.05909	10.37189	9.75563	9.20141	8.70162	8.24967	5.81219
13.08532	12.60765	12.15812	11.33560	10.60360	9.95011	9.36492	8.83929	8.36578	5.84350
13.46221	12.95038	12.46992	11.59401	10.81815	10.12855	9.51356	8.96333	8.46944	5.86958
14.79864	14.15170	13.55036	12.46933	11.52876	10.70661	9.98474	9.34814	8.78432	5.93710
16.14107	15.33310	14.59072	13.27767	12.15841	11.19828	10.36961	9.65011	9.02181	5.97472
18.01704	16.92866	15.94907	14.26493	12.87858	11.72552	10.75696	9.93567	9.23303	5.99592

Questions for Review of Key Topics

Question	6–1	Define interest.
Question	6–2	Explain compound interest.
Question	6–3	What would cause the annual interest rate to be different from the annual effective rate or yield?
Question	6–4	Identify the three items of information necessary to calculate the future value of a single amount.
Question	6–5	Define the present value of a single amount.
Question	6–6	Explain the difference between monetary and nonmonetary assets and liabilities.
Question	6–7	What is an annuity?
Question	6–8	Explain the difference between an ordinary annuity and an annuity due.
Question	6–9	Explain the relationship between Table 6A–2, Present Value of $1, and Table 6A–4, Present Value of an Ordinary Annuity.
Question	6–10	Prepare a time diagram for the present value of a four-year ordinary annuity of $200. Assume an interest rate of 10% per year.
Question	6–11	Prepare a time diagram for the present value of a four-year annuity due of $200. Assume an interest rate of 10% per year.
Question	6–12	What is a deferred annuity?
Question	6–13	Assume that you borrowed $500 from a friend and promised to repay the loan in five equal annual installments beginning one year from today. Your friend wants to be reimbursed for the time value of money at an 8% annual rate. Explain how you would compute the required annual payment.
Question	6–14	Compute the required annual payment in Question 6-13.
Question	6–15	Explain how the time value of money concept is incorporated into the valuation of long-term leases.

Exercises

Exercise 6–1
Future value; single amount

Determine the future value of the following single amounts:

	Invested Amount	Interest Rate	No. of Periods
1.	$10,000	6%	12
2.	20,000	8	10
3.	30,000	12	20
4.	50,000	10	12

Exercise 6–2
Present value; single amount

Determine the present value of the following single amounts:

	Future Amount	Interest Rate	No. of Periods
1.	$20,000	7%	10
2.	10,000	8	12
3.	25,000	12	20
4.	40,000	10	12

Exercise 6–3
Present value; multiple, unequal amounts

Determine the combined present value as of December 31, 1997, of the following four payments to be received at the *end* of each of the designated years, assuming an annual interest rate of 8%.

Payment	Year Received
$5,000	1998
6,000	1999
8,000	2001
7,000	2003

Exercise 6–4
Future value; single amounts

Determine the future value of $10,000 under each of the following sets of assumptions:

	Annual Rate	Period Invested	Interest Compounded
1.	10%	10 years	Semiannually
2.	12	5 years	Quarterly
3.	24	30 months	Monthly

Exercise 6–5

Future value; annuities

Wiseman Video plans to make four annual deposits of $2,000 each to a special building fund. The fund's assets will be invested in mortgage instruments expected to pay interest at 12% on the fund's balance. Using the appropriate annuity table, determine how much will be accumulated in the fund on December 31, 2000, under each of the following situations:

1. The first deposit is made on December 31, 1997, and interest is compounded annually.
2. The first deposit is made on December 31, 1996, and interest is compounded annually.
3. The first deposit is made on December 31, 1996, and interest is compounded quarterly.
4. The first deposit is made on December 31, 1996, interest is compounded annually, *and* interest earned is withdrawn at the end of each year.

Exercise 6–6

Present value; annuities

Using the appropriate present value table and assuming a 12% annual interest rate, determine the present value on December 31, 1997, of a five-period annual annuity of $5,000 under each of the following situations:

1. The first payment is received on December 31, 1998, and interest is compounded annually.
2. The first payment is received on December 31, 1997, and interest is compounded annually.
3. The first payment is received on December 31, 1998, and interest is compounded quarterly.

Exercise 6–7

Solving for unknowns; single amounts

For each of the following situations involving single amounts, solve for the unknown (?). Assume that interest is compounded annually. (i = interest rate, and n = number of years)

	Present Value	Future Value	i	n
1.	?	$30,000	10%	5
2.	$36,289	65,000	?	10
3.	15,884	40,000	8	?
4.	46,651	100,000	?	8
5.	15,376	?	7	20

Exercise 6–8

Solving for unknowns; annuities

For each of the following situations involving annuities, solve for the unknown (?). Assume that interest is compounded annually and that all annuity amounts are received at the *end* of each period. (i = interest rate, and n = number of years)

	Present Value	Annuity Amount	i	n
1.	?	$ 3,000	8%	5
2.	$242,980	75,000	?	4
3.	161,214	20,000	9	?
4.	500,000	80,518	?	8
5.	250,000	?	10	4

Exercise 6–9

Future value; solving for annuities and single amount

John Rider wants to accumulate $100,000 to be used for his daughter's college education. He would like to have the amount available on December 31, 2002. Assume that the funds will accumulate in a certificate of deposit paying 8% interest compounded annually.

Required:

Answer each of the following independent questions.

1. If John were to deposit a single amount, how much would he have to invest on December 31, 1997?
2. If John were to make five equal deposits on each December 31, beginning on December 31, 1998, what is the required deposit?
3. If John were to make five equal deposits on each December 31, beginning on December 31, 1997, what is the required deposit?

Exercise 6-10

Future and present value

Answer each of the following independent questions.

1. Alex Meir recently won a lottery and has the option of receiving one of the following three prizes: (1) $50,000 cash immediately, (2) $20,000 cash immediately and a five-period annuity of $8,000 beginning one year from today, or (3) a five-period annuity of $13,000 beginning one year from today. Assuming an interest rate of 6%, which option should Alex choose?
2. The Weimer Corporation wants to accumulate a sum of money to repay certain debts due on December 31, 2006. Weimer will make annual deposits of $100,000 into a special bank account at the end of each of 10 years beginning December 31, 1997. Assuming that the bank account pays 7% interest compounded annually, what will be the fund balance after the last payment is made on December 31, 2006?

Exercise 6–11
Noninterest-bearing note; single payment

The Field Detergent Company sold merchandise to the Abel Company on June 30, 1997. Payment was made in the form of a noninterest-bearing note requiring Abel to pay $85,000 on June 30, 1999. Assume that a 9% interest rate properly reflects the time value of money in this situation.

Required:
Calculate the amount at which Field should record the note receivable and corresponding sales revenue on June 30, 1997.

Exercise 6–12
Solving for unknown annuity payment

Don James purchased a new automobile for $20,000. Don made a cash down payment of $6,000 and agreed to pay the remaining balance in 30 monthly installments, beginning one month from the date of purchase. Financing is available at a 24% *annual* interest rate.

Required:
Calculate the amount of the required monthly payment.

Exercise 6–13
Solving for unknown interest rate

Lang Warehouses borrowed $100,000 from a bank and signed a note requiring 20 annual payments of $13,388 beginning one year from the date of the agreement.

Required:
Determine the interest rate implicit in this agreement.

Exercise 6–14
Deferred annuities

The Lincoln Company purchased merchandise from Grandville Corp. on September 30, 1997. Payment was made in the form of a noninterest-bearing note requiring Lincoln to make six annual payments of $5,000 on each September 30, beginning on September 30, *2000*.

Required:
Calculate the amount at which Lincoln should record the note payable and corresponding purchases on September 30, 1997, assuming that an interest rate of 10% properly reflects the time value of money in this situation.

Exercise 6–15
Deferred annuities; solving for annuity amount

On April 1, 1997, John Vaughn purchased appliances from the Acme Appliance Company for $1,200. In order to increase sales, Acme allows customers to pay in installments and will defer any payments for six months. John will make 18 equal monthly payments, beginning October 1, 1997. The annual interest rate implicit in this agreement is 24%.

Required:
Calculate the monthly payment necessary for John to pay for his purchases.

Exercise 6–16
Lease payments

On June 30, 1997, Fly-By-Night Airlines leased a jumbo jet from Boeing Corporation. The terms of the lease require Fly-By-Night to make 20 annual payments of $250,000 on each June 30. Accounting standards require this lease to be recorded as a liability for the present value of scheduled payments. Assume that a 7% interest rate properly reflects the time value of money in this situation.

Required:

1. At what amount should Fly-By-Night record the lease liability on June 30, 1997, assuming that the first payment will be made on June 30, 1998.
2. At what amount should Fly-By-Night record the lease liability on June 30, 1997, *before* any payments are made, assuming that the first payment will be made on June 30, 1997.

Exercise 6–17
Concepts; terminology

Listed below are several terms and phrases associated with concepts discussed in the chapter. Pair each item from List A (by letter) with the item from List B that is most appropriately associated with it.

List A	List B
_____ 1. Interest	a. First cash flow occurs one period after agreement begins.
_____ 2. Monetary asset	
_____ 3. Compound interest	b. The rate at which money will actually grow during a year.
_____ 4. Simple interest	
_____ 5. Annuity	c. First cash flow occurs on the first day of the agreement.
_____ 6. Present value of a single amount	
_____ 7. Annuity due	d. The amount of money that a dollar will grow to.
_____ 8. Future value of a single amount	e. Amount of money paid/received in excess of amount borrowed/lent.
_____ 9. Ordinary annuity	
_____ 10. Effective rate or yield	f. Obligation to pay a sum of cash, the amount of which is fixed
_____ 11. Nonmonetary asset	

_____ 12. Time value of money
_____ 13. Monetary liability

g. Money can be invested today and grow to a larger amount.
h. No fixed dollar amount attached.
i. Computed by multiplying an invested amount by the interest rate.
j. Interest calculated on invested amount plus accumulated interest.
k. A series of equal sized cash flows.
l. Amount of money required today that is equivalent to a given future amount.
m. Claim to receive a fixed amount of money.

Problems

Problem 6–1
Analysis of alternatives

The Esquire Company needs to acquire a molding machine to be used in its manufacturing process. Two types of machines that would be appropriate are presently on the market. The company has determined the following:

Machine A could be purchased for $48,000. It will last 10 years with annual maintenance costs of $1,000 per year. After 10 years the machine can be sold for $5,000.

Machine B could be purchased for $40,000. It also will last 10 years and will require maintenance costs of $4,000 in year three, $5,000 in year six, and $6,000 in year eight. After 10 years, the machine will have no salvage value.

Required:
Determine which machine Esquire should purchase. Assume an interest rate of 8% properly reflects the time value of money in this situation and that maintenance costs are paid at the end of each year. Ignore income tax considerations.

Problem 6–2
Present and future value

The Johnstone Company is facing several decisions regarding investing and financing activities. Address each decision independently.

1. On June 30, 1997, the Johnstone Company purchased equipment from Genovese Corp. Johnstone agreed to pay Genovese $10,000 on the purchase date and the balance in five annual installments of $8,000 on each June 30 beginning June 30, 1998. Assuming that an interest rate of 10% properly reflects the time value of money in this situation, at what amount should Johnstone value the equipment?
2. Johnstone needs to accumulate sufficient funds to pay a $400,000 debt that comes due on December 31, 2002. The company will accumulate the funds by making five equal annual deposits to an account paying 6% interest compounded annually. Determine the required annual deposit if the first deposit is made on December 31, 1997.
3. On January 1, 1997, Johnstone leased an office building. Terms of the lease require Johnstone to make 20 annual lease payments of $120,000 beginning on January 1, 1997. A 10% interest rate is implicit in the lease agreement. At what amount should Johnstone record the lease liability on January 1, 1997, _before_ any lease payments are made?

Problem 6–3
Analysis of alternatives

The Harding Company is in the process of purchasing several large pieces of equipment from Danning Machine Corporation. Several financing alternatives have been offered by Danning:

1. Pay $1,000,000 in cash immediately.
2. Pay $420,000 immediately and the remainder in 10 annual installments of $80,000, with the first installment due in one year.
3. Make 10 annual installments of $135,000 with the first payment due immediately.
4. Make one lump-sum payment of $1,500,000 five years from date of purchase.

Required:
Determine the best alternative for Harding, assuming that Harding can borrow funds at an 8% interest rate.

Problem 6–4
Investment analysis

John Wiggins is contemplating the purchase of a small restaurant. The purchase price listed by the seller is $800,000. John has used past financial information to estimate that the net cash flows (cash inflows less cash outflows) generated by the restaurant would be as follows:

Years	Amount
1–6	$80,000
7	70,000
8	60,000
9	50,000
10	40,000

If purchased, the restaurant would be held for 10 years and then sold for an estimated $700,000.

Required:
Assuming that John desires a 10% rate of return on this investment, should the restaurant be purchased? (Assume that all cash flows occur at the end of the year.)

Problem 6–5

Investment decision; varying rates

John and Sally Claussen are contemplating the purchase of a hardware store from John Duggan. The Claussen's anticipate that the store will generate cash flows of $70,000 per year for 20 years. At the end of 20 years, they intend to sell the store for an estimated $400,000. The Claussen's will finance the investment with a variable rate mortgage. Interest rates will increase twice during the 20-year life of the mortgage. Accordingly, the Claussen's desired rate of return on this investment varies as follows:

Years 1–5	8%
Years 6–10	10%
Years 11–20	12%

Required:
What is the maximum amount the Claussen's should pay John Duggan for the hardware store? (Assume that all cash flows occur at the end of the year.)

Problem 6–6

Solving for unknowns

The following situations should be considered independently.

1. John Jamison wants to accumulate $60,000 for a down payment on a small business. He will invest $30,000 today in a bank account paying 8% interest compounded annually. Approximately how long will it take John to reach his goal?
2. The Jasmine Tea Company purchased merchandise from a supplier for $28,700. Payment was a noninterest-bearing note requiring Jasmine to make five annual payments of $7,000 beginning one year from the date of purchase. What is the interest rate implicit in this agreement?
3. Sam Robinson borrowed $10,000 from a friend and promised to pay the loan in 10 equal annual installments beginning one year from the date of the loan. Sam's friend would like to be reimbursed for the time value of money at a 9% annual rate. What is the annual payment Sam must make to pay back his friend?

Problem 6–7

Solving for unknowns

The Lowlife Company defaulted on a $250,000 loan that was due on December 31, 1997. The bank has agreed to allow Lowlife to repay the $250,000 by making a series of equal annual payments beginning on December 31, 1998.

Required:

1. Calculate the required annual payment if the bank's interest rate is 10% and four payments are to be made.
2. Calculate the required annual payment if the bank's interest rate is 8% and five payments are to be made.
3. If the bank's interest rate is 10%, how many annual payments of $51,351 would be required to repay the debt?
4. If three payments of $104,087 are to be made, what interest rate is the bank charging Lowlife?

Problem 6–8

Deferred annuities

On January 1, 1997, the Montgomery company agreed to purchase a building by making six payments. The first three are to be $25,000 each, and will be paid on December 31, 1997, 1998, and 1999. The last three are to be $40,000 each and will be paid on December 31, 2000, 2001, and 2002. Montgomery recently borrowed other money at a 10% annual rate.

Required:

1. At what amount should Montgomery record the note payable and corresponding cost of the building on January 1, 1997?
2. How much interest expense on this note will Montgomery recognize in 1997?

Problem 6–9

Deferred annuities

John Roberts is 55 years old and has been asked to accept early retirement from his company. The company has offered John three alternative compensation packages to induce John to retire:

1. $180,000 cash payment to be paid immediately.
2. A 20-year annuity of $16,000 beginning immediately.
3. A 10-year annuity of $50,000 beginning at age 65.

Required:
Which alternative should John choose assuming that he is able to invest funds at a 7% rate?

Problem 6–10

Noninterest-bearing note; annuity and lump-sum payment

On January 1, 1997, The Barrett Company purchased merchandise from a supplier. Payment was a non-interest-bearing note requiring five annual payments of $20,000 on each December 31 beginning on December 31, 1997, and a lump-sum payment of $100,000 on December 31, 2001. A 10% interest rate properly reflects the time value of money in this situation.

Required:
Calculate the amount at which Barrett should record the note payable and corresponding merchandise purchased on January 1, 1997.

Problem 6–11

Solving for unknown lease payment

The Benning Manufacturing Company is negotiating with a customer for the lease of a large machine manufactured by Benning. The machine has a cash price of $800,000. Benning wants to be reimbursed for financing the machine at an 8% annual interest rate.

Required:

1. Determine the required lease payment if the lease agreement calls for 10 equal annual payments beginning immediately.
2. Determine the required lease payment if the first of 10 annual payments will be made one year from the date of the agreement.
3. Determine the required lease payment if the first of 10 annual payments will be made immediately and Benning will be able to sell the machine to another customer for $50,000 at the end of the 10 year lease.

Problem 6–12

Lease vs. buy alternatives

The Kiddy Toy Corporation needs to acquire the use of a machine to be used in its manufacturing process. The machine needed is manufactured by Lollie Corp. The machine can be used for 10 years and then sold for $10,000 at the end of its useful life. Lollie has presented Kiddy with the following options:

1. *Buy machine*   The machine could be purchased for $160,000 in cash. All maintenance and insurance costs, which approximate $5,000 per year, would be paid by Kiddy.
2. *Lease machine*   The machine could be leased for a 10-year period for an annual lease payment of $25,000 with the first payment due immediately. All maintenance and insurance costs will be paid for by the Lollie Corp. and the machine will revert back to Lollie at the end of the 10-year period.

Required:
Assuming that a 12% interest rate properly reflects the time value of money in this situation and that all maintenance and insurance costs are paid at the end of each year, determine which option Kiddy should choose. Ignore income tax considerations.

Problem 6–13

Deferred annuities; pension obligation

Three employees of the Horizon Distributing Company will receive annual pension payments from the company when they retire. The employees will receive their annual payments for as long as they live. Life expectancy for each employee is 15 years beyond retirement. Their names, the amount of their annual pension payments, and the date they will receive their first payment are shown below:

Employee	Annual Payment	Date of First Payment
Tinkers	$20,000	12/31/00
Evers	25,000	12/31/01
Chance	30,000	12/31/02

Required:

1. Compute the present value of the pension obligation to these three employees as of December 31, 1997. Assume an 11% interest rate.
2. The company wants to have enough cash invested at December 31, 2000, to provide for all three employees. To accumulate enough cash, they will make three equal annual contributions to a fund that will earn 11% interest compounded annually. The first contribution will be made on December 31, 1997. Compute the amount of this required annual contribution.

Cases

Discussion Case 6–1
Bonus alternatives; present value analysis

Sally Hamilton has performed well as the chief financial officer of the Maxtech Computer Company and has earned a bonus. She has a choice among the following three bonus plans:

1. A $50,000 cash bonus paid now.
2. A $10,000 annual cash bonus to be paid each year over the next six years, with the first $10,000 paid now.
3. A three-year $22,000 annual cash bonus with the first payment due three years from now.

Required:
Evaluate the three alternative bonus plans. Sally can earn a 6% annual return on her investments.

Writing Case 6–2
Present value of annuities

Harvey Alexander, an all-league professional football player, has just declared free agency. Two teams, the San Francisco 49ers and the Dallas Cowboys, have made Harvey the following offers to obtain his services:

49ers: $1 million signing bonus payable immediately and an annual salary of $1.5 million for the five-year term of the contract.

Cowboys: $2.5 million signing bonus payable immediately and an annual salary of $1 million for the five-year term of the contract.

With both contracts, the annual salary will be paid in one lump-sum at the end of the football season.

Required:
You have been hired as a consultant to Harry's agent, Phil Marks, to evaluate the two contracts. Write a short letter to Phil with your recommendation including the method you used to reach your conclusion. Assume that Harry has no preference between the two teams and that the decision will be based entirely on monetary considerations. Also assume that Harry can invest his money and earn an 8% annual return.

Ethics Case 6–3

The Damon Investment Company manages a mutual fund composed mostly of speculative stocks. You recently saw an add claiming that investments in the funds have been earning a rate of return of 21%. This rate seemed quite high so you called a friend who works for one of Damon's competitors. The friend told you that the 21% return figure was determined by dividing the two-year appreciation on investments in the fund by the average investment. In other words, $100 invested in the fund two years ago would have grown to $121 ($21 ÷ $100 = 21%).

Required:
Discuss the ethics of the 21% return claim made by the Damon Investment Company.

Critical Thought Case 6–4
Replacement decision

The Hughes Corporation is considering replacing a machine used in the manufacturing process with a new, more efficient model. The purchase price of the new machine is $150,000 and the old machine can be sold for $100,000. Output for the two machines is identical; they will both be used to produce the same amount of product for five years. However, the annual operating costs of the old machine are $18,000 compared to $10,000 for the new machine. Also, the new machine has a salvage value of $25,000, but the old machine will be worthless at the end of the five years.

Required:
Should the company sell the old machine and purchase the new model? Assume that an 8% rate properly reflects the time value of money in this situation and that all operating costs are paid at the end of the year. Ignore the effect of the decision on income taxes.

Real World Case 6–5
Zero-coupon notes

Solectron Corporation, headquartered in Milpitas, California, is a provider of customized, integrated manufacturing services to original equipment manufacturers in the electronics industry. The company's 1994 financial statements included the following information in the long-term debt disclosure note :

	($ in thousands)	
	1994	**1993**
Zero-coupon subordinated notes, due 2012	$135,848	$127,137

Zero-coupon notes pay no interest. The note disclosed that 460,000 notes were issued in May 1992 and have a maturity value of $1,000 each in May 2012. The company is accreting the issue price to maturity value using the note's effective interest rate.

Required:

1. Determine the approximate effective interest rate on the notes (round to the nearest whole %).
2. Determine the issue price of one, $1,000 maturity value note.

Financial Analysis Case 6–6
Time value of money
applications

**Federal Express
Corporation**

Refer to the financial statements and related disclosure notes of Federal Express Corporation in the appendix to Chapter 1.

Required:

1. Identify the various liabilities that are valued by applying the time value of money concept.
2. What rate is used to value pension obligations?

2

ECONOMIC RESOURCES

7

CASH AND RECEIVABLES

OVERVIEW

We begin our study of assets by looking at cash and receivables — the two assets typically listed first in a balance sheet. Internal control and classification on the balance sheet are key issues we address in consideration of cash. For receivables, the key issues are valuation and the related income statement effects of transactions involving accounts receivable and notes receivable.

LEARNING OBJECTIVES   **After studying this chapter, you should be able to:**

1. Define what is meant by internal control and describe some key elements of an internal control system for cash receipts and disbursements.
2. Prepare a bank reconciliation and explain its value as an internal control tool.
3. Explain the possible restrictions on cash and their implications for classification on the balance sheet.
4. Distinguish between the gross and net methods of accounting for cash discounts.
5. Describe the accounting treatment for merchandise returns.
6. Describe the accounting treatment of anticipated uncollectible accounts receivable.
7. Describe the two approaches to estimating bad debts.
8. Describe the accounting treatment of short-term notes receivable.
9. Differentiate between the use of receivables in financing arrangements accounted for as a loan and those accounted for as a sale.
10. List and explain the four-step process used to account for a discounted note receivable.

You Give the Lecture

"Didn't anyone ever tell you not to volunteer? And you're a senior!" your friend chided.

"I know," you sigh, "I'm beginning to have second thoughts."

It seemed so natural to raise your hand when Professor Henley asked for a volunteer. Professor Henley is the faculty advisor to Beta Alpha Psi, the national honorary fraternity for accounting majors. The tutoring session the group is organizing has a section on the concept of accounting for uncollectible accounts receivable. After all, you understood that topic really well last year, and Professor Henley promised she would review your outline for the tutoring session. You set yourself to the task of preparing the outline, silently praying that no one will ask any questions.

QUESTION

As the hesitant volunteer, what will your outline look like for a tutoring session on accounting for uncollectible accounts receivable?

In the beginning chapters of this text, we studied the underlying measurement and reporting concepts for the basic financial statements presented to external decision makers. Now we turn our attention to the elements of those financial statements. Specifically, we further explore the elements of the balance sheet including the income statement effects of transactions involving these elements. We first address assets, then liabilities, and finally shareholders' equity. This chapter focuses on the current assets **cash and cash equivalents** and **receivables**.

PART

A CASH AND CASH EQUIVALENTS

Cash includes currency and coins, balances in checking accounts, and items acceptable for deposit in these accounts, such as checks and money orders received from customers.

Managers typically invest temporarily idle cash to earn interest on those funds rather than keep an unnecessarily large checking account. These amounts are essentially equivalent to cash because they can quickly become available for use as cash. So, short-term, highly liquid investments that can be readily converted to cash with little risk of loss are viewed by the FASB as cash equivalents. For financial reporting we make no distinction between cash in the form of currency or bank account balances and amounts held in cash equivalent investments.

Cash equivalents include such things as certain money market funds, short-term certificates of deposit, treasury bills, and commercial paper. To be classified as cash equivalents, these investments must have a maturity date no longer than three months from the date of purchase. Companies are permitted flexibility in designating cash equivalents and must establish individual policies regarding which short-term, highly liquid investments are classified as cash equivalents. A company's policy should be consistent with the usual motivation for acquiring certain types of investments. The policy should be disclosed in the notes to the financial statements. Graphic 7–1 shows a note from a recent annual report of the Colgate-Palmolive Company that provides a description of the company's cash equivalents.

A company's policy concerning which short-term, highly liquid investments it classifies as cash equivalents should be described in a disclosure note.

GRAPHIC   7–1

Disclosure of cash equivalents—Colgate-Palmolive Company

> *Note 1: Cash and Cash Equivalents (in part)*
> The company considers all highly liquid investments with maturities of three months or less when purchased to be cash equivalents for the purpose of the Consolidated Balance Sheet and the Consolidated Statement of Cash Flows. Investments in securities which do not meet the definition of cash equivalents are classified as marketable securities.

The measurement and reporting of cash and cash equivalents is largely straightforward because cash generally presents no measurement problems. Cash and cash equivalents usually are combined and reported as a single amount on the balance sheet. However, cash that is not available for use in current operations because it is restricted for a special purpose usually is classified in one of the noncurrent asset categories. Restricted cash is discussed later in this chapter.

All assets must be safeguarded against possible misuse. However, cash is the most liquid asset and the asset most easily expropriated. As a result, a system of internal control of cash is a key accounting issue.

Internal Control of Cash

The success of any business enterprise depends on an effective system of **internal control**. Internal control refers to a company's plan to (a) encourage adherence to company policies and procedures, (b) promote operational efficiency, (c) minimize errors and theft, and (d) enhance the reliability and accuracy of accounting data. From a financial accounting perspective, the focus is on controls intended to improve the accuracy and reliability of accounting information and to safeguard the company's assets.

A critical aspect of an internal control system is the *separation of duties*. Individuals that have physical responsibility for assets should not also have access to accounting records. For exam-

Learning objective 1
Define what is meant by internal control and describe some key elements of an internal control system for cash receipts and disbursements.

ple, if the same individual has control of both the supplies inventory and the accounting records, the theft of supplies could be concealed by a reduction of the supplies account.

As cash is the most liquid of all assets, a well-designed and functioning system of internal control must surround all cash transactions. Separation of duties is critical. Ideally, those who handle cash should not be involved in or have access to accounting records nor be involved in the reconciliation of cash book balances to bank balances.

> Employees involved in recordkeeping should not also have physical access to the assets.

Internal Control Procedures—Cash Receipts

Consider the cash receipt process. Most nonretail businesses receive payment for goods by checks received through the mail. An approach to internal control over cash receipts might include the following steps:

1. Employee A opens the mail each day and prepares a multicopy listing of all checks including the amount and payor's name.
2. Employee B takes the checks, along with one copy of the listing, to the person responsible for depositing the checks in the company's bank account.
3. A second copy of the check listing is sent to the accounting department where the receipts are entered into the records.

The amount received should equal the amount deposited as verified by comparison with the bank-generated deposit slip and the amount recorded in the accounting records. This helps ensure accuracy as well as safeguard cash against theft.

Internal Control Procedures—Cash Disbursements

Proper controls for cash disbursements should be designed to prevent any unauthorized payments and ensure that disbursements are recorded in the proper general ledger and subsidiary ledger accounts. Important elements of a cash disbursement control system include:

1. All disbursements, other than very small disbursements from petty cash, should be made by check. This provides a permanent record of all disbursements.
2. All expenditures should be *authorized* before a check is prepared. For example, a vendor invoice for the purchase of inventory should be compared with the purchase order and receiving report to ensure the accuracy of quantity, price, part numbers, and so on. This process should include verification of the proper ledger accounts to be debited.
3. Checks should be signed only by authorized individuals.

Responsibilities for check signing, check writing, check mailing, cash disbursement documentation, and recordkeeping ideally should be separated whenever possible.

An important part of any system of internal control of cash is the periodic reconciliation of book balances and bank balances to the correct balance. In addition, a petty cash system is employed by many business enterprises. We now turn to these two topics.

Bank Reconciliation

One of the most important tools used in the control of cash is the **bank reconciliation**. Since all cash receipts are deposited into the bank account and cash disbursements are made by check, the bank account provides a separate record of cash. It's desirable to periodically compare the bank balance with the balance in the company's own records and reconcile any differences.

> **Learning objective 2**
> Prepare a bank reconciliation and explain its value as an internal control tool.

From your own personal experience, you know that the ending balance in your checking account reported on the monthly bank statement you receive rarely equals the balance you have recorded in your checkbook. Differences arise from two types of items: timing differences and errors.

Timing differences occur when the company and the bank record transactions at different times. At any point in time the company may have adjusted the cash balance for items of which the bank is not yet aware. Likewise, the bank may have adjusted its record of that balance by items of which the company is not yet aware. For example, checks written and cash deposits are not all processed by the bank in the same month that they are recorded by the company. Also, the bank may adjust the company's account for items such as service charges that the company is not aware of until the bank statement is received.

> Differences between the cash book and bank balance occur due to differences in the timing of recognition of certain transactions.

Differences between book and bank cash balances are caused by errors made by either the bank or the company.

Step 1:   Adjust the bank balance to the corrected cash balance.

Step 2:   Adjust the book balance to the corrected cash balance.

Errors can be made either by the company or the bank. For example, a check might be written for $210 but recorded on the company's books as a $120 disbursement; a deposit of $500 might be processed incorrectly by the bank as a $50 deposit. In addition to serving as a safeguard of cash, the bank reconciliation also uncovers errors such as these and helps ensure that the proper cash balance is reported on the balance sheet.

Bank reconciliations include adjustments to the balance per bank for timing differences involving transactions already reflected in the company's accounting records that have not yet been processed by the bank. These adjustments usually include *checks outstanding* and *deposits outstanding*. In addition, the balance per bank would be adjusted for any bank errors discovered. These adjustments produce an adjusted bank balance that represents the corrected cash balance.

The balance per books is similarly adjusted for timing differences involving transactions already reflected by the bank of which the company is unaware until the bank statement is received. These would include service charges, charges for NSF (nonsufficient funds) checks, and collections made by the bank on the company's behalf. In addition, the balance per books is adjusted for any company errors discovered, resulting in an adjusted book balance that will also represent the corrected cash balance. *Each of these adjustments requires a journal entry to correct the book balance.* Only adjustments to the book balance require journal entries. Graphic 7–2 recaps these reconciling items.

GRAPHIC   7 - 2

Bank reconciliation— reconciling items

Bank balance
+ Deposits outstanding
− Checks outstanding
± Errors
_____
Corrected balance

Book balance
+ Collections by bank
− Service charges
− NSF checks
± Errors
_____
Corrected balance

Step 1:   Adjustments to Bank Balance:

1. *Add deposits outstanding.* These represent cash received by the company and debited to cash that have not been deposited in the bank by the bank statement cutoff date and cash deposited in the bank near the end of the period that are not recorded by the bank until after the cutoff date.
2. *Deduct checks outstanding.* These represent checks written and recorded by the company as credits to cash that have not yet been processed by the bank before the cutoff date.
3. *Bank errors.* These will either be increases or decreases depending on the nature of the error.

Step 2:   Adjustments to Book Balance:

1. *Add collections made by the bank* on the company's behalf and other increases in cash that the company is unaware of until the bank statement is received.
2. *Deduct service and other charges* made by the bank that the company is unaware of until the bank statement is received.
3. *Deduct NSF* (nonsufficient funds) *checks.* These are checks previously deposited for which the payors do not have sufficient funds in their accounts to cover the amount of the checks. The checks are returned to the company whose responsibility it is to seek payment from payors.
4. *Company errors.* These will either be increases or decreases depending on the nature of the error.

To demonstrate the bank reconciliation process, consider Illustration 7–1.

The next step is to prepare adjusting journal entries to reflect each of the adjustments to the balance per books. These represent amounts the company was not previously aware of. No adjusting entries are needed for the adjustments to the balance per bank because the company has already recorded these items. However, the bank needs to be notified of any errors discovered.

To record the receipt of principal and interest on note collected directly by the bank.

Cash	1,120	
Notes receivable		1,000
Interest revenue		120

To record credits to cash revealed by the bank reconciliation.

Miscellaneous expense (bank service charges)	80	
Accounts receivable (NSF checks)	2,187	
Accounts payable (error in check to supplier)	1,000	
Cash		3,267

After these entries are posted, the general ledger cash account will equal the corrected balance of $33,129.

The Hawthorne Manufacturing Company maintains a general checking account at the First Pacific Bank. First Pacific provides a bank statement and canceled checks once a month. The cutoff date is the last day of the month. The bank statement for the month of May is summarized as follows:

Balance, May 1, 1997	$ 32,120
Deposits	82,140
Checks processed	(78,433)
Service charges	(80)
NSF checks	(2,187)
Note payment collected by bank (includes $120 interest)	1,120
Balance, May 31, 1997	$ 34,680

The company's general ledger cash account has a balance of $35,276 at the end of May. A review of the company records and the bank statement reveals the following:

1. Cash and checks on hand from customers recorded but not deposited totaled $2,965.
2. A deposit of $1,020 was made on May 31 that was not credited to the company's account until June.
3. All checks written in April have been processed by the bank. Checks written in May that had not been processed by the bank total $5,536.
4. A check written for $1,790 was incorrectly recorded by the company as a $790 disbursement. The check was for payment to a supplier of raw materials.

The bank reconciliation prepared by the company appears as follows:

Step 1:   Bank Balance to Corrected Balance

Balance per bank statement	$34,680
Add: Deposits outstanding	3,985*
Deduct: Checks outstanding	(5,536)
Corrected cash balance	$33,129

Step 2:   Book Balance to Corrected Balance

Balance per books	$35,276
Add: Note collected by bank	1,120
Deduct:	
Service charges	(80)
NSF checks	(2,187)
Error—understatement of check	(1,000)
Corrected cash balance	$33,129

* $2,965 + 1,020 = $3,985

Petty Cash

Most companies keep a small amount of cash on hand to pay for low cost items such as postage, office supplies, delivery charges, and entertainment expenses. It would be inconvenient, time consuming, and costly to process a check each time these small payments are made. A petty cash fund provides a more efficient way to handle these payments.

A petty cash fund is established by transferring a specified amount of cash from the company's general checking account to an employee designated as the petty cash custodian. The amount of the fund should approximate the expenditures made from the fund during a relatively short period of time (say a week or a month). The custodian disburses cash from the fund when the appropriate documentation is presented, such as a receipt for the purchase of office supplies. At any point in time, the custodian should be in possession of cash and appropriate receipts that sum to the amount of the fund. The receipts serve as the basis for recording appropriate expenses each time the fund is replenished. Consider the example in Illustration 7–2.

In journal entry form, the transaction to establish the fund would be recorded as follows:

> The petty cash fund always should have cash and receipts that together equal the amount of the fund.

> A petty cash fund is established by writing a check to the custodian.

May 1, 1997

Petty Cash	200	
Cash (checking account)		200

ILLUSTRATION   7-2

Petty cash fund

On May 1, 1997, the Hawthorne Manufacturing Company established a $200 petty cash fund. John Ringo is designated as the petty cash custodian. The fund will be replenished at the end of each month. On May 1, 1997, a check is written for $200 made out to John Ringo, petty cash custodian. During the month of May, John paid bills totaling $160 summarized as follows:

Postage	$ 40
Office supplies	35
Delivery charges	55
Entertainment	30
Total	$160

No entries are recorded at the time the actual expenditures are made from the fund. The expenditures are recorded when reimbursement is requested at the end of the month. At that time, a check is written to John Ringo, petty cash custodian, for the total of the fund receipts, $160 in this case. John cashes the check and replenishes the fund to $200. In journal entry form, replenishing the fund would be recorded as follows:

The appropriate expense accounts are debited when the petty cash fund is reimbursed.

May 31, 1997

Postage expense	40	
Office supplies expense	35	
Delivery expense	55	
Entertainment expense	30	
Cash (checking account)		160

The petty cash account is not debited when replenishing the fund. If, however, the size of the fund is increased at time of replenishment, the account is debited for the increase. Similarly, petty cash would be credited if the size of the fund is decreased.

To maintain the control objective of separation of duties, the petty cash custodian should not be involved in the process of writing or approving checks, nor in recordkeeping. In addition, management should arrange for surprise counts of the fund.

Restricted Cash and Compensating Balances

We discussed the classification of assets and liabilities in Chapter 5. You should recall that only cash available for current operations or to satisfy current liabilities is classified as a current asset. Cash that is restricted in some way and not available for current use usually is reported as *investments and funds* or *other assets*.

Learning objective 3
Explain the possible restrictions on cash and their implications for classification on the balance sheet.

Restrictions on cash can be informal, arising from management's intent to use a certain amount of cash for a specific purpose. For example, a company may set aside funds for future plant expansion. This cash, if material, should be classified as investments and funds or other assets. Sometimes restrictions are contractually imposed. Debt instruments, for instance, frequently require the borrower to set aside funds for the future payment of a debt. In these instances, the restricted cash is classified as investments and funds or other assets if the debt is classified as noncurrent. On the other hand, if the liability is current, the restricted cash also is classified as current. Disclosure notes should describe any material restrictions of cash.

Banks frequently require cash restrictions in connection with loans or loan commitments (lines of credit). Typically, the borrower is asked to maintain a specified balance in a low-interest or noninterest-bearing account at the bank (creditor). The required balance usually is some percentage of the committed amount (say 2% to 5%). These are known as **compensating balances** because they compensate the bank for granting the loan or extending the line of credit.

The effect of a **compensating balance** is a higher effective interest rate on the debt.

A compensating balance results in the borrower's paying an effective interest rate higher than the stated rate on the debt. For example, suppose that a company borrows $10,000,000 from a bank at an interest rate of 12%. If the bank requires a compensating balance of $2,000,000 to be held in a noninterest-bearing checking account, the company really is borrowing only $8,000,000 (the loan less the compensating balance). This means an effective interest rate of 15% ($1,200,000 interest divided by $8,000,000 cash available for use).

The classification and disclosure of a compensating balance depends on the nature of the restriction and the classification of the related debt.[1] If the restriction is legally binding, the cash is classified as either current or noncurrent (investments and funds or other assets) depending on the classification of the related debt. In either case, note disclosure is appropriate.

> A material compensating balance must be disclosed regardless of the classification of the cash.

If the compensating balance arrangement is informal with no contractual agreement that restricts the use of cash, the compensating balance can be reported as part of cash and cash equivalents, with note disclosure of the arrangement. Graphic 7–3 provides an example of a note disclosure of a compensating balance for Kmart Corporation. Because the company is "free to withdraw the entire balance...," the cash is reported as a current asset.

GRAPHIC   7-3

Disclosure of compensating balances—Kmart Corporation

Note K: Compensating Balances

($ in millions)

At January 26, 1994, Kmart corporation had bank lines of credit aggregating $1,473 which provide for interest rates not exceeding the "prime" lending rate on any borrowings thereunder. In support of certain lines of credit, it is expected that compensating balances will be maintained on deposit with the banks, which will average 10% of the line to the extent that it is not in use and an additional 10% on the portion in use, whereas other lines require fees in lieu of compensating balances. Kmart is free to withdraw the entire balance in its accounts at any time.

PART

B CURRENT RECEIVABLES

Receivables represent a company's claims to the future collection of cash, other assets, or services. Receivables resulting from the sale of goods or services on account are called **accounts receivable** and often are referred to as *trade receivables*. *Nontrade receivables* are those other than trade receivables and include tax refund claims, advances to affiliated companies, and loans by the company to other entities including stockholders and employees. When a receivable, trade or nontrade, is accompanied by a formal promissory note, it's referred to as a note receivable. We consider notes receivable after first discussing accounts receivable.

Accounts Receivable

Most businesses provide credit to their customers, either because it's not practical to require immediate cash payment or to encourage customers to purchase the company's product or service. Accounts receivable are *informal* credit arrangements supported by an invoice and normally are due in 30 to 60 days after the sale. They almost always are classified as *current* assets because their normal collection period, even if longer than a year, is part of, and therefore less than, the operating cycle.

> Accounts receivable are current assets because, by definition, they will be converted to cash within the normal operating cycle.

The point at which accounts receivable are recognized depends on the earnings process of the company. We discussed the realization principle in Chapter 3 and the criteria that must be met before revenue can be recognized. Recall that revenue can be recognized only after the earnings process is *virtually complete* and *collection* from the customer *is reasonably certain*. For the typical credit sale, these criteria are satisfied at the point of delivery of the product or service, so revenue and the related receivable are recognized at that time.

> Typically, revenue and related accounts receivable are recognized at the point of delivery of the product or service.

Initial Valuation of Accounts Receivable

We know from prior discussions that receivables should be recorded at the present value of future cash receipts using a realistic interest rate. So, a $10,000 sale on credit due in 30 days should result in a receivable valued at the present value of the $10,000. In other words, the interest portion of the $10,000 due in 30 days should be removed and recognized as interest revenue over the

---

[1]"Amendments to Regulations S-X and Related Interpretations and Guidelines Regarding the Disclosure of Compensating Balances and Short-Term Borrowing Arrangements," *Accounting Series Release No. 148,* Securities and Exchange Commission (November 13, 1973).

30-day period, not as sales revenue at date of delivery of the product. If the monthly interest rate is 2%, the receivable would be valued at $9,804, calculated by multiplying the future cash payment of $10,000 by the present value of $1 factor for one period at 2% (.98039).

The typical account receivable is valued at the amount expected to be received, not the present value of that amount.

However, because the difference between the future and present values of accounts receivable often is immaterial, *APBO 21* specifically excludes accounts receivable from the general rule that receivables be recorded at present value.[2] Therefore, accounts receivable initially are valued at the exchange price agreed on by the buyer and seller. In our example, both the account receivable and sales revenue would be recorded at $10,000. Let's discuss two aspects of accounts receivable related to their initial valuation—trade discounts and cash discounts.

Trade Discounts.   Companies frequently offer **trade discounts** to customers, usually a percentage reduction from the list price. Trade discounts can be a way to change prices without publishing a new catalog or to disguise real prices from competitors. They also are used to give quantity discounts to large customers. For example, a manufacturer might list a machine part at $2,500 but sell it to a customer at list less a 10% discount. The trade discount of $250 is not recognized directly when recording the transaction. The discount is recognized indirectly by recording the sale at the net of discount price of $2,250, not at the list price.

Cash Discounts.   Be careful to distinguish a *trade* discount from a *cash* discount. **Cash discounts** represent reductions not in the selling price of a good or service but in the amount to be paid by a credit customer if paid within a specified period of time. It is a discount intended to provide incentive for quick payment.

The amount of the discount and the time period within which it's available usually are conveyed by cryptic terms like 2/10, n/30 (meaning a 2% discount if paid within 10 days, otherwise full payment within 30 days). There are two ways to record cash discounts, the gross method and the net method. Conceptually, the **gross method** views a discount not taken by the customer as part of sales revenue. On the other hand, the **net method** considers sales revenue to be the net amount, after discount, and any discounts not taken by the customer as interest revenue. The discounts are viewed as compensation to the seller for providing financing to the customer. With both methods, discounts *taken* are subtracted from gross sales to arrive at net sales. Consider the example in Illustration 7–3.

Cash discounts reduce the amount to be paid if remittance is made within a specified short period of time.

Learning objective 4
Distinguish between the gross and net methods of accounting for cash discounts.

ILLUSTRATION   7–3

Cash discounts

By either method, net sales is reduced by discounts *taken*.

Discounts *not* taken are included in sales revenue using the gross method and interest revenue using the net method.

The Hawthorne Manufacturing Company offers credit customers a 2% cash discount if the sales price is paid within 10 days. Any amounts not paid within 10 days are due in 30 days. These repayment terms are stated as 2/10, n/30. On October 5, 1997, Hawthorne sold merchandise at a price of $20,000. The customer paid $13,720 ($14,000 less the 2% cash discount) on October 14 and the remaining balance of $6,000 on November 4.

The appropriate journal entries to record the sale and cash collection, comparing the gross and net methods are as follows:

Gross Method			Net Method		
October 5, 1997					
Accounts receivable	20,000		Accounts receivable	19,600	
Sales revenue		20,000	Sales revenue		19,600
October 14, 1997					
Cash	13,720		Cash	13,720	
Sales discounts	280		Accounts receivable		13,720
Accounts receivable		14,000			
November 4, 1997					
Cash	6,000		Cash	6,000	
Accounts receivable		6,000	Accounts receivable		5,880
			Interest revenue		120

[2]"Interest on Receivables and Payables," *Accounting Principles Board Opinion No. 21* (New York: AICPA, 1971).

The **gross method** views cash discounts *not* taken as part of sales revenue.

Notice that by using the gross method, we record the revenue and related receivable at the full $20,000 price. On remittance within the discount period, the $280 discount is recorded as a debit to an account called *sales discounts*. This is a valuation (contra) account to sales revenue and is deducted from sales revenue to derive the net sales reported on the income statement. For payments made after the discount period, cash is simply increased and accounts receivable decreased by the gross amount originally recorded.

The **net method** considers cash discounts *not* taken as interest revenue.

Under the net method, we record revenue and the related accounts receivable at the agreed on price *less* the 2% discount applied to the entire price. Payments made within the discount period are recorded as debits to cash and credits to accounts receivable for the amount received. If a customer loses a discount by failing to pay within the discount period, the discount not taken is recorded as interest revenue. In this case, $120 in cash (2% × $6,000) is interest.

Total revenue on the 1997 income statement would be the same by either method:

Revenue comparison of the gross method and the net method

	Gross Method	Net Method
Sales	$20,000	$19,600
Less: Sales discounts	(280)	- 0 -
Net sales revenue	19,720	19,600
Interest revenue	- 0 -	120
Total revenue	$19,720	$19,720

Which is correct? Conceptually, the net method usually reflects the reality of the situation—the real price is $19,600 and $120 is an interest penalty for not paying promptly. The net price usually is the price expected by the seller because the discount usually reflects a hefty interest cost that prudent buyers are unwilling to bear. Consider Illustration 7–3. Although the discount rate is stated as 2%, the effective rate really is 36.5%. The buyer must pay 2% of the price to delay payment an additional 20 days beyond the 10-day discount period. To convert this 20-day rate to an annual rate, we multiply by 365/20:

$$2\% \times 365/20 = 36.5\% \text{ effective rate}$$

Understandably, most buyers try to take the discount if at all possible.

The difference between the two methods, in terms of the effect of the transactions on income, is in the timing of the recognition of any discounts not taken. The gross method recognizes discounts not taken as revenue when the sale is made. The net method recognizes them as revenue after the discount period has passed and the cash is collected. These two measurement dates could be in different reporting periods.

From a practical standpoint, the effect on the financial statements of the difference between the two methods usually is immaterial. As a result, most companies use the gross method because it's easier and doesn't require adjusting entries for discounts not taken.

Subsequent Valuation of Accounts Receivable

Following the initial valuation of an account receivable, two situations possibly could cause the cash ultimately collected to be less than the initial valuation of the receivable: (1) the customer could return the product, or (2) the customer could default and not pay the agreed on sales price. When accounting for sales and accounts receivable, we anticipate these possibilities.

Learning objective 5
Describe the accounting treatment for merchandise returns.

Sales Returns.   Customers frequently are given the right to return the merchandise they purchase if they are not satisfied. We discussed how this policy affects revenue recognition in Chapter 4. We now discuss it from the perspective of asset valuation.

Recognizing sales returns when they occur could result in an overstatement of income in the period of the related sale.

When merchandise is returned for a refund or for credit to be applied to other purchases the situation is called a **sales return**. When practical, a dissatisfied customer might be given a special price reduction as an incentive to keep the merchandise purchased.[3] Returns are common and often substantial in some industries such as food products, publishing, and retailing. In these cases, recognizing returns and allowances only as they occur could cause profit to be overstated in the

---

[3]Price reductions sometimes are referred to as *sales allowances* and are distinguished from situations when the products actually are returned for a refund or credit (sales returns).

period of the sale and understated in the return period. For example, assume merchandise is sold to a customer for $10,000 in December 1997, the last month in the selling company's fiscal year, and that the merchandise cost $6,000. If all of the merchandise is returned in 1998 after financial statements for 1997 are issued, gross profit will be overstated in 1997 and understated in 1998 by $4,000. Assets at the end of 1997 also will be overstated by $4,000 because a $10,000 receivable would be recorded instead of $6,000 in inventory.

To avoid misstating the financial statements, when amounts are material, returns should be anticipated by subtracting an allowance for estimated returns. For an example, refer to Illustration 7–4.

ILLUSTRATION   7–4

Sales returns

During 1997, its first year of operations, the Hawthorne Manufacturing Company sold merchandise on account for $2,000,000. This merchandise cost $1,200,000 (60% of the selling price). Industry experience indicates that 10% of all sales will be returned. Customers returned $130,000 in sales during 1997, prior to making payment.

The entries to record sales and merchandise returned during the year, *assuming that a perpetual inventory system is used*, are as follows:

Sales

Accounts receivable	2,000,000	
Sales		2,000,000
Cost of goods sold (60% × $2,000,000).................................	1,200,000	
Inventory...		1,200,000

Returns — actual return

Sales returns (actual return)...	130,000	
Accounts receivable		130,000
Inventory...	78,000	
Cost of goods sold (60% × $130,000)		78,000

At the end of 1997, the company would anticipate the remaining estimated returns using the following adjusting entries :

Adjusting entries — estimate return

Sales returns ([10% × $2,000,000] – 130,000) ....(contra sales)	70,000	
Allowance for sales returns .....(contra asset)		70,000
Inventory—estimated returns	42,000	
Cost of goods sold (60% × $70,000)		42,000

> If sales returns are material, they should be estimated and recorded in the same period of the related sales.

The allowance for sales returns is a contra account to accounts receivable. When returns actually occur in the following reporting period, the allowance for sales returns is debited. In this way, income is not reduced in the return period but in the period of the sales revenue.[4] The inventory of $78,000 in the first set of entries represents merchandise on hand, while the inventory of $42,000 in the second set of entries represents an estimate of the cost of merchandise expected to be returned.

Assuming that the estimates of future returns are correct, the following (summary) journal entry would be recorded in 1998:

Allowance for sales returns	70,000	
Accounts receivable		70,000

> If sales returns are immaterial, they can be recorded as they occur.

In some industries, returns are typically small and infrequent. Companies in these industries usually simply record returns in the period they occur because the effect on income measurement

---

[4]Of course, if the allowance for sales returns is estimated incorrectly, income in both the period of the sale and the return will be misstated.

and asset valuation is immaterial. In a few situations, significant uncertainty as to future collection is created by the right of return. In those cases, revenue recognition is deferred until the uncertainty is resolved. We discussed this possibility in Chapter 4.

Uncollectible Accounts Receivable.   Companies that extend credit to customers know that it's unlikely that all customers will fully pay their accounts. **Bad debt expense** is an inherent cost of granting credit. It's an operating expense incurred to boost sales. As a result, even when specific customer accounts haven't been proven uncollectible by the end of the reporting period, the expense properly should be matched with sales revenue on the income statement for that period.[5] Likewise, as it's not expected that all accounts receivable will be collected, the balance sheet should report only the expected net realizable value of that asset. So, to record the bad debt expense and the related reduction of accounts receivable when the amount hasn't yet been determined, an estimate is needed. In an adjusting entry, we record bad debt expense and reduce accounts receivable indirectly by crediting a contra account (valuation account) to accounts receivable for an estimate of the amount that eventually will prove uncollectible. This approach to accounting for bad debts is known as the **allowance method**.

There are two ways commonly used to arrive at this estimate of future bad debts, the income statement approach and the balance sheet approach. Illustration 7–5 demonstrates both approaches.

Learning objective 6
Describe the accounting treatment of anticipated uncollectible accounts receivable.

OPENING CASE
Question 1

Learning objective 7
Describe the two approaches to estimating bad debts.

ILLUSTRATION   7–5
Bad debts

The Hawthorne Manufacturing Company sells its products offering 30 days credit to its customers. During 1997, its first year of operations, the following events occurred:

Sales on credit	$1,200,000
Cash collections from credit customers	(895,000)
Accounts receivable, end of year	$ 305,000

There were no specific accounts determined to be uncollectible in 1997. The company anticipates that 2% of all credit sales will ultimately become uncollectible.

Income Statement Approach.   Using the **income statement approach,** we estimate bad debt expense as a percentage of each period's net credit sales. This percentage usually is determined by reviewing the company's recent history of the relationship between credit sales and actual bad debts. For a relatively new company, this percentage may be obtained by referring to other sources such as industry averages.

Under the income statement approach, the Hawthorne Manufacturing Company would make the following adjusting journal entry at the end of 1997:

Bad debt expense is estimated as a percentage of net credit sales.

Bad debt expense (2% × $1,200,000)	24,000	
Allowance for uncollectible accounts *(contra asset)*		24,000

Allowance for uncollectible accounts is a contra account (valuation account) to accounts receivable. In the current asset section of the 1997 balance sheet, accounts receivable would be reported *net* of the allowance, as follows:

Accounts receivable	$305,000
Less: Allowance for uncollectible accounts	(24,000)
Net accounts receivable	$281,000

Quite often, companies report the allowance for uncollectible accounts (sometimes called *allowance for doubtful accounts*) parenthetically or alongside the accounts receivable account title separated by a dash or a comma. For example, Federal Express Corporation reported the following under current assets in its comparative balance sheets for 1996 and 1995:

Federal Express Corporation

---

[5]Some consider bad debts to be a contra (reduction) to revenue rather than an operating expense.

($ in thousands)

	1996	1995
Receivables - less allowance for doubtful accounts of $30,809 and $31,173	$1,271,599	$1,130,254

The $1,271,599,000 figure at the end of 1996 is the company's estimate of the net realizable value of accounts receivable. Actual (gross) accounts receivable at the end of 1996 were $1,302,408,000 ($1,271,599,000 + $30,809,000).

It's important to notice that the income statement approach focuses on the current year's credit sales. The effect on the balance sheet—the allowance for uncollectible accounts and hence net accounts receivable—is an incidental result of estimating the expense. An alternative is to focus on the balance sheet amounts instead. We look at this approach next.

Balance Sheet Approach.   Using the **balance sheet approach** to estimate future bad debts, we determine bad debt expense by estimating the net realizable value of accounts receivable to be reported on the balance sheet. In other words, the allowance for uncollectible accounts is determined. Bad debt expense is an indirect outcome of adjusting the allowance account to the desired balance.

For the Hawthorne Manufacturing Company example in Illustration 7–5, the company would estimate the amount of uncollectible accounts that will result from the $305,000 in accounts receivable outstanding at the end of 1997. This could be done by analyzing each customer account, by applying a percentage to the entire outstanding receivable balance, or by applying different percentages to accounts receivable balances depending on the length of time outstanding. This latter approach normally employs an **accounts receivable aging schedule**. For example, the aging schedule for Hawthorne's 1997 year-end accounts receivable is shown in Illustration 7–5a.

> Using the income statement approach, the balance sheet amount is an indirect outcome of estimating bad debt expense.

> Using the balance sheet approach, bad debt expense is an incidental result of estimating the net realizable value of accounts receivable.

> An aging of accounts receivable is a grouping of receivable balances according to length of time outstanding.

ILLUSTRATION   7–5a

Accounts receivable aging schedule

> The schedule assumes older accounts are more likely to prove uncollectible.

> Higher estimated default percentages are applied to groups of older receivables.

Customer	Accounts Receivable 12/31/97	0–60 Days	61–90 Days	91–120 Days	Over 120 Days
Axel Manufacturing Co.	$ 20,000	$ 14,000	$ 6,000		
Banner Corporation	33,000		20,000	$10,000	$ 3,000
Dando Company	60,000	50,000	10,000		
ˋ ˋ ˋ ˋ			ˋ ˋ	ˋ ˋ	ˋ ˋ
ˋ ˋ	ˋ ˋ	ˋ ˋ	ˋ ˋ	ˋ ˋ	ˋ ˋ
Xicon Company	18,000	10,000	4,000	3,000	1,000
Totals	$305,000	$220,000	$50,000	$25,000	$10,000

Summary

Age Group	Amount	Estimated Percent Uncollectible	Estimated Allowance
0–60 days	$220,000	5%	$11,000
61–90 days	50,000	10%	5,000
91–120 days	25,000	20%	5,000
Over 120 days	10,000	45%	4,500
Allowance for uncollectible accounts			$25,500

The schedule classifies the year-end receivable balances according to their length of time outstanding. Presumably, the longer an account has been outstanding the more likely it will prove uncollectible. Based on past experience or other sources of information, a percentage is applied to age group totals.

The 1997 entry to record bad debts adjusts the balance in the allowance for uncollectible accounts to this required amount of $25,500. Because it is the first year of operations for Hawthorne and the beginning balance in the allowance account is zero, the adjusting entry would *debit* bad debt expense and *credit* allowance for uncollectible accounts for $25,500.

To illustrate the concept further, let's suppose that this was not the first year of operations and the allowance account prior to the adjusting entry had a *credit* balance of $4,000. Then the amount of the entry would be $21,500—the amount necessary to adjust a credit balance of $4,000 to a credit

Allowance	
Beg. bal.	4,000
Adj. entry	21,500
Bal.	25,500

balance of $25,500. Similarly, if the allowance account prior to the adjusting entry had a *debit* balance of $4,000, then the amount of the entry would be $29,500.

Some companies use a combination of approaches in estimating bad debts. For example, Hawthorne could decide to accrue bad debts on a monthly basis using the income statement approach and then employ the balance sheet approach at the end of the year based on an aging of receivables. Each month an adjusting entry would record a debit to bad debt expense and a credit to allowance for uncollectible accounts equal to 2% of credit sales. In our illustration, the monthly accruals for 1997 would result in the following account balances at the end of 1997:

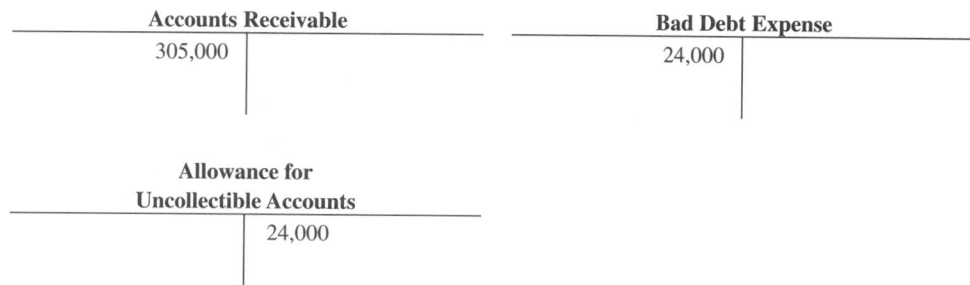

Accounts Receivable		Bad Debt Expense	
305,000		24,000	

Allowance for Uncollectible Accounts	
	24,000

At the end of the year, if the aging revealed a required allowance of $25,500, the following adjusting entry would be recorded:

Bad debt expense	1,500	
Allowance for uncollectible accounts		1,500

This entry adjusts the allowance account to the required amount.

In the 1997 balance sheet, accounts receivable would be reported net of the allowance, as follows:

Accounts receivable	$305,000
Less: Allowance for uncollectible accounts	(25,500)
Net accounts receivable	$279,500

ETHICAL DILEMMA

The management of the Auto Parts Division of the Santana Corporation receives a bonus if the division's income achieves a specific target. For 1997 the target will be achieved by a wide margin. Mary Beth Williams, the controller of the division, has been asked by Philip Stanton, the head of the division's management team, to try to reduce this year's income and "bank" some of the profits for future years. Mary Beth suggests that the division's bad debt expense as a percentage of net credit sales for 1997 be increased from 3% to 5%. She believes that 3% is the more accurate estimate but knows that both the corporation's internal auditors as well as the external auditors allow some flexibility when estimates are involved. Does Mary Beth's proposal present an ethical dilemma?

When Accounts Are Deemed Uncollectible. The actual write-off of a receivable using the allowance method is recorded as a debit to allowance for uncollectible accounts and a credit to accounts receivable. In our illustration, assume that actual bad debts in 1998 were $25,000. These bad debts would be recorded (in a summary journal entry) as follows:

Allowance for uncollectible accounts	25,000	
Accounts receivable		25,000

The write-off of an account receivable reduces both receivables and the allowance, thus having no effect on income or financial position.

Net realizable value is not affected directly by the write-offs.

Accounts receivable	$280,000
Less: Allowance for uncollectible accounts	(500)
Net accounts receivable	$279,500

Of course, actual bad debts will tend to differ from estimates. However, the year in which the estimate is made, 1997 in this case, is unaffected by the incorrect estimate. If the prior year's estimate of bad debts is too low, then, using the balance sheet approach, bad debt expense in the subsequent year will be increased. If the estimate is too high, then bad debt expense in the subsequent year will be decreased. For example, in our illustration, the allowance at the end of 1997 is $25,500. Actual bad debts related to 1997 receivables are $25,000. 1997's financial information cannot be changed. Instead, the $500 credit balance in allowance for uncollectible accounts will cause 1998's bad debt expense to be less than if 1997's estimate of bad debts had been correct.

> Recoveries of accounts receivable previously written off require the reinstatement of both the receivable and the allowance.

When Previously Written-Off Accounts Are Collected.   Occasionally, a receivable that has been written off will be collected in part or in full. When this happens, the receivable and the allowance should be reinstated. In other words, the entry to write off the account simply is reversed. The collection is then recorded the usual way as a debit to cash and a credit to accounts receivable. This process ensures that the company will have a complete record of the payment history of the customer. For example, assume that in our illustration, $1,200 that was previously written off is collected. The following journal entries record the event:

To reinstate the receivable previously written off.	Accounts receivable	1,200
	Allowance for uncollectible accounts	1,200
To record the cash collection.	Cash	1,200
	Accounts receivable	1,200

Direct Write-Off of Uncollectible Accounts.   If uncollectible accounts are not anticipated or are immaterial, or if it's not possible to reliably estimate uncollectible accounts, an allowance for uncollectible accounts is not appropriate. In these few cases, adjusting entries are not recorded and any bad debts that do arise simply are written off as bad debt expense. A $750 uncollectible account would be recorded as follows:

Bad debt expense	750
Accounts receivable	750

Of course, if the sale that generated this receivable occurred in a previous reporting period, this violates the matching principle. Operating expenses would have been understated and assets overstated that period. This is why the direct write-off of uncollectible accounts is not permitted by GAAP except in limited circumstances. Specifically, the allowance method must be used if it is probable that a material amount of receivables will not be collected and the amount can be reasonably estimated.[6]

Graphic 7–4 summarizes the key issues involving measuring and reporting accounts receivable.

GRAPHIC   7–4

Measuring and reporting accounts receivable

Recognition	Depends on the earnings process; for most credit sales, revenue and the related receivables are recognized at the point of delivery.
Initial valuation	Initially recorded at the exchange price agreed on by the buyer and seller.
Subsequent valuation	Initial valuation reduced by: 1. Allowance for sales returns. 2. Allowance for uncollectible accounts.
Classification	Almost always classified as a current asset.

---

[6]"Accounting for Contingencies," *Statement of Financial Accounting Standards No. 5* (Stamford, Conn.: FASB, 1975), par. 8.

CONCEPT REVIEW EXERCISE   UNCOLLECTIBLE ACCOUNTS RECEIVABLE

The Righter Company sells its products, offering 30 days credit to its customers. Uncollectible amounts are estimated by accruing a monthly charge to bad debt expense equal to 2% of credit sales. At the end of the year, the allowance for uncollectible accounts is adjusted based on an aging of accounts receivable. The company began 1998 with the following balances in its accounts:

Accounts receivable	$305,000
Allowance for uncollectible accounts	(25,500)

During 1998, sales on credit were $1,300,000, cash collections from customers were $1,250,000, and actual write-offs of accounts were $25,000. An aging of accounts receivable at the end of 1998 indicates a required allowance of $30,000.

Required:
1. Determine the balances in accounts receivable and allowance for uncollectible accounts at the end of 1998.
2. Determine bad debt expense for 1998.
3. Prepare journal entries for the monthly accrual of bad debts (in summary form), the write-off of receivables, and the year-end adjusting entry for bad debts.

CONCEPT REVIEW EXERCISE   SOLUTION

1. Determine the balances in accounts receivable and allowance for uncollectible accounts at the end of 1998.

Accounts receivable:	
Beginning balance	$ 305,000
Add: Credit sales	1,300,000
Less: Cash collections	(1,250,000)
Write-offs	(25,000)
Ending balance	$ 330,000
Allowance for uncollectible accounts:	
Beginning balance	$ 25,500
Add: Bad debt expense recorded monthly	
(2% × $1,300,000)	26,000
Less: Write-offs	(25,000)
Balance before year-end adjustment	26,500
Year-end adjustment	3,500*
Ending balance	$ 30,000

* Required allowance of $30,000 less 26,500 already in allowance account.

2. Determine bad debt expense for 1998.

Bad debt expense would be $29,500 (monthly accrual of $26,000 plus year-end adjustment of an additional $3,500).

3. Prepare journal entries for the monthly accrual of bad debts (in summary form), the write-off of receivables, and the year-end adjusting entry for bad debts.

Bad debt expense (2% × $1,300,000)	26,000	
Allowance for uncollectible accounts		26,000
Monthly accrual of 2% of credit sales—summary entry.		
Allowance for uncollectible accounts	25,000	
Accounts receivable		25,000
Write-off of accounts receivable as they are determined uncollectible.		
Bad debt expense	3,500	
Allowance for uncollectible accounts		3,500
Year-end adjusting entry for bad debts.		

Notes Receivable

Notes receivable are formal credit arrangements between a creditor (lender) and a debtor (borrower). Notes arise from loans to other entities including affiliated companies and to stockholders and employees, from the extension of the credit period to trade customers, and occasionally from the sale of merchandise, other assets, or services. Notes receivable are classified as either current or noncurrent depending on the expected payment date(s).

Interest-Bearing Notes

Learning objective 8
Describe the accounting treatment of short-term notes receivable.

The typical note receivable requires the payment of a specified face amount, also called *principal*, at a specified maturity date or dates. In addition, interest is paid at a stated percentage of the face amount. Interest on notes is calculated as:

$$\text{Face amount} \times \text{Annual rate} \times \text{Time to maturity}$$

For an example, consider Illustration 7–6.

ILLUSTRATION   7–6

Note receivable

The Stridewell Wholesale Shoe Company manufactures athletic shoes which it sells to retailers. On May 1, 1997, the company sold shoes to Harmon Sporting Goods. Stridewell agreed to accept a $700,000, 6-month, 12% note in payment for the shoes. Interest is payable at maturity.
   Stridewell would account for the note as follows:*

May 1, 1997

Notes receivable	700,000	
Sales revenue		700,000
To record the sale of goods in exchange for a note receivable.		

November 1, 1997

Cash ($700,000 + 42,000)	742,000	
Interest revenue ($700,000 × 12% × $^6/_{12}$)		42,000
Notes receivable		700,000
To record the collection of the note at maturity.		

*To focus on recording the note we intentionally omit the entry required for the cost of the goods sold if the perpetual inventory system is used.

If the sale in the preceding illustration occurs on August 1, 1997, and the company's fiscal year-end is December 31, a year-end adjusting entry accrues interest earned.

December 31, 1997		
Interest receivable	35,000	
Interest revenue ($700,000 × 12% × $^5/_{12}$)		35,000

The February 1 collection is then recorded as follows:

February 1, 1998		
Cash ($700,000 + [$700,000 × 12% × $^{6}/_{12}$])	742,000	
Interest revenue ($700,000 × 12% × $^{1}/_{12}$)		7,000
Interest receivable (accrued at December 31)		35,000
Note receivable		700,000

Noninterest-Bearing Notes

Sometimes a receivable assumes the form of a so-called **noninterest-bearing note**. The name is a misnomer, though. Noninterest-bearing notes actually do bear interest, but the interest is deducted (or discounted) from the face amount to determine the cash proceeds made available to the borrower at the outset. For example, the preceding note could be packaged as a $700,000 noninterest-bearing note, with a 12% discount rate. In that case, the $42,000 interest would be discounted at the outset rather than explicitly stated. As a result, the selling price of the shoes would have been only $658,000. Assuming a May 1, 1997 sale, the transaction is recorded as follows:[7]

May 1, 1997		
Note receivable (face amount)	700,000	
Discount on note receivable ($700,000 × 12% × $^{6}/_{12}$)		42,000
Sales revenue (difference)		658,000
November 1, 1997		
Discount on note receivable	42,000	
Interest revenue		42,000
Cash	700,000	
Note receivable (face amount)		700,000

> The discount becomes interest revenue in a noninterest-bearing note.

> When interest is discounted from the face amount of a note, the effective interest rate is higher than the stated discount rate.

The sales revenue under this arrangement is only $658,000, but the interest is calculated as the discount rate times the $700,000 face amount. This causes the *effective* interest rate to be higher than the 12% stated rate:

$ 42,000	Interest for 6 months
÷ $658,000	Sales price
= 6.38%	Rate for 6 months
× $^{12}/_{6}$	To annualize the rate
= 12.76%	Effective interest rate

If the sale occurs on August 1, the December 31, 1997, adjusting entry and the entry to record the cash collection on February 1, 1998, are recorded as follows:

---

[7]The entries shown assume the note is recorded by the gross method. By the net method, the interest component is netted against the face amount of the note as follows:

May 1, 1997		
Note receivable	658,000	
Sales revenue		658,000
November 1, 1997		
Cash	700,000	
Note receivable		658,000
Interest revenue ($700,000 × 12% × $^{6}/_{12}$)		42,000

December 31, 1997		
Discount on note receivable	35,000	
Interest revenue ($700,000 × 12% × $\frac{5}{12}$)		35,000

February 1, 1998		
Discount on note receivable	7,000	
Interest revenue ($700,000 × 12% × $\frac{1}{12}$)		7,000
Cash	700,000	
Note receivable (face amount)		700,000

On the December 31, 1997, balance sheet, the note receivable is shown at $693,000, face amount ($700,000) less remaining discount ($7,000).

Notes Received Solely for Cash.   If a note with an unrealistic interest rate—even a noninterest-bearing note—is received *solely* in exchange for cash, the cash paid to the issuer is considered to be its present value.[8] Even if this means recording interest at a ridiculously low or zero rate, the amount of cash exchanged is the basis for valuing the note. When a noncash asset is exchanged for a note with a low stated rate, we can argue that its real value is less than it's purported to be, but we can't argue that the present value of a sum of cash currently exchanged is less than that sum. If the noninterest-bearing note in the previous example had been received solely in exchange for $700,000 cash, the transaction would be recorded as follows:

When a noninterest-bearing note is received solely in exchange for cash, the amount of cash exchanged is the basis for valuing the note.

Note receivable (face amount)	700,000	
Cash (given)		700,000

Our examples above illustrate short-term notes. When the term of a note is longer than a year, it is reported as a long-term note. Long-term notes receivable are discussed in conjunction with long-term notes payable in Chapter 14.

Subsequent Valuation of Notes Receivable

Similar to accounts receivable, if a company anticipates bad debts on short-term notes receivable, it uses an allowance account to reduce the receivable to net realizable value. The process of recording bad debt expense is the same as with accounts receivable.

Long-term notes present a more significant measurement problem. The longer the duration of the note, the more likely are bad debts. One of the more difficult measurement problems facing banks and other lending institutions is the estimation of bad debts on its long-term notes (loans). As an example, Wells Fargo & Company, a large California bank, reported the following in the asset section of a recent balance sheet:

	December 31,	
(in millions)	**1995**	**1994**
Loans	$35,582	$36,347
Allowance for loan losses	(1,794)	(2,082)
Net loans	$33,788	$34,265

A disclosure note, reproduced in Graphic 7–5, describes Wells Fargo's loan loss policy.

---

[8]This assumes that no other present or future considerations are included in the agreement. For example, a noninterest-bearing note might be given to a vendor in exchange for cash *and* a promise to provide future inventories at prices lower than anticipated market prices. The issuer values the note at the present value of cash payments using a realistic interest rate, and the difference between present value and cash payments is recognized as interest revenue over the life of the note. This difference also increases future inventory purchases to realistic market prices.

GRAPHIC   7 – 5

Disclosure of allowance for loan losses—Wells Fargo & Company

Allowance For Loan Losses (in part)

The Company's determination of the level of the allowance for loan losses rests upon various judgments and assumptions, including general economic conditions, loan portfolio composition, prior loan loss experience, evaluation of credit risk related to certain individual borrowers and the Company's ongoing examination process and that of its regulators.

When it becomes probable that a creditor will be unable to collect all amounts due according to the contractual terms of a note, the receivable is considered **impaired**. When a creditor's investment in a note receivable becomes impaired for any reason, the receivable is remeasured as the discounted present value of currently expected cash flows at the loan's original effective rate. Impairments of receivables are discussed in Appendix 12C.

Financing with Receivables

Receivables, like any other asset, can be sold or used as collateral for debt. In fact, retailers often avoid the difficulties of servicing (billing and collecting) receivables by transferring them to financial institutions. This also shortens the operating cycle by providing cash to the retailer immediately rather than making the company wait until the credit customer pays the amount due. Of course, the financial institution will require compensation for providing this service, such as interest and/or a finance charge.

Learning objective 9
Differentiate between the use of receivables in financing arrangements accounted for as a loan and those accounted for as a sale.

Financial institutions have developed a wide variety of ways for companies to use their receivables to obtain immediate cash. The methods differ with respect to which rights and risks are retained by the *transferor* (the original holder of the receivable) and those passed on to the *transferee* (the new holder, usually a financial institution). Despite this diversity, any of these methods can be described by one of two basic arrangements:

1. The **assigning** of receivables, usually accounts receivable, as collateral against cash borrowed by the company.
2. The transfer of receivables, known as **factoring** in the case of accounts receivable or **discounting** in the case of notes receivable, in an outright exchange for cash.

The accounting question with any of these financing arrangements is whether the transaction should be considered (1) a *loan* for which receivables are pledged as collateral or (2) an *outright sale* of the receivables. If treated as a loan, the difference between the cash transferred and the receivables involved is considered interest on the loan.[9] On the other hand, if treated as a sale, the transferor considers the difference between the cash proceeds received and the receivables involved a loss on the sale of receivables, and the transferee recognizes the receivables obtained and measures them at their fair value.

In deciding between a loan and a sale, the critical element is the extent to which the transferor surrenders control over the assets transferred. The distinction for some arrangements is obvious. In a *pledging* of accounts receivable, for example, ownership interests in the receivables are retained; the receivables merely are made available as collateral for a loan. Likewise, a *factoring* of accounts receivable or *discounting* of notes receivable without recourse is an outright exchange of receivables for cash in which the transferee obtains complete control over the receivables. It clearly is a sale. For other arrangements, though, the distinction is not clear. Sometimes, receivables are transferred, but the transferee is given recourse to collect from the transferor in the event of uncollectibility. These arrangements possess characteristics of both a sale and a loan. Before we consider these various financing arrangements individually, you should study the overview provided by Graphic 7–6.

Assigning of Accounts Receivable

The **assigning** of receivables is merely a promise by the borrower (the owner of the receivables) that any failure to repay debt owed to the lender in accordance with the debt agreement will cause the proceeds from collecting the receivables to go directly toward repayment of the debt. This arrangement is no different from the use of a building as collateral for a mortgage loan. In case of default, the building can be sold to provide the necessary cash to repay the loan.

---

[9]Initially recorded as a discount on the associated liability, then allocated to interest expense over the term of the loan.

GRAPHIC 7-6

Accounting for the financing of receivables

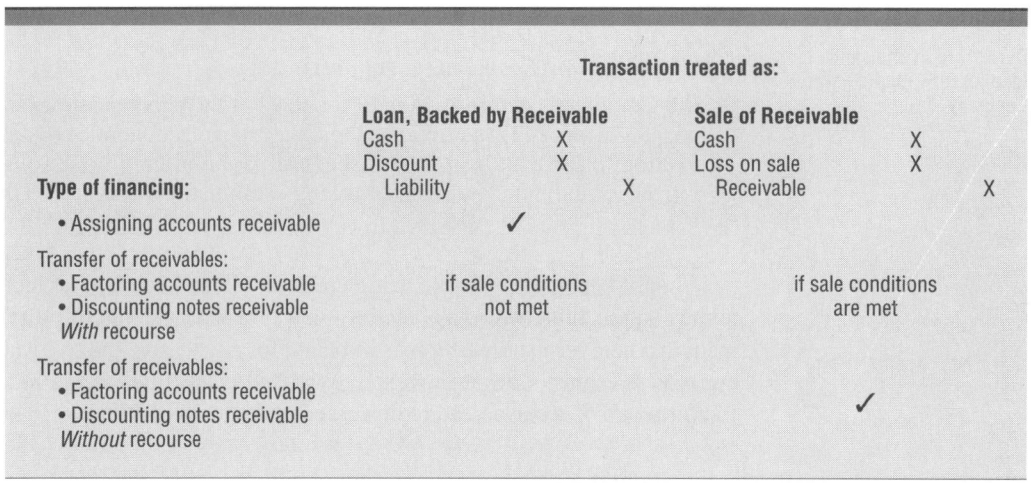

> An **assignment** involves the pledging of specific accounts receivable as collateral for a debt.

The assignor (borrower) assigns the assignee (lender) the rights to specific receivables as collateral for a loan. The assignor still is responsible for collecting and servicing the accounts. However, the agreement often allows the assignee to seek payment of the receivable directly from the customers if the loan is not repaid on time.

Usually, the amount borrowed is less than the amount of receivables assigned. The difference provides some protection for the lender to allow for possible uncollectible accounts. Also, the assignee usually charges the assignor an up-front finance charge in addition to stated interest on the collateralized loan. Both amounts (up-front charge and stated interest) are recognized as interest expense over the life of the loan. The assignor records the up-front charge as a discount to be allocated to interest in addition to the stated interest. Receivables assigned are reclassified as accounts receivable assigned.

This can be seen easier by reference to Illustration 7–7.

ILLUSTRATION 7–7

Assignment of accounts receivable

At the end of November 1997, Santa Teresa Glass Company had outstanding accounts receivable of $750,000. On December 1, 1997, the company borrowed $500,000 from Finance Affiliates and signed a promissory note. Interest at 12% is payable monthly. The company pledged specific receivables totaling $620,000 as collateral for the loan. Finance Affiliates charges a finance fee equal to 1.5% of the accounts receivable assigned.

The borrowing and the assignment are recorded on the books of Santa Teresa Glass as follows:

> The up-front finance charge is recorded as a discount to be allocated to interest over the life of the loan.

Cash (difference)	490,700	
Discount on liability (1.5% × $620,000)	9,300	
Liability—financing arrangement		500,000
Accounts receivable assigned	620,000	
Accounts receivable		620,000

In the financial statements, the accounts receivable assigned are shown *net* of the related liability and the arrangement is disclosed in a note.

Santa Teresa will continue to collect the receivables but remit the cash to the lender, usually on a monthly basis. If $400,000 of the receivables assigned are collected in December, the following entries are recorded:

Cash	400,000	
Accounts receivable assigned		400,000

> Interest expense includes the stated interest and an allocated portion of the up-front finance charge.

Interest expense ($500,000 × 12% × $1/12$)	5,000	
Liability — financing arrangement	400,000	
Cash		405,000
Interest expense ($9,300 × $400,000/$500,000)	7,440	
Discount on liability		7,440

On Santa Teresa's December 31, 1997, balance sheet, the receivables and note payable would be reported together as follows:

Current assets:
Accounts receivable pledged	$ 220,000
Less: Liability—financing arrangement	(100,000)
Equity in accounts receivable pledged	$ 120,000

Netting a liability against a related asset generally is not allowed by GAAP. However, in this case, the note payable is deducted from the accounts receivable assigned because by contractual agreement, the note will be paid with cash collected from the receivables.

A variation of assigning receivables is when trade receivables in general rather than specific receivables are pledged as collateral. This variation is referred to as **pledging** accounts receivable. No special accounting treatment is needed when the borrower's accounts receivable in general serve as collateral for a loan. The pledging arrangement is simply described in a disclosure note. For example, Graphic 7–7 shows the Chock Full O'Nuts Corporation note included in its 1996 financial statements.

GRAPHIC   7–7

Disclosure of receivables used as collateral—Chock Full O'Nuts Corporation

Note 3: Long-Term Debt (in part)

Under the Company's amended and restated revolving credit and term loan agreements (collectively the "Loan Agreements") with Fleet Bank, N.A. and The Chase Manhattan Bank (the "Banks"), the Company may, from time to time, borrow funds from the Banks, provided that the total principal amount of all such loans outstanding through December 31, 1996 may not exceed $40,000,000 and after such date may not exceed $20,000,000. Interest (8.25% at July 31, 1996) on all such loans is equal to the prime rate, subject to adjustment based on the level of loans outstanding. Outstanding borrowings under the Loan Agreements may not exceed certain percentages of and are collateralized by, among other things, the trade accounts receivable...

Transfer of Receivables

Another way companies get cash from their receivables without having to wait for collection is to *transfer* the receivables to a bank or finance company. When accounts receivable are transferred, this is called **factoring** accounts receivable. When notes receivable are transferred, the transaction is referred to as **discounting** notes receivable.

Factoring Accounts Receivable.   Very often the finance company is a financial subsidiary of the seller. The Unocal Corporation, for instance, established a financial subsidiary for this purpose and disclosed the appropriate information in the note shown in Graphic 7–8.

GRAPHIC   7–8

Disclosure of factoring arrangement through a finance subsidiary—Unocal Corporation

Note 14: Consolidated Finance Subsidiary (in part)

The company's consolidated financial statements include the accounts of Union Oil Corporation (UOCC), a wholly owned finance subsidiary. Business operations consist primarily of financing certain customer obligations of Union Oil resulting from retail sales of petroleum products, automotive accessories and other merchandise charged on credit cards.

Factoring can be made without recourse or with recourse.

Actually, credit cards like VISA are forms of factoring arrangements. The seller relinquishes all rights to the future cash receipts in exchange for cash from the buyer (known as the *factor*). The appropriate accounting treatment for factoring arrangements depends on the amount of risk assumed by the factor. Transfers can be made without recourse or with recourse.

Factoring without Recourse.   When accounts receivable are factored (sold) **without recourse**, the buyer assumes the risk of uncollectibility. This means the buyer has no recourse to the seller if the receivables are not paid. The seller simply accounts for the transaction as a sale of an asset. The buyer charges a fee for providing this service, usually a percentage of the book value of receivables. Because the fee reduces the proceeds received from selling the asset, it is recorded by the seller as a loss on sale of assets. Illustration 7–8 provides an example.

ILLUSTRATION   7–8

Accounts receivable factored without recourse

At the end of November, 1997, the Santa Teresa Glass Company had outstanding accounts receivable of $750,000. In December 1997, the company transferred $600,000 of accounts receivable to Finance Affiliates. The transfer was made without recourse. The buyer charges a fee equal to 4% of receivables transferred.

The transfer is recorded on the books of Santa Teresa Glass as follows:

Cash (difference)	576,000	
Loss on sale of receivables (4% × $600,000)	24,000	
Accounts receivable (balance sold)		600,000

Factoring with Recourse.   Sometimes receivables are transferred **with recourse**, meaning the seller retains the risk of uncollectibility. In effect, the seller guarantees that the buyer will be paid even if some receivables prove to be uncollectible. In this type of arrangement, it's not clear that an outright sale has occurred because not all the risks of ownership have been transferred. These transfers usually resemble a loan of cash, with receivables serving as collateral for the loan, much like the assigning of accounts receivable we discussed earlier. On the other hand, even with recourse, the terms of a transfer of receivables may convey a degree of finality that causes the transaction to more closely resemble a sale than a borrowing.

The FASB has provided guidance for these situations. Recall that the transfer is accounted for as a sale if the transferor surrenders control over the receivables transferred. The transferor has surrendered control if and only if all of the following conditions are met:[10]

1. The transferred assets have been isolated from the transferor.
2. Either (a) each transferee obtains the right to pledge or exchange the transferred assets, or (b) the transferee is a qualifying special-purpose entity and the holders of beneficial interests in that entity have the right to pledge or exchange those interests.
3. The transferor does not maintain effective control over the transferred assets.

The intent of these criteria is to provide guidelines for determining whether the transferor has retained any beneficial interest in the transferred assets.

Accounting for the transaction as a sale would be the same as that in the without recourse example above.[11]

If these criteria are *not* met, the transfer is accounted for as a loan. That is, the cash proceeds from the transfer are reported as a liability. The seller retains the receivables on its books. The difference between the accounts receivable transferred and the cash proceeds represents interest on the loan rather than a loss on a sale as it is when the transfer is viewed as a sale. The interest amount is recorded initially as a discount on the liability and then is allocated to interest expense over the term of the loan. Consider Illustration 7–9.

[10]"Accounting for Transfers and Servicing of Financial Assets and Extinguishments of Liabilities," *Statement of Financial Accounting Standards No. 125* (Norwalk, Conn.: FASB, 1996). The standard supersedes SFAS No. 77, "Reporting by Transferors for Transfers of Receivables with Recourse."

[11]Note disclosure may be required for the contingent liability created by the seller's guaranty of payment. This is discussed in Chapter 13.

ILLUSTRATION   7-9

Accounts receivable factored with recourse—sale conditions *not* met

At the end of November 1997, the Santa Teresa Glass Company had outstanding accounts receivable of $750,000. In December 1997, the company transferred $600,000 of accounts receivable to Finance Affiliates. The transfer was made **with** recourse. The buyer charges a fee equal to 4% of receivables transferred. Finance Affiliates can require Santa Teresa Glass to repurchase the receivables under certain conditions.

The transfer is recorded as a loan by Santa Teresa Glass as follows:

Cash (difference)	576,000	
Discount on liability (4% × $600,000)	24,000	
Liability — financing arrangement		600,000
Accounts receivable factored	600,000	
Accounts receivable		600,000

Finance Affiliates will collect the receivables. If $450,000 of the receivables transferred are collected in December, the following entries are recorded by Santa Teresa Glass as follows:

Liability—financing arrangement	450,000	
Accounts receivable factored		450,000
Interest expense ($24,000 × $450,000/$600,000)	18,000	
Discount on liability		18,000

> The buyer's fee, the difference between the asset and the amount borrowed, is recorded as a discount.

> Interest expense is an allocated portion of the discount.

The discount on the liability is recognized by the transferor as interest expense over the period that the liability is outstanding. Because $450,000, or ¾ of the total receivables, is collected in 1997, ¾ of the discount is expensed that year. Notice that in this arrangement, the liability is actually paid by the customers when they make payments on the receivables. So, as the receivables are collected by the factor, Santa Teresa's liability is reduced.

The Chrysler Corporation maintains factoring relationships (as the buyer) on both a recourse and nonrecourse basis. Graphic 7–9 contains the company's note disclosure of these relationships.

GRAPHIC   7-9

Disclosure of factoring arrangement—The Chrysler Corporation

Note 2: Financing and Accounts Receivable (in part)

CFC purchases automotive retail installment contracts from dealers on a recourse and a nonrecourse basis. For contracts acquired with full or partial recourse provisions, the dealer agrees to repurchase the automotive retail installment contract upon the customer's default and return of the repossessed vehicle. A portion of the proceeds due to the dealer is withheld to provide CFC a reserve for the dealer's contingent liability.

Discounting a Note Receivable.   Similar to accounts receivable, notes receivable can be used to obtain immediate cash from a financial institution either by pledging the note as collateral for a loan or by selling the note. A common practice is to *discount* a note receivable. The financial institution, usually a bank, accepts the note and gives the seller cash equal to the maturity value of the note reduced by a discount. The discount is computed by applying a discount rate to the maturity value and represents the financing fee the bank charges for the transaction.

Most notes are discounted with recourse, meaning the transferor is obligated to pay the note if the debtor defaults. As with accounts receivable factored with recourse, if certain criteria are met (see page 292), the transferor will account for a note receivable discounted as a sale. Otherwise, it's recorded as a loan. Of course, if the note is sold without recourse, the discounting also is recorded as a sale.

Consider the example in Illustration 7–10.

> The sale of a note receivable to a financial institution is called **discounting**.
>
> *not covered*

ILLUSTRATION 7–10

Discounting a note receivable

Learning objective 10
List and explain the four-step process used to account for a discounted note receivable.

Step 1: Accrue interest earned on the note receivable prior to its being discounted.

Step 2: Add interest to maturity to calculate maturity value.

Step 3: Deduct discount to calculate cash proceeds.

On December 31, 1997, the Stridewell Wholesale Shoe Company sold land in exchange for a nine-month, 10% note. The note requires the payment of $200,000 *plus* interest on September 30, 1998. The company's fiscal year-end is December 31. The 10% rate properly reflects the time value of money for this type of note. On March 31, 1998, Stridewell discounted the note at the Bank of the East. The Bank's discount rate is 12%.

Because the note has been outstanding for three months before being discounted at the bank, Stridewell first records the interest that has accrued prior to being discounted:

March 31, 1998

Interest receivable	5,000	
Interest revenue ($200,000 × 10% × $^3/_{12}$)		5,000

Next, the value of the note if held to maturity is calculated. Then the discount for the time remaining to maturity is deducted to determine the cash proceeds from discounting the note:

$200,000	Face amount
15,000	Interest to maturity ($200,000 × 10% × $^9/_{12}$)
215,000	Maturity value
(12,900)	Discount ($215,000 × 12% × $^6/_{12}$)
$202,100	Cash proceeds

If the note is discounted without recourse, or with recourse when the sale criteria are met, Stridewell records the transaction as the sale of the note receivable as shown in Illustration 7–10a.

ILLUSTRATION 7–10a

Discounted note treated as a sale:

Step 4: Record a loss (or gain) for difference between the cash proceeds and the note's book value.

Cash (proceeds determined above)	202,100	
Loss on sale of note receivable (difference)	2,900	
Note receivable (face amount)		200,000
Interest receivable (accrued interest determined above)		5,000

Sometimes a note is discounted with recourse and the sale criteria are not met. In that case, Stridewell records the transaction as a loan for which the note receivable is pledged as collateral, as shown in Illustration 7–10b.

ILLUSTRATION 7–10b

Discounted note treated as a loan:

Step 4: Record interest for difference between the cash proceeds and the note's book value.

Cash (proceeds determined above)	202,100	
Discount (difference)	2,900	
Liability—discounted note receivable (face amount)		205,000
Note receivable discounted	205,000	
Note receivable		200,000
Interest receivable		5,000

Because a sale hasn't occurred in this case, no loss or gain can occur. Instead, the difference between the cash proceeds and the book value represents interest. If the cash proceeds are less than book value, as in this example, the interest amount is recorded initially as a discount on the liability and then allocated to interest expense over the remaining term of the loan. If cash proceeds are higher than book value, the difference represents interest revenue to be recognized over the remaining term of the loan.

If a note is discounted with recourse, the transferor should describe its potential liability in a note to the financial statements.

Additional Consideration

If a note receivable that has been discounted with recourse is not paid on the maturity date, it is considered dishonored, or in default. The company must pay cash to the bank equal to the maturity value of the note plus any fees the bank might charge. A receivable is recorded for the maturity value of the note plus any fees charged by the bank. For the illustration above, the following entries would be made on September 30, 1998, assuming the bank charges a $100 protest fee:

Receivable past due	215,100	
Cash ($215,000 + 100)		215,100

CONCEPT REVIEW EXERCISE

FINANCING WITH RECEIVABLES

The Hollywood Lumber Company obtains financing from the Midwest Finance Company by factoring (or discounting) its receivables. During June 1997, the company transferred $1,000,000 of accounts receivable to Midwest. The transfer was made with recourse. The buyer, Midwest Finance, charges a fee equal to 3% of receivables transferred.

In addition, on June 30, 1997, Hollywood discounted a note receivable. The note, which originated on March 31, 1997, requires the payment of $150,000 plus interest at 8% on March 31, 1998. Midwest's discount rate is 10% and the transfer was made with recourse. The company's fiscal year-end is December 31.

Required:
1. Prepare journal entries for Hollywood Lumber for the transfer of accounts receivables and the note receivable discounted on June 30. Assume that the required criteria are met and the transfers are accounted for as sales.
2. Repeat requirement 1, assuming that the sale criteria are not met and the transfers are accounted for as loans.

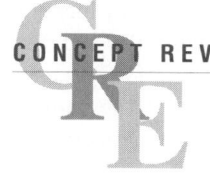

CONCEPT REVIEW EXERCISE

SOLUTION

1. Prepare journal entries for Hollywood Lumber for the transfer of accounts receivables and the note receivable discounted on June 30. Assume that the required criteria are met and the transfers are accounted for as sales.

The transfer of receivables:		
Cash (difference)	970,000	
Loss on sale of receivables (3% × $1,000,000)	30,000	
Accounts receivable (balance sold)		1,000,000
The note receivable discounted:		
Interest receivable	3,000	
Interest revenue ($150,000 × 8% × 3/12)		3,000
Cash (proceeds determined below)	149,850	
Loss on sale of note receivable (difference)	3,150	
Note receivable (face amount)		150,000
Interest receivable (accrued interest determined above)		3,000

Add interest to maturity to calculate maturity value.

Deduct discount to calculate cash proceeds.

$150,000	Face amount
12,000	Interest to maturity ($150,000 × 8%)
162,000	Maturity value
(12,150)	Discount ($162,000 × 10% × 9/12)
$149,850	Cash proceeds

2. Repeat requirement 1. assuming that the sale criteria are not met and the transfers are accounted for as loans.

The transfer of receivables:		
Cash (difference)	970,000	
Discount on liability (3% × $1,000,000)	30,000	
Liability—financing arrangement		1,000,000
Accounts receivable factored	1,000,000	
Accounts receivable		1,000,000
The note receivable discounted:		
Interest receivable	3,000	
Interest revenue ($150,000 × 8% × 3/12)		3,000
Cash (proceeds determined above)	149,850	
Discount (difference)	3,150	
Liability—discounted note receivable (face amount)		153,000
Note receivable discounted	153,000	
Note receivable		150,000
Interest receivable (accrued interest determined above)		3,000

Decision Makers' Perspective

A company's investment in receivables is influenced by several variables, including the level of sales, the nature of the product or service sold, and credit and collection policies. These variables are, of course, related. For example, a change in credit policies could affect sales. In fact, more liberal credit policies—allowing customers a longer time to pay or offering cash discounts for early payment—often are initiated with the specific objective of increasing sales volume.

Management's choice of credit and collection policies often involves trade-offs. For example, offering cash discounts may increase sales volume, accelerate customer payment, and reduce bad debts. These benefits are not without cost. The cash discounts reduce the amount of cash collected from customers who take advantage of the discounts. Extending payment terms also may increase sales volume. However, this creates an increase in the required investment in receivables and may increase bad debts.

The ability to use receivables as a method of financing also offers management alternatives. Assigning, factoring, and discounting receivables are alternative methods of financing operations that must be evaluated relative to other financing methods such as lines of credit or other types of short-term borrowing.

Investors, creditors, and financial analysts can gain important insights by monitoring a company's investment in receivables. Chapter 4 introduced the receivables turnover ratio and the related average collection period, ratios designed to monitor receivables. Recall that these ratios are calculated as follows:

> Management must evaluate the costs and benefits of any change in credit and collection policies.

$$\text{Receivables turnover ratio} = \frac{\text{Net sales}}{\text{Average accounts receivable (net)}}$$

$$\text{Average collection period} = \frac{365 \text{ days}}{\text{Receivables turnover ratio}}$$

The turnover ratio shows the number of times during a period that the average accounts receivable balance is collected, and the average collection period is an approximation of the number of days the average accounts receivable balance is outstanding.

As a company's sales grow, receivables also will increase. If the percentage increase in receivables is greater than the percentage increase in sales, the receivables turnover ratio will decline (the average collection period will increase). This could indicate customer dissatisfaction with the product or that the company has extended too generous payment terms in order to attract new customers, which, in turn, could increase sales returns and bad debts.

These ratios also can be used to compare the relative effectiveness of companies in managing the investment in receivables. Of course, it would be meaningless to compare the receivables turnover ratio of a computer products company such as IBM with that of, say, a food products company like Sara Lee. A company selling high-priced, low-volume products like mainframe computers generally will grant customers longer payment terms than a company selling lower priced, higher volume food products. Graphic 7–10 lists the 1995 receivables turnover ratio for some well-known companies. The differences are as expected, given the nature of the companies' products.

GRAPHIC   7-10

Receivables turnover ratios

Company	1995 Receivables Turnover Ratio
Caterpillar	3.60
IBM	4.72
Hewlett-Packard	5.36
Johnson & Johnson	6.84
Hershey	11.22
Sara Lee	11.34

Let's compute the 1995 receivables turnover ratio and the average collection period for two companies in the same industry, Maytag and Whirlpool.

Balance sheet and income statement information— Maytag and Whirlpool

($ in millions)

	Maytag 1995	Maytag 1994	Whirlpool 1995	Whirlpool 1994
Accounts receivable (net)	$ 417	$ 568	$1,031	$1,001
Two-year averages:	$492.5		$1,016	
Net sales—1995	$3,040		$8,163	

Receivables turnover and average collection period— Maytag and Whirlpool

	Maytag	Whirlpool
Receivables turnover	$= \frac{3,040}{492.5} = 6.2$	$\frac{8,163}{1,016} = 8.0$
Average collection period	$= \frac{365}{6.2} = 59$ days	$\frac{365}{8.0} = 46$ days

On average, it takes Maytag 13 days longer than Whirlpool to collect its receivables.

Academic research also has shown receivables information to be useful in financial statement analysis. Professors Lev and Thiagarajan empirically demonstrated the importance of a set of 12 fundamental variables in valuing companies' common stock. The set of variables included accounts receivable (change in accounts receivable minus change in sales) and allowance for uncollectible accounts (change in accounts receivable minus change in the allowance). Motivation for the receivables variable was that disproportionate increases in accounts receivable (relative to sales increases) can indicate difficulties in selling products, reflected in more lenient credit policies. The allowance variable was expected to indicate inadequate bad debt provisions. Both were found to be significant indicators of stock returns during high inflation years.[12]

Solution to Financial Reporting Case (at the opening of the chapter)

Accounting for Uncollectible Accounts Receivable

1. As the hesitant volunteer, what will your outline look like for a tutoring session on accounting for uncollectible accounts receivable?

A. Allowance method
   1. The allowance method attempts to estimate future bad debts and match them with related revenues.
   2. There are two approaches to estimating bad debts, the income statement approach and the balance sheet approach.

[12]B. Lev and S. R. Thiagarajan, "Fundamental Information Analysis," *Journal of Accounting Research*, 31, no. 2, Autumn 1993. The main conclusion of the study was that fundamental variables, not just earnings, are useful in firm valuation, particularly when examined in the context of macroeconomic conditions such as inflation.

3. With either approach, accounts receivable are reduced indirectly to net realizable value by an adjusting entry in which bad debt expense is debited and an allowance account is credited.

4. Actual bad debt write-offs reduce both accounts receivable and the allowance account.

B. Income statement approach

1. Bad debt expense is a percentage of the period's net credit sales.

2. The amount recorded ignores any prior balance in the allowance account.

C. Balance sheet approach

1. The net realizable value of receivables is determined. An accounts receivable aging schedule often is used.

2. Bad debt expense is equal to the required adjustment to the allowance account to bring net receivables to realizable value.

D. Direct write-off method

1. This is a method not generally permitted by GAAP.

2. Bad debt expense is simply the actual bad debt write-offs during the period.

The Bottom Line

1. Internal control refers to the plan designed to encourage adherence to company policies and procedures; promote operational efficiency; minimize irregularities, errors, thefts or fraud; and maximize the reliability and accuracy of accounting data. Key elements of an internal control system for cash receipts and disbursements include separation of recordkeeping from control of cash duties and the periodic preparation of a bank reconciliation.

2. A two-step bank reconciliation first adjusts the bank balance for outstanding deposits, outstanding checks, and bank errors. The second step adjusts the book balance for collections made on the company's behalf, charges made by the bank, including NSF check charges, and any company errors discovered. The adjusted balances should each be equal to the corrected cash balance.

3. Cash can be informally restricted by management for a particular purpose. Restrictions also can be contractually imposed. If restricted cash is available for current operations or to pay current liabilities, it's classified as a current asset; otherwise, it's classified as investments and funds or other assets.

4. The gross method of accounting for cash discounts considers a discount not taken as part of sales revenue. The net method considers a discount not taken as interest revenue.

5. When merchandise returns are anticipated, an allowance for sales returns should be recorded as a contra account to accounts receivable and sales revenue also should be reduced by the anticipated sales returns.

6. Uncollectible accounts receivable should be anticipated in order to match bad debt expense with revenues generated. Likewise, accounts receivable should be reduced by an allowance for uncollectible accounts to report accounts receivable at net realizable value.

7. There are two approaches to estimating future bad debts. The income statement approach estimates bad debt expense based on the notion that a certain percentage of each period's credit sales will prove to be uncollectible. The balance sheet approach to estimating future bad debts indirectly determines bad debt expense by directly estimating the net realizable value of accounts receivable at the end of the period.

8. Notes receivable are formal credit arrangements between a creditor (lender) and a debtor (borrower). The typical note receivable requires the payment of a specified face amount, also called principal, at a specified maturity date or dates. In addition, interest is paid at a stated percentage of the face amount. Interest on notes is calculated by multiplying the face amount by the annual rate by the time to maturity.

9. A wide variety of methods exists for companies to use their receivables to obtain immediate cash. These methods can be described as either:

a. The assigning of receivables, usually accounts receivable, as collateral against cash borrowed by the company, or

b. The transfer of receivables, known as factoring in the case of accounts receivable or discounting in the case of notes receivable, in an outright exchange for cash.

The conditions of these financing arrangements determine whether they are accounted for as (a) a loan for which receivables are pledged as collateral or (b) an outright sale of the receivables.

10. To account for a discounted note receivable we: (a) accrue interest revenue earned to date of discounting, (b) compute the maturity value, (c) compute the proceeds to be received from the bank, and (d) compute the difference between proceeds and book value of the note.

Questions for Review of Key Topics

Question   7–1   Define cash equivalents.

Question   7–2   Explain the primary functions of internal controls procedures in the accounting area. What is meant by separation of duties?

Question   7–3   How is a petty cash fund established? How is the fund replenished?

Question   7–4   In a two-step bank reconciliation, identify the items that might be necessary to adjust the bank balance to the corrected cash balance. Identify the items that might be necessary to adjust the book balance to the corrected cash balance.

Question   7–5   Define a compensating balance. How are compensating balances reported in financial statements?

Question   7–6   Explain the difference between a trade discount and a cash discount.

Question   7–7   Distinguish between the gross and net methods of accounting for cash discounts.

Question   7–8   Briefly explain the accounting treatment for sales returns.

Question   7–9   Explain the typical way companies account for uncollectible accounts receivable (bad debts). When is it permissible to write off accounts receivable only when they actually prove uncollectible?

Question   7–10   Briefly explain the difference between the income statement approach and the balance sheet approach to estimating bad debts.

Question   7–11   Is any special accounting treatment required for the assigning of accounts receivable in general as collateral for debt?

Question   7–12   Explain any possible differences between accounting for accounts receivable factored without recourse and those factored with recourse.

Question   7–13   What is meant by the discounting of a note receivable? Describe the four-step process used to account for discounted notes.

Exercises

Exercise 7–1
Cash and cash equivalents;
restricted cash

The controller of the Red Wing Corporation is in the process of preparing the company's 1997 financial statements. She is trying to determine the correct balance of cash and cash equivalents to be reported as a current asset on the balance sheet. The following items are being considered:

a. Balances in the company's accounts at the First National Bank; checking $13,500, savings $22,100.
b. Undeposited customer checks of $3,200.
c. Currency and coins on hand of $580.
d. Savings account at the East Bay Bank with a balance of $400,000. This account is being used to accumulate cash for future plant expansion (in 1999).
e. Petty cash of $200.
f. $20,000 in a checking account at the East Bay Bank. The balance in the account represents a 20% compensating balance for a $100,000 loan with the bank. Red Wing may not withdraw the funds until the loan is due in 2000.
g. U.S. treasury bills; 2-month maturity bills totaling $15,000, and 7-month bills totaling $20,000.

Required:
1. Determine the correct balance of cash and cash equivalents to be reported in the current asset section of the 1997 balance sheet.
2. For each of the items not included in your answer to requirement 1, explain the correct classification of the item.

Exercise 7–2
Petty cash

The Loucks Company established a $200 petty cash fund on October 2, 1997. The fund is replenished at the end of each month. At the end of October 1997, the fund contained $37 in cash and the following receipts:

Office supplies	$76
Lunch with client	48
Postage	20
Miscellaneous	19

Required:
Prepare the necessary general journal entries to establish the petty cash fund on October 2 and to replenish the fund on October 31.

Exercise 7–3
Bank reconciliation

The Jansen Company's general ledger showed a checking account balance of $23,820 at the end of May 1997. The May 31 cash receipts of $2,340, included in the general ledger balance, were placed in the night depository at the bank on May 31 and were processed by the bank on June 1. The bank statement dated May 31, 1997, showed bank service charges of $38. All checks written by the company had been processed by the bank by May 31 and were listed on the bank statement except for checks totaling $1,890.

Required:
Prepare a bank reconciliation as of May 31, 1997. [Hint: You will need to compute the balance that would appear on the bank statement.]

Exercise 7–4
Bank reconciliation and adjusting entries

The Harrison Company maintains a checking account at the First National City Bank. The bank provides a bank statement along with canceled checks on the last day of each month. The July 1997 bank statement included the following information:

Balance, July 1, 1997	$ 55,678
Deposits	179,500
Checks processed	(192,610)
Service charges	(30)
NSF checks	(1,200)
Monthly loan payment deducted directly by bank from account	
(includes $320 in interest)	(3,320)
Balance, July 31, 1997	$ 38,018

The company's general ledger account had a balance of $38,918 at the end of July. Deposits outstanding totaled $6,300 and all checks written by the company were processed by the bank except for those totaling $8,420. In addition, a $2,000 July deposit from a credit customer was recorded as a $200 debit to cash and credit to accounts receivable, and a check correctly recorded by the company as a $30 disbursement was incorrectly processed by the bank as a $300 disbursement.

Required:
1. Prepare a bank reconciliation for the month of July.
2. Prepare the necessary journal entries at the end of July to adjust the general ledger cash account.

Exercise 7–5
Multiple choice; cash

The following questions dealing with cash are adapted from questions that appeared on recent CPA examinations. Determine the response that best completes the statements or questions.

1. In preparing its August 31, 1997 bank reconciliation, Apex Corp. has available the following information:

Balance per bank statement, 8/31/97	$18,050
Deposit in transit, 8/31/97	3,250
Return of customer's check for insufficient funds, 8/31/97	600
Outstanding checks	2,750
Bank service charges for August	100

At August 31, 1997, Apex's correct cash balance is
   a. $18,550
   b. $17,950
   c. $17,850
   d. $17,550

2. Poe, Inc., had the following bank reconciliation at March 31, 1997:

Balance per bank statement, 3/31/97	$46,500
Add: deposit in transit	10,300
	56,800
Less: outstanding checks	12,600
Balance per books, 3/31/97	$44,200
Data per bank for the month of April:	
Deposits	$58,400
Disbursements	49,700

All reconciling items at March 31, 1997, were processed by the bank in April. Outstanding checks at April 30, 1997, totaled $7,000. There were no deposits in transit at April 30, 1997. What is the cash balance per books at April 30, 1997?
   a. $48,200
   b. $52,900
   c. $55,200
   d. $58,500

3.   At December 31, 1997, Kale Co. had the following balances in the accounts it maintains at First State Bank:

Checking account #101	$175,000
Checking account #102	(10,000)
Money market account	25,000
90-day certificate of deposit, due 2/28/98	50,000
180-day certificate of deposit, due 3/15/98	80,000

Kale classifies investments with original maturities of three months or less as cash equivalents. In its December, 31, 1997, balance sheet, what amount should Kale report as cash and cash equivalents?

a. $190,000
b. $200,000
c. $240,000
d. $320,000

Exercise 7–6

Trade and cash discounts; the gross method and the net method compared

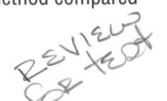

Tracy Company, a manufacturer of air conditioners, sold 100 units to Thomas Company on November 17, 1997. The units have a list price of $500 each, but Thomas was given a 30% trade discount. The terms of the sale were 2/10, n/30.

take of original amount
Recoded after discount

Required:

1. Prepare the journal entries to record the sale on November 17 (ignore cost of goods) and payment on November 26, 1997, assuming that the gross method of accounting for cash discounts is used.
2. Prepare the journal entries to record the sale on November 17 (ignore cost of goods) and payment on December 15, 1997, assuming that the gross method of accounting for cash discounts is used.
3. Repeat requirements 1 and 2 assuming that the net method of accounting for cash discounts is used.

Exercise 7–7

Cash discounts; the gross method

Harwell Company manufactures automobile tires. On July 15, 1997, the company sold 1,000 tires to the Nixon Car Company for $50 each. The terms of the sale were 2/10, n/30. Harwell uses the gross method of accounting for cash discounts.

Required:

1. Prepare the journal entries to record the sale on July 15 (ignore cost of goods) and payment on July 23, 1997.
2. Prepare the journal entries to record the sale on July 15 (ignore cost of goods) and payment on August 15, 1997.

Exercise 7–8

Cash discounts; the net method

[This is a variation of the previous exercise modified to focus on the net method of accounting for cash discounts.]

Harwell Company manufactures automobile tires. On July 15, 1997, the company sold 1,000 tires to the Nixon Car Company for $50 each. The terms of the sale were 2/10, n/30. Harwell uses the net method of accounting for cash discounts.

Required:

1. Prepare the journal entries to record the sale on July 15 (ignore cost of goods) and payment on July 23, 1997.
2. Prepare the journal entries to record the sale on July 15 (ignore cost of goods) and payment on August 15, 1997.

Exercise 7–9

Uncollectible accounts; allowance method vs. direct write-off method

The Johnson Company uses the allowance method to account for uncollectible accounts receivable. Bad debt expense is established as a percentage of credit sales. For 1997, net credit sales totaled $4,500,000, and the estimated bad debt percentage is 1.2%. The allowance for uncollectible accounts had a credit balance of $32,000 at the beginning of 1997 and $40,000, after adjusting entries, at the end of 1997.

Required:

1. What is bad debt expense for 1997?
2. Determine the amount of accounts receivable written off during 1997.
3. If the company uses the direct write-off method, what would bad debt expense be for 1997?

Exercise 7-10

Uncollectible accounts; allowance method; balance sheet approach

The Colorado Rocky Cookie Company offers credit terms to its customers. At the end of 1997, accounts receivable totaled $625,000. The allowance method is used to account for uncollectible accounts. The allowance for uncollectible accounts had a credit balance of $32,000 at the beginning of 1997 and $21,000 in receivables were written off during the year as uncollectible. Also, $1,200 in cash was received in

December from a customer whose account previously had been written off. The company estimates bad debts by applying a percentage of 10% to accounts receivable at the end of the year.

Required:

1. Prepare journal entries to record the write-off of receivables, the collection of $1,200 for previously written off receivables, and the year-end adjusting entry for bad debt expense.
2. How would accounts receivable be shown in the 1997 year-end balance sheet?

Exercise 7–11
Uncollectible accounts; allowance method and direct write-off method compared; solving for unknown

The Castle Company provides estimates for its uncollectible accounts. The allowance for uncollectible accounts had a credit balance of $17,280 at the beginning of 1997 and a $22,410 credit balance at the end of 1997 (after adjusting entries). If the direct write-off method had been used to account for uncollectible accounts, the income statement for 1997 would have included bad debt expense of $14,800 and revenue of $2,200 from the collection of previously written off bad debts.

Required:

Determine bad debt expense for 1997 according to the allowance method.

Exercise 7–12
Note receivable

On June 30, 1997, the Esquire Company sold some merchandise to a customer for $30,000. In payment, Esquire agreed to accept a 8% note requiring the payment of interest and principal on March 31, 1998.

Required:

Prepare journal entries to record the sale of merchandise (omit any entry that might be required for the cost of the goods sold), the December 31, 1997, interest accrual, and the March 31 collection.

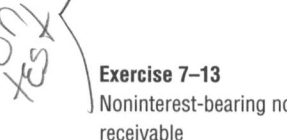

Exercise 7–13
Noninterest-bearing note receivable

[This is a variation of the previous exercise modified to focus on a noninterest-bearing note.]

On June 30, 1997, the Esquire Company sold some merchandise to a customer for $30,000 and agreed to accept as payment a noninterest-bearing note with an 8% discount rate requiring the payment of $30,000 on March 31, 1998.

Required:

1. Prepare journal entries to record the sale of merchandise (omit any entry that might be required for the cost of the goods sold), the December 31, 1997, interest accrual, and the March 31 collection.
2. What is the *effective* interest rate on the note?

Exercise 7–14
Interest-bearing note receivable; solving for unknown rate

On January 1, 1997, the Apex Company exchanged some shares of common stock it had been holding as an investment for a note receivable. The note principal plus interest is due on January 1, 1998. The 1997 income statement reported $2,200 in interest revenue from this note and a $6,000 gain on sale of investment in stock. The stock's book value was $16,000. The company's fiscal year ends on December 31.

Required:

1. What is the note's effective interest rate?
2. Reconstruct the journal entries to record the sale of the stock on January 1, 1997, and the adjusting entry to record interest revenue at the end of 1997. The company records adjusting entries only at year-end.

Exercise 7–15
Multiple choice; accounts receivable

The following questions dealing with accounts receivable are adapted from questions that appeared on recent CPA examinations. Determine the response that best completes the statements or questions.

1. When the allowance method of recognizing uncollectible accounts is used, the entry to record the write-off of a specific account:
   a. Decreases both accounts receivable and the allowance for uncollectible accounts.
   b. Decreases accounts receivable and increases the allowance for uncollectible accounts.
   c. Increases the allowance for uncollectible accounts and decreases net income.
   d. Decreases both accounts receivable and net income.
2. The following information pertains to Tara Co.'s accounts receivable at December 31, 1997:

Days Outstanding	Amount	Estimated % Uncollectible
0–60	$120,000	1%
61–120	90,000	2
Over 120	100,000	6
	$310,000	

During 1997, Tara wrote off $7,000 in receivables and recovered $4,000 that had been written off in prior years. Tara's December 31, 1996, allowance for uncollectible accounts was $22,000. Under the aging method, what amount of allowance for uncollectible accounts should Tara report at December 31, 1997?

  a. $ 9,000
  b. $10,000
  c. $13,000
  d. $19,000

3. Mill Co.'s allowance for uncollectible accounts was $100,000 at the end of 1997 and $90,000 at the end of 1996. For the year ended December 31, 1997, Mill reported bad debt expense of $16,000 in its income statement. What amount did Mill debit to the appropriate account in 1997 to write off actual bad debts?

  a. $ 6,000
  b. $10,000
  c. $16,000
  d. $26,000

4. At January 1, 1997, Jamin Co. had a credit balance of $260,000 in its allowance for uncollectible accounts. Based on past experience, 2% of Jamin's credit sales have been uncollectible. During 1997, Jamin wrote off $325,000 of uncollectible accounts. Credit sales for 1997 were $9,000,000. In its December 31, 1997, balance sheet, what amount should Jamin report as allowance for uncollectible accounts?

  a. $115,000
  b. $180,000
  c. $245,000
  d. $440,000

Exercise 7–16
Assigning of specific accounts receivable

On June 30, 1997, the High Five Surfboard Company had outstanding accounts receivable of $600,000. On July 1, 1997, the company borrowed $400,000 from the Equitable Finance Corporation and signed a promissory note. Interest at 10% is payable monthly. The company assigned specific receivables totaling $500,000 as collateral for the loan. Equitable Finance charges a finance fee equal to 1.5% of the accounts receivable assigned.

Required:
Prepare the journal entries to record the borrowing and the assignment of receivables on the books of High Five Surfboard.

Exercise 7–17
Factoring of accounts receivable without recourse

The Mountain High Ice Cream Company transferred $50,000 of accounts receivable to the Prudential Bank. The transfer was made without recourse. Prudential assesses a finance charge equal to 2% of accounts receivable transferred. The bank will collect the receivables directly from Mountain High's customers.

Required:
Prepare the journal entry to record the transfer on the books of Mountain High.

Exercise 7–18
Factoring of accounts receivable with recourse

[This is a variation of the previous exercise modified to focus on factoring with recourse.]
The Mountain High Ice Cream Company transferred $50,000 of accounts receivable to the Prudential Bank. The transfer was made with recourse. Prudential assesses a finance charge equal to 2% of accounts receivable transferred. The bank will collect the receivables directly from Mountain High's customers.

Required:
1. Prepare the journal entry to record the transfer on the books of Mountain High assuming that the sale criteria are met.
2. Repeat requirement 1 assuming that the sale criteria are *not* met.

Exercise 7–19
Discounting a note receivable

The Selkirk Company obtained a $10,000 note receivable from a customer on January 1, 1997. The note, along with interest at 12%, is due on July 1, 1997. On February 28, 1997, Selkirk discounted the note at Unionville Bank. The bank's discount rate is 14%.

Required:
1. Prepare the journal entries required on February 28, 1997, to accrue interest and to record the discounting (round all calculations to the nearest dollar) for Selkirk. Assume that the discounting is accounted for as a sale.
2. Record the discounting assuming that it is accounted for as a loan.

Exercise 7–20
Multiple choice; notes receivable

The following questions dealing with financing with receivables are adapted from questions that appeared on recent CPA examinations. Determine the response that best completes the statements or questions.
1. Gar Co. factored its receivables without recourse with Ross Bank. Gar received cash as a result of this transaction, which is best described as a:

    a. Loan from Ross collateralized by Gar's accounts receivable.

    b. Loan from Ross to be repaid by the proceeds from Gar's accounts receivable.

    c. Sale of Gar's accounts receivable to Ross, with the risk of uncollectible accounts retained by Gar.

    d. Sale of Gar's accounts receivable to Ross, with the risk of uncollectible accounts transferred to Ross.

2. Roth, Inc. received from a customer a one-year, $500,000 note bearing annual interest of 8%. After holding the note for six months, Roth discounted the note at Regional Bank at an effective interest rate of 10%. What amount of cash did Roth receive from the bank?

    a. $540,000

    b. $523,810

    c. $513,000

    d. $495,238

Exercise 7–21
Concepts; terminology

Listed below are several terms and phrases associated with cash and receivables. Pair each item from List A (by letter) with the item from List B that is most appropriately associated with it.

List A	List B
____ 1. Internal control	a. Restriction on cash.
____ 2. Bank service charges	b. Deducted from balance per bank.
____ 3. Trade discount	c. Cash discount not taken is sales revenue.
____ 4. Cash equivalents	d. Includes separation of duties.
____ 5. Allowance for uncollectibles	e. Bad debt expense a % of credit sales.
____ 6. Cash discount	f. Deducted from balance per books.
____ 7. Balance sheet approach	g. Recognizes bad debts as they occur.
____ 8. Outstanding checks	h. Sale of receivables to a financial institution.
____ 9. Income statement approach	i. Include highly liquid investments.
____ 10. Net method	j. Estimate of bad debts.
____ 11 Compensating balance	k. Reduction in amount paid by credit customer.
____ 12. Discounting	l. Reduction below list price.
____ 13. Gross method	m. Cash discount not taken is interest revenue.
____ 14. Direct write-off method	n. Bad debt expense determined by estimating realizable value.
____ 15. Factoring	o. Sale of note receivable to a financial institution.

Exercise 7–22
Receivables; transaction analysis

The Weldon Corporation's fiscal year ends December 31. The following is a list of transactions involving receivables that occurred during 1997:

March 17 – Accounts receivable of $1,700 were written off as uncollectible. The company uses the allowance method.

March 30 – Loaned an officer of the company $20,000 and received a note requiring principal and interest at 7% to be paid on March 30, 1998.

May 30 – Discounted the $20,000 note at a local bank. The bank's discount rate is 8%. The note was discounted without recourse.

June 30 – Sold merchandise to the Blankenship Company for $12,000. Terms of the sale are 2/10, n/30. Weldon uses the gross method to account for cash discounts.

July 8 – The Blankenship Company paid its account in full.

Aug. 31 – Sold stock in a nonpublic company with a book value of $5,000 and accepted a $6,000 noninterest-bearing note with a discount rate of 8%. The $6,000 payment is due on February 28, 1998. The stock has no ready market value.

Dec. 31 – Bad debt expense is estimated to be 2% of credit sales for the year. Credit sales for 1997 were $700,000.

Required:

1. Prepare journal entries for each of the above transactions (round all calculations to the nearest dollar).

2. Prepare any additional year-end adjusting entries indicated.

Exercise 7–23
Ratio analysis; solve for unknown

The current asset section of the Moorcroft Outboard Motor Company's balance sheet reported the following amounts:

	12/31/97	12/31/96
Accounts receivable, net	$400,000	$300,000

The average collection period for 1997 is 50 days.

Required:

Determine net sales for 1997.

Problems

Problem 7–1
Bank reconciliation and
adjusting entries; determining
cash and cash equivalents

The bank statement for the checking account of Management Systems, Inc. (MSI) showed a December 31, 1997, balance of $14,632.12. Information that might be useful in preparing a bank reconciliation is as follows:

a. Outstanding checks were $1,320.25.
b. The December 31, 1997, cash receipts of $575 were not deposited in the bank until January 2, 1998.
c. One check written in payment of rent for $246 was correctly recorded by the bank but was recorded by MSI as a $264 disbursement.
d. In accordance with prior authorization, the bank withdrew $450 directly from the checking account as payment on a mortgage note payable. The interest portion of that payment was $350. MSI has made no entry to record the automatic payment.
e. Bank service charges of $14 were listed on the bank statement.
f. A deposit of $875 was recorded by the bank on December 13, but it did not belong to MSI. The deposit should have been made to the checking account of MSI, Inc.
g. The bank statement included a charge of $85 for an NSF check. The check was returned with the bank statement and the company will seek payment from the customer.
h. MSI maintains a $200 petty cash fund that was appropriately reimbursed at the end of December.
i. According to instructions from MSI on December 30, the bank withdrew $10,000 from the account and purchased U.S. Treasury bills for MSI. MSI recorded the transaction in its books on December 31 when it received notice from the bank. Half of the treasury bills mature in two months and the other half in six months.

Required:
1. Prepare a bank reconciliation for the MSI checking account at December 31, 1997. You will have to compute the balance per books.
2. Prepare any necessary adjusting journal entries indicated.
3. What amount would MSI report as cash and cash equivalents in the current asset section of the December 31, 1997, balance sheet?

The El Gato Painting Company maintains a checking account at American Bank. Bank statements are prepared at the end of each month. The November 30, 1997, reconciliation of the bank balance is as follows:

Balance per bank, November 30		$3,231
Add: Deposits outstanding		1,200
Less: Checks outstanding		
#363	$123	
#365	201	
#380	56	
#381	86	
#382	340	(806)
Adjusted balance per bank, November 30		$3,625

The company's general ledger checking account showed the following for December:

Balance, December 1	$ 3,625
Receipts	42,650
Disbursements	(41,853)
Balance, December 31	$ 4,422

The December bank statement contained the following information:

Balance, December 1	$ 3,231
Deposits	43,000
Checks processed	(41,918)
Service charges	(22)
NSF checks	(440)
Balance, December 31	$ 3,851

The checks that were processed by the bank in December include all of the outstanding checks at the end of November except for check #365. In addition, there are some December checks that had not been processed by the bank by the end of the month. Also, you discover that check #411 for $320 was correctly recorded by the bank but was incorrectly recorded on the books as a $230 disbursement for advertising expense. Included in the bank's deposits is a $1,300 deposit incorrectly credited to the company's account. The deposit should have been posted to the credit of the Los Gatos Company. The NSF checks have not been redeposited and the company will seek payment from the customers involved.

Required:

1. Prepare a bank reconciliation for the El Gato checking account at December 31, 1997.
2. Prepare any necessary adjusting journal entries indicated.

Problem 7–3

Uncollectible accounts;
allowance method; income
statement and balance sheet
approach

The Swathmore Clothing Corporation grants its customers 30 days' credit. The company uses the allowance method for its uncollectible accounts receivable. During the year, a monthly bad debt accrual is made by multiplying 3% times the amount of credit sales for the month. At the fiscal year-end of December 31, an aging of accounts receivable schedule is prepared and the allowance for uncollectible accounts is adjusted accordingly.

At the end of 1996, accounts receivable were $574,000 and the allowance account had a credit balance of $54,000. Accounts receivable activity for 1997 was as follows:

Beginning balance	$ 574,000
Credit sales	2,620,000
Collections	(2,483,000)
Write-offs	(68,000)
Ending balance	$ 643,000

The company's controller prepared the following aging summary of year-end accounts receivable:

Summary

Age Group	Amount	Percent Uncollectible
0–60 days	$430,000	4%
61–90 days	98,000	15
91–120 days	60,000	25
Over 120 days	55,000	40
Total	$643,000	

Required:

1. Prepare a summary journal entry to record the monthly bad debt accrual and the write-offs during the year.
2. Prepare the necessary year-end adjusting entry for bad debt expense.
3. What is total bad debt expense for 1997? How would accounts receivable appear in the 1997 balance sheet?

Problem 7–4

Uncollectible accounts

The Amdahl Corporation manufactures large-scale, high performance computer systems. In a recent annual report, the balance sheet included the following information (dollars in thousands):

	Current year	Previous year
Current assets:		
Receivables, net of allowances of $5,042 and $6,590 in the previous year	$504,944	$580,640

In addition, the income statement reported sales revenue of $2,158,755 (dollars in thousands) for the current year. All sales are made on a credit basis. The statement of cash flows indicates that cash collected from customers during the current year was $2,230,065 (dollars in thousands). There were no recoveries of accounts receivable previously written off.

Required:

1. Compute the following (dollar amounts in thousands):
   a. The amount of uncollectibles written off by Amdahl during the current year.
   b. The amount of bad debt expense that Amdahl would include in its income statement for the current year.
   c. The approximate percentage that Amdahl used to estimate uncollectibles for the current year, assuming that it uses the income statement approach.
2. Suppose that Amdahl had used the direct write-off method to account for uncollectibles. Compute the following (dollars in thousands):
   a. The accounts receivable information that would be included in the year-end balance sheet.
   b. The amount of bad debt expense that Amdahl would include in its income statement for the current year.

Problem 7–5

Uncollectible accounts

The Raintree Cosmetic Company sells its products to customers on a credit basis. An adjusting entry for bad debt expense is recorded only at December 31, the company's fiscal year-end. The 1996 balance sheet disclosed the following:

Current assets:	
Receivables, net of allowance for uncollectible accounts of $30,000	$432,000

During 1997, credit sales were $1,750,000, cash collections from customers $1,830,000, and $35,000 in accounts receivable were written off. In addition, $3,000 was collected from a customer whose account was written off in 1996. An aging of accounts receivable at December 31, 1997, reveals the following:

Age Group	Percentage of Year-End Receivables in Group	Percent Uncollectible
0–60 days	65%	4%
61–90 days	20	15
91–120 days	10	25
Over 120 days	5	40

Required:
1. Prepare summary journal entries to account for the 1997 write-offs and the collection of the receivable previously written off.
2. Prepare the year-end adjusting entry for bad debts according to each of the following situations:
   a. Bad debt expense is estimated to be 3% of credit sales for the year.
   b. Bad debt expense is estimated by computing net realizable value of the receivables. The allowance for uncollectible accounts is estimated to be 10% of the year-end balance in accounts receivable.
   c. Bad debt expense is estimated by computing net realizable value of the receivables. The allowance for uncollectible accounts is determined by an aging of accounts receivable.
3. For situations (a)–(c) in requirement 2 above, what would be the net amount of accounts receivable reported in the 1997 balance sheet.

Problem 7–6
Notes receivable; solving for unknowns

The Cypress Oil Company's December 31, 1997, balance sheet listed $645,000 of notes receivable and $16,000 of interest receivable included in current assets. The following notes make up the notes receivable balance:

Note 1   Dated 8/31/97, principal of $300,000 and interest at 10% due on 2/28/98.
Note 2   Dated 6/30/97, principal of $150,000 and interest due 3/31/98.
Note 3 $200,000 face value noninterest-bearing note dated 9/31/97, due 3/31/98. Note was issued in exchange for merchandise.

The company records adjusting entries only at year-end. There were no other notes receivable outstanding during 1997.

Required:
1. Determine the rate used to discount the noninterest-bearing note.
2. Determine the explicit interest rate on Note 2.
3. What is the amount of interest revenue that appears in the company's 1997 income statement related to these notes?

Problem 7–7
Factoring versus assigning of accounts receivable

The Lonergan Company occasionally uses its accounts receivable to obtain immediate cash. At the end of June 1997, the company had accounts receivable of $780,000. Lonergan needs approximately $500,000 to capitalize on a unique investment opportunity. On July 1, 1997, a local bank offers Lonergan the following two alternatives:
a. Borrow $500,000, sign a note payable, and assign the entire receivable balance as collateral. At the end of each month, a remittance will be made to the bank that equals the amount of receivables collected plus 12% interest on the unpaid balance of the note at the beginning of the period.
b. Transfer $550,000 of specific receivables to the bank without recourse. The bank will charge a 2% finance charge on the amount of receivables transferred. The bank will collect the receivables directly from customers.

Required:
1. Prepare the journal entries that would be recorded on July 1 for each of the alternatives.
2. Assuming that 80% of all June 30 receivables are collected during July, prepare the necessary journal entries to record the collection and the remittance to the bank.
3. For each alternative, explain any required note disclosures that would be included in the July 31, 1997, financial statements.

Problem 7–8
Factoring of accounts receivable; with and without recourse

The Samson Wholesale Beverage Company regularly factors its accounts receivable with the Milpitas Finance Company. On April 30, 1997, the company transferred $800,000 of accounts receivable to Milpitas. The transfer was made without recourse. Milpitas charges a fee equal to 4% of receivables transferred. During May, $600,000 of the transferred receivables were collected by Milpitas. The company's fiscal year-end is December 31.

Required:
1. Prepare journal entries for Samson Wholesale Beverage for the transfer of accounts receivable on April 30.
2. Repeat requirement 1 assuming that the receivables were transferred with recourse and the sale criteria are not met. Also prepare the journal entries to reflect the cash collection in May.

Problem 7–9
Miscellaneous receivable transactions

The Evergreen Company sells lawn and garden products to wholesalers. The company's fiscal year-end is December 31. During 1997, the following transactions related to receivables occurred:

Feb. 28	Sold merchandise to Lennox, Inc. for $10,000 and accepted a 10%, 7-month note. 10% is an appropriate rate for this type of note.
March 31	Sold merchandise to Maddox Co. and accepted a noninterest-bearing note with a discount rate of 10%. The $8,000 payment is due on March 31, 1998.
April 3	Sold merchandise to Carr Co. for $7,000 with terms 2/10, n/30. Evergreen uses the gross method to account for cash discounts.
April 11	Collected the entire amount due from Carr Co.
April 17	A customer returned merchandise costing $3,200. Evergreen reduced the customer's receivable balance by $5,000, the sales price of the merchandise. Sales returns are recorded by the company as they occur.
April 30	Transferred receivables of $50,000 to a factor without recourse. The factor charged Evergreen a 1% finance charge on the receivables transferred.
June 30	Discounted the Lennox, Inc., note at the bank. The bank's discount rate is 12%. The note was discounted without recourse.
August 31	Lennox, Inc., paid the note amount plus interest to the bank.

Required:
1. Prepare the necessary journal entries for Evergreen for each of the above dates. For transactions involving the sale of merchandise, ignore the entry for the cost of goods sold (Round all calculations to the nearest dollar).
2. Prepare any necessary adjusting entries at December 31, 1997. Adjusting entries are only recorded at year-end (Round all calculations to the nearest dollar).
3. Prepare a schedule showing the effect of the journal entries in requirements 1 and 2 on 1997 income before taxes.

Problem 7–10
Discounting a note receivable

Descriptors are provided below for six situations involving notes receivable being discounted at a bank. In each case, the maturity date of the note is December 31, 1997, and the principal and interest are due at maturity. For each, determine the proceeds received from the bank on discounting the note.

Note	Note Face Value	Date of Note	Interest Rate	Date Discounted	Discount Rate
1	$50,000	3/31/97	8%	6/30/97	10%
2	50,000	3/31/97	8	9/30/97	10
3	50,000	3/31/97	8	9/30/97	12
4	80,000	6/30/97	6	10/31/97	10
5	80,000	6/30/97	6	10/31/97	12
6	80,000	6/30/97	6	11/30/97	10

Cases

Discussion Case 7–1
Accounts and notes receivable

Magrath Company has an operating cycle of less than one year and provides credit terms for all of its customers. On April 1, 1997, the company factored, without recourse, some of its accounts receivable.

Magrath uses the allowance method to account for uncollectible accounts. During 1997, some accounts were written off as uncollectible and other accounts previously written off as uncollectible were collected.

Required:
1. How should Magrath account for and report the accounts receivable factored on April 1, 1997? Why is this accounting treatment appropriate?
2. How should Magrath account for the collection of the accounts previously written off as uncollectible?
3. What are the two basic approaches to estimating uncollectible accounts under the allowance method? What is the rationale for each approach?

(AICPA adapted)

Writing Case 7–2
Uncollectible accounts

You have been hired as a consultant by a parts manufacturing firm to provide advice as to the proper accounting methods the company should use in some key areas. In the area of receivables, the company president does not understand your recommendation to use the allowance method for uncollectible accounts. She stated, "Financial statements should be based on objective data rather than the guesswork required for the allowance method. Besides, since my uncollectibles are fairly constant from period to period, with significant variations occurring infrequently, the direct write-off method is just as good as the allowance method."

Required:

Draft a one-page response in the form of a memo to the president in support of your recommendation for the company to use the allowance method.

Discussion Case 7–3
Accounts receivable

Hogan Company uses the net method of accounting for sales discounts. Hogan offers trade discounts to various groups of buyers.

On August 1, 1997, Hogan factored some accounts receivable on a without recourse basis. Hogan incurred a finance charge.

Hogan also has some notes receivable bearing an appropriate rate of interest. The principal and total interest are due at maturity. The notes were received on October 1, 1997, and mature on September 30, 1998. Hogan's operating cycle is less than one year.

Required:

1. a. Using the net method, how should Hogan account for the sales discounts at the date of sale? What is the rationale for the amount recorded as sales under the net method?
    b. Using the net method, what is the effect on Hogan's sales revenues and net income when customers do not take the sales discounts?
2. What is the effect of trade discounts on sales revenues and accounts receivable? Why?
3. How should Hogan account for the accounts receivable factored on August 1, 1997? Why?
4. How should Hogan report the effects of the interest-bearing notes receivable on its December 31, 1997, balance sheet and its income statement for the year ended December 31, 1997? Why?

(AICPA adapted)

Ethics Case 7–4
Uncollectible accounts

You have recently been hired as the assistant controller for Stanton Industries, a large, publicly held manufacturing company. Your immediate superior is the controller who, in turn, is responsible to the vice president of finance.

The controller has assigned you the task of preparing the year-end adjusting entries. In the receivables area, you have prepared an aging of accounts receivable and have applied historical percentages to the balances of each of the age categories. The analysis indicates that an appropriate balance for the allowance for uncollectible accounts is $180,000. The existing balance in the allowance account prior to any adjusting entry is a $20,000 credit balance.

After showing your analysis to the controller, he tells you to change the aging category of a large account from over 120 days to current status and to prepare a new invoice to the customer with a revised date that agrees with the new aging category. This will change the required allowance for uncollectible accounts from $180,000 to $135,000. Tactfully, you ask the controller for an explanation for the change and he tells you "We need the extra income, the bottom line is too low."

Required:

1. What is the effect on income before taxes of the change requested by the controller?
2. Discuss the ethical dilemma you face. Consider your options and responsibilities along with the possible consequences of any action you might take.

Critical Thought Case 7–5
Internal control

For each of the following independent situations, indicate the apparent internal control weaknesses and suggest alternative procedures to eliminate the weaknesses.

1. John Smith is the petty cash custodian. John approves all requests for payment out of the $200 fund which is replenished at the end of each month. At the end of each month, John submits a list of all accounts and amounts to be charged and a check is written to him for the total amount. John is the only person ever to tally the fund.
2. All of the company's cash disbursements are made by check. Each check must be supported by an approved voucher which is in turn supported by the appropriate invoice and, for purchases, a receiving document. The vouchers are approved by Dean Leiser, the chief accountant, after reviewing the supporting documentation. Betty Hanson prepares the checks for Leiser's signature. Leiser also maintains the company's check register (the cash disbursements journal) and reconciles the bank account at the end of each month.
3. Fran Jones opens the company's mail and makes a listing of all checks and cash received from customers. A copy of the list is sent to Jerry McDonald who maintains the general ledger accounts. Fran prepares and makes the daily deposit at the bank. Fran also maintains the subsidiary ledger for accounts receivable which is used to generate monthly statements to customers.

Discussion Case 7–6
Sales returns

Many of the products sold by King Company give customers the right to return the merchandise if they are not satisfied. For the seller, these are called sales returns.

Required:
Explain three different approaches that might be used to account for sales returns and describe the circumstances that would dictate the use of the alternative methods.

Real World Case 7–7
Bad debts

Read-Rite Corporation, located in Milpitas, California, is the leading independent supplier of thin film recording heads for computer disk drives. The company's 1995 financial statements contained the following information:

Balance Sheets ($ in thousands)	1995	1994
Current assets:		
Accounts receivable, net of allowances of $3,017 in 1995 and $1,627 in 1994	$ 147,277	$ 95,687

Income Statements ($ in thousands)	1995	1994
Net sales	$1,003,040	$638,589

In addition, the statement of cash flows disclosed that accounts receivable increased during 1995 by $54,911,000. This indicates that cash received from customers was $54,911,000 less than accrual sales revenue.

Required:
1. What is the amount of accounts receivable due from customers at the end of 1995 and 1994?
2. Assuming that all sales are made on a credit basis and that the company provides no allowances for sales returns, determine the amount of bad debt expense for 1995 and the amount of actual bad debt write-offs made in 1995.

Internet Case 7–8
Receivables; bad debts

EDGAR, the Electronic Data Gathering, Analysis, and Retrieval system, performs automated collection, validation, indexing, and forwarding of submissions by companies and others who are required by law to file forms with the U.S. Securities and Exchange Commission (SEC). All publicly traded domestic companies use EDGAR to make the majority of their filings. (Some foreign companies file voluntarily.) Form 10-K or 10-KSB, which include the annual report, is required to be filed on EDGAR. The SEC makes this information available on the Internet.

Required:
1. Access EDGAR on the Internet. You can use a web browser or anonymous FTP. The web address is http://www.sec.gov/. To use anonymous FTP, use your File Transfer Protocol software to connect to sec.gov and log in as user "anonymous" with a password of your electronic mail address.
2. Search for Ben & Jerry's Homemade, Inc. Access the 10-K filing for the most recent fiscal year. Search or scroll to find the financial statements.
3. Answer the following questions related to the company's accounts receivable and bad debts:
   a. What is the amount of gross trade accounts receivable at the end of the year?
   b. What is the amount of bad debt expense for the year? (Hint: check the statement of cash flows.)
   c. Determine the amount of actual bad debt write-offs made during the year. Assume that all bad debts relate only to trade accounts receivable.
   d. Using only information from the balance sheets, income statements, and your answer to requirement 3.c., determine the amount of cash collected from customers during the year. Assume that all sales are made on a credit basis, that the company provides no allowances for sales returns, that no previously written-off receivables were collected, and that all sales relate to trade accounts receivable.

Integrating Case 7–9
Change in estimate of bad debts

The McLaughlin Corporation uses the allowance method to account for bad debts. At the end of the company's fiscal year, accounts receivable are analyzed and the allowance for uncollectible accounts is adjusted. At the end of 1997, the company reported the following amounts:

Accounts receivable	$10,850,000
Less: Allowance for uncollectible accounts	(450,000)
Accounts receivable, net	$10,400,000

In 1998, it was determined that $1,825,000 of year-end 1997 receivables had to be written off as uncollectible. This was due in part to the fact that Hughes Corporation, a long-standing customer that had always paid its bills, unexpectedly declared bankruptcy in 1998. Hughes owed McLaughlin $1,400,000. At the end of 1997, none of the Hughes receivable was considered uncollectible.

Required:

Describe the appropriate accounting treatment and required disclosures for McLaughlin's underestimation of bad debts at the end of 1997.

Discussion Case 7–10
Financing with receivables

Financial institutions have developed a wide variety of methods for companies to use their receivables to obtain immediate cash. The methods differ with respect to which rights and risks are retained by the transferor (the original holder of the receivable) and those passed on to the transferee (the new holder, usually a financial institution).

Required:
1. Describe the alternative methods available for companies to use their receivables to obtain immediate cash.
2. Discuss the alternative accounting treatments for these methods.

Financial Analysis Case 7–11
Compare receivables management using ratios

The table below contains selected financial information included in the 1995 financial statements of Sara Lee Corporation and Tyson Foods, Inc.:

	Sara Lee		Tyson Foods	
(dollars in millions)	**1995**	**1994**	**1995**	**1994**
Balance sheet: Accounts receivable, net	$1,653	$1,472	$495	$444
Income statement: Net sales	$17,719	$15,536	$5,511	$5,110

Required:
1. Calculate the 1995 receivables turnover ratio and average collection period for both companies. Evaluate the management of each company's investment in receivables.
2. Obtain annual reports from three corporations in the same primary industry and compare the management of each company's investment in receivables.

   Note: You can obtain copies of annual reports from your library, from friends who are shareholders, from the investor relations department of the corporations, from a friendly stockbroker, or from EDGAR (Electronic Data Gathering Retrieval) on the Internet (http://www.sec.gov).

Financial Analysis Case 7–12
Reporting cash and receivables

Federal Express Corporation

Refer to the financial statements and related disclosure notes of Federal Express Corporation in the appendix to Chapter 1.

Required:
1. What is Federal Express' policy for designating investments as cash equivalents?
2. Determine the gross amount of receivables outstanding at the end of 1996 and 1995.
3. What amount of receivables were written off during 1996? Assume that no previously written-off receivables were collected during the year. (Hint: check the statement of cash flows.)

8

INVENTORIES: MEASUREMENT

OVERVIEW

The next two chapters continue our study of assets by investigating the measurement and reporting issues involving inventories and the related expense—cost of goods sold. Inventory refers to the assets a company (1) intends to sell in the normal course of business, (2) has in production for future sale, or (3) uses currently in the production of goods to be sold.

LEARNING OBJECTIVES   After studying this chapter, you should be able to:

1. Explain the difference between a perpetual inventory system and a periodic inventory system.
2. Explain which physical quantities of goods should be included in inventory.
3. Determine the expenditures that should be included in the cost of inventory.
4. Differentiate between the specific identification, FIFO, LIFO, and average cost methods used to determine the cost of ending inventory and cost of goods sold.
5. Discuss the factors affecting a company's choice of inventory method.
6. Determine ending inventory using the dollar-value LIFO inventory method.

INVENTORY MEASUREMENT AT GENERAL MOTORS

By the time you finish this chapter, you should be able to respond appropriately to the questions posed in this case. Compare your response to the solution provided at the end of the chapter.

A recent article in the financial section of your local newspaper reported on the labor negotiations between General Motors Corporation (GM) and the United Auto Workers. When you showed the article to a friend, he said "I'll bet GM uses LIFO to value its inventories. That way they can report lower profits and give them an edge in the negotiations." This aroused your curiosity and led you to download GM's most recent financial statements from the Internet which contained the following disclosure note:

Note 5. Inventories

	December 31	
(Dollars in millions)	**1995**	**1994**
Productive material, work in process, and supplies	$ 6,570.4	$ 5,478.3
Finished product, service parts, etc.	4,959.1	4,649.5
Total	$11,529.5	$10,127.8
Memo: Increase in LIFO inventories if valued at FIFO	$ 2,424.4	$ 2,535.9

Inventories are stated generally at cost, which is not in excess of market. The cost of substantially all U.S. inventories other than the inventories of Saturn Corporation (Saturn) and Hughes is determined by the last-in, first-out (LIFO) method. The cost of non-U.S., Saturn, and Hughes inventories is determined generally by the first-in, first-out (FIFO) or average cost methods.

As a result of decreases in U.S. inventories, certain inventory quantities carried at lower LIFO costs prevailing in prior years, as compared with current purchases, were liquidated in 1993. This inventory adjustment improved pretax operating results by approximately $134.4 million in 1993, primarily from the sale of AGT.

QUESTIONS

1. What inventory methods does GM use to value its inventories? Is this permissible according to GAAP?
2. What is the purpose of the memo that reports the increase in LIFO inventories if valued at FIFO?
3. What is the purpose of the last paragraph in the note that discusses a liquidation of inventories?
4. Is your friend correct in his assertion that by using LIFO, GM is able to report lower profits?

PART A

RECORDING AND MEASURING INVENTORY

Inventory refers to the assets a company (1) intends to sell in the normal course of business, (2) has in production for future sale, or (3) uses currently in the production of goods to be sold. The computers produced by Apple Computer that are intended for sale to customers are inventory, as are partially completed components in the assembly lines of Apple's Cupertino facility, and the computer chips and memory modules that will go into computers produced later. The computers *used* by Apple to maintain its accounting system, however, are classified and accounted for as plant and equipment. Similarly, the stocks and bonds a securities dealer holds for sale are inventory, whereas Apple would classify the securities it holds as investments.

> Inventories consist of assets that a retail or wholesale company acquires for resale or goods that manufacturers produce for sale.

Proper accounting for inventories is essential for manufacturing, wholesale, and retail companies (enterprises that earn revenue by selling goods). Inventory usually is one of the most valuable assets listed on the balance sheet for these firms. Cost of goods sold—the expense recorded when inventory is sold—typically is the largest expense on the income statement. For example, a recent balance sheet for Sara Lee Corporation reported inventories of $2.830 billion which represented 23% of total assets. The company's income statement reported cost of goods sold of $11 billion representing 67% of all expenses.

This and the following chapter focus on the measurement and reporting issues involving the asset **inventory** and the corresponding expense, **cost of goods sold**.

Types of Inventory

Merchandising Inventory

Wholesale and retail companies purchase goods that are primarily in finished form. These companies are intermediaries in the process of moving goods from the manufacturer to the end-user. They often are referred to as merchandising companies and their inventory as merchandise inventory. The cost of merchandise inventory includes the purchase price plus any other costs necessary to get the goods in condition and location for sale. We discuss the concept of condition and location and the types of costs that typically constitute inventory later in this chapter.

Manufacturing Inventories

> Inventory for a manufacturing company consists of **raw materials**, **work in process**, and **finished goods**.

Unlike merchandising companies, manufacturing companies actually produce the goods they sell to wholesalers, retailers, or other manufacturers. Inventory for a manufacturer consists of (1) raw materials, (2) work in process, and (3) finished goods. **Raw materials** represent the cost of components purchased from other manufacturers that will become part of the finished product. For example, Apple's raw materials inventory includes semiconductors, circuit boards, plastic, and glass that go into the production of personal computers.

> The cost of **work in process** and **finished goods** includes the cost of raw materials, direct labor, and an allocated portion of manufacturing overhead.

Work-in-process inventory refers to the products that are not yet complete. The cost of work in process includes the cost of raw materials used in production, the cost of labor that can be directly traced to the goods in process, and an allocated portion of other manufacturing costs, called *manufacturing overhead*. Overhead costs include electricity and other utility costs to operate the manufacturing facility, depreciation of manufacturing equipment, and many other manufacturing costs that cannot be directly linked to the production of specific goods. Once the manufacturing process is completed, these costs that have accumulated in work in process are transferred to **finished goods**.

Manufacturing companies generally disclose, either in a note or directly on the balance sheet, the dollar amount of each inventory category. For example, IBM Corporation's note disclosure of inventory categories was shown on page 195. Sara Lee Corporation reports inventory categories directly on the balance sheet, as illustrated in Graphic 8–1.

The inventory accounts and the cost flows for a typical manufacturing company are shown using T-accounts in Graphic 8–2. The costs of raw materials used, direct labor applied, and manufacturing overhead applied, flow into work in process and then to finished goods. When the goods are sold, the cost of those goods flow to cost of goods sold.

GRAPHIC   8–1

Inventories Disclosure—
Sara Lee Corporation

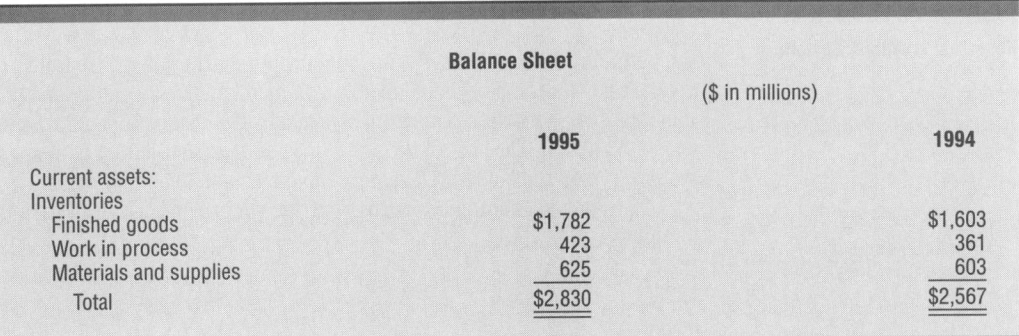

	Balance Sheet	
		($ in millions)
	1995	**1994**
Current assets:		
Inventories		
Finished goods	$1,782	$1,603
Work in process	423	361
Materials and supplies	625	603
Total	$2,830	$2,567

GRAPHIC   8–2

**Inventory Components and
Cost Flow for a
Manufacturing Company**

The costs of inventory units
follow their physical
movement from one stage
of activity to another.

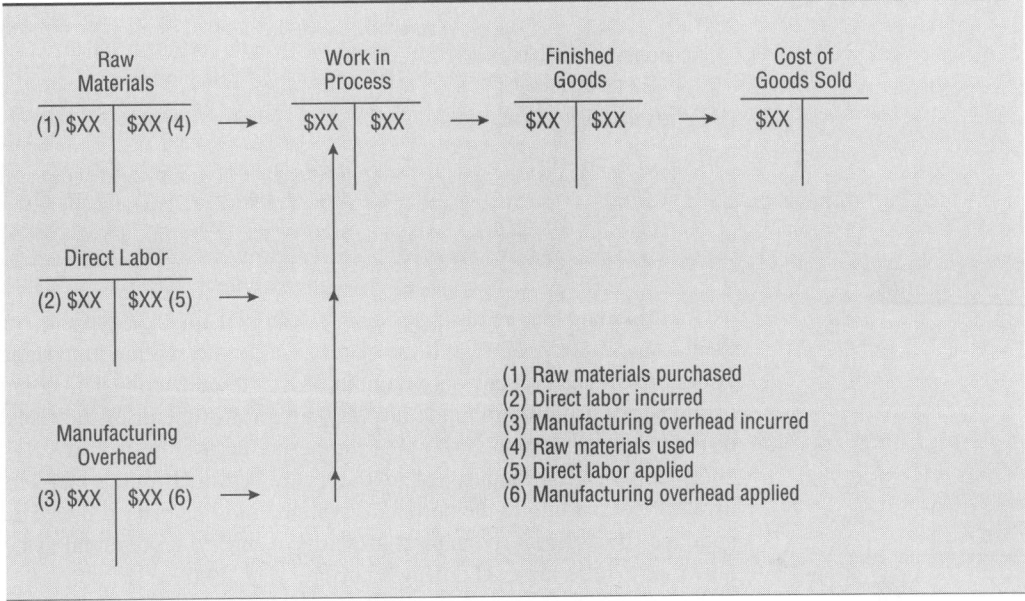

We focus here primarily on merchandising companies (wholesalers and retailers). Still, most of the accounting principles and procedures discussed here also apply to manufacturing companies. The unique problems involved with accumulating the direct costs of raw materials and labor and with allocating manufacturing overhead are addressed in managerial and cost accounting textbooks.

Perpetual Inventory System

Two accounting systems are used to record transactions involving inventory: the **perpetual inventory system** and the **periodic inventory system**. The perpetual system was introduced in Chapter 2. The system is aptly termed perpetual because the account *inventory* is continuously adjusted for each change in inventory, whether it's caused by a purchase, a sale, or a return of merchandise by the company to its supplier (a *purchase return* for the buyer, a *sales return* for the seller).[1] The cost of goods sold account, along with the inventory account, is adjusted each time goods are sold or are returned by a customer. This concept is applied to the Lothridge Wholesale Beverage Company for which inventory information is provided in Illustration 8–1. This hypothetical company also will be used in the next several illustrations.

A **perpetual inventory
system** continuously
records both changes in
inventory quantity and
inventory cost.

---

[1]We discussed accounting for sales returns in Chapter 7.

The Lothridge Wholesale Beverage Company purchases soft drinks from producers and then sells them to retailers. The company begins 1997 with merchandise inventory of $120,000 on hand. During 1997 additional merchandise is purchased on account at a cost of $600,000. Sales for the year, all on account, totaled $820,000. The cost of the soft drinks sold is $540,000. Lothridge uses the perpetual inventory system to keep track of both inventory quantities and inventory costs.

     The following summary journal entries record the inventory transactions for the Lothridge Company:

1997

Inventory	600,000	
Accounts payable		600,000
To record the purchase of merchandise inventory.		

1997

Accounts receivable	820,000	
Sales revenue		820,000
To record sales on account.		
Cost of goods sold	540,000	
Inventory		540,000
To record the cost of sales.		

An important feature of a perpetual system is that it is designed to track inventory quantities from their acquisition to their sale. If the system is accurate, it allows management to determine how many goods are on hand on any date without having to take a physical count. However, physical counts of inventory usually are made anyway, either at the end of the fiscal year or on a sample basis throughout the year, to verify that the perpetual system is correctly tracking quantities. Differences between the quantity of inventory determined by the physical count and the quantity of inventory according to the perpetual system could be caused by system errors, theft, breakage, or spoilage. In addition to keeping up with inventory, a perpetual system also directly determines how many items are sold during a period.

     You are probably familiar with the scanning mechanisms used at grocery store checkout counters. The scanners not only record the sale on the cash register but also can be used to track the sale of merchandise for inventory management purposes. For a company to use the perpetual inventory system to record inventory and cost of goods sold transactions, merchandise cost data also must be included on the system. That is, when merchandise is purchased/sold, the system must be able to record not only the addition/reduction in inventory quantity but also the addition/reduction in the *cost* of inventory.

> A perpetual inventory system tracks both inventory quantities and inventory costs.

Periodic Inventory System

A **periodic inventory system** is not designed to track either the quantity or cost of merchandise. The merchandise inventory account balance is not adjusted as purchases and sales are made but only periodically at the end of a reporting period. A physical count of the period's ending inventory is made and costs are assigned to the quantities determined. Merchandise purchases, purchase returns, purchase discounts, and freight-in (purchases plus freight-in less returns and discounts equals net purchases) are recorded in temporary accounts and the period's cost of goods sold is determined at the end of the period by combining the temporary accounts with the inventory account:

> A **periodic inventory system** adjusts inventory and records cost of goods sold only at the end of each reporting period.

Beginning inventory + Net purchases – Ending inventory = Cost of goods sold

> Cost of goods sold equation

The cost of goods sold equation assumes that all inventory quantities not on hand at the end of the period were sold. This may not be the case if inventory items were either damaged or stolen. If damaged and stolen inventory are identified, they must be removed from beginning inventory and purchases before calculating cost of goods sold and then classified as a separate expense item.

     Illustration 8–2 looks at the periodic system using the Lothridge Wholesale Beverage Company example.

ILLUSTRATION   8–2

Periodic Inventory System

The Lothridge Wholesale Beverage Company purchases soft drinks from producers and then sells them to retailers. The company began 1997 with merchandise inventory of $120,000 on hand. During 1997 additional merchandise was purchased on account at a cost of $600,000. Sales for the year, all on account, totaled $820,000. Lothridge uses a periodic inventory system. A physical count determined the cost of inventory at the end of the year to be $180,000.

   The following journal entries summarize the inventory transactions for 1997. Of course, each individual transaction would actually be recorded as incurred.

1997

Purchases	600,000	
Accounts payable		600,000

To record the purchase of merchandise inventory.

1997

Accounts receivable	820,000	
Sales revenue		820,000

To record sales on account.

No entry is recorded for the cost of inventory sold.

Because cost of goods sold isn't determined automatically and continuously by the periodic system, it must be determined indirectly after a physical inventory count. Cost of goods sold for 1997 is determined as follows:

Beginning inventory	$120,000
Plus: Purchases	600,000
Cost of goods available for sale	720,000
Less: Ending inventory (per physical count)	(180,000)
Cost of goods sold	$540,000

The following journal entry combines the components of cost of goods sold into a single expense account and updates the balance in the inventory account:

December 31, 1997

Cost of goods sold	540,000	
Inventory (ending)	180,000	
Inventory (beginning)		120,000
Purchases		600,000

To adjust inventory, close the purchases account, and record cost of goods sold.

This entry adjusts the inventory account to the correct period-end amount, closes the temporary purchases account, and records the residual as cost of goods sold. Now let's compare the two inventory accounting systems.

A Comparison of the Perpetual and Periodic Inventory Systems

Beginning inventory plus net purchases during the period is the cost of goods available for sale. The main difference between a perpetual and a periodic system is that the periodic system allocates cost of goods available for sale between ending inventory and cost of goods sold only (periodically) *at the end of the period*. In contrast, the perpetual system performs this allocation by decreasing inventory and increasing cost of goods sold (perpetually) *each time goods are sold*.

   The impact on the financial statements of choosing one system over the other generally is not significant. The choice between the two approaches usually is motivated by management control considerations as well as the comparative costs of implementation. Perpetual systems can provide more information about the dollar amounts of inventory levels on a continuous basis. They

Learning objective 1
Explain the difference between a perpetual inventory system and a periodic inventory system.

also facilitate the preparation of interim financial statements by providing fairly accurate information without the necessity of a physical count of inventory.

A perpetual system provides more timely information but generally is more costly.

On the other hand, a perpetual system may be more expensive to implement than a periodic system. This is particularly true for inventories consisting of large numbers of low-cost items. Perpetual systems are more workable with inventories of high-cost items such as construction equipment or automobiles. However, with the help of computers and electronic sales devices such as cash register scanners, the perpetual inventory system is now available to many small businesses that previously could not afford them and is economically feasible for a broader range of inventory items than before.

The periodic system is less costly to implement during the period but requires a physical count before ending inventory and cost of goods sold can be determined. This makes the preparation of interim financial statements more costly unless an inventory estimation technique is used.[2] And, perhaps most importantly, the inventory monitoring features provided by a perpetual system are not available. However, it is important to remember that a perpetual system involves the tracking of both inventory quantities *and* costs. Many companies that determine costs only periodically employ systems to constantly monitor inventory quantities.

What is Included in Inventory?

Physical Quantities Included in Inventory

Learning objective 2
Explain which physical quantities of goods should be included in inventory.

Regardless of the system used, the measurement of inventory and cost of goods sold starts with determining the physical quantities of goods. Typically, determining the physical quantity that should be included in inventory is a simple matter because it consists of items in the possession of the company. However, in some situations the identification of items that should be included in inventory is more difficult. Consider, for example, goods in transit and goods on consignment.

Goods in Transit.   At the end of a reporting period, it's important to ensure a proper inventory cutoff. This means determining the ownership of goods that are in transit between the company and its customers as well as between the company and its suppliers. For example, in December 1997, the Lothridge Wholesale Beverage Company sold goods to the Jabbar Company. The goods were shipped on December 29, 1997, and arrived at Jabbar's warehouse on January 3, 1998. The fiscal year-end for both companies is December 31.

Inventory shipped **f.o.b. shipping point** is included in the purchaser's inventory as soon as the merchandise is shipped.

Should the merchandise shipped to Jabbar be recorded as a sale by Lothridge and a purchase by Jabbar in 1997 and thus included in Jabbar's 1997 ending inventory? Should recording the sale/purchase be delayed until 1998 and the merchandise be included in Lothridge's 1997 ending inventory? The answer depends on who owns the goods at December 31. Ownership depends on the terms of the agreement between the two companies. If the goods are shipped **f.o.b. (free on board) shipping point**, then legal title to the goods changes hands at the point of shipment when the seller delivers the goods to the common carrier (for example, a trucking company), and the purchaser is responsible for shipping costs and transit insurance. In that case, Lothridge records the sale in 1997 and Jabbar records a 1997 purchase and includes the goods in 1997 ending inventory even though the company is not in physical possession of the goods on the last day of the fiscal year.

Inventory shipped **f.o.b. destination** is included in the purchaser's inventory only after it reaches the purchaser's location.

On the other hand, if the goods are shipped **f.o.b. destination**, the seller is responsible for shipping and legal title does not pass until the goods arrive at their destination (the customer's location). In our example, Lothridge includes the merchandise in its 1997 ending inventory and the sale is recorded in 1998. Jabbar records the purchase in 1998.

Goods on Consignment.   Sometimes a company arranges for another company to sell its product under **consignment**. The goods are physically transferred to the other company (the consignee), but the transferor (consignor) retains legal title. If the consignee can't find a buyer, the goods are returned to the consignor. If a buyer is found, the consignee remits the selling price (less commission and approved expenses) to the consignor.

[2]In Chapter 9 we discuss inventory estimation techniques that avoid the necessity of a physical count to determine ending inventory and cost of goods sold.

Because risk is retained by the consignor, the sale is not complete until an eventual sale to a third party occurs. As a result, goods held on consignment generally are not included in the consignee's inventory. While in stock, they belong to the consignor and should be included in inventory of the consignor even though not in the company's physical possession. A sale is recorded by the consignor only when the goods are sold by the consignee and title passes to the customer.

Now that we've considered which goods are part of inventory, let's examine the types of costs that should be associated with those inventory quantities.

Expenditures Included in Inventory

As mentioned earlier, the cost of inventory includes all necessary expenditures to acquire the inventory and bring it to its desired condition and location for sale or for use in the manufacturing process. Obviously, the cost includes the purchase price of the goods. But usually the cost of acquiring inventory also includes freight charges on incoming goods borne by the buyer,[3] insurance costs incurred by the buyer while the goods are in transit (if shipped f.o.b. shipping point), and the costs of unloading, unpacking, and preparing merchandise inventory for sale or raw materials inventory for use. For practical reasons, though, some of these expenditures often are not included in inventory cost but are expensed as incurred if they are immaterial or impractical to associate with particular units of inventory (for example, unloading and unpacking costs).

Freight-In on Purchases.   Freight-in on purchases is commonly included in the cost of inventory. These costs clearly are necessary to get the inventory in location for sale or use and can generally be associated with particular goods. Freight costs are added to the inventory account in a perpetual system. In a periodic system, freight costs generally are added to a temporary account called **freight-in** or **transportation-in**, which is added to purchases in determining net purchases. The account is closed to cost of goods sold along with purchases and other components of cost of goods sold at the end of the reporting period (See Illustration 8–4 on page 322). From an accounting system perspective, freight-in also could be added to the purchases account. From a control perspective, by recording freight-in as a separate item, management can more easily track its freight costs. The same perspectives pertain to purchases returns and purchase discounts, which are discussed below.

Purchase Returns.   In Chapter 7 we discussed merchandise returns from the perspective of the selling company. We now address returns from the buyer's point of view. You may recall that the seller views a return as a reduction of net sales. Likewise, a buyer views a return as a reduction of net purchases. When the buyer returns goods to the seller, a **purchase return** is recorded. In a perpetual inventory system, this means a reduction in both inventory and accounts payable (if the account has not yet been paid) at the time of the return. In a periodic system an account called *purchase returns* temporarily accumulates these amounts. Purchase returns are subtracted from purchases when determining net purchases. The account is closed to cost of goods sold at the end of the reporting period.

Purchase Discounts.   Cash discounts also were discussed from the seller's perspective in Chapter 7. These discounts really are quick-payment discounts because they represent reductions in the amount to be paid by the buyer in the event payment is made within a specified period of time. The amount of the discount and the time period within which it's available are conveyed by cryptic terms like 2/10, n/30 (meaning a 2% discount if paid within 10 days, otherwise full payment within 30 days). As with the seller, the purchaser can record these **purchase discounts** using either the **gross method** or the **net method**. Consider Illustration 8–3 which is similar to the cash discount illustration in Chapter 7.

Goods held on **consignment** are included in the inventory of the consignor until sold by the consignee.

Learning objective 3
Determine the expenditures that should be included in the cost of inventory.

Expenditures necessary to bring inventory to its condition and location for sale or use are included in its cost.

The cost of **freight-in** paid by the purchaser generally is part of the cost of inventory.

A **purchase return** represents a reduction of net purchases.

Purchase discounts represent reductions in the amount to be paid if remittance is made within a designated period of time.

---

[3]Shipping charges on outgoing goods are related to the selling activity and are reported as a selling expense when incurred, not as part of inventory cost.

ILLUSTRATION   8–3

Purchase Discounts

PERIODIC INVENTORY

On October 5, 1997, the Lothridge Wholesale Beverage Company purchased merchandise at a price of $20,000. The repayment terms are stated as 2/10, n/30. Lothridge paid $13,720 ($14,000 less the 2% cash discount) on October 14 and the remaining balance of $6,000 on November 4. Lothridge employs a periodic inventory system.

The gross and net methods of recording the purchase and cash payment are compared as follows:

Gross Method			Net Method		
October 5, 1997					
Purchases*	20,000		Purchases*	19,600	
Accounts payable		20,000	Accounts payable		19,600
October 14, 1997					
Accounts payable	14,000		Accounts payable	13,720	
Purchase discounts* . . .		280	Cash		13,720
Cash		13,720			
November 4, 1997					
Accounts payable	6,000		Accounts payable	5,880	
Cash		6,000	Interest expense	120	
			Cash		6,000

*The inventory account is used in a perpetual system.

> By either method, net purchases is reduced by discounts taken.

> Discounts not taken are included as purchases using the gross method and as interest expense using the net method.

> The **gross method** views discounts not taken as part of inventory cost.

> The **net method** considers discounts not taken as interest expense.

Conceptually, the gross method views a discount not taken as part of the cost of inventory. The net method considers the cost of inventory to include the net, after-discount amount and any discounts not taken are reported as *interest expense*.[4] The discount is viewed as compensation to the seller for providing financing to the buyer.

Purchase discounts recorded under the gross method are subtracted from purchases when determining net purchases. The account is a temporary account that is closed to cost of goods sold at the end of the reporting period. Under the perpetual inventory system, purchase discounts are treated as a reduction in the inventory account.

The effect on the financial statements of the difference between the two methods usually is immaterial. Net income over time will be the same using either method. There will, however, be a difference in gross profit between the two methods equal to the amount of discounts not taken. In the preceding illustration, $120 in discounts not taken is included as interest expense using the net method and cost of goods sold using the gross method.

Illustration 8–4 compares the perpetual and periodic inventory systems, using the net method.

ILLUSTRATION   8–4

**Inventory Transactions—
Perpetual and Periodic
Systems**

The Lothridge Wholesale Beverage Company purchases soft drinks from producers and then sells them to retailers. The company began 1997 with merchandise inventory of $120,000 on hand. During 1997 additional merchandise is purchased on account at a cost of $600,000. Lothridge's suppliers offer credit terms of 2/10, n/30. All discounts were taken. Lothridge uses the net method to record purchase discounts. All purchases are made f.o.b. shipping point. Freight charges paid by Lothridge totaled $16,000. Merchandise costing $20,000 (net of discounts) was returned to suppliers for credit. Sales for the year, all on account, totaled $830,000. The cost of the soft drinks sold is $550,000. $154,000 of inventory remained on hand at the end of 1997.

The above transactions are recorded in summary form according to both the perpetual and periodic inventory systems as follows:

Perpetual System		Periodic System	
Purchases	($ in 000s)		
Inventory ($600 × 98%) . . .	588	Purchases ($600 × 98%) . .	588
Accounts payable	588	Accounts payable	588

---

[4]An alternative treatment is to debit an expense account called *purchase discounts lost* rather than interest expense. This enables a company to more easily identify the forgone discounts.

ILLUSTRATION   8-4

**Inventory Transactions—
Perpetual and Periodic
Systems—continued**

Perpetual System			Periodic System		
Freight					
Inventory	16		Freight-in	16	
Cash		16	Cash		16
Returns					
Accounts payable	20		Accounts payable	20	
Inventory		20	Purchase returns		20
Sales					
Accounts receivable	830		Accounts receivable	830	
Sales revenue		830	Sales revenue		830
Cost of goods sold	550		No entry		
Inventory		550			
End of period					
No Entry			Cost of goods sold (below)	550	
			Inventory (ending)	154	
			Purchase returns	20	
			Inventory (beginning) ..		120
			Purchases		588
			Freight-in		16

Supporting schedule:

Cost of goods sold:		
Beginning inventory		$ 120
Purchases	$588	
Less: Returns	(20)	
Plus: Freight-in	16	
Net purchases		584
Cost of goods available		704
Less: Ending inventory		(154)
Cost of goods sold		$ 550

Inventory Cost Flow Assumptions

Regardless of whether the perpetual or periodic system is used, it's necessary to assign dollar amounts to the physical quantities of goods sold and goods remaining in ending inventory. Unless each item of inventory is specifically identified and traced through the system, assigning dollars is accomplished by making an assumption regarding how goods (and their associated costs) flow through the system. We examine the common cost flow assumptions next. In previous illustrations, dollar amounts of the cost of goods sold and the cost of ending inventory were assumed known. However, if various portions of inventory are acquired at different costs, we need a way to decide which units were sold and which remain in inventory. Illustration 8–5 will help explain.

ILLUSTRATION   8-5

Cost Flow

> Goods available for sale
> include beginning
> inventory plus purchases.

The Browning Company began 1997 with $22,000 of inventory. The cost of beginning inventory (BI) is composed of 4,000 units purchased for $5.50 each. Merchandise transactions during 1997 were as follows:

	Purchases		
Date of Purchase	Units	Unit Cost*	Total Cost
Jan. 17	1,000	$6.00	$ 6,000
Mar. 22	3,000	7.00	21,000
Oct. 15	3,000	7.50	22,500
Totals	7,000		$49,500

*includes purchase price and cost of freight.

Sales	
Date of Sale	Units
Jan. 10	2,000
Apr. 15	1,500
Nov. 20	3,000
Total	6,500

As the data show, 7,000 units were purchased during 1997 at various prices and 6,500 units were sold. What is the cost of the 6,500 units sold? If all units, including beginning inventory, were purchased at the same price, then the answer would be simple. However, that rarely is the case.

The year started with 4,000 units, 7,000 units were purchased, and 6,500 units were sold. This means 4,500 units remain in ending inventory. This allocation of units available for sale is depicted in Graphic 8–3.

GRAPHIC   8 – 3

Allocation of Units Available

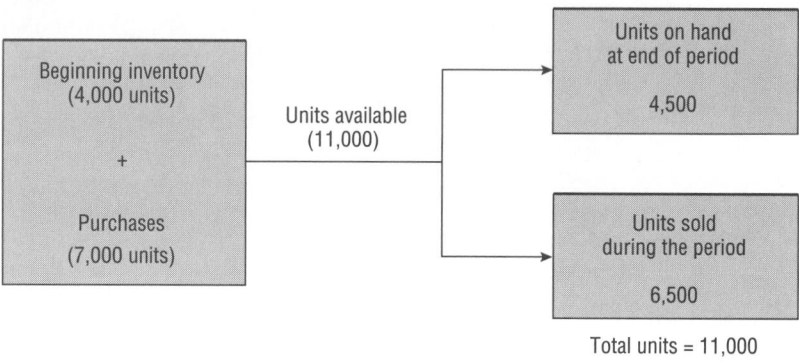

If a periodic system is used, what is the cost of the 4,500 units in ending inventory? In other words, which of the 11,000 (4,000 + 7,000) units available for sale were sold? Are they the more expensive ones bought toward the end of the year, or the less costly ones acquired before prices increased? Using the numbers given, let's consider the question as follows:

Beginning inventory (4,000 units @ $5.50)	$22,000
Plus: Purchases (7,000 units @ various prices)	49,500
Cost of goods available for sale (11,000 units)	$71,500
Less: Ending inventory (4,500 units @ ?)	?
Cost of goods sold (6,500 units @ ?)	?

The $71,500 in cost of goods available for sale must be allocated to ending inventory and cost of goods sold. The allocation decision is depicted in Graphic 8–4.

GRAPHIC   8 – 4

Allocation of Cost of Goods Available

Let's turn our attention now to the various inventory methods that can be used to achieve this allocation.

Specific Identification

It's sometimes possible for each unit sold during the period or each unit on hand at the end of the period to be matched with its actual cost. Actual costs can be determined by reference to the invoice representing the purchase of the item. This method is used frequently by companies

Learning objective 4
Differentiate between the specific identification, FIFO, LIFO, and average cost methods used to determine the cost of ending inventory and cost of goods sold.

The **specific identification method** is not feasible for most inventories.

selling unique, expensive products with low sales volume which makes it relatively easy and economically feasible to associate each item with its actual cost. For example, automobiles have unique serial numbers that can be used to match a specific auto with the invoice identifying the actual purchase price.

The **specific identification method,** however, is not feasible for many types of products either because items are not uniquely identifiable or because it is too costly to match a specific purchase price with each item sold or each item remaining in ending inventory. Most companies use cost flow methods to determine cost of goods sold and ending inventory. Cost flow methods are based on assumptions about how inventory might flow in and out of a company. However, it's important to note that the actual flow of a company's inventory does not have to correspond to the cost flow assumed. The various motivating factors that influence management's choice among alternative methods are discussed later in this chapter. We now explore the three most common cost flow methods: average cost, first-in, first-out (FIFO) and last-in, first-out (LIFO).

Average Cost

The **average cost method** assumes that items sold and items in ending inventory come from a mixture of all the goods available for sale.

The **average cost method** assumes that cost of goods sold and ending inventory consist of a mixture of all the goods available for sale. The average unit cost applied to goods sold or to ending inventory is not simply an average of the various unit costs of purchases during the period but an average unit cost *weighted* by the number of units acquired at the various unit prices.

Periodic Average Cost.   In a periodic inventory system, this weighted average is calculated at the end of the period as follows:

$$\text{Weighted-average unit cost} = \frac{\text{Cost of goods available for sale}}{\text{Quantity available for sale}}$$

The calculation of average cost is demonstrated in Illustration 8–5a using data from Illustration 8–5.

ILLUSTRATION   8–5a

Average Cost—Periodic Inventory System

Beginning inventory (4,000 units @ $5.50)	$22,000
Plus: Purchases (7,000 units @ various prices)	49,500
Cost of goods available for sale (11,000 units)	71,500
Less: Ending inventory (determined below)	(29,250)
Cost of goods sold (6,500 units)	$42,250

Cost of ending inventory:

$$\text{Weighted-average unit cost} = \frac{\$71,500}{11,000 \text{ units}} = \$6.50$$

4,500 units $\times$ $6.50 = $29,250

Cost of goods sold also could be determined directly by multiplying the weighted-average unit cost of $6.50 by the number of units sold ($6.50 $\times$ 6,500 = $42,250).

Perpetual Average Cost.   The weighted-average unit cost in a perpetual inventory system becomes a moving-average unit cost. A new weighted-average unit cost is calculated each time additional units are *purchased.* The average is determined after each purchase by dividing the cost of goods available for sale by the total number of units available for sale. This average is then used to cost any units sold before the next purchase is made. The moving-average concept is applied in Illustration 8–5b.

ILLUSTRATION   8–5b

Average Cost—Perpetual Inventory System

In a perpetual inventory system, the average cost method is applied by computing a moving-average unit cost each time additional inventory is purchased.

Date	Purchased	Sold	Balance
Beginning inventory	4,000 @ $5.50 = $22,000		4,000 @ $5.50 $22,000
Jan. 10		2,000 @ $5.50 = $11,000	
			2,000 @ $5.50 $11,000
Jan. 17	1,000 @ $6.00 = $6,000		$11,000 + $6,000 = $17,000
			2,000 + 1,000 = 3,000 units
	$\frac{\$17,000}{3,000 \text{ units}}$ = $5.667/unit		
Mar. 22	3,000 @ $7.00 = $21,000		$17,000 + $21,000 = $38,000
			3,000 + 3,000 = 6,000 units
	$\frac{\$38,000}{6,000 \text{ units}}$ = $6.333/unit		
Apr. 15		1,500 @ $6.333 = $9,500	
			4,500 @ $6.333 = $28,500
Oct. 15	3,000 @ $7.50 = $22,500		$28,500 + $22,500 = $51,000
			4,500 + 3,000 = 7,500 units
	$\frac{\$51,000}{7,500 \text{ units}}$ = $6.80/unit		
Nov. 20		3,000 @ $6.80 = $20,400	
			4,500 @ $6.80 = **$30,600**
	Total cost of goods sold	= **$40,900**	

On January 17, the new average of $5.667 (rounded) is calculated by dividing the $17,000 cost of goods available ($11,000 from beginning inventory + $6,000 purchased on January 17) by the 3,000 units available (2,000 units from beginning inventory + 1,000 units acquired on January 17). The average is updated to $6.333 (rounded) with the March 22 purchase. The 1,500 units sold on April 15 are then costed at the average cost of $6.333.

Periodic average cost and perpetual average cost generally produce different allocations to cost of goods sold and ending inventory.

First-In, First-Out (FIFO)

The **first-in, first-out (FIFO)** method assumes that items sold are those that were acquired first.

Ending inventory applying FIFO consists of the most recently acquired items.

The **first-in, first-out (FIFO)** method assumes that units sold are the first units acquired. Beginning inventory is sold first, followed by purchases during the period in the chronological order of their acquisition. In our illustration, 6,500 units were sold during 1997. Applying FIFO, these would be the 4,000 units in beginning inventory, the 1,000 units purchased on January 17, and 1,500 of the 3,000 units from the March 22 purchase. By default, ending inventory consists of the most recently acquired units. In this case, the 4,500 units in ending inventory consist of the 3,000 units purchased on October 15, and 1,500 of the 3,000 units purchased on March 22. Graphically, the flow is as follows:

FIFO flow

```
                Units Available
        BI          4,000  ⎫
        Jan. 17     1,000  ⎬  6,500 units sold
        Mar. 22     1,500  ⎭

        Mar. 22     1,500  ⎫
                           ⎬  4,500 units in ending inventory
        Oct. 15     3,000  ⎭
        Total      11,000
```

Periodic FIFO.   Recall that we determine physical quantities on hand in a periodic inventory system by taking a physical count. Costing the 4,500 units in ending inventory this way automatically gives us the cost of goods sold as well. Using the numbers from our illustration, we determine cost of goods sold to be $38,500 by subtracting the $33,000 ending inventory from $71,500 cost of goods available for sale as shown in Illustration 8–5c.

ILLUSTRATION   8–5c

FIFO—Periodic Inventory System

Beginning inventory (4,000 units @ $5.50)	$22,000
Plus: Purchases (7,000 units @ various prices)	49,500
Cost of goods available for sale (11,000 units)	71,500
Less: Ending inventory (determined below)	(33,000)
Cost of goods sold (6,500 units)	$38,500

Cost of ending inventory:

Date of Purchase	Units	Unit Cost	Total Cost
Mar. 22	1,500	$7.00	$10,500
Oct. 15	3,000	7.50	22,500
Total	4,500		$33,000

Of course, the 6,500 units sold could be costed directly as follows:

Date of Purchase	Units	Unit Cost	Total Cost
Beg. inv.	4,000	$5.50	$22,000
Jan. 17	1,000	6.00	6,000
Mar. 22	1,500	7.00	10,500
Total	6,500		$38,500

Perpetual FIFO. The same ending inventory and cost of goods sold amounts are always produced in a perpetual inventory system as in a periodic inventory system when FIFO is used. This is because the same units and costs are first in and first out whether cost of goods sold is determined as each sale is made or at the end of the period as a residual amount. The application of FIFO in a perpetual system is shown in Illustration 8–5d.

ILLUSTRATION   8–5d

FIFO—Perpetual Inventory System

Date	Purchased	Sold	Balance	
Beginning inventory	4,000 @ $5.50 = $22,000		4,000 @ $5.50	$22,000
Jan. 10		2,000 @ $5.50 = $11,000	2,000 @ $5.50	$11,000
Jan. 17	1,000 @ $6.00 = $ 6,000		2,000 @ $5.50 1,000 @ $6.00	$17,000
Mar. 22	3,000 @ $7.00 = $21,000		2,000 @ $5.50 1,000 @ $6.00 3,000 @ $7.00	$38,000
Apr. 15		1,500 @ $5.50 = $ 8,250	500 @ $5.50 1,000 @ $6.00 3,000 @ $7.00	$29,750
Oct. 15	3,000 @ $7.50 = $22,500		500 @ $5.50 1,000 @ $6.00 3,000 @ $7.00 3,000 @ $7.50	$52,250
Nov. 20		500 @ $5.50 + 1,000 @ $6.00 + 1,500 @ $7.00 = $19,250	1,500 @ $7.00 3,000 @ $7.50	**$33,000**
	Total cost of goods sold	= **$38,500**		

Last In, First Out (LIFO)

The **last-in, first-out (LIFO) method** assumes that items sold are those that were most recently acquired.

Ending inventory applying LIFO consists of the items acquired first.

The **last-in, first-out (LIFO) method** assumes that the units sold are the most recent units purchased. In our illustration, the 6,500 units assumed sold would be the 6,500 units acquired most recently: the 3,000 units acquired on October 15, the 3,000 units acquired on March 22, and 500 of the 1,000 units purchased on January 17. Ending inventory, then, consists of the units acquired first; in this case, the 4,000 units from beginning inventory and 500 of the 1,000 units purchased on January 17. Graphically, the flow is as follows:

LIFO flow

Units Available

BI	4,000
Jan. 17	500

} 4,500 units in ending inventory

Jan. 17	500
Mar. 22	3,000
Oct. 15	3,000

} 6,500 units sold

Total	11,000

Periodic LIFO.   The cost of ending inventory, determined to be $25,000 (calculated below) by the LIFO assumption and using a periodic system is subtracted from cost of goods available for sale to arrive at the cost of goods sold of $46,500 as shown in Illustration 8–5e.

ILLUSTRATION   8–5e

LIFO—Periodic Inventory System

Beginning inventory (4,000 units @ $5.50) $22,000
Plus: Purchases (7,000 units @ various prices)   49,500
Cost of goods available for sale (11,000 units)   71,500
Less: Ending inventory (determined below)   (25,000)
Cost of goods sold (6,500 units) $46,500

Cost of ending inventory:

Date of Purchase	Units	Unit Cost	Total Cost
Beginning inventory	4,000	$5.50	$22,000
Jan. 17	500	6.00	3,000
Total	4,500		$25,000

The 6,500 sold could be costed directly as follows:

Date of Purchase	Units	Unit Cost	Total Cost
Jan. 17	500	$6.00	$ 3,000
Mar. 22	3,000	7.00	21,000
Oct. 15	3,000	7.50	22,500
Total	6,500		$46,500

Perpetual LIFO.   The application of LIFO in a perpetual system is shown in Illustration 8–5f. Each time inventory is purchased or sold, the LIFO layers are adjusted. For example, after the March 22 purchase, we have three layers of inventory at different prices listed in the chronological order of their purchase. When 1,500 units are sold on April 15, we assume they come from the most recent layer of 3,000 units purchased at $7.00.

ILLUSTRATION   8–5f

LIFO—Perpetual Inventory System

Date	Purchased	Sold	Balance	
Beginning inventory	4,000 @ $5.50 = $22,000		4,000 @ $5.50	$22,000
Jan. 10		2,000 @ $5.50 = $11,000	2,000 @ $5.50	$11,000
Jan. 17	1,000 @ $6.00 = $ 6,000		2,000 @ $5.50	
			1,000 @ $6.00	$17,000
Mar. 22	3,000 @ $7.00 = $21,000		2,000 @ $5.50	
			1,000 @ $6.00	$38,000
			3,000 @ $7.00	
Apr. 15		1,500 @ $7.00 = $10,500	2,000 @ $5.50	
			1,000 @ $6.00	$27,500
			1,500 @ $7.00	
Oct. 15	3,000 @ $7.50 = $22,500		2,000 @ $5.50	
			1,000 @ $6.00	
			1,500 @ $7.00	$50,000
			3,000 @ $7.50	
Nov. 20		3,000 @ $7.50 = $22,500	2,000 @ $5.50	
			1,000 @ $6.00	**$27,500**
			1,500 @ $7.00	
	Total cost of goods sold	= **$44,000**		

Perpetual LIFO generally
results in cost of goods sold
and inventory amounts that
are different from those
obtained by applying
periodic LIFO.

Notice that $44,000 of the cost of goods available for sale is allocated to cost of goods sold by LIFO and $27,500 to ending inventory (the balance after the last transaction), which is different from the periodic LIFO result of $46,500 and $25,000. Unlike FIFO, applying LIFO in a perpetual inventory system will generally result in an ending inventory and cost of goods sold different from the allocation arrived at applying LIFO in a periodic system. Periodic LIFO applies the last-in, first-out concept to total sales and total purchases only at the conclusion of the reporting period. Perpetual LIFO applies the same concept, but several times during the period—every time a sale is made.

For example, when 2,000 units are sold on January 10, perpetual LIFO costs those units at $5.50, the beginning inventory unit cost. Periodic LIFO, by contrast, would be applied at year-end. By the end of the year, enough purchases have been made that the beginning inventory would be assumed to remain intact, and the January 10 units sold would be costed at a more recent price.

Comparison of Cost Flow Methods

The three cost flow methods are compared below assuming a periodic inventory system.

Comparison of cost flow
methods

	Average	FIFO	LIFO
Cost of goods sold	$42,250	$38,500	$46,500
Ending inventory	29,250	33,000	25,000
Total	$71,500	$71,500	$71,500

Notice that the average cost method in this example produces amounts that fall in between the FIFO and LIFO amounts for both cost of goods sold and ending inventory. This will usually be the case. Whether it will be FIFO or LIFO that produces the highest or lowest value of cost of goods sold and ending inventory depends on the pattern of the actual unit cost changes during the period.

If unit costs are increasing,
LIFO will result in a higher
cost of goods sold and
lower ending inventory than
FIFO.

During periods of generally rising costs, as in our example, FIFO results in a lower cost of goods sold than LIFO because the lower costs of the earliest purchases are assumed sold. LIFO cost of goods sold will include the more recent higher unit cost purchases. On the other hand, FIFO ending inventory includes the most recent higher cost purchases which results in a higher ending inventory than LIFO. LIFO ending inventory includes the lower costs of the earliest purchases. Conversely, if costs are declining, then FIFO will result in a higher cost of goods sold and lower ending inventory than LIFO.[5]

OPENING CASE

Question 1

Each of the three methods is permissible according to generally accepted accounting principles and are used frequently. Also, a company need not use the same method for all of its inventory. For example, Federal Paper Company, Inc., uses LIFO for its bleached paperboard, pulp, and wood products, and the FIFO method for recycled paperboard. Graphic 8–5 shows the results of a survey of inventory methods used by large public companies in 1994 and 1973. FIFO is the most popular method in both periods, but there has been a dramatic increase in the use of LIFO since the earlier period.[6]

GRAPHIC   8–5

**Inventory cost flow methods
used in practice**

	1994		1973	
Methods	# of Companies	% of Companies	# of Companies	% of Companies
FIFO	417	42%	394	43%
LIFO	351	35	150	16
Average	192	19	235	25
Other*	42	4	148	16
Total	1,002	100%	927	100%

*"Other" includes the specific identification method, the retail inventory method (which is discussed in Chapter 9), and miscellaneous less popular methods.

---

[5]The differences between the various methods also hold when a perpetual inventory system is used.
[6]*Accounting Trends and Techniques—1995* and *1974* (New York: AICPA, 1995 and 1974).

Inventory measurement techniques vary widely across different countries. For example, in Germany both LIFO and FIFO are permitted if they correspond to the physical flow of goods. In the United Kingdom, Norway, Denmark, Hong Kong, Israel, and Australia, LIFO is either not permitted or not commonly used for financial reporting purposes. In Japan and Mexico an acceptable technique is to use the latest purchase price to measure ending inventory.

Decision Makers' Perspective—Factors Influencing Method Choice

Learning objective 5
Discuss the factors affecting a company's choice of inventory method.

What factors motivate companies to choose one method over another? What factors have caused the increased popularity of LIFO? Choosing among alternative accounting methods is a complex issue. Often such choices are not made in isolation but in such a way that the combination of inventory cost flow assumptions, depreciation methods, pension assumptions, and other choices meet a particular objective. Also, many believe managers sometimes make these choices to maximize their own personal benefits rather than those of the company or its external constituents. But regardless of the motive, the impact on reported numbers is an important consideration in each choice of method. The inventory choice determines (a) how closely reported costs reflect the actual physical flow of inventory, (b) the timing of reported income and income tax expense, and (c) how well costs are matched with associated revenues.

Physical Flow.   If a company wanted to choose a method that most closely approximates specific identification, then the actual physical flow of inventory in and out of the company would motivate the choice of method.

For example, companies often attempt to sell the oldest goods in inventory first for some of their products. This certainly is the case with perishable goods such as many grocery items. The FIFO method best mirrors the physical flow in these situations. LIFO might be used for products like coal that are stored in piles or bins. In these cases, when inventory is sold or used, the items taken from the top of the pile are the most recent items acquired. The average cost method might be used for liquids such as chemicals where items sold are taken from a mixture of inventory acquired at different times and different prices. There is no requirement that companies choose an inventory method that approximates actual physical flow and few companies make the choice on this basis.

> A company is not required to choose an inventory method that approximates actual physical flow.

Income Taxes and Net Income.   If the unit cost of inventory changes during a period, the inventory method chosen can have a significant effect on the amount of income reported by the company to external parties and also on the amount of income taxes paid to the Internal Revenue Service (IRS) and state and local taxing authorities. Over the entire life of a company, cost of goods sold for all years will equal actual costs of items sold regardless of the inventory method used. However, as we have discussed, different inventory methods can produce significantly different results in each particular year.

When prices rise and inventory quantities are not decreasing, LIFO produces a higher cost of goods sold and therefore lower net income than the other methods. The company's income tax returns will report a lower taxable income using LIFO and lower taxes will be paid currently. Taxes are not reduced permanently, only deferred. The reduced amount will be paid to the taxing authorities when either the unit cost of inventory or the quantity of inventory subsequently declines. However, we know from our discussion of the time value of money that it is advantageous to save a dollar today even if it must be paid back in the future. Recall from the recent survey results exhibited earlier that the popularity of LIFO increased significantly between 1973 and 1994. The main reason for this increased popularity is attributable to high inflation (increasing prices) during the 1970s which motivated many companies to switch to LIFO in order to gain this tax benefit.

> Many companies choose LIFO in order to reduce income taxes in periods when prices are rising.

A corporation's taxable income comprises revenues, expenses (including cost of goods sold), gains, and losses as measured according to the regulations of the appropriate taxing authority.

If a company uses LIFO to measure its taxable income, IRS regulations require that LIFO also be used to measure income reported to investors and creditors (the **LIFO conformity rule**).

OPENING CASE

Question 2

Income before tax as reported on the income statement does not always equal taxable income. In some cases, differences are caused by the use of different measurement methods.[7] However, IRS regulations, which determine federal taxable income, require that if a company uses LIFO to measure taxable income, the company also must use LIFO for external financial reporting. This is known as the **LIFO conformity rule** with respect to inventory methods.

Because of the LIFO conformity rule, to obtain the tax advantages of using LIFO in periods of rising prices, lower net income is reported to shareholders, creditors, and other external parties. The income tax motivation for using LIFO may be offset by a desire to report higher net income. Reported net income could have an effect on a corporation's share price[8], on bonuses paid to management, or on debt agreements with lenders. For example, research has indicated that the managers of companies with bonus plans tied to income measures are more likely to choose accounting methods that maximize their bonuses (often those that increase net income).[9]

In 1981, the LIFO conformity rule was liberalized to permit LIFO users to present designated supplemental disclosures, allowing a company to report in a note the effect of using another method on inventory valuation rather than LIFO. For example, Graphic 8–6 shows the note disclosure provided by the Sara Lee Corporation included in the summary of significant accounting policies in its 1995 financial statements.[10]

GRAPHIC   8–6

Inventories disclosure—Sara Lee Corporation

Inventory valuation (in part)

(dollars in millions)
Inventories are valued at the lower of cost (in 1995, approximately 35% at last-in, first-out [LIFO] and the remainder at first-in, first-out [FIFO]) or market. Inventories recorded at LIFO were approximately $18 at July 1, 1995, $24 at July 2, 1994, and $38 at July 3, 1993, lower than if they had been valued at FIFO.

Proponents of LIFO argue that it results in a better match of revenues and expenses.

LIFO Liquidations.   Earlier in the text, we demonstrated the importance of matching revenues and expenses in creating an income statement that is useful in predicting future cash flows. If prices change during a period, then LIFO generally will provide a better match of revenues and expenses. Sales reflects the most recent selling prices, and cost of goods sold includes the costs of the most recent purchases. Graphic 8–7 shows the Vulcan Materials Company disclosure that was included in its summary of significant accounting policies.

[7]For example, a corporation can take advantage of incentives offered by Congress by deducting more depreciation in the early years of an asset's life on its federal income tax return than it reports on its income statement.

[8]The concept of capital market efficiency has been debated for many years. In an efficient capital market, the market is not fooled by differences in accounting method choice that do not translate into real cash flow differences. The only apparent cash flow difference caused by different inventory methods is the amount of income taxes paid currently. In an efficient market, we would expect the share price of a company that switched its method to LIFO and saved tax dollars to increase even though it reported lower net income than if LIFO had not been adopted. Research on this issue is mixed. For example, see William E. Ricks, "Market's Response to the 1974 LIFO Adoptions," *Journal of Accounting Research* (Autumn 1982), and Robert Moren Brown, "Short-Range Market Reaction to Changes to LIFO Using Preliminary Earnings Announcement Dates," *Journal of Accounting Research* (Spring 1980).

[9]For example, see P. M., Healy, "The Effect of Bonus Schemes on Accounting Decisions," *Journal of Accounting and Economics* (April 1985), and D. Dhaliwal, G. Salamon, and E. Smith, "The Effect of Owner Versus Management Control on the Choice of Accounting Methods," *Journal of Accounting and Economics* (July 1982).

[10]Sara Lee uses both the LIFO and FIFO inventory methods. Earlier in the chapter we pointed out that a company need not use the same inventory method for all of its inventory.

GRAPHIC   8–7

Inventory policy disclosure— Vulcan Materials Company

1 Inventories (in Part)

The Company uses the last-in, first-out (LIFO) method for most of its inventories because it results in a better matching of costs with revenues.

OPENING CASE

Question 3

A decline in inventory quantity results in LIFO liquidation profit in periods of rising costs.

For the same reason, though, inventory costs on the balance sheet with LIFO generally are out of date because they reflect old purchase transactions. It is not uncommon for a company's LIFO inventory balance to be based on unit costs actually incurred several years earlier.

This distortion sometimes carries over to the income statement as well. When inventory quantities decline during a period, then these out-of-date inventory layers are liquidated and the cost of goods sold will partially match noncurrent costs with current selling prices. If costs have been rising, LIFO liquidations produce higher net income than would have resulted if the liquidated inventory were included in cost of goods sold at current costs. The paper profits caused by including out-of-date, low costs in cost of goods sold is referred to as the effect on income of liquidations of LIFO inventory.

To illustrate this problem, consider the example in Illustration 8–6.

ILLUSTRATION   8–6

LIFO Liquidation

National Distributors, Inc., uses the LIFO inventory method. The company began 1997 with inventory of 10,000 units which cost $20 per unit. During 1997 30,000 units were purchased for $25 each and 35,000 units were sold.

National's LIFO cost of goods sold for 1997 consists of:

30,000 units @ $25 per unit =	$750,000
5,000 units @ $20 per unit =	100,000
35,000	$850,000

A material effect on net income of LIFO layer liquidation must be disclosed in a note.

Included in cost of goods sold are 5,000 units from beginning inventory that have now been liquidated. If the company had purchased at least 35,000 units, no liquidation would have occurred. Then cost of goods sold would have been $875,000 (35,000 units × $25 per unit) instead of $850,000. The difference between these two cost of goods sold figures is $25,000 ($875,000 – 850,000). This is the before tax income effect of the LIFO liquidation. Assuming a 40% income tax rate, the net effect of the liquidation is to increase net income by $15,000 [$25,000 × (1–.40)]. The lower the costs of the units liquidated, the more severe the effect on income.

A company must disclose in a note any material effect of **LIFO liquidation** on net income. For example, Graphic 8–8 shows the disclosure that accompanied recent financial statements of Shell Oil.

GRAPHIC   8–8

LIFO liquidation disclosure— Shell Oil

6. Inventories of Oils and Chemicals (in Part)

Partial liquidations of inventories valued on a LIFO basis improved 1995 and 1994 net income by $167 million and $29 million, respectively, . . .

In our illustration, National Distributors, Inc., would disclose that LIFO liquidations increased income by $15,000 in 1997, assuming that this effect on income is considered material.

We've discussed several factors that influence companies in their choice of inventory method. A company could be influenced by the actual physical flow of its inventory, by the effect of inventory method on reported net income and the amount of income taxes payable currently, or by a desire to provide a better match of expenses with revenues. You've seen that the direction of the change in unit costs determines the effect of using different methods on net income and income taxes. While the United States has experienced persistent inflation for many years (increases in the general price-level), the prices of many goods and services have experienced periods of declining prices (for example, personal computers).

Additional Consideration

LIFO Reserves

Many companies use LIFO for external reporting and income tax purposes but maintain their internal records using FIFO or average cost. The reasons for doing this might include: (1) the high recordkeeping costs of the LIFO method, (2) the existence of contractual agreements such as bonus or profit sharing plans that prohibit the use of LIFO in the calculation of net income, and (3) the need for FIFO or average cost information for pricing decisions.

Generally, the conversion to LIFO is performed at the end of the period and not entered into the company's records. However, some companies enter the results of the conversion—the difference between the internal method and LIFO—directly into the accounts as a contra (valuation) account to inventory. This contra account is called either the LIFO reserve or the LIFO allowance.

Occasionally, such companies report ending inventory valued using the internal method less the LIFO reserve to arrive at LIFO inventory reported on the balance sheet. For example, J.C. Penney Company, Inc., recently reported the following note:

Merchandise inventories ($ in millions)	1995	1994
Merchandise inventories, at lower of cost (FIFO) or market	$4,161	$4,123
LIFO reserve	(226)	(247)
Merchandise inventories, at LIFO cost	$3,935	$3,876

Note that this is merely another way of presenting the supplemental non-LIFO disclosures discussed previously.

CONCEPT REVIEW EXERCISE   INVENTORY COST FLOW METHODS

The Rogers Company began 1997 with an inventory of 10 million units of its principle product. These units cost $5 each. The following inventory transactions occurred during the first six months of 1997:

Date	Transaction
Feb. 15	Purchased, on account, 5 million units at a cost of $6.50 each.
March 20	Sold, on account, 8 million units at a selling price of $12 each.
April 30	Purchased, on account, 5 million units at a cost of $7 each.

On June 30, 1997, 12 million units were on hand.

Required:

1. Prepare journal entries to record the above transactions. The company uses a periodic inventory system.
2. Prepare the required adjusting entry on June 30, 1997, applying each of the following inventory methods:
   a. Average
   b. FIFO
   c. LIFO
3. Repeat requirement 1 assuming that the company uses a perpetual inventory system.

CONCEPT REVIEW EXERCISE   SOLUTION

1. Prepare journal entries to record the above transactions. The company uses a periodic inventory system.

Feb. 15	($ in millions)	
Purchases (5 million 3 $6.50)	32.5	
Accounts payable		32.5
To record the purchase of inventory.		

March 20		($ in millions)
Accounts receivable (8 million × $12)	96	
Sales revenue		96
To record sales on account.		

No entry is recorded for the cost of inventory sold

April 30		
Purchases (5 million × $7)	35	
Accounts payable		35
To record the purchase of inventory.		

2. Prepare the required adjusting entry on June 30, 1997, applying each method.

			($ in millions)	
Date	**Journal entry**	**Average**	**FIFO**	**LIFO**
June 30	Cost of goods sold (determined below)	47.0	40.0	54.5
	Inventory (ending – determined below)	70.5	77.5	63.0
	Inventory (beginning – [10 million 3 $5])	50.0	50.0	50.0
	Purchases ($32.5 million + $35 million)	67.5	67.5	67.5

Calculation of ending inventory and cost of goods sold: ($ in millions)

a. Average:

Beginning inventory (10 million units @ $5.00)	$ 50.0
Plus: Purchases (10 million units @ various prices)	67.5
Cost of goods available for sale (20 million units)	117.5
Less: Ending inventory (determined below)	(70.5)
Cost of goods sold	$ 47.0

Cost of ending inventory:

$$\text{Weighted average unit cost} = \frac{\$117.5 \text{ million}}{20 \text{ million units}} = \$5.875$$

12 million units × $5.875 = **$70.5 million**

b. FIFO:

Cost of goods available for sale (20 million units)	$117.5
Less: Ending inventory (determined below)	(77.5)
Cost of goods sold	$ 40.0

Cost of ending inventory:

Date of purchase	Units	Unit cost	Total cost
April 30	5 million	$7.00	$35.0
Feb. 15	5 million	6.50	32.5
Beg. inv.	2 million	5.00	10.0
Total	12 million		**$77.5**

c. LIFO:

Cost of goods available for sale (20 million units)	$117.5
Less: Ending inventory (determined below)	(63.0)
Cost of goods sold	$ 54.5

Cost of ending inventory:

Date of purchase	Units	Unit cost	Total cost
Beg. inv.	10 million	$5.00	$50.0
Feb. 15	2 million	6.50	13.0
Total	12 million		**$63.0**

3. Repeat requirement 1 assuming that the company uses a perpetual inventory system.

Feb. 15	($ in millions)
Inventory (5 million units × $6.50)	32.5
Accounts payable	32.5
To record the purchase of inventory.	
April 30	
Inventory (5 million units × $7.00)	35.0
Accounts payable	35.0
To record the purchase of inventory.	

($ in millions)

Journal entries—March 20	Average		FIFO		LIFO	
Accounts receivable (8 million × $12)	96.0		96.0		96.0	
Sales revenue		96.0		96.0		96.0
To record sales on account.						
Cost of goods sold (determined below)	44.0		40.0		47.5	
Inventory (determined below)		44.0		40.0		47.5
To record cost of goods sold.						

Calculation of cost of goods sold: ($, except unit costs, in millions)

a. Average:
    Cost of goods sold:

Date	Purchased	Sold	Balance
Beg. inv.	10 million @ $5.00		10 million @ $5.00 = $50.0
Feb. 15	5 million @ $6.50		

$$\frac{\$82.5 \text{ million}}{15 \text{ million units}} = \$5.50/\text{unit}$$

March 20	8 million @ $5.50 = **$44.0**	

b. FIFO:
    Cost of goods sold:

Units sold	Cost of Units Sold	Total Cost
8 million (from BI)	$5.00	$40.0

c. LIFO:
    Cost of goods sold:

Units sold	Cost of Units Sold	Total Cost
5 million (from Feb. 15 purchase)	$6.50	$32.5
3 million (from Beg. inventory)	5.00	15.0
8 million		**$47.5**

Decision Makers' Perspective— Financial Analysis

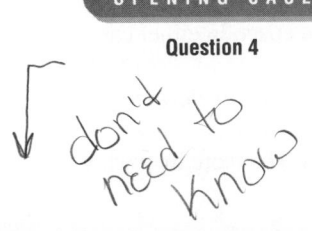

OPENING CASE

Question 4

The choice of inventory method is an important and complex management decision. The many factors affecting this decision were discussed in a previous section. The inventory method also affects the analysis of a company's liquidity and profitability by investors, creditors, and financial analysts. Analysts must make adjustments when evaluating companies that use different inventory methods. During periods of rising prices, we would expect a company using FIFO to report higher income than a LIFO or average cost company. If one of the companies being analyzed uses LIFO, precise adjustments can often be made using the supplemental disclosures provided by many LIFO companies. Recall that the LIFO conformity rule was liberalized to permit LIFO users to report in a note the effect of using a method other than LIFO for inventory valuation.

For example, the disclosure note exhibited on page 331 reveals that Sara Lee Corporation uses both the FIFO and LIFO inventory methods with 35% of its inventories valued using LIFO. Tyson Foods, Inc., values all of its inventory using FIFO. Both of these companies derive a significant portion of their revenues from the sale of food products. 1995 financial statement values for the two companies are as follows:

(dollars in millions)	Sara Lee Corporation		Tyson Foods, Inc.	
	1995	1994	1995	1994
Balance sheet:				
Inventories	$2,830	$2,567	$949	$754
	1995		1995	
Income statement:				
Net sales	$17,719		$5,511	
Cost of goods sold	11,023		4,423	

Supplemental LIFO disclosures can be used to convert LIFO inventory and cost of goods sold amounts.

We can convert Sara Lee's inventory and cost of goods sold to a 100% FIFO basis before comparing the two companies by using the information provided in Sara Lee's note on page 331. Inventories recorded at LIFO were approximately $18 million at July 1, 1995, and $24 million at July 2, 1994, lower than if they had been valued at FIFO:

	1995	1994
Inventories (as reported)	$2,830	$2,567
Add: Conversion to FIFO	18	24
Inventories (100% FIFO)	$2,848	$2,591

Cost of goods sold for 1995 would have been $6 million higher had Sara Lee used FIFO instead of LIFO. While beginning inventory would have been $24 million higher, ending inventory also would have been higher by $18 million. An increase in beginning inventory causes an increase in cost of goods sold, but an increase in ending inventory causes a decrease in cost of goods sold. Purchases for 1995 are the same regardless of the inventory valuation method used. 1995 cost of goods sold would have been $11,029 million ($11,023 + 6) if FIFO had been used for all inventories.

We can now use the 100% FIFO amounts to compare the two companies. Because cost of goods sold is higher by $6 million, income taxes and net income require adjustment before calculating any profitability ratio. Also, the converted inventory amounts can be used to compute liquidity ratios.

One important profitability indicator using cost of goods sold is **gross profit** or **gross margin,** which highlights the important relationship between net sales revenue and cost of goods sold. The **gross profit ratio** is computed as follows:

$$\text{Gross profit ratio} = \frac{\text{Gross profit}}{\text{Net sales}}$$

The gross profit ratio indicates the percentage of each sales dollar available to cover other expenses and provide a profit.

The higher the ratio, the higher the markup a company is able to achieve on its products. For example, a product that costs $100 that is sold for $150 provides a gross profit of $50 ($150 – 100) and a gross profit ratio of 33% ($50 ÷ $150). If that same product can be sold for $200, the gross profit increases to $100 and the gross profit ratio increases to 50% ($100 ÷ $200) and more dollars are available to cover expenses other than cost of goods sold.

The 1995 gross profit for Sara Lee, using the 100% FIFO amounts, is $6,690 ($17,719 – 11,029) and the gross profit ratio is 38% ($6,690 ÷ $17,719). The ratio for Tyson Foods is 20% ($5,511 – 4,423 = $1,088 ÷ $5,511), indicating that Sara Lee is able to sell its products at significantly higher markups than Tyson Foods. Sara Lee's percentage of each sales dollar available to cover other expenses and provide a profit is nearly twice as much as that of Tyson Foods.

Monitoring this ratio over time can provide valuable insights. For example, a declining ratio could indicate that the company is unable to offset rising costs with corresponding increases in sales price, or that sales prices are declining without a commensurate reduction in costs. In either case, the decline in the ratio has important implications for future profitability.

Chapter 4 introduced an important ratio, the **inventory turnover ratio,** which is designed to evaluate a company's effectiveness in managing its investment in inventory. The ratio shows the number of times the average inventory balance is sold during a reporting period. The more frequently a business is able to sell, or turn over its inventory, the lower its investment in inventory must be for a given level of sales. Usually, the higher the ratio the more profitable a company will be. Monitoring the inventory turnover ratio over time can highlight potential problems. A declining ratio generally is unfavorable and could be caused by the presence of obsolete or slow-moving products, or poor marketing and sales efforts.

Recall that the ratio is computed as follows:

$$\text{Inventory turnover ratio} = \frac{\text{Cost of goods sold}}{\text{Average inventory}}$$

We can divide the inventory turnover ratio into 365 days to compute the **average days in inventory**, which indicates the average number of days it normally takes to sell inventory.

For Sara Lee, the inventory turnover ratio for 1995 is 4.06 {$11,029 ÷ [($2,848 + 2,591) ÷ 2]} and the average days inventory is 90 days (365 ÷ 4.06). This compares to a turnover ratio of 5.19 {$4,423 ÷ [($949 + 754) ÷ 2]} and an average days inventory of 70 days (365 days ÷ 5.19) for Tyson Foods. It takes nearly 1.3 times as long for Sara Lee to turn over its inventory. Sara Lee's products command a higher markup (higher gross profit ratio) but take longer to sell (lower inventory turnover ratio) than the products of Tyson Foods.

Inventory increases that outrun increases in cost of goods sold might indicate difficulties in generating sales. These inventory buildups may also indicate that a company has obsolete or slow-moving inventory. This proposition was tested in an important academic research study. Professors Lev and Thiagarajan empirically demonstrated the importance of a set of 12 fundamental variables in valuing companies' common stock. The set of variables included inventory (change in inventory minus change in sales). The inventory variable was found to be a significant indicator of stock returns, particularly during high and medium inflation years.[11]

PART

B METHODS OF SIMPLIFYING LIFO

The recordkeeping costs of unit LIFO can be significant.

The LIFO method described and illustrated to this point is called *unit LIFO*[12] because the last-in, first-out concept is applied to individual units of inventory. One problem with unit LIFO is that it can be very costly to implement. It requires records of each unit of inventory. The costs of maintaining these records can be significant, particularly when a company has numerous individual units of inventory and when unit costs change often during a period.

Another disadvantage of unit LIFO is the possibility of LIFO liquidation.

In the previous section, a second disadvantage of unit LIFO was identified—the possibility that LIFO layers will be liquidated if the quantity of a particular inventory unit declines below its beginning balance. Even if a company's total inventory quantity is stable or increasing, if the quantity of any particular inventory unit declines, unit LIFO will liquidate all or a portion of a LIFO layer of inventory. When inventory quantity declines in a period of rising costs, noncurrent lower costs will be included in cost of goods sold and matched with current selling prices, resulting in LIFO liquidation profit.

This part of the chapter discusses techniques that can be used to significantly reduce the recordkeeping costs of LIFO and to minimize the probability of LIFO inventory layers being liquidated. Specifically, we discuss the use of inventory pools and the dollar-value LIFO method.

LIFO Inventory Pools

A pool consists of inventory units grouped according to natural physical similarities.

The objectives of using **LIFO inventory pools** are to simplify recordkeeping by grouping inventory units into pools based on physical similarities of the individual units and to reduce the risk of LIFO layer liquidation. For example, a glass company might group its various grades of window glass into a single window pool. Other pools might be auto glass and sliding door glass. A lumber company might pool its inventory into hardwood, framing lumber, paneling, and so on.

---

[11]B. Lev and S. R. Thiagarajan, " Fundamental Information Analysis," *Journal of Accounting Research* (Autumn 1993). The main conclusion of the study was that fundamental variables, not just earnings, are useful in firm valuation, particularly when examined in the context of macroeconomic conditions such as inflation.

[12]Unit LIFO sometimes is called *specific goods LIFO*.

The average cost for all of the pool purchases during the period is applied to the current year's LIFO layer.

This allows a company to account for a few inventory pools rather than every specific type of inventory separately. Within pools, all purchases during a period are considered to have been made at the same time and at the same cost. Individual unit costs are converted to an average cost for the pool. If the quantity of ending inventory for the pool increases, then ending inventory will consist of the beginning inventory plus a single layer added during the period at the average acquisition cost for that pool.

Despite the advantages of LIFO inventory pools, it's easy to imagine situations in which its benefits are not achieved. Suppose, for instance, that a company discontinues a certain product included in one of its pools. The old costs that existed in prior layers of inventory would be recognized as cost of goods sold and produce LIFO liquidation profit. Even if the product is replaced with another product, the replacement may not be similar enough to be included in the same inventory pool. In fact, the process itself of having to periodically redefine pools as changes in product mix occur, can be expensive and time consuming. The **dollar-value LIFO** approach helps overcome these problems.

Dollar-Value LIFO

Dollar-value LIFO (DVL) gained such widespread popularity during the 1960s and 1970s that most LIFO applications are now based on this approach. DVL extends the concept of inventory pools by allowing a company to combine a large variety of goods into one pool. Physical units are not used in calculating ending inventory. Instead, the inventory is viewed as a quantity of value instead of a physical quantity of goods. Instead of layers of units from different purchases, the DVL inventory pool is viewed as comprising layers of dollar value from different years.

Learning objective 6 Determine ending inventory using the dollar-value LIFO inventory method.

A DVL pool is made up of items that are likely to face the same cost change pressures.

Because the physical characteristics of inventory items are not relevant to DVL, an inventory pool is identified in terms of economic similarity rather than physical similarity. Specifically, a pool should consist of those goods that are likely to be subject to the same cost change pressures.

Advantages of DVL

The DVL method has important advantages. First, it simplifies the recordkeeping procedures compared to unit LIFO because no information is needed about unit flows. Second, it minimizes the probability of the liquidation of LIFO inventory layers, even more so than the use of pools alone, through the aggregation of many types of inventory into larger pools. In addition, the method can be used by firms that do not replace units sold with new units of the same kind. For firms whose products are subject to annual model changes, for example, the items in one year's inventory are not the same as the prior year's. Under pooled LIFO, the new replacement items must be substantially identical to previous models to be included in the same pool. Under DVL, no distinction is drawn between the old and new merchandise on the basis of their physical characteristics, so a much broader range of goods can be included in the pool. That is, the acquisition of the new items is viewed as replacement of the dollar value of the old items. Because the old layers are maintained, this approach retains the benefits of LIFO by matching the most recent acquisition cost of goods with sales measured at current selling prices.

Cost Indexes

In either the unit LIFO approach or the pooled LIFO approach, we determine whether a new LIFO layer was added by comparing the ending quantity with the beginning quantity. The focus is on *units* of inventory. Under DVL, we determine whether a new LIFO layer was added by comparing the ending dollar amount with the beginning dollar amount. The focus is on inventory *value*, not units. However, if the price level has changed, we need a way to determine whether an observed increase is a real increase (an increase in the quantity of inventory) or one caused by an increase in prices. So before we compare the beginning and ending inventory amounts, we need to deflate inventory amounts by any increase in prices so that both the beginning and ending amounts are measured in terms of the same price level. We accomplish this by using cost indexes. A cost index for a particular layer year is determined as follows:

$$\text{Cost index in layer year} = \frac{\text{Cost in layer year}}{\text{Cost in base year}}$$

The base year is the year in which the DVL method is adopted and the layer year is any subsequent year in which an inventory layer is created. The cost index for the base year is set at 1.00. Subsequent years' indices reflect cost changes relative to the base year. For example, if a "basket" of inventory items cost $120 at the end of the current year, and $100 at the end of the base year, the cost index for the current year would be: $120 ÷ $100 = 120%. This index simply tells us that costs in the layer year are 120% of what they were in the base year (i.e., costs increased by 20%).

> The cost index for the base year (the year DVL is initially adopted) is set at 1.00.

There are several techniques that can be used to determine an index for a DVL pool. An external index like the Consumer Price Index or the Producer Price Index can be used, or an internal index can be calculated using one of several techniques such as the *double-extension method* or the *link-chain method*. A discussion of these methods is beyond the scope of this text. In our examples and illustrations, we assume cost indexes are given.

> An external index or an internally generated index can be used.

The DVL Inventory Estimation Technique

> The starting point in DVL is determining the current year's ending inventory valued at year-end costs.

DVL estimation begins with the determination of the current year's ending inventory valued in terms of year-end costs. It's not necessary for a company using DVL to track the item-by-item cost of purchases during the year. All that's needed is to take the physical quantities of goods on hand at the end of the year and apply year-end costs. Let's say the Hanes Company adopted the dollar-value LIFO method on January 1, 1997, when the inventory value was $400,000. The 1997 ending inventory valued at year-end costs is $441,000, and the cost index for the year is 1.05 (105%).

What is the 1997 ending inventory valued at DVL cost? The first step is to convert the ending inventory from year-end costs to base year costs so we can see if there was a real increase in inventory rather than an illusory one caused by price increases. We divide the ending inventory by the year's cost index to get an amount that can be compared directly with beginning inventory.

> Step 1: Convert ending inventory valued at year-end cost to base year cost.

$$\text{Ending inventory at } base\ year \text{ cost} = \frac{\$441,000}{1.05} = \$420,000$$

The $420,000 reflects the 1997 ending inventory deflated to base year cost.

Next we compare the $420,000 ending inventory at base year cost to the beginning inventory, also at base year cost, of $400,000. The $20,000 increase in base-year dollars signifies a real increase in inventory quantity during the year. Applying the LIFO concept, ending inventory at base year cost consists of the beginning inventory layer of $400,000 plus a $20,000 1997 layer. These are the hypothetical costs of the layers as if each was acquired at base year prices.

> Step 2: Identify the layers of ending inventory and the years they were created.

Once the layers are identified, each is restated to prices existing when the layers were acquired. Each layer is multiplied by the cost index for the year it was acquired. The costs are totaled to obtain ending inventory at DVL cost.[13]

> Step 3: Convert each layer's base year cost to layer year cost using the cost index for the year it was acquired.

Date	Ending Inventory at Base Year Cost	×	Cost Index	=	Ending Inventory at DVL Cost
1/1/97	$400,000		1.00		$400,000
1997 layer	20,000		1.05		21,000
Totals	$420,000				$421,000

If we determined that inventory quantity had decreased during the year, then there would have been no 1997 layer added. The most recently added layer, in this case the beginning inventory layer, would be decreased to the inventory valuation determined in step 1. Once a layer of inventory or a portion of a layer is used (that is, sold) it cannot be replaced. In our example, if the base year layer is reduced to $380,000, it will never be increased. Future increases in inventory quantity will result in new layers being added.

CONCEPT REVIEW EXERCISE   DOLLAR-VALUE LIFO

On January 1, 1997, the Johnson Company adopted the dollar-value LIFO method. The inventory value on this date was $500,000. Inventory data for 1997 through 2000 is as follows:

---

[13]It is important to note that the costs of the year's layer is only an approximation of actual acquisition cost. DVL assumes that all inventory quantities added during a particular year were acquired at a single cost.

Date	Ending Inventory at Year-End Costs	Cost Index
12/31/97	$556,500	1.05
12/31/98	596,200	1.10
12/31/99	615,250	1.15
12/31/00	720,000	1.25

Required:

Calculate Johnson's ending inventory for the years 1997 through 2000.

CONCEPT REVIEW EXERCISE

SOLUTION

JOHNSON COMPANY

Date	Ending Inventory at Year-End Cost	Step 1 Ending Inventory at Base Year Cost	Step 2 Inventory Layers at Base Year Cost	Step 3 Inventory Layers Converted to Acquisition Year Cost	Ending Inventory At DVL Cost
1/1/97	$500,000 (base year)	$\frac{\$500,000}{1.00} = \$500,000$	$500,000 (base)	$500,000 \times 1.00 = \$500,000$	**$500,000**
12/31/97	556,500	$\frac{\$556,500}{1.05} = \$530,000$	$500,000 (base) 30,000 (1997)	$500,000 \times 1.00 = \$500,000$ $30,000 \times 1.05 = \ \ 31,500$	**531,500**
12/31/98	596,200	$\frac{\$596,200}{1.10} = \$542,000$	$500,000 (base) 30,000 (1997) 12,000 (1998)	$500,000 \times 1.00 = \$500,000$ $30,000 \times 1.05 = \ \ 31,500$ $12,000 \times 1.10 = \ \ 13,200$	**544,700**
12/31/99	615,250	$\frac{\$615,250}{1.15} = \$535,000^*$	$500,000 (base) 30,000 (1997) 5,000 (1998)	$500,000 \times 1.00 = \$500,000$ $30,000 \times 1.05 = \ \ 31,500$ $5,000 \times 1.10 = \ \ \ \ 5,500$	**537,000**
12/31/00	720,000	$\frac{\$720,000}{1.25} = \$576,000$	$500,000 (base) 30,000 (1997) 5,000 (1998) 41,000 (1999)	$500,000 \times 1.00 = \$500,000$ $30,000 \times 1.05 = \ \ 31,500$ $5,000 \times 1.10 = \ \ \ \ 5,500$ $41,000 \times 1.25 = \ \ 51,250$	**588,250**

*Since inventory declined during 1999 (from $542,000 to $535,000 at base year prices), no new layer is added. Instead the most recently acquired layer, 1998, is reduced to arrive at the $535,000 ending inventory at base year price.

Solution to Financial Reporting Case (at the opening of the chapter)

1. What inventory methods does GM use to value its inventories? Is this permissible according to GAAP?

GM uses the LIFO inventory method to value most of its U.S. inventories. The company uses the FIFO and average cost methods for its Saturn, Hughes, and non-U.S. inventories. Yes, all three methods are permissible according to generally accepted accounting principles.

2. What is the purpose of the Memo that reports the increase in LIFO inventories if valued at FIFO?

The LIFO conformity rule requires that if a company uses LIFO to measure taxable income, it also must use LIFO for external financial reporting. GM does this. However, in 1981, the LIFO conformity rule was liberalized to allow LIFO users to provide supplemental disclosure of the effect on inventories of using a method other than LIFO for inventory valuation. GM's memo in the disclosure note offers this additional information.

3. What is the purpose of the last paragraph in the note that discusses a liquidation of inventories?

Using LIFO means that ending inventory costs could easily be out of date because they reflect old purchase transactions. When inventory quantities decline during a period, some of these out-of-date costs are liquidated and included in cost of goods sold. If costs have been rising, these liquidations produce higher net income than would have resulted if the cost of goods sold reflected more current costs. These profits caused by including out-of-date, low costs in cost of goods sold is referred to as the effect on income of liquidations of LIFO inventory. If these effects are material, they must be disclosed. GM felt its LIFO liquidation profits of $134.4 million were material.

4. Is your friend correct in his assertion that by using LIFO, GM is able to report lower profits?

Yes and no. If GM had used FIFO instead of LIFO for its LIFO inventories, income before taxes in all prior years, including 1995, would have been higher by $2,424.4 million (the increase in 1995 ending inventory). However, in 1995 alone, income before taxes would have been lower by $111.5 million. Here's why. The increase in ending inventory of $2,424.4 decreases cost of goods sold, but the increase in beginning inventory of $2,535.9 increases cost of goods sold, resulting in a net increase in cost of goods sold of $111.5 million.

The Bottom Line

1. In a perpetual inventory system, inventory is continuously adjusted for each change in inventory. Cost of goods sold is adjusted each time goods are sold or returned by a customer. A periodic inventory system adjusts inventory and records cost of goods sold only at the end of a reporting period.

2. Generally, determining the physical quantity that should be included in inventory is a simple matter, because it consists of items in the possession of the company. However, at the end of a reporting period it's important to determine the ownership of goods that are in transit between the company and its customers as well as between the company and its suppliers. Also, goods on consignment should be included in inventory of the consignor even though the company doesn't have physical possession of the goods.

3. The cost of inventory includes all expenditures necessary to acquire the inventory and bring it to its desired condition and location for sale or use. Generally, these expenditures include the purchase price of the goods reduced by any returns and purchase discounts, plus freight-in charges.

4. Once costs are determined, the cost of goods available for sale must be allocated between cost of goods sold and ending inventory. Unless each item is specifically identified and traced through the system, the allocation requires an assumption regarding the flow of costs. First-in, first-out (FIFO) assumes that units sold are the first units acquired. Last-in, first-out (LIFO) assumes that the units sold are the most recent units purchased. The average cost method assumes that cost of goods sold and ending inventory consist of a mixture of all the goods available for sale.

5. A company's choice of inventory method will affect (a) how closely cost flow reflects the actual physical flow of its inventory, (b) the timing of income tax expenses; and (c) how costs are matched with revenues.

6. The dollar-value LIFO method converts ending inventory at year-end cost to base year cost using a cost index. After identifying the layers in ending inventory with the years they were created, each year's base year cost measurement is converted to layer year cost measurement using the layer year's cost index. The layers are then summed to obtain total ending inventory at cost.

Questions for Review of Key Topics

Question	8–1	Describe the three types of inventory of a manufacturing company.
Question	8–2	What is the main difference between a perpetual inventory system and a periodic inventory system?
Question	8–3	The Cloud Company employs a perpetual inventory system and the McKenzie Corporation uses a periodic system. Describe the differences between the two systems in accounting for the following events: (1) purchase of merchandise, (2) sale of merchandise, (3) return of merchandise to supplier, and (4) payment of freight charge on merchandise purchased. Indicate which accounts would be debited and credited for each event.
Question	8–4	The Bockner Company shipped merchandise to Laetner Corporation on December 28, 1997. Laetner received the shipment on January 3, 1998. December 31 is the fiscal year-end for both companies. The merchandise was shipped f.o.b. shipping point. Explain the difference in the accounting treatment of the merchandise if the shipment had instead been designated f.o.b. destination.
Question	8–5	What is a consignment arrangement? Explain the accounting treatment of goods held on consignment.
Question	8–6	Distinguish between the gross and net methods of accounting for purchase discounts.
Question	8–7	The Esquire Company employs a periodic inventory system. Indicate the effect (increase or decrease) of the following items on cost of goods sold:

1. Beginning inventory
2. Purchases
3. Ending inventory
4. Purchase returns
5. Freight-in

Question	8–8	Identify four methods of assigning cost to ending inventory and cost of goods sold and briefly explain the difference in the methods.
Question	8–9	It's common in the electronics industry for unit costs of raw materials inventories to decline over time. In this environment, explain the difference between LIFO and FIFO, in terms of the effect on income and financial position. Assume that inventory quantities remain the same for the period.
Question	8–10	Explain why proponents of LIFO argue that it provides a better match of revenue and expenses. In what situation would it not provide a better match?

Question	8–11	Explain what is meant by the Internal Revenue Service conformity rule with respect to inventory method choice.
Question	8–12	What is a LIFO inventory pool? How is the cost of ending inventory determined when pools are used?
Question	8–13	Identify two advantages of dollar-value LIFO compared with unit LIFO.
Question	8–14	The Austin Company uses the dollar-value LIFO inventory method with internally developed price indexes. Assume that ending inventory at year-end cost has been determined. Outline the remaining steps used in the dollar-value LIFO computations.

Exercises

Exercise 8–1
Perpetual inventory system; journal entries

John's Specialty Store uses a perpetual inventory system. The following are some inventory transactions for the month of May, 1997:

1. John's purchased merchandise on account for $4,000. Freight charges of $300 were paid in cash.
2. John's returned some of the merchandise purchased in (1). The cost of the merchandise was $600 and John's account was credited by the supplier.
3. Merchandise costing $2,800 was sold for $5,000 in cash.

Required:
Prepare the necessary journal entries to record these transactions.

Exercise 8–2
Periodic inventory system; journal entries

[This is a variation of the previous exercise modified to focus on the periodic inventory system.]
John's Specialty Store uses a periodic inventory system. The following are some inventory transactions for the month of May, 1997:

1. John's purchased merchandise on account for $4,000. Freight charges of $300 were paid in cash.
2. John's returned some of the merchandise purchased in (1). The cost of the merchandise was $600 and John's account was credited by the supplier.
3. Merchandise costing $2,800 was sold for $5,000 in cash.

Required:
Prepare the necessary journal entries to record these transactions.

Exercise 8–3
Determining cost of goods sold; periodic inventory system

The Askew Company uses a periodic inventory system. The June 30, 1997, year-end trial balance for the company contained the following information:

Account	Debit	Credit
Merchandise inventory, 7/1/96	32,000	
Sales		380,000
Sales returns	12,000	
Purchases	230,000	
Purchase discounts		6,000
Purchase returns		8,000
Freight-in	16,000	
Freight-out	13,000	

In addition, you determine that the June 30, 1997, inventory balance is $40,000.

Required:
1. Calculate the cost of goods sold for the Askew Company for the year ending June 30, 1997.
2. Prepare the year-end adjusting entry to record cost of goods sold.

Exercise 8–4
Perpetual and periodic inventory systems compared

The following information is available for the Johnson Corporation for 1997:

Beginning inventory	$ 25,000
Merchandise purchases (on account)	150,000
Freight charges on purchases (paid in cash)	10,000
Merchandise returned to supplier (for credit)	12,000
Ending inventory	30,000
Sales (on account)	250,000
Cost of merchandise sold	143,000

Required:
Applying both a perpetual and a periodic inventory system, prepare the journal entries that summarize the transactions that created these balances. Include all end-of-period adjusting entries indicated.

Exercise 8–5
Periodic inventory system;
missing data

The Playa Company uses a periodic inventory system. The following information is taken from Playa's records. Certain data have been intentionally omitted. ($ in thousands)

	1997	1998	1999
Beginning inventory	?	?	225
Cost of goods sold	627	621	?
Ending inventory	?	225	216
Cost of goods available for sale	876	?	800
Purchases (gross)	630	?	585
Purchase discounts	18	15	?
Purchase returns	24	30	14
Freight-in	13	32	16

Required:
Determine the missing numbers. Show computations where appropriate.

Exercise 8–6
Purchase discounts; the gross
method

On July 15, 1997, the Nixon Car Company purchased 1,000 tires from the Harwell Company for $50 each. The terms of the sale were 2/10, n/30. Nixon uses a periodic inventory system and the gross method of accounting for purchase discounts.

Required:
1. Prepare the journal entries to record the purchase on July 15 and payment on July 23, 1997.
2. Prepare the journal entries to record the purchase on July 15 and payment on August 15, 1997.
3. If Nixon instead uses a perpetual inventory system, explain any changes to the journal entries created in requirements 1 and 2.

Exercise 8–7
Purchase discounts; the net
method

[This is a variation of the previous exercise modified to focus on the net method of accounting for purchase discounts.]

On July 15, 1997, the Nixon Car Company purchased 1,000 tires from the Harwell Company for $50 each. The terms of the sale were 2/10, n/30. Nixon uses a periodic inventory system, and the net method of accounting for purchase discounts.

Required:
1. Prepare the journal entries to record the purchase on July 15 and payment on July 23, 1997.
2. Prepare the journal entries to record the purchase on July 15 and payment on August 15, 1997.
3. If Nixon instead uses a perpetual inventory system, explain any changes to the journal entries created in requirements 1 and 2.

Exercise 8–8
Trade and purchase
discounts; the gross method
and the net method compared

Tracy Company, a manufacturer of air conditioners, sold 100 units to Thomas Company on November 17, 1997. The units have a list price of $500 each, but Thomas was given a 30% trade discount. The terms of the sale were 2/10, n/30. Thomas uses a periodic inventory system.

Required:
1. Prepare the journal entries to record the purchase by Thomas on November 17 and payment on November 26, 1997, using the gross method of accounting for purchase discounts.
2. Prepare the journal entries to record the purchase on November 17 and payment on December 15, 1997, using the gross method of accounting for purchase discounts.
3. Repeat requirements 1 and 2 using the net method of accounting for purchase discounts.

Exercise 8–9
Goods in transit

The Kwok Company's inventory balance on December 31, 1997, was $165,000 (based on a physical count) *before* considering the following transactions:
1. Goods shipped to Kwok f.o.b. destination on December 20, 1997, were received on January 4, 1998. The invoice cost was $30,000.
2. Goods shipped to Kwok f.o.b. shipping point on December 28, 1997, were received on January 5, 1998. The invoice cost was $17,000.
3. Goods shipped from Kwok to a customer f.o.b. destination on December 27, 1997, were received by the customer on January 3, 1998. The sales price was $40,000 and the merchandise cost $22,000.
4. Goods shipped from Kwok to a customer f.o.b. destination on December 26, 1997, were received by the customer on December 30, 1997. The sales price was $20,000 and the merchandise cost $13,000.
5. Goods shipped from Kwok to a customer f.o.b. shipping point on December 28, 1997, were received by the customer on January 4, 1998. The sales price was $25,000 and the merchandise cost $12,000.

Required:

Determine the correct inventory amount to be reported on Kwok's 1997 balance sheet.

Exercise 8–10
Goods in transit; consignment

The December 31, 1997, year-end inventory balance of the Raymond Corporation is $220,000. You have been asked to review the following transactions to determine if they have been correctly recorded.

1. Goods shipped to Raymond f.o.b. destination on December 26, 1997, were received on January 2, 1998. The invoice cost of $30,000 *is* included in the preliminary inventory balance.
2. At year-end, Raymond held $12,000 of merchandise on consignment from the Harrison Company. This merchandise *is* included in the preliminary inventory balance.
3. On December 29, merchandise costing $6,000 was shipped to a customer f.o.b. shipping point and arrived at the customer's location on January 3, 1998. The merchandise is *not* included in the preliminary inventory balance.
4. At year-end, Raymond had merchandise costing $15,000 on consignment with the Joclyn Corporation. The merchandise is *not* included in the preliminary inventory balance.

Required:

Determine the correct inventory amount to be reported on Raymond's 1997 balance sheet.

Exercise 8–11
Inventory cost flow methods; periodic system

Altira Corporation uses a periodic inventory system. The following information related to its merchandise inventory during the month of August 1997 is available:

August 1 — Inventory on hand—2,000 units; cost $6.10 each.
          8 — Purchased 10,000 units for $5.50 each.
      14 — Sold 8,000 units for $12.00 each.
      18 — Purchased 6,000 units for $5.00 each.
      25 — Sold 7,000 units for $11.00 each.
      31 — Inventory on hand—3,000 units.

Required:

Determine the inventory balance Altira would report on its August 31, 1997, balance sheet and the cost of goods sold it would report on its August 1997 income statement using each of the following cost flow methods:

1. First-in, first-out (FIFO)
2. Last-in, first-out (LIFO)
3. Average cost

Exercise 8–12
Inventory cost flow methods; perpetual system

[This is a variation of the previous exercise modified to focus on the perpetual inventory system and alternative cost flow methods.]

Altira Corporation uses a perpetual inventory system. The following transactions affected its merchandise inventory during the month of August 1997:

August 1 — Inventory on hand—2,000 units; cost $6.10 each.
          8 — Purchased 10,000 units for $5.50 each.
      14 — Sold 8,000 units for $12.00 each.
      18 — Purchased 6,000 units for $5.00 each.
      25 — Sold 7,000 units for $11.00 each.
      31 — Inventory on hand—3,000 units.

Required:

Determine the inventory balance Altira would report on its August 31, 1997, balance sheet and the cost of goods sold it would report on its August 1997 income statement using each of the following cost flow methods:

1. First-in, first-out (FIFO)
2. Last-in, first-out (LIFO)
3. Average cost

Exercise 8–13
Comparison of FIFO and LIFO; periodic system

Alta Ski Company's inventory records contained the following information regarding its latest ski model. The company uses a periodic inventory system.

Beginning inventory, January 1, 1997	600 units @ $ 80 each
Purchases:	
January 15	1,000 units @ $ 90 each
January 21	800 units @ $100 each

Sales:
January 5	400 units @ $120 each
January 22	800 units @ $130 each
January 29	400 units @ $135 each
Ending inventory, January 31, 1997	800 units

Required:

1. Which method, FIFO or LIFO, will result in the highest cost of goods sold figure for January 1997? Why? Which method will result in the highest ending inventory balance? Why?
2. Compute cost of goods sold for January and the ending inventory using both the FIFO and LIFO methods.

Exercise 8–14
Average cost method; periodic and perpetual systems

The following information is taken from the inventory records of the CNB Company:

Beginning inventory, 9/1/97	5,000 units @ $10.00
Purchases:	
9/7	3,000 units @ $10.40
9/25	8,000 units @ $10.75
Sales:	
9/10	4,000 units
9/29	5,000 units

7,000 units were on hand at the end of September.

Required:

1. Assuming that CNB uses a periodic inventory system and employs the average cost method, determine cost of goods sold for September and September's ending inventory.
2. Repeat requirement 1 assuming that the company uses a perpetual inventory system.

Exercise 8–15
FIFO, LIFO, and average cost methods

The Causwell Company began 1997 with 10,000 units of inventory on hand. The cost of each unit was $5.00. During 1997 an additional 30,000 units were purchased at a single unit cost, and 20,000 units remained on hand at the end of 1997 (20,000 units therefore were sold during 1997). Causwell uses a periodic inventory system. Cost of goods sold for 1997, applying the average cost method, is $115,000. The company is interested in determining what cost of goods sold would have been if the FIFO or LIFO methods were used.

Required:

1. Determine the cost of goods sold for 1997 using the FIFO method. [Hint: Determine the cost per unit of 1997 purchases.]
2. Determine the cost of goods sold for 1997 using the LIFO method.

Exercise 8–16
Multiple choice; inventory measurement

The following questions dealing with inventory measurement are adapted from questions that appeared on recent CPA examinations. Determine the response that best completes the statements or questions.

1. Herc Co.'s inventory at December 31, 1997, was $1,500,000 based on a physical count priced at cost, and before any adjustment for the following:

   - Merchandise costing $90,000, shipped FOB shipping point from a vendor on December 30, 1997, was received and recorded on January 5, 1998.
   - Goods in the shipping area were excluded from inventory although shipment was not made until January 4, 1998. The goods, billed to the customer FOB shipping point on December 30, 1997, had a cost of $120,000

   What amount should Herc report as inventory in its December 31, 1997, balance sheet?

   a. $1,500,000
   b. $1,590,000
   c. $1,620,000
   d. $1,710,000

   Items 2 and 3 are based on the following:
   During 1997, Metro Co., which maintains a perpetual inventory system, recorded the following information pertaining to its inventory:

	Units	Unit Cost	Total Cost	Units on Hand
Balance on 1/1/97	1,000	$1	$1,000	1,000
Purchased on 1/7/97	600	3	1,800	1,600
Sold on 1/20/97	900			700
Purchased on 1/25/97	400	5	2,000	1,100

2. Under the moving-average inventory method, what amount should Metro report as inventory at January 31, 1997?
    a. $2,640
    b. $3,225
    c. $3,300
    d. $3,900

3. Under the LIFO method, what amount should Metro report as inventory at January 31, 1997?
    a. $1,300
    b. $2,700
    c. $3,900
    d. $34,100

4. According to the net method, which of the following items would be included in the cost of inventory?

	Freight Costs	Purchase Discounts not Taken
a.	Yes	No
b.	Yes	Yes
c.	No	Yes
d.	No	No

Exercise 8–17
LIFO liquidation

The Reuschel Company began 1997 with inventory of 10,000 units at a cost of $7 per unit. During 1997, 50,000 units were purchased for $9 each. Sales for the year totaled 56,000 units leaving 4,000 units on hand at the end of 1997. Reuschel uses a periodic inventory system and the LIFO inventory cost method.

Required:
1. Calculate cost of goods sold for 1997.
2. From a financial reporting perspective, what problem is created by the use of LIFO in this situation? Describe the disclosure required to report the effects of this problem.

Exercise 8–18
Ratio analysis

The table below contains selected financial information from the 1995 financial statements of Maytag Corporation and Whirlpool Corporation (dollars in millions):

	Maytag		Whirlpool	
	1995	1994	1995	1994
Net sales	$3,040	$3,373	$8,163	$7,949
Cost of goods sold	2,251	2,496	6,245	5,952
Year-end inventory	265	387	1,029	838

Required:
Calculate and compare the 1995 gross profit ratio, the inventory turnover ratio, and the average days in inventory for the two companies.

Exercise 8–19
Dollar-value LIFO

On January 1, 1997, the Haskins Company adopted the dollar-value LIFO method for its one inventory pool. The pool's value on this date was $660,000. The 1997 and 1998 ending inventory valued at year-end costs were $690,000 and $770,000, respectively. The appropriate cost indexes are 1.03 for 1997 and 1.10 for 1998.

Required:
Calculate the inventory value at the end of 1997 and 1998 using the dollar-value LIFO method.

Exercise 8–20
Dollar-value LIFO

The Mercury Company has only one inventory pool. On December 31, 1997, Mercury adopted the dollar-value LIFO inventory method. The inventory on that date using the dollar-value LIFO method was $200,000. Inventory data are as follows:

Year	Inventory at Year-End Costs	Inventory at Base Year Costs
1998	$231,000	$220,000
1999	299,000	260,000
2000	300,000	250,000

Required:
Compute the inventory at December 31, 1998, 1999, and 2000, using the dollar-value LIFO method.

(AICPA adapted)

Exercise 8–21
Multiple choice; dollar-value LIFO

The following questions dealing with dollar-value LIFO are adapted from questions that appeared on recent CPA examinations. Determine the response that best completes the statements or questions.

1. Walt Co. adopted the dollar-value LIFO inventory method as of January 1, 1997, when its inventory was valued at $500,000. Walt's entire inventory constitutes a single pool. Using a relevant price index of 1.10, Walt determined that its December 31, 1997, inventory was $577,500 at current year cost, and $525,000 at base year cost. What was Walt's dollar-value LIFO inventory at December 31, 1997??
    a. $525,000
    b. $527,500
    c. $552,500
    d. $577,500

2. Brock Co. adopted the dollar-value LIFO inventory method as of January 1, 1996. A single inventory pool and an internally computed price index are used to compute Brock's LIFO inventory layers. Information about Brock's dollar value inventory follows:

| | Inventory | | |
Date	At Base Year Cost	At Current Year Cost	At Dollar-Value LIFO
1/1/96	$40,000	$40,000	$40,000
1996 layer	5,000	14,000	6,000
12/31/96	45,000	54,000	46,000
1997 layer	15,000	26,000	?
12/31/97	$60,000	$80,000	?

What was Brock's dollar-value LIFO inventory at December 31, 1997?
    a. $80,000
    b. $74,000
    c. $66,000
    d. $60,000

Exercise 8–22
Concepts; terminology

Listed below are several terms and phrases associated with inventory measurement. Pair each item from List A (by letter) with the item from List B that is most appropriately associated with it.

List A	List B
____ 1. Perpetual inventory system	a. Legal title passes when goods are delivered to common carrier.
____ 2. Periodic inventory system	b. Goods are transferred to another company but title remains with transferor.
____ 3. F.o.b. shipping point	c. Purchase discounts not taken are included in inventory cost.
____ 4. Gross method	d. If LIFO is used for taxes, it must be used for financial reporting.
____ 5. Net method	e. Items sold are those acquired first.
____ 6. Cost inde	f. Items sold are those acquired last.
____ 7. F.o.b. destination	g. Purchase discounts not taken are considered interest expense.
____ 8. FIFO	h. Used to convert ending inventory at year-end cost to base year cost.
____ 9. LIFO	i. Continuously records changes in inventory.
____ 10. Consignment	j. Items sold come from a mixture of goods acquired during the period.
____ 11. Average cost	k. Legal title passes when goods arrive at location.
____ 12. IRS conformity rule	l. Adjusts inventory at the end of the period.

Problems

Problem 8–1
Various inventory transactions; journal entries

The James Company began the month of October with inventory of $15,000. The following inventory transactions occurred during the month:

a. The company purchased merchandise on account for $22,000 on October 12, 1997. Terms of the purchase were 2/10, n/30. James uses the net method to record purchases. The merchandise was shipped f.o.b. shipping point and freight charges of $500 were paid in cash.

b. On October 18 the company returned merchandise costing $3,000. The return reduced the amount owed to the supplier. The merchandise returned came from beginning inventory, not from the October 12 purchase.

c. On October 31, James paid for the merchandise purchased on October 12.

d. During October merchandise costing $18,000 was sold on account for $28,000.

e. It was determined that inventory on hand at the end of October cost $16,060.

Required:

1. Assuming that the James Company uses a periodic inventory system, prepare journal entries for the above transactions including the adjusting entry at the end of October to record cost of goods sold.

2. Assuming that the James Company uses a perpetual inventory system, prepare journal entries for the above transactions.

Problem 8–2
Items to be included in inventory

The following inventory transactions took place near December 31, 1997, the end of the Rasul Company's fiscal year-end:

1. On December 27, 1997, merchandise costing $2,000 was shipped to the Myers Company on consignment. The shipment arrived at Myers's location on December 29, but none of the merchandise was sold by the end of the year. The merchandise was *not* included in the 1997 ending inventory.

2. On January 5, 1998, merchandise costing $8,000 was received from a supplier and recorded as a purchase on that date and *not* included in the 1997 ending inventory. The invoice revealed that the shipment was made f.o.b. shipping point on December 28, 1997.

3. On December 29, 1997, the company shipped merchandise costing $12,000 to a customer f.o.b. destination. The goods, which arrived at the customer's location on January 4, 1998, were *not* included in Rasul's 1997 ending inventory. The sale was recorded in 1997.

4. Merchandise costing $4,000 was received on December 28, 1997, on consignment from the Aborn Company. A purchase was *not* recorded and the merchandise was *not* included in 1997 ending inventory.

5. Merchandise costing $6,000 was received and recorded as a purchase on January 8, 1998. The invoice revealed that the merchandise was shipped from the supplier on December 28, 1997, f.o.b. destination. The merchandise was *not* included in 1997 ending inventory.

Required:

State whether the company correctly accounted for each of the above transactions. Give the reason for your answer.

Problem 8–3
Costs included in inventory

The Reagan Corporation is a wholesale distributor of truck replacement parts. Initial amounts taken from Reagan's records are as follows:

Inventory at December 31 (based on a physical count of goods in Reagan's warehouse on December 31) $1,250,000

Accounts payable at December 31:

Vendor	Terms	Amount
Baker Company	2%,10 days, net 30	$ 265,000
Charlie Company	Net 30	210,000
Dolly Company	Net 30	300,000
Eagler Company	Net 30	225,000
Full Company	Net 30	—
Greg Company	Net 30	—
		$1,000,000

Sales for the year $9,000,000

Additional information:

1. Parts held by Reagan on consignment from Charlie, amounting to $155,000, were included in the physical count of goods in Reagan's warehouse and in accounts payable at December 31.

2. Parts totaling $22,000, which were purchased from Full and paid for in December, were sold in the last week of the year and appropriately recorded as sales of $28,000. The parts were included in the physical count of goods in Reagan's warehouse on December 31 because the parts were on the loading dock waiting to be picked up by customers.

3. Parts in transit on December 31 to customers, shipped f.o.b. shipping point on December 28, amounted to $34,000. The customers received the parts on January 6 of the following year. Sales of $40,000 to the customers for the parts were recorded by Reagan on January 2.

4. Retailers were holding goods on consignment from Reagan, which had a cost of $210,000 and a retail value of $250,000.

5. Goods were in transit from Greg to Reagan on December 31. The cost of the goods was $25,000, and they were shipped f.o.b. shipping point on December 29.

6. A freight bill in the amount of $2,000 specifically relating to merchandise purchased in December, all of which was still in the inventory at December 31, was received on January 3. The freight bill was not included in either the inventory or in accounts payable at December 31.

7. All the purchases from Baker occurred during the last seven days of the year. These items have been recorded in accounts payable and accounted for in the physical inventory at cost before discount. Reagan's policy is to pay invoices in time to take advantage of all discounts, adjust inventory accordingly, and record accounts payable net of discounts.

Required:

Prepare a schedule of adjustments to the initial amounts using the format shown below. Show the effect, if any, of each of the transactions separately and if the transactions would have no effect on the amount shown, state *none*.

	Inventory	Accounts Payable	Sales
Initial amounts	$1,250,000	$1,000,000	$9,000,000
Adjustments–increase (decrease):			
1.			
2.			
3.			
4.			
5.			
6.			
7.			
Total adjustments			
Adjusted amounts	$_____	$_____	$_____

(AICPA adapted)

Problem 8–4
Various inventory transactions; determining inventory and cost of goods

The Johnson Corporation began 1997 with inventory of 10,000 units of its only product. The units cost $8 each. The company uses a periodic inventory system and the LIFO cost method. The following transactions occurred during 1997:

a. Purchased 50,000 additional units at a cost of $10 per unit. Terms of the purchases were 2/10, n/30, and 60% of the purchases were paid for within the 10-day discount period. The company uses the gross method to record purchase discounts. The merchandise was purchased f.o.b. shipping point and freight charges of $.50 per unit were paid by Johnson.

b. 1,000 units purchased during the year were returned to suppliers for credit. Johnson was also given credit for the freight charges of $.50 per unit it had paid on the original purchase. The units were defective and were returned two days after they were received.

c. Sales for the year totaled 45,000 units at $18 per unit.

d. On December 28, 1997, Johnson purchased 5,000 additional units at $10 each. The goods were shipped f.o.b. destination and arrived at Johnson's warehouse on January 4, 1998.

e. 14,000 units were on hand at the end of 1997.

Required:

1. Determine ending inventory and cost of goods sold for 1997.

2. Assuming that operating expenses other than those indicated in the above transactions amounted to $150,000, determine income before income taxes for 1997.

Problem 8–5
Various inventory costing methods

The Ferris Company began 1997 with 6,000 units of its principal product. The cost of each unit is $8. Merchandise transactions for the month of January 1997 are as follows:

Purchases			
Date of Purchase	Units	Unit Cost*	Total Cost
Jan. 10	5,000	$ 9	$ 45,000
Jan. 18	6,000	10	60,000
Totals	11,000		$105,000

* Includes purchase price and cost of freight.

Sales	
Date of Sale	Units
Jan. 5	3,000
Jan. 12	2,000
Jan. 20	4,000
Total	9,000

8,000 units were on hand at the end of the month.

Required:

Calculate January's ending inventory and cost of goods sold for the month using each of the following alternatives:

1. FIFO, periodic system
2. LIFO, periodic system
3. LIFO, perpetual system
4. Average cost, periodic system
5. Average cost, perpetual system

Problem 8–6
Various inventory costing methods

Carlson Auto Dealers Inc. sells a handmade automobile as its only product. Each automobile is identical; however, they can be distinguished by their unique ID number. At the beginning of 1997, Carlson had three cars in inventory, as follows:

Car ID	Cost
203	$60,000
207	60,000
210	63,000

During 1997, each of the three autos sold for $90,000. Additional purchases (listed in chronological order) and sales for the year were as follows:

Car ID	Cost	Selling Price
211	$63,000	$ 90,000
212	63,000	93,000
213	64,500	not sold
214	66,000	96,000
215	69,000	100,500
216	70,500	not sold
217	72,000	105,000
218	72,300	106,500
219	75,000	not sold

Required:
1. Compute 1997 ending inventory and cost of goods sold assuming the company uses the specific identification inventory method.
2. Compute ending inventory and cost of goods sold assuming FIFO and a periodic inventory system.
3. Compute ending inventory and cost of goods sold assuming LIFO and a periodic inventory system.
4. Compute ending inventory and cost of goods sold assuming the average cost method and a periodic inventory system.

Problem 8–7
Supplemental LIFO disclosures

The Ford Motor Company uses both the LIFO and the average cost method for its inventories. The following disclosure note is included in the company's 1995 financial statements:

Note 4. Inventories – Automotive

(in millions)	1995	1994
Raw materials, work in process and supplies	$3,717	$3,192
Finished products	3,445	3,295
Total inventories	$7,162	$6,487

Inventories are stated at the lower of cost or market. The cost of most U.S. inventories is determined by the last-in, first-out ("LIFO") method. The cost of the remaining inventories is determined primarily by the first-in, first-out ("FIFO") method.

If the FIFO method had been used instead of the LIFO method, inventories would have been higher by $1,406 million and $1,383 million at December 31, 1995 and 1994, respectively.

Ford's 1995 income statement reported ($ in millions) cost of goods sold of $101,171 and income before income taxes of $6,705.

Required:
1. Calculate cost of goods sold and income before income taxes for 1995 assuming Ford had used the FIFO inventory method for all of its inventory.
2. Why might the information obtained in step 1 be useful to a financial analyst?
3. Assuming a 40% income tax rate, how much higher (lower) would retained earnings have been at the end of 1995 if Ford had used the FIFO inventory method for all of its inventory?

Problem 8–8
LIFO liquidation

The Taylor Corporation has used a periodic inventory system and the LIFO cost method since its inception in 1977. The company began 1997 with the following inventory layers (listed in chronological order of acquisition):

10,000 units @ $15	$150,000
15,000 units @ $20	300,000
Beginning inventory	$450,000

During 1997, 30,000 units were purchased for $25 per unit. Due to unexpected demand for the company's product, 1997 sales totaled 40,000 units at various prices, leaving 15,000 units in ending inventory.

Required:
1. Calculate cost of goods sold for 1997.
2. Determine the amount of LIFO liquidation profit that the company must report in a disclosure note to its 1997 financial statements. Assume an income tax rate of 40%.
3. If the company decided to purchase an additional 10,000 units at $25 per unit at the end of the year, how much income tax currently payable would be saved?

Problem 8–9
Dollar-value LIFO

On January 1, 1997, the Taylor Company adopted the dollar-value LIFO method. The inventory value for its one inventory pool on this date was $400,000. Inventory data for 1997 through 1999 is as follows:

Date	Ending Inventory at Year-End Costs	Cost Index
12/31/97	$441,000	1.05
12/31/98	487,200	1.12
12/31/99	510,000	1.20

Required:
Calculate Taylor's ending inventory for 1997, 1998, and 1999.

Problem 8–10
Dollar-value LIFO

The Kingston Company uses the dollar-value LIFO method of computing inventory. An external price index is used to convert ending inventory to base year. The company began operations on January 1, 1997, with an inventory of $150,000. Year-end inventories at year-end costs and price indexes for its one inventory pool were as follows:

Year Ended December 31	Inventory at Year-End Costs	Cost Index (Relative to Base Year)
1997	$200,000	1.08
1998	245,700	1.17
1999	235,980	1.14
2000	228,800	1.10

Required:
Compute inventory amounts at the end of each year.

Cases

Critical Thought Case 8–1
Riding the Merry-Go-Round

Merry-Go-Round Enterprises, the clothing retailer for dedicated followers of young men's and women's fashion, was looking natty as a company. It was March 1993, and the Joppa, Maryland-based outfit had just announced the acquisition of Chess King, a rival clothing chain, a move that would give it the biggest share of the young men's clothing market. Merry-Go-Round told brokerage firm analysts that the purchase would add $13 million, or 15 cents a share, to profits for the year. So some Wall Street analysts raised their earnings estimates for Merry-Go-Round. The company's stock rose $2.25, or 15 percent, to $17 on the day of the Chess King news. Merry-Go-Round was hot—$100 of its stock in January 1988 was worth $804 five years later. In 1993 the chain owned 1,460 stores in 44 states, mostly under the Cignal, Chess King, and Merry-Go-Round names.

Merry-Go-Round's annual report for the fiscal year ended January 30, 1993, reported a 15% sales growth, to $877.50 million from $761.2 million. A portion of the company's balance sheet is reproduced below:

	January 30, 1993	February 1, 1992
Assets:		
Cash and cash equivalents	$40,115,000	$29,781,000
Marketable securities	——	9,703
Receivables	6,466,000	6,195
Merchandise inventories	82,197,000	59,971,000

But Merry-Go-Round spun out. The company lost $544,000 in the first six months of 1993, compared with earnings of $13.5 million in the first half of 1992. In the fall of 1992, Leonard "Boogie" Weinglass, Merry-Go-Round's flamboyant founder and chairman who started the company in 1968, boarded up his Merry-Go-Ranch in Aspen, Colorado, and returned to management after a 12-year hiatus. But the ponytailed, shirtsleeved entrepreneur—the inspiration for the character Boogie in the movie Diner—couldn't save his company from bankruptcy. In January 1994, the company filed for Chapter 11 protection in Baltimore. Shares crumbled below $3.

Required:

In retrospect, can you identify any advance warning at the date of the financial statements of the company's impending bankruptcy?

[Adapted from Jonathan Burton, "Due Diligence," *Worth,* June 1994, pp. 89–96]

Discussion Case 8–2
The specific identification inventory method; inventoriable costs

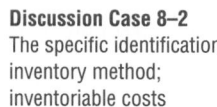

Happlia Co. imports household appliances. Each model has many variations and each unit has an identification number. Happlia pays all costs for getting the goods from the port to its central warehouse in Des Moines. After repackaging, the goods are consigned to retailers. A retailer makes a sale, simultaneously buys the appliance from Happlia, and pays the balance due within one week.

To alleviate the overstocking of refrigerators at a Minneapolis retailer, some were reshipped to a Kansas City retailer where they were still held in inventory at December 31, 1997. Happlia paid the costs of this reshipment. Happlia uses the specific identification inventory costing method.

Required:

1. In regard to the specific identification inventory costing method:
   a. Describe its key elements.
   b. Discuss why it is appropriate for Happlia to use this method.
2. a. What general criteria should Happlia use to determine inventory carrying amounts at December 31, 1997?
   b. Give four examples of costs included in these inventory carrying amounts.
3. What costs should be reported in Happlia's 1997 income statement? Ignore lower of cost or market considerations.

(AICPA adapted)

Writing Case 8–3
LIFO versus FIFO

You have just been hired as a consultant to Tangier Industries, a newly formed company. The company president, John Meeks, is seeking your advice as to the appropriate inventory method Tangier should use to value its inventory and cost of goods sold. Mr. Meeks has narrowed the choice to LIFO and FIFO. He has heard that LIFO might be better for tax purposes, but FIFO has certain advantages for financial reporting to investors and creditors. You have been told that the company will be profitable in its first year and for the foreseeable future.

Required:

Prepare a report for the president describing the factors that should be considered by Tangier in choosing between LIFO and FIFO.

Discussion Case 8–4
LIFO versus FIFO

An accounting intern for a local CPA firm was reviewing the financial statements of a client in the electronics industry. The intern noticed that the client used the FIFO method of determining ending inventory and cost of goods sold. When she asked a colleague why the firm used FIFO instead of LIFO, she was told that the client used FIFO to minimize its income tax liability. This response puzzled the intern because she thought that LIFO would minimize income tax liability.

Required:

What would you tell the intern to resolve the confusion?

Discussion Case 8–5
Goods in transit

At the end of 1997, the Biggie Company performed its annual physical inventory count. John Lawrence, the manager in charge of the physical count, was told that an additional $22,000 in inventory that had been sold and was in transit to the customer should be included in the ending inventory balance. John was of the opinion that the merchandise shipped should be excluded from the ending inventory since Biggie was not in physical possession of the merchandise.

Required:

Discuss the situation and indicate why John's opinion might be incorrect.

Ethics Case 8–6
Profit manipulation

In 1996 the Moncrief Company purchased from Jim Lester the right to be the sole distributor in the western states of a product called Zelenex. In payment, Moncrief agreed to pay Lester 20% of the gross profit recognized from the sale of Zelenex in 1997.

Moncrief uses a periodic inventory system and the LIFO inventory method. Late in 1997, the following information is available concerning the inventory of Zelenex:

Beginning inventory, 1/1/97 (10,000 units @ $30)	$ 300,000
Purchases (40,000 units @ $30)	1,200,000
Sales (35,000 units @ $60)	$2,100,000

By the end of the year, the purchase price of Zelenex had risen to $40 per unit. On December 28, 1997, three days before year-end, Moncrief is in a position to purchase 20,000 additional units of Zelenex at the $40 per unit price. Due to the increase in purchase price, Moncrief will increase the selling price in 1998 to $80 per unit. Inventory on hand before the purchase, 15,000 units, is sufficient to meet the next six months' sales and the company does not anticipate any significant changes in purchase price during 1998.

Required:
1. Determine the effect of the purchase of the additional 20,000 units on the 1997 gross profit from the sale of Zelenex and the payment due to Jim Lester.
2. Discuss the ethical dilemma Moncrief faces in determining whether or not the additional units should be purchased.

Real World Case 8–7
Effects of inventory valuation methods; LIFO and FIFO

Income statement and balance sheet information abstracted from a recent annual report of Safeway, Inc., one of the world's largest food retailers, appears below:

Balance Sheets ($ in millions)

Current assets:	1995	1994
Merchandise inventories	$1,191.8	$1,136.0

Income Statements ($ in millions)

	1995	1994
Net sales	$16,397.5	$15,626.6
Cost of goods sold	(11,943.7)	(11,376.6)
Gross profit	$ 4,453.8	$ 4,250.0

The significant accounting policies note disclosure contained the following:

Merchandise Inventories (in part)

At year-end 1995 and 1994, merchandise inventory of $693 million and $660 million, respectively, is valued at the lower of cost on a last-in, first-out ("LIFO") basis or market value. Such LIFO inventory had a replacement cost or current cost of $767 million and $724 million at year-end 1995 and 1994, respectively. The remaining inventory is valued at the lower of cost on a first-in, first-out ("FIFO") basis or market value.

Required:
1. Why is Safeway disclosing the replacement or current cost of its LIFO inventory?
2. Assuming that year-end replacement/current cost figures approximate FIFO inventory values, estimate what the beginning and ending inventory balances for the 1995 fiscal year would have been if Safeway had used FIFO instead of LIFO.
3. Estimate the effect on cost of goods sold (that is, would it have been greater or less and by how much?) for the 1995 fiscal year if Safeway had used FIFO instead of LIFO.

Internet Case 8–8
Effects of inventory valuation methods

EDGAR, the Electronic Data Gathering, Analysis, and Retrieval system, performs automated collection, validation, indexing, and forwarding of submissions by companies and others who are required by law to file forms with the U.S. Securities and Exchange Commission (SEC). All publicly traded domestic companies use EDGAR to make the majority of their filings. (Some foreign companies file voluntarily.) Form 10-K or 10-KSB, which include the annual report, is required to be filed on EDGAR. The SEC makes this information available on the Internet.

Required:
1. Access EDGAR on the Internet. You can use a web browser or anonymous FTP. The web address is http://www.sec.gov/. To use anonymous FTP, use your File Transfer Protocol software to connect to sec.gov and log in as user "anonymous" with a password of your electronic mail address.
2. Search for Varian Associates, Inc. Access the 10-K filing for the most recent fiscal year. Search or scroll to find the financial statements and related notes.
3. Answer the following questions related to the company's inventories:
   a. What method(s) does the company use to value its inventories?

b. Calculate what cost of sales would have been for the year if the company had used FIFO to value its inventories.

c. Calculate inventory turnover for the year using the reported numbers.

Research Case 8–9
The use of LIFO inventory pools

An inventory pool consists of inventory units grouped according to natural physical similarities. The objectives of using LIFO inventory pools is to simplify recordkeeping by grouping inventory units into pools based on physical similarities of the individual units and to reduce the risk of LIFO layer liquidation. Professors Reeve and Stanga in "The LIFO Pooling Decision: Some Empirical Results from Accounting Practice," conducted a survey to investigate the number of pools companies use in practice.

Required:

1. In your library or from some other source, locate the indicated article in *Accounting Horizons*, June, 1987.
2. For the companies included in the sample, what is the median and mean number of pools used by retail and nonretail companies?
3. What are the authors' six conclusions?

International Case 8–10
Comparison of inventory valuation in Denmark and the U.S.A.

Nova Nordisk A/S, located in Denmark, is a large, international conglomerate with significant markets in the bioindustrial and agricultural industries. The inventory disclosure included in recent financial statements of the company is reproduced below:

Significant Accounting Policies (in part)

I. Inventories

Inventories are stated at cost or market, whichever is lower. Cost is determined on the first-in-first-out basis and comprises direct material and energy but does not include direct labour and production overheads.

Required:
On the basis of the information the disclosures provide, compare inventory valuation in Denmark with that in the United States.

Discussion Case 8–11
Dollar-value LIFO method

The Maxi Corporation uses the unit LIFO inventory method. The costs of the company's products have been steadily rising since the company began operations in 1990 and cost increases are expected to continue. The chief financial officer of the company would like to continue using LIFO because of its tax advantages. However, the controller, Sally Hamel, would like to reduce the recordkeeping costs of LIFO that have steadily increased over the years as new products have been added to the company's product line. Sally suggested the use of the dollar-value LIFO method. The chief financial officer has asked Sally to describe the dollar-value LIFO procedure.

Required:
Describe the dollar-value LIFO procedure.

Financial Analysis Case 8–12
Compare inventory management using ratios

The table below contains selected financial information included in the 1995 financial statements of General Motors and Ford Motor Company:

(dollars in millions)	General Motors		Ford Motor Company	
	1995	**1994**	**1995**	**1994**
Balance sheet:				
Inventories	$11,530	$10,128	$7,162	$6,487
	1995		**1995**	
Income statement:				
Net sales	$143,666		$110,496	
Cost of goods sold	126,535		101,171	

Disclosure notes reveal that both companies use the LIFO inventory method to value the majority of their inventories.

1. Calculate the 1995 gross profit ratio, inventory turnover ratio, and average days in inventory for both companies. Evaluate the management of each company's investment in inventory.
2. Obtain annual reports from three corporations in the same primary industry (but not autos) and compare the management of each company's investment in inventory.

Note: You can obtain copies of annual reports from your library, from friends who are shareholders, from the investor relations department of the corporations, from a friendly stockbroker, or from EDGAR (Electronic Data Gathering Retrieval) on the Internet (http://www.sec.gov).

**Financial Analysis
Case 8–13**
Reporting of inventories
Federal Express Corporation

**Federal Express
Corporation**

Refer to the financial statements and related disclosure notes of Federal Express Corporation in the appendix to Chapter 1.

Required:
1. Why does merchandise inventory not appear on Federal Express's balance sheet? Does the balance sheet report any type of inventory?
2. What method does Federal Express use to value its inventory?

INVENTORIES: ADDITIONAL ISSUES

OVERVIEW

We covered most of the principal measurement and reporting issues involving the asset inventory and the corresponding expense cost of goods sold in the previous chapter. In this chapter we complete our discussion of inventory measurement by explaining the lower-of-cost-or-market rule used to value inventories. In addition, we investigate inventory estimation techniques, methods of simplifying LIFO, changes in inventory method, and inventory errors.

LEARNING OBJECTIVES   After studying this chapter, you should be able to:

1. Understand and apply the lower-of-cost-or-market rule used to value inventories.
2. Estimate ending inventory and cost of goods sold using the gross profit method.
3. Estimate ending inventory and cost of goods sold using the retail inventory method, applying the various cost flow methods.
4. Explain how the retail inventory method can be made to approximate the lower-of-cost-or-market rule.
5. Determine ending inventory using the dollar-value LIFO retail inventory method.
6. Explain the appropriate accounting treatment required when a change in inventory method is made.
7. Explain the appropriate accounting treatment required when an inventory error is discovered.

DOES IT COUNT?

Today you drove over to Kmart to pick up a few items. Yesterday, your accounting professor had discussed inventory measurement issues and the different methods (FIFO, LIFO, and average) used by companies to determine ending inventory and cost of goods sold. You can't imagine actually counting the inventory in all of the Kmart stores around the country. "There must be some way they can avoid counting all of that inventory every time they want to make financial statements," you tell your dog when you get home. "I think I'll go check their financial statements on the Internet to see what kind of inventory method they use." You find the following in the summary of significant accounting policies included in Kmart's most recent financial statements:

Inventories (in part)
Inventories are stated at the lower of cost or market, primarily using the retail method. As of year end 1995, 1994, and 1993, the last-in, first-out (LIFO) method, utilizing internal inflation indices, was used to determine cost . . . .

QUESTIONS

1. Kmart values its inventory at the lower of cost or market. What does that mean? Under what circumstances might Kmart be justified in reporting its inventory at less than cost?
2. How does Kmart avoid counting all its inventory every time it makes financial statements? What are internal inflation indices used for?

A REPORTING—LOWER OF COST OR MARKET

 Learning objective 1
Understand and apply the
lower-of-cost-or-market
rule used to value
inventories.

It's important for a company to disclose the inventory method that it uses. Otherwise, investors and creditors would be unable to meaningfully compare accounting information from company to company. This disclosure typically is made in the summary of significant accounting policies accompanying the financial statements. IBM Corporation's inventory method disclosure is shown in Graphic 9–1.

GRAPHIC 9–1

Disclosure of Inventory Method—IBM Corporation

> *Significant Accounting Policies (in part)*
> Inventories
> Raw materials, work in process, and finished goods are stated at the lower of average cost or market.

OPENING CASE

Question 1

The **lower-of-cost-or-market** approach to valuing inventory recognizes losses in the period when the value of inventory declines below its cost.

The disclosure indicates that IBM uses the average cost inventory method to determine the cost of its inventories. Notice that inventories actually are stated (valued) at the lower of average cost or market. Assets usually are reported at their historical costs, but a departure from cost is warranted when the utility of an asset (its probable future economic benefits) is no longer as great as its cost. The utility or benefits from inventory result from the ultimate sale of the goods. So, deterioration, obsolescence, changes in price levels, or any situation that might compromise the inventory's saleability impairs utility. To avoid reporting inventory at an amount greater than the benefits it can provide, the **lower-of-cost-or-market (LCM)** approach to valuing inventory was developed. Reporting inventories at LCM causes losses to be recognized when the value of inventory declines below its cost rather than in the period in which the goods ultimately are sold.

In the late 1970s, Polaroid Corporation developed a new product called Polavision. Polavision was an instant movie system that allowed the user to film moving pictures and then view the movies instantly without having to wait for the film to be developed. Inventories of Polavision products were manufactured in anticipation of consumer demand. However, at approximately the same time, VCR technology was developed, rendering Polavision an obsolete product that would have to be sold at significantly reduced prices, or a product that could not be sold at all. The LCM rule caused Polaroid Corporation to lower the value of the Polavision inventory and recognize a loss in 1979, the period the decline in value became apparent, rather than wait until some future period when the product might be sold.

POLAROID SLICES BOOK **Cambridge,**
VALUE OF POLAVISION **Mass.**

Polaroid Corp. announced yesterday it will reduce by $68 million the book value of its inventory of Polavision products and the remaining purchase commitments to its supplier of equipment for the instant movie system.

Company spokesman Don Dery said the company will charge the revaluation to Polaroid's third quarter profits. "We'll probably show a loss for the third quarter," Dery said. [Excerpt from article appearing in the *San Jose Mercury News* (September 1979)]

Determining Market Value

From the preceding discussion, you might interpret the term *market* to mean the amount that could be realized if the inventory were sold. However, *Accounting Research Bulletin No. 43* defines market for LCM purposes as the inventory's current replacement cost (by purchase or reproduction) except that market should not:

a. Exceed the net realizable value (that is, estimated selling price in the ordinary course of business less reasonably predictable costs of completion and disposal).
b. Be less than net realizable value reduced by an allowance for an approximately normal profit margin.

Replacement cost (RC) generally means the cost to replace the item by purchase or manufacture.

In effect, we have a ceiling and a floor between which market (that is, replacement cost) must fall. **Net realizable value (NRV)** represents the upper limit and **net realizable value less a nor-**

The ceiling of **net realizable value (NRV)** and the floor of **net realizable value less a normal profit margin (NRV – NP)** establish a range within which the market must fall.

mal profit margin (**NRV – NP**) provides the lower limit. If **replacement cost (RC)** is within the range, it represents market; if it is above the ceiling or below the floor, the ceiling or the floor becomes market. As a result, the designated market value is the number that falls in the middle of the three possibilities; RC, NRV, and NRV – NP. The designated market value is compared with cost, and the lower of the two is used to value inventory.

Let's see how the LCM rule is applied in Illustration 9–1 and then we will discuss its theoretical merit.

ILLUSTRATION   9–1

Lower of Cost or Market

The Collins Company has five inventory items on hand at the end of 1997. The year-end unit costs (determined by applying the average cost method), current unit selling prices, and estimated disposal (selling) costs for each of the items are presented below. The gross profit ratio for each of the products is 20% of selling price.

Item	Cost	Replacement Cost	Selling Price	Estimated Disposal Costs
A	$ 50	$55	$100	$15
B	100	90	120	20
C	80	70	85	20
D	90	37	100	24
E	95	92	110	24

The determination of inventory value is a two-step process: first, determine the designated market value and second, compare the designated market value to cost. The lower of the two is the LCM inventory value.

Inventory is valued at the lower of cost or the designated market value.

	(1)	(2)	(3)	(4) Designated Market Value [Middle value of (1)–(3)]	(5)	Inventory Value [Lower of (4) or (5)]
Item	RC	NRV	NRV-NP		Cost	
A	$55	$ 85	**$65**	$65	$ 50	$50
B	**90**	100	76	90	100	90
C	70	**65**	48	65	80	65
D	37	76	**56**	56	90	56
E	92	**86**	64	86	95	86

RC = Current replacement cost.
NRV = Estimated selling price less estimated disposal costs.
NRV – NP = NRV less a normal profit margin.

Example for item B:

Selling price	$120	
Less: Disposal costs	(20)	
NRV	100	
Less: Normal profit	(24)	($120 selling price × 20%)
NRV – NP	$ 76	

Notice that the designated market value is the middle amount of the three market possibilities. This number is then compared to cost and the lower of the two is the final inventory value. For item A, cost is lower than market. For each of the other items, the designated market is lower than cost, requiring an adjustment to the carrying value of inventory. We discuss the adjustment procedure later in the chapter. First though, let's consider the conceptual justification of the LCM rule.

GLOBAL PERSPECTIVE

The technique of valuing inventories at the lower of cost or market is fairly standard around the globe. However, differences exist in the designation of market. In the United States, market is defined as replacement cost, constrained by the ceiling of net realizable value and the floor of net realizable value less a normal profit margin. In many other countries, for example the United Kingdom, Denmark, Finland, and New Zealand, market is defined as net realizable value. In Sweden, inventories are carried at the lower of cost or real value. Real value is defined as net realizable value, but replacement cost is permissible for raw materials and semi-finished products.

Theoretical Merits.   What is the logic for designating replacement cost as the principal meaning of market value in the LCM rule? First, a change in replacement cost usually is a good indicator of the direction of change in selling price. If replacement cost declines, selling price usually will decline, or already has declined. Another reason is that if previously acquired inventory is revalued at its replacement cost, then the profit margin realized on its sale will likely approximate the profit margin realizable on the sale of newly acquired items.

> The upper and lower limits placed on replacement cost prevent certain types of profit distortion.

The upper limit placed on replacement cost prevents inventory from being valued at an amount above what can be realized from its sale. The lower limit prevents inventory from being valued at an amount below what can be realized from its sale after considering normal profit margin. For example, consider item D in our illustration. If item D is valued at its replacement cost of $37 without considering the ceiling or floor, a loss of $53 ($90 cost less $37) would be recognized. If the item is subsequently sold at its current selling price less usual disposal costs (NRV = $76), then a gross profit of $39 ($76 less $37) would be recognized. This is much higher than its normal profit of $20 (20% × $100) and causes a shifting of income from the period the inventory loss is recognized to the period the item is sold. The ceiling and floor prohibit this kind of profit distortion.

> Some accountants complain that LCM promotes conservatism at the expense of consistency.

On the other hand, critics of LCM contend that the method causes losses to be recognized that haven't actually occurred. Others maintain that it introduces needless inconsistency in order to be conservative. Inconsistency is created because LCM recognizes decreases in market value as they occur, but not increases.

The LCM rules stated in *ARB No. 43* are intended as a guide rather than a literal rule. In practice, companies frequently define market as net realizable value. This is a number that often is easier to estimate than replacement cost. Also, assuming the NRV does not change, when the item is sold, there will be neither gross profit nor additional loss. The entire effect on income is recognized in the period the realizable value drops below cost.

ETHICAL DILEMMA

The Hartley Paper Company, owned and operated by Bill Hartley, manufactures and sells different types of computer paper. The company has reported profits in the majority of years since the company's inception in 1962 and is projecting a profit in 1997 of $65,000, down from $96,000 in 1996.

Near the end of 1997, the company is in the process of applying for a bank loan. The loan proceeds will be used to replace manufacturing equipment necessary to modernize the manufacturing operation. In preparing the financial statements for the year, the chief accountant, Don Davis, mentioned to Bill Hartley that approximately $40,000 of paper inventory has become obsolete and should be written off as a loss in 1997. Bill is worried that the write-down would lower 1997 income to a level that might cause the bank to refuse the loan. Without the loan, it would be difficult for the company to compete. This could cause decreased future business and employees might have to be laid off. Bill is considering waiting until 1998 to write down the inventory. Don Davis is contemplating his responsibilities in this situation.

Applying Lower of Cost or Market

Lower of cost or market can be applied to individual inventory items, to logical categories of inventory, or to the entire inventory. A major product line can be considered a logical category of inventory. For example, Polaroid applied the LCM rule to its entire line of Polavision products. For income tax purposes, the lower-of-cost-or-market rule must be applied on an individual item basis.

> The LCM rule can be applied to individual inventory items, logical inventory categories, or the entire inventory.

Let's return to our illustration and assume the unit amounts pertain to 10,000 units of each inventory item. Also, let's say items A–B and items C–E are two collections of similar items that can be considered logical categories of inventory. Illustration 9–1a compares the LCM valuation according to each of three possible applications.

ARB No. 43   **The most common practice is to apply the *lower of cost or market rule* separately to each item of the inventory. However, if there is only one end-product category the cost utility of the total stock—the inventory in its entirety—may have the greatest significance for accounting purposes.**

Similarly, where more than one major product or operational category exists, the application of the *lower of cost or market, whichever is lower* rule to the total of items included in such major categories may result in the most useful determination of income.[1]

[1]"Restatement and Revision of Accounting Research Bulletins," *Accounting Research Bulletin No. 43* (New York: AICPA, 1953), Ch. 4, par 11.

ILLUSTRATION   9–1A

LCM Determination—
Application at Different
Levels of Aggregation

Item	Cost	Designated Market Value	Lower-of-cost-or-market By Individual Items	By Product Line	By Total Inventory
A	$ 50,000	$ 65,000	$ 50,000		
B	100,000	90,000	90,000		
Total A + B	$150,000	$155,000		$150,000	
C	$ 80,000	$ 65,000	65,000		
D	90,000	56,000	56,000		
E	95,000	86,000	86,000		
Total C, D & E	$265,000	$207,000		207,000	
Total	$415,000	$362,000	$347,000	$357,000	$362,000

The final LCM inventory value is different for each of the three applications. The inventory value is $347,000 if LCM is applied to each item, $357,000 if it is applied to product line categories, and $362,000 if applied to the entire inventory. Applying LCM to groups of inventory items will usually cause a higher inventory valuation than if applied on an item-by-item basis because group application permits decreases in the market value of some items to be offset by increases in others. Each approach is acceptable but should be applied consistently from one period to another.

Adjusting Cost to Market

When the LCM rule is applied and a material write-down of inventory is required, the most popular method of recording the reduction is to recognize the loss as a separate item on the income statement. An alternative is to include the loss in cost of goods sold.

Loss on reduction to LCM ... xx		Cost of goods sold xx
Inventory*	xx or	Inventory* xx

*Alternatively, inventory can be reduced indirectly with a credit to an allowance account

Usually a loss from the write-down of inventory is reported as a separate item on the income statement.

Recording the write-down as a separate item more accurately reports the event that occurred—a loss from holding inventory during a period when inventory value declined. Including this holding loss as part of cost of goods sold distorts the relationship between sales and cost of goods sold. Cost of goods sold should include only the cost of goods actually sold during the period.[2] Regardless of the method used to record the write-down, the reduced inventory value is considered to be the new cost for future LCM determinations. Any subsequent recovery of value is ignored.

Additional Consideration

In very limited circumstances, businesses are allowed under GAAP to carry inventory at a market value above cost. *ARB 43* restricted this approach generally to companies that deal in precious metals, and "... agricultural, mineral, and other products, units of which are interchangeable and have an immediate marketability at quoted prices ..."[3] Writing inventory *up* to market value means recognizing revenue for the increase. This is called the *production basis* of recognizing revenue. In rare cases when the method is appropriate, full disclosure of the fact that inventory is valued at market is required.

[2]Inventory write-downs that are not material quite often are included in cost of goods sold.
[3]"Restatement and Revision of Accounting Research Bulletins," *Accounting Research Bulletin No. 43* (New York: AICPA, 1953), Ch. 4, par. 16.

CONCEPT REVIEW EXERCISE   LOWER-OF-COST-OR-MARKET

The Strand Company sells four products that can be grouped into two major categories. Information necessary to apply the LCM rule at the end of 1997 for each of the four products is presented below. The normal profit margin for each of the products is 25% of selling price. The company records any losses from adjusting cost to market as separate income items and reduces inventory directly.

Product	Replacement Cost	Cost	Selling Price	Disposal Costs
101	$ 80,000	$ 85,000	$160,000	$30,000
102	175,000	160,000	200,000	25,000
201	160,000	140,000	180,000	50,000
202	45,000	20,000	60,000	22,000

Products 101 and 102 are in category A and products 201 and 202 are in category B.

Required:

1. Determine the designated market value for each of the four products according to the LCM rule.
2. Determine the amount of the loss from write-down of inventory that would be required, applying the LCM rule to:
   a. Individual items
   b. Major categories
   c. The entire inventory

CONCEPT REVIEW EXERCISE   SOLUTION

1. Determine the designated market value for each of the four products according to the LCM rule.

Product	(1) RC	(2) NRV Selling Price Less Disposal Costs	(3) NRV – NP	(4) Designated Market Value [Middle value of (1)–(3)]
101	$ 85,000	$130,000	$ 90,000	$ 90,000
102	160,000	175,000	125,000	160,000
201	140,000	130,000	85,000	130,000
202	20,000	38,000	23,000	23,000

Calculation of NRV – NP:

Product	NRV	NP	NRV-NP
101	$130,000	$40,000 (25% × $160,000)	$ 90,000
102	175,000	50,000 (25% × $200,000)	125,000
103	130,000	45,000 (25% × $180,000)	85,000
104	38,000	15,000 (25% × $60,000)	23,000

2. Determine the amount of the loss from write-down of inventory that would be required.

Product	Cost	Designated Market Value	Lower-of-Cost-or-Market By Individual Products	By Category	By Total Inventory
101	$ 80,000	$ 90,000	$ 80,000		
102	175,000	160,000	160,000		
Total 101+102	$255,000	$250,000		$250,000	
201	$160,000	$130,000	130,000		
202	45,000	23,000	23,000		
Total 201+202	$205,000	$153,000		153,000	
Total	$460,000	$403,000	$393,000	$403,000	$403,000

The LCM value for both the category application and the entire inventory application are identical because, in this particular case, market is below cost for both of the categories.

Amount of loss from write-down using individual items:

$$\$460,000 - 393,000 = \mathbf{\$67,000}$$

Amount of loss from write-down using categories or the entire inventory:

$$\$460,000 - 403,000 = \mathbf{\$57,000}$$

PART B   INVENTORY ESTIMATION TECHNIQUES

The Southern Wholesale Company distributes approximately 100 products throughout the state of Mississippi. Southern uses a periodic inventory system and takes a physical count of inventory once a year at its fiscal year-end. A recent fire destroyed the entire inventory in one of Southern's warehouses. How can the company determine the dollar amount of inventory destroyed when submitting an insurance claim to obtain reimbursement for the loss?

Home Improvement Stores, Inc., sells over 1,000 different products to customers in each of its 17 retail stores. The company uses a periodic inventory system and takes a physical count of inventory once a year at its fiscal year-end. Home Improvement's bank has asked for monthly financial statements as a condition attached to a recent loan. Can the company avoid the costly procedure of counting inventory at the end of each month to determine ending inventory and cost of goods sold?

These are just two examples of situations when it is either impossible or infeasible to determine the dollar amount of ending inventory by taking a count of the physical quantity of inventory on hand at the end of a period. Fortunately, companies can estimate inventory in these situations by either the gross profit method or the retail inventory method.

The Gross Profit Method

Learning objective 2
Estimate ending inventory and cost of goods sold using the gross profit method.

The **gross profit method,** also known as the **gross margin method**, is useful in situations where estimates of inventory are desirable. The technique is valuable in a variety of situations:

1. In determining the cost of inventory that has been lost, destroyed, or stolen.
2. In estimating inventory and cost of goods sold for interim reports, avoiding the expense of a physical inventory count.
3. In auditors' testing of the overall reasonableness of inventory amounts reported by clients.
4. In budgeting and forecasting.

The **gross profit method** is not acceptable for the preparation of annual financial statements.

However, the gross profit method provides only an approximation of inventory and is not acceptable according to generally accepted accounting principles for annual financial statements.

The technique relies on a relationship you learned in the previous chapter—ending inventory and cost of goods sold always equal the cost of goods available for sale. Even when inventory is unknown, we can estimate it because accounting records usually indicate the cost of goods available for sale (beginning inventory plus net purchases), and the cost of goods sold can be estimated from available information. So by subtracting the cost of goods sold estimate from the cost of goods available for sale, we obtain an estimate of ending inventory. Let's compare that with the way inventory and cost of goods sold normally are determined.

Usually, in a periodic inventory system, ending inventory is known from a physical count and cost of goods sold is *derived* as follows:

Beginning inventory	(from the accounting records)
Plus: Net purchases	(from the accounting records)
Goods available for sale	
Less: Ending inventory	(from a physical count)
Cost of goods sold	

However, when using the gross profit method, the ending inventory is *not* known. Instead, the amount of sales is known—from which we can estimate the cost of goods sold—and ending inventory is the amount calculated.

Beginning inventory	(from the accounting records)
Plus: Net purchases	(from the accounting records)
Goods available for sale	
Less: Cost of goods sold	(estimated)
Ending inventory	(estimated)

So, a first step in estimating inventory is to estimate cost of goods sold. This estimate relies on the historical relationship among (a) net sales, (b) cost of goods sold, and (c) gross profit. Gross profit, you will recall, is simply net sales minus cost of goods sold. So, if we know what net sales are, and if we know what percentage of net sales the gross profit is, we can fairly accurately estimate cost of goods sold. Companies often sell products that have similar gross profit ratios. As a result, accounting records usually provide the information necessary to estimate the cost of ending inventory, even when a physical count is impractical. Let's use the gross profit method to solve the problem of Southern Wholesale Company introduced earlier in the chapter. Suppose the company began 1997 with inventory of $600,000, and on March 17 a warehouse fire destroyed the entire inventory. Company records indicate net purchases of $1,500,000 and net sales of $2,000,000 prior to the fire. The gross profit ratio in each of the previous three years has been very close to 40%. Illustration 9–2 shows how Southern can estimate the cost of the inventory destroyed for its insurance claim.

ILLUSTRATION 9–2

Gross Profit Method

Beginning inventory (from records)		$ 600,000
Plus: Net purchases (from records)		1,500,000
Goods available for sale		2,100,000
Less: Cost of goods sold:		
Net sales	$2,000,000	
Less: Estimated gross profit of 40%	(800,000)	
Estimated cost of goods sold*		(1,200,000)
Estimated ending inventory		$ 900,000

*Alternatively, cost of goods sold can be calculated as $2,000,000 × (1 − .40) = $1,200,000.

A Word of Caution

> The key to obtaining accurate estimates is the reliability of the gross profit ratio.

The gross profit method provides only an estimate. The key to obtaining accurate estimates is the reliability of the gross profit ratio. The ratio usually is estimated from relationships between sales and cost of goods sold. However, the current relationship may differ from the past. In that case, all available information should be used to make necessary adjustments. For example, the company may have made changes in the markup percentage of some of its products. Very often different products have different markups. In these situations, a blanket ratio should not be applied across the board. The accuracy of the estimate can be improved by grouping inventory into pools of products that have similar gross profit relationships rather than using one gross profit ratio for the entire inventory.

The company's cost flow assumption should be implicitly considered when estimating the gross profit ratio. For example, if LIFO is used and the relationship between cost and selling price has changed for recent acquisitions, this would suggest a ratio different from one where the average cost method was used. Another difficulty with the gross profit method is that it does not explicitly consider possible theft or spoilage of inventory. The method assumes that if the inventory was not sold, then it must be on hand at the end of the period. Suspected theft or spoilage would require an adjustment to estimates obtained using the gross profit method.

Additional Consideration

The gross profit ratio is, by definition, a percentage of sales. Sometimes, though, information provided will state the gross profit as a percentage of cost instead. In that case, it will be referred to as the **markup on cost**. For instance, a 66⅔% markup on cost is equivalent to a gross profit ratio of 40%. Here's why:
A gross profit ratio of 40% can be formulated as:

$$\text{Sales} = \text{Cost} + \text{Gross Profit}$$
$$100\% = 60\% + 40\%$$

Now, expressing gross profit as a percentage of cost we get:

$$\frac{\text{Gross Profit}}{\text{Cost}} = \frac{40\%}{60\%} = 66\,{}^{2}/_{3}\%$$

As a result, it's necessary to be careful to note which way the percentage is being stated. If stated as a markup on cost, it can be converted to the gross profit ratio, and the gross profit method can be applied the usual way.

The Retail Inventory Method

Learning objective 3
Estimate ending inventory and cost of goods sold using the retail inventory method, applying the various cost flow methods.

The **retail inventory method** is similar to the gross profit method in that it relies on the relationship between cost and selling price to estimate ending inventory and cost of goods sold. As the name implies, the method is used by many retail companies such as Kmart, Dayton Hudson, and May Department Stores. Certain retailers like auto dealers and jewelry stores, whose inventory consists of few, high-priced items can economically use the specific identification inventory method. However, high-volume retailers selling many different items at low unit prices find the retail inventory method ideal, although with the advent of bar coding on more and more retail merchandise, use of the method is declining. Similar to the gross profit method, its principal benefit is that a physical count of inventory is not required to estimate ending inventory and cost of goods sold.

The retail method tends to provide a more accurate estimate than the gross profit method because it's based on the current **cost-to-retail percentage** (the reciprocal of the gross profit ratio) rather than on a historical gross profit ratio.

The **retail inventory method** uses the **cost-to-retail percentage** based on a current relationship between cost and selling price.

The increased reliability in the estimate of the cost percentage is achieved by comparing cost of goods available for sale with goods available for sale *at current selling prices*. So, to use the technique, a company must maintain records of inventory and purchases not only at cost, but also at current selling price. We refer to this as *retail information*. In its simplest form, the retail inventory method estimates the amount of ending inventory (at retail) by subtracting sales (at retail) from goods available for sale (at retail). This estimated ending inventory at retail is then converted to cost by multiplying it by the cost-to-retail percentage. This ratio is found by dividing goods available for sale at *cost* by goods available for sale at *retail*.

Let's use the retail inventory method to solve the problem of the Home Improvement Store introduced earlier in the chapter. Suppose the company's bank has asked for monthly financial statements as a condition attached to a loan dated May 31, 1997. To avoid a physical count of inventory, the company intends to use the retail inventory method to estimate ending inventory and cost of goods sold for the month of June. Using data available in its accounting records, Illustration 9–3 shows how Home Improvement can estimate ending inventory and cost of goods sold for June.

ILLUSTRATION   9–3

Retail Method

By keeping records of both cost and retail, a company can easily calculate the cost-to-retail percentage.

Goods available for sale (at retail) minus net sales equals estimated ending inventory (at retail).

	Cost	Retail
Beginning inventory	$ 60,000	$100,000
Plus: Net purchases	287,200	460,000
Goods available for sale	347,200	560,000
Cost-to-retail percentage: $\frac{\$347,200}{\$560,000} = 62\%$		
Less: Net sales		(400,000)
Estimated ending inventory at retail		$160,000
Estimated ending inventory at cost (62% × $160,000)	(99,200)	
Estimated cost of goods sold—goods available for sale (at cost) minus ending inventory (at cost) equals cost of goods sold	$248,000	

The retail inventory method can be used for financial reporting and income tax purposes.

Unlike the gross profit method, the retail inventory method is acceptable for external financial reporting if the results of applying the method are sufficiently close to what would have been achieved using a more rigorous determination of the cost of ending inventory. Also, it's allowed by the Internal Revenue Service as a method that can be used to determine cost of goods sold for income tax purposes.[4] Another advantage of the method is that different cost flow methods can be explicitly incorporated into the estimation technique. In other words, we can modify the application of the method to estimate ending inventory and cost of goods sold to approximate average cost, lower-of-average-cost-or-market (conventional method) and LIFO. (The FIFO retail method is possible but rarely used in practice.) We illustrate these variations later in the chapter.

Like the gross profit method, the retail inventory method also can be used to estimate the cost of inventory lost, stolen, or destroyed; for testing the overall reasonableness of physical counts; in budgeting and forecasting as well as in generating information for interim financial statements. Even though the retail method provides fairly accurate estimates, a physical count of inventory usually is performed at least once a year to verify accuracy and detect spoilage, theft, and other irregularities.

Retail Terminology

> Changes in the selling prices must be included in the determination of ending inventory at retail.

Our example above is simplified in that we implicitly assumed that the selling prices of beginning inventory and of merchandise purchased did not change from date of acquisition to the end of the period. This frequently is an unrealistic assumption. The terms in Graphic 9–2 are associated with changing retail prices of merchandise inventory.

GRAPHIC 9–2

Terminology Used in Applying the Retail Method

Initial markup	Original amount of markup from cost to selling price.
Additional markup	Increase in selling price subsequent to initial markup.
Markup cancellation	Elimination of an additional markup.
Markdown	Reduction in selling price below the original selling price.
Markdown cancellation	Elimination of a markdown.

To illustrate, assume that a product purchased for $6 is initially marked up $4 to $10. This $10 is our original selling price. If the selling price is subsequently increased to $12, the additional markup is $2. If the selling price is then subsequently decreased to $10.50, the markup cancellation is $1.50. We refer to the net effect of the changes ($2.00 – 1.50 = $.50) as the **net markup**.

> **Net markups** and **net markdowns** are included in the retail column to determine ending inventory

Now let's say the selling price of the product purchased for $6 and initially marked up to $10, is decreased to $7. The markdown is $3. If the selling price is later increased to $8, the markdown cancellation is $1. The net effect of the change ($3 – 1 = $2) is the **net markdown**. When applying the retail inventory method, *net markups and net markdowns must be included in the determination of ending inventory at retail*. Graphic 9–3 demonstrates the retail inventory method terminology.

GRAPHIC 9–3

Retail Inventory Method Terminology

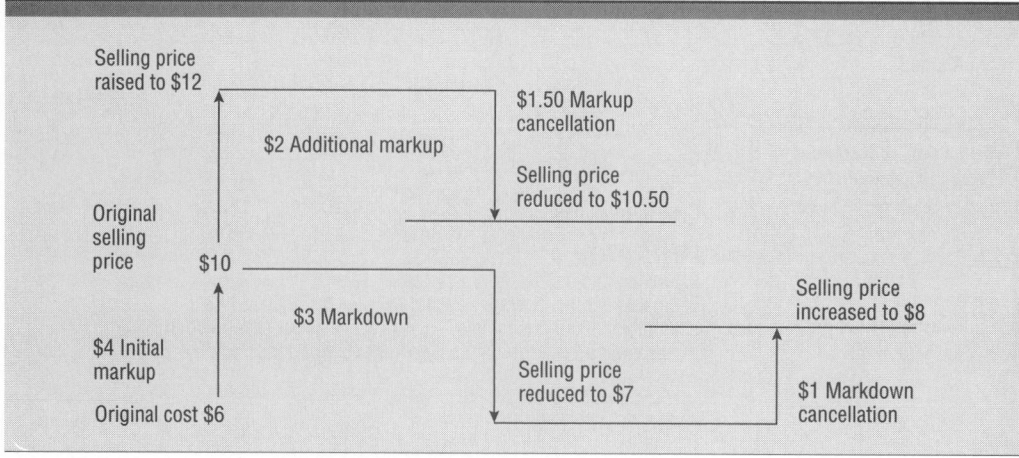

---

[4]The retail method is acceptable for external reporting and for tax purposes because it tends to provide a more accurate estimate than the gross profit method. The retail method uses a current cost-to-retail percentage rather than a historical gross profit ratio.

We now continue our illustration of the retail inventory method but expand it to incorporate markups and markdowns as well as to approximate cost by each of the alternative inventory cost flow methods.

Cost Flow Methods

Let's continue the Home Improvement Stores example into July with Illustration 9–4 and see how the retail inventory method can be used to approximate different cost flow assumptions. We'll also use the same illustration to see how the retail method can be modified to approximate lower of cost or market.

ILLUSTRATION   9–4

The Retail Inventory Method—Various Cost Flow Methods

Home Improvement Stores, Inc., uses a periodic inventory system and the retail inventory method to estimate ending inventory and cost of goods sold. The following data are available from the company's records for the month of July 1997:

	Cost	Retail
Beginning inventory	$ 99,200	$160,000
Net purchases	305,280[1]	470,000[2]
Net markups		10,000
Net markdowns		8,000
Net sales		434,000[3]

[1]Purchases at cost less returns, plus freight-in.
[2]Original selling price of purchased goods less returns at retail.
[3]Gross sales less returns.

Approximating Average Cost.   Recall that the average cost method assumes that cost of goods sold and ending inventory each consist of a *mixture* of all the goods available for sale. So when we use the retail method to approximate average cost, the cost-to-retail percentage should be based on the weighted averages of the costs and retail amounts for *all* goods available for sale. This is achieved by calculating the cost-to-retail percentage by dividing the total cost of goods available for sale by total goods available for sale at retail. When this average percentage is applied to ending inventory at retail, we get an estimate of ending inventory at average cost. If you look back to our simplified example for the month of June, you'll notice that we used this approach there. So, our ending inventory and cost of goods sold estimates for June were estimates of average cost.[5]

> To approximate average cost, the cost-to-retail percentage is determined for *all* goods available for sale.

Now, we use the retail inventory method to approximate average costs for July. Notice in Illustration 9–5 that both markups and markdowns are included in the determination of goods available for sale at retail.

ILLUSTRATION   9–5

Retail Method—Average Cost

	Cost	Retail
Beginning inventory	$ 99,200	$160,000
Plus: Net purchases	305,280	470,000
Net markups		10,000
Less: Net markdowns		(8,000)
Goods available for sale	404,480	632,000
Cost-to-retail percentage: $\frac{\$404,480}{\$632,000} = \underline{64\%}$		
Less: Net sales		(434,000)
Estimated ending inventory at retail		$198,000
Estimated ending inventory at cost (64% × $198,000)	(126,720)	
Estimated cost of goods sold	$277,760	

Approximating Average LCM—The Conventional Retail Method.   Recall from our discussion earlier in the chapter that, however costs are determined, inventory should be reported on the balance sheet at LCM. Fortunately, we can apply the retail inventory method in such a way that LCM is approximated. This is the method most commonly used by retailers and often is referred to as

> **Learning objective 4**
> Explain how the retail inventory method can be made to approximate the lower-of-cost-or-market rule.

[5]We also implicitly assumed no net markups or markdowns.

To approximate LCM, markdowns are not included in the calculation of the cost-to-retail percentage.

the **conventional retail method**. We apply the method by *excluding markdowns from the calculation of the cost-to-retail percentage*. Markdowns still are subtracted in the retail column but only *after* the percentage is calculated. To approximate lower of average cost or market, the retail method is modified as shown in Illustration 9–6.

ILLUSTRATION 9–6

Retail Method—Average Cost, LCM

	Cost	Retail
Beginning inventory	$ 99,200	$160,000
Plus: Net purchases	305,280	470,000
Net markups		10,000
		640,000
Cost to retail percentage: $\frac{\$404,480}{\$640,000} = 63.2\%$		
Less: Net markdowns		(8,000)
Goods available for sale	404,480	632,000
Less: Net sales		(434,000)
Estimated ending inventory at retail		$198,000
Estimated ending inventory at cost (63.2% × $198,000)	(125,136)	
Estimated cost of goods sold	$279,344	

The logic for using this approximation is that a markdown is evidence of a reduction in the utility of inventory.

Notice that by not subtracting net markdowns from the denominator, the cost-to-retail percentage is lower than it was previously (63.2% versus 64%). This always will be the case when markdowns exist. As a result, the cost approximation of ending inventory always will be less when markdowns exist. To understand why this lower amount approximates LCM, we need to realize that markdowns usually occur when obsolescence, spoilage, overstocking, price declines, or competition has lessened the utility of the merchandise. To recognize this decline in utility in the period it occurs, as LCM does, we exclude net markdowns from the calculation of the cost-to-retail (market) percentage. It should be emphasized that this approach provides only an *approximation* of what ending inventory might be as opposed to applying the LCM rule in the more exact way described earlier in the chapter.

Also notice that the ending inventory at retail is the same using both approaches ($198,000). This will be the case regardless of the cost flow method used because in all approaches this amount reflects the ending inventory at current retail prices.

The LCM variation also could be applied to the FIFO method, but LCM is not generally used in combination with LIFO. This does not mean that a company using LIFO ignores the LCM rule. Any obsolete or slow-moving inventory that has not been marked down by year-end can be written down to market after the estimation of inventory using the retail method. This is usually not a significant problem. If prices are rising, LIFO ending inventory includes old lower priced items whose costs are likely to be lower than current market.

The LIFO Retail Method. The last-in, first-out (LIFO) method assumes that units sold are those most recently acquired. When there's a net increase in inventory quantity during a period, the use of LIFO results in ending inventory that includes the beginning inventory as well as one or more additional layers added during the period. When there's a net decrease in inventory quantity, LIFO layer(s) are liquidated. In applying LIFO to the retail method in the simplest way, we assume that the retail prices of goods remained stable during the period. This assumption, which is relaxed later in the chapter, allows us to look at the beginning and ending inventory in dollars to determine if inventory quantity has increased or decreased.

If inventory at retail increases during the year, a new layer is added.

We'll use the numbers from our previous example to illustrate using the retail method to approximate LIFO so we can compare the results with those of the conventional retail method. Recall that beginning inventory at retail is $160,000 and ending inventory at retail is $198,000. If we assume stable retail prices, inventory quantity must have increased during the year. This means ending inventory includes the beginning inventory layer of $160,000 ($99,200 at cost) as well as some additional merchandise purchased during the period. To estimate total ending inventory at LIFO cost, we also need to determine the inventory layer added during the period. When using the LIFO retail method, we assume no more than one inventory layer is added per year if inventory increases.[6] Each layer will carry its own cost-to-retail percentage. In our illustration, the beginning inventory layer carries a cost-to-retail percentage of 62% ($99,200 ÷ $160,000). The layer of inventory added during the period is $38,000 at retail, which is determined by subtracting beginning inventory at retail from ending inventory at retail ($198,000 − 160,000). This layer will be converted to cost by multiplying it by its own cost-to-retail percentage reflecting the *current* period's ratio of cost to retail amounts.

Illustration 9–7 shows how Home Improvement Stores would estimate total ending inventory and cost of goods sold for the period using the LIFO retail method.

ILLUSTRATION   9–7

LIFO Retail Method

	Cost	Retail
Beginning inventory	$ 99,200	$160,000
Plus: Net purchases	305,280	470,000
Net markups		10,000
Less: Net markdowns		(8,000)
Goods available for sale (excluding beginning inventory)	305,280	472,000
Goods available for sale (including beginning inventory)	404,480	632,000

Cost-to-retail percentage: $\frac{\$305,280}{\$472,000} = 64.68\%$

		Retail
Less: Net sales		(434,000)
Estimated ending inventory at retail		$198,000

Estimated ending inventory at cost:

	Retail	Cost	
Beginning inventory	$160,000 × 62.00%*	$ 99,200	
Current period's layer	38,000 × 64.68%	24,578	
Total	$198,000	$123,778	(123,778)
Estimated cost of goods sold			$280,702

*$99,200 ÷ $160,000 = 62%

The July layer's cost-to-retail percentage of 64.68% is the same as the percentage that results using retail FIFO. This is because in both cases, beginning inventory is excluded from the calculation. The next period's (August's) beginning inventory will include the two distinct layers (June and July), each of which carries its own unique cost-to-retail percentage. Notice in the illustration that both net markups and net markdowns are included in the calculation of the current period's cost-to-retail percentage.

Other Issues Pertaining to the Retail Method

To focus on the key elements of the retail method, we've so far ignored some of the details of the retail process. Fundamental elements such as returns and allowances, discounts, freight, spoilage, and shortages can complicate the retail method.

Recall that net purchases is found by adding freight-in to purchases and subtracting both purchase returns and purchase discounts. When these components are considered separately in the retail method, purchase returns are deducted from purchases on both the cost and retail side (at different amounts) and freight-in is added only to the cost side in determining net purchases. If the gross method is used to record purchases, purchase discounts taken also are deducted in determining the cost of net purchases.

Likewise, net sales is found by subtracting sales returns from sales. However, sales discounts are *not* subtracted because to do so would cause the inventory to be overstated. Sales discounts do not represent an adjustment in selling price but a financial incentive for customers to pay early. On the other hand, when sales are recorded net of employee discounts, the discounts are *added* to net sales before sales are deducted in the retail column.

If sales are recorded net of employee discounts, the discounts are added to sales.

[6]Of course, any number of layers at different costs can actually be added through the years. When using the regular LIFO method, rather than LIFO retail, we would keep track of each of those layers.

For example, suppose an item of merchandise purchased for $6 is initially marked up to $10. Original selling price is therefore $10. When the item is sold, we deduct sales of $10 from the retail column. But if the item is sold to an employee for $7 (a $3 employee discount) and recorded as a $7 sale, the $3 employee discount must be added back to sales so the full $10 is deducted from goods available at retail to arrive at ending inventory at retail.

We also need to consider spoilage, breakage, and theft. So far we've assumed that by subtracting goods sold from goods available for sale, we find ending inventory. It's possible, though, that some of the goods available for sale were lost to such shortages and therefore do not remain in ending inventory.

> Normal shortage is deducted in the retail column *after* the calculation of the cost-to-retail percentage.

To take these shortages into account when using the retail method, we deduct the retail value of inventory lost due to spoilage, breakage, or theft in the retail column. These losses are expected for most retail ventures so they are referred to as *normal shortage* and are deducted in the retail column *after* the calculation of the cost to retail percentage. Because these losses are anticipated, they are included implicitly in the determination of selling prices. Including normal spoilage in the calculation of the percentage would distort the normal relationship between cost and retail. *Abnormal shortage* should be deducted in the retail column *before* the calculation of the cost to retail percentage. These losses are not anticipated and are not included in the determination of selling prices.

> Abnormal shortage is deducted in the retail column *before* the calculation of the cost-to-retail percentage.

The following concept review exercise considers some of these previously ignored elements.

CONCEPT REVIEW EXERCISE   RETAIL INVENTORY METHOD

The Henderson Company uses the retail inventory method to estimate ending inventory and cost of goods sold. The following data for 1997 is available in Henderson's accounting records:

	Cost	Retail
Beginning inventory	$ 8,000	$12,000
Purchases	68,000	98,000
Freight-in	3,200	
Purchase returns	3,000	4,200
Net markups		6,000
Net markdowns		2,400
Normal spoilage		1,800
Net sales		92,000

The company records sales net of employee discounts. These discounts for 1997 totaled $2,300.

Required:

1. Estimate Henderson's ending inventory and cost of goods sold for the year using the conventional retail method (LCM, average cost).
2. Estimate Henderson's ending inventory and cost of goods sold for the year using the LIFO retail method.

CONCEPT REVIEW EXERCISE   SOLUTION

1. Estimate Henderson's ending inventory and cost of goods sold for the year using the conventional retail method (LCM, average cost).

		Cost	Retail
Beginning inventory		$ 8,000	$12,000
Plus:	Purchases	68,000	98,000
	Freight-in	3,200	
Less:	Purchase returns	(3,000)	(4,200)
Plus:	Net markups		6,000
			111,800

Cost to retail percentage: $\dfrac{\$76,200}{\$111,800} = \underline{\underline{68.16\%}}$

		Cost	Retail
Less: Net markdowns			(2,400)
Goods available for sale		76,200	109,400
Less: Normal spoilage			(1,800)
Sales:			
Net sales	$92,000		
Add back employee discounts	2,300		(94,300)
Estimated ending inventory at retail			$ 13,300
Estimated ending inventory at cost (68.16% × $13,300)		(9,065)	
Estimated cost of goods sold		$67,135	

2. Estimate Henderson's ending inventory and cost of goods sold for the year using the LIFO retail method.

		Cost	Retail
Beginning inventory		$ 8,000	$ 12,000
Plus: Purchases		68,000	98,000
Freight-in		3,200	
Less: Purchase returns		(3,000)	(4,200)
Plus: Net markups			6,000
Less: Net markdowns			(2,400)
Goods available for sale (excluding beginning inventory)		68,200	97,400
Goods available for sale (including beginning inventory)		76,200	109,400

Cost to retail percentage: $\dfrac{\$68,200}{\$97,400} = 70.02\%$

		Cost	Retail
Less: Normal spoilage			(1,800)
Sales:			
Net sales	$92,000		
Add back employee discounts	2,300		(94,300)
Estimated ending inventory at retail			$ 13,300
Estimated ending inventory at cost:			

	Retail		Cost
Beginning inventory	$12,000	× 66.67%*	$8,000
Current period's layer	1,300	× 70.02%	910
Total	$13,300		$8,910

		Cost	Retail
Total		(8,910)	
Estimated cost of goods sold		$67,290	

*$8,000 ÷ $12,000 = 66.67%

PART

Learning objective 5
Determine ending inventory using the dollar-value LIFO retail inventory method.

OPENING CASE

Question 2

Using the *retail method* to approximate *LIFO* is referred to as the **dollar-value LIFO retail method**.

C DOLLAR-VALUE LIFO RETAIL

In our earlier illustration of the LIFO retail method, we assumed that the retail prices of the inventory remained stable during the period. If you recall, we compared the ending inventory (at retail) with the beginning inventory (at retail) to see if inventory had increased. If the dollar amount of ending inventory exceeded the beginning amount we assumed a new LIFO layer had been added. But this isn't necessarily true. It may be that the dollar amount of ending inventory exceeded the beginning amount simply because prices increased, without an actual change in the quantity of goods. So, to see if there's been a "real" increase in quantity, we need a way to eliminate the effect of any price changes before we compare the ending inventory with the beginning inventory. Fortunately, we can accomplish this by combining two methods we've already discussed—the LIFO retail method (Part B of this chapter) and dollar-value LIFO (previous chapter). The combination is called the **dollar-value LIFO retail method**.

To illustrate, we return to the Home Improvement Stores situation (Illustration 9–7) in which we applied LIFO retail. Now, though, in Illustration 9–7a let's assume that retail prices did not remain stable during 1997, but instead the price level (as measured by a retail price index) increased from 1 to 1.10. We follow the LIFO retail procedure up to the point of comparing the ending inventory with the beginning inventory. However, because prices have risen, the apparent increase in inventory is only partly due to an additional layer of inventory and partly due to the increase in retail prices. The real increase is found by deflating the ending inventory amount to beginning of the year prices before comparing beginning and ending amounts. We did this with the dollar-value LIFO technique discussed in the previous chapter.[7]

	Cost	Retail
Beginning inventory	$ 99,200	$160,000
Plus: Net purchases	305,280	470,000
Net markups		10,000
Less: Net markdowns		(8,000)
Goods available for sale (excluding beginning inventory)	305,280	472,000
Goods available for sale (including beginning inventory)	404,480	632,000

Base layer cost-to-retail percentage: $\frac{\$\,99{,}200}{\$160{,}000}$ = 62%

1997 layer cost-to-retail percentage: $\frac{\$305{,}280}{\$472{,}000}$ = 64.68%

Less: Net sales		(434,000)
Ending inventory at current year retail prices		$198,000
Estimated ending inventory at cost (calculated below)	(113,430)	
Estimated cost of goods sold	$291,050	

Ending Inventory at Year-end Retail Prices	Step 1 Ending Inventory at Base Year Retail Prices	Step 2 Inventory Layers at Base Year Retail Prices	Step 3 Inventory Layers Converted to Cost
$198,000 (determined above)	$\frac{\$198{,}000}{1.10}$ = $180,000	$180,000	
		160,000 (base) × 1.00 × .62 =	$ 99,200
		$ 20,000 (1997) × 1.10 × .6468 =	14,230
	Total ending inventory at dollar-value LIFO retail cost		$113,430

In this illustration, a $20,000 1997 layer is added to the base layer. Two adjustments are needed to convert this amount to LIFO cost. Multiplying by the 1997 price index (1.10) converts it from its base year retail to 1997 retail. Multiplying by the 1997 cost-to-retail percentage (.6468) converts it from its 1997 retail to 1997 cost. The two steps are combined in our illustration. The base year inventory also is converted to cost. The two layers are added to derive ending inventory at dollar-value LIFO retail cost.

When additional layers are added in subsequent years, their LIFO amounts are determined the same way. For illustration, let's assume ending inventory in 1998 is $226,200 at current retail prices and the price level has risen to 1.16. Also assume that the cost-to-retail percentage for 1998 net purchases is 63%. In Illustration 9–7b, the ending inventory is converted to base year retail (step 1). This amount is apportioned into layers, each at base year retail (step 2). Layers then are converted to layer year costs (step 3).

Ending Inventory at Year-end Retail Prices	Step 1 Ending Inventory at Base Year Retail Prices	Step 2 Inventory Layers at Base Year Retail Prices	Step 3 Inventory Layers Converted to LIFO Cost
$226,200 (assumed)	$\frac{\$226{,}200}{1.16}$ = $195,000	$195,000	
		160,000 (base) × 1.00 × .62 =	$ 99,200
		$ 20,000 (1997) × 1.10 × .6468 =	14,230
		$ 15,000 (1998) × 1.16 × .63 =	10,962
	Total ending inventory at dollar-value LIFO retail cost		$124,392

[7]The index used here is analogous to the cost index used in regular DVL except that it reflects the change in retail prices rather than in acquisition costs.

Now let's assume that ending inventory in 1998 is $204,160 at current retail prices (instead of $226,200) and the price level has risen to 1.16. Also assume that the cost-to-retail percentage for 1998 net purchases is 63%. Step 1 converts the ending inventory to a base year price of $176,000 ($204,160 ÷ 1.16). A comparison to the beginning inventory at base year prices of $180,000 ($160,000 base year layer + $20,000 1997 layer) indicates that inventory *decreased* during 1998. In this case, no 1998 layer is added and 1998 ending inventory at dollar-value LIFO retail of $110,584 is determined in Illustration 9–7c.

ILLUSTRATION 9–7c	
The Dollar-Value LIFO Retail Inventory Method	

Ending Inventory at Year-end Retail Prices	Step 1 Ending Inventory at Base Year Retail Prices	Step 2 Inventory Layers at Base Year Retail Prices	Step 3 Inventory Layers Converted to LIFO Cost
$204,160 (assumed)	$\dfrac{\$204,160}{1.16}$ = $176,000 →	$176,000	
		160,000 (base) × 1.00 × .62 =	$ 99,200
		16,000 (1997) × 1.10 × .6468 =	11,384
	Total ending inventory at dollar-value LIFO retail cost		$110,584

A portion of the 1997 inventory layer has been liquidated—reduced from $20,000 to $16,000 at base year prices—to reduce total inventory at base year prices to $176,000.

CONCEPT REVIEW EXERCISE   DOLLAR-VALUE LIFO RETAIL METHOD

On January 1, 1997, the Nicholson Department Store adopted the dollar-value LIFO retail inventory method. Inventory transactions at both cost and retail and cost indexes for 1997 and 1998 are as follows:

	1997		1998	
	Cost	Retail	Cost	Retail
January 1, 1997	$16,000	$24,000		
Net purchases	42,000	58,500	45,000	58,700
Net markups		3,000		2,400
Net markdowns		1,500		1,100
Net sales		56,000		57,000
Price Index:				
January 1, 1997	1.00			
December 31, 1997	1.08			
December 31, 1998	1.15			

Required:
Estimate the 1997 and 1998 ending inventory and cost of goods sold using the dollar-value LIFO retail inventory method.

CONCEPT REVIEW EXERCISE   SOLUTION

	1997		1998	
	Cost	Retail	Cost	Retail
Beginning inventory	$16,000	$24,000	$17,456	$28,000
Plus: Net purchases	42,000	58,500	45,000	58,700
Net markups		3,000		2,400
Less: Net markdowns		(1,500)		(1,100)
Goods available for sale (excluding beg. inv.)	42,000	60,000	45,000	60,000
Goods available for sale (including beg. inv.)	58,000	84,000	62,456	88,000

Base layer
Cost-to-retail percentage: $\dfrac{\$16,000}{\$24,000}$ = 66.67%

1997
Cost-to-retail percentage: $\dfrac{\$42,000}{\$60,000} = \underline{70\%}$

1998
Cost-to-retail percentage: $\dfrac{\$45,000}{\$60,000} = \underline{75\%}$

Less: Net sales		(56,000)	(57,000)
Estimated ending inv. at current year retail prices		$28,000	$31,000
Less: Estimated ending inventory at cost (below)	17,456		18,345
Estimated cost of goods sold	$40,544		$44,111

1997

Ending Inventory at Year-end Retail Prices	Step 1 Ending Inventory at Base Year Retail Prices	Step 2 Inventory Layers at Base Year Retail Prices	Step 3 Inventory Layers Converted to Cost
$28,000 (above)	$\dfrac{\$28,000}{1.08} = \$25,926$	$24,000 (base) × 1.00 × 66.67% =	$16,000
		1,926 (1997) × 1.08 × 70.00% =	1,456
			$17,456

Total ending inventory at dollar-value LIFO retail cost

1998

Ending Inventory at Year-end Retail Prices	Step 1 Ending Inventory at Base Year Retail Prices	Step 2 Inventory Layers at Base Year Retail Prices	Step 3 Inventory Layers Converted to Cost
$31,000 (above)	$\dfrac{\$31,000}{1.15} = \$26,957$	$24,000 (base) × 1.00 × 66.67% =	$16,000
		1,926 (1997) × 1.08 × 70.00% =	1,456
		1,031 (1998) × 1.15 × 75.00% =	889
			$18,345

Total ending inventory at dollar-value LIFO retail cost

PART

D CHANGE IN INVENTORY METHOD AND INVENTORY ERRORS

Change in Accounting Principle

Learning objective 6
Explain the appropriate accounting treatment required when a change in inventory method is made.

Accounting principles should be applied consistently from period to period to allow for comparability of operating results. However, changes within a company as well as changes in the external economic environment may require a company to change an accounting method. As we mentioned in Chapter 8, high inflation in the 1970s motivated many companies to switch to the LIFO inventory method.

Specific accounting treatment and disclosures are prescribed for companies that change accounting principles. Chapter 3 introduced the subject of accounting changes and Chapter 21 provides in-depth coverage of the topic. Here we provide an overview of how changes in inventory methods are reported.

Changes Not Involving LIFO

For changes not involving LIFO, the cumulative after-tax effect on prior years' income is reported as a separate item of income.

For most accounting changes, the effect of the change is accounted for by reporting it on the income statement in the year of change rather than by restating prior years' financial statements to the new method. Changes in inventory method that don't involve LIFO are treated this way. The amount reported is the cumulative effect of the change, which is the difference between retained earnings at the beginning of the year of the change as reported and the beginning of year retained earnings that would have resulted if the new accounting method had been used in all prior years. The cumulative after-tax effect is reported on the income statement immediately below any discontinued operations and extraordinary items. Consider Illustration 9–8.

ILLUSTRATION   9 – 8

Change in Inventory Method

In early 1997, the Xavier Company changed its method of valuing inventory from the average cost method to the FIFO cost method. At December 31, 1996, and December 31, 1995, Xavier's inventories were $46 million and $43 million, respectively. Xavier's records indicated that inventories would have totaled $58 million at December 31, 1996, and $50 million at December 31, 1995, if FIFO had been used. Xavier's financial statements include the current year and one prior year for comparative purposes.

For inventory to reflect the FIFO cost method, its balance must be increased by $12 million (from $46 million to $58 million). Prior years' cost of goods sold would have been lower and income before income tax higher by $12 million if FIFO had been used. Of course, income tax expense also would have been higher. With a 40% tax rate, the after-tax effect would be $7.2 million. The cumulative effect reported in the 1997 income statement is the net of tax effect on prior years' income. The change is reported on Xavier's income statement as follows:

	($ in millions) 1997
Income before extraordinary item and accounting change	$xxx
Extraordinary gain (loss), net of tax	xx
Cumulative effect of accounting change (net of $4.8 tax)	7.2
Net income	$xxx

The effect of the change on certain key income numbers is disclosed for all periods reported.

Previous financial statements are not restated. However, the effect of the change on certain key income numbers is disclosed on a pro forma (as if) basis for financial statements of all prior periods that are included for comparison purposes with the current financial statements. Specifically, income statements should include pro forma restatement of (a) income before extraordinary items, (b) net income, and (c) earnings per share for both income amounts. In addition, a disclosure note describes the change and justification for the change along with the effect of the change on the current year's income numbers. The pro forma information allows for a comparison of current and prior years' operating results using the new method. The disclosure note information indicates the effect of the change on the current year's income numbers permitting the same comparison using the old method.

For changes that involve LIFO, reporting requirements are different from the usual way changes in accounting principles are reported. As we see next, accounting treatment depends on whether the change is *to* LIFO or *from* LIFO.

Change to the LIFO Method

Accounting records usually are inadequate for a company changing *to LIFO* to report the cumulative income effect.

When a company changes to the LIFO inventory method from any other method, it usually is impossible to calculate the cumulative effect. To do so would require assumptions as to when specific LIFO inventory layers were created in years prior to the change. As a result, a company changing to LIFO does not report the cumulative income effect. Instead, the LIFO method simply is used from that point on. The base year inventory for all future LIFO determinations is the beginning inventory in the year the LIFO method is adopted.[8]

A disclosure note is needed to explain (a) the nature of and justification for the change, (b) the effect of the change on current year's income and earnings per share, and (c) why the cumulative income effect was omitted. When Chesapeake Corporation adopted the LIFO inventory method, it reported the change in the note shown in Graphic 9–4.

As mentioned in Chapter 8, inflation was extremely high in 1974 causing hundreds of companies to switch to LIFO. With costs rising, LIFO produces a higher cost of goods sold and lower net income than does FIFO, accounting for the decline in reported net income of the switch for all of these companies. Each of these companies paid significantly lower income taxes in 1974 than they would have if not for the switch to LIFO. Graphic 9–5 lists the earnings per share (EPS) effect of the switch from FIFO to LIFO for just a few of the hundreds of companies that switched to LIFO in 1974.

---

[8]A change to LIFO is handled the same way for income tax purposes.

GRAPHIC   9 – 4

Change in Inventory Method Disclosure—Chesapeake Corporation

Note 6 : Change in Accounting Principle (in part)
Effective January 1, 1994, the Company changed the method of valuation of raw materials, work-in-process and finished goods of its Wisconsin Tissue Mills Inc. subsidiary from the average cost method to the LIFO method and expanded the use of the LIFO method to include all of the work-in-process and finished goods of its Chesapeake Packing Co. subsidiary. The Company believes that, in periods of rapid cost increases, such as were experienced by the paper industry during 1994, use of the LIFO method will result in a better matching of current costs with current revenues. The effects of adopting the LIFO method at Wisconsin Tissue and expanding the use of the LIFO method at Chesapeake Packing were to reduce consolidated year-end inventories by $4.4 million and to decrease net income by $2.8 million ($.12 per share). The cumulative effect of this change to the LIFO method on the operating results as of the beginning of 1994 and the pro forma effects on the operating results of prior years have not been presented, as the effects are not readily determinable.

GRAPHIC   9 – 5

Income Effect of Change to LIFO—1974 Examples

Company	FIFO EPS	LIFO EPS	% Effect of the Switch
DuPont	$6.27	$5.10	−18.7
Eastman Kodak	1.68	1.54	− 8.3
Firestone Tire	2.40	1.53	−36.2
Florida Steel	4.61	3.96	−14.1
Marathon Oil	4.84	4.32	−10.8
Std. Oil of Ohio	2.27	2.02	−11.0
Stokely Van Camp	3.69	2.70	−26.8

Change from the LIFO Method

Because of their unique nature, some changes in accounting principle are accounted for by restating prior years' financial statements for the income effect of the change, rather than by reporting that effect as part of net income in the year the change occurs. Usually the effect of these changes is quite large. If the total effect is recognized currently, net income would be distorted in the year of the change. Also, previous financial statements would lose meaning if not restated for such large changes.

A change from the LIFO inventory method to any other inventory method is one of these changes in accounting principle that is accounted for retroactively. We *restate* financial statements for each year reported for comparative purposes to reflect the use of the new method. Each financial statement is thereby presented on a comparable basis. Also, a description of the change and justification for the change, along with the effect of the change on income for all years presented, should be provided in the disclosure notes to the financial statements.

> A change *from* the LIFO method to another inventory method is a change in accounting principle requiring retroactive restatement.

Additional Consideration

When changing from one generally accepted accounting principle to another, a company must justify that the change results in financial information that more properly portrays operating results and financial position. For income tax purposes, a company generally must obtain consent from the Internal Revenue Service before changing an accounting method. A special form also must be filed with the IRS when a company intends to adopt the LIFO inventory method.

Inventory Errors

Learning objective 7
Explain the appropriate accounting treatment required when an inventory error is discovered.

Accounting errors must be corrected when they are discovered. In Chapter 3 we briefly discussed the correction of accounting errors and Chapter 21 provides in-depth coverage. Here we overview the accounting treatment and disclosures in the context of inventory errors. Inventory errors include the over- or understatement of ending inventory due to a mistake in a physical count or a mistake in pricing inventory quantities. Also, errors include the over- or understatement of purchases, which could be caused by the cutoff errors described in Chapter 8.

If an inventory error is discovered in the same accounting period it occurred, the original erroneous entry should simply be reversed and the appropriate entry recorded. This situation presents no particular reporting problem.

If a *material* inventory error is discovered in an accounting period subsequent to the period in which the error was made, any previous years' financial statements that were incorrect as a result of the error are retroactively restated to reflect the correction.[9] And, of course, any account balances that are incorrect as a result of the error are corrected by journal entry. If, due to an error affecting net income, retained earnings is one of the incorrect accounts, the correction is reported as a prior period adjustment to the beginning balance on the statement of shareholders' equity.[10] In addition, a disclosure note is needed to describe the nature of the error and the impact of its correction on net income, income before extraordinary item, and earnings per share.

When analyzing inventory errors, it's helpful to visualize the way cost of goods sold, net income and retained earnings are determined. (See Graphic 9–6.) Of course, errors that affect income also will affect income taxes. In the illustration that follows, we ignore the tax effects of the errors and focus on the errors themselves rather than their tax aspects.

> Previous years' financial statements are retroactively restated.
>
> Incorrect balances are corrected.
>
> A correction of retained earnings is reported as a prior period adjustment.
>
> A disclosure note describes the nature and the impact of the error.

GRAPHIC   9–6

Visualizing the Effect of Inventory Errors

Let's look at an example in Illustration 9–9.

ILLUSTRATION   9–9

Inventory Error Correction

The Halliburton Company uses a periodic inventory system. At the end of 1996, a mathematical error caused an $800,000 overstatement of ending inventory. Ending inventories for 1997 and 1998 are correctly determined.

The way we correct this error depends on when the error is discovered. Assuming that the error is not discovered until after 1997, the 1996 and 1997 effects of the error, ignoring income tax effects, are shown below. The overstated and understated amounts are $800,000 in each instance.

Analysis: U = Understated   O = Overstated

1996		1997	
Beginning inventory		Beginning inventory	O
Plus: Net purchases		Plus: Net purchases	
Less: Ending inventory	O	Less: Ending inventory	
Cost of goods sold	U	Cost of goods sold	O
Revenues		Revenues	
Less: Cost of goods sold	U	Less: Cost of goods sold	O
Less: Other expenses		Less: Other expenses	
Net income	O	Net income	U
↓		↓	
Retained earnings	O	Retained earnings	*corrected*

---

[9]If the effect of the error is not material, it is simply corrected in the year of discovery.

[10]The prior period adjustment is applied to beginning retained earnings for the year following the error, or for the earliest year being reported in the comparative financial statements when the error occurs prior to the earliest year presented. The retained earnings balances in years after the first year also are adjusted to what those balances would be if the error had not occurred, but a company may choose not to explicitly report those adjustments as separate line items.

When the Inventory Error Is Discovered the Following Year

First, let's assume the error is discovered in 1997. The 1996 financial statements that were incorrect as a result of the error are retroactively restated to reflect the correct inventory amount, cost of goods sold, net income, and retained earnings when those statements are reported again for comparative purposes in the 1997 annual report. The following journal entry, ignoring income taxes, corrects the error:

Retained earnings	800,000	
Inventory		800,000

Because retained earnings is one of the accounts that is incorrect when the error is discovered in 1997, the correction to that account is reported as a prior period adjustment to the 1997 beginning retained earnings balance in Halliburton's statement of shareholders' equity (or statement of retained earnings). Prior period adjustments do not flow through the income statement but directly adjust retained earnings. This adjustment is illustrated in Chapter 21.

When the Inventory Error Is Discovered Subsequent to the Following Year

If the error isn't discovered until 1998, the 1997 financial statements also are retroactively restated to reflect the correct cost of goods sold and net income even though no correcting entry would be needed at that point. Inventory and retained earnings would not require adjustment. The error has self-corrected and no prior period adjustment is needed.

Also, a disclosure note in Halliburton's annual report should describe the nature of the error and the impact of its correction on each year's net income (overstated by $800,000 in 1996; understated by $800,000 in 1997), income before extraordinary items (same as net income in this case), and earnings per share.

Solution to Financial Reporting Case (at the opening of the chapter)

A departure from historical cost is warranted when the probable benefits to be received from any asset drop below the asset's cost. The benefits from inventory result from the ultimate sale of the goods. Deterioration, obsolescence, and changes in price levels are situations that might cause the benefits to be received from sale to drop below cost. The lower-of-cost-or-market approach recognizes losses in the period when the value of the inventory declines below its cost rather than in the period in which the goods ultimately are sold.

Kmart uses the dollar-value LIFO retail inventory method. The retail inventory estimation technique avoids the counting of ending inventory by keeping track of goods available for sale not only at cost but also at retail prices. Each period's sales, at sales prices, are deducted from the retail amount of goods available for sale to arrive at ending inventory at retail. This amount is then converted to cost using a cost-to-retail percentage.

The dollar-value LIFO retail method uses a price index to first convert ending inventory at retail to base year prices. Yearly LIFO layers are then determined and each layer is converted to that year's current year retail prices using the year's price index and then to cost using the layer's cost-to-retail percentage. For the price index, Kmart uses an internally generated index rather than an external price index.

The Bottom Line

1. Inventory is valued at the lower of cost or market (LCM). The designated market value in the LCM rule is the middle number of replacement cost (RC), net realizable value (NRV), and net realizable value less a normal profit margin (NRV – NP).

2. The gross profit method estimates cost of goods sold which is then subtracted from cost of goods available for sale to estimate ending inventory. The estimate of cost of goods sold is determined by subtracting an estimate of gross profit from net sales. The estimate of gross profit is determined by multiplying the historical gross profit ratio times net sales.

3. The retail inventory method determines the amount of ending inventory at retail by subtracting sales for the period from goods available for sale at retail. Ending inventory at retail is then converted to *cost* by multiplying it by the cost-to-retail percentage, which is based on a current relationship between cost and selling price.

4. By the conventional retail method, we estimate average cost at lower of cost or market. Average cost is estimated by including beginning inventory in the calculation of the cost-to-retail percentage. LCM is estimated by excluding markdowns from the calculation. Markdowns are subtracted in the retail column after the percentage is calculated.

5. By the LIFO retail method, ending inventory includes the beginning inventory plus the current year's layer. To determine layers, we compare ending inventory at retail to beginning inventory at retail and assume that no more than one inventory layer is added if inventory increases. Each layer carries its own cost-to-retail percentage which is used to convert each layer from retail to cost. The dollar-value LIFO retail inventory method combines the LIFO retail method and the dollar-value LIFO method (Chapter 8) to estimate LIFO from retail prices when the price level has changed.

6. When a company changes its inventory method, the accounting treatment depends on whether or not the LIFO method is involved. For changes not involving LIFO, the event is accounted for as a normal change in accounting principle with the cumulative effect of the change reported on the income statement in the year of the change. When a company changes to LIFO, no cumulative effect is reported. A change from the LIFO method is a change in accounting principle requiring retroactive restatement.

7. If a material inventory error is discovered in an accounting period subsequent to the period in which the error is made, previous years' financial statements that were incorrect as a result of the error are retroactively restated to reflect the correction. Account balances are corrected by journal entry. A correction of retained earnings is reported as a prior period adjustment to the beginning balance on the statement of shareholders' equity. In addition, a disclosure note is needed to describe the nature of the error and the impact of its correction on income.

not on test?

APPENDIX

9

PURCHASE COMMITMENTS

Purchase commitments protect the buyer against price increases and provide a supply of product.

Purchase commitments are contracts that obligate a company to purchase a specified amount of merchandise or raw materials at specified prices on or before specified dates. Companies enter into these agreements to make sure they will be able to obtain important inventory as well as to protect against increases in purchase price. However, if the purchase price decreases before the agreement is exercised, the commitment has the disadvantage of requiring the company to purchase inventory at a higher than market price. If this happens, a loss on the purchase commitment is recorded.

Purchases made pursuant to a purchase commitment are recorded at the lower of contract price or market price on the date the contract is executed.

Because purchase commitments create the possibility of this kind of loss, the loss occurs when the market price falls below the commitment price rather than when the inventory eventually is sold. This means recording the loss when the product is purchased or, if the commitment is still outstanding, at the end of the reporting period. In other words, purchases are recorded at market price when that price is lower than the contract price, and a loss is recognized for the difference. Also, losses are recognized for any purchase commitments outstanding at the end of a reporting period when market price is less than contract price. In effect, the LCM rule is applied to purchase commitments. This is best understood by the example in Illustration 9A-1.

ILLUSTRATION   9A–1

Purchase Commitments

> In July 1997, the Lassiter Company signed two purchase commitments. The first requires Lassiter to purchase inventory for $500,000 by November 15, 1997. The second requires the company to purchase inventory for $600,000 by February 15, 1998. Lassiter's fiscal year-end is December 31. The company uses a perpetual inventory system.

Contract Period within Fiscal Year

The contract period for the first commitment is contained within a single fiscal year. Lassiter would record the purchase at the contract price if the market price at date of acquisition is at least *equal to* the contract price of $500,000.[11]

If market price is equal to or greater than the contract price, the purchase is recorded at the contract price.

Inventory (contract price)	500,000	
Cash (or accounts payable)		500,000

If the market price at acquisition is *less* than the contract price, inventory is recorded at the market price and a loss is recognized.[12] For example, if the market price is $425,000, the following entry records the purchase:

If market price is less than the contract price, the purchase is recorded at the market price.

Inventory (market price)	425,000	
Loss on purchase commitment	75,000	
Cash (or accounts payable)		500,000

The objective of this treatment is to associate the loss with the period in which the price declines rather than with the period in which the company eventually sells the inventory. This is the same objective as the LCM rule you studied in the chapter.

Contract Period Extends beyond Fiscal Year

Now let's consider Lassiter's second purchase commitment that is outstanding at the end of the fiscal year 1997 (that is, the purchases have not yet been made). If the market price at the end of the year is at least *equal to* the contract price of $600,000, no entry is recorded. However, if the market price at year-end is *less* than the contract price, a loss must be recognized to satisfy the LCM objective of associating the loss with the period in which the price declines rather than with the period in which the company eventually sells the inventory. Let's say the year-end market price of the inventory for Lassiter's second purchase commitment is $540,000. The following adjusting entry is recorded:

If the market price at year-end is less than the contract price for outstanding purchase commitments, a loss is recorded for the difference.

December 31, 1997

Estimated loss on purchase commitment ($600,000 – 540,000)	60,000	
Estimated liability on purchase commitment		60,000

A liability is credited for estimated losses on purchase commitments.

At this point, the loss is an *estimated* loss. The actual loss, if any, will not be known until the inventory actually is purchased. The best estimate of the market price on date of purchase is the

---

[11]In each of the following situations, if a periodic inventory system is used *purchases* is debited instead of *inventory*.

[12]Recall from the LCM discussion in the chapter that the preferred method of recording losses from inventory write-downs is to recognize the loss as a separate item on the income statement, rather than as an increase in cost of goods sold.

current market price, in this case $540,000. Because no inventory has been acquired, we can't credit inventory for the LCM loss. Instead, a liability is credited because, in a sense, the loss represents an obligation to the seller of the inventory to purchase inventory above market price.

Earlier in this chapter, the Polavision inventory write-down for Polaroid Corporation provided an example of the application of the LCM rule. Notice in the newspaper article that the $68 million loss includes not only a reduction in the book value of inventory but also losses on remaining purchase commitments.

The entry to record the actual purchase on or before February 15, 1998, will vary depending on the market price of the inventory at date of purchase. If the market price is unchanged or has increased from the year-end price, the following entry is made:

> POLAROID SLICES BOOK **CAMBRIDGE, MASS.** VALUE OF POLAVISION   **Polaroid Corp.** announced yesterday it will reduce by **$68 million the book value of its inventory of Polavision products and the remaining purchase commitments to its supplier of equipment for the instant movie system.**
>
> Company spokesman Don Dery said the company will charge the revaluation to Polaroid's third quarter profits. "We'll probably show a loss for the third quarter," Dery said. (Excerpt from article appearing in the *San Jose Mercury News,* September 1979.)

If market price on purchase date has not declined from year-end price, the purchase is recorded at the year-end market price.

Inventory (accounting cost)	540,000	
Estimated liability on purchase commitment	60,000	
Cash (or accounts payable)		600,000

Even if the market price of the inventory increases, there is no recovery of the $60,000 loss recognized in 1997. Remember that when the LCM rule is applied, the reduced inventory value, in this case the reduced value of purchases, is considered to be the new cost and any recovery of value is ignored.

If the market price declines even further from year-end levels, an additional loss is recognized. For example, if the market price of the inventory covered by the commitment declines to $510,000, the following entry is recorded:

If market price on purchase date declines from year-end price, the purchase is recorded at the market price.

Inventory (market price)	510,000	
Loss on purchase commitment ($540,000 – 510,000)	30,000	
Estimated liability on purchase commitment	60,000	
Cash (or accounts payable)		600,000

The total loss on this purchase commitment of $90,000 is thus allocated between 1997 and 1998 according to when the decline in value of the inventory covered by the commitment occurred.

If there are material amounts of purchase commitments outstanding at the end of a reporting period, the contract details are disclosed in a note. This disclosure is required even if no loss estimate has been recorded.

▌Questions for Review of Key Topics

Question	9–1	Explain the lower-of-cost-or-market approach to valuing inventory.
Question	9–2	What is the meaning of market in the lower-of-cost-or-market rule?
Question	9–3	What are the various ways the LCM determination can be made?
Question	9–4	Describe the preferred method of adjusting from cost to market for material inventory write-downs.
Question	9–5	Explain the gross profit method of estimating ending inventory.
Question	9–6	The Rider Company uses the gross profit method to estimate ending inventory and cost of goods sold. The cost percentage is determined based on historical data. What factors could cause the estimate of ending inventory to be overstated?
Question	9–7	Explain the retail inventory method of estimating ending inventory.
Question	9–8	Both the gross profit method and the retail inventory method provide a way to estimate ending inventory. What is the main difference between the two estimation techniques?
Question	9–9	Define each of the following retail terms: initial markup, additional markup, markup cancellation, markdown, markdown cancellation.

Question	9–10	Explain how to estimate the average cost of inventory when using the retail inventory method.
Question	9–11	What is the conventional retail method?
Question	9–12	Explain the LIFO retail inventory method.
Question	9–13	Discuss the treatment of freight-in, net markups, normal spoilage, and employee discounts in the application of the retail inventory method.
Question	9–14	Explain the difference between the retail inventory method using LIFO and the dollar-value LIFO retail method.
Question	9–15	Describe the accounting treatment of a change in inventory method that does not involve LIFO.
Question	9–16	When a company changes its inventory method to or from LIFO, an exception is made for the way accounting changes usually are reported. Explain the difference in the accounting treatment of a change *to* the LIFO inventory method and a change *from* LIFO.
Question	9–17	Explain the accounting treatment of material inventory errors discovered in an accounting period subsequent to the period in which the error is made.
Question	9–18	It is discovered in 1997 that ending inventory in 1995 was understated. What is the effect of the understatement on the following:

        1995:   Cost of goods sold
                   Net income
                   Ending retained earnings
        1996:   Net purchases
                   Cost of goods sold
                   Net income
                   Ending retained earnings

Question	9–19	Define purchase commitments. What is the advantage(s) of these agreements to buyers?
[based on Appendix 9]		
Question	9–20	Explain how the lower-of-cost-or-market rule is applied to purchase commitments.
[based on Appendix 9]		

Exercises

Exercise 9–1
Lower of cost or market

The Herman Company has three products in its ending inventory. Specific per unit data for each of the products is as follows:

	Product 1	Product 2	Product 3
Cost	$20	$ 90	$50
Replacement cost	18	85	40
Selling price	40	150	70
Disposal costs	6	40	10
Normal profit margin	5	30	12

(handwritten: on exam)

Required:

What unit values should Herman use for each of its products when applying the LCM rule to ending inventory?

Exercise 9–2
Lower of cost or market

The Tatum Company has four products in its inventory. Information about the December 31, 1997, inventory is as follows:

Product	Total Cost	Total Replacement Cost	Total Net Realizable Value
101	$120,000	$110,000	$100,000
102	90,000	85,000	110,000
103	60,000	40,000	50,000
104	30,000	28,000	50,000

(handwritten: PM 30,000 / 22,500 / 15,000 / 7,500)

(handwritten left margin: Re-do for test study)

The normal gross profit percentage is 25 percent of *cost*.

Required:

1.   Determine the balance sheet inventory carrying value at December 31, 1997, assuming the LCM rule is applied to individual products.
2.   Assuming that Tatum recognizes an inventory write-down as a separate income statement item, determine the amount of the loss.

(handwritten bottom left: Loss on LCM Inv.)

(handwritten bottom center: $42,500)

Exercise 9–3
Gross profit method

On September 22, 1997, a flood destroyed the entire merchandise inventory on hand in a warehouse owned by the Rocklin Sporting Goods Company. The following information is available from the records of the company's periodic inventory system:

Inventory, January 1, 1997	$120,000
Net purchases, January 1 through September 22	370,000
Net sales, January 1 through September 22	500,000
Gross profit ratio	20%

Required:
Estimate the cost of inventory destroyed in the flood using the gross profit method.

Exercise 9–4
Gross profit method

On November 21, 1997, a fire at Hodge Company's warehouse caused severe damage to its entire inventory of Product Tex. Hodge estimates that all usable damaged goods can be sold for $10,000. The following information was available from the records of Hodge's periodic inventory system:

Inventory, November 1	$100,000
Net purchases from November 1, to the date of the fire	140,000
Net sales from November 1, to the date of the fire	220,000

Based on recent history, Hodge's gross profit ratio on Product Tex is 30% of net sales.

Required:
Calculate the estimated loss on the inventory from the fire, using the gross profit method.

(AICPA adapted)

Exercise 9–5
Gross profit method

A fire destroyed a warehouse of the Goren Group, Inc., on May 4, 1997. Accounting records on that date indicated the following:

Merchandise inventory, January 1, 1997	$1,800,000
Purchases to date	5,800,000
Freight-in	400,000
Sales to date	9,200,000

The gross profit ratio has averaged 30% of sales for the past four years.

Required:
Use the gross profit method to estimate the cost of the inventory destroyed in the fire.

Exercise 9–6
Gross profit method; solving for unknown cost percentage

The National Distributing Company uses a periodic inventory system to track its merchandise inventory and the gross profit method to estimate ending inventory and cost of goods sold for interim periods. Net purchases for the month of August were $31,000. The July 31 and August 31, 1997, financial statements contained the following information:

Income Statements
For the Months Ending

	August 31, 1997	July 31, 1997
Net sales	$50,000	$40,000

Balance Sheets
For the Months Ending

	August 31, 1997	July 31, 1997
Assets:		
Merchandise inventory	$28,000	$27,000

Required:
Determine the company's cost percentage.

Exercise 9–7
Retail inventory method; average cost

The San Lorenzo General Store uses a periodic inventory system and the retail inventory method to estimate ending inventory and cost of goods sold. The following data is available for the month of October 1997:

	Cost	Retail
Beginning inventory	$35,000	$50,000
Net purchases	20,760	31,600
Net markups		1,200
Net markdowns		800
Net sales		31,000

Required:

Estimate the average cost of ending inventory and cost of goods sold for October. Do not approximate LCM.

Exercise 9–8

Conventional retail method

Campbell Corporation uses the retail method to value its inventory. The following information is available for the year 1997:

	Cost	Retail
Merchandise inventory, January 1, 1997	$190,000	$280,000
Purchases	600,000	840,000
Freight-in	~~8,000~~	
Net markups		~~20,000~~
Net markdowns		~~4,000~~
Net sales		800,000

[handwritten in margin: use format shown in class notes on exam]

Required:

[handwritten: Est. End Inv   227,200]

Determine the December 31, 1997, inventory that approximates average cost, lower of cost or market. *[handwritten: Est]*

Exercise 9–9

Retail inventory method; LIFO

The Crosby Company owns a chain of hardware stores throughout the state. The company uses a periodic inventory system and the retail inventory method to estimate ending inventory and cost of goods sold. The following data is available for the three months ending March 31, 1997:

	Cost	Retail
Beginning inventory	$160,000	$280,000
Net purchases	599,200	840,000
Net markups		20,000
Net markdowns		4,000
Net sales		820,000

Required:

Estimate the LIFO cost of ending inventory and cost of goods sold for the three months ending March 31, 1997. Assume stable retail prices during the period.

Exercise 9–10

Conventional retail method; normal spoilage

The Almaden Valley Variety Store uses the retail inventory method to estimate ending inventory and cost of goods sold. Data for 1997 is as follows:

	Cost	Retail
Beginning inventory	$ 12,000	$ 20,000
Purchases	102,600	165,000
Freight-in	3,480	
Purchase returns	4,000	7,000
Net markups		6,000
Net markdowns		3,000
Normal spoilage		4,200
Net sales		156,000

Required:

Estimate the ending inventory and cost of goods sold for 1997, applying the conventional retail method (average, LCM).

Exercise 9–11

Conventional retail method; employee discounts

The LeMay Department Store uses the retail inventory method to estimate ending inventory for its monthly financial statements. The following data pertain to one of its largest departments for the month of March 1997:

	Cost	Retail
Beginning inventory	$ 40,000	$ 60,000
Purchases	201,000	400,000
Freight-in	10,752	
Purchase returns	4,000	6,000
Net markups		4,800
Net markdowns		3,500
Normal breakage		6,000
Net sales		270,000
Employee discounts		1,800

Sales are recorded net of employee discounts.

Required:

1. Compute estimated ending inventory and cost of goods sold for March applying the conventional retail method (average, LCM).
2. Recompute the cost-to-retail percentage using the average cost method and ignoring LCM considerations.

Exercise 9–12
Retail inventory method; solving for unknowns

The Adams Corporation uses a periodic inventory system and the retail inventory method to estimate ending inventory and cost of goods sold. The following data is available for the month of September 1997:

	Cost	Retail
Beginning inventory	$21,000	$35,000
Net purchases	10,500	?
Net markups		4,000
Net markdowns		1,000
Net sales		?

The company used the average cost flow method and estimated inventory at the end of September to be $17,437.50. If the company had used the LIFO cost flow method, the cost-to-retail percentage would have been 50%.

Required:
Compute net purchases at retail and net sales for the month of September.

Exercise 9–13
Multiple choice; LCM; inventory estimation techniques

The following questions dealing with the lower-of-cost-or-market rule for valuing inventory and inventory estimation techniques are adapted from questions that appeared on recent CPA examinations. Determine the response that best completes the statements or questions.

1. Which of the following statements are correct when a company applying the lower-of-cost-or-market method reports its inventory at replacement cost?
   I. The original cost is less than replacement cost.
   II. The net realizable value is greater than replacement cost.

   a. I only.
   b. II only.
   c. Both I and II.
   d. Neither I nor II.

2. Moss Co. has determined its December 31, 1997, inventory on a FIFO basis to be $400,000. Information pertaining to that inventory follows:

Estimated selling price	$408,000
Estimated cost of disposal	20,000
Normal profit margin	60,000
Current replacement cost	360,000

   Moss records losses that result from applying the lower-of-cost-or-market rule. At December 31, 1997, what should be the net carrying amount of Moss' inventory?
   a. $400,000
   b. $388,000
   c. $360,000
   d. $328,000

3. Hutch, Inc. uses the conventional retail inventory method to account for inventory. The following information relates to 1997 operations:

	Average	
	Cost	Retail
Beginning inventory and purchases	$600,000	$920,000
Net markups		40,000
Net markdowns		60,000
Sales		780,000

   What amount should be reported as cost of goods sold for 1997?
   a. $480,000
   b. $487,500
   c. $520,000
   d. $525,000

4. The following information is available for Cooke Company for 1997:

Net sales	$1,800,000
Freight-in	45,000
Purchase discount	25,000
Ending inventory	120,000

   The gross margin is 40% of net sales. What is the cost of goods available for sale?
   a. $ 840,000
   b. $ 960,000
   c. $1,200,000
   d. $1,220,000

Exercise 9–14
Dollar-value LIFO retail

On January 1, 1997, the Brunswick Hat Company adopted the dollar-value LIFO retail method. The following data is available for 1997:

	Cost	Retail
Beginning inventory	$ 71,280	$132,000
Net purchases	120,000	255,000
Net markups		6,000
Net markdowns		11,000
Net sales		230,000
Retail price index, 12/31/97		1.04

Required:
Calculate the estimated ending inventory and cost of goods sold for 1997.

Exercise 9–15
Dollar-value LIFO retail

The Canova Corporation adopted the dollar-value LIFO retail method on January 1, 1997. On that date, the cost of the inventory on hand was $15,000 and its retail value was $18,750. Information for 1997 and 1998 is as follows:

Date	Ending Inventory at Retail	Retail Price Index	Cost-to-Retail Percentage
12/31/97	$25,000	1.25	82%
12/31/98	28,600	1.30	85

Required:
1. What is the cost-to-retail percentage for the inventory on hand at 1/1/97?
2. Calculate the inventory value at the end of 1997 and 1998 using the dollar-value LIFO retail method.

Exercise 9–16
Dollar-value LIFO retail

Lance-Hefner Specialty Shoppes decided to use the dollar-value LIFO retail method to value its inventory. Accounting records provide the following information:

	Cost	Retail
Merchandise inventory, January 1, 1997	$160,000	$250,000
Net purchases	360,500	510,000
Net markups		7,000
Net markdowns		2,000
Net sales		380,000

Pertinent retail price indexes are as follows:

January 1, 1997	100
December 31, 1997	110

Required:
Determine ending inventory and cost of goods sold.

Exercise 9–17
Dollar-value LIFO retail;
solving for unknowns

The Bosco Company adopted the dollar-value LIFO retail method at the beginning of 1997. Information for 1997 and 1998 is as follows, with certain data intentionally omitted:

	Inventory		Retail Price Index	Cost-to-Retail Percentage
Date	Cost	Retail		
Inventory, 1/1/97	$21,000	$28,000	1.00	?
Inventory, 12/31/97	22,792	33,600	1.12	?
1998 net purchases	60,000	88,400		
1998 net sales		80,000		
Inventory, 12/31/98	?	?	1.20	

Required:
Determine the missing data.

Exercise 9–18
Change in inventory costing
methods

Exercise 21–6 deals with changes in inventory costing methods.

Exercise 9–19
Change in inventory costing
methods

Goddard Company has used the FIFO method of inventory valuation since it began operations in 1994. Goddard decided to change to the average cost method for determining inventory costs at the beginning of 1997. The following schedule shows year-end inventory balances under the FIFO and average cost methods:

Year	FIFO	Average cost
1994	$45,000	$54,000
1995	78,000	71,000
1996	83,000	78,000

Required:

1. What amount, before income taxes, should be reported in the 1997 income statement as the cumulative effect of the change in accounting principle?
2. What is the pro forma effect of the change in method on 1996's income before taxes?

(AICPA adapted)

Exercise 9–20
Error correction; inventory error

Exercise 21–19 deals with the correction of an inventory error.

Exercise 9–21
Inventory errors

For each of the following inventory errors occurring in 1997, determine the effect of the error on 1997's cost of goods sold, net income, and retained earnings. Assume that the error is not discovered until 1998 and that a periodic inventory system is used. Ignore income taxes.

U = understated   O = overstated   NE = no effect

	Cost of Goods Sold	Net Income	Retained Earnings
(Example)			
1. Overstatement of ending inventory	U	O	O
2. Overstatement of purchases			
3. Understatement of beginning inventory			
4. Freight-in charges are understated			
5. Understatement of ending inventory			
6. Understatement of purchases			
7. Overstatement of beginning inventory			
8. Understatement of purchases plus understatement of ending inventory by the same amount			

Exercise 9–22
Inventory error

In 1997, the internal auditors of Development Technologies, Inc. discovered that a $3 million purchase of merchandise in 1997 was recorded in 1996 instead. The physical inventory count at the end of 1996 was correct.

Required:

Prepare the journal entry needed in 1997 to correct the error. Also, briefly describe any other measures Development Technologies would take in connection with correcting the error. (Ignore income taxes.)

Exercise 9–23
Multiple choice; dollar-value LIFO retail, inventory errors, accounting changes

The following questions dealing with dollar-value LIFO retail, inventory errors, and changes in inventory methods are adapted from questions that appeared on recent CPA examinations. Determine the response that best completes the statements or questions.

1. On December 31, 1996, Jason Company adopted the dollar-value LIFO retail inventory method. Inventory data for 1997 are as follows:

	LIFO Cost	Retail
Inventory, 12/31/96	$360,000	$500,000
Inventory, 12/31/97	?	660,000
Increase in price level for 1997		10%
Cost to retail ratio for 1997		70%

Under the LIFO retail method, Jason's inventory at December 31, 1997, should be
a. $437,000
b. $462,000
c. $472,000
d. $483,000

2. Bren Co.'s beginning inventory at January 1, 1997, was understated by $26,000, and its ending inventory was overstated by $52,000. As a result, Bren's cost of goods sold for 1997 was
a. Understated by $26,000.
b. Overstated by $26,000.
c. Understated by $78,000.
d. Overstated by $78,000.

3. On December 31, 1997, Rapp Co. changed inventory cost methods to FIFO from LIFO for financial statement and income tax purposes. The change will result in a $175,000 increase in the beginning inventory at January 1, 1997. Assuming a 30% income tax rate, the cumulative effect of this accounting change reported on the income statement for the year ended December 31, 1997, is
a. $175,000
b. $122,000

   c. $52,500
   d. $0

Exercise 9–24
Concepts; terminology

Listed below are several terms and phrases associated with inventory measurement. Pair each item from List A (by letter) with the item from List B that is most appropriately associated with it.

List A	List B
____ 1. Gross profit ratio	a. Reduction in selling price below the original selling price.
____ 2. Cost-to-retail percentage	b. Beginning inventory is not included in the calculation of the cost-to-retail percentage.
____ 3. Additional markup	
____ 4. Markdown	c. Deducted in the retail column after the calculation of the cost-to-retail percentage.
____ 5. Net markup	
____ 6. Retail method, FIFO and LIFO	d. Requires base year retail to be converted to layer year retail and then to cost.
____ 7. Conventional retail method	
____ 8. Change from LIFO	e. Gross profit divided by net sales.
____ 9. Dollar-value LIFO retail	f. Material inventory error discovered in a subsequent year.
____ 10. Normal spoilage	
____ 11. Requires retroactive restatement	g. Must be added to sales if sales are recorded net of discounts.
____ 12. Employee discounts	
____ 13. Net markdowns	h. Deducted in the retail column to arrive at ending inventory at retail.
____ 14. Net realizable value	
	i. Divide cost of goods available for sale by goods available at retail.
	j. Average cost, LCM.
	k. Added to the retail column to arrive at ending inventory at retail.
	l. Increase in selling price subsequent to initial markup.
	m. Ceiling in the determination of market.
	n. Accounting change requiring retroactive restatement.

Exercise 9–25
[based on Appendix 9]
Purchase commitments

On October 6, 1997, the Elgin Corporation signed a purchase commitment to purchase inventory for $60,000 on or before March 31, 1998. The company's fiscal year-end is December 31. The contract was exercised on March 21, 1998, and the inventory was purchased for cash at the contract price. On the purchase date of March 21, the market price of the inventory was $54,000. The market price of the inventory on December 31, 1997, was $56,000. The company uses a perpetual inventory system.

Required:
1. Prepare the necessary adjusting journal entry (if any is required) on December 31, 1997.
2. Prepare the journal to record the purchase on March 21, 1998.

Exercise 9–26
[based on Appendix 9]
Purchase commitments

In March 1997, the Phillips Tool Company signed two purchase commitments. The first commitment requires Phillips to purchase inventory for $100,000 by June 15, 1997. The second commitment requires the company to purchase inventory for $150,000 by August 20, 1997. The company's fiscal year-end is June 30. Phillips uses a periodic inventory system.

The first commitment is exercised on June 15, 1997, when the market price of the inventory purchased was $85,000. The second commitment was exercised on August 20, 1997, when the market price of the inventory purchased was $120,000.

Required:
Prepare the journal entries required on June 15, June 30, and August 20, 1997, to account for the two purchase commitments. Assume that the market price of the inventory related to the outstanding purchase commitment was $140,000 at June 30.

Problems

Problem 9–1
Lower of cost or market

The Decker Company has five products in its inventory. Information about the December 31, 1997, inventory follows.

Product	Quantity	Unit Cost	Unit Replacement Cost	Unit Selling Price
A	1,000	$10	$12	$16
B	800	15	11	18
C	600	3	2	8
D	200	7	4	6
E	600	14	12	13

The selling cost for each product consists of a 15 percent sales commission. The normal profit percentage for each product is 40 percent of the selling price.

Required:

1. Determine the balance sheet inventory carrying value at December 31, 1997, assuming the LCM rule is applied to individual products.
2. Determine the balance sheet inventory carrying value at December 31, 1997, assuming the LCM rule is applied to the entire inventory. Also, assuming that Decker recognizes an inventory write-down as a separate income statement item, determine the amount of the loss.

Problem 9–2
Lower of cost or market

The Almaden Hardware Store sells two distinct types of products, tools and paint products. Information pertaining to its 1997 year-end inventory is as follows:

Inventory, by product type	Quantity	Per Unit Cost	Designated Market
Tools:			
Hammers	100	$ 5.00	$5.50
Saws	200	10.00	9.00
Screwdrivers	300	2.00	2.60
Paint products:			
1-gallon cans	500	6.00	5.00
Paint brushes	100	4.00	4.50

Required:

1. Determine the balance sheet inventory carrying value at year-end, assuming the LCM rule is applied to (a) individual products, (b) product type, and (c) total inventory.
2. Assuming that the company recognizes an inventory write-down as a separate income statement item, for each of the LCM applications determine the amount of the loss.

Problem 9–3
Gross profit method

Smith Distributors, Inc., supplies ice cream shops with various toppings for making sundaes. On November 17, 1997, a fire resulted in the loss of all of the toppings stored in one section of the warehouse. The company must provide its insurance company with an estimate of the amount of inventory lost. The following information is available from the company's accounting records:

	Fruit Toppings	Marshmallow Toppings	Chocolate Toppings
Inventory, January 1, 1997	$ 20,000	$ 7,000	$ 3,000
Net purchases through Nov. 17	150,000	36,000	12,000
Net sales through Nov. 17	200,000	55,000	20,000
Historical gross profit ratio	20%	30%	35%

Required:

1. Calculate the estimated cost of each of the toppings lost in the fire.
2. What factors could cause the estimates to be over or understated?

Problem 9–4
Retail inventory method; various cost methods

The Sparrow Company uses the retail inventory method to estimate ending inventory and cost of goods sold. Data for 1997 is as follows:

	Cost	Retail
Beginning inventory	$ 90,000	$180,000
Purchases	355,000	580,000
Freight-in	9,000	
Purchase returns	7,000	11,000
Net markups		16,000
Net markdowns		12,000
Normal spoilage		3,000
Abnormal spoilage		8,000
Sales		540,000
Sales returns		10,000

The company records sales net of employee discounts. Discounts for 1997 totaled $4,000.

Required:

Estimate Sparrow's ending inventory and cost of goods sold for the year using the retail inventory method and the following applications:

1. Average cost.
2. Conventional (average, LCM)

Problem 9–5
Retail inventory method;
conventional and LIFO

The Alquist Company uses the retail method to estimate its ending inventory. Selected information about its 1997 operations is as follows:

a. January 1, 1997, beginning inventory had a cost of $100,000 and a retail value of $150,000.
b. Purchases during 1997 cost $1,387,500 with an original retail value of $2,000,000.
c. Freight costs were $10,000 for incoming merchandise and $25,000 for outgoing (sold) merchandise.
d. Net additional markups were $300,000 and net markdowns were $150,000.
e. Based on prior experience, shrinkage due to shoplifting was estimated to be $15,000 of retail value.
f. Merchandise is sold to employees at a 20% of selling price discount. Employee sales are recorded in a separate account at the net selling price. The balance in this account at the end of 1997 is $250,000.
g. Sales to customers totaled $1,750,000 for the year.

Required:

1. Estimate ending inventory and cost of goods sold using the conventional retail method (average, LCM).
2. Estimate ending inventory and cost of goods sold using the LIFO retail method. (Assume stable prices.)

Problem 9–6
Retail inventory method

The Grand Department Store, Inc., uses the retail inventory method to estimate ending inventory for its monthly financial statements. The following data pertain to a single department for the month of October 1997:

Inventory, October 1, 1997:	
At cost	$ 20,000
At retail	30,000
Purchases (exclusive of freight and returns):	
At cost	100,151
At retail	146,495
Freight-in	5,100
Purchase returns:	
At cost	2,100
At retail	2,800
Additional markups	2,500
Markup cancellations	265
Markdowns (net)	800
Normal spoilage and breakage	4,500
Sales	135,730

Required:

1. Using the conventional retail method, prepare a schedule computing estimated lower-of-cost-or-market inventory for October 31, 1997.
2. A department store using the conventional retail inventory method estimates the cost of its ending inventory as $29,000. An accurate physical count reveals only $22,000 of inventory at lower of cost or market. List the factors that may have caused the difference between computed inventory and the physical count.

(AICPA adapted)

Problem 9–7
Retail method—average cost
and LCM

The Smith-Kline Company maintains inventory records at selling prices as well as at cost. For 1997, the records indicate the following data:

($ in 000s)	Cost	Retail
Beginning inventory	$ 80	$ 125
Purchases	671	1,006
Freight-in on purchases	30	
Purchase returns	1	2
Net markups		4
Net markdowns		8
Net sales		916

Required:
Use the retail method to approximate cost of ending inventory in each of the following ways:

1. Average cost
2. Average (LCM) cost

Problem 9–8
Dollar-value LIFO retail method

[This is a variation of the previous problem, modified to focus on the dollar-value LIFO retail method.]
    The Smith-Kline Company maintains inventory records at selling prices as well as at cost. For 1997, the records indicate the following data:

($ in 000s)	Cost	Retail
Beginning inventory	$ 80	$ 125
Purchases	671	1,006
Freight-in on purchases	30	
Purchase returns	1	2
Net markups		4
Net markdowns		8
Net sales		916

Required:
Assuming the price level increased from 1.00 at January 1 to 1.10 at December 31, 1997, use the dollar-value LIFO retail method to approximate cost of ending inventory and cost of goods sold.

Problem 9–9
Dollar-value LIFO retail

On January 1, 1997, the HGC Camera Store adopted the dollar-value LIFO retail inventory method. The following information was available at December 31, 1997, the company's fiscal year-end:

	Cost	Retail
Beginning inventory	$28,000	$ 40,000
Purchases (net of returns)	85,000	108,000
Freight-in	2,000	
Net markups		10,000
Net markdowns		2,000
Sales to customers		100,000
Sales to employees (net of 20% discount)		2,400

The retail prices for cameras increased by 6% from January 1 to December 31, 1997.

Required:
Estimate HGC's ending inventory at December 31 and cost of goods sold for the year using the dollar-value LIFO retail inventory method.

Problem 9–10
Retail inventory method; various applications

The Raleigh Department Store converted from the conventional retail method to the LIFO retail method on January 1, 1995, and is now considering converting to the dollar-value LIFO retail inventory method. Management requested, during your examination of the financial statements for the year ended December 31, 1997, that you furnish a summary showing certain computations of inventory costs for the past three years. Available information follows:

a. The inventory at January 1, 1995, had a retail value of $45,000 and a cost of $27,500 based on the conventional retail method.
b. Transactions during 1995 were as follows:

	Cost	Retail
Gross purchases	$282,000	$490,000
Purchase returns	6,500	10,000
Purchase discounts	5,000	
Gross sales		492,000
Sales returns		5,000
Employee discounts		3,000
Freight-in	26,500	
Net markups		25,000
Net markdowns		10,000

Sales to employees are recorded net of discounts.

c. The retail value of the December 31, 1996, inventory was $56,100, the cost-to-retail percentage for 1996 under the LIFO retail method was 62%, and the appropriate price index was 102% of the January 1, 1996, price level.
d. The retail value of the December 31, 1997, inventory was $48,300, the cost-to-retail percentage for 1997 under the LIFO retail method was 61%, and the appropriate price index was 105% of the January 1, 1996, price level.

Required:
1. Prepare a schedule showing the computation of the cost of inventory at December 31, 1995, based on the conventional retail method.
2. Prepare a similar schedule as in requirement 1 based on the LIFO retail method.
3. Same requirement as (1) for December 31, 1996 and 1997, based on the dollar-value LIFO retail method.

(AICPA adapted)

Problem 9–11
Change in methods

The Rockwell Corporation uses a periodic inventory system and has used the FIFO cost method since inception of the company in 1968. In 1997, the company decided to switch to the average cost method. Data for 1997 is as follows:

Beginning inventory, FIFO (5,000 units @ $30)		$150,000
Purchases:		
5,000 units @ $36	$180,000	
5,000 units @ $40	200,000	380,000
Cost of goods available for sale		$530,000
Sales for 1997 (8,000 units @ $70)		$560,000

Additional information:

a. The company's effective income tax rate is 40% for all years.
b. If the company had used the average cost method prior to 1997, ending inventory for 1996 would have been $130,000.
c. 7,000 units remained in inventory at the end of 1997.

Required:
1. What is the cumulative effect of the change in inventory methods that will appear in the 1997 income statement?
2. What is the effect of the change in methods on 1997 income before the cumulative effect?

Problem 9–12
Inventory errors

You have been hired as the new controller for the Ralston Company. Shortly after joining the company in 1997, you discover the following errors related to the 1995 and 1996 financial statements:

a. Inventory at 12/31/95 was understated by $6,000.
b. Inventory at 12/31/96 was overstated by $9,000.
c. On 12/26/96, inventory was purchased for $3,000. The company did not record the purchase until the inventory was paid for early in 1997. At that time, the purchase was recorded by debit to purchases and a credit to cash.

The company uses a periodic inventory system.

Required:
1. Assuming that the errors were discovered after the 1996 financial statements were issued, analyze the effect of the errors on 1996 and 1995 cost of goods sold, net income, and retained earnings. (Ignore income taxes.)
2. Prepare a journal entry to correct the errors.
3. What other step(s) would be taken in connection with the error?

Problem 9–13
[based on Appendix 9]
Purchase commitments

In November 1997, the Brunswick Company signed two purchase commitments. The first commitment requires Brunswick to purchase 10,000 units of inventory at $10 per unit by December 15, 1997. The second commitment requires the company to purchase 20,000 units of inventory at $11 per unit by March 15, 1998. Brunswick's fiscal year-end is December 31. The company uses a periodic inventory system. Both contracts were exercised on their expiration date.

Required:
1. Prepare the journal entry to record the December 15 purchase for cash assuming the following alternative unit market prices on that date:
   a. $10.50
   b. $ 9.50
2. Prepare any necessary adjusting entry at December 31, 1997, for the second purchase commitment, assuming the following alternative unit market prices on that date:
   a. $12.50
   b. $10.30

3. Assuming that the unit market price on December 31 was $10.30, prepare the journal to record the purchase on March 15, 1998, assuming the following alternative unit market prices on that date:
    a. $11.50
    b. $10.00

Cases

Critical Thought Case 9–1
Inventoriable costs; lower of cost or market; retail inventory method

Hudson Company, which is both a wholesaler and a retailer, purchases its inventories from various suppliers.

Additional facts for Hudson's wholesale operations are as follows:

a. Hudson incurs substantial warehousing costs.
b. Hudson uses the lower-of-cost-or-market method. The replacement cost of the inventories is below the net realizable value and above the net realizable value less the normal profit margin. The original cost of the inventories is above replacement cost and below the net realizable value.

Additional facts for Hudson's retail operations are as follows:

a. Hudson determines the estimated cost of its ending inventories held for sale at retail using the conventional retail inventory method, which approximates lower of average cost or market.
b. Hudson incurs substantial freight-in costs.
c. Hudson has net markups and net markdowns.

Required:
1. Theoretically, how should Hudson account for the warehousing costs related to its wholesale inventories? Why?
2. a. In general, why is the lower-of-cost-or-market method used to report inventory?
    b. At which amount should Hudson's wholesale inventories be reported in the balance sheet? Explain the application of the lower-of-cost-or-market method in this situation.
3. In the calculation of the cost-to-retail percentage used to determine the estimated cost of its ending retail inventories, how should Hudson treat
    a. Freight-in costs?
    b. Net markups?
    c. Net markdowns?
4. Why does Hudson's retail inventory method approximate lower of average cost or market?

(AICPA adapted)

Group Interaction Case 9–2
Lower of cost or market

The lower-of-cost-or-market approach to valuing inventory is a departure from the accounting principle of reporting assets at their historical costs. There are those who believe that inventory, as well as other assets, should be valued at market, regardless of whether market is above or below cost.

The focus of this case is the justification for the lower-of-cost-or-market rule for valuing inventories. Your instructor will divide the class into from two to six groups depending on the size of the class. The mission of your group is to defend the lower-of-cost-or-market approach against the alternatives of valuing inventory at either historical cost or market value.

Required:
1. Each group member should consider the situation independently and draft a tentative argument prior to the class session for which the case is assigned.
2. In class, each group will meet for 10 to 15 minutes in different areas of the classroom. During that meeting, group members will take turns sharing their suggestions for the purpose of arriving at a single group argument.
3. After the allotted time, a spokesperson for each group (selected during the group meetings) will share the group's solution with the class. The goal of the class is to incorporate the views of each group into a consensus approach to the situation.

Integrating Case 9–3
Unit LIFO and LCM

York Co. sells one product, which it purchases from various suppliers. York's trial balance at December 31, 1997, included the following accounts:

Sales (33,000 units @ $16)			$528,000
Sales discounts			7,500
Purchases			368,900
Purchase discounts			18,000
Freight-in			5,000
Freight-out			11,000

York Co.'s inventory purchases during 1997 were as follows:

	Units	Cost per Unit	Total Cost
Beginning inventory	8,000	$8.20	$ 65,600
Purchases, quarter ended March 31	12,000	8.25	99,000
Purchases, quarter ended June 30	15,000	7.90	118,500
Purchases, quarter ended September 30	13,000	7.50	97,500
Purchases, quarter ended June 30	7,000	7.70	53,900
	55,000		$434,500

Additional information:

a. York's accounting policy is to report inventory in its financial statements at the lower of cost or market, applied to total inventory. Cost is determined under the last-in, first-out (LIFO) method.

b. York has determined that, at December 31, 1997, the replacement cost of its inventory was $8 per unit and the net realizable value was $8.80 per unit. York's normal profit margin is $1.05 per unit.

Required:
1. Prepare York's schedule of cost of goods sold, with a supporting schedule of ending inventory. York uses the direct method of reporting losses from market decline of inventory.
2. Explain the rule of lower of cost or market and its application in this situation.

(AICPA adapted)

Critical Thought Case 9–4
The dollar-value LIFO method; the retail inventory method

Huddell Company, which is both a wholesaler and retailer, purchases merchandise from various suppliers. The dollar-value LIFO method is used for the wholesale inventories.

Huddell determines the estimated cost of its retail ending inventories using the conventional retail inventory method, which approximates lower of average cost or market.

Required:
1. a. What are the advantages of using the dollar-value LIFO method as opposed to the traditional LIFO method?
    b. How does the application of the dollar-value LIFO method differ from the application of the traditional LIFO method?
2. a. In the calculation of the cost to retail percentage used to determine the estimated cost of its ending inventories, how should Huddell use

    ⑦ Net markups?
    ⑦ Net markdowns?

    b. Why does Huddell's retail inventory method approximate lower of average cost or market?

(AICPA adapted)

Writing Case 9–5
Retail inventory method

The Brenly Paint Company, your client, manufactures paint. The company's president, Mr. Brenly, decided to open a retail store to sell paint as well as wallpaper and other items that would be purchased from other suppliers. He has asked you for information about the retail method of pricing inventories at the retail store.

Required:
Prepare a report to the president explaining the retail method of pricing inventories.

Discussion Case 9–6
Change in inventory method

Generally accepted accounting principles should be applied consistently from period to period. However, changes within a company, as well as changes in the external economic environment, may force a company to change an accounting method. The specific reporting requirements when a company changes from one generally accepted inventory method to another depend on the methods involved.

Required:
Explain the accounting treatment and disclosures required for a change in inventory method (1) not involving LIFO, (2) to the LIFO method, and (3) from the LIFO method.

Real World Case 9–7
Change in inventory method

Champion Industries, Inc., included the following disclosure note in its financial statements for the fiscal year ending February 29, 1992:

Note 3: Inventories (in part)

During the fourth quarter of fiscal 1992, the Company changed its method of accounting for inventory from the Last-In, First-Out (LIFO) method to the First-In, First-Out (FIFO) method. Management believes that the FIFO method provides a more meaningful presentation of the Company's financial position, including significant financial statement amounts and ratios, as well as shareholders' equity. As required by generally accepted accounting principles, the Company retroactively adjusted prior years' financial statements for this change. The effect of the restatement was to increase retained earnings at March 4, 1989, by $10,522,000. The restatement reduced net income in 1991 by $2,120,000, or $.31 per share, and increased the net loss in 1990 by $517,000, or $.07 per share.

Required:

1. Why does GAAP require Champion Industries to retroactively adjust prior years' financial statements for this type of accounting change?
2. Assuming that the quantity of inventory remained stable during 1991, did the cost of Champion's inventory move up or down during that year?

Internet Case 9–8
Change in inventory method

EDGAR, the Electronic Data Gathering, Analysis, and Retrieval system, performs automated collection, validation, indexing, and forwarding of submissions by companies and others who are required by law to file forms with the U.S. Securities and Exchange Commission (SEC). All publicly traded domestic companies use EDGAR to make the majority of their filings. (Some foreign companies file voluntarily.) Form 10-K or 10-KSB, which include the annual report, is required to be filed on EDGAR. The SEC makes this information available on the Internet.

Required:

1. Access EDGAR on the Internet. You can use a web browser or anonymous FTP. The web address is http://www.sec.gov/. To use anonymous FTP, use your File Transfer Protocol software to connect to sec.gov and log in as user "anonymous" with a password of your electronic mail address.
2. Search for Fluke Corporation. Access the 10-K filing for the fiscal year ended April 28, 1995. Search or scroll to find the financial statements and related notes.
3. Answer the following questions related to the company's inventories:
   a. Describe the change made in 1993 in the company's method of applying overhead costs to inventory.
   b. What is the net-of-tax cumulative effect of the change reported on the income statement for the period ended April 30, 1993?
   c. What is the impact of the change on 1993 income?
   d. What is the pro forma effect of the change on 1992 net income? (That is, by how much would net income have differed in 1992 if the new method had been used in 1992?)

Discussion Case 9–9
Inventory errors

Some inventory errors are said to be self-correcting in that the error has the opposite financial statement effect in the period following the error, thereby correcting the original account balance errors.

Required:

Despite this self-correcting feature, discuss why these errors should not be ignored and describe the steps required to account for the error correction.

Ethics Case 9–10
Overstatement of ending inventory

Danville Bottlers is a wholesale beverage company. Danville uses the FIFO inventory method to determine the cost of its ending inventory. Ending inventory quantities are determined by a physical count. For the fiscal year-end June 30, 1997, ending inventory was originally determined to be $3,265,000. However, on July 17, 1997, John Howard, the company's controller, discovered an error in the ending inventory count. He determined that the correct ending inventory amount should be $2,600,000.

Danville is a privately owned corporation with significant financing provided by a local bank. The bank requires annual audited financial statements as a condition of the loan. By July 17, the auditors had completed their review of the financial statements which are scheduled to be issued on July 25. They did not discover the inventory error.

John's first reaction was to communicate his finding to the auditors and to revise the financial statements before they are issued. However, he knows that his and his fellow workers' profit-sharing plans are based on annual pretax earnings and that if he revises the statements, everyone's profit-sharing bonus will be significantly reduced.

Required:

1. Why will bonuses be negatively affected? What is the effect on pretax earnings?
2. If the error is not corrected in the current year and is discovered by the auditors during the following year's audit, how will it be reported in the company's financial statements?
3. Discuss the ethical dilemma Howard faces.

Discussion Case 9–11
[based on Appendix 9]
Purchase commitments

The management of the Esquire Oil Company believes that the wholesale price of heating oil that they sell to homeowners will increase again as the result of increased political problems in the Mideast. The company is currently paying $.80 a gallon. If they are willing to enter an agreement in November 1997 to purchase a million gallons of heating oil during the winter of 1998, their supplier will guarantee the price at $.80 per gallon. However, if the winter is a mild one, Esquire would not be able to sell a million gallons unless they reduced their retail price and thereby increased the risk of a loss for the year. On the other hand, if the wholesale price did increase substantially, they would be in a favorable position with respect to their competitors. The company's fiscal year-end is December 31.

Required:

Discuss the accounting issues related to the purchase commitment that Esquire is considering.

10

OPERATIONAL ASSETS: ACQUISITION

OVERVIEW

This chapter and the one that follows address the measurement and reporting issues involving operational assets. Operational assets include tangible and intangible long-term assets that are used in the production of goods and services.

This chapter covers the valuation of these assets at date of acquisition. In Chapter 11 we discuss the treatment of expenditures made over the life of these assets to maintain and improve them, the disposition of operational assets, and the allocation of the cost of operational assets to the periods benefited by their use.

LEARNING OBJECTIVES   **After studying this chapter, you should be able to:**

1. Identify the various costs included in the initial cost of property, plant, and equipment, natural resources, and intangible assets.
2. Determine the initial cost of individual operational assets acquired as a group for a lump-sum purchase price.
3. Determine the initial cost of an operational asset acquired in exchange for a deferred payment contract.
4. Determine the initial cost of operational assets acquired in exchange for equity securities, through donation, or in exchange for other nonmonetary assets.
5. Identify the items included in the cost of a self-constructed asset and determine the amount of capitalized interest.
6. Explain the difference in the accounting treatment of costs incurred to purchase intangible assets versus the costs incurred to internally develop intangible assets.

A QUESTION OF INTEREST

By the time you finish this chapter, you should be able to respond appropriately to the questions posed in this case. Compare your response to the solution provided at the end of the chapter.

"Now I'm really confused," confessed Stan, your study partner. "I thought that interest was always expensed on the income statement in the period incurred. Now you're telling me that sometimes interest is capitalized. I'm not even quite sure what *capitalize* means!" "That's right," you tell Stan, "and if you hadn't missed class today, we wouldn't be having this conversation. Here, take a look at this example of a disclosure note for The Walt Disney Company that our professor passed out today. I'll try to explain it all to you."

"While we're at it, we can go over the rest of today's lecture," Stan added hopefully.

Long-term debt (in part):
The Company capitalizes interest on assets constructed for its theme parks, resort and other property, and on theatrical and television productions in process. In 1995, 1994, and 1993, respectively, total interest costs incurred were $236.3, $171.9, and $183.7 million, of which $58.1, $52.0, and $26.0 million were capitalized.

QUESTIONS

1. What does it mean to capitalize an expenditure? What is the general rule for determining which costs are capitalized when an operational asset is acquired?
2. Describe to Stan which costs might be included in the initial cost of equipment.
3. In what situations is interest capitalized?
4. What is the three-step process used to determine the amount of interest capitalized?

General Motors Corporation has significant investments in the production facilities it uses to manufacture the automobiles it sells. On the other hand, the principal revenue-producing assets of Microsoft Corporation are the copyrights on its computer software that permit it the exclusive rights to earn profits from those products. Timber reserves provide major revenues to Boise Cascade. From a reporting perspective, we classify GM's production facilities as property, plant, and equipment;[1] Microsoft's copyrights as intangible assets, and Boise Cascade's timber reserves as natural resources. Together, these three noncurrent assets constitute **operational assets**, a term used to describe the broad category of *long-term, revenue-producing assets*. Unlike manufacturers, many service firms and merchandising companies rely primarily on people or investments in inventories rather than on operational assets to generate revenues. Even nonmanufacturing firms, though, typically have at least modest investments in buildings, equipment, and other operational assets.

The two financial reporting issues pertaining to this group of assets are (1) how to value these assets at the date they are either acquired in an exchange transaction or self-constructed and (2) how to account for these assets subsequent to acquisition to include maintenance, disposition, and the allocation of the assets' costs to reporting periods that benefit from their use.[2] We focus on the first issue in this chapter and the second issue in the next chapter.

PART A   VALUATION AT ACQUISITION

Types of Operational Assets

For financial reporting purposes, operational assets typically are classified in two categories:

1. **Property, plant, and equipment**. Assets in this category include land, buildings, equipment, machinery, autos, and trucks. **Natural resources** such as oil and gas deposits, timber tracts, and mineral deposits also are included.
2. **Intangible assets**. Unlike other operational assets, these lack physical substance and the extent and timing of their future benefits typically are highly uncertain. They include patents, copyrights, trademarks, franchises, organization costs, and goodwill.

Of course, every company maintains its own unique mix of operational assets. The way these assets are classified and combined for reporting purposes also varies from company to company. As an example, a recent Tyson Foods, Inc., balance sheet reported net property, plant, and equipment of $2,013.5 million and $1,610.0 million at the end of fiscal 1995 and 1994, respectively. A disclosure note, shown in Graphic 10–1, provided the details.

GRAPHIC 10–1

Property, Plant, and Equipment— Tyson Foods, Inc.

Property, Plant, and Equipment (in part):

(In millions)	September 30, 1995	October 1, 1994
Property, plant, and equipment and accumulated depreciation, at cost are as follows:		
Land	$ 56.7	$ 56.1
Buildings and improvements	866.4	676.1
Machinery and equipment	1,725.9	1,452.2
Vessels	110.0	111.7
Land improvements and other	86.9	70.5
Buildings and equipment under construction	200.7	143.2
	3,046.6	2,509.8
Less: accumulated depreciation	1,033.1	899.8
Net property, plant, and equipment	$2,013.5	$1,610.0

---

[1]These are sometimes called *plant assets* or *fixed assets*.

[2]Allocation of asset cost to expense over time is called *depreciation* for plant and equipment, *amortization* for intangible assets, and *depletion* for natural resources.

In practice, some companies report intangibles as part of property, plant, and equipment. Some include intangible assets in the other asset category on the balance sheet, and others show intangibles as a separate balance sheet category. For example, Duracell International, Inc., reported intangibles as a separate category in a recent balance sheet:

ASSETS (in part):	($ in millions)	
	1996	**1995**
Intangibles, net	$1,271.7	$1,208.9

The disclosure note shown in Graphic 10–2 provided the details.

GRAPHIC 10–2 **Intangible Assets— Duracell International, Inc.**	**8. Intangibles** ($ in millions) The following summarizes intangible assets, net of accumulated amortization of $374.3 and $328.5 at June 30, 1996 and 1995, respectively:

	1996	1995
Goodwill	$ 590.7	$ 499.2
Trademarks and trade names	406.6	417.4
Patents and computer software	40.9	50.4
Other	233.5	241.9
	$1,271.7	$1,208.9

Before we examine the various operational assets one by one, you should find it helpful to study the overview provided by Graphic 10–3 (on the following page).

Costs to Be Capitalized

Learning objective 1
Identify the various costs included in the initial cost of property, plant, and equipment, natural resources, and intangible assets.

OPENING CASE

Question 1

Costs are capitalized if they are expected to produce benefits beyond the current period.

OPENING CASE

Question 2

Operational assets can be acquired through purchase, exchange, lease, donation, self-construction, or a business combination. We address acquisitions through leasing in Chapter 15 and acquisitions through business combinations in Chapter 12. We discuss the other means of acquisition here.

The initial valuation of operational assets usually is quite simple. We know from prior study that assets are valued on the basis of their original costs. In Chapter 8 we introduced the concept of condition and location in determining the cost of inventory. This concept applies to the valuation of operational assets as well. The initial cost of an operational asset includes the purchase price and all expenditures necessary to bring the asset to its desired condition and location for use.

Our objective in identifying the costs of an asset is to distinguish the expenditures that produce future benefits from those that produce benefits only in the current period. The costs in the second group are recorded as expenses, but those in the first group are *capitalized*. That is, they are recorded as an asset and expensed in future periods.[3]

Property, Plant, and Equipment

Cost of Equipment. Equipment is a broad term that encompasses machinery used in manufacturing, computers and other office equipment, vehicles, furniture, and fixtures. The cost of equipment includes the purchase price plus any sales tax (less any discounts received from the seller), transportation costs paid by the buyer to transport the asset to the location in which it will be used, expenditures for installation, testing, legal fees to establish title, and any other costs of bringing the asset to its condition and location for use. To the extent that these costs can be identified and measured, they should be included in the asset's initial valuation rather than expensed currently.

Although most costs can be identified easily, others are more difficult. For example, the costs of training personnel to operate machinery could be considered a cost necessary to make the asset ready for use. However, because it is difficult to measure the amount of training costs associated with specific assets, these costs usually are expensed. Consider Illustration 10–1.

---

[3]An exception is land. Costs to acquire land also produce future benefits and therefore are capitalized, but unlike other assets, the cost of land is not expensed in future periods because land doesn't depreciate.

GRAPHIC   10–3

Operational Assets and Their Acquisition Costs

Asset	Description	Typical Acquisition Costs
Property, plant, and equipment	Productive assets that derive their value from long-term use in operations rather than from resale.	All expenditures necessary to get the asset in condition and location for its intended use.
Equipment	Broad term that includes machinery, computers and other office equipment, vehicles, furniture, furnishings, and fixtures.	Purchase price (less discounts), taxes, transportation, installation, testing, trial runs, reconditioning.
Land	Real property used in operations (land held for speculative investment or future use is reported as investments or other assets).	Purchase price, attorney's fees, title, recording fees, commissions, back taxes, mortgages, liens, clearing, filling, draining, removing old buildings.
Land improvements	Enhancements to property such as parking lots, driveways, private roads, fences, landscaping, and sprinkler systems.	Separately identifiable costs.
Buildings	Structures that include warehouses, plant facilities, and office buildings.	Purchase price, attorney's fees, commissions, reconditioning.
Natural resources	Productive assets that are physically consumed in operations such as timber, mineral deposits, and oil and gas reserves.	Acquisition, exploration, and development costs.
Intangible assets	Productive assets that lack physical substance and have long-term but typically uncertain benefits.	All expenditures necessary to get the asset in the location and condition for its intended use.
Patents	Exclusive 17-year right to manufacture a product or use a process.	Purchase price, legal fees, filing fees, not including internal R&D.
Copyrights	Exclusive right to benefit from a creative work such as a song, film, painting, photograph, or book.	Purchase price, legal fees, filing fees, not including internal R&D.
Trademarks (tradenames)	Exclusive right to display a word, a slogan, a symbol, or an emblem that distinctively identifies a company, product, or a service.	Purchase price, legal fees, filing fees, not including internal R&D.
Organization costs	The right to operate as a corporation.	Legal fees, state filing fees, fees to underwriters.
Franchises	A contractual arrangement under which a franchisor grants the franchisee the exclusive right to use the franchisor's trademark or tradename.	Franchise fee plus any legal fees.
Goodwill	The unique value of the company as a whole over and above all identifiable assets.	Excess of the purchase price of the company over the fair value of the net assets acquired.

ILLUSTRATION   10–1

Initial Cost of Equipment

Central Machine Tools purchased an industrial lathe to be used in its manufacturing process. The purchase price was $62,000. Central paid a freight company $1,000 to transport the machine to its plant location plus $300 shipping insurance. In addition, the machine had to be installed and mounted on a special platform built specifically for the machine at a cost of $1,200. After installation, several trial runs were made to ensure proper operation. The cost of these trials including wasted materials was $600. At what amount should Central capitalize the lathe?

Purchase price	$62,000
Freight and handling	1,000
Insurance during shipping	300
Special foundation	1,200
Trial runs	600
	$65,100

Each of the expenditures described was necessary to bring the machine to its condition and location for use and should be capitalized and expensed in the future periods in which the asset is used.

Cost of Land. The cost of land also should include each expenditure needed to get the land ready for its intended use. These include the purchase price plus closing costs such as fees for the attorney, title and title search, and recording. If the property is subject to back taxes, liens, mortgages, or other obligations, these amounts are included also. In addition, any expenditures such as clearing, filling, draining, and even removing old buildings that are needed to prepare the land for its intended use are part of the land's cost. This is demonstrated in Illustration 10–2.

ILLUSTRATION   10–2

Initial Cost of Land

The Byers Structural Metal Company purchased a six-acre tract of land and an existing building for $500,000. The company plans to raze the old building and construct a new office building on the site. In addition to the purchase price, the company made the following expenditures at closing of the purchase:

Title insurance	$3,000
Escrow fees	1,000
Property taxes	6,000

Shortly after closing, the company paid a contractor $10,000 to tear down the old building and remove it from the site. An additional $5,000 was paid to grade the land. Property taxes included $4,000 of delinquent taxes paid by Byers on behalf of the seller and $2,000 attributable to the portion of the current fiscal year after the purchase date. What should be the capitalized cost of the land?

Capitalized cost of land:	
Purchase price of land (and building to be razed)	$500,000
Title insurance	3,000
Escrow fees	1,000
Delinquent property taxes	4,000
Cost of removing old building	10,000
Cost of grading	5,000
Total cost of land	$523,000

Two thousand dollars of the property taxes relate only to the current period and should be expensed. Other costs were necessary to acquire the land and are capitalized.

> The costs of **land improvements** are capitalized and depreciated.

Land Improvements.   It's important to distinguish between the cost of land and the cost of **land improvements** because land has an indefinite life and land improvements usually do not. Examples of land improvements include the cost of parking lots, driveways, and private roads and the costs of fences and lawn and garden sprinkler systems. Costs of these assets are separately identified and capitalized. We depreciate their cost over periods benefited by their use.

Cost of Buildings.   The cost of acquiring a building usually includes realtor commissions and legal fees in addition to the purchase price. Quite often a building must be refurbished, remodeled, or otherwise modified to suit the needs of the new owner. These reconditioning costs are part of the building's acquisition cost. When a building is constructed rather than purchased, unique accounting issues are raised. We discuss these in the "Self-Constructed Assets" section.

> Natural resources provide benefits through their physical *consumption* in the production of goods and services.

Cost of Natural Resources.   **Natural resources** that provide long-term benefits are reported as property, plant, and equipment. These include timber tracts, mineral deposits, and oil and gas deposits. They can be distinguished from other assets by the fact that their benefits are derived from their physical consumption. For example, mineral deposits are physically diminishing as the minerals are extracted from the ground and either sold or used in the production process.[4] On the contrary, equipment, land, and buildings produce benefits for a company through their *use* in the production of goods and services. Unlike those of natural resources, their physical characteristics usually remain unchanged during their useful lives.

> The cost of a natural resource includes the **acquisition costs** for the use of land and the **exploration** and **development costs** incurred before production begins.

Natural resources sometimes are purchased from another company. In that case, initial valuation is simply the purchase price plus any other costs necessary to bring the asset to condition and location for use. More frequently, these assets are developed. In these situations, initial valuation can include (a) acquisition costs, (b) exploration costs, and (c) development costs. **Acquisition costs** are the amounts paid to acquire the rights to explore for undiscovered natural resources or to extract proven natural resources. **Exploration costs** are expenditures such as drilling a well or excavating a mine as well as any other costs of searching for natural resources. **Development**

---

[4]Because of this characteristic, natural resources sometimes are called *wasting assets*.

costs are incurred after the resource has been discovered but before production has begun. They include the costs of tunnels, wells, and shafts. The costs of heavy equipment and other assets used during drilling or excavation usually are not considered part of the cost of the natural resource. Instead, they are considered depreciable plant and equipment. Of course, if an asset used in the development of a natural resource cannot be moved and has no alternative use, its depreciable life is limited by the useful life of the natural resource. Consider Illustration 10–3.

ILLUSTRATION   10–3

Cost of Natural Resources

The Jackson Mining Company paid $100,000 for the right to explore for a coal deposit on 500 acres of land in Pennsylvania. Costs of exploring for the coal deposit totaled $200,000 and intangible development costs incurred in digging and erecting the mine shaft were $500,000. In addition, the company purchased new excavation equipment for the project at a cost of $600,000. After the coal is removed from the site, the equipment will be sold.

Total capitalized cost for the coal deposit is:

Purchase of rights to explore	$100,000
Exploration costs	200,000
Development costs	500,000
Total cost of coal deposit	$800,000

As we will discuss in Chapter 11, this cost is allocated to future periods as depletion expense by calculating a depletion rate based on the estimated amount of coal discovered. The $600,000 cost of the excavation equipment is recorded as a plant asset and depreciated.

If it proved to be economically infeasible to remove the discovered minerals from the mine, the $800,000 cost of the coal deposit would be expensed rather than capitalized. In the oil and gas industry, there are two generally accepted accounting alternatives for the treatment of the acquisition, exploration, and development costs incurred when projects prove unsuccessful. An unsuccessful project, or dry hole, results when there is insufficient oil or gas discovered to warrant incurring the additional extraction costs. These alternatives were discussed in Chapter 1 and are reviewed in Appendix 10.

Intangible Assets

Intangible assets generally represent exclusive rights that provide benefits to the owner.

Intangible assets include such items as patents, copyrights, trademarks, franchises, and goodwill. Despite their lack of physical substance, these assets can be extremely valuable resources for a company. For example, in 1993 the *Financial World* magazine estimated the value of the Coca-Cola trademark to be $24 billion.[5] In general, intangible assets refer to the ownership of exclusive rights that provide benefits to the owner in the production of goods and services.

The issues involved in accounting for intangibles are similar to those of other operational assets. One key difference, though, is that the future benefits that we attribute to intangible assets usually are much less certain than those attributed to tangible operational assets. For example, will the new toy for which a company acquires a patent be accepted by the market? If so, will it be a blockbuster like Hula Hoops or Rubic's Cube, or will it be only a moderate success? Will it have lasting appeal like Barbie dolls, or will it be a short-term fad? In short, it's often very difficult to anticipate the timing, and even the existence, of future benefits attributable to most intangible assets. In fact, this uncertainty is a discriminating characteristic of intangible assets that perhaps better distinguishes them from tangible assets than their lack of physical substance. After all, other assets, too, do not exist physically but are not considered intangible assets. Accounts receivable and prepaid expenses, for example, have no physical substance and yet are reported among tangible assets.

Companies can either (1) *purchase* intangible assets in exchange transactions with other entities (existing patent, copyright, trademark, or franchise rights) or (2) *develop* intangible assets internally (development of a new product or process that is then patented). Let's discuss the costs of purchased intangibles next and the costs of developing intangibles in a later section.

---

[5]This $24 billion represents an estimate of the market value to the company at the time the estimate was made, not the historical cost valuation that appears on the balance sheet of Coca-Cola.

Purchased intangibles are valued at their original cost.

The initial valuation of purchased intangibles usually is quite simple. Purchased intangibles are valued at their original cost to include the purchase price and all other necessary costs to bring the asset to condition and location for use. For example, if a patent is purchased from another entity, legal fees and filing fees might have to be paid in addition to the purchase price. Intangible assets acquired in exchange for stock, for other nonmonetary assets, or with deferred payment contracts are valued exactly as other operational assets. Let's look briefly at the costs typically associated with some of the more common intangible assets.

Patents.   A **patent** is an exclusive right to manufacture a product or to use a process. This right is granted by the U.S. Patent Office for a period of 17 years. In essence, the holder of a patent has a monopoly on the use, manufacture, or sale of the product or process. If a patent is purchased from an inventor or another individual or company, the amount paid is its initial valuation. The cost might also include such other costs as legal and filing fees to secure the patent. Holders of patents often need to defend a patent in court against infringement. Any attorney fees and other costs of successfully defending a patent are added to the patent account.

When a patent is developed internally, the research and development costs of doing so are expensed as incurred. We discuss research and development in more detail in a later section. Legal and filing fees to secure the patent, even if internally developed, are capitalized.

Copyrights.   A **copyright** is an exclusive right of protection given to a creator of a published work such as a song, film, painting, photograph, or book. Copyrights are protected by law and give the creator the exclusive right to reproduce and sell the artistic or published work for the life of the creator plus 50 years, or if the copyright is held by a corporation, 75 years from the date of first publication. Accounting for the costs of copyrights is virtually identical to that for patents and trademarks, which we discuss next.

Trademark.   A **trademark,** also called **tradename,** is an exclusive right to display a word, a slogan, a symbol, or an emblem that distinctively identifies a company, product, or a service. The trademark can be registered with the U.S. Patent Office which protects the trademark from use by others for a period of 20 years. The registration can be renewed for an indefinite number of 20-year periods, so a trademark has no legally limited life.

A trademark or tradename can be very valuable. The estimated value of $24 billion for the Coca-Cola trademark mentioned previously is a good example. Note that the cost of the trademark reported on the balance sheet is far less than the estimate of its worth to the company. The Coca-Cola Company's 1993 balance sheet disclosed goodwill and other intangibles at a cost of only $549 million.

Franchise operations are among the most common way of doing business.

Franchises.   A **franchise** is a contractual arrangement under which the franchisor grants the franchisee the exclusive right to use the franchisor's trademark or tradename within a geographical area usually for a specified period of time. Many popular retail businesses such as fast food outlets, automobile dealerships, and motels are franchises. For example, the last time you ordered a hamburger at McDonald's, you were probably dealing with a franchise. The owner of that McDonald's outlet paid McDonald's Corporation a sum of money in exchange for the exclusive right to use the McDonald's name and to sell its products within a specified geographical area. In addition, many franchisors provide other benefits to the franchisee, such as participation in the construction of the retail outlet, training of employees, and national advertising.

Payments to the franchisor usually include an initial payment plus periodic payments over the life of the franchise agreement. The initial franchise fee plus any legal costs associated with the contract agreement are capitalized as an intangible asset, franchise, which is then amortized over the life of the franchise agreement. The periodic payments usually relate to services such as advertising provided by the franchisor on a continuing basis and are expensed as incurred.

Organization costs include only those costs incurred in the formation of the corporation.

Organization Costs.   The costs incurred to organize a business as a corporation include legal fees, state filing fees, and fees to underwriters for undertaking stock issues and are referred to as **organization costs**. These costs are fairly limited in nature and do not include normal operating expenses incurred in the development stage of a business (before revenues are generated). *SFAS 7* provides specific accounting guidelines for companies that are in their development stage.[6]

Additional Consideration

Development Stage Enterprises
A development stage enterprise is a new business that has either not commenced its principal operations or has begun its principal operations but has not generated significant revenues. Prior to *SFAS 7*, many of these companies recorded an asset for the normal operating costs incurred during the development stage. This asset was then expensed over a period of time beginning with the commencement of operations.

SFAS 7 requires that these enterprises comply with the same generally accepted accounting principles that apply to established operating companies in determining whether a cost is to be charged to expense when incurred or capitalized and expensed in future periods. Therefore, normal operating costs incurred during the development stage are expensed, not capitalized. *SFAS 7* does allow development stage enterprises to provide items of supplemental information to help financial statement readers more readily assess their future cash flows.

Most purchased intangibles are *specifically identifiable*. That is, cost can be directly associated with a specific intangible right. In contrast, the intangible asset called *goodwill* does not relate to any specifically identifiable right.

Goodwill.   Goodwill is a unique intangible asset in that its cost can't be directly associated with any specifically identifiable right and is not separable from the company as a whole. It represents the unique value of the company as a whole over and above all identifiable tangible and intangible assets. Goodwill can emerge from a company's clientele and reputation, its trained employees and management team, its favorable business location, and any other unique features of the company that can't be associated with a specific asset.

> The existence of **goodwill** indicates that the whole is worth more than the sum of its parts.

> **Goodwill** can only be purchased through the acquisition of another company.

> **Goodwill** is the excess of the purchase price over the fair value of the net assets acquired.

Because goodwill can't be separated from a company, it's not possible for a buyer to acquire it without also acquiring the whole company or a substantial portion of it. Goodwill will appear as an asset on a balance sheet only when it was paid for in connection with the acquisition of another company. In that case, the capitalized cost of goodwill equals the purchase price of the company less the fair value of the net assets acquired. The fair value of the net assets equals the fair value of all identifiable tangible and intangible assets less the fair value of any liabilities of the selling company assumed by the buyer. Goodwill is a residual asset; it's the amount left after other assets are identified. Consider Illustration 10–4.

Additional Consideration

It is possible for the fair value of net assets to be greater than the purchase price. The fact that the sum of the separate values of the assets is greater than their combined value indicates that the act of bringing them together actually reduced their value. This effect is rare and often is referred to as *negative goodwill*. Some accountants have argued that this negative amount should be disclosed on the balance sheet as a deduction from other assets. GAAP generally requires the simpler treatment of recognizing the acquired assets at their combined purchase price instead of their individual fair values.

Of course, a company can develop its own goodwill through advertising, training, and other efforts. In fact, most do. However, a company must expense all such costs incurred in the internal generation of goodwill. Imagine how difficult it would be to associate these expenditures with any objective measure of goodwill. For this reason, though, it's difficult to compare two companies when one has purchased goodwill and the other has not.

In Chapter 11 we discuss the amortization of goodwill, and in Chapter 12 we discuss the concept of goodwill in greater detail.

---

[6]"Accounting and Reporting by Development Stage Enterprises," *Statement of Financial Accounting Standards No. 7* (Stamford, Conn: FASB, 1975).

ILLUSTRATION   10-4

Goodwill

The Smithson Corporation acquired all of the outstanding common stock of the Rider Corporation in exchange for $1,800,000 in cash.* Smithson assumed all of Rider's long-term debt which had a fair value of $1,200,000 at date of acquisition. The fair values of all identifiable assets of Rider are:

Receivables	$ 500,000
Inventory	700,000
Property, plant, and equipment	950,000
Patent	350,000
Total	$2,500,000

The cost of the goodwill resulting from the acquisition is $500,000, determined as follows:

Purchase price		$1,800,000
Less: Fair value of net assets		
Assets	$2,500,000	
Less: Liabilities assumed	(1,200,000)	(1,300,000)
Goodwill		$ 500,000

The Smithson Company records the acquisition as follows:

Receivables (fair value)	500,000	
Inventory (fair value)	700,000	
Property, plant, and equipment (fair value)	950,000	
Patent (fair value)	350,000	
Goodwill (difference)	500,000	
Liabilities (fair value)		1,200,000
Cash (purchase price)		1,800,000

*The determination of the amount a purchaser is willing to pay for a company in excess of the identifiable net assets is a question of determining the value of a company as a whole. This question is addressed in most introductory and advanced finance textbooks.

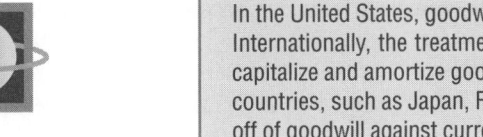

GLOBAL PERSPECTIVE

In the United States, goodwill is capitalized and amortized over a period of time no longer than 40 years. Internationally, the treatment of goodwill varies widely. Countries such as Australia and Sweden also capitalize and amortize goodwill, but the maximum amortization periods vary from 5 to 20 years. Other countries, such as Japan, France, Germany, Italy, and the United Kingdom, permit the immediate write-off of goodwill against current earnings, but as an extraordinary or nonrecurring item. Switzerland is the only major industrialized country that allows companies to capitalize goodwill without amortization.

Lump-Sum Purchases

Learning objective 2
Determine the initial cost of individual operational assets acquired as a group for a lump-sum purchase price.

It's not unusual for a group of operational assets to be acquired for a single sum. If these assets are indistinguishable, for example 10 identical delivery trucks purchased for a lump-sum price of $150,000, valuation is obvious. Each of the trucks would be valued at $15,000 ($150,000 ÷ 10). However, if the lump-sum purchase involves different assets, it's necessary to allocate the lump-sum acquisition price among the separate items, usually in proportion to the individual assets' relative market values. This is best explained by the example in Illustration 10–5.

The relative market value percentages are multiplied by the lump-sum purchase price to determine the initial valuation of each of the separate assets. Notice that the lump-sum purchase includes inventories, which is not an operational asset. The procedure used here to allocate the purchase price in a lump-sum acquisition pertains to any type of asset mix, not just to operational assets.

ILLUSTRATION   10-5

Lump-Sum Purchase

The Smyrna Hand & Edge Tools Company purchased an existing factory for a single sum of $2,000,000. The price included title to the land, the factory building, and the manufacturing equipment in the building, a patent on a process the equipment uses, and inventories of raw materials. An independent appraisal estimated the market values of the assets (if purchased separately) at $330,000 for the land, $550,000 for the building, $660,000 for the equipment, $440,000 for the patent and $220,000 for the inventories. The lump-sum purchase price of $2,000,000 is allocated to the separate assets as follows:

ILLUSTRATION   10–5

continued

	Market values	
Land	$ 330,000	15%
Building	550,000	25
Equipment	660,000	30
Patent	440,000	20
Inventories	220,000	10
Total	$2,200,000	100%

> The total purchase price is allocated in proportion to the relative market values of the assets acquired.

Land	(15% × $2,000,000)	300,000
Building	(25% × $2,000,000)	500,000
Equipment	(30% × $2,000,000)	600,000
Patent	(20% × $2,000,000)	400,000
Inventories	(10% × $2,000,000)	200,000
Cash	....	2,000,000

ETHICAL DILEMMA

Grandma's Cookie Company purchased a factory building. The company Controller, Don Nelson, is in the process of allocating the lump-sum purchase price between land and building. Don suggests to the company's chief financial officer, Judith Prince, that they fudge a little by allocating a disproportionately higher share of the price to land. Don reasons that this will reduce depreciation expense, boost income, increase their profit-sharing bonus and, hopefully, increase the price of the company's stock. Judith has some reservations about this because the higher reported income will also cause income taxes to be higher than they would have been if a correct allocation of the purchase price is made.

What are the ethical issues? What stakeholders' interests are in conflict?

Noncash Acquisitions

Companies sometimes acquire operational assets without paying cash but instead by issuing debt or equity securities, receiving donated assets, or exchanging other assets. The controlling principle in each of these situations is that in any noncash transaction (not just those dealing with operational assets), the components of the transaction are recorded at their fair values. The first indicator of fair value is the fair value of the assets, debt, or equity securities given. Sometimes the fair value of the assets received is used when their fair value is more clearly evident than the fair value of the assets given.

> Assets acquired in noncash transactions are valued at the fair value of the assets given or the fair value of the assets received, whichever is more clearly evident.

Deferred Payments

> **Learning objective 3**
> Determine the initial cost of an operational asset acquired in exchange for a deferred payment contract.

A company can acquire an operational asset by giving the seller a promise to pay cash in the future and thus creating a liability, usually a note payable. The initial valuation of the asset is, again, quite simple as long as the note payable explicitly requires the payment of interest at a realistic interest rate. For example, suppose a machine is acquired for $15,000 and the buyer signs a note requiring the payment of $15,000 sometime in the future *plus* interest in the meantime at a realistic interest rate. The machine would be valued at $15,000 and the transaction recorded as follows:

Machine	15,000	
Note payable		15,000

We know from our discussion of the time value of money in Chapter 6 that most liabilities are valued at the present value of future cash payments, reflecting an appropriate time value of money. As long as the note payable explicitly contains a realistic interest rate, the present value will equal the face value of the note, $15,000 in our previous example. This also should be equal to the fair value of the machine purchased. On the other hand, when an interest rate is not specified or is unrealistic, determining the cost of the asset is less straightforward. In that case, the accountant should look beyond the form of the transaction and record its substance. Consider Illustration 10–6.

not covered

ILLUSTRATION   10–6

Deferred Payment Contract

> On June 30, 1997, the Midwestern Steam Gas Corporation purchased an industrial furnace. Midwestern paid $10,000 on the purchase date and signed a noninterest-bearing note requiring the balance to be paid in five annual installments of $10,000 beginning June 30, 1998. An interest rate of 10% would be reasonable in this situation.

Some portion of the payments required by a noninterest-bearing note in reality is interest.

On the surface, it might appear that Midwestern is paying $60,000 for the furnace, the sum of the eventual cash payments. However, when you note that the agreement specifies no interest even though the final payment won't be made for five years, it becomes obvious that a portion of the payments is not actually payment for the furnace but instead is interest on the note. At what amount should Midwestern value the furnace and the related note payable?

Noncash transactions are recorded at the fair value of the items exchanged.

Midwestern could either (1) determine the fair value of the note payable by computing the present value of the cash payments at the appropriate interest rate of 10% or (2) determine the fair value of the furnace on the date of purchase. Theoretically, both alternatives should lead to the same valuation. In this case, because we can determine an appropriate interest rate for the note, we determine the fair value of the note by computing its present value. The amount actually paid for the machine is the present value of the cash flows called for by the loan agreement, discounted at the market rate—assumed in this case to be 10%.

$$PV = \$10,000 \, (3.79079^*) = \$37,908$$

*Present value of an ordinary annuity of $1: n=5, i=10% (from Table 6A–4).

So, the furnace should be recorded at its *real* cost, $47,908, as follows:[7]

The economic essence of a transaction should prevail over its outward appearance.

Machine ($37,908 + 10,000)	47,908	
Cash (payment on purchase date)		10,000
Note payable (determined above)		37,908

Sometimes, the fair value of an asset acquired in a noncash transaction is readily available from price lists, previous purchases, or otherwise. In that case, this fair value may be more clearly evident than the fair value of the note and it would serve as the best evidence of the exchange value of the transaction. As an example, let's look at Illustration 10–7.

ILLUSTRATION   10–7

Noninterest-Bearing Note— Fair Value Known

> On January 1, 1997, Dennison, Inc., purchased a machine and signed a noninterest-bearing note in payment. The note requires the company to make five annual payments of $20,000 beginning on December 31, 1997. Dennison is not sure what interest rate appropriately reflects the time value of money. However, price lists indicate the machine could have been purchased for cash at a price of $79,854.
>
> Dennison records the following entry on January 1:
>
> | | | |
> |---|---|---|
> | Machine (cash price) . . . . | 79,854 | |
> | Note payable . . . . | | 79,854 |

In this situation, we infer the present value of the note from the fair value of the asset. Again, the difference between the note's $79,854 present value and the total of the cash payments to be made—$20,000 × 5 = $100,000 in this case—represents interest. We can determine the interest rate that is implicit in the agreement as follows:

$$\frac{\$79,854}{\$20,000} = 3.99271^*$$

*Present value of an ordinary annuity of $1: n=5, i = ? (from Table 6A–4, i = **8%**)

---

[7]The entry shown assumes the note is recorded by the net method. By the gross method, the note is recorded at its present value of $37,908 by using a contra account, called *discount on note payable*, to offset note payable for the difference between the face value of the note and its present value. The difference of $12,092 is recognized as interest expense over the life of the note.

Machine	47,908	
Discount on note payable	12,092	
Cash		10,000
Note payable (face amount)		50,000

We refer to the 8% rate as the *implicit rate of interest,* which also is the implied market rate. Dennison records interest after one year at 8% multiplied by $79,854, the balance of the liability outstanding during that first year:

The effective interest on debt is the market rate of interest multiplied by the outstanding balance of the debt (during the interest period).

December 31, 1997

Interest expense (8% × $79,854)	6,388	
Note payable (difference)	13,612	
Cash (annual installment payment)		20,000

Because $6,388 of the $20,000 payment is determined to be interest, this leaves $13,612 to reduce the carrying amount of the note from $79,854 to $66,242. Interest in the second year is 8% × $66,242 = $5,299. We discuss this concept in greater depth in Chapter 14.

We now turn our attention to the acquisition of operational assets acquired in exchange for equity securities, through donation, or in exchange for other nonmonetary assets.

Issuance of Equity Securities

Learning objective 4
Determine the initial cost of operational assets acquired in exchange for equity securities, through donation, or in exchange for other nonmonetary assets.

The most common situation in which equity securities are issued for operational assets occurs when small companies incorporate and the owner or owners contribute assets to the new corporation in exchange for ownership securities, usually common stock. Because the common shares are not publicly traded, it's difficult to determine their fair value. In that case, the fair value of the assets received by the corporation is probably the better indicator of the transaction's exchange value. In other situations, particularly those involving corporations whose stock is actively traded, the market value of the shares is the best indication of fair value. Consider Illustration 10–8.

ILLUSTRATION   10–8

Asset Acquired by Issuing Equity Securities

Assets acquired by issuing common stock are valued at the fair value of the securities or the fair value of the assets, whichever is more clearly evident.

On March 31, 1997, the Elcorn Company issued 10,000 shares of its nopar common stock in exchange for land. On the date of the transaction, the market value of the common stock was $20 per share. The journal entry to record this transaction is:

Land	200,000	
Common stock (10,000 shares × $20)		200,000

If the market value of the common stock had not been reliably determinable, the value of the land as determined through an independent appraisal would be used as the cost of the land and the value of the common stock.

Donated Assets

On occasion, companies acquire operational assets through donation. A local government unit might provide land or pay all or some of the cost of a new office building or manufacturing plant to entice a company to locate in its geographical boundaries. For example, the city of San Jose, California, recently paid a significant portion of the cost of a new office building for IBM Corporation. The new office building, located in downtown San Jose, brought jobs to a revitalized downtown area and increased revenues to the city.

Donated assets are valued at their fair values.

Assets donated by unrelated parties should be recorded at their fair value based on either an available market price or an appraisal value. This is not a departure from historical cost valuation. The treatment of the transaction is equivalent to the donor contributing cash to the company and the company using the cash to acquire the asset.

SFAS 116 requires that on receipt of the asset the company must record revenue at an amount equal to the value of the **donated asset**.[8] Recall that revenues generally are inflows of assets from delivering or producing goods, rendering services, or performing activities that constitute the

---

[8]"Accounting for Contributions Received and Contributions Made," *Statement of Financial Accounting Standards No. 116* (Norwalk, Conn: FASB, 1993).

entity's ongoing major or central operations. The company receiving the donation is performing a service for the donor (like building an office building within the donor city boundaries) in exchange for the asset donated. Let's look at Illustration 10–9.

ILLUSTRATION   10–9

Asset Donation

Revenue is credited for the amount paid by an unrelated party.

The Elcorn Company decided to relocate its office headquarters to the city of Westmont. The city agreed to pay 40% of the $3 million cost of the building to entice Elcorn to relocate. The building was completed on May 3, 1997. Elcorn paid its portion of the cost of the building in cash. The journal entry to record this transaction is:

Building	3,000,000	
Cash (60% × $3 million)		1,800,000
Revenue—donation of asset (40% × $3 million)		1,200,000

Acquisition by Exchange

An asset received in a nonmonetary exchange generally is recorded at the cash equivalent value of the assets exchanged.

Sometimes a company will acquire an operational asset in exchange for another operational asset. This frequently involves a trade-in by which a new asset is acquired in exchange for an old asset, and cash is given to equalize the fair values of the assets exchanged. The basic principle followed in these nonmonetary exchanges is to value the asset received at fair value.[9] This can be the fair value of the asset given up or the fair value of the asset received plus (or minus) any cash exchanged.[10] We first look to the fair value of the asset given up. However, in a trade-in, quite often the fair value of the new asset is more clearly evident than the second-hand value of the asset traded in.

If we cannot determine the fair value of either asset in the exchange, the asset received is valued at the book value of the asset given.

An important exception to the fair value principle relates to certain exchanges involving similar productive assets. We consider this exception later in the chapter. Another exception is situations when we cannot determine the fair value of either the asset given up or the asset received. In these cases, the asset received is valued at the book value of the asset given. This would be an unusual situation when we could not reasonably determine fair value.

Exchanges of Dissimilar Assets.   When dissimilar assets are exchanged, four possibilities arise regarding whether a loss or gain is created and whether cash is paid or received. By varying the terms of a single exchange transaction, we can compare the effect of the four possibilities.

ILLUSTRATION   10–10

Nonmonetary Exchange— Dissimilar Assets

The Elcorn Company traded land it had been holding as an investment in exchange for equipment. The land had a book value of $100,000.

If the fair value of the asset given up, the land, is determinable, it is used to value the transaction. The difference between that amount and the book value of the land would determine whether a gain or loss is indicated. The equipment is valued at the fair value of the land plus (minus) any cash paid (received) regardless of whether a gain or loss is indicated. If we cannot determine the fair value of the land, then we use the fair value of the asset received, the equipment.

The fair value of the land is $80,000, and $10,000 cash is given.

Situation D1:
Dissimilar assets; loss indicated; cash given

The $10,000 cash is given to equate the fair values of the exchanged assets. In this case, because the land's fair value is $80,000, and the Elcorn Company paid $10,000 in cash to equalize the transaction, the equipment apparently has a fair value of $90,000. The equipment is recorded at this amount, and a $20,000 loss is recognized for the difference between the fair value and book value of the land.

Equipment ($80,000 + 10,000)	90,000	
Loss ($100,000 – 80,000)	20,000	
Cash (amount paid)		10,000
Land (book value)		100,000

---

[9]Monetary items are assets and liabilities whose amounts are fixed, by contract or otherwise, in terms of a specific number of dollars. Others are considered nonmonetary.

[10]"Accounting for Nonmonetary Transactions," *Opinion of the Accounting Principles Board No. 29* (New York: AICPA, 1973).

Situation D2:
Dissimilar assets; loss
indicated; cash received

The fair value of the land is $80,000, and $10,000 cash is *received*.

Because cash is received in this case to equalize fair values, the new equipment's fair value must be less than the fair value of the land.

Equipment ($80,000 – 10,000)	70,000	
Cash (amount received)	10,000	
Loss ($100,000 – 80,000)	20,000	
Land (book value)		100,000

Notice that in each of the first two situations the loss is the same, the $20,000 difference between the fair value and book value of the land.

Situation D3:
Dissimilar assets; gain
indicated; cash given

The fair value of the land is $140,000, and $10,000 cash is *given*.

In this situation, a gain is indicated because the fair value of the land is higher than its book value. Again, the equipment is valued at the fair value of the land plus the cash paid.

Equipment ($140,000 + 10,000)	150,000	
Cash (amount paid)		10,000
Land (book value)		100,000
Gain ($140,000 – 100,000)		40,000

Situation D4:
Dissimilar assets; gain
indicated; cash received

The fair value of the land is $140,000, and $10,000 cash is *received*.

The equipment is valued at $130,000, the fair value of the land less cash received, and the indicated gain is recognized.

Equipment ($140,000 – 10,000)	130,000	
Cash (amount received)	10,000	
Land (book value)		100,000
Gain ($140,000 – 100,000)		40,000

Notice that in situations D3 and D4, the gain is the same, the $40,000 difference between the fair value and book value of the land.

Exchanges of Similar Assets. When an exchange involves similar assets—say an old delivery truck for a new delivery truck or old factory equipment for new factory equipment—the accounting treatment depends on (1) whether a gain or loss is indicated by the fair value of the asset given up compared to its book value and (2) whether or not cash is received. Specifically, gains are not recognized unless cash is received in the exchange. Let's consider why.

An exchange of *similar*
assets is viewed as a
continuation of the earnings
process using the same
operational assets rather
than the culmination of an
earnings process.

To record a gain implies that an earning process has been completed. When similar assets are exchanged, the earning process in which the assets are employed typically continues. On the contrary, in an exchange of *dissimilar* assets such as land for equipment or inventory for a computer, the transaction is considered to be the culmination of an earning process. Stated differently, since the old asset isn't being replaced, it is viewed as having been sold. This is not the case when *similar* assets are exchanged, *unless cash is received*. Then it's assumed that part of the old asset is *traded* for the new asset and part of the old asset is *sold* for cash. In such a case, a gain is recorded on the sale portion of the transaction if the cash received exceeds the book value of the portion of the asset considered sold. This is best understood through the example provided in Illustration 10–11.

ILLUSTRATION 10–11

Exchange of Similar Assets

The Elcorn Company exchanged equipment used in the production process for new equipment to be used for a similar purpose. The old equipment has a book value of $100,000 (original cost of $140,000 less accumulated depreciation of $40,000) on the date of the exchange.

As before, we'll vary the terms of this single transaction in order to compare four different scenarios.

Situation S1:
Similar assets; loss indicated; cash given

The fair value of the old equipment is $80,000, and $10,000 cash is *given*.

A loss is indicated in this situation because the fair value of the old equipment ($80,000) relinquished is less than its book value ($100,000). The basic principle of using fair value of the assets given up is used to value the new equipment. The new equipment is recorded at the fair value of old equipment plus cash paid and a $20,000 loss is recognized.

Equipment—new ($80,000 + 10,000)	90,000	
Loss ($100,000 – 80,000)	20,000	
Accumulated depreciation (account balance)	40,000	
Cash (amount paid)		10,000
Equipment—old (account balance)		140,000

Situation S2:
Similar assets; loss indicated; cash received

The fair value of the old equipment is $80,000, and $10,000 cash is *received*.

Again, a loss is indicated. The market value of the old equipment minus the cash received is the initial valuation of the new equipment.

Equipment—new ($80,000 – 10,000)	70,000	
Cash (amount received)	10,000	
Loss ($100,000 – 80,000)	20,000	
Accumulated depreciation (account balance)	40,000	
Equipment—old (account balance)		140,000

Notice again that in situations S1 and S2 the loss is the same, the $20,000 difference between the fair value and book value of the equipment.

Situation S3:
Similar assets; gain indicated; cash given

The fair value of the old equipment is $110,000, and $10,000 cash is *given*.

A $10,000 gain is indicated by the excess of the fair value of old equipment of $110,000 over its book value of $100,000. As we discussed earlier, it is inappropriate to record this gain because the exchange of similar assets is considered to be a trade rather than the culmination of an earning process. As a result, the new equipment is valued at the book value of the old asset plus the cash paid. No gain is recognized.[11]

Equipment—new ($100,000 + 10,000)	110,000	
Accumulated depreciation (account balance)	40,000	
Cash (amount paid)		10,000
Equipment—old (account balance)		140,000

To better understand the reasoning behind the nonrecognition of gain, consider the effect of the exchange. The company has exchanged similar assets and is in no better position economically than before the exchange. Whatever benefits the old asset provided, the new asset will continue to provide. That is, the new equipment replaces the old equipment in an ongoing earning process (the production of merchandise for sale).

Situation S4:
Similar assets; gain indicated; cash received

The fair value of the old equipment is $150,000, and $15,000 cash is *received*.

[11]*APBO 29* considers nonmonetary transactions to be those that involve little or no monetary assets. If monetary consideration is significant, the exchange is considered a monetary exchange by both parties and fair values are used to value assets and measure gains and losses. This distinction is important only in situations S3 and S4 when a departure from using fair values is otherwise appropriate. The Emerging Issues Task Force in *EITF Issue No. 86-29,* "Nonmonetary Transactions: Magnitude of Boot and the Exception to the Use of Fair Value," stated that if monetary consideration represents 25% or more of the total consideration received, the transaction is monetary. In our illustrations and concept review, cash received is less than 25% and the transactions are treated as nonmonetary.

An apparent gain of $50,000 is indicated because the exchange gives Elcorn credit for the old equipment's fair value of $150,000 while its book value is only $100,000. In the previous situation, we did not recognize the gain because similar assets were exchanged. In this situation, though, in addition to receiving the *similar* asset—equipment—the company also receives a *dissimilar* asset—cash. In a sense, part of the old equipment is *sold* for cash, and part is *exchanged* for a similar asset. We can recognize a gain on the portion sold because it represents the completion of an earning process. To do this, we need to allocate the book value of the old asset between the part that is sold and the part that is traded. The allocation is based on the proportional relationship between the fair value of the new asset and the cash received. This is the same technique we used earlier to allocate a lump-sum purchase price among the individual asset accounts.

The proportion of the asset considered sold is the proportion of the total fair value received represented by cash.

$$\frac{\text{Cash received}}{\text{Cash received} + \text{Fair value of similar asset received*}}$$

$$\frac{\$15,000}{\$15,000 + \$135,000} = 10\%$$

*Indicated in this case by the fair value of the equipment surrendered ($150,000) minus the cash received ($15,000).

Calculation of the Gain.

Determine Relative Fair Values of Assets Received:	Fair Values	Relative Proportions
Cash	$ 15,000	10%
New equipment* ($150,000 – 15,000)	135,000	90
Total	$150,000	100%

10% of the fair value received is cash.

Determine Portion of Old Equipment Sold :	
Portion sold (10% × $100,000)	$ 10,000
Portion traded (90% × $100,000)	90,000
Total book value ($140,000 – 40,000)	$100,000

10% of the old equipment is considered sold.

Determine Gain on Portion of Old Equipment Sold :	
Cash received	$ 15,000
Portion sold (10% × $100,000)	(10,000)
Gain recognized on portion sold	$ 5,000

A gain can be recognized only on the portion of the old equipment considered sold.

*Fair value of old equipment minus the cash received.

You should note that the total gain is more than the amount recognized:

Cash received	$ 15,000
New equipment ($150,000 – 15,000)	135,000
Total received (fair value of old equipment)	150,000
Total given up (book value of old equipment)	(100,000)
Total gain	$ 50,000

Another way to calculate the portion of the gain to be recognized is by multiplying the sold percentage by the total gain:

Total gain	$50,000
Portion of old asset considered sold	× 10%
Gain recognized on portion sold	$ 5,000

The journal entry to record the exchange is as follows:

Equipment—new (to balance)	90,000	
Cash (amount received)	15,000	
Accumulated depreciation (account balance)	40,000	
Equipment—old (account balance)		140,000
Gain (determined above)		5,000

The cost of the new equipment can be calculated as the fair value of the new equipment minus the portion of the gain not recognized, as follows:

Fair value of the new equipment	$135,000
Less: Gain not recognized ($50,000 – 5,000)	(45,000)
Cost of new equipment	$ 90,000

Cost also can be determined by adding the book value of the old equipment less any cash received plus the gain recognized, as follows:

Book value of the old equipment	$100,000
Less: Cash received	(15,000)
Plus: Gain recognized	5,000
Cost of new equipment	$ 90,000

Additional Consideration

For illustration, you might find it helpful to separate the entry into its two components:

Portion sold:

Cash (amount received)	15,000	
Accumulated depreciation (10% × $40,000)	4,000	
Equipment—old (10% × $140,000)		14,000
Gain (difference: also calculated above)		5,000

Portion traded:

Equipment—new (plug: book value of portion traded)	90,000	
Accumulated depreciation (90% × $40,000)	36,000	
Equipment—old (90% × $140,000)		126,000

CONCEPT REVIEW EXERCISE   NONMONETARY EXCHANGES

PART A:

The MD Corporation recently acquired new equipment to be used in its production process. In exchange, the company traded in an existing asset that had an original cost of $60,000 and accumulated depreciation on the date of the exchange of $45,000. In addition, MD paid $40,000 cash to the equipment manufacturer. The fair value of the old equipment is $10,000.

Required:
1. Prepare the journal entry to record the exchange transaction assuming that the old and new equipment are considered dissimilar assets.
2. Prepare the journal entry to record the exchange transaction assuming that the old and new equipment are considered similar assets.

PART B:

The MD Corporation recently acquired new equipment to be used in its production process. In exchange, the company traded in an existing asset that had an original cost of $100,000 and accumulated depreciation on the date of the exchange of $60,000. In addition, MD received $10,000 in cash from the equipment manufacturer. The fair value of the old equipment is $80,000, which means the fair value of the new equipment is $70,000 ($80,000 – cash received of $10,000).

Required:
1. Prepare the journal entry to record the exchange transaction assuming that the old and new equipment are considered dissimilar assets.
2. Prepare the journal entry to record the exchange transaction assuming that the old and new equipment are considered similar assets.

C R E

CONCEPT REVIEW EXERCISE   SOLUTION

PART A:

1. Prepare the journal entry to record the exchange transaction assuming that the old and new equipment are considered dissimilar assets.

Equipment—new ($10,000 + 40,000)	50,000	
Loss ($15,000 – 10,000)	5,000	
Accumulated depreciation (account balance)	45,000	
Cash (amount paid)		40,000
Equipment—old (account balance)		60,000

2. Prepare the journal entry to record the exchange transaction assuming that the old and new equipment are considered similar assets.

    Answer is the same as requirement 1.

PART B:

1. Prepare the journal entry to record the exchange transaction assuming that the old and new equipment are considered dissimilar assets.

Equipment—new ($80,000 – 10,000)	70,000	
Cash (amount received)	10,000	
Accumulated depreciation (account balance)	60,000	
Gain ($80,000 – 40,000)		40,000
Equipment—old (account balance)		100,000

2. Prepare the journal entry to record the exchange transaction assuming that the old and new equipment are considered similar assets.

The proportion of the asset considered sold is the proportion of the total fair value received represented by cash.

$$\frac{\text{Cash received}}{\text{Cash received + fair value of similar asset received}}$$

$$\frac{\$10,000}{\$10,000 + \$70,000} = 12.5\%$$

Calculation of the gain
12.5% of the old equipment is considered sold.

Cash received	$10,000
Portion sold [12.5% × ($100,000 – 60,000)]	(5,000)
Gain recognized on portion sold	$ 5,000

Equipment—new (to balance*)	35,000	
Cash (amount received)	10,000	
Accumulated depreciation (account balance)	60,000	
Equipment—old (account balance)		100,000
Gain (determined above)		5,000

*The cost of the new equipment can also be calculated as the fair value of the new equipment minus the portion of the gain not recognized, as follows:

Fair value of the new equipment	$70,000
Less: Gain not recognized ($40,000 – 5,000)	(35,000)
Cost of new equipment	$35,000

Decision Makers' Perspective

The operational asset acquisition decision is among the most significant decisions that management must make. A decision to acquire a new fleet of airplanes or to build or purchase a new office building or manufacturing plant could influence a company's performance for many years.

These decisions, often referred to as **capital budgeting** decisions, require management to forecast all future net cash flows (cash inflows minus cash outflows) generated by the operational asset(s). These cash flows are then used in a model to determine if the future cash flows are sufficient to warrant the capital expenditure. One such model, the net present value model, compares the present value of future net cash flows with the required initial acquisition cost of the asset(s). If the present value is higher than the acquisition cost, the asset is acquired. You have studied or will study capital budgeting in considerable depth in a financial management course. The introduction to the time value of money concept in Chapter 6 provided you with important tools necessary to evaluate capital budgeting decisions.

> The **fixed-asset turnover ratio** measures a company's effectiveness in managing property, plant, and equipment.

A key to profitability is how well a company manages and utilizes its assets. Financial analysts often use activity, or turnover, ratios to evaluate a company's effectiveness in managing assets. This concept was illustrated with receivables and inventory in previous chapters. Operational assets—particularly property, plant, and equipment (PP&E)—usually are a company's primary revenue-generating assets. Their efficient use is critical to generating a satisfactory return to owners. One ratio analysts often use to measure how effectively managers use PP&E is the **fixed-asset turnover ratio**. This ratio is calculated as follows:

$$\text{Fixed-asset turnover ratio} = \frac{\text{Net sales}}{\text{Average fixed assets}}$$

The ratio indicates the level of sales generated by the company's investment in fixed assets. The denominator usually is the book value (cost less accumulated depreciation and depletion) of property, plant, and equipment.[12]

As with other turnover ratios, we can compare a company's fixed-asset turnover ratio with that of its competitors, with an industry average, or with the same company's ratio over time. Let's compare the fixed-asset turnover ratios for Maytag and Whirlpool, the same two companies we used in Chapter 7 to illustrate accounts receivable turnover.

	($ in millions)			
	Maytag		**Whirlpool**	
	1995	**1994**	**1995**	**1994**
Property, plant, and equipment (net)	$ 701	$ 749	$1,779	$1,440
Net sales—1995	$3,040		$8,163	

The fixed-asset turnover ratio for 1995 for Maytag is 4.19 {$3,040 ÷ [($701 + 749) ÷ 2]} compared to Whirlpool's turnover of 5.07 {$8,163 ÷ [($1,779 + 1,440) ÷ 2]}. Whirlpool is able to generate $.88 more in sales dollars for each dollar of investment in fixed assets than does Maytag.

PART

B SELF-CONSTRUCTED ASSETS AND RESEARCH AND DEVELOPMENT

Two types of expenditures relating to operational assets whose accounting treatment has generated considerable controversy are interest costs pertaining to self-constructed assets and amounts spent for research and development. We now consider those expenditures and why those controversies have developed.

Self-Constructed Assets

> **Learning objective 5**
> Identify the items included in the cost of a self-constructed asset and determine the amount of capitalized interest.

A company might decide to construct an asset for its own use rather than buy an existing one. For example, a construction company might decide to build its own office building rather than purchase an existing building. A manufacturing company could construct its own machinery rather than purchase it from an equipment manufacturer. The critical accounting issue in these instances is identifying the cost of the self-constructed asset. The task is more difficult than for purchased assets because there is no external transaction to establish an exchange price. Actually, two difficulties arise in connection with assigning costs to self-constructed assets:

---

[12]If intangible assets are significant, their book value could be added to the denominator to produce a turnover that reflects all operational assets. The use of book value provides an approximation of the company's current investment in these assets.

(1) determining the amount of the company's indirect manufacturing costs (overhead) to be allocated to the construction and (2) deciding on the proper treatment of interest (actual or implicit) incurred during construction.

Overhead Allocation

The cost of a self-constructed asset includes identifiable materials and labor and a portion of the company's manufacturing overhead costs.

One difficulty of associating costs with self-constructed assets is the same difficulty encountered when determining cost of goods manufactured for sale. The costs of material and direct labor usually are easily identified with a particular construction project and are included in cost. However, the treatment of manufacturing overhead cost and its allocation between construction projects and normal production is a controversial issue.

Some accountants advocate the inclusion of only the *incremental* overhead costs in the total cost of construction. That is, the asset's cost would include only those additional costs that are incurred because of the decision to construct the asset. This would exclude such indirect costs as depreciation and the salaries of supervisors that would be incurred whether or not the construction project is undertaken. If, however, a new construction supervisor was hired specifically to work on the project, then that salary would be included in asset cost.

Others advocate assigning overhead on the same basis that is used for a regular manufacturing process. That is, all overhead costs are allocated both to production and to self-constructed assets based on the relative amount of a chosen cost driver (for example, labor hours) incurred. This is known as the *full-cost approach* and is the generally accepted method used to determine the cost of a self-constructed asset.

Interest Capitalization

OPENING CASE

Question 3

To reiterate, the cost of an asset includes all costs necessary to get the asset ready for its intended use. Unlike one purchased from another company, a self-constructed asset requires time to create it. During this construction period, the project must be financed in some way. This suggests the question as to whether interest costs during the construction period are one of the costs of acquiring the asset itself or simply costs of financing the asset. On the one hand, we might point to interest charges to finance inventories during their period of manufacture or to finance the purchase of plant assets from others and argue that construction period interest charges are merely costs of financing the asset that should be expensed as incurred like all other interest costs. On the other hand, we might argue that self-constructed assets are different in that during the construction period, they are not yet ready for their intended use for producing revenues. And, so, in keeping with both the historical cost principle and the matching concept, all costs during this period, including interest, should be capitalized and then allocated as depreciation expense during later periods when the assets are providing benefits.

Only assets that are constructed as discrete projects qualify for interest capitalization.

Generally accepted accounting principles are consistent with the second argument. Specifically, interest is capitalized during the construction period for (a) assets built for a company's own use as well as for (b) assets constructed *as discrete projects* for sale or lease (a ship or a real estate development, for example). This excludes from interest capitalization consideration inventories that are routinely manufactured in large quantities on a repetitive basis and assets that already are in use or are ready for their intended use.[13] Interest costs incurred during the productive life of the asset are expensed as incurred.

Only interest incurred during the construction period is eligible for capitalization.

Prior to 1979, when this treatment was mandated by *SFAS 34*, many companies treated construction-period interest costs as a cost of obtaining funds and not a cost of obtaining an asset. Accordingly, interest costs were expensed rather than capitalized. In fact, prior to the early 1970s, few companies other than utilities capitalized interest. Utilities have long been motivated to do so by the desire to increase their asset bases on which regulated utility rates are determined. Nonregulated companies began to follow suit during the economic slowdown of the early 1970s as a way to decrease expenses and bolster profits. *SFAS 34* was an attempt to address the diversity of accounting practice. Now all companies capitalize interest incurred during the construction of a qualified asset.

---

[13]"Capitalization of Interest Costs," *Statement of Financial Accounting Standards No. 34* (Stamford, Conn: FASB, 1979).

The interest capitalization period begins when construction begins and the first expenditure is made as long as interest costs are actually being incurred.

don't read

Average accumulated expenditures approximates the average debt necessary for construction.

Period of Capitalization.   The capitalization period for a self-constructed asset starts with the first expenditure (materials, labor, or overhead) and ends either when the asset is substantially complete and ready for use or when interest costs no longer are being incurred. Interest costs incurred can pertain to borrowings other than those obtained specifically for the construction project. However, interest costs can't be imputed; actual interest costs must be incurred.

Average Accumulated Expenditures.   Because we consider interest to be a necessary cost of getting a self-constructed asset ready for use, the amount capitalized is only that portion of interest cost incurred during the construction period that *could have been avoided* if expenditures for the asset had not been made. In other words, if construction had not been undertaken, debt incurred for the project would not have been necessary and/or other interest-bearing debt could have been liquidated or employed elsewhere.

As a result, interest should be determined for only the construction expenditures actually incurred during the capitalization period. And unless all expenditures are made at the outset of the period, it's necessary to determine the *average* amount outstanding during the period. This is the amount of debt that would be required to finance the expenditures and thus the amount on which interest would accrue. For instance, if a company accumulated $1,500,000 of construction expenditures fairly evenly throughout the construction period, the average expenditures would be:

Total accumulated expenditures incurred evenly throughout the period	$1,500,000
	÷ 2
Average accumulated expenditures	$ 750,000

At the beginning of the period, no expenditures have accumulated, so no interest has accrued (on the equivalent amount of debt). But, by the end of the period interest is accruing on the total amount, $1,500,000. On average, then, interest accrues on half the total or $750,000.

If expenditures are not incurred evenly throughout the period, a simple average is insufficient. In that case, a weighted average is determined by time-weighting individual expenditures or groups of expenditures by the number of months from their incurrence to the end of the construction period or the end of the reporting period, whichever comes first. This is demonstrated in Illustration 10–12.

ILLUSTRATION 10–12

Interest Capitalization

On January 1, 1997, the Mills Conveying Equipment Company began construction of a building to be used as its office headquarters. The building was completed on June 30, 1998. Expenditures on the project were as follows:

January 3, 1997	$ 500,000
March 31, 1997	400,000
September 30, 1997	600,000
Accumulated expenditures at Dec. 31, 1997 (before interest capitalization)	$1,500,000
January 31, 1998	600,000
April 30, 1998	300,000

On January 2, 1997, the company obtained a $1 million construction loan with an 8% interest rate. The loan was outstanding during the entire construction period. The company's other interest-bearing debt included two long-term notes of $2,000,000 and $4,000,000 with interest rates of 6% and 12%, respectively. Both notes were outstanding during the entire construction period.

OPENING CASE

Question 4

Step 1: Determine the average accumulated expenditures.

The weighted-average accumulated expenditures by the end of 1997 are:

January 3, 1997	$500,000 × $^{12}/_{12}$	=	$500,000
March 31, 1997	400,000 × $^{9}/_{12}$	=	300,000
September 30, 1997	600,000 × $^{3}/_{12}$	=	150,000
Average accumulated expenditures for 1997		=	$950,000

Again notice that the average accumulated expenditures are less than the total accumulated expenditures of $1,500,000. If Mills had borrowed exactly the amount necessary to finance the project, it would not have incurred interest on a loan of $1,500,000 for the whole year but only on an average loan of $950,000. The next step is to determine the interest to be capitalized for the average accumulated expenditures.

Interest Rates. In this situation, debt financing was obtained specifically for the construction project, and the amount borrowed is sufficient to cover the average accumulated expenditures. To determine the interest capitalized, then, we simply multiply the construction loan rate of 8% by the average accumulated expenditures.

$$\text{Interest capitalized for 1997} = \$950,000 \times 8\% = \$76,000$$

Notice that this is the same answer we would get by assuming separate 8% construction loans were made for each expenditure at the time each expenditure was made:

Loans		Annual Rate		Portion of Year Outstanding		Interest
$500,000	×	8%	×	$12/12$	=	$40,000
400,000	×	8%	×	$9/12$	=	24,000
600,000	×	8%	×	$3/12$	=	12,000
Interest capitalized for 1997						$76,000

The interest of $76,000 is added to the cost of the building, bringing accumulated expenditures at December 31, 1997, to $1,576,000 ($1,500,000 + 76,000). The remaining interest cost incurred but not capitalized is expensed.

It should be emphasized that interest capitalization does not require that funds actually be borrowed for this specific purpose, only that the company does have outstanding debt. The presumption is that even if the company doesn't borrow specifically for the project, funds from other borrowings must be diverted to finance the construction. Either way—directly or indirectly—interest costs are incurred. In our illustration, for instance, even without the construction loan, interest would be capitalized because other debt was outstanding. The capitalized interest would be the average accumulated expenditures multiplied by the weighted-average rate on these other loans. The weighted-average interest rate on all debt other than the construction loan would be 10%, calculated as follows:[14]

Loans		Rate		Interest
$2,000,000	×	6%	=	$120,000
4,000,000	×	12%	=	480,000
$6,000,000				$600,000

$$\text{Weighted-average rate: } \frac{\$600,000}{\$6,000,000} = 10\%$$

This is a weighted average because total interest is $600,000 on total debt of $6,000,000.

[14]The same result can be obtained simply by multiplying the individual debt interest rates by the relative amount of debt at each rate. In this case, one-third of total debt is at 6% and two-thirds of the total debt is at 12% (1/3 × 6% + 2/3 × 12% = 10%).

Interest capitalized is limited to interest incurred.

It's possible that the amount of interest calculated to be capitalized exceeds the amount of interest actually incurred. If that's the case, we limit the interest capitalized to the actual interest incurred. In our illustration, total interest cost incurred during 1997 far exceeds the $76,000 of capitalized interest calculated, so it's not necessary to limit the capitalized amount.

Step 3: Compare calculated interest with actual interest incurred.

Loans		Rate		Actual Interest	Calculated Interest
$1,000,000	×	8%	=	$ 80,000	
2,000,000	×	6%	=	120,000	
4,000,000	×	12%	=	480,000	
				$680,000	$76,000

↑
Use lower amount

Continuing the example based on the information in Illustration 10–12, let's determine the amount of interest capitalized during 1998 for the building. The total accumulated expenditures by the end of the project are:

Accumulated expenditures at the beginning of 1998 (including interest capitalization)	$1,576,000
January 31, 1998	600,000
April 30, 1998	300,000
Accumulated expenditures at June 30, 1998 (before 1998 interest capitalization)	$2,476,000

The weighted-average accumulated expenditures by the end of the project are:

Step 1: Determine the average accumulated expenditures

January 1, 1998	$1,576,000 × $6/6$ =	$1,576,000
January 31, 1998	600,000 × $5/6$ =	500,000
April 30, 1998	300,000 × $2/6$ =	100,000
Average accumulated expenditures for 1998		$2,176,000

Notice that the 1998 expenditures are weighted relative to the construction period of six months because the project was finished on June 30, 1998. Interest capitalized for 1998 would be $98,800, calculated as follows:

Step 2: Calculate the amount of interest to be capitalized.

	Average Accumulated Expenditures		Annual Rate		Fraction of Year		Interest
	$2,176,000						
Specific borrowing	1,000,000	x	8%	x	$6/12$	=	$40,000
Excess	$1,176,000	x	10%	x	$6/12$	=	58,800
Capitalized interest							$98,800

Multiplying by six-twelfths reflects the fact that the interest rates are annual rates (12-month rates) and the construction period is only 6 months.

Step 3: Compare calculated interest with actual interest incurred.

Loans		Annual Rate				Actual Interest	Calculated Interest
$1,000,000	×	8%	×	$6/12$	=	$ 40,000	
2,000,000	×	6%	×	$6/12$	=	60,000	
4,000,000	×	12%	×	$6/12$	=	240,000	
						$340,000	$98,800

↑
Use lower amount

For the first six months of 1998, $98,800 interest would be capitalized, bringing the total capitalized cost of the building to $2,574,800 ($2,476,000 + 98,800), and $241,200 in interest would be expensed ($340,000 − 98,800).

The method of determining interest to capitalize that we've discussed is called the **specific interest method** because we use rates from specific construction loans to the extent of specific borrowings before using the average rate of other debt. Sometimes, though, it's difficult to associate specific borrowings with projects. In these situations, it's acceptable to just use the weighted-average rate on all interest-bearing debt, including all construction loans. This is known as the **weighted-average method**. In our illustration, for example, if the $1,000,000, 8% loan had not been specifically related to construction, we would calculate a single weighted-average rate as shown on the following page.

Weighted-average method

Loans		Rate		Interest
$1,000,000	×	8%	=	$ 80,000
2,000,000	×	6%	=	120,000
4,000,000	×	12%	=	480,000
$7,000,000				$680,000

Weighted-average rate: $\dfrac{\$680,000}{\$7,000,000} = 9.7\%$

If we were using the weighted-average method rather than the specific method, we would simply multiply this single rate times the average accumulated expenditures to determine capitalizable interest.

Disclosure.   For an accounting period in which interest costs are capitalized, both the total amount of interest costs incurred and the amount that has been capitalized should be disclosed. Graphic 10–4 shows an interest capitalization disclosure note that was included in a recent annual report of Tyson Foods, Inc.

If material, the amount of interest capitalized during the period must be disclosed.

GRAPHIC   10–4

Capitalized Interest Disclosure—Tyson Foods, Inc.

Property, Plant and Equipment and Depreciation (in Part):

The Company capitalized interest costs of $3.1 million in 1995, $2 million in 1994, and $1.6 million in 1993 as part of the cost of major asset construction projects. Approximately $104.3 million will be required to complete construction projects in progress at September 30, 1995.

Research and Development (R&D)

Learning objective 6
Explain the difference in the accounting treatment of costs incurred to purchase intangible assets versus the costs incurred to internally develop intangible assets.

For years the practice was to allow companies to either expense or capitalize R&D costs, but in 1974 the FASB issued *SFAS 2* which now requires all research and development costs to be charged to expense when incurred.[15] This was a controversial standard opposed by many companies who preferred delaying the recognition of these expenses until later years when presumably the expenditures bear fruit.

A company undertakes an R&D project because it believes the project will eventually provide benefits that exceed the current expenditures. Unfortunately, though, it's difficult to predict which individual research and development projects will ultimately provide benefits. In fact, only 1 in 10 actually reach commercial production. Moreover, even for those projects that pan out, a direct

Most R&D costs are expensed in the periods incurred.

[15]"Accounting for Research and Development Costs," *Statement of Financial Accounting Standards No. 2* (Stamford, Conn: FASB, 1974), par. 12.

relationship between research and development costs and specific future revenue is difficult to establish. In other words, even if R&D costs do lead to future benefits, it's difficult to objectively determine the size of the benefits and in which periods the costs should be expensed if they are capitalized. These are the issues that prompted the FASB to require immediate expensing.

> R&D costs entail a high degree of uncertainty of future benefits and are difficult to match with future revenues.

The FASB's approach is certain in most cases to understate assets and overstate current expense because at least some of the R&D expenditures will likely produce future benefits.

Determining R&D Costs.   *SFAS 2* distinguishes research and development as follows:

Research is planned search or critical investigation aimed at discovery of new knowledge with the hope that such knowledge will be useful in developing a new product or service or a new process or technique or in bringing about a significant improvement to an existing product or process.

Development is the translation of research findings or other knowledge into a plan or design for a new product or process or for a significant improvement to an existing product or process whether intended for sale or use.[16]

R&D costs include salaries, wages, and other labor costs of personnel engaged in R&D activities, the costs of materials consumed, equipment, facilities, and intangibles used in R&D projects, the costs of services performed by others in connection with R&D activities, and a reasonable allocation of indirect costs related to those activities. General and administrative costs should not be included unless they are clearly related to the R&D activity.

> R&D expense includes the depreciation and amortization of operational assets used in R&D activities.

If an operational asset is purchased specifically for a single R&D project, its cost is considered R&D and expensed immediately even though the asset's useful life extends beyond the current year. However, the cost of an operational asset that has an alternative future use beyond the current R&D project is *not* a current R&D expense. Instead, the depreciation or amortization of these alternative-use assets is included as R&D expenses in the current and future periods the assets are used for R&D activities.

In general, R&D costs pertain to activities that occur prior to the start of commercial production, and costs of starting commercial production and beyond are not R&D costs. Graphic 10–5 captures this concept with a time line beginning with the start of an R&D project and ending with the ultimate sale of a developed product or the use of a developed process. The graphic also provides examples of activities typically included as R&D and examples of activities typically excluded from R&D.[17]

Costs incurred before the start of commercial production are all expensed as R&D. The costs incurred after commercial production begins would be either expensed or treated as manufacturing overhead and included in the cost of inventory. Let's look at an example in Illustration 10–13.

> Filing and legal costs for patents, copyrights, and other developed intangibles are capitalized and amortized in future periods.

The salaries and wages, supplies consumed, and payments to others for R&D services are expensed in 1997 as R&D. The equipment is capitalized and the 1997 depreciation is expensed as R&D. Even though the costs to develop the patented product are expensed, the filing and legal costs for the patent are capitalized and amortized in future periods just as similar costs are capitalized for purchased intangibles. Amortization of the patent is discussed in Chapter 11.

---

[16]Ibid., par. 8.

[17]Ibid., par. 9 and 10.

GRAPHIC   10-5

Research and Development Expenditures

Costs incurred *before* the start of commercial production are all expensed as R&D.

Costs incurred *after* commercial production begins would be either expensed or included in the cost of inventory.

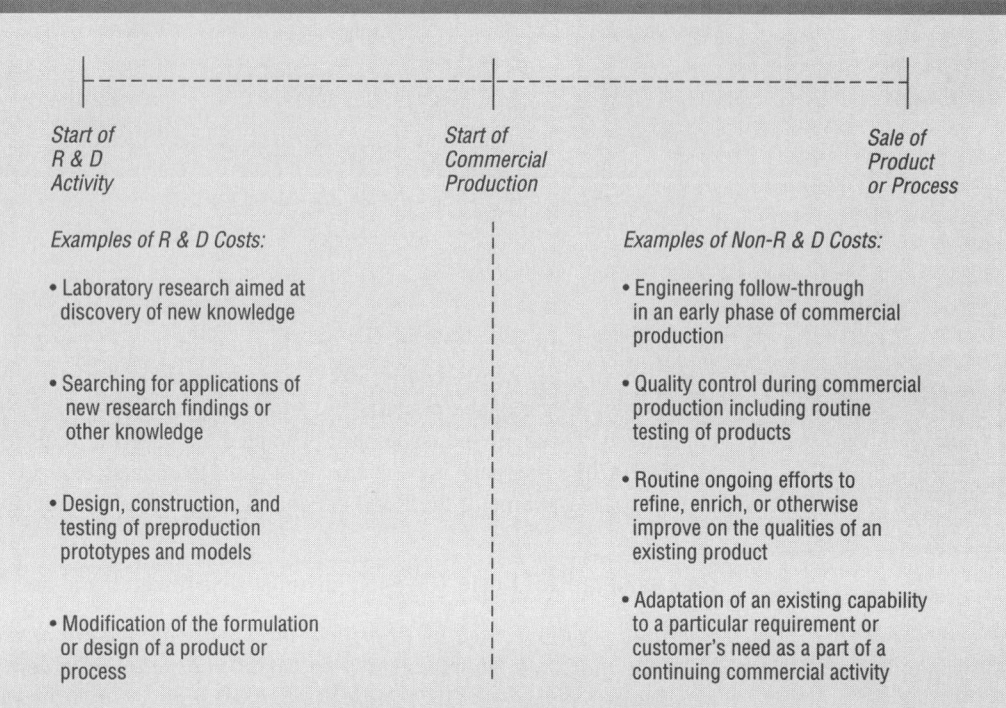

Start of R & D Activity	Start of Commercial Production	Sale of Product or Process

Examples of R & D Costs:

• Laboratory research aimed at discovery of new knowledge

• Searching for applications of new research findings or other knowledge

• Design, construction, and testing of preproduction prototypes and models

• Modification of the formulation or design of a product or process

Examples of Non-R & D Costs:

• Engineering follow-through in an early phase of commercial production

• Quality control during commercial production including routine testing of products

• Routine ongoing efforts to refine, enrich, or otherwise improve on the qualities of an existing product

• Adaptation of an existing capability to a particular requirement or customer's need as a part of a continuing commercial activity

ILLUSTRATION   10-13

Research and Development Costs

The Askew Company made the following cash expenditures during 1997 related to the development of a new industrial plastic:

R&D salaries and wages	$10,000,000
R&D supplies consumed during 1997	3,000,000
Purchase of R&D equipment	5,000,000
Patent filing and legal costs	100,000
Payments to others for services performed in connection with R&D activities	1,200,000
Total	$19,300,000

The project resulted in a new product to be manufactured in 1998. A patent was filed with the U.S. Patent Office. The equipment purchased will be employed in other projects. Depreciation on the equipment for 1997 was $500,000.

The various expenditures would be recorded as follows:

R&D expense ($10,000,000 + 3,000,000 + 1,200,000)	14,200,000	
Cash		14,200,000
To record R&D expenses.		
Equipment	5,000,000	
Cash		5,000,000
To record the purchase of equipment.		
R&D expense	500,000	
Accumulated depreciation—equipment		500,000
To record R&D depreciation.		
Patent	100,000	
Cash		100,000
To capitalize the patent filing and legal costs.		

Expenditures reconciliation:	
Recorded as R&D	$14,200,000
Capitalized as equipment	5,000,000
Capitalized as patent	100,000
Total expenditures	$19,300,000

<table>
<tr><td style="width:25%; vertical-align:top;">

GAAP require disclosure of total R&D expense incurred during the period.

</td><td>

GAAP require that total R&D expense incurred must be disclosed either as a line item on the income statement or in a disclosure note. For example, IBM reported $6,010 million of R&D expense on the face of its 1995 income statement. In our illustration, total R&D expense disclosed in 1997 would be $14,700,000 ($14,200,000 in expenditures and $500,000 in depreciation). Note that if Askew later sells this patent to another company for, say, $15 million, the buyer would capitalize the entire purchase price rather than only the filing and legal costs. Once again, the reason for the apparent inconsistency in accounting treatment of internally generated intangibles and externally purchased intangibles is the difficulty of associating costs and benefits.

</td></tr>
</table>

R&D Performed for Others.   The requirements of *SFAS 2* do not apply to companies that perform R&D for other companies under contract. In these situations, the R&D costs are capitalized as inventory and carried forward into future years until the project is completed. Of course, justification is that the benefits of these expenditures are the contract fees which are determinable and are earned over the term of the project. Income from these contracts can be recognized using either the percentage-of-completion or completed contract method. We discussed these alternatives in Chapter 4.

Another exception pertains to a company that develops computer software. Expenditures made after the software is determined to be technologically feasible but before it is ready for commercial production are capitalized. Costs incurred before technological feasibility is established are expensed as incurred. We discuss software development costs next.

GLOBAL PERSPECTIVE

Unlike the United States, the capitalization of research and development costs as an intangible asset is permitted in most other industrialized countries. Germany and Mexico are two countries that do follow the U.S. treatment of expensing all R & D costs in the period incurred.

Software Development Costs.   The computer software industry has become a large and important U.S. business over the last two decades. Relative newcomers such as Microsoft and Lotus, as well as traditional hardware companies like IBM, are leaders in this multibillion dollar industry. A significant expenditure for these companies is the cost of developing software. Prior to 1985, some companies were capitalizing software development costs and expensing them in future periods and others were expensing these costs in the period incurred.

<table>
<tr><td style="width:25%; vertical-align:top;">

GAAP require the capitalization of software development costs incurred after **technological feasibility** is established.

</td><td>

In 1985, the FASB issued *SFAS 86* which requires all companies to expense costs incurred to develop or purchase computer software to be sold, leased, or otherwise marketed as R&D costs until **technological feasibility** of the product or process has been established.[18] The Statement does not address the accounting treatment of costs incurred to develop computer software to be used internally. Most companies expense these costs as R&D. The cost of computer software purchased for internal use generally is capitalized.

</td></tr>
</table>

Technological feasibility is established "when the enterprise has completed all planning, designing, coding, and testing activities that are necessary to establish that the product can be produced to meet its design specifications including functions, features, and technical performance requirements."[19] Costs incurred after technological feasibility but before commercial production of the product begins are capitalized as an intangible asset. These costs include coding and testing costs and the production of product masters. Similar to the treatment of such costs under *SFAS 2*, costs incurred after commercial production begins usually are not R&D expenditures. Graphic 10–6 shows the R&D time line introduced earlier in the chapter and adds the point of establishment of

---

[18]"Accounting for the Costs of Computer Software to be Sold, Leased, or Otherwise Marketed," *Statement of Financial Accounting Standards No. 86* (Stamford, Conn: FASB, 1985).

[19]Ibid., par. 4.

technological feasibility. Only the costs incurred between technological feasibility and the start of commercial production are capitalized.

The amortization of capitalized computer software development costs begins with the start of commercial production. The periodic amortization percentage is the greater of (1) the ratio of current revenues to current and anticipated revenues (percentage-of-revenue method) or (2) the straight-line percentage over the useful life of the asset, as shown in Illustration 10–14.

The Astro Corporation develops computer software graphics programs for sale. A new development project begun in 1996 reached technological feasibility at the end of June 1997, and commercial production began early in 1998. Development costs incurred in 1997 prior to June 30 were $1,200,000 and costs incurred from June 30 to the start of commercial production were $800,000. 1998 revenues from the sale of the new product were $3,000,000 and the company anticipates an additional $7,000,000 in revenues. The economic life of the software is estimated at four years.

The Astro company would expense the $1,200,000 in costs incurred prior to the establishment of technological feasibility and capitalize the $800,000 in costs incurred between technological feasibility and the start of commercial production. 1998 amortization of the intangible asset, software development costs, is calculated as follows:

1. Percentage-of-revenue method:

$$\frac{\$3,000,000}{\$3,000,000 + \$7,000,000} = 30\% \times \$800,000 = \$240,000$$

2. Straight-line method:

$$^1/_4 \text{ or } 25\% \times \$800,000 = \$200,000.$$

The percentage-of-revenue method is used because it produces the greater amortization, $240,000.

Graphic 10–7 shows the software disclosure included in a recent IBM Corporation annual report. The note provides a good summary of the accounting treatment of software development costs.

Software (in Part):

Costs related to the conceptual formulation and design of licensed programs are expensed as research and development. Costs incurred subsequent to establishment of technological feasibility to produce the finished product are generally capitalized. The annual amortization of the capitalized amounts is the greater of the amount computed based on the estimated revenue distribution over the product's revenue-producing lives, or the straight-line method, and is applied over periods ranging up to four years.

Solution to Financial Reporting Case (at the opening of the chapter)

1. What does it mean to capitalize an expenditure? What is the general rule for determining which costs are capitalized when an operational asset is acquired?

To capitalize an expenditure simply means to record it as an asset. All expenditures other than payments to shareholders and debt repayments are either expensed as incurred or capitalized. In general, the choice is determined by whether the expenditure benefits more than just the current period. Exceptions to this general principle are discussed in the chapter. The initial cost of an operational asset includes all expenditures necessary to bring the asset to its desired condition and location for use.

2. Describe to Stan which costs might be included in the initial cost of equipment.

3. In what situations is interest capitalized?

4. What is the three-step process used to determine the amount of interest capitalized?

In addition to the purchase price, the cost of equipment might include the cost of transportation, installation, testing, and legal fees to establish title.

Interest is capitalized only for assets constructed for a company's own use or for assets constructed as discrete projects for sale or lease. For example, Walt Disney capitalizes interest on assets constructed for its theme parks, resort, and other property and on theatrical and television productions in process. During the construction period, interest is considered a cost necessary to get the asset ready for its intended use.

The first step is to determine the average accumulated expenditures for the period. The second step is to multiply the average accumulated expenditures by an appropriate interest rate or rates to determine the amount of interest capitalized. A final step compares the interest determined in step two with actual interest incurred. Interest capitalized is limited to the amount of interest incurred.

The Bottom Line

1. The initial cost of an operational asset acquired in an exchange transaction includes the purchase price and all expenditures necessary to bring the asset to its desired condition and location for use. The cost of a natural resource includes the acquisition costs for the use of land and the exploration and development costs incurred before production begins. Purchased intangibles are valued at their original cost to include the purchase price and legal and filing fees.

2. If a lump-sum purchase involves different assets, it is necessary to allocate the lump-sum acquisition price among the separate items according to some logical allocation method. A widely used allocation method is to divide the lump-sum purchase price according to the individual assets' relative market values.

3. Assets acquired in exchange for deferred payment contracts are valued at their fair value or the present value of payments using a realistic interest rate.

4. Assets acquired through the issuance of equity securities are valued at the fair value of the securities if known; if not known, the fair value of the assets received is used. Donated assets are valued at their fair value. The basic principle used for other nonmonetary exchanges is to value the asset(s) received based on the fair value of the asset(s) given up.

5. The cost of a self-constructed asset includes identifiable materials and labor and a portion of the company's manufacturing overhead costs. In addition, GAAP provides for the capitalization of interest incurred during construction. The amount of interest capitalized is equal to the average accumulated expenditures for the period multiplied by the appropriate interest rates, not to exceed actual interest incurred.

6. Research and development costs incurred to internally develop an intangible asset are expensed in the period incurred. Filing and legal costs for developed intangibles are capitalized.

APPENDIX

10

OIL AND GAS ACCOUNTING

Chapter 1 characterized the establishment of accounting and reporting standards as a political process. Standards, particularly changes in standards, can have significant differential effects on companies, investors and creditors, and other interest groups. The FASB must consider potential economic consequences of a change in an accounting standard or the introduction of a new standard. The history of oil and gas accounting provides a good example of this political process and the effect of possible adverse economic consequences on the standard-setting process.

There are two generally accepted methods that companies can use to account for oil and gas exploration costs. The **successful efforts method** requires that exploration costs that are known *not* to have resulted in the discovery of oil or gas (sometimes referred to as *dry holes*) be included as expenses in the period the expenditures are made. The alternative, the **full-cost method,** allows costs incurred in searching for oil and gas within a large geographical area to be capitalized as assets and expensed in the future as oil and gas from the successful wells are removed from that area. Both of these methods are widely used.

ILLUSTRATION   10A–1

Oil and Gas Accounting

The Shannon Oil Company incurred $2,000,000 in exploration costs for each of 10 oil wells drilled in 1997 in West Texas. Eight of the 10 wells were dry holes.

The accounting treatment of the $20 million in total exploration costs will vary significantly depending on the accounting method used. The summary journal entries using each of the alternative methods are as follows:

Successful Efforts			Full Cost		
Oil deposit	4,000,000		Oil deposit	20,000,000	
Exploration expense	16,000,000		Cash		20,000,000
Cash		20,000,000			

Using the full-cost method, Shannon would capitalize the entire $20 million which is expensed as oil from the two successful wells is depleted. On the other hand, using the successful efforts method, the cost of the unsuccessful wells is expensed in 1997, and only the $4 million cost related to the successful wells is capitalized and expensed in future periods as the oil is depleted.

In 1977 the FASB attempted to establish uniformity in the accounting treatment of oil and gas exploration costs. *SFAS 19* was issued requiring all companies to use the successful efforts method.[20]

SFAS 19 met with criticism from the oil and gas companies that were required to switch from full cost to successful efforts accounting. These companies felt that the switch would seriously depress their reported income over time. As a result, they argued, their ability to raise capital in the securities markets would be inhibited, which would result in a cutback of new exploration. The fear that the standard would cause domestic companies to significantly reduce oil and gas exploration and thus increase our dependence on foreign oil was compelling to the U.S. Congress, the SEC, and the Department of Energy.

Extensive pressure from Congress, the SEC, and affected companies forced the FASB to rescind *Standard 19.* Presently, oil and gas companies can use either the successful efforts or full-cost method to account for oil and gas exploration costs. Of course, the method used must be disclosed. For example, Graphic 10A–1 shows how Texaco, Inc., disclosed their use of the successful efforts method in a note to recent financial statements.

> Many feared that the implementation of *SFAS 19* would cause a significant cutback in the exploration for new oil and gas in the United States.

GRAPHIC   10A–1

Oil and Gas Accounting Disclosure—Texaco, Inc.

Properties, Plant and Equipment (in Part):

Texaco follows the "successful efforts" method of accounting for its oil and gas exploration and producing operations.

Questions for Review of Key Topics

Question	10–1	Define operational assets and explain the difference between tangible and intangible operational assets.
Question	10–2	What is included in the original cost of an operational asset acquired in an exchange transaction?
Question	10–3	Identify the costs associated with the initial valuation of a developed natural resource.
Question	10–4	Briefly summarize the accounting treatment for intangible assets, explaining the difference between purchased and internally developed intangible assets.
Question	10–5	What is goodwill and how is it measured?
Question	10–6	Explain the method generally used to allocate the cost of a lump-sum purchase to the individual assets acquired.
Question	10–7	When an operational asset is acquired and a note payable is assumed, explain how acquisition cost of the asset is determined when the interest rate for the note is less than the current market rate for similar notes.
Question	10–8	Explain how operational assets acquired in exchange for equity securities are valued.
Question	10–9	Explain how operational assets acquired through donation are valued.
Question	10–10	What is the basic principle for valuing operational assets acquired in exchange for another nonmonetary asset?

---

[20]"Financial Accounting and Reporting by Oil and Gas Producing Companies," *Statement of Financial Accounting Standards No. 19* (Stamford, Conn: FASB, 1977).

Question	10–11	Identify the three exceptions to valuing assets acquired in nonmonetary exchanges at the fair market value of the asset(s) given up.
Question	10–12	In what situations is interest capitalized?
Question	10–13	Define average accumulated expenditures and explain how it is computed.
Question	10–14	Explain the difference between the specific interest method and the weighted-average method in determining the amount of interest to be capitalized.
Question	10–15	Define R&D according to *SFAS 2*.
Question	10–16	Explain the accounting treatment of equipment acquired for use in R&D projects.
Question	10–17	Explain the accounting treatment of costs incurred to develop computer software.
Question	10–18 [based on Appendix 10]	Explain the difference between the successful efforts and the full-cost methods of accounting for oil and gas exploration costs.

Exercises

Exercise 10–1
Acquisition costs; land and building

On March 1, 1997, Beldon Corporation purchased land as a factory site for $50,000. An old building on the property was demolished, and construction began on a new building which was completed on December 15, 1997. Costs incurred during this period are listed below:

Demolition of old building	$ 4,000
Architect's fees (for new building)	10,000
Legal fees for title investigation of land	2,000
Property taxes on land (for period beginning March 1, 1997)	3,000
Construction costs	500,000
Interest on construction loan	5,000

Salvaged materials resulting from the demolition of the old building were sold for $2,000.

Required:
Determine the amounts that Beldon should capitalize as the cost of the land and the new building.

Exercise 10–2
Acquisition cost; machinery

The Oaktree Company purchased a new machine and made the following expenditures:

Purchase price	$40,000
Freight charges for shipment of machine	700
Insurance on the machine for the first year	800
Installation of machine	1,000

The machine was purchased on open account, with payment due in 30 days. The other expenditures listed above were paid in cash.

Required:
Prepare the necessary journal entries to record the above expenditures.

Exercise 10–3
Intangibles

The Freitas Corporation was organized early in 1997. The following expenditures were made during the first few months of the year:

Attorneys' fees in connection with the organization of the corporation	$12,000
State filing fees and other incorporation costs	3,000
Purchase of a patent	20,000
Legal and other fees for transfer of the patent	2,000
Purchase of furniture	30,000
Total	$67,000

Required:
Prepare a summary journal entry to record the $67,000 in cash expenditures.

Exercise 10–4
Goodwill

On March 31, 1997, the Wolfson Corporation acquired all of the outstanding common stock of Barney Corporation for $16,000,000 in cash. The book values and fair values of Barney's assets and liabilities were as follows:

	Book Value	Fair Value
Current assets	$ 6,000,000	7,500,000
Property, plant, and equipment	11,000,000	14,000,000
Other assets	1,000,000	1,500,000
Current liabilities	4,000,000	4,000,000
Long-term liabilities	6,000,000	5,500,000

Required:

Calculate the amount paid for goodwill.

Exercise 10–5
Goodwill

The Johnson Corporation purchased all of the outstanding common stock of Smith Corporation for $11,000,000 in cash. The book value of Smith's net assets (assets minus liabilities) was $7,800,000. The fair values of all of Smith's assets and liabilities were equal to their book values with the following exceptions:

	Book Value	Fair Value
Receivables	$1,300,000	$1,100,000
Property, plant, and equipment	8,000,000	9,200,000
Intangible assets	200,000	1,200,000

Required:

Calculate the amount paid for goodwill.

Exercise 10–6
Multiple choice; operational assets

The following questions dealing with operational assets are adapted from questions that appeared on recent CPA examinations. Determine the response that best completes the statements or questions.

1. On December 1, 1997, Boyd Co. purchased a $400,000 tract of land for a factory site. Boyd razed an old building on the property and sold the materials it salvaged from the demolition. Boyd incurred additional costs and realized salvage proceeds during December 1997 as follows:

Demolition of old building	$50,000
Legal fees for purchase contract and recording of ownership	10,000
Title guarantee insurance	12,000
Proceeds from sale of salvaged materials	8,000

   In its December 31, 1997, balance sheet, Boyd should report a balance in the land account of
   a. $464,000
   b. $460,000
   c. $442,000
   d. $422,000

2. On October 1, 1997, Shaw Corp. purchased a machine for $126,000 that was placed in service on November 30, 1997. Shaw incurred additional costs for this machine, as follows:

Shipping	$3,000
Installation	4,000
Testing	5,000

   In Shaw's December 31, 1997, balance sheet, the machine's cost should be reported as
   a. $126,000
   b. $129,000
   c. $133,000
   d. $138,000

3. Hy Corp. bought Patent A for $40,000 and Patent B for $60,000. Hy also paid acquisition costs of $5,000 for Patent A and $7,000 for Patent B. Both patents were challenged in legal actions. Hy paid $20,000 in legal fees for a successful defense of Patent A and $30,000 in legal fees for an unsuccessful defense of Patent B. What amount should Hy capitalize for patents?
   a. $162,000
   b. $112,000
   c. $ 65,000
   d. $ 45,000

Exercise 10–7
Lump-sum acquisition

The Pinewood Company purchased two buildings on four acres of land. The lump-sum purchase price was $900,000. According to independent appraisals, the fair market values were $450,000 (building A) and $250,000 (building B) for the buildings and $300,000 for the land.

Required:

Determine the initial valuation of the buildings and the land.

Exercise 10–8
Acquisition cost; noninterest-bearing note

On January 1, 1997, the Byner Company purchased a used tractor. Byner paid $5,000 down and signed a noninterest-bearing note requiring five annual installments of $5,000 to be paid on each December 31 beginning December 31, 1997. The fair value of the tractor is not determinable. An interest rate of 10% properly reflects the time value of money in this situation.

Required:

1. Prepare the journal entry to record the acquisition of the tractor. Round computations to the nearest dollar.

2. Prepare the journal entry to record the first payment on December 31, 1997. Round computations to the nearest dollar.

3. Prepare the journal entry to record the second payment on December 31, 1998. Round computations to the nearest dollar.

Exercise 10–9
Acquisition cost; issuance of equity securities and donation

On February 1, 1997, the Xilon Corporation issued 5,000 shares of its nopar common stock in exchange for five acres of land located in the city of Monrovia. On the date of the acquisition, Xilon's common stock had a market value of $18 per share. An office building was constructed on the site by an independent contractor. The building was completed on November 2, 1997, at a cost of $600,000. Xilon paid $400,000 in cash and the remainder was paid by the city of Monrovia.

Required:
Prepare the journal entries to record the acquisition of the land and the building.

Exercise 10–10
Nonmonetary exchange; similar assets

The Cedric Company recently traded in an older model computer for a new model. The old model's book value was $180,000 (original cost of $400,000 less $220,000 in accumulated depreciation) and its fair value was $200,000. Cedric paid $50,000 to complete the exchange.

Required:
Prepare the journal entry to record the exchange.

Exercise 10–11
Nonmonetary exchange; similar assets

[This is a variation of the previous exercise.]

Required:
Assume the same facts as in Exercise 10–10, except that the fair value of the old equipment is $170,000. Prepare the journal entry to record the exchange.

Exercise 10–12
Nonmonetary exchange; dissimilar assets

The Bronco Corporation exchanged land for a patent. The land had a carrying value of $120,000 and a fair value of $150,000. Bronco paid the owner of the patent $10,000 to complete the exchange.

Required:
1. What is the fair value of the patent?
2. Prepare the journal entry to record the exchange.

Exercise 10–13
Nonmonetary exchange; dissimilar assets

[This is a variation of the previous exercise.]

Required:
Assume the same facts as in Exercise 10–12 except that Bronco *received* $10,000 from the owner of the patent to complete the exchange.

1. What is the fair value of the patent?
2. Prepare the journal entry to record the exchange.

Exercise 10–14
Nonmonetary exchange; similar assets

The Tinsley Company exchanged land that it had been holding for future plant expansion for a more suitable parcel located farther from residential areas. Tinsley carried the land at its original cost of $30,000. According to an independent appraisal, the land currently is worth $60,000. Tinsley received $10,000 in cash to complete the transaction.

Required:
1. What is the fair value of the new parcel of land received by Tinsley?
2. Prepare the journal entry to record the exchange.

Exercise 10–15
Acquisition cost; multiple methods

The Connors Corporation acquired manufacturing equipment for use in its assembly line. Below are four *independent* situations relating to the acquisition of the equipment.

1. The equipment was purchased on account for $25,000. Credit terms were 2/10, n/30. Payment was made within the discount period and the company records the purchases of equipment net of discounts.

2. Connors gave the seller a noninterest-bearing note. The note required payment of $27,000 one year from date of purchase. The fair value of the equipment is not determinable. An interest rate of 10% properly reflects the time value of money in this situation.

3. Connors traded in old, similar equipment that had a book value of $6,000 (original cost of $14,000 and accumulated depreciation of $8,000) and paid cash of $22,000. The old equipment had a fair value of $2,500 on the date of the exchange.

4. Connors issued 1,000 shares of its nopar common stock in exchange for the equipment. The market value of the common stock was not determinable. The equipment could have been purchased for $24,000 in cash.

Required:

For each of the above situations, prepare the journal entries required to record the acquisition of the equipment. Round computations to the nearest dollar.

Exercise 10–16
Interest capitalization

On January 1, 1997, the Marjlee Company began construction of an office building to be used as its corporate headquarters. The building was completed early in 1998. Construction expenditures for 1997, which were incurred evenly throughout the year, totaled $5,000,000. Marjlee had the following debt obligations which were outstanding during all of 1997:

Construction loan, 10%	$1,000,000
Long-term note, 9%	2,000,000
Long-term note, 6%	4,000,000

Required:

Calculate the amount of interest capitalized for the building using the specific interest method.

Exercise 10–17
Interest capitalization

On January 2, 1997, the Shagri Company began construction on a new manufacturing facility for its own use. The building was completed in 1998. The only interest-bearing debt the company had outstanding during 1997 was long-term bonds with a carrying value of $10,000,000 and an effective interest rate of 8%. Construction expenditures incurred during 1997 were as follows:

January 2	$500,000
March 1	600,000
July 31	480,000
September 30	600,000
December 31	300,000

Required:

Calculate the amount of interest capitalized for 1997.

Exercise 10–18
Interest capitalization

On January 2, 1997, the Highlands Company began construction on a new manufacturing facility for its own use. The building was completed in 1998. The company borrowed $1,500,000 at 10% on January 2 to help finance the construction. In addition to the construction loan, Highlands had the following debt outstanding throughout 1997:

$5,000,000, 12% bonds
$3,000,000, 8% long-term note

Construction expenditures incurred during 1997 were as follows:

January 2	$ 400,000
March 31	1,200,000
June 30	800,000
September 30	600,000
December 31	400,000

Required:

Calculate the amount of interest capitalized for 1997 using the specific interest method.

Exercise 10–19
Research and development

In 1997, Space Technology Company modified its model Z2 satellite to incorporate a new communication device. The company made the following expenditures:

Basic research to develop the technology	$2,000,000
Engineering design work	600,000
Development of a prototype device	300,000
Acquisition of equipment	60,000
Testing and modification of the prototype	200,000
Legal and other fees for patent application on the new communication system	40,000
Legal fees for successful defense of the new patent	30,000
Total	$3,230,000

The equipment will be used on this and other research projects. Depreciation on the equipment for 1997 is $10,000.

During your year-end review of the accounts related to intangibles, you discover that the company has capitalized all of the above as costs of the patent. Management contends that the device simply represents an improvement of the existing communication system of the satellite and, therefore, should be capitalized.

Required:

Prepare correcting entries that reflect the appropriate treatment of the expenditures.

Exercise 10–20
Research and development

The Delaware Company incurred the following research and development costs during 1997:

Salaries and wages for lab research	$ 400,000
Materials used in R&D projects	200,000
Purchase of equipment	900,000
Fees paid to outsiders for R&D projects	320,000
Patent filing and legal costs for a developed product	65,000
Salaries, wages, and supplies for R&D work performed	
for another company under a contract	350,000
Total	$2,235,000

The equipment has a seven-year life and will be used for a number of research projects. Depreciation for 1997 is $120,000.

Required:
Calculate the amount of research and development expense that Delaware should report in its 1997 income statement.

Exercise 10–21
Multiple choice; operational assets

The following questions dealing with operational assets are adapted from questions that appeared on recent CPA examinations. Determine the response that best completes the statements or questions.

1. Dahl Co. traded a delivery van and $5,000 cash for a newer van owned by West Corp. The following information relates to the values of the vans on the exchange date:

	Carrying Value	Fair Value
Old van	$30,000	$45,000
New van	40,000	50,000

Dahl's income tax rate is 30%. What amount should Dahl report as gain on exchange of the vans?
   a. $15,000
   b. $ 1,000
   c. $ 700
   d. $ 0

2. Heller Co. incurred the following costs in 1997:

Research and development services performed by Kay Corp. for Heller	$150,000
Testing for evaluation of new products	125,000
Laboratory research aimed at discovery of new knowledge	185,000

What amount should Heller report as research and development costs in its income statement for the year ended December 31, 1997?
   a. $125,000
   b. $150,000
   c. $335,000
   d. $460,000

3. During 1997, Bay Co. constructed machinery for its own use and for sale to customers. Bay Co. routinely manufactures machinery for sale. Bank loans financed these assets both during construction and after construction was complete. How much of the interest incurred should be reported as interest expense in the 1997 income statement?

	Interest Incurred for Machinery for Own Use	Interest Incurred for Machinery Held for Sale
a.	All interest incurred	All interest incurred
b.	All interest incurred	Interest incurred after completion
c.	Interest incurred after completion	Interest incurred after completion
d.	Interest incurred after completion	All interest incurred

4. Cole Co. began constructing a new building for its own use in January 1997. During 1997, Cole incurred interest of $50,000 on specific construction debt and $20,000 on other borrowings. Interest computed on the weighted-average amount of accumulated expenditures for the building during 1997 was $40,000. What amount of interest cost should Cole capitalize?
   a. $20,000
   b. $40,000
   c. $50,000
   d. $70,000

Exercise 10–22
Concepts; terminology

Listed below are several terms and phrases associated with operational assets. Pair each item from List A (by letter) with the item from List B that is most appropriately associated with it.

List A	List B
_____ 1. Depreciation	a. Exclusive right to display a word, a symbol, or an emblem.
_____ 2. Depletion	
_____ 3. Amortization	b. Represents the right to operate as a corporation.
_____ 4. Average accumulated expenditures	c. Exclusive right to benefit from a creative work.
_____ 5. Revenue — donation of asset	d. Operational assets that represent rights.
_____ 6. Nonmonetary exchange	e. The allocation of cost for natural resources.
_____ 7. Natural resources	f. Purchase price less fair market value of net identifiable assets.
_____ 8. Intangible assets	
_____ 9. Copyright	g. The allocation of cost for plant and equipment.
_____ 10. Trademark	h. Approximation of average amount of debt if all construction funds were borrowed.
_____ 11. Organization costs	
_____ 12. Goodwill	i. Account credited when assets are donated to a corporation.
	j. The allocation of cost for intangible assets.
	k. Basic principle is to value assets acquired using fair value of assets given.
	l. Wasting assets.

Exercise 10–23
Software development costs

Early in 1997, the Excalibur Company began developing a new software package to be marketed. The project was completed in December 1997 at a cost of $4 million. Of this amount, $3 million was spent before technological feasibility was established. Excalibur expects a useful life of five years for the new product with total revenues of $10 million. During 1998, revenue of $4 million was recognized.

Required:
1. Prepare a journal entry to record the 1997 development costs.
2. Calculate the required amortization for 1998.
3. At what amount should the computer software costs be reported in the December 31, 1998, balance sheet?

Exercise 10–24
Full-cost and successful efforts methods compared [based on Appendix 10A]

The Manguino Oil Company incurred exploration costs in 1997 searching and drilling for oil as follows:

Well 101	$ 50,000
Well 102	60,000
Well 103	80,000
Wells 104–108	260,000
Total	$450,000

It was determined that Wells 104–108 were dry holes and were abandoned. Wells 101, 102, and 103 were determined to have sufficient oil reserves to be commercially successful.

Required:
1. Prepare a summary journal entry to record the indicated costs assuming that the company uses the full-cost method of accounting for exploration costs. All of the exploration costs were paid in cash.
2. Prepare a summary journal entry to record the indicated costs assuming that the company uses the successful efforts method of accounting for exploration costs. All of the exploration costs were paid in cash.

Problems

Problem 10–1
Acquisition costs

Tristar Production Company began operations on September 1, 1997. Listed below are a number of transactions that occurred during its first four months of operations.

1. On September 1, the company acquired five acres of land with a building that will be used as a warehouse. Tristar paid $100,000 in cash for the property. According to appraisals, the land had a fair market value of $75,000 and the building had a fair market value of $45,000.
2. On September 1, Tristar entered into a five-payment noninterest-bearing installment contract to purchase equipment. The first annual $9,000 payment was made on the date of purchase. Assume that 8% is a reasonable interest rate.
3. On September 15, the president of the company donated a truck to the corporation. Similar trucks were selling for $2,500.

4. On September 18, the company paid its lawyer $3,000 for organizing the corporation.
5. On October 10, Tristar purchased machinery for cash. The purchase price was $15,000 and $500 in freight charges also were paid.
6. On December 2, Tristar acquired various items of office equipment. The company was short of cash and could not pay the $5,500 normal cash price. The supplier agreed to accept 200 shares of the company's nopar common stock in exchange for the equipment. The market value of the stock is not readily determinable.
7. On December 10, the company acquired a tract of land at a cost of $20,000. It paid $2,000 down and signed a 10% note with both principal and interest due in one year. Ten percent is an appropriate rate of interest for this note.

Required:
Prepare journal entries to record each of the above transactions.

Problem 10–2
Acquisition costs; land and building

On January 1, 1997, the Blackstone Corporation purchased a tract of land (site number 11) with a building for $600,000. Additionally, Blackstone paid a real estate broker's commission of $36,000, legal fees of $6,000, and title insurance of $18,000. The closing statement indicated that the land value was $500,000 and the building value was $100,000. Shortly after acquisition, the building was razed at a cost of $75,000.

Blackstone entered into a $3,000,000 fixed-price contract with Barnett Builders, Inc., on March 1, 1997, for the construction of an office building on land site 11. The building was completed and occupied on September 30, 1998. Additional construction costs were incurred as follows:

Plans, specifications, and blueprints	$12,000
Architects' fees for design and supervision	95,000

To finance the construction cost, Blackstone borrowed $3,000,000 on March 1, 1997. The loan is payable in 10 annual installments of $300,000 plus interest at the rate of 14%. Blackstone's average amounts of accumulated building construction expenditures were as follows:

For the period March 1 to December 31, 1997	$ 900,000
For the period January 1 to September 30, 1998	2,300,000

Required:
1. Prepare a schedule that discloses the individual costs making up the balance in the land account in respect of land site 11 as of September 30, 1998.
2. Prepare a schedule that discloses the individual costs that should be capitalized in the office building account as of September 30, 1998.

(AICPA adapted)

Problem 10–3
Acquisition costs

The plant asset and accumulated depreciation accounts of Pell Corporation had the following balances at December 31, 1996:

	Plant Asset	Accumulated Depreciation
Land	$ 350,000	$ —
Land improvements	180,000	45,000
Building	1,500,000	350,000
Machinery and equipment	1,158,000	405,000
Automobiles	150,000	112,000

Transactions during 1997 were as follows:

a. On January 2, 1997, machinery and equipment were purchased at a total invoice cost of $260,000, which included a $5,500 charge for freight. Installation costs of $27,000 were incurred.
b. On March 31, 1997, a machine purchased for $58,000 in 1993 was sold for $36,500. Depreciation recorded through the date of sale totaled $24,650.
c. On May 1, 1997, expenditures of $50,000 were made to repave parking lots at Pell's plant location. The work was necessitated by damage caused by severe winter weather.
d. On November 1, 1997, Pell acquired a tract of land with an existing building in exchange for 10,000 shares of Pell's common stock that had a market price of $38 per share. Pell paid legal fees and title insurance totaling $23,000. Shortly after acquisition, the building was razed at a cost of $35,000 in anticipation of new building construction in 1998.
e. On December 31, 1997, Pell purchased a new automobile for $15,250 cash and trade-in of an old automobile purchased for $18,000 in 1996. Depreciation on the old automobile recorded through December 31, 1997, totaled $13,500. The market value of the old automobile was $3,750.

Required:

1. Prepare a schedule analyzing the changes in each of the plant assets during 1997, with detailed supporting computations.
2. Prepare a schedule showing the gain or loss from each asset disposal that would be recognized in Pell's income statement for the year ended December 31, 1997.

(AICPA adapted)

Problem 10–4
Intangibles

The Horstmeyer Corporation commenced operations early in 1997. A number of expenditures were made during 1997 that were debited to one account called *intangible asset.* A recap of the $644,000 balance in this account at the end of 1997 is as follows:

Date	Transaction	Amount
2/3/97	State incorporation fees and legal costs related to organizing the corporation	$ 7,000
3/1/97	Fire insurance premium for three-year period	6,000
3/15/97	Purchased a copyright	20,000
4/3/97	Improvements made to leased office building	8,000
4/30/97	Research and development costs	32,000
6/15/97	Legal fees for filing a patent on a new product resulting from an R&D project	3,000
9/30/97	Legal fee for successful defense of patent developed above	12,000
10/13/97	Entered into a 10-year franchise agreement with franchisor	40,000
Various	Advertising costs	16,000
11/30/97	Purchase of all of the outstanding common stock of Stiltz Corp.	500,000
	Total	$644,000

The total purchase price of the Stiltz Corp. stock was debited to this account. The market value of Stiltz Corp.'s assets and liabilities on the date of the purchase were as follows:

Receivables	$100,000
Equipment	350,000
Patent	150,000
Total assets	600,000
Note payable assumed	(220,000)
Market value of net assets	$380,000

Required:
Prepare the necessary journal entries to clear the intangible asset account and to set up accounts for separate intangibles, other types of assets, and expenses indicated by the transactions.

Problem 10–5
Acquisition costs; journal entries

Consider each of the transactions below. All of the expenditures were made in cash.

1. The Edison Company spent $12,000 during the year for experimental purposes in connection with the development of a new product.
2. In April, the Marshall Company lost a patent infringement suit and paid the plaintiff $7,500.
3. In March, the Cleanway Laundromat bought equipment on an installment note. The contract price was $24,000, payable $6,000 down, and $2,000 a month for the next nine months. The cash price for this equipment was $23,000.
4. On June 1, the Jamsen Corporation installed a sprinkler system throughout the building at a cost of $28,000.
5. The Mayer Company, plaintiff, paid $12,000 in legal fees in November, in connection with a successful infringement suit on its patent.
6. The Johnson Company traded its old machine with an original cost of $7,400 and a net book value of $3,000 plus cash of $8,000 for a new one that had a fair value of $10,000.

Required:
Prepare journal entries to record each of the above transactions.

Problem 10–6
Nonmonetary exchange; similar assets

Southern Company owns a building that it leases. The building's fair value is $1,400,000 and its book value is $800,000 (original cost of $2,000,000 less accumulated depreciation of $1,200,000). Southern exchanges this for another building owned by the Eastern Company. The building's book value on Eastern's books is $950,000 (original cost of $1,600,000 less accumulated depreciation of $650,000). Eastern also gives Southern $140,000 to complete the exchange.

Required:

Prepare the journal entries to record the exchange on the books of both Southern and Eastern assuming that the buildings are considered to be similar assets by both companies.

Problem 10–7
Nonmonetary exchange;
dissimilar assets

[This is a variation of the previous problem modified to focus on the exchange of dissimilar assets.]
  Southern Company owns a building that it leases. The building's fair value is $1,400,000 and its book value is $800,000 (original cost of $2,000,000 less accumulated depreciation of $1,200,000). Southern exchanges this for another building owned by the Eastern Company. The building's book value on Eastern's books is $950,000 (original cost of $1,600,000 less accumulated depreciation of $650,000). Eastern also gives Southern $140,000 to complete the exchange.

Required:

Prepare the journal entries to record the exchange on the books of both Southern and Eastern assuming that the buildings are considered to be dissimilar assets by both companies.

Problem 10–8
Nonmonetary exchange

On September 3, 1997, the Robers Company exchanged operational assets with Phifer Corporation. The facts of the exchange are as follows:

	Rober's Asset	Phifer's Asset
Original cost	$120,000	$140,000
Accumulated depreciation	55,000	63,000
Fair value	75,000	70,000

To equalize the exchange, Phifer paid Robers $5,000 in cash.

Required:

1. Assuming that the assets exchanged are considered dissimilar for both companies, record the exchange for both Robers and Phifer.
2. Assuming that the assets exchanged are considered similar for both companies, record the exchange for both Robers and Phifer.

Problem 10–9
Interest capitalization; specific
interest method

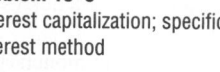

On January 1, 1997, the Mason Manufacturing Company began construction of a building to be used as its office headquarters. The building was completed on September 30, 1998.
  Expenditures on the project were as follows:

January 3, 1997	$1,000,000
March 1, 1997	600,000
June 30, 1997	800,000
October 1, 1997	600,000
January 31, 1998	270,000
April 30, 1998	585,000
August 31, 1998	900,000

On January 2, 1997, the company obtained a $3 million construction loan with a 10% interest rate. The loan was outstanding all of 1997 and 1998. The company's other interest-bearing debt included two long-term notes of $4,000,000 and $6,000,000 with interest rates of 6% and 8%, respectively. Both notes were outstanding during all of 1997 and 1998. The company's fiscal year-end is December 31.

Required:

1. Calculate the amount of interest that Mason should capitalize in 1997 and 1998 using the specific interest method.
2. What is the total cost of the building?
3. Calculate the amount of interest expense that will appear on the 1997 and 1998 income statements.

Problem 10–10
Interest capitalization;
weighted-average method

[This is a variation of the previous problem, modified to focus on the weighted-average interest method.]

Required:

Refer to the facts in Problem 10–9 and answer the following questions:
1. Calculate the amount of interest that Mason should capitalize in 1997 and 1998 using the weighted-average interest method.
2. What is the total cost of the building?
3. Calculate the amount of interest expense that will appear on the 1997 and 1998 income statements.

Problem 10–11
Research and development

In 1997, Starsearch Corporation began work on three research and development projects. One of the projects was completed and commercial production of the developed product began in December. The company's fiscal year-end is December 31. All of the following 1997 expenditures were included in the R&D expense account:

Salaries and wages for:	
Lab research	$ 300,000
Design and construction of preproduction prototype	160,000
Quality control during commercial production	20,000
Materials and supplies consumed for:	
Lab research	60,000
Construction of preproduction prototype	30,000
Purchase of equipment	600,000
Patent filing and legal fees for completed project	40,000
Payments to others for research	120,000
Total	$1,330,000

$200,000 of equipment was purchased solely for use in one of the projects. After the project is completed, the equipment will be abandoned. The remaining $400,000 in equipment will be used on future R&D projects. The useful life of equipment is five years. Assume that all of the equipment was acquired at the beginning of the year.

Required:
Prepare journal entries to reflect the appropriate treatment of the expenditures.

Cases

Discussion Case 10–1
Acquisition costs

A company may acquire operational assets for cash, in exchange for a deferred payment contract, by exchanging other operational assets, or by a combination of these methods.

Required:
1. Identify six types of costs that should be capitalized as the cost of a parcel of land. For your answer, assume that the land has an existing building that is to be removed in the immediate future in order that a new building can be constructed on the site.
2. At what amount should a company record an operational asset acquired in exchange for a deferred payment contract?
3. In general, at what amount should operational assets received in exchange for other nonmonetary assets be valued? Specifically, at what amount should a company value a new machine acquired by exchanging an older, similar machine and paying cash?

(AICPA adapted)

Trueblood Accounting Case 10–2
Cost capitalization

The following Robert M. Trueblood case is recommended for use with this chapter. The case provides an excellent opportunity for class discussion, group projects, and writing assignments. The case, along with Professor's Discussion Material, can be obtained from the Deloitte & Touche Foundation.

Case 90-1: *To Capitalize or Not to Capitalize*
The objective of this case is to consider whether costs incurred to convert previously developed commercial cookware for use in outerspace are eligible for capitalization under the provisions of *SFAS 2*.

Discussion Case 10–3
Self-constructed assets

Chilton Peripherals manufactures printers, scanners, and other computer peripheral equipment. In the past, the company purchased equipment used in manufacturing from an outside vendor. In March 1997, Chilton decided to design and build equipment to replace some obsolete equipment. A section of the manufacturing plant was set aside to develop and produce the equipment. Additional personnel were hired for the project. The equipment was completed and ready for use in September.

Required:
1. In general, what costs should be capitalized for a self-constructed asset?
2. Discuss two alternatives for the inclusion of overhead costs in the cost of the equipment constructed by Chilton. Which alternative is generally accepted for financial reporting purposes?
3. Under what circumstance(s) would interest be included in the cost of the equipment?

Discussion Case 10–4
Interest capitalization

SFAS 34 provides guidelines for the inclusion of interest in the initial cost of an operational asset.

Required:
1. What assets qualify for interest capitalization? What assets do not qualify for interest capitalization?
2. Over what period should interest be capitalized?
3. Explain average accumulated expenditures.
4. Explain the two methods that could be used to determine the appropriate interest rate(s) to be used in capitalizing interest.
5. Describe the three steps used to determine the amount of interest capitalized during a reporting period.

Research Case 10–5
Interest capitalization

The cost of an asset includes all expenditures necessary to bring the asset to the condition and location of its intended use. The FASB, in *SFAS 34*, took the position that interest is an acquisition cost and should be included as part of the cost of assets constructed for an enterprise's own use or produced as discrete projects that are intended for sale or lease to others. Professors Means and Kazenski in "*SFAS 34*: A Recipe for Diversity," point out some internal inconsistencies in *SFAS 34*.

Required:
1. In your library or from some other source, locate the indicated article in *Accounting Horizons*, September 1988.
2. Briefly explain the problem the two authors describe in the article. What are the conditions that could lead to more than one correct answer to an interest capitalization situation?
3. Briefly explain the authors' solution to the problem.

Real World Case 10–6
Property, plant, and equipment; intangibles

Hershey Foods Corporation produces and distributes a broad line of chocolate, confectionery, grocery, and pasta products. The company reported the following amounts in the asset section of its balance sheets for the years ended December 31, 1993 and 1992:

(in thousands of dollars)	1993	1992
Property, Plant and Equipment, Net	$1,460,904	$1,295,989
Intangibles Resulting from Business Acquisitions	473,408	399,768

In addition, the 1993 statement of cash flows reported the following items (in thousands of dollars):

Depreciation and amortization	$113,064
Additions to property, plant, and equipment	211,621

Required:
1. What is another name for the asset described as "Intangibles Resulting from Business Acquisitions"?
2. Assuming that no items of property, plant, and equipment nor any previously acquired businesses were sold during the year, what amount of intangibles resulting from business acquisitions was capitalized during the year?

Discussion Case 10–7
Goodwill

The Athena Paper Corporation acquired for cash 100% of the outstanding common stock of Georgia, Inc., a supplier of wood pulp. The purchase price of $4,500,000 was significantly higher than the book value of Georgia's net assets (assets less liabilities) of $2,800,000. The Athena controller recorded the difference of $1,700,000 as an asset, goodwill.

Required:
1. Discuss the meaning of the term *goodwill*.
2. In what situation would the Athena controller be correct in her valuation of goodwill?

Critical Thought Case 10–8
Research and development

Prior to 1974, accepted practice was for companies to either expense or capitalize R&D costs. In 1974, the FASB issued *SFAS 2* which now requires all research and development costs to be charged to expense when incurred. This was a controversial standard, opposed by many companies who preferred delaying the recognition of these expenses until later years when presumably the expenditures bear fruit.

Several research studies have been conducted to determine if the standard had any impact on the behavior of companies. One interesting finding was that, prior to *SFAS 2*, companies that expensed R&D costs were significantly larger than those companies that capitalized R&D costs.

Required:
1. Explain the FASB's logic in deciding to require all companies to expense R&D costs in the period incurred.
2. Identify possible reasons to explain why, prior to *SFAS 2*, companies that expensed R&D costs were significantly larger than those companies that capitalized R&D costs.

Discussion Case 10–9
Research and development

Clonal, Inc., a biotechnology company, developed and patented a diagnostic product called Trouver. Clonal purchased some research equipment to be used exclusively for Trouver and subsequent research projects. Clonal defeated a legal challenge to its Trouver patent, and began production and marketing operations for the product.

Corporate headquarters' costs were allocated to Clonal's research division as a percentage of the division's salaries.

Required:

1. How should the equipment purchased for Trouver be reported on Clonal's income statements and statements of financial position.
2. a. Describe the matching principle.
   b. Describe the accounting treatment of research and development costs and consider whether this is consistent with the matching principle. What is the justification for the accounting treatment of research and development costs?
3. How should corporate headquarters' costs allocated to the research division be classified on Clonal's income statements? Why?
4. How should the legal expenses incurred in defending Trouver's patent be reported in Clonal's financial statements?

(AICPA adapted)

**Group Interaction
Case 10–10**
Research and development

The focus of this case is the situation described in Case 10–9. What is the appropriate accounting for R&D costs? Do you believe that (1) capitalization is the correct treatment of R&D costs, (2) expensing is the correct treatment of R&D costs, or (3) that companies should be allowed to choose between expensing and capitalizing R&D costs?

Required:

1. Develop a list of arguments in support of your view prior to the class session for which the case is assigned. Do not be influenced by the method required by the FASB. Base your opinion on the conceptual merit of the options.
2. In class, your instructor will pair you (and everyone else) with a classmate who also has independently developed a position.
   a. You will be given three minutes to argue your view to your partner. Your partner likewise will be given three minutes to argue his or her view to you. During these three-minute presentations, the listening partner is not permitted to speak.
   b. Then after each person has had a turn attempting to convince his or her partner, the two partners will have a three-minute discussion in which they will decide which alternative is more convincing and arguments will be merged into a single view for each pair.
3. After the allotted time, a spokesperson for each of the three alternatives will be selected by the instructor. Each spokesperson will field arguments from the class as to the appropriate alternative. The class will then discuss the merits of the alternatives and attempt to reach a consensus view, though a consensus is not necessary.

**Trueblood Accounting
Case 10–11**
Accounting for purchased
R&D

The following Robert M. Trueblood case is recommended for use with this chapter. The case provides an excellent opportunity for class discussion, group projects, and writing assignments. The case, along with Professor's Discussion Material, can be obtained from the Deloitte & Touche Foundation.

Case 90-2: *Accounting for Purchased R&D*
This case is intended to expose students to the issue of accounting for purchased R&D and to the use of NAARS data as a decision aid.

Writing Case 10–12
Research and development

The Thomas Plastics Company is in the process of developing a revolutionary new plastic valve. A new division of the company was formed to develop, manufacture, and market this new product. As of year-end (December 31, 1997), the new product has not been manufactured for sale; however, prototype units were built and are in operation.

Throughout 1997, the new division incurred a variety of costs. These costs included expenses (including salaries of administrative personnel) and market research costs. In addition, approximately $500,000 in equipment (estimated useful life of 10 years) was purchased for use in developing and manufacturing the new valve. Approximately $200,000 of this equipment was built specifically for developing the design of the new product; the remaining $300,000 of the equipment was used to manufacture the preproduction prototypes and will be used to manufacture the new product once it is in commercial production.

The president of the company, Sally Rogers, has been told that research and development costs must be expensed as incurred, but she does not understand this treatment. She believes the research will lead to a profitable product and to increased future revenues. Also, she wonders how to account for the $500,000 of equipment purchased by the new division. "I thought I understood accounting," she growled. "Explain to me why expenditures that benefit our future revenues are expensed rather than capitalized!"

Required:
Write a one- to two-page report to Sally Rogers explaining the generally accepted accounting principles relevant to this issue. The report should also address the treatment of the equipment purchases.

(AICPA adapted)

Ethics Case 10–13
Research and development

Mayer Biotechnical, Inc., develops, manufacturers, and sells pharmaceuticals. Significant research and development (R&D) expenditures are made for the development of new drugs and the improvement of existing drugs. During 1997, $220 million was spent on R&D. Of this amount, $30 million was spent on the purchase of equipment to be used in a research project involving the development of a new antibiotic.

The controller, Alice Cooper, is considering capitalizing the equipment and depreciating it over the five-year useful life of the equipment at $6 million per year, even though the equipment likely will be used on only one project. The company president has asked Alice to make every effort to increase 1997 earnings because in 1998 the company will be seeking significant new financing from both debt and equity sources. "I guess we might use the equipment in other projects later," Alice wondered to herself.

Required:
1. Assuming that the equipment was purchased at the beginning of 1997, by how much would Alice's treatment of the equipment increase before tax earnings as opposed to expensing the equipment cost?
2. Discuss the ethical dilemma Alice faces in determining the treatment of the $30 million equipment purchase.

International Case 10–14
Comparison of operational asset valuation in the Netherlands and the U.S.A.

Heineken, based in Amsterdam, is one of the world's largest international beverage companies, selling its products in some 150 countries. Operational asset disclosures accompanying a recent annual report are reproduced below. The term *Group funds* used in the note is equivalent to retained earnings in the U.S.A.

Intangible Assets
The differences between the price paid and the valuation calculated according to these policies upon acquisition of participants are offset against Group funds. Costs of other intangible assets, including brands, patents, licenses, software, research and development, are charged directly to the statement of income.

Fixed Assets (in part)
Tangible fixed assets have been valued on the basis of replacement cost and, with the exception of sites, after deduction of cumulative depreciation. The replacement cost is based on valuations by internal and external experts, taking technical and economic developments into account. They are supported by the experience gained in the construction of establishments all over the world.

Required:
On the basis of the information the disclosures provide, compare operational asset valuation in the Netherlands with that in the United States.

Financial Analysis Case 10–15
Fixed-asset turnover ratio

National Semiconductor Corporation, headquartered in Santa Clara, California, is a global semiconductor manufacturer. The company's 1995 fixed-asset turnover ratio, using the average book value of property, plant, and equipment (PP&E) as the denominator, was approximately 2.92. Additional information taken from the company's 1995 annual report is as follows:

	($ in millions)
Book value of PP&E—beginning of 1995	$668
Purchases of PP&E during 1995	479
Depreciation of PP&E for 1995	185

There were no dispositions of PP&E during 1995.

Required:
1. How is the fixed-asset turnover ratio computed? How would you interpret National's ratio of 2.92?
2. Use the data to determine National's net sales for 1995.
3. Obtain annual reports from three corporations in the same primary industry as National (Intel Corporation and Advanced Micro Devices are two well-known competitors) and compare the management of each company's investment in property, plant, and equipment.

   Note: You can obtain copies of annual reports from your library, from friends who are shareholders, from the investor relations department of the corporations, from a friendly stockbroker, or from EDGAR (Electronic Data Gathering and Retrieval) on the Internet (http://www.sec.gov).

Discussion Case 10–16
Computer software costs

The Elegant Software Company recently completed the development and testing of a new software program that provides the ability to transfer data from among a variety of operating systems. The company believes this product will be quite successful and capitalized all of the costs of designing, developing, coding, and testing the software. These costs will be amortized over the expected useful life of the software on a straight-line basis.

Required:

1. Was Elegant correct in its treatment of the software development costs? Why?
2. Explain the appropriate method for determining the amount of periodic amortization for any capitalized software development costs.

Internet Case 10–17
Operational assets

EDGAR, the Electronic Data Gathering, Analysis, and Retrieval system, performs automated collection, validation, indexing, and forwarding of submissions by companies and others who are required by law to file forms with the U.S. Securities and Exchange Commission (SEC). All publicly traded domestic companies use EDGAR to make the majority of their filings. (Some foreign companies file voluntarily.) Form 10-K or 10-KSB, which include the annual report, is required to be filed on EDGAR. The SEC makes this information available on the Internet.

Required:

1. Access EDGAR on the Internet. You can use a web browser or anonymous FTP. The web address is http://www.sec.gov/. To use anonymous FTP, use your File Transfer Protocol software to connect to sec.gov and log in as user "anonymous" with a password of your electronic mail address.
2. Search for Raychem Corporation. Access the 10–K filing for the most recent fiscal year. Search or scroll to find the financial statements and related notes.
3. Answer the following questions related to the company's operational assets:
   a. Name the four types of operational assets the company lists on its balance sheet under property, plant, and equipment.
   b. How much cash was used for the acquisition of property, plant, and equipment during the year?
   c. What is the amount of capitalized software development costs at the end of the year?
   d. What is the company's policy for amortizing software development costs?
   e. Compute the fixed-asset turnover ratio for the fiscal year.

Financial Analysis Case 10–18
Reporting operational assets

Refer to the financial statements and related disclosure notes of Federal Express Corporation in the Appendix to Chapter 1.

Required:

1. What categories of operational assets does Federal Express report on its 1996 balance sheet?
2. How much interest did Federal Express capitalize in 1996?
3. How much cash was used in 1996 to purchase property and equipment? How does this compare with purchases in previous years?
4. The fixed-asset turnover ratio for United Parcel Service, Federal Express's chief competitor, for the year ended December 31, 1995, is 2.51. How does this compare with Federal Express's ratio? What is the ratio intended to measure?

11

OPERATIONAL ASSETS: UTILIZATION AND DISPOSITION

OVERVIEW

This chapter completes our discussion of accounting for operational assets. We address the allocation of the cost of these assets to the periods benefited by their use.

The usefulness of operational assets (other than land) is consumed as the assets are applied to the production of goods or services. Cost allocation corresponding to this consumption of usefulness is known as *depreciation* for plant and equipment, *depletion* for natural resources, and *amortization* for intangibles.

We also consider the accounting treatment of expenditures incurred subsequent to acquisition as well as the disposition of operational assets.

LEARNING OBJECTIVES   After studying this chapter, you should be able to:

1. Explain the concept of cost allocation as it pertains to operational assets.
2. Determine periodic depreciation using both time-based and activity-based methods.
3. Calculate the periodic depletion of a natural resource.
4. Calculate the periodic amortization of an intangible asset.
5. Explain the appropriate accounting treatment required when a change is made in the service life or residual value of an operational asset.
6. Explain the appropriate accounting treatment required when a change in depreciation method is made.
7. Explain the appropriate treatment required when an error in accounting for an operational asset is discovered.
8. Identify situations that involve a significant impairment of the value of operational assets and describe the required accounting procedures.
9. Discuss the accounting treatment of repairs and maintenance, additions, improvements, and rearrangements to operational assets.
10. Explain how to account for the disposition of operational assets.

WHAT'S IN A NAME?

"I don't understand this at all," your friend Penny Lane moaned. "Depreciation, depletion, amortization; what's the difference? Aren't they all the same thing?" Penny and you are part of a class team working on a case involving Boise Cascade Corporation. "Look at these disclosure notes. The notes use all of those terms. And what's this business about asset impairment in the goodwill note?" Penny showed you a disclosure note from the annual report of Boise Cascade Corporation.

Property (in part)

Substantially all of the Company's paper and wood products manufacturing facilities determine depreciation by the units-of-production method, and other operations use the straight-line method.

Estimated service lives of principal items of property and equipment range from 3 to 40 years.

Depletion of the cost of company timber harvested and amortization of logging roads are determined on the basis of the annual amount of timber cut in relation to the total amount of recoverable timber.

Goodwill (in part)

Goodwill represents the excess of purchase price and related costs over the value assigned to the net tangible assets of businesses acquired. Goodwill is amortized on a straight-line basis generally over 40 years. Annually, the Company reviews the recoverability of goodwill. The measurement of possible impairment is based primarily on the ability to recover the balance of the goodwill from expected future operating cash flows on an undiscounted basis.

QUESTIONS

1. Is Penny correct? Do the terms depreciation, depletion, and amortization all mean the same thing?
2. What is the units-of-production method? How is it used by Boise Cascade?
3. Why do you suppose Boise Cascade chose a 40-year period to amortize goodwill?
4. What does Boise Cascade mean when it states that the measurement of possible goodwill impairment is based on undiscounted cash flows?

P A R T

A   DEPRECIATION, DEPLETION, AND AMORTIZATION

Cost Allocation— An Overview

| Learning objective 1
Explain the concept of cost allocation as it pertains to operational assets.

Operational assets are purchased with the expectation that they will provide future benefits, usually for several years. Specifically, they are acquired to be used as part of the revenue-generating operations. Logically, then, the costs of acquiring the assets should be allocated to expense during the reporting periods benefited by their use. That is, their costs are matched with the revenues they help generate.

Let's suppose that a company purchases a delivery truck for $8,200 to be used to deliver product to customers. The company estimates that five years from the acquisition date the truck will be sold for $2,200. The cost of using the truck during the five-year period is $6,000 ($8,200 – $2,200). The situation is portrayed in Graphic 11–1.

G R A P H I C   1 1 – 1

Cost Allocation for an Operational Asset

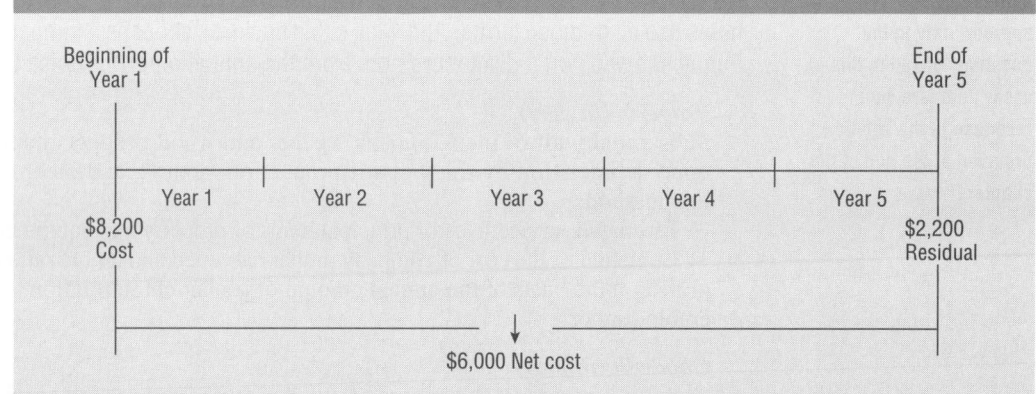

Theoretically, the matching principle requires that the $6,000 be allocated to the five individual years of asset use in direct proportion to the role the asset played in revenue production. However, very seldom is there a clear-cut relationship between the use of operational assets and revenue production. In other words, we can't tell precisely the portion of the total benefits of the asset that were consumed in any particular period. As a consequence, we must resort to arbitrary allocation methods to approximate a matching of expense with revenue. Contrast this situation with the $24,000 prepayment of two years' rent on an office building at $2,000 per month. In that case, we know precisely that the benefits of the asset, prepaid rent, are consumed at a rate of $2,000 per month.

Question 1

| Depreciation refers to a process of cost allocation, not valuation.

| Depreciation, depletion, and amortization for an asset used to manufacture a product is an overhead cost included in the cost of inventory.

Cost allocation for operational assets is known as **depreciation** for plant and equipment, **depletion** for natural resources, and **amortization** for intangibles. The process often is confused with measuring a decline in fair value of an asset. For example, let's say our delivery truck purchased for $8,200 can be sold for $5,000 at the end of one year but we intend to keep it for the full five-year estimated life. It has experienced a decline in value of $3,200 ($8,200 – $5,000). However, *depreciation is a process of cost allocation, not valuation.* We would not record depreciation expense of $3,200 for year one of the truck's life. Instead, we would distribute the cost of the asset, less any anticipated residual value, over the estimated useful life in a systematic and rational manner that attempts to match revenues with the *use* of the asset, not the decline in its value. After all, the truck is purchased to be used in operations, not to be sold.

The specific accounting treatment depends on the intended use of the asset. For assets used in the manufacture of a product, for example, depreciation, depletion, or amortization is considered a product cost to be included as part of the cost of inventory. Eventually, when the product is sold, it becomes part of the cost of goods sold. For assets *not* used in production, primarily plant and equipment and certain intangibles used in the selling and administrative functions of the company, periodic depreciation or amortization is reported as expense on the income statement. You might recognize this distinction as the difference between a product cost and a period cost. When a product cost is reported as an expense (cost of goods sold) depends on when the product is sold; when a period cost is reported as an expense depends on the reporting period in which it is incurred.

Measuring Cost Allocation

The process of cost allocation for operational assets requires that three factors be established at the time the asset is put into use. These factors are:

1. **Service life**—the estimated use that the company expects to receive from the asset.
2. **Allocation base**—the value of the usefulness that is expected to be consumed.
3. **Allocation method**—the pattern in which the usefulness is expected to be consumed.

Let's consider these one at a time.

Service Life

The service life, or useful life, of an operational asset can be expressed in units of time or in units of activity.

The **service life**, or **useful life**, of an operational asset is the amount of use that the company expects to obtain from the asset before disposing of it. This use can be expressed in units of time, or in units of activity. For example, the estimated service life of a delivery truck could be expressed in terms of years or in terms of the number of miles that the company expects the truck to be driven before disposition.

Physical life provides the upper bound for service life. Physical life will vary according to the purpose for which the asset is acquired and the environment in which it is operated. For example, a diesel powered electric generator may last for many years if it is used only as an emergency backup or for only a few years if it is used regularly.

Expected obsolescence can shorten service life below physical life.

The service life of a tangible operational asset may be less than physical life for a variety of reasons. For example, the expected rate of technological change may shorten service life. If suppliers are expected to develop new technologies that are more efficient, the company may keep an asset for a period of time much shorter than physical life. Likewise, if the company sells its product in a market that frequently demands new products, the machinery and equipment used to produce products may be useful only for as long as its output can be sold. Similarly, a mineral deposit might be projected to contain 4 million tons of a mineral, but it may be economically feasible with existing extraction methods to mine only 2 million tons. For intangible assets, legal life often is a limiting factor. For instance, a patent might be capable of providing enhanced profitability for 50 years, but the legal life of a patent is only 17 years.

Management intent also may shorten the period of an asset's usefulness below its physical or legal life. For example, a company may have a policy of using its delivery trucks for a three-year period and then trading the trucks for new models.

Companies quite often disclose the range of service lives for different categories of operational assets. For example, Graphic 11–2 shows how Ford Motor Company disclosed its service lives in a note accompanying recent financial statements.

GRAPHIC   11–2

Service Life Disclosure—Ford Motor Company

> *Depreciation and Amortization (in Part):*
>
> On average, buildings and land improvements are depreciated based on a 30-year life; automotive machinery, equipment, and office furniture are depreciated based on a 14-year life.

Allocation Base

Allocation base is the difference between the cost of the asset and its anticipated residual value.

The total amount of cost to be allocated over an asset's service life is called its **allocation base**. The amount is the difference between the initial value of the asset at its acquisition (its cost) and its **residual value**. Residual or salvage value is the amount the company expects to receive for the asset at the end of its service life less any anticipated disposal costs. In our delivery truck example above, the allocation base is $6,000 ($8,200 cost less $2,200 anticipated residual value).

In certain situations, residual value can be estimated by referring to a company's prior experience or to publicly available information concerning resale values of various types of assets. For example, if a company intends to trade its delivery trucks in three years for the new model, approximations of the three-year residual value for that type of truck can be obtained from used truck blue books.

However, estimating residual value for many operational assets can be very difficult due to the uncertainty about the future. For this reason, along with the fact that residual values often are immaterial, many companies simply assume a residual value of zero. Companies usually do not disclose residual values.

Allocation Method

The **allocation method** used should be systematic and rational and correspond to the pattern of asset use.

In determining how much cost to allocate to periods of an asset's use, a method should be selected that corresponds to the pattern of the loss of the asset's usefulness. *ARB 43* states that the chosen method should allocate the asset's cost "as equitably as possible to the periods during which services are obtained from [its] use." The bulletin further specifies that the method should produce a cost allocation in a "systematic and rational manner."[1] The objective is to try to allocate cost to the period in an amount that is proportional to the amount of benefits generated by the asset relative to the total benefits provided by the asset during its life.

In practice, there are two general approaches that attempt to obtain this systematic and rational allocation. The first approach allocates the cost base according to the *passage of time*. Methods following this approach are referred to as **time-based** methods. The second approach allocates an asset's cost base using a measure of the asset's *output*. This is an **activity-based** method. We compare these approaches first in the context of depreciation. Later we see that depletion of natural resources typically follows an activity-based approach and the amortization of intangibles typically follows a time-based approach.

Depreciation of Operational Assets

To demonstrate and compare the most common depreciation methods, we refer to the situation described in Illustration 11–1.

ILLUSTRATION   11–1

Depreciation Methods

Learning objective 2
Determine periodic depreciation using both **time-based** and **activity-based** methods.

The Hogan Manufacturing Company purchased a machine for $250,000. The company expects the service life of the machine to be five years. During that time, it is expected that the machine will produce 140,000 units. The anticipated residual value is $40,000. The machine was disposed of after five years of use. Actual production during the five years of the asset's life was:

Year	Units Produced
1	24,000
2	36,000
3	46,000
4	8,000
5	16,000
Total	130,000

Time-Based Depreciation Methods

The **straight-line depreciation method** allocates an equal amount of depreciable base to each year of the asset's service life.

Straight-line Method. By far the most easily understood and widely used depreciation method is **straight line**. By this approach, an equal amount of depreciable base is allocated to each year of the asset's service life. The depreciable base is simply divided by the number of years in the asset's life to determine annual depreciation. In our illustration, the straight-line annual depreciation is $42,000, calculated as follows:

$$\frac{\$250,000 - \$40,000}{5 \text{ years}} = \$42,000 \text{ per year}$$

---

[1]"Restatement and Revision of Accounting Research Bulletins," *Accounting Research Bulletin No. 43* (New York: AICPA, 1953), Ch. 9.

Accelerated Methods.   Using the straight-line method implicitly assumes that the benefits derived from the use of the asset are the same each year. In some situations it might be more appropriate to assume that the asset will provide greater benefits in the early years of its life than in the later years. In these cases, a more appropriate matching of depreciation with revenues is achieved with a declining pattern of depreciation, with higher depreciation in the early years of the asset's life and lower depreciation in later years. An accelerated depreciation method also would be appropriate when benefits derived from the asset are approximately equal over the asset's life, but repair and maintenance costs increase significantly in later years. The early years incur higher depreciation and lower repairs and maintenance expense, while the later years have lower depreciation and higher repairs and maintenance. Two commonly used ways to achieve such a declining pattern are the sum-of-the-years' digits method and declining balance methods.

> **Accelerated depreciation methods** are appropriate when the asset is more useful in its earlier years.

Sum-of-the-Years'-Digits Method.   The **sum-of-the-years'-digits (SYD) method** has no logical foundation other than the fact that it accomplishes the objective of accelerating depreciation in a systematic manner. This is achieved by multiplying the depreciable base by a fraction that declines each year and results in depreciation that decreases by the same amount each year. The denominator of the fraction remains constant and is the sum of the digits from one to n, where n is the number of years in the asset's service life. For example, if there are five years in the service life, the denominator is the sum of 1, 2, 3, 4, and 5, which equals 15.[2] The numerator decreases each year; it begins with the value of n in the first year and decreases by one each year until it equals one in the final year of the asset's estimated service life. The annual fractions for an asset with a five-year life are: $5/15$, $4/15$, $3/15$, $2/15$, and $1/15$. We calculate depreciation for the five years of the machine's life using the sum-of-the-years' digits method in Illustration 11–1a.

> The **SYD method** multiplies depreciable base by a declining fraction.

ILLUSTRATION 11–1a

Sum-of-the-Years'-Digits Depreciation

Year	Depreciable Base	×	Depreciation Rate per Year	=	Depreciation	Book Value End of Year
1	$210,000		$5/15$*		$ 70,000	$180,000
2	210,000		$4/15$		56,000	124,000
3	210,000		$3/15$		42,000	82,000
4	210,000		$2/15$		28,000	54,000
5	210,000		$1/15$		14,000	40,000
Totals			$15/15$		$210,000	

$$*\frac{n(n+1)}{2} = \frac{5(5+1)}{2} = 15$$

Declining Balance Methods.   As an alternative, an accelerated depreciation pattern can be achieved by various declining balance methods. Rather than multiplying a constant balance by a declining fraction as we do in SYD depreciation, we multiply a constant fraction by a declining balance each year. Specifically, we multiply a constant percentage rate times the decreasing book value (cost less accumulated depreciation) of the asset (*not depreciable base*) at the beginning of the year. Because the rate remains constant while the book value declines, annual depreciation is less each year.

> **Declining balance depreciation methods** multiply beginning of year book value, not depreciable base, by an annual rate that is a multiple of the straight-line rate.

The rates used are multiples of the straight-line rate. The straight-line rate is simply one, divided by the number of years in the asset's service life. For example, the straight-line rate for an asset with a five-year life is one-fifth, or 20%. Various multiples used in practice are 125%, 150%, or 200% of the straight-line rate. When 200% is used as the multiplier, the method is known as the **double-declining-balance (DDB) method** because the rate used is twice the straight-line rate.

In our illustration, the double-declining-balance rate would be 40% (two times the straight-line rate of 20%). Depreciation is calculated in Illustration 11–1b for the five years of the machine's life using the double-declining-balance method.

---

[2]A formula useful when calculating the denominator is $n(n+1)/2$.

ILLUSTRATION 11-1b

Double-Declining-Balance
Depreciation

Year	Book Value Beginning of Year	×	Depreciation Rate per Year	=	Depreciation	Book Value End of Year
1	$250,000		40%		$100,000	$150,000
2	150,000		40%		60,000	90,000
3	90,000		40%		36,000	54,000
4	54,000				14,000*	40,000
5	40,000				—	40,000
Total					$210,000	

* Amount necessary to reduce book value to residual value

Notice that in the fourth year depreciation expense is a plug amount that reduces book value to the expected residual value. There is no depreciation expense in year 5 since book value has already been reduced to the expected residual value. Declining balance methods often allocate the asset's depreciable base over fewer years than the expected service life.

Switch from Accelerated to Straight Line.   The result of applying the double-declining-balance method in our illustration produces an awkward result in the later years of the asset's life. By using the double-declining-balance method in our illustration, no depreciation expense is recorded in year 5 even though the asset is still producing benefits. In practice, many companies switch to the straight-line method approximately half way through an asset's useful life.

> It is not uncommon for a company to switch from accelerated to straight line approximately half way through an asset's useful life.

In our illustration, the company would switch to straight-line in either year 3 or year 4. Assuming the switch is made at the beginning of year 4, because the book value at the beginning of that year is $54,000, an additional $14,000 ($54,000 – $40,000 in residual value) of depreciation must be recorded. Applying the straight-line concept, $7,000 ($14,000 divided by two remaining years) in depreciation is recorded in both year 4 and year 5.

It should be noted that this switch to straight line is not a change in depreciation method requiring reporting as a change in an accounting principle. The switch is part of the company's planned depreciation approach.

Activity-Based Depreciation Methods

> **Activity-based depreciation methods** estimate service life in terms of some measure of productivity.

The most logical way to allocate an asset's cost to periods of an asset's use is to measure the usefulness of the asset in terms of its productivity. For example, we could measure the service life of a machine in terms of its *output* (for example, the estimated number of units it will produce) or in terms of its *input* (for example, the number of hours it will operate). We have already mentioned that one way to measure the service life of a vehicle is to estimate the number of miles it will operate. The most common activity-based method is called the **units-of-production method**.

OPENING CASE

Question 2

> The **units-of-production method** computes a depreciation rate per measure of output and then multiplies this rate by actual output to determine periodic depreciation.

The measure of output used is the estimated number of units (pounds, items, barrels, etc.) to be produced by the machine. We could also use a measure of input such as the number of hours the machine is expected to operate. By the units-of-production method, we first compute the average depreciation rate per unit by dividing the depreciable base by the number of units expected to be produced. This per unit rate is then multiplied by the number of units produced each period. In our illustration, the depreciation rate per unit is $1.50, computed as follows:

$$\frac{\$250,000 - \$40,000}{140,000 \text{ units}} = \$1.50 \text{ per unit}$$

Each unit produced will require an additional $1.50 of depreciation to be recorded. As we are estimating service life based on units produced rather than in years, depreciation is not constrained by time. However, total depreciation is constrained by the asset's cost and the anticipated residual amount. In our illustration, suppose the company intended to dispose of the asset at the end of five years. Depreciation for year five must be modified. Depreciation expense would be a residual amount necessary to bring the book value of the asset down to residual value. Depreciation for the five years is determined in Illustration 11–1c using the units-of-production method. Notice that the last year's depreciation expense is a plug amount that reduces book value to the expected residual value.

ILLUSTRATION   11–1c

Units-of-Production Depreciation

Year	Units Produced	×	Depreciation Rate per Year	=	Depreciation	Book Value End of Year
1	24,000		$1.50		$ 36,000	$214,000
2	36,000		1.50		54,000	160,000
3	46,000		1.50		69,000	91,000
4	8,000		1.50		12,000	79,000
5	16,000				39,000*	40,000
Totals	130,000				$210,000	

* Amount necessary to reduce book value to residual value

Decision Makers' Perspective— Selecting A Depreciation Method

Illustration 11–1d compares periodic depreciation calculated using each of the alternatives we discussed and illustrated.

ILLUSTRATION   11–1d

Comparison of Various Depreciation Methods

Year	Straight Line	Sum-of-the-Years' Digits	Double-Declining Balance	Units of Production
1	$ 42,000	$ 70,000	$100,000	$ 36,000
2	42,000	56,000	60,000	54,000
3	42,000	42,000	36,000	69,000
4	42,000	28,000	14,000	12,000
5	42,000	14,000	0	39,000
Total	$210,000	$210,000	$210,000	$210,000

> All methods provide the same total depreciation over an asset's life.

> Activity-based methods are theoretically superior to time-based methods but often are impractical to apply in practice.

Theoretically, using an activity-based depreciation method provides a better matching of revenues and expenses. Clearly, the productivity of a plant asset is more closely associated with the benefits provided by that asset than the mere passage of time. Also, these methods allow for random patterns of depreciation to correspond with random patterns of asset use.

However, activity-based methods quite often are either infeasible or too costly to use. For example, buildings don't have an identifiable measure of productivity. Even for machinery, there may be an identifiable measure of productivity such as machine hours or units produced, but it frequently is more costly to determine each period than it is to simply measure the passage of time. For these reasons, most companies use time-based depreciation methods.

Graphic 11–3 shows the results of a recent survey of depreciation methods used by large public companies.[3]

GRAPHIC   11–3

Use of Various Depreciation Methods

Depreciation Method	Number of Companies
Straight line	573
Declining balance	27
Sum-of-the-years' digits	9
Accelerated method—not specified	49
Units of production	49
Other	11

Why do so many companies use the straight-line method as opposed to other time-based methods? Many companies perhaps consider the benefits derived from the majority of plant assets to be realized approximately evenly over these asset's useful lives. Certainly a contributing factor is that straight line is the easiest method to understand and apply.

---

[3]*Accounting Trends and Techniques—1995* (New York, New York: AICPA, 1995).

Another motivation is the positive effect on reported income. Straight-line depreciation produces a higher net income than accelerated methods in the early years of an asset's life. In Chapter 8 we pointed out that reported net income can affect bonuses paid to management or debt agreements with lenders.

Conflicting with the desire to report higher profits is the desire to reduce taxes by reducing taxable income. An accelerated method serves this objective by reducing taxable income more in the early years of an asset's life than straight line. You probably recall a similar discussion from Chapter 8 in which the benefits were described of using the LIFO inventory method during periods of increasing costs. However, remember that the LIFO conformity rule requires companies using LIFO for income tax reporting to also use LIFO for financial reporting. *No such conformity rule exists for depreciation methods.* Income tax regulations allow firms to use different approaches to computing depreciation in their tax returns and in their financial statements. The method used for tax purposes is therefore not a constraint in the choice of depreciation methods for financial reporting. As a result, most companies use the straight-line method for financial reporting and the Internal Revenue Service's prescribed accelerated method (discussed later in this chapter) for income tax purposes. For example, Graphic 11–4 shows Merck & Co.'s depreciation policy as reported in a disclosure note accompanying recent financial statements.

> A company does not have to use the same depreciation method for both financial reporting and income tax purposes.

GRAPHIC   11–4

Depreciation Method Disclosure—Merck & Co.

Summary of Accounting Policies (in Part):

Depreciation—Depreciation is provided over the estimated useful lives of the assets, principally using the straight-line method. For tax purposes, accelerated methods are used.

GLOBAL PERSPECTIVE

In the United States, income tax regulations allow firms to use different approaches to computing depreciation in their tax returns and financial statements. Internationally, in a number of countries, such as Japan and Germany, depreciation rates for financial reporting must be the same as those used for income tax purposes.

It is not unusual for a company to use different depreciation methods for different classes of assets. For example, Graphic 11–5 illustrates the International Paper Company depreciation policy disclosure contained in a note accompanying recent financial statements.

GRAPHIC   11–5

Depreciation Method Disclosure – International Paper Company

Summary of Accounting Policies (in Part):

Plants, Properties, and Equipment

Plants, properties, and equipment are stated at cost, less accumulated depreciation. For financial reporting purposes, the Company uses the unit-of-production method for depreciating its major pulp and paper mills and certain wood products facilities, and the straight-line method for other plants and equipment.

CONCEPT REVIEW EXERCISE   DEPRECIATION METHODS

The Sprague Company purchased a fabricating machine on January 1, 1997, at a net cost of $130,000. At the end of its four-year useful life, the company estimates that the machine will be worth $30,000. Sprague also estimates that the machine will run for 25,000 hours during its four-year life. The company's fiscal year ends on December 31.

Required:

Compute depreciation for 1997 through 2000 using each of the following methods:

1. Straight line.
2. Sum-of-the-years' digits.
3. Double-declining balance.
4. Units of production (using machine hours). Actual production was as follows:

Year	Machine hours
1997	6,000
1998	8,000
1999	5,000
2000	7,000

CONCEPT REVIEW EXERCISE   SOLUTION

1. Straight line.

$$\frac{\$130,000 - \$30,000}{4 \text{ years}} = \$25,000 \text{ per year}$$

2. Sum-of-the-years' digits.

Year	Depreciable Base	×	Depreciation Rate per Year	=	Depreciation
1	$100,000		$4/10$		$ 40,000
2	100,000		$3/10$		30,000
3	100,000		$2/10$		20,000
4	100,000		$1/10$		10,000
Total					$100,000

3. Double-declining balance.

Year	Book Value Beginning of Year	×	Depreciation Rate per Year	=	Depreciation	Book Value End of Year
1	$130,000		50%		$ 65,000	$65,000
2	65,000		50%		32,500	32,500
3	32,500				2,500*	30,000
4	30,000				—	30,000
Total					$100,000	

*Amount necessary to reduce book value to residual value

4. Units of production (using machine hours).

Year	Machine Hours	×	Depreciation Rate per Hour	=	Depreciation	Book Value End of Year
1	6,000		$4 *		$ 24,000	$106,000
2	8,000		4		32,000	74,000
3	5,000		4		20,000	54,000
4	7,000				24,000†	30,000
Total					$100,000	

$$*\frac{(\$130,000 - \$30,000)}{25,000 \text{ hours}} = \$4 \text{ per hour}$$

†Amount necessary to reduce book value to residual value

Group and Composite Depreciation Methods

Group and **composite** depreciation methods aggregate assets to reduce the recordkeeping costs of determining periodic depreciation.

As you might imagine, depreciation records could become quite cumbersome and costly if a company has hundreds, or maybe thousands, of depreciable assets. However, the burden can be lessened if the company uses the group or composite method to depreciate assets collectively rather than individually. The two methods are the same except for the way the collection of assets is aggregated for depreciation. The **group depreciation method** defines the collection as depreciable assets that share similar service lives and other attributes. For example, group depreciation could be used for fleets of vehicles or collections of machinery. The **composite depreciation method** is used when assets are physically dissimilar but are aggregated anyway to gain the convenience of group depreciation. For instance, composite depreciation can be used for all of the depreciable assets in one manufacturing plant, even though individual assets in the composite may have widely diverse service lives.

Both approaches are similar in that they involve applying a single straight-line rate based on the average service lives of the assets in the group or composite.[4] The process is demonstrated using Illustration 11–2.

ILLUSTRATION 11–2

Group Depreciation

The Express Delivery Company began operations in 1997. It will depreciate its fleet of delivery vehicles using the group method. The cost of vehicles purchased early in 1997, along with residual values, estimated lives, and straight-line depreciation per year by type of vehicle are as follows:

Asset	Cost	Residual Value	Depreciable Base	Estimated Life (yrs.)	Depreciation per Year (straight line)
Vans	$150,000	$30,000	$120,000	6	$20,000
Trucks	120,000	16,000	104,000	5	20,800
Wagons	60,000	12,000	48,000	4	12,000
Totals	$330,000	$58,000	$272,000		$52,800

The *group depreciation* rate is determined by dividing the depreciation per year by the total cost. The group's *average service* life is calculated by dividing the depreciable base by the depreciation per year:

$$\text{Group depreciation rate} = \frac{\$52,800}{\$330,000} = 16\%$$

$$\text{Average service life} = \frac{\$272,000}{\$52,800} = 5.15 \text{ years (rounded)}$$

The depreciation rate is applied to the total cost of the group or composite for the period.

If there are no changes in the assets contained in the group, depreciation of $52,800 per year (16% × $330,000) will be recorded for 5.15 years. This means the depreciation in the sixth year will be $7,920 (.15 of a full year's depreciation = 15% × $52,800) which depreciates the cost of the group down to its estimated residual value. In other words, the group will be depreciated over the average service life of the assets in the group.

In practice, there very likely will be changes in the assets constituting the group as new assets are added and others are retired or sold. Additions are recorded by increasing the group asset account for the cost of the addition. Depreciation is determined by multiplying the group rate by the total cost of assets in the group for that period. Because depreciation records are not kept on an individual asset basis, dispositions are recorded under the assumption that the book value of the disposed item exactly equals any proceeds received and no gain or loss is recorded. For example, if a delivery truck in the above illustration that cost $15,000 is sold for $3,000 in the year 2000, the following journal entry is recorded:

No gain or loss is recorded when a group or composite asset is retired or sold.

Cash	3,000	
Accumulated depreciation (difference)	12,000	
Vehicles		15,000

Any actual gain or loss is included in the accumulated depreciation account. This practice generally will not distort income as the unrecorded gains tend to offset unrecorded losses. Once the group or composite rate and the average service life are determined, they normally are continued despite the addition and disposition of individual assets. This implicitly assumes that the service lives of new assets approximate those of individual assets they replace.

The group and composite methods simplify the recordkeeping of depreciable assets. This simplification justifies any immaterial errors in income determination.

Depletion of Natural Resources

Allocation of the cost of natural resources is called **depletion**. Because the usefulness of natural resources generally is directly related to the amount of the resources extracted, the activity-based units-of-production method is widely used to calculate periodic depletion.

---

[4]A declining balance method could also be used with either the group or composite methods by applying a multiple (e.g., 200%) to the straight-line group or composite rate.

Learning objective 3
Calculate the periodic depletion of a natural resource.

Service life is therefore the estimated amount of natural resource to be extracted (for example, tons of mineral or barrels of oil).

Depletion base is cost less any anticipated residual value. Residual value could be significant if cost includes land that has a value after the natural resource has been extracted.

The example in Illustration 11–3 was first introduced in Chapter 10.

ILLUSTRATION   11–3

Depletion of Natural Resources

In 1997, the Jackson Mining Company paid $100,000 for the right to explore for a coal deposit on 500 acres of land in Pennsylvania. Costs of exploring for the coal deposit totaled $200,000 and intangible development costs incurred in digging and erecting the mine shaft were $500,000. In addition, the company purchased new excavation equipment for the project at a cost of $600,000. After the coal is removed from the site, the equipment will be sold for its anticipated residual value of $60,000. It is estimated that the land will have a residual value of $100,000 after 1,000,000 tons of coal are extracted over a four-year period. During 1997, 300,000 tons were extracted.

In Chapter 10 on page 402 we determined that the capitalized cost of the natural resource, coal deposit, is $800,000. The depletion base is $700,000 ($800,000 – residual of $100,000), and the depletion rate per ton is calculated as follows:

Depletion of the cost of natural resources usually is determined using the units-of-production method.

$$\text{Depletion per ton} = \frac{\text{Depletion base}}{\text{Estimated extractable tons}}$$

$$\text{Depletion per ton} = \frac{\$700,000}{1,000,000 \text{ tons}} = \$.70 \text{ per ton}$$

For each ton of coal extracted, $.70 in depletion is recorded. In 1997, the following journal entry records depletion.

Depletion ($.70 × 300,000 tons)	210,000	
Coal deposit		210,000

Notice that the credit is to the asset, coal deposit, rather than to a contra account, accumulated depletion. Although this approach is traditional, the use of a contra account is acceptable.

Depletion is a product cost and is included in the cost of the inventory of coal, just as the depreciation on manufacturing equipment is included in inventory cost. The depletion is then included in cost of goods sold on the income statement when the coal is sold.

What about depreciation on the $600,000 cost of excavation equipment? If the equipment can be moved from the site and used on future projects, the equipment's depreciable base should be allocated over its useful life. If the asset is not movable, as in our illustration, then it should be depreciated over its useful life or the life of the natural resource, whichever is shorter.

The units-of-production method often is used to determine depreciation on assets used in the extraction of natural resources.

Quite often, companies use the units-of-production method to calculate depreciation on assets used in the extraction of natural resources. The activity base used is the same as that used to calculate depletion, the estimated recoverable natural resource. In our illustration, the depreciation rate would be $.54 per ton, calculated as follows:

$$\text{Depreciation per ton} = \frac{\$600,000 - \$60,000}{1,000,000 \text{ tons}} = \$.54 \text{ per ton}$$

In 1997, $162,000 in depreciation ($.54 × 300,000 tons) is recorded and also included as part of the cost of the coal inventory.

The property, plant, and equipment disclosure accompanying recent financial statements of the Coastal Corporation shown in Graphic 11–6 provides a good summary of depletion and depreciation for natural resource properties.

GRAPHIC 11-6

Depletion Method Disclosure—Coastal Corporation

Summary of Accounting Policies (in Part):

Plants, Properties, and Equipment

Depreciation, depletion, and amortization of gas and oil properties are provided on the unit-of-production basis whereby the unit rate for depreciation, depletion and amortization is determined by dividing the total unrecovered carrying value of gas and oil properties plus estimated future development costs by the estimated proved reserves included therein, as estimated by an independent engineer.

Additional Consideration

Percentage Depletion

Depletion of cost less residual value required by GAAP should not be confused with percentage depletion (also called *statutory depletion*) allowable for income tax purposes for oil, gas, and most mineral natural resources. Under these tax provisions, a producer is allowed to deduct a fixed percentage of gross income as depletion expense without regard to the cost of the natural resource. Over the life of the asset, percentage depletion could exceed the asset's cost. The percentage allowed varies according to the type of natural resource.

Because percentage depletion usually differs from cost depletion, a difference between taxable income and financial reporting income before tax results. These differences are discussed in Chapter 16.

Amortization of Intangible Assets

Learning objective 4
Calculate the periodic amortization of an intangible asset.

OPENING CASE

Question 3

GAAP require that the service life of an intangible not exceed 40 years.

Allocating the cost of intangible assets is called **amortization**. The capitalized cost of an intangible asset must be allocated to the periods in which the asset is expected to contribute to the company's revenue-generating activities. Intangibles typically have no residual values, so the amortization base is simply cost.

Intangible assets generally represent exclusive rights that provide benefits to the owner. These assets have no physical life to provide an upper bound to service life. However, most intangibles have a legal or contractual life that limits service life. For example, a **patent** has a legal life of 17 years and a **franchise** has a contractual life indicated in the franchise agreement.

Of course, estimated service life can be less than the legal or contractual life of the asset. For example, the useful life of a patent would be considerably shorter than its legal life of 17 years if obsolescence is expected to limit the longevity of a protected product. Some intangibles, such as **goodwill**, have neither a legal nor contractual life. *APBO 17* states that the service life of any intangible asset should not exceed 40 years.[5] Remember, this is a maximum service life. Most companies amortize goodwill over periods shorter than 40 years. For example, IBM amortizes goodwill over a five-year period.

The 40-year rule also applies to intangibles that have a legal life of greater than 40 years. For example, a **copyright** gives the creator exclusive right to reproduce and sell artistic or published work for the life of the creator plus 50 years. Its cost, though, must be amortized over no more than 40 years.

Duracell International, Inc., reported a number of intangible assets on a recent balance sheet. A note, illustrated in Graphic 11–7, disclosed the range of estimated useful lives for each type of intangible.

GRAPHIC 11-7

Intangible Asset Service Life Disclosure—Duracell International, Inc.

Summary of Significant Accounting Policies (in Part):

Intangibles

Patents are amortized on a straight-line basis over periods ranging up to 15 years and computer software is amortized over 5 years. All other intangibles are amortized on a straight-line basis over 40 years.

[5]"Intangible Assets," *Accounting Principles Board Opinion No. 17* (New York, New York: APB, 1970), par. 29.

The cost of an intangible asset is amortized by the straight-line method

The selection of an allocation method for computing periodic amortization theoretically is subject to the same considerations that apply to depreciation. However, *APBO 17* specifies that the straight-line approach "should be applied unless a company demonstrates that another systematic method is more appropriate."[6] Like depletion, amortization expense is traditionally credited to the asset account rather than to accumulated amortization. However, the use of a contra account is acceptable. Let's look at an example in Illustration 11–4.

ILLUSTRATION   11–4

Amortization of Intangibles

> Hollins Corporation began operations early in 1997. Expenditures of $5,000 were made for legal fees and state filing fees necessary to form the corporation. In addition, a patent was purchased in January for $50,000. The remaining legal life of the patent is 13 years. However, due to expected technological obsolescence, the company estimates that the useful life of the patent is only eight years. Straight-line amortization is used for all intangible assets. The company's fiscal year-end is December 31.

Organization costs usually are amortized over a five-year period.

The service life of the patent clearly is eight years. But what about the service life of the intangible asset organization costs? This $5,000 cost, which represents the right to operate as a corporate entity, provides benefits to a company over its entire life. However, we know that the maximum period to amortize any intangible is 40 years. In practice, most companies amortize organization costs over a much shorter period, usually five years, which corresponds to the required amortization period for income tax reporting.

The journal entries to record a full year of amortization for these intangibles are as follows:

Amortization expense ($5,000 ÷ 5 years)	1,000	
Organization costs		1,000
To record amortization of organization costs.		
Amortization expense ($50,000 ÷ 8 years)	6,250	
Patent		6,250
To record amortization of patent.		

Similar to depreciation, amortization is either a product cost or a period cost depending on the use of the asset. For intangibles used in the manufacture of product, amortization is a product cost and is included in the cost of inventory. For intangibles not used in production, such as the organization costs in our illustration, periodic amortization is expensed in the period incurred.

PART B ADDITIONAL ISSUES

In this part of the chapter, we discuss the following issues related to cost allocation:

1. Partial periods
2. Changes in estimates
3. Change in depreciation method
4. Error correction
5. Comparison with MACRS
6. Impairment of value

Partial Periods

Only in textbooks are operational assets purchased and disposed of at the very beginning or very end of a company's fiscal year. When acquisition and disposal occur at other times, a company theoretically must determine how much depreciation, depletion, and amortization to record for the part of the year that each asset actually is used.

Let's repeat the Hogan Manufacturing Company illustration used earlier in the chapter but modify it in Illustration 11–5 to assume that the asset was acquired *during* the company's fiscal year.

---

[6]"Intangible Assets," *Accounting Principles Board Opinion No. 17* (New York, New York: APB, 1970), par. 30.

ILLUSTRATION   11–5

**Depreciation Methods—
Partial Year**

On April 1, 1997, the Hogan Manufacturing Company purchased a machine for $250,000. The company expects the service life of the machine to be five years and the anticipated residual value is $40,000. The machine was disposed of after five years of use. The company's fiscal year-end is December 31. Partial-year depreciation is recorded based on the number of months the asset is in service.

Notice that no information is provided on the estimated output of the machine. Partial-year depreciation presents a problem only when time-based depreciation methods are used. In an activity-based method, the rate per unit of output simply is multiplied by the actual output for the period, regardless of the length of that period.

Depreciation per year of the asset's life calculated earlier in the chapter for the various time-based depreciation methods is shown in Illustration 11–5a.

ILLUSTRATION   11–5a

Yearly Depreciation

Year	Straight Line	Sum-of-the-Years' Digits	Double-Declining Balance
1	$ 42,000	$ 70,000	$100,000
2	42,000	56,000	60,000
3	42,000	42,000	36,000
4	42,000	28,000	14,000
5	42,000	14,000	0
Total	$210,000	$210,000	$210,000

Illustration 11–5b shows how Hogan would depreciate the machinery by these three methods assuming an April 1 acquisition date.

ILLUSTRATION   11–5b

Partial-Year Depreciation

Year	Straight Line	Sum-of-the-Years' Digits	Double-Declining Balance
1997	$42,000 × 3/4 = **$ 31,500**	$70,000 × 3/4 = **$ 52,500**	$100,000 × 3/4 = **$ 75,000**
1998	**$ 42,000**	$70,000 × 1/4 = $ 17,500 +56,000 × 3/4 = 42,000 **$ 59,500**	$100,000 × 1/4 = $ 25,000 + 60,000 × 3/4 = 45,000 **$ 70,000***
1999	**$ 42,000**	$56,000 × 1/4 = $ 14,000 +42,000 × 3/4 = 31,500 **$ 45,500**	$ 60,000 × 1/4 = $ 15,000 + 36,000 × 3/4 = 27,000 **$ 42,000**
2000	**$ 42,000**	$42,000 × 1/4 = $ 10,500 +28,000 × 3/4 = 21,000 **$ 31,500**	$ 36,000 × 1/4 = $ 9,000 + 14,000 × 3/4 = 10,500 **$ 19,500**
2001	**$ 42,000**	$28,000 × 1/4 = $ 7,000 +14,000 × 3/4 = 10,500 **$ 17,500**	$ 14,000 × 1/4 = **$ 3,500**
2002	$42,000 × 1/4 = **$ 10,500**	$14,000 × 1/4 = **$ 3.500**	
Totals	**$210,000**	**$210,000**	**$210,000**

* Could also be determined by multiplying the book value at the beginning of the year by twice the straight-line rate: ($250,000 – $75,000) × 40% = $70,000.

Notice that 1997 depreciation is three-quarters of the full year's depreciation for the first year of the asset's life, because the asset was used 9 months, or 3/4 of the year. The remaining one-quarter of the first year's depreciation is included in 1998's depreciation along with 3/4 of the depreciation for the second year of the asset's life. This calculation is not necessary for the straight-line method because a full year's depreciation is the same for each year of the asset's life.

Usually, the above procedure is impractical or at least cumbersome. As a result, most companies adopt a simplifying assumption, or convention, for computing partial year's depreciation and use it consistently. A common convention is to record one-half of a full year's depreciation in the year of acquisition and another half year in the year of disposal. This is known as the **half-year convention**.[7]

Changes in Estimates

The calculation of depreciation, depletion, or amortization requires estimates of both service life and residual value. It's inevitable that at least some estimates will prove incorrect. Chapter 3 introduced the topic of changes in estimates along with coverage of changes in accounting principles and the correction of errors. Here and in subsequent sections of this chapter, we provide overviews of the accounting treatment and disclosures required for these changes and errors when they involve operational assets.

Changes in estimates are accounted for prospectively. When a company revises a previous estimate based on new information, prior financial statements are not restated. Instead, the company merely incorporates the new estimate in any related accounting determinations from then on. So, it usually will affect some aspects of both the balance sheet and the income statement in the current and future periods. And a disclosure note should describe the effect of a change in estimate on income before extraordinary items, net income, and related per-share amounts for the current period.

Consider this example of a change in the estimated service life of a depreciable asset. On January 1, 1995, the Hogan Manufacturing Company purchased a machine for $250,000. The company expects the service life of the machine to be five years and its anticipated residual value to be $40,000. The company's fiscal year-end is December 31 and the straight-line depreciation method is used for all depreciable assets. During 1997, the company revised its estimate of service life from five to eight years and also revised estimated residual value to $22,000.

For 1995 and 1996, depreciation is $42,000 per year [($250,000 − $40,000) ÷ 5 years] or $84,000 for the two years. However, with the revised estimate, depreciation for 1997 and subsequent years is determined by allocating the book value remaining at the beginning of 1997 less the revised residual value equally over the remaining service life of six years (8 − 2). The remaining book value at the beginning of 1997 is $166,000 ($250,000 − $84,000) and depreciation for 1997 and subsequent years is recorded as follows:

Depreciation expense [($166,000 − 22,000) ÷ 6 years]	24,000	
Accumulated depreciation—machinery		24,000

The asset's book value is depreciated down to the anticipated residual value of $22,000 at the end of the revised eight-year service life. In addition, a note discloses the effect of the change in estimate on income, if material. The before-tax effect is an increase in income of $18,000 (depreciation of $42,000 if the change had not been made, less $24,000 depreciation after the change).

The Brown & Sharpe Manufacturing Company recently revised the service lives for certain depreciable assets. Graphic 11–8 shows the note that disclosed the change.

1 Significant Accounting Policies (in Part):

Property, Plant, and Equipment
($ in thousands, except per share amounts)

The Company extended the estimated useful lives of machinery and equipment at its Swiss subsidiary, based upon the current low rate of utilization. The effect of this change was to reduce [current year] depreciation expense and net loss by $921 or $.19 per share.

---

[7]Another common method is the modified half-year convention. This method records a full year's depreciation when the asset is acquired in the first half of the year or sold in the second half. No depreciation is recorded if the asset is acquired in the second half of the year or sold in the first half. These half-year conventions are simple and, in most cases, will not result in material differences from a more precise calculation.

Change in Depreciation Method

A change in depreciation method is accounted for as a normal change in accounting principle. The cumulative after-tax effect on prior years' income is reported on the income statement in the year of the change. The cumulative effect is the difference between retained earnings at the beginning of the year of the change as reported, and the beginning-of-year retained earnings that would have resulted if the new accounting method had been used in all prior years.

In addition, the effect of the change on income before extraordinary items, net income, and related per-share amounts, if material, should be reported for the current period and on a pro forma basis for the financial statements of all prior periods included with the current financial statements. These disclosures allow for comparisons between periods using both the old and new accounting method. Consider the example in Illustration 11–6.

A change in depreciation method is considered a normal change in accounting principle.

ILLUSTRATION 11–6

Change in Depreciation Method

On January 1, 1995, the Hogan Manufacturing Company purchased a machine for $250,000. The company expects the service life of the machine to be five years and its anticipated residual value to be $40,000. The company's fiscal year-end is December 31 and the double-declining-balance (DDB) depreciation method is used. During 1997, the company switched from the DDB to the straight-line method.

Cumulative effect of the change:

($ in thousands)

	DDB	Straight Lline
1995 depreciation	$100 ($250 × 40%)	$42 ($210 ÷ 5)
1996 depreciation	60 ($150 × 40%)	42 ($210 ÷ 5)
Accumulated depreciation and 1995–96 reduction in income	$160	$84

difference
$76

The $76,000 before-tax increase in retained earnings caused by switching from DDB to straight line would be reported, net of tax, on the income statement as a cumulative effect of an accounting change. The journal entry to record the change, ignoring income tax considerations, is:

Accumulated depreciation (determined above)	76,000	
Cumulative effect of accounting change		76,000

The effect of the change on 1997 income before extraordinary items, net income, and related earnings per share figures for the current year, along with the nature and justification for the change, should be described in a disclosure note. Depreciation for 1997 using DDB would have been $36,000. Compared to straight-line depreciation of $42,000, the effect of the switch is to *decrease* before-tax income by $6,000.

Also, because the company's 1997 financial statements will probably include 1996's statements for comparative purposes, 1996's income numbers must be presented as if the straight-line method had been used to calculate depreciation.

Frequently, when a company changes depreciation methods, the change will be effective only for assets placed in service after that date. Of course, that means there would be no cumulative effect on prior years' earnings because the change doesn't affect assets depreciated in prior periods. Graphic 11–9 provides an example of this type of change in depreciation method.

GRAPHIC 11–9

Change in Depreciation Method for Newly Acquired Assets—Rohm and Haas Company

Note 12: Land, Buildings, and Equipment, Net (in part)

... the company changed its method of depreciation for newly acquired buildings and equipment to the straight-line method. The change had no cumulative effect on prior years' earnings but did increase [current year] net earnings by $9 million, or $.14 per share. ...

Error Corrections

Learning objective 7
Explain the appropriate
treatment required when an
error in accounting for an
operational asset is
discovered.

Errors involving operational assets include computational errors in the calculation of depreciation, depletion, or amortization and mistakes made in determining whether expenditures should be capitalized or expensed. These errors can affect many years. For example, let's say a major addition to an operational asset should be capitalized but incorrectly is expensed. Not only is income in the year of the error understated, but subsequent years' income is overstated because depreciation is omitted.

Recall from our discussion of inventory errors that if a material error is discovered in an accounting period subsequent to the period in which the error is made, any previous years' financial statements that were incorrect as a result of the error are retroactively restated to reflect the correction. Any account balances that are incorrect as a result of the error are corrected by journal entry. If retained earnings is one of the incorrect accounts, the correction is reported as a prior period adjustment to the beginning balance on the statement of shareholders' equity.[8] In addition, a disclosure note is needed to describe the nature of the error and the impact of its correction on net income, income before extraordinary items, and earnings per share. Consider Illustration 11–7.

> For material errors
> occurring in a previous
> year:
>   Previous years' financial
>   statements are
>   retroactively restated.
>   Account balances are
>   corrected.
>   If retained earnings
>   requires correction, the
>   correction is reported as
>   a prior period
>   adjustment.
>   A note describes the
>   nature of the error and
>   the impact of the
>   correction on income.

The 1995 and 1996 financial statements that were incorrect as a result of the error are retroactively restated to report the addition to the patent and to reflect the correct amount of amortization expense, assuming both statements are reported again for comparative purposes in the 1997 annual report.

Because retained earnings is one of the accounts incorrect as a result of the error, a correction to that account of $180,000 is reported as a prior period adjustment to the 1997 beginning retained earnings balance in Hathaway's comparative statements of shareholders' equity. Assuming that 1996 is included with 1997 in the comparative statements, a correction would be made to the *1996* beginning retained earnings balance as well. That prior period adjustment, though, would be for the pre-1996 difference: $300,000 – $60,000 = $240,000.

Also, a disclosure note accompanying Hathaway's 1997 financial statements should describe the nature of the error and the impact of its correction on each year's net income (understated by

ILLUSTRATION   11–7

Error Correction

> Sometimes, the analysis is
> easier if you recreate the
> entries actually recorded
> incorrectly and those that
> would have been recorded
> if the error hadn't occurred,
> and then compare them.

In 1997, the controller of the Hathaway Corporation discovered an error in recording $300,000 in legal fees to successfully defend a patent infringement suit in 1995. The $300,000 was charged to legal fee expense but should have been capitalized and amortized over the five-year remaining life of the patent. Straight-line amortization is used by Hathaway for all intangibles.

Analysis:

($ in thousands)

	Correct (should have been recorded)			Incorrect (as recorded)		
1995	Patent	300		Expense	300	
	Cash		300	Cash		300
1995	Expense	60		Amortization entry omitted		
	Patent		60			
1996	Expense	60		Amortization entry omitted		
	Patent		60			

During the two-year period, amortization expense was *understated* by $120 thousand, but other expenses were *overstated* by $300 thousand, so net income during the period was *understated* by $180 thousand (ignoring income taxes). This means retained earnings is currently *understated* by that amount.

Patent is understated by $180 thousand.

	($ in thousands)	
Patent	180	
Retained earnings		180
To correct incorrect accounts.		

---

[8]The prior period adjustment is applied to beginning retained earnings for the year following the error, or for the earliest year being reported in the comparative financial statements when the error occurs prior to the earliest year presented. The retained earnings balances in years after the first year also are adjusted to what those balances would be if the error had not occurred, but a company may choose not to explicitly report those adjustments as separate line items.

$240,000 in 1995 and overstated by $60,000 in 1996), income before extraordinary items (same as net income), and earnings per share.

Comparison with MACRS (Tax Depreciation)

Depreciation for financial reporting purposes is an attempt to distribute the cost of the asset, less any anticipated residual value, over the estimated useful life in a systematic and rational manner that attempts to match revenues with the use of the asset. Depreciation for income tax purposes is influenced by the revenue needs of government as well as the desire to influence economic behavior. For example, accelerated depreciation schedules currently allowed are intended to provide incentive for companies to expand and modernize their facilities thus stimulating economic growth.

The federal income tax code allows taxpayers to compute depreciation for their tax returns on assets acquired after 1986 using the **modified accelerated cost recovery system (MACRS)**.[9] Key differences between the calculation of depreciation for financial reporting and the calculation using MACRS are:

1. Estimated useful lives and residual values are not used in MACRS.
2. Firms can't choose among various accelerated methods under MACRS.
3. A half-year convention is used in determining the MACRS depreciation rates.

Under MACRS, each asset is placed within a recovery period category. The six categories for personal property are 3, 5, 7, 10, 15, and 20 years. For example, the 5-year category includes most machinery and equipment, automobiles, and light trucks.

Depending on the category, fixed percentage rates are applied to the original cost of the asset. The rates for the 5-year asset category are as follows:

Year	Rate
1	20.00%
2	32.00
3	19.20
4	11.52
5	11.52
6	5.76
Total	100.00%

These rates are equivalent to applying the double-declining-balance method with a switch to straight-line in the year straight line yields an equal or higher deduction than DDB. Also, the half-year convention is used regardless of when the asset is placed in service. The first-year rate of 20% for the five-year category is one-half of the DDB rate for an asset with a five-year life (2 × 20%). The sixth year rate of 5.76% is one-half of the straight-line rate established in year 4, the year straight-line depreciation exceeds DDB depreciation.

Companies have the option to use the straight-line method for the entire tax life of the asset, applying the half-year convention, rather than using MACRS depreciation schedules. Because of the differences discussed above, tax depreciation for a given year will likely be different than GAAP depreciation.

Impairment of Value

Learning objective 8
Identify situations that involve a significant impairment of the value of operational assets and describe the required accounting procedures.

Depreciation, depletion, and amortization reflect a gradual consumption of the benefits inherent in an operational asset. An implicit assumption in allocating the cost of an asset over its useful life is that there has been no significant reduction in the anticipated total benefits or service potential of the asset. Situations can arise, however, that cause a significant decline or impairment of those benefits or service potentials. An extreme case would be the destruction of a plant asset—say a building destroyed by fire—before the asset is fully depreciated. The remaining carrying value of the asset in that case should be written off as a loss.

An increasingly common occurrence in practice is the partial write-down of operational assets that remain in use. For example, Philip Morris recently reduced the carrying value of a $450 mil-

---

[9]For assets acquired between 1981 and 1986, tax depreciation is calculated using the accelerated cost recovery system (ACRS), which is similar to MACRS. For assets acquired before 1981, tax depreciation can be calculated using any of the depreciation methods discussed in the chapter. Residual values are used in the calculation of depreciation for pre-1981 assets.

lion Miller brewery (Miller is a subsidiary of Philip Morris) to $170 million and recognized a loss for the $280 million write-down because of lack of product demand.

> An operational asset should be written-down if there has been a significant and permanent impairment of value.

Conceptually, there is considerable merit for a policy requiring the write-down of an operational asset when there has been a significant and permanent decline in value below book value. The write-down provides important information about the future cash flows to be generated from the use of the asset. However, in practice this policy is very subjective. Even if it appears certain that there has been a permanent impairment of value, it often is difficult to measure the amount of the required write-down.

For example, suppose a company purchased $2,000,000 of equipment to be used in the production of a new type of laser printer. The useful life of the equipment is six years, residual value is estimated at $200,000, and the straight-line method is used to determine depreciation. At the beginning of year three, the machine's book value has been reduced by accumulated depreciation to $1,400,000 [$2,000,000 − ($300,000 × 2)]. At that time, new technology is developed causing a significant reduction in the selling price of the new laser printer as well as a reduction in anticipated demand for the product. Management estimates that the equipment will be useful for only two more years and will have no significant residual value.

This situation is not simply a matter of a change in the estimates of useful life and residual value of the equipment. Management must decide if the events occurring in year 3 warrant a write-down of the book value of the asset below $1,400,000. A write-down would be appropriate if the company decided that it would be unable to fully recover this amount through future use.

SFAS 121 establishes guidance for when to recognize and how to measure impairment losses of long-lived assets and certain identifiable intangibles.[10] The standard identifies a three-step process for determining if an impairment loss is required and how that loss is to be measured. Graphic 11–10 outlines this process.

GRAPHIC   11–10

Identifying and Measuring Impairment Loss—Three-Step Process

Step 1: Triggering Event
An event or change in circumstance that indicates that the carrying amount of an asset may not be recoverable.

Examples of triggering events:
1. Significant decrease in market value of asset.
2. Significant change in extent or manner in which asset is used.
3. Significant physical change in asset.
4. Significant adverse change in legal factors or business climate.
5. Projection or forecast demonstrating continuing losses.

Step 2: Test to Determine if Recognition Required
Recognition is required if the book value of the asset exceeds the sum of undiscounted expected cash flows.

Step 3: Measurement of Impairment
The amount of impairment loss is the excess of the book value of the asset over fair value of the asset. Fair value is based on:
1. Market price of the asset, if available.
2. Otherwise, estimate fair value using best information available:
a. Prices of similar assets
b. Other valuation techniques, such as:
1) Present value of estimated expected future cash flows using a discount rate commensurate with risks involved
2) Option-pricing models, matrix pricing, and fundamental analysis

> **OPENING CASE**
> **Question 4**

The FASB realized that it would be impractical to test all assets or asset groups for impairment at the end of every reporting period. *SFAS 121* requires investigation of possible impairment only if a triggering event occurs—step 1. Determining whether to record an impairment loss and actually recording the loss are two distinct calculations. An impairment loss is required only when the undiscounted sum of estimated future cash flows from an asset is less than the asset's book

[10] "Accounting for the Impairment of Long-Lived Assets and for Long-Lived Assets to Be Disposed Of," *Statement of Financial Accounting Standards No. 121* (Norwalk, Conn: FASB, 1995).

An impairment loss is recognized when the undiscounted sum of estimated future cash flows from an asset is less than the asset's book value.

value—step 2. For purposes of this estimation, assets are grouped at the lowest level for which there are cash flows that can be separated from the cash flows of other asset groups. The measurement of impairment loss—step 3—is the difference between asset book value and fair value. As the graphic illustrates, if fair value is not determinable, it must be estimated. One method that can be used to estimate fair value is to compute the discounted present value of future cash flows from the asset or group of assets. Notice that *undiscounted* estimates of cash flows are used to determine whether an impairment loss is indicated, but *discounted* estimates of cash flows can be used to determine the amount of the loss.

In addition, a description of the impaired asset or asset group, the reasons that the asset is impaired, and a description of the measurement assumptions included in the calculation of the loss should be disclosed.[11] As an example, Graphic 11–11 shows the disclosure note included in the January 31, 1996, financial statements of Kmart describing an asset impairment loss of $532 million. The loss appeared on the income statement as a separate line item included in income from continuing operations.

GRAPHIC   11–11

Asset Impairment Loss—Kmart

5. Asset Impairment Charge

($ in millions)

Kmart adopted Financial Accounting Standard No. 121 "Accounting for the Impairment of Long-Lived Assets and for Long-Lived Assets to Be Disposed Of" (*FAS 121*) in the fourth quarter of 1995. This statement requires companies to record impairments of long-lived assets, certain identifiable intangibles, and associated goodwill on an exception basis, when there is evidence that events or changes in circumstances have made recovery of an asset's carrying value unlikely. In conducting its review, management considered, among other things, its current and expected operating cash flows together with a judgment as to the fair value the Company could receive upon sale of its investment. Based on this review, Kmart recorded a $532 pretax charge, $390 after tax, relating to Builders Square and certain international operations.

PART

C SUBSEQUENT EXPENDITURES AND DISPOSITION

Now that we have acquired and measured operational assets, we can address accounting problems incurred subsequent to their acquisition. This part of the chapter deals with the treatment of expenditures made over the life of these assets to maintain and/or improve them and the disposition of operational assets.

GLOBAL PERSPECTIVE

In the United States, accounting for operational assets subsequent to initial acquisition is based on the historical cost of the asset, and revaluations to reflect changes in market values, other than in asset impairment situations, generally are not permitted. Internationally, the International Accounting Standards Committee has issued IAS 16, *Accounting for Property, Plant and Equipment*. The requirements of IAS 16 conform to U.S. GAAP except that a revaluation of property, plant, and equipment is permitted. Countries such as Germany, Canada, and Japan adhere strictly to historical cost valuation. However, other countries, including Australia and France allow the periodic revaluation of property, plant, and equipment to current market value.

---

[11]This is true even when the fair value of the asset is determinable. In that case, the discounted present value of future cash flows is implicit in the fair value.

Expenditures Subsequent to Acquisition

Learning objective 9
Discuss the accounting treatment of repairs and maintenance, additions, improvements, and rearrangements to operational assets.

Many operational assets require expenditures to repair, maintain, or improve them. These expenditures can present accounting problems if they are material. In general, a choice must be made between capitalizing the expenditures by either increasing the asset's book value or creating a new asset, or expensing them in the period in which they are incurred. Conceptually, we can refer to the matching principle which requires the capitalization of expenditures that are expected to produce benefits beyond the current fiscal year. Expenditures that simply maintain a given level of benefits are expensed in the period they are incurred.

Expenditures related to operational assets can increase future benefits in the following ways:

1. An extension of the *useful life* of the asset.
2. An increase in the *operating efficiency* of the asset resulting in either an increase in the quantity of goods or services produced or a decrease in future operating costs.
3. An increase in the *quality* of the goods or services produced by the asset.

Theoretically, expenditures that cause any of these results should be capitalized initially and then expensed in future periods through depreciation, depletion, or amortization. This permits the matching of the expenditure with the future benefits. Of course, materiality is an important factor in the practical application of this approach.

Many companies do not capitalize any expenditure unless it exceeds a predetermined amount that is considered material.

For expediency, many companies set materiality thresholds for the capitalization of any expenditure. For example, a company might decide to expense all expenditures under $200 regardless of whether or not future benefits are increased. Judgment is required to determine the appropriate materiality threshold as well as the appropriate treatment of expenditures over $200. There often are practical problems in capitalizing these expenditures. For example, even if future benefits are increased by the expenditure, it may be difficult to determine how long the benefits will last. It's important for a company to establish a policy for treating these expenditures and apply it consistently.

We classify subsequent expenditures as (1) repairs and maintenance, (2) additions, (3) improvements, or (4) rearrangements.

Repairs and Maintenance

Expenditures for **repairs and maintenance** generally are expensed when incurred.

These expenditures are made to *maintain* a given level of benefits provided by the asset and do not *increase* future benefits. For example, the cost of an engine tune-up or the repair of an engine part for a delivery truck allows the truck to continue its productive activity. If the maintenance is not performed, the truck will not provide the benefits originally anticipated. In that sense, future benefits are provided; without the repair, the truck will no longer operate. The key, though, is that future benefits are not provided *beyond those originally anticipated*. Expenditures for these activities should be expensed in the period incurred.

Additional Consideration

If repairs and maintenance costs are seasonal, interim financial statements may be misstated. For example, suppose annual maintenance is performed on a company's fleet of delivery trucks. The annual income statement correctly includes one year's maintenance expense. However, for interim reporting purposes, if the entire expenditure is made in one quarter, should that quarter's income statement include as expense the entire cost of the annual maintenance? If these expenditures can be anticipated, they should be accrued evenly throughout the year by crediting an allowance account. The allowance account is then debited when the maintenance is performed.

Additions

The costs of **additions** usually are capitalized.

As the term implies, **additions** involve adding a new major component to an existing asset and should be capitalized because future benefits are increased. For example, adding a refrigeration unit to a delivery truck increases the capability of the truck, thus increasing its future benefits. Other examples include the construction of a new wing on a building and the addition of a security system to an existing building.

The capitalized cost includes all necessary expenditures to bring the addition to a condition and location for use. For a building addition, this might include the costs of tearing down and removing a wall of the existing building. The capitalized cost of additions are depreciated over the remaining useful life of the original asset or its own useful life, whichever is shorter.

Improvements

The costs of **improvements** usually are capitalized.

Expenditures classified as **improvements** involve the replacement of a major component of an operational asset. The replacement can be a new component with the same characteristics as the old component or a new component with enhanced operating capabilities. For example, an existing refrigeration unit in a delivery truck could be replaced with a new but similar unit or with a new and improved refrigeration unit. In either case, the cost of the improvement usually increases future benefits and should be capitalized by increasing the book value of the related asset (the delivery truck). There are three methods used to record the cost of improvements.

1. **Substitution.** The improvement can be recorded as both (1) a disposition of the old component and (2) the acquisition of the new component. This approach is conceptually appealing but is practical only if the original cost and accumulated depreciation of the old component can be separately identified.
2. **Capitalization of new cost.** Another way to record an improvement is to include the cost of the improvement (net of any consideration received from the disposition of the old component) as a debit to the related asset account, without removing the original cost and accumulated depreciation of the original component. This approach is acceptable only if the book value of the original component has been reduced to an immaterial amount through prior depreciation.
3. **Reduction of accumulated depreciation.** Another way to increase an asset's book value is to leave the asset account unaltered but decrease its related accumulated depreciation. The argument for this method is that many improvements extend the useful life of an asset and are equivalent to a partial recovery of previously recorded depreciation. This approach produces the same book value as the capitalization of cost to the asset account. Cost and accumulated depreciation will differ under the two methods.

The three methods are compared in Illustration 11–8.

ILLUSTRATION   11–8

Improvements

Substitution
1. Disposition of old component.
2. Acquisition of new component.

Capitalization of new cost

Reduction of accumulated depreciation

The Palmer Corporation replaced the air conditioning system in one of its office buildings that it leases to tenants. The cost of the old air conditioning system, $200,000, is included in the cost of the building. However, the company has separately depreciated the air conditioning system. Depreciation recorded up to the date of replacement totaled $160,000. The old system was removed and the new system installed at a cost of $230,000, which was paid in cash. Parts from the old system were sold for $12,000. Accounting for the improvement differs depending on the alternative chosen.		
Cash	12,000	
Accumulated depreciation – buildings	160,000	
Loss on disposal (difference)	28,000	
Buildings		200,000
Buildings	230,000	
Cash		230,000
Buildings	218,000	
Cash ($230,000 – 12,000)		218,000
Accumulated depreciation – buildings	218,000	
Cash ($230,000 – 12,000)		218,000

Rearrangements

The costs of material **rearrangements** should be capitalized if they clearly increase future benefits.

Expenditures made to restructure an asset without addition, replacement, or improvement are termed **rearrangements**. The objective is to create a new capability for the asset and not necessarily to extend its useful life. Examples include the rearrangement of machinery on the production line to increase operational efficiency and the relocation of a company's operating plant or office building. If these expenditures are material and they clearly increase future benefits, they should be capitalized and expensed in the future periods benefited. If the expenditures are not material or if it's not certain that future benefits have increased, they should be expensed in the period incurred.

Costs of Defending Intangible Rights

The costs incurred to *successfully* defend an intangible right should be capitalized.

Repairs, additions, improvements, and rearrangements generally relate to tangible operational assets. A possible significant expenditure incurred subsequent to the acquisition of intangible assets is the cost of defending the right that gives the asset its value. If an intangible right is *successfully* defended, the litigation costs should be capitalized and amortized over the remaining useful life of the related intangible. This is the appropriate treatment of these expenditures even if the intangible asset was originally developed rather than purchased.

The costs incurred to *unsuccessfully* defend an intangible right should be expensed.

If the defense of an intangible right is *unsuccessful*, then the litigation costs should be expensed as incurred because they provide no future benefit. In addition, the book value of any intangible asset should be reduced to realizable value. For example, if a company is unsuccessful in defending a patent infringement suit, the patent's value may be eliminated. The book value of the patent should be written off as a loss.

Disposition of Operational Assets

Learning objective 10
Explain how to account for the disposition of operational assets.

Operational assets may be sold, exchanged, or retired. In each case, depreciation, depletion, or amortization should be recorded up to the date of disposition. Exchanges were discussed in the previous chapter. For outright sales for monetary consideration (cash or a receivable), a gain or loss is recognized for the difference between the consideration received and the book value of the asset. Illustration 11–9 provides an example.

Retirements and abandonments are treated similarly. The only difference is that there will be no monetary consideration received. A loss is recorded for the remaining book value of the asset.

ILLUSTRATION   11–9

Sale of Operational Asset

When operational assets are sold, a gain or loss is recognized for the difference between the consideration received and the asset's book value.

The Robosport Company sold machinery that originally cost $20,000 for $6,000. Depreciation of $12,000 had been recorded up to the date of sale. Because the asset's book value of $8,000 ($20,000 – $12,000) is more than the $6,000 consideration received, a $2,000 loss is recognized. The sale is recorded as follows:

Cash	6,000	
Accumulated depreciation	12,000	
Loss on disposal of machinery (difference)	2,000	
Machinery		20,000

Additional Consideration

Involuntary conversions

Occasionally operational assets are disposed of involuntarily. These so-called involuntary conversions include destruction by fire, earthquake, flood, or other catastrophe and expropriation by a governmental body.

Usually, the company receives a cash settlement from the insurance company for destroyed assets or from the governmental body for expropriated assets. This cash quite often is immediately reinvested in similar assets. Nevertheless, involuntary conversions are treated just as voluntary conversions. The proceeds are recorded, the book values of the lost assets are removed, and a gain or loss is recognized for the difference.

Solution to Financial Reporting Case (at the opening of the chapter)

1. Is Penny correct? Do the terms depreciation, depletion, and amortization all mean the same thing?

2. What is the units-of-production method? How is it used by Boise Cascade?

Penny is correct. Each of these terms refers to the cost allocation of operational assets over their service lives. The term depreciation is used for plant and equipment, depletion for natural resources, and amortization for intangibles.

The units-of-production method is an activity-based method that computes a depreciation (or depletion or amortization) rate per measure of output and then multiplies this rate by actual output to determine periodic cost allocation. Boise Cascade uses this method to (1) depreciate its paper and wood products manufacturing facilities, (2) measure depletion of the cost of timber harvested, and (3) measure amortization of the cost of logging roads. The cost of logging roads is an intangible asset because the company does not own the roads. Boise Cascade has incurred costs to upgrade the roads to make them serviceable and has the right to use them in its timber operations.

3. Why do you suppose Boise Cascade chose a 40-year period to amortize goodwill?

4. What does Boise Cascade mean when it states that the measurement of possible goodwill impairment is based on undiscounted cash flows?

Certain intangible assets, like goodwill, have no legal nor contractual life. GAAP require that the service life of an intangible asset not exceed 40 years. Boise Cascade has decided to amortize its goodwill over the maximum allowable period.

SFAS 121 requires the recording of an asset impairment loss anytime the undiscounted sum of estimated future cash flows from an asset is less than the asset's book value. If an impairment is indicated, then the loss is measured as the difference between the asset's fair value and book value.

The Bottom Line

1. The use of operational assets represents a consumption of benefits, or service potentials, inherent in the assets. The matching principle requires that the cost of these inherent benefits or service potentials that were consumed be recognized as expense. As there very seldom is a direct relationship between the use of operational assets and revenue production, accounting resorts to arbitrary allocation methods to achieve a matching of expenses with revenues.

2. The allocation process for plant and equipment is called depreciation. Time-based depreciation methods estimate service life in years and then allocate depreciable base, cost less estimated residual value, using either a straight-line or accelerated pattern. Activity-based depreciation methods allocate the depreciable base by estimating service life according to some measure of productivity.

3. The allocation process for natural resources is called depletion. The activity-based method called units-of-production usually is used to determine periodic depletion.

4. The allocation process for intangible assets is called amortization. The cost of intangible assets is amortized using the straight-line method over estimated service life which is limited to 40 years or the legal/contractual life of the asset, whichever is shorter.

5. A change in either the service life or residual value of an operational asset should be reflected in the financial statements of the current period and future periods by recalculating periodic depreciation, depletion, or amortization.

6. A change in depreciation method is considered a change in accounting principle that requires the cumulative effect of the change to be reported on the income statement in the year of the change.

7. A material error in accounting for an operational asset that is discovered in a year subsequent to the year of the error requires that previous years' financial statements that were incorrect as a result of the error are retroactively restated to reflect the correction. Any account balances that are incorrect as a result of the error are corrected by journal entry. If retained earnings is one of the incorrect accounts, the correction is reported as a prior period adjustment to the beginning balance on the statement of shareholders' equity. In addition, a disclosure note is needed to describe the nature of the error and the impact of its correction on income.

8. Conceptually, there is considerable merit for a policy requiring the write-down of an operational asset when there has been a *significant* and *permanent* decline in value below carrying value. The write-down provides important information about the future cash flows to be generated from the use of the asset. However, in practice this policy is very subjective. *SFAS 121* establishes guidance for when to recognize and how to measure impairment losses of long-lived assets and certain identifiable intangibles.

9. Expenditures for repairs and maintenance generally are expensed when incurred. The costs of additions and improvements usually are capitalized. The costs of material rearrangements should be capitalized if they clearly increase future benefits.

10. When an operational asset is sold, a gain or loss is recognized for the difference between the consideration received and the asset's book value. Retirements and abandonments are handled in a similar fashion. The only difference is that there will be no monetary consideration received. A loss is recorded for the remaining book value of the asset.

11

RETIREMENT AND REPLACEMENT METHODS OF DEPRECIATION

Retirement and **replacement** depreciation methods occasionally are used to depreciate relatively low-valued assets with short service lives. Under either approach, an aggregate asset account that represents a group of similar assets is increased at the time the initial collection is acquired.

Retirement Method

> The **retirement depreciation method** records depreciation when assets are disposed of and measures depreciation as the difference between the proceeds received and cost.

Using the **retirement depreciation method,** the asset account also is increased for the cost of subsequent expenditures. When an item is disposed of, the asset account is credited for its cost, and depreciation expense is recorded for the difference between cost and proceeds received, if any. No other entries are made for depreciation. As a consequence, one or more periods may pass without any expense recorded. For example, the following entry records the purchase of 100 hand-held calculators at $50 acquisition cost each:

Calculators (100 × $50)	5,000	
Cash		5,000
To record the acquisition of calculators.		

If 20 new calculators are acquired at $45 each, the asset account is increased.

Calculators (20 × $45)	900	
Cash		900
To record additional calculator acquisitions.		

Thirty calculators are disposed of (retired) by selling them second-hand to a bookkeeping firm for $5 each. The following entry reflects the retirement method:

Cash (30 × $5)	150	
Depreciation expense (difference)	1,350	
Calculators (30 × $50)		1,500
To record the sale/depreciation of calculators.		

Notice that the retirement system assumes a FIFO cost flow approach in determining the cost of assets, $50 each, that were disposed.

Replacement Method

> By the **replacement method,** depreciation is recorded when assets are replaced.

By the **replacement depreciation method,** the initial acquisition of assets is recorded the same way as by the retirement method; that is, the aggregate cost is increased. However, depreciation expense is the amount paid for new or replacement assets. Any proceeds received from asset dispositions reduces depreciation expense. For our example, the acquisition of 20 new calculators at $45 each is recorded as depreciation as follows:

Depreciation expense (20 × $45)	900	
Cash		900
To record the replacement/depreciation of calculators.		

The sale of the old calculators is recorded as a reduction of depreciation:

Cash (30 × $5) 150

    Depreciation expense 150

To record the sale of calculators.

    The asset account balance remains the same throughout the life of the aggregate collection of assets.

    Because these methods are likely to produce aggregate expense measurements that differ from individual calculations, retirement and replacement methods are acceptable only in situations where the distortion in depreciation expense does not have a material effect on income. These methods occasionally are encountered in regulated industries such as utilities.

Questions for Review of Key Topics

Question	11–1	Explain the similarities in and differences among depreciation, depletion, and amortization.
Question	11–2	Depreciation is a process of cost allocation, not valuation. Explain this statement.
Question	11–3	Identify and define the three characteristics of an asset that must be established to determine periodic depreciation, depletion, or amortization.
Question	11–4	Discuss the factors that influence the estimation of service life for a depreciable asset.
Question	11–5	What is meant by depreciable base? How is it determined?
Question	11–6	Briefly differentiate between activity-based and time-based allocation methods.
Question	11–7	Briefly differentiate between the straight-line depreciation method and accelerated depreciation methods.
Question	11–8	Why are time-based depreciation methods used more frequently than activity-based methods?
Question	11–9	What are some factors that could explain the predominate use of the straight-line depreciation method.
Question	11–10	Briefly explain the differences and similarities between the group approach and composite approach to depreciating aggregate assets.
Question	11–11	Define depletion and compare it with depreciation.
Question	11–12	Compare and contrast amortization of intangible assets with depreciation and depletion.
Question	11–13	What are some of the simplifying conventions a company can use to calculate depreciation for partial years.
Question	11–14	Explain the accounting treatment required when a change is made to the estimated service life of a machine.
Question	11–15	Explain the accounting treatment and disclosures required when a change is made in depreciation method.
Question	11–16	Explain the steps required to correct an error in accounting for an operational asset that is discovered in a year subsequent to the year the error was made.
Question	11–17	Explain what is meant by the impairment of value of an operational asset. How should these impairments be accounted for?
Question	11–18	Explain the differences in the accounting treatment of repairs and maintenance, additions, improvements, and rearrangements.
Question	11–19	When an operational asset is disposed of, how is the gain or loss on disposal computed?

Exercises

Exercise 11–1
Depreciation methods

    On January 1, 1997, the Excel Delivery Company purchased a delivery van for $22,000. At the end of its five-year useful life, it is estimated that the van will be worth $2,000. During the five-year period, the company expects to drive the van 100,000 miles.

Required:
Calculate annual depreciation for the five-year life of the van using each of the following methods. Round all computations to the nearest dollar.

    1.   Straight line.
    2.   Sum-of-the-years' digits.
    3.   Double-declining balance.
    4.   Units of production using miles driven as a measure of output, and the following actual mileage:

Year	Miles
1997	22,000
1998	24,000
1999	15,000
2000	20,000
2001	21,000

Exercise 11–2
Depreciation methods

On January 1, 1997, the Alleghany Corporation purchased machinery for $115,000. The estimated useful life of the machinery is 10 years and the estimated residual value is $5,000. The machine is expected to produce 220,000 units during its useful life.

Required:

Calculate depreciation for 1997 and 1998 using each of the following methods. Round all computations to the nearest dollar.

1. Straight line.
2. Sum-of-the-years' digits.
3. Double-declining balance.
4. One hundred fifty percent declining balance.
5. Units of production (units produced in 1997, 30,000; units produced in 1998, 25,000).

Exercise 11–3
Depreciation methods;
partial years

[This is a variation of the previous exercise modified to focus on depreciation for partial years.]

On October 1, 1997, the Alleghany Corporation purchased machinery for $115,000. The estimated useful life of the machinery is 10 years and the estimated residual value is $5,000. The machine is expected to produce 220,000 units during its useful life.

Required:

Calculate depreciation for 1997 and 1998 using each of the following methods. Partial-year depreciation is calculated based on the number of months the asset is in service. Round all computations to the nearest dollar.

1. Straight line.
2. Sum-of-the-years' digits.
3. Double-declining balance.
4. One hundred fifty percent declining balance.
5. Units of production (units produced in 1997, 10,000; units produced in 1998, 25,000).

Exercise 11–4
Depreciation methods; asset
addition

The Funseth Company purchased a five-story office building on January 1, 1995, at a cost of $4,400,000. The building has a residual value of $200,000 and a 30-year useful life. The straight-line depreciation method is used. On June 30, 1997, construction of a sixth floor was completed at a cost of $1,100,000.

Required:

Calculate the depreciation on the building and building addition for 1997 and 1998 assuming that the addition did not change the useful life or residual value of the building.

Exercise 11–5
Depreciation methods; solving
for unknowns

For each of the following depreciable assets, determine the missing amount (?). Abbreviations for depreciation methods are SL for straight line, SYD for sum-of-the-years' digits, and DDB for double-declining balance.

Asset	Cost	Residual Value	Service Life (years)	Depreciation Method	Depreciation (year 2)
A	?	$20,000	5	DDB	$24,000
B	$ 40,000	?	8	SYD	7,000
C	65,000	5,000	?	SL	6,000
D	230,000	10,000	10	?	22,000
E	200,000	20,000	8	150% DB	?

Exercise 11–6
Multiple choice; cost
allocation

The following questions dealing with depreciation, depletion, and amortization are adapted from questions that appeared on recent CPA examinations. Determine the response that best completes the statements or questions.

1. In January 1997, Vorst Co. purchased a mineral mine for $2,640,000 with removable ore estimated at 1,200,000 tons. After it has extracted all the ore, Vorst will be required by law to restore the land to its original condition at an estimated cost of $180,000. Vorst believes it will be able to sell the property afterwards for $300,000. During 1997, Vorst incurred $360,000 of development costs preparing the mine for production and removed and sold 60,000 tons of ore. In its 1997 income statement, what amount should Vorst report as depletion?

    a. $135,000
    b. $144,000
    c. $150,000
    d. $159,000

2. South Co. purchased a machine that was installed and placed in service on January 1, 1997, at a cost of $240,000. Salvage value was estimated at $40,000. The machine is being depreciated over 10 years by the double-declining-balance method. For the year ended December, 31, 1998, what amount should South report as depreciation expense?

    a. $48,000
    b. $38,400
    c. $32,000
    d. $21,600

3. A machine with a five-year estimated useful life and an estimated 10% residual value was acquired on January 1, 1995. On December 31, 1998, accumulated depreciation, using sum-of-the-years'-digits method, would be

    a. (Original cost less residual value) multiplied by 1/15.
    b. (Original cost less residual value) multiplied by 14/15.
    c. Original cost multiplied by 14/15.
    d. Original cost multiplied by 1/15.

4. Mark Co. bought a franchise from Fred Co. on January 1, 1997, for $204,000. An independent consultant retained by Mark estimated that the remaining useful life of the franchise was 50 years. Its unamortized cost on Fred's books at January 1, 1997, was $68,000. Mark has decided to amortize the franchise over the maximum period allowed. What amount should be amortized for the year ended December 31, 1997?

    a. $5,100
    b. $4,080
    c. $4,000
    d. $1,700

Exercise 11–7
Group depreciation

Highsmith Rental Company purchased an apartment building early in 1997. There are 20 apartments in the building and each is furnished with major kitchen appliances. The company has decided to use the group depreciation method for the appliances. The following data is available:

Appliance	Cost	Residual Value	Useful Life (in years)
Stoves	$15,000	$3,000	6
Refrigerators	10,000	1,000	5
Dishwashers	8,000	500	4

In 2000, three new refrigerators costing $2,700 were purchased for cash. The old refrigerators, which originally cost $1,500, were sold for $200.

Required:
1. Calculate the group depreciation rate, group life, and depreciation for 1997.
2. Prepare the journal entries to record the purchase of the new refrigerators and the sale of the old refrigerators.

Exercise 11–8
Double-declining-balance method; switch to straight line.

On January 2, 1997, the Jackson Company purchased equipment to be used in its manufacturing process. The equipment has an estimated useful life of eight years and an estimated residual value of $30,000. The expenditures made to acquire the asset were as follows:

Purchase price	$135,000
Freight charges	1,000
Installation charges	4,000

Jackson uses the double-declining-balance (DDB) method of depreciation in the early years of the equipment's life and then switches to straight line half way through the equipment's life.

Required:
1. Calculate depreciation for each year of the asset's eight-year life.
2. Discuss the accounting treatment of the depreciation on the equipment.

Exercise 11–9
Depletion

On April 17, 1997, the Loadstone Mining Company purchased the rights to a coal mine. The purchase price plus additional costs necessary to prepare the mine for extraction of the coal totaled $3,600,000. The company expects to extract 900,000 tons of coal during a four-year period. During 1997, 220,000 tons were extracted and sold immediately.

Required:

1. Calculate depletion for 1997.
2. Discuss the accounting treatment of the depletion calculated in requirement 1.

Exercise 11–10
Depletion and depreciation

The Jackpot Mining Company operates a copper mine in central Montana. The company paid $1,000,000 in 1997 for the mining site and spent an additional $400,000 to prepare the mine for extraction of the copper. The company estimates that the property can be sold for $100,000 after extraction is completed in six years. The company expects to extract 10,000,000 tons of copper from the mine. Actual production was 800,000 tons in 1997 and 2,000,000 tons in 1998.

To aid extraction, Jackpot purchased some new equipment on July 1, 1997. The equipment cost $120,000 and has an estimated physical life of eight years. After the copper is removed from this mine, the equipment will be sold for an estimated $10,000.

Required:

1. Compute depletion and depreciation on the mine and mining equipment for 1997 and 1998. The units-of-production method is used to calculate depreciation.
2. Discuss the accounting treatment of the depletion and depreciation on the mine and mining equipment.

Exercise 11–11
Amortization

The Janes Company provided the following information on intangible assets:

a. A patent was purchased from the Lou Company for $600,000 on January 1, 1995. Janes estimated the remaining useful life of the patent to be 10 years. The patent was carried on Lou's accounting records at a net book value of $350,000 when Lou sold it to Janes.

b. During 1997, a franchise was purchased from the Rink Company for $500,000. The contractual life of the franchise is 10 years and Janes records a full year of amortization in the year of purchase.

c. Janes incurred research and development costs in 1997 as follows:

Materials and supplies	$140,000
Personnel	180,000
Indirect costs	60,000
Total	$380,000

d. Effective January 1, 1997, based on new events that have occurred, Janes estimates that the remaining life of the patent purchased from Lou is only five more years.

Required:

1. Prepare the entries necessary in 1995 and 1997 to reflect the above information.
2. Prepare a schedule showing the intangible asset section of Janes' December 31, 1997, balance sheet.

Exercise 11–12
Patent amortization

On January 2, 1997, David Corporation purchased a patent for $500,000. The remaining legal life is 12 years, but the company estimated that the patent will be useful only for eight years. In January 1999, the company incurred legal fees of $45,000 in successfully defending a patent infringement suit. The successful defense did not change the company's estimate of useful life.

Required:

Prepare journal entries related to the patent for 1997, 1998, and 1999.

Exercise 11–13
Change in estimate; useful life of patent

Van Frank Telecommunications has a patent on a cellular transmission process. The company has amortized the patent on a straight-line basis since 1993, when it was acquired at a cost of $18 million at the beginning of that year. Due to rapid technological advances in the industry, management decided that the patent would benefit the company over a total of six years rather than the nine-year life being used to amortize its cost. The decision was made at the end of 1997 (before adjusting and closing entries).

Required:

Prepare the appropriate adjusting entry for patent amortization in 1997 to reflect the revised estimate.

Exercise 11–14
Change in estimate; useful life and residual value of equipment

Wardell Company purchased a minicomputer on January 1, 1995, at a cost of $40,000. The computer was depreciated using the straight-line method over an estimated five-year useful life with an estimated residual value of $4,000. On January 1, 1997, the estimate of useful life was changed to a total of 10 years, and the estimate of residual value was changed to $900.

Required:

1. Prepare the appropriate adjusting entry for depreciation in 1997 to reflect the revised estimate.
2. Repeat requirement 1 assuming that the company uses the sum-of-the-years'-digits method instead of the straight-line method.

Exercise 11–15
Change in depreciation methods

Exercise 21–2 deals with a change in depreciation methods.

Exercise 11–16
Change in principle; change in depreciation methods

Clinton Poultry Farms has used the declining-balance method of depreciation for conveyor equipment acquired at the beginning of 1994 for financial reporting. At the beginning of 1997, Clinton decides to change to the straight-line method. There is no change in the method used for tax reporting. Clinton's tax rate is 40%.

The effect of this change on depreciation for each year is as follows:

($ in 000s) Year	Straight Line	Declining Balance	Difference
1994	$ 400	$ 640	$240
1995	400	550	150
1996	400	460	60
	$1,200	$1,650	$450

Required:
1. Prepare the journal entry to record the change in principle. (Ignore income tax effects.)
2. Briefly describe any other steps Clinton should take to report this accounting change in the 1996–1997 comparative financial statements.

Exercise 11–17
Error correction

In 1997, internal auditors discovered that PKE Displays, Inc., had debited an expense account for the $350,000 cost of a machine purchased on January 1, 1994. The machine's useful life was expected to be five years with no residual value. Straight-line depreciation is used by the PKE.

Required:
1. Prepare the appropriate correcting entry assuming the error was discovered in 1997 before the adjusting and closing entries. (Ignore income taxes.)
2. Assume the error was discovered in 2000 before the adjusting and closing entries. Prepare the appropriate correcting entry.

Exercise 11–18
Subsequent expenditures

The Belltone Company made the following expenditures related to its 10-year-old manufacturing facility:

1. The heating system was replaced at a cost of $300,000. The cost of the old system was not known. The company accounts for improvements as reductions of accumulated depreciation.
2. A new wing was added at a cost of $750,000. The new wing substantially increases the productive capacity of the plant.
3. Annual building maintenance was performed at a cost of $12,000.
4. All of the machinery on the assembly line in the plant was rearranged at a cost of $50,000. The rearrangement clearly increases the productive capacity of the plant.

Required:
Prepare journal entries to record each of the above expenditures.

Exercise 11–19
Disposal of operational asset

Funseth Farms, Inc., purchased a tractor in 1994 at a cost of $30,000. The tractor was sold for $6,000 in 1997. Depreciation recorded through the disposal date totaled $22,000.

Required:
1. Prepare the journal entry to record the sale.
2. Assuming that the tractor was sold for $10,000, prepare the journal entry to record the sale.

Exercise 11–20
Depreciation methods; disposal of operational asset

The Howarth Manufacturing company purchased a lathe on June 30, 1993, at a cost of $80,000. The residual value of the lathe was estimated to be $5,000 at the end of a five-year useful life. The lathe was sold on March 31, 1997, for $17,000. Howarth uses the straight-line depreciation method for all of its plant and equipment. Partial-year depreciation is calculated based on the number of months the asset is in service.

Required:
1. Prepare the journal entry to record the sale.
2. Assuming that Howarth had instead used the sum-of-the-years'-digits depreciation method, prepare the journal entry to record the sale.

Exercise 11–21
Multiple choice; changes in estimates; asset impairment

The following questions dealing with changes in estimates involving operational assets and changes in depreciation methods are adapted from questions that appeared on recent CPA examinations. Determine the response that best completes the statements or questions.

1. In January 1995, Winn Corp. purchased equipment at a cost of $500,000. The equipment had an estimated residual value of $100,000, an estimated eight-year useful life, and was being depreciated by the straight-line method. Two years later, it became apparent to Winn that this equipment suffered a permanent impairment of value. In January 1997, management determined the carrying amount should be only $175,000, with a two-year remaining useful life, and the residual value should be reduced to $25,000. In Winn's December 31, 1997, balance sheet, the equipment should be reported at a carrying amount of
   a. $350,000
   b. $175,000
   c. $150,000
   d. $100,000

2. On January 1, 1994, Lane, Inc., acquired equipment for $100,000 with an estimated 10-year useful life. Lane estimated a $10,000 residual value and used the straight-line method of depreciation. During 1998, after its 1997 financial statements had been issued, Lane determined that, due to obsolescence, this equipment's remaining useful life was only four years and its residual value would be $4,000. In Lane's December 31, 1998, balance sheet, what was the carrying amount of this asset?
   a. $51,500
   b. $49,000
   c. $41,500
   d. $39,000

3. On January 1, 1994, Taft Co. purchased a patent for $714,000. The patent is being amortized over its remaining legal life of 15 years expiring on January 1, 2009. During 1997, Taft determined that the economic benefits of the patent would not last longer than 10 years from the date of acquisition. What amount should be reported on the balance sheet for the patent, net of accumulated amortization, at December 31, 1997?
   a. $428,400
   b. $489,600
   c. $504,000
   d. $523,600

4. During 1996, Yvo Corp. installed a production assembly line to manufacture furniture. In 1997, Yvo purchased a new machine and rearranged the assembly line to install this machine. The rearrangement did not increase the estimated useful life of the assembly line, but it did result in significantly more efficient production. The following expenditures were incurred in connection with this project:

Machine	$75,000
Labor to install machine	14,000
Parts added in rearranging the assembly line to provide future benefits	40,000
Labor and overhead to rearrange the assembly line	18,000

   What amount of the above expenditures should be capitalized in 1997?
   a. $147,000
   b. $107,000
   c. $ 89,000
   d. $ 75,000

Exercise 11–22
Concepts; terminology

Listed below are several terms and phrases associated with depreciation, depletion, and amortization. Pair each item from List A (by letter) with the item from List B that is most appropriately associated with it.

List A	List B
_____ 1. Depreciation	a. Cost allocation for natural resource.
_____ 2. Service life	b. Accounted for prospectively.
_____ 3. Depreciable base	c. When there has been a significant and permanent decline in value.
_____ 4. Activity-based methods	d. The amount of use expected from an operational asset.
_____ 5. Time-based methods	e. Service life of an intangible asset.
_____ 6. Double-declining balance	f. Estimates service life in units of output.
_____ 7. Group method	g. Cost less residual value.
_____ 8. Composite method	h. Cost allocation for plant and equipment.
_____ 9. Depletion	i. Does not subtract residual value from cost.
_____ 10. Amortization	j. Requires the cumulative effect to be reported on the income statement.
_____ 11. Change in useful life	k. Aggregates assets that are similar.
_____ 12. Change in depreciation method	l. Aggregates assets that are physically unified.
_____ 13. Write-down of asset	m. Cost allocation for an intangible asset.
_____ 14. Maximum of 40 years	n. Estimates service life in years.

Exercise 11–23
[based on Appendix 11]
Retirement and replacement
depreciation

The Cadillac Construction Company uses the retirement method to determine depreciation on its small tools. During 1995, the first year of the company's operations, tools were purchased at a cost of $8,000. In 1997, tools originally costing $2,000 were sold for $250 and replaced with new tools costing $2,500.

Required:
1. Prepare journal entries to record each of the above transactions.
2. Repeat requirement 1 assuming that the company uses the replacement depreciation method instead of the retirement method.

Problems

Problem 11–1
Depreciation methods; change
in methods

The fact that generally accepted accounting principles allow companies flexibility in choosing between certain allocation methods can make it difficult for a financial analyst to compare periodic performance from firm to firm.

Suppose you were a financial analyst trying to compare the performance of two companies. Company A uses the double-declining-balance depreciation method. Company B uses the straight-line method. You have the following information taken from the 12/31/97 year-end financial statements for Company B:

Income Statement

Depreciation expense	$ 10,000

Balance Sheet

Assets:	
Plant and equipment, at cost	$200,000
Less: Accumulated depreciation	(40,000)
Net	$160,000

You also determine that all of the assets constituting the plant and equipment of Company B were acquired at the same time, and that all of the $200,000 represents depreciable assets. Also, all of the depreciable assets have the same useful life and residual values are zero.

Required:
1. In order to compare performance with Company A, estimate what B's depreciation expense would have been for 1997 if the double-declining-balance depreciation method had been used by Company B since acquisition of the depreciable assets.
2. If Company B decided to switch depreciation methods in 1997 from the straight line to the double-declining-balance method, prepare the journal entry to record the cumulative effect of the switch. Ignore income taxes.

Problem 11–2
Comprehensive problem;
Chapters 10 and 11

At December 31, 1996, Cord Company's plant asset and accumulated depreciation and amortization accounts had balances as follows:

Category	Plant Asset	Accumulated Depreciation and Amortization
Land	$ 175,000	$ —
Buildings	1,500,000	328,900
Machinery and equipment	1,125,000	317,500
Automobiles and trucks	172,000	100,325
Leasehold improvements	216,000	108,000
Land improvements	—	—

Depreciation methods and useful lives:
Buildings—150% declining balance; 25 years.
Machinery and equipment—Straight line; 10 years.
Automobiles and trucks—150% declining balance; 5 years, all acquired after 1993.
Leasehold improvements—Straight line.
Land improvements—Straight line.

Depreciation is computed to the nearest month and residual values are immaterial.

Transactions during 1997 and other information:

a. On January 6, 1997, a plant facility consisting of land and building was acquired from King Corp. in exchange for 25,000 shares of Cord's common stock. On this date, Cord's stock had a market price of $50 a share. Current assessed values of land and building for property tax purposes are $187,500 and $562,500, respectively.

b. On March 25, 1997, new parking lots, streets, and sidewalks at the acquired plant facility were completed at a total cost of $192,000. These expenditures had an estimated useful life of 12 years.

c. The leasehold improvements were completed on December 31, 1993, and had an estimated useful life of eight years. The related lease, which would have terminated on December 31, 1999, was renewable for an additional four-year term. On April 29, 1997, Cord exercised the renewal option.

d. On July 1, 1997, machinery and equipment were purchased at a total invoice cost of $325,000. Additional costs of $10,000 for delivery and $50,000 for installation were incurred.

e. On August 30, 1997, Cord purchased a new automobile for $12,500.

f. On September 30, 1997, a truck with a cost of $24,000 and a carrying amount of $9,100 on date of sale was sold for $11,500. Depreciation for the nine months ended September 30, 1997, was $2,650.

g. On November 4, 1997, Cord purchased for $350,000 a tract of land as a potential future building site.

h. On December 20, 1997, a machine with a cost of $17,000 and a carrying amount of $2,975 at date of disposition was scrapped without cash recovery.

Required:

1. Prepare a schedule analyzing the changes in each of the plant asset accounts during 1997. This schedule should include columns for beginning balance, increase, decrease, and ending balance for each of the plant asset accounts. Do not analyze changes in accumulated depreciation and amortization.

2. For each asset category, prepare a schedule showing depreciation or amortization expense for the year ended December 31, 1997. Round computations to the nearest whole dollar.

(AICPA adapted)

Problem 11–3
Depreciation methods

(This problem is a continuation of Problem 10–3 in Chapter 10 focusing on depreciation)

Required:

For each asset classification, prepare a schedule showing depreciation expense for the year ended December 31, 1997, using the following depreciation methods and useful lives:

Land improvements—Straight line; 15 years.
Building—150% declining balance; 20 years.
Machinery and equipment—Straight-line; 10 years.
Automobiles—150% declining balance; 3 years.

Depreciation is computed to the nearest month and no residual values are used.

(AICPA adapted)

Problem 11–4
Partial-year depreciation; asset addition; increase in useful life

On April 1, 1995, the KB Toy Company purchased equipment to be used in its manufacturing process. The equipment cost $48,000, has an eight-year useful life and no residual value. The company uses the straight-line depreciation method for all manufacturing equipment.

On January 4, 1997, $12,350 was spent to repair the equipment and to add a feature that increased its operating efficiency. Of the total expenditure, $2,000 represented ordinary repairs and annual maintenance and $10,350 represented the cost of the new feature. In addition to increasing operating efficiency, the total useful life of the equipment was extended to 10 years.

Required:

Prepare journal entries for the following:
1. Depreciation for 1995 and 1996.
2. The 1997 expenditure.
3. Depreciation for 1997.

Problem 11–5
Operational assets; comprehensive

The Thompson Corporation, a manufacturer of steel products, began operations on October 1, 1995. The accounting department of Thompson has started the fixed-asset and depreciation schedule presented below. You have been asked to assist in completing this schedule. In addition to ascertaining that the data already on the schedule are correct, you have obtained the following information from the company's records and personnel:

a. Depreciation is computed from the first of the month of acquisition to the first of the month of disposition.

b. Land A and Building A were acquired from a predecessor corporation. Thompson paid $812,500 for the land and building together. At the time of acquisition, the land had an appraised value of $72,000 and the building had an appraised value of $828,000.

c. Land B was acquired on October 2, 1995, in exchange for 3,000 newly issued shares of Thompson's common stock. At the date of acquisition, the stock had a par value of $5 per share and a fair market value of $25 per share. During October 1995, Thompson paid $10,400 to demolish an existing building on this land so it could construct a new building.

d. Construction of Building B on the newly acquired land began on October, 1, 1996. By September 30, 1997, Thompson had paid $210,000 of the estimated total construction costs of $300,000. Estimated completion and occupancy are July 1998.

e. Certain equipment was donated to the corporation by a local university. An independent appraisal of the equipment when donated placed the fair value at $16,000 and the residual value at $2,000.

f. Machine A's total cost of $110,000 includes installation charges of $550 and normal repairs and maintenance of $11,000. Residual value is estimated at $5,500. Machine A was sold on February 1, 1997.

g. On October 1, 1996, Machine B was acquired with a down payment of $4,000 and the remaining payments to be made in 10 annual installments of $4,000 each beginning October 1, 1997. The prevailing interest rate was 8%.

THOMPSON CORPORATION
Fixed Asset and Depreciation Schedule
For Fiscal Years Ended September 30, 1996, and September 30, 1997

Assets	Acquisition Date	Cost	Residual	Depreciation Method	Estimated Life in Years	Depreciation for Year Ended 9/30 1996	1997
Land A	10/1/95	$(1)	N/A	N/A	N/A	N/A	N/A
Building A	10/1/95	(2)	$47,500	SL	(3)	$14,000	$(4)
Land B	10/2/95	(5)	N/A	N/A	N/A	N/A	N/A
Building B	Under Construction	210,000 to date	—	SL	30	—	(6)
Donated Equipment	10/2/95	(7)	2,000	150% Declining Balance	10	(8)	(9)
Machine A	10/2/95	(10)	5,500	Sum-of-the-years' digits	10	(11)	(12)
Machine B	10/1/96	(13)	—	SL	15	—	(14)

N/A = not applicable

Required:

Supply the correct amount for each numbered item on the schedule. Round each answer to the nearest dollar.

(AICPA adapted)

Problem 11–6
Depreciation methods; partial-year depreciation; sale of assets

On March 31, 1997, the Herzog Company purchased a factory complete with machinery and equipment. The allocation of the total purchase price of $1,000,000 to the various types of assets along with estimated useful lives and residual values are as follows:

Asset	Cost	Estimated Residual Value	Estimated Useful Life in Years
Land	$ 100,000	N/A	N/A
Building	500,000	none	25
Machinery	240,000	10% of cost	8
Equipment	160,000	$13,000	6
Total	$1,000,000		

On June 29, 1998, machinery included in the March 31, 1997, purchase that cost $100,000 was sold for $80,000. Herzog uses the straight-line depreciation method for buildings and machinery and the sum-of-the-years'-digits method for equipment. Partial-year depreciation is calculated based on the number of months an asset is in service.

Required:

1. Compute depreciation expense on the building, machinery, and equipment for 1997.
2. Prepare the journal entries to record (1) depreciation on the machinery sold on June 29, 1998, and (2) the sale of machinery.
3. Compute depreciation expense on the building, remaining machinery, and equipment for 1998.

Problem 11–7
Depletion; change in estimate

In 1997, the Marion Company purchased land containing a mineral mine for $1,600,000. Additional costs of $600,000 were incurred to develop the mine. Geologists estimated that 400,000 tons of ore would be extracted. After the ore is removed, the land will have a resale value of $100,000.

To aid in the extraction, Marion built various structures and small storage buildings on the site at a cost of $150,000. These structures have a useful life of 10 years. The structures cannot be moved after the ore has been removed and will be left at the site. In addition, new equipment costing $80,000 was purchased and installed at the site. Marion does not plan to move the equipment to another site, but estimates that it can be sold at auction for $4,000 after the mining project is completed.

In 1997, 50,000 tons of ore were extracted and sold. In 1998, the estimate of total tons of ore in the mine was revised from 400,000 to 487,500. During 1998, 80,000 tons were extracted, of which 60,000 tons were sold.

Required:

1. Compute depletion and depreciation of the mine and the mining facilities and equipment for 1997 and 1998. Marion uses the units-of-production method to determine depreciation on mining facilities and equipment.
2. Compute the book value of the mineral mine, structures, and equipment as of December 31, 1998.
3. Discuss the accounting treatment of the depletion and depreciation on the mine and mining facilities and equipment.

Problem 11–8
Amortization

The following information concerns the intangible assets of Epstein Corporation:

a. The company was organized early in 1995. Expenditures for legal fees and state licensing fees totaling $22,000 were incurred in the formation of the corporation. Epstein amortizes organization costs over a five-year period.
b. On June 30, 1997, Epstein completed the purchase of the Johnstone Corporation for $2,000,000 in cash. The fair value of the net identifiable assets of Johnstone was $1,700,000. Marion amortizes the minimum amount of goodwill allowable by generally accepted accounting principles.
c. Included in the assets purchased from Johnstone was a patent that was valued at $80,000. The remaining legal life of the patent was 13 years, but Epstein believes that the patent will only be useful for another eight years.
d. Epstein acquired a franchise on October 1, 1997, by paying an initial franchise fee of $200,000. The contractual life of the franchise is 10 years.

Required:

1. Prepare year-end adjusting journal entries to record amortization expense on the intangibles at December 31, 1997.
2. Prepare the intangible asset section of the December 31, 1997, balance sheet. Assume a full year's amortization was recorded on the organization costs in 1995.

Problem 11–9
Straight-line depreciation; change in useful life and residual value

The property, plant and equipment section of the Jasper Company's December 31, 1996, balance sheet contained the following:

Property, plant, and equipment:		
Land		$120,000
Building	$840,000	
Less: Accumulated depreciation	(200,000)	640,000
Equipment	$180,000	
Less: Accumulated depreciation	?	?
Total property, plant and equipment		?

The land and building were purchased at the beginning of 1992. Straight-line depreciation is used and a residual value of $40,000 for the building is anticipated.

The equipment is comprised of the following three machines:

Machine	Cost	Date Acquired	Residual Value	Life in years
101	$70,000	1/1/94	$7,000	10
102	80,000	6/30/95	8,000	8
103	30,000	9/1/96	3,000	9

The straight-line method is used to determine depreciation on the equipment. On March 31, 1997, Machine 102 was sold for $52,500. Early in 1997, the useful life of machine 101 was revised to seven years in total, and the residual value was revised to zero.

Required:

1. Calculate the accumulated depreciation on the equipment at December 31, 1996.
2. Prepare the journal entry to record the sale of machine 102. Also prepare the journal entry to record 1997 depreciation on machine 102 up to the date of sale.

3. Prepare the 1997 year-end adjusting journal entries to record depreciation on the building and equipment.

Problem 11–10
Accounting changes; three accounting situations

Described below are three independent and unrelated situations involving accounting changes. Each change occurs during 1997 before any adjusting entries or closing entries are prepared.

a. On December 30, 1993, Rival Industries acquired its office building at a cost of $1,000,000. It has been depreciated on a straight-line basis assuming a useful life of 40 years and no residual value. However, plans were finalized in 1997 to relocate the company headquarters at the end of 2002. The vacated office building will have a residual value at that time of $700,000.

b. At the beginning of 1993, the Hoffman Group purchased office equipment at a cost of $330,000. Its useful life was estimated to be 10 years with no residual value. The equipment has been depreciated by the sum-of-the-years'-digits method. On January 1, 1997, the company changed to the straight-line method.

c. At the beginning of 1997, the Jantzen Specialties, which uses the sum-of-the-years'-digits method changed to the straight-line method for newly acquired buildings and equipment. The change increased current year net income by $445,000.

Required:
For each situation:
1. Identify the type of change.
2. Prepare any journal entry necessary as a direct result of the change as well as any adjusting entry for 1997 related to the situation described. (Ignore income tax effects.)
3. Briefly describe any other steps that should be taken to appropriately report the situation.

Problem 11–11
Error correction; change in depreciation method

The Collins Corporation purchased office equipment at the beginning of 1995 and capitalized a cost of $2,000,000. This cost figure included the following expenditures:

Purchase price	$1,850,000
Freight charges	30,000
Installation charges	20,000
Annual maintenance charge	100,000
Total	$2,000,000

The company estimated an eight-year useful life for the equipment. No residual value is anticipated. The double-declining-balance method was used to determine depreciation expense for 1995 and 1996.

In 1997, after the 1996 financial statements were issued, the company decided to switch to the straight-line depreciation method for this equipment. At that time, the company's controller discovered that the original cost of the equipment incorrectly included one year of annual maintenance charges for the equipment.

Required:
1. Ignoring income taxes, prepare the appropriate correcting entry for the equipment capitalization error discovered in 1997.
2. Ignoring income taxes, prepare the journal entry to record the cumulative effect of the change in depreciation methods.
3. Ignoring income taxes, what is the effect of the change in methods on 1997 income before the cumulative effect?

Cases

Discussion Case 11–1
Depreciation, depletion, and amortization

The terms depreciation, depletion, and amortization all refer to the process of allocating the cost of an operational asset to the periods the asset is used.

Required:
Discuss the differences between depreciation, depletion, and amortization as the terms are used in accounting for operational assets.

Writing Case 11–2
Depreciation

At a recent luncheon, you were seated next to Mr. Hopkins, the president of a local company that manufactures bicycle parts. He heard that you were a CPA and made the following comments to you:

Why is it that I am forced to recognize depreciation expense in my company's income statement when I know that I could sell many of my operational assets for more than I paid for them? I thought that the purpose of the balance sheet was to reflect the value of my business and that the purpose of the income statement was to report the net change in value or wealth of a company. It just doesn't make sense to penalize my profits when there hasn't been any loss in value from using the operational assets.

At the conclusion of the luncheon, you promised to send him a short explanation of the rationale for current depreciation practices.

Required:

Prepare a letter to Mr. Hopkins. Explain the accounting concept of depreciation and include a brief example in your explanation showing that over the life of the asset the change in value approach to depreciation and the allocation of cost approach will result in the same total effect on income.

Discussion Case 11–3
Straight-line method; composite depreciation

Portland Co. uses the straight-line depreciation method for depreciable assets. All assets are depreciated individually except manufacturing machinery, which is depreciated by the composite method.

Required:

1. What factors should have influenced Portland's selection of the straight-line depreciation method?
2. a. What benefits should derive from using the composite method rather than the individual basis for manufacturing machinery?
    b. How should Portland have calculated the manufacturing machinery's annual depreciation in its first year of operation?

(AICPA adapted)

Trueblood Accounting Case 11–4
Tenant relocation costs; depreciation for building renovation

The following Robert M. Trueblood case is recommended for use with this chapter. The case provides an excellent opportunity for class discussion, group projects, and writing assignments. The case, along with Professor's Discussion Material, can be obtained from the Deloitte & Touche Foundation.

Case 91–3: *Accounting for Tenant Relocation Costs*

This case deals with two issues: (1) Accounting for tenant relocation costs and (2) the timing of depreciation for costs incurred to renovate an existing building while it is in use and the allocation and depreciation of costs to construct a common plaza.

Discussion Case 11–5
Depreciation

At the beginning of the year, Patrick Company acquired a computer to be used in its operations. The computer was delivered by the supplier, installed by Patrick, and placed into operation. The estimated useful life of the computer is five years, and its estimated residual value is significant.

Required:

1. a. What costs should Patrick capitalize for the computer?
    b. What is the objective of depreciation accounting?
2. What is the rationale for using accelerated depreciation methods?

(AICPA adapted)

Critical Thought Case 11–6
Capitalize or expense; materiality

Redline Publishers, Inc., produces various manuals ranging from computer software instructional booklets to manuals explaining the installation and use of large pieces of industrial equipment. At the end of 1997, the company's balance sheet reported total assets of $62 million and total liabilities of $40 million. The income statement for 1997 reported net income of $1.1 million which represents an approximate 3% increase from the prior year. The company's effective income tax rate is 30%.

Near the end of 1997, a variety of expenditures were made to overhaul the company's manufacturing equipment. None of these expenditures exceeded $750, the materiality threshold the company has set for the capitalization of any such expenditure. Even though the overhauls extended the service life of the equipment, the expenditures were expensed, not capitalized.

John Henderson, the company's controller, is worried about the treatment of the overhaul expenditures. Even though no individual expenditure exceeded the $750 materiality threshold, total expenditures were $70,000.

Required:

Should the overhaul expenditures be capitalized or expensed?

Group Interaction Case 11–7
Capitalize or expense; materiality

The focus of the case is the situation described in the previous case. Your instructor will divide the class into from two to six groups depending on the size of the class. The mission of your group is to determine the treatment of the overhaul expenditures.

Required:

1. Each group member should deliberate the situation independently and draft a tentative argument prior to the class session for which the case is assigned.

2. In class, each group will meet for 10 to 15 minutes in different areas of the classroom. During the meeting, group members will take turns sharing their suggestions for the purpose of arriving at a single group treatment.
3. After the allotted time, a spokesperson for each group (selected during the group meetings) will share the group's solution with the class. The goal of the class is to incorporate the views of each group into a consensus approach to the situation.

Integrating Case 11–8
Errors; change in estimate; change in principle; inventory and operational assets

Whaley Distributors is a wholesale distributor of electronic components. Financial statements for the year ended December 31, 1997, reported the following amounts and subtotals ($ in millions):

	Assets	Liabilities	Shareholders' Equity	Net Income	Expenses
1996	$640	$330	$310	$210	$150
1997	$820	$400	$420	$230	$175

In 1998 the following situations occurred or came to light:
a. Internal auditors discovered that ending inventories reported in the financial statements the two previous years were misstated due to faulty internal controls. The errors were in the following amounts:

1996 inventory	Overstated by $12 million
1997 inventory	Understated by $10 million

b. A patent costing $18 million at the beginning of 1996, expected to benefit operations for a total of six years, has not been amortized since acquired.
c. Whaley's conveyer equipment has been depreciated by the sum-of-the-years'-digits (SYD) method since constructed at the beginning of 1996 at a cost of $30 million. It has an expected useful life of five years and no expected residual value. At the beginning of 1998, Whaley decided to switch to straight-line depreciation.

Required:
For each situation:
1. Prepare any journal entry necessary as a direct result of the change or error correction as well as any adjusting entry for 1998 related to the situation described. (Ignore tax effects.)
2. Determine the amounts to be reported for each of the items shown above from the 1996 and 1997 financial statements when those amounts are reported again in the 1998, 1997, and 1996 comparative financial statements.

Discussion Case 11–9
Accounting changes

There are various types of accounting changes, each of which is required to be reported differently.

Required:
1. What type of accounting change is a change from the sum-of-the -years'-digits method of depreciation to the straight-line method for previously recorded assets? Under what circumstances does this type of accounting change occur?
2. What type of accounting change is a change in the expected service life of an asset arising because of more experience with the asset? Under what circumstances does this type of accounting change occur?
3. With respect to a change in accounting principle,
   a. How should a company calculate the effect?
   b. How should a company report the effect? (Do not discuss earnings per share requirements.)

(AICPA adapted)

Research Case 11–10
Asset impairment

The text discusses the issue of impairment of asset value. There are those who feel that the costs of complying with asset impairment standards outweigh the benefits. Professor Kimberly Smith in "Asset Impairment Disclosures," explores the costs and benefits of providing asset impairment information.

Required:
1. In your library or from some other source, locate the indicated article in the *Journal of Accountancy*, December 1994.
2. Professor Smith discusses a process referred to as *postauditing*. Describe how postauditing is used by industrial companies.
3. How does Professor Smith recommend that postauditing be used in determining asset impairments?

Ethics Case 11–11
Asset impairment

At the beginning of 1995, the Healthy Life Food Company purchased equipment for $42 million to be used in the manufacture of a new line of gourmet frozen foods. The equipment was estimated to have a 10-year service life and no residual value. The straight-line depreciation method was used to measure depreciation for 1995 and 1996.

Late in 1997, it became apparent that sales of the new frozen food line were significantly below expectations. The company decided to continue production for two more years (1998 and 1999) and then discontinue the line. At that time, the equipment will be sold for minimal scrap values.

The controller, Heather Meyer, was asked by Harvey Dent, the company's chief executive officer (CEO), to determine the appropriate treatment of the change in the service life of the equipment. Heather determined that there has been an impairment of value requiring an immediate write-down of the equipment of $12,900,000. The remaining book value would then be depreciated over the equipment's revised service life.

The CEO does not like Heather's conclusion because of the effect it would have on 1997 income. "Looks like a simple revision in service life from 10 years to 5 years to me," Dent concluded. "Let's go with it that way, Heather."

Required:

1. What is the difference in before-tax income between the CEO's and Heather's treatment of the situation?
2. Discuss Heather Meyer's ethical dilemma.

**Critical Thought
Case 11–12**
Subsequent expenditures

The Cummings Company charged various expenditures made during 1997 to an account called repairs and maintenance expense. You have been asked by your supervisor in the company's internal audit department to review the expenditures to determine if they were appropriately recorded. The amount of each of the transactions included in the account is considered material.

1. Engine tune-up and oil change on the company's 12 delivery trucks—$1,300.
2. Rearrangement of machinery on the main production line—$5,500. It is not evident that the rearrangement will increase operational efficiency.
3. Installation of aluminum siding on the manufacturing plant—$32,000.
4. Replacement of the old air conditioning system in the manufacturing plant with a new system—$120,000.
5. Replacement of broken parts on three machines—$1,500.
6. Annual painting of the manufacturing plant—$11,000.
7. Purchase of new forklift to move finished product to the loading dock—$6,000.
8. Patching leaks in the roof of the manufacturing plant—$6,500. The repair work did not extend the useful life of the roof.

Required:

For each of the transactions listed above, indicate whether the expenditure is appropriately charged to the repair and maintenance expense account, and if not, indicate the proper account to be charged.

Real World Case 11–13
Disposition and depreciation

International Business Machines Corporation (IBM) reported the following in the asset section of its balance sheets for the years ended December 31, 1995 and 1994:

(Dollars in millions)	1995	1994
Plant, Rental Machines, and Other Property	$43,981	$44,820
Less: Accumulated depreciation	27,402	28,156
Plant, Rental Machines, and Other Property —Net	$16,579	$16,664

The following note was included as a part of the Significant Accounting Policies disclosure note in IBM's 1995 financial statements:

Depreciation

Plant, rental machines, and other property are carried at cost, and depreciated over their estimated useful lives using the straight-line method.

Also, Note E disclosed that the total cost of plant, rental machines, and other property included $1,348 and $1,437 (dollars in millions) in land and land improvements at the end of 1995 and 1994, respectively. In addition, the statement of cash flows for the year ended December 31, 1995, reported the following as cash flows from investing activities:

(Dollars in millions)	
Payments for plant, rental machines, and other property	$(4,744)
Proceeds from disposition of plant, rental machines, and other property	1,561

The statement of cash flows also reported 1995 depreciation of $3,955 (dollars in millions).

Required:

1. Assume that all plant, rental machines, and other property acquired during 1995 were purchased for cash. Determine the amount of gain or loss from dispositions of plant, rental machines, and other property recognized during 1995.
2. Assume that the entire amount reported in Note E as land and land improvements represents assets that are not depreciated. What is the approximate average service life of IBM's depreciable assets?

Internet Case 11–14
Depreciation and depletion method; asset impairment; subsequent expenditures

EDGAR, the Electronic Data Gathering, Analysis, and Retrieval system, performs automated collection, validation, indexing, and forwarding of submissions by companies and others who are required by law to file forms with the U.S. Securities and Exchange Commission (SEC). All publicly traded domestic companies use EDGAR to make the majority of their filings. (Some foreign companies file voluntarily.) Form 10-K or 10-KSB, which include the annual report, is required to be filed on EDGAR. The SEC makes this information available on the Internet.

Required:

1. Access EDGAR on the Internet. You can use a web browser or anonymous FTP. The web address is http://www.sec.gov/. To use anonymous FTP, use your File Transfer Protocol software to connect to sec.gov and log in as user "anonymous" with a password of your electronic mail address.
2. Search for Chevron Corporation. Access the 10-K filing for the fiscal year ended December 31, 1995. Search or scroll to find the financial statements and related notes.
3. Answer the following questions related to the company's operational assets:
    a. Describe the company's depreciation and depletion policies.
    b. Effective October 1, 1995, the company adopted *SFAS 121*. What is the amount of the impairment write-downs recorded in 1995? What asset(s) were written down?
    c. Describe the company's policy for subsequent expenditures made for operational assets.

Financial Analysis Case 11–15
Depreciation and amortization

Federal Express Corporation

Refer to the financial statements and related disclosure notes of Federal Express Corporation in the appendix to Chapter 1.

Required:

1. What amount of depreciation and amortization did the company report in 1996?
2. What depreciation method is used for financial reporting purposes and what are the service lives and residual values of depreciable assets? What depreciation method is used for income tax purposes?
3. What amortization method is used for goodwill? Over what period?

FINANCIAL INSTRUMENTS

12

INVESTMENTS

In this chapter, you will learn that investments that companies make in the stock and debt securities of other companies are accounted for differently depending on the nature of the investments. For instance, you'll see that investment securities categorized as securities held to maturity are reported at amortized cost, while securities available for sale and trading securities are reported at their fair values.

In the second part of the chapter, we discuss the equity method—a completely different way to record and report investments in stock when specific characteristics indicate that the investor can significantly influence the operating and financial policies of the investee.

This chapter concludes our presentation of assets and begins our coverage of financial instruments.

LEARNING OBJECTIVES   **After studying this chapter, you should be able to:**

1. Explain how to identify and account for investments classified for reporting purposes as held to maturity.
2. Explain how to identify and account for investments classified for reporting purposes as available for sale.
3. Explain how to identify and account for investments classified for reporting purposes as trading securities.
4. Explain what constitutes significant influence by the investor over the operating and financial policies of the investee.
5. Understand the way investments are recorded and reported by the equity method.
6. Explain the adjustments made in the equity method when the cost of an investment exceeds the book value of the underlying net assets.

CRACKER BARREL OLD COUNTRY STORE

By the time you finish this chapter, you should be able to respond appropriately to the questions posed in this case. Compare your response to the solution provided at the end of the chapter.

You are the lone accounting major in your five-member group in your Business Policy class. A part of the case your group is working on is the analysis of the financial statements of Cracker Barrel Old Country Store. The company operates stores that provide a combination of restaurant and gift shop services to the motoring public.

The marketing major in the group is confused by the following disclosure note from Cracker Barrel's 1995 annual report:

3. Short-term and Long-term Investments (in part)

Effective July 30, 1993, the Company adopted *SFAS No. 115,* "Accounting for Certain Investments in Debt and Equity Securities". The Company's investment securities are classified as held-to-maturity under *SFAS No. 115* and, as a result, are carried at amortized cost. Unrealized holding gains and losses are not reported in the Company's financial statements, since the investments are classified as held-to-maturity under *SFAS No. 115*. The adoption of *SFAS No. 115* had no effect on the Company's financial statements.

The amortized cost and fair values of securities held-to-maturity at July 28, 1995, were as follows:

	Amortized Cost	Unrealized Gains	Unrealized Losses	Fair Value
U.S. Treasury and U.S. Government Agencies	$11,167,970	—	$129,415	$11,038,555
Obligations of states and political subdivisions	806,948	$1,313	—	808,261
Corporate debt securities	3,166,537	889	22,703	3,144,723
Short-term and long-term investments	$15,141,455	$2,202	$152,118	$14,991,539

The following table shows the maturity distribution of the Company's investment securities at July 28, 1995:

Maturity (Fiscal Years)	Amortized Cost	Fair Value
1996	$11,103,625	$11,030,272
1997–2000	3,975,806	3,899,200
2001–2005	62,024	62,067
Short-term and long-term investments	$15,141,455	$14,991,539

"What does 'unrealized holding gains and losses are not reported in the company financial statements' mean?" he wondered. "Didn't the value of the company's investments change by those amounts?"

QUESTIONS

1. How should you respond?
2. Suppose Cracker Barrel classified all of its investments as available for sale. How would the unrealized gains and losses be reported?

Most companies invest in financial instruments issued by other companies. For some investors, these investments represent ongoing affiliations with the companies whose securities are acquired. For instance, RJR Nabisco acquired all the common stock of Kraft General Foods to become a major player in the food industry. Kimberly-Clark Corp. acquired Scott Paper Co. in 1995 to create the no. 2-ranked personal-care company in the United States and to create a far more formidable competitor for Procter & Gamble Co. Some investments, though, are made not to obtain a favorable business relationship with another firm but simply to earn a return from the dividends or interest the securities pay or from increases in the market prices of the securities—the same prospective rewards that might motivate you to buy stocks, bonds, or other investment securities. With such diversity in investment objectives, it's understandable that no single accounting method is adequate to report every investment. As you'll discover when reading this chapter, investments are accounted for in six ways, depending on the nature of the investment relationship. Before we discuss these in detail, see the quick overview of the six approaches in Graphic 12–1.

GRAPHIC   12–1

Reporting Categories for Investments

Types of Securities	Characteristics	Reporting Category	Reported at
Debt	Investor has the "positive intent and ability" to hold to maturity.	Held to maturity	Amortized cost
Debt or equity	Held in active trading account for immediate resale.	Trading securities	Fair value (with unrealized gains and losses included in earnings)
Debt or equity	Investments not classified in another category.	Securities available for sale	Fair value (with unrealized gains and losses excluded from earnings and reported in shareholders' equity)
Equity	Fair value not determinable and the equity method is not appropriate.	Cost method	Cost
Equity	The investor can *significantly influence* the operating and financial policies of the investee.	Equity method	Cost, adjusted for subsequent growth of the investee
Equity	The investor *controls* the investee.	Consolidation	Financial statements are combined as if a single company

We discuss the first four categories in Part A of the chapter. Part B contains a description of the equity method as well as an abbreviated discussion of consolidated statements.

PART A ACCOUNTING FOR INVESTMENT SECURITIES

To finance its operations and often the expansion of those operations, a corporation raises funds by selling equity securities (common and preferred stock) and debt securities (bonds and notes). These securities are purchased as investments by individual investors, mutual funds, and also by other corporations. In later chapters we discuss equity and debt securities from the perspective of the issuing company. Our focus in this chapter is on the corporations that invest in securities issued by other corporations as well as those issued by governmental units (bonds, Treasury bills, and Treasury bonds).

For reporting purposes, all investments in *debt* securities and investments in *equity* securities that have readily determinable fair values (except those for which the equity method or consolidation is appropriate) are classified in three categories and accounted for differently depending on the classification as shown in Graphic 12–2.[1]

---

[1]"Accounting for Certain Investments in Debt and Equity Securities," *Statement of Financial Accounting Standards No. 115* (Norwalk, Conn.: FASB, 1993).

GRAPHIC   12–2

Reporting Categories for Investments in Marketable Equity and Debt Securities

Reporting Category	Classification Criteria
Held to maturity	Debt securities the investor has the positive intent and ability to hold to maturity
Trading securities	Debt or equity securities held for immediate resale
Securities available for sale	Debt or equity securities not classified as either securities held to maturity or trading securities

As you know, the purpose of accounting is to provide information useful in making decisions. What's most relevant for that purpose is not necessarily the same for each investment a company might make. For example, day-to-day changes in market value are less descriptive of investment success for an investment in corporate bonds that management *fully intends to hold until the bonds mature* than for an investment in the common stock of another corporation *acquired with the hope of profiting from market price changes*. Let's examine the three reporting classifications, one by one.

When an Investment Security Is Acquired to Be Held to Maturity

Learning objective 1
Explain how to identify and account for investments classified for reporting purposes as held to maturity.

OPENING CASE

Question 1

Changes in market value are irrelevant to an investor who will hold a security to its maturity regardless of those changes.

Unlike a share of stock, a bond or other debt security has a specified date on which it matures. On its maturity date, its face amount is paid to investors. In the meantime, interest equal to a specified percentage of the face amount is paid to investors on specified interest dates. However, just because the maturity amount is fixed and interest payments are fixed, this doesn't mean the market value of the security doesn't change. On the contrary, if market rates of interest *rise* after a fixed-rate security is purchased, the value of the now-below-market, fixed-interest payments declines. So, the market value of the investment falls. Conversely, if market rates of interest *fall* after a fixed-rate security is purchased, the fixed interest payments become relatively attractive, so the market value of the investment rises.

Are these movements in market price relevant? Not if the investor has no intention of selling the investment before maturity. Increases and decreases in the market value between the time a debt security is acquired and the day it matures to a prearranged maturity value aren't important if sale before maturity isn't an alternative. For this reason, if an investor has the positive intent and ability to hold the securities to maturity, investments in debt securities are classified as **held to maturity** and reported at amortized *cost* in the balance sheet.

A debt security is *not* classified as held to maturity if the investor might sell it in response to changes in market prices or interest rates, to meet the investor's liquidity needs, or similar factors. For instance, an investment would not be classified as held to maturity if the investor might sell it to achieve favorable tax treatment.

Accounting and reporting for investments in debt securities to be held to maturity will be described in Chapter 14 "Bonds and Long-Term Notes." This way we can more readily see that accounting by the company that issues bonds and by the company that invests in those bonds is opposite but parallel. Also, accounting for investments in a debt security whose cost is more or less than the security's maturity amount entails an understanding of procedures best explained in the context of accounting for the issuance of the securities. That will be the focus of our discussion in Chapter 14. For now, just note that these investments are recorded at cost, and holding gains or losses from market price changes are ignored. Only realized gains and losses are reported. Graphic 12–3 provides an example from the annual report of Midland Financial Group, Inc.

The Board (FASB) deliberately chose to make the held-to-maturity category restrictive because it believes that the use of amortized cost must be justified for each investment in a debt security. At acquisition, an entity should establish the positive intent and ability to hold a security to maturity, which is distinct from the mere absence of an intent to sell.[2]

[2]"Accounting for Certain Investments in Debt and Equity Securities," *Statement of Financial Accounting Standards No. 115* (Norwalk, Conn.: FASB, 1993), par. 46.

490

GRAPHIC   12-3

Investments in Securities
to Be Held to Maturity—
Midland Financial
Group, Inc.

Note (in Part): Investment Securities
Company holds both investment securities held to maturity and held for resale. . . . Investment securities held to maturity are stated at amortized cost, as the Company has the ability and intent to hold such securities to maturity. Realized gains and losses on the sale of investments are recognized in the determination of net income or loss on the basis of specific identification.

> Investments to be held to maturity are described in Chapter 14.

Because our discussion of investments in debt securities to be held to maturity is deferred until a later chapter, our focus in the first part of this chapter is accounting and reporting for investments referred to as securities available for sale and trading securities. These include investments in *debt* securities that are not classified as held to maturity and *equity* securities that have *readily determinable fair values*. Investments in both categories are reported at their fair values.

When the Fair Value Isn't Readily Determinable

The fair value of equity securities is considered readily determinable if selling prices (or bid-and-asked quotations) are currently available on a securities exchange.[3]

> An investment is carried and reported at cost when its fair value is *not* readily determinable.

If the fair value of an equity security is *not* readily determinable, an investment in that security is carried and reported at cost.[4] Any dividends received would be recognized as investment revenue, and a gain or loss would be reported only when actually realized, which is when the investment is sold.

Having a readily determinable fair value is not a requirement for *debt* securities to be reported at fair value. Even though quoted market prices aren't available for debt securities that don't trade regularly, the fair values of these securities can be reasonably estimated by determining the discounted present value of their interest and principal payments. You learned how to do this in Chapter 6 and will gain considerably more exposure to the process in Chapter 14.

When an Investment Is to be Held for an Unspecified Period of Time

Obviously, not all investments are held to maturity. When an investment is acquired to be held for an *unspecified period of time*, it is reported at the fair value of the investment securities on the reporting date. For these investments, fair value information is more relevant than for investments to be *held to maturity*.[5] For instance, consider an investment in debt. As interest rates rise or fall, the fair value of the investment will decrease or increase. Movements in fair values are irrelevant if the investment is to be held to maturity; the investor receives the same contracted interest payments and principal at maturity, regardless of changes in fair value.

> Investments in securities to be held for an *unspecified period of time* are reported at their fair values.

> Fair values are irrelevant for investments to be held to maturity.

On the other hand, for investments of unspecified length, changes in fair values and thus market returns provide an indication of management's success in deciding when to acquire the investment, when to sell it, whether to invest in fixed-rate or variable-rate securities, and whether to invest in long-term or short-term securities. This is demonstrated in Illustration 12–1.

> **The Board concluded that fair value information is more relevant than amortized cost information, in part because it reflects the effects of management decision to buy a financial asset at a specific time and then continue to hold it for an unspecified period of time.[6]**

---

[3]This includes the over-the-counter market when prices or quotations are publicly reported by the National Association of Securities Dealers Automated Quotations (NASDAQ) systems or by the National Quotation Bureau. If the security is traded only in a foreign market, fair value is readily determinable only if that foreign market is of a breadth and scope comparable to U.S. markets. "Accounting for Certain Investments in Debt and Equity Securities," *Statement of Financial Accounting Standards No. 115* (Norwalk, Conn.: FASB, 1993).

[4]An exception to this occurs when the equity method described in Part B of this chapter is appropriate.

[5]Investments to be held to maturity, of course, includes only debt securities.

[6]"Accounting for Certain Investments in Debt and Equity Securities," *Statement of Financial Accounting Standards No. 115* (Norwalk, Conn.: FASB, 1993), par. 51.

ILLUSTRATION   12–1

Investments Held for
Unspecified Periods

good example ↓

American Capital buys and sells both debt and equity securities of other companies as investments. The following transactions during December 1997 pertain to the investment portfolio. The company's fiscal year-end is December 31.

December	18	Received cash dividends of $2 million on an investment in ABM Corporation common shares, the only securities in the investment portfolio.
	20	Sold the ABM Corporation common shares for $13 million. These were purchased for $12 million.
	21	Acquired two new investments costing:

| | | Millington-Frazier bonds | $30 million |
| | | Bartlett Corporation common shares | 20 million |

| | 31 | The market prices of the investments are: |

| | | Millington-Frazier bonds | $33 million |
| | | Bartlett Corporation common shares | 19 million |

Investment Revenue.   The journal entry to record the cash dividend is:

Dividend and interest income from all investment securities is included in earnings.

December 18	($ in millions)	
Cash	2	
Investment revenue		2

Sale of Investments.   The journal entry to record the sale of the ABM Corporation common shares is:

Realized gains and losses are included in earnings.

December 20	($ in millions)	
Cash	13	
Investment in ABM Corporation shares		12
Gain on sale of investments		1

Purchase of Investments.   The journal entry to record the purchase of investment securities is:

All investment securities are initially recorded at cost.

December 21	($ in millions)	
Investment in Millington-Frazier bonds	30	
Investment in Bartlett Corporation shares	20	
Cash		50

Adjusting Investments to Fair Value.   Reporting investments at their fair values means adjusting their carrying amounts for changes in fair value after their acquisition (or since the last reporting date if they were held at that time). These changes are called *unrealized holding gains and losses* because they haven't yet been realized through the sale of the securities. They must be recorded (or updated) any time financial statements are prepared for external use. The journal entry to adjust the investments in our illustration to fair value at year-end is:

All investment securities (except those held to maturity) are adjusted to their fair values on each reporting date.

December 31	($ in millions)	
Investment in Millington-Frazier bonds	3	
Unrealized holding gain on investments ($33 – 30)		3
Unrealized holding loss on investments ($19 – 20)	1	
Investment in Bartlett Corporation shares		1

The way we report unrealized holding gains and losses in the financial statements depends on whether the investments are classified as securities available for sale or as trading securities. The trading securities category concerns primarily banks and other financial institutions who frequently buy and sell securities expecting to earn profits on short-term differences in price, particularly differences in "bid" and "ask" prices, and who actively maintain trading accounts to manage those investments. On the other hand, securities available for sale is a more general classification that includes all investments other than trading securities or securities to be held to maturity. So, we'll discuss the less restrictive securities-available-for-sale category first.

When Investment Securities Are Classified as Available for Sale

Learning objective 2
Explain how to identify and account for investments classified for reporting purposes as available for sale.

OPENING CASE

Question 2

All investments in debt and equity securities that don't fit the definitions of the other reporting categories are classified as **available for sale.** Individual securities available for sale are classified as either current or noncurrent assets, depending on how long they're likely to be held.

Investments in securities available for sale are reported at fair value. Holding gains and losses from retaining securities during periods of price change are *not* included in the determination of income for the period. Instead, they are accumulated and reported as a separate component of shareholders' equity. That is, an unrealized holding gain would increase shareholders' equity; an unrealized holding loss would decrease shareholders' equity. By definition, these securities are not acquired for the purpose of profiting from short-term market price changes, so gains and losses from holding these securities while prices change are not considered relevant performance measures to be included in earnings.

Illustration 12–2 offers an example:

ILLUSTRATION   12–2

Investments in Securities Available for Sale

Refer to Illustration 12–1. Assume American Capital buys securities not intending to profit from short-term differences in price or necessarily to hold debt securities to maturity but to have them available for sale when circumstances warrant.

The journal entries to record the cash dividend, the sale of the ABM Corporation common shares, and the purchase of the investment securities and to adjust the investments to fair value at year-end would be precisely the same regardless of whether the investments are available for sale or are trading securities.

Reporting Investments in Securities Available for Sale.   On the 1997 balance sheet, investments available for sale are reported at the fair value of the investment securities ($33 million + $19 million), but the *net* unrealized holding gain is not reported on the income statement. Instead, it's reported as a separate component of shareholders' equity:

Balance Sheet

($ in millions)

Securities **available for sale** are reported at fair value.

Assets:	
Cash and cash equivalents	$xx
Short-term investments at fair value (cost $50)*	52
Accounts receivable	xx
✦	✦
✦	✦

Net unrealized holding gains or losses are reported as a separate component of shareholders' equity.

Shareholders' Equity:	
✦	✦
✦	✦
Net unrealized holding gain on investments	2
✦	✦

*Assumes both securities are intended to be held less than one year; otherwise long-term investments.

An example from the 1995 annual report of Cisco Systems is shown in Graphic 12–4.

4. Investments

Effective August 1, 1994, the Company adopted *SFAS No. 115,* "Accounting for Certain Investments in Debt and Equity Securities." This statement requires the company to classify debt and equity securities into one of three categories: held-to-maturity, trading, or available-for-sale. At July 30, 1995, substantially all of the Company's investments were classified as available-for-sale, and the difference between the cost and fair market value of those securities, net of the tax effect, is shown as a separate component of shareholders' equity.

The following table summarizes the Company's securities at July 30, 1995:

Issue	Amortized Cost	Unrealized Gains	Unrealized Losses	Market Value
U.S. government notes and bonds	$200,902	$ 665	$(2,963)	$198,604
State, municipal, and county government notes and bonds	425,225	1,599	(4,995)	421,829
Foreign government notes and bonds	38,841	433	—	39,274
Corporate notes and bonds	61,052	77	(242)	60,887
Corporate equity securities	2,900	88,115	—	91,015
Short-term and long-term investments	$728,920	$90,889	$(8,200)	$811,609

Additional Consideration

Be sure to note that the effect on *total* shareholders' equity is precisely the same as if the holding gains and losses had been included in earnings. The difference is that, if included in earnings, the impact would be an increase or decrease in retained earnings rather than a separate component of shareholders' equity.

Selling Securities Previously Adjusted to Fair Value.   To see how to record the sale of a security that was previously adjusted to fair value, let's assume the Millington-Frazier bonds are sold on January 29, 1998, for $34 million. The fair value of the bonds has risen $4 million since the investment was acquired. Three million dollars of that rise occurred in 1997 but wasn't recognized in 1997 earnings because it wasn't yet realized by selling the investment. Now, the entire $4 million gain is recognized in 1998 when it is actually realized:

Holding gains and losses from securities available for sale are included in earnings when they are realized by selling the securities.

January 29, 1998	($ in millions)	
Cash	34	
Unrealized holding gain on investments (balance)	3	
Gain on sale of investments (to balance)		4
Investment in Millington-Frazier bonds ($30 + 3)		33

Now suppose, the market price of the Bartlett Corporation common shares has risen by $1 million to the original price American Capital paid for the investment ($20 million), and the shares are sold on February 13. Because the investment is sold at cost, the holding loss in 1997 is offset by a subsequent holding gain during 1998. As a result, no gain or loss is realized:

Unrealized holding gains or losses often are offset by subsequent holding losses or gains.

February 13, 1998	($ in millions)	
Cash	20	
Unrealized holding loss on investments		1
Investment in Bartlett Corporation shares ($20 – 1)		19

Impairment of Securities Available for Sale.

Occasionally, the fair value of a security will decline for a specific reason that's judged to be other than temporary. For instance, a bankruptcy filing might indicate a degradation in the creditworthiness of the issuer of bonds. An investor holding the bonds as an investment might conclude that a concurrent drop in the market price of the bonds is an other-than-temporary impairment. In that case, when the investment is written down to its fair value, the amount of the write-down should be treated as though it were a realized loss (meaning it's included in income for the period.) After the other-than-temporary write-down, the normal treatment of unrealized gains or losses is resumed; that is, changes in fair value are reported as a separate component of shareholders' equity. The accounting treatment of an impairment due to a troubled debt restructuring is described in Appendix B.

When Investment Securities Are Classified as Trading Securities

The approach used to account for securities available for sale is modified somewhat when the securities a company invests in are classified as **trading securities.** Specifically, unrealized holding gains or losses on trading securities are reported on the income statement as if they actually had been realized. Keep in mind as you study this section that relatively few investments are classified this way because only banks and other financial operations invest in securities in the manner and for the purpose necessary to be categorized as trading securities.

Some companies—primarily financial institutions—actively and frequently buy and sell securities expecting to earn profits on short-term differences in price. Investments in debt or equity securities acquired principally for the purpose of selling them in the near term are classified as trading securities. By definition, these are short-term investments to be reported among the investor's current assets.

Why Report Holding Gains and Losses in Earnings?

When securities are actively managed, as trading securities are, with the expressed intent of profiting from short-term market price changes, the gains and losses that result from holding securities during market price changes are appropriate measures of success or lack of success in that endeavor. For that reason, it's appropriate to report these holding gains and losses in earnings for the period of change, even if they haven't yet been realized through the sale of the securities. To see how, let's modify our illustration to assume the investment securities we considered earlier are trading securities, rather than securities available for sale. Consider Illustration 12–3:

> Refer to Illustration 12–2. Assume American Capital frequently and actively buys and sells both debt and equity securities, intending to profit from short-term differences in price. The transactions during December 1997 that were described earlier pertain to the trading account.

As mentioned earlier, the cash dividend, the sale of the ABM Corporation common shares, the purchase of the investment securities, and the adjustments to fair value are recorded in precisely the same way as for investments classified as available for sale. Only the way the holding gains and losses are reported differs.

Reporting Investments in Trading Securities.

For trading securities, unrealized holding gains and losses are included in earnings of the period the changes in value occur. On the 1997 balance sheet, the investments in our illustration are reported at the fair value of the investment securities ($33 million + $19 million), and the *net* unrealized holding gain is reported on the income statement:

Balance Sheet

	($ in millions)
Assets:	
Cash and cash equivalents	$xx
Short-term investments at fair value (cost $50)	52
Accounts receivable	xx
✦	✦
✦	✦

Income Statement

◆	◆
◆	◆
Net unrealized holding gain on investments	2
◆	◆

> Unrealized holding gains and losses are included in earnings for trading securities only.

Selling Trading Securities Previously Adjusted to Fair Value. Now assume the same scenario we used to illustrate the sale of securities available for sale. The Millington-Frazier bonds are sold on January 29, 1998, for $34 million. The fair value of the bonds has risen $4 million since the investment in trading securities was acquired. Three million dollars of that rise occurred in 1997 and was recognized in 1997 earnings, even though the gain wasn't actually realized at that point. Now, the remaining $1 million of the gain is recognized in 1998 as the entire gain is realized by selling the trading securities:

> Because holding gains and losses are included in earnings when they occur, only gains and losses that occur since the last reporting date are recognized during the current reporting period.

January 29	($ in millions)
Cash	34
Investment in Millington-Frazier bonds ($30 + 3)	33
Gain on sale of investments	1

Also assume the market price of the Bartlett Corporation common shares rises by $1 million to the original price American Capital paid for the investment, and the shares are sold on February 13. Although the investment is sold at cost, market changes produced a holding loss in 1997 that was not realized because management chose not to sell the investment. That loss was recognized in 1997 earnings. Now, when the investment is sold, the subsequent price rise during 1998 has produced a gain:

February 13	($ in millions)
Cash	20
Investment in Bartlett Corporation shares ($20 – 1)	19
Gain on sale of investments	1

Transfers between Reporting Categories

> A transfer of a security between reporting categories is accounted for at fair value and in accordance with the new reporting classification.

At acquisition, an investor assigns debt and equity securities to one of the three reporting classifications—held to maturity, available for sale, or trading. At each reporting date, the appropriateness of the classification is reassessed. For instance, if the investor no longer has the ability to hold certain securities to maturity and will now hold them for resale, those securities would be reclassified. When a security is reclassified between two reporting categories, the security is transferred at its fair value on the date of transfer. Any unrealized holding gain or loss at reclassification should be accounted for *in a manner consistent with the classification into which the security is being transferred.* Reclassifications are quite unusual, so when they occur, footnote disclosures should describe the circumstances that resulted in the transfers. Other footnote disclosures are described in a later section.

CONCEPT REVIEW EXERCISE

VARIOUS INVESTMENT SECURITIES

Diversified Services, Inc., offers a variety of business services, including financial services through its escrow division. Diversified entered into the following investment activities during the last month of 1997 and the first week of 1998. Diversified's fiscal year ends on December 31. The only securities held by Diversified at December 1 were 12 million common shares of Shelby Laminations, Inc., purchased in November for $48 million.

December 1	Purchased $30 million of 12% bonds of Vince-Gill Amusement Corporation and $24 million of 10% bonds of Eastern Waste Disposal Corporation, both at face value and both to be held until they mature. Interest on each bond issue is payable semiannually on November 30 and May 31.
9	Sold one-half of the Shelby Laminations common shares for $25 million.
29	Received cash dividends of $1.5 million from the Shelby Laminations common shares.
30	Purchased U.S. Treasury bonds for $5.8 million as trading securities, hoping to earn profits on short-term differences in prices.
31	Recorded the necessary adjusting entry(s) relating to the investments.

The market price of the Shelby Lamination's common stock was $4.25 per share. The fair values of the bond investments were $32 million for Vince-Gill Amusement Corporation and $20 million for Eastern Waste Disposal Corporation. A sharp rise in short-term interest rates on the last day of the year caused the fair value of the Treasury bonds to fall to $5.7 million.

1998

January	7	Sold the remaining Shelby Laminations common shares for $26 million.

Required:
Prepare the appropriate journal entry for each transaction or event and show the amounts that would be reported on the company's 1997 income statement relative to these investments.

CONCEPT REVIEW EXERCISE   SOLUTION

December 1	Purchased $30 million of 12% bonds of Vince-Gill Amusement Corporation and $24 million of 10% bonds of Eastern Waste Disposal Corporation, both at face value and both to be held until they mature. Interest on each bond issue is payable semiannually on November 30 and May 31.

	($ in millions)	
Investment in Vince-Gill Amusement bonds	30	
Investment in Eastern Waste Disposal bonds	24	
Cash		54

December 9   Sold one-half of the Shelby Laminations common shares for $25 million.

	($ in millions)	
Cash (selling price)	25	
Investment in Shelby Laminations common shares ($48 × 1/2)		24
Gain on sale of investments (difference)		1

December 29   Received cash dividends of $1.5 million from the Shelby Laminations common shares.

	($ in millions)	
Cash	1.5	
Investment revenue		1.5

December 30   Purchased U.S. Treasury bonds for $5.8 million as trading securities, hoping to earn profits on short-term differences in prices.

	($ in millions)	
Investment in U.S. Treasury bonds	5.8	
Cash		5.8

December 31   Recorded the necessary adjusting entry(s) relating to the investments.

Accrued interest (one month):		($ in millions)
Investment revenue receivable—Vince-Gill Amusement		
($30 million × 12% × ¹/₁₂)	0.3	
Investment revenue receivable—Eastern Waste Disposal		
($24 million × 10% × ¹/₁₂)	0.2	
Investment revenue		0.5
Fair value adjustments:		
Unrealized holding loss on investments ($5.7 – $5.8 million)	0.1	
Investment in U.S. Treasury bonds		0.1
Investment in Shelby Laminations common shares	1.5	
Unrealized holding gain on investments		
([12 million shares 3 ½ × $4.25] – [$48 million × ½])		1.5

Note: Securities held to maturity are not adjusted to fair value.

Reported on the 1997 income statement:	($ in millions)
Investment revenue ($1.5 + 0.5)	$2.0
Gain on sale of investments (Shelby)	1.0
Unrealized holding loss on investments (Treasury bonds)	(0.1)

Note: The unrealized holding gain for the Shelby Laminations common shares is not included in income because it pertains to securities available for sale rather than trading securities.

1998

January   7   Sold the remaining Shelby Laminations common shares for $26 million.

	($ in millions)
Cash (selling price)	26.0
Unrealized holding gain on investments	
(balance after adjusting entry)	1.5
Investment in Shelby Laminations common shares	
(balance after adjusting entry)	25.5
Gain on sale of investments (difference)	2.0

Financial Statement Presentation and Disclosure

Trading securities are current assets by definition. Held-to-maturity and available-for-sale securities are either current or noncurrent depending on when they are expected to mature or to be sold. However, it's not necessary that a company report individual amounts for the three categories of investments—held to maturity, available for sale, or trading—on the face of the balance sheet as long as that information is presented in the disclosure notes.[7]

On the statement of cash flows, inflows and outflows of cash from buying and selling trading securities are considered operating activities. But because held-to-maturity and available-for-sale securities are not purchased and held principally to be sold in the near term, cash flows from the purchase, sale, and maturity of these securities are considered investing activities.

Investors should disclose the following in the disclosure notes for each year presented:

- Aggregate fair value.
- Gross realized and unrealized holding gains.

---

[7]"Accounting for Certain Investments in Debt and Equity Securities," *Statement of Financial Accounting Standards No. 115* (Norwalk, Conn.: FASB, 1993), par. 18.

- Gross realized and unrealized holding losses.
- Change in net unrealized holding gains and losses.
- Amortized cost basis by major security type.

Information about maturities should be reported for debt securities by disclosing the fair value and cost for at least four maturity groupings: (a) within 1 year, (b) after 1 year through 5 years, (c) after 5 years through 10 years, and (d) after 10 years.[8]

PART B — THE EQUITY METHOD

When a company invests in the equity securities (primarily common or preferred stock) of another company, the investor can benefit either (a) *directly* through dividends and/or market price appreciation or (b) *indirectly* through the creation of desirable operating relationships with the investee. The way we report a company's investment in the stock of another company depends on the nature of the relationship between the investor and the investee.

For reporting purposes, we classify the investment relationship in one of three ways, and account for the investment differently depending on the classification, as shown in Graphic 12–5:

GRAPHIC   12–5

Reporting Classifications for Investment Relationships

> The **equity method** is used when an investor can't control, but can significantly influence the investee.

Classification	Reporting Method
The investor *cannot* significantly influence the investee (usually <20% equity ownership)	Varies by reporting category (see Part A of this chapter)
The investor can significantly influence the operating and financial policies of the investee (usually 20%–50% equity ownership)	Equity method
The investor controls the investee (usually >50% equity ownership)	Consolidation

We focused on the first classification in Part A of the chapter. Now, let's turn our attention to the second classification—the **equity method**. A detailed discussion of the third classification—consolidated financial statements—is beyond the scope of this book. That discussion often is a major focus of the advanced accounting course or is taught as a separate consolidations course. In this chapter, we'll briefly overview the subject only to provide perspective to aspects of the equity method that purposely mimic some effects of consolidation. Let's do that now, before addressing the specifics of the equity method.

How the Equity Method Relates to Consolidated Financial Statements

If a company acquires 51% or more of the voting stock of another company, it's said to have a controlling interest because by voting those shares, the investor actually can control the company acquired. The investor is referred to as the *parent;* the investee is termed the *subsidiary.* For reporting purposes (although not legally), the parent and subsidiary are considered to be a single reporting entity, and their financial statements are *consolidated.* Both companies continue to operate as separate legal entities and therefore report separate financial statements. However, because of the controlling interest, the parent company also reports consolidated financial statements. So, the parent prepares two sets of financial statements—one as a separate entity and another as a consolidated entity.

> **Consolidated financial statements** combine the individual elements of the parent and subsidiary statements.

Consolidated financial statements combine the separate financial statements of the parent and the subsidiary each period into a single aggregate set of financial statements as if there were only one company. This entails an item-by-item combination of the parent and subsidiary statements (after first eliminating any amounts that are shared by the separate financial statements).[9]

---

[8]Ibid., par. 20.

[9]This avoids double counting those amounts in the consolidated statements. For example, amounts owed by one company to the other are represented by accounts payable in one set of financial statements and accounts receivable in the other. These amounts are not included in the statements of the consolidated entity because a company can't "owe itself."

The acquired company's assets are included in consolidated financial statements at their fair values and the difference between the acquisition price and the fair value of the acquired net assets is recorded as goodwill.

For instance, if the parent has $8 million cash and the subsidiary has $3 million cash, the consolidated balance sheet would report $11 million cash.

Two aspects of the consolidation process are of particular interest to us in understanding the equity method. In consolidated financial statements in which an acquisition is viewed as a purchase of the acquired company, the acquired company's assets are included in the financial statements at their fair values rather than their book values.[10] Secondly, if the acquisition price is more than the fair value of the acquired net assets (assets less liabilities), that difference is recorded as an intangible asset—goodwill.[11] We'll return to the discussion of these two aspects when we reach the point in our discussion of the equity method where their influence is felt. As we'll see, the equity method is in many ways a partial consolidation.

We use the equity method when the investor owns less than 51% of the voting shares and therefore can't control the investee but can exercise significant influence over the operating and financial policies of an investee.

What Is Significant Influence?

Usually an investor can exercise **significant influence** over the investee when it owns between 20% and 50% of the investee's voting shares.

When effective control is absent because the investor owns less than 51% of the voting shares, the investor still may be able to exercise significant influence over the operating and financial policies of the investee. This would be the case if the investor owns a large percentage of the outstanding shares relative to other shareholders. By voting those shares as a block, decisions often can be swayed in the direction the investor desires. When significant influence exists, the investment should be accounted for by the equity method. It should be presumed, in the absence of evidence to the contrary, that the investor exercises **significant influence** over the investee when it owns between 20% and 50% of the investee's voting shares.[12]

Additional Consideration

It's possible that a company that owns over 20% of the voting shares cannot exercise significant influence over the investee. If, for instance, another company or a small group of shareholders owns 51% or more of the shares, that company controls the investee regardless of how other investors vote their shares. *FASB Interpretation No. 35* provides this and other examples of indications that an investor may be unable to exercise significant influence:

- The investee challenges the investor's ability to exercise significant influence (through litigation or complaints to regulators).
- The investor surrenders significant shareholder rights in a signed agreement.
- The investor is unable to acquire sufficient information about the investee to apply the equity method.
- The investor tries and fails to obtain representation on the board of directors of the investee.[13]

In such cases, the equity method would be inappropriate.

Conversely, it's also possible that a company that owns *less than* 20% of the voting shares *is* able to exercise significant influence over the investee. Ability to exercise significant influence with less than 20% ownership might be indicated, for example, by having an officer of the investor corporation on the board of directors of the investee corporation or by having, say, 18% of the voting shares while no other investor owns more than $1/2$%. In such cases the equity method would be appropriate.

---

[10]In your consolidations course, you'll learn that when specific conditions are met, an acquisition is viewed as a pooling of interests rather than a purchase. In that case, the acquired company's assets are included in the financial statements at their book values rather than their fair market values. Pooling of interests accounting is irrelevant to the equity method.

[11]This is the usual case because most companies are worth more than the sum of the values of individual components of the company due to reputation, longevity, managerial expertise, customer loyalty, or a host of other possibilities.

[12]Shareholders are the owners of the corporation. By voting their shares, it is they who determine the makeup of the board of directors—who, in turn, appoint officers—who, in turn, manage the company. Common stock usually is the class of shares given voting privileges. However, a corporation can create classes of preferred shares that also have voting rights. This is discussed at greater length in Chapter 19.

[13]"Criteria for Applying the Equity Method of Accounting for Investments in Common Stock," *FASB Interpretation No. 35* (Stamford, Conn.: FASB, 1981).

A Single Entity Concept

Much like consolidation, the equity method views the investor and investee collectively as a special type of single entity (as if the two companies were one company). However, using the equity method, the investor doesn't include separate financial statement items of the investee on an item-by-item basis as in consolidation. Instead, the investor reports its equity interest in the investee as a single investment account.

Under the equity method, the investor recognizes investment income equal to its percentage share (based on share ownership) of the net income earned by the investee rather than the portion of that net income received as cash dividends. The rationale for this approach is the presumption of the equity method that the fortunes of the investor and investee are sufficiently intertwined that as the investee prospers, the investor prospers proportionately. Stated differently, as the investee earns additional net assets, the investor's share of those net assets increases.

Initially, the investment is recorded at cost. The carrying amount of this investment subsequently is:

- Increased by the investor's percentage share of the investee's net income (or decreased by its share of a loss).
- Decreased by dividends declared.

Let's look at the example in Illustration 12–4.

Further Adjustments

When the investor's expenditure to acquire an investment exceeds the book value of the underlying net assets acquired, additional adjustments to both the investment account and investment revenue are needed. The purpose is to approximate the effects of consolidation, without actually consolidating financial statements. More specifically, both the investment account and investment revenue are adjusted for differences between net income reported by the investee and what that amount would have been if consolidation procedures had been followed. Let's look closer at what that means.

As mentioned earlier, consolidated financial statements report (a) the acquired company's assets at their fair market values rather than their book values and (b) goodwill for the excess of the acquisition price over the fair value of the acquired net assets.

Each of these two consequences of the consolidation process has an effect on income, and it's the income effect that we're interested in when applying the equity method. First, increasing asset balances to their fair values usually will result in higher expenses. For instance, if buildings, equipment, or other depreciable assets are written up to higher values, depreciation expense will be higher during their remaining useful lives. Likewise, if the recorded amount of inventory is increased, cost of goods sold will be higher when the inventory is sold.

Similarly, recording goodwill will result in higher expenses. Goodwill is an intangible asset whose cost is amortized as goodwill amortization expense during the years expected to benefit from its acquisition, not to exceed 40 years. As a consequence, then, of both (a) increasing asset balances to fair value and (b) recording goodwill, expenses will rise and income will fall. It is this negative effect on income that the equity method seeks to imitate.

Recall that our illustration provides the following information regarding Embassy Message Corporation's net assets at the time American Capital Corporation pays $200 million for a 25% interest in the company:

Net assets at acquisition:	($ in millions)
Fair value:	$600
Book value	480

If we assume the difference between the book value of the net assets and their fair market value is attributable to depreciable assets having a fair market value in excess of their undepreciated cost, we can determine the additional amounts to be expensed as shown in Graphic 12–6.

In other words, American Capital paid $200 million for identifiable net assets worth $150 million, and the $50 million difference is attributable to goodwill.

Amortization of Purchased Goodwill   Recall from Chapter 11 that goodwill (or any other intangible asset) should be amortized over its estimated useful life, not to exceed 40 years. Let's suppose 25 years is an appropriate amortization period. Both investment revenue and the investment would be reduced by $2 million as follows:

Goodwill Amortization

($ in millions)

Investment revenue ($50 million ÷ 25 years) 2

   Investment in equity securities 2

ILLUSTRATION   12–4

Equity Method

good examples ↓

On January 2, 1997, American Capital Corporation purchased 25% of the outstanding common shares of Embassy Message Corporation for $200 million. The following information is available regarding Embassy Message Corporation during 1997:

	($ in millions)
Net assets at acquisition:*	
Fair value	$600
Book value	480
1997 net income	100
1997 dividends declared and paid	20

When a company invests in shares of another corporation, the asset initially is recorded at cost. In accordance with the cost principle, the recorded amount includes any brokerage fees or commissions paid to acquire the shares.

Initial Acquisition

($ in millions)

Investment in equity securities (cost of shares) 200

  Cash 200

Following the acquisition, the investment account is adjusted for the investor's percentage share of net income reported by the investee.†

Investee Net Income

Investment in equity securities 25

  Investment revenue (25% share of $100 million earned) 25

Adjusting the investment account reflects the equity method's presumption that as the investee earns additional net assets, the investor's equity interest in those net assets increases proportionately. This reasoning also supports recognizing investment revenue as the investee earns net income, not when those earnings actually are distributed as dividends.

In fact, when the investor actually receives dividends, the investment account is *reduced* accordingly:

Dividends

Cash (25% share of $20 million dividends paid) 5

  Investment in equity securities 5

Because investment revenue is recognized as it is earned by the investee, it would be inappropriate to recognize revenue again as earnings are distributed as dividends. Instead, the dividend distribution is viewed as a *reduction of the investee's net assets,* indicating that the investor's equity interest in those net assets declines proportionately.

*Recall that net assets are equivalent to shareholders' equity. Each is what's left over after creditor claims have been subtracted from assets: $\underbrace{\text{Assets} - \text{Liabilities}}_{\text{Net assets}}$ = Shareholders' equity

†If any portion of the investee's net income was reported by the investee as an extraordinary item, the investor also would report the same proportion of its share as an extraordinary item. In this illustration, for instance, if $4 million, or 4%, of Embassy Message Corporation's income had been reported as an extraordinary gain, then American Capital Corporation would report 4% of its $25 million share, or $1 million, as an extraordinary gain as well.

> The *cost principle* governs the acquisition of assets.

> As the investee earns additional net assets, the investment in those net assets increases.

> As the investee prospers, the investor prospers proportionately.

> As the investee distributes net assets as dividends, the investment in those net assets declines.

GRAPHIC   12–6

Determining Amounts to Amortize

	Investee Net Assets ↓	Net Assets Purchased ↓	Difference Attributed to ↓
		($ in millions)	
Cost		$200	
Fair value:	$600 × 25% =	$150	Goodwill: $50
Book value:	$480 × 25% =	$120	Undervaluation of assets: $30

Amortization of Additional Depreciation. Let's also assume that the depreciable assets whose fair value exceeds book value have an average remaining useful life of 10 years and are being depreciated by the straight-line method. Investment revenue and the investment both would be reduced by the negative income effect of the extra depreciation the higher fair value would cause:

Additional Depreciation:	($ in millions)
Investment revenue ($30 million ÷ 10 years)	3
Investment in equity securities	3

Reporting the Investment

The market value of the investment shares at the end of the reporting period is irrelevant when using the equity method. The investment account is not reported at market as it is for investments not accounted for by the equity method.

The investment account is reported at its original cost, increased by the investor's share of the investee's net income (adjusted for additional expenses like depreciation and amortization), and decreased by the portion of those earnings actually received as dividends. In other words, the investment account represents the investor's share of the investee's net assets initially acquired, adjusted for the investor's share of the subsequent increase in the investee's net assets (net assets earned and not yet distributed as dividends).

Investment in Equity Securities

			($ in millions)	
Cost	200			
Share of income	25			
		5	Dividends	
		2	Goodwill amortization	
		3	Depreciation	
Balance	215			

> The carrying amount of the investment is its initial cost plus the investor's equity in the undistributed earnings of the investee.

When the Investee Reports a Net Loss. Our illustration assumed the investee earned net income. If the investee reports a *net loss* instead, the investment account would be *decreased* by the investor's share of the investee's net loss (adjusted for additional expenses).

When the Investment Is Acquired in Mid-Year. Obviously, we've simplified the illustration by assuming the investment was acquired at the beginning of 1997, entailing a full year's income, dividends, and amortization. In the more likely event that an investment is acquired sometime after the beginning of the year, the application of the equity method is easily modified to include the appropriate fraction of each of those amounts. For example, if the investment in our illustration had been acquired on October 1 rather than January 2, we would simply record income, dividends, and amortization for three months, or $3/12$ of the year. This would result in the following adjustments to the investment account:

Investment in Equity Securities

			($ in millions)	
Cost	200.00			
Share of income ($3/12 \times \$25$)	6.25			
		1.25 ($3/12 \times \$5$)	Dividends*	
		.50 ($3/12 \times \$2$)	Goodwill amortization	
		.75 ($3/12 \times \$3$)	Depreciation	
Balance	203.75			

> Adjustments to the investment account the first year are adjusted for fraction of the year the investor has owned the investment.

*This example assumes quarterly dividends and that the dividend was declared for the October 1–December 31 quarter. Investors receive the entire amount of any dividends declared while they own stock, regardless of how long they have held the shares.

Additional Consideration

It's possible that the investor's proportionate share of investee losses could exceed the carrying amount of the investment. If this happens, the investor should discontinue applying the equity method until the investor's share of subsequent investee earnings has equaled losses not recognized during the time the equity method was discontinued. This avoids reducing the investment account below zero.

Owens-Corning Fiberglass Corporation reported its investments in affiliated companies for which it exercised significant influence as shown in Graphic 12–7.

GRAPHIC   12–7

Equity Method—Owens-Corning Fiberglass Corporation

	(In millions of dollars)	
	1994	**1993**
Total current assets	$ 930	$ 827
Other Assets:		
Goodwill, less accumulated amortization of $14 million in 1994 and $12 million in 1993 (Note 4)	151	77
Investments in affiliates (Note 13)	74	63
Deferred income taxes (Note 9)	308	428
Insurance for asbestos litigation claims (Note 21)	556	643
Other noncurrent assets	122	81
Total other assets	$1,211	$1,292

Summary of Significant Accounting Policies

Investments in Affiliates

Investments in affiliates are accounted for by using the equity method, under which the Company's share of earnings of these affiliates is reflected in incomes as earned and dividends are credited against the investment in affiliates when received.

What if Conditions Change?

A Change from the Equity Method to Another Method. When the investor's level of influence changes, it may be necessary to change from the equity method to another method. This could happen, for instance, if a sale of shares causes the investor's ownership interest to fall from, say, 25% to 15%, resulting in the equity method's no longer being appropriate.[14] When this situation happens, *no adjustment* is made to the remaining carrying amount of the investment. Instead, the equity method is simply discontinued and the new method applied from then on. The balance in the investment account when the equity method is discontinued would serve as the new cost basis for writing the investment up or down to market value on the next set of financial statements.

> When the investor changes from another method to the equity method, the investment account is retroactively adjusted to the equity method.

A Change from Another Method to the Equity Method. On the other hand, when a change *to* the equity method is appropriate, because the investor's ownership interest rises from 15% to 25%, the investment account should be retroactively adjusted to the balance that would have existed if the equity method always had been used. As income also would have been different, retained earnings would be adjusted as well. For example, assume it's determined that an investor's share of investee net income, reduced by dividends, was $4 million during a period when the equity method was not used, but additional purchases of shares cause the equity method to be appropriate now. The following journal entry would record the change:

> Both the investment and retained earnings would be increased by the investor's share of the undistributed earnings in years prior to a change to the equity method.

	($ in millions)	
Investment in equity securities	4	
Retained earnings (investment revenue from the equity method)		4

---

[14]When a portion of an equity method investment is sold, the investor removes from the investment account the appropriate proportion of the carrying value and records a gain or loss for the difference between that amount and the selling price.

In addition to the adjustment of account balances, financial statements would be restated to the equity method for each year reported in the annual report for comparative purposes. Also, the income effect for years prior to those shown in the comparative statements is reported on the statement of retained earnings as an adjustment to beginning retained earnings of the earliest year reported. A disclosure note also should describe the change. Reporting accounting changes is described in more detail in Chapter 21.

Additional Consideration

Effect on Deferred Income Taxes:

Investment revenue is recorded by the equity method when income is earned by the investee, but that revenue is not taxed until it's actually received as cash dividends. This creates a temporary difference between book income and taxable income. You will learn in Chapter 16 that the investor must report a deferred tax liability for the income tax that eventually will be paid when the income eventually is received as dividends.

You also should note that corporations that own stock in other corporations are permitted by tax laws to exclude from taxation 70% of the dividends they receive. In other words, only 30% of the amounts received as dividends are taxable. Therefore, when a deferred tax liability is recorded for undistributed earnings of an equity-method investee, the liability should be determined by multiplying the tax rate times 30% of the income that eventually will be received as dividends.

If an Equity Method Investment Is Sold

When an investment being reported by the equity method is sold, a gain or loss is recognized if the selling price is more or less than the carrying amount (book value) of the investment. For example, let's continue our illustration and assume American Capital Corporation sells its investment in Embassy Message Corporation at the end of 1997 for $234 million. A journal entry would record a gain as follows:

	($ in millions)	
Cash (proceeds from sale)	234	
Investment in equity securities (balance)		215
Gain on sale of investment (difference)		19

When an equity method investment is sold, a gain or loss is recognized for the difference between its selling price and its carrying amount.

CONCEPT REVIEW EXERCISE   THE EQUITY METHOD

Delta Apparatus bought 40% of Clay Crating Corp.'s outstanding common shares on January 2, 1997, for $540 million. The carrying amount of Clay Crating's net assets (shareholders' equity) at the purchase date totaled $900 million. Book values and fair values were the same for all financial statement items except for inventory and buildings, for which fair values exceeded book values by $25 million and $225 million, respectively. All inventory on hand at the acquisition date was sold during 1997. The buildings have average remaining useful lives of 18 years. Any goodwill is to be amortized over 40 years. During 1997, Clay Crating reported net income of $220 million and paid an $80 million cash dividend.

Required:

1. Prepare the appropriate journal entries during 1997 for the investment.
2. Determine the amounts relating to the investment that Delta Apparatus should report in the 1997 financial statements:
    a. As an investment on the balance sheet.
    b. As investment revenue on the income statement.
    c. Among investing activities on the statement of cash flows.

CONCEPT REVIEW EXERCISE

SOLUTION

1. Prepare the appropriate journal entries during 1997 for the investment.

Purchase	($ in millions)	
Investment in Clay Crating shares	540	
Cash		540
Net income		
Investment in Clay Crating shares (40% × $220 million)	88	
Investment revenue		88
Dividends		
Cash (40% × $80 million)	32	
Investment in Clay Crating shares		32
Inventory		
Investment revenue (higher cost of goods sold during 1997 if beginning inventory had been adjusted to fair value)	10	
Investment in Clay Crating shares (40% × $25 million)		10
Buildings		
Investment revenue ([$225 million × 40%] ÷ 18 years)	5	
Investment in Clay Crating shares		5
Goodwill		
Investment revenue [$80 million (calculation below*) ÷ 40 years]	2	
Investment in Clay Crating shares		2

*Goodwill calculation:

	Investee Net Assets	Net Assets Purchased	Difference Attributed to:	
Cost		$540		
			Goodwill:	$80 [difference]
Fair value:	$1,150† × 40% =	$460		
			Undervaluation of inventory:	$10 [$25 × 40%]
			Undervaluation of buildings:	$90 [$225 × 40%]
Book value:	$900 × 40% =	$360		

†($900 + 25 + 225)

2. Determine the amounts that Delta Apparatus should report in the 1997 financial statements:

   a. As an investment on the balance sheet

   Investment in Clay Crating shares

		($ in millions)	
Cost	540		
Share of income	88		
		32	Dividends
		10	Inventory
		5	Buildings
		2	Goodwill
Balance	579		

   b. As investment revenue on the income statement.

   $88 million (share of income) − [$10+5+2] million (amortization) = $71 million

   c. On the statement of cash flows:
   - Among investing activities: $540 million
   - Among operating activities: $32 million

Joint Ventures

Sometimes a company will join forces with another company to share resources or expertise to accomplish a specific purpose. Typically, each company in such an arrangement has a specified equity interest in the joint venture but does not otherwise own any portion of the company with which the joint venture is formed. For example, IBM and Apple Computer got together in 1990 to jointly develop a new software platform that would compete with a common competitor, Microsoft Corporation. Joint ventures also are a common way for American companies to do business abroad. Forming such an arrangement with an existing company is an efficient way to gain access to foreign markets or suppliers. In fact, some countries require joint ventures with local companies as a requisite for American (or other) firms operating in those countries.

Each party contributes something to a joint venture. The contribution may be some combination of expertise, cash, or other assets. This contribution constitutes the investment's cost. See Graphic 12–8 for a disclosure example.

GRAPHIC   12–8

Joint Ventures—Ecolab, Inc.

> *Note 2 (in Part): Transaction with Henkel KGaA*
>
> On July 11, 1991, the company and Henkel KGaA, Dusseldorf, Germany, (Henkel) completed the formation of Henkel-Ecolab, a joint venture of their respective European institutional and industrial cleaning and sanitizing businesses. . . . . In consideration for a 50 percent economic interest in the European joint venture and the outright purchase of Henkel's non-European operations, Ecolab contributed its European cleaning and sanitizing businesses to the joint venture, issued approximately 3.8 million common shares, and paid approximately $138 million cash and other consideration, subject to adjustment.

Typically, joint ventures between two companies are 50/50 arrangements, giving each firm significant influence but not control of its operations. In such cases, each company applies the equity method when reporting the joint venture. Pentair, Inc., uses the equity method for a joint venture in Lake Superior Paper Industries which manufactures paper in Duluth, Minnesota (see Graphic 12–9).

GRAPHIC   12–9

Joint Ventures—Pentair, Inc.

> *Note 1 (in Part): Summary of Significant Accounting Policies*
> The equity method is used for the 50/50 joint venture.

Decision-Makers' Perspective

The way we account for investments has considerable impact on both the valuation of corporate assets and income determination. Consequently, it is critical that both managers and external decision makers clearly understand those impacts and make decisions accordingly.

| Corporations invest in other corporations for a variety of reasons.

Managerial decisions concerning investments in other corporations are motivated by a variety of factors. Short-term investments in actively traded securities are common among banks, insurance companies, and other financial institutions. Manufacturing, merchandising, and nonfinancial service firms are more likely to make short-term investments to optimize the use of temporarily idle cash. Substantial portfolios of long-term securities are prominent among financial institutions who must keep large amounts of funds invested for long periods. Other firms, though, invest long term to derive any number of operating benefits such as creating desirable relationships with suppliers or customers. The way we report a company's investment in the stock of another company depends on the nature of the relationship between the investor and the investee. That is, the choice is dictated by the situation; it's not a discretionary matter.

| The way an investment is accounted for impacts reported income as well as various financial ratios.

By and large, the way we account for an investment has little effect on a company's cash flows. On the other hand, profits companies report often are significantly impacted by methods used to account for investments. For example, suppose Investor Company owns 20% of Investee Company. Investee's net income is $1 million. Suppose also that Investee distributes one-half its earnings as dividends. (Thus, Investor receives 20% × $1 million × $1/_2$ = $100,000.) The fair value of Investor's investment in Investee's common stock increased by $250,000 during the year. The investment revenue Investor includes on its income statement varies greatly depending on whether the investment is reported as a trading security, a security held for sale, or an investment accounted for by the equity method. The variation is shown in Graphic 12–10.

GRAPHIC   12–10

Variation in Earnings by Method Used to Account for Investments

Which accounting method causes reported income to be highest?

	Accounting Method Used:		
	Trading Security	Security Held for Sale	Equity Method
Share of Investee income*	$100,000	$100,000	$200,000
Increase in Investee's fair value†	250,000	0	0
Investor's investment income	$350,000	$100,000	$200,000

*Recognized whether received as dividends or not by the equity method; only if received as dividends otherwise.
†Reported in income for trading securities, component of shareholders' equity for securities available for sale, and not recognized at all for equity-method investments.

Accounting methods intended to limit the opportunities for income manipulation sometimes actually create other opportunities.

Thus, despite the lack of real impact on cash flows, the accounting method affects net income, including calculations of earnings per share and any rate of return ratios. When analyzing a company's profitability, lenders and investors should be alert to the way accounting methods affect reported net income. As an analyst, you would want to be particularly wary if the method changes from one year to the next. Companies have been known to adjust their ownership percentage, and therefore their method of accounting, suspiciously in concert with the prosperity of an investee.

Actually, the equity method was designed in part to prevent the manipulation of income that would be possible if investing corporations recognized income only when received as dividends, even when they have significant influence over investees. This would create the possibility that an investing corporation can dictate when and if dividends are paid, effectively manipulating the timing of income recognition. The equity method limits that potential method of managing earnings but given the discretion management has in classifying investments, creates other potential abuses.

GLOBAL PERSPECTIVE

No other country reports its investments exactly like we do in the United States. Most countries report short-term investments at lower of cost or market. Some, including Argentina and Israel, report at fair value. They are reported at current cost (usually replacement cost) in the United Kingdom.

Most countries report noncurrent investments (other than equity method investees) at some variation of cost, but methods vary widely, ranging from unadjusted historical cost (China) to fair market value (New Zealand).

Solution to Financial Reporting Case (at the opening of the chapter)

1. How should you respond?

You should explain that if an investor has the positive intent and ability to hold the securities to maturity, investments in debt securities are classified as held to maturity and reported at amortized cost in the balance sheet. Increases and decreases in market value are not reported in the financial statements. The reasoning is that the changes are irrelevant to an investor who will hold a security to its maturity regardless of those changes. Changes in the market value between the time a debt security is acquired and the day it matures to a prearranged maturity value aren't important if sale before maturity isn't an alternative.

2. Suppose Cracker Barrel classified all of its investments as available for sale. How would the unrealized gains and losses be reported?

Investments in securities available for sale are reported at fair value. However, holding gains and losses from retaining securities during periods of price change are not included in the determination of income for the period. Instead, they are accumulated and reported as a separate component of shareholders' equity. Thus an unrealized holding gain would increase shareholders' equity; and an unrealized holding loss would decrease shareholders' equity. Because these securities are *not* acquired for the purpose of profiting from short-term market price changes, gains and losses from holding these securities while prices change are not considered relevant performance measures to be included in earnings.

The Bottom Line

1. Investment securities are classified for reporting purposes as held to maturity, available for sale, or trading securities. If an investor has the positive intent and ability to hold the securities to maturity, investments in debt securities are classified as held to maturity and reported at amortized cost in the balance sheet. These investments are recorded at cost, and holding gains or losses from market price changes are ignored.

2. Investments in debt and equity securities that don't fit the definitions of the other reporting categories are classified as available for sale. They are reported at their fair values. Holding gains and losses from retaining securities during periods of price change are not included in the determination of income for the period; they are reported as a separate component of shareholders' equity.

3. Investments in debt or equity securities acquired principally for the purpose of selling them in the near term are classified as trading securities. They are reported at their fair values. Holding gains and losses for trading securities are included in earnings.

4. When an investor still is able to exercise significant influence over the operating and financial policies of the investee, the investment should be accounted for by the equity method. Usually an investor can exercise significant influence when it owns between 20% and 50% of the investee's voting shares.

5. By the equity method, the investor recognizes investment income equal to its percentage share (based on share ownership) of the net income earned by the investee, rather than the portion of that net income received as cash dividends. The investment account is adjusted for the investor's percentage share of net income reported by the investee. When the investor actually receives dividends, the investment account is reduced accordingly.

6. When the cost of an investment exceeds the book value of the underlying net assets acquired, both the investment account and investment revenue are adjusted for differences between net income reported by the investee and what that amount would have been if consolidation procedures had been followed.

Read - but not Responsible   **APPENDIX**

12A

INVESTMENTS IN DERIVATIVES

This is the first of eight chapters that deal with financial instruments. A **financial instrument** is defined as:

- Cash.
- Evidence of an *ownership interest* in an entity.[15]
- A contract that (a) imposes on one entity an obligation to *deliver* cash (say accounts payable) or another financial instrument and (b) conveys to a second entity a right to *receive* cash (say accounts receivable) or another financial instrument.
- A contract that (a) imposes on one entity an obligation to *exchange* financial instruments on potentially unfavorable terms (say the issuer of a stock option) and (b) conveys to a second entity a right to *exchange* other financial instruments on potentially favorable terms (say the holder of a stock option).[16]

Derivatives are financial instruments that derive their values from some other security or index.

An entirely new class of financial instruments has emerged in recent years in response to the desire of firms to manage risks. In fact, these financial instruments would not exist in their own right but have been created solely to hedge against risks created by other financial instruments or by transactions that have yet to occur but are anticipated. Financial futures, interest rate swaps, forward contracts, and options have become commonplace.[17] These financial instruments often are called **derivatives** because they derive their values or contractually required cash flows from some other security or index. Their rapid acceptance as indispensable components of the corporate capital structure has left the accounting profession scrambling to keep pace.

---

[15]This category includes not just shares of stock, but also partnership agreements and stock options.

[16]"Disclosure of Information about Financial Instruments with Off-Balance-Sheet Risk and Financial Instruments with Concentrations of Credit Risk," *Statement of Financial Accounting Standards No. 105* (Norwalk, Conn.: FASB, 1990), par. 6.

[17]Interest rate futures were traded for the first time in 1975 on the Chicago Board of Trade. Interest rate swaps were invented in the early 1980s.

The urgency has been accelerated by headline stories in the financial press reporting multimillion dollar losses on exotic derivatives by Procter & Gamble, Orange County California, Piper Jaffray, and Gibson Greetings, to mention a few. The headlines have tended to focus attention on the misuse of these financial instruments rather than their legitimate use in managing risk. Derivatives have been so maligned in the press that in a 1995 conference, James Leisenring, the FASB's vice chairman, facetiously defined a derivative as "any investment that lost money this year."

> The FASB's ongoing financial instruments project is expected to lead to a consistent framework for accounting for all financial instruments.

Actually, the FASB has been involved since 1986 in a project to provide a consistent framework for resolving financial instrument accounting issues, including those related to derivatives and other off-balance-sheet instruments. The financial instruments project has three separate but related parts: disclosure, recognition and measurement, and distinguishing between liabilities and equities. Unfortunately, issues to be resolved are extremely complex and will likely require several years to resolve. To help fill the disclosure gap in the meantime, the FASB has offered a series of temporary, patchwork solutions. These are primarily in the form of additional disclosures for financial instruments. More recently, the FASB has tackled the issues of recognition and measurement. We discuss these requirements next.

Derivative Financial Instruments

The amounts reported for financial instruments sometimes provide inadequate disclosure about the degree to which a company is exposed to risk of loss. Relatedly, some business arrangements that do not appear as specific assets or liabilities also expose companies to off-balance-sheet risk. In fact, some financial instruments are created specifically for the purpose of hedging against some of these risks, and the hedging instruments themselves expose the company to new risks.

> Hedging means taking a risk position that is opposite to an actual position that is exposed to risk.

Derivatives Used to Hedge Risk.   Hedging means taking an action that is expected to produce exposure to a particular type of risk that's precisely the *opposite* of an actual risk to which the company already is exposed. For instance, the volatility of interest rates creates exposure to interest rate risk for companies that issue debt—which, of course, includes most companies. So, a company that frequently arranges short-term loans from its bank under a floating (variable) interest rate agreement is exposed to the risk that interest rates might increase and adversely affect borrowing costs. Similarly, a company that regularly reissues commercial paper as it matures faces the possibility that new rates will be higher and cut into forecasted income. When borrowings are large, the potential cost can be substantial. So, the firm might choose to hedge its position by entering into a transaction that would produce a *gain* of roughly the same amount as the potential loss if interest rates do, in fact, increase.

Hedging is used to deal with three areas of risk: interest rate risk, commodity price risk, and foreign currency risk. The following is a brief description of some of the more common derivatives.

> A **futures contract** allows a firm to sell (or buy) a financial instrument at a designated future date, at today's price.

Financial Futures.   A futures contract is an agreement between a seller and a buyer that the seller will deliver a particular commodity (say corn, gold, or pork bellies) at a designated future date, at a *predetermined* price. These contracts are actively traded on regulated futures exchanges. When the commodity is a financial instrument such as a Treasury bond, Treasury bill, commercial paper, or a CD, the agreement is referred to as a **financial futures contract**.[18] The way a transaction is created on the Futures Exchange is diagrammed in Graphic 12A–1.

> The seller in a futures contract realizes a gain (loss) when interest rates rise (decline).

To appreciate the way these hedges work, you need to understand that when interest rates rise, the market price of interest-bearing securities goes down. For instance, if you have a 10% note and market interest rates go up to, say, 12%, your 10% note is less valuable relative to other notes. Conversely, when interest rates decline, the market price of interest-bearing securities goes up.

Now let's look at the effect on the contract to sell or buy securities at preset prices. One who is contracted to sell securities at a preset price after their market price has fallen, benefits from the interest rate increase. Consequently, the value of the contract that gives one the right to sell securities at a preset price goes up as the market price declines. The seller in a futures contract derives a gain (loss) when interest rates rise (decline).[19] Conversely, the one obligated to buy securities at a preset price experiences a loss.

For illustration, consider a company in April that will replace its $10 million of 8.5% bank notes when they mature in June. The company is exposed to the risk that interest rates in June will have risen, increasing borrowing costs. To counteract that possibility, the firm might enter a contract in April to deliver (sell) bonds in June at their current price. Because there are no corporate bond futures contracts, the company buys Treasury bond futures, which will accomplish essentially the same purpose. In essence, the firm agrees

---

[18]Note that a financial futures contract meets the definition of a financial instrument because it entails the exchange of financial instruments (cash for Treasury bonds, for instance). But, a futures contract for the sale or purchase of a nonfinancial commodity like corn or gold does not meet the definition because one of the items to be exchanged is not a financial instrument.

[19]The *seller* of a futures contract is obligated to *sell* the bonds at a future date. The *buyer* of a futures contract is obligated to *buy* the bonds at a future date. The company in our example, then, is the seller of the futures contract.

GRAPHIC   12A-1

How a Futures Transaction is Created

Seller
1 5 $
↓ ↑ ↓

Buyer
1 5 $
↓ ↑ ↓

Broker   2 →   Futures Exchange   ← 2   Broker
                          ← 4   (price agreed to   4 →
                                     on exchange floor)

$ 3 $
↓   ↓   ↓

Clearing   Clearinghouse   Clearing
Firm $ →   (intermediates and   ← $ Firm
                                     guarantees each trade)

1   Seller and buyer each instruct brokers to enter a futures contract.
2   Each broker asks its respective commission broker on exchange floor to execute the transaction.
3   Trade price and other information reported to the clearinghouse.
4   Trade price reported to the brokers.
5   Trade price reported to the seller and buyer.
$ Seller and buyer each deposit initial margin with clearinghouse through the broker and broker's clearing firm.

to sell Treasury bonds in June at a price established now (April). Let's say it's April 6 and the price of Treasury bond futures on the International Monetary Market of the Chicago Mercantile Exchange is quoted as 95.24.[20] As the trading unit of Treasury bond futures is a 15-year, $100,000, 8% Treasury bond, the company might sell 105 Treasury bond futures to hedge the June issuance of debt. This would effectively provide a hedge of $105 \times \$100,000 \times 95.24\% = \$10,000,200$.[21]

Here's what happens then. If interest rates rise, borrowing costs will go up for our example company because it will have to sell debt securities at a higher interest cost (or lower price). But that loss will be offset (approximately) by the gain produced by being in the opposite position on Treasury bond futures. Take note, though, this works both ways. If interest rates go down, causing debt security prices to rise, the potential benefit of being able to issue debt at that lower interest rate (higher price) will be offset by a *loss* on the futures position.

A very important point about futures contracts is that the seller does not need to have actual possession of the commodity (the Treasury bonds, in this case), nor is the purchaser of the contract required to take possession of the commodity. In fact, virtually all financial futures contracts are netted out before the actual transaction is to take place. This is simply a matter of reversing the original position. A seller closes out his transaction with a purchase. Likewise, a purchaser would close out her transaction with a sale. After all, the objective is not to actually buy or sell Treasury bonds (or whatever the commodity might be) but to incur the financial impact of movements in interest rates as reflected in changes in Treasury bond prices. Specifically, it will buy at the lower price (to reverse the original seller position) at the same time it's selling its new bond issue at that same lower price. The financial futures market is an artificial exchange in that its reason for existing is to provide a mechanism to transfer risk from those exposed to it to those willing to accept the risk, not to actually buy and sell the underlying financial instruments.

If the impending debt issue being hedged is a short-term issue, the company may attain a more effective hedge by selling Treasury bill futures because Treasury bills are 90-day securities, or maybe certificate of deposit (CD) futures which also are traded in futures markets. The object is to get the closest association between the financial effects of interest rate movements on the actual transaction and the effects on the financial instrument used as a hedge. Because financial futures contracts usually are bought and sold to hedge against interest rate risk, they often are called interest rate futures.

Interest Rate Swaps.   About 80% of derivatives are interest rate swaps. These contracts exchange fixed-interest payments for floating rate payments, or vice versa, without exchanging the underlying principal amounts. For example, suppose you owe $100,000 on a 10% fixed-rate home loan. You envy your neighbor who also is paying 10% on her $100,000 mortgage because hers is a floating rate loan, so if market rates fall, so will her loan rate. To the contrary, she is envious of your fixed rate, fearful that rates will rise, increasing her

> The effectiveness of the hedge is influenced by the closeness of the match between the item being hedged and the financial instrument chosen as a hedge.

> **Interest rate swaps** hedge the risk associated with interest rate movements by exchanging fixed interest payments for floating rate payments, or vice versa, without exchanging the underlying principal amounts.

[20]Price quotes are expressed as a percent of par.
[21]This is a simplification of the more sophisticated way financial managers determine the optimal number of futures.

payments. A solution would be for the two of you to effectively swap interest payments using an interest-rate swap agreement. The way a swap works, you both would continue to actually make your own interest payments but would exchange the net cash difference between payments at specified intervals. So, in this case, if market rates (and thus floating payments) increase, you would pay your neighbor; if rates fall, she pays you. The net effect is to exchange the consequences of rate changes.

Of course, this technique is not dependent on happening into such a fortuitous pairing of two borrowers with opposite philosophies on interest rate risk. Instead, banks or other intermediaries offer, for a fee, one-sided swap agreements to companies desiring to be either fixed-rate payers or variable-rate payers. Intermediaries usually strive to maintain a balanced portfolio of matched, offsetting swap agreements.

Financial Forward Contracts.   A **forward contract** is similar to a futures contract but differs in three ways:

1. A forward contract calls for delivery on a specific date, whereas a futures contract permits the seller to decide later which specific day within the specified month will be the delivery date (if it gets as far as actual delivery before it is closed out).
2. Unlike a futures contract, a forward contract usually is not traded on a market exchange.
3. Unlike a futures contract, a forward contract does not call for a daily cash settlement for price changes in the commodity underlying the contract. Gains and losses on forward contracts are paid only when they are closed out.

Options.   **Options** frequently are purchased to hedge interest rate risk. Options serve the same purpose as futures in that respect but are fundamentally different. An option on a financial instrument, say a Treasury bill, gives its holder the *right* either to buy or to sell the Treasury bill at a specified price and within a given time period. Importantly, though, the option holder has *no obligation* to exercise the option. On the other hand, the holder of a futures contract *must* buy or sell within a specified period unless the contract is closed out before delivery comes due.

From an accounting standpoint, the central issue is not the operational differences among various hedge instruments but their similarities in functioning as hedges against interest rate risk.

Foreign Currency Futures.   Foreign loans frequently are denominated in the currency of the lender (Japanese yen, Swiss franc, German mark, and so on). When loans must be repaid in foreign currencies, a new element of risk is introduced. This is because if exchange rates change, the dollar equivalent of the foreign currency that must be repaid differs from the dollar equivalent of the foreign currency borrowed.

To hedge against foreign exchange risk exposure, some firms buy or sell foreign currency futures contracts. These are similar to financial futures except specific foreign currencies are specified in the futures contracts rather than specific debt instruments. They work the same way to protect against foreign exchange risk as financial futures protect against interest rate risk.

> Foreign exchange risk often is hedged in the same manner as interest rate risk.

Accounting for Derivatives

As this text went to press, the FASB had outstanding a proposal for improved standards for accounting for derivative financial instruments and hedging transactions. As planned, the new standard would require all derivatives to be carried on the balance sheet as either assets or liabilities at fair (or market) value. Accounting for the gain or loss on a derivative would depend on how it is used.

1. For a **derivative that hedges forecasted transactions**, the gain or loss would be deferred and included in earnings when the transaction is projected to occur but recognized currently in other comprehensive income outside earnings along with such items as foreign currency translation adjustments and unrealized gains and losses on securities.
2. For a **derivative that hedges an asset, liability, or firm commitment,** the gain or loss would be included currently in earnings, but would be offset by recording the corresponding loss or gain on the item being hedged.
3. For a **derivative that hedges the foreign currency exposure** of a company's net investment in a foreign operation, the foreign currency transaction gain or loss would be reported in other comprehensive income with the rest recognized in earnings.
4. For a **derivative not designated as a hedge,** gains or losses would be included currently in earnings.

Derivative Disclosures

A key to understanding financial instruments, particularly derivatives, is knowing the purpose for which a company holds those instruments. Derivatives, for instance, may be held for risk management (hedging activities). The desired effect, and often the real effect, is a reduction in risk. On the other hand, derivatives sometimes are held for speculative position taking, hoping for large profits. The effect of this activity usually is to increase risk. Also, some firms, primarily financial institutions, hold derivatives for dealing or other trading activities. To help investors and creditors understand what firms are trying to accomplish with the derivatives, descriptive information should be reported in disclosure notes to financial statements.

read-but not responsible

12B

OTHER INVESTMENTS (SPECIAL PURPOSE FUNDS, INVESTMENT IN LIFE INSURANCE POLICIES)

Special Purpose Funds

> Some special purchase funds—like petty cash—are current assets.

It's often convenient for companies to set aside money to be used for specific purposes. You learned about one such special purpose fund in Chapter 7 when we discussed petty cash funds. Recall that a petty cash fund is money set aside to conveniently make small expenditures using currency rather than having to follow the time-consuming, formal procedures normally used to process checks. Similar funds sometimes are used to pay interest, payroll, or other short-term needs. Like petty cash, these short-term special purpose funds are reported as current assets.

> A special purchase fund can be established for virtually any purpose.

> Noncurrent special purchase funds are reported within the category *investments and funds.*

Special purpose funds also are sometimes established to serve longer term needs. It's common, for instance, to periodically set aside cash into a fund designated to repay bonds and other long-term debt. Such funds usually accumulate cash over the debt's term to maturity and are composed of the company's periodic contributions plus interest or dividends from investing the money in various return-generating investments. In fact, some debt contracts require the borrower to establish such a fund to repay the debt. In similar fashion, management might voluntarily choose to establish a fund to accumulate money to expand facilities, provide for unexpected losses, to buy back shares of stock, or any other special purpose that might benefit from an accumulation of funds. Of course, these funds that won't be used within the upcoming operating cycle are noncurrent assets. They are reported as part of investments and funds. The same criteria for classifying securities into reporting categories that we discussed previously should be used to classify securities in which funds are invested. Any investment revenue from these funds is reported as such on the income statement.

Investments in Life Insurance Policies

> Certain life insurance policies can be surrendered while the insured is still alive in exchange for its **cash surrender value**.

Companies frequently buy life insurance policies on the lives of their key officers. Under normal circumstances, the company pays the premium for the policy and as beneficiary, receives the proceeds when the officer dies. Of course, the objective is to compensate the company for the untimely loss of a valuable resource in the event the officer dies. However, some types of life insurance policies can be surrendered while the insured is still alive in exchange for a determinable amount of money, called the **cash surrender value**. In effect, a portion of each premium payment is not used by the insurance company to pay for life insurance coverage, but instead is invested on behalf of the insured company in a fixed-income investment. Accordingly, the cash surrender value increases each year by the portion of premiums invested plus interest on the previous amount invested. This is simply a characteristic of whole life insurance, unlike term insurance whose lower premiums provide death benefits only.

> Part of each insurance premium represents an increase in the cash surrender value.

From an accounting standpoint, the periodic insurance premium should not be expensed in its entirety. Rather, part of each premium payment, the investment portion, is recorded as an asset. Illustration 12B–1 provides an example.

ILLUSTRATION   12B-1

Cash Surrender Value

> Several years ago, American Capital acquired a $1 million insurance policy on the life of its chief executive officer, naming American Capital as beneficiary. Annual premiums are $18,000, payable at the beginning of each year. In 1997, the cash surrender value of the policy increased according to the contract from $5,000 to $7,000. The CEO died at the end of 1997.

Insurance expense (difference)	16,000	
Cash surrender value of life insurance ($7,000 − 5,000)	2,000	
Cash (1997 premium)		18,000

To record insurance expense and the increase in the investment.

> The cash surrender value is considered to be a noncurrent investment and would be reported in the investments and funds section of the balance sheet. Of course when the insured officer dies, the corporation receives the death benefit of the insurance policy, and the cash surrender value ceases to exist because canceling the policy no longer is an option. The corporation recognizes a gain for the amount of the death benefit less the cash surrender value:

Cash (death benefit)	1,000,000	
Cash surrender value of life insurance (balance)		7,000
Gain on life insurance settlement (difference)		993,000

To record the proceeds at death.

> Part of the annual premium represents a build-up in the cash surrender value.

> When the death benefit is paid, the cash surrender value becomes null and void.

READ - but not RESPONSIBLE

APPENDIX

12C

IMPAIRMENT OF AN INVESTMENT IN A RECEIVABLE DUE TO A TROUBLED DEBT RESTRUCTURING

When a creditor's investment in a receivable becomes impaired due to a troubled debt restructuring or for any other reason, the receivable is remeasured based on the discounted present value of currently expected cash flows at the loan's original effective rate (regardless of the extent to which expected cash receipts have been reduced).

When the original terms of a debt agreement are changed as a result of financial difficulties experienced by the debtor (borrower), the new arrangement is referred to as a **troubled debt restructuring**. We discuss troubled debt restructurings in much more detail in Chapter 14. The essential point here is that such an arrangement involves some concessions on the part of the creditor (lender), resulting in the impairment of the creditor's asset: the investment in a receivable.

When the Receivable Is Settled Outright

Sometimes a receivable in a troubled debt restructuring is actually settled at the time of the restructuring with the receipt of cash (or a noncash asset), or even shares of the debtor's stock. In that case, the creditor simply records a loss for the difference between the carrying amount of the receivable and the fair value of the asset(s) or equity securities received. Illustration 12C–1 provides an example.

When the Receivable Is Continued, but with Modified Terms

In the previous example we assumed that First Prudent Bank agreed to accept property in full settlement of the receivable. In a troubled debt restructuring, it is more likely that the bank would allow the receivable to continue but with the terms of the debt agreement modified to make it easier for the debtor to comply. The

ILLUSTRATION 12C–1

Debt Settled at the Time of a Restructuring

First Prudent Bank is owed $30 million by Brillard Properties under a 10% note with two years remaining to maturity. Due to financial difficulties of the developer, the previous year's interest ($3 million) was not received. The bank agrees to settle the receivable (and accrued interest receivable) in exchange for property having a fair market value of $20 million.

		($ in millions)
Land (fair market value)	20	
Loss on troubled debt restructuring	13	
Accrued interest receivable (10% × $30 million)		3
Note receivable (balance)		30

For most active lenders, a troubled debt restructuring unfortunately is not both unusual and infrequent; so usually the loss is not reported as an extraordinary loss.

> The carrying amount of the receivable is $33 million.

lender might agree to reduce or delay the scheduled interest payments. Or, it may agree to reduce or delay the maturity amount. Often a troubled debt restructuring will call for some combination of these concessions.

As one of many possibilities, suppose the bank agrees to (1) forgive the interest accrued from last year, (2) reduce the two remaining interest payments from $3 million each to $2 million each, and (3) reduce the face amount from $30 million to $25 million. Clearly, the bank's investment in the receivable has been impaired. The extent of impairment is the difference between the $33 million carrying amount of the receivable (the present value of the receivable's cash flows prior to the restructuring) and the present value of the revised cash flows discounted at the loan's original effective rate (10%). See Illustration 12C–2 for a demonstration.

After restructuring, the lender still records interest annually at the 10% effective rate.

ILLUSTRATION 12C–2

Receivable Impaired by Troubled Debt Restructuring— Terms Modified

Brillard Properties owes First Prudent Bank $30 million under a 10% note with two years remaining to maturity. Due to financial difficulties of the developer, the previous year's interest ($3 million) was not paid. First Prudent Bank agrees to:

1. Forgive the interest accrued from last year.
2. Reduce the remaining two interest payments to $2 million each.
3. Reduce the principal to $25 million.

Analysis

Previous Value:			
Accrued interest	(10% × $30,000,000)	$ 3,000,000	
Principal		30,000,000	
Carrying amount of the receivable			$33,000,000
New Value:			
Interest	$2 million × 1.73554* =	$ 3,471,080	
Principal	$25 million × 0.82645† =	20,661,250	
Present value of the receivable			(24,132,330)
Loss:			$ 8,867,670

*Present value of an ordinary annuity of $1: *n*=2, *i*=10%
†Present value of $1: n=2, i=10%

Journal Entry

Loss on troubled debt restructuring (to balance)	8,867,670	
Accrued interest receivable (10% × $30,000,000)		3,000,000
Note receivable ($30,000,000 – $24,132,330)		5,867,670

> The discounted present value of the cash flows prior to the restructuring was the same as the receivable's carrying amount.

> The discounted present value of the cash flows after the restructuring is less.

> The difference is a loss.

Questions for Review of Key Topics

Question   12–1   All investments in *debt* securities and investments in *equity* securities that have readily determinable fair values (except those for which the equity method or consolidation is appropriate) are classified for reporting purposes in one of three categories and accounted for differently depending on the classification. What are these three categories?

Question   12–2   When market rates of interest *rise* after a fixed-rate security is purchased, the value of the now-below-market, fixed-interest payments declines, so the market value of the investment falls. On the other hand, if market rates of interest *fall* after a fixed-rate security is purchased, the fixed-interest payments become relatively attractive, and the market value of the investment rises. How are these price changes reflected in the investment account for a security classified as held to maturity?

Question   12–3   When is the fair value of an equity security considered to be readily determinable? How is an investment in an equity security reported if its fair value is *not* readily determinable?

Question   12–4   When an investment is acquired to be held for an unspecified period of time as opposed to being held to maturity, it is reported at the fair value of the investment securities on the reporting date. Why?

Question   12–5   Reporting an investment at its fair value means adjusting its carrying amount for changes in fair value after its acquisition (or since the last reporting date if it was held at that time). Such changes are called unrealized holding gains and losses because they haven't yet been realized through the sale of the security. If the security is classified as available for sale, how are unrealized holding gains and losses reported?

Question   12–6   Why are holding gains and losses treated differently for trading securities and securities available for sale?

Question   12–7   The market value of Helig Forestry and Mining Corporation common stock dropped $6^1/_8$ points when the Federal government passed new legislation banning one of the company's primary techniques for extracting ore. Harris Corporation owns shares of Helig and classifies its investment as securities available for sale. How should the decline in market value be handled by Harris?

Question   12–8   Western Die-casting Company holds an investment in unsecured bonds of LGB Heating Equipment, Inc. When the investment was acquired, management's intention was to hold the bonds for resale. Now management has the positive intent and ability to hold the bonds to maturity. How should the reclassification of the investment be accounted for?

Question   12–9   Is it necessary for an investor to report individual amounts for the three categories of investments—held to maturity, available for sale, or trading—in the financial statements? What information should be disclosed about these investments?

Question   12–10   Under what circumstances is the equity method used to account for an investment in stock?

Question   12–11   The equity method has been referred to as a *one-line consolidation.* What might prompt this description?

Question   12–12   In the application of the equity method, how should dividends from the investee be accounted for? Why?

Question   12–13   Under the equity method, both the investment account and investment revenue are adjusted for the amortization of goodwill—the excess of the acquisition price over the fair value of the acquired net assets. Explain.

Question   12–14   The fair value of depreciable assets of Penner Packaging Company exceeds their book value by $12 million and have an average remaining useful life of 10 years. They are being depreciated by the straight-line method. Finest Foods Industries buys 40% of Penner's common shares. When adjusting investment revenue and the investment by the equity method, how will the situation described affect those two accounts?

Question   12–15   Superior Company owns 40% of the outstanding stock of Bernard Company. During 1997, Bernard paid a $100,000 cash dividend on its common shares. What effect did this dividend have on Superior's 1997 financial statements?

Question   12–16   Sometimes an investor's level of influence changes, making it necessary to change from the equity method to another method. How should the investor account for this change in accounting method?

Question   12–17   (based on Appendix 12A)   Define a financial instrument. Provide three examples of current liabilities that represent financial instruments.

Question   12–18   (based on Appendix 12A)   Some financial instruments are called derivatives. Why?

Question   12–19   (based on Appendix 12B)   Northwest Carburetor Company established a fund in 1997 to accumulate money for a new plant scheduled for construction in 2003. How should this special purpose fund be reported in Northwest's balance sheet?

Question   12–20   (based on Appendix 12B)   Whole-life insurance policies typically can be surrendered while the insured is still alive in exchange for a determinable amount of money called the *cash surrender value.* When a company buys a life insurance policy on the life of a key officer to protect the company against the untimely loss of a valuable resource in the event the officer dies, how should the company account for the cash surrender value?

Question   12–21   (based on Appendix 12C   Marshall Companies, Inc., holds a note receivable from a former subsidiary. Due to financial difficulties, the former subsidiary has been unable to pay the previous year's interest on the note. Marshall agreed to restructure the debt by both delaying and reducing remaining cash payments. The concessions impair the creditor's investment in the receivable. How is this impairment recorded?

Exercises

Exercise 12–1
Securities held to maturity

FF&T Corporation is a confectionery wholesaler that frequently buys and sells securities to meet various investment objectives. The following selected transactions relate to FF&T's investment activities during the last two months of 1997. At November 1, FF&T held $48 million of 20-year, 10% bonds of Convenience, Inc., purchased May 1, 1977, at face value. Management has the positive intent and ability to hold the bonds until maturity. FF&T's fiscal year ends on December 31.

[handwritten: adjusting → 48mil × 10% × 2/12 = interest for Nov + Dec]

November	1	Received semiannual interest of $2.4 million from the Convenience, Inc., bonds.
December	1	Purchased 12% bonds of Facsimile Enterprises at their $30 million face value, to be held until they mature in 2016. Semiannual interest is payable May 31 and November 30.
	31	Purchased U.S. Treasury bills that mature in two months for $8.9 million.
	31	Recorded any necessary adjusting entry(s) relating to the investments.

[handwritten: adjusting entry for interest revenue]

[handwritten: 30mil × 12% × 1/12 interest for Dec. adjusting entry]

The fair values of the investments at December 31 were:

Convenience bonds	$44.7 million
Facsimile Enterprises bonds	30.9 million
U.S. Treasury bills	8.9 million

Required:
Prepare the appropriate journal entry for each transaction or event.

Exercise 12–2
Purchase and sale of investment securities

Shott Farm Supplies Corporation purchased 800 shares of General Motors stock at $50 per share and paid a brokerage fee of $1,200. Two months later, the shares were sold for $53 per share. The brokerage fee on the sale was $1,300.

Required:
Prepare entries for the purchase and the sale.

Exercise 12–3
Securities available for sale; adjusting entries

Loreal-American Corporation purchased several marketable securities during 1997. At December 31, 1997, the company had the investments in common stock listed below. None was held at the last reporting date, and all are considered securities available for sale.

[handwritten: Cost > FV = loss; Cost < FV = gain]

	Cost	Fair Value	Unrealized Holding Gain (Loss)
Short term:			
Blair, Inc.	$ 480,000	$ 405,000	$(75,000)
ANC Corporation	450,000	480,000	30,000
Totals	$ 930,000	$ 885,000	$(45,000)
Long term:			
Drake Corporation	$ 480,000	$ 560,000	$ 80,000
Aaron Industries	720,000	660,000	(60,000)
Totals	$1,200,000	$1,220,000	$ 20,000

Required:
1. Prepare appropriate adjusting entries at December 31, 1997.
2. What amounts would be reported on the income statement at December 31, 1997, as a result of these adjusting entries?

Exercise 12–4
Classification of securities; adjusting entries

On February 18, 1997, Union Corporation purchased 10,000 shares of IBM common stock as a long-term investment at $60 per share. On December 31, 1997, and December 31, 1998, the market value of IBM stock is $58 and $61 per share, respectively.

Required:
1. What is the appropriate reporting category for this investment? Why?
2. Prepare the adjusting entry for December 31, 1997.
3. Prepare the adjusting entry for December 31, 1998.

Exercise 12–5
Various transactions related to securities available for sale

Construction Forms Corporation buys securities to be available for sale when circumstances warrant, not to profit from short-term differences in price and not necessarily to hold debt securities to maturity. The following selected transactions relate to investment activities of Construction Forms whose fiscal year ends on December 31. No investments were held by Construction Forms at the beginning of the year.

1997

March	2	Purchased 1 million Platinum Gauges, Inc., common shares for $31 million, including brokerage fees and commissions.

April	12	Purchased $20 million of 10% bonds at face value from Zenith Wholesale Corporation.
July	18	Received cash dividends of $2 million on the investment in Platinum Gauges, Inc., common shares.
September	1	Received semiannual interest of $1 million on the investment in Zenith bonds.
	2	Sold the Zenith bonds for $21 million.
November	1	Purchased 500,000 LTD International preferred shares for $40 million, including brokerage fees and commissions.
December	31	Recorded the necessary adjusting entry(s) relating to the investments. The market prices of the investments are $32 per share for Platinum Gauges, Inc., and $74 per share for LTD International preferred shares.
1998		
January	23	Sold half the Platinum Gauges, Inc., shares for $32 per share.
March	1	Sold the LTD International preferred shares for $76 per share.

Required:

1. Prepare the appropriate journal entry for each transaction or event.
2. Show the amounts that would be reported on the company's 1997 income statement relative to these investments.

Exercise 12–6
Securities available for sale; journal entries

Purchase
N I
Dividend
Year-end adj

On January 2, 1997, Sanborn Tobacco, Inc., bought 5% of Jackson Industry's capital stock for $90 million as a temporary investment. Sanborn classified the securities acquired as available for sale. Jackson Industry's net income for the year ended December 31, 1997, was $120 million. The fair value of the shares held by Sanborn was $98 million at December 31, 1997. During 1997, Jackson declared a dividend of $60 million.

Required:

1. Prepare all appropriate journal entries related to the investment during 1997.
2. Indicate the effect of this investment on 1997 income before taxes.

Trading Sec.

Exercise 12–7
Various transactions relating to trading securities

Purchase
Dividends
Year-end adj
Sale of stock

Rantzow-Lear Company buys and sells securities expecting to earn profits on short-term differences in price. The company's fiscal year ends on December 31. The following selected transactions relating to Rantzow-Lear's trading account occurred during December, 1997, and the first week of 1998.

1997		
December	17	Purchased 100,000 Grocers' Supply Corporation preferred shares for $350,000.
	28	Received cash dividends of $2,000 from the Grocers' Supply Corporation preferred shares.
	31	Recorded any necessary adjusting entry relating to the Grocers' Supply Corporation preferred shares. The market price of the stock was $4 per share.
1998		
January	5	Sold the Grocers' Supply Corporation preferred shares for $395,000.

compare FV 400,000 to cash 395,000 loss of 5,000

Required:

1. Prepare the appropriate journal entry for each transaction.
2. Indicate any amounts that Rantzow-Lear Company would report on its 1997 balance sheet and income statement as a result of these investments.

Exercise 12–8
Various investment securities

At December 31, 1997, Hull-Meyers Corp. had the following investments that were purchased during 1997, its first year of operations:

		Cost	Fair value
Trading Securities:			
Security	A	$ 900,000	$ 910,000
	B	105,000	100,000
Totals		$1,005,000	$1,010,000
Securities Available for Sale:			
Security	C	$ 700,000	$ 780,000
	D	900,000	915,000
Totals		$1,600,000	$1,695,000
Securities to Be Held to Maturity:			
Security	E	$ 490,000	$ 500,000
	F	615,000	610,000
Totals		$1,105,000	$1,110,000

No investments were sold during 1997. All securities except Security D and Security F are considered short-term investments. None of the market changes is considered permanent.

Required:

Determine the following amounts at December 31, 1997:

1. Investments reported as current assets.

2. Investments reported as noncurrent assets.
3. Unrealized gain (or loss) component of income before taxes.
4. Unrealized gain (or loss) component of shareholders' equity.

Exercise 12–9
Securities available for sale; adjusting entries

The accounting records of Jamaican Importers, Inc., at January 1, 1997, included the following:

Assets:

Investment in Yucatan Growers common shares $1,200,000

Shareholders' Equity:

Unrealized holding loss on investment in Yucatan Growers common shares $ 145,000

No changes occurred during 1997 in the investment portfolio.

Required:
Prepare appropriate adjusting entry(s) at December 31, 1997, assuming the market value of the Yucatan Growers common shares was:

1. $1,175,000.
2. $1,275,000.
3. $1,375,000.

Exercise 12–10
Multiple choice; investment securities

The following questions dealing with investments are adapted from questions that appeared in the Financial Accounting & Reporting—Business Enterprises section of recent CPA examinations. Determine the response that best completes the statements or questions.

1. Nola Co. has adopted *Statement of Financial Accounting Standards No. 115*, "Accounting for Certain Investments in Debt and Equity Securities." Nola has a portfolio of marketable equity securities that it does not intend to sell in the near term. How should Nola classify these securities, and how should it report unrealized gains and losses from these securities?

Classify as	Report as a
a. Trading securities	Component of income from continuing operations
b. Available for sale	Separate component of stockholders' equity
c. Trading securities	Separate component of stockholders' equity
d. Available for sale	Components of income from continuing operations

2. Kale Co. has adopted *Statement of Financial Accounting Standards No. 115*, "Accounting for Certain Investments in Debt and Equity Securities." Kale purchased bonds at a discount on the open market as an investment and intends to hold these bonds to maturity. Kale should account for these bonds at:
   a. Cost
   b. Amortized cost
   c. Fair value
   d. Lower of cost or market

Exercise 12–11
Investment securities and equity method investments compared

REVIEW for exam

As a long-term investment, Painters' Equipment Company purchased 20% of AMC Supplies, Inc.'s, 400,000 shares for $480,000 at the beginning of the fiscal year of both companies. On the purchase date, the fair value and book value of AMC's net assets were equal. During the year, AMC earned net income of $250,000 and distributed cash dividends of 25 cents per share. At year-end, the fair value of the shares is $505,000.

Required: FV, Avail for Sale
1. Assume <u>no significant influence</u> was acquired. Prepare the appropriate journal entries from the purchase through the end of the year.
2. Assume <u>significant influence</u> was acquired. Prepare the appropriate journal entries from the purchase through the end of the year.   Equity

Exercise 12–12
Equity method; purchase; investee income; dividends

As a long-term investment at the beginning of the fiscal year, Florists International purchased <u>30%</u> of Nursery Supplies, Inc.'s, 8 million shares for $56 million. The fair value and book value of the shares were the same at that time. During the year, Nursery Supplies earned net income of $40 million and distributed cash dividends of $1.25 per share. At the end of the year, the fair value of the shares is $52 million.

Required:
Prepare the appropriate journal entries from the purchase through the end of the year.

Exercise 12–13
Change in principle; change to the equity method

The Trump Companies, Inc., has ownership interests in several public companies. At the beginning of 1997, the company's ownership interest in the common stock of Milken Properties increased to the point that it became appropriate to begin using the equity method of accounting for the investment. The balance in the investment account was $31 million at the time of the change. Accountants working with company records determined that the balance would have been $48 million if the account had been adjusted for investee net income and dividends as prescribed by the equity method.

Required:
1. Prepare the journal entry to record the change in principle.
2. Briefly describe other steps Trump should take to report the change.
3. Suppose Trump is changing *from* the equity method rather than *to* the equity method. How would your answers to requirements 1 and 2 differ?

Exercise 12–14
Error corrections; investment

Exercise 21–22 deals with the correction of an error in recording investments.

Exercise 12–15
Equity method; adjustments for depreciation and goodwill

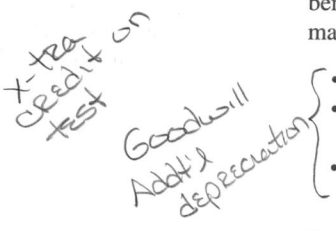

Fizer Pharmaceutical paid $68 million on January 2, 1997, for 4 million shares of Carne Cosmetics common stock. The investment represents a 25% interest in the net assets of Carne and gave Fizer the ability to exercise significant influence over Carne's operations. Fizer received dividends of $1 per share on December 21, 1997, and Carne reported net income of $40 million for the year ended December 31, 1997. The market value of Carne's common stock at December 31, 1997, was $18.50 per share. $17/share

-   The book value of Carne's net assets was $192 million.
-   The fair market value of Carne's depreciable assets exceeded their book value by $32 million. These assets had an average remaining useful life of 8 years.
-   The remainder of the excess of the cost of the investment over the book value of net assets purchased was attributable to goodwill to be amortized over 40 years. $92 M

Required:
Prepare all appropriate journal entries related to the investment during 1997.

Exercise 12–16
Equity method; adjustment for goodwill

On January 1, 1997, Cameron, Inc., bought 20% of the outstanding common stock of Lake Construction Company for $300 million cash. At the date of acquisition of the stock, Lake's net assets had a book value and fair value of $900 million. Any purchased goodwill should be amortized over an estimated life of 30 years. Lake's net income for the year ended December 31, 1997, was $150 million. During 1997, Lake declared and paid cash dividends of $30 million.

Required:
1. Prepare all appropriate journal entries related to the investment during December 31, 1997, assuming Cameron accounts for this investment by the equity method.
2. Determine the amounts to be reported by Cameron:
    a. As an investment on Cameron's 1997 balance sheet.
    b. As investment revenue on the income statement.
    c. Among investing activities on the statement of cash flows.

Exercise 12–17
Multiple choice; equity method

The following questions dealing with the equity method are adapted from questions that appeared on recent CPA examinations. Determine the response that best completes the statements or questions.

Questions 1–3 are based on the following information.

Grant, Inc., acquired 30% of South Co's voting stock for $200,000 on January 2, 1997. Grant's 30% interest in South gave Grant the ability to exercise significant influence over South's operating and financial policies. During 1997, South earned $80,000 and paid dividends of $50,000. South reported earnings of $100,000 for the six months ended June 30, 1998, and $200,000 for the year ended December 31, 1998. On July 1, 1998, Grant sold half of its stock in South for $150,000 cash. South paid dividends of $60,000 on October 1, 1998.

1. Before income taxes, what amount should Grant include in its 1997 income statement as a result of the investment?
    a. $15,000
    b. $24,000
    c. $50,000
    d. $80,000

2. In Grant's December 31, 1997, balance sheet, what should be the carrying amount of this
    investment?
    a. $200,000
    b. $209,000
    c. $224,000
    d. $230,000
3. In its 1998 income statement, what amount should Grant report as gain from the sale of half of its
    investment?
    a. $24,500
    b. $30,500
    c. $35,000
    d. $45,500

Exercise 12–18
Life insurance policy
(based on Appendix12B)

Edible Chemicals Corporation owns a $4 million whole life insurance policy on the life of its CEO, nam-
ing Edible Chemicals as beneficiary. The annual premiums are $70,000 and are payable at the beginning of
each year. The cash surrender value of the policy was $21,000 at the beginning of 1997.

Required:
1. Prepare the appropriate 1997 journal entry to record insurance expense and the increase in the
    investment assuming the cash surrender value of the policy increased according to the contract to
    $27,000.
2. The CEO died at the end of 1997. Prepare the appropriate journal entry.

Exercise 12–19
Life insurance policy
(based on Appendix12B)

Below are two unrelated situations relating to life insurance.

Required:
Prepare the appropriate journal entry for each situation.

1. Ford Corporation owns a whole life insurance policy on the life of its president. Ford Corporation is
    the beneficiary. The insurance premium is $25,000. The cash surrender value increased during the
    year from $2,500 to $4,600.
2. Petroleum Corporation received a $250,000 life insurance settlement when its CEO died. At that
    time, the cash surrender value was $16,000.

Exercise 12–20
Impairment of securities
available for sale; troubled
debt restructuring
(based on Appendix 12C)

At January 1, 1997, Clayton Hoists, Inc., owed Third BancCorp $12 million, under a 10% note due
December 31, 1998. Interest was paid last on December 31, 1995. Clayton was experiencing severe finan-
cial difficulties and asked Third BancCorp to modify the terms of the debt agreement. After negotiation
Third BancCorp agreed to:

*   Forgive the interest accrued for the year just ended.
*   Reeduce the remaining two years' interest payments to $1 million each.
*   Reduce the principal amount to $11 million.

Required:
Prepare the journal entries by Third BancCorp necessitated by the restructuring of the debt at

1. January 1, 1997.
2. December 31, 1997.
3. December 31, 1998.

Exercise 12–21
Impairment of securities
available for sale; troubled
debt restructuring
(based on Appendix 12C)

At January 1, 1997, NCI Industries, Inc., was indebted to First Federal Bank under a $240,000, 10%
unsecured note. The note was signed January 1, 1993, and was due December 31, 1998. Annual interest was
last paid on December 31, 1995. NCI was experiencing severe financial difficulties and negotiated a restructuring of the terms of the debt agreement. First Federal agreed to reduce last year's interest and the remaining two years' interest payments to $11,555 each and delay all payments until December 31, 1998, the
maturity date.

Required:
Prepare the journal entries by First Federal Bank necessitated by the restructuring of the debt at

1. January 1, 1997.
2. December 31, 1997.
3. December 31, 1998.

Problems

Problem 12–1
Various transactions related to securities available for sale

The following selected transactions relate to investment activities of Ornamental Insulation Corporation. The company buys securities, *not* intending to profit from short-term differences in price and *not* necessarily to hold debt securities to maturity but to have them available for sale when circumstances warrant. Ornamental's fiscal year ends on December 31. No investments were held by Ornamental on December 31, 1996.

1997

February	21	Acquired Distribution Transformers Corporation common shares costing $400,000.
March	18	Received cash dividends of $8,000 on the investment in Distribution Transformers common shares.
September	1	Acquired $900,000 of American Instruments' 10% bonds at face value.
October	20	Sold the Distribution Transformers shares for $425,000.
November	1	Purchased M&D Corporation common shares costing $1,400,000.
December	31	Recorded any necessary adjusting entry(s) and closing entries relating to the investments. The market prices of the investments are:

American Instruments bonds	$ 850,000
M&D Corporation shares	$1,460,000

(Hint: Interest must be accrued for the American Instruments' bonds.)

1998

January	20	Sold the M&D Corporation shares for $1,485,000.
March	1	Received semiannual interest of $45,000 on the investment in American Instruments bonds.

Required:

1. Prepare the appropriate journal entry for each transaction or event during 1997.
2. Indicate any amounts that Ornamental Insulation would report on its 1997 balance sheet and income statement as a result of these investments.
3. Prepare the appropriate journal entry for each transaction or event during 1998.

Problem 12–2
Various transactions relating to trading securities

American Surety and Fidelity buys and sells securities expecting to earn profits on short-term differences in price. The following selected transactions relate to American's trading account during December, 1997, and the first week of 1998. The company's fiscal year ends on December 31. No trading securities were held by American on December 1, 1997. For the first 11 months of the year, gains from selling trading securities totaled $8 million, losses were $11 million, and the company had earned $5 million in investment revenue.

December	12	Purchased FF&G Corporation bonds for $12 million.
	13	Purchased 2 million Ferry Intercommunications common shares for $22 million.
	15	Sold the FF&G Corporation bonds for $12.1 million.
	22	Purchased U.S. Treasury bills for $56 million and Treasury bonds for $65 million.
	23	Sold half the Ferry Intercommunications common shares for $10 million.
	26	Sold the U.S. Treasury bills for $57 million.
	27	Sold the Treasury bonds for $63 million.
	28	Received cash dividends of $200,000 from the Ferry Intercommunications common shares.
	31	Recorded any necessary adjusting entry(s) and closing entries relating to the investments. The market price of the Ferry Intercommunications stock was $10 per share.
1998		
January	2	Sold the remaining Ferry Intercommunications common shares for $10.2 million.
	5	Purchased Warehouse Designs Corporation bonds for $34 million.

Required:

1. Prepare the appropriate journal entry for each transaction or event during 1997.
2. Indicate any amounts that American would report on its 1997 balance sheet and income statement as a result of these investments.
3. Prepare the appropriate journal entry for each transaction or event during 1998.

Problem 12–3
Securities held to maturity, securities available for sale, and trading securities

Amalgamated General Corporation is a consulting firm that also offers financial services through its credit division. From time to time the company buys and sells securities intending to earn profits on short-term differences in price. The following selected transactions relate to Amalgamated's investment activities during the last quarter of 1997 and the first month of 1998. The only securities held by Amalgamated at October 1 were $30 million of 10% bonds of Kansas Abstractors, Inc., purchased on May 1 at face value. The company's fiscal year ends on December 31.

1997

October	18	Purchased 2 million preferred shares of Millwork Ventures Company for $58 million as a speculative investment to be sold under suitable circumstances.
	31	Received semiannual interest of $1.5 million from the Kansas Abstractors bonds.
November	1	Purchased 10% bonds of Holistic Entertainment Enterprises at their $18 million face value, to be held until they mature in 2007. Semiannual interest is payable April 30 and October 31.

November	1	Sold the Kansas Abstractors bonds for $28 million because rising interest rates are expected to cause their fair value to continue to fall.
December	1	Purchased 12% bonds of Household Plastics Corporation at their $60 million face value, to be held until they mature in 2017. Semiannual interest is payable May 31 and November 30.
	20	Purchased U.S. Treasury bonds for $5.6 million as trading securities, hoping to earn profits on short-term differences in prices.
	21	Purchased 4 million common shares of NXS Corporation for $44 million as trading securities, hoping to earn profits on short-term differences in prices.
	23	Sold the Treasury bonds for $5.7 million.
	29	Received cash dividends of $3 million from the Millwork Ventures Company preferred shares.
	31	Recorded any necessary adjusting entry(s) and closing entries relating to the investments. The market price of the Millwork Ventures Company preferred stock was $27.50 per share and $11.50 per share for the NXS Corporation common. The fair values of the bond investments were $58.7 million for Household Plastics Corporation and $16.7 million for Holistic Entertainment Enterprises.

1998

| January | 7 | Sold the NXS Corporation common shares for $43 million. |

Required:
Prepare the appropriate journal entry for each transaction or event.

Problem 12–4
Investment securities and equity method investments compared

On January 4, 1997, Runyan Bakery paid $324 million for 10 million shares of Lavery Labeling Company common stock. The investment represents a 30% interest in the net assets of Lavery and gave Runyan the ability to exercise significant influence over Lavery's operations. Runyan received dividends of $2.00 per share on December 15, 1997, and Lavery reported net income of $160 million for the year ended December 31, 1997. The market value of Lavery's common stock at December 31, 1997, was $31 per share. The book value of Lavery's net assets was $800 million and:

a.   The fair market value of Lavery's depreciable assets, with an average remaining useful life of 6 years, exceeded their book value by $80 million.

b.   The remainder of the excess of the cost of the investment over the book value of net assets purchased was attributable to goodwill to be amortized over 20 years.

Required:
1.   Prepare all appropriate journal entries related to the investment during 1997, assuming Runyan accounts for this investment by the equity method.
2.   Prepare the journal entries required by Runyan, assuming that the 10 million shares represents a 10% interest in the net assets of Lavery rather than a 30% interest.

Problem 12–5
Equity method

Northwest Paperboard Company, a paper and allied products manufacturer, was seeking to gain a foothold in Canada. Toward that end, the company bought 40% of the outstanding common shares of Vancouver Timber and Milling, Inc., on January 2, 1997, for $400 million.

At the date of purchase, the book value of Vancouver's net assets was $775 million. The book values and fair values for all balance sheet items were the same except for inventory and plant facilities. The fair value exceeded book value by $5 million for the inventory and by $20 million for the plant facilities.

The estimated useful life of the plant facilities is 16 years. Goodwill, if any, is to be amortized by Northwest over 40 years. All inventory acquired was sold during 1997.

Vancouver reported net income of $140 million for the year ended December 31, 1997. Vancouver paid a cash dividend of $30 million.

Required:
1.   Prepare all appropriate journal entries related to the investment during 1997.
2.   What amount should Northwest report as its income from its investment in Vancouver for the year ended December 31, 1997?
3.   What amount should Northwest report on its balance sheet as its investment in Vancouver?
4.   What should Northwest report on its statement of cash flows regarding its investment in Vancouver?

Problem 12–6
Equity method

On January 2, 1997, Miller Properties paid $19 million for 1 million shares of Marlon Company's 6 million outstanding common shares. Miller's CEO became a member of Marlon's board of directors during the first quarter of 1997.

The carrying amount of the Marlon's net assets was $90 million. Miller attributed the excess of cost over carrying amount to goodwill. Miller amortizes intangibles over 20 years.

Marlon reported earnings of $12 million and paid dividends of $6 million during 1997. On December 31, 1997, Marlon's common stock was trading on the NYSE at $18.50 per share.

Required:

1. When considering whether to account for its investment in Marlon under the equity method, what criteria should Miller's management apply?
2. Assume Miller accounts for its investment in Marlon using the equity method. Ignoring income taxes, determine the amounts related to the investment to be reported on its 1997:
   a. Income statement.
   b. Balance sheet.
   c. Statement of cash flows.

Problem 12–7
Classifying investments

Indicate (by letter) the way each of the investments listed below most likely should be accounted for based on the information provided.

Item	Reporting Category
____ 1. 35% of the nonvoting preferred stock of American Aircraft Company.	T. Trading securities
____ 2. Treasury bills to be held to maturity.	M. Securities held to maturity
____ 3. Two-year note receivable from affiliate.	A. Securities available for sale
____ 4. Accounts receivable.	E. Equity method
____ 5. Treasury bond maturing in one week.	C. Consolidation
____ 6. Common stock held in trading account for immediate resale.	N. None of these
____ 7. Bonds acquired to profit from short-term differences in price.	
____ 8. 35% of the voting common stock of Computer Storage Devices Company.	
____ 9. 90% of the voting common stock of Affiliated Peripherals, Inc.	
____ 10. Corporate bonds of Primary Smelting Company to be sold if interest rates fall $1/2$%.	
____ 11. 25% of the voting common stock of Smith Foundries Corporation: 51% family-owned by Smith family; fair value determinable.	
____ 12. 17% of the voting common stock of Shipping Barrels Corporation: Investor's CEO on the board of directors of Shipping Barrels Corporation.	

Problem 12–8
Impairment of securities available for sale; troubled debt restructuring
(based on Appendix 12C)

At January 1, 1997, Rothschild Chair Company, Inc., was indebted to First Lincoln Bank under a $20 million, 10% unsecured note. The note was signed January 1, 1991, and was due December 31, 2000. Annual interest was last paid on December 31, 1995. Rothschild Chair Company was experiencing severe financial difficulties and negotiated a restructuring of the terms of the debt agreement.

Required:

Prepare all journal entries by First Lincoln Bank to record the restructuring and any remaining transactions relating to the debt under each of the independent circumstances below:

1. First Lincoln Bank agreed to settle the debt in exchange for land having a fair market value of $16 million but carried on Rothschild Chair Company's books at $13 million.
2. First Lincoln Bank agreed to (a) forgive the interest accrued from last year, (b) reduce the remaining four interest payments to $1 million each, and (c) reduce the principal to $15 million.
3. First Lincoln Bank agreed to defer all payments (including accrued interest) until the maturity date and accept $27,775,000 at that time in settlement of the debt.

Cases

Real World Case 12–1
Securities available for sale

The following disclosure note appeared in the 1993 annual report of the Sprint Corporation.

INVESTMENTS IN COMMON STOCKS

Effective December 31, 1993, Sprint changed its method of accounting for its portfolio of marketable equity securities by adopting *SFAS No. 115,* "Accounting for Certain Investments in Debt and Equity Securities." Accordingly, such investments in common stocks are classified as available for sale and reported at fair value (estimated based on quoted market prices) as of December 31, 1993 and at cost as of December 31, 1992. As of December 31, 1993, the cost of such investments is $202 million, with the gross unrealized holding gains of $101 million reflected as an addition to other shareholders' equity, net of related income taxes. As of December 31, 1992, the market value of such investments was $278 million.

Required:

1. From the information provided by the disclosure note, determine the amount at which Sprint reported its investment in common stock in its 1993 balance sheet.
2. What would have been Sprint's journal entry to reflect the 1993 fair value of the investments?
3. If the requirements of *SFAS No. 115* had been applied in 1992 also, what would have been the journal entry to reflect the 1993 fair value of the investments.

Research Case 12–2
Reporting securities available for sale; obtain and critically evaluate an annual report

Investments in common stocks potentially affect each of the various financial statements as well as the disclosure notes that accompany those statements.

Required:

1. Locate a recent annual report of a public company that includes a footnote that describes an investment in securities available for sale.
2. Under what caption are the investments reported on the comparative balance sheets? Are they reported as current or noncurrent assets?
3. Are realized gains or losses reported in the comparative income statements?
4. Are unrealized gains or losses reported in the comparative statements of shareholders' equity?
5. Are unrealized gains or losses identifiable in the comparative balance sheets? If so, under what caption? Why are unrealized gains or losses reported here rather than on the income statements?
6. Are cash flow effects of these investments reflected in the company's comparative statements of cash flows? If so, what information is provided by this disclosure?
7. Does the footnote provide information not available in the financial statements?

Note: You can obtain copies of annual reports from the investor relations department of the corporation, from a friendly stockbroker, from Public Register's Annual Report Service on the Internet at http://www.PRARS.com. or from EDGAR, the Electronic Data Gathering and Retrieval service of the SEC, at http://www.sec.gov/.

Integrating Case 12–3
How was the adoption of *SFAS 115* an exception to the usual method of accounting for changes in accounting principle?

In Chapter 3 you learned that most changes in accounting principle require reporting the cumulative income effect of the change as part of earnings in the year of the change, but that a few exceptions require retroactive restatement of prior years' financial statements. Also, some changes mandated by new FASB accounting standards require neither of those approaches, and instead require or permit *prospective* application of the new standard. An example of this exception is *SFAS 115*, "Accounting For Certain Investments in Debt and Equity Securities." Recall that the standard requires that certain investments that previously were reported at lower of cost or market were required by the new standard to be reported instead at their fair values.

Required:

Explain how *SFAS 115* is an exception to the general method of accounting for changes in accounting principle.

Trueblood Accounting Case 12–4
Provisions of *SFAS 115*

The following Robert M. Trueblood case is recommended for use with this chapter. The case provides an excellent opportunity for class discussion, group projects, and writing assignments. The case, along with Professor's Discussion Material, can be obtained from the Deloitte & Touche Foundation.

Case 94-10: *Hold That Gain*

This case focuses on the provisions of *SFAS 115* and requires consideration of whether large unrealized gains can result from simply implementing the standard.

International Case 12–5
Comparison of investment accounting in France and the United States

Renault is the largest automobile manufacturer in France. The investment disclosures accompanying the financial statements in Renault's 1993 annual report are reproduced below:

Accounting Policies (in part)

B. Investments

Investments in controlled subsidiaries are accounted for by the equity method:

- this method is applied to all companies within the scope of consolidation, including fully consolidated companies and financial companies over which Regie Renault exercises direct or indirect majority control;
- shareholders' equity in these companies is determined according to the accounting principles applied in the Renault Group's consolidated financial statements;

- in valuing a subsidiary, its shareholdings in companies wholly controlled by the group are valued in the same manner;
- The change during the year in the total percentage of shareholders' equity corresponding to these interests is not an income or loss item; it is entered under shareholders' equity, in "equity valuation surplus." This amount cannot be distributed or offset against losses. If the amount becomes negative, a general provision against investments is set up, by a charge to income.

Investments in companies which are not controlled are valued at the lower of cost or fair market value.

Balance sheets (partial) in millions of French francs	1993	1992
Shareholders' Equity		
Capital stock	3,401	3,401
Excess over par value	14,578	14,578
Revaluation surplus	72	73
Equity method valuation surplus	12,739	13,674
Legal reserves	340	179
Other reserves	2,413	2,413
Retained earnings, beg. of year	3,812	1,672
Net income (loss) for the period	(5,225)	3,251
Investment subsidies received	1	1
Tax basis reserves	4,086	3,301
Total shareholders' equity	36,219	42,543

Required:

On the basis of the information the disclosures provide, compare accounting for investments in France with that in the United States.

Internet Case 12–6
Researching the way investments are reported; retrieving information from the Internet

EDGAR, the Electronic Data Gathering, Analysis, and Retrieval system, performs automated collection, validation, indexing, acceptance, and forwarding of submissions by companies and others who are required by law to file forms with the U.S. Securities and Exchange Commission (SEC). All publicly traded domestic companies use EDGAR to make the majority of their filings. (Filings by foreign companies are not required to be filed on EDGAR, but some of these companies do so voluntarily.) Form 10-K or 10-KSB, which include the annual report, are required to be filed on EDGAR. The SEC makes this information available on the Internet.

Required:

1. Access EDGAR on the Internet. The web address is http://www.sec.gov/.
2. Search for a public company with which you are familiar. Access its most recent 10-K filing. Search or scroll to find the financial statements and related notes.
3. Answer the following questions. (If the chosen company does not report investments in the securities of other companies, choose another company.)
   a. What is the amount and classification of any investment securities reported on the balance sheet? Are unrealized gains or losses reported in the shareholders' equity section?
   b. Are any investments reported by the equity method?
   c. What amounts from these investments are reported on the comparative income statements? Has that income increased or decreased over the years reported?
   d. Are any acquisitions or disposals of investments reported on the statement of cash flows?

Research Case 12–7
Disclosure of derivative risk; research article in *Accounting Horizons*
(based on Appendix 12A)

The objective of *SFAS 105, SFAS 107,* and *SFAS 119* is to provide disclosures useful in assessing risk associated with off-balance-sheet financial instruments. Some of those off-balance-sheet financial instruments are derivatives related to foreign exchange transactions. Professors Goldberg, Tritschler, and Godwin, in "Financial Reporting for Foreign Exchange Derivatives," surveyed actual disclosures on foreign exchange derivatives to examine the extent and usefulness of those disclosures.

Required:

1. In your library or from some other source, locate the indicated article in *Accounting Horizons*, June 1995.
2. What are the three conclusions the authors reach regarding avoiding large derivative losses like those reported recently by Proctor & Gamble and Gibson Greetings, or at least avoiding being surprised by them?

Group Interaction
Case 12–8
Derivatives; hedge accounting
(based on Appendix 12A)

An unsettled question in accounting for derivatives is: Should gains and losses on a hedge instrument be recorded as they occur, or should they be recorded to coincide (match) with income effects of the item being hedged?

ABI Wholesalers plans to issue long-term notes in May that will replace its $20 million of 9.5% bonds when they mature in July. ABI is exposed to the risk that interest rates in July will have risen, increasing borrowing costs (reducing the selling price of its notes). To hedge that possibility, ABI entered a (Treasury bond) futures contract in May to deliver (sell) bonds in July at their *current* price.

As a result, if interest rates rise, borrowing costs will go up for ABI because it will sell notes at a higher interest cost (or lower price). But that loss will be offset (approximately) by the gain produced by being in the opposite position on Treasury bond futures.

Two opposing viewpoints are:

View 1: Gains and losses on instruments designed to hedge anticipated transactions should be recorded as they occur.

View 2: Gains and losses on instruments designed to hedge anticipated transactions should be recorded to coincide (match) with income effects of the item being hedged.

In considering this question, focus on conceptual issues regarding the practicable and theoretically appropriate treatment, unconstrained by GAAP. Your instructor will divide the class into from two to six groups depending on the size of the class. The mission of your group is to reach consensus on the appropriate accounting for the gains and losses on instruments designed to hedge anticipated transactions.

Required:

1. Each group member should deliberate the situation independently and draft a tentative argument prior to the class session for which the case is assigned.
2. In class, each group will meet for 10 to 15 minutes in different areas of the classroom. During that meeting, group members will take turns sharing their suggestions for the purpose of arriving at a single group treatment.
3. After the allotted time, a spokesperson for each group (selected during the group meetings) will share the group's solution with the class. The goal of the class is to incorporate the views of each group into a consensus approach to the situation.

Internet Case 12–9
Researching the way interest rate futures prices are quoted on the Chicago Mercantile Exchange; retrieving information from the Internet (based on Appendix 12A)

The Chicago Mercantile Exchange, or Merc, at 30 S. Wacker Drive in Chicago, is the world's largest financial exchange, an international marketplace enabling institutions and businesses to trade futures and options contracts including currencies, interest rates, stock indices, and agricultural commodities.

Required:

1. Access the Merc on the Internet. The web address is http://www.cme.com/.
2. Access the daily settlement prices within the site. Scroll to find the 13-week Treasury bill futures.
3. What are the settlement prices for March, June, September, and December futures contracts?
4. In terms of dollars, how can we interpret the settlement price?

13 CHAPTER

CURRENT LIABILITIES AND CONTINGENCIES

OVERVIEW

With the discussion of investments in the previous chapter, we concluded our six-chapter coverage of assets that began in Chapter 7 with cash and receivables. This is the first of six chapters devoted to liabilities. Here, we focus on short-term liabilities. Bonds and long-term notes are discussed in the next chapter. Obligations relating to leases, income taxes, pensions, and other postretirement benefits are the subjects of the following four chapters. In Part A of this chapter, we discuss open accounts and notes, accrued liabilities, and other liabilities that are classified appropriately as current. In Part B we turn our attention to situations in which there is uncertainty as to whether an obligation really exists. These are designated as loss contingencies.

LEARNING OBJECTIVES   After studying this chapter, you should be able to:

1. Define liabilities and distinguish between current and long-term liabilities.
2. Account for the issuance and payment of various forms of notes and record the interest on the notes.
3. Characterize accrued liabilities and liabilities from advance collection and describe when and how they should be recorded.
4. Determine when a liability can be classified as a noncurrent obligation.
5. Identify situations that constitute contingencies and the circumstances under which they should be accrued.
6. Describe the appropriate accounting treatment for contingencies, including unasserted claims and assessments.

WENTWORTH'S WIFE

By the time you finish this chapter, you should be able to respond appropriately to the questions posed in this case. Compare your response to the solution provided at the end of the chapter.

"My wife is confused," your friend Buzz Wentworth proclaims at the office one morning. "You see, we're competing against each other in that investment game I told you about, and one of her hot investments is Alt Microsystems. When she got their annual report yesterday afternoon, she started analyzing it, you know, really studying it closely. Then she asked me about this part here." Buzz pointed to the current liability section of the balance sheet and related disclosure note:

Alt Microsystems, Inc.
Balance Sheet ($ in millions)
December 31, 1997 and 1996

Current Liabilities:	1997	1996
Accounts payable	$233.5	$241.6
Short-term borrowings (Note 3)	187.0	176.8
Accrued liabilities	65.3	117.2
Accrued loss contingency	76.9	—
Other current liabilities	34.6	45.2
Current portion of long-term debt	44.1	40.3
Total current liabilities	641.4	621.1

Note 3: Short-term borrowings (in part)

The components of short-term borrowings and their respective weighted average interest rates at the end of the period are as follows:

In millions:	1997		1996	
	Amount	Average Interest Rate	Amount	Average Interest Rate
Commercial paper	$ 34.0	5.2%	$ 27.1	5.3%
Bank loans	218.0	5.5	227.7	5.6
Amount reclassified to long-term liabilities	(65.0)	—	(78.0)	—
Total short-term borrowings	$187.0		$176.8	

The Company maintains bank credit lines sufficient to cover outstanding short-term borrowings. As of December 31, 1997, the Company had $200.0 million fee-paid lines available.

At December 31, 1997 and 1996, the Company classified $65.0 million and $78.0 million, respectively, of commercial paper and bank notes as long-term debt. The Company has the intent and ability, through formal renewal agreements, to renew these obligations into future periods.

Note 6: Contingencies (in part)

Between 1995 and 1996, the Company manufactured cable leads which, the Company has learned, contribute to corrosion of linked components with which they are installed. At December 31, 1997, the Company accrued 132.0 million in anticipation of remediation and claims settlement deemed probable, of which $76.9 million is considered a current liability.

"So, what's the problem?" you asked.

"Well, she thinks I'm some sort of financial wizard because I'm in the business."

"And because you tell her so all the time," you interrupted.

"Maybe so, but she's been told that current liabilities are riskier than long-term liabilities, and now she's focusing on that. She can't see why some long-term debt is reported here in the current section. And it also looks like some is reported the other way around; some current liabilities reported as long term. Plus, the contingency amount seems like it's not even a contractual liability. Then she wants to know what some of those terms mean. Lucky for me, we had to leave before I had to admit I didn't know the answers. You're the accounting graduate; help me out."

QUESTIONS

1. What are accrued liabilities? What is commercial paper?
2. Why did Alt Microsystems include some long-term debt in the current liability section?
3. Did they also report some current amounts as long-term debt? Explain.
4. Must obligations be known contractual debts to be reported as liabilities?
5. Is it true that current liabilities are riskier than long-term liabilities?

PART

CURRENT LIABILITIES

Before a business can invest in an asset it first must acquire the money to pay for it. This can happen in either of two ways—funds can be provided by owners, or the funds must be borrowed. You may recognize this as a description of the basic accounting equation: liabilities and owners' equity on the right-hand side of the equation represent the two basic sources of the assets on the left-hand side. You studied assets in the chapters leading to this one and you will study owners' equity later. This chapter and the next four describe the various liabilities that constitute creditors' claims on a company's assets.

> Liabilities and owners' equity accounts represent specific sources of a company's assets.

Characteristics of Liabilities

You already know what liabilities are. You encounter them every day. The multibillion dollar national debt we hear discussed almost daily is a liability of all of us. Our creditors are the individuals and institutions that have bought debt securities from (loaned money to) our government. Similarly, when businesses issue notes and bonds, their creditors are the banks, individuals, and organizations that exchange cash for those securities. If you are paying for a car or a home with monthly payments, you have a personal liability. Each of these obligations represents the most common type of liability—one to be paid in cash and for which the amount and timing are specified by a legally enforceable contract.

> Most liabilities obligate the debtor to pay cash at specified times and result from legally enforceable agreements.

> **Entities routinely incur most liabilities to acquire the funds, goods, and services they need to operate and just as routinely settle the liabilities they incur.[1]**

However, to be reported as a **liability**, an obligation need not be payable in cash. Instead, it may require the company to transfer other assets or to provide services. It also need not be represented by a written agreement nor be legally enforceable. Even the amount and timing of repayment need not be precisely known. From a financial reporting perspective, a liability has three essential characteristics. Liabilities:

> Some liabilities are not contractual obligations and may not be payable in cash.

> **Learning objective 1**
> Define liabilities and distinguish between current and long-term liabilities.

1. Are *probable, future* sacrifices of economic benefits.
2. Arise from *present* obligations (to transfer goods or provide services) to other entities.
3. Result from *past* transactions or events.[2]

Notice that the definition of a liability involves the present, the future, and the past. It is a present responsibility to sacrifice assets in the future because of a transaction or other event that already has happened.

> A **liability** is a present obligation to sacrifice assets in the future because of something that already has occurred.

---

[1]"Elements of Financial Statements," *Statement of Financial Accounting Concepts No. 6*, par. 36 (Stamford, Conn.: FASB, 1985), par. 38.
[2]Ibid.

Later in the chapter we'll discuss several liabilities that possess these characteristics but have elements of uncertainty regarding the amount and timing of payments and sometimes even their existence.

What Is A Current Liability?

In a classified balance sheet, liabilities are categorized as either **current liabilities** or long-term liabilities. Listing financial statement elements by classification provides additional clarification concerning the nature of those elements. In the case of liabilities, the additional information provided by the classification relates to their relative riskiness. Will payment require the use of current assets and reduce the amount of liquid funds available for other uses? If so, are sufficient liquid funds available to pay currently maturing obligations in addition to meeting current operating needs? Or is the due date comfortably in the future, permitting resources to be used for other purposes without risking default or without compromising operating efficiency? Classifying liabilities as either current or long term helps investors and creditors assess the riskiness of a business's obligations in this regard. In this chapter, we focus on current liabilities. The next three chapters address liabilities classified as long term.

> Classifying liabilities as either current or long term helps investors and creditors assess the relative risk of a business's liabilities.

We often characterize current liabilities as obligations payable within one year or within the firm's operating cycle, whichever is longer. This general definition usually applies. However, a more discriminating definition identifies current liabilities as those expected to be satisfied with *current assets* or by the creation of other *current liabilities*.[3]

> **Current liabilities** are expected to require current assets and usually are payable within one year.

As you study the liabilities discussed in this chapter, you should be aware that a practical expediency usually affects the way current liabilities are reported on the balance sheet. Conceptually, liabilities should be recorded at their present values. In other words, the amount recorded is the present value of all anticipated future cash payments resulting from the debt (specifically, principal and interest payments). This is due to the time value of money.[4] However, in practice liabilities payable within one year ordinarily are recorded instead at their maturity amounts.[5] The inconsistency usually is inconsequential because the relatively short-time maturity of current liabilities makes the interest or time value component immaterial.

> Current liabilities ordinarily are reported at their maturity amounts.

The most common obligations reported as current liabilities are accounts payable, notes payable, commercial paper, income tax liability, accrued liabilities, and contingencies. Liabilities related to income taxes are the subject of Chapter 16. We discuss the others here.

Before we examine specific current liabilities, let's use the current liability section of the balance sheet of General Mills, Inc., and related disclosure notes to overview the chapter and to provide perspective on the liabilities we discuss (Graphic 13–1).

You may want to refer back to portions of Graphic 13–1 as corresponding liabilities are described later in the chapter. We discuss accounts payable and notes payable first.

Open Accounts and Notes

Many businesses buy merchandise or supplies on credit. Most also find it desirable to borrow cash from time to time to finance their activities. In this section we discuss the liabilities these borrowing activities create: namely, trade accounts and trade notes, bank loans, and commercial paper.

Accounts Payable and Trade Notes Payable

> Buying merchandise on account in the ordinary course of business creates **accounts payable**.

Accounts payable are obligations to suppliers of merchandise or of services purchased on *open account*. Most trade credit is offered on open account. This means that the only formal credit instrument is the invoice. Because the time until payment usually is short (often 30, 45, or 60 days), these liabilities typically are noninterest-bearing and are reported at their face amounts. As shown in Graphic 13–1, General Mills' largest current liability in 1996 was accounts payable, $591 million. The key accounting considerations relating to accounts payable are determining their existence and ensuring that they are recorded in the appropriate accounting period. You stud-

---

[3]Committee on Accounting Procedure, American Institute of CPAs, *Accounting Research and Terminology Bulletin, Final Edition* (New York: AICPA, August 1961), p. 21.

[4]You learned the concept of the time value of money and the mechanics of present value calculations in Chapter 6.

[5]In fact, those arising in connection with suppliers in the normal course of business and due within a year are specifically exempted from present value reporting by "Interest on Receivables and Payables," *Accounting Principles Board Opinion No 21* (New York: AICPA, August 1971), par. 3.

GRAPHIC   13–1

Current Liabilities— General Mills

In practice, there is little uniformity regarding precise captions used to describe current liabilities or in the extent to which accounts are combined into summary captions. These are representative and fairly typical.

Amounts reported on the face of the balance sheet seldom are sufficient to adequately describe current liabilities. Additional descriptions are provided in disclosure notes.

About 50% of General Mills' current liabilities are in the form of trade credit.

GENERAL MILLS, INC.
BALANCE SHEET ($ IN MILLIONS)
MAY 26, 1996, AND MAY 28, 1995

Assets
(by classification)

Liabilities

Current Liabilities:	1996	1995
Accounts payable	$ 590.7	$ 494.0
Current portion of long-term debt	75.4	93.7
Notes payable	141.6	112.9
Accrued taxes	124.3	108.8
Accrued payroll	124.7	118.2
Other current liabilities	135.2	293.3
Total current liabilities	1,191.9	1,220.9

Long-term Liabilities:

(listed individually)

Shareholders' Equity
(by source)

Note Eight: Notes Payable

The components of notes payable and their respective weighted average interest rates at the end of the period are as follows:

In millions	1996		1995	
	Note Payable	Weighted-Average Interest Rate	Note Payable	Weighted-Average Interest Rate
U.S. commercial paper	$ 15.0	5.2%	$ 78.3	6.1%
Canadian commercial paper	19.9	4.8	22.8	7.7
Financial institutions	281.7	5.4	261.8	6.4
Amount reclassified to long-term debt	(175.0)	—	(250.0)	—
Total notes payable	$141.6		$112.9	

To ensure availability of funds, we maintain bank credit lines sufficient to cover our outstanding short-term borrowings. As of May 26, 1996, we had $350.0 million fee-paid lines and $64.6 million uncommitted, no-fee lines available in the U.S. and Canada. In addition, other foreign subsidiaries had no-fee lines of $122.7 million of which $55.3 million are unused.

We have a revolving credit agreement expiring in December 2000 that provides for the fee-paid credit lines. This agreement provides us with the ability to refinance short-term borrowings on a long-term basis, and therefore we have reclassified a portion of our notes payable to long-term debt.

ied these issues and learned how cash discounts are handled during your study of inventories in Chapter 8.

Trade notes payable differ from accounts payable in that they are formally recognized by a written promissory note. Often these are of a somewhat longer term than open accounts and sometimes they bear interest.

Short-Term Notes Payable

The most common way for a corporation to obtain temporary financing is to arrange a short-term bank loan. When a company borrows cash from a bank and signs a promissory note (essentially an IOU), the firm's liability is reported as *notes payable* (sometimes *bank loans* or *short-term borrowings*). About two-thirds of bank loans are short term, but because many are routinely renewed, some tend to resemble long-term debt. In fact, in some cases we report them as long-term financing (as you'll see later in the chapter).

Very often, smaller firms are unable to tap into the major sources of long-term financing to the extent necessary to provide for their capital needs. So they must rely heavily on short-term financing. Even large companies typically utilize short-term debt as a significant and indispensable component of their capital structure. One reason is that short-term funds usually offer lower interest rates than long-term debt. Perhaps most importantly, corporations desire flexibility. As a rule, managers want as many financing alternatives as possible.

A **line of credit** allows a company to borrow cash without having to follow formal loan procedures and paperwork.

Credit Lines.   Usually short-term bank loans are arranged under an existing **line of credit** with a bank or group of banks. These can be noncommitted or committed lines of credit. A *noncommitted* line of credit is an informal agreement that permits a company to borrow up to a prearranged limit without having to follow formal loan procedures and paperwork. Banks sometimes require the company to maintain a compensating balance on deposit with the bank, say, 5% of the line of credit.[6] The 1996 annual report of Campbell Soup Company illustrates a noncommitted line of credit (Graphic 13–2).

GRAPHIC   13–2

Disclosure of Short-term Borrowings—Campbell Soup Company

Note 15 Notes Payable and Long-Term Debt (in part): ($ in millions)

The amount of unused lines of credit at July 28, 1996, approximates $856. The lines of credit are unconditional and generally cover loans for a period of one year at prime commercial rates.

A *committed* line of credit is a formal arrangement usually requiring a commitment fee and sometimes a compensating balance.

A *committed* line of credit is a more formal agreement that usually requires the firm to pay a commitment fee to the bank. A typical annual commitment fee is ¼% of the total committed funds. Banks often require smaller firms to keep compensating balances in the bank. A recent disclosure note of the Black and Decker Corporation describes a committed line of credit as shown in Graphic 13–3.

GRAPHIC   13–3

Disclosure of Committed Line of Credit—Black and Decker Corporation

Note 5: Short-term Borrowings (in part)

The Corporation also has a revolving credit facility in the amount of $90,000,000 with several commercial banks. This facility is at various interest rates at the Corporation's option based on the prime London interbank borrowing, certificates of deposit, bankers' acceptance, or other negotiated rates; and it also can be used to support the issuance of commercial paper in the United States and in European markets through dealers at the best available open market rates. Commitment fees are .25% on the unused balance during the availability period.

General Mills' disclosure notes that we looked at in Graphic 13–1 indicate the company has both noncommitted and committed lines of credit.

Interest.   Interest on notes is calculated as:

$$\text{Face amount} \times \text{Annual rate} \times \text{Time to maturity}$$

This is demonstrated in Illustration 13–1.

ILLUSTRATION   13–1

Note Issued for Cash

Learning objective 2
Account for the issuance and payment of various forms of notes and record the interest on the notes.

Interest on notes is calculated as:

$$\frac{\text{Face}}{\text{amount}} \times \frac{\text{Annual}}{\text{rate}} \times \frac{\text{Time to}}{\text{maturity}}$$

On May 1, 1997, Affiliated Technologies, Inc., a consumer electronics firm, borrowed $700,000 cash from First BancCorp under a noncommitted short-term line of credit arrangement and issued a six-month, 12% promissory note. Interest was payable at maturity.

May 1, 1997		
Cash	700,000	
Notes payable		700,000
November 1, 1997		
Interest expense ($700,000 × 12% × 6/12)	42,000	
Notes payable	700,000	
Cash ($700,000 + 42,000)		742,000

---

[6]A compensating balance is a deposit kept by a company in a low-interest or noninterest-bearing account at the bank. The required deposit usually is some percentage of the committed amount or the amount used (say, 2% to 5%). The effect of the compensating balance is to increase the borrowers effective interest rate and the bank's effective rate of return.

Sometimes a bank loan assumes the form of a so-called **noninterest-bearing note.** Obviously, though, no bank will lend money without interest. Noninterest-bearing loans actually do bear interest, but the interest is deducted (or discounted) from the face amount to determine the cash proceeds made available to the borrower at the outset. For example, the preceding note could be packaged as a $700,000 noninterest-bearing note, with a 12% discount rate. In that case, the $42,000 interest would be discounted at the outset, rather than explicitly stated:[7]

> When interest is discounted from the face amount of a note, the effective interest rate is higher than the stated discount rate.

> The proceeds of the note are reduced by the interest in a noninterest-bearing note.

May 1, 1997		
Cash (difference)	658,000	
Discount on notes payable ($700,000 × 12% × $^{6}/_{12}$])	42,000	
Notes payable (face amount)		700,000
November 1, 1997		
Interest expense	42,000	
Discount on notes payable		42,000
Notes payable (face amount)	700,000	
Cash		700,000

Notice that the amount borrowed under this arrangement is only $658,000, but the interest is calculated as the discount rate times the $700,000 face amount. This causes the *effective* interest rate to be higher than the 12% stated rate:

$$\frac{\$42,000 \text{ Interest for 6 months}}{\$658,000 \text{ Amount borrowed}} = 6.38\% \text{ Rate for 6 months}$$

To annualize:

$$6.38\% \times {}^{12}/_6 = 12.76\% \text{ Effective interest rate}$$

We studied short-term notes from the perspective of the lender (note receivable) in Chapter 7.

Secured Loans. Sometimes short-term loans are *secured,* meaning a specified asset of the borrower is pledged as collateral or security for the loan. Although many kinds of assets can be pledged, the secured loans most frequently encountered in practice are secured by inventory or accounts receivable. For example, Collins Industries, Inc., which sells vehicle chassis to major vehicle manufacturers, disclosed the secured notes described in Graphic 13–4.

> Inventory or accounts receivable often are pledged as security for short-term loans.

GRAPHIC 13–4

Disclosure of Notes Secured by Inventory— Collins Industries, Inc.

Note 4: Chassis Floorplan Notes Payable (in part)

Chassis floorplan notes are payable to a financing subsidiary of a chassis manufacturer. These notes are secured by the related chassis and are payable upon the earlier of the date the Company sells the chassis or 180 days from the date of the note.

When accounts receivable serve as collateral, we refer to the arrangement as *pledging* accounts receivable. Sometimes, the receivables actually are sold outright to a finance company as a means of short-term financing. This is called *factoring* receivables.[8]

---

[7]The entries shown assume the note is recorded by the gross method. By the net method, the interest component is netted against the face amount of the note as follows:

May 1, 1997		
Cash	658,000	
Notes payable		658,000
November 1, 1997		
Interest expense ($700,000 × 12% × $^{6}/_{12}$)	42,000	
Notes payable	658,000	
Cash		700,000

[8]Both methods of accounts receivable financing were discussed in Chapter 7, "Cash and Receivables."

The financial market is becoming increasingly multinational. World markets have grown dramatically in the last decade. The commercial unification of European countries, the emergence of Japan as the country having the largest value of securities traded, and the fall of communism in portions of Europe and Asia are both causes and symptoms of the heightened globalization of the capital marketplace.

Companies wishing to reduce their exposure to risk and to widen their choices of funding sources are taking advantage of the broader opportunities the global environment provides. Increasingly, U.S. corporate debt is displaying a multinational dimension, with statements of financial position often reporting short-term to intermediate-term loans in several different countries. Loans from foreign banks that are denominated in dollars are called Eurodollar loans. Also, foreign loans frequently are denominated in the currency of the lender (Swiss franc, German mark, and so on). When loans must be repaid in foreign currencies a new element of risk is introduced. This is because if exchange rates change, the number of dollars representing the foreign currency that must be repaid differs from the number of dollars representing the foreign currency borrowed. We discussed hedging against this risk exposure in the previous chapter.[9]

> Corporations often have loans from banks in many different countries.

Commercial Paper

> Large, highly rated firms sometimes sell **commercial paper** to borrow funds at a lower rate than through a bank loan.

> OPENING CASE
>
> Question 1

Some large corporations obtain temporary financing by issuing **commercial paper,** often purchased by other companies as a short-term investment. Commercial paper refers to unsecured notes sold in minimum denominations of $25,000 with maturities ranging from 30 to 270 days (beyond 270 days the firm would be required to file a registration statement with the SEC). Interest often is discounted at the issuance of the note. Usually commercial paper is issued directly to the buyer (lender) and is backed by a line of credit with a bank (see the Black & Decker disclosure note in Graphic 13–3). This allows the interest rate to be lower than in a bank loan. Commercial paper has become an increasingly popular way for large companies to raise funds, the total amount having expanded over fivefold in the last decade.

The name *commercial paper* refers to the fact that a paper certificate traditionally is issued to the lender to signify the obligation, although there is a trend toward total computerization of paper sold directly to the lender so that no paper is created. Since commercial paper is a form of notes payable, recording its issuance and payment is exactly the same as our earlier illustration. We discuss long-term notes in the next chapter.

Accrued Liabilities

> **Learning objective 3**
> Characterize accrued liabilities and liabilities from advance collection and describe when and how they should be recorded.

> Liabilities accrue for expenses that are incurred but not yet paid.

Accrued liabilities represent expenses already incurred but for which cash has yet to be paid (accrued expenses). These are recorded by adjusting entries at the end of the reporting period, prior to preparing financial statements. You learned how to record accrued liabilities in your study of introductory accounting and you reinforced your understanding in Chapter 2. Common examples are salaries and wages payable, income taxes payable, and interest payable.

Accrued Interest Payable

Accrued interest payable arises in connection with notes like those discussed earlier in this chapter (as well as other forms of debt). For example, to continue Illustration 13–1, let's assume the fiscal period for Affiliated Technologies ends on June 30, two months after the six-month note is issued. The issuance of the note, intervening adjusting entry, and note payment would be recorded as shown in Illustration 13–1a (shown at the top of the next page).

Salaries, Commissions, and Bonuses

Compensation for employee services can be in the form of hourly wages, salary, commissions, bonuses, stock compensation plans, or pensions.[10] Accrued liabilities arise in connection with

---

[9]Elsewhere in your accounting curriculum, often in advanced accounting, you will learn how foreign-currency-denominated loans are translated into dollars in U.S. financial statements, as well as how to account for gains and losses resulting from changes in exchange rates.

[10]Pensions are discussed in Chapter 17, and stock-based compensation plans and bonuses are discussed in Chapter 18.

[handwritten margin note: "on exam ✓"]

[handwritten margin note: "7/1 Reversing Entry"]

ILLUSTRATION 13–1a

Note with Accrued Interest

> At June 30, two months' interest has accrued and is recorded to avoid misstating expenses and liabilities on the June 30 financial statements.

Issuance of note May 1, 1997

Cash	700,000	
Note payable		700,000

Accrual of interest on June 30, 1997

Interest expense ($700,000 $\times$ 12% $\times$ $^2/_{12}$)	14,000	
Interest payable		14,000

Note payment November 1, 1997 *[handwritten: 6/12]*

Interest expense ($700,000 $\times$ 12% $\times$ $^4/_{12}$) *[handwritten: 81,000]*	~~28,000~~ *[handwritten: 42,000]*	
~~Interest payable~~ (from adjusting entry)	~~14,000~~	
Note payable	700,000	
Cash ($700,000 + 42,000)		~~742,000~~

[handwritten: 84,000]

compensation expense when employee services have been performed as of a financial statement date, but employees have yet to be paid. These accrued expenses/accrued liabilities are recorded by adjusting entries at the end of the reporting period, prior to preparing financial statements.

Liabilities From Advance Collections

Liabilities are created when amounts are received that will be returned or remitted to others. Deposits and advances from customers and collections for third parties are cases in point.

Deposits and Advances from Customers

Collecting cash from a customer as a refundable deposit or as an advance payment for products or services creates a liability to return the deposit or to supply the products or services.[11]

Refundable Deposits.   In some businesses it's typical to require customers to pay cash as a deposit that will be refunded when a specified event occurs. You probably have encountered such situations. When apartments are rented, security or damage deposits often are collected. Utility companies frequently collect deposits when service is begun. Similarly, deposits sometimes are required on returnable containers, to be refunded when the containers are returned. The situation is demonstrated in Illustration 13–2.

ILLUSTRATION 13–2

Refundable Deposits

> When a deposit becomes nonrefundable, inventory should be reduced to reflect the fact that the containers won't be returned.

Rancor Chemical Company sells combustible chemicals in expensive, reusable containers. Customers are charged a deposit for each container delivered and receive a refund when the container is returned. Deposits collected on containers delivered in 1997 were $300,000. Deposits are forfeited if containers are not returned within one year. Ninety percent of the containers were returned within the allotted time. Deposits charged are twice the actual cost of containers. The inventory of containers remains on the company's books until deposits are forfeited.

When deposits are collected

Cash	300,000	
Liability—refundable deposits		300,000

When containers are returned*

Liability—refundable deposits	270,000	
Cash		270,000

When deposits are forfeited*

Liability—refundable deposits	30,000	
Revenue—sale of containers		30,000
Cost of goods sold	15,000	
Inventory of containers		15,000

* Of course, not all containers are returned at the same time, nor does the allotted return period expire at the same time for all containers not returned. These entries summarize the several individual returns and forfeitures.

---

[11]*SFAC 6* specifically identifies customer advances and deposits as liabilities under the definition provided in that statement. "Elements of Financial Statements," *Statement of Financial Accounting Concepts No. 6* (Stamford, Conn.: FASB, 1985), par. 197.

Advances From Customers.   At times, businesses require advance payments from customers that will be applied to the purchase price when goods are delivered or services provided. Gift certificates, magazine subscriptions, layaway deposits, special order deposits, and airline tickets are examples. These customer advances represent liabilities until the related product or service is provided. For instance, the largest liability reported by Readers Digest Association, Inc., is deferred revenue from the sale of magazine subscriptions ($354.9 million in 1996). Advances are demonstrated in Illustration 13–3.

ILLUSTRATION   13–3

Customer Advance

> A customer advance produces an obligation that is satisfied when the product or service is provided.

Tomorrow Publications collects magazine subscriptions from customers at the time subscriptions are sold. Subscription revenue is recognized over the term of the subscription. Tomorrow collected $20 million in subscription sales during 1997, its first year of operations. At December 31, 1997, the average subscription was one-fourth expired.

	($ in millions)	
When advance is collected		
Cash	20	
Liability—subscriptions paid *(or customer deposits)*		20
When product is delivered		
Liability—subscriptions paid	5	
Subscriptions revenue		5

The New York Times Company described its recognition of revenue from newspaper subscriptions in the disclosure note shown in Graphic 13–5.

GRAPHIC   13–5

Disclosure of Advances from Customers—The New York Times Company

Note 1: Summary of Significant Accounting Policies (in part)

Proceeds from subscriptions are deferred at the times of sale as unexpired subscriptions and are included in revenues on a pro rata basis over the terms of the subscriptions.

Like refundable deposits, customer advances forfeited (for instance, gift certificates not redeemed) create gains when they are deemed forfeited. Liability accounts produced by customer deposits and advances are classified as current or long-term liabilities depending on when the obligation is expected to be satisfied.

Collections for Third Parties

Companies often make collections for third parties from customers or from employees and periodically remit these amounts to the appropriate governmental (or other) units. Amounts collected this way represent liabilities until remitted.

An example is sales taxes. For illustration, assume a state sales tax rate of 4% and local sales tax rate of 3%. Adding the tax to a $100 sale creates a $7 liability until the tax is paid:

> Sales taxes collected from customers represent liabilities until remitted.

Cash (or accounts receivable)	107	
Sales revenue		100
Sales taxes payable ([4% + 3%] × $100)		7

> Amounts collected from employees in connection with payroll also represent liabilities until remitted.

Payroll-related deductions such as withholding taxes, social security taxes, employee insurance, employee contributions to retirement plans, and union dues also create current liabilities until the amounts collected are paid to appropriate parties. These payroll-related liabilities are explored further in the Appendix to this chapter.

Although recorded in separate liability accounts, accrued liabilities usually are combined and reported under a single caption or perhaps two accrued liability captions in the balance sheet.

A Closer Look at the Current and Noncurrent Classification

█ **Learning objective 4**
Determine when a liability can be classified as a noncurrent obligation.

Given a choice, do you suppose management would prefer to report an obligation as a current liability or as a noncurrent liability? Other things being equal, most would opt for the noncurrent classification. The reason is that in most settings outsiders (like banks, bondholders, and shareholders) consider debt that is payable currently to be riskier than debt that need not be paid for some time. Relatedly, the long-term classification enables the company to report higher working capital (current assets minus current liabilities) and a higher current ratio (current assets / current liabilities). Working capital and the current ratio often are explicitly restricted in loan contracts. As you study this section, you should view the classification choice from this perspective. That is, the question is not so much "What amount should be reported as a current liability?" but rather "What amount can be excluded from classification as a current liability?"

Current Maturities of Long-Term Debt

OPENING CASE

Question 2

█ The currently maturing portion of a long-term debt must be reported as a current liability.

Long-term obligations (bonds, notes, lease liabilities, deferred tax liabilities) usually are reclassified and reported as current liabilities when they become payable within the upcoming year (or operating cycle, if longer than a year). For example, a 20-year bond issue is reported as a long-term liability for 19 years but normally is reported as a current liability on the balance sheet prepared during the 20th year of its term to maturity.[12] General Mills reported $75.4 million of its long-term debt as a current liability in 1996 (see Graphic 13–1, page 532).

Obligations Callable by the Creditor

█ Long-term liabilities that are due on demand—by terms of the contract or violation of contract covenants—must be reported as current liabilities.

The requirement to classify currently maturing debt as a current liability includes debt that is *callable* (in other words, due on demand) *by the creditor* in the upcoming year (or operating cycle, if longer), even if the debt is not expected to be called. The current liability classification also is intended to include situations in which the creditor has the right to demand payment because an *existing violation* of a provision of the debt agreement makes it callable (say, working capital has fallen below a contractual minimum). This also includes situations in which debt is not yet callable but will be callable within the year if an existing violation is not corrected within a specified grace period (unless it's probable the violation will be corrected within the grace period).[13]

When Short-Term Obligations Are Expected to Be Refinanced

OPENING CASE

Question 3

█ Short-term obligations can be reported as noncurrent liabilities if the company (a) *intends* to refinance on a long-term basis and (b) demonstrates the *ability* to do so by a refinancing agreement or by actual financing.

Reconsider the 20-year bond issue we discussed earlier. Normally we would reclassify it as a current liability on the balance sheet prepared during its 20th year. But suppose a second 20-year bond issue is sold to refund the first issue at maturity. Do we have a long-term liability for 19 years, a current liability for a year, and then another long-term liability? Or, do we have a single 40-year, long-term liability? If we look beyond the outward form of the transactions, the substance of the events obviously supports a single, continuing, noncurrent obligation. The concept of substance over form motivates the classification of obligations expected to be refinanced.

Short-term obligations (including the callable obligations we discussed in the previous section) that are expected to be refinanced on a long-term basis can be reported as noncurrent, rather than current, liabilities only if two conditions are met. The firm (1) must intend to refinance on a long-term basis and (2) must actually have demonstrated the ability to do so. Ability to refinance on a long-term basis can be demonstrated by either an existing refinancing agreement or by actual financing prior to the issuance of the financial statements.[14] An example will provide perspective (Illustration 13–4).

If shares of stock had been issued to refinance the bonds in the illustration, the bonds still would be excluded from classification as a current liability. The specific form of the long-term refinancing (bonds, bank loans, equity securities) is irrelevant when determining the appropriate

---

[12]Debt to be refinanced is an exception we discuss later.

[13]"Classification of Obligations that Are Callable by the Creditor," *Statement of Financial Accounting Standards No 78* (Stamford, Conn.: FASB, 1983).

[14]"Classification of Obligations Expected To Be Refinanced," *Statement of Financial Accounting Standards No 6* (Stamford, Conn.: FASB, 1975).

ILLUSTRATION 13–4

Short-Term Obligations that Are Expected to Be Refinanced on a Long-Term Basis

Brahm Bros. Ice Cream had $12 million of notes that mature in May 1998 and also had $4 million of bonds issued in 1975 that mature in February 1998. On December 31, 1997, the company's fiscal year-end, management intended to refinance both on a long-term basis.

On February 7, 1998, the company issued $4 million of 20-year bonds, applying the proceeds to repay the bond issue that matured that month. In early March, prior to the actual issuance of the 1997 financial statements, Brahm Bros. negotiated a line of credit with a commercial bank for up to $7 million any time during 1998. Any borrowings will mature two years from the date of borrowing. Interest is at the prime London interbank borrowing rate.*

Classification:	December 31, 1997
	($ in 000)
Current liabilities:	
Notes payable	$5,000
Long-term liabilities:	
Notes payable	$7,000
Bonds payable	4,000

Management's ability to refinance the bonds on a long-term basis was demonstrated by actual financing prior to the issuance of the financial statements. Ability to refinance $7 million of the notes is demonstrated by a refinancing agreement. The remaining $5 million must be reported as a current liability.

* This is a widely available rate often used as a basis for establishing interest rates on lines of credit.

classification. Requiring companies to actually demonstrate the ability to refinance on a long-term basis in addition to merely intending to do so avoids intentional or unintentional understatements of current liabilities.

It's important to remember that several weeks usually pass between the end of a company's fiscal year and the date the financial statements for that year actually are issued. Events occurring during that period can be used to clarify the nature of financial statement elements at the reporting date. Here we consider refinancing agreements and actual securities transactions to support a company's ability to refinance on a long-term basis. Later in the chapter we use information that becomes available during this period to decide how loss contingencies are reported.

CONCEPT REVIEW EXERCISE

CURRENT LIABILITIES

The following selected transactions relate to liabilities of Southern Communications, Inc., for portions of 1997 and 1998. Southern's fiscal year ends on December 31.

Required:

Prepare the appropriate journal entries for these transactions.

1997

July	1	Arranged an uncommitted short-term line of credit with First City Bank amounting to $25,000,000 at the bank's prime rate (11.5% in July). The company will pay no commitment fees for this arrangement.
Aug.	9	Received a $30,000 refundable deposit from a major customer for copper-lined mailing containers used to transport communications equipment.
Oct.	7	Received most of the mailing containers covered by the refundable deposit and a letter stating that the customer will retain containers represented by $2,000 of the deposit and forfeits that amount. The cost of the forfeited containers was $1,500.
Nov.	1	Borrowed $7 million cash from First City Bank under the line of credit arranged in July and issued a nine-month promissory note. Interest at the prime rate of 12% was payable at maturity.
Dec.	31	Recorded appropriate adjusting entries for the liabilities described above.

1998

Feb.	12	Using the unused portion of the credit line as support, issued $9 million of commercial paper and issued a six-month promissory note. Interest was discounted at issuance at a 10% discount rate.
Aug.	1	Paid the 12% note at maturity.
	12	Paid the commercial paper at maturity.

Good Review Exercise

CRE

CONCEPT REVIEW EXERCISE

SOLUTION

1997

July 1 No entry is made for a line of credit until a loan actually is made. The existence and terms of the line would be described in a disclosure note.

Aug. 9

Cash	30,000	
Liability—refundable deposits		30,000

Oct. 7

Liability—refundable deposits	30,000	
Cash		28,000
Revenue—sale of containers		2,000
Cost of goods sold	1,500	
Inventory of containers		1,500

Nov. 1

Cash	7,000,000	
Notes payable		7,000,000

Dec. 31

Interest expense ($7,000,000 \times 12\% \times {}^{2}/_{12}$)	140,000	
Interest payable		140,000

1998

Feb. 12

Cash ($\$9,000,000 - [\$9,000,000 \times 10\% \times {}^{6}/_{12}]$)	8,550,000	
Note payable		8,550,000

Note that the effective interest rate is ($[\$9,000,000 \times 10\% \times {}^{6}/_{12}] \div \$8,550,000) \times {}^{12}/_{6} = \$450,000 \div \$8,550,000 \times 2 = 10.53\%$.

Aug. 1

Interest expense ($7,000,000 \times 12\% \times {}^{7}/_{12}$)	490,000	
Interest payable (from adjusting entry)	140,000	
Note payable (face amount)	7,000,000	
Cash ($7,000,000 + 630,000)		7,630,000

Aug. 12

Interest expense ($9,000,000 \times 10\% \times {}^{6}/_{12}$)	450,000	
Note payable (face amount)	8,550,000	
Cash ($8,550,000 + 450,000)		9,000,000

PART

B

CONTINGENCIES

Learning objective 5
Identify situations that constitute contingencies and the circumstances under which they should be accrued.

The feature that distinguishes the contingencies we discuss in this part of the chapter from the liabilities we discussed previously is uncertainty as to whether an obligation really exists. The existing uncertainty will be resolved only when some future event occurs (or doesn't occur). We will discuss gain contingencies, too, because of their similarity to loss contingencies.

Loss Contingencies

Ford Motor Company's financial statements recently indicated potential obligations from pending lawsuits (shown in Graphic 13–6).

GRAPHIC   13–6

Disclosure of Pending Litigation—Ford Motor Company

Note 13: Litigation and Claims (in part)

Various legal actions, governmental investigations and proceedings and claims are pending or may be instituted or asserted in the future against the company and its subsidiaries, including those arising out of alleged defects in the company's products, governmental regulations relating to safety, emissions and fuel economy, financial services, intellectual property rights, product warranties and environmental matters. Certain of the pending legal actions are, or purport to be, class actions. Some of the foregoing matters involve or may involve compensatory, punitive, or antitrust or other treble damage claims in very large amounts, or demands for recall campaigns, environmental remediation programs, sanctions, or other relief which, if granted, would require very large expenditures.

The disclosure indicates that if certain events occur, "very large expenditures" would result. Do these contingencies represent liabilities of Ford? Certainly the liabilities *may* exist on the date of the financial statements. But how likely is an unfavorable outcome? Also, precise amounts of any obligations Ford may have are unknown. But can the amounts be estimated? These are the key questions addressed by accounting standards for loss contingencies.

A **loss contingency** is an existing, uncertain situation involving potential loss depending on whether some future event occurs. Whether a contingency is accrued and reported as a liability depends on (a) the likelihood that the confirming event will occur and (b) what can be determined about the amount of loss. Consider an IRS assessment of back taxes, pending at year-end, for which the outcome will not be known until after the financial statements are issued. The likelihood must be assessed that the company will pay the back taxes and if so, what the payment amount will be.

> A **loss contingency** involves an existing uncertainty as to whether a loss really exists, where the uncertainty will be resolved only when some future event occurs.

Note that the cause of the uncertainty must occur before the statement date. In this case, the prior years' operations for which the tax liability is questioned occurred before the current accounting period ended. Otherwise, regardless of the likelihood of the eventual outcome, no liability could have existed at the statement date. Recall that one of the essential characteristics of a liability is that it results "from past transactions or events."

Accounting standards require that the likelihood that the future event(s) will confirm the incurrence of the liability be (somewhat arbitrarily) categorized as probable, reasonably possible, or remote:[15]

OPENING CASE

Question 4

Likelihood That a Liability Exists

> **Learning objective 6**
> Describe the appropriate accounting treatment for contingencies, including unasserted claims and assessments.

Probable—Confirming event is likely to occur.
Reasonably possible—The chance the confirming event will occur is more than remote but less than likely.
Remote—The chance the confirming event will occur is slight.

Also key to reporting a contingent liability is its dollar amount. The amount of the potential loss is classified as either known, reasonably estimable, or not reasonably estimable. A liability is accrued if it is both probable that the confirming event will occur and the amount can be at least reasonably estimated.[16] A general depiction of the accrual of a loss contingency is:

Accrual of a Loss Contingency—Liability

Loss (or expense)	x,xxx	
Liability		x,xxx

In a recent annual report (Graphic 13–7), Motorola reported a loss contingency it had accrued for a claim against it by the Environmental Protection Agency for which the company deemed payment was both probable and reasonably estimable.

---

[15]"Accounting for Contingencies," *Statement of Financial Accounting Standards No 5* (Stamford, Conn.: FASB, 1975).

[16]If one amount within a range of possible loss appears better than other amounts within the range, that amount is accrued. When no amount within the range appears more likely than others, the *minimum* amount should be *recorded* and the possible *additional loss* should be *disclosed*. "Reasonable Estimation of the Amount of the Loss," *FASB Interpretation No. 14* (Stamford, Conn.: FASB, 1976).

GRAPHIC   13–7

Accrual of Litigation Contingency—Motorola, Inc.

(In millions, except as noted)

Note 6: Commitments and Contingencies (in part)

Environmental and Legal: Under the Comprehensive Environmental Response Compensation and Liability Act of 1980, as amended (CERCLA, or Superfund), the Company has been designated as a potentially responsible party by the United States Environmental Protection Agency with respect to certain waste sites with which the Company may have had direct or indirect involvement. Such designations are made regardless of the extent of the Company's involvement. These claims are in various stages of administrative or judicial proceedings. They include demands for recovery of past governmental costs and for future investigations or remedial actions. In many cases, the dollar amounts of the claims have not been specified, and have been asserted against a number of other entities for the same cost recovery or other relief as was asserted against the Company. The Company accrues cost associated with environmental matters when they become probable and reasonably estimable, which totaled $70 million as of December 31, 1994.

It's important to note that some loss contingencies don't involve liabilities at all. Some contingencies when resolved cause a noncash asset to be impaired, so accruing it means reducing the related asset rather than recording a liability:

Accrual of a Loss Contingency—Asset Impairment

| Loss (or expense) .... | X,XXX | |
| Asset (or valuation account) .... | | X,XXX |

The most common loss contingency of this type is an uncollectible receivable. You have recorded these before without knowing you were accruing a loss contingency (*Debit*: bad debt expense; *Credit*: allowance for uncollectible accounts).

If one or both of these criteria is not met, but there is at least a reasonable possibility that the loss will occur, a disclosure note should describe the contingency. It also should provide an estimate of the possible loss or range of loss, if possible. If an estimate cannot be made, a statement to that effect is needed.

> A loss contingency is disclosed in notes to the financial statements if there is at least a reasonable possibility that the loss will occur.

Ford Motor Company felt the loss contingency from the lawsuits described in the disclosure note above fit the reasonably possible and not reasonably estimable combination and accordingly did not accrue a liability but provided the information noted in Graphic 13–8.

GRAPHIC   13–8

Disclosure of Loss Contingencies—Ford Motor Company

Note 13: Litigation and Claims (continued)

Litigation is subject to many uncertainties, and the outcome of individual litigated matters is not predictable with assurance. It is reasonably possible that some of the matters discussed in the foregoing paragraph could be decided unfavorably to the company or the subsidiary involved and could require the company or such subsidiary to pay damages or make other expenditures in amounts or a range of amounts that at December 31, 1994 cannot reasonably be estimated. Although the final resolution of any such matters could have a material effect on the company's consolidated financial results for a particular reporting period, the company believes that, based on its analysis, any resulting liability should not materially affect the company's consolidated financial position at December 31, 1994.

Graphic 13–9 highlights appropriate accounting treatment for each possible combination of (a) the likelihood of an obligation's being confirmed and (b) the determinability of its dollar amount.

Product Warranties and Guarantees

> Most consumer products are accompanied by a guarantee.

Manufacturer's Original Warranty.   Satisfaction guaranteed! Your money back if not satisfied! If anything goes wrong in the first five years or 50,000 miles . . .! 3-year guarantee! These and sim-

GRAPHIC   1 3 – 9

Accounting Treatment of Loss Contingencies

A loss contingency is accrued only if a loss is probable and the amount can reasonably be estimated.

	Dollar Amount of Potential Loss		
Likelihood	Known	Reasonably Estimable	Not Reasonably Estimable
Probable	Liability accrued and disclosure note	Liability accrued and disclosure note	Disclosure note only
Reasonably Possible	Disclosure note only	Disclosure note only	Disclosure note only
Remote	No disclosure required*	No disclosure required*	No disclosure required*

*Except for certain guarantees and other specified off-balance-sheet risk situations discussed in a later section.

ilar promises accompany most consumer goods. The reason—to boost sales. It follows, then, that any costs of making good on such guarantees should be recorded as expenses in the same accounting period the products are sold. The obstacle is that much of the cost usually occurs later, sometimes years later. This is a loss contingency. There may be a future sacrifice of economic benefits (cost of satisfying the guarantee) due to an existing circumstance (the guaranteed products have been sold) that depends on an uncertain future event (customer claim).

As you might expect, meeting the accrual criteria is more likely for some types of loss contingencies than for others. For instance, the outcome of pending litigation is particularly difficult to predict. On the other hand, the criteria for accrual almost always are met for some types of loss contingencies. Product warranties (or product guarantees) inevitably entail costs. And while we usually can't predict the liability associated with an individual sale, reasonably accurate estimates of the *total* liability for a period usually are possible, based on prior experience. So the contingent liability for warranties and guarantees usually is accrued. The estimated warranty (guarantee) liability is credited and warranty (guarantee) expense is debited in the reporting period in which the product under warranty is sold. This is demonstrated in Illustration 13–5.

The contingent liability for product warranties almost always is accrued.

ILLUSTRATION   1 3 – 5

Product Warranty

The costs of satisfying guarantees should be recorded as expenses in the same accounting period the products are sold.

Caldor Health, a supplier of in-home health care products, introduced a new therapeutic chair carrying a two-year warranty against defects. Estimates based on industry experience indicate warranty costs of 3% of sales during the first 12 months following the sale and 4% the next 12 months. During December 1997, its first month of availability, Caldor sold $2 million of the chairs.

During December

Cash (and accounts receivable)	2,000,000	
Sales revenue		2,000,000

December 31, 1997 (adjusting entry)

Warranty expense ([3% + 4%] × $2,000,000)	140,000	
Estimated warranty liability		140,000

When customer claims are made and costs are incurred to satisfy those claims, the liability is reduced (let's say $61,000 in 1998):

Estimated warranty liability	61,000	
Cash, wages payable, parts and supplies, etc.		61,000

Estimates of warranty costs cannot be expected to be precise. However, if the estimating method is monitored and revised when necessary, overestimates and underestimates should cancel each other over time. The estimated liability may be classified as current or as part current and part long-term, depending on when costs are expected to be incurred.

Extended Warranty Contracts.   It's difficult these days to buy a CD player, or a microwave oven, or a car, or almost any durable consumer product without being asked to buy an extended warranty agreement. An extended warranty provides warranty protection beyond the manufacturer's original warranty. Because an extended warranty is priced and sold separately from the warranted product, it essentially constitutes a separate sales transaction. The accounting question is "when should the revenue from the sale be recognized?"

By the accrual concept, revenue is recognized when earned, not necessarily when cash is received. Because the earning process for an extended warranty continues during the contract period, revenue should be recognized over the same period. So, revenue from separately priced extended warranty contracts is deferred as a liability at the time of sale and recognized on a straight-line basis over the contract period. Notice that this is similar to an advance payment for products or services that, as we discussed earlier, creates a liability to supply the products or services. We demonstrate accounting for extended warranties in Illustration 13–6.

ILLUSTRATION 13–6

Extended Warranty

The manufacturer's warranty covers 1997. Revenue from the extended warranty is recognized during the three years of the contract period.

Brand Name Appliances sells major appliances that carry a one-year manufacturer's warranty. Customers are offered the opportunity at the time of purchase to also buy a three-year extended warranty for an additional charge. On January 3, 1997, Brand Name sold a $60 extended warranty.

January 3, 1997

Cash (or accounts receivable)	60	
Unearned revenue—extended warranties		60

December 31, 1998, 1999, 2000 (adjusting entries)

Unearned revenue—extended warranties	20	
Revenue—extended warranties ($60 ÷ 3)		20

Remember that the costs incurred to satisfy customer claims under the extended warranties also will be recorded during the same three-year period, achieving a proper matching of revenues and expenses. If sufficient historical evidence indicates that the costs of satisfying customer claims will be incurred on other than a straight-line basis, revenue should be recognized by the same pattern (proportional to the costs).[17]

Premiums

Cash rebates have become commonplace. Cash register receipts, bar codes, rebate coupons, or other proofs of purchase often can be mailed to the manufacturer for cash rebates. Sometimes promotional offers promise premiums other than cash (like toys, dishes, and utensils) to buyers of certain products. Of course the purpose of these premium offers is to stimulate sales. So it follows that the estimated amount of the cash rebates or the cost of noncash premiums estimated to be given out represents both an expense and an estimated liability in the reporting period the product is sold. Like a manufacturer's warranty, this loss contingency almost always meets accrual criteria. Premiums are illustrated in Illustration 13–7.

ILLUSTRATION   13–7

Premiums

The costs of promotional offers should be recorded as expenses in the same accounting period the products are sold.

CMX Corporation offered $2 cash rebates on a particular model of hand-held hair dryers. To receive the rebate, customers must mail in a rebate certificate enclosed in the package plus the cash register receipt. Previous experience indicates that 30% of coupons will be redeemed. One million hair dryers were sold in 1997 and total payments to customers were $225,000.

Promotional expense (30% × $2 × 1,000,000)	600,000	
Estimated premium liability		600,000
To record the estimated liability for premiums.		
Estimated premium liability	225,000	
Cash		225,000
To record payments to retailers for coupons.		

---

[17]"Accounting for Separately Priced Extended Warranty and Product Maintenance Contracts," *FASB Technical Bulletin 90-1*, 1990.

The remaining liability of $375,000 is reported on the 1997 balance sheet and is reduced as future rebates are paid. The liability should be classified as current or long term depending on when future rebates are expected to be paid.

Of course, if premiums actually are included in packages of products sold, no contingent liability is created. For example, the costs of toys in Cracker Jack boxes and cereal boxes, towels in detergent boxes, and compact discs in drink cartons are simply expenses of the period the product is sold, for which the amount is readily determinable.

Additional Consideration

Cents-off coupons are an increasingly popular marketing tool. Coupons clipped from newspapers, from mail offers, or included in packages are redeemable for cash discounts at the time promoted items are purchased. Issuing the coupons creates a contingent liability to be recorded in the period the coupons are issued. However, because the hoped-for sales don't materialize until later, a question arises as to when the related expense should be recognized. Logically, since the purpose of coupon offers is to stimulate sales, the expense properly should be deferred until the coupons are redeemed (when the sales occur).

Illustration

On December 18, 1997, Craft Foods distributed coupons in newspaper inserts offering 50 cents off the purchase price of one of its cereal brands when coupons are presented to retailers. Retailers are reimbursed by Craft for the face amount of coupons plus 10% for handling. Previous experience indicates that 20% of coupons will be redeemed. Coupons issued had a total face amount of $1,000,000 and total payments to retailers in 1997 were $50,000. Retailers were paid $170,000 in 1998.

Promotional expense (redeemed in 1997)	50,000	
Cash		50,000

To record payments to retailers for coupons in 1997.

Deferred promotional expense	170,000	
Estimated coupon liability ([20% × $1,000,000 × 1.10] − $50,000)		170,000

To record the estimated liability for coupons in 1997.

Estimated coupon liability	170,000	
Cash		170,000
Promotional expense (redeemed in 1998)	170,000	
Deferred promotional expense		170,000

To record payments to retailers for coupons in 1998.

This situation, though prevalent, is not addressed by promulgated accounting standards. In practice, most firms either (a) recognize the entire expense with the liability in the period the coupons are issued, like we record premiums, or (b) recognize no liability in the period the coupons are issued, recording the expense when reimbursements are made. One reason is that the same coupons are reissued periodically, making it difficult to associate specific reimbursements with specific offers. Another reason is that the time lag between the time a merchant receives coupons from customers and the time it's presented to the manufacturer for reimbursement prevents appropriate apportionment of the expense.

Litigation Claims

Pending litigation similar to that disclosed by Ford in Graphic 13–8 on page 542 is not unusual. In fact, the majority of medium and large corporations annually report loss contingencies due to litigation. By far the most common disclosure is nonspecific regarding the actual litigation but uses wording similar to this contingency disclosure from an annual report of Hasbro, Inc. (Graphic 13–10).

GRAPHIC 13–10

Disclosure of Litigation Contingencies—Hasbro, Inc.

Note 14: Commitments and Contingencies (in part)

The Company is involved in various claims and legal actions arising in the ordinary course of business. In the opinion of management, the ultimate disposition of these matters will not have a material adverse effect on the Company's consolidated financial position.

You are chief financial officer of Camp Industries. Camp is the defendant in a $44 million class action suit. The company's legal counsel informally advises you that chances are remote that the company will emerge victorious in the lawsuit. Counsel feels the company will probably lose $30 million. You recall that under the provisions of "Accounting For Contingencies," *Statement of Financial Accounting Standards No. 5,* a loss contingency should be accrued if a loss is probable and the amount can reasonably be estimated. A colleague points out that, in practice, *accrual* of a loss contingency for unsettled litigation is rare. After all, disclosure that management feels it is probable that the company will lose a specified dollar amount would be welcome ammunition for the opposing legal counsel. He suggests that a loss not be recorded until after the ultimate settlement has been reached. What do you think?

Subsequent Events

It's important to remember several weeks usually pass between the end of a company's fiscal year and the date the financial statements for that year actually are issued. Events occurring during this period can be used to clarify the nature of financial statement elements at the report date. This situation can be represented by the following time line:

> When the cause of a loss contingency occurs before the year-end, a clarifying event before financial statements are issued can be used to determine how the contingency is reported.

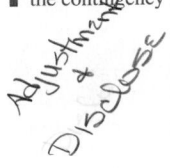

For instance, if information becomes available that sheds light on a lawsuit that existed when the fiscal year ended, that information should be used in determining the probability of a loss contingency materializing and in estimating the amount of the loss. The settlement of a lawsuit after the May 31 report date of Dean Foods Company apparently influenced its accrual of a loss contingency at May 31 (Graphic 13–11).

GRAPHIC   13–11

Accrual of Litigation Contingency—Dean Foods

(Dollar amounts in thousands unless otherwise noted)

Notes: Litigation (in part)

In February 1988, a civil antitrust action was filed by the Florida Attorney General on behalf of school boards located in thirty-two Florida counties. The complaint alleged that several dairies and distributors, including three of the Company's subsidiaries, conspired to rig bids and allocate contracts to supply milk from at least 1977 to 1987. In addition to this civil action, a federal grand jury is investigating the pricing of certain dairy products sold in Florida during the same period.

On August 1, 1988, the Company announced that it had reached a settlement with state authorities on this matter. As a result, the Company, based upon discussions with legal counsel, has accrued and charged to operations in the fourth quarter, $9,025 to cover the anticipated cost of all Florida pricing actions. The Company believes that the ultimate settlement of these and other unrelated claims and lawsuits will not have a material adverse effect on the Company's financial position.

For a loss contingency to be accrued, the cause of the lawsuit must have occurred before the accounting period ended. It's not necessary that the lawsuit actually was filed during that reporting period.

Sometimes, the cause of a loss contingency occurs after the end of the year but before the financial statements are issued:

> If an event giving rise to a contingency occurs after the year-end, a liability should not be accrued.

When a contingency comes into existence after the year-end, a liability cannot be accrued because it didn't exist at the end of the year. However, if the failure to disclose the possible loss would cause the financial statements to be misleading, the situation should be described in a disclosure note, including the effect of the possible loss on key accounting numbers affected.[18]

In fact, *any* event occurring after the fiscal year-end but before the financial statements are issued that has a material effect on the company's financial position must be disclosed in a subsequent events disclosure note. Examples are an issuance of debt or equity securities, a business combination, and discontinued operations. A disclosure note of the Campbell Soup Company from its 1996 annual report is shown in Graphic 13–12 and describes an event that will occur in the first quarter of fiscal 1997.

GRAPHIC   13–12

**Subsequent Events—
Campbell Soup Company**

Note 21: Subsequent Events (in part)   *($ in millions)*

On September 4, 1996, the company's Board of Directors approved a divestiture and restructuring program which includes the divestiture of several non-strategic businesses and the sale of various plant operations. An after-tax charge of approximately $160 is expected to be recorded in the first quarter of fiscal 1997 for this program.

Unasserted Claims and Assessments

It must be probable that an unasserted claim or assessment or an unfiled lawsuit will occur before considering whether and how to report the possible loss.

Even if a claim has yet to be made when the financial statements are issued, a contingency may warrant accrual or disclosure. However, an unfiled lawsuit or an unasserted claim or assessment need not be disclosed unless it is *probable that the suit, claim, or assessment will occur.* If it is probable, then the likelihood of an unfavorable outcome and the feasibility of estimating a dollar amount should be considered in deciding whether and how to report the possible loss.

For example, the IRS may be in the process of auditing a company's tax returns and has not proposed a deficiency assessment. If management feels an assessment is probable, reporting the possible tax assessment would be warranted if an unfavorable settlement is at least reasonably possible. That is, an estimated loss and contingent liability would be accrued if an unfavorable outcome is probable and the amount can be reasonably estimated, otherwise footnote disclosure would be appropriate. Notice that when the claim or assessment is unasserted as yet, a two-step process is involved in deciding how it should be reported:

1. Is a claim or assessment probable? {If not, no disclosure is needed.}
2. Only if a claim or assessment is probable should we evaluate (a) the likelihood of an unfavorable outcome and (b) whether the dollar amount can be estimated.

If the conclusion of step 1 is that the claim or assessment *is not* probable, no further action is required. If the conclusion of step 1 is that the claim or assessment *is* probable, the decision as to whether or not a liability is accrued or disclosed is precisely the same as when the claim or assessment already has been asserted.

Accrued loss contingencies meet the SFAC 6 definition of liabilities.

Notice that the treatment of contingent liabilities is consistent with the accepted definition of liabilities as (a) probable, future sacrifices of economic benefits (b) that arise from present obligations to other entities and (c) that result from past transactions or events.[19] The inherent uncertainty involved with contingent liabilities means additional care is required to determine whether future sacrifices of economic benefits are probable and whether the amount of the sacrifices can be quantified.

Gain Contingencies

Gain contingencies are not accrued.

A gain contingency is an uncertain situation that might result in a gain. For example, in a pending lawsuit, one side—the defendant—faces a loss contingency; the other side—the plaintiff—has a gain contingency. As we discussed earlier, loss contingencies are accrued when the event confirming the obligation is probable and the amount can reasonably be estimated. However, gain contingencies are not accrued. The nonparallel treatment of gain contingencies follows

---

[18]"Accounting for Contingencies," *Statement of Financial Accounting Standards No 5* (Stamford, Conn.: FASB, 1975), par. 11.

[19]"Elements of Financial Statements," *Statement of Financial Accounting Concepts No. 6* (Stamford, Conn.: FASB, 1985).

the same conservative reasoning that motivates reporting some assets at lower of cost or market. Specifically, it's desirable to anticipate losses, but recognizing gains should await their realization.

Though gain contingencies are not recorded in the accounts, they should be disclosed in notes to the financial statements. Care should be taken that the disclosure note not give "misleading implications as to the likelihood of realization."[20]

CONCEPT REVIEW EXERCISE   CONTINGENCIES

Hanover Industries manufactures and sells food products and food processing machinery. While preparing December 31, 1997, financial statements for Hanover, the following information was discovered relating to contingencies and possible adjustments to liabilities. Hanover's 1997 financial statements were issued on April 1, 1998.

a. On November 12, 1997, a former employee filed a lawsuit against Hanover alleging age discrimination and asking for damages of $750,000. At December 31, 1997, Hanover's attorney indicated that the likelihood of losing the lawsuit was possible but not probable. On March 5, 1998, Hanover agreed to pay the former employee $125,000 in return for withdrawing the lawsuit.

b. After a tax audit of the 1996 return, the IRS has questioned some expenses paid to a major stockholder. At April, 1998, the IRS has not yet made an assessment of additional taxes, but Hanover feels it will. Hanover's accountants and legal counsel believe the deductions were appropriate but that if an assessment is made, there is a reasonable possibility that subsequent court action would result in an additional tax liability of $55,000.

c. Hanover grants a one-year warranty for each processing machine sold. Past experience indicates that the costs of satisfying warranties are approximately 2% of sales. During 1997, sales of processing machines totaled $21,300,000. 1997 expenditures for warranty repair costs were $178,000 related to 1997 sales and $220,000 related to 1996 sales. The January 1, 1997, balance of the warranty liability account was $250,000.

d. Hanover is the plaintiff in a $600,000 lawsuit filed in 1996 against Ansdale Farms for failing to deliver on contracts for produce. The suit is in final appeal. Legal counsel advises that it is probable that Hanover will prevail and will be awarded $300,000.

e. Included with certain food items sold in 1997 were coupons redeemable for a kitchen appliance at the rate of five coupons per appliance. During 1997, 30,000 coupons were issued and 5,000 coupons were redeemed. Although this is the first such promotion in years, past experience indicates that 60% of coupons are never redeemed. An inventory of kitchen appliances is maintained, and a count shows that 1,000 are on hand at December 31, 1997, with a normal retail value of $20,000 and a cost to Hanover of $8,000.

Required:

1. Determine the appropriate means of reporting each situation. Briefly explain your reasoning.
2. Prepare any necessary journal entries and state whether a disclosure note is needed.

CONCEPT REVIEW EXERCISE   SOLUTION

a. This is a loss contingency. Hanover can use the information occurring after the end of the year in determining appropriate disclosure. The cause for the suit existed at the end of the year. Hanover should accrue the $125,000 loss because an agreement has been reached confirming the loss and the amount is known.

| Loss—litigation .... | 125,000 | |
| Liability—litigation .... | | 125,000 |

[20]"Accounting For Contingencies," *Statement of Financial Accounting Standards No 5* (Stamford, Conn.: FASB, 1975), par. 17.

A disclosure note also is appropriate.

b. At the time financial statements are issued, an IRS claim is as yet unasserted. However, an assessment is probable. Thus, (a) the likelihood of an unfavorable outcome and (b) whether the dollar amount can be estimated are considered. No accrual is necessary because an unfavorable outcome is not probable. But because an unfavorable outcome is reasonably possible, a disclosure note is appropriate.

Note: If the likelihood of a claim being asserted is not probable, disclosure is not required even if an unfavorable outcome is thought to be probable in the event of an assessment and the amount is estimable.

c. The contingency for warranties should be accrued because it is probable that expenditures will be made and the amount can be estimated from past experience. When customer claims are made and costs are incurred to satisfy those claims the liability is reduced.

Warranty expense (2% × $21,300,000)	426,000	
Estimated warranty liability		426,000
Estimated warranty liability ($178,000 + $220,000)	398,000	
Cash, wages payable, parts and supplies, etc.		398,000

The liability at December 31, 1997, would be reported as $278,000:

Warranty Liability
(in 000s)

		250	Balance, Jan. 1
		426	1997 expense
1997 expenditures	398		
		278	Balance, Dec. 31

A disclosure note also is appropriate.

d. This is a gain contingency. Gain contingencies cannot be accrued even if the gain is probable and reasonably estimable. The gain should be recognized only when realized. It can be disclosed, but care should be taken to avoid misleading language regarding the realizability of the gain.

e. The contingency for premiums should be accrued because it is probable that coupons will be redeemed and the amount can be estimated from past experience. When coupons are redeemed and appliances are issued, the liability is reduced.

Promotional expense (40% × [30,000 ÷ 5] × $8*)	19,200	
Estimated premium liability		19,200
Estimated premium liability ([5,000 ÷ 5] × $8*)	8,000	
Inventory of premiums		8,000
*$8,000 ÷ 1,000 = $8		

The liability at December 31, 1997, would be reported as $11,200:

Premium Liability

		19,200	1997 expense
1997 expenditures	8,000		
		11,200	Balance, Dec. 31

A disclosure note also is appropriate.

Decision-Makers' Perspective

Current liabilities impact a company's liquidity. Liquidity refers to a company's cash position and overall ability to obtain cash in the normal course of business. A company is said to be liquid if it has sufficient cash or is capable of converting its other assets to cash in a relatively short period of time so that currently maturing debts can be paid. Because the lack of liquidity can

OPENING CASE

Question 5

An analyst of risk should be concerned with a company's ability to meet its short-term obligations.

cause the demise of an otherwise healthy company, it is critical that managers as well as outside investors and creditors maintain close scrutiny of this aspect of a company's well-being.

Keeping track of the current ratio is one of the most common ways of doing this. The current ratio is intended as a measure of short-term solvency and is determined by dividing current assets by current liabilities.

When we compare liabilities that must be satisfied in the near term with assets that either are cash or will be converted to cash in the near term, we get a useful measure of a company's liquidity. A ratio of 1 to 1 or higher often is considered a rule-of-thumb standard, but like other ratios, acceptability should be evaluated in the context of the industry in which the company operates and other specific circumstances. Keep in mind, though, that industry averages are only one indication of adequacy and that the current ratio is but one indication of liquidity.

A manager should actively monitor the company's liquidity.

We can adjust for the implicit assumption of the current ratio that all current assets are equally liquid. The acid-test, or quick, ratio is similar to the current ratio but is based on a more conservative measure of assets available to pay current liabilities. Specifically, the numerator, quick assets, includes only cash and cash equivalents, short-term investments, and accounts receivable. By eliminating current assets such as inventories and prepaid expenses that are less readily convertible into cash, the acid-test ratio provides a more rigorous indication of a company's short-term solvency than does the current ratio.

A liquidity ratio is but one indication of a company's liquidity.

If either of these liquidity ratios is less than that of the industry as a whole, does that mean that liquidity is a problem? Perhaps; perhaps not. It does, though, raise a red flag that suggests caution when assessing other areas. It's important to remember that each ratio is but one piece of the puzzle. For example, profitability is probably the best long-run indication of liquidity. Also, management may be very efficient in managing current assets so that some current assets—receivables or inventory—are more liquid than they otherwise would be and more readily available to satisfy liabilities. The turnover ratios discussed in earlier chapters help measure the efficiency of asset management in this regard.

Outside analysts as well as managers should actively monitor risk management activities.

Relatedly, most companies attempt to actively manage the risk associated with these and other obligations as discussed in previous sections of this chapter. It is important for top management to understand and closely monitor risk management strategies. Some of the financial losses that have grabbed headlines in recent years were permitted by a lack of oversight and scrutiny by senior management of companies involved. It is similarly important for investors and creditors to become informed about risks companies face and how well-equipped those companies are in managing that risk. The risk disclosures and derivative disclosures we discussed in this and the previous chapter contribute to that understanding.

In the next chapter, we continue our discussion of liabilities. Our focus will shift from current liabilities to long-term liabilities in the form of bonds and long-term notes.

Solution to Financial Reporting Case (at the opening of the chapter)

1. What are accrued liabilities? What is commercial paper?

Accrued liabilities are reported for expenses already incurred but not yet paid (accrued expenses). These include salaries and wages payable, income taxes payable, and interest payable. Commercial paper is a form of notes payable sometimes used by large corporations to obtain temporary financing. It is sold to other companies as a short-term investment. It represents unsecured notes sold in minimum denominations of $25,000 with maturities ranging from 30 to 270 days. Typically, commercial paper is issued directly to the buyer (lender) and is backed by a line of credit with a bank.

2. Why did Alt Microsystems include some long-term debt in the current liability section?

Alt Microsystems did include some long-term debt in the current liability section. The currently maturing portion of a long-term debt must be reported as a current liability. Amounts are reclassified and reported as current liabilities when they become payable within the upcoming year.

3. Did they also report some current amounts as long-term debt?

Yes they did. It is permissible to report short-term obligations as noncurrent liabilities if the company (a) intends to refinance on a long-term basis and (b) demonstrates the ability to do so by a refinancing agreement or by actual financing. As the disclosure note explains, this is the case for a portion of Alt's currently payable debt.

4. Must obligations be known contractual debts to be reported as liabilities?

No. From an accounting perspective, it is not necessary that obligations be known, legally enforceable debts to be reported as liabilities. They must only be probable and the dollar amount reasonably estimable.

5. Is it true that current liabilities are riskier than long-term liabilities?

Other things being equal, current liabilities generally are considered riskier than long-term liabilities. For that reason, management usually would rather report a debt as long term. Current debt, though, is not necessarily risky. The liquidity ratios we discussed in the chapter attempt to measure liquidity. Remember, any such measure must be assessed in the context of other factors: industry standards, profitability, turnover ratios, and risk management activities, to name a few.

The Bottom Line

1. Liabilities are present obligations to sacrifice assets in the future because of something that already has occurred. Current liabilities are expected to require current assets (or the creation of other current liabilities) and usually are payable within one year.

2. Short-term bank loans usually are arranged under an existing line of credit with a bank or group of banks. When interest is discounted from the face amount of a note (a so-called noninterest-bearing note), the effective interest rate is higher than the stated discount rate. Large, highly rated firms sometimes sell commercial paper directly to the buyer (lender) to borrow funds at a lower rate than through a bank loan.

3. Accrued liabilities are recorded by adjusting entries for expenses already incurred, but for which cash has yet to be paid (accrued expenses). Familiar examples are salaries and wages payable, income taxes payable, and interest payable.

4. Short-term obligations can be reported as noncurrent liabilities if the company (a) intends to refinance on a long-term basis and (b) demonstrates the ability to do so by actual financing or a formal agreement to do so.

5. A loss contingency is an existing, uncertain situation involving potential loss depending on whether some future event occurs. Whether a contingency is accrued and reported as a liability depends on (a) the likelihood that the confirming event will occur and (b) what can be determined about the amount of loss. It is accrued if it is both probable that the confirming event will occur and the amount can be at least reasonably estimated.

6. A clarifying event before financial statements are issued, but after the year-end, can be used to determine how the contingency is reported. An unasserted suit, claim, or assessment warrants accrual or disclosure if it is probable it will be asserted. A gain contingency is a contingency that might result in a gain. A gain contingency usually is not recognized until it actually is realized.

APPENDIX

13

PAYROLL-RELATED LIABILITIES

All firms incur liabilities in connection with their payrolls. These arise primarily from legal requirements to withhold taxes from employees' paychecks and from payroll taxes on the firms themselves. Some payroll-related liabilities result from voluntary payroll deductions of amounts payable to third parties.

Employees' Withholding Taxes

Employers are required by law to withhold federal (sometimes state) income taxes and social security taxes from employees' paychecks and remit these to the Internal Revenue Service. The amount withheld for federal income taxes is determined by a tax table furnished by the IRS and varies according to the amount earned and the number of exemptions claimed by the employee. Also, the Federal Insurance Contributions Act (FICA) requires employers to withhold a percentage of each employee's earnings up to a specified maximum. Both the percentage and the maximum are changed intermittently. As this text went to print, the deduction for social security was 6.2% of the first $65,400 an employee earns. Additionally, a deduction for Medicare tax was 1.45% with no limit on the base amount. The employer also must pay an equal (matching) amount on behalf of the employee.

Voluntary Deductions

Besides the required deductions for income taxes and social security taxes, employees often authorize their employers to deduct other amounts from their paychecks. These deductions might include union dues, contributions to savings or retirement plans, and insurance premiums. Amounts deducted this way represent liabilities until paid to the appropriate organizations.

Employers' Payroll Taxes

One payroll tax mentioned earlier is the employer's matching amount of FICA taxes. The employer also must pay federal and state unemployment taxes on behalf of its employees. The Federal Unemployment Tax Act (FUTA) requires a tax of 6.2% of the first $7,000 (as of 1997) earned by each employee. This amount is reduced by a 5.4% (maximum) credit for contributions to state unemployment programs, so the net federal rate often is .8%.[21] In many states the state rate is 5.4% but may be reduced by merit ratings affected by the employer's employment experience.

Fringe Benefits

In addition to salaries and wages, withholding taxes, and payroll taxes, many companies provide employees a variety of fringe benefits. Most commonly, employers pay all or part of employees' insurance premiums and/or contributions to retirement income plans.

Representative payroll-related liabilities are presented in Illustration 13A–1.

ILLUSTRATION   13A–1

Payroll-Related Liabilities

Crescent Lighting and Fixtures' payroll for the second week in January was $100,000. The following deductions, fringe benefits, and taxes apply:

Federal income taxes to be withheld	$20,000
State income taxes to be withheld	3,000
Medical insurance premiums (Blue Cross) – 70% paid by employer	1,000
Employee contribution to voluntary retirement plan (Fidelity Investments)—contributions matched by employer	4,000
Union dues (Local No. 222)—paid by employees	100
Life insurance premiums (Prudential Life)—100% paid by employer	200
Social security (FICA) tax rate	7.65%
Federal unemployment tax rate (after state deduction)	0.80%
State unemployment tax rate	5.40%

Salaries and wages expense (total amount earned)	100,000	
Withholding taxes payable (federal income tax)		20,000
Withholding taxes payable (state income tax)		3,000
FICA taxes payable (social security tax: 7.65%)		7,650 ←
Payable to Blue Cross (insurance premiums – 30%)		300 ←
Payable to Fidelity Investments (employees' investment)		4,000 ←
Payable to Local No. 222 (union dues)		100
Salaries and wages payable (net pay)		64,950
Payroll tax expense (total)	13,850	
FICA taxes payable (employer's matching amount)		7,650 ←
FUTA payable (federal unemployment tax: .8%)		800
State unemployment tax payable (5.4%)		5,400
Salaries and wages expense (fringe benefits)	4,900	
Payable to Blue Cross (insurance premiums – 70%)		700 ←
Payable to Fidelity Investments (matching amount)		4,000 ←
Payable to Prudential Life (insurance premiums)		200

Amounts withheld from paychecks represent liabilities until remitted to third parties.

The employer's share of FICA and unemployment taxes constitute the employer's payroll tax expense.

Fringe benefits are part of salaries and wages expense and represent liabilities until remitted to third parties.

As you study the illustration, you should note the similarity among all payroll-related liabilities. Amounts withheld—voluntarily or involuntarily—from paychecks are liabilities until turned over to appropriate third parties. Payroll taxes and expenses for fringe benefits are incurred as a result of services performed by employees and also are liabilities until paid to appropriate third parties.

---

[21]All states presently have unemployment tax programs.

Questions for Review of Key Topics

Question	13–1	What are the essential characteristics of liabilities for purposes of financial reporting?
Question	13–2	What distinguishes current liabilities from long-term liabilities?
Question	13–3	Bronson Distributors owes a supplier $100,000 on open account. The amount is payable in three months. What is the theoretically correct way to measure the reportable amount for this liability? In practice, how will it likely be reported? Why?
Question	13–4	Bank loans often are arranged under existing lines of credit. What is a line of credit? How does a noncommitted line of credit differ from a committed line?
Question	13–5	Banks sometimes loan cash under noninterest-bearing notes. Is it true that banks lend money without interest?
Question	13–6	How does commercial paper differ from a bank loan? Why is the interest rate often less for commercial paper?
Question	13–7	Salaries of $5,000 have been earned by employees by the end of the period but will not be paid to employees until the following period. How should the expense and related liability be recorded? Why?
Question	13–8	How are refundable deposits and customer advances similar? How do they differ?
Question	13–9	Amounts collected for third parties represent liabilities until remitted. Provide several examples of this kind of collection.
Question	13–10	Consider the following liabilities of Future Brands, Inc., at December 31, 1997, the company's fiscal year-end. Should they be reported as current liabilities or long-term liabilities?

1. $77 million of 8% notes are due on May 31, 2001. The notes are callable by the Company's bank, beginning March 1, 1998.
2. $102 million of 8% notes are due on May 31, 2001. A debt covenant requires Future to maintain a current ratio (ratio of current assets to current liabilities) of at least 2 to 1. Future is in violation of this requirement but has obtained a waiver from the bank until May 1998, since both companies feel Future will correct the situation during the first half of 1998.

Question	13–11	Long-term obligations usually are reclassified and reported as current liabilities when they become payable within the upcoming year (or operating cycle, if longer than a year). So, a 25-year bond issue is reported as a long-term liability for 24 years but normally is reported as a current liability on the balance sheet prepared during the 25th year of its term to maturity. Name a situation in which this would not be the case.
Question	13–12	Define a loss contingency. Provide three examples.
Question	13–13	List and briefly describe the three categories of likelihood that a future event(s) will confirm the incurrence of the liability for a loss contingency.
Question	13–14	Under what circumstances should a loss contingency be accrued?
Question	13–15	Suppose the analysis of a loss contingency indicates that an obligation is not probable. What accounting treatment if any is warranted?
Question	13–16	Name two loss contingencies that almost always are accrued.
Question	13–17	Distinguish between the accounting treatment of a manufacturer's warranty and an extended warranty. Why the difference?
Question	13–18	At December 31, the end of the reporting period, the analysis of a loss contingency indicates that an obligation is only reasonably possible, though its dollar amount is readily estimable. During February, before the financial statements are issued, new information indicates the loss is probable. What accounting treatment is warranted?
Question	13–19	After the end of the reporting period, a contingency comes into existence. Under what circumstances, if any, should the contingency be reported in the financial statements for the period ended?
Question	13–20	Suppose the Environmental Protection Agency is in the process of investigating Ozone Ruination Limited for possible environmental damage but has not proposed a penalty as of December 31, 1997, the company's fiscal year-end. Describe the two-step process involved in deciding how this unasserted assessment should be reported.
Question	13–21	You are the plaintiff in a lawsuit. Your legal counsel advises that your eventual victory is inevitable. "You will be awarded $12 million," your attorney confidently asserts. Describe the appropriate accounting treatment.

Exercises

Exercise 13–1
Bank loan; accrued interest

On November 1, 1997, Quantum Technology, a geothermal energy supplier, borrowed $8 million cash to fund a geological survey. The loan was made by Nevada BancCorp under a noncommitted short-term line of credit arrangement. Quantum issued a nine-month, 12% promissory note. Interest was payable at maturity. Quantum's fiscal period is the calendar year.

Required:

1. Prepare the journal entry for the issuance of the note by Quantum Technology.
2. Prepare the appropriate adjusting entry for the note by Quantum on December 31, 1997.
3. Prepare the journal entry for the payment of the note at maturity.

Exercise 13–2
Determining accrued interest in various situations

On July 1, 1997, Ross-Livermore Industries issued nine-month notes in the amount of $200 million. Interest is payable at maturity.

Required:

Determine the amount of interest expense that should be recorded in a year-end adjusting entry under each of the following independent assumptions:

	Interest Rate	Fiscal Year-End
1.	12%	December 31
2.	10%	September 30
3.	9%	October 31
4.	6%	January 31

Exercise 13–3
Multiple choice; current liabilities

The following questions dealing with current liabilities are adapted from questions that appeared on recent CPA examinations. Determine the response that best completes the statements or questions.

1. Black Co. requires advance payments with special orders for machinery constructed to customer specifications. These advances are nonrefundable. Information for 1997 is as follows:

Customer advances—balance 12/31/96	$118,000
Advances received with orders in 1997	184,000
Advances applied to orders shipped in 1997	164,000
Advances applicable to order canceled in 1997	50,000

In Black's December 31, 1997, balance sheet, what amount should be reported as a current liability for advances from customer?
   a. $0.
   b. $88,000.
   c. $138,000.
   d. $148,000.

2. Which of the following is generally associated with payables classified as accounts payable?

	Periodic Payment of Interest	Secured by Collateral
a.	No	No
b.	No	Yes
c.	Yes	No
d.	Yes	Yes

Exercise 13–4
Short-term notes

The following selected transactions relate to liabilities of United Insulation Corporation. United's fiscal year ends on December 31.

Required:

Prepare the appropriate journal entries through the maturity of each liability.

1997
Jan. 13   Negotiated a revolving credit agreement with Parish Bank that can be renewed annually upon bank approval. The amount available under the line of credit is $20,000,000 at the bank's prime rate.
Feb. 1   Arranged a three-month bank loan of $5 million with Parish Bank under the line of credit agreement. Interest at the prime rate of 10% was payable at maturity.
May 1   Paid the 10% note at maturity.
Dec. 1   Supported by the credit line, issued $10 million of commercial paper on a nine-month note. Interest was discounted at issuance at a 9% discount rate.
Dec. 31   Recorded any necessary adjusting entry(s).

1998
Sept. 1   Paid the commercial paper at maturity.

Exercise 13–5
Customer advances; sales taxes

Bavarian Bar and Grill opened for business in November 1997. During its first two months of operation, the restaurant sold gift certificates in various amounts totaling $5,200, mostly as Christmas presents. They are redeemable for meals within two years of the purchase date, although experience within the industry indicates that 80% of gift certificates are redeemed within one year. Certificates totaling $1,300 were presented for redemption during 1997 for meals having a total price of $2,100. The sales tax rate on restaurant sales is 4%, assessed at the time meals (not gift certificates) are purchased. Sales taxes will be remitted in January.

Required:
1. Prepare the appropriate journal entries (in summary form) for the gift certificates during 1996 (keeping in mind that, in actuality, each sale of a gift certificate or a meal would be recorded individually).
2. Determine the liability for gift certificates to be reported on the December 31, 1997, balance sheet.
3. What is the appropriate classification (current or noncurrent) of the liabilities at December 31, 1997? Why?

Exercise 13–6
Customer deposits

Diversified Semiconductors sells perishable electronic components. Some must be shipped and stored in reusable protective containers. Customers pay a deposit for each container received. The deposit is equal to the container's cost. They receive a refund when the container is returned. During 1997, deposits collected on containers shipped were $850,000.

Deposits are forfeited if containers are not returned within 18 months. Containers held by customers at January 1, 1997, represented deposits of $530,000. In 1997, $790,000 was refunded and deposits forfeited were $35,000.

Required:
1. Prepare the appropriate journal entries for the deposits received and returned during 1997.
2. Determine the liability for refundable deposits to be reported on the December 31, 1997, balance sheet.

Exercise 13–7
Various transactions involving advance collections

The following selected transactions relate to liabilities of Interstate Farm Implements for December of 1997. Interstate's fiscal year ends on December 31.

Required:
Prepare the appropriate journal entries for these transactions.

1. On December 15, received $7,500 from Bradley Farms toward the purchase of a $98,000 tractor to be delivered on January 6, 1998.
2. During December, received $25,500 of refundable deposits relating to containers used to transport equipment parts.
3. During December, credit sales totaled $800,000. The state sales tax rate is 5% and the local sales tax rate is 2%. (This is a summary journal entry for the many individual sales transactions for the period.)

Exercise 13–8
Current – noncurrent classification of debt

A recent annual report of Sprint Corporation contained a rather lengthy narrative entitled "Review of Segmental Results of Operation." The narrative noted that short-term notes payable and commercial paper outstanding at the end of the year aggregated $756 million and that during the following year "This entire balance will be replaced by the issuance of long-term debt or will continue to be refinanced under existing long-term credit facilities."

Required:
How did Sprint report the debt in its balance sheet? Why?

Exercise 13–9
Current – noncurrent classification of debt

At December 31, 1997, Newman Engineering's liabilities include the following:

1. $10 million of 9% bonds were issued for $10 million on May 31, 1976. The bonds mature on May 31, 2008, but bondholders have the option of calling (demanding payment on) the bonds on May 31, 1998. However, the call option is not expected to be exercised, given prevailing market conditions.
2. $14 million of 8% notes are due on May 31, 2001. A debt covenant requires Newman to maintain current assets at least equal to 175% of its current liabilities. On December 31, 1997, Newman is in violation of this covenant. Newman obtained a waiver from National City Bank until June 1998, having convinced the bank that the company's normal 2 to 1 ratio of current assets to current liabilities will be reestablished during the first half of 1998.
3. $7 million of noncallable 11% bonds were issued for $7 million on August 31, 1966. The bonds mature on July 31, 1998. Sufficient cash is expected to be available to retire the bonds at maturity.

Required:
What portion of the debt can be excluded from classification as a current liability (that is, reported as a noncurrent liability)? Explain.

Exercise 13–10
Warranties

Cupola Awning Corporation introduced a new line of commercial awnings in 1997 that carry a two-year warranty against manufacturer's defects. Based on their experience with previous product introductions, warranty costs are expected to approximate 3% of sales. Sales and actual warranty expenditures for the first year of selling the product were:

	Sales	Actual Warranty Expenditures
	$5,000,000	$37,500

Required:

1. Does this situation represent a loss contingency? Why or why not? How should it be accounted for?
2. Prepare journal entries that summarize sales of the awnings (assume all credit sales) and any aspects of the warranty that should be recorded during 1997.
3. What amount should Cupola report as a liability at December 31, 1997?

Exercise 13–11
Extended warranties

Carnes Electronics sells consumer electronics that carry a 90-day manufacturer's warranty. At the time of purchase, customers are offered the opportunity to also buy a two-year extended warranty for an additional charge. During 1997, Carnes received $412,000 for these extended warranties (approximately evenly throughout the year).

Required:

1. Does this situation represent a loss contingency? Why or why not? How should it be accounted for?
2. Prepare journal entries that summarize sales of the extended warranties (assume all credit sales) and any aspects of the warranty that should be recorded during 1997.

Exercise 13–12
Various transactions involving contingencies

The following selected transactions relate to contingencies of Classical Tool Makers, Inc., which began operations in July 1997. Classical's fiscal year ends on December 31. Financial statements are published in April, 1998.

Required:

Prepare the appropriate journal entries to record any amounts that should be recorded as a result of each of these contingencies.

1. Classical's products carry a one-year warranty against manufacturer's defects. Based on previous experience, warranty costs are expected to approximate 4% of sales. Sales were $2 million (all credit) for 1997. Actual warranty expenditures were $30,800 and were recorded as warranty expense when incurred.
2. Although no customer accounts have been shown to be uncollectible, Classical estimates that 2% of credit sales will eventually prove uncollectible.
3. In December 1997, the State of Tennessee filed suit against Classical, seeking penalties for violations of clean air laws. On January 23, 1998, Classical reached a settlement with state authorities to pay $1.5 million in penalties.
4. Classical is the plaintiff in a $4 million lawsuit filed against a supplier. The suit is in final appeal and attorneys advise that it is virtually certain that Classical will win the case and be awarded $2.5 million.
5. In November 1997, Classical became aware of a design flaw in an industrial saw that poses a potential electrical hazard. A product recall appears unavoidable. Such an action would likely cost the company $500,000.
6. Classical offered $25 cash rebates on a new model of jigsaw. Customers must mail in a proof-of-purchase seal from the package plus the cash register receipt to receive the rebate. Experience suggests that 60% of the rebates will be claimed. Ten thousand of the jigsaws were sold in 1997. Total rebates to customers in 1997 were $105,000 and were recorded as promotional expense when paid.

Exercise 13–13
Multiple choice; contingencies

The following questions dealing with current liabilities are adapted from questions that appeared on recent CPA examinations. Determine the response that best completes the statements or questions.

1. During 1997, Smith Co. filed suit against West, Inc., seeking damages for patent infringement. At December 31, 1997, Smith's legal counsel believed that it was probable that Smith would be successful against West for an estimated amount in the range of $75,000 to $150,000, with all amounts in the range considered equally likely. In March 1998, Smith was awarded $100,000 and received full payment thereof. In its 1997 financial statements, issued in February 1998, how should this award be reported?
   a. As a receivable and revenue of $100,000.

   b. As a receivable and deferred revenue of $100,000.
   c. As a disclosure of a contingent gain of $100,000.
   d. As a disclosure of a contingent gain of an undetermined amount in the range of $75,000
      to $150,000.

2. Vadis Co. sells appliances that include a three-year warranty. Service calls under the warranty are
   performed by an independent mechanic under a contract with Vadis. Based on experience, warranty
   costs are estimated at $30 for each machine sold. When should Vadis recognize these warranty
   costs?
   a. Evenly over the life of the warranty.
   b. When the service calls are performed.
   c. When payments are made to the mechanic.
   d. When the machines are sold.

3. Management can estimate the amount of loss that will occur if a foreign government expropriates
   some company assets. If expropriation is reasonably possible, a loss contingency should be
   a. Disclosed but not accrued as a liability.
   b. Disclosed and accrued as a liability.
   c. Accrued as liability but not disclosed.
   d. Neither accrued as a liability nor disclosed.

4. In December 1997, Mill Co. began including one coupon in each package of candy that it sells and
   offering a toy in exchange for 50 cents and five coupons. The toys cost Mill 80 cents each.
   Eventually 60% of the coupons will be redeemed. During December, Mill sold 110,000 packages of
   candy and no coupons were redeemed. In its December 31, 1997, balance sheet, what amount
   should Mill report as estimated liability for coupons?
   a. $ 3,960
   b. $10,560
   c. $19,800
   d. $52,800

Exercise 13–14
Disclosures of liabilities

Indicate (by letter) the way each of the items listed below should be reported on a balance sheet at December 31, 1997.

Item	Reporting Method
_____ 1. Commercial paper.	N. Not reported
_____ 2. Noncommitted line of credit.	C. Current liability
_____ 3. Customer advances.	L. Long-term liability
_____ 4. Estimated warranty cost.	D. Disclosure note only
_____ 5. Accounts payable.	A. Asset

   _____ 6. Long-term bonds that will be callable by the creditor in the upcoming year unless an existing
           violation is not corrected (there is a reasonable possibility the violation will be corrected within
           the grace period).
   _____ 7. Note due March 3, 1998.
   _____ 8. Interest accrued on note, Dec. 31, 1997.
   _____ 9. Short-term bank loan to be paid with proceeds of sale of common stock.
   _____ 10. A determinable gain that is contingent on a future event that appears extremely likely to occur
           in three months.
   _____ 11. Unasserted assessment of back taxes that probably will be asserted, in which case there would
           probably be a loss in six months.
   _____ 12. Unasserted assessment of back taxes with a reasonable possibility of being asserted, in which
           case there would probably be a loss in 13 months.
   _____ 13. A determinable loss that is contingent on a future event that appears extremely likely to occur
           in three months.
   _____ 14. Bond sinking fund.
   _____ 15. Long-term bonds callable by the creditor in the upcoming year that are not expected to be
           called.

Exercise 13–15
Change in accounting
estimate

Exercise 21–12 deals with a change in estimated warranty expense.

Exercise 13–16
Change in accounting
estimate

The Commonwealth of Virginia filed suit in October 1995, against Northern Timber Corporation, seeking civil penalties and injunctive relief for violations of environmental laws regulating forest conservation. When the financial statements were issued in 1996, Northern had not reached a settlement with state authorities, but legal counsel advised Northern Timber that it was probable the ultimate settlement would be $1,000,000 in penalties. The following entry was recorded:

Loss—litigation	1,000,000	
Liability—litigation		1,000,000

Late in 1997, a settlement was reached with state authorities to pay a total of $600,000 to cover the cost of violations.

Required:

1. Prepare any journal entries related to the change.
2. Briefly describe other steps Northern should take to report the change.

Exercise 13–17
Contingency; *Wall Street Journal* article

The following quote is taken from an article that appeared in *The Wall Street Journal* on Thursday, November 14, 1996:

Darling International Inc.

Darling International Inc. said a $5.9 million loss provision from the expected settlement of federal and state environmental claims caused a net loss of $1.3 million, or 24 cents a share, for its fiscal third quarter ended Sept. 28. The Irving, Texas, food-waste recycling concern said the environmental claims involved wastewater violations at its plant in Blue Earth, Minn. On the Nasdaq Stock Market yesterday, Darling closed at $30.50, unchanged.

Required:

Does the excerpt describe a loss contingency? Under what conditions would Darling accrue such a contingency? What journal entry did Darling use to record the provision (loss)?

Exercise 13–18
Payroll-related liabilities (based on Appendix 13)

Lee Financial Services pays employees monthly. Payroll information is listed below for January 1997, the first month of Lee's fiscal year. Assume that none of the employees exceeded any relevant wage base.

Salaries	$500,000
Federal income taxes to be withheld	100,000
Federal unemployment tax rate	0.80%
State unemployment tax rate (after FUTA deduction)	5.40%
Social security (FICA) tax rate	7.65%

Required:

Prepare the appropriate journal entries to record salaries and wages expense and payroll tax expense for the January 1997 pay period.

Problems

Problem 13–1
Bank loan: accrued interest

Blanton Plastics, a household plastic product manufacturer, borrowed $14 million cash on October 1, 1997, to provide working capital for year-end production. Blanton issued a four-month, 12% promissory note to N,C&I Bank under a prearranged short-term line of credit. Interest on the note was payable at maturity. Each firm's fiscal period is the calendar year.

Required:

1. Prepare the journal entries to record (a) the issuance of the note by Blanton Plastics and (b) N,C&I Bank's receivable on October 1, 1997.
2. Prepare the journal entries by both firms to record all subsequent events related to the note through January 31, 1998.
3. Suppose the face amount of the note was adjusted to include interest (a noninterest-bearing note) and 12% is the bank's stated discount rate. Prepare the journal entries to record the issuance of the noninterest-bearing note by Blanton Plastics on October 1, 1997. What would be the effective interest rate?

Problem 13–2
Various transactions involving liabilities

Camden Biotechnology began operations in September 1997. The following selected transactions relate to liabilities of the company for September 1997 through March 1998. Camden's fiscal year ends on December 31. Its financial statements are issued in April.

1997

a. On September 5, opened checking accounts at Second Commercial Bank and negotiated a short-term line of credit of up to $15,000,000 at the bank's prime rate (10.5% at the time). The company will pay no commitment fees.

b. On October 1 borrowed $12 million cash from Second Commercial Bank under the line of credit and issued a five-month promissory note. Interest at the prime rate of 10% was payable at maturity. Management planned to issue 10-year bonds in February to repay the note.

c. Received $2,600 of refundable deposits in December for reusable containers used to transport and store chemical-based products.

d. For the September–December period, credit sales totaled $4,100,000. The state sales tax rate is 3% and the local sales tax rate is 3%. (This is a summary journal entry for the many individual sales transactions for the period.)

e. Recorded the adjusting entry for accrued interest.

1998

f. In February, issued $10 million of 10-year bonds at face value and paid the bank loan on the March 1 due date.

g. Half of the storage containers covered by refundable deposits were returned in March. The remaining containers are expected to be returned during the next six months.

Required:

1. Prepare the appropriate journal entries for these transactions.
2. Prepare the current and long-term liability sections of the December 31, 1997, balance sheet. Trade accounts payable on that date were $252,000.

Problem 13–3
Current – noncurrent classification of debt

The balance sheet at December 31, 1997, for Nevada Harvester Corporation includes the liabilities listed below:

a. 11% bonds with a face amount of $40 million were issued for $40 million on October 31, 1988. The bonds mature on October 31, 2008. Bondholders have the option of calling (demanding payment on) the bonds on October 31, 1998, at a redemption price of $40 million. Market conditions are such that the call option is not expected to be exercised.

b. Management intended to refinance $6 million of notes that mature in May 1998. In early March, prior to the actual issuance of the 1997 financial statements, Nevada Harvester negotiated a line of credit with a commercial bank for up to $5 million any time during 1998. Any borrowings will mature two years from the date of borrowing.

c. Noncallable 12% bonds with a face amount of $20 million were issued for $20 million on September 30, 1976. The bonds mature on September 30, 1998. Sufficient cash is expected to be available to retire the bonds at maturity.

d. A $12 million 9% bank loan is payable on October 31, 2003. The bank has the right to demand payment after any fiscal year-end in which Nevada Harvester's ratio of current assets to current liabilities falls below a contractual minimum of 1.7 to 1 and remains so for six months. That ratio was 1.45 on December 31, 1997, due primarily to an intentional temporary decline in inventory levels. Normal inventory levels will be reestablished during the first quarter of 1998.

Required:

1. Determine the amount that can be excluded from classification as a current liability (that is, reported as a noncurrent liability) for each. Explain the reasoning behind your classifications.
2. Prepare the liability section of a classified balance sheet and any necessary footnote disclosure for Nevada Harvester at December 31, 1997. Accounts payable and accruals are $22 million.

Problem 13–4
Various liabilities

The unadjusted trial balance of the Manufacturing Equitable at December 31, 1997, the end of its fiscal year, included the following account balances. Manufacturing's 1997 financial statements were issued on April 1, 1998.

Accounts receivable	$ 92,500
Accounts payable	35,000
Bank notes payable	600,000
Mortgage note payable	1,200,000

Other information:

a. The bank notes, issued August 1, 1997, are due on July 31, 1998, and pay interest at a rate of 10%, payable at maturity.

b.   The mortgage note is due on March 1, 1998. Interest at 9% has been paid up to December 31 (assume 9% is a realistic rate). Manufacturing intended at December 31, 1997, to refinance the note on its due date with a new 10-year mortgage note. In fact, on March 1, Manufacturing paid $250,000 in cash on the principal balance and refinanced the remaining $950,000.

c.   Included in the accounts receivable balance at December 31, 1997, were two subsidiary accounts that had been overpaid and had credit balances totaling $18,000. The accounts were of two major customers who were expected to order more merchandise from Manufacturing and apply the overpayments to those future purchases.

d.   On November 1, 1997, Manufacturing rented a portion of its factory to a tenant for $30,000 per year, payable in advance. The payment for the 12 months ended October 31, 1998, was received as required and was credited to rent revenue.

Required:

1.   Prepare any necessary adjusting journal entries at December 31, 1997, pertaining to each item of other information (a–d).

2.   Prepare the current and long-term liability sections of the December 31, 1997, balance sheet.

Problem 13–5
Various contingencies

   Eastern Manufacturing is involved with several situations that possibly involve contingencies. Each is described below. Eastern's fiscal year ends December 31, and the 1997 financial statements are issued on March 15, 1998.

a.   Eastern is involved in a lawsuit resulting from a dispute with a supplier. On February 3, 1998, judgment was rendered against Eastern in the amount of $107 million plus interest, a total of $122 million. Eastern plans to appeal the judgment and is unable to predict its outcome though it is not expected to have a material adverse effect on the company.

b.   In November, 1996, the State of Nevada filed suit against Eastern, seeking civil penalties and injunctive relief for violations of environmental laws regulating hazardous waste. On January 12, 1998, Eastern reached a settlement with state authorities. Based upon discussions with legal counsel, the Company feels it is probable that $140 million will be required to cover the cost of violations. Eastern believes that the ultimate settlement of this claim will not have a material adverse effect on the company.

c.   Eastern is the plaintiff in a $200 million lawsuit filed against United Steel for damages due to lost profits from rejected contracts and for unpaid receivables. The case is in final appeal and legal counsel advises that it is probable that Eastern will prevail and be awarded $100 million.

d.   At March 15, 1998, the IRS is in the process of auditing Eastern's tax returns for 1995-1997, but has not proposed a deficiency assessment. Management feels an assessment is reasonably possible, and if an assessment is made an unfavorable settlement of up to $33 million is reasonably possible.

Required:

1.   Determine the appropriate means of reporting each situation. Explain your reasoning.

2.   Prepare any necessary journal entries and disclosure notes.

Problem 13–6
Various contingencies

   Western Manufacturing is involved with several situations that possibly involve contingencies. Each is described below. Western's fiscal year is the calendar year 1997, and the 1997 financial statements are issued on March 15, 1998.

a.   During 1997, Western experienced labor disputes at three of its plants. Management hopes an agreement will soon be reached. However negotiations between the Company and the unions have not produced an acceptable settlement and, as a result, strikes have been ongoing at these facilities since March 1, 1998. It is virtually certain that material costs will be incurred but the amount of possible costs cannot be reasonably ascertained.

b.   In accordance with a 1995 contractual agreement with A. J. Conner Company, Western is entitled to $37 million for certain fees and expense reimbursements. These were written off as bad debts in 1996. A. J. Conner has filed for bankruptcy. The bankruptcy court on February 4, 1998, ordered A. J. Conner to pay $23 million immediately upon consummation of a proposed merger with Garner Holding Group.

c.   Western warrants most products it sells against defects in materials and workmanship for a period of a year. Based on their experience with previous product introductions, warranty costs are expected to approximate 2% of sales. A warranty liability of $39 million was reported at December 31, 1996. Sales of warranted products during 1997 were $2,100 million and actual warranty expenditures were $40 million. Expenditures in excess of the existing liability were debited to warranty expense.

d.   Western is involved in a suit filed in January 1998 by Crump Holdings seeking $88 million, as an adjustment to the purchase price in connection with the Company's sale of its textile business in 1997. The suit alleges that Western misstated the assets and liabilities used to calculate the purchase price for the textile division. Legal counsel advises that it is reasonably possible that Western could end up losing an indeterminable but material amount not expected to have a material adverse effect on the Company's financial position.

Required:
1.   Determine the appropriate means of reporting each situation. Explain your reasoning.
2.   Prepare any necessary journal entries and disclosure notes.

Problem 13–7
Subsequent events

  Lincoln Chemicals became involved in investigations by the U.S. Environmental Protection Agency in regard to damages connected to waste disposal sites. Below are four possibilities regarding the timing of (A) the alleged damage caused by Lincoln, (B) an investigation by the EPA, (C) the EPA assessment of penalties, and (D) ultimate settlement. In each case, assume that Lincoln is unaware of any problem until an investigation is begun. Also assume that once the EPA investigation begins, it is probable that a damage assessment will ensue and that once an assessment is made by the EPA, it is reasonably possible that a determinable amount will be paid by Lincoln.

Required:
For each case, decide whether (a) a loss should be accrued in the financial statements with an explanatory note, (b) a disclosure note only should be provided, or (c) no disclosure is necessary.

Case 1

Case 2

Case 3

Case 4

Problem 13–8
Concepts; terminology

Listed below are several terms and phrases associated with current liabilities. Pair each item from List A (by letter) with the item from List B that is most appropriately associated with it.

	List A		List B
J	1. Face amount × interest rate × time.	a.	Informal agreement
G	2. Payable with current assets.	b.	Secured loan
	3. Short-term debt to be refinanced with common stock.	c.	Refinancing prior to the issuance of the financial statements
H	4. Present value of interest plus present value of principal.	d.	Accounts payable
B	5. Noninterest-bearing.	e.	Accrued liabilities
A	6. Noncommitted line of credit.	f.	Commercial paper
	7. Pledged accounts receivable.	g.	Current liabilities
C	8. Reclassification of debt.	h.	Long-term liability
F	9. Purchased by other corporations.	i.	Usual valuation of liabilities
E	10. Expenses not yet paid.	j.	Interest on debt
L	11. Liability until refunded.	k.	Customer advances
K	12. Applied against purchase price.	l.	Customer deposits

Problem 13–9
(based on Appendix 13)
Payroll-related liabilities

Alamar Petroleum Company offers its employees the option of contributing up to 5% of their wages or salaries, with the contribution being matched by Alamar. The company also pays 80% of medical and life insurance premiums. Deductions relating to these plans and other payroll information for the first biweekly payroll period of February are listed below.

Wages and salaries	$2,000,000
Employee contribution to voluntary retirement plan	84,000
Medical insurance premiums	42,000
Life insurance premiums	9,000
Federal income taxes to be withheld	400,000
Local income taxes to be withheld	53,000
Payroll taxes:	
Federal unemployment tax rate	0.80%
State unemployment tax rate (after FUTA deduction)	5.40%
Social security (FICA) tax rate	7.65%

Required:
Prepare the appropriate journal entries to record salaries and wages expense and payroll tax expense for the biweekly pay period. Assume that no employee's cumulative wages exceed the relevant wage bases.

Cases

Research Case 13–1
Bank loan: accrued interest
SFAS

A fellow accountant has solicited your opinion regarding the classification of short-term obligations repaid prior to being replaced by a long-term security. Cheshire Foods, Inc., issued $5,000,000 of short-term commercial paper during 1996 to finance construction of a plant. At September 30, 1997, Cheshire's fiscal year-end, the company intends to refinance the commercial paper by issuing long-term bonds. However, because Cheshire temporarily has excess cash, in November 1997 it liquidates $2,000,000 of the commercial paper as the paper matures. In December 1997, the company completes a $10,000,000 long-term bond issue. Later during December, it issues its September 30, 1997 financial statements. The proceeds of the long-term bond issue are to be used to replenish $2,000,000 in working capital, to pay $3,000,000 of commercial paper as it matures in January 1998, and to pay $5,000,000 of construction costs expected to be incurred later that year to complete the plant.

You initially are hesitant because you don't recall encountering a situation in which short-term obligations were repaid prior to being replaced by a long-term security. However, you are encouraged by remembering that this general topic is covered by an FASB pronouncement to which you have access: "Classification of Obligations Expected To Be Refinanced," *Statement of Financial Accounting Standards No 6*, (Stamford, Conn.: FASB, 1975). And "Classification of Obligation Repaid Prior to Being Replaced by a Long-Term Security," *FASB Interpretation No 8*, addresses this situation specifically.

Required:
Determine how the $5,000,000 of commercial paper should be classified by consulting the FASB standard. Before doing so, formulate your own opinion on the proper treatment.

Real World
Case 13–2
Returnable containers

The Zoo Doo Compost Company processes a premium organic fertilizer made with the help of the animals at the Memphis Zoo. Zoo Doo is sold in a specially designed plastic pail that may be kept and used for household chores or returned to the seller. The fertilizer is sold for $12.50 per two-gallon pail (including the

$1.76 cost of the pail). For each pail returned, Zoo Doo donates $1 to the Memphis Zoo and the pail is used again.[22]

Required:

The founder and president of this start-up firm has asked your opinion on how to account for the donations to be made when fertilizer pails are returned. (Ignore any tax implications.)

Research Case 13–3
Relationship of liabilities to assets and owners' equity
SFAC

SFAC No. 6 states that "an entity's assets, liabilities, and equity (net assets) all pertain to the same set of probable future economic benefits." Explain this statement.

Ethics Case 13–4
Outdoors R Us

Outdoors R Us owns several membership-based campground resorts throughout the Southwest. The company sells campground sites to new members, usually during a get-acquainted visit and tour. The campgrounds offer a wider array of on-site facilities than most. New members sign a multiyear contract, pay a down payment, and make monthly installment payments. Because no credit check is made and many memberships originate on a spur-of-the-moment basis, cancellations are not uncommon.

Business has been brisk during its first three years of operations, and since going public in 1995, the market value of its stock has tripled. The first sign of trouble came in 1997 when the new sales dipped sharply.

One afternoon, two weeks before the end of the fiscal year, Diane Rice, CEO, and Gene Sun, controller, were having an active discussion in Sun's office.

Sun: I've thought more about our discussion yesterday. Maybe something can be done about profits.
Rice: I hope so. Our bonuses and stock value are riding on this period's performance.
Sun: We've been recording unearned revenues when new members sign up. Rather than recording liabilities at the time memberships are sold, I think we can justify reporting sales revenue for all memberships sold.
Rice: What will be the effect on profits?
Sun: I haven't run the numbers yet, but let's just say very favorable.

Required:
1. Why do you think liabilities had been recorded previously?
2. Is the proposal ethical?
3. Who would be affected if the proposal is implemented?

Trueblood Accounting Case 13–5
Reclassification of long-term debt as current

The following Robert M. Trueblood case is recommended for use with this chapter. The case provides an excellent opportunity for class discussion, group projects, and writing assignments. The case, along with Professor's Discussion Material, can be obtained from the Deloitte & Touche Foundation.

Case 92-4: *Classification of Debt*

This case provides a vehicle for consideration of the requirements for the reclassification of long-term debt as current. It emphasizes the need for professional judgment.

Group Interaction Case 13–6
Exceptions to the general classification guideline

Domestic Transfer and Storage is a large trucking company headquartered in the Midwest. Rapid expansion in recent years has been financed in large part by debt in a variety of forms. In preparing the financial statements for 1998, questions have arisen regarding the way certain of the liabilities are to be classified in the company's classified balance sheet.

A meeting of several members of the accounting area is scheduled for tomorrow, April 22, 1998. You are confident that discussions during that meeting will include the topic of debt classification. You want to appear knowledgeable at the meeting, but realizing it's been a few years since you have dealt with classification issues, you have sought out information you think relevant. Questionable liabilities at the company's fiscal year-end (January 31, 1998) include the following:

a. $15 million of 9% commercial paper is due on July 31, 1998. Management intends to refinance the paper on a long-term basis. In early April, 1998, Domestic negotiated a credit agreement with a commercial bank for up to $12 million any time during the next 3 years, any borrowings from which will mature two years from the date of borrowing.

b. $17 million of 11% notes were issued on June 30, 1995. The notes are due on November 30, 1998. The company has investments of $20 million classified as "available for sale."

c. $25 million of 10% notes were due on February 28, 1998. On February 21, 1998, the company issued 30-year, 9.4% bonds in a private placement to institutional investors.

d. Recently, company management has considered reducing debt in favor of a greater proportion of equity financing. $20 million of 12% bonds mature on July 31, 1998. Discussions with underwriters which began on January 4, 1998, resulted in a contractual arrangement on March 15 under which new common shares will be sold in July for approximately $20 million.

In order to prepare notes to yourself in preparation for the meeting concerning the classification of these items, you decide to discuss them with a colleague. Specifically, you want to know what portion of the debt can be excluded from classification as a current liability (that is, reported as a noncurrent liability) and why.

Required:

1. What is the appropriate classification of each liability? Develop a list of arguments in support of your view prior to the class session for which the case is assigned.

2. In class, your instructor will pair you (and everyone else) with a classmate (who also has independently developed a position). You will be given three minutes to argue your view to your partner. Your partner likewise will be given three minutes to argue his or her view to you. During these three minute presentations, the listening partner is not permitted to speak.

3. Then after each person has had a turn attempting to convince his or her partner, the two partners will have a three-minute discussion in which they will decide which classifications are more convincing and arguments will be merged into a single view for each pair.

4. After the allotted time, a spokesperson for each of the four liabilities will be selected by the instructor. Each spokesperson will field arguments from the class as to the appropriate classification. The class then will discuss the merits of the classification and attempt to reach a consensus view, though a consensus is not necessary.

Discussion Case 13–7
Contingencies

Spackenki Il Company is a manufacturer of household appliances. During the year, the following information became available:

a. Potential costs due to the discovery of a safety hazard related to one of its products—these costs are probable and can be reasonably estimated.

b. Potential new product warranty costs—these costs are probable but cannot be reasonably estimated.

c. Potential costs due to the discovery of a possible product defect related to one of its products—these costs are reasonably possible and can be reasonably estimated.

Required:

1. How should Spackenki Il report the potential costs due to the discovery of a safety hazard? Why?

2. How should Spackenki Il report the potential warranty costs? Why?

3. How should Spackenki ll report the potential costs due to the discovery of a possible product defect? Why?

(AICPA adapted)

Critical Thought Case 13–8
Loss contingency and full disclosure

In the March 1998 meeting of Valleck Corporation's board of directors, a question arose as to the way a possible obligation should be disclosed in the forthcoming financial statements for the year ended December 31. A veteran board member brought to the meeting a draft of a disclosure note that had been prepared by the controller's office for inclusion in the annual report. Here is the note:

On May 9, 1997, the United States Environmental Protection Agency (EPA) issued a Notice of Violation (NOV) to Valleck alleging violations of the Clean Air Act. Subsequently, in June 1997, the EPA commenced a civil action with respect to the foregoing violation seeking civil penalties of approximately $853,000. The EPA alleges that Valleck exceeded applicable volatile organic substance emission limits. The Company estimates that the cost to achieve compliance will be $190,000; in addition the Company expects to settle the EPA lawsuit for a civil penalty of $205,000 which will be paid in 2000.

"Where did we get the $205,000 figure?" he asked. On being informed that this is the amount negotiated last month by company attorneys with the EPA, the director inquires, "Aren't we supposed to report a liability for that in addition to the note?"

Required:

Explain whether Valleck should report a liability in addition to the note. Why or why not? For full disclosure, should anything be added to the disclosure note itself?

Trueblood Accounting Case 13–9
Gain contingencies; revenue recognition criteria; accrual concept

The following Robert M. Trueblood case is recommended for use with this chapter. The case provides an excellent opportunity for class discussion, group projects, and writing assignments. The case, along with Professor's Discussion Material, can be obtained from the Deloitte & Touche Foundation.

Case 91-4: *Accounting for an Insurance Settlement or Are They All Washed Up?*

This case provides an opportunity to consider whether and when it may be appropriate to accrue gain contingencies. It requires consideration of how the basic revenue recognition criteria and the accrual concept are used to resolve issues in practice.

Writing Case 13–10
Change in loss contingency; write a memo

Writing Case 21–6 deals with a change in a loss contingency.

Internet Case 13–11
Researching the way contingencies are reported; retrieving information from the Internet

EDGAR, the Electronic Data Gathering, Analysis, and Retrieval system, performs automated collection, validation, indexing, acceptance, and forwarding of submissions by companies and others who are required by law to file forms with the U.S. Securities and Exchange Commission (SEC). All publicly traded domestic companies use EDGAR to make the majority of their filings. (Filings by foreign companies are not required to be filed on EDGAR, but some of these companies do so voluntarily.) Form 10-K or 10-KSB, which include the annual report, is required to be filed on EDGAR. The SEC makes this information available on the Internet.

Required:
1. Access EDGAR on the Internet. The web address is http://www.sec.gov/.
2. Search for a public company with which you are familiar. Access its most recent 10-K filing. Search or scroll to find the financial statements and related notes.
3. Specifically, look for any contingency(s) reported in the disclosure notes. Identify the nature of the contingency(s) described and explain the reason(s) the loss or losses was or was not accrued.
4. Repeat requirements 2 and 3 for two additional companies.

Trueblood Accounting Case 13–12
Unasserted claims

The following Robert M. Trueblood case is recommended for use with this chapter. The case provides an excellent opportunity for class discussion, group projects, and writing assignments. The case, along with Professor's Discussion Material, can be obtained from the Deloitte & Touche Foundation.

Case 89-2: *Creative Crockery—A Company Going to Pot*

The primary issue in this case is the consideration of accounting for an unasserted claim related to an EPA investigation.

Writing Case 13–13
Accounting changes

Kevin Brantly is a new hire in the controller's office of Fleming Home Products. Two events occurred in late 1997 that the company had not previously encountered. The events appear to affect two of the company's liabilities, but there is some disagreement concerning whether they also affect financial statements of prior years. Each change occurred during 1997 before any adjusting entries or closing entries were prepared. The tax rate for Fleming is 40% in all years.

- Fleming Home Products introduced a new line of commercial awnings in 1996 that carry a one-year warranty against manufacturer's defects. Based on industry experience, warranty costs were expected to approximate 3% of sales. Sales of the awnings in 1996 were $3,500,000. Accordingly, warranty expense and a warranty liability of $105,000 were recorded in 1996. In late 1997, the company's claims experience was evaluated and it was determined that claims were far fewer than expected—2% of sales rather than 3%. Sales of the awnings in 1997 were $4,000,000 and warranty expenditures in 1997 totaled $91,000
- In November 1995, the State of Minnesota filed suit against the company, seeking penalties for violations of clean air laws. When the financial statements were issued in 1996, Huggins had not reached a settlement with state authorities, but legal counsel advises Fleming that it was probable the company would have to pay $200,000 in penalties. Accordingly, the following entry was recorded:

Loss—litigation	200,000	
Liability—litigation		200,000

Late in 1997, a settlement was reached with state authorities to pay a total of $350,000 in penalties.

Required:

Kevin's supervisor, perhaps unsure of the answer, perhaps wanting to test Kevin's knowledge, emails the following message, "Kevin, send me a memo on how we should handle our awning warranty and that clean air suit." Wanting to be accurate, he consults his reference materials. What will he find? Prepare the memo requested.

Real World Case 13–14
Frequent flyer miles

In 1994, Northwest Airlines Corporation issued 20 million shares of common stock as an initial public offering. Financial statements that accompanied the prospectus describing the stock offering included the following information:

Frequent Flyer Program (in Part)

Northwest operates a frequent flyer marketing program known as "WORLDPERKS" under which mileage credits are earned by flying on Northwest or participating airlines and by using the services of participating bank credit cards, hotels and car rental firms. The program was designed to retain and increase the business of frequent travelers by offering incentives for their continued patronage. KLM is the larger other airline participating in the WORLDPERKS program. The combined route networks of Northwest and KLM offer the opportunity to earn and redeem miles on flights to more than 350 cities in over 80 countries on six continents. See "Strategic Repositioning-KLM Alliance." WORLDPERKS has had an 84% increase in its membership from year-end 1990 to year-end 1993. The program has certain restrictive provisions, including flight blackout dates and capacity control of reservations, which substantially limit the use of the awards on certain flights. Awards are issued to members at the 20,000 miles level. All awards have an expiration date three years from the date earned.

Northwest accounts for its frequent flyer obligation on the accrual basis using the incremental cost method. Northwest's frequent flyer liability is accrued for financial accounting purposes on all outstanding free travel awards earned and issued (20,000 miles) and expected to be used on Northwest. Northwest includes food and beverage, fuel, insurance, security, miscellaneous claims and WORLDPERKS service center expense in its incremental cost calculation. Thus incremental costs do not include any contribution to overhead or profit. Food, beverage and other cost per passenger is based on engineering formulas to determine the average fuel cost per pound per hour. Current fuel price and estimated average weight of each added onboard passenger and luggage are factored into the computation and converted to a rate per passenger per award.

	1994	1993
Current Liabilities:		
Air traffic liability	$ 798.7	$ 721.2
Accounts payable and other liabilities	520.3	672.3
Accrued compensation and benefits	390.2	346.1
Accrued commissions	146.1	189.6
Accrued aircraft rent	167.6	161.9
Current maturities of long-term debt	244.9	115.6
Current obligations under capital leases	46.3	42.3
Short-term borrowings	9.5	4.0
	2,323.6	2,253.0

Required:

1. Why does Northwest's frequent flyer program produce a liability?
2. Is incremental cost the appropriate measure of the liability? Why?
3. Is the liability current, long-term, or both?
4. Prepare journal entries appropriate to recognize Northwest's expense and liability making the following additional assumptions:
   a. The entire liability is considered current and 80% of the Air Traffic Liability pertains to the frequent flyer program.
   b. Revenue received for travel sold to companions of award recipients is recognized when the transportation is provided.
   c. In 1994, Northwest provided $100 million of travel under its frequent flyer program of which $20 million was travel sold to companions of award recipients.

Real World Case 13–15
Breast implant liability

In the early 1990s, major manufacturers of silicone breast implants faced extensive litigation regarding health risks associated with the devices. Most of the leading makers, defendants in a class action lawsuit, entered into a global settlement agreement. In 1994, Bristol-Myers Squibb Company, maker of health and personal care products reported the following information pertaining to its involvement in the suit:

Note 2: Special Charge (in Part)

As described in Note 18, the company is party to a settlement concerning pending and future breast implant product liability claims (related to a previously discontinued business of a subsidiary) brought against it, its Medical Engineering Corporation subsidiary, certain other subsidiaries. In the fourth quarter of 1993, the company recorded a special charge of $500 million before taxes, $310 million after taxes, or $.60 per share. The charge consisted of $1.5 billion in anticipation of its share of the pending settlement and costs of the litigation ($1.4 billion recorded as a long-term liability in Product Liability and $100 million recorded as a current liability in Accrued Expenses), offset by $1 billion of expected insurance proceeds (recorded as Insurance Recoverable). Although the company is currently engaged in coverage litigation with certain of its insurers, expected insurance proceeds represent the amount of insurance which the company considers appropriate to record as recoverable at this time. The company believes that ultimately it will obtain substantial additional amounts of insurance proceeds.

Ethics Case 13–16
Profits guaranteed

Required:

1. From an accounting perspective, what necessitated the special charge?
2. Bristol-Myers Squibb did not report the charge as an extraordinary item on its income statement. Which of the amounts mentioned in the note is the appropriate income statement line item? Why?
3. Relying on the information provided by the disclosure note, recreate the journal entry Bristol-Myers Squibb recorded to accrue the charge.

This was Joel Craig's first visit to the controller's corner office since being recruited for his senior accountant position in May. Because he'd been directed to bring with him his preliminary report on year-end adjustments, Craig presumed he'd done something wrong in preparing the report. That he had not was Craig's first surprise. His second surprise was his boss's request to reconsider one of the estimated expenses.

S & G Fasteners was a new company, specializing in plastic industrial fasteners. All products carry a generous long-term warranty against manufacturer's defects. "Don't you think 4% of sales is a little high for our warranty expense estimate?" his boss wondered. "After all, we're new at this. We have little experience with product introductions. I just got off the phone with Blanchard (the company president). He thinks we'll have trouble renewing our credit line with the profits we're projecting. The pressure's on."

Required:

1. Should Craig follow his boss's suggestion?
2. Does revising the warranty estimate pose an ethical dilemma?
3. Who would be affected if the suggestion is followed?

International Case 13–17
Accounting for current liabilities and contingencies in other countries

The International Accounting Standards Committee (IASC) seeks to narrow worldwide differences in accounting practices and the presentation of financial information. The IASC has worked toward uniformity since 1973, but harmonization has by no means been achieved. In the area of accounting for current liabilities and contingencies, significant differences exist from country to country. The differences impact the financial position and the ability of analysts to assess risk in countries where these benefits are significant.

Required

Choose a country other than the United States and:

1. Locate a recent annual report of a non-U.S. company.
2. Determine the way that country reports current liabilities on its balance sheet. Include in your analysis:
   a. Whether they are reported as a separate classification of liabilities or whether they are netted against current assets.
   b. Whether and how details are reported in disclosure notes.
3. Determine the way that country reports contingencies. Include in your analysis:
   a. Under what conditions are loss contingencies accrued.
   b. Whether gain contingencies can be accrued or reported in disclosure notes.

Note: You can obtain copies of annual reports by contacting the investor relations department of the corporation, from a friendly stockbroker, from Public Register's Annual Report Service, available on the Internet at http://www.PRARS.com. or from EDGAR, the Electronic Data Gathering and Retrieval service of the SEC, at http://www.sec.gov/.

**Financial Analysis
Case 13–18**
Analyzing financial
statements; liquidity ratios

IGF Foods Company is a large, primarily domestic, consumer foods company involved in the manufacture, distribution and sale of a variety of food products. Industry averages are derived from Troy's *The Almanac of Business and Industrial Financial Ratios.* Following are the 1997 and 1996 comparative balance sheets for IGF. (The financial data we use are from actual financial statements of a well-known corporation, but the company name used is fictitious and the numbers and dates have been modified slightly.)

IGF Foods Company
Years Ended December 31, 1997 and 1996

($ in millions)	1997	1996
Comparative Balance Sheets		
Assets		
Current assets:		
Cash	$ 48	$ 142
Accounts receivable	347	320
Marketable securities	358	–
Inventories	914	874
Prepaid expenses	212	154
Total current assets	$1,879	$1,490
Property, plant, and equipment (net):	2,592	2,291
Intangibles (net):	800	843
Other assets	74	60
Total assets	$5,345	$4,684
Liabilities and Shareholders' Equity		
Current liabilities:		
Accounts payable	$ 254	$ 276
Accrued liabilities	493	496
Notes payable	518	115
Current portion of long-term debt	208	54
Total current liabilities	$1,473	$ 941
Long-term debt	534	728
Deferred income taxes	407	344
Total liabilities	2,414	2,013
Shareholders' equity:		
Common stock	180	180
Additional paid-in capital	21	63
Retained earnings	2,730	2,428
Total shareholders' equity	2,931	2,671
Total liabilities and shareholders' equity	$5,345	$4,684

Liquidity refers to a company's cash position and overall ability to obtain cash in the normal course of business. A company is said to be liquid if it has sufficient cash or is capable of converting its other assets to cash in a relatively short period of time so that currently maturing debts can be paid.

Required:
1. Calculate the current ratio for IGF. The average ratio for the stocks listed on the New York Stock Exchange in a comparable time period was 1.5. What information does your calculation provide an investor?
2. Calculate IGF's acid-test or quick ratio. The ratio for the stocks listed on the New York Stock Exchange in a comparable time period was .80. What does your calculation indicate about IGF's liquidity?

**Financial Analysis
Case 13–19**
Reporting current liabilities;
liquidity

**Federal Express
Corporation**

Refer to the financial statements and related disclosure notes of Federal Express Corporation in the Appendix to Chapter 1. At the end of its 1996 fiscal year, Federal Express reported current liabilities of $1.6 billion on its balance sheet.

Required:
1. What are the three components of current liabilities?
2. Are current assets sufficient to cover current liabilities? What is the current ratio for 1996? How does the ratio compare with 1995?
3. Federal Express has a revolving credit facility with a number of financial institutions. What amount is available to Federal Express under this credit line?

14

BONDS AND LONG-TERM NOTES

OVERVIEW

This chapter continues the presentation of liabilities. Specifically, the discussion focuses on the accounting treatment of long-term liabilities. Long-term notes and bonds are discussed, as well as the extinguishment of debt and troubled debt restructuring.

LEARNING OBJECTIVES   After studying this chapter, you should be able to:

1. Identify the underlying characteristics of debt instruments and describe the basic approach to accounting for debt.
2. Account for bonds issued at par, at a discount, or at a premium, recording interest at the effective rate or by the straight-line method.
3. Describe innovative financial instruments used to attract lenders and how each is accounted for.
4. Characterize the accounting treatment of notes, including installment notes, issued for cash or for noncash consideration.
5. Record the retirement of debt at maturity and by early extinguishment.
6. Describe troubled debt restructuring and the three accounting methods used to record the restructuring under specific circumstances.
7. Describe the disclosures appropriate to long-term debt in its various forms.

SERVICE LEADER, INC.

The mood is both upbeat and focused on this cool October morning. Executives and board members of Service Leader, Inc., are meeting with underwriters and attorneys to discuss the company's first bond offering in its 20-year history. You are attending in the capacity of company controller and two-year member of the board of directors. The closely held corporation has been financed entirely by equity, internally generated funds, and short-term bank borrowings.

Bank rates of interest, though, have risen recently and the company's unexpectedly rapid, but welcome, growth has prompted the need to look elsewhere for new financing. Under consideration are 15-year, 10.25% first mortgage bonds with a principal amount of $70 million. The bonds would be callable at 103 any time after June 30, 2002, and convertible into Service Leader common stock at the rate of 45 shares per $1,000 bond.

Other financing vehicles have been discussed over the last two months, including the sale of additional stock, nonconvertible bonds, and unsecured notes. This morning *The Wall Street Journal* indicated that market rates of interest for debt similar to the bonds under consideration is about 10.5%.

QUESTIONS

1. What does it mean that the bonds are "first mortgage" bonds? What effect does that have on financing?
2. From Service Leader's perspective, why are the bonds callable? What does that mean?
3. How will it be possible to sell bonds paying investors 10.25% when other, similar investments will provide the investors a return of 10.5%?
4. Why might the company choose to make the bonds convertible into common stock?
5. Would accounting differ if the debt were designated as notes rather than bonds?

PART A

BONDS AND NOTES

The Nature of Long-Term Debt

Learning objective 1
Identify the underlying characteristics of debt instruments and describe the basic approach to accounting for debt.

Liabilities signify **creditors' interest** in a company's assets

A note payable and a note receivable are two sides of the same coin.

Periodic interest is the effective interest rate times the amount of the debt outstanding during the interest period.

A company must raise funds to finance its operations and often the expansion of those operations. Presumably, at least some of the necessary funding can be provided by the company's own operations, though some funds must be provided by external sources. Ordinarily, external financing includes some combination of equity and debt funding. We explore debt financing first.

In the present chapter, we focus on debt in the form of bonds and notes. The following four chapters deal with liabilities also, namely those arising in connection with leases (Chapter 15), deferred income taxes (Chapter 16), pensions (Chapter 17), and employee benefits (Chapter 18). Some employee benefits create equity rather than debt, which also are discussed in Chapter 18. Then, in Chapter 19, we examine shareholders' interest arising from external *equity* financing. In Chapter 22, we see that cash flows from both debt and equity financing are reported together in a statement of cash flows as "cash flows from financing activities."

As you read this chapter, you will find the focus to be on the liability side of the transactions we examine. Realize, though, that the mirror image of a liability is an asset (bonds payable / investment in bonds, note payable/note receivable, etc.). So as we discuss accounting for debts from the viewpoint of the issuers of the debt instruments, we also will take the opportunity to see how the lender deals with the corresponding asset. Studying the two sides of the same transaction in tandem will emphasize their inherent similarities.

Accounting for a liability is a relatively straightforward concept. This is not to say that all debt instruments are unchallenging, "plain vanilla" loan agreements. Quite the contrary, the financial community continuously devises increasingly exotic ways to flavor financial instruments in the attempt to satisfy the diverse and evolving tastes of both debtors and creditors.

Packaging aside, a liability requires the future payment of cash in specified (or estimated) amounts, at specified (or projected) dates. As time passes, interest accrues on debt. As a general rule, the periodic interest is the effective interest rate times the amount of the debt outstanding during the period. This same principle applies regardless of the specific form of the liability—note payable, bonds payable, lease liability, pension obligation, or other debt instrument. Also, as a general rule, long-term liabilities are reported at their present values. The present value of a liability is the present value of its related cash flows (principal and/or interest payments), discounted at the effective rate of interest at issuance.

We begin our study of long-term liabilities by examining accounting for bonds. We follow that section by examining debt in the form of notes. Although particulars of the two forms of debt differ, the basic approach to accounting for each type is precisely the same.

Bonds

A bond issue divides a large liability into many smaller liabilities.

Corporations issuing bonds are obligated to repay a stated amount at a specified *maturity date* and periodic *interest* between the issue date and maturity.

A company can borrow cash from a bank or other financial institution by signing a promissory note. We discuss notes payable later in the chapter. Medium- and large-sized corporations often choose to borrow cash by issuing bonds. In fact, the most common form of corporate debt is bonds. A bond issue, in effect, breaks down a large debt (large corporations often borrow hundreds of millions of dollars at a time) into manageable parts—usually $1,000 units. This avoids the necessity of finding a single lender who is both willing and able to loan a large amount of money at a reasonable interest rate. So rather than signing a $400 million note to borrow cash from a financial institution, a company may find it more practical to sell 400,000 $1,000 bonds to many lenders—theoretically up to 400,000 lenders.

Bonds obligate the issuing corporation to repay a stated amount (variously referred to as the *principal, par value, face amount*, or *maturity value*) at a specified *maturity date*. Maturities for bonds typically range from 10 to 40 years. In return for the use of the money borrowed, the company also agrees to pay *interest* to bondholders between the issue date and maturity. The periodic interest is a stated percentage of face amount (variously referred to as the *stated rate, coupon rate, or nominal rate*). Ordinarily, interest is paid semiannually on designated interest dates beginning six months after the day the bonds are "dated."

The Bond Indenture

The specific promises made to bondholders are described in a document called a **bond indenture**. Because it would be impractical for the corporation to enter into a direct agreement with each of the many bondholders, the bond indenture is held by a trustee, usually a commercial bank or other financial institution, appointed by the issuing firm to represent the rights of the bondholders. If the company fails to live up to the terms of the bond indenture, the trustee may bring legal action against the company on behalf of the bondholders.

Most corporate bonds are debenture bonds. A **debenture bond** is secured only by the "full faith and credit" of the issuing corporation. No specific assets are pledged as security. Investors in debentures usually have the same standing as the firm's other general creditors. So in case of bankruptcy, debenture holders and other general creditors would be treated equally.

A **mortgage bond**, on the other hand, is backed by a lien on specified real estate owned by the issuer. Because a mortgage bond is considered less risky than debentures, it typically will command a lower interest rate.

A **subordinated debenture**, as the name implies, is not entitled to receive any liquidation payments until the claims of other specified debt issues are satisfied.

The method used to pay interest depends on whether the bonds are **registered bonds** or **coupon bonds** (sometimes called *bearer bonds*). Interest checks are mailed directly to the owner of a registered bond, whose name is registered with the issuing company. The name of the owner of a coupon bond is not registered. Instead, to collect interest on a coupon bond the holder must actually clip an attached coupon and redeem it in accordance with instructions in the indenture. Today most corporate bonds are registered bonds.

Bonds are not always retired by a single-sum payment at a specific maturity date. The bond indenture also might provide for their redemption through a call feature, by serial payments, through sinking fund provisions, or by conversion.

Most corporate bonds are **callable** (or redeemable). The call feature allows the issuing company to buy back, or call, outstanding bonds from bondholders before their scheduled maturity date. This feature affords the company some protection against being stuck with relatively high-cost debt in the event interest rates fall during the period to maturity. The call price must be prespecified and often exceeds the bond's face amount (a call premium), sometimes declining as maturity is approached.

For example, recent financial statements of Emhart Corporation included this footnote disclosure:

The Company's $9^1/4\%$ (9.65% effective interest rate, after discount) sinking fund debentures are callable at prices decreasing from 105 percent of face amount currently to 100 percent in 2006.

"No call" provisions usually prohibit calls during the first few years of a bond's life. Very often, calls are mandatory. That is, the corporation may be required to redeem the bonds on a prespecified, year-by-year basis. Bonds requiring such sinking fund redemptions often are labeled *sinking fund debentures*. Emhart's disclosures regarding its sinking fund debentures also included:

…Commencing in 1997, sinking fund redemptions are required in the amount of $8.0 million each year.

The **sinking fund** typically is administered by a trustee who repurchases bonds in the open market. If insufficient willing sellers are found, the trustee must exercise the bonds' call feature to buy the required amount of bonds, using a lottery approach to select bonds for call from among existing bondholders.

Serial bonds provide a more structured (and less popular) way to retire bonds on a piecemeal basis. Serial bonds are retired in installments during all or part of the life of the issue. Each bond has its own specified maturity date. So for a typical 30-year serial issue, 25 to 30 separate maturity dates might be assigned to specific portions of the bond issue.

Convertible bonds are retired as a consequence of bondholders choosing to convert them into shares of stock. We look closer at convertible bonds a little later in the chapter.

A bond indenture describes the specific promises made to bondholders.

OPENING CASE

Question 1

Liquidation rights affect a bond issue's effective interest rate.

know definitions →

OPENING CASE

Question 2

Mandatory sinking fund redemptions retire a bond issue gradually over its term to maturity.

Learning objective 2

Account for bonds issued at par, at a discount, or at a premium, recording interest at the effective rate or by the straight-line method.

Recording Bonds at Issuance

Bonds represent a liability to the corporation that issues the bonds and an asset to a company that buys the bonds as an investment. Each side of the transaction is the mirror image of the other.[1] This is demonstrated in Illustration 14–1.

ILLUSTRATION 14–1

Bonds Sold at Face Amount

On January 1, 1997, Masterwear Industries issued $700,000 of 12% bonds. Interest of $42,000 is payable semiannually on June 30 and December 31. The bonds mature in three years (an unrealistically short maturity to shorten the illustration). The entire bond issue was sold in a private placement to United Intergroup, Inc., at face amount.

At Issuance (January 1)

Masterwear (Issuer)

Cash	700,000	
Bonds payable (face amount)		700,000

United (Investor)

Investment in bonds (face amount)	700,000	
Cash		700,000

Bonds Issued Between Interest Dates.   We assumed that the bonds in the previous example were sold on the day they were dated (date printed in the indenture contract). But suppose a weak market caused a delay in selling the bonds until two months after that date (four months before semi-annual interest was to be paid). In that case, the buyer would be asked to pay the seller **accrued interest** for two months in addition to the price of the bonds. For illustration, assume Masterwear was unable to sell the bonds in the previous example until March 1—two months after they are dated. This variation is shown in Illustration 14–1a. United would pay the price of the bonds ($700,000) plus $14,000 accrued interest:

All bonds sell at their price plus any interest that has accrued since the last interest date.

$$\underset{\substack{\text{Face}\\\text{amount}}}{\$700{,}000} \times \underset{\substack{\text{Annual}\\\text{rate}}}{12\%} \times \underset{\substack{\text{Fraction of the}\\\text{annual period}}}{^2/_{12}} = \underset{\substack{\text{Accrued}\\\text{interest}}}{\$14{,}000}$$

ILLUSTRATION 14–1a

Bonds Sold at Face Amount between Interest Dates

Since the investor will hold the bonds for only four months before receiving six months' interest, two months' accrued interest must be added to the price paid.

At Issuance (March 1)

Masterwear (Issuer)

Cash (price plus accrued interest)	714,000	
Bonds payable (face amount)		700,000
Interest payable (accrued interest determined above)		14,000

United (Investor)

Investment in bonds (face amount)	700,000	
Interest receivable (accrued interest determined above)	14,000	
Cash (price plus accrued interest)		714,000

When Masterwear pays semiannual interest on June 30, a full six months' interest is paid. But having received two months' accrued interest in advance, Masterwear's *net* interest expense will be four months' interest, for the four months the bonds have been outstanding at that time. Likewise, when United receives six month's interest—after holding the bonds for only four months—United will net only the four months' interest to which it is entitled:

The issuer incurs interest expense, and the investor earns interest revenue, for only the four months the bonds are outstanding.

At the First Interest Date (June 30)

Masterwear (Issuer)

Interest expense (6 mo. – 2 mo. = 4 mo.)	28,000	
Interest payable[2] (accrued interest determined above)	14,000	
Cash (stated rate × face amount)		42,000

---

[1]You should recall from Chapter 12 that investments in bonds that are to be held to maturity by the investor are reported at amortized cost, which is the method described here. However, also remember that investments in debt securities *not* to be held to maturity are reported at the fair value of the securities held, as described in Chapter 12.

United (Investor)

Cash (stated rate × face amount)	42,000	
Interest receivable (accrued interest determined above)		14,000
Interest revenue (6 mo. – 2 mo. = 4 mo.)		28,000

OPENING CASE

Question 3

Determining the Selling Price.   The price of a bond issue at any particular time is not necessarily equal to its face amount. The $700,000, 12% bond issue in the previous illustration, for example, may sell for more than face amount (at a **premium**) or less than face amount (at a **discount**), depending on how the 12% *stated* interest rate compares with the prevailing *market* or *effective rate* of interest (for securities of similar risk and maturity). For instance, if the 12% bonds are competing in a market in which similar bonds are providing a 14% return, the bonds could be sold only at a price less than $700,000. On the other hand, if the market rate is only 10%, the 12% stated rate would seem relatively attractive and the bonds would sell at a premium over face amount.

In addition to the characteristic terms of a bond agreement as specified in the indenture, the market rate for a specific bond issue is influenced by the creditworthiness of the company issuing the bonds. To evaluate the risk and quality of an individual bond issue, investors rely heavily on bond ratings provided by Standard & Poor's Corporation and by Moody's Investors Service, Inc. See the following bond ratings Graphic 14–1.

> Other things being equal, the lower the perceived riskiness of the corporation issuing bonds, the higher the price those bonds will command.

GRAPHIC 14–1

Bond Ratings*

	S&P	Moody's
Investment Grades:		
Highest	AAA	Aaa
High	AA	Aa
Medium	A	A
Minimum investment grade	BBB	Baa
"Junk" Ratings:		
Speculative	BB	Ba
Very speculative	B	B
Default or near default:	CCC	Caa
	CC	Ca
	C	C
	D	

*Adapted from: *Bond Record* (New York: Moody's Investor Services, monthly) and *Bond Guide* (New York: Standard & Poor's Corporation, monthly).

> A bond issue will be priced by the marketplace to yield the market rate of interest for securities of similar risk and maturity.

Forces of supply and demand cause a bond issue to be *priced to yield the market rate*. In other words, an investor paying that price will earn an effective rate of return on the investment equal to the market rate. The price is calculated as the present value of all the cash flows required of the bonds, where the discount rate used in the present value calculation is the market rate. Specifically, the price will be the present value of the periodic cash interest payments (face amount × stated rate) plus the present value of the principal payable at maturity, both discounted at the market rate.

Bonds priced at a discount are described in Illustration 14–2.

---

[2]Some accountants prefer to credit interest expense, rather than interest payable, when the bonds are sold. When that is done, this entry would require simply a debit to interest expense and a credit to cash for $42,000. The interest expense account would then reflect the same *net* debit of four months' interest ($42,000 – 14,000).

	Interest Expense	
		2 months
6 months		
4 months		

Similarly, the investor could debit interest revenue, rather than interest receivable when buying the bonds.

ILLUSTRATION 14–2

Bonds Sold at a Discount

Because interest is paid semiannually, the present value calculations use:
a. one-half the stated rate (6%),
b. one-half the market rate (7%), and
c. 6 (3 × 2) semi-annual periods.

On January 1, 1997, Masterwear Industries issued $700,000 of 12% bonds, dated January 1. Interest of $42,000 is payable semiannually on June 30 and December 31. The bonds mature in three years. The market yield for bonds of similar risk and maturity is 14%. The entire bond issue was purchased by United Intergroup, Inc.

Calculation of the price of the bonds:

						Present Values
Interest	$42,000	×	4.76654*	=		$200,195
Principal	$700,000	×	0.66634†	=		466,438
	Present value (price) of the bonds					$666,633

*Present value of an ordinary annuity of $1: n=6, i=7% (Table 6A–4).
†Present value of $1: n=6, i=7% (Table 6A–2).

The calculation is illustrated in Graphic 14–2.

GRAPHIC 14–2

Cash Flows from a Bond Issue

Dates of Cash Flows			
1. June 30, 1997	$ 42,000		
2. December 31, 1997	42,000		
3. June 30, 1998	42,000		
4. December 31, 1998	42,000		
5. June 30, 1999	42,000		**Total Future**
6. December 31, 1999	42,000	$700,000	**Cash Flows**
	$252,000	$700,000 =	**$952,000**

Discounted at 7%

Because of the time value of money, the present value of the future cash flows is less than $952,000.

January 1, 1997	$200,195	+	466,438	=	**Present Value of Cash Flows** **$666,633**

Although the cash flows total $952,000, the present value of those future cash flows as of January 1, 1997, is only $666,633. This is due to the time value of money.

Journal Entries at Issuance—Bonds Sold at Discount

Masterwear (Issuer)

Cash (price calculated above)	666,633	
Discount on bonds payable (difference)	33,367	
Bonds payable (face amount)		700,000

United (Investor)

Investment in bonds (face amount)	700,000	
Discount on bond investment (difference)		33,367
Cash (price calculated above)		666,633

When bond prices are quoted in financial media, they typically are stated in terms of a percentage of face amount. Thus, a price quote of 98 means a $1,000 bond will sell for $980; a bond priced at 101 will sell for $1,010.

Determining Interest—Effective Interest Method

Interest accrues on an outstanding debt at a constant percentage of the debt each period. Of course, under the concept of accrual accounting, the periodic effective interest is not affected by the time at which the cash interest actually is paid. Recording interest each period as the *effective market rate of interest multiplied by the outstanding balance of the debt* (during the interest period) is referred to as the **effective interest method**. Although giving this a label—the effective interest method—implies some specialized procedure, this simply is an application of the accrual concept, consistent with accruing all expenses as they are incurred.

The **effective interest** on debt is the market rate of interest multiplied by the outstanding balance of the debt.

Continuing our example, we determined that the amount of debt when the bonds are issued is $666,633. Since the effective interest rate is 14%, interest recorded (as expense to the issuer and revenue to the investor) for the first six-month interest period is $46,664:

$$\underset{\text{Outstanding balance}}{\$666,633} \quad \times \quad \underset{\text{Effective rate}}{[14\% \div 2]} \quad = \quad \underset{\text{Effective interest}}{\$46,664}$$

However, the bond indenture calls for semiannual interest payments of only $42,000—the *stated* rate (6%) times the *face amount* ($700,000). As always, when only a portion of an expense is paid, the remainder becomes a liability—in this case an addition to the already outstanding liability. So the difference, $4,664, increases the liability and is reflected as a reduction in the discount (a valuation account). This is illustrated in Graphic 14–3.

GRAPHIC 14–3

Change in Debt When Effective Interest Exceeds Cash Paid

The unpaid portion of the effective interest increases the existing liability.

		Account Balances				
		Outstanding Balance		Bonds Payable (face amount)		Discount on Bonds Payable
January 1		$666,633	=	$700,000	less	33,367
Interest accrued at 7%		46,664				
Portion of interest paid		(42,000)				(4,664)
June 30		$671,297	=	$700,000	less	28,703

Interest accrues on the outstanding debt at the effective rate. Interest paid is the amount specified in the bond indenture—the stated rate times the face amount. These amounts and the change in the outstanding debt are recorded as follows:

Journal Entries— The Interest Method

The effective interest is calculated each period as the market rate times the amount of the debt outstanding during the interest period.

At the First Interest Date (June 30)		
Masterwear (Issuer)		
Interest expense (market rate × outstanding balance)	46,664	
Discount on bonds payable (difference)		4,664
Cash (stated rate × face amount)		42,000
United (Investor)		
Cash (stated rate × face amount)	42,000	
Discount on bond investment (difference)	4,664	
Interest revenue (market rate × outstanding balance)		46,664

Because the balance of the debt changes each period, the dollar amount of interest (balance × rate) also will change each period. To keep up with the changing amounts, it usually is convenient to prepare a schedule that reflects the changes in the debt over its term to maturity. An amortization schedule for the situation under discussion is shown in Graphic 14–4.

GRAPHIC 14–4

Amortization Schedule— Discount

Since less cash is paid each period than the effective interest, the unpaid difference increases the outstanding balance of the debt.

	Cash Interest (6% × Face amount)	Effective Interest (7% × Outstanding balance)	Increase in Balance (Discount reduction)	Outstanding Balance
				666,633
1	42,000	.07(666,633) = 46,664	4,664	671,297
2	42,000	.07(671,297) = 46,991	4,991	676,288
3	42,000	.07(676,288) = 47,340	5,340	681,628
4	42,000	.07(681,628) = 47,714	5,714	687,342
5	42,000	.07(687,342) = 48,114	6,114	693,456
6	42,000	.07(693,456) = 48,544*	6,544	700,000
	252,000	285,367	33,367	

*Rounded.

Amounts for the journal entries each interest date are found in the first three columns of the schedule. Traditionally, this schedule has been referred to as an **amortization schedule**—a reference to alleged amortization of the discount.[3] This is an apparent carryover from earlier days when the dis-

---

[3]You learned in earlier chapters that amortization is the accounting process of reducing an asset or liability by periodic write-downs or payments [*SFAC 6*, par. 142.].

count was considered to be an asset to be amortized. To the contrary, the discount is a valuation account, having no existence apart from the related debt. As you learned in the previous paragraphs, changes in its balance are the derived result of changes in the outstanding debt, when portions of periodic accrued interest go unpaid.[4]

However, because this terminology is so prevalent in practice, we too will use the label *amortization schedule*. Be sure to realize, though, that this label is a misnomer—nothing is being amortized. The essential point to remember is that the effective interest method is a straightforward application of the accrual concept, whereby interest expense (or revenue) is accrued periodically at the effective rate. It involves neither deferring expenses (or revenues) nor amortizing deferrals.

> Terms such as unamortized or deferred discount or premium and to amortize discount or premium are carryovers from the days when debt discount was considered to be an amortizable asset and do not describe accurately either the assets or liabilities and events involved or the interest method of accounting for them.[5]

> A liability should be reported at its present value.

Determining interest in this manner has a convenient side effect. It results in reporting the liability at the present value of future cash payments—the appropriate valuation method for any liability.[6] This is obvious at issuance; we actually calculated the present value to be $666,633. What perhaps is not quite as obvious is that the outstanding amount of debt each subsequent period (shown in the right-hand column of the amortization schedule) is still the present value of the remaining cash flows, discounted at the original rate.

Additional Consideration

Although the reported amount each period is the **present value** of the bonds, at any date after issuance this amount is not necessarily equal to the **market value** of the bonds. This is because the **market** rate of interest will not necessarily remain the same as the rate implicit in the original issue price (the effective rate). Of course, for negotiable financial instruments, the issue price is the market price at any given time. Differences between market values and present values based on the original rate are holding gains and losses. If we were to use the market rate to revalue bonds on each reporting date—that is, recalculate the present value using the market rate—the reported amount always would be the market value. Some accountants contend that reporting market values and resultant holding gains and losses would provide more meaningful information than reporting debt at its present value, discounted at the original rate. Reporting debt at market values is not presently permitted by GAAP except in certain specialized industries like the mutual fund and insurance industries. Certainly the market value of existing debt is information considered by management in refinancing decisions.

When Financial Statements Are Prepared Between Interest Dates.   When an accounting period ends between interest dates, it is necessary to record interest that has accrued since the last interest date. For instance, if the fiscal years of Masterwear and United end on October 31 and interest was last paid and recorded on June 30, four months' interest must be accrued in a year-end adjusting entry. Because interest is recorded for only a portion of a semiannual period, amounts recorded are simply the amounts shown in the amortization schedule times the appropriate fraction of the semiannual period (in this case $4/6$).

> Any interest that has accrued since the last interest date must be recorded by an adjusting entry prior to preparing financial statements.

> **Adjusting Entries—To Accrue Interest**
> To avoid understating interest on the financial statements, four months' interest is recorded at the end of the reporting period.

At October 31		
Masterwear (Issuer)		
Interest expense ($4/6 \times 46,991$)	31,327	
Discount on bonds payable ($4/6 \times 4,991$)		3,327
Interest payable ($4/6 \times 42,000$)		28,000

---

[4]Or as we see later, the debt changes when periodic interest is overpaid. This occurs when debt is sold at a premium, rather than at a discount.

[5]Elements of Financial Statements," *Statement of Financial Accounting Concepts No. 6,* par. 36 (Stamford, Conn.: FASB, 1985), par. 239.

[6] "Interest on Receivables and Payables," *APB Opinion No. 21,* (New York: AICPA), 1971.

United (Investor)		
Interest receivable ($^4/_6$ × 42,000)	28,000	
Discount on bond investment ($^4/_6$ × 4,991)	3,327	
Interest revenue ($^4/_6$ × 46,991)		31,327

Two months later, when semiannual interest is paid next, the remainder of the semiannual interest is allocated to the first two months of the next accounting year—November and December:

At the December 31 Interest Date		
Masterwear (Issuer)		
Interest expense ($^2/_6$ × 46,991)	15,664	
Interest payable (from adjusting entry)	28,000	
Discount on bonds payable ($^2/_6$ × 4,991)		1,664
Cash (stated rate × face amount)		42,000
United (Investor)		
Cash (stated rate × face amount)	42,000	
Discount on bond investment ($^2/_6$ × 4,991)	1,664	
Interest receivable (from adjusting entry)		28,000
Interest revenue ($^2/_6$ × 46,991)		15,664

Of the six-months' interest paid December 31, only the November and December interest is expensed in the new fiscal year.

The Straight-Line Method—A Practical Expediency

In some circumstances the profession permits an exception to the conceptually appropriate method of determining interest for bond issues. A company is allowed to determine interest indirectly by allocating a discount or a premium equally to each period over the term to maturity—if doing so produces results that are not materially different from the usual (and preferable) interest method.[7] The decision should be guided by whether the **straight-line method** would tend to mislead investors and creditors in the particular circumstance.

By the straight-line method, the discount in the earlier illustration would be allocated equally to the six semiannual periods (three years):

$$\$33,367 \div 6 \text{ periods} = \$5,561 \text{ per period}$$

Journal Entries— Straight-Line Method

At Each of the Six Interest Dates		
Masterwear (Issuer)		
Interest expense (to balance)	47,561	
Discount on bonds payable (discount ÷ 6 periods)		5,561
Cash (stated rate × face amount)		42,000
United (Investor)		
Cash (stated rate × face amount)	42,000	
Discount on bond investment (discount ÷ 6 periods)	5,561	
Interest revenue (to balance)		47,561

By the straight-line method, interest (expense and revenue) is a plug figure, resulting from calculating the amount of discount reduction.

Allocating the discount or premium equally over the life of the bonds by the straight-line method results in a constant dollar amount of interest each period. An amortization schedule, then, would serve little purpose. For example, if we prepared one for the straight-line method in this situation, it would provide the same amounts each period as shown in Graphic 14–5.

---

[7]"Interest on Receivables and Payables," *APB Opinion No. 21,* AICPA, 1971.

GRAPHIC 14-5

Amortization Schedule—
Straight-Line Method

By the straight-line method, the amount of the discount to be reduced periodically is calculated, and the recorded interest is the plug figure.

	Cash Interest	Recorded Interest	Increase in Balance	Outstanding Balance
	(6% × Face amount)	(Cash plus Discount reduction)	($33,367 ÷ 6)	
				666,633
1	42,000	(42,000 + 5,561) = 47,561	5,561	672,194
2	42,000	(42,000 + 5,561) = 47,561	5,561	677,755
3	42,000	(42,000 + 5,561) = 47,561	5,561	683,316
4	42,000	(42,000 + 5,561) = 47,561	5,561	688,877
5	42,000	(42,000 + 5,561) = 47,561	5,561	694,438
6	42,000	(42,000 + 5,561) = 47,561	5,561	700,000*
	252,000	285,366	33,366	

*Rounded.

Remember, constant dollar amounts are not produced when the effective interest method is used. By that method, the dollar amounts of interest vary over the term to maturity because the percentage rate of interest remains constant but is applied to a changing debt balance.

Determining interest by allocating the discount (or premium) on a straight-line basis is a practical expediency permitted in some situations by the materiality concept.

Also, be sure to realize that the straight-line method is not an alternative method of determining interest in a conceptual sense. Instead, it is an application of the materiality concept, by which an appropriate application of GAAP (e.g., the effective interest method) can be bypassed for reasons of practical expediency in situations when doing so has no material effect on the results.

Bonds Sold at a Premium. In Illustration 14–2, Masterwear Industries sold the bonds at a price that would yield an effective rate higher than the stated rate. The result was a discount. On the other hand, if the 12% bonds had been issued when the market yield for bonds of similar risk and maturity was *lower* than the stated rate, say 10%, the issue would have been priced at a *premium*. Because the 12% rate would seem relatively attractive in a 10% market, the bonds would command an issue price of more than $700,000, calculated in Illustration 14–3.

ILLUSTRATION 14-3

Bonds Sold at a Premium

Because interest is paid *semiannually*, the present value calculations use:
a. one-half the stated rate (6%),
b. one-half the market rate (5%), and
c. 6 (3 × 2) semi-annual periods.

On January 1, 1997, Masterwear Industries issued $700,000 of 12% bonds, dated January 1. Interest of $42,000 is payable semiannually on June 30 and December 31. The bonds mature in three years. The market yield for bonds of similar risk and maturity is 10%. The entire bond issue was purchased by United Intergroup, Inc.

Calculation of the price of the bonds:

					Present Values
Interest	$42,000	×	5.07569*	=	$213,179
Principal	$700,000	×	0.74622†	=	522,354
	Present value (price) of the bonds				$735,533

*Present value of an ordinary annuity of $1: n=6, i=5%.
†Present value of $1: n=6, i=5%.

Journal Entries at Issuance—Bonds Sold at Premium

Masterwear (Issuer)

Cash (price calculated above)	735,533	
Bonds payable (face amount)		700,000
Premium on bonds payable (difference)		35,533

United (Investor)

Investment in bonds (face amount)	700,000	
Premium on bond investment (difference)	35,533	
Cash (price calculated above)		735,533

Interest on bonds sold at a premium is determined in precisely the same manner as on bonds sold at a discount. Again, interest is the effective interest rate applied to the debt outstanding during each period (balance at the end of the previous interest period), and the cash paid is the stated rate times the face amount, as shown in Graphic 14–6:

GRAPHIC   14–6

Amortization Schedule—Premium

Date I	Cash Interest	Effective Interest	Decrease in Balance	Outstanding Balance
	(6% × Face amount)	(5% × Outstanding balance)	(Premium reduction)	
				735,533
1	42,000	.05(735,533) = 36,777	5,223	730,310
2	42,000	.05(730,310) = 36,516	5,484	724,826
3	42,000	.05(724,826) = 36,241	5,759	719,067
4	42,000	.05(719,067) = 35,953	6,047	713,020
5	42,000	.05(713,020) = 35,651	6,349	706,671
6	42,000	.05(706,671) = 35,329*	6,671	700,000
	252,000	216,467	35,533	

*Rounded.

> Since *more* cash is paid each period than the effective interest, the debt outstanding is reduced by the overpayment.

Notice that the debt declines each period. This is because the effective interest each period is less than the cash interest paid. The overpayments each period reduce the amount owed. Remember, this is precisely the opposite of when debt is sold at a discount, when the effective interest each period is more than the cash paid, and the underpayment of interest adds to the amount owed.

Additional Consideration

The preceding illustrations describe bonds sold at a discount and at a premium. The same concepts apply to bonds sold at face amount. But some of the procedures would be unnecessary. For instance, calculating the present value of the interest and the principal always will give us the face amount when the effective rate and the stated rate are the same:

Calculation of the price of the bonds:

					Present Values
Interest	$42,000	×	4.91732*	=	$206,528
Principal	$700,000	×	0.70496†	=	493,472
	Present value (price) of the bonds				$700,000

*Present value of an ordinary annuity of $1: *n*=6, *i*=6%.
†Present value of $1: *n*=6, *i*=6%.

CONCEPT REVIEW EXERCISE   ISSUING BONDS AND RECORDING INTEREST

On January 1, 1997, the Meade Group issued $8,000,000 of 11% bonds, dated January 1. Interest is payable semiannually on June 30 and December 31. The bonds mature in four years. The market yield for bonds of similar risk and maturity is 10%.

Required:
1. Determine the price these bonds sold for to yield the 10% market rate and record their issuance by the Meade Group.
2. Prepare an amortization schedule that determines interest at the effective rate and record interest on the first interest date, June 30, 1997.

CONCEPT REVIEW EXERCISE   SOLUTION

1. Determine the price these bonds sold for to yield the 10% market rate and record their issuance by the Meade Group.

Calculation of the price of the bonds:
There are eight semiannual periods and one-half the market rate is 5%.

Interest	$440,000 × 6.46321*	=	$2,843,812
Principal	$8,000,000 × 0.67684†	=	5,414,720
	Present value (price) of the bonds		$8,258,532

*Present value of an ordinary annuity of $1: *n*=8, *i*=5%.
†Present value of $1: *n*=8, *i*=5%.

Journal Entry at Issuance

Cash (price calculated above) 8,258,532	
Bonds payable (face amount)	8,000,000
Premium on bonds payable (difference)	258,532

2. Prepare an amortization schedule that determines interest at the effective rate and record interest on the first interest date, June 30, 1997.

Amortization Schedule

Date	Cash Interest (5.5% × Face amount)	Effective Interest (5% × Outstanding balance)	Decrease in Balance (Premium reduction)	Outstanding Balance
				8,258,532
1	440,000	.05(8,258,532) = 412,927	27,073	8,231,459
2	440,000	.05(8,231,459) = 411,573	28,427	8,203,032
3	440,000	.05(8,203,032) = 410,152	29,848	8,173,184
4	440,000	.05(8,173,184) = 408,659	31,341	8,141,843
5	440,000	.05(8,141,843) = 407,092	32,908	8,108,935
6	440,000	.05(8,108,935) = 405,446	34,554	8,074,381
7	440,000	.05(8,074,381) = 403,719	36,281	8,038,100
8	440,000	.05(8,038,100) = 401,900*	38,100	8,000,000
	3,520,000	3,261,468	258,532	

*Rounded.

More cash is paid each period than the effective interest, so the debt *outstanding is reduced by the "overpayment."*

Interest expense (5% × $8,258,529)	412,927	
Premium on bonds payable (difference)	27,073	
Cash (5.5% × $8,000,000)		440,000
To record interest		

Debt Issue Costs

Rather than sell bonds directly to the public, corporations usually sell an entire issue to an underwriter who then resells them to other security dealers and the public. By committing to purchase bonds at a set price, an investment house such as Salomon Brothers, First Boston, and Merrill Lynch is said to underwrite any risks associated with a new issue. The underwriting fee is the spread between the price the underwriter pays and the resale price.

Alternatively, the issuing company may choose to sell the debt securities directly to a single investor (as we assumed in previous illustrations)—often a pension fund or an insurance company. This is referred to as *private placement*. Issue costs are less because privately placed securities are not subject to the costly and lengthy process of registering with the SEC that is required of public offerings. Underwriting fees also are avoided.

With either publicly or privately sold debt, the issuing company will incur costs in connection with issuing bonds or notes, such as legal and accounting fees and printing costs, in addition to registration and underwriting fees. These **debt issue costs** are recorded *separately* and are amortized over the term of the related debt. GAAP requires a debit to an asset account—debt issue costs. The asset is allocated to expense, usually on a straight-line basis.

For example, let's assume issue costs in Illustration 14–3 had been $12,000. The entries for the issuance of the bonds would include a separate asset account for the issue costs:

Costs of issuing debt securities are recorded as a debit to an asset account, "debt issue costs," and amortized to expense over the term to maturity.

The premium (or discount) is unaffected by debt issue costs because they are recorded in a separate account.

Cash (price minus issue costs)	723,533	
Debt issue costs	12,000	
Bonds payable (face amount)		700,000
Premium on bonds payable (price minus face amount)		35,533

Semiannual amortization of the asset would be:

Debt issue expense ($12,000 ÷ 6)	2,000	
Debt issue costs		2,000

Additional Consideration

The treatment of issue costs just described is required by *APB Opinion No. 21*. A conceptually more appealing treatment would be to reduce the recorded amount of the debt by the debt issue costs instead of recording the costs separately as an asset. The cost of these services reduces the net cash the issuing company receives from the sale of the financial instrument. A lower [net] amount is borrowed at the same cost, increasing the effective interest rate. Unless the recorded amount of the debt is reduced by the issue costs, the higher rate is not reflected in a higher recorded interest expense.[8] The actual increase in the effective interest rate would be reflected in the interest expense if the issue cost is allowed to reduce the premium (or increase the discount) on the debt:

Cash (price calculated above)	723,533	
Bonds payable (face amount)		700,000
Premium on bonds payable (difference)		23,533

Also, this approach is consistent with the treatment of issue costs when equity securities are sold. You will see in Chapter 19 that the effect of share issue costs is to reduce the amount credited to stock accounts.

This treatment also is suggested by the FASB in *SFAC 6*. Remember, though, that concept statements do not constitute GAAP, so until a new FASB standard is issued to supersede *APB Opinion 21*, the generally accepted practice is to record debt issue costs as assets.

Variations in Debt Instruments

I Learning objective 3
Describe innovative financial instruments used to attract lenders and how each is accounted for.

Some financial instruments that include traditional characteristics of bonds are modified to achieve specific purposes of the corporations that issue them. Three of the most popular bond variations are (1) zero-coupon bonds, (2) convertible bonds, and (3) bonds issued with detachable warrants. We discuss these in this section.

Zero-Coupon Bonds

A zero-coupon bond pays no interest. Instead, it offers a return in the form of a "deep discount" from the face amount. For illustration, let's look at the zero-coupon bond issue offered by PepsiCo, Inc. in 1982. One million dollars face amount of the 30-year bonds sold for $26,430. As the amortization schedule in Graphic 14–7 demonstrates, the bonds were priced to yield 12.875%.

GRAPHIC   14–7

Zero-Coupon Bonds—
PepsiCo

A single bond from Pepsi's zero-coupon issue selling for $26.43 in 1983 pays $1,000 at maturity in 2012.

Dec. 31	Cash Interest	Effective Interest	Increase in Balance	Outstanding Balance*
	(0% × Face amount)	(12.875% × Outstanding debt)	(Discount reduction)	
				26,430
1983	0	.12875(26,430) = 3,403	3,403	29,831
1984	0	.12875(29,831) = 3,841	3,841	33,672
1985	0	.12875(33,672) = 4,335	4,335	38,007
•	•	•	•	•
•	•	•	•	•
•	•	•	•	•
2011	0	.12875(784,882) = 101,054	101,054	885,936
2012	0	.12875(885,936) = 114,064	114,064	1,000,000
	0	973,570	973,570	

*Some numbers appear not to total because the underlying calculations are not rounded.

---

[8]When the same amortization method is used for both, the net income is unaffected by whether the cost is amortized as a separate debt issue expense or is reflected in a higher interest expense.

An advantage of issuing zero-coupon bonds is that the corporation can deduct for tax purposes the annual interest expense (see schedule) but has no related cash outflow until the bonds mature. However, the reverse is true for investors in zeros. Investors receive no periodic cash interest, even though annual interest revenue is reportable for tax purposes. So those who invest in zero-coupon bonds usually have tax-deferred or tax-exempt status, such as pension funds, individual retirement accounts (IRAs), and charitable organizations. Zero-coupon bonds and notes are gaining popularity but still constitute a relatively small proportion of corporate debt.

Convertible Bonds

OPENING CASE

Question 4

Convertible bonds can be exchanged for shares of stock at the option of the investor.

Convertible bonds have features of both debt and equity.

Sometimes corporations include a convertible feature as part of a bond offering. **Convertible bonds** can be converted into (that is, exchanged for) shares of stock at the option of the bondholder. Among the reasons for issuing convertible bonds rather than straight debt are (a) to sell the bonds at a higher price (which means a lower effective interest cost),[9] (b) to use as a medium of exchange in mergers and acquisitions, and (c) to enable smaller firms or debt-heavy companies to obtain access to the bond market. Sometimes convertible bonds serve as an indirect way to issue stock when there is shareholder resistance to direct issuance of additional equity.

Central to each of these reasons for issuing convertible debt is that the conversion feature is attractive to investors. This hybrid security has features of both debt and equity. The owner has a fixed-income security that can become common stock if and when the firm's prosperity makes that feasible. This increases the investor's upside potential while limiting the downside risk. The conversion feature has monetary value. Just how valuable it is depends on both the conversion terms and market conditions. But from an accounting perspective the question raised is how to account for its value. To evaluate the question, consider Illustration 14–4.

ILLUSTRATION   14–4

Convertible Bonds

> On January 1, 1997, HTL Manufacturers issued $100 million of 8% convertible debentures due 2007 at 102 (102% of face value). The bonds are convertible at the option of the holder into $1 par common stock at a conversion ratio of 40 shares per $1,000 bond. HTL recently issued nonconvertible, 20-year, 8% debentures at 98.

Because of the inseparability of their debt and equity features, the entire issue price of convertible bonds is recorded as debt, as if they are nonconvertible bonds.

It would appear that the conversion feature is valued by the market at $4 million—the difference between the market value of the convertible bonds, $102 million, and the market value of the nonconvertible bonds, $98 million. Some accountants argue that we should record the value of the conversion option in a shareholders' equity account ($4 million in this case) and the debt value in the bond accounts ($100 million bonds payable less $2 million discount).[10] However, the currently accepted practice is to record the entire issue price as debt in precisely the same way as for nonconvertible bonds.[11] This approach is supported by the view that the two features of the security, the debt and the conversion option, are physically inseparable—the option cannot be exercised without surrendering the debt. Treating the features as two inseparable parts of a single security also avoids the practical difficulty of trying to measure the separate values of the debt and the conversion option. We sidestepped this difficulty in our illustration by assuming that HTL had recently issued nonconvertible bonds that were otherwise similar to the convertible bonds.

Journal Entry at Issuance— Convertible Bonds

The value of the conversion feature is not separately recorded.

	($ in millions)	
Cash (102% × $100 million)	102	
Convertible bonds payable (face amount)		100
Premium on bonds payable (difference)		2

---

[9]Remember, there is an inverse relationship between bond prices and interest rates. When the price is higher, the rate (yield) is lower, and vice versa.

[10]These arguments are summarized in the FASB *Discussion Memorandum,* "Distinguishing between Liability and Equity Instruments and Accounting for Instruments with Characteristics of Both," 1990.

[11]"Accounting for Convertible Debt and Debt Issued with Stock Purchase Warrants," *Accounting Principles Board Opinion No. 14,* (New York: APB, 1969).

Since we make no provision for the separate value of the conversion option, all subsequent entries, including the periodic reduction of the premium, are exactly the same as if these were nonconvertible bonds. So the illustrations and examples of bond accounting we discussed earlier would pertain equally to nonconvertible or convertible bonds.

When the Conversion Option Is Exercised.

If and when the bondholder exercises his or her option to convert the bonds into shares of stock, the bonds are removed from the accounting records and the new shares issued are recorded at the same amount (in other words, at the book value of the bonds). To illustrate, assume that half the convertible bonds issued by HTL Manufacturers are converted at a time when the remaining unamortized premium is $2 million:

Journal Entry at Conversion

The 2 million shares issued are recorded at the $51 million book value of the bonds retired.

	($ in millions)	
Convertible bonds payable (½ the account balance)	50	
Premium on bonds payable (½ the account balance)	1	
Common stock ([50,000 bonds × 40 shares] × $1 par)		2
Paid-in capital – excess of par (to balance)		49

Additional Consideration

The method just described is referred to as the *book value method*, since the new shares are recorded at the book value of the bonds being redeemed. It is by far the most popular method in practice. Another acceptable approach, the *market value method*, records the new shares at the market value of the shares themselves or of the bonds, whichever is more determinable. Because the market value most likely will differ from the book value of the bonds, a gain or loss on conversion will result. Assume for illustration that the market value of HTL's stock is $30 per share at the time of the conversion:

	($ in millions)	
Convertible bonds payable (½ the account balance)	50	
Premium on bonds payable (½ the account balance)	1	
Loss on conversion of bonds (to balance)	9	
Common stock [(50,000 bonds × 40 shares) × $1 par]		2
Paid-in capital in excess of par [(50,000 × 40 shares) × $29]		58

If a single investor had purchased the 50,000 bonds being converted, that company would record the conversion as follows:

	($ in millions)	
Investment in common stock	51	
Investment in convertible bonds (account balance)		50
Premium on bond investment (account balance)		1

Induced Conversion.

Investors often are reluctant to convert bonds to stock, even when share prices have risen significantly since the convertible bonds were purchased. This is because the market price of the convertible bonds will rise along with market prices of the stock. So companies sometimes try to induce conversion. The motivation might be to reduce debt and become a better risk to potential lenders or achieve a lower debt-to-equity ratio.

One way is through the call provision. As we noted earlier, most corporate bonds are callable by the issuing corporation. When the specified call price is less than the conversion value of the bonds (the market value of the shares), calling the convertible bonds provides bondholders with incentive to convert. Bondholders will choose the shares rather than the lower call price.

586

Any additional consideration provided to induce conversion of convertible debt is recorded as an expense of the period.

Occasionally, corporations may try to encourage voluntary conversion by offering an added inducement in the form of cash, stock warrants, or a more attractive conversion ratio. When additional consideration is provided to induce conversion, the fair value of that consideration is considered an expense incurred to bring about the conversion.[12]

Bonds with Detachable Warrants

Another way to sweeten a bond issue is to include **detachable stock purchase warrants** as part of the security issue. A stock warrant gives the investor an option to purchase a stated number of shares of common stock at a specified *option price*, often within a given period of time. Like a conversion feature, warrants usually mean a lower interest rate and often enable a company to issue debt when borrowing would not be feasible otherwise.

The issue price of bonds with detachable warrants is allocated between the two different securities on the basis of their market values.

However, unlike a conversion feature, warrants can be separated from the bonds. This means they can be exercised independently or traded in the market separately from bonds, having their own market price. In essence, two different securities—the bonds and the warrants—are sold as a package for a single issue price. Accordingly, the issue price is allocated between the two different securities on the basis of their market values. If the independent market value of only one of the two securities is reliably determinable, that value establishes the allocation. This is demonstrated in Illustration 14–5.

ILLUSTRATION 14–5

Bonds with Detachable Warrants

x-tra credit

On January 1, 1997, HTL Manufacturers issued $100 million of 8% debentures due 2007 at 102 (102% of face value). Accompanying each bond were 20 warrants. Each warrant permitted the holder to buy one share of $1 par common stock at $25 per share. Shortly after issuance, the warrants were listed on the exchange at $3 per warrant.

	($ in millions)	
Cash (102% × $100 million)	102	
Discount on bonds payable (difference)	4	
Bonds payable (face amount)		100
Paid-in capital—stock warrants outstanding		
(100,000 bonds × 20 warrants × $3)		6

Additional Consideration

Market imperfections may cause the separate market values not to sum to the issue price of the package. In this event, allocation is achieved on the basis of the **relative market values** of the two securities. Let's say the bonds have a separate market price of $940 per bond (priced at 94):

Market Values

Bonds (100,000 bonds × $940)	$ 94	94%
Warrants (100,000 bonds × 20 warrants × $3)	6	6
Total	$100	100%

Proportion of issue price allocated to bonds:

$$\$102 \times 94\% = \$95,880,000$$

Proportion of issue price allocated to warrants:

$$\$102 \times 6\% = \$6,120,000$$

	($ in millions)	
Cash (102% × $100 million)	102.00	
Discount on bonds payable ($100 million – 95.88 million)	4.12	
Bonds payable (face amount)		100.00
Paid-in capital—stock warrants outstanding		6.12

Notice that this is the same approach we used in Chapter 10 to allocate a single purchase price to two or more assets bought for that single price. We also will allocate the total selling price of two equity securities sold for a single issue in proportion to their relative market values in Chapter 19.

---

[12]"Induced Conversions of Convertible Debt," *Statement of Financial Accounting Standards No. 84* (Stamford Conn.: FASB, 1985).

If one-half of the warrants (1 million) are exercised when the market value of HTL's common stock is $30 per share, 1 million shares would be issued for one warrant each plus the option price of $25 per share.

Journal Entry at Exercise of Detachable Warrants

		($ in millions)
Cash (1,000,000 warrants × $25)	25	
Paid-in capital—stock warrants outstanding		
(1,000,000 warrants × $3)	3	
Common stock (1,000,000 shares × $1 par per share)		1
Paid-in capital in excess of par (to balance)		27

The $30 market value at the date of exercise is not used in valuing the additional shares issued. The new shares are recorded at the total of the previously measured values of both the warrants and the shares.

The corporate bond is the basic long-term debt instrument for most large companies. But for many small and medium-sized firms, the debt instrument often used is a *note*. We discuss notes next.

Long-Term Notes

When a company borrows cash from a bank and signs a promissory note (essentially an IOU), the firm's liability is reported as a *note payable*. Or a note might be issued in exchange for a noncash asset—perhaps to purchase equipment on credit. In concept, notes are accounted for in precisely the same way as bonds. In fact, we could properly substitute notes payable for bonds payable in each of our previous illustrations.

▌ **Learning objective 4**
Characterize the accounting treatment of notes, including installment notes, issued for cash or for noncash consideration.

OPENING CASE

Question 5

Note Issued for Cash

The interest rate stated in a note is likely to be equal to the market rate because the rate usually is negotiated at the time of the loan. So discounts and premiums are less likely than on bonds. Accounting for a note issued for cash is demonstrated in Illustration 14–6.

ILLUSTRATION 14–6

Note Issued for Cash

On January 1, 1997, Skill Graphics, Inc., a product-labeling and graphics firm, borrowed 700,000 cash from First BancCorp and issued a three-year, $700,000 promissory note. Interest of $42,000 was payable semiannually on June 30 and December 31.

At Issuance

Skill Graphics (Borrower)

Cash	700,000	
Notes payable (face amount)		700,000

First BancCorp (Lender)

Notes receivable (face amount)	700,000	
Cash		700,000

At Each of the Six Interest Dates

Skill Graphics (Borrower)

Interest expense	42,000	
Cash (stated rate × face amount)		42,000

First BancCorp (Lender)

Cash (stated rate × face amount)	42,000	
Interest revenue		42,000

At Maturity

Skill Graphics (Borrower)

Notes payable	700,000	
Cash (face amount)		700,000

First BancCorp (Lender)

Cash (face amount)	700,000	
Notes receivable		700,000

[handwritten margin note: On Exam general J.E. & concept]

Note Exchanged for Assets or Services

Occasionally the *stated* interest rate is not indicative of the *market* rate at the time a note is negotiated. The value of the asset (cash or noncash) or service exchanged for the note establishes the market rate.[13] For example, let's assume Skill Graphics purchased a package-labeling machine from Hughes–Barker Corporation by issuing a 12%, $700,000, three-year note that requires interest to be paid semiannually. Let's also assume that the machine could have been purchased at a cash price of $666,633. You probably recognize this numerical situation as the one used earlier to illustrate bonds sold at a discount (Illustration 14–2). Reference to the earlier example will confirm that exchanging this $700,000 note for a machine with a cash price of $666,633 implies an annual market rate of interest of 14%. That is, 7% is one-half the discount rate that yields a present value of $666,633 for the note's cash flows (interest plus principal):

			Present Values
Interest	$42,000 × 4.76654*	=	$200,195
Principal	$700,000 × 0.66634†	=	466,438
Present value of the note			$666,633

*Present value of an ordinary annuity of $1: $n=6$, $i=7\%$.
†Present value of $1: $n=6$, $i=7\%$.

This is referred to as the **implicit rate of interest**—the rate implicit in the agreement. It may be that the implicit rate is not apparent. Sometimes the value of the asset (or service) is not readily determinable, but the interest rate stated in the transaction is unrealistic relative to the rate that would be expected in a similar transaction under similar circumstances. Deciding what the appropriate rate should be is called *imputing* an interest rate.

For example, suppose the machine exchanged for the 12% note is custom-made for Skill Graphics so that no customary cash price is available with which to work backwards to find the implicit rate. In that case, the appropriate rate would have to be found externally. It might be determined, for instance, that a more realistic interest rate for a transaction of this type, at this time, would be 14%. Then it would be apparent that Skill Graphics actually paid less than $700,000 for the machine and that part of the face amount of the note in effect makes up for the lower than normal interest rate. You learned early in your study of accounting that the economic essence of a transaction should prevail over its outward appearance. In keeping with this basic precept, the accountant should look beyond the *form* of this transaction and record its *substance*. The amount actually paid for the machine is the present value of the cash flows called for by the loan agreement, discounted at the market rate—imputed in this case to be 14%. So both the asset acquired and the liability used to purchase it should be recorded at the real cost, $666,633.

A basic concept of accounting is *substance over form*.

Additional Consideration

For another example, let's assume the more realistic interest rate for a transaction of this type is, say, 16%. In that case we would calculate the real cost of the machine by finding the present value of both the interest and the principal, discounted at half the 16% rate:

					Present Values
Interest	$42,000	×	4.62288*	=	$194,161
Principal	$700,000	×	0.63017†	=	441,119
Present value of the note					$635,280

*Present value of an ordinary annuity of $1: $n=6$, $i=8\%$.
†Present value of $1: $n=6$, $i=8\%$.

Both the asset acquired and the liability used to purchase it would be recorded at $635,280.

The accounting treatment is the same whether the amount is determined directly from the market value of the machine (and thus the note) or indirectly as the present value of the note (and thus the value of the asset):[14]

---

[13]If the debt instrument is negotiable and a dependable exchange price is readily available, the market value of the debt may be better evidence of the value of the transaction than the value of a noncash asset, particularly if it has no established cash selling price. The value of the asset or the debt, whichever is considered more reliable, should be used to record the transaction (*APB 21*).

Journal Entries at Issuance—Note With Unrealistic Interest Rate

Skill Graphics (Buyer/Issuer)		
Machinery (cash price)	666,633	
Discount on note (difference)	33,367	
Notes payable (face amount)		700,000
Hughes–Barker (Seller/Lender)		
Notes receivable (face amount)	700,000	
Discount on note (difference)		33,367
Sales revenue (cash price)		666,633

Likewise, whether the effective interest rate is determined as the rate implicit in the agreement, given the asset's market value, or whether the effective rate is imputed as the appropriate interest rate if the asset's value is unknown, both parties to the transaction should record periodic interest (interest expense to the borrower, interest revenue to the lender) at the effective rate, rather than the stated rate.

Journal Entries—The Interest Method

The effective interest (expense to the issuer; revenue to the investor) is calculated each period as the market rate times the amount of the debt outstanding during the interest period.

At the First Interest Date (June 30)		
Skill Graphics (Borrower)		
Interest expense (market rate × outstanding balance)	46,664	
Discount on notes payable (difference)		4,664
Cash (stated rate × face amount)		42,000
Hughes–Barker (Seller/Lender)		
Cash (stated rate × face amount)	42,000	
Discount on notes receivable (difference)	4,664	
Interest revenue (market rate × outstanding balance)		46,664

The interest expense (interest revenue for the lender) varies as the balance of the note changes over time. See the amortization schedule in Graphic 14–8.[15]

GRAPHIC   14–8

Amortization Schedule—Note

Since less cash is paid each period than the effective interest, the unpaid difference (the discount reduction) increases the outstanding balance of the debt.

	Cash Interest	Effective Interest	Increase in Balance	Outstanding Balance
	(6% × Face amount)	(7% × Outstanding balance	(Discount reduction)	
				666,633
1	42,000	.07(666,633) = 46,664	4,664	671,297
2	42,000	.07(671,297) = 46,991	4,991	676,288
3	42,000	.07(676,288) = 47,340	5,340	681,628
4	42,000	.07(681,628) = 47,714	5,714	687,342
5	42,000	.07(687,342) = 48,114	6,114	693,456
6	42,000	.07(693,456) = 48,544*	6,544	700,000
	252,000	285,367	33,367	

*Rounded.

---

[14]The method shown is the *gross method*. Alternatively, the *net method* can be used as follows:

Skill Graphics (Buyer / Issuer)

Machinery (cash price)	666,633	
Notes payable (face amount)		666,633

Hughes–Barker (Seller / Lender)

Notes receivable (face amount)	666,633	
Sales revenue (cash price)		666,633

Under the gross method the note is recorded at the face amount and a contra account, called *discount on note,* is recorded for the difference between face value and present value. This discount represents the interest to be recognized over the term of the loan. As payments are made, the note is reduced by the full amount of the payment. Interest revenue (and interest expense) are recognized by a reduction in the discount on note and a credit to interest revenue (debit to interest expense). After the last payment, the discount and note accounts both will be zero. Over the term of the note, the note is shown net of the discount on the balance sheet.

[15]The creation of amortization schedules is simplified by an electronic spreadsheet such as Microsoft Excel.

Installment Notes

Notes often are paid in installments, rather than by a single amount at maturity. Typically, installment payments are equal amounts each period. Each payment includes both an amount that represents interest and an amount that represents a reduction of principal. The periodic reduction of principal is sufficient that at maturity the note is completely paid. This amount is easily calculated by dividing the amount of the loan by the appropriate discount factor for the present value of an annuity. The installment payment amount that would pay the note above is:

$$\underset{\text{Amount of loan}}{\$666,633} \quad \div \quad \underset{\substack{\text{(from Table 6A–4} \\ n=6, \ i=7.0\%)}}{4.76654} \quad = \quad \underset{\text{Installment payment}}{\$139,857}$$

Consider Graphic 14–9:

GRAPHIC   14–9

Amortization Schedule— Installment Note

Each installment payment includes interest on the outstanding debt at the effective rate. The remainder of each payment reduces the outstanding balance.

Date	Cash Payment	Effective Interest (7% × Outstanding balance)	Decrease in Debt	Outstanding Balance
				666,633
1	139,857	.07(666,633) = 46,664	93,193	573,440
2	139,857	.07(573,440) = 40,141	99,716	473,724
3	139,857	.07(473,724) = 33,161	106,696	367,028
4	139,857	.07(367,028) = 25,692	114,165	252,863
5	139,857	.07(252,863) = 17,700	122,157	130,706
6	139,857	.07(130,706) = 9,151*	130,706	0
	839,142	172,509	666,633	

*Rounded.

The procedure is the same as for a note whose principal is paid at maturity, but the periodic cash payments are larger and there is no lump-sum payment at maturity. We calculated the amount of the payments so that after covering the interest on the existing debt each period, the excess would exactly amortize the debt to zero at maturity (rather than to a designated maturity amount.)

For installment notes, the outstanding balance of the note does not eventually become its face amount as it does for notes with designated maturity amounts. Instead, at the maturity date the balance is zero. Consequently, the significance is lost of maintaining separate balances for the face amount (in a note account) and the discount (or premium) is lost. So installment notes typically are recorded at their net carrying amount in a single note payable (or receivable) account:

Journal Entries at Issuance—Installment Note

Skill Graphics (Buyer / Issuer)

Machinery	666,633	
Note payable		666,633

Hughes–Barker (Seller / Lender)

Note receivable	666,633	
Sales revenue		666,633

At the First Interest Date (June 30)

Skill Graphics (Borrower)

Interest expense (market rate × outstanding balance)	46,664	
Note payable (difference)	93,193	
Cash (installment payment calculated above)		139,857

Hughes–Barker (Seller / Lender)

Cash (installment payment calculated above)	139,857	
Note receivable (difference)		93,193
Interest revenue (market rate × outstanding balance)		46,664

Each payment includes both an amount that represents interest and an amount that represents a reduction of principal.

Additional Consideration

You will learn in the next chapter that the liability associated with a capital lease is accounted for the same way as this installment note. In fact, if the asset described above had been leased rather than purchased, the cash payments would be designated lease payments rather than installment loan payments, and a virtually identical amortization schedule would apply.

The reason for the similarity is that we view a capital lease as being, in substance, equivalent to an installment purchase/sale. Naturally, then, accounting treatment of the two essentially identical transactions should be consistent. Be sure to notice the parallel treatment as you study leases in the next chapter.

CONCEPT REVIEW EXERCISE

NOTE WITH AN UNREALISTIC INTEREST RATE

Cameron-Brown, Inc., constructed for Harmon Distributors a warehouse that was completed and ready for occupancy on January 2, 1997. Harmon paid for the warehouse by issuing a $900,000, four-year note that required 7% interest to be paid on December 31 of each year. The warehouse was custom-built for Harmon, so its cash price was not known. By comparison with similar transactions, it was determined that an appropriate interest rate was 10%.

Required:

1. Prepare the journal entry for Harmon's purchase of the warehouse on January 2, 1997.
2. Prepare (a) an amortization schedule for the four-year term of the note and (b) the journal entry for Harmon's first interest payment on December 31, 1997.
3. Suppose Harmon's note had been an installment note to be paid in four equal payments. What would be the amount of each installment if payable (a) at the end of each year, beginning December 31, 1997? or (b) at the beginning of each year, beginning on January 2, 1997?

CONCEPT REVIEW EXERCISE

SOLUTION

1. Prepare the journal entry for Harmon's purchase of the warehouse on January 2, 1997.

			Present Values
Interest	$ 63,000 × 3.16987*	=	$199,702
Principal	$900,000 × 0.68301†	=	614,709
	Present value of the note		$814,411

*Present value of an ordinary annuity of $1: $n=4$, $i=10\%$.
†Present value of $1: $n=4$, $i=10\%$.

Warehouse (price determined above)	814,411	
Discount on notes payable (difference)	85,589	
Notes payable (face amount)		900,000

2. Prepare (a) an amortization schedule for the four-year term of the note and (b) the journal entry for Harmon's first interest payment on December 31, 1997.

a.

Dec. 31	Cash Interest	Effective Interest	Decrease in Balance	Outstanding Balance
	(7% × Face amount)	(10% × Outstanding balance)	(Discount reduction)	
				814,411
1997	63,000	.10(814,411) = 81,441	18,441	832,852
1998	63,000	.10(832,852) = 83,285	20,285	853,137
1999	63,000	.10(853,137) = 85,314	22,314	875,451
2000	63,000	.10(875,451) = 87,549*	24,549	900,000
	252,000	337,589	85,589	

*Rounded.

Each period the unpaid interest increases the outstanding balance of the debt.

b.

The effective interest is the market rate times the amount of the debt outstanding during the year.

Interest expense (market rate × outstanding balance) 81,441	
Discount on notes payable (difference)	18,441
Cash (stated rate × face amount)	63,000

3. Suppose Harmon's note had been an installment note to be paid in four equal payments. What would be the amount of each installment if payable (a) at the end of each year, beginning December 31, 1997? or (b) at the beginning of each year, beginning on January 2, 1997?

Because money has a time value, installment payments delayed until the end of each period must be higher than if the payments are made at the beginning of each period.

a. $814,411   ÷   3.16987   = $256,922
       Amount of loan   (from Table 6A-4   Installment payment
                     $n=4, i=10\%$)

b. $814,411   ÷   3.48685   = $233,566
       Amount of loan   (from Table 6A-6   Installment payment
                     $n=4, i=10\%$)

PART

B RETIREMENT, RESTRUCTURING, AND DISCLOSURE OF DEBT

Retirement of Debt   Retirement on the Maturity Date

Learning objective 5
Record the retirement of debt at maturity and by early extinguishment.

As the previous illustration demonstrated, debt paid in installments is systematically retired over the term to maturity so that at the designated maturity date the outstanding balance is zero. When a maturity amount is specified as in our earlier illustrations, any discount or premium has been systematically reduced to zero as of the maturity date and the debt is retired simply by paying the maturity amount. However, a gain or a loss may result when debt is retired before its scheduled maturity.

Early Extinguishment

Earlier we noted that a call feature accompanies most bonds to protect the issuer against declining interest rates. Even when bonds are not callable, the issuing company can retire bonds early by purchasing them on the open market. Regardless of the method, when debt of any type is retired prior to its scheduled maturity date, the transaction is referred to as **early extinguishment of debt**.

To record the extinguishment, the account balances pertinent to the debt obviously must be removed from the books. Of course cash is credited for the amount paid – the call price or market price. The difference between the carrying amount of the debt and the reacquisition price represents either a gain or a loss on the early extinguishment of debt. Let's continue an earlier example to illustrate the retirement of debt prior to its scheduled maturity (Illustration 14–7):

ILLUSTRATION 14–7

Early Extinguishment of Debt

Any difference between the outstanding debt and the amount paid to retire that debt represents either a gain or a loss.

On January 1, 1998, Masterwear Industries called its $700,000, 12% bonds when their carrying amount was $676,290. The indenture specified a call price of $685,000. The bonds were issued previously at a price to yield 14%.

Bonds payable (face amount)	700,000	
Loss on early extinguishment ($685,000 − 676,290)	8,710	
Discount on bonds payable ($700,000 − 676,290)		23,710
Cash (call price)		685,000

The FASB requires that the gain or loss be classified on the income statement as an extraordinary item whether or not the situation meets the usual criteria of being both unusual and infrequent.[16] The Maytag Corporation reported an extraordinary loss on early extinguishment of debt in 1995 as follows:

Notes Payable (in part)

In 1995, the Company retired $116.5 million of long-term debt. Included in this amount was $22.6 million of the 9.75 percent notes due May 15, 2002, $26.4 million of the 8.875 percent notes due July 15, 1999, $46.3 million of the 8.875 percent notes due July 1, 1997 and $21.2 million of medium-term notes ranging in maturities from November 15, 2001, to February 23, 2010. As a result of these early retirements, the Company recorded an after-tax charge of $5.5 million (net of income tax benefit of $3.6 million), which has been reflected in the consolidated statement of income (loss) as an extraordinary item.

CONCEPT REVIEW EXERCISE   ISSUANCE AND EARLY EXTINGUISHMENT OF DEBT

The disclosure notes to the 1997 financial statements of the Park-Reserve Corporation included the following:

Note 11: 14% Subordinated Debentures

On October 3, 1995, the Corporation sold debentures with an aggregate principal amount of $250,000,000 bearing a 14% interest rate. The debentures will mature on September 15, 2005 and are unsecured subordinated obligations of the Corporation. Interest is payable semiannually on March 15 and September 15. The Corporation may redeem the debentures at any time beginning September 15, 1995, as a whole or from time to time in part, through maturity, at specified redemption prices ranging from 113.0% of principal in declining percentages of principal amount through 2002 when the percentage is set at 100% of principal amount. The cost of issuing the debentures, totaling $5,505,000, and the discount of $2,500,000 are being amortized over the life of the debentures, using the straight-line method and the interest method, respectively. Amortization of these items for the year ended January 31, 1997, was $480,000 and $126,000, respectively, and $172,000 and $37,000, respectively, for the year ended January 31, 1996.

During the year ended January 31, 1997, the Corporation repurchased, in open market transactions, $100,050,000 in face amount of the debentures for $111,998,000, including accrued interest. The unamortized cost of issuing these debentures and the unamortized discount, $1,987,000 and $946,000, respectively, and the redemption premium paid have been expensed in the current period, and classified as an extraordinary item, net of applicable income tax benefits.

From the information provided by the Park-Reserve Corporation in Note 11, you should be able to recreate some of the journal entries the company recorded in connection with this bond issue.

Required:

1. Prepare the journal entry for the issuance of these bonds on October 3, 1995. (Be sure to include accrued interest for the one-half month period between September 15 and October 3.)
2. Prepare the journal entry for the repurchase of these bonds, assuming the date of repurchase was November 15, 1997. The accrued interest for the two-month period between September 15 and November 15 would be $100,050,000 \times 14\% \times {}^2/_{12} = $2,335,000. Assume the entry to record accrued interest was recorded separately, so the cash paid to repurchase the bonds was $109,663,000 [$111,998,000 (amount given) − $2,335,000].

---

[16] "Reporting Gains and Losses from Extinguishment of Debt," *Statement of Financial Accounting Standards No. 4* (Stamford, Conn.: FASB, 1975).

1. Prepare the journal entry for the issuance of these bonds on October 3, 1995.

	($ in 000s)	
Cash (to balance)	243,453	
Bond issue costs (given in note)	5,505	
Discount on bonds payable (given in note)	2,500	
Bonds payable (face amount - given in note)		250,000
Interest payable (accrued interest–see below)		1,458
Accrued interest: $250,000 \times 14\% \times {}^{0.5}/_{12} = \$1,458$		

2. Prepare the journal entry for the repurchase of these bonds, assuming the date of repurchase was November 15, 1997.

	($ in 000s)	
Bonds payable (face amount repurchased)	100,050	
Loss on early extinguishment * (to balance)	12,546	
Discount on bonds payable (given in note)		946
Bond issue costs (given in note)		1,987
Cash (given in note)		109,663
*Reported as an extraordinary loss, net of any tax savings from deducting the loss.		

Troubled Debt Restructuring

A respected real estate developer, Brillard Properties, was very successful developing and managing a number of properties in the southeastern United States. To finance these investments, the developer had borrowed hundreds of millions of dollars from several regional banks. For years, events occurred as planned. The investments prospered. Cash flow was high. Interest payments on the debt were timely and individual loans were repaid as they matured.

Almost suddenly, however, the real estate climate in the region soured. Investments that had provided handsome profits now did not provide the cash flow necessary to service the debt. Bankers who had loaned substantial funds to Brillard now faced a dilemma. Because contractual interest payments were unpaid, the bankers had the legal right to demand payment, which would force the developer to liquidate all or a major part of the properties to raise the cash. Sound business practice? Not necessarily.

If creditors force liquidation, they then must share among themselves the cash raised from selling the properties—at forced sale prices. Believing the developer's financial difficulties were caused by temporary market forces, not by bad management, the bankers felt they could minimize their losses by *restructuring* the debt agreements, rather than by forcing liquidation.

When changing the original terms of a debt agreement is motivated by financial difficulties experienced by the debtor (borrower), the new arrangement is referred to as a **troubled debt restructuring**. By definition, a troubled debt restructuring involves some concessions on the part of the creditor (lender). A troubled debt restructuring may be achieved in either of two ways:

1. The debt may be *settled* at the time of the restructuring.
2. The debt may be *continued*, but with *modified terms*.

Debt Is Settled

In the situation described above, one choice the bankers had was to try to actually settle the debt outright at the time of the troubled debt restructuring. For instance, a bank holding a $30 million note from the developer might agree to accept a property valued at, let's say, $20 million as final

> **Learning objective 6**
> Describe troubled debt restructuring and the three accounting methods used to record the restructuring under specific circumstances.

In all areas of accounting, a noncash transaction is recorded at fair value.

settlement of the debt. In that case, the developer has a $10 million gain equal to the difference between the carrying amount of the debt and the fair value of the property transferred. The debtor may need to adjust the carrying amount of an asset to its fair value prior to recording its exchange for a debt. The developer in our example, for instance, would need to change the recorded amount for the property specified in the exchange agreement if it is carried at an amount other than its $20 million fair market value. In such an instance, an ordinary gain or loss on disposition of assets should be recorded as shown in Illustration 14–8.

ILLUSTRATION 14–8

Debt Settled

An asset is adjusted to fair value prior to recording its exchange for a debt.

First Prudent Bank agrees to settle Brillard's $30 million debt in exchange for property having a fair market value of $20 million. The carrying amount of the property on Brillard's books is $17 million:

	($ in millions)	
Land ($20 million minus $17 million)	3	
Gain (ordinary) on disposition of assets		3
Note payable (carrying amount)	30	
Gain (extraordinary) on troubled debt restructuring		10
Land (fair value)		20

A gain from a troubled debt restructuring is reported as an extraordinary gain.

The FASB stipulates that the gain be reported by the debtor as an *extraordinary gain*.[17] Notice that this is consistent with the way we classify a gain on an "early extinguishment of debt" (see prior section). Indeed, the outright settlement of a debt by a troubled debt restructuring is merely a special case of an early extinguishment of debt.

The payment to settle a debt in a troubled debt restructuring might be cash, or a noncash asset (as in the example here), or even shares of the debtor's stock. An example of shares of stock being given in exchange for debt forgiveness is the celebrated reorganization of TWA in 1992, when creditors received a 55% stake in the company's common shares in return for forgiving about $1 billion of the airline's $1.5 billion debt. In any case, the debtor's gain is the difference between the carrying amount of the debt and the fair value of the asset(s) or equity securities transferred.

concept only-no J.E.

→ ## Debt Is Continued, but with Modified Terms

We assumed in the previous example that First Prudent Bank agreed to accept property in full settlement of the debt. A more likely occurrence would be that the bank allows the debt to continue, but modifies the terms of the debt agreement to make it easier for the debtor to comply. The bank might agree to reduce or delay the scheduled *interest payments*. Or, it may agree to reduce or delay the *maturity amount*. Often a troubled debt restructuring will call for some combination of these concessions.

The carrying amount of a debt is the current balance of the primary debt plus any accrued (unpaid) interest.

Let's say the stated interest rate on the note in question is *10%* and annual interest payments of $3 million (10% × $30 million) are payable in December of each of two remaining years to maturity. Also assume that the developer was unable to pay the $3 million interest payment for the year just ended. This means that the amount owed—the carrying amount (or book value) of the debt—is $33 million ($30 million plus one year's accrued interest).

According to generally accepted accounting principles, the way the debtor accounts for the restructuring depends on the extent of the reduction in cash payments called for by the restructured arrangement. More specifically, the accounting procedure depends on whether, under the new agreement, total cash payments—(a) are *less than* the carrying amount of the debt or (b) still *exceed* the carrying amount of the debt.

Two quite different situations are created when the terms of a debt are modified, depending on whether the cash payments are reduced to the extent that interest is eliminated.

When Total Cash Payments Are Less than the Carrying Amount of the Debt.

By the original agreement, the debtor was to pay at maturity the $30 million loaned, plus enough periodic interest to provide a 10% effective rate of return. If the new agreement calls for less cash than the $33 million now owed, interest is presumed to have been eliminated.

---

[17] "Accounting by Debtors and Creditors for Troubled Debt Restructurings," *Statement of Financial Accounting Standards No. 15,* (Stamford, Conn.: FASB, 1977), par. 21.

As one of many possibilities, suppose the bank agrees to (1) forgive the interest accrued from last year, (2) reduce the two remaining interest payments from $3 million each to $2 million each, and (3) reduce the face amount from $30 million to $25 million. Clearly, the debtor will pay less by the new agreement than by the original one. In fact, if we add up the total payments called for by the new agreement, the total [($2 million × 2) plus $25 million] is less than the $33 million carrying amount. Because the $29 million does not exceed the amount owed, the restructured debt agreement no longer provides interest on the debt. Actually, the new payments are $4 million short of covering the debt itself. So, after the debt restructuring, no interest expense is recorded. All subsequent cash payments are considered to be payment of the debt itself. Consider Illustration 14–9:

ILLUSTRATION   14–9

Cash Payments Less than the Debt

The carrying amount of the debt is reduced from $33 million to the $29 million to be paid under the revised agreement, producing a gain for the debtor.

Carrying Amount

Before restr.	Adj.	After restr.
$30	(1)	$29
3	(3)	0
$33	(4)	$29

Brillard Properties owes First Prudent Bank $30 million under a 10% note with two years remaining to maturity. Due to financial difficulties of the developer, the previous year's interest ($3 million) was not paid. First Prudent Bank agrees to:

1. Forgive the interest accrued from last year.
2. Reduce the remaining two interest payments to $2 million each.
3. Reduce the principal to $25 million.

Analysis: Carrying amount: $30 million + $3 million = $33 million
Future payments: ($2 million × 2) + $25 million = 29 million
Gain $ 4 million

($ in millions)

Accrued interest payable (10% × $30 million)	3
Note payable ($30 million – $29 million)	1
Gain (extraordinary) on debt restructuring	4

When the total future cash payments are less than the carrying amount of the debt, the difference is recorded as a gain at the date of restructure. The gain is reported as an extraordinary item. No interest should be recorded thereafter. That is, all subsequent cash payments result in reductions of principal.

After restructuring, no interest expense is recorded. All cash payments are considered to be payment of the note itself.

The $25 million payment at maturity reduces the note to zero.

At Each of the Two Interest Dates

($ in millions)

Note payable	2	
Cash (revised "interest" amount)		2

At Maturity

Note payable	25	
Cash (revised principal amount)		25

When Total Cash Payments Exceed the Carrying Amount of the Debt.   Let's modify the example in the previous section. Now suppose the bank agrees to delay the due date for all cash payments until maturity and accept $34,333,200 at that time in full settlement of the debt. Rather than just reducing the cash payments as in the previous illustration, the payments are delayed. It is not the nature of the change that creates the need to account differently for this situation, but the amount of the total cash payments under the agreement relative to the carrying amount of the debt. This situation is demonstrated in Illustration 14–10.

As long as cash payments exceed the amount owed there will be interest—although at a lower effective rate.

Now the total payments called for by the new agreement, $34,333,200, exceed the $33 million carrying amount. Because the payments exceed the amount owed, the restructured debt agreement still provides interest on the debt—but less than before the agreement was revised. No longer is the effective rate 10%. The accounting objective now is to determine what the new effective rate is and *record interest for the remaining term of the loan at that new, lower rate,* as shown in Illustration 14–10.

Because the total future cash payments are not less than the carrying amount of the debt, no reduction of the existing debt is necessary and no entry is required at the time of the debt restructuring. Even though no cash is paid until maturity under the restructured debt agreement, interest expense still is recorded annually—but at the new rate.

ILLUSTRATION 14–10

Cash Payments More than the Debt

> The discount rate that equates the present value of the debt ($33 million) and its future value ($34,333,200) is the effective rate of interest.

Brillard Properties owes First Prudent Bank $30 million under a 10% note with two years remaining to maturity. Due to Brillard's financial difficulties, the previous year's interest ($3 million) was not paid. First Prudent Bank agrees to:

1. Delay the due date for all cash payments until maturity.
2. Accept $34,333,200 at that time in full settlement of the debt.

	Analysis:		
	Future payments:		$34,333,200
	Carrying amount:	$30 million + $3 million =	33,000,000
	Interest		$ 1,333,200

Calculation of the new effective interest rate:

- $33,000,000 ÷ $34,333,200 = .9612, the Table 6A-2 value for n = 2, i = ?
- In row 2 of Table 6A-2, the number .9612 is in the 2% column. So, this is the new effective interest rate.

> Unpaid interest is accrued at the effective rate times the carrying amount of the note.

At the End of the First Year

Interest expense (2% × [$30,000,000 + 3,000,000])	660,000	
Accrued interest payable		660,000

> The carrying amount of the debt is increased by the unpaid interest from the previous year.

At the End of the Second Year

Interest expense (2% × [$30,000,000 + 3,660,000])	673,200	
Accrued interest payable		673,200

> The total of the accrued interest account plus the note account is equal to the amount scheduled to be paid at maturity.

At Maturity (End of the Second Year)

Note payable	30,000,000	
Accrued interest payable ($3,000,000 + $660,000 + $673,200)		4,333,200
Cash (required by new agreement)		34,333,200

Additional Consideration

To keep up with the changing amounts, it may be convenient to prepare an amortization schedule for the debt.

Year	Cash Interest	Effective Interest (2% × Outstanding balance)		Increase in Balance	Outstanding Balance
					33,000,000
1	0	.02 (33,000,000) =	660,000	660,000	33,660,000
2	0	.02 (33,660,000) =	673,200	673,200	34,333,200
	0		1,333,200	1,333,200	

An amortization schedule is particularly helpful if there are several remaining years to maturity.

In our example, the restructured debt agreement called for a single cash payment at maturity ($34,333,200). If more than one cash payment is required (as in the agreement in our earlier example), calculating the new effective rate is more difficult. The concept would remain straightforward: (1) determine the interest rate that provides a present value of all future cash payments that is equal to the current carrying amount and (2) record the interest at that rate thereafter. Mechanically, though, the computation would be cumbersome, requiring a time-consuming trial-and-error calculation. Since our primary interest is understanding the concepts involved, we will avoid the mathematical complexities of such a situation.

You also should be aware that when a restructuring involves modification of terms, accounting for a liability by the debtor, as described in this section, and accounting for a receivable by the creditor, which was described in Chapter 12, are inconsistent. You may recall that when a creditor's investment in a receivable becomes impaired, due to a troubled debt restructuring or for any other reason, the receivable is remeasured based on the discounted present value of currently expected cash flows at the loan's original effective rate (regardless of the extent to which expected cash receipts have been reduced). For ease of comparison, the example in this chapter (Illustration 14–10) describes the same situation as the example in Chapter 12 (Illustration 12C–2). There is no conceptual justification for the asymmetry between debtors' and creditors' accounting for troubled debt restructurings. The FASB will likely reconsider debtors' accounting in the future.[18]

Financial Statement Disclosures

| **Learning objective 7**
Describe the disclosures appropriate to long-term debt in its various forms.

| Supplemental disclosure is required of the fair value of bonds, notes, and other financial instruments.

On the balance sheet, long-term debt (liability for the debtor; asset for the creditor) can be reported either as a single amount, net of any discount or increased by any premium, or at its face amount accompanied by a separate valuation account for the discount or premium. Any portion of the debt to be paid (received) during the upcoming year, or operating cycle if longer, should be reported as a current amount.

The fair value of financial instruments must be disclosed either in the body of the financial statements or in disclosure notes. For bonds and other securities traded on market exchanges, quoted market prices are available to measure market value. Financial instruments not traded on market exchanges require other evidence of market value. For example, the market value of a note payable might be approximated by the present value of principal and interest payments using a current discount rate commensurate with the risks involved. Fair value disclosure requirements are described in more detail in Chapter 13.

For all long-term borrowings, disclosures also should include the aggregate amounts maturing and sinking fund requirements (if any) for each of the next five years.[19] To comply, Proctor & Gamble's 1997 annual report stated:

| The fair value and scheduled amounts should be disclosed for the next five years.

($ in millions)

The fair value of the long-term debt was $5,014 and $5,662 June 30, 1996 and 1995, respectively. The following payments are required the next five years:

1997, $420; 1998, $344; 1999, $87; 2000, $240; and 2001, $338

Risk Disclosures

For some liabilities, the amounts reported on the face of the financial statements provide inadequate disclosure about the degree to which a company is exposed to risk of loss. Additionally, some financial instruments that do not appear as specific liabilities also expose companies to off-balance-sheet risk.

To provide adequate disclosure about a company's exposure to risk, additional information is provided about (a) off-balance-sheet credit or market risk, (b) concentrations of credit risk, and (c) the market value of financial instruments. These supplemental disclosures were discussed extensively in the previous chapter.

Decision-Makers' Perspective

Business decisions involve risk. Failure to properly consider risk in those decisions is one of the most costly, yet one of the most common, mistakes investors and creditors can make. Long-term debt is one of the first places decision makers should look when trying to get a handle on risk.

| Generally speaking, debt increases risk.

In general, debt increases risk. As an owner, debt would place you in a subordinate position relative to creditors because the claims of creditors must be satisfied first in case of liquidation. In addition, debt requires payment, usually on specific dates. Failure to pay debt interest and principal on a timely basis may result in default and perhaps even bankruptcy. The debt to equity ratio, total liabilities/shareholders' equity, often is calculated to measure the degree of risk. Other things being equal, the higher the debt to equity ratio, the higher the risk. The type of risk this ratio measures is called *default risk* because it presumably indicates the likelihood a company will default on its obligations.

| To evaluate a firm's risk, you might start by calculating its debt to equity ratio.

Debt also can be an advantage. It can be used to enhance the return to shareholders. This concept, known as leverage, was described and illustrated in Chapter 5. If a company earns a return

---

[18]"Accounting by Creditors for Impairment of a Loan," *Statement of Financial Accounting Standards No. 114* (Norwalk, Conn.: FASB, 1993), par. 63.

[19]"Disclosure of Long-Term Obligations," *Statement of Financial Accounting Standards No. 47* (Stamford, Conn.: FASB, 1981), par. 10b.

on borrowed funds in excess of the cost of borrowing the funds, shareholders are provided with a total return greater than what could have been earned with equity funds alone. This desirable situation is called *favorable financial leverage*. Unfortunately, leverage is not always favorable. Sometimes the cost of borrowing the funds exceeds the returns they generate. This illustrates the typical risk-return trade-off faced by shareholders.

Creditors demand interest payments as compensation for the use of their capital. Failure to pay interest as scheduled may cause several adverse consequences, including bankruptcy. Therefore, another way to measure a company's ability to pay its obligations is by comparing interest payments with income available to pay those charges. The times interest earned ratio does this by dividing income before subtracting interest expense or income tax expense by interest expense.

Two points about this ratio are important. First, because interest is deductible for income tax purposes, income before interest and taxes is a better indication of a company's ability to pay interest than is income after interest and taxes (i.e., net income). Second, income before interest and taxes is a rough approximation for cash flow generated from operations. The primary concern of decision makers is, of course, the cash available to make interest payments. In fact, this ratio often is computed by dividing cash flow generated from operations by interest payments.

For illustration, let's compare the ratios for Coca-Cola and PepsiCo. Graphic 14–10 provides condensed financial statements adapted from recent annual reports of those companies.

GRAPHIC 14–10

Condensed Financial Statements—Coca-Cola, PepsiCo

Balance Sheets

	($ in millions)	
	Coca-Cola	PepsiCo
Assets:		
Current assets	$1,203.0	$1,478.7
Property, plant, and equipment (net)	2,608.2	2,064.6
Intangibles and other assets	210.3	464.7
Total assets	$4,021.5	$4,008.0
Liabilities and Shareholders' Equity:		
Current liabilities	$1,280.2	$1,787.1
Long-term liabilities	1,024.2	1,248.1
Total liabilities	$2,304.4	$3,035.2
Common stock (par and additional paid-in capital)	144.9	335.0
Retained earnings	2,476.9	1,601.9
Less: Treasury stock	(904.7)	(964.1)
Total liabilities and shareholders' equity	$4,021.5	$4,008.0

Income Statements

	Coca-Cola	PepsiCo
Net sales	$5,698.0	$7,768.2
Cost of goods sold	(2,909.0)	(4,481.7)
Gross profit	$2,789.0	$3,286.5
Operating expenses	(1,743.7)	(2,539.2)
Interest expense	(56.8)	(46.6)
Income before taxes	$ 988.5	$ 700.7
Tax expense	(394.7)	(276.1)
Net income	$ 593.8	$ 424.6

The debt equity ratio is higher for PepsiCo:

$$\text{Debt to equity ratio} = \frac{\text{Total liabilities}}{\text{Shareholders' equity}}$$

$$\text{Coca-Cola} = \frac{\$2,304.4}{\$144.9 + 2,476.9 - 904.7} = 1.34$$

$$\text{PepsiCo} = \frac{\$3,035.2}{\$335.0 + 1,601.9 - 964.1} = 3.12$$

Remember, that's not necessarily a positive or a negative. Let's look closer. When the return on shareholders' equity is greater than the return on assets, management is using debt funds to enhance the earnings for stockholders. Both firms do this. We calculate return on assets as follows:

$$\text{Rate of return on assets} = \frac{\text{Net income}}{\text{Total assets}}$$

$$\text{Coca-Cola} = \frac{\$593.8}{\$4,021.5} = 14.8\%$$

$$\text{PepsiCo} = \frac{\$424.6}{\$4,008.0} = 10.6\%$$

The rate of return on assets indicates profitability without regard to how resources are financed.

The return on assets indicates a company's overall profitability, ignoring specific sources of financing. In this regard, Coca-Cola's profitability exceeds that of PepsiCo. That advantage shifts when we compare return to shareholders:

$$\text{Rate of return on shareholders' equity} = \frac{\text{Net income}}{\text{Shareholders' equity}}$$

$$\text{Coca-Cola} = \frac{\$593.8}{\$144.9 + 2,476.9 - 904.7} = 34.6\%$$

$$\text{PepsiCo} = \frac{\$424.6}{\$335.0 + 1,601.9 - 964.1} = 43.6\%$$

The rate of return on shareholders' equity indicates the effectiveness of employing resources provided by owners.

PepsiCo's higher leverage has been used to provide a higher return to shareholders than Coca-Cola, even though its return on assets is less. PepsiCo increased it's return to shareholders 4.11 times (43.6%/10.6%) the return on assets. Coca-Cola increased its return to shareholders 2.34 times (34.6%/14.8%) the return on assets. Interpret this with caution, though. PepsiCo's higher leverage means higher risk as well. In down times, PepsiCo's return to shareholders will suffer proportionally more than will Coca-Cola's.

From the perspective of a creditor, we might look at which company offers the most comfortable margin of safety in terms of its ability to pay fixed interest charges:

$$\text{Times interest earned ratio} = \frac{\text{Net income plus interest plus taxes}}{\text{Interest}}$$

$$\text{Coca-Cola} = \frac{\$593.8+56.8+394.7}{\$56.8} = 18.4 \text{ times}$$

$$\text{PepsiCo} = \frac{\$424.6+46.6+276.1}{\$46.6} = 16.0 \text{ times}$$

The times interest earned ratio indicates the margin of safety provided to creditors.

In this regard, both firms provide an adequate margin of safety. The interest coverage ratios seem to indicate an ample safety cushion for creditors, particularly when considered in conjunction with their debt-equity ratios.

Liabilities also can have misleading effects on the income statement. Decision makers should look carefully at gains and losses produced by early extinguishment of debt. These have nothing to do with a company's normal operating activities. Unchecked, corporate management can be tempted to schedule debt buybacks to provide discretionary income in down years or even losses in up years to smooth income over time. Fortunately, the requirement described in the chapter to report such gains and losses as extraordinary items makes their identification and proper interpretation easier.

Decision makers should be alert to gains and losses that have nothing to do with a company's normal operating activities.

GLOBAL PERSPECTIVE

Capital markets are operating more and more as a global marketplace. Firms competing for international resources, such as debt funding, include domestic corporations, multinational corporations, as well as foreign corporations and joint ventures. This poses several problems for lenders and other resource providers attempting to evaluate alternatives across international boundaries.

One persistent problem is the lack of uniformity in accounting standards used to produce the financial statements being compared. The gap has narrowed in recent years, but analysts must be aware of differences in accounting methods from country to country. Other considerations are being familiar with the accounting consequences of translating results from abroad into dollars, institutional, political, cultural, and tax differences, and identifying appropriate international industry standards for comparison.

> Off-balance-sheet financing and other commitments can increase risk.

Alert investors and lenders also look outside the financial statements for risks associated with off-balance-sheet financing and other commitments that don't show up on the face of financial statements but nevertheless expose a company to risk. We discussed supplemental disclosures designed to communicate the degree of risk associated with derivatives and other financial instruments in this and the previous two chapters. We examine the significance of lease commitments in the next chapter.

Solution to Financial Reporting Case (at the opening of the chapter)

1. What does it mean that the bonds are first mortgage bonds? What effect does that have on financing?
2. From Service Leader's perspective, why are the bonds callable? What does that mean?

3. How will it be possible to sell bonds paying investors 10.25 % when other, similar investments will provide the investors a return of 10.5%?

4. Why might the company choose to make the bonds convertible into common stock?

5. Would accounting differ if the debt were designated as notes rather than bonds?

A mortgage bond is backed by a lien on specified real estate owned by the issuer. This makes it less risky than unsecured debt, so Service Leader can expect to be able to sell the bonds at a higher price (lower interest rate).

The call feature gives Service Leader some protection against being stuck with relatively high-cost debt in case interest rates fall during the 15 years to maturity. Service Leader can buy back, or call, the bonds from bondholders before the 15-year maturity date, after June 30, 2003. The call price is prespecified at 103 percent of face value—$1,030 per $1,000 bond.

Service Leader will be able to sell its 10.25% bonds in a 10.5% market only by selling them at a discounted price, below face amount. Bonds are priced by the marketplace to yield the market rate of interest for securities of similar risk and maturity. The price will be the present value of all the periodic cash interest payments (face amount × stated rate) plus the present value of the principal payable at maturity, both discounted at the market rate.

Convertible bonds can be converted at the option of the bondholders into shares of stock. Sometimes the motivation for issuing convertible bonds rather than straight debt is to use the bonds as a medium of exchange in mergers and acquisitions, as a way for smaller firms or debt-heavy companies to obtain access to the bond market, or as an indirect way to issue stock when there is shareholder resistance to direct issuance of additional equity. None of these seems pertinent to Service Leader. The most likely reason is to sell at a higher price. The conversion feature is attractive to investors. Investors have a fixed-income security that can become common stock if circumstances make that attractive. The investor has additional possibilities for higher returns, with downside risk limited by the underlying debt.

No. Other things being equal, whether they're called bonds, notes, or some other form of debt, the same accounting principles apply. They will be recorded at present value and interest will be recorded at the market rate over the term to maturity.

| **The Bottom Line** | **1.** A liability requires the future payment of cash in specified amounts at specified dates. As time passes, interest accrues on debt at the effective interest rate times the amount of the debt outstanding during the period. This same principle applies regardless of the specific form of the liability. |

2. Forces of supply and demand cause a bond to be priced to yield the market rate, calculated as the present value of all the cash flows required, where the discount rate is the market rate. Interest accrues at the effective market rate of interest multiplied by the outstanding balance (during the interest period). A company is permitted to allocate a discount or a premium equally to each period over the term to maturity if doing so produces results that are not materially different from the interest method.

3. Convertible bonds are accounted for as straight debt, but the value of the equity feature is recorded separately for bonds issued with detachable warrants.

4. In concept, notes are accounted for in precisely the same way as bonds. When a note is issued with an unrealistic interest rate, the effective market rate is used both to determine the amount recorded in the transaction and to record periodic interest thereafter.

5. A gain or loss on early extinguishment of debt should be recorded for the difference between the reacquisition price and the carrying amount of the debt. The gain or loss should be classified on the income statement as an extraordinary item.

6. The way a troubled debt restructuring is recorded depends on whether (1) the debt is settled at the time of the restructuring, or (2) the debt is continued, but with modified terms where the total cash to be paid (a) is less than the carrying amount of the debt or (b) exceeds the carrying amount of the debt.

7. On the balance sheet, disclosure should include, for all long-term borrowings, the aggregate amounts maturing and sinking fund requirements (if any) for each of the next five years. Supplemental disclosures are needed for (a) off-balance-sheet credit or market risk, (b) concentrations of credit risk, and (c) the fair value of financial instruments.

Questions for Review of Key Topics

Question	14–1	How is periodic interest determined for outstanding liabilities? For outstanding receivables? How does the approach compare from one form of debt instrument (say bonds payable) to another (say notes payable)?
Question	14–2	As a general rule, how should long-term liabilities be reported on the debtor's balance sheet?
Question	14–3	How are bonds and notes the same? How do they differ?
Question	14–4	What information is contained in a bond indenture? What purpose does it serve?
Question	14–5	Why will bonds always sell at their price plus any interest that has accrued since the last interest date?
Question	14–6	On January 1, 1997, Brandon Electronics issued $85 million of 11.5% bonds, dated January 1. The market yield for bonds of maturity issued by similar firms in terms of riskiness is 12.25%. How can Brandon sell debt paying only 11.5% in a 12.25% market?
Question	14–7	How is the price determined for a bond (or bond issue)?
Question	14–8	Compare the two commonly used methods of determining interest on bonds.
Question	14–9	When bonds are issued at a premium the debt declines each period. Explain.
Question	14–10	*APB Opinion No. 21* requires that debt issue costs be recorded separately and amortized over the term of the related debt. Describe a logical alternative to this accounting treatment.
Question	14–11	A zero-coupon bond pays no interest. Explain.
Question	14–12	Both convertible bonds and bonds issued with detachable warrants have features of both debt and equity. How does the accounting treatment differ for the two hybrid securities? Why is the accounting treatment different?
Question	14–13	At times, companies try to induce voluntary conversion by offering an added incentive—maybe cash, stock warrants, or a more favorable conversion ratio. How is such an inducement accounted for? How is it measured?
Question	14–14	When a note's stated rate of interest is unrealistic relative to the market rate, the concept of substance over form should be employed. Explain.
Question	14–15	How does an installment note differ from a note for which the principal is paid as a single amount at maturity?
Question	14–16	Early extinguishment of debt often produces a gain or a loss. How is the gain or loss determined?
Question	14–17	What criteria are used to classify a gain or loss on early extinguishment of debt as an extraordinary item on the income statement?
Question	14–18	When the original terms of a debt agreement are changed because of financial difficulties experienced by the debtor (borrower), the new arrangement is referred to as a *troubled debt restructuring*. Such a restructuring can take a variety of forms. For accounting purposes, these possibilities are categorized. What are the accounting classifications of troubled debt restructurings?
Question	14–19	Pratt Industries owes First National Bank $5 million but, due to financial difficulties, is unable to comply with the original terms of the loan. The bank agrees to settle the debt in exchange for land having a fair market value of $3 million. The carrying amount of the property on Pratt's books is $2 million. For the reporting period in which the debt is settled, what amount(s) will Pratt report on its income statement in connection with the troubled debt restructuring?
Question	14–20	The way a debtor accounts for the restructuring depends on the extent of the reduction in cash payments called for by the restructured arrangement. Describe, in general, the accounting procedure for the two basic cases: when, under the new agreement, total cash payments (a) are less than the carrying amount of the debt or (b) still exceed the carrying amount of the debt.
Question	14–21	Long-term debt can be reported either (a) as a single amount, net of any discount or increased by any premium or (b) at its face amount accompanied by a separate valuation account for the discount or premium. Any portion of the debt to be paid during the upcoming year, or operating cycle if longer, should be reported as a current amount. Regarding amounts to be paid in the future, what additional disclosures should be made in connection with long-term debt?

Exercises

Exercise 14–1
Accrued interest

On March 1, 1997, Brown-Ferring Corporation issued $100 million of 12% bonds, dated January 1, 1997, for $99 million (plus accrued interest). The bonds mature on December 31, 2016, and pay interest semi-annually on June 30 and December 31. Brown-Ferring's fiscal period is the calendar year.

Required:

1. Determine the amount of accrued interest that was included in the proceeds received from the bond sale.
2. Prepare the journal entry for the issuance of the bonds by Brown-Ferring.

Exercise 14–2
Bond valuation

Your investment department has researched possible investments in corporate debt securities. Among the available investments are the following $100 million bond issues, each dated January 1, 1997. Prices were determined by underwriters at different times during the last few weeks.

	Company	Bond Price	Stated rate
1.	BB Corp.	$109 million	11%
2.	DD Corp.	$100 million	10%
3.	GG Corp.	$ 91 million	9%

Each of the bond issues matures on December 31, 2016, and pays interest semiannually on June 30 and December 31. For bonds of similar risk and maturity, the market yield at January 1, 1997, is 10%.

Required:
Other things being equal, which of the bond issues offers the most attractive investment opportunity at the prices stated? the least attractive? Why?

Exercise 14–3
Determining the price of bonds in various situations

Determine the price of a $1 million bond issue under each of the following independent assumptions:

	Maturity	Interest paid	Stated rate	Effective (market) rate
1.	10 years	annually	10%	12%
2.	10 years	semiannually	10%	12%
3.	10 years	semiannually	12%	10%
4.	20 years	semiannually	12%	10%
5.	20 years	semiannually	12%	12%

Exercise 14–4
Determine the price of bonds; issuance; effective interest; no amortization schedule

The Bradford Company issued 10% bonds, dated January 1, with a face amount of $80 million on January 1, 1997. The bonds mature in 2007 (10 years). For bonds of similar risk and maturity, the market yield is 12%. Interest is paid semiannually on June 30 and December 31.

Required:

1. Determine the price of the bonds at January 1, 1997.
2. Prepare the journal entry to record their issuance by The Bradford Company on January 1, 1997.
3. Prepare the journal entry to record interest on June 30, 1997 (at the effective rate). (Do not prepare an amortization schedule.)
4. Prepare the journal entry to record interest on December 31, 1997 (at the effective rate). (Do not prepare an amortization schedule.)

on Exam

Exercise 14–5
Investor; effective interest; no amortization schedule

The Bradford Company sold the entire bond issue described in the previous exercise to Saxton-Bose Corporation.

Required:

1. Prepare the journal entry to record the purchase of the bonds by Saxton-Bose on January 1, 1997.
2. Prepare the journal entry to record interest revenue on June 30, 1997 (at the effective rate). (Do not prepare an amortization schedule.)
3. Prepare the journal entry to record interest revenue on December 31, 1997 (at the effective rate). (Do not prepare an amortization schedule.)

Exercise 14–6
Determine the price of bonds; issuance; effective interest; no amortization schedule

The Gorman Group issued $900,000 of 13% bonds on June 30, 1997. The bonds were dated on June 30 and mature on June 30, 2017 (20 years). The market yield for bonds of similar risk and maturity is 12%. Interest is paid semiannually on December 31 and June 30.

Required:

1. Determine the price of the bonds at June 30, 1997.
2. Prepare the journal entry to record their issuance by The Gorman Group on June 30, 1997.
3. Prepare the journal entry to record interest on December 31, 1997 (at the effective rate). (Do not prepare an amortization schedule.)
4. Prepare the journal entry to record interest on June 30, 1998 (at the effective rate). (Do not prepare an amortization schedule.)

on Exam

Exercise 14–7
Determine the price of bonds; issuance; straight-line method

Universal Foods issued 10% bonds, dated January 1, with a face amount of $150 million on January 1, 1997. The bonds mature on December 31, 2014 (15 years). The market rate of interest for similar issues was 12%. Interest is paid semiannually on June 30 and December 31. Universal uses the straight-line method.

Required:
1. Determine the price of the bonds at January 1, 1997.
2. Prepare the journal entry to record their issuance by Universal Foods on January 1, 1997.
3. Prepare the journal entry to record interest on June 30, 1997.
4. Prepare the journal entry to record interest on December 31, 2004.

Exercise 14–8
Investor; straight-line method

Universal Foods sold the entire bond issue described in the previous exercise to Wang Communications.

Required:
1. Prepare the journal entry to record the purchase of the bonds by Wang Communications on January 1, 1997.
2. Prepare the journal entry to record interest revenue on June 30, 1997.
3. Prepare the journal entry to record interest revenue on December 31, 2004.

Exercise 14–9
Issuance of bonds; effective interest; no amortization schedule

Federal Semiconductors issued 11% bonds, dated January 1, with a face amount of $800 million on January 1, 1997. The bonds sold for $739,814,813 and mature in 2016 (20 years). For bonds of similar risk and maturity the market yield was 12%. Interest is paid semiannually on June 30 and December 31.

Required:
1. Prepare the journal entry to record their issuance by Federal on January 1, 1997.
2. Prepare the journal entry to record interest on June 30, 1997 (at the effective rate). (Do not prepare an amortization schedule.)
3. Prepare the journal entry to record interest on December 31, 1997 (at the effective rate). (Do not prepare an amortization schedule.)

Exercise 14–10
Issuance of bonds; effective interest; amortization schedule

National Orthopedics, Co., issued 9% bonds, dated January 1, with a face amount of $500,000 on January 1, 1997. The bonds mature in 2001 (4 years). For bonds of similar risk and maturity the market yield was 10%. Interest is paid semiannually on June 30 and December 31.

Required:
1. Determine the price of the bonds at January 1, 1997.
2. Prepare the journal entry to record their issuance by National on January 1, 1997.
3. Prepare an amortization schedule that determines interest at the effective rate each period.
4. Prepare the journal entry to record interest on June 30, 1997.
5. Prepare the appropriate journal entries at maturity on December 31, 2001.

Exercise 14–11
Bonds; effective interest; no amortization schedule; adjusting entry

On February 1, 1997, Strauss-Lombardi issued 9% bonds, dated February 1, with a face amount of $800,000. The bonds sold for $731,364 and mature on January 31, 2017 (20 years). The market yield for bonds of similar risk and maturity was 10%. Interest is paid semiannually on July 31 and January 31. Strauss-Lombardi's fiscal year ends December 31.

Required:
1. Prepare the journal entry to record their issuance by Strauss-Lombardi on February 1, 1997.
2. Prepare the journal entry to record interest on July 31, 1997 (at the effective rate). (Do not prepare an amortization schedule.)
3. Prepare the adjusting entry to accrue interest on December 31, 1997.
4. Prepare the journal entry to record interest on January 31, 1998.

Exercise 14–12
Bonds; straight-line method; adjusting entry

On March 1, 1997, Stratford Lighting issued 14% bonds, dated March 1, with a face amount of $300,000. The bonds sold for $294,000 and mature on February 28, 2017 (20 years). Interest is paid semiannually on August 31 and February 28. Stratford uses the straight-line method and its fiscal year ends December 31.

Required:
1. Prepare the journal entry to record the issuance of the bonds by Stratford Lighting on March 1, 1997.
2. Prepare the journal entry to record interest on August 31, 1997.
3. Prepare the adjusting entry to accrue interest on December 31, 1997.
4. Prepare the journal entry to record interest on February 28, 1998.

Exercise 14–13
Convertible bonds

On January 1, 1997, Gless Textiles issued $12 million of 9%, 10-year convertible bonds at 101. The bonds pay interest on June 30 and December 31. Each $1,000 bond is convertible into 40 shares of Gless's $1 par common stock. Century Services purchased 10% of the issue as an investment.

Required:

1. Prepare the journal entries for the issuance of the bonds by Gless and the purchase of the bond investment by Century.
2. Prepare the journal entries for the June 30, 2001, interest payment by both Gless and Century assuming both use the straight-line method.
3. On July 1, 2002, when Gless's common stock had a market price of $33 per share, Century converted the bonds it held. Prepare the journal entries by both Gless and Century for the conversion of the bonds (book value method).

Exercise 14–14
Bonds with detachable warrants

On August 1, 1997, Limbaugh Communications issued $30 million of 10% nonconvertible bonds at 104. The bonds are due on July 31, 2017. Each $1,000 bond was issued with 20 detachable stock warrants, each of which entitled the bondholder to purchase, for $60, one share of Limbaugh Communications' $10 par common stock. Interstate Containers purchased 20% of the bond issue. On August 1, 1997, the market value of the common stock was $58 per share and the market value of each warrant was $8.

In February, 2008, when Limbaugh's common stock had a market price of $72 per share and the unamortized premium balance was $1 million, Interstate Containers exercised the warrants it held.

Required:

1. Prepare the journal entries on August 1, 1997, to record (a) the issuance of the bonds by Limbaugh and (b) the investment by Interstate.
2. Prepare the journal entries for both Limbaugh and Interstate in February, 2008, to record the exercise of the warrants.

Exercise 14–15
Multiple choice; bonds

The following questions dealing with bonds are adapted from recent CPA examinations. Determine the response that best completes the statements or questions.

1. On January 1, 1998, Oak Co. issued 400 of its 8%, $1,000 bonds at 97 plus accrued interest. The bonds are dated October 1, 1997, and mature on October 1, 2003. Interest is payable semiannually on April and October 1. Accrued interest for the period October 1, 1997, to January 1, 1998, amounted to $8,000. On January 1, 1998, what amount should Oak report as bonds payable, net of discount?
   a. $380,000
   b. $388,000
   c. $388,300
   d. $392,000
2. On December 31, 1997, Moss Co. issued $1,000,000 of 11% bonds at 109. Each $1,000 bond was issued with 50 detachable stock warrants, each of which entitled the bondholder to purchase one share of $5 par common stock for $25. Immediately after issuance, the market value of each warrant was $4. On December 31, 1997, what amount should Moss record as discount or premium for issuance of bonds?
   a. $40,000 premium
   b. $90,000 premium
   c. $110,000 discount
   d. $200,000 discount
3. A bond issued on June 1, 1997, has interest payment dates of April 1 and October 1. Bond interest expense for the year ended December 31, 1997, is for a period of
   a. Three months
   b. Four months
   c. Six months
   d. Seven months

Exercise 14–16
Note with unrealistic interest rate

Farrow Mining and Milling, Inc., contracted with Truax Corporation to have constructed a custom-made lathe. The machine was completed and ready for use on January 1, 1997. Farrow paid for the lathe by issuing a $600,000, three-year note that specified 4% interest, payable annually on December 31 of each year. The cash market price of the lathe was unknown. It was determined by comparison with similar transactions that 12% was a reasonable rate of interest.

Required:

1. Prepare the journal entry on January 1, 1997, for Farrow Mining and Milling's purchase of the lathe.

2. Prepare an amortization schedule for the three-year term of the note.
3. Prepare the journal entries to record (a) interest for each of the three years and (b) payment of the note at maturity.

Exercise 14–17
Installment note

American Food Services, Inc., acquired a packaging machine from Barton and Barton Corporation. Barton and Barton completed construction of the machine on January 1, 1997. In payment for the $4 million machine, American Food Services issued a four-year installment note to be paid in four equal payments at the end of each year. The payments include interest at the rate of 10%.

Required:
1. Prepare the journal entry for American Food Services' purchase of the machine on January 1, 1997.
2. Prepare an amortization schedule for the four-year term of the installment note.
3. Prepare the journal entry for the first installment payment on December 31, 1997.
4. Prepare the journal entry for the third installment payment on December 31, 1999.

Exercise 14–18
Early extinguishment

The balance sheet of Indian River Electronics Corporation as of December 31, 1996, included 12.25% bonds having a face amount of $90 million. The bonds had been issued in 1989 and had a remaining discount of $3 million at December 31, 1996. On January 1, 1997, Indian River Electronics called the bonds before their scheduled maturity at the call price of 102.

Required:
Prepare the journal entry by Indian River Electronics to record the redemption of the bonds at January 1, 1997.

Exercise 14–19
Troubled debt restructuring; debt settled

At January 1, 1997, Transit Developments owed First City Bank Group $600,000, under an 11% note with three years remaining to maturity. Due to financial difficulties, Transit was unable to pay the previous year's interest.

First City Bank Group agreed to settle Transit's debt in exchange for land having a fair market value of $450,000. Transit purchased the land in 1993 for $325,000.

Required:
Prepare the journal entry(s) to record the restructuring of the debt by Transit Developments.

Exercise 14–20
Troubled debt restructuring; modification of terms

At January 1, 1997, Brainard Industries, Inc., owed Second BancCorp $12 million under a 10% note due December 31, 1998. Interest was paid last on December 31, 1995. Brainard was experiencing severe financial difficulties and asked Second BancCorp to modify the terms of the debt agreement. After negotiation Second BancCorp agreed to:

- Forgive the interest accrued for the year just ended.
- Reduce the remaining two years' interest payments to $1 million each and delay the first payment until December 31, 1998.
- Reduce the principal amount to $11 million.

Required:
Prepare the journal entries by Brainard Industries, Inc. necessitated by the restructuring of the debt at (1) January 1, 1997, (2) December 31, 1998, and (3) December 31, 1999.

Exercise 14–21
Troubled debt restructuring; modification of terms

At January 1, 1997, NCI Industries, Inc., was indebted to First Federal Bank under a $240,000, 10% unsecured note. The note was signed January 1, 1993, and was due December 31, 1998. Annual interest was last paid on December 31, 1995. NCI was experiencing severe financial difficulties and negotiated a restructuring of the terms of the debt agreement. First Federal agreed to reduce last year's interest and the remaining two years' interest payments to $11,555 each and delay all payments until December 31, 1998, the maturity date.

Required:
Prepare the journal entries by NCI Industries, Inc. necessitated by the restructuring of the debt at (1) January 1, 1997, (2) December 31, 1997, and (3) December 31, 1998.

Exercise 14–22
Error in amortization schedule

Exercise 21-23 deals with correcting an error in an amortization schedule.

Exercise 14–23
Error correction; accrued interest on bonds

At the end of 1996, Majors Furniture Company failed to accrue $61,000 of interest expense that accrued during the last five months of 1996 on bonds payable. The bonds mature in 2010. The discount on the bonds is amortized by the straight-line method. The following entry was recorded on February 1, 1997, when the semiannual interest was paid:

Interest expense	73,200	
Discount on bonds payable		1,200
Cash		72,000

Required:
Prepare any journal entry necessary to correct the error as well as any adjusting entry for 1997 related to the situation described. (Ignore income taxes.)

Exercise 14–24
New debt issues; *Wall Street Journal* announcement

Periodically, *The Wall Street Journal* lists new security issues that include corporate debt issues and stock issues. The following were among the debt offerings reported in the November 19, 1996, issue:

NEW SECURITIES ISSUES

The following were among yesterday's offerings and pricings in the U.S. and non-U.S. capital markets, with terms and syndicate manner, based on information provided by Dow Jones Capital Markets Report.

CORPORATE

Federal Home Loan Bank System—$100 million bonds via lead managers First Tennessee Bank N.A. and Goldman, Sachs & Co., according to Bond Data Corporate Service. Terms: maturity, Dec. 10, 1999; coupon 6.33%; issue price, par; yield, 6.33%; noncallable after three months.

Comdisco Inc.—$250 million of notes via lead manager Salomon Brothers, Inc., according to a syndicate official. Terms: maturity, Nov. 30, 2001; coupon, 6.375%; Issue price, 99.638; yield, 6.46%; call date, NC; debt ratings: Baa-1 (Moody's Investor's Service, Inc.), BBB+ (Standard & Poor's).

WSJ Nov. 19, 1996

Required:
1. Prepare the appropriate journal entries to record the sale of both issues to underwriters. Ignore share issue costs and assume no accrued interest.
2. Prepare the appropriate journal entries to record the first semiannual interest payment for both issues.

Problems

Problem 14–1
Determining the price of bonds—discount and premium—issuer and investor

On January 1, 1997, Instaform, Inc., issued 10% bonds with a face amount of $50 million, dated January 1. The bonds mature in 2016 (20 years). The market yield for bonds of similar risk and maturity is 12%. Interest is paid semiannually.

Required:
1. Determine the price of the bonds at January 1, 1997, and prepare the journal entry to record their issuance by Instaform.
2. Assume the market rate was 9%. Determine the price of the bonds at January 1, 1997, and prepare the journal entry to record their issuance by Instaform.
3. Assume Broadcourt Electronics purchased the entire issue in a private placement of the bonds. Using the data in requirement 2, prepare the journal entry to record their purchase by Broadcourt.

Problem 14–2
Straight-line and effective interest compared

On January 1, 1997, Bradley Recreational Products issued $100,000, 9%, four-year bonds. Interest is paid semiannually on June 30 and December 31. The bonds were issued at $96,768 to yield an annual return of 10%.

Required:
1. Prepare an amortization schedule that determines interest at the effective interest rate.
2. Prepare an amortization schedule by the straight-line method.
3. Prepare the journal entries to record interest expense on June 30, 1999, by each of the two approaches.
4. Explain why the pattern of interest differs between the two methods.
5. Assuming the market rate is still 10%, what price would a second investor pay the first investor on June 30, 1999, for $10,000 of the bonds?

Problem 14–3
Bond amortization schedule

On January 1, 1997, Tennessee Harvester Corporation issued debenture bonds that pay interest semiannually on June 30 and December 31. Portions of the bond amortization schedule appear below:

Payment	Cash Interest	Effective Interest	Increase in Balance	Outstanding Balance
				6,627,273
1	320,000	331,364	11,364	6,638,637
2	320,000	331,932	11,932	6,650,569
3	320,000	332,528	12,528	6,663,097
4	320,000	333,155	13,155	6,676,252
5	320,000	333,813	13,813	6,690,065
6	320,000	334,503	14,503	6,704,568
~	~	~	~	~
~	~	~	~	~
~	~	~	~	~
38	320,000	389,107	69,107	7,851,247
39	320,000	392,562	72,562	7,923,809
40	320,000	396,191	76,191	8,000,000

Required:
1. What is the face amount of the bonds?
2. What is the initial selling price of the bonds?
3. What is the term to maturity in years?
4. Interest is determined by what approach?
5. What is the stated annual interest rate?
6. What is the effective annual interest rate?
7. What is the total cash interest paid over the term to maturity?
8. What is the total effective interest expense recorded over the term to maturity?

Problem 14–4
Issuer and investor; effective interest; amortization schedule; adjusting entries

On February 1, 1997, Cromley Motor Products issued 9% bonds, dated February 1, with a face amount of $80 million. The bonds mature on January 31, 2001 (4 years). The market yield for bonds of similar risk and maturity was 10%. Interest is paid semiannually on July 31 and January 31. Barnwell Industries acquired $80,000 of the bonds as a long-term investment. The fiscal years of both firms end December 31.

Required:
1. Determine the price of the bonds issued on February 1, 1997.
2. Prepare amortization schedules that indicate (a) Cromley's effective interest expense and (b) Barnwell's effective interest revenue for each interest period during the term to maturity.
3. Prepare the journal entries to record (a) the issuance of the bonds by Cromley and (b) Barnwell's investment on February 1, 1997.
4. Prepare the journal entries by both firms to record all subsequent events related to the bonds through January 31, 1999.

Problem 14–5
Issuer and investor; straight-line method; adjusting entries

On April 1, 1997, Western Communications, Inc., issued 12% bonds, dated March 1, 1997, with a face amount of $30 million. The bonds sold for $29.3 million and mature on February 28, 2000. Interest is paid semiannually on August 31 and February 28. Stillworth Corporation acquired $30,000 of the bonds as a long-term investment. The fiscal years of both firms end December 31, and both firms use the straight-line method.

Required:
1. Prepare the journal entries to record (a) the issuance of the bonds by Western and (b) Stillworth's investment on April 1, 1997.
2. Prepare the journal entries by both firms to record all subsequent events related to the bonds through maturity.

Problem 14–6
Issuer and investor; effective interest; no amortization schedule

McWherter Instruments sold $400 million of 8% bonds, dated January 1, on January 1, 1997. The bonds mature on December 31, 2016 (20 years). For bonds of similar risk and maturity, the market yield was 10%. Interest is paid semiannually on June 30 and December 31. Blanton Technologies, Inc., purchased $400,000 (10%) of the bonds as a long-term investment.

Required:
1. Determine the price of the bonds issued on January 1, 1997.
2. Prepare the journal entries to record (a) their issuance by McWherter and (b) Blanton's investment on January 1, 1997.
3. Prepare the journal entries by (a) McWherter and (b) Blanton to record interest on June 30, 1997 (at the effective rate). (Do not prepare an amortization schedule.)
4. Prepare the journal entries by (a) McWherter and (b) Blanton to record interest on December 31, 1997 (at the effective rate). (Do not prepare an amortization schedule.)

Problem 14–7
Zero-coupon bonds

On January 1, 1997, Darnell Window and Pane issued $18 million of 10-year, zero-coupon bonds for $5,795,518.

Required:

1. Prepare the journal entry to record the bond issue.
2. Determine the effective rate of interest.
3. Prepare the journal entry to record annual interest expense at December 31, 1997.
4. Prepare the journal entry to record annual interest expense at December 31, 1998.
5. Prepare the journal entry to record the extinguishment at maturity.

Problem 14–8
Convertible bonds; induced conversion; bonds with detachable warrants

Bradley-Link's December 31, 1997, balance sheet included the following items :

Long-Term Liabilities:	($ in millions)
9.6% convertible bonds, callable at 101 beginning in 1998, due 2004 (net of unamortized discount of $2) [note 8]	$198
10.4% registered bonds callable at 104 beginning in 2007, due 2014 (net of unamortized discount of $1) [note 8]	49
Shareholders' Equity:	
Paid-in capital—stock warrants outstanding	4

Note 8: Bonds (in part)

The 9.6% bonds were issued in 1984 at 97.5 to yield 10%. Interest is paid semiannually on June 30 and December 31. Each $1,000 bond is convertible into 40 shares of the Company's $1 par common stock.

The 10.4% bonds were issued in 1988 at 102 to yield 10%. Interest is paid semiannually on June 30 and December 31. Each $1,000 bond was issued with 40 detachable stock warrants, each of which entitles the holder to purchase one share of the Company's $1 par common stock for $25, beginning 1998.

On January 3, 1998, when Bradley-Link's common stock had a market price of $32 per share, Bradley-Link called the convertible bonds to force conversion. 90% were converted; the remainder were acquired at the call price. When the common stock price reached an all-time high of $37 in December of 1998, 40% of the warrants were exercised.

Required:

1. Show the journal entries that were recorded when each of the two bond issues was originally sold in 1984 and 1988.
2. Prepare the journal entry to record (book value method) the conversion of 90% of the convertible bonds in January 1998 and the retirement of the remainder.
3. Assume Bradley-Link induced conversion by offering $150 cash for each bond converted. Prepare the journal entry to record (book value method) the conversion of 90% of the convertible bonds in January 1998.
4. Assume Bradley-Link induced conversion by modifying the conversion ratio to exchange 45 shares for each bond rather than the 40 shares provided in the contract. Prepare the journal entry to record (book value method) the conversion of 90% of the convertible bonds in January 1998.
5. Prepare the journal entry to record the exercise of the warrants in December 1998.

Problem 14–9
Notes exchanged for assets

At the beginning of the year, Lambert Motors issued the three notes described below.

1. The company issued a two-year, 12%, $600,000 note in exchange for a tract of land. The current market rate of interest is 12%.
2. Lambert acquired some office equipment with a fair market value of $94,643 by issuing a one-year, $100,000 note. The stated interest on the note is 6%.
3. The company purchased a building by issuing a three-year installment note. The note is to be repaid in equal installments of $1 million per year beginning one year hence. The current market rate of interest is 12%.

Required:
Prepare the journal entries to record each of the three transactions and the interest expense at the end of the first year for each.

Problem 14–10
Note with unrealistic interest rate

At January 1, 1997, Brant Cargo acquired equipment by issuing a five-year, $150,000 (payable at maturity), 4% note. The market rate of interest for notes of similar risk is 10%.

Required:

1. Prepare the journal entry for Brant Cargo to record the purchase of the equipment.

2. Prepare the journal entry for Brant Cargo to record the interest at December 31, 1997.
3. Prepare the journal entry for Brant Cargo to record the interest at December 31, 1998.

Problem 14–11
Noninterest-bearing
installment note

At the beginning of 1997, VHF Industries acquired a machine with a fair market value of $6,074,700 by issuing a four-year, noninterest-bearing note in the face amount of $8 million. The note is payable in four annual installments of $2 million at the end of each year.

Required:
1. What is the effective rate of interest implicit in the agreement?
2. Prepare the journal entry to record the purchase of the machine.
3. Prepare the journal entry to record the first installment payment at December 31, 1997.
4. Prepare the journal entry to record the second installment payment at December 31, 1998.
5. Suppose the market value of the machine was unknown at the time of purchase, but the market rate of interest for notes of similar risk was 11%. Prepare the journal entry to record the purchase of the machine.

Problem 14–12
Note and installment note with
unrealistic interest rate

Braxton Technologies, Inc., constructed a conveyor for A&G Warehousers that was completed and ready for use on January 1, 1997. A&G paid for the conveyor by issuing a $100,000, four-year note that specified 5% interest to be paid on December 31 of each year. The conveyor was custom-built for A&G, so its cash price was unknown. By comparison with similar transactions it was determined that a reasonable interest rate was 10%.

Required:
1. Prepare the journal entry for A&G's purchase of the conveyor on January 1, 1997.
2. Prepare an amortization schedule for the four-year term of the note.
3. Prepare the journal entry for A&G's third interest payment on December 31, 1999.
4. If A&G's note had been an installment note to be paid in four equal payments at the end of each year beginning December 31, 1997, what would be the amount of each installment?
5. Prepare an amortization schedule for the four-year term of the installment note.
6. Prepare the journal entry for A&G's third installment payment on December 31, 1999.

Problem 14–13
Early extinguishment of debt

Three years ago American Insulation Corporation issued 10 percent, $800,000, 10-year bonds for $770,000. Debt issue costs were $3,000. American Insulation exercised its call privilege and retired the bonds for $790,000. The corporation uses the straight-line method both to determine interest and to amortize debt issue costs.

Required:
Prepare the journal entry to record the call of the bonds.

Problem 14–14
Early extinguishment;
effective interest

The long-term liability section of Twin Digital Corporation's balance sheet as of December 31, 1996, included 12% bonds having a face amount of $20 million and a remaining discount of $1 million. Disclosure notes indicate the bonds were issued to yield 14%.

Interest is recorded at the effective interest rate and paid on January 1 and July 1 of each year. On July 1, 1997, Twin Digital retired the bonds at 102 ($20.4 million) before their scheduled maturity.

Required:
1. Prepare the journal entry by Twin Digital to record the semiannual interest on July 1, 1997.
2. Prepare the journal entry by Twin Digital to record the redemption of the bonds on July 1, 1997.

Problem 14–15
Investments in bonds;
accrued interest; sale

The following transactions relate to bond investments of Livermore Laboratories. The company's fiscal year ends on December 31. Livermore uses the straight-line method to determine interest.

1997

July	1	Purchased $16 million of Bracecourt Corporation 10% debentures, due in 20 years (June 30, 2017), for $15.7 million. Interest is payable on January 1 and July 1 of each year.
Oct.	1	Purchased $30 million of 12% Framm Pharmaceuticals debentures, due May 31, 2007, for $31,160,000 plus accrued interest. Interest is payable on June 1 and December 1 of each year.
Dec.	1	Received interest on the Framm bonds
	31	Accrued interest

1998

Jan.	1	Received interest on the Bracecourt bonds
June	1	Received interest on the Framm bonds.
July	1	Received interest on the Bracecourt bonds
Sept.	1	Sold $15 million of the Framm bonds at 101 plus accrued interest

Dec.   1   Received interest on the remaining Framm bonds
     31   Accrued interest

1999

Jan.   1   Received interest on the Bracecourt bonds
Feb.   28   Sold the remainder of the Framm bonds at 102 plus accrued interest
Dec.   31   Accrued interest

Required:

Prepare the appropriate journal entries for these long-term bond investments. Determine interest at the effective rate.

Problem 14–16
Debt issue costs; issuance; expensing; early extinguishment

Cupola Fan Corporation issued 10%, $400,000, 10-year bonds for $385,000 on June 30, 1997. Debt issue costs were $1,500. Interest is paid semiannually on December 31 and June 30. One year from the issue date (July 1, 1998), the corporation exercised its call privilege and retired the bonds for $395,000. The corporation uses the straight-line method both to determine interest and to amortize debt issue costs.

Required:

1. Prepare the journal entry to record the issuance of the bonds.
2. Prepare the journal entries to record the payment of interest and amortization of debt issue costs on December 31, 1997.
3. Prepare the journal entries to record the payment of interest and amortization of debt issue costs on June 30, 1998.
4. Prepare the journal entries to record the call of the bonds.

Problem 14–17
Early extinguishment

The long-term liability section of Eastern Post Corporation's balance sheet as of December 31, 1996, included 10% bonds having a face amount of $40 million and a remaining premium of $6 million. On January 1, 1997, Eastern Post retired some of the bonds before their scheduled maturity.

Required:

Prepare the journal entry by Eastern Post to record the redemption of the bonds under each of the independent circumstances below:

1. Eastern Post called half the bonds at the call price of 102 (102% of face amount).
2. Eastern Post repurchased $10 million of the bonds on the open market at their market price of $10.5 million.

Problem 14–18
Troubled debt restructuring

At January 1, 1997, Rothschild Chair Company, Inc., was indebted to First Lincoln Bank under a $20 million, 10% unsecured note. The note was signed January 1, 1991, and was due December 31, 2000. Annual interest was last paid on December 31, 1995. Rothschild Chair Company was experiencing severe financial difficulties and negotiated a restructuring of the terms of the debt agreement.

Required:

Prepare all journal entries by Rothschild Chair Company, Inc., to record the restructuring and any remaining transactions relating to the debt under each of the independent circumstances below:

1. First Lincoln Bank agreed to settle the debt in exchange for land having a fair market value of $16 million but carried on Rothschild Chair Company's books at $13 million.
2. First Lincoln Bank agreed to (a) forgive the interest accrued from last year, (b) reduce the remaining four interest payments to $1 million each, and (c) reduce the principal to $15 million.
3. First Lincoln Bank agreed to defer all payments (including accrued interest) until the maturity date and accept $27,775,000 at that time in settlement of the debt.

Problem 14–19
Concepts; terminology

Listed below are several terms and phrases associated with long-term debt. Pair each item from List A (by letter) with the item from List B that is most appropriately associated with it.

List A	List B
____ 1. Effective rate times balance.	a. Straight-line method.
____ 2. Promises made to bondholders.	b. Discount.
____ 3. Interest determined at new, lower rate.	c. Restructured cash payments less than carrying amount of debt.
____ 4. Present value of interest plus present value of principal.	d. Restructured cash payments exceed carrying amount of debt.
____ 5. Call feature.	e. Name of owner not registered.
____ 6. Debt issue costs.	f. Premium.
____ 7. Market rate higher than stated rate.	g. Checks are mailed directly.
____ 8. Coupon bonds.	h. No specific assets pledged.
____ 9. Convertible bonds.	i. Bond indenture.
____ 10. Market rate less than stated rate.	j. Backed by a lien.
____ 11. Stated rate times face amount.	

____ 12. Registered bonds.
____ 13. Debenture bond.
____ 14. Mortgage bond.
____ 15. Materiality concept.
____ 16. Recording of interest discontinued.
____ 17. Subordinated debenture.

k. Interest expense.
l. May become stock.
m. Legal, accounting, printing.
n. Protection against falling rates.
o. Periodic cash payments.
p. Bond price.
q. Liquidation payments after other claims satisfied.

Cases

Writing Case 14–1
Convertible securities and warrants; concepts

It is not unusual to issue long-term debt in conjunction with an arrangement under which lenders receive an option to buy common stock during all or a portion of the time the debt is outstanding. Sometimes the vehicle is convertible bonds; sometimes warrants to buy stock accompany the bonds and are separable. Interstate Chemical is considering these options in conjunction with a planned debt issue.

"You mean we have to report $7 million more in liabilities if we go with convertible bonds? Makes no sense to me," your CFO said. "Both ways seem pretty much the same transaction. Explain it to me, will you?"

Required:

Write a memo. Include in your explanation each of the following:
1. The differences in accounting for proceeds from the issuance of convertible bonds and of debt instruments with separate warrants to purchase common stock.
2. The underlying rationale for the differences.
3. Arguments that could be presented for the alternative accounting treatment.

Research Case 14–2
Alternative ways to measure interest income; research article in *Accounting Horizons*

As described in Chapter 12, *SFAS 115* requires that certain investment securities be reported on the balance sheet at fair value.[20] Nevertheless, the required approach is to continue to measure interest income as the original effective rate times the unadjusted outstanding balance, as described in this chapter. That is, the new fair value is ignored. Professor Means, in "Effective Interest ... On What Basis?," compares this approach with two alternatives and suggests a theoretically correct solution.

Required:

1. In your library or from some other source, locate the indicated article in *Accounting Horizons*, June 1994.
2. What are the two alternative ways to measure interest income described in the article?
3. What is the author's conclusion as to the theoretically correct alternative?
4. What is the primary reason for her conclusion?

Group Interaction Case 14–3
Is convertible debt a liability or is it shareholders' equity?

Some financial instruments can be considered compound instruments in that they have features of both debt and shareholders' equity. The most common example encountered in practice is convertible debt—bonds or notes convertible by the investor into common stock. A topic of debate for several years has been whether:

View 1: Issuers should account for an instrument with both liability and equity characteristics entirely as a liability or entirely as an equity instrument depending on which characteristic governs.
View 2: Issuers should account for an instrument as consisting of a liability component and an equity component that should be accounted for separately.

In considering this question, you should disregard what you know about the current position of the FASB on the issue. Instead, focus on conceptual issues regarding the practicable and theoretically appropriate treatment, unconstrained by GAAP. Also, focus your deliberations on convertible bonds as the instrument with both liability and equity characteristics.

Required:

1. Which view do you favor? Develop a list of arguments in support of your view prior to the class session for which the case is assigned.
2. In class, your instructor will pair you (and everyone else) with a classmate (who also has independently developed an argument).
   a. You will be given three minutes to argue your view to your partner. Your partner likewise will be given three minutes to argue his or her view to you. During these three-minute presentations, the listening partner is not permitted to speak.

---

[20] "Accounting for Certain Investments in Debt and Equity Securities," *Statement of Financial Accounting Standards No. 115,* (Norwalk, Conn.: FASB, 1993). The standard became effective in 1994.

b.   Then after each person has had a turn attempting to convince his or her partner, the two partners will have a three-minute discussion in which they will decide which view is more convincing and arguments will be merged into a single view for each pair.

3. After the allotted time, a spokesperson for each of the two views will be selected by the instructor. Each spokesperson will field arguments from the class in support of that view's position and list the arguments on the board. The class then will discuss the merits of the two lists of arguments and attempt to reach a consensus view, though a consensus is not necessary.

Trueblood Accounting Case 14–4
Accounting for warrants issued to bondholders; ambiguity and professional judgment

The following Robert M. Trueblood case is recommended for use with this chapter. The case provides an excellent opportunity for class discussion, group projects, and writing assignments. The case, along with Professor's Discussion Material, can be obtained from the Deloitte & Touche Foundation.

Case 94-4: *Stock Warrants*

The primary issue in this case is the accounting for warrants issued to bondholders. The approach is not addressed in current authoritative literature, so students will need to consider related analogous literature in solving the case. The impact on accounting decisions of attorneys and investment bankers also is considered.

Real World Case 14–5
Issuance of notes

The following appeared in the November 14, 1996 , issue of *The Wall Street Journal*:

This announcement is not an offer of securities for sale or an offer to buy securities.

New Issue   November 14, 1996

$250,000,000

ANHEUSER-BUSCH COMPANIES, INC.

6.75% Notes Due November 1, 2006

Price 99.467%

plus accrued interest if any from date of issuance

Copies of the prospectus and the related prospectus supplement may be obtained from such of the undersigned as may legally offer these securities under applicable securities laws.

Dillon, Read & Co. Inc.
   Goldman, Sachs & Co.
      Merrill Lynch & Co.
         J.P. Morgan & Co.

Required:

1. Explain what is being described by the announcement.
2. Can you think of a psychological reason for the securities to be priced as they are?
3. What are the accounting considerations for Anheuser-Busch Companies, Inc.? Describe how Anheuser-Busch recorded the sale.

Critical Thought Case 14–6
Noninterest-bearing debt

While reading a recent issue of *Health & Fitness*, a trade journal, Brandon Wilde noticed an ad for equipment he had been seeking for use in his business. The ad offered oxygen therapy equipment under the following terms:

> Model BL 44582
> $204,000 zero interest loan
> Quarterly payments of $17,000 for only 3 years

The ad captured Wilde's attention, in part because he recently had been concerned that the interest charges incurred by his business were getting out of line. The price, though, was somewhat higher than prices for this model he had seen elsewhere.

Required:
Advise Mr. Wilde on the purchase he is considering.

Critical Thought Case 14–7
Noninterest bearing note exchanged for cash and other privileges

The Jaecke Group, Inc., manufacturers various kinds of hydraulic pumps. In June 1995, the company signed a four-year purchase agreement with one of its main parts suppliers, Hydraulics, Inc. Over the four-year period, Jaecke has agreed to purchase 100,000 units of a key component used in the manufacture of its pumps. The agreement allows Jaecke to purchase the component at a price lower than the prevailing market price at the time of purchase. As part of the agreement, Jaecke will lend hydraulics $200,000 to be repaid after four years with no stated interest (the prevailing market rate of interest for a loan of this type is 10%).

Jaecke's chief accountant has proposed recording the note receivable at $200,000. The parts inventory purchased from Hydraulics over the next four years will then be recorded at the actual prices paid.

Required:

Do you agree with the accountant's valuation of the note and his intention to value the parts inventory acquired over the four-year period of the agreement at actual prices paid? If not, how would you account for the initial transaction and the subsequent inventory purchases?

Group Interaction Case 14–8
Note receivable exchanged for cash and other services

The Pastel Paint Company recently loaned $300,000 to KIX 96, a local radio station. The radio station signed a noninterest-bearing note requiring the $300,000 to be repaid in three years. As part of the agreement, the radio station will provide Pastel with a specified amount of free radio advertising over the three-year term of the note.

The focus of this case is the valuation of the note receivable by Pastel Paint Company and the treatment of the "free" advertising provided by the radio station. Your instructor will divide the class into from two to six groups depending on the size of the class. The mission of your group is to reach consensus on the appropriate note valuation and accounting treatment of the free advertising.

Required:

1. Each group member should deliberate the situation independently and draft a tentative argument prior to the class session for which the case is assigned.
2. In class, each group will meet for 10 to 15 minutes in different areas of the classroom. During that meeting, group members will take turns sharing their suggestions for the purpose of arriving at a single group treatment.
3. After the allotted time, a spokesperson for each group (selected during the group meetings) will share the group's solution with the class. The goal of the class is to incorporate the views of each group into a consensus approach to the situation.

Discussion Case 14–9
Issuance, extinguishment, and conversion of bonds

On January 1, 1996, Brewster Company issued 2,000 of its five-year, $1,000 face amount, 11% bonds dated January 1 at an effective annual interest rate (yield) of 9%. Brewster uses the effective interest method of amortization. On December 31, 1997, the 2,000 bonds were extinguished early through acquisition in the open market by Brewster for $1,980,000. On July 1, 1996, Brewster issued 5,000 of its six-year, $1,000 face amount, 10% convertible bonds dated July 1 at an effective annual interest rate (yield) of 12%. The convertible bonds are convertible at the option of the investor into Brewster's common stock at a ratio of 10 shares of common stock for each bond. Brewster uses the effective interest method of amortization. On July 1, 1997, an investor in Brewster's convertible bonds tendered 1,500 bonds for conversion into 15,000 shares of Brewster's common stock which had a market value of $105 per share at the date of the conversion.

Required:

1. a. Were the 11% bonds issued at par, at a discount, or at a premium? Why?
   b. Would the amount of interest expense for the 11% bonds using the effective interest method of amortization be higher in the first or second year of the life of the bonds issue? Why?
2. a. How should gain or loss on early extinguishment of debt be determined? Does the early extinguishment of the 11% bonds result in a gain or loss? Why?
   b. How should Brewster report the early extinguishment of the 11% bonds on the 1997 income statement?
3. a. Would recording the conversion of the 10% convertible bonds into common stock under the book value method affect net income? What is the rationale for the book value method?
   b. Would recording the conversion of the 10% convertible bonds into common stock under the market value method affect net income? What is the rationale for the market value method?

(AICPA adapted)

Trueblood Accounting Case 14–10
Troubled debt restructurings; ambiguity and professional judgment

The following Robert M. Trueblood case is recommended for use with this chapter. The case provides an excellent opportunity for class discussion, group projects, and writing assignments. The case, along with Professor's Discussion Material, can be obtained from the Deloitte & Touche Foundation.

Case 90-3: *Accounting for a Gain on a Debt Restructuring*

The objective of this case is to point out the ambiguity involved in reporting gains related to troubled debt restructurings for firms in bankruptcy. It therefore emphasizes the role of professional judgment in dealing with these situations.

Ethics Case 14–11
Debt for equity swaps; have
your cake and eat it too

The cloudy afternoon mirrored the mood of the conference of division managers. Claude Meyer, assistant to the controller for Hunt Manufacturing, wore one of the gloomy faces that was just emerging from the conference room. "Wow, I knew it was bad, but not that bad," Claude thought to himself. "I don't look forward to sharing those numbers with shareholders."

The numbers he discussed with himself were fourth quarter losses which more than offset the profits of the first three quarters. Everyone had known for some time that poor sales forecasts and production delays had wreaked havoc on the bottom line, but most were caught off guard by the severity of damage.

Later that night he sat alone in his office, scanning and rescanning the preliminary financial statements on his computer monitor. Suddenly his mood brightened. "This may work," he said aloud, though no one could hear. Fifteen minutes later he congratulated himself, "Yes!"

The next day he eagerly explained his plan to Susan Barr, controller of Hunt for the last six years. The plan involved $300 million in convertible bonds issued three years earlier.

Meyer: By swapping stock for the bonds, we can eliminate a substantial liability from the balance sheet, wipe out most of our interest expense, and reduce our loss. In fact, the book value of the bonds is significantly less than the market value of the stock we'd issue. I think we can produce a profit.

Barr: But Claude, our bondholders are not inclined to convert the bonds.

Meyer: Right. But, the bonds are callable. As of this year, we can call the bonds at a call premium of 1%. Given the choice of accepting that redemption price or converting to stock, they'll all convert. We won't have to pay a cent. And, since no cash will be paid, we won't pay taxes either.

Required:
Do you perceive an ethical dilemma? What would be the impact of following up on Claude's plan? Who would benefit? Who would be injured?

**Financial Analysis
Case 14–12**
Analyzing financial
statements; financial leverage;
interest coverage

IGF Foods Company is a large, primarily domestic, consumer foods company involved in the manufacture, distribution, and sale of a variety of food products. Industry averages are derived from Troy's The *Almanac of Business and Industrial Financial Ratios*. Following are the 1997 and 1996 comparative income statements and balance sheets for IGF. (The financial data we use are from actual financial statements of a well-known corporation, but the company name is fictitious and the numbers and dates have been modified slightly to disguise the company's identity.)

IGF FOODS COMPANY
Years Ended December 31, 1997 and 1996

($ in millions)	1997	1996
Comparative Income Statements		
Net sales	$6,440	$5,800
Cost of goods sold	(3,667)	(3,389)
Gross profit	2,773	2,411
Operating expenses	(1,916)	(1,629)
Operating income	857	782
Interest expense	(54)	(53)
Income from operations before tax	803	729
Income taxes	(316)	(287)
Net income	$ 487	$ 442
Comparative Balance Sheets		
Assets		
Total current assets	$1,879	$1,490
Property, plant, and equipment (net):	2,592	2,291
Intangibles (net):	800	843
Other assets	74	60
Total assets	$5,345	$4,684
Liabilities And Shareholders' Equity		
Total current liabilities	$1,473	$ 941
Long-term debt	534	728
Deferred income taxes	407	344
Total liabilities	2,414	2,013
Shareholders' equity:		
Common stock	180	180
Additional paid-in capital	21	63
Retained earnings	2,730	2,428
Total shareholders' equity	2,931	2,671
Total liabilities and shareholders' equity	$5,345	$4,684

Long-term solvency refers to a company's ability to pay its long-term obligations. Financing ratios provide investors and creditors with an indication of this element of risk.

Required:

1. Calculate the debt to equity ratio for IGF. The average ratio for the stocks listed on the New York Stock Exchange in a comparable time period was 1.0. What information does your calculation provide an investor?
2. Is IGF experiencing favorable or unfavorable financial leverage?
3. Calculate IGF's times interest earned ratio. The coverage for the stocks listed on the New York Stock Exchange in a comparable time period was 5.1. What does your calculation indicate about IGF's risk?

Internet Case 14–13
Researching the way long-term debt is reported; retrieving information from the Internet

EDGAR, the Electronic Data Gathering, Analysis, and Retrieval system, performs automated collection, validation, indexing, acceptance, and forwarding of submissions by companies and others who are required by law to file forms with the U.S. Securities and Exchange Commission (SEC). All publicly traded domestic companies use EDGAR to make the majority of their filings. (Some foreign companies do so voluntarily.) Form 10-K or 10-KSB, including the annual report, is required to be filed on EDGAR. The SEC makes this information available on the Internet.

Required:

1. Access EDGAR on the Internet. The web address is http://www.sec.gov/.
2. Search for Quaker Oats. Access its most recent 10-K filing. Search or scroll to find the financial statements and related notes.
3. What is the total debt (including current liabilities and deferred taxes) reported on the balance sheet? How has that amount changed over the most recent three years?
4. Compare the total liabilities (including current liabilities and deferred taxes) with the shareholders' equity and calculate the debt to equity ratio for the most recent three years. Has the proportion of debt financing and equity financing changed recently?
5. Does Quaker obtain more financing through bonds or notes? Are required debt payments increasing or decreasing over time? Is any short-term debt classified as long term? Why?

Financial Analysis Case 14–14
Reporting long-term debt

Refer to the financial statements of Federal Express Corporation in the appendix to Chapter 1.

Required:

1. The long-term debt section of Federal Express's balance sheet reports an increase in long-term liabilities from 1995 to 1996. The statement of cash flows, however, shows 1996 payments on debt exceeding proceeds from debt issuances by quite a bit. Explain this apparent discrepancy.
2. What is Federal Express's primary form of long-term debt?
3. During the five-year period following 1996, in which year will the highest amount be required to pay maturity amounts of debt?
4. Note 3 indicates that the fair value of debt exceeds the carrying value of debt in both years reported. What does that tell us about interest rates since the debt was issued?

15

LEASES

OVERVIEW

In the previous chapter, we saw how companies account for their long-term debt. The focus of that discussion was *bonds* and *notes*. In this chapter we continue our discussion of debt, but we now turn our attention to liabilities arising in connection with *leases*. Leases that produce such debtor/creditor relationships are referred to as *capital* leases by the lessee and as either *direct financing* or *sales-type* leases by the lessor. We also will see that some leases do not produce debtor/creditor relationships, but instead are accounted for as rental agreements. These are designated *operating* leases.

LEARNING OBJECTIVES   After studying this chapter, you should be able to:

1. Identify and describe the operational, financial, and tax objectives that motivate leasing.
2. Explain why some leases constitute rental agreements and some represent purchases/sales accompanied by debt financing.
3. Explain the basis for each of the criteria and conditions used to classify leases.
4. Record all transactions associated with operating leases by both the lessor and lessee.
5. Describe and demonstrate how both the lessee and lessor account for a nonoperating lease.
6. Describe and demonstrate how the lessor accounts for a sales-type lease.
7. Explain how lease accounting is affected by the residual value of a leased asset.
8. Describe the way a bargain purchase option affects lease accounting.
9. Explain sale leaseback arrangements and their accounting treatment.

IT'S A HIT!

A recent *Wall Street Journal* news brief commented on estimated lease revenues for IBM Corporation which leases its computers to some customers and sells them to others. An excerpt follows:

> IBM's quarterly profit was a bit better than expected, but an IBM executive made cautious statements about the future that prompted some analysts to cut profit forecasts. IBM's finance chief warned that IBM is taking a revenue hit as more customers lease mainframes rather than buy them.

"What's News," *The Wall Street Journal,* Tuesday, October 22, 1996.

QUESTIONS

1. How would IBM's revenues "take a hit" as a result of more customers leasing than buying mainframes?
2. Under what kind of leasing arrangements would the "hit" not occur?

Focus on pgs 620-629, 632-633, 641 (bottom), 648-650

PART **A**

ACCOUNTING BY THE LESSOR AND LESSEE

We all are familiar with leases. If you ever have leased an apartment, you know that a lease is a contractual arrangement by which a **lessor** (owner) provides a **lessee** (user) the right to use an asset for a specified period of time. In return for this right, the lessee agrees to make stipulated, periodic cash payments during the term of the lease. An apartment lease is a typical rental agreement in which the fundamental rights and responsibilities of ownership are retained by the lessor; the lessee merely uses the asset temporarily. Businesses, too, lease assets under similar arrangements. These are referred to as **operating leases**. Many contracts, though, are formulated outwardly as leases, but in reality are installment purchases/sales. These are called **capital leases** (**direct financing** or **sales-type leases** to the lessor). Graphic 15–1 compares the possibilities.

> An apartment lease is a typical rental agreement referred to as an **operating lease**.

GRAPHIC   15–1

Basic Lease Classifications

Lessee	Lessor
Operating lease	Operating lease
Capital lease	Direct financing lease
	Sales-type lease

After looking at some of the possible advantages of leasing assets rather than buying them in certain circumstances, we will explore differences in leases further.

Advantages of Leasing: A Decision-Makers' Perspective

> **Learning objective 1**
> Identify and describe the operational, financial, and tax objectives that motivate leasing.

When a young entrepreneur started a computer training center a few years ago, she had no idea how fast her business would grow. While she knows she needs computers, she doesn't know how many. Just starting out, she also has little cash with which to buy them.

The mutual funds department of a large investment firm often needs new computers and peripherals—fast. The department manager knows he can't afford to wait up to a year, the time it sometimes takes, to go through company channels to obtain purchase approval.

An established computer software publisher recently began developing a new line of business software. The senior programmer has to be certain he's testing the company's products on the latest versions of computer hardware. And yet he views large expenditures on equipment subject to rapid technological change and obsolescence as risky business.

> Leasing can facilitate asset acquisition.

Each of these individuals is faced with different predicaments and concerns. The entrepreneur is faced with uncertainty and cash flow problems, the department manager with time constraints and bureaucratic control systems, the programmer with

> The U.S. Navy once leased a fleet of tankers to avoid asking Congress for appropriations.

fear of obsolescence. Though their specific concerns differ, these individuals have all met their firms' information technology needs with the same solution: each has decided to lease their computers rather than buy them.

> The number one method of external financing by U.S. businesses is leasing.

Computers are by no means the only assets obtained through leasing arrangements. To the contrary, leasing has grown to be the most popular method of external financing of corporate assets in America. The airplane in which you last flew probably was leased, as was the gate from which it departed. Your favorite retail outlet at the local shopping mall likely leases the space it operates. Many companies actually exist for the sole purpose of acquiring assets and leasing them to others. And, leasing often is a primary method of "selling" a firm's products. IBM and Boeing are familiar examples.

In light of its popularity, you may be surprised that leasing usually is more expensive than buying. Of course, the higher apparent cost of leasing is because the lessor usually shoulders at least some of the financial and risk burdens that a purchaser normally would assume. So, why the popularity?

> Tax incentives often motivate leasing.

The lease decisions described above are motivated by operational incentives. Tax and market considerations also motivate firms to lease. Sometimes leasing offers tax saving advantages over outright purchases. For instance, a company with little or no taxable income—maybe a business just getting started, or one experiencing an economic downturn—will get little benefit from depreciation deductions. But the company can benefit *indirectly* by leasing assets rather than buying. By allowing the *lessor* to retain ownership and thus benefit from depreciation deductions, the lessee often can negotiate lower lease payments. Lessees with sufficient taxable income to take advantage of the depreciation deductions, but still in lower tax brackets than lessors, also can achieve similar indirect tax benefits.

The desire to obtain "off-balance-sheet financing" also is sometimes a leasing stimulus. When funds are borrowed to purchase an asset, the liability has a detrimental effect on the company's debt-equity ratio and other mechanical indicators of riskiness. Similarly, the purchased asset increases total assets and correspondingly lowers calculations of the rate of return on assets. Despite research that indicates otherwise, management actions continue to reflect a belief that the financial market is naive, and is fooled by off-balance-sheet financing.[1] Managers continue to avoid reporting assets and liabilities by leasing rather than buying and by constructing lease agreements in such a way that capitalizing the assets and liabilities is not required.[2]

Whether or not there is any real effect on security prices, sometimes off-balance-sheet financing helps a firm avoid exceeding contractual limits on designated financial ratios (like the debt to equity ratio, for instance).[3] When the operational, tax, and financial market advantages are considered, the *net* cost of leasing often is less than the cost of purchasing.

> Leasing sometimes is used as a means of off-balance-sheet financing.

> Operational, tax, and financial market incentives often make leasing an attractive alternative to purchasing.

Capital Leases and Installment Notes Compared

> **Learning objective 2**
> Explain why some leases constitute rental agreements and some represent purchases/sales accompanied by debt financing.

You learned in the previous chapter how to account for an installment note. To a great extent, then, you already have learned how to account for a capital lease. To illustrate, let's recall the situation described in the previous chapter. We assumed that Skill Graphics purchased a package-labeling machine from Hughes–Barker Corporation by issuing a three-year installment note that required six semiannual installment payments of $139,857 each. That arrangement provided for the purchase of the $666,634 machine as well as interest at an annual rate of 14% (7% twice each year). Remember, too, that each installment payment consisted of part interest (7% times the outstanding balance) and part payment for the machine (the remainder of each payment).

Now let's suppose that Skill Graphics instead acquired the package-labeling machine from Hughes–Barker Corporation under a three-year *lease* that required six semiannual rental payments of $139,857 each. Obviously, the fundamental nature of the transaction remains the same regardless of whether it is negotiated as an installment purchase or as a lease. So, it would be inconsistent to account for this lease in a fundamentally different way than for an installment purchase:

> **Comparison of a Note and Capital Lease**
> In keeping with the basic accounting concept of substance over form, accounting for a capital lease parallels that for an installment purchase.

At Inception (January 1)		
Installment Note		
Machinery	666,634	
Note payable		666,634
Capital Lease		
Leased machinery	666,634	
Lease payable		666,634

---

[1]A comprehensive research study commissioned by the FASB offers strong evidence that managers try to structure leases as operating leases to avoid balance sheet effects, but also that the securities market behaves as if it sees through these attempts. That is, leases have the same effect on the market whether they are reflected as assets and liabilities on the balance sheet or are merely reported in the disclosure notes. These are conclusions of A. Rashad Abdel-khalik, "The Economic Effects on Leases of FASB *Statement No. 13*, Accounting for Leases," *Research Report* (Stamford, Conn.: FASB, 1981).

[2]You will learn later in the chapter that accounting standards are designed to identify lease arrangements that, despite their outward appearance, are in reality purchases of assets. Assets acquired by these arrangements, *capital leases*, are required to be recorded as well as the related lease liability. Managers often structure lease terms so that capitalization requirements are avoided.

[3]It is common for debt agreements, particularly long-term ones, to include restrictions on the debtor as a way to provide some degree of protection to the creditor. Sometimes a minimum level is specified for current assets relative to current liabilities, net assets, debt as a ratio of equity, or many other financial ratios. Often a restriction is placed on dividend payments, share repurchases, or other activities that might impede the debtor's ability to repay the debt. Typically, the debt becomes due on demand when the debtor becomes in violation of such a debt covenant, often after a specified grace period.

Consistent with the nature of the transaction, interest expense accrues each period at the effective rate times the outstanding balance:

At the First Semiannual Payment Date (June 30)		
Installment Note		
Interest expense (7% × $666,634)	46,664	
Note payable (difference)	93,193	
Cash (installment payment)		139,857
Capital Lease		
Interest expense (7% × $666,634)	46,664	
Lease payable (difference)	93,193	
Cash (rental payment)		139,857

Interest Compared for a Note and Capital Lease Each payment includes both an amount that represents interest and an amount that represents a reduction of principal.

Because the lease payable balance declines with each payment, the interest becomes less each period. An amortization schedule is convenient to track the changing amounts as shown in Graphic 15–2.

GRAPHIC   15–2
Lease Amortization Schedule

Each rental payment includes interest on the outstanding balance at the effective rate. The remainder of each payment reduces the outstanding balance.

Date	Payments	Effective Interest (7% × Outstanding balance)	Decrease in Balance	Outstanding Balance
				666,634
1	139,857	.07(666,634) = 46,664	93,193	573,441
2	139,857	.07(573,441) = 40,141	99,716	473,725
3	139,857	.07(473,725) = 33,161	106,696	367,029
4	139,857	.07(367,029) = 25,692	114,165	252,864
5	139,857	.07(252,864) = 17,700	122,157	130,707
6	139,857	.07(130,707) = 9,150	130,707	0
	839,142	172,508	666,634	

You should recognize this as essentially the same amortization schedule we used in the previous chapter in connection with our installment note example. The reason for the similarity is that we view a capital lease as being, in substance, equivalent to an installment purchase. So naturally the accounting treatment of the two essentially identical transactions should be consistent.

Lease Classification

A lease is accounted for as either a rental agreement or a purchase/sale accompanied by debt financing. The choice of accounting method hinges on the nature of the leasing arrangement.

A basic concept of accounting is substance over form.

Capital leases are agreements that we identify as being formulated outwardly as leases, but which are in reality installment purchases. Sometimes the true nature of an arrangement is obvious. For example, a 10-year noncancelable lease of a computer with a 10-year useful life, by which title passes to the lessee at the end of the lease term, obviously more nearly represents a purchase than a rental agreement. But what if the terms of the contract do not transfer title, and the lease term is for only seven years of the asset's 10-year life? Suppose contractual terms permit the lessee to obtain title under certain prearranged conditions? What if compensation provided by the lease contract is nearly equal to the value of the asset under lease? These situations are less clear-cut.

Accounting for leases attempts to see through the legal form of the agreements to determine their economic substance.

Professional judgment is needed to differentiate between leases that represent rental agreements and those that in reality are installment purchases/sales. The essential question is whether the usual risks and rewards of ownership have been transferred to the lessee. But judgment alone is likely to lead to inconsistencies in practice. The desire to encourage consistency in practice motivated the FASB to provide guidance for distinguishing between the two fundamental types of leases.[4] As you study the classification criteria in the following paragraphs, keep in mind that

[4]"Accounting for Leases," *Statement of Financial Accounting Standards No. 13*, (Stamford, Conn.: FASB, 1980), par. 7.

some leases clearly fit the classifications we give them, but others fall more in a gray area somewhere between the two extremes. For those, we end up forcing them into one category or the other by somewhat arbitrary criteria.

Classification Criteria

Learning objective 3
Explain the basis for each of the criteria and conditions used to classify leases.

A lessee should classify a lease transaction as a capital lease if it includes a noncancelable lease term and one or more of the four criteria listed in Graphic 15–3 are met.[5] Otherwise, it is an operating lease.

GRAPHIC   15–3

Criteria for Classification as a Capital Lease

1. The agreement specifies that ownership of the asset transfers to the lessee.
2. The agreement contains a **bargain purchase option.**
3. The noncancelable lease term is equal to 75% or more of the expected economic life of the asset.
4. The present value of the minimum lease payments is equal to or greater than 90% of the fair value of the asset.

Let's look closer at these criteria.

Since our objective is to determine when the risks and rewards of ownership have been transferred to the lessee, the first criterion is self-evident. If legal title passes to the lessee during, or at the end of, the lease term, obviously ownership attributes are transferred.

Criterion 1: Transfer of ownership

A **bargain purchase option (BPO)** is a provision in the lease contract that gives the lessee the option of purchasing the leased property at a bargain price. This is defined as a price sufficiently lower than the expected fair value of the property (when the option becomes exercisable) that the exercise of the option appears reasonably assured at the inception of the lease. Because exercise of the option appears reasonably assured, transfer of ownership is expected. So the logic of the second criterion is similar to that of the first. Applying criterion 2 in practice, though, often is more difficult because it is necessary to make a judgment now about whether a future option price will be a bargain.

Criterion 2: Bargain purchase option

If an asset is leased for most of its useful life, then most of the benefits and responsibilities of ownership are transferred to the lessee. We presume, quite arbitrarily, that 75% or more of the expected economic life of the asset is an appropriate threshold point for this purpose.

Criterion 3: Lease term is 75% of economic life

Although the intent of this criterion is fairly straightforward, implementation sometimes is troublesome. First, the lease term may be uncertain. It may be renewable beyond its initial term. Or the lease may be cancelable after a designated noncancelable period. When either is an issue, we ordinarily consider the lease term to be the noncancelable[6] term of the lease plus any periods covered by **bargain renewal options.**[7] A bargain renewal option gives the lessee the option to renew the lease at a bargain rate. That is, the rental payment is sufficiently lower than the expected fair rental of the property at the date the option becomes exercisable that exercise of the option appears reasonably assured.

[5]Noncancelable in this context does not preclude the agreement from specifying that the lease is cancelable after a designated noncancelable lease term. If no portion of the lease term is noncancelable, it is an operating lease. Later in this section, we discuss treatment of any cancelable portion of the lease term.

[6]Noncancelable in this context is a lease that is cancelable only by (a) the occurrence of some remote contingency, (b) permission of the lessor, (c) a new lease with the same lessor, or (d) payment by the lessee of a penalty in an amount such that continuation of the lease appears, at inception, reasonably assured. "Accounting for Leases: Sale and Leaseback Transactions Involving Real Estate, Sales-Type Leases of Real Estate, Definition of the Lease Term, Initial Direct Costs of Direct Financing Leases," *Statement of Financial Accounting Standards No. 98*, (Stamford, Conn.: FASB, 1988), par. 22.

[7]If applicable, the lease term also should include (a) periods for which failure to renew the lease imposes a penalty on the lessee in an amount such that renewal appears reasonably assured, (b) periods covered by ordinary renewal options during which a guarantee by the lessee of the lessor's debt directly or indirectly related to the leased property is expected to be in effect or a loan from the lessee to the lessor directly or indirectly related to the leased property is expected to be outstanding, (c) periods covered by ordinary renewal options preceding the date that a bargain purchase option is exercisable, or (d) periods representing renewals or extensions of the lease at the lessor's option. "Accounting for Leases: Sale and Leaseback Transactions Involving Real Estate, Sales-Type Leases of Real Estate, Definition of the Lease Term, Initial Direct Costs of Direct Financing Leases," *Statement of Financial Accounting Standards No. 98*, (Stamford, Conn.: FASB, 1988), par. 22.

Additional Consideration

Periods covered by bargain renewal options are not included in the lease term if a **bargain purchase option** is present. This is because the lease term should not extend beyond the date a bargain purchase option becomes exercisable. For example, assume a BPO allows a lessee to buy a leased delivery truck at the end of the noncancelable five-year lease term. Even if an option to renew the lease beyond that date is considered to be a bargain renewal option, that extra period would not be included as part of the lease term. Remember, we presume the BPO will be exercised after the initial five-year term, making the renewal option irrelevant.

Another implementation issue is estimating the **economic life** of the leased property. This is the estimated remaining time the property is expected to be economically usable for its intended purpose, with normal maintenance and repairs, at the inception of the lease. Estimates of the economic life of leased property are subject to the same uncertainty limitations of most estimates. This uncertainty presents the opportunity to arrive at estimates that cause this third criterion not to be met.

Finally, if the inception of the lease occurs during the last 25% of an asset's economic life, this third criterion does not apply. This is consistent with the basic premise of this criterion that most of the risks and rewards of ownership occur during the first 75% of an asset's life.

If the lease payments required by a lease contract substantially pay for a leased asset, it is logical to identify the arrangement as a lease equivalent to an installment purchase. This situation is

| Criterion 4: Present value of payments is 90% of fair value |

considered to exist when the present value of the **minimum lease payments** is equal to or greater than 90% of the fair value of the asset at the inception of the lease. In general, minimum lease payments are payments the lessee is required to make in connection with the lease. We look closer at the make-up of minimum lease payments later in the chapter.

The 90% recovery criterion often is the decisive one. As mentioned earlier, lessees often try to avoid writing a lease agreement that will require recording an asset and liability. When this is an objective, it usually is relatively easy to avoid meeting the first three criteria. However, when the underlying motive for the lease agreement is that the lessee substantively acquire the asset, it is more difficult to avoid meeting the 90% recovery criterion without defeating that motive. New ways, though, continually are being devised to structure leases to avoid meeting this criterion. Later we will look at some popular devices that are used.

Again consistent with the basic premise that most of the risks and rewards of ownership occur during the first 75% of an asset's life, this fourth criterion does not apply if the inception of the lease occurs during the last 25% of an asset's economic life.

Additional Lessor Conditions

As we saw in the previous section, the lessee accounts for a capital lease as if an asset were purchased—records both an asset and a liability at the inception of the lease. Consistency would suggest that the lessor in the same lease transaction should record the sale of an asset. Indeed, consistency is a goal of the FASB's lease accounting standards. The four classification criteria discussed in the previous section apply to both parties to the transaction, lessees and lessors. However, a fundamental difference is that for a lessor to record the sale side of the transaction, it is necessary also to satisfy the conditions of the realization principle we discussed in Chapter 4. In particular, the FASB specifies that for the lessor to record a lease as a direct financing lease or a sales-type lease, two conditions must be met in addition to one of the four classification criteria. These are listed in Graphic 15–4.

GRAPHIC   15–4

Additional Conditions for Classification as a Nonoperating Lease by the Lessor

1. The collectibility of the lease payments must be reasonably predictable.
2. If any costs to the lessor have yet to be incurred, they are reasonably predictable. (Performance by the lessor is substantially complete.)

In the case of a sales-type lease in which the lessor recognizes sales revenue, the reason for these additional conditions is apparent; collectibility of payments and substantial completion of the

Additional lessor conditions for classification as a nonoperating lease are consistent with criteria of the revenue realization principle.

earnings process are conditions of the revenue realization principle. This logic is extended to agreements classified as direct financing leases. Although sales revenue is not recorded in a direct financing lease, the leased asset is removed from the lessor's books and is replaced by a receivable.

Although uniformity of classification is a goal of lease accounting standards, it is obvious that the additional conditions allow inconsistencies.[8] Indeed, in lease negotiations an objective of the parties involved often is to devise terms that will result in a sale by the lessor but an operating lease by the lessee.[9]

In the remaining sections of Part A of this chapter we consider, in order, operating leases, direct financing leases (capital leases to the lessee), and sales-type leases (capital leases to the lessee).

Operating Leases

OPENING CASE

Question 1

Learning objective 4
Record all transactions associated with operating leases by both the lessor and lessee.

If a lease does not meet any of the criteria for a capital lease it is considered to be more in the nature of a rental agreement and is referred to as an **operating lease.**[10] We assume that the fundamental rights and responsibilities of ownership are retained by the lessor and that the lessee merely is using the asset temporarily. In keeping with that presumption, a sale is not recorded by the lessor; a purchase is not recorded by the lessee. Instead, the periodic rental payments are accounted for merely as rent by both parties to the transaction—rent revenue by the lessor, rent expense by the lessee.

Let's look at an example that illustrates the relatively straightforward accounting for operating leases. The earlier illustration comparing a capital lease to an installment purchase assumed rental payments at the *end* of each period. A more typical leasing arrangement requires rental payments at the *beginning* of each period. This more realistic payment schedule is assumed in Illustration 15–1.

ILLUSTRATION   15–1

Application of Classification Criteria

On January 1, 1997, Sans Serif Publishers, Inc., a computer services and printing firm, leased a color copier from CompuDec Corporation.

The lease agreement specifies four annual payments of $100,000 beginning January 1, 1997, the inception of the lease, and at each January 1 through 2000. The useful life of the copier is estimated to be six years.

Before deciding to lease, Sans Serif considered purchasing the copier for its cash price of $479,079. If funds were borrowed to buy the copier, the interest rate would have been 10%.

How should this lease be classified? We apply the four classification criteria:

1. Does the agreement specify that ownership of the asset transfers to the lessee?	No
2. Does the agreement contain a bargain purchase option?	No
3. Is the lease term equal to 75% or more of the expected economic life of the asset?	No (4 yrs < 75% of 6 yrs)
4. Is the present value of the minimum lease payments equal to or greater than 90% of the fair value of the asset?	No ($348,685 < 90% of $479,079)

$100,000 × 3.48685* = $348,685

Lease	Present
payments	value

Since none of the four classification criteria is met, this is an operating lease.

* Present value of an annuity due of $1: *n*=4, *i*=10%. Recall from Chapter 6 that we refer to periodic payments at the beginning of each period as an *annuity due.*

Journal entries for Illustration 15–1 are shown in Illustration 15–1a.

ILLUSTRATION   15–1a

Journal Entries for an Operating Lease

The operating lease described in Illustration 15–1 is recorded as follows:

At Each of the Four Payment Dates

Sans Serif Publishers, Inc. (Lessee)

Prepaid rent	100,000	
Cash		100,000

---

[8]"Accounting for Leases," *Statement of Financial Accounting Standards No. 13*, (Stamford, Conn.: FASB, 1980).

[9]Later in the chapter we discuss ways this is done.

[10]The term operating lease got its name long ago when a lessee routinely received from the lessor an operator along with leased equipment.

ILLUSTRATION 15-1a

continued

At the beginning of the year, the rent payments are prepaid rent to the lessee and unearned rent to the lessor.

The lessor retains the asset on its books, and accordingly records depreciation on the asset.

CompuDec Corporation (Lessor)		
Cash	100,000	
Unearned rent revenue		100,000
At the End of Each Year		
Sans Serif Publishers, Inc. (Lessee)		
Rent expense	100,000	
Prepaid rent		100,000
CompuDec Corporation (Lessor)		
Unearned rent revenue	100,000	
Rent revenue		100,000
Depreciation expense	x,xxx	
Accumulated depreciation		x,xxx

In an operating lease, rent is recognized on a straight-line basis unless another systematic method more clearly reflects the benefits of the asset's use. So, if rental payments are uneven—for instance, if rent increases are scheduled—the total scheduled payments ordinarily would be expensed equally (straight-line basis) over the lease term.[11]

Advance Payments

Advance payments are considered prepayments of rent. They are deferred and allocated to rent over the lease term.

Often lease agreements call for advance payments to be made at the inception of the lease that represent prepaid rent. For instance, it is common for a lessee to pay a bonus in return for negotiating more favorable lease terms. Such payments are recorded as prepaid rent and allocated (normally on a straight-line basis) to rent expense/rent revenue over the lease term. So the rent that is periodically reported in those cases consists of the periodic rent payments themselves plus an allocated portion of prepaid rent. This is demonstrated in Illustration 15-1b.

ILLUSTRATION 15-1b

Journal Entries—Operating Lease with Advance Payment

Advance payments in operating leases are deferred and allocated to rent over the lease term.

Rent comprises the periodic rent payments plus an allocated portion of the advance payment.

Assume Sans Serif paid a $40,000 bonus (advance payment) at the inception of the lease described in Illustration 15-1 in return for lower periodic payments – $90,000 each.

At the Inception of the Lease		
Sans Serif Publishers, Inc. (Lessee)		
Prepaid rent (bonus payment)	40,000	
Cash		40,000
CompuDec Corporation (Lessor)		
Cash	40,000	
Unearned rent revenue (bonus payment)		40,000
At Each of the Four Payment Dates		
Sans Serif Publishers, Inc. (Lessee)		
Prepaid rent (annual rent payment)	90,000	
Cash		90,000
CompuDec Corporation (Lessor)		
Cash	90,000	
Unearned rent revenue (annual rent payment)		90,000
At the End of Each Year		
Sans Serif Publishers, Inc. (Lessee)		
Rent expense (annual rent)	90,000	
Prepaid rent		90,000
Rent expense (bonus allocation)	10,000	
Prepaid rent ($40,000 ÷ 4)		10,000
CompuDec Corporation (Lessor)		
Unearned rent revenue	90,000	
Rent revenue (annual rent)		90,000
Unearned rent revenue ($40,000 ÷ 4)	10,000	
Rent revenue (bonus allocation)		10,000
Depreciation expense	x,xxx	
Accumulated depreciation		x,xxx

---

[11]"Accounting for Operating Leases With Scheduled Rent Increases," *FASB Technical Bulletin 85-3* (Stamford, Conn.: FASB, 1985), par. 1.

Sometimes advance payments include security deposits that are refundable at the expiration of the lease or prepayments of the last period's rent. A refundable security deposit is recorded as a long-term receivable (by the lessee) and liability (by the lessor) unless it is not expected to be returned. A prepayment of the last period's rent is recorded as prepaid rent and allocated to rent expense/rent revenue during the last period of the lease term.

At times, lease agreements call for uneven rent payments during the term of the lease. One way this can occur is when the initial payment (or maybe several payments) is waived. This is called a **rent abatement**.

Alternatively, rent payments may be scheduled to increase periodically over the lease term. In any event, the total rent over the term of the lease is allocated to individual periods on a straight-line basis. This means the (temporarily) unpaid portion of rent expense must be credited to deferred rent expense payable until later in the lease term when rent payments exceed rent expense.

Leasehold Improvements

> The cost of a **leasehold improvement** is depreciated over its useful life to the lessee.

Sometimes a lessee will make improvements to leased property that reverts back to the lessor at the end of the lease. If a lessee constructs a new building or makes modifications to existing structures, that cost represents an asset just like any other capital expenditure. Like other assets, its cost is allocated as depreciation expense over its useful life to the lessee, which will be the shorter of the physical life of the asset or the lease term.[12] Theoretically, such assets can be recorded in accounts descriptive of their nature, such as buildings or plant. In practice, the traditional account title used is **leasehold improvements**.[13] In any case, the undepreciated cost usually is reported in the balance sheet under the caption *property, plant, and equipment.* Moveable assets like office furniture and equipment that are not attached to the leased property are not considered leasehold improvements.

Let's turn our attention now to accounting for leases that meet the criteria and conditions for classification as nonoperating leases by both the lessee and the lessor.

Nonoperating Leases – Lessee and Lessor

> **Learning objective 5**
> Describe and demonstrate how both the lessee and lessor account for a nonoperating lease.

In the operating lease illustration, we assumed Sans Serif leased a copier directly from its manufacturer. Now let's assume a financial intermediary provided financing by acquiring the copier and leasing it to the user. And to temporarily avoid unnecessary confusion that adjusting entries might create, the example in Illustration 15–2 assumes that the inception of the lease, as well as subsequent rental payments, are made at the end of both companies' fiscal years:[15]

> A lease that transfers substantially all of the benefits and risks incident to ownership of property should be accounted for as the acquisition of an asset and the incurrence of an obligation by the lessee and as a sale or financing by the lessor.[14]

> **ILLUSTRATION   15–2**
>
> **Nonoperating Leases**

On December 31, 1996, Sans Serif Publishers, Inc., leased a copier from First LeaseCorp. First LeaseCorp purchased the equipment from CompuDec Corporation at a cost of $479,079.

The lease agreement specifies annual payments beginning December 31, 1996, the inception of the lease, and at each December 31 through 2001. The six-year lease term is equal to the estimated useful life of the copier.

First LeaseCorp routinely acquires electronic equipment for lease to other firms. The interest rate in these financing arrangements is 10%.

Since the lease term is equal to the expected useful life of the copier (>75%), the transaction must be recorded by the lessee as a **capital lease**.[16] If we assume also that collectibility of the lease payments and any costs to the lessor that are yet to be incurred are reasonably predictable, this qualifies also as a **direct financing lease** to First LeaseCorp. To achieve its objectives, First LeaseCorp must (a) recover its $479,079 investment as well as (b) earn interest revenue at a rate of 10%. So, the lessor determined that annual rental payments would be $100,000:

---

[12]If the agreement contains an option to renew, and the likelihood of renewal is uncertain, the renewal period is ignored.

[13]Also, traditionally, depreciation sometimes is labeled amortization when in connection with leased assets and leasehold improvements. This is of little consequence. Remember, both depreciation and amortization refer to the process of allocating an asset's cost over its useful life.

[14]"Accounting for Leases," *Statement of Financial Accounting Standards No. 13*, (Stamford, Conn.: FASB, 1980).

[15]We relax this assumption and consider accrued interest in a later section.

[16]The fourth criterion also is met. The present value of lease payments ($479,079) is 100% (>90%) of the fair value of the computers ($479,079). Meeting any one of the four criteria is sufficient.

ILLUSTRATION   15-2

continued

Rental payments are calculated such that their present value is equal to the lessor's cost.

Journal Entries at Inception— Direct Financing Lease

LESSEE

		Net Payable
		$479,079

LESSOR

Gross Rec'ble	Unearned Interest	Net Rec'ble
$600,000	(120,921)	$479,079

LESSEE

		Net Payable
		$479,079
		(100,000)
		$379,079

LESSOR

Gross Rec'ble	Unearned Interest	Net Rec'ble
$600,000	(120,921)	$479,079
(100,000)	0	(100,000)
$500,000	(120,921)	$379,079

$$\$479,079 \div 4.79079^* = \$100,000$$
Lessor's cost   Rental payments

* Present value of an annuity due of $1: $n=6$, $i=10\%$.

Of course, Sans Serif Publishers, Inc., views the transaction from the other side. The price the lessee pays for the copier is the present value of the rental payments:

$$\$100,000 \times 4.79079^* = \$479,079$$
Rental Payments   Lessee's cost

* Present value of an annuity due of $1: $n=6$, $i=10\%$.

Direct Financing Lease (December 31, 1996)*

Sans Serif Publishers, Inc. (Lessee)

Leased equipment (present value of lease payments)	479,079	
Lease payable (present value of lease payments)		479,079

First LeaseCorp (Lessor)

Lease receivable (gross sum of lease payments)*	600,000	
Unearned interest revenue (difference)		120,921
Inventory of equipment (lessor's cost)		479,079

First Lease Payment (December 31, 1996)†

Sans Serif Publishers, Inc. (Lessee)

Lease payable	100,000	
Cash		100,000

First LeaseCorp (Lessor)

Cash	100,000	
Lease receivable		100,000

*In the disclosure notes, the lease receivable is reported as the lessor's gross investment in the lease.
†Of course, the entries to record the lease and the first payment could be combined into a single entry since they occur at the same time.

Traditionally, the lessee uses the **net method** to record leases, and the lessor uses the **gross method**.[17] As you study the entries in Illustration 15–2, keep in mind that both methods achieve the same result, and theoretically either method could be used.

The amount recorded (capitalized) by the lessee is the present value of the **minimum lease payments**. However, if the fair value of the asset is lower than this amount, the recorded value of the asset should be limited to fair value. Unless the lessor is a manufacturer or dealer, the fair value typically will be the lessor's cost ($479,079 in this case). However, if considerable time has elapsed between the purchase of the property by the lessor and the inception of the lease, the fair value might be different. When the lessor is a manufacturer or dealer, the fair value of the property at the inception of the lease ordinarily will be its normal selling price (reduced by any volume or trade discounts). We study this situation (a sales-type lease) later. In unusual cases, market conditions may cause fair value to be less than the normal selling price.

Be sure to note that the entire $100,000 first rental payment is applied to principal reduction.[18] Because it occurred at the inception of the lease, no interest had yet accrued. Subsequent rental payments include interest on the outstanding balance as well as a residual portion that reduces that outstanding balance. As of the second rental payment date, one year's interest has accrued on the $379,079 balance outstanding during 1997, recorded as in Illustration 15–2a.

Notice that by either the net method (lessee) or the gross method (lessor), the outstanding balance is reduced by $62,092—the portion of the $100,000 payment remaining after interest is covered. The lease liability is reduced directly; the reduction in the net receivable is the combined effect of reducing the gross receivable by $100,000 and unearned interest revenue, a valuation (contra) account, by $37,908.[19]

A leased asset is recorded by the lessee at the present value of the **minimum lease payments** or the asset's fair value, whichever is lower.

Interest is a function of time. It accrues at the effective rate on the balance outstanding during the period.

Unearned interest revenue is a valuation (contra) account that indirectly reduces the lessor's net receivable.

---

[17]*SFAS 13* does not specifically mandate the methods to be used, but illustrations provided in the standard portray the net method for the lessee and the gross method for the lessor. As indicated later in the chapter, both the lessee and the lessor must report in disclosure notes *both* the gross and net amounts of the lease.

[18]Another way to view this is to think of the first $100,000 as a down payment with the remaining $379,079 financed by 5 (i.e., 6 - 1) *year-end* lease payments.

[19]Note that unearned interest revenue is not a liability, as you might assume from the account title. Unlike other unearned revenue accounts for which the cash is received in advance of the revenue being earned (and thus a liability), this account represents interest revenue that will be both received and earned periodically over the lease term. The account is analogous to the discount on notes receivable or on bond investment when those investments are recorded by the gross method.

ILLUSTRATION   15-2a

Journal Entries for the Second Lease Payment

LESSEE

	Net Payable
	$479,079
	(100,000)
	$379,079
	(62,092)
	$316,987

LESSOR

Gross Rec'ble	Unearned Interest	Net Rec'ble
$600,000	(120,921)	$479,079
(100,000)	0	(100,000)
$500,000	(120,921)	$379,079
(100,000)	37,908	(62,092)
$400,000	(83,013)	$316,987

Second Lease Payment (December 31, 1997)		
Sans Serif Publishers, Inc. (Lessee)		
Interest expense [10% × ($479,079 – 100,000)]	37,908	
Lease payable (difference)	62,092	
Cash (rental payment)		100,000
First LeaseCorp (Lessor)		
Cash (rental payment)	100,000	
Lease receivable		100,000
Unearned interest revenue	37,908	
Interest revenue [10% × ($600,000 – 120,921 – 100,000)]		37,908

The amortization schedule in Graphic 15–5 shows how the lease balance and the effective interest change over the six-year lease term.

Lease Amortization Schedule

The first rental payment includes no interest.

The total of the cash payments ($600,000) provides for:
1. Payment for the copier ($479,079).
2. Interest ($120,921) at an effective rate of 10%.

Dec.31	Payments	Effective Interest	Decrease in Balance	Outstanding Balance
		(10% × Outstanding balance)		
1996				479,079
1996	100,000		100,000	379,079
1997	100,000	.10(379,079) = 37,908	62,092	316,987
1998	100,000	.10(316,987) = 31,699	68,301	248,686
1999	100,000	.10(248,686) = 24,869	75,131	173,555
2000	100,000	.10(173,555) = 17,355	82,645	90,910
2001	100,000	.10(90,910) = 9,090*	90,910	0
	600,000	120,921*	479,079	

* Adjusted for rounding of other numbers in the schedule.

Each rental payment after the first includes both an amount that represents interest and an amount that represents a reduction of principal. The periodic reduction of principal is sufficient that, at the end of the lease term, the outstanding balance is zero.

An interesting aspect of the amortization schedule that you may want to note at this point relates to a disclosure requirement that we discuss at the end of the chapter. Among other things, the lessee and lessor must report separately the current and noncurrent portions of the outstanding lease balance. Both amounts are provided by the amortization schedule. For example, if we want the amounts to report on the 1997 balance sheet, refer to the next row of the schedule. The portion of the 1998 payment that represents principal ($68,301) is the *current* (as of December 31, 1997) balance. The *noncurrent* amount is the balance outstanding after the 1998 reduction ($248,686). These amounts are the current and noncurrent lease liability for the lessee and the current and noncurrent net investment for the lessor.

Depreciation

Depreciation is recorded for leased assets in a manner consistent with the lessee's usual policy for depreciating its operational assets.

Because a capital lease assumes the lessee purchased the asset, the lessee depreciates its cost.

End of Each Year		
Sans Serif Publishers, Inc. (Lessee)		
Depreciation expense ($479,079 ÷ 6 years*)	79,847	
Accumulated depreciation		79,847
*If the lessee depreciates assets by the straight-line method.		

The depreciation period is restricted to the lease term unless the lease provides for transfer of title or a BPO.

Depreciation Period.   The lessee normally should depreciate a leased asset over the term of the lease. However, if ownership transfers or a bargain purchase option is present (i.e., either of the first two classification criteria is met), the asset should be depreciated over its useful life. This means depreciation is recorded over the useful life of the asset to the lessee.

A description of leased assets and related depreciation provided in a recent disclosure note (Graphic 15–6) of Fruit of the Loom, Inc., is representative of leased asset disclosures.

Disclosure of Leased Assets—Fruit of the Loom, Inc.

(In Part): Lease Commitments
Assets recorded under capital leases are included in Property, Plant and Equipment as follows (in thousands of dollars):

	December 31	
	1995	1994
Land	$ 10,200	$ 9,800
Buildings, structures and improvements	71,700	72,900
Machinery and equipment	95,800	94,800
	177,700	177,500
Less accumulated depreciation	(85,700)	(78,500)
	$ 92,000	$ 99,000

Rental expense for operating leases amounted to $30,200,000, $20,200,000, and $11,600,000 in 1995, 1994, and 1993, respectively.

Accrued Interest

If a company's reporting period ends at any time between payment dates, it is necessary to record (as an adjusting entry) any interest that has accrued since interest was last recorded. We purposely avoided this step in the previous illustration by assuming that the lease agreement specified rental payments on December 31—the end of the reporting period. But if payments were made on another date, or if the company's fiscal year ended on a date other than December 31, accrued interest would be recorded prior to preparing financial statements. For example, if the inception of the lease had been a day later (January 1, 1997) and rental payments were made on January 1 of each year, the effective interest amounts shown in the lease amortization schedule still would be appropriate but would be recorded one day prior to the actual rental payment. For instance, the second cash payment of $100,000 would occur on January 1, 1998, but the interest component of that payment ($37,908) would be accrued a day earlier as shown in Illustration 15–2b.

> At each financial statement date, any interest that has accrued since interest was last recorded must be accrued for all liabilities and receivables, including those relating to leases.

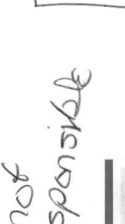

Read-not Responsible

ILLUSTRATION   15–2b

Journal Entries When Interest Is Accrued Prior to the Lease Payment

LESSEE

	Net Payable
	$479,079
	(100,000)
	$379,079
	(62,092)
	$316,987

LESSOR

Gross Rec'ble	Unearned Interest	Net Rec'ble
$600,000	(120,921)	$479,079
(100,000)	0	(100,000)
$500,000	(120,921)	$379,079
(100,000)	37,908	(62,092)
$400,000	(83,013)	$316,987

December 31, 1997 (to accrue interest)		
Sans Serif Publishers, Inc. (Lessee)		
Interest expense [10% × ($479,079 − 100,000)]	37,908	
Interest payable		37,908
First LeaseCorp (Lessor)		
Unearned interest revenue	37,908	
Interest revenue [10% × ($479,079 − 100,000)]		37,908
Second Lease Payment (January 1, 1998)		
Sans Serif Publishers, Inc. (Lessee)		
Interest payable (from adjusting entry above)	37,908	
Lease payable (difference)	62,092	
Cash (rental payment)		100,000
First LeaseCorp (Lessor)		
Cash (rental payment)	100,000	
Lease receivable		100,000

Notice that this is consistent with recording accrued interest on any debt, whether in the form of a note, a bond, or a lease.

We assumed in this illustration that First LeaseCorp bought the copier for $479,079 and then leased it for the same price. There was no profit on the "sale" itself. The only income derived by the lessor was interest revenue earned over the lease term. In effect, First LeaseCorp financed the purchase of the computer by Sans Serif Publishers. This type of lease is a direct financing lease. This kind of leasing is a thriving industry. It is a profitable part of operations for banks and other financial institutions (Citicorp is one of the largest). Some leasing companies do nothing else. Often leasing companies, like IBM Credit Corporation, are subsidiaries of larger corporations, formed for the sole purpose of conducting financing activities for their parent corporations.

CONCEPT REVIEW EXERCISE   DIRECT FINANCING LEASE

United Cellular Systems leased a satellite transmission device from Pinnacle Leasing Services on January 1, 1998. Pinnacle paid $625,483 for the transmission device. Its fair market value is $625,483.   PV↗

Terms of the lease agreement and related information:

Lease term   3 years (6 semiannual periods)
Semiannual rental payments $120,000 – beginning of each period
Economic life of asset   3 years
Implicit interest rate   12% ÷2 = 6%
(Also lessee's incremental borrowing rate)

Required:
1. Prepare the appropriate entries for both United Cellular Systems and Pinnacle Leasing Services on January 1, the inception of the lease.
2. Prepare an amortization schedule that shows the pattern of interest expense for United Cellular Systems and interest revenue for Pinnacle Leasing Services over the lease term.
3. Prepare the appropriate entries to record the second lease payment on July 1, 1998, and adjusting entries on December 31, 1998 (the end of both companies' fiscal years).

CONCEPT REVIEW EXERCISE   SOLUTION

1. Prepare the appropriate entries for both United Cellular Systems and Pinnacle Leasing Services on January 1, the inception of the lease.

Present value of periodic rental payments:

Calculation of the present value of minimum lease payments

$$($120,000 \times 5.21236^*) = $625,483$$
*Present value of an annuity due of $1: n=6, i=6%.

January 1, 1998		
United Cellular Systems (Lessee)		
Leased equipment (calculated above)	625,483	
Lease payable (calculated above)		625,483
Lease payable	120,000	
Cash (rental payment)		120,000
Pinnacle Leasing Services (Lessor)		
Lease receivable ($120,000 × 6)	720,000	
Unearned interest revenue ($720,000 – 625,483)		94,517
Inventory of equipment (lessor's cost)		625,483
Cash (rental payment)	120,000	
Lease receivable		120,000

2. Prepare an amortization schedule that shows the pattern of interest expense for United Cellular Systems and interest revenue for Pinnacle Leasing Services over the lease term.

	Payments	Effective Interest	Decrease in Balance	Outstanding Balance
		(6% × Outstanding balance)		
1/1/98				625,483
1/1/98	120,000		120,000	505,483
7/1/98	120,000	.06(505,483) = 30,329	89,671	415,812
1/1/99	120,000	.06(415,812) = 24,949	95,051	320,761
7/1/99	120,000	.06(320,761) = 19,246	100,754	220,007
1/1/00	120,000	.06(220,007) = 13,200	106,800	113,207
7/1/00	120,000	.06(113,207) = 6,793*	113,207	0
	720,000	94,517	625,483	

* Adjusted for rounding of other numbers in the schedule.

3. Prepare the appropriate entries to record the second lease payment on July 1, 1998, and adjusting entries on December 31, 1998 (the end of both companies' fiscal years).

July 1, 1998

United Cellular Systems (Lessee)

Interest expense (6% × [$625,483 − 120,000])	30,329	
Lease payable (difference)	89,671	
Cash (rental payment)		120,000

Pinnacle Leasing Services (Lessor)

Cash (rental payment)	120,000	
Lease receivable (payment less executory costs)		120,000
Unearned interest revenue	30,329	
Interest revenue (6% × [$625,483 − 120,000])		30,329

December 31, 1998

United Cellular Systems (Lessee)

Interest expense (6% × $415,812: from schedule)	24,949	
Interest payable		24,949
Depreciation expense ($625,483 ÷ 3 years)	208,494	
Accumulated depreciation		208,494

Pinnacle Leasing Services (Lessor)

Unearned interest revenue	24,949	
Interest revenue (6% × $415,812: from schedule)		24,949

Let's turn our attention now to situations in which the lessors are manufacturers or retailers and use lease arrangements as a means of selling their products.

Sales-Type Leases

Learning objective 6
Describe and demonstrate how the lessor accounts for a sales-type lease.

OPENING CASE

Question 2

A **sales-type lease** differs from a direct financing lease in only one respect. In addition to interest revenue earned over the lease term, the lessor receives a manufacturer's or dealer's profit on the "sale" of the asset.[20] This additional profit exists when the fair value of the asset (usually the present value of the minimum lease payments, or "selling price") exceeds the cost or carrying value of the asset sold. Accounting for a sales-type lease is the same as for a direct financing lease except for recognizing the profit at the inception of the lease.[21]

For illustration, let's modify our previous illustration. Assume all facts are the same except Sans Serif Publishers leased the copier directly from CompuDec Corporation, rather than through the financing intermediary. Also assume CompuDec's cost of the copier was $300,000. If you recall that the lease payments (their present value) provide a selling price of $479,079, you see that CompuDec receives a gross profit on the sale of $479,079 − 300,000 = $179,079. This sales-type lease is demonstrated in Illustration 15–3.

---

[20]A lessor need not be a manufacturer or a dealer for the arrangement to qualify as a sales-type lease. The existence of a profit (or loss) on the sale is the distinguishing factor.

[21]It is possible that the asset's carrying value will exceed its fair value, in which case a dealer's loss should be recorded.

ILLUSTRATION   15–3

Sales-Type Lease

**Lessor's Entries at
Inception—
Sales-Type Lease**

Sales revenue	$479,079
– COGS	300,000
Dealer's profit	$179,079

Remember, no interest has accrued when the first payment is made at the inception of the lease.

On December 31, 1996, Sans Serif Publishers, Inc., leased a copier from CompuDec Corporation at a price of $479,079.

The lease agreement specifies annual payments of $100,000 beginning December 31, 1996, the inception of the lease, and at each December 31 through 2001. The six-year lease term is equal to the estimated useful life of the copier.

CompuDec manufactured the copier at a cost of $300,000.

CompuDec's interest rate for financing the transaction is 10%.

Sales-Type Lease*

CompuDec Corporation (Lessor)

Lease receivable ($100,000 × 6)	600,000	
Cost of goods sold (lessor's cost)	300,000	
Sales revenue (present value of the minimum lease payments)		479,079
Unearned interest revenue ($600,000 - 479,079)		120,921
Inventory of equipment (lessor's cost)		300,000

First Lease Payment*

CompuDec Corporation (Lessor)

Cash	100,000	
Lease receivable		100,000

*Of course, the entries to record the lease and the first payment could be combined into a single entry:

Lease receivable ($600,000 - 100,000)	500,000	
Cost of goods sold	300,000	
Cash	100,000	
Unearned interest revenue		120,921
Sales revenue		479,079
Inventory of equipment		300,000

Recording a sales-type lease is similar to recording a sale of merchandise on account:

A/R . . . . {price}
  Sales rev. . . .   {price}
COGS . . . . {cost}
  Inventory . . .   {cost}

You should recognize the similarity between recording both the revenue and cost components of this sale by lease and recording the same components of other sales transactions. As in the sale of any product, gross profit is the difference between sales revenue and cost of goods sold.

All entries other than the entry at the inception of the lease, which includes the gross profit on the sale, are the same for a sales-type lease and a direct financing lease.

Accounting by the lessee is not affected by how the lessor classifies the lease. All lessee entries are precisely the same as in the previous illustration of a direct financing lease.

Graphic 15–7 shows the relationships among various lease components, using dollar amounts from the previous illustration.

GRAPHIC   15–7

Lease Payment Relationships

The difference between the total payments and their present value (selling price of the asset) represents interest.

If the price is higher than the cost to the lessor, the lessor realizes a profit on the sale.

Lessor: SALES-TYPE LEASE		Lessee: CAPITAL LEASE
Gross Investment in Lease*	$600,000	Minimum Lease Payments
	Less: Interest during Lease Term ($120,921)	
Selling Price (present value of payments)	Equals: $479,079	Purchase Price (present value of payments)
	Less: Profit on Sale† ($179,079)	
Cost to Lessor	Equals: $300,000	(Irrelevant to Lessee)

*The lessor's gross investment in the lease also would include any *unguaranteed* residual value in addition to the minimum lease payments. Also, any residual value guaranteed by the lessee is included in the minimum lease payments (both companies). We address these issues later in the chapter.
†If profit is zero, this would be a direct financing lease.

PART B   OTHER LEASE ACCOUNTING ISSUES

read, but not going thru in class

Residual Value

Learning objective 7
Explain how lease accounting is affected by the residual value of a leased asset.

The **residual value** of leased property is an estimate of what its commercial value will be at the end of the lease term. In our previous examples of nonoperating leases, we assumed that the residual value was negligible. But now let's consider the economic effect of a leased asset that does have a residual value and how that will affect the way both the lessee and the lessor account for the lease agreement.

Suppose the copier leased in Illustration 15–3 was expected to be worth $60,000 at the end of the six-year lease term. Should this influence the lessor's (CompuDec) calculation of periodic rental payments? Other than the possible influence on rental payments, should the lessee (Sans Serif Publishers) be concerned with the residual value of the leased assets? The answer to both questions is maybe. We'll use modified Illustration 15–4 to see why.

ILLUSTRATION   15–4

Residual Value

On December 31, 1996, Sans Serif Publishers, Inc., leased a color copier from CompuDec Corporation at a price of $479,079. The lease agreement specifies annual payments beginning December 31, 1996, the inception of the lease, and at each December 31 through 2001. The estimated useful life of the copier is seven years. At the end of the six-year lease term the copier is expected to be worth $60,000.

CompuDec manufactured the copier at a cost of $300,000.*
CompuDec's interest rate for financing the transaction is 10%.

*This provision is to be consistent with Illustration 15-3 which described a sales-type lease. However, our discussion of the effect of a residual value would be precisely the same if our illustration were of a direct financing lease (for instance, if the lessor's cost were $479,079) except that, of course, neither sales revenue nor cost of goods sold would be recorded in a direct financing lease.

In deciding whether the residual value affects how the lease is recorded, the first question that influences the answer is "Who gets the residual value?"

Who Gets the Residual Value?

If the *lessee* obtains title, the lessor's computation of rental payments is unaffected by any residual value.

Lessee Obtains Title.   Consider CompuDec (the lessor) first. Suppose Sans Serif will own the copier at the end of the lease term—by transfer of title or the expected exercise of a bargain purchase option. In that case, it is Sans Serif, not CompuDec, who will benefit by the residual value. So the lessor can't count on the $60,000 residual value to help recover its $479,079 investment. The lessor's computation of rental payments of $100,000 therefore is unaffected by the residual value.

On the other side of the transaction, the residual value influences the lessee only by the fact that depreciation calculations reflect a reduced depreciable amount. However, in determining the amount to capitalize as a leased asset and to record as a lease liability, the residual value is ignored. The capitalized amount is simply the present value of the minimum lease payments.

If the lessor retains title, the amount to be recovered through periodic lease payments is reduced by the present value of the residual amount.

Lessor Retains Title.   On the other hand, if CompuDec retains title to the asset, then it would anticipate receiving the $60,000 residual value at the conclusion of the lease term. That amount would contribute to the total amount to be recovered by the lessor and would reduce the amount needed to be recovered from the lessee through periodic rental payments. The amount of each payment would be reduced from $100,000 to $92,931, calculated in Illustration 15–4a.

ILLUSTRATION 15–4a

Lessor's Calculation of Rental Payments When Lessor Retains Residual Value

Amount to be recovered (fair market value)	$479,079
Less: Present value of the residual value ($60,000 × .56447*)	(33,868)
Amount to be recovered through periodic rental payments	$445,211
Rental payments at the beginning of each of the next six years: ($445,211 ÷ 4.79079†)	$ 92,931

*Present value of $1: n=6, i=10%
†Present value of an annuity due of $1: n=6, i=10%

On the other side of the transaction, the lessee (Sans Serif Publishers) considers the purchase price of the copier to include, at a minimum, the present value of the periodic rental payments ($445,211):

$$\$92,931 \times 4.79079^* = \$445,211†$$

Rental   Present

payments   value

*Present value of an annuity due of $1: n=6, i=10%.

†The multiplication actually produces $445,212.9. We use $445,211 to be consistent with the lessor's calculation ($445,211 ÷ 4.79079 = $92,931). The difference is due to rounding.

Whether or not the lessee's cost also includes an amount due to the residual value depends on whether the residual value is viewed as an additional "payment" by the lessee. It is viewed as an additional payment when the lessee *guarantees* the residual value to be a particular amount at the end of the lease term.

When the Residual Value Is Guaranteed

Sometimes the lease agreement includes a guarantee by the lessee that the lessor will recover a specified residual value when custody of the asset reverts back to the lessor at the end of the lease term. This not only reduces the lessor's risk but also provides incentive to the lessee to exercise a higher degree of care in maintaining the leased asset than it otherwise might. The lessee promises to return not only the property but also sufficient cash to provide the lessor with a minimum combined value. In effect, the guaranteed residual value is an additional lease payment that is to be paid in property, or cash, or both. As such, it is included in the minimum lease payments and affects the amount the lessee records as both a leased asset and a lease liability:

ILLUSTRATION 15–4b

Lessee's Calculation of the Present Value of Minimum Lease Payments Including a Guaranteed Residual Value

Present value of periodic rental payments ($92,931 × 4.79079*)	$445,211†
Plus: Present value of the residual value ($60,000 × .56447)	33,868
Present value of minimum lease payments	
(Recorded as a leased asset and a lease liability)	$479,079

*Present value of an annuity due of $1: n=6, i=10%.
†Present value of $1: n=6, i=10%.

You should notice that the lessee's calculation of the amount to capitalize is precisely the reverse of the lessor's calculation of periodic rental payments. This is because when the residual value is guaranteed, both view it as an additional lease payment. In accordance with *SFAS 13*, the guaranteed residual value is a component of the minimum lease payments for both the lessor and lessee.[22] We see in Graphic 15–8 how this affects the accounting for the lease as reflected in the lease amortization schedule for CompuDec and Sans Serif.

---

[22]Later you will see that when the residual value is *not* guaranteed, it is *not* considered a component of minimum lease payments for either the lessor or the lessee; but it still is considered a part of the lessor's gross investment in the lease and affects the amount of periodic lease payments.

Dec.31	Payments	Effective Interest	Decrease in Balance	Outstanding Balance
		(10% × Outstanding balance)		
1996				479,079
1996	92,931		92,931	386,148
1997	92,931	.10(386,148) = 38,615	54,316	331,832
1998	92,931	.10(331,832) = 33,183	59,748	272,084
1999	92,931	.10(272,084) = 27,208	65,723	206,361
2000	92,931	.10(206,361) = 20,636	72,295	134,066
2001	92,931	.10(134,066) = 13,407	79,524	54,542
2002	60,000	.10(54,542) = 5,458*	54,542	0
	617,586	138,507	479,079	

* Adjusted for rounding of other numbers in the schedule.

You should notice several points the amortization schedule reveals. First, the six periodic cash payments are now $92,931 as we calculated previously. Notice also that we now include the $60,000 residual value as an additional lease payment. Despite the different composition of the minimum lease payments, their present value ($479,079) is the same as when we assumed $100,000 periodic payments and no residual value. However, the effective interest that will be recorded over the lease term (as interest expense by the lessee and interest revenue by the lessor) now is more: $138,507. (It was $120,921 before.) The higher interest reflects the fact that payments are farther in the future, causing the outstanding lease balances (and interest on those balances) to be higher during the lease term. Also, note that the total of the lease payments now is more: $617,586. (It was $600,000 before.) This total is referred to as the lessor's **gross investment in the lease** and initially is recorded by the lessor as the lease receivable:[23]

Sales revenue	$479,079
–COGS	300,000
Dealer's profit	$179,079

Sales-Type Lease, December 31, 1996

Sans Serif Publishers, Inc. (Lessee)

Leased equipment (present value of lease payments)	479,079	
Lease payable (present value of lease payments)		479,079

CompuDec Corporation (Lessor)

Lease receivable [($92,931 × 6) + $60,000]	617,586	
Cost of goods sold (lessor's cost)	300,000	
Sales revenue (present value of minimum lease payments*)		479,079
Unearned interest revenue ($617,586 – 479,079)		138,507
Inventory of equipment (lessor's cost)		300,000

First Lease Payment, December 31, 1996

Sans Serif Publishers, Inc. (Lessee)

Lease payable	92,931	
Cash		92,931

CompuDec Corporation (Lessor)

Cash	92,931	
Lease receivable		92,931

*Minimum lease payments include the residual value because it's guaranteed.

Notice, too, that the timing of the $60,000 payment is December 31, 2002, the end of the lease term. Remember, the final periodic cash payment on December 31, 2001, is at the beginning of the final year. The journal entries that accompany this final cash payment are shown in Illustration 15–4d.

---

[23]Under the net method, the net investment in the lease ($479,079) would be recorded as the lessor's lease receivable.

ILLUSTRATION   15–4d

Entries to Accompany Final Periodic Payment

The residual value reduces the asset's depreciable cost to $419,079.

As the outstanding balance becomes less toward the end of the lease term, the portion of each payment that represents interest also becomes less.

December 31, 2001		
Sans Serif Publishers, Inc. (Lessee)		
Depreciation expense [($479,079 – 60,000)* ÷ 6 years]	69,847	
Accumulated depreciation		69,847
Interest expense (10% × outstanding balance)	13,407	
Lease payable (difference)	79,524	
Cash (rental payment)		92,931
CompuDec Corporation (Lessor)		
Cash (rental payment)	92,931	
Lease receivable		92,931
Unearned interest revenue	13,407	
Interest revenue (10% × outstanding balance)		13,407

* The depreciable cost is reduced by the lessee-guaranteed residual value.

At December 31, 2002, the lessee's book value of the fully depreciated copier is its $60,000 estimated residual value. If we assume that the actual residual value also is at least $60,000, then the lessee is not obligated to pay cash in addition to returning the copier to the lessor (demonstrated in Illustration 15–4e).[24]

ILLUSTRATION   15–4e

End of Lease Term—Actual Residual Value Equals The Guaranteed Amount

The sixth and final depreciation charge increases the balance in accumulated depreciation to $419,079.

The copier is reinstated on the books of the lessor at its fair value at the end of the lease term.

December 31, 2002		
Sans Serif Publishers, Inc. (Lessee)		
Depreciation expense [($479,079 – 60,000)* ÷ 6 years]	69,847	
Accumulated depreciation		69,847
Interest expense (10% × outstanding balance)	5,458	
Lease payable (difference)	54,542	
Accumulated depreciation (account balance)	419,079	
Leased equipment (account balance)		479,079
CompuDec Corporation (Lessor)		
Inventory of equipment (residual value)	60,000	
Lease receivable (account balance)		60,000
Unearned interest revenue (account balance)	5,458	
Interest revenue (10% × outstanding balance)		5,458

*The depreciable cost is reduced by the lessee-guaranteed residual value.

However, if we assume that the actual residual value at December 31, 2002, is only $25,000, then the lessee is obligated to pay $35,000 cash to the lessor in addition to returning the copier. The lessee records this payment as a loss.[25]

When the Residual Value Is Not Guaranteed

If the lessee doesn't guarantee the residual value, the asset and liability are recorded as the PV of periodic rental payments only.

The previous example demonstrates that when the residual value is guaranteed, both the lessor and lessee view it as a component of minimum lease payments. But what if the lessee does *not* guarantee the residual value? In that case, the lessee is not obligated to make any payments other than the periodic rental payments. As a result, the present value of the minimum lease payments—recorded as a leased asset and a lease liability—is simply the present value of periodic rental payments ($445,211). The same is true when the residual value is guaranteed by a third-party guarantor. (Insurance companies sometimes assume this role.)

From the lessor's perspective, the residual value is a component of minimum lease payments only if it is guaranteed (by either the lessee or a third-party guarantor). Yet, even if it is not guar-

---

[24]If the actual value is *more* than the estimated residual value, the lessor may realize a gain if and when the asset subsequently is sold, but the potential gain does not affect the entries at the end of the lease term.

[25]Sometimes by mutual agreement the lessee will sell the leased asset at the end of the lease term and remit the proceeds (plus any deficiency under the guarantee) to the lessor.

anteed, the residual value is viewed as a component of the lessor's gross investment in the lease. So, if we modify the previous illustration to assume the residual value is not guaranteed, the lessor's gross investment still is $617,586 [($92,931 × 6) + $60,000], but the sales revenue is only $445,211—the present value of the minimum lease payments. In other words, sales revenue includes the present value only of the periodic rental payments, not the unguaranteed residual value. Cost of goods sold is similarly reduced by present value of the unguaranteed residual value, as shown in Illustration 15–4f.

ILLUSTRATION   15–4f

Sales-Type Lease with Unguaranteed Residual Value

Dealer's profit is the same as when the residual value is guaranteed because both sales revenue and COGS are reduced by the same amounts.

Sales-Type Lease		
Sans Serif Publishers, Inc. (Lessee)		
Leased equipment (present value of lease payments)	445,211	
Lease payable (present value of lease payments)		445,211
CompuDec Corporation (Lessor)		
Lease receivable ([$92,931 × 6] + $60,000)	617,586	
Cost of goods sold ($300,000 – 33,868)	266,132	
Sales revenue ($479,079 – 33,868)*		445,211
Unearned interest revenue ($617,586 – 479,079)		138,507
Inventory of equipment (lessor's cost)		300,000
First Lease Payment		
Sans Serif Publishers, Inc. (Lessee)		
Lease payable	92,931	
Cash		92,931
CompuDec Corporation (Lessor)		
Cash	92,931	
Lease receivable		92,931

*Also can be calculated as the present value of the lessor's minimum lease payments, which do not include the unguaranteed residual value.

Sales revenue does not include the unguaranteed residual value because the revenue to be recovered from the lessee is lease payments only. The remainder of the lessor's gross investment is to be recovered—not from payment by the lessee (as is presumed when the residual value is guaranteed), but by selling, re-leasing, or otherwise obtaining value from the asset when it reverts back to the lessor. You might want to view the situation this way: The portion of the asset sold is the portion not represented by the unguaranteed residual value. So, both the asset's cost and its selling price are reduced by the present value of the portion not sold.

The lessor's net lease receivable is $479,079, as described in an earlier amortization schedule, even when the residual value is not guaranteed. However, the lessee's lease liability would be only $445,211 at the inception of the lease and would become zero with the final payment at the beginning of the final year, with reductions occurring in accordance with the pattern described by the schedule in Graphic 15–9.

GRAPHIC   15–9

Lessee's Amortization Schedule—Residual Value Not Guaranteed

Because the lessee does not guarantee the residual value, the lessee does not consider it to be an additional lease payment.

Dec. 31	Payments	Effective Interest	Decrease in Balance	Outstanding Balance
		(10% × Outstanding balance)		
1996				445,211
1996	92,931		92,931	352,280
1997	92,931	.10(352,280) = 35,228	57,703	294,577
1998	92,931	.10(294,577) = 29,458	63,473	231,104
1999	92,931	.10(231,104) = 23,110	69,821	161,283
2000	92,931	.10(161,283) = 16,128	76,803	84,480
2001	92,931	.10(84,480) = 8,451*	84,480	0
	557,586	112,375*	445,211*	

* Adjusted for rounding of other numbers in the schedule.

When the residual value is not guaranteed, the lessor bears any loss that results from the actual residual value of the leased asset being less than the original estimate.

Graphic 15–10 summarizes the effect of the residual value of a leased asset for each of the various possibilities regarding the nature of the residual value.

GRAPHIC   15–10

Effect of a Residual Value: A Summary

Is the **residual value** of a leased asset included in (a) the lessor's gross investment in the lease (thus affecting the computation by the **lessor** of the amount of the periodic rental payments), (b) the lessor's minimum lease payments (the present value is sales revenue in a sales-type lease), or (c) the lessee's minimum lease payments (the present value is the amount to be capitalized)?

| | Lessor's | | Lessee's |
	(a) Gross Investment in Lease *Computation of Payments*	(b) Minimum Lease Payments *Sales Revenue*	(c) Minimum Lease Payments *Asset & Liability*
Lessee gets the residual value—by transfer of title or the expected exercise of a bargain purchase option	No	No	No
Lessor gets the residual value—title does *not* transfer; *no* bargain purchase option			
• Residual value is not guaranteed	Yes	No	No
• Residual value is guaranteed by the lessee.	Yes	Yes	Yes
• Residual value is guaranteed by a third party guarantor.	Yes	Yes	No

(handwritten: general definition only)

Bargain Purchase Options

We stipulated earlier that a **bargain purchase option (BPO)** is a provision of some lease contracts that gives the lessee the option of purchasing the leased property at a bargain price. We discussed BPOs in the context of how they affect the classification of leases, but none of our earlier illustrations included a situation in which a BPO was present. You should have noted that a bargain price is defined in such a way that an additional cash payment is expected when a BPO is included in the agreement. Remember, a bargain price is one that is sufficiently below the property's expected fair value that the exercise of the option appears reasonably assured. Because exercise of the option appears at the inception of the lease to be reasonably assured, payment of the option price is expected to occur when the option becomes exercisable.

> **Learning objective 8**
> Describe the way a bargain purchase option affects lease accounting.

> When a BPO is present, both the lessor and the lessee view the option price as an additional lease payment.

The logic applied to lessee-guaranteed residual values in the previous section applies here too. The expectation that the option price will be paid effectively adds an additional cash flow to the lease for both the lessee and the lessor. That additional payment is included as a component of minimum lease payments for both the lessor and the lessee. It therefore (a) reduces the amount of the periodic rent payments the *lessor* must receive from the lessee and (b) is included in the computation of the amount to be capitalized (as an asset and liability) by the *lessee*. In fact, the way a BPO is included in these calculations is precisely the same way that a lessee-guaranteed residual value is included. This is demonstrated in Graphic 15–11.

GRAPHIC   15–11

Effect of a Bargain Purchase Option

✔ The lessor, when computing periodic rental payments, subtracts the present value of the BPO price from the amount to be recovered (fair market value) to determine the amount that must be recovered from the lessee through the periodic rent payments.

✔ The lessee adds the present value of the BPO price to the present value of periodic payments when computing the amount to be recorded as a leased asset and a lease liability.

To emphasize the similarity in the way a lessee-guaranteed[26] residual value and a BPO affect the calculations, let's assume the $60,000 in our last illustration is an option price that could be paid by Sans Serif at the conclusion of the lease to purchase the copier. To make this a "bargain" purchase option let's say the residual value at the same time is expected now to be $75,000. This situation is assumed in Illustration 15–5.

---

[26]The lessee-guaranteed qualification here refers to what you learned in the previous section: a residual value is part of the lessee's minimum lease payments only when guaranteed by the lessee; the lessor includes in its computation of rent payments any residual values that revert to the lessor—guaranteed or not.

ILLUSTRATION   15-5

Bargain Purchase Option

On December 31, 1996, Sans Serif Publishers, Inc., leased a color copier from CompuDec Corporation at a price of $479,079. The lease agreement specifies annual payments beginning December 31, 1996, the inception of the lease, and at each December 31 through 2001. The estimated useful life of the copier is seven years. At the end of the six-year lease term the copier is expected to be worth $75,000 and Sans Serif has the option to purchase it for $60,000 on that date. The residual value after seven years is zero.[27]

CompuDec manufactured the copier at a cost of $300,000.
CompuDec's interest rate for financing the transaction is 10%.

> The lessor's selling price is reduced by the present value of the BPO price to determine the amount that must be recovered from the periodic rental payments.

Amount to be recovered (fair market value)	$479,079
Less: Present value of the BPO price ($60,000 × .56447*)	(33,868)
Amount to be recovered through periodic rental payments	$445,211
Rental payments at the beginning of each of the next six years: ($445,211 ÷ 4.79079†)	$ 92,931

*Present value of $1: $n=6$, $i=10\%$.
†Present value of an annuity due of $1: $n=6$, $i=10\%$.

When you compare the way the *BPO* affected the lessor's (CompuDec's) calculation with the way the lessee-guaranteed residual value affected the calculation earlier, you see that they are exactly the same. That's the case also for the lessee (Sans Serif Publishers) as shown in Illustration 15–5a.

ILLUSTRATION   15-5a

Lessee's Calculation of the Present Value of Minimum Lease Payments When a BPO Is Present

> Because a BPO is expected to be exercised, its exercise price is viewed as one more cash payment.

Present value of periodic rental payments ($92,931 × 4.79079*)	$445,211
Plus: Present value of the BPO price ($60,000 × .56447†)	33,868
Present value of minimum lease payments (recorded as a leased asset and a lease liability)	$479,079

*Present value of an annuity due of $1: $n=6$, $i=10\%$.
†Present value of $1: $n=6$, $i=10\%$.

You should recognize this as the same calculation we used when there was no BPO but the residual value was guaranteed and so was considered an additional lease payment. A question you might have at this point is: Why are we now ignoring the residual value? Earlier it was considered an additional lease payment. Yet, now we view the BPO price as an additional lease payment but ignore the residual value. The reason is obvious when you recall an essential characteristic of a BPO—it's expected to be exercised. So, when it is exercised, title to the leased asset passes to the lessee and with title, any residual value. And remember, when the lessee gets the residual value it is ignored by both parties to the lease.

> When a BPO is present, the residual value becomes irrelevant.

The lease amortization schedule for CompuDec and Sans Serif when a BPO is included in the lease agreement (Graphic 15–12) should look familiar to you also.

GRAPHIC   15-12

Amortization Schedule—with BPO

> Both the lessor and lessee view the BPO price ($60,000) as an additional cash payment.

Dec. 31	Payments	Effective Interest	Decrease in Balance	Outstanding Balance
		(10% × Outstanding balance)		
1996				479,079
1996	92,931		92,931	386,148
1997	92,931	.10(386,148) = 38,615	54,316	331,832
1998	92,931	.10(331,832) = 33,183	59,748	272,084
1999	92,931	.10(272,084) = 27,208	65,723	206,361
2000	92,931	.10(206,361) = 20,636	72,295	134,066
2001	92,931	.10(134,066) = 13,407	79,524	54,542
2002	60,000	.10(54,542) = 5,458*	54,542	0
	617,586	138,507	479,079	

* Adjusted for rounding of other numbers in the schedule.

---

[27]Our discussion of the effect of a bargain purchase option would be precisely the same if our illustration were of a direct financing lease (for instance, if the lessor's cost were $479,079) except that, of course, neither sales revenue nor cost of goods sold would be recorded in a direct financing lease.

Recording the exercise of the option is similar to recording the periodic rent payments. That is, a portion of the payment covers interest for the year, and the remaining portion reduces the outstanding balance (to zero with this last payment), as shown in Illustration 15–5b.

ILLUSTRATION 15–5b

Journal Entries—with BPO

December 31, 2002		
Sans Serif Publishers, Inc. (Lessee)		
Depreciation expense ($479,079* ÷ 7 years)	68,440	
Accumulated depreciation		68,440
Interest expense (10% × $54,542)	5,458	
Lease payable (difference)	54,542	
Cash (BPO price)		60,000
CompuDec Corporation (Lessor)		
Cash (BPO price)	60,000	
Lease receivable (account balance)		60,000
Unearned interest revenue (account balance)	5,458	
Interest revenue (10% × outstanding balance)		5,458

*The residual value is zero after the full seven-year useful life.

> The depreciation entries reflect the fact that the lessee anticipates using the copier for its full seven-year life.

> The cash payment expected when the BPO is exercised represents part interest, part principal just like the other cash payments.

Note that depreciation also is affected by the BPO. As pointed out earlier, the lessee normally depreciates a leased asset over the term of the lease. But if ownership transfers by contract or by the expected exercise of a bargain purchase option, the asset should be depreciated over the asset's useful life. This reflects the fact that the lessee anticipates using the leased asset for its full useful life. In this illustration, the copier is expected to be useful for seven years, so depreciation is $68,440 ($479,079 ÷ 7 years).

When a BPO Is Exercisable before the End of the Lease Term

We assumed in this example that the BPO was exercisable on December 31, 2002—the end of the lease term. This assumption was convenient to illustrate the similarity between how a residual value and a BPO are dealt with when accounting for leases. It also is a very realistic assumption. Sometimes, though, the lease contract specifies that a BPO becomes exercisable before the designated lease term ends. Since a BPO is expected to be exercised, the lease term ends for accounting purposes when the option becomes exercisable. For example, let's say the BPO in the previous example could be exercised a year earlier—at the end of the fifth year. The effect this would have on accounting for the lease is to change the lease term from six years to five. All calculations would be modified accordingly. Stated differently, minimum lease payments include only the periodic cash payments specified in the agreement that occur prior to the date a BPO becomes exercisable. (We assume the option is exercised at that time and the lease ends.)

> The length of the lease term is limited to the time up to when a bargain purchase option becomes exercisable.

We have seen how minimum lease payments are affected by a residual value and by a bargain purchase option. Let's now consider how maintenance, insurance, taxes, and other costs usually associated with ownership (called *executory costs*) affect minimum lease payments.

ETHICAL DILEMMA

"I know we had discussed that they're supposed to be worth $24,000 when our purchase option becomes exercisable," Ferris insisted. "That's why we agreed to the lease terms. But, Jenkins, you know how fast computers become dated. We can make a good case that they'll be worth only $10,000 in three years."

The computers to which Ferris referred were acquired by lease. The lease meets none of the criteria for classification as a capital lease except that it contains an apparent bargain purchase option. Under the lease option, the computers can be purchased for $10,000 after three years.

"We could avoid running up our debt that way," Jenkins agreed. How could debt be avoided? Do you perceive an ethical problem?

✓ **Executory Costs**

need to know

One of the responsibilities of ownership that is transferred to the lessee in a capital lease is the responsibility to pay for maintenance, insurance, taxes, and any other costs usually associated with ownership. These are referred to as **executory costs**. Lease agreements usually are written in such a way that these costs are borne by the lessee. These expenditures simply are expensed by the lessee as incurred: repair expense, insurance expense, property tax expense, and so on. Let's return, for example, to Illustration 15–2. Now, suppose that a $2,000 per year maintenance agreement was arranged with an outside service for the leased copier. Sans Serif (the lessee) would expense this fee each year as incurred:

The lessee simply expenses executory costs as incurred.

Maintenance expense	2,000	
Cash (annual fee)		2,000

The lessor is unaffected by executory costs paid by the lessee.

Sometimes, as an expediency, a lease contract will specify that the lessor is to pay executory costs, but that the lessee will reimburse the lessor through higher rental payments. When rental payments are inflated for this reason, these executory costs are excluded in determining the minimum lease payments. They still are expensed by the lessee, even though paid through the lessor. For demonstration, let's modify Illustration 15–2 to assume the periodic rental payments were increased to $102,000 with the provision the lessor (First LeaseCorp) pays the maintenance fee. We do this in Illustration 15–6.

Any portion of rental payments that represents maintenance, insurance, taxes, or other executory costs is not considered part of minimum lease payments.

ILLUSTRATION 15–6

Rental Payments Including Executory Costs Paid by the Lessor

On December 31, 1996, Sans Serif Publishers, Inc., leased a copier from First LeaseCorp. First LeaseCorp purchased the equipment from CompuDec Corporation at a cost of $479,079.

- Six annual payments of $102,000 beginning December 31, 1996.
- Payments include $2,000 which First LeaseCorp will use to pay an annual maintenance fee.
- The interest rate in these financing arrangements is 10%.
- Capital lease to Sans Serif.
- Direct financing lease to First LeaseCorp.
- Interest rate: 10%.

Second Payment (December 31, 1997)

Sans Serif Publishers, Inc. (Lessee)

Maintenance expense (1997 fee)	2,000	
Prepaid maintenance (paid in 1996)		2,000
Interest expense [10% × ($479,079 − 100,000)]	37,908	
Lease payable (difference)	62,092	
Prepaid maintenance (1998 fee)	2,000	
Cash (rental payment)		102,000

First LeaseCorp (Lessor)

Cash (rental payment)	102,000	
Lease receivable		100,000
Maintenance fee payable*		2,000
Unearned interest revenue	37,908	
Interest revenue (10% × [$600,000 − 120,921 − 100,000])		37,908

*This assumes the $2,000 maintenance fee has not yet been paid to the outside maintenance service.

Executory costs that are included in periodic rental payments to be paid by the lessor are, in effect, indirectly paid by the lessee—and expensed by the lessee.

Amounts recorded for periodic interest and the periodic reduction of principal are unaffected by executory costs.

Discount Rate

An important factor in the overall lease equation that we've glossed over until now is the discount rate used in present value calculations. Because lease payments occur in future periods, we must consider the time value of money when evaluating their present value. The rate is important because it influences virtually every amount reported in connection with the lease by both the lessor and the lessee.

One rate is implicit in the lease agreement. This is the effective interest rate the lease payments provide the lessor over and above the price at which the asset is sold under the lease. It is the desired rate of return the lessor has in mind when deciding the size of the rental payments. (Refer to our earlier calculations of the periodic rental payments.) Usually the lessee is aware of the lessor's implicit rate or can infer it from the asset's fair market value. When the lessor's implicit rate is unknown, the lessee should use its own incremental borrowing rate. This is the rate the lessee would be expected to pay a bank if funds were borrowed to buy the asset.[28] When the lessor's implicit rate *is* known, the lessee should use the lower of the two rates.

The lessee uses the lower of the interest rate implicit in the lease or the lessee's own incremental borrowing rate.

---

[28]*Incremental borrowing rate* refers to the fact that lending institutions tend to view debt as being increasingly risky as the level of debt increases. Thus, additional (i.e., incremental) debt is likely to be loaned at a higher interest rate than existing debt, other things being equal.

When the Lessee's Incremental Borrowing Rate Is Less than the Lessor's Implicit Rate

Instances are few in which the lessee actually would use its incremental borrowing rate. Here's why. We noted earlier that, like any other asset, a leased asset should not be recorded at more than its fair market value. Look what happens to the present value of lease payments if Sans Serif uses a discount rate less than the 10% rate implicit in Illustration 15–6 (let's say 9%):

$$\underset{\substack{\text{Rental} \\ \text{payments}}}{\$100{,}000} \times 4.88965^* = \underset{\substack{\text{Lessee's} \\ \text{cost}}}{\$488{,}965}$$

*Present value of an annuity due of $1: $n=6$, $i=9\%$.

But remember, the fair market value of the copier was $479,079. The $100,000 amount for the rental payments was derived by the lessor, contemplating a market value of $479,079 and a desired interest rate of return (implicit rate) of 10%. So, using a discount rate lower than the lessor's implicit rate usually would result in the present value of minimum lease payments being more than the fair market value.

This conclusion does not hold when the leased asset has an unguaranteed residual value. You will recall that the lessor's determinations always include any residual value that accrues to the lessor; but when the lessee doesn't guarantee the residual value, it is *not* included in the lessee's present value calculations. Combining two previous examples, let's modify our demonstration of an unguaranteed residual value (Illustration 15–6) to assume the lessee's incremental borrowing rate was 9%. Because the residual value was expected to contribute to the lessor's recovery of the $479,079 fair market value, the rental payments were only $92,931. But, the lessee would ignore the unguaranteed residual value and calculate its cost of the leased asset to be $454,400.

$$\underset{\substack{\text{Rental} \\ \text{payments}}}{\$92{,}931} \times 4.88965^* = \underset{\substack{\text{Lessee's} \\ \text{cost}}}{\$454{,}400}$$

* Present value of an annuity due of $1: $n=6$, $i=9\%$.

In this case, the present value of minimum lease payments would be *less than* the fair market value even though a lower discount rate is used. But again, if there is no residual value, or if the lessee guarantees the residual value, or if the unguaranteed residual value is relatively small, a discount rate lower than the lessor's implicit rate will result in the present value of minimum lease payments being more than the fair market value.

When the Lessor's Implicit Rate Is Unknown

What if the lessee's discount rate is higher than the lessor's implicit rate? This is a logical question in light of the rule that says the lessee should use its own incremental borrowing rate when the lessor's implicit rate is unknown to the lessee. But in practice the lessor's implicit rate usually is known. Even if the lessor chooses not to explicitly disclose the rate, the lessee usually can deduce the rate using information he knows about the value of the leased asset and the lease payments. After all, in making the decision to lease rather than buy, the lessee typically becomes quite knowledgeable about the asset.

Even so, it is possible that a lessee might be unable to derive the lessor's implicit rate. This might happen, for example, if the leased asset has a relatively high residual value. Remember, a residual value (guaranteed or not) is an ingredient in the lessor's calculation of the rental payments. Sometimes it may be hard for the lessee to identify the residual value estimated by the lessor if the lessor chooses not to make it known.[29] The longer the lease term or the more risk of obsolescence the leased asset is subject to, the less of a factor the residual value typically is.

---

[29]Disclosure requirements provide that the lessor must disclose the components of their investments in nonoperating leases, which would include any estimated residual values. But the disclosures are aggregate amounts, not amounts of individual leased assets.

Additional Consideration

As pointed out earlier, the management of a lessee company sometimes will try to structure a lease to avoid the criteria that would cause the lease to be classified as a capital lease in order to gain the questionable advantages of off-balance-sheet financing. On the other hand, a lessor normally would prefer recording a **nonoperating** lease, other things being equal. Two ways sometimes used to structure a lease to qualify as an operating lease by the lessee, but as a nonoperating lease by the lessor are: (1) cause the two parties to use different interest rates and (2) avoid including the residual value in the lessee's minimum lease payments. Let's see how they work:

1. Cause the two parties to use different interest rates.

It was pointed out earlier that a lessee sometimes can claim to be unable to determine the lessor's implicit rate. Not knowing the lessor's implicit rate would permit the lessee to use its own incremental borrowing rate. If higher than the lessor's implicit rate, the present value it produces may cause the 90% of fair value criterion **not** to be met for the lessee (thus an operating lease) even though the criterion is met for the lessor (thus a nonoperating lease).

2. Avoid including the residual value in the lessee's minimum lease payments.

The residual value, if guaranteed by the lessee or by a third party guarantor, is included in the minimum lease payments by the lessor when applying the 90% of fair value criterion and thus increases the likelihood that it is met. However, when the residual value is guaranteed by a third-party guarantor and not by the lessee, it is **not** included in the lessee's minimum lease payments. So, if a residual value is sufficiently large and guaranteed by a third-party guarantor, it may cause the 90% of fair value criterion to be met by the lessor, but not by the lessee.

Both schemes are unintentionally encouraged by lease accounting rules. As long as arbitrary cutoff points are used (90% of fair value in this case), maneuvers will be devised to circumvent them.

Lessor's Initial Direct Costs

The costs incurred by the lessor that are associated directly with originating a lease and are essential to acquire that lease are referred to as **initial direct costs**. They include legal fees, commissions, evaluating the prospective lessee's financial condition, and preparing and processing lease documents. The method of accounting for initial direct costs depends on the nature of the lease. Remember, a lessor can classify a lease as (1) an operating lease, (2) a direct financing lease, or (3) a sales-type lease. The accounting treatment for initial direct costs by each of the three possible lease types is summarized below.

1. For *operating leases,* initial direct costs are recorded as assets and amortized over the term of the lease. Since the only revenue an operating lease produces is rental revenue, and that revenue is recognized over the lease term, initial direct costs also are automatically recognized over the lease term to match these costs with the rent revenues they help generate.

2. In *direct financing leases,* interest revenue is earned over the lease term, so initial direct costs are matched with the interest revenues they help generate. Therefore, initial direct costs are not expensed at the outset but are deferred and recognized over the lease term. This can be accomplished by reducing the lessor's *unearned interest revenue* by the total of initial direct costs. Then, as unearned interest revenue is recognized over the lease term at a constant effective rate, the initial direct costs are recognized at the same rate (that is, proportionally).

3. For *sales-type leases,* initial direct costs are expensed at the inception of the lease. Since the usual reason for a sales-type lease is for a manufacturer or a dealer to sell its product, it's reasonable to recognize the costs of creating the transaction as a selling expense in the period of the sale.

Contingent Rentals

Sometimes rental payments may be increased (or decreased) at some future time during the lease term, depending on whether or not some specified event occurs. Usually the contingency is related to revenues or profitability above some designated level. For example, a recent annual report of Kmart Corporation included the note recreated in Graphic 15–13.

Disclosure of Contingent Rentals—Kmart

> *Note L (in Part): Leases*
>
> . . . Certain leases provide for additional rental payments based on a percentage of sales in excess of a specified base. . . .

Contingent rentals are *not* included in the minimum lease payments because they are not determinable at the inception of the lease. Instead, they are included as components of income when (and if) they occur. Increases or decreases in rental payments that are dependent only on the passage of time are not contingent rentals; these are part of minimum lease payments.

Although contingent rentals are not included in minimum lease payments, they are reported in disclosure notes by both the lessor and lessee.

A Brief Summary

Leasing arrangements often are complex. In studying this chapter you've encountered several features of lease agreements that alter the way we make several of the calculations needed to account for leases. Graphic 15–14 provides a concise review of the essential lease accounting components, using calculations from a hypothetical lease situation to provide a numerical perspective.

Lease Terms and Concepts: A Summary

Lease Situation for Calculations

($ in 000s)

Lease term (years)	4	Lessor's cost	$300
Asset's useful life (years)	5	Residual value:	
Lessor's implicit rate (known by lessee)	12%	Guaranteed by lessee	$8
Lessee's incremental borrowing rate	13%	Guaranteed by third party[a]	$6
Rental payments (including executory		Unguaranteed	$5
costs) at the beginning of each year	$102	Executory costs paid annually by lessor	$2
		Bargain purchase option	none
		Initial direct costs	3

Amount	Description	Calculation
LESSOR'S:		
Gross investment in the lease[b]	Total of periodic rental payments[c] plus any residual value that reverts to the lessor (guaranteed or not) or plus BPO price[d]	($100 × 4) + ($8 + 6 + 5) = $419
Net investment in the lease	Present value of the gross investment (discounted at lessor's rate) plus any initial direct costs in a direct financing lease	($100 × 3.40183[e]) + ($19 × .63552[f]) = $352[g]
Unearned interest revenue	Gross investment – Net investment	$419 – 352 = $67
Minimum lease payments	Total of periodic rental payments[c] plus residual value guaranteed to the lessor (by lessee and/or by third party) or plus BPO price[d]	($100 × 4) + ($8 + 6) = $414
Sales revenue	Present value of lessor's minimum lease payments; also, net investment – present value of unguaranteed residual value	($100 × 3.40183[e]) + ($14 × .63552[f]) = $349; also: $352 – ($5 × .63552) = $349
Cost of goods sold	Lessor's cost – present value of unguaranteed residual value	$300 – ($5 × .63552[f]) = $297
Dealer's profit	Sales revenue – cost of goods sold; also, net investment – lessor's cost	$349 – 297 = $52; also, $352 – 300 = $52
LESSEE'S:		
Minimum lease payments	Total of periodic rental payments[c] plus residual value guaranteed by lessee or plus BPO price[d]	($100 × 4) + $8 = $408
Leased asset	Present value of minimum lease payments (using lower of lessor's rate and lessee's incremental borrowing rate); cannot exceed fair value	($100 × 3.40183[e]) + ($8 × .63552[f]) = $345

GRAPHIC   15-14
continued

Amount	Description	Calculation
Lease liability at inception	Same as leased asset	($100 × 3.40183[e]) + ($8 × .63552[f]) = $345

[a]Beyond any amount guaranteed by the lessee (amount guaranteed is $8 + $6 minus any amount paid by the lessee).
[b]This is the amount to be recovered by the lessor and therefore is used in the calculation of periodic lease payments. It also is the lease receivable at the inception of lease.
[c]Any portion of rental payments that represents maintenance, insurance, taxes, or other executory costs is not considered part of minimum lease payments. In this case, rentals are reduced as follows: $102 − 2 = $100.
[d]In this context, a residual value and a BPO price are mutually exclusive: if a BPO exists, any residual value is expected to remain with the lessee and is not considered an additional payment.
[e]Present value of an annuity due of $1: $n=4, i=12\%$.
[f]Present value of $1: $n=4, i=12\%$.
[g]Since this is a sales-type lease ($352 − 300 = $52 dealer's profit), initial direct costs are expensed at the lease's inception and do not increase the net investment in the lease.

don't do

CONCEPT REVIEW EXERCISE

VARIOUS LEASE ACCOUNTING ISSUES

(This is an extension of the previous Concept Review Exercise.)

United Cellular Systems leased a satellite transmission device from Satellite Technology Corporation on January 1, 1998. Satellite Technology paid $500,000 for the transmission device. Its retail value is $653,681.

Terms of the lease agreement and related information:

Lease term	3 years (6 semiannual periods)
Semiannual rental payments	$123,000—beginning of each period
Economic life of asset	4 years
Implicit interest rate	12%
(Also lessee's incremental borrowing rate)	
Unguaranteed residual value	$40,000
Regulatory fees paid by lessor	$3,000 / twice each year (included in rentals)
Lessor's initial direct costs	$4,500
Contingent rental payments	Additional $4,000 if revenues exceed a specified base

Required:

1. Prepare an amortization schedule that describes the pattern of interest expense over the lease term for United Cellular Systems.
2. Prepare an amortization schedule that describes the pattern of interest revenue over the lease term for Satellite Technology.
3. Prepare the appropriate entries for both United Cellular Systems and Satellite Technology on January 1 and June 30, 1998.
4. Prepare the appropriate entries for both United Cellular Systems and Satellite Technology on December 31, 2000 (the end of the lease term), assuming the device is returned to the lessor and its actual residual value is $14,000 on that date.

CONCEPT REVIEW EXERCISE

SOLUTION

1. Prepare an amortization schedule that describes the pattern of interest expense over the lease term for United Cellular Systems.

Calculation of the Present Value of Minimum Lease Payments

Present value of periodic rental payments excluding executory costs of $3,000:

$$(\$120,000 \times 5.21236^*) = \$625,483$$

*Present value of an annuity due of $1: $n=6, i=6\%$.
Note: The *unguaranteed* residual value is excluded from minimum lease payments for both the lessee and lessor.

	Payments	Effective Interest	Decrease in Balance	Outstanding Balance
		(6% × Outstanding balance)		
1/1/98				625,483
1/1/98	120,000		120,000	505,483
6/30/98	120,000	.06(505,483) = 30,329	89,671	415,812
1/1/99	120,000	.06(415,812) = 24,949	95,051	320,761
6/30/99	120,000	.06(320,761) = 19,246	100,754	220,007
1/1/00	120,000	.06(220,007) = 13,200	106,800	113,207
6/30/00	120,000	.06(113,207) = 6,793*	113,207	0
	720,000	94,517	625,483	

* Adjusted for rounding of other numbers in the schedule.

2. Prepare an amortization schedule that describes the pattern of interest revenue over the lease term for Satellite Technology.

Calculation of the Lessor's Net Investment

Present value of periodic rental payments excluding executory costs of $3,000 ($120,000 × 5.21236*)	$625,483
Plus: Present value of the unguaranteed residual value ($40,000 × .70496†)	28,198
Lessor's net investment in lease	$653,681

* Present value of an annuity due of $1: n=6, i=6%.
†Present value of $1: n=6, i=6%.
Note: The *unguaranteed* residual value is excluded from minimum lease payments, but is part of the lessor's gross and net investment in the lease.

	Payments	Effective Interest	Decrease in Balance	Outstanding Balance
		(6% × Outstanding balance)		
1/1/98				653,681
1/1/98	120,000		120,000	533,681
6/30/98	120,000	.06 (533,681) = 32,021	87,979	445,702
1/1/99	120,000	.06 (445,702) = 26,742	93,258	352,444
6/30/99	120,000	.06 (352,444) = 21,147	98,853	253,591
1/1/00	120,000	.06 (253,591) = 15,216	104,784	148,807
6/30/00	120,000	.06 (148,807) = 8,928	111,072	37,735
12/31/00	40,000	.06(37,735) = 2,265*	37,735	0
	760,000	106,319	653,681	

*Adjusted for rounding of other numbers in the schedule.

3. Prepare the appropriate entries for both United Cellular Systems and Satellite Technology on January 1 and June 30, 1998.

January 1, 1998

United Cellular Systems (Lessee)

Leased equipment (calculated above)	625,483	
Lease payable (calculated above)		625,483
Lease payable (payment less executory costs)	120,000	
Regulatory fees expense (executory costs)	3,000	
Cash (rental payment)		123,000

Satellite Technology (Lessor)

Lease receivable [($120,000 × 6) + $40,000[a]]	760,000	
Cost of goods sold [$500,000 − ($40,000[a] × .70496)]	471,802	
Sales revenue (present value of minimum lease payments[b])		625,483
Unearned interest revenue ($760,000 − 653,681)		106,319
Inventory of equipment (lessor's cost)		500,000
Selling expense	4,500	
Cash (initial direct costs)		4,500
Cash (rental payment)	123,000	
Regulatory fees payable (or cash)		3,000
Lease receivable (payment less executory costs)		120,000

[a] This is the unguaranteed residual value.
[b] Also, $653,681 − ($40,000[a] × .70496)

June 30, 1998		
United Cellular Systems (Lessee)		
Interest expense (6% × [$625,483 – 120,000])	30,329	
Lease payable (difference)	89,671	
Regulatory fees expense (annual fee)	3,000	
Cash (rental payment)		123,000
Satellite Technology (Lessor)		
Cash (lease payment)	123,000	
Regulatory fees payable (or cash)		3,000
Lease receivable (payment less executory costs)		120,000
Unearned interest revenue	32,021	
Interest revenue [6% × ($653,681 – 120,000)]		32,021

4. Prepare the appropriate entries for both United Cellular Systems and Satellite Technology on December 31, 2000 (the end of the lease term), assuming the device is returned to the lessor and its actual residual value is $14,000 on that date.

December 31, 2000		
United Cellular Systems (Lessee)		
Depreciation expense ($625,483 ÷ 3 years)	208,494	
Accumulated depreciation		208,494
Accumulated depreciation (account balance)	625,483	
Leased equipment (account balance)		625,483
Satellite Technology (Lessor)		
Inventory of equipment (actual residual value)	14,000	
Loss on leased assets ($40,000 – $14,000)	26,000	
Lease receivable (account balance)		40,000
Unearned interest revenue (account balance)	2,264	
Interest revenue (6% × $37,735: from schedule)		2,264

Sale-Leaseback Arrangements

Learning objective 9
Explain sale-leaseback arrangements and their accounting treatment.

In a sale-leaseback transaction, the owner of an asset sells it and immediately leases it back from the new owner. Sound strange? Maybe, but this arrangement is common. In a sale-lease-back transaction two things happen:

1. The seller-lessee receives cash from the sale of the asset.
2. The seller-lessee pays periodic rent payments to the buyer-lessor to retain the use of the asset.

What motivates this kind of arrangement? The two most common reasons are: (1) If the asset had been financed originally with debt and interest rates have fallen, the sale-leaseback transaction can be used to effectively refinance at a lower rate. (2) The most likely motivation for a sale-leaseback transaction is to generate cash.

Capital Leases

Illustration 15–7 (shown at the top of the next page) demonstrates a sale-leaseback involving a capital lease.

Recording a sale-leaseback transaction follows the basic accounting concept of substance over form.

The sale and simultaneous leaseback of the warehouses should be viewed as a single borrowing transaction. Although there appear to be two separate transactions, look closer at the substance of the agreement. Teledyne still retains the use of the warehouses that it had prior to the sale-leaseback. What is different? Teledyne has $900,000 cash and a noncancelable obligation to make annual payments of $133,155. In substance, Teledyne simply has borrowed $900,000 to be repaid over 10 years along with 10% interest. From the perspective of substance over form, we do not imme-

ILLUSTRATION   15–7

Sale-Leaseback

Teledyne Distribution Center was in need of cash. Its solution: sell its four warehouses for $900,000, then lease back the warehouses to obtain their continued use. The warehouses had a carrying value on Teledyne's books of $600,000 (original cost $950,000). Other information:

1. The sale date is December 31, 1997.
2. The noncancelable lease term is 10 years and requires annual payments of $133,155 beginning December 31, 1997. The estimated remaining useful life of the warehouses is 10 years.
3. The annual rental payments (present value $900,000) provide the lessor with a 10% rate of return on the financing arrangement.* Teledyne's incremental borrowing rate is 10%.
4. Teledyne depreciates its warehouses on a straight-line basis.

*$133,155	×	6.75902	=	$900,000 ($899,997.30 rounded)
Rent		(from Table 6A–6)		Present
payments		$n=10, i=10\%$		value

diately recognize the $300,000 gain on the sale of the warehouses but defer the gain to be recognized over the term of the lease (or the useful life of the asset if title is expected to transfer outright or by the exercise of a BPO), demonstrated in Illustration 15–7a.

ILLUSTRATION   15–7a

Recording a Sale-Leaseback

The gain on sale-leaseback is deferred and recognized over the lease term as a reduction of depreciation expense.

December 31, 1997		
Cash	900,000	
Accumulated depreciation ($950,000 − 600,000)	350,000	
Warehouses (cost)		950,000
Deferred gain on sale-leaseback (difference)		300,000
Leased warehouses (present value of lease payments)	900,000	
Lease payable (present value of lease payments)		900,000
Lease payable	133,155	
Cash		133,155
December 31, 1998		
Interest expense (10% × [$900,000 − 133,155])	76,684	
Lease payable (difference)	56,471	
Cash (rental payment)		133,155
Depreciation expense ($900,000 ÷ 10 years)	90,000	
Accumulated depreciation		90,000
Deferred gain on sale-leaseback ($300,000 ÷ 10 years)	30,000	
Depreciation expense		30,000

Since the lease term is equal to the expected useful life of the warehouses (>75%), the leaseback must be recorded by the lessee as a capital lease.[30] There typically is an interdependency between the lease terms and the price at which the asset is sold. The earnings process is not complete at the time of sale but is completed over the term of the lease. So, viewing the sale and the leaseback as a single transaction is consistent with the realization principle. Look closely at the 1997 entries to see the net effect of recording the sale leaseback this way. Amortizing the deferred gain over the lease term as a reduction of depreciation expense decreases depreciation each year to $60,000.[31] Interest expense is $76,684. If Teledyne had *not* sold the warehouses ($600,000 carrying value) and had borrowed $900,000 cash by issuing an installment note, the 1997 effect would have been virtually identical:

Depreciating the carrying value of the warehouses over their remaining useful life produces depreciation equal to the net depreciation recorded in a sale-leaseback.

December 31, 1998		
Interest expense (10% × [$900,000 − 133,155])	76,684	
Note payable (difference)	56,471	
Cash (installment payment)		133,155
Depreciation expense ($600,000 ÷ 10 years)	60,000	
Accumulated depreciation		60,000

[30]The fourth criterion also is met. The present value of lease payments ($900,000) is 100% (>90%) of the fair value of the warehouses ($900,000). Meeting any one of the four criteria is sufficient.

[31]If depreciation is over the useful life of the leased asset rather than the lease term because ownership is expected to transfer to the lessee, amortization of the deferred gain also would be over the useful life. If a leaseback of land is a capital lease, the amortization of the deferred gain is recorded as revenue.

The deferred gain is reported on the balance sheet as a valuation (contra) account, offsetting the leased asset. The 1998 balance sheet effect of the sale-leaseback transaction and a $900,000 installment note are compared in Graphic 15–15. Once again, the effect is virtually identical.

GRAPHIC   15–15

Comparison of a Sale-Leaseback and a Purchase

	Sale-Leaseback	Retain Asset; Borrow Cash
Assets:		
Leased asset	$900,000	$950,000
Less: Accumulated depreciation	(90,000)	(410,000)
Less: Deferred gain ($300,000 – 30,000)	(270,000)	
	$540,000	$540,000
Liabilities:		
Lease payable ($900,000 – 133,155 – 56,471)	$710,374	
Note payable ($900,000 – 133,155 – 56,471)		$710,374

Accounting by the buyer/lessor is no different in a sale-leaseback transaction than another lease transaction. That is, it records a lease in accordance with the usual lease guidelines.

Operating Leases — Read, not Responsible

If the leaseback portion of the previous sale-leaseback transaction were classified as an operating lease, the gain still would be deferred but would be recognized as a reduction of rent expense rather than depreciation. (There is no leased asset to depreciate.[32]):

December 31, 1998		
Deferred gain on sale-leaseback ($300,000 ÷ 10 years)	30,000	
Rent expense		30,000

Those of you with a healthy sense of skepticism will question whether the leaseback portion of our sale-leaseback situation could qualify as an operating lease. After all, the 10-year lease term is equal to the 10-year remaining useful life. But when you remember that neither the third (75% of economic life) nor the fourth (90% recovery) classification criterion applies if the inception of the lease occurs during the last 25% of an asset's economic life, you see the possibility of an operating lease. Suppose, for instance, that the original useful life of the warehouses was 40 years. In that case, the current lease term would occur during the last 25% of an asset's economic life and we would have an operating lease.

defer + amortize loss over life of lease

Losses on Sale-Leasebacks

In a sale-leaseback, any gain on the sale of the asset is deferred and amortized. However, a real loss on the sale of the property is recognized immediately—not deferred. A real loss means the fair value is less than the carrying amount of the asset. On the other hand, if the fair value exceeds the carrying amount, but the asset is sold to the buyer/lessor for less than the carrying amount, an artificial loss is produced that is probably in substance a prepayment of rent and should be deferred and amortized.

Real Estate Leases   Some leases involve land—exclusively, or in part. The concepts we discussed in the chapter also relate to real estate leases. But the fact that land has an unlimited life causes us to modify how we account for some leases involving real estate.

Leases of Land Only

Because the useful life of land is indefinite, the risks and rewards of ownership cannot be presumed transferred from the lessor to the lessee unless title to the land is expected to transfer—out-

---

[32]The deferred gain would be reported as a deferred liability since it could not be offset against a leased asset.

right or by the expected exercise of a bargain purchase option (criterion 1 or criterion 2). Since the useful life is undefined, the third and fourth criteria are not applicable. Relatedly, because the leased asset is land, depreciation is inappropriate.

> Only the first (title transfers) and second (BPO) classification criteria apply in a land lease.

Leases of Land and Building

When the leased property includes both land and a building and the lease transfers ownership or is expected to by exercise of a BPO, the lessee should record each leased asset separately. The present value of the minimum lease payments is allocated between the leased land and leased building accounts on the basis of their relative market values.

> When (a) the leased property includes both land and a building, (b) neither of the first two criteria is met, and (c) the fair value of the land is 25% or more of the combined fair value, both the lessee and the lessor treat the land as an operating lease and the building as any other lease.

When neither of the first two criteria is met, the question arises as to whether the third and fourth criteria apply. Because they logically should apply to the building (because its life is limited) but not to the land (because its life is unlimited), the profession employs an arbitrary guideline. If the fair value of the land is less than 25% of the combined fair value, it is in effect ignored and both the lessee and the lessor treat the land and building as a single unit. The single leased asset is depreciated as if land were not involved. If the fair value of the land is 25% or more of the combined fair value, both the lessee and the lessor treat the land and building as two separate leases. Thus, the land lease is an operating lease, and the building lease is classified and accounted for in the manner described in the chapter.

Leases of Only Part of a Building

> Usual lease accounting procedures apply to leases that involve only part of a building, although extra effort may be needed to arrive at reasonable estimates of cost and fair value.

Some of the most common of leases involve leasing only part of a building. For instance, businesses frequently lease space in an office building or individual stores in a shopping mall. Practical difficulties arise when applying lease accounting procedures in these situations. What is the cost of the third shop from the entrance in a $14 million mall? What is the fair value of a sixth floor office suite in a 40-floor office complex? Despite practical difficulties, usual lease accounting treatment applies. It may, however, be necessary to employ real estate appraisals or replacement cost information to arrive at reasonable estimates of cost or fair value.

Leveraged Leases

> A **leveraged lease** involves significant long-term, nonrecourse financing by a third-party creditor.

In a **leveraged lease**, a third-party, long-term creditor provides nonrecourse financing for a lease agreement between a lessor and lessee. The term *leveraged* refers to the fact that the lessor acquires title to the asset after borrowing a large part of the investment.

> A lessor records its investment (receivable) net of the nonrecourse debt and reports income from the lease only in those years when the receivable exceeds the liability.

From the lessee's perspective, accounting for a leveraged lease is not distinguishable from accounting for a nonleveraged lease. Accounting for leveraged leases by the lessor is similar to that for nonleveraged leases. A lessor records its investment (receivable) net of the nonrecourse debt. The lessor's liability to the lender should be offset against its lease receivable from the lessee because its role is in substance that of a mortgage broker. That is, the lessor earns income by serving as an agent for a firm wishing to acquire property and a lender seeking an investment. The lessor borrows enough cash from the lender to acquire the property, which is in turn leased to the lessee under a capital lease. Payments from the lessee are applied to the note held by the lender. The note may be assumed by the lessee *without recourse* such that the lessor is absolved of responsibility for its payment. In order to qualify for favorable treatment under the tax code, the lessor must maintain at least a minimum percentage of equity position in the asset. Also, the lessor should report income from the lease only in those years when the receivable exceeds the liability.

Lease Disclosures

Lease disclosure requirements are quite extensive for both the lessor and lessee. Virtually all aspects of the lease agreement must be disclosed. For *all* leases (a) a general description of the leasing arrangement is required as well as (b) minimum future payments, in the aggregate and for each of the five succeeding fiscal years. Other required disclosures are specific to the type of lease and include: residual values, contingent rentals, unearned interest, sublease rentals, and executory costs. Some representative examples are shown in Graphics 15–16 and 15–17.

IBM is a manufacturer that relies heavily on leasing as a means of selling its products. Its disclosure of sales-type leases is shown in Graphic 15–16.

GRAPHIC   15–16

Lessor Disclosure of Sales-Type Leases—IBM Corporation

F: Investments and Sundry Assets

	1995	1994
(Dollars in millions)		
Net investment in sales-type leases†	$14,007	$14,751
Less: Current portion (net)	5,961	6,351

†These leases relate principally to IBM equipment and are for terms generally ranging from three to five years. Net investment in sales-type leases includes unguaranteed residual values of approximately $470 million and $535 million at December 31, 1994 and 1993, and is reflected net of unearned income at these dates of approximately $2,100 million and $2,600 million, respectively. Scheduled maturities of minimum lease payments outstanding at December 31, 1995, expressed as a percentage of the total, are approximately as follows: 1996, 45 percent; 1997, 30 percent; 1998, 17 percent; 1999, 7 percent; 2000 and after, 1 percent.

Wal-Mart Stores leases facilities under both operating and capital leases. Its long-term obligations under these lease agreements are disclosed in a note to their financial statements (see Graphic 15–17).

GRAPHIC   15–17

Lessee Disclosure of Leases—Wal-Mart Stores

Note 7. Long-Term Lease Obligations

The Company and certain of its subsidiaries have long-term leases for stores and equipment. Rentals (including, for certain leases, amounts applicable to taxes, insurance, maintenance, other operating expenses, and contingent rentals) under all operating leases were $479 million in 1995, $361 million in 1994, and $313 million in 1993. Aggregate minimum annual rentals at January 31, 1995, under non-cancelable leases are as follows (in millions):

Fiscal years	Operating leases	Capital leases
1996	$ 386	$ 252
1997	403	251
1998	386	251
1999	334	249
2000	318	247
Thereafter	3,155	2,785
Total minimum rentals	$4,982	4,035
Less estimated executory costs		80
Net minimum lease payments		3,955
Less imputed interest at rates ranging from 6.1% to 14.0%		2,053
Present value of net minimum lease payments		$1,902

Certain of the leases provide for contingent additional rentals based on percentage of sales. Such additional rentals amounted to $42 million, $27 million, and $30 million in 1995, 1994, and 1993, respectively. Substantially all of the store leases have renewal options for additional terms from five to 25 years at the same or lower minimum rentals.

The Company has entered into lease commitments for land and buildings for 62 future locations. These lease commitments with real estate developers or through sale/leaseback arrangements provide for minimum rentals for 20 to 25 years, excluding renewal options, which, if consummated based on current cost estimates, will approximate $58 million annually over the lease terms.

A Decision-Makers' Perspective: Financial Statement Impact

As indicated in the Decision-Makers' Perspective at the beginning of the chapter, leasing can allow a firm to conserve assets, to avoid some risks of owning assets, and to obtain favorable tax benefits.

| Leasing sometimes is used as a means of off-balance-sheet financing.

These advantages are desirable. It also was pointed out earlier that some firms try to obscure the realities of their financial position through off-balance-sheet financing or by avoiding violating terms of contracts that limit the amount of debt a company can have. Accounting guidelines are designed to limit the ability of firms to hide financial realities. Nevertheless, investors and creditors should be alert to the impact leases can have on a company's financial position and on its risk.

Balance Sheet and Income Statement

Lease transactions identified as nonoperating impact several of a firm's financial ratios. Because we record liabilities for capital leases, the debt-equity ratio (liabilities divided by shareholders' equity) is immediately impacted. Because we also record leased assets, the immediate impact on the rate of return on assets (net income divided by assets) is negative, but the lasting effect depends on how leased assets are utilized to enhance future net income. As illustrated in this chapter, the financial statement impact of a capital lease is no different from that of an installment purchase.

> **Lease liabilities affect the debt-equity ratio and the rate of return on assets.**

Even operating leases, though, can significantly affect risk. Operating leases represent long-term commitments that can become a problem if business declines and cash inflows drop off. For example, long-term lease commitments became a big problem for Businessland in the early 1990s. The company's revenues declined but it was saddled with lease commitments for numerous facilities the company no longer occupied. Its stock's market price declined from $11.88 in 1990 to $.88 in 1991.

> **Do operating leases create long-term commitments equivalent to liabilities?**

Whether leases are capitalized or treated as operating leases affects the income statement as well as the balance sheet. However, the impact generally is not significant. Over the life of a lease, total expenses are equal regardless of the accounting treatment of a lease. If the lease is capitalized, total expenses comprise interest and depreciation. The total of these equals the total amount of rental payments, which would constitute rent expense if not capitalized. There is, however, a timing difference between lease capitalization and operating lease treatment, but the timing difference usually isn't great.

> **The net income difference between treating a lease as a capital lease versus an operating lease generally is not significant.**

The more significant difference between capital leases and operating leases is the impact on the balance sheet. As mentioned above, a capital lease adds to both the asset and liability side of the balance sheet; operating leases do not affect the balance sheet at all. How can external financial statement users adjust their analysis to incorporate the balance sheet differences between capital and operating leases? A frequently offered suggestion is to capitalize all noncancelable lease commitments, including those related to operating leases. Some financial analysts, in fact, do this on their own to get a better feel for a company's actual debt position.

> **The difference in impact on the balance sheet between capital leases and operating leases is significant.**

To illustrate, refer to Graphic 15–17 which reveals the operating lease commitments disclosed by Wal-Mart Stores. If these lease arrangements were considered nonoperating, these payments would be capitalized (reported at the present value of all future payments). By making some reasonable assumptions, we can estimate the present value of all future payments to be made on existing operating leases. For example, the interest rates used by Wal-Mart to discount rental payments on capital leases range from 6.1% to 14.0%. If we use the approximate average rate of 10%, and make certain other assumptions, we can determine the debt equivalent of the operating lease commitments as shown in Graphic 15–18.

GRAPHIC   15–18

Estimating the Debt Equivalent of Operating Lease Commitments

Capitalized Value or Debt Equivalent of Wal-Mart's Operating Leases

Fiscal Years	Operating Leases	PV Factor 10%	Present Value
1996	$ 386	.909	$ 351
1997	403	.826	333
1998	386	.751	290
1999	334	.683	228
2000	318	.621	197
Thereafter	3,155	.386*	1,218
Total minimum rentals	$4,982		$2,617

*This is the PV factor for i=10%, n=10, which treats payments after 2000 as occurring in 2005, an assumption due to not knowing precise dates of specific payments after 2000.

If capitalized, these operating lease commitments would add $2,617 million to Wal-Mart's liabilities and approximately $2,617 million to the company's assets.[33] Let's look at the impact this

---

[33]If these operating leases were capitalized, both assets and liabilities would increase by the same amount at inception of the lease. However, in later years, the leased asset account balance and the lease liability account will, generally, not be equal. The leased asset account is reduced by depreciation and the lease liability account is reduced (amortized) down to zero using the effective interest method.

would have on the company's debt to equity ratio and its return on assets ratio using selected financial statement information taken from Wal-Mart's 1995 annual report, shown below:

	($ in millions)
Total assets	$32,819
Total liabilities	20,093
Total shareholders' equity	12,726
Net income for 1995	2,681

The debt to equity and return on assets ratios are calculated below without considering the capitalization of operating leases and then again after adding $2,617 million to both total assets and total liabilities. In the calculation of return on assets, we use only the 1995 year-end total assets rather than the average total assets for the year. Also, we assume no impact on net income.

Ratios with and without capitalization of operating leases

($ in millions)	Without Capitalization	With Capitalization
Debt to equity ratio	$\dfrac{\$20,093}{\$12,726} = 1.58$	$\dfrac{\$22,710}{\$12,726} = 1.78$
Return on assets	$\dfrac{\$2,681}{\$32,819} = 8.2\%$	$\dfrac{\$2,681}{\$35,436} = 7.6\%$

The debt to equity ratio rises from 1.58 to 1.78, a 13% increase, and the return on assets ratio declines from 8.2% to 7.6%, a 7% decrease.

Statement of Cash Flow Impact

Operating leases are not reported on a statement of cash flows at the leases' inception.

On a statement of cash flows, lease payments (operating or nonoperating) are reported as cash flows from financing activities by the lessee and cash flows from investing activities by the lessor. The principal difference between an operating or a nonoperating lease is that the lease at its inception would be reported as a noncash investing/financing activity if treated as nonoperating, but not reported at all if treated as an operating lease.

Solution to Financial Reporting Case (at the opening of the chapter)

1. How would IBM's revenues "take a hit" as a result of more customers leasing than buying mainframes?

When IBM leases computers under operating leases, it reports revenue as it collects "rent" over the term lease. When IBM sells computers, on the other hand, it recognizes revenue "up front" in the year of sales. Actually, total revenues are not necessarily less with a lease, but are spread out over the several years of the lease term. This delays the recognition of revenues, creating the "hit" in the reporting periods in which a shift to leasing occurs.

2. Under what kind of leasing arrangements would the "hit" not occur?

The hit will not occur when IBM leases its computers under sales-type leases. In those cases, despite the fact that the contract specifies a lease, in effect, IBM actually sells its computers under the arrangement. Consequently, IBM will recognize sales revenue (and cost of goods sold) at the inception of the lease. The amount recognized is roughly the same as if customers actually buy the computers. As a result, the income statement will not receive the hit created by the substitution of operating leases for outright sales.

The Bottom Line

1. Leasing is used as a means of off-balance-sheet financing and to achieve operational and tax objectives.

2. In keeping with the concept of substance over form a lease is accounted for as either a rental agreement or a purchase/sale accompanied by debt financing.

3. A lessee should classify a lease transaction as a capital lease if it is noncancelable and if one or more of four classification criteria are met. Otherwise, it is an operating lease. A lessor records a lease as a direct financing lease or a sales-type lease only if two conditions relating to revenue realization are met in addition to one of the four classification criteria.

4. In an operating lease a sale is not recorded by the lessor; a purchase is not recorded by the lessee. Instead, the periodic rental payments are accounted for merely as rent revenue by the lessor, rent expense by the lessee.

5. In a capital lease the lessee records a leased asset at the present value of the minimum lease payments. A nonoperating lease is recorded by the lessor as a sales-type lease or direct financing lease, depending on whether the lease provides the lessor a dealer's profit.

6.   A sales-type lease requires recording sales revenue and cost of goods sold by the lessor at the inception of the lease. All other entries are the same as in a direct financing lease.

7.   A lessee-guaranteed residual value is included as a component of minimum lease payments for both the lessor and the lessee. An unguaranteed residual value is not (but is part of the lessor's gross investment in the lease).

8.   A bargain purchase option is included as a component of minimum lease payments for both the lessor and the lessee. The lease term effectively ends when the BPO is exercisable.

9.   A gain on the sale of an asset in a sale leaseback arrangement is deferred and amortized over the lease term (or asset life if title is expected to transfer to the lessee). The lease portion of the transaction is evaluated and accounted for like any lease.

Questions for Review of Key Topics

Question	15–1	The basic concept of "substance over form" influences lease accounting. Explain.
Question	15–2	How is interest determined in a nonoperating lease transaction. How does the approach compare to other forms of debt (say bonds payable or notes payable)?
Question	15–3	How are leases and installment notes the same? How do they differ?
Question	15–4	A lessee should classify a lease transaction as a capital lease if it is noncancelable and one or more of four classification criteria are met. Otherwise, it is an operating lease. What are these criteria?
Question	15–5	What is a bargain purchase option? How does it differ from other purchase options?
Question	15–6	Lukawitz Industries leased equipment to Seminole Corporation for a four-year period, at which time possession of the leased asset will revert back to Lukawitz. The equipment cost Lukawitz $4 million and has an expected useful life of six years. Its normal sales price is $5.6 million. The present value of the minimum lease payments for both the lessor and lessee is $5.2 million. The first payment was made at the inception of the lease. Collectibility of the remaining lease payments is reasonably assured, and Lukawitz has no material cost uncertainties. How should this lease be classified (a) by Lukawitz Industries (the lessor) and (b) by Seminole Corporation (the lessee)? Why?
Question	15–7	Can the present value of minimum lease payments differ between the lessor and lessee? If so, how?
Question	15–8	Compare the way a bargain purchase option and a residual value are treated by the lessee when determining minimum lease payments.
Question	15–9	What are executory costs? How are they accounted for by the lessee in a capital lease when paid by the lessee? When paid by the lessor? Explain.
Question	15–10	The discount rate influences virtually every amount reported in connection with a lease by both the lessor and the lessee. What is the lessor's discount rate when determining the present value of minimum lease payments? What is the lessee's discount rate?
Question	15–11	A lease might specify that rental payments may be increased (or decreased) at some future time during the lease term depending on whether or not some specified event occurs such as revenues or profits exceeding some designated level. Under what circumstances are contingent rentals included or excluded from minimum lease payments? If excluded, how are they recognized in income determination?
Question	15–12	The lessor's initial direct costs often are substantial. What are initial direct costs?
Question	15–13	When are initial direct costs recognized in an operating lease? In a direct financing lease? In a sales-type lease? Why?
Question	15–14	In a sale-leaseback transaction the owner of an asset sells it and immediately leases it back from the new owner. This dual transaction should be viewed as a single borrowing transaction. Why?
Question	15–15	Explain how the general classification criteria are applied to leases that involve land.
Question	15–16	What are the guidelines for determining when a material amount of land is involved in a lease?
Question	15–17	How does a leveraged lease differ from a nonleveraged lease?

Exercises

Exercise 15–1
Operating lease

On January 1, 1997, Nath-Langstrom Services, Inc., a computer software training firm, leased several computers from ComputerWorld Corporation under a two-year operating lease agreement. The contract calls for four rent payments of $10,000 each, payable semiannually on June 30 and December 31 each year. The computers were acquired by ComputerWorld at a cost of $90,000 and were expected to have a useful life of six years with no residual value.

Required:

Prepare the appropriate entries for both (a) the lessee and (b) the lessor from the inception of the lease through the end of 1997. (Use straight-line depreciation.)

Exercise 15–2
Operating lease; advance payment; leasehold improvement

[handwritten notes: adj Rent exp 80,000; Prepaid Rent 80,000; Rent exp (bonus) 33,000; Prepaid Rent 33,000]

On January 1, 1997, Winn Heat Transfer leased office space under a three-year operating lease agreement. The arrangement specified three annual rent payments of $80,000 each, beginning January 1, 1997, the inception of the lease, and at each January 1 through 1999. Winn also paid a $96,000 advance payment at the inception of the lease in addition to the first $80,000 rent payment. With permission of the owner, Winn made structural modifications to the building before occupying the space at a cost of $180,000. The useful life of the building and the structural modifications were estimated to be 30 years with no residual value.

Required:

Prepare the appropriate entries for Winn Heat Transfer from the inception of the lease through the end of 1997. Winn's fiscal year is the calendar year. Winn uses straight-line depreciation.

Exercise 15–3
Multiple choice; operating leases

The following questions dealing with various topics in this chapter appeared in the Theory and Practice sections of recent CPA examinations. Determine the response that best completes the statements or questions.

1. On January 2, 1996, Ral Co. leased land and building from an unrelated lessor for a 10-year term. The lease has a renewal option for an additional 10 years, but Ral has not reached a decision with regard to the renewal option. In early January 1996, Ral completed the following improvements to the property:

Description	Estimated Life	Cost
Sales office	10 years	$47,000
Warehouse	25 years	75,000
Parking lot	15 years	18,000

   Amortization of leasehold improvements for 1997 should be
   a. $7,000
   b. $8,900
   c. $12,200
   d. $14,000

2. As an inducement to enter a lease, Graf Co., a lessor, granted Zep, Inc., a lessee, 12 months of free rent under a five-year operating lease. The lease was effective on January 1, 1997, and provides for monthly rental payments to begin January 1, 1998. Zep made the first rental payment on December 30, 1997. In its 1997 income statement, Graf should report rental revenue in an amount equal to
   a. Zero.
   b. Cash received during 1997.
   c. One-fourth of the total cash to be received over the life of the lease.
   d. One-fifth of the total cash to be received over the life of the lease.

(Note: Exercises 4,5, and 6 are three variations of the same basic situation.)

Exercise 15–4
Capital lease; lessee

[handwritten notes: Lease Entry; Payment 1; Payment 2; Depreciation]

Manufacturers Southern leased high-tech electronic equipment from Edison Leasing on January 1, 1998. Edison purchased the equipment from International Machines at a cost of $112,080.

Related information:

Lease term	2 years (8 quarterly periods)
Quarterly rental payments	$15,000—beginning of each period
Economic life of asset	2 years
Fair value of asset	$112,080
Implicit interest rate	8% *← annual*
(Also lessee's incremental borrowing rate)	*quarterly rate = 2%*

Required:

~~Prepare a lease amortization schedule~~ and appropriate entries for Manufacturers Southern from the inception of the lease through January 1, 1999. Depreciation is recorded at the end of each fiscal year (December 31) on a straight-line basis.

Exercise 15–5

Direct financing lease; lessor

[handwritten: Lease Entry, Payment 1, Payment 2]

Edison Leasing leased high-tech electronic equipment to Manufacturers Southern on January 1, 1998. Edison purchased the equipment from International Machines at a cost of $112,080.

Related information:

Lease term	2 years (8 quarterly periods)
Quarterly rental payments	$15,000—beginning of each period
Economic life of asset	2 years
Fair value of asset	$112,080
Implicit interest rate	8%
(Also lessee's incremental borrowing rate)	*[handwritten: quarterly is 2%]*

Required:

~~Prepare a lease amortization schedule~~ and appropriate entries for Edison Leasing from the inception of the lease through January 1, 1999. Edison's fiscal year ends December 31.

Exercise 15–6

Sales-type lease; lessor

Manufacturers Southern leased high-tech electronic equipment from International Machines on January 1, 1998. International Machines manufactured the equipment at a cost of $85,000.

Related information:

Lease term	2 years (8 quarterly periods)
Quarterly rental payments	$15,000—beginning of each period
Economic life of asset	2 years
Fair value of asset	$112,080
Implicit interest rate	8%
(Also lessee's incremental borrowing rate)	

Required:

1. Show how International Machines determined the $15,000 quarterly rental payments.
✓2. Prepare appropriate entries for International Machines to record the lease at its inception, January 1, 1998, and the second rental payment on April 1, 1998.

Exercise 15–7

Capital lease *[handwritten: REVIEW for test]*

American Food Services, Inc., leased a packaging machine from Barton and Barton Corporation. Barton and Barton completed construction of the machine on January 1, 1998. The lease agreement for the $4 million (fair market value) machine specified four equal payments at the ~~end~~ of each year. The useful life of the machine was expected to be four years with no residual value. Barton and Barton's implicit interest rate was 10% (also American Food Services' incremental borrowing rate). *[handwritten: → PV of lease payment]*

Required: *[handwritten: $1,261,881.00 = lease payments beginning]*

✓1. Prepare the journal entry for American Food Services at the inception of the lease on January 1, 1998.
~~2. Prepare an amortization schedule for the four-year term of the lease.~~
✓3. Prepare the journal entry for the first lease payment on ~~December 31, 1998~~. *[handwritten: 1/1/98]*
✓4. Prepare the journal entry for the ~~third~~ *[handwritten: 2nd]* lease payment on ~~December 31, 2000~~. *[handwritten: 1/1/99]*

[handwritten left margin: think about diff between end vs begin year payments]

(Note: You may wish to compare your solution to this exercise with that of Exercise 14-17 which deals with a parallel situation in which the packaging machine was acquired with an installment note.)

Exercise 15–8

Lessor calculation of annual rental payments; lessee calculation of asset and liability

Each of the three independent situations below describes a nonoperating lease in which annual rental payments are payable at the beginning of each year. The lessee is aware of the lessor's implicit rate of return.

	Situation		
	1	2	3
Lease term (years)	10	20	4
Lessor's rate of return	11%	9%	12%
Lessee's incremental borrowing rate	12%	10%	11%
Fair market value of leased asset	$600,000	$980,000	$185,000

Required:

For each situation, determine:
a. The amount of the annual rental payments as calculated by the lessor.
b. The amount the lessee would record as a leased asset and a lease liability.

Exercise 15–9
Lessor calculation of annual rental payments; lessee calculation of asset and liability

(This is a variation of the previous exercise modified to assume rental payments are at the end of each period.)

Each of the three independent situations below describes a nonoperating lease in which annual rental payments are payable at the *end* of each year. The lessee is aware of the lessor's implicit rate of return.

	Situation		
	1	2	3
Lease term (years)	10	20	4
Lessor's rate of return	11%	9%	12%
Lessee's incremental borrowing rate	12%	10%	11%
Fair market value of leased asset	$600,000	$980,000	$185,000

Required:

For each situation, determine:

a. The amount of the annual rental payments as calculated by the lessor.
b. The amount the lessee would record as a leased asset and a lease liability.

Exercise 15–10
Calculation of annual lease payments; residual value

Each of the four independent situations below describes a nonoperating lease in which annual rental payments are payable at the beginning of each year. Determine the annual rental payments for each:

	Situation			
	1	2	3	4
Lease term (years)	4	7	5	8
Lessor's rate of return	10%	11%	9%	12%
Fair market value of leased asset	$50,000	$350,000	$75,000	$465,000
Lessor's cost of leased asset	$50,000	350,000	$45,000	$465,000
Residual value:				
Guaranteed by lessee	0	$ 50,000	0	$ 30,000
Unguaranteed	0	0	$ 7,000	$ 15,000

Exercise 15–11
Lease concepts; direct financing leases; guaranteed and unguaranteed residual value

Each of the four independent situations below describes a direct financing lease in which annual rental payments of $100,000 are payable at the beginning of each year. Each is a capital lease for the lessee. Determine the following amounts at the inception of the lease:

A. The lessor's:
    1. Minimum lease payments
    2. Gross investment in the lease
    3. Net investment in the lease
    4. Unearned interest revenue
B. The lessee's:
    5. Minimum lease payments
    6. Leased asset
    7. Lease liability

	Situation			
	1	2	3	4
Lease term (years)	7	7	8	8
Lessor's and lessee's discount rate	9%	11%	10%	12%
Residual value:				
Guaranteed by lessee	0	$50,000	0	$40,000
Unguaranteed	0	0	$50,000	$60,000

Exercise 15–12
Calculation of annual lease payments; BPO

For each of the three independent situations below determine the amount of the annual rental payments. Each describes a nonoperating lease in which annual rental payments are payable at the beginning of each year. Each lease agreement contains an option that permits the lessee to acquire the leased asset at an option price sufficiently lower than the expected market value that the exercise of the option appears reasonably certain.

	Situation		
	1	2	3
Lease term (years)	5	12	4
Lessor's rate of return	12%	11%	9%
Fair market value of leased asset	$60,000	$420,000	$185,000
Lessor's cost of leased asset	$50,000	420,000	$145,000
Bargain purchase option:			
Option price	$10,000	$50,000	$22,000
Exercisable at end of year:	5	5	3

Exercise 15–13
Capital lease; bargain purchase option; lessee

Federated Fabrications leased a tooling machine on December 31, 1996, for a three-year period. The lease agreement specified annual payments of $36,000 beginning with the first payment at the inception of the lease, and each December 31 through 1998. The company had the option to purchase the machine on December 30, 1999, for $45,000 when its fair value was expected to be $60,000. The machine's estimated useful life was six years with no salvage value. Federated depreciates assets by the straight-line method. The company was aware that the lessor's implicit rate of return was 12%, which was less than Federated's incremental borrowing rate.

Required:

1. Calculate the amount Federated should record as a leased asset and lease liability for this capital lease.
2. Prepare an amortization schedule that describes the pattern of interest expense for Federated over the lease term.
3. Prepare the appropriate entries for Federated from the inception of the lease through the end of the lease term.

Exercise 15–14
Bargain purchase option; lessor; direct financing lease

Universal Leasing leases electronic equipment to a variety of businesses. The company's primary service is providing alternate financing by acquiring equipment and leasing it to customers under long-term direct financing leases. Universal earns interest under these arrangements at a 10% annual rate.

The company leased an electronic typesetting machine purchased for $30,900 to a local publisher, Desktop Inc. on December 31, 1996. The lease contract specified annual payments of $8,000 beginning December 31, 1996, the inception of the lease, and each December 31 through 1998 (three-year lease term). The publisher had the option to purchase the machine on December 30, 1999, for $12,000 when it was expected to have a residual value of $16,000.

Required:

1. Show how Universal calculated the $8,000 annual rental payments for this direct financing lease.
2. Prepare an amortization schedule that describes the pattern of interest revenue for Universal Leasing over the lease term.
3. Prepare the appropriate entries for Universal Leasing from the inception of the lease through the end of the lease term.

Exercise 15–15
Executory costs; lessor and lessee

On December 31, 1996, NRC Credit Corporation leased equipment to Brand Services under a direct financing lease designed to earn NRC a 12% rate of return for providing long-term financing. The lease agreement specified:

a. 10 annual payments of $55,000 (including executory costs) beginning December 31, 1996, the inception of the lease.
b. The estimated useful life of the leased equipment is 10 years with no residual value. Its cost to NRC was $316,412.
c. The lease qualifies as a capital lease to Brand.
d. A 10-year service agreement with Quality Maintenance Company was negotiated to provide maintenance of the equipment as required. Payments of $5,000 per year are specified, beginning December 31, 1996. NRC was to pay this executory cost as incurred, but lease payments reflect this expenditure.
e. A partial amortization schedule, appropriate for both the lessee and lessor, follows:

Dec. 31	Payments	Effective Interest	Decrease in Balance	Outstanding Balance
		(12% × Outstanding balance)		
				316,412
1996	50,000		50,000	266,412
1997	50,000	.12(266,412) = 31,969	18,031	248,381
1998	50,000	.12(248,381) = 29,806	20,194	228,188

Required:
Prepare the appropriate entries for both the lessee and lessor to record:

1. The lease at its inception.
2. The second lease payment and depreciation (straight line) on December 31, 1997.

Exercise 15–16
Executory costs plus management fee; lessor and lessee

Refer to the lease agreement described in the previous exercise. Assume the contract specified that NRC (the lessor) was to pay, not only the $5,000 maintenance fees, but also insurance of $700 per year, and was to receive a $250 management fee for facilitating service and paying executory costs. The lessee's rental payments were increased to include an amount sufficient to reimburse executory costs plus NRC's fee.

Required:
Prepare the appropriate entries for both the lessee and lessor to record the **second** lease payment, executory costs, and depreciation (straight line) on December 31, 1997.

Exercise 15–17
Multiple choice; nonoperating leases

The following questions dealing with various topics in this chapter are adapted from recent CPA examinations. Determine the response that best completes the statements or questions.

1. On December 31, 1996, Roe Co. leased a machine from Colt for a five-year period. Equal annual payments under the lease are $105,000 (including $5,000 annual executory costs) and are due on December 31 of each year. The first payment was made on December 31, 1996, and the second payment was made on December 31, 1997. The five lease payments are discounted at 10% over the lease term. The present value of minimum lease payments at the inception of the lease and before the first annual payment was $417,000. The lease is appropriately accounted for as a capital lease by Roe. In its December 31, 1997, balance sheet, Roe should report a lease liability of
    a. $317,000
    b. $315,000
    c. $285,300
    d. $248,700

2. Winn Co. manufactures equipment that is sold or leased. On December 31, 1997, Winn leased equipment to Bart for a five-year period ending December 31, 2002, at which date ownership of the leased asset will be transferred to Bart. Equal payments under the lease are $22,000 (including $2,000 executory costs) and are due on December 31 of each year. The first payment was made on December 31, 1997. Collectibility of the remaining lease payments is reasonably assured, and Winn has no material cost uncertainties. The normal sales price of the equipment is $77,000, and cost is $60,000. For the year ended December 31, 1997, what amount of income should Winn realize from the lease transaction?
    a. $17,000
    b. $22,000
    c. $23,000
    d. $33,000

3. At the inception of a capital lease, the guaranteed residual value should be
    a. Included as part of minimum lease payments at present value.
    b. Included as part of minimum lease payments at future value.
    c. Included as part of minimum lease payments only to the extent that guaranteed residual value is expected to exceed estimated residual value.
    d. Excluded from minimum lease payments.

Exercise 15–18
Lessor's initial direct costs; operating, direct financing and sales-type leases

Terms of a lease agreement and related facts were:
    a. Leased asset had a retail cash selling price of $100,000. Its useful life was six years with no residual value (straight-line depreciation).
    b. Annual rental payments at the beginning of each year were $20,873, beginning January 1.
    c. Lessor's implicit rate when calculating annual rental payments was 10%.
    d. Costs of negotiating and consummating the completed lease transaction incurred by the lessor were $2,062.
    e. Collectibility of the rent payments by the lessor was reasonably predictable and there were no costs to the lessor that were yet to be incurred.

Required:
Prepare the appropriate entries for the lessor to record the lease, the initial payment at its inception, and at the December 31 fiscal year-end under each of the following three independent assumptions:

1. The lease term is three years and the lessor paid $100,000 to acquire the asset (operating lease).
2. The lease term is six years and the lessor paid $100,000 to acquire the asset (direct financing lease) Also assume that adjusting the net investment by initial direct costs reduces the effective rate of interest to 9%.
3. The lease term is six years and the lessor paid $85,000 to acquire the asset (sales-type lease).

Exercise 15–19
Lessor's initial direct costs; operating lease

The following relate to an operating lease agreement:
    a. The lease term is 3 years, beginning January 1, 1997.
    b. The leased asset cost the lessor $800,000 and had a useful life of eight years with no residual value. The lessor uses straight-line depreciation for its depreciable assets.
    c. Annual rental payments at the beginning of each year were $137,000.
    d. Costs of negotiating and consummating the completed lease transaction incurred by the lessor were $2,400.

Required:
Prepare the appropriate entries for the lessor from the inception of the lease through the end of the lease term.

Exercise 15–20
Lessor's initial direct costs; direct financing lease

Terms of a lease agreement and related facts were:

a. Costs of negotiating and consummating the completed lease transaction incurred by the lessor were $4,242.

b. The retail cash selling price of the leased asset was $500,000. Its useful life was three years with no residual value.

c. Collectibility of the rent payments by the lessor was reasonably predictable and there were no costs to the lessor that were yet to be incurred.

d. The lease term is three years and the lessor paid $500,000 to acquire the asset (direct financing lease).

e. Annual rental payments at the beginning of each year were $184,330.

f. Lessor's implicit rate when calculating annual rental payments was 11%.

Required:

1. Prepare the appropriate entries for the lessor to record the lease and related payments at its inception, January 1, 1998.
2. Calculate the effective rate of interest revenue after adjusting the net investment by initial direct costs.
3. Record any entry(s) necessary at December 31, 1998, the fiscal year-end.

Exercise 15–21
Lessor's initial direct costs; sales-type lease

The lease agreement and related facts indicate the following:

a. Leased equipment had a retail cash selling price of $300,000. Its useful life was five years with no residual value.

b. Collectibility of the rent payments by the lessor was reasonably predictable and there were no costs to the lessor that were yet to be incurred.

c. The lease term is five years and the lessor paid $265,000 to acquire the equipment (sales-type lease).

d. Lessor's implicit rate when calculating annual rental payments was 8%.

e. Annual rental payments beginning January 1, 1998, the inception of the lease, were $69,571.

f. Costs of negotiating and consummating the completed lease transaction incurred by the lessor were $7,500.

Required:
Prepare the appropriate entries for the lessor to record:

1. The lease and the initial payment at its inception.
2. Any entry(s) necessary at December 31, 1998, the fiscal year-end.

Exercise 15–22
Sale-leaseback; capital lease

also PV of lease payments

To raise operating funds, Signal Aviation sold an airplane on January 1, 1998, to a finance company for $770,000. Signal immediately leased the plane back for a 13-year period, at which time ownership of the airplane will transfer to Signal. The airplane has a fair value of $800,000. Its cost and its carrying value were $620,000. Its useful life is estimated to be 15 years. The lease requires Signal to make payments of $102,771 to the finance company each January 1. Signal depreciates assets on a straight-line basis. The lease has an implicit rate of 11%.

Required:
Prepare the appropriate entries for Signal on :

1. January 1, 1998, to record the sale-leaseback.
2. December 31, 1998, to record necessary adjustments.

Exercise 15–23
Sale-leaseback; operating lease

To raise operating funds, National Distribution Center sold its office building to an insurance company on January 1, 1998, for $800,000 and immediately leased the building back. The operating lease is for the final 12 years of the building's estimated 50-year useful life. The building has a fair value of $800,000 and a carrying amount of $650,000 (its original cost was $1,000,000). The rental payments of $100,000 are payable to the insurance company each December 31. The lease has an implicit rate of 9%.

Required:
Prepare the appropriate entries for National Distribution Center on:

1. January 1, 1998, to record the sale-leaseback.
2. December 31, 1998, to record necessary adjustments.

Exercise 15–24
Multiple choice; other lease accounting issues

The following questions dealing with various topics in this chapter are adapted from recent CPA examinations. Determine the response that best completes the statements or questions.

1. Able sold its headquarters building at a gain and simultaneously leased back the building. The lease was reported as a capital lease. At the time of sale, the gain should be reported as
   a. Operating income.
   b. An extraordinary item, net of income tax.
   c. A separate component of stockholders' equity.
   d. An asset valuation allowance.

2. On January 1, 1997, Wren Co. leased a building to Brill under an operating lease for 10 years at $50,000 per year, payable the first day of each lease year. Wren paid $15,000 to a real estate broker as a finder's fee. The building is depreciated $12,000 per year. For 1997, Wren incurred insurance and property tax expense totaling $9,000. Wren's net rental income for 1997 should be
   a. $27,500
   b. $29,000
   c. $35,000
   d. $36,500

Exercise 15–25
Concepts; terminology

Listed below are several terms and phrases associated with leases. Pair each item from List A (by letter) with the item from List B that is most appropriately associated with it.

List A	List B
___ 1. Effective rate times balance.	a. PV of BPO price.
___ 2. Realization principle.	b. Lessor's net investment.
___ 3. Minimum lease payments plus unguaranteed residual value.	c. Lessor's gross investment.
	d. Operating lease.
___ 4. Periodic rent payments plus lessee-guaranteed residual value.	e. Depreciable assets.
	f. Loss to lessee.
___ 5. PV of minimum lease payments plus PV of unguaranteed residual value.	g. Executory costs.
	h. Depreciation longer than lease term.
___ 6. Initial direct costs.	i. Disclosure only.
___ 7. Rent revenue.	j. Interest expense.
___ 8. Bargain purchase option.	k. Additional lessor conditions.
___ 9. Leasehold improvements.	l. Lessee's minimum lease payments.
___ 10. Cash to satisfy residual value guarantee.	m. Purchase price less than fair market value.
___ 11. Capital lease expense.	n. Sales-type lease selling expense.
___ 12. Deducted in lessor's computation of rental payments.	o. Lessor's minimum lease payments.
___ 13. Title transfers to lessee.	
___ 14. Contingent rentals.	
___ 15. Rent payments plus lessee-guaranteed and third-party-guaranteed residual value.	

Exercise 15–26
Real estate lease; land and building

On January 1, 1998, Cook Textiles leased a building with two acres of land from Peck Development. The lease is for 10 years at which time Cook has an option to purchase the property for $100,000. The building has an estimated life of 20 years with a residual value of $150,000. The lease calls for Cook to assume all costs of ownership and to make annual payments of $200,000 due at the beginning of each year. On January 1, 1998, the estimated value of the land was $400,000. Cook uses the straight-line method of depreciation and pays 10% interest on borrowed money. Peck's implicit rate is unknown.

Required:
Prepare Cook Company's journal entries related to the lease in 1998.

Problems

Problem 15–1
Operating lease; scheduled rent increases

On January 1, 1997, Sweetwater Furniture Company leased office space under a 21-year operating lease agreement. The contract calls for annual rent payments on December 31 of each year. The payments are $10,000 the first year and increase by $500 per year. Benefits expected from using the office space are expected to remain constant over the lease term.

Required:

Record Sweetwater's rent payment at December 31, 2001 (the fifth rent payment) and December 31, 2011 (the fifteenth rent payment).

Problem 15–2

Lease amortization schedule

On January 1, 2000, National Insulation Corporation (NIC) leased office space under a capital lease. Rental payments are made annually. Title does not transfer to the lessee and there is no bargain purchase option. Portions of the lessee's lease amortization schedule appear below:

January 1	Payments	Effective Interest	Decrease in Balance	Outstanding Balance
1997				192,501
1997	20,000		20,000	172,501
1998	20,000	17,250	2,750	169,751
1999	20,000	16,975	3,025	166,726
2000	20,000	16,673	3,327	163,399
2001	20,000	16,340	3,660	159,739
2002	20,000	15,974	4,026	155,713
~	~	~	~	~
~	~	~	~	~
~	~	~	~	~
2014	20,000	7,364	12,636	61,006
2015	20,000	6,101	13,899	47,107
2016	20,000	4,711	15,289	31,818
2017	35,000	3,182	31,818	0

Required:

1. What is NICs lease liability at the inception of the lease (after the first payment)?
2. What amount would NIC record as a leased asset?
3. What is the lease term in years?
4. What is the asset's residual value expected at the end of the lease term?
5. How much of the residual value is guaranteed by the lessee?
6. What is the effective annual interest rate?
7. What is the total amount of minimum lease payments?
8. What is the total effective interest expense recorded over the term of the lease?

Problem 15–3

Direct financing and sales-type lease; lessee and lessor

Rand Medical manufactures lithotripters. Lithotripsy uses shock waves instead of surgery to eliminate kidney stones. Physicians' Leasing purchased a lithotripter from Rand for $2,000,000 and leased it to Mid-South Urologists Group, Inc., on January 1, 1998.

PV of lease payments

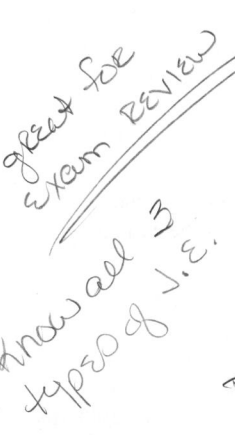

Lease description:

Quarterly rental payments	$130,516 – beginning of each period *x 20 pymnts = Lease Receivable*
Lease term	5 years (20 quarters)
No residual value; no BPO	
Economic life of lithotripter	5 years
Implicit interest rate and lessee's incremental borrowing rate	12% *12 ÷ 4 = 3% quarterly*
Fair value of asset	$2,000,000

Collectibility of the rental payments is reasonably assured, and there are no lessor costs yet to be incurred.

Required:

1. How should this lease be classified by Mid-South Urologists Group and by Physicians' Leasing?
2. Prepare appropriate entries for both Mid-South Urologists Group and Physicians' Leasing from the inception of the lease through the second rental payment on April 1, 1998. Depreciation is recorded at the end of each fiscal year (December 31). *Direct financing*
3. Assume Mid-South Urologists Group leased the lithotripter directly from the manufacturer, Rand Medical, which produced the machine at a cost of $1,700,000. Prepare appropriate entries for Rand Medical from the inception of the lease through the second rental payment on April 1, 1998. *Sales-type*

PV as well

Problem 15–4

Capital lease

At the beginning of 1998, VHF Industries acquired a machine with a fair market value of $6,074,700 by signing a four-year lease. Rentals are payable in four annual payments of $2 million at the end of each year.

Required:

1. What is the effective rate of interest implicit in the agreement?
2. Prepare the lessee's journal entry at the inception of the lease.
3. Prepare the journal entry to record the first lease payment at December 31, 1998.
4. Prepare the journal entry to record the second lease payment at December 31, 1999.

5. Suppose the market value of the machine and the lessor's implicit rate were unknown at the time of the lease, but that the lessee's incremental borrowing rate of interest for notes of similar risk was 11%. Prepare the lessee's entry at the inception of the lease.

(Note: You may wish to compare your solution to this exercise with that of Problem 14-11, which deals with a parallel situation in which the machine was acquired with an installment note.)

Problem 15–5
Guaranteed residual value; direct financing lease

(Note: Problems 5, 6, and 7 are three variations of the same basic situation.)

On December 31, 1997, Rhone-Metro Industries leased equipment to Western Soya Co. for a four-year period ending December 31, 2001, at which time possession of the leased asset will revert back to Rhone-Metro. The equipment cost Rhone-Metro $365,760 and has an expected useful life of six years. Its normal sales price is $365,760. The lessee-guaranteed residual value at December 31, 2001, is $25,000. Equal payments under the lease are $100,000 and are due on December 31 of each year. The first payment was made on December 31, 1997. Collectibility of the remaining lease payments is reasonably assured, and Rhone-Metro has no material cost uncertainties. Western Soya's incremental borrowing rate is 12%. Western Soya knows the interest rate implicit in the lease payments is 10%. Both companies use straight-line depreciation.

Required:

1. Show how Rhone-Metro calculated the $100,000 annual rental payments.
2. How should this lease be classified (a) by Western Soya Co. (the lessee) and (b) by Rhone-Metro Industries (the lessor)? Why?
3. Prepare the appropriate entries for both Western Soya Co. and Rhone-Metro on December 31, 1997.
4. Prepare an amortization schedule(s) that describes the pattern of interest over the lease term for the lessee and the lessor.
5. Prepare all appropriate entries for both Western Soya and Rhone-Metro on December 31, 1998 (the second rent payment and depreciation).
6. Prepare the appropriate entries for both Western Soya and Rhone-Metro on December 31, 2001 (the end of the lease), assuming the equipment is returned to Rhone-Metro and the actual residual value on that date is $1,500.

Problem 15–6
Unguaranteed residual value; executory costs; sales-type lease

Rhone-Metro Industries manufactures equipment that is sold or leased. On December 31, 1997, Rhone-Metro leased equipment to Western Soya Co. for a four-year period ending December 31, 2001, at which time possession of the leased asset will revert back to Rhone-Metro. The equipment cost $300,000 to manufacture and has an expected useful life of six years. Its normal sales price is $365,760. The expected residual value of $25,000 at December 31, 2001, is not guaranteed. Equal payments under the lease are $104,000 (including $4,000 executory costs) and are due on December 31 of each year. The first payment was made on December 31, 1997. Collectibility of the remaining lease payments is reasonably assured, and Rhone-Metro has no material cost uncertainties. Western Soya's incremental borrowing rate is 12%. Western Soya knows the interest rate implicit in the lease payments is 10%. Both companies use straight-line depreciation.

Required:

1. Show how Rhone-Metro calculated the $104,000 annual rental payments.
2. How should this lease be classified (a) by Western Soya Co. (the lessee) and (b) by Rhone-Metro Industries (the lessor)? Why?
3. Prepare the appropriate entries for both Western Soya Co. and Rhone-Metro on December 31, 1997.
4. Prepare an amortization schedule(s) that describes the pattern of interest over the lease term for the lessee and the lessor.
5. Prepare the appropriate entries for both Western Soya and Rhone-Metro on December 31, 1998 (the second rent payment and depreciation).
6. Prepare the appropriate entries for both Western Soya and Rhone-Metro on December 31, 2001, assuming the equipment is returned to Rhone-Metro and the actual residual value on that date is $1,500.

Problem 15–7
Bargain purchase option exercisable before lease term ends; executory costs; sales-type lease

Rhone-Metro Industries manufactures equipment that is sold or leased. On December 31, 1997, Rhone-Metro leased equipment to Western Soya Co. for a noncancelable stated lease term of four years ending December 31, 2001, at which time possession of the leased asset will revert back to Rhone-Metro. The equipment cost $300,000 to manufacture and has an expected useful life of six years. Its normal sales price is $365,760. The expected residual value of $25,000 at December 31, 2001, is not guaranteed. Western Soya Co. can exercise a bargain purchase option on December 30, 2000, at an option price of $10,000. Equal payments under the lease are $134,960 (including $4,000 annual executory costs) and are due on December 31 of each year. The first payment was made on December 31, 1997. Collectibility of the remaining lease payments is reasonably assured, and Rhone-Metro has no material cost uncertainties. Western Soya's incremental borrowing rate is 12%. Western Soya knows the interest rate implicit in the lease payments is 10%. Both companies use straight-line depreciation.

    Hint: A lease term ends for accounting purposes when an option becomes exercisable if it's expected to be exercised (i.e., a BPO).

Required:
1. Show how Rhone-Metro calculated the $134,960 annual rental payments.
2. How should this lease be classified (a) by Western Soya Co. (the lessee) and (b) by Rhone-Metro Industries (the lessor)? Why?
3. Prepare the appropriate entries for both Western Soya Co. and Rhone-Metro on December 31, 1997.
4. Prepare an amortization schedule(s) that describes the pattern of interest over the lease term for the lessee and the lessor.
5. Prepare the appropriate entries for both Western Soya and Rhone-Metro on December 31, 1998 (the second rent payment and depreciation).
6. Prepare the appropriate entries for both Western Soya and Rhone-Metro on December 30, 2000, assuming the BPO is exercised on that date.

Problem 15–8
Operating lease to lessee—nonoperating lease to lessor

Allied Industries manufactures high performance conveyers that often are leased to industrial customers. On December 31, 1997, Allied leased a conveyer to Poole Carrier Corporation for a three-year period ending December 31, 2000, at which time possession of the leased asset will revert back to Allied. Equal payments under the lease are $200,000 and are due on December 31 of each year. The first payment was made on December 31, 1997. Collectibility of the remaining lease payments is reasonably assured, and Allied has no material cost uncertainties. The conveyer cost $450,000 to manufacture and has an expected useful life of six years. Its normal sales price is $659,805. The expected residual value of $150,000 at December 31, 2000, is guaranteed by United Assurance Group. Poole Carrier's incremental borrowing rate and the interest rate implicit in the lease payments are 10%.

Required:
1. Show how Allied Industries calculated the $200,000 annual rental payments.
2. How should this lease be classified (a) by Allied (the lessor) and (b) by Poole (the lessee)? Why?
3. Prepare the appropriate entries for both Poole and Allied on December 31, 1997.
4. Prepare an amortization schedule(s) that describes the pattern of interest over the lease term.
5. Prepare the appropriate entries for both Poole and Allied on December 31, 1998, 1999, and 2000, assuming the conveyer is returned to Allied at the end of the lease and the actual residual value on that date is $105,000.

Problem 15–9
Lease concepts; direct financing leases; guaranteed and unguaranteed residual value

Each of the four independent situations below describe direct financing leases in which annual rental payments of $10,000 are payable at the beginning of each year. Each is a capital lease for the lessee. Determine the following amounts at the inception of the lease:

A.   The lessor's:
    1. Minimum lease payments
    2. Gross investment in the lease
    3. Net investment in the lease
    4. Unearned interest revenue
B.   The lessee's:
    5. Minimum lease payments
    6. Leased asset
    7. Lease liability

	Situation			
	1	2	3	4
Lease term (years)	4	4	4	4
Asset's useful life (years)	4	5	5	5
Lessor's implicit rate (known by lessee)	11%	11%	11%	11%
Lessee's incremental borrowing rate	11%	12%	11%	12%
Residual value:				
Guaranteed by lessee	0	$4,000	0	0
Guaranteed by third party	0	0	$4,000	0
Unguaranteed	0	0	0	$4,000

Problem 15–10
Lease concepts

Four independent situations are described below. For each, annual rental payments of $100,000 (not including any executory costs paid by lessor) are payable at the beginning of each year. Each is a nonoperating lease for both the lessor and lessee. Determine the following amounts at the inception of the lease:

A.   The lessor's:
    1. Minimum lease payments
    2. Gross investment in the lease
    3. Net investment in the lease
    4. Unearned interest revenue
    5. Sales revenue
    6. Cost of goods sold
    7. Dealer's profit
B. The lessee's:
    8. Minimum lease payments
    9. Leased asset
    10. Lease liability

	Situation			
	1	**2**	**3**	**4**
Lease term (years)	4	5	6	4
Lessor's cost	$369,176	$433,809	$500,000	$400,000
Asset's useful life (years)	6	7	7	5
Lessor's implicit rate (known by lessee)	10%	12%	9%	10%
Lessee's incremental borrowing rate	9%	10%	11%	12%
Residual value:				
Guaranteed by lessee	0	$ 53,000	$ 40,000	$ 60,000
Guaranteed by third party*	0	0	0	$ 50,000
Unguaranteed	$ 30,000	0	$ 35,000	$ 40,000
Executory costs paid annually by lessor	$ 1,000	$ 8,000	$ 5,000	$ 10,000

*Over and above any amount guaranteed by the lessee (after a deductible equal to any amount guaranteed by the lessee)

Problem 15–11
Executory costs; lessor and lessee

Branif Leasing leases mechanical equipment to industrial consumers under direct financing leases that earn Branif a 10% rate of return for providing long-term financing. A lease agreement with Branson Construction specified 20 annual payments of $100,000 beginning December 31, 1996, the inception of the lease. The estimated useful life of the leased equipment is 20 years with no residual value. Its cost to Branif was $936,500. The lease qualifies as a capital lease to Branson. Maintenance of the equipment was contracted for through a 20-year service agreement with Midway Service Company requiring 20 annual payments of $3,000 beginning December 31, 1996. Both companies use straight-line depreciation.

Required:

Prepare the appropriate entries for both the lessee and lessor to record the **second** lease payment and depreciation on December 31, 1997, under each of three independent assumptions:

1.   The lessee pays executory costs as incurred.
2.   The contract specifies that the lessor pays executory costs as incurred. The lessee's rental payments were increased to $103,000 to include an amount sufficient to reimburse these costs.
3.   The contract specifies that the lessor pays executory costs as incurred. The lessee's rental payments were increased to $103,300 to include an amount sufficient to reimburse these costs plus a 10% management fee for Branif.

Problem 15–12
Sales-type lease; bargain purchase option exercisable before lease term ends; lessor and lessee

Mid-South Auto Leasing leases vehicles to consumers. The attraction to customers is that the company can offer competitive prices due to volume buying and requires an interest rate implicit in the lease that is one percent below alternate methods of financing. On September 30, 1997, the company leased a delivery truck to a local florist, Anything Grows.

The lease agreement specified quarterly payments of $3,000 beginning September 30, 1997, the inception of the lease, and each quarter (December 31, March 31, and June 30) through June 30, 2000 (three-year lease term). The florist had the option to purchase the truck on September 29, 1999, for $6,000 when it was expected to have a residual value of $10,000. The estimated useful life of the truck is four years. Mid-South Auto Leasing's quarterly interest rate for determining payments was 3% (approximately 12% annually). Mid-South paid $25,000 for the truck. Both companies use straight-line depreciation.

Hint: A lease term ends for accounting purposes when an option becomes exercisable if it's expected to be exercised (i.e., a BPO)

Required:

1. Calculate the amount of dealer's profit that Mid-South would recognize in this sales-type lease. (Be careful to note that, although payments occur on the last calendar day of each quarter, since the first payment was at the inception of the lease, payments represent an annuity due.)
2. Prepare the appropriate entries for Anything Grows and Mid-South on September 30, 1997.
3. Prepare an amortization schedule(s) that describes the pattern of interest expense for Anything Grows and interest revenue for Mid-South Auto Leasing over the lease term.
4. Prepare the appropriate entries for Anything Grows and Mid-South Auto Leasing on December 31, 1997.
5. Prepare the appropriate entries for Anything Grows and Mid-South on September 29, 1999, assuming the bargain purchase option was exercised on that date.

Problem 15–13

Lessee-guaranteed residual value; third-party-guaranteed residual value; unguaranteed residual value; executory costs; different interest rates for lessor and lessee

On December 31, 1996, Yard Art Landscaping leased a delivery truck from Branch Motors. Branch paid $40,000 for the truck. Its retail value is $45,114.

The lease agreement specified annual payments of $11,000 beginning December 31, 1996, the inception of the lease, and at each December 31 through 1999. Branch Motors' interest rate for determining payments was 10%. At the end of the four-year lease term (December 31, 2000) the truck was expected to be worth $15,000. The estimated useful life of the truck is five years with no salvage value. Both companies use straight-line depreciation.

Yard Art guaranteed a residual value of $6,000. Guarantor Assurance Corporation was engaged to guarantee a residual value of $11,000, but with a deductible equal to any amount paid by the Lessee ($11,000 reduced by any amount paid by the Lessee). Yard Art's incremental borrowing rate is 9%.

A $1,000 per year maintenance agreement was arranged for the truck with an outside service firm. As an expediency, Branch Motors agreed to pay this fee. It is, however, reflected in the $11,000 rental payments.

Collectibility of the rent payments by Yard Arts is reasonably predictable and there are no costs to the lessor that are yet to be incurred.

Required:

1. How should this lease be classified by Yard Art Landscaping (the lessee)? Why?
2. Calculate the amount Yard Arts Landscaping would record as a leased asset and a lease liability.
3. How should this lease be classified by Branch Motors (the lessor)? Why?
4. Show how Branch Motors calculated the $11,000 annual rental payments.
5. Calculate the amount Branch Motors would record as sales revenue.
6. Prepare the appropriate entries for both Yard Arts and Branch Motors on December 31, 1996.
7. Prepare an amortization schedule that describes the pattern of interest expense over the lease term for Yard Arts.
8. Prepare an amortization schedule that describes the pattern of interest revenue over the lease term for Branch Motors.
9. Prepare the appropriate entries for both Yard Arts and Branch Motors on December 31, 1997.
10. Prepare the appropriate entries for both Yard Arts and Branch Motors on December 31, 1999 (the final rent payment).
11. Prepare the appropriate entries for both Yard Arts and Branch Motors on December 31, 2000 (the end of the lease term), assuming the truck is returned to the lessor and the actual residual value of the truck was $4,000 on that date.

Problem 15–14

Initial direct costs; direct financing lease

Bidwell Leasing purchased a single-engine plane for its fair market value of $645,526 and leased it to Red Baron Flying Club on December 31, 1996.

Terms of the lease agreement and related facts were:

a. Eight annual payments of $110,000 beginning December 31, 1996, the inception of the lease, and at each December 31 through 2003. Bidwell Leasing's implicit interest rate was 10%. The estimated useful life of the plane is eight years. Payments were calculated as follows:

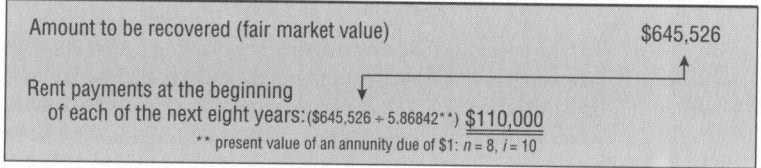

Amount to be recovered (fair market value)	$645,526
Rent payments at the beginning of each of the next eight years: ($645,526 ÷ 5.86842**)	$110,000
** present value of an annuity due of $1: $n = 8, i = 10$	

b. Red Baron's incremental borrowing rate is 11%.

c. Costs of negotiating and consummating the completed lease transaction incurred by Bidwell Leasing were $18,099.
d. Collectibility of the rent payments by Bidwell Leasing is reasonably predictable and there are no costs to the lessor that are yet to be incurred.

Required:

1. How should this lease be classified (a) by Bidwell Leasing (the lessor) and (b) by Red Baron (the lessee)?
2. Prepare the appropriate entries for both Red Baron Flying Club and Bidwell Leasing on December 31, 1996.
3. Prepare an amortization schedule that describes the pattern of interest expense over the lease term for Red Baron Flying Club.
4. Determine the effective rate of interest for Bidwell Leasing for the purpose of recognizing interest revenue over the lease term.
5. Prepare an amortization schedule that describes the pattern of interest revenue over the lease term for Bidwell Leasing .
6. Prepare the appropriate entries for both Red Baron and Bidwell Leasing on December 31, 1997 (the second rent payment). Both companies use straight-line depreciation.
7. Prepare the appropriate entries for both Red Baron and Bidwell Leasing on December 31, 2003 (the final rent payment).

Problem 15–15
Initial direct costs; sales-type lease

(Note: This problem is a variation of the preceding problem, modified to cause the lease to be a sales-type lease.)
Bidwell Leasing purchased a single-engine plane for $400,000 and leased it to Red Baron Flying Club for its fair market value of $645,526 on December 31, 1996.

Terms of the lease agreement and related facts were:

a. Eight annual payments of $110,000 beginning December 31, 1996, the inception of the lease, and at each December 31 through 2003. Bidwell Leasing's implicit interest rate was 10%. The estimated useful life of the plane is eight years. Payments were calculated as follows:

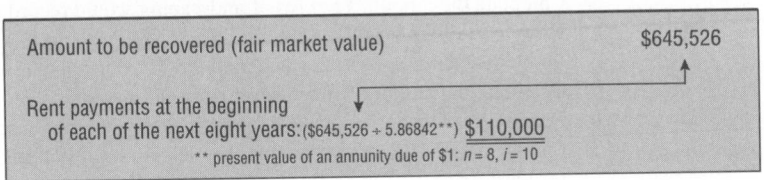

| Amount to be recovered (fair market value) | $645,526 |

Rent payments at the beginning of each of the next eight years: ($645,526 ÷ 5.86842**) $110,000
** present value of an annuity due of $1: $n = 8, i = 10$

b. Red Baron's incremental borrowing rate is 11%.
c. Costs of negotiating and consummating the completed lease transaction incurred by Bidwell Leasing were $18,099.
d. Collectibility of the rent payments by Bidwell Leasing is reasonably predictable and there are no costs to the lessor that are yet to be incurred.

Required:

1. How should this lease be classified (a) by Bidwell Leasing (the lessor) and (b) by Red Baron (the lessee)?
2. Prepare the appropriate entries for both Red Baron Flying Club and Bidwell Leasing on December 31, 1996.
3. Prepare an amortization schedule that describes the pattern of interest expense over the lease term for Red Baron Flying Club.
4. Prepare the appropriate entries for both Red Baron and Bidwell Leasing on December 31, 1997 (the second rent payment). Both companies use straight-line depreciation.
5. Prepare the appropriate entries for both Red Baron and Bidwell Leasing on December 31, 2003 (the final rent payment).

Problem 15–16
Sale-leaseback

To raise operating funds, North American Courier Corporation sold its building on January 1, 1998, to an insurance company for $500,000 and immediately leased the building back. The lease is for a 10-year period ending December 31, 2004, at which time ownership of the building will revert to North American Courier. The building has a carrying amount of $400,000 (original cost $1,000,000). The lease requires North American to make payments of $88,492 to the insurance company each December 31. The building had a total original useful life of 30 years with no residual value and is being depreciated on a straight-line basis. The lease has an implicit rate of 12%.

Required:

1. Prepare the appropriate entries for North American on (a) January 1, 1998, to record the sale-leaseback and (b) December 31, 1998, to record necessary adjustments.
2. Show how North American's December 31, 1998, balance sheet and income statement would reflect the sale-leaseback.

Problem 15–17
Real estate lease; land and building

On January 1, 1998, Cook Textiles leased a building with two acres of land from Peck Development. The lease is for 10 years. No purchase option exists and the property will revert to Peck at the end of the lease. The building and land combined have a fair market value on January 1, 1998, of $1,450,000 and the building has an estimated life of 20 years with a residual value of $150,000. The lease calls for Cook to assume all costs of ownership and to make annual payments of $200,000 due at the beginning of each year. On January 1, 1998, the estimated value of the land was $400,000. Cook uses the straight-line method of depreciation and pays 10% interest on borrowed money. Peck's implicit rate is unknown.

Required:

1. Prepare journal entries for Cook Textiles for 1998. Assume the land could be rented without the building for $59,000 each year.
2. Assuming the land had a fair market value on January 1, 1998, of $200,000 and could be rented alone for $30,000, prepare journal entries for Cook Textiles for 1998.

Cases

Financial Analysis Case 15–1
Reporting leases; off balance sheet financing

Refer to the financial statements and related disclosure notes of Federal Express Corporation in the appendix to Chapter 1. Management's Discussion and Analysis states that "Generally, management's practice in recent years with respect to funding new aircraft acquisitions has been to finance such aircraft through long-term lease transactions that qualify as off balance sheet operating leases under applicable accounting rules."

Required:

1. What does Federal Express's management mean when it says some leases "qualify as off-balance-sheet" financing?
2. See Note 4 in the disclosure notes. What is Federal Express's capital lease liability?
3. If the operating leases were capitalized, approximately how much would that increase the capital lease liability?
4. What effect would that have on the company's debt-equity ratio?

Discussion Case 15–2
Capital Leases

Von Company entered into two noncancelable leases for new machines to be used in its manufacturing operations. The first lease does not contain a bargain purchase option; the lease term is equal to 80 percent of the estimated economic life of the machine. The second lease contains a bargain purchase option; the lease term is equal to 50 percent of the estimated economic life of the machine.

Required:

1. What is the theoretical basis for requiring lessees to capitalize certain long-term leases? Do not discuss the specific criteria classifying a lease as a capital lease.
2. How should a lessee account for a capital lease at its inception?
3. How should a lessee record each minimum lease payment for a capital lease?
4. How should Von classify each of the two leases? Why?

(AICPA adapted)

Writing Case 15–3
Where's the gain?

General Tools is seeking ways to maintain and improve cash balances. As company controller, you have proposed the sale and leaseback of much of the company's equipment. As seller-lessee, General Tools would retain the right to substantially all of the remaining use of the equipment. The term of the lease would be six years. A gain would result on the sale portion of the transaction. The lease portion would be classified appropriately as a capital lease.

You previously convinced your CFO of the cash flow benefits of the arrangement, but now he doesn't understand the way you will account for the transaction. "I really had counted on that gain to bolster this period's earnings. What gives?" he wondered. "Put it in a memo, will you? I'm having trouble following what you're saying to me."

Required:

Write a memo to your CFO. Include discussion of each of these points:

1. How the sale portion of the sale-leaseback transaction should be accounted for at the lease's inception.
2. How the gain on the sale portion of the sale-leaseback transaction should be accounted for during the lease.
3. How the leaseback portion of the sale-leaseback transaction should be accounted for at the lease's inception.
4. The conceptual basis for capitalizing certain long-term leases.

Group Interaction Case 15–4
Classification issues; lessee accounting

Interstate Automobiles Corporation leased 40 vans to VIP Transport under a four-year noncancelable lease on December 30, 1997. Information concerning the lease and the vans follows:

a. Equal annual lease payments of $300,000 are due on December 31 each year. The first payment was made December 31, 1997. Interstate's implicit interest rate is 10% and known by VIP.
b. VIP has the option to purchase all of the vans at the end of the lease for a total of $290,000. The vans' estimated residual value is $300,000 at the end of the lease term and $50,000 at the end of 7 years, the estimated life of each van.
c. VIP estimates the fair value of the vans to be $1,240,000. Interstate's cost was $1,050,000.
d. VIP's incremental borrowing rate is 11%.
e. VIP will pay the executory costs (maintenance, insurance, and other fees not included in the annual lease payments) of $1,000 per year. The depreciation method is straight-line.
f. The collectibility of the lease payments is reasonably predictable, and there are no important cost uncertainties.

Your instructor will divide the class into from two to six groups depending on the size of the class. The mission of your group is to assess the proper recording and reporting of the lease described.

Required:
1. Each group member should deliberate the situation independently and draft a tentative argument prior to the class session for which the case is assigned.
2. In class, each group will meet for 10 to 15 minutes in different areas of the classroom. During that meeting, group members will take turns sharing their suggestions for the purpose of arriving at a single group treatment.
3. After the allotted time, a spokesperson for each group (selected during the group meetings) will share the group's solution with the class. The goal of the class is to incorporate the views of each group into a consensus approach to the situation.

Specifically, you should address:
a. Identify potential advantages to VIP of leasing the vans rather than purchasing them.
b. How should the lease be classified by VIP? by Interstate?
c. Regardless of your response to previous requirements, suppose VIP recorded the lease on December 31, 1997, as a capital lease in the amount of $1,100,000. What would be the appropriate journal entries related to the capital lease for the second lease payment on December 31, 1998.

Discussion Case 15–5
Lease classification and reporting

On January 1, 1997, Hendrick Company entered into two noncancelable leases for machines to be used in its manufacturing operations. The first lease transfers ownership of the machine to the lessee by the end of the lease term. The second lease contains a bargain purchase option. Payments have been made on both leases during 1997.

Required:
1. How should Hendrick classify each of the two leases? Why?
2. How should a lessee report a capital lease on its balance sheet and income statement?
3. How should a lessee report an operating lease on its balance sheet and income statement?

(AICPA adapted)

International Case 15–6
Comparison of lease accounting in the U.K. and the United States

One of the world's largest petroleum and petrochemical groups is the British Petroleum Company p.l.c. (BP), based in London. Lease disclosures accompanying BP's 1993 financial statements are reproduced below:

Accounting Policies (in part)

Leases

Assets held under leases which result in group companies receiving substantially all risks and rewards of ownership (finance leases) are capitalized as tangible fixed assets at the estimated present value of underlying lease payments. The corresponding finance lease obligation is included with borrowings. Rentals under operating leases are charged against income as incurred.

Note 24: Finance debt (in part) Obligations under finance leases	£ million	
	1993	1992
Minimum future lease payments payable within:		
1 year	99	81
2 to 5 years	491	487
Thereafter	3,286	3,591
	3,876	4,159
Less finance charges	2,581	2,836
Net obligations	1,295	1,323

Required:

On the basis of the information the disclosures provide, compare lessee accounting for leases in the United Kingdom with that in the United States.

Critical Thought Case 15–7
Debt equivalent of operating leases

At December 31, 1994, American Airlines had 216 jet aircraft under operating leases and 82 jet aircraft under capital leases. Lease disclosures accompanying American's 1994 financial statements are reproduced below:

4. Leases

American leases various types of equipment and property, including aircraft, passenger terminals, equipment and various other facilities. The future minimum lease payments required under capital leases, together with the present value of net minimum lease payments, and future minimum lease payments required under operating leases that have initial or remaining non-cancelable lease terms in excess of one year as of December 31, 1994, were (in millions):

Year Ending December 31,	Capital Leases	Operating Leases
1995	$ 228	$ 887
1996	254	883
1997	236	884
1998	231	902
1999	226	889
2000 and subsequent	2,148	15,321
	3,323 (1)	$19,766 (2)
Less amount representing interest	1,249	
Present value of net minimum lease payments	$2,074	

(1) Future minimum payments required under capital leases include $390 million and $216 million guaranteed by AMR and American, respectively, relating to special facility revenue bonds issued by municipalities.
(2) Future minimum payments required under operating leases include $6.3 billion guaranteed by AMR relating to special facility revenue bonds issued by municipalities.

American's capital lease liability is reported among other debt on the balance sheet. The company's debt to equity ratio is 4.51, calculated as $14,583 / $3,233. Some analysts might consider operating lease commitments as equivalent to debt when assessing financial risk. If American's operating leases were considered capital leases, lease payments would be capitalized at the present value of all future payments.

Required:

1. If the interest rates used by American to discount rental payments on capital leases is 12% and rentals after 1999 are payable approximately evenly over the following 17 years (approximated as $15,321 ÷ $889), what is the debt equivalent of the operating lease commitments?
2. If operating lease commitments are considered equivalent to debt, what is American's debt to equity ratio?

Real World Case 15–8
Lease concepts

Safeway, Inc., is one of the world's largest food retailers, operating 1,062 stores in the United States and Canada. A majority of the premises that the company occupies are leased. 1994 financial statements and disclosure notes revealed the following information ($ in millions):

Balance Sheet		
Assets	1994	1993
Property:		
Property under capital lease	$291.7	$310.4
Less: Accumulated depreciation	(150.1)	(148.1)
Liabilities		
Current liabilities:		
Current obligations under capital leases	19.3	19.3
Long-term debt:		
Obligation under capital leases	174.8	193.6

The minimum rental payments applicable to capital leases for 1995 is $40.9 million and depreciation expense for property under capital leases was $20.6 million in 1994.

Required:
1. Discuss some possible reasons why Safeway leases rather than purchases most of its premises.
2. The net asset "property under capital lease" has a 1994 balance of $141.6 million ($291.7 – 150.1). Liabilities for capital leases total $194.1 ($19.3 + 174.8). Why do the asset and liability amounts differ?
3. Prepare a 1995 summary entry to record the $40.9 million in rental payments.
4. Assuming that all property under capital lease is depreciated over the life of the lease, what is the average life of Safeway's capital leases?
5. What is the approximate average interest rate on Safeway's capital leases?

Ethics Case 15–9
Leasehold improvements

American Movieplex, a large movie theater chain, leases most of its theater facilities. In conjunction with recent operating leases, the company spent $28 million for seats and carpeting. The question being discussed over breakfast on Wednesday morning was the length of the depreciation period for these leasehold improvements. The company Controller, Sarah Keene, was surprised by the suggestion of Larry Person, her new assistant.

Keene: Why 25 years? We've never depreciated leasehold improvements for such a long period.
Person: I noticed that in my review of back records. But during our expansion to the Midwest, we don't need expenses to be any higher than necessary.
Keene: But isn't that a pretty rosy estimate of these assets' actual life? Trade publications show an average depreciation period of 12 years.

Required:
1. How would increasing the depreciation period affect American Movieplex's income?
2. Does revising the estimate pose an ethical dilemma?
3. Who would be affected if Person's suggestion is followed?

Internet Case 15–10
Researching lease disclosures; retrieving information from the Internet

EDGAR, the Electronic Data Gathering, Analysis, and Retrieval system, performs automated collection, validation, indexing, acceptance, and forwarding of submissions by companies and others who are required by law to file forms with the U.S. Securities and Exchange Commission (SEC). All publicly traded domestic companies use EDGAR to make the majority of their filings. (Some foreign companies do so voluntarily.) Form 10-K or 10-KSB, which include the annual report, is required to be filed on EDGAR. The SEC makes this information available on the Internet.

Required:
1. Access EDGAR on the Internet. The web address is http://www.sec.gov/.
2. Search for a company with which you are familiar and which you believe leases some of its facilities. (Retail firms and airlines are good candidates). Access the company's most recent 10-K filing. Search or scroll to find the financial statements and related notes.
3. From the disclosure notes, determine the total capital lease obligation of the firm. What percentage does this represent of total liabilities (including current liabilities and deferred taxes) reported on the balance sheet?
4. Compare the company's rental commitments over the next five years and beyond five years for capital leases and operating leases. If operating leases were capitalized, would the company's reported debt change significantly?
5. Repeat steps 2-4 for another firm in the same industry. Are leasing practices similar between the two firms?

ACCOUNTING FOR INCOME TAXES

OVERVIEW

In this chapter we explore the financial accounting and reporting standards for the effects of income taxes. The discussion defines and illustrates temporary differences, which are the basis for recognizing deferred tax assets and deferred tax liabilities, as well as nontemporary differences, which have no deferred tax consequences. You will learn how to adjust deferred tax assets and deferred tax liabilities when tax laws or rates change. We also discuss accounting for operating loss carrybacks and carryforwards and intraperiod tax allocation.

LEARNING OBJECTIVES
After studying this chapter, you should be able to:

1. Describe the types of temporary differences that cause deferred tax liabilities and determine the amounts needed to record periodic income taxes.
2. Identify and describe the types of temporary differences that cause deferred tax assets.
3. Describe when and how a valuation allowance is recorded for deferred tax assets.
4. Explain why nontemporary differences have no deferred tax consequences.
5. Explain how a change in tax rates affects the measurement of deferred tax amounts.
6. Determine income tax amounts when multiple temporary differences exist.
7. Describe when and how an operating loss carryforward and an operating loss carryback are recognized in the financial statements.
8. Explain how deferred tax assets and deferred tax liabilities are classified and reported in a classified balance sheet and describe related disclosures.
9. Explain intraperiod tax allocation.

WHAT'S THE DIFFERENCE?

The board of directors for Times-Lehrer Industries is meeting for the first time since Laura Little-john was asked to join the board. Laura was the director of the regional office of United Charities. Although she has broad experience with the tax advantages of charitable giving and the vast array of investment vehicles available to donors, her 30 years of experience with not-for-profit organizations has not exposed her to the issues involved with corporate taxation. This gap in her considerable business knowledge causes her to turn to you, Times-Lehrer's CFO and long-time friend, who recommended Laura for appointment to the board.

"I must say," Laura confided, "I've looked long and hard at these statements, and I can't quite grasp why the amount reported for income tax expense is not the same as the amount of income taxes we paid. What's the difference?"

QUESTIONS

1. What's the difference? Explain to Laura how differences between financial reporting standards and income tax rules might cause the two tax amounts to differ.
2. What is the conceptual advantage of determining income tax expense as we do?
3. Are there differences between financial reporting standards and income tax rules that will not contribute to the difference between income tax expense and the amount of income taxes paid?

PART

A

DEFERRED TAX ASSETS AND DEFERRED TAX LIABILITIES

OPENING CASE

Question 1

A manufacturer of leather accessories in the Midwest is obligated to pay the Internal Revenue Service $24 million in income taxes as determined by its 1997 income tax return. Another $9 million in income taxes also is attributable to 1997 activities. Conveniently, though, tax laws permit the company to defer paying the additional $9 million until subsequent tax years by reporting certain revenues and expenses on the tax return in years other than when reported on the income statement. Does the company have only a current income tax liability of $24 million? Or does it also have a deferred income tax liability for the other $9 million? To phrase the question differently: Should the company report a 1997 income tax expense of the $24 million tax payable for the current year, or $33 million to include the future tax effects of events already recognized? For perspective on this question, we should look closer at the circumstances that might create the situation. Such circumstances are called *temporary differences.*

Conceptual Underpinning

OPENING CASE

Question 2

> The goals of financial accounting and tax accounting are not the same.

> Accounting for income taxes is consistent with the accrual concept of accounting.

> *APB 11* focused on the income statement and the matching principle.

> *SFAS 109* focuses on the balance sheet and the recognition of liabilities and assets.

When a company prepares its tax return for a particular year, the revenues and expenses (and gains and losses) included on the return are, by and large, the same as those reported on the company's income statement for the same year. However, in some instances tax laws and financial accounting standards differ. The reason they differ is that the fundamental objectives of financial reporting and those of taxing authorities are not the same. Financial accounting standards are established to provide useful information to investors and creditors. Congress, through the Internal Revenue Service, on the other hand, is primarily concerned with raising public revenues in a socially acceptable manner and, frequently, with influencing the behavior of taxpayers. In pursuing the latter objective, Congress uses tax laws to encourage activities it deems desirable, such as investment in productive assets, and to discourage activities it deems undesirable, such as violations of law.

A consequence of differences between GAAP and tax rules is that tax payments frequently occur in years different from when the revenues and expenses that cause the taxes are generated. The financial reporting issue is *when* the tax expense should be recognized. The issue has generated considerable controversy for decades. In 1967 the profession, through *APB 11,* embraced the concept of reporting income tax expense in the same period as events that give rise to the expense, regardless of when the tax actually is paid.[1] You may recognize this approach as being consistent with the accrual concept of accounting. The primary focus of that pronouncement was the matching principle. Income tax expense was calculated on the basis of pretax income reported on the income statement. Differences between the expense and the tax currently paid were reported on the balance sheet not as deferred tax liabilities (or assets) but as nebulous deferred credits (or debits).[2]

APB 11 was replaced in 1987 by *SFAS 96,* which reiterated the objective of reporting deferred taxes but redirected the focus to an asset-liability approach.[3] This balance sheet focus emphasizes reporting the future tax sacrifice or benefit attributable to temporary differences between the reported amount of an asset or liability in the financial statements and its tax basis.[4] Plagued by implementation complexities, *SFAS 96* was delayed three times and then replaced in 1992 with *SFAS 109* before ever becoming mandatory.[5] The current standard modified some of the more troublesome measurement and recognition requirements but retained the essential flavor of *SFAS 96.* That is, the objective of accounting for income taxes is to recognize a deferred tax liability or deferred tax asset for the tax consequences of amounts that will become taxable or deductible in future years as a result of transactions or events that already have occurred. Future taxable amounts and future deductible amounts arise as a result of temporary differences. We discuss those now.

---

[1]"Accounting for Income Taxes," *Accounting Principles Board Opinion 11,* (New York: AICPA, 1967).

[2]Some critics at the time referred to these amounts as "UGOs: Unidentified Growing Objects."

[3]"Accounting for Income Taxes," *Statement of Financial Accounting Standards No. 96,* (Stamford, Conn.: FASB, 1987).

[4]Research supports the notion that deferred tax liabilities are, in fact, viewed by investors as a real liability.

[5]"Accounting for Income Taxes," *Statement of Financial Accounting Standards No. 109,* (Norwalk, Conn.: FASB, 1992).

Temporary Differences

The differences in the rules for computing taxable income and those for financial reporting often cause amounts to be included in taxable income in a year later—or earlier—than the year in which they are recognized for financial reporting purposes, or not to be included in taxable income at all. For example, you learned in Chapter 4 that income from selling merchandise on an installment basis is reported for financial reporting purposes in the year of the sale. But tax laws permit installment income to be reported on the tax return as it actually is received (by the installment method). This means taxable income might be less than accounting income in the year of an installment sale but higher than accounting income in later years when installment income is collected.

Learning objective 1
Describe the types of temporary differences that cause deferred tax liabilities and determine the amounts needed to record periodic income taxes.

The situation just described creates what's referred to as a **temporary difference** between pretax *accounting* income and *taxable* income and, consequently, between the reported amount of an asset or liability in the financial statements and its tax basis. In our example, the asset for which the temporary difference exists is the installment receivable that's recognized for financial reporting purposes, but not for tax purposes.

Deferred Tax Liabilities

It's important to understand that a temporary difference *originates* in one period and *reverses*, or turns around, in one or more subsequent periods. The temporary difference described in the previous section originates in the year the installment sales are made and are reported on the *income statement* and then reverses when the installments are collected and income is reported on the *tax return*. An example is provided in Illustration 16–1.

ILLUSTRATION   16–1

Revenue Reported on the Tax Return after the Income Statement

In 1997, taxable income is less than accounting income because income from installment sales is not reported on the tax return until 1998–1999.

Audio-Video World reported pretax income in 1997, 1998, and 1999 of $100 million, plus additional 1997 income of $40 million from installment sales. However, the installment sales income is reported on the tax return when collected, in 1998 ($10 million) and 1999 ($30 million). The enacted tax rate is 40% each year.*

($ in millions)	Temporary Difference:			
	Originates	Reverses		
	1997	1998	1999	Total
Accounting Income	$140	$100	$100	$340
Installment sale income on the income statement	(40)	0	0	(40)
Installment sale income on the tax return	0	10	30	40
Taxable income	$100	$110	$130	$340

* The enacted rate refers to the tax rate indicated by currently enacted tax legislation (as distinguished from anticipated legislation). This is discussed later in the chapter.

Notice that accounting income and taxable income total the same amount over the three-year period but are different in each individual year. In 1997 taxable income is $40 million *less* than accounting income because it does not include income from installment sales. The difference is temporary, though. That situation reverses over the next two years. In 1998 and 1999 taxable income is *more* than accounting income because income on the installment sales, reported on the income statement in 1997, becomes taxable during the next two years as installments are collected.

Because tax laws permit the company to delay reporting this income as part of taxable income, the company is able to defer paying the tax on that income. The tax is not avoided, just deferred. In the meantime, the company has a liability for the income tax deferred. The liability originates in 1997 and is paid over the next two years as follows:

Deferred Tax Liability

The 1997 tax liability is paid in the next two years.

		($ in millions)	
		16	1997 ($40 × 40%)
1998 ($10 × 40%)	4		
1999 ($13 × 40%)	12		
		0	Balance after 3 years

At the end of 1997, financial and taxable income for 1998 and 1999 are, of course, not yet known. We assumed knowledge of that information above so we could compare the three-year effect of the temporary difference, but seeing the future is unnecessary to determine amounts needed to record income taxes in 1997. This is demonstrated in Illustration 16–1a.

ILLUSTRATION 16–1a

Determining and Recording Income Taxes—1997

($ in millions)	Current Year 1997	Future Taxable Amounts 1998	1999	Future Taxable Amounts (total)
↗GAAP (book) Accounting income	140			
Temporary difference: Installment income	(40)	10	30	40
Taxable income	100			
Enacted tax rate	40%			40%
Tax payable currently	40			
Deferred tax liability				16 ↓
Deferred tax liability:				
Desired ending balance				$16
Less: Beginning balance				0
Change in balance				$16

Journal entry at the end of 1997   140 × 40%

Income tax expense ~~(to balance)~~ ↗	56	
Income tax payable ~~(determined above)~~ 100 × 40%		40
Deferred tax liability ~~(determined above)~~		16
56 − 40		

With future taxable amounts of $40 million, taxable at 40%, a $16 million deferred tax liability is indicated. Since no previous balance exists, this amount is added to the liability.

Each year, income tax expense comprises both the current and the deferred tax consequences of events and transactions already recognized. This means we:

a.   Calculate the income tax that is payable currently.
b.   Separately calculate the change in the deferred tax liability (or asset).
c.   Combine the two to get the income tax expense.

Using the 1998 and 1999 income numbers, the journal entries to record income taxes those years would be:

1998	($ in millions)
Income tax expense (to balance)	40
Deferred tax liability [($30 million × 40%) – 16 million]	4
Income tax payable ($110 million × 40%)	44
1999	
Income tax expense (to balance)	40
Deferred tax liability ($0 million – 12 million)	12
Income tax payable ($130 million × 40%)	52

At the end of 1998, the deferred tax liability should have a balance of $12 million. Because the balance from 1997 is $16 million, we reduce it by $4 million.

At the end of 1999, the deferred tax liability should have a balance of zero. So, we eliminate the $12 million balance.

The FASB's Balance Sheet Approach

Our perspective in this example so far has centered around the income effects of the installment sales and thus on the changes in the deferred tax liability as the temporary difference reverses. Another perspective is to consider the balance sheet effect. From this viewpoint, we regard a deferred tax liability (or asset) to be the tax effect of the temporary difference between the *financial statement carrying amount* of an asset or liability and its *tax basis*. The tax basis of an asset or liability is its original value for tax purposes reduced by any amounts included to date on tax returns. In our example, a temporary book-tax difference exists for a receivable from installment sales that's recognized for financial reporting purposes but not for tax purposes. When a company sells something on an installment basis, it reports a receivable. From a tax perspective,

An installment receivable has no tax basis.

though, there is no receivable because a "taxable sale" doesn't occur until installments are collected. This is shown in Illustration 16–1b.

ILLUSTRATION 16–1b

Balance Sheet Perspective

> The deferred tax liability each year is the tax rate times the temporary difference between the financial statement carrying amount of the receivable and its tax basis.

		1997		1998		1999
Receivable from installment sales:						
Accounting basis	40	$40	(10)	$30	(30)	$ 0
Tax basis	0	0	(0)	0	(0)	0
Temporary difference	40	40	(10)	30	(30)	0
Tax rate		×40%		×40%		×40%
Deferred tax liability		$16		$12		$ 0

($ in millions)
December 31

Originating difference

Reversing differences

> *SFAS 109* takes a balance sheet approach to establishing deferred tax assets and liabilities that meet the definitions of assets and liabilities provided by the FASB's conceptual framework.

Of course, the income statement view and the balance sheet view are two different perspectives on the very same event. In this example, we derive the same deferred tax liability whether we view it as a result of a temporary difference (a) between accounting and taxable income or (b) between the financial statement carrying amount of an installment receivable and its tax basis. Conceptually, though, the balance sheet approach strives to establish deferred tax assets and liabilities that meet the definitions of assets and liabilities provided by the FASB's conceptual framework. As specified by *SFAC 6,* assets represent "probable future economic benefits obtained or controlled by a particular entity as a result of past transactions or events," and liabilities are "probable future sacrifices of economic benefits as a result of past transactions or events."[6] In our example, the probable future sacrifices of economic benefits are the payments of $4 million in 1998 and $12 million in 1999. The past transactions or events resulting in the future tax payments are the installment sales in 1997.

Types of Temporary Differences

Examples of temporary differences are provided in Graphic 16–1.

GRAPHIC   16–1

Types of Temporary Differences

	Revenues (or gains)	Expenses (or losses)
Items Reported on the Tax Return *after* the Income Statement	• Installment sale income (installment method for taxes). • Unrealized gain from recording investments at fair value (taxable when asset is sold).	• Estimated expenses and losses (tax deductible when paid). • Unrealized loss from recording investments at fair value or inventory at LCM (tax deductible when asset is sold).
Items Reported on the Tax Return *before* the Income Statement	• Rent collected in advance. • Subscriptions collected in advance. • Other revenue collected in advance.	• Accelerated depreciation on tax return (straight-line depreciation on the income statement). • Prepaid expenses (tax deductible when paid).

- The temporary differences shown in the diagonal unshaded areas create *deferred tax liabilities* because they result in *taxable* amounts in some future year(s) when the related assets are recovered or the related liabilities are settled (when the temporary differences reverse).
- The temporary differences in the opposite diagonal (shaded) areas create *deferred tax assets* because they result in *deductible* amounts in some future year(s) when the related assets are recovered or the related liabilities are settled (when the temporary differences reverse).

---

[6]"Elements of Financial Statements," *Statement of Financial Accounting Concepts No. 6,* (Stamford, Conn.: FASB, 1985), par. 25, 35.

Additional Consideration

Temporary differences between the reported amount of an asset or liability in the financial statements and its tax basis are primarily caused by revenues, expenses, gains, and losses being included in taxable income in a year earlier or later than the year in which they are recognized for financial reporting purposes as illustrated in Graphic 16–1. Other events also can cause temporary differences between the reported amount of an asset or liability in the financial statements and its tax basis. Three other such events that are beyond the scope of this textbook are briefly described in "Accounting for Income Taxes," *Statement of Financial Accounting Standards No. 109,* (Norwalk, Conn.: FASB, 1992), par. 11 e–h. Our discussions in this chapter focus on temporary differences caused by the timing of revenue and expense recognition, but it's important to realize that the concept of temporary differences embraces all differences that will result in taxable or deductible amounts in future years.

Be sure to notice that deferred tax liabilities can arise from either (a) a revenue being reported on the tax return after the income statement or (b) an expense being reported on the tax return before the income statement. Our previous illustration was of the first type. Now, let's look at the second.

ILLUSTRATION   16–2

Expense Reported on the Tax Return before the Income Statement

To determine taxable income, we add back to accounting income the actual depreciation taken in the income statement and then subtract the depreciation deduction allowed on the tax return.

Woods Temporary Services reported pretax income in 1997, 1998, 1999, and 2000 of $100 million. In 1997, an asset was acquired for $100 million. The asset is depreciated for financial reporting purposes over four years on a straight-line basis (no residual value). For tax purposes the asset's cost is deducted (by MACRS) over 1997–2000 as follows: $33 million, $44 million, $15 million, and $8 million. No other depreciable assets were acquired. The enacted tax rate is 40% each year.

($ in millions)	Originates 1997	1998	Reverses 1999	2000	Total
Accounting Income	$100	$100	$100	$100	$400
Depreciation on the income statement	25	25	25	25	100
Depreciation on the tax return	(33)	(44)	(15)	(8)	(100)
Taxable income	$ 92	$ 81	$110	$117	$400

Notice, too, that this temporary difference originates during more than a single year before it begins to reverse. This usually is true when depreciation is the cause of the temporary difference. Tax laws typically permit the cost of a depreciable asset to be deducted on the tax return sooner than it is reported as depreciation on the income statement.[7] This means taxable income will be less than accounting income during the years the tax deduction is higher than income statement depreciation, but higher than accounting income in later years when the situation reverses.

1997 income taxes would be recorded as follows:

ILLUSTRATION   16–2a

Determining and Recording Income Taxes—1997

Taxable income is $8 million less than accounting income because that much more depreciation is deducted on the 1997 tax return ($33 million) than is reported on the income statement ($25 million).

($ in millions)	Current Year 1997	1998	Future Taxable Amounts 1999	2000	Future Taxable Amounts (total)
Accounting income	100				
Temporary difference: Depreciation	(8)	(19)	10	17	8
Taxable income	92				
Enacted tax rate	40%				40%
Tax payable currently	36.8				
Deferred tax liability					3.2 ↓

Deferred tax liability:	
Ending balance	$3.2
Less: Beginning balance	0.0
Change in balance	$3.2

---

[7]Presently, the accelerated depreciation method prescribed by the tax code is the modified accelerated cost recovery system (MACRS). The method is described in Chapter 11.

ILLUSTRATION 16–2a

continued

Income tax expense is comprised of two components: the amount payable now and the amount deferred until later.

Journal entry at the end of 1997		
Income tax expense (to balance)	40	
Income tax payable (determined above)		36.8
Deferred tax liability (determined above)		3.2

Let's follow the determination of income taxes for this illustration all the way through the complete reversal of the temporary difference. We assume accounting income is $100 million each year and that the only difference between financial and taxable income is caused by depreciation. 1998 income taxes would be determined as shown in Illustration 16–2b.

ILLUSTRATION 16–2b

Determining and Recording Income Taxes—1998

The cumulative temporary difference between the book basis ($50 million) and tax basis ($23 million) is both (a) the sum of the amounts originating in 1997 ($8 million) and in 1998 ($19 million) and (b) the sum of the amounts reversing in 1999 ($10 million) and in 2000 ($17 million).

Since a balance of $3.2 million already exists, $7.6 million must be added.

($ in millions)	1997	Current Year 1998	Future Taxable Amounts 1999	Future Taxable Amounts 2000	Future Taxable Amounts (total)
Accounting income	100				
Temporary difference:					
Depreciation	(8)	(19)	10	17	27
Taxable income		81			
Enacted tax rate		40%			40%
Tax payable currently		32.4			
Deferred tax liability					10.8 ↓

Deferred tax liability:

Ending balance	$10.8
Less: Beginning balance	(3.2)
Change in balance	$ 7.6

Journal entry at the end of 1998		
Income tax expense (to balance)	40	
Income tax payable (determined above)		32.4
Deferred tax liability (determined above)		7.6

Notice that each year the appropriate balance is determined for the deferred tax liability. That amount is compared with any existing balance to determine whether the account must be either increased or decreased.

Income taxes for 1999 would be recorded as shown in Illustration 16–2c.

ILLUSTRATION 16–2c

Determining and Recording Income Taxes—1999

A credit balance of $6.8 million is needed in the deferred tax liability account.

Since a credit balance of $10.8 million already exists, $4 million must be deducted (debited).

A portion of the tax deferred from 1997 and 1998 is now being paid in 1999.

($ in millions)	1997	1998	Current Year 1999	Future Taxable Amounts 2000	Future Taxable Amounts (total)
Accounting income	100				
Temporary difference:					
Depreciation	(8)	(19)	10	17	27
Taxable income			110		
Enacted tax rate			40%		40%
Tax payable currently			44		
Deferred tax liability					6.8 ↓

Deferred tax liability:

Ending balance	$ 6.8
Less: Beginning balance	(10.8)
Change in balance	$ (4.0)

Journal entry at the end of 1999		
Income tax expense (to balance)	40	
Deferred tax liability (determined above)	4	
Income tax payable (determined above)		44

Income taxes for 2000 would be recorded as shown in Illustration 16–2d.

ILLUSTRATION 16–2d

Determining and Recording Income Taxes—2000

Because the entire temporary difference has now reversed, there is a zero cumulative temporary difference, and the balance in the deferred tax liability should be zero.

Since a credit balance of $6.8 million exists, that amount must be deducted (debited).

The final portion of the tax deferred from 1997 and 1998 is paid in 2000.

($ in millions)	1997	1998	1999	Current Year 2000	Future Taxable Amounts (total)
Accounting income				100	
Temporary difference:					
Depreciation	(8)	(19)	10	17	0
Taxable income				117	
Enacted tax rate				40%	40%
Tax payable currently				46.8	
Deferred tax liability					0.0 ↓

Deferred tax liability:

Ending balance	$ 0.00
Less: Beginning balance	(6.8)
Change in balance	$ (6.8)

Journal entry at the end of 2000

Income tax expense (to balance)	40.0	
Deferred tax liability (determined above)	6.8	
Income tax payable (determined above)		46.8

The deferred tax liability is increased in 1997–1998 and decreased in 1999–2000:

Deferred Tax Liability

			($ in millions)
		3.2	1997 ($8 × 40%)
		7.6	1998 ($19 × 40%)
1999 ($10 × 40%)	4.0		
2000 ($17 × 40%)	6.8		
		0	Balance after 4 years

The deferred tax liability increases the first two years and is paid over the next two years.

We can see this result from the alternate perspective of looking at the temporary book–tax difference that exists for the depreciable asset. Its carrying amount is its cost minus accumulated straight-line depreciation. Its tax basis is cost minus the accumulated cost recovery for tax purposes:

A balance sheet perspective focuses on the difference between the carrying amount at the tax basis.

($ in millions)			December 31						
	1997		**1998**		**1999**		**2000**		
Depreciable asset:									
Accounting basis	$100	(25)	$75	(25)	$50	(25)	$25	(25)	$0
Tax basis	100	(33)	67	(44)	23	(15)	8	(8)	0
Temporary difference		8	8	19	27	(10)	17	(17)	0
Enacted tax rate			40%		40%		40%		40%
Deferred tax liability			$ 3.2		$10.8		$6.8		$0
		↑		↑		↑		↑	
		Originating differences				**Reversing differences**			

Deferred Tax Assets

Learning objective 2
Identify and describe the types of temporary differences that cause deferred tax assets.

Deferred tax assets are recognized for the future tax benefits of temporary differences that create future deductible amounts.

The temporary differences illustrated to this point produce future taxable amounts when the temporary differences reverse. Future taxable amounts means taxable income will be increased relative to accounting income in one or more future years. Sometimes, though, the future tax consequence of a temporary difference will be to decrease taxable income relative to accounting income. Such situations produce what's referred to as *future deductible amounts*. These have favorable tax consequences that are recognized as deferred tax assets.

Two examples indicated in Graphic 16–1 are (1) estimated expenses that are recognized on income statements when incurred but deducted on tax returns in later years when actually paid and (2) revenues that are taxed when collected but recognized on income statements in later years when actually earned. An example of the first type is provided in Illustration 16–3.

ILLUSTRATION 16-3

Expense Reported on the Tax Return *after* the Income Statement

In 1997, taxable income is more than accounting income because the warranty expense is not deducted on the tax return until paid.

Lane Electronics reported pretax income in 1997, 1998, and 1999 of $70 million, $100 million, and $100 million, respectively. The 1997 income statement includes a $30 million warranty expense that is deducted for tax purposes when paid in 1998 ($15 million) and 1999 ($15 million).* The income tax rate is 40% each year.

| ($ in millions) | Temporary Difference: | | | |
| | Originates | Reverses | | |
	1997	1998	1999	Total
Accounting income	$70	$100	$100	$270
Warranty expense on the income statement	30			30
Warranty expense on the tax return	___	(15)	(15)	(30)
Taxable income	$100	$ 85	$ 85	$270

*Remember from Chapter 13 that warranty expense is estimated for the period the products are sold even though the actual cost isn't incurred until later periods.

At the end of 1997, the amounts needed to record income tax for 1997 would be determined as shown in Illustration 16–3a.

ILLUSTRATION 16-3a

Determining and Recording Income Taxes—1997

Because the warranty expense was subtracted on the 1997 income statement but isn't deductible on the 1997 tax return, it is added back to accounting income to find taxable income.

The amounts deductible in 1998 and 1999 will produce tax benefits that are recognized now as a deferred tax asset.

The deferred tax benefit of the 1997 warranty expense is combined with the tax payable currently to find the 1997 tax expense.

($ in millions)	Current Year 1997	Future Deductible Amounts 1998	Future Deductible Amounts 1999	Future Deductible Amounts (total)
Accounting income	70			
Temporary difference:				
Warranty expense	30	(15)	(15)	(30)
Taxable income	100		(30)	
Enacted tax rate	40%			40%
Tax payable currently	40			(12)
Deferred tax asset				↓

Deferred tax asset:

Ending balance	$12
Less: Beginning balance	0
Change in balance	$12

Journal entry at the end of 1997

Income tax expense (to balance) (70 × 40%)	28	
Deferred tax asset (determined above) (40 − 28)	12	
Income tax payable (determined above) (100 × 40%)		40

At the end of 1997 and 1998, the company reports a deferred tax asset for future income tax benefits.

Deferred Tax Asset

Income taxes payable in 1998 and 1999 are less than otherwise payable because of the taxes "prepaid" in 1997.

1997 ($30 × 40%)	12	($ in millions)	
		6	1998 ($15 × 40%)
		6	1999 ($15 × 40%)
Balance after 3 years	0		

If we continue the assumption of $85 million taxable income in each of 1998 and 1999, income tax those years would be recorded this way:

1998

Income tax expense (to balance)	40	
Deferred tax asset ($15 million × 40%)		6
Income tax payable ($85 million × 40%)		34

1999		
Income tax expense (to balance)	40	
Deferred tax asset ($15 million × 40%)		6
Income tax payable ($85 million × 40%)		34

The deferred tax asset represents the future tax benefit from the reversal of a temporary difference between the financial statement carrying amount of the warranty liability and its tax basis.

A liability is recognized for financial reporting purposes when the guaranteed product is sold:

1997	Warr. exp	30	
	Liability		30

and reduced when the expense is paid:

1998	Liability	15	
	Cash		15
1999	Liability	15	
	Cash		15

From a tax perspective, there is no liability.

($ in millions)		December 31				
		1997		**1998**		**1999**
Warranty liability:						
Accounting basis	30	$30	(15)	$15	(15)	$ 0
Tax basis	0	0	(0)	0	(0)	0
Temporary difference	30	30	(15)	15	(15)	0
Tax rate		× 40%		× 40%		× 40%
Deferred tax asset	12	$12	(6)	$ 6	(6)	$ 0

Originating differences ↑   **Reversing differences** ↑   ↑

The preceding was an illustration of an estimated expense that is reported on the income statement when incurred but deducted on tax returns in later years when actually paid. A second type of temporary difference that gives rise to a deferred tax asset is a revenue that is taxed when collected but recognized on income statements in later years when actually earned. Illustration 16–4 demonstrates this second type.

ILLUSTRATION 16–4

Revenue Reported on the Tax Return *before* the Income Statement

Tomorrow Publications reported pretax income in 1997, 1998, and 1999 of $80 million, $115 million, and $105 million, respectively. The 1997 income statement does *not* include $20 million of magazine subscriptions received that year for one- and two-year subscriptions. The subscription revenue is reported for tax purposes in 1997. The revenue will be earned in 1998 ($15 million) and 1999 ($5 million). The income tax rate is 40% each year.

In 1997, taxable income is more than accounting income because subscription revenue is not reported on the income statement until 1998–1999.

($ in millions)		Temporary Difference:		
	Originates	Reverses		
	1997	**1998**	**1999**	**Total**
Accounting income	$80	$115	$105	$300
Subscription revenue on the income statement		(15)	(5)	(20)
Subscription revenue on the tax return	20	0	0	20
Taxable income	$100	$100	$100	$300

A deferred tax asset is recognized when an existing temporary difference will produce future deductible amounts.

Notice that this temporary difference produces future *deductible* amounts. In 1997, taxable income is $20 million *more* than accounting income because it includes the unearned subscriptions revenue not yet reported on the income statement. However, in 1998 and 1999 taxable income is *less* than accounting income because the subscription revenue is earned and reported on the income statements but not on the tax returns of those two years.

In effect, tax laws require the company to prepay the income tax on this revenue, which is a sacrifice now but will benefit the company later when it avoids paying the taxes when the revenue is earned. In the meantime, the company has an asset representing this future income tax benefit.

At the end of 1997, the amounts needed to record income tax for 1997 would be determined as shown at the top of the next page.

ILLUSTRATION 16–4a

Determining and Recording Income Taxes—1997

($ in millions)	Current Year 1997	Future Deductible Amounts 1998	1999	Future Deductible Amounts (total)
Accounting income	80			
Temporary difference:				
Subscription revenue	20	(15)	(5)	(20)
Taxable income	100			
Enacted tax rate	40%			40%
Tax payable currently	40			
Deferred tax asset				(8) ↓

Deferred tax asset:	
Ending balance	$8
Less: Beginning balance	0
Change in balance	$8

Journal entry at the end of 1997

Income tax expense (to balance)	32	
Deferred tax asset (determined above)	8	
Income tax payable (determined above)		40

At the end of 1997 and 1998, the company reports a deferred tax asset for future tax benefits.

Deferred Tax Asset

			($ in millions)
1997 ($20 × 40%)	8		
		6	1998 ($15 × 40%)
		2	1999 ($5 × 40%)
Balance after 3 years	0		

> Income taxes payable in 1998 and 1999 are less than otherwise payable because of the taxes prepaid in 1997.

Again, we could determine the deferred tax asset as the future tax benefit from the reversal of a temporary difference between the financial statement carrying amount of the subscription liability and its tax basis.[8]

> A liability is recognized for financial reporting purposes when the cash is received:
>
> **1997** Cash   20
>   Liability   20
>
> and reduced when the revenue is earned:
>
> **1998** Liability   15
>   Revenue   15
> **1999** Liability   5
>   Revenue   5
> From a tax perspective, there is no liability.

($ in millions)		December 31				
		1997		1998		1999
Liability—subscriptions:						
Accounting basis	20	$20	(15)	$ 5	(5)	$ 0
Tax basis	0	0	(0)	0	(0)	0
Temporary difference	20	20	(15)	5	(5)	0
Tax rate		× 40%		× 40%		× 40%
Deferred tax asset		$ 8		$ 2		$ 0

↑ Originating differences   Reversing differences

Valuation Allowance

Deferred tax assets are recognized for all deductible temporary differences. However, a deferred tax asset is then reduced by a valuation allowance if it is "more likely than not" that some portion or all of the deferred tax asset will not be

Learning objective 3
Describe when and how a valuation allowance is recorded for deferred tax assets.

---

[8]It is less intuitive to view an unearned revenue (Illustration 16–4) as producing future deductible amounts when the unearned revenue liability is settled than it is to view the future deductibility of an estimated expense (Illustration 16–3) as a future deductible amount. Nevertheless, the recognition of deferred tax assets for the future tax benefits of unearned revenue liability temporary differences is consistent with the asset/liability approach of *SFAS 109* because these unearned revenue liabilities are reported as if they represent future refundable amounts and therefore future deductible amounts. This point is argued persuasively by Hugo Nurnberg, "Deferred Tax Assets under FASB Statement No. 96," *Accounting Horizons*, December 1989.

realized.[9] Remember, a future deductible amount reduces taxable income and saves taxes only if there is taxable income to be reduced when the future deduction is available. So, a valuation allowance is needed if taxable income is anticipated to be insufficient to realize the tax benefit.

For example, let's say that in the previous illustration management determines that it's more likely than not that $3 million of the deferred tax asset will not ultimately be realized. The deferred tax asset would be reduced by the creation of a valuation allowance as follows:

	($ in millions)
Income tax expense	3
Valuation allowance—deferred tax asset	3

> A valuation allowance is needed if it is more likely than not that some portion or all of a deferred tax asset will not be realized.

The effect is to increase the income tax expense as a result of reduced expectations of future tax savings. On the 1997 balance sheet, the deferred tax asset would be reported at its estimated net realizable value:

Deferred tax asset	$8
Less: Valuation allowance—deferred tax asset	3
	$5

> A deferred tax asset is reported at its estimated net realizable value.

Additional Consideration

The decision as to whether a valuation allowance is needed should be based on the weight of all available evidence. The real question is whether or not there will be sufficient taxable income in future years for the anticipated tax benefit to be realized. The benefit of future deductible amounts can be realized only if future income is at least equal to the deferred deductions. After all, a deduction reduces taxes only if it reduces taxable income.

All evidence—both positive and negative—should be considered. For instance, operating losses in recent years or anticipated circumstances that would adversely affect future operations would constitute negative evidence. On the other hand, a strong history of profitable operations or sizable, existing contracts would constitute positive evidence of sufficient taxable income to be able to realize the deferred tax asset.

Managerial actions that could be taken to reduce or eliminate a valuation allowance when deferred tax assets are not otherwise expected to be realized must be considered. These tax-planning strategies include any prudent and feasible actions management might take to realize a tax benefit while it is available.

At the end of each reporting period, the valuation allowance is reevaluated. The appropriate balance is decided on and the balance is adjusted—up or down—to create that balance. For instance, let's say that at the end of the following year, 1998, available evidence indicates that $500,000 of the deferred tax asset at the end of 1998 will not be realized. We would adjust the valuation allowance to reflect the indicated amount:

	($ in millions)
Valuation allowance—deferred tax asset ($3 million – 0.5 million)	2.5
Income tax expense	2.5

> Each period, the valuation allowance is adjusted to reflect the appropriate balance at the time.

The disclosure note shown in Graphic 16–2 accompanied the 1995 annual report of Unigene Laboratories, Inc., indicating that none of its deferred tax asset was expected to be realized:

---

[9]"More likely than not" means a likelihood of more than 50%, "Accounting for Income Taxes," *Statement of Financial Accounting Standards No. 109,* (Norwalk, Conn.: FASB, 1992), par. 17.

GRAPHIC   16–2

Valuation Allowance—
Unigene Laboratories, Inc.

> Given the Company's past history of incurring operating losses, any deferred tax assets that are recognizable under *SFAS 109* have been fully reserved. As of January 1, 1995, and 1994, under *SFAS 109,* the Company had deferred tax assets of approximately $11,100,000 and $8,400,000, respectively, subject to a valuation allowance of 11,100,000 and $8,400,000, respectively.

Nontemporary Differences

Learning objective 4
Explain why nontemporary differences have no deferred tax consequences.

OPENING CASE

Question 3

Permanent differences are disregarded when determining both the tax payable currently and the deferred tax asset or liability.

So far, we've dealt with temporary differences between the reported amount of an asset or liability in the financial statements and its tax basis. You learned that temporary differences result in future taxable or deductible amounts when the related asset or liability is recovered or settled. However, some differences are caused by transactions and events that under existing tax law will never affect taxable income or taxes payable. Interest received from investments in bonds issued by state and municipal governments, for instance, is exempt from taxation. Interest revenue of this type is, of course, reported as revenue on the recipient's income statement but not on its tax return—not now, not later. Accounting income exceeds taxable income. This situation will not reverse in a later year. Taxable income in a later year will not exceed accounting income because the tax-free income will never be reported on the tax return.

These permanent differences are disregarded when determining the tax payable currently, the deferred tax effect, and therefore the income tax expense.[10] This is why we adjust accounting income in the illustrations that follow to eliminate any permanent differences from taxable income. Graphic 16–3 provides examples of differences with no deferred tax consequences.

GRAPHIC   16–3

Differences without Deferred Tax Consequences

Provisions of the tax laws, in some instances, dictate that the amount of a revenue that is taxable or expense that is deductible permanently differs from the amount reported on the income statement.

- Interest received from investments in bonds issued by state and municipal governments (not taxable).
- Investment expenses incurred to obtain tax-exempt income (not tax deductible).
- Life insurance proceeds on the death of an insured executive (not taxable).
- Premiums paid for life insurance policies when the payer is the beneficiary (not tax deductible).
- Compensation expense pertaining to some employee stock option plans (not tax deductible).
- Expenses due to violations of the law (not tax deductible).
- Portion of dividends received from U.S. corporations that is not taxable due to the dividends received deduction.[11]
- Tax deduction for depletion of natural resources (percentage depletion) that permanently exceeds the income statement depletion expense (cost depletion).[12]

To compare temporary and nontemporary differences, we can modify Illustration 16–1 to include nontaxable income in Audio-Video World's 1997 pretax accounting income. We do this in Illustration 16–5.

ILLUSTRATION   16–5

Temporary and Permanent Differences

Audio-Video World reported pretax income in 1997, 1998, and 1999 of $100 million except for additional income of $40 million from installment sales **and $5 million interest from investments in municipal bonds** in 1997. The installment sales income is reported for tax purposes in 1998 ($10 million) and 1999 ($30 million). The enacted tax rate is 40% each year.

[10]The term permanent difference was used in *APB 11* to describe differences with no deferred tax consequences. Although the term itself is not used in more recent pronouncements (*SFAS 96* and *SFAS 109*), it still is useful to describe nontemporary differences.

[11]When a corporation owns shares of another U.S. corporation, a percentage of the dividends from those shares is exempt from taxation due to the dividends received deduction. The percentage is 70% if the investor owns less than 20% of the investee's shares, 80% for 20% to 80% ownership, and 100% for more than 80% ownership.

[12]The cost of natural resources is reported as depletion expense over their extraction period for financial reporting purposes; but tax rules prescribe specific percentages of cost to be deducted for tax purposes. There usually is a difference between the cost depletion and percentage depletion that doesn't eventually reverse.

ILLUSTRATION   16–5

continued

Because interest on municipal bonds is tax exempt, it is reported only on the income statement. This difference between accounting income and taxable income does not reverse later.

($ in millions)	Current Year 1997	Future Taxable Amounts		Future Taxable Amounts (total)
		1998	1999	
Accounting income	145			
Permanent difference:				
Municipal bond interest	(5)			
Temporary difference:				
Installment income	(40)	10	30	40
Taxable income	100			
Enacted tax rate	40%			40%
Tax payable currently	40			
Deferred tax liability				16
				↓

Deferred tax liability:

Ending balance	$16
Less: Beginning balance	0
Change in balance	$16

Journal entry at the end of 1997

Income tax expense (to balance)	56	
Income tax payable (determined above)		40
Deferred tax liability (determined above)		16

Note that the existence of an amount that causes a permanent difference has no effect on income taxes payable, deferred taxes, or income tax expense.

To this point, we've seen that our objective in accounting for income taxes is to recognize the tax consequences of amounts that will become taxable or deductible in future years as a result of transactions or events that already have occurred. To achieve the objective, we record a deferred tax liability or deferred tax asset for future taxable amounts or future deductible amounts that arise as a result of temporary differences. Permanent differences, on the other hand, do not create future taxable amounts and future deductible amounts and therefore have no tax consequences.

GLOBAL PERSPECTIVE

The extent of differences between accounting income and taxable income varies widely from country to country. In fact, in France and Germany financial accounting and tax accounting must coincide. There also is little uniformity as to how to handle these differences. In many countries, Finland for instance, income taxes are not deferred. Instead, tax expense is simply the actual tax paid. Under standards of the International Accounting Standards Committee (IASC), income taxes are deferred, but if differences are not expected to reverse for at least three years, these amounts can be excluded from tax expense. The United Kingdom, among others, subscribes to this approach.

CONCEPT REVIEW EXERCISE   TEMPORARY AND PERMANENT DIFFERENCES

Mid-South Cellular Systems began operations in 1997. That year the company reported pretax accounting income of $70 million, which included the following amounts:

1. Compensation expense of $3 million related to employee stock option plans granted to organizers was reported on the 1997 income statement. This expense is not deductible for tax purposes.

2. An asset with a four-year useful life was acquired last year. It is depreciated by the straight-line method on the income statement. MACRS is used on the tax return, causing deductions for depreciation to be more than straight-line depreciation the first two years but less than straight-line depreciation the next two years ($ in millions):

	Depreciation		
	Income Statement	Tax Return	Difference
1997	$150	$198	$ (48)
1998	150	264	(114)
1999	150	90	60
2000	150	48	102
	$600	$600	0

The enacted tax rate is 40%.

Required:

Prepare the journal entry to record Mid-South Cellular's income taxes for 1997.

CONCEPT REVIEW EXERCISE   SOLUTION

Because the compensation expense is not tax deductible, taxable income does not include that $3 million deduction and is higher by that amount than accounting income.

($ in millions)	Current Year 1997	1998	Future Taxable Amounts 1999	2000	Future Taxable Amounts (total)
Accounting income	70				
Permanent difference:					
Compensation expense	3				
Temporary differences:					
Depreciation	(48)	(114)	60	102	48
Taxable income	25				
Enacted tax rate	40%				40%
Tax payable	10				
Deferred tax liability					19.2
					↓
Deferred tax liability:					
Ending balance					$19.2
Less: Beginning balance					0.0
Change in balance					$19.2

Income tax expense is composed of: (1) the tax payable now and (2) the tax deferred until later.

Journal entry at the end of 1997

Income tax expense (to balance)	29.2	
Income tax payable (determined above)		10.0
Deferred tax liability (determined above)		19.2

PART **B** # OTHER TAX ACCOUNTING ISSUES – *not going to cover*

Tax Rate Considerations

Learning objective 5
Explain how a change in tax rates affects the measurement of deferred tax amounts.

A deferred tax liability (or asset) is based on enacted tax rates and laws.

To measure the deferred tax liability or asset, we multiply the temporary difference by the currently *enacted* tax rate that will be effective in the year(s) the temporary difference reverses.[13] We do not base calculations on *anticipated* legislation that would alter the company's tax rate. A conceptual case can be made that expected rate changes should be anticipated when measuring the deferred tax liability or asset. However, this is one of many examples of the frequent trade-off between relevance and reliability. In this case, the FASB chose to favor reliability by waiting until an anticipated change actually is enacted into law before recognizing its tax consequences.

---

[13]The current U.S. corporate tax rate is 34%, or 35% for corporations with taxable income over $75,000. Most states tax corporate income at rates less than 10%. We use 40% in most of our illustrations to simplify calculations.

When Enacted Tax Rates Differ

Existing tax laws may call for enacted tax rates to be different in two or more future years in which a temporary difference is expected to reverse. When a phased-in change in rates is scheduled to occur, the specific tax rates of each future year are multiplied by the amounts reversing in each of those years. The total is the deferred tax liability or asset.

To illustrate, let's again modify our Audio-Video World illustration, this time to assume a scheduled change in tax rates. See Illustration 16–6.

ILLUSTRATION 16–6

Scheduled Change in Tax Rates

The tax effects of the future taxable amounts depend on the tax rates at which those amounts will be taxed.

Audio-Video World reported pretax income in 1997, 1998, and 1999 of $100 million except for additional income of $40 million from installment sales and $5 million interest from investments in municipal bonds in 1997. The installment sales income is reported for tax purposes in 1998 ($10 million) and 1999 ($30 million). **The enacted tax rates are 40% for 1997 and 1998, and 35% for 1999.**

($ in millions)	Current Year 1997	Future Taxable Amounts		(total)
		1998	1999	
Accounting income	145			
Permanent difference:				
Municipal bond interest	(5)			
Temporary difference:				
Installment income	(40)	10	30	
Taxable income	100			
Enacted tax rate	40%	40%	35%	
Tax payable currently	40			
Deferred tax liability		4	10.5	14.5 ↓

Deferred tax liability:

Ending balance	$14.5
Less: Beginning balance	0.0
Change in balance	$14.5

Journal entry at the end of 1997

Income tax expense (to balance)	54.5	
Income tax payable (determined above)		40.0
Deferred tax liability (determined above)		14.5

Be sure to note that the 1998 rate (40%) as well as the 1999 rate (35%) already is enacted into law as of 1997 when the deferred tax liability is established. In the next section we discuss how to handle a change resulting from new legislation.

Changes in Tax Laws or Rates

Tax laws sometimes change. If a change in a tax law or rate occurs, the deferred tax liability or asset must be adjusted. Remember, the deferred tax liability or asset is meant to reflect the amount to be paid or recovered in the future. When legislation changes that amount, the deferred tax liability or asset also should change. The effect is reflected in operating income in the year of the enactment of the change in the tax law or rate.

As a result of [a change in tax law or rate] deferred tax consequences become larger or smaller.[14]

For clarification, reconsider the previous illustration. Without a change in tax rates and assuming that accounting income in 1998 is $100 million (with no additional temporary or permanent differences), the 1998 income tax amounts would be determined as shown in Illustration 16–6a.

Now assume Congress passed a new tax law in 1998 that will cause the 1999 tax rate to be 30% instead of the previously scheduled 35% rate. Because a deferred tax liability was estab-

14"Accounting for Income Taxes," *Statement of Financial Accounting Standards No. 109,* (Norwalk, Conn.: FASB, 1992), par. 112.

ILLUSTRATION   16–6a

Reversal of Temporary Difference without a Tax Rate Change

The 40% 1998 rate and the 35% 1999 rate are established by previously enacted legislation.

($ in millions)	Current Year 1998	Future Taxable Amount 1999	
Accounting income	100		
Temporary difference:			
Installment income	10	30	
Taxable income	110		
Enacted tax rate	40%	35%	
Tax payable currently	44		
Deferred tax liability		10.5	10.5
			↓
Deferred tax liability:			
Ending balance			$10.5
Less: Beginning balance			(14.5)
Change in balance			$(4.0)

Journal entry at the end of 1998

Income tax expense (to balance)	40	
Deferred tax liability (determined above)	4	
Income tax payable (determined above)		44

lished in 1997 with the expectation that the 1999 taxable amount would be taxed at 35%, it would now be adjusted to reflect taxation at 30%, instead. This is demonstrated in Illustration 16–6b.

ILLUSTRATION   16–6b

Reversal of Temporary Difference with a Tax Rate Change

The deferred tax liability would have been $10.5 million ($30 million × 35%) if the tax rate had not changed.

($ in millions)	Current Year 1998	Future Taxable Amounts 1999	
Accounting income	100		
Temporary difference:			
Installment income	10	30	
Taxable income	110		
Enacted tax rate	40%	30%*	
Tax payable currently	44		
Deferred tax liability		9	9.0
*1999 rate enacted into law in 1998			↓
Deferred tax liability:			
Ending balance			$ 9.0
Less: Beginning balance			(14.5)
Change in balance			$ (5.5)

Journal entry at the end of 1998

Income tax expense (to balance)	38.5	
Deferred tax liability (determined above)	5.5	
Income tax payable (determined above)		44.0

When a tax rate changes, the deferred tax liability or asset should be adjusted with the effect reflected in operating income in the year of the change.

Notice that the methods used to determine the deferred tax liability and the change in that balance are the same as without the rate change—the calculation merely uses the new rate (30%) rather than the old rate (35%). So recalculating the desired balance in the deferred tax liability each period and comparing that amount with any previously existing balance automatically takes into account tax rate changes.

Also notice that the income tax expense ($38.5 million) is $1.5 million less than it would have been without the tax rate change ($40 million). The effect of the change is included in income tax expense. In fact, this is highlighted if we separate the previous entry into its component parts: (1) record the income tax expense without the tax rate change and (2) separately record the adjustment of the deferred tax liability for the change:

Journal entries at the end of 1998	($ in millions)	
Income tax expense	40	
Deferred tax liability	4	
Income tax payable		44
Deferred tax liability ($30 million × [35% – 30%])	1.5	
Income tax expense		1.5

The tax consequence of a change in a tax law or rate is recognized in the period the change is enacted. In this case, the consequence of a lower tax rate is a reduced deferred tax liability, recognized as a reduction in income tax expense in 1998 when the change occurs.

Multiple Temporary Differences

It would be unusual for any but a very small company to have only a single temporary difference in any given year. Having multiple temporary differences, though, doesn't change any of the principles you've learned so far in connection with single differences. All that's necessary is to categorize all temporary differences according to whether they create (a) future taxable amounts or (b) future deductible amounts. The total of the future taxable amounts is multiplied by the future tax rate to determine the appropriate balance for the deferred tax liability, and the total of the future deductible amounts is multiplied by the future tax rate to determine the appropriate balance for the deferred tax asset. This is demonstrated in Illustration 16–7.

Learning objective 6
Determine income tax amounts when multiple temporary differences exist.

Temporary differences are classified according to whether they create future taxable amounts or future deductible amounts.

ILLUSTRATION   16–7

Multiple Temporary Differences

1997
During 1997, its first year of operations, Eli-Wallace Distributors reported pretax accounting income of $200 million which included the following amounts:

1. Income from installment sales in 1997 of $9 million to be reported for tax purposes in 1998 ($5 million) and 1999 ($4 million).
2. Depreciation is reported by the straight-line method on an asset with a four-year useful life. On the tax return, deductions for depreciation will be more than straight-line depreciation the first two years but less than straight-line depreciation the next two years ($ in millions):

	Income Statement	Tax Return	Difference
1997	$ 50	$ 66	$(16)
1998	50	88	(38)
1999	50	30	20
2000	50	16	34
	$200	$200	0

3. Estimated warranty expense that will be deductible on the tax return when actually paid during the next two years. Estimated deductions are as follows ($ in millions):

	Income Statement	Tax Return	Difference
1997	$7		$7
1998		$4	(4)
1999		3	(3)
	$7	$7	0

1998
During 1998, pretax accounting income of $200 million included an estimated loss of $1 million from having accrued a loss contingency. The loss is expected to be paid in 2000 at which time it will be tax deductible.
   The enacted tax rate is 40% each year.

Income tax amounts for 1997 would be determined as shown in Illustration 16–7a.

ILLUSTRATION 16–7a

Multiple Temporary Differences—1997

Temporary differences are grouped according to whether they create future **taxable** amounts or future **deductible** amounts.

The desired balances in the deferred tax liability and the deferred tax asset are separately determined.

Income tax expense is composed of three components: (1) the tax payable now plus (2) the tax deferred until later, reduced by (3) the deferred tax benefit.

($ in millions)	Current Year 1997	Future Taxable (Deductible) Amounts 1998	1999	2000	Future Taxable Amounts (total)	Future Deductible Amounts (total)
Accounting income	200					
Temporary differences:						
Installment sales	(9)	5	4		9	
Depreciation	(16)	(38)	20	34	16	
Warranty expense	7	(4)	(3)			(7)
Taxable income	182				25	(7)
Enacted tax rate	40%				40%	40%
Tax payable currently	72.8					
Deferred tax liability					10	
Deferred tax asset						(2.8)
					↓	↓
					Deferred Tax Liability	Deferred Tax Asset
Ending balances:					$10	$2.8
Less: Beginning balances:					0	(0.0)
Change in balances					$10	$2.8

Journal entry at the end of 1997

Income tax expense (to balance)	80.0	
Deferred tax asset (determined above)	2.8	
Deferred tax liability (determined above)		10.0
Income tax payable (determined above)		72.8

Income tax amounts for 1998 would be determined as shown in Illustration 16–7b.

ILLUSTRATION 16–7b

Multiple Temporary Differences—1998

The future taxable amount of installment sales ($4 million) is equal to the cumulative temporary book-tax difference in the installment receivable ($9 million – $5 million).

Similarly, the total of other future taxable and deductible amounts are equal to the cumulative temporary differences in the related assets and liabilities.

Analysis indicates that the deferred tax liability should be increased further and the deferred tax asset should be reduced.

($ in millions)	1997	Current Year 1998	Future Taxable (Deductible) Amounts 1999	2000	Future Taxable Amounts (total)*	Future Deductible Amounts (total)*
Accounting income		200				
Temporary differences:						
Installment sales	(9)	5	4		4	
Depreciation	(16)	(38)	20	34	54	
Warranty expense	7	(4)	(3)			(3)
Estimated loss		1		(1)		(1)
Taxable income		164			58	(4)
Enacted tax rate		40%			40%	40%
Tax payable currently		65.6				
Deferred tax liability					23.2	
Deferred tax asset						(1.6)
					↓	↓
					Deferred Tax Liability	Deferred Tax Asset
Ending balances:					$23.2	$1.6
Less: Beginning balances:					(10.0)	(2.8)
Change in balances					$13.2	$(1.2)

Journal entry at the end of 1998

Income tax expense (to balance)	80.0	
Deferred tax asset (determined above)		1.2
Deferred tax liability (determined above)		13.2
Income tax payable (determined above)		65.6

*Total future taxable and deductible amounts also are equal to the cumulative temporary differences in the related assets and liabilities.

After the journal entry, the balances of both the deferred tax asset and the deferred tax liability reflect the desired amounts as follows ($ in millions):

The deferred tax asset declines and the deferred tax liability increases during 1998.

Deferred Tax Asset			Deferred Tax Liability	
2.8		1997 balance		10.0
	1.2	Adjustment		13.2
1.6		1998 balance		23.2

Of course, if a phased-in change in rates is scheduled to occur, it would be necessary to determine the total of the future taxable amounts and the total of the future deductible amounts for each future year as outlined previously. Then the specific tax rates of each future year would be multiplied by the two totals in each of those years. Those annual tax effects would then be summed to get the deferred tax liability and the deferred tax asset.

Operating Losses

An **operating loss** is negative taxable income: tax-deductible expenses exceed taxable revenues. Of course, there is no tax payable for the year an operating loss occurs because there's no taxable income. In addition, tax laws permit the operating loss to be used to reduce taxable income in other, profitable years. Offsetting operating profits with operating losses is achieved by either a carryback of the loss to prior years or a carryforward of the loss to later years, or both. In essence, the tax deductible expenses that can't be deducted this year because they exceed taxable revenues can be deducted in other years. Specifically, the operating loss can be carried back 3 years and forward up to 15 years:

Carryforward → up to 15 years

| 1994 | 1995 | 1996 | LOSS | 1998 | 1999 | 2000 | → | 2011 | 2012 |

3 years ← Carryback

Tax laws permit a choice. A company can elect an **operating loss carryback** if taxable income was reported in any of the three previous years. By reducing taxable income of a previous year, the company can receive an immediate refund of taxes paid that year.

If taxable income was not reported in any of the three previous years or higher tax rates are anticipated in the future, a company can elect to forgo the operating loss carryback and carry the loss forward for up to 15 years to offset taxable income of those years. Even if a loss carryback is elected, any loss that remains after the three-year carryback can be carried forward. The carryback election is a choice that must be made in the year of the operating loss and the choice is irrevocable. It usually is advantageous to carry back losses because by filing an amended tax return to get a refund, a company can realize the benefit much sooner than if the loss is carried forward.

The accounting question is: *When* should the tax benefit created by an operating loss be recognized on the income statement? The answer is: In the year the loss occurs.

Operating Loss Carryforward

First consider a loss carryforward. You have learned in this chapter that a deferred tax asset is recognized for the future tax benefit of temporary differences that create future deductible amounts. An operating loss carryforward also creates future deductible amounts. Logically, then, a deferred tax asset is recognized for an operating loss carryforward also. This is demonstrated in Illustration 16–8.

ILLUSTRATION   16–8

Operating Loss Carryforward

An **operating loss carryforward** can be deducted from taxable income in future years.

During 1997, its first year of operations, American Laminating Corporation reported an operating loss of $125 million for financial reporting and tax purposes. The enacted tax rate is 40%.

($ in millions)	Current Year 1997	Future Deductible Amounts (total)
Operating loss	(125)	
Loss carryforward	125	(125)
	0	
Enacted tax rate	40%	40%
Tax payable	0	
Deferred tax asset		(50)
		↓

Deferred tax asset:

Ending balance	$50
Less: Beginning balance	0
Change in balance	$50

ILLUSTRATION   16-8

continued

The tax benefit of being able to deduct amounts in the future represents a deferred tax asset.

Journal entry at the end of 1997		
Deferred tax asset (determined above)	50	
Income tax benefit—operating loss (to balance)		50

The income tax benefit of an operating loss carryforward is recognized for accounting purposes in the year the operating loss occurs. The net after-tax operating loss reflects the future tax savings that the operating loss is expected to create:

The income tax benefit of an operating loss carryforward is recognized in the year the operating loss occurs.

Income Statement (partial)

($ in millions)	
Operating loss before income taxes	$125
Less: Income tax benefit—operating loss	(50)
Net operating loss	$ 75

Valuation Allowance.   Just as for all deductible temporary differences, deferred tax assets are recognized for any operating loss without regard to the likelihood of having taxable income in future years sufficient to absorb future deductible amounts. However, the deferred tax asset is then reduced by a valuation allowance if it is more likely than not that some portion or all of the deferred tax asset will not be realized. Remember, a valuation allowance both reduces the net deferred tax asset and increases the income tax expense just as if that portion of the deferred tax asset had not been recognized.

Operating Loss Carryback

An operating loss must be applied to the earliest year first and then brought forward to the second and first years.

To compare the treatment of an operating loss carryback, let's modify the illustration to assume that there was taxable income in the three years prior to the operating loss and that American Laminating elected a loss carryback. Note that the operating loss must be applied to the earliest year first and then brought forward to second and first years. If any of the loss remains after reducing taxable income to zero in the three previous years, the remainder is carried forward to future years as an operating loss carryforward.

ILLUSTRATION   16-9

Operating Loss Carryback and Carryforward

An **operating loss carryback** can be deducted from taxable income in the three prior years, creating a refund of taxes paid those years.

During 1997, American Laminating Corporation reported an operating loss of $125 million for financial reporting and tax purposes. The enacted tax rate is 40% for 1997. Taxable income, tax rates, and income taxes paid in the three previous years were as follows:

	Taxable Income	Tax Rates	Income Taxes Paid
1994	$20 million	45%	$ 9 million
1995	40 million	40%	16 million
1996	15 million	40%	6 million

Here's how the income tax benefit of the operating loss carryback and the operating loss carryforward is determined:

($ in millions)	Prior Years			Current Year	Future Taxable Amounts
	1994	1995	1996	1997	(total)
Operating loss				(125)	
Loss carryback	(20)	(40)	(15)	75	
Loss carryforward				50	(50)
				0	
Enacted tax rate	45%	40%	40%	40%	40%
Tax payable (refundable)	(9)	(16)	(6)	0	
Deferred tax asset					(20) ↓

The portion of an operating loss that remains after a carryback is carried forward.

Deferred tax asset:	
Ending balance	$20
Less: Beginning balance	0
Change in balance	$20

The income tax benefit of an operating loss carryback, like a carryforward, is recognized in the year the operating loss occurs.

Journal entry at the end of 1997		
Receivable—income tax refund ($9 + 16 + 6)	31	
Deferred tax asset (determined above)	20	
Income tax benefit—operating loss (to balance)		51

The income tax benefit of both an operating loss carryback and an operating loss carryforward are recognized for accounting purposes in the year the operating loss occurs. The net after-tax operating loss reflects the reduction of past taxes from the loss carryback and future tax savings that the loss carryforward is expected to create:

($ in millions)		
Operating loss before income taxes		$125
Less: Income tax benefit:		
Tax refund from loss carryback	$31	
Future tax savings from loss carryforward	20	51
Net operating loss		$ 74

Notice that the income tax benefit ($51 million) is higher than it was when we assumed a carryforward only ($50 million). This is because the tax rate in one of the carryback years (1994) was higher than the carryforward rate (40%).

Let's carry the illustration forward one year and assume a performance turnaround in 1998 resulted in pretax accounting income of $15 million.

ILLUSTRATION 16–9a

Determining and Recording Income Taxes—1998

$15 million of the carryforward can be used to offset 1998 income. The remaining $35 million is carried forward up to 14 more years.

The $20 million deferred tax asset is reduced to $14 million.

The income tax expense reflects the tax consequence of 1998 accounting income even though none actually is paid this year.

($ in millions)	1997	Current Year 1998	Future Deductible Amounts (total)
Accounting income		15	
Temporary difference:			
Loss carryforward	50	(15)	(35)
Taxable income		0	
Enacted tax rate		40%	40%
Tax payable currently		0	
Deferred tax asset			(14)
			↓
Deferred tax asset:			
Ending balance			$14.0
Less: Beginning balance			(20.0)
Change in balance			$(6.0)
Journal entry at the end of 1998			
Income tax expense (to balance)		6	
Deferred tax asset (determined above)			6

Financial Statement Presentation

Balance Sheet Classification

Learning objective 8
Explain how deferred tax assets and deferred tax liabilities are classified and reported in a classified balance sheet and describe related disclosures.

In a classified balance sheet, deferred tax assets and deferred tax liabilities are classified as either current or noncurrent according to how the related assets or liabilities are classified for financial reporting. For instance, a deferred tax liability arising from different depreciation methods being used for tax and book purposes would be classified as noncurrent because depreciable assets are reported in one of the noncurrent categories. A deferred tax asset or deferred tax liability is considered to be related to an asset or liability if reduction (including amortization) of that asset or liability will cause the temporary difference to reverse.

A net current amount and a net noncurrent amount are reported as either an asset or a liability.

Most companies will have several different types of temporary differences that give rise to deferred tax amounts. The several deferred tax assets and liabilities should not be reported individually but combined instead into two summary amounts. Current deferred tax assets and liabilities should be offset (netted together), with the *net current* amount reported as either a current asset (if deferred tax assets exceed deferred tax liabilities) or current liability (if deferred tax liabilities exceed deferred tax assets). Similarly, a single *net noncurrent* amount should be reported as a net noncurrent asset or a net noncurrent liability. This is demonstrated in Illustration 16–10.

ILLUSTRATION 16-10

Balance Sheet Classification and Presentation

> The current or noncurrent classification of deferred tax assets and deferred tax liabilities is the same as that of the related assets or liabilities.

Warren Fabrics, Inc. had future taxable amounts and future deductible amounts relating to temporary differences between the tax bases of the assets and liabilities indicated below and their financial reporting amounts:

($ in millions)

Related Balance Sheet Account	Classification current-C noncurrent-N	Future Taxable (Deductible) Amounts	Tax Rate	Deferred Tax (Asset) Liability C	N
Receivable—installment sales	C	10	× 40%	4	
Receivable—installment sales	N	5	× 40%		2
Depreciable assets	N	105	× 40%		42
Allowance—uncollectible accounts	C	(15)	× 40%	(6)	
Liability—subscriptions received	C	(20)	× 40%	(8)	
Estimated warranty liability	C	(30)	× 40%	(12)	
Net current liability (asset)				(22)	
Net noncurrent liability (asset)					44

Balance Sheet Presentation:

Current Assets:	
Deferred tax asset	$22
Long-Term Liabilities:	
Deferred tax liability	$44

Note: Before offsetting assets and liabilities within the current and noncurrent categories, the **total** deferred tax assets is $26 ($6 + 8 + 12) and the **total** deferred tax liabilities is $48 ($4 + 2 + 42).

> A deferred tax asset or liability that is not related to a specific asset or liability should be classified according to when the underlying temporary difference is expected to reverse.

Deferred Tax Amount Not Related To A Specific Asset Or Liability.   Sometimes, a deferred tax asset or a deferred tax liability cannot be identified with a specific asset or liability. When that's the case, it should be classified according to when the underlying temporary difference is expected to reverse. For instance, some organization costs are recognized as expenses for financial reporting purposes when incurred, but are deducted for tax purposes in later years. When such expenditures are made, an expense is recorded, but no asset or liability is recognized on the balance sheet. The deferred tax asset recognized for the future deductible amounts is classified as a current asset for the tax effect of the deduction expected next year, and as a noncurrent asset for the tax effect of the deductions expected in later years. Operating loss carryforwards also are unrelated to a specific asset or liability and so are classified as current or noncurrent according to when future income is expected to be sufficient to realize the benefit of the carryforward.

> A valuation allowance is allocated between current and noncurrent on a pro rata basis.

Valuation Allowance.   Any valuation allowance for deferred tax assets should be allocated between the current and noncurrent amount in proportion to the amounts of deferred tax assets that are classified as current and noncurrent. In our illustration, all three deferred tax assets were classified as current, so any valuation allowance would be reported with the net current deferred tax asset.

Disclosure Notes

Deferred Tax Assets and Deferred Tax Liabilities.   Additional disclosures are required pertaining to amounts reported on the balance sheet. Disclosure notes should reveal the:

- Total of all deferred tax liabilities ($48 million in Illustration 16–10).
- Total of all deferred tax assets ($26 million in our Illustration 16–10).
- Total valuation allowance recognized for deferred tax assets.
- Net change in the valuation allowance.
- Approximate tax effect of each type of temporary difference (and carryforward).

In its 1996 balance sheet, the Procter & Gamble Company reported current deferred tax assets (all assets) of $598 million and net deferred tax liabilities of $638 million. The composition of these amounts was provided in the disclosure note shown in Graphic 16–4.

Note 9. Income Taxes (in part)

Deferred Income Tax Assets and Liabilities

(millions of dollars)

June 30	1996	1995
Current deferred tax assets:		
Restructuring reserve	$ 267	$ 293
Other	331	511
Noncurrent deferred tax assets (liabilities):	598	804
Depreciation	(1,005)	(1,164)
Postretirement benefits	492	550
Restructuring reserve	–	170
Loss carryforwards	166	276
Other	(291)	(363)
	(638)	(531)

Included in the above are total valuation allowances of $252 and $263 in 1996 and 1995, respectively.

Operating Loss Carryforwards.   In addition, the amounts and expiration dates should be revealed for any operating loss carryforwards. Remember, operating losses can be carried forward for reduction of future taxable income for 15 years. This potential tax benefit can foreshadow desirable cash savings for the company if earnings sufficient to absorb the loss carryforwards are anticipated before their expiration date. The presence of large operating loss carryforwards also can make an unprofitable company an attractive target for acquisition by a company that could use those loss carryforwards to shelter its own earnings from taxes with that loss deduction. If the IRS determines that an acquisition is made solely to obtain the tax benefits of operating loss carryforwards, the deductions will not be allowed. However, motivation is difficult to determine, so it is not uncommon for companies to purchase operating loss carryforwards.

Income Tax Expense.   Disclosures also are required pertaining to the income tax expense reported on the income statement. Disclosure notes should reveal the:

- Current portion of the tax expense (or tax benefit).
- Deferred portion of the tax expense (or tax benefit), with separate disclosure of amounts attributable to:
  - ↪ Portion that does not include the effect of the following separately disclosed amounts.
  - ↪ Operating loss carryforwards.
  - ↪ Adjustments due to changes in tax laws or rates.
  - ↪ Adjustments to the beginning-of-the-year valuation allowance due to revised estimates.
  - ↪ Investment tax credits.

Tax Effects of Accounting Changes and Error Correction

You were introduced to accounting changes and the correction of errors early in this course and exposed to their applicability in the context of various accounting topics as they were encountered in later chapters. You may have noticed, though, that we avoided extensive discussion of income tax effects during those discussions. The reason, of course, is that the appropriate foundation had yet to be laid. Now that you are familiar with income tax accounting we reconsider accounting changes and the correction of errors with tax effects in mind.

Change in an Accounting Principle

Recall the general treatment of a change in an accounting principle. For most such changes, the cumulative effect of the change is reported on the income statement as a separate item of income, between extraordinary items and net income. It is reported net of the tax effect of the change. In other words, it should be increased or decreased by the difference between income tax expense as reported in previous years and what it would have been if the new accounting method had been used in those years.[15]

In Chapter 3, an illustration we used described a change from accelerated to straight-line depreciation that resulted in a before-tax cumulative income effect of $12 million. That is to say, if the new method had been used in the two prior years the depreciable assets were in service, depreciation would have been $12 million less and pretax income $12 million more.[16] With a tax rate of 30%, the cumulative tax effect of the depreciation change would be $3.6 million ($12 million × 30%). The explanation is that under straight-line depreciation, the reduction of income for depreciation would be $12 million less, causing tax expense to be higher by that amount times the tax rate. The higher tax expense partially offsets the lower depreciation expense when determining the net, after-tax, cumulative effect of the change.

> The cumulative after-tax effect on prior years' income is a separate item of income between extraordinary items and net income.

Reported as a separate component of income:

	($ in millions)	
	1997	1996
Income before extraordinary items and accounting change	$xxx	$xxx
Extraordinary gain (loss), net of tax	xx	xx
Cumulative effect of accounting change (net of $3.6 tax)	8.4	
Net income	$xxx	$xxx

Besides income, other financial statement amounts would have been different if the new method had been applied in previous years. In our illustration, accumulated depreciation would have been less if straight-line rather than accelerated depreciation had been used. The balance in this account should be adjusted to reflect the new method:

> Accumulated depreciation would have been $12 million less and net income $8.4 million more if straight-line rather than accelerated depreciation had been used.

	($ in millions)
Accumulated depreciation (cumulative effect described above)	12.0
Deferred tax liability ($12 × 40%)	4.8
Cumulative effect of accounting change (net effect)	7.2

The reason for the credit to deferred tax liability requires some explanation. Remember from our earlier discussions that when taxable income is less than pretax accounting income because of a temporary difference, a deferred tax liability is recorded. This liability reflects the tax that eventually will be paid when the difference later reverses and taxable income is *higher* than pretax accounting income. In our illustration, tax depreciation would have been more than accelerated depreciation during the two previous years, but the temporary difference would have been greater still if accounting income had been based on straight-line depreciation.[17] So we need to increase the deferred tax liability from what it is now to what it would have been if straight-line depreciation had been used the two previous years. It's not necessary to know what the old or new balance is—only that the new balance should be $4.8 million higher.

Correction of an Error

Let's also use depreciation to illustrate the tax effect of correcting errors. Recall that when material errors are discovered in a year subsequent to the year the error is made, the correction of these errors is considered to be a prior period adjustment. A prior period adjustment refers to an addition to or reduction in the beginning retained earnings balance in a statement of shareholders' equity (or statement of retained earnings if that's presented instead).

When it's discovered that the ending balance of retained earnings in the period prior to the discovery of an error was incorrect as a result of that error, the balance must be corrected at the time it appears as the beginning balance the following year. Illustration 16–11 offers an example.

---

[15]Reporting the income amount net of its tax effect is consistent with the way we report other special items on the income statement net of tax. Recall that extraordinary gains and losses are reported separately on the income statement, net of their tax impact, as are discontinued operations.

[16]A detailed calculation is provided in Chapter 3.

[17]Presently, the accelerated depreciation method prescribed by the tax code is the Modified Accelerated Cost Recovery System (MACRS). The method is described in Chapter 11. For our purposes now, recall that this method produces tax deductions higher in the first years of an asset's useful life than does straight-line (and usually SYD) depreciation. The opposite is true in the later years of the asset's useful life.

ILLUSTRATION 16–11

Tax Effect of Error Corrections

In early 1997, internal auditors discovered that XL Transportation, Inc., had neglected to record $2 million of depreciation on a conveyor system acquired in early 1996. The tax rate is 40%.

Analysis:

($ in millions)

	Correct (Should Have Been Recorded)		**Incorrect** (as Recorded)
1996	Depreciation expense	2	adjusting entry omitted
	Accumulated depreciation	2	

Depreciation expense was understated, so 1996 net income was overstated, which means retained earnings is currently overstated.

Accumulated depreciation was understated and continues to be understated.

To consider taxes, we need to know whether depreciation was also omitted from the tax return, the depreciation methods used for both financial reporting and tax reporting, and whether the tax liability has been paid. Let's say that depreciation was also omitted from the tax return, straight-line depreciation is used by XL for both tax and financial reporting, and the 1996 tax liability has not yet been paid.

Depreciation expense still would have been *understated* by $2 million in 1996, but that would have caused taxable income to be overstated and the tax liability and income tax expense to be *overstated* by 40% of $2 million. So 1996 net income and retained earnings would have been overstated by only $1.2 million:

Depreciation expense understated	$2.0 million
Income tax expense overstated	.8 million
Net income overstated	$1.2 million

To correct incorrect accounts:

	($ in millions)
Retained earnings ($2 million – [40% × $2 million])	1.2
Income tax payable (40% × $2 million)	.8
Accumulated depreciation	2.0

If the tax bill already had been paid, the debit to income tax payable in the correcting entry would be replaced by a debit to refund—overpayment of income taxes. If depreciation had been omitted from the income statement but not from the tax return, or if accelerated depreciation was used for tax reporting but straight-line depreciation for financial reporting, the debit to income tax payable in the correcting entry would be replaced by a debit to deferred tax liability.

The 1996 financial statements that were incorrect as a result of the error are retroactively restated to reflect the correct amount of depreciation expense, accumulated depreciation, and income taxes when those statements are reported again for comparative purposes in the 1997 annual report.

Also, a disclosure note in XL's 1997 annual report should describe the nature of the error and the impact of its correction on each year's net income, income before extraordinary items ($1.2 million in 1996), and earnings per share.

Intraperiod Tax Allocation

Learning objective 9
Explain intraperiod tax allocation.

You should recall that an income statement reports certain items separately from income (or loss) from continuing operations when such items are present. Specifically, (a) discontinued operations, (b) extraordinary items, and (c) changes in accounting principle are given a place of their own on the income statement to better allow the user of the statement to isolate irregular components of net income from those that represent ordinary, recurring business operations. Presumably, this permits the user to more accurately project future operations without neglecting events that affect current performance.[18] Following this logic, each component of net income should reflect the income tax effect directly associated with that component.

---

[18]This was discussed in Chapter 3.

Consequently, the total income tax expense for a reporting period should be allocated among the financial statement items that gave rise to it. Each of the following items should be reported net of its respective income tax effects:

- Income (or loss) from continuing operations.
- Discontinued operations.
- Extraordinary items.
- Changes in accounting principle.
- Prior period adjustments (to the beginning retained earnings balance).

The related tax effect can be either a tax expense or a tax benefit. For example, an extraordinary gain adds to a company's tax expense, while an extraordinary loss produces a tax reduction because it reduces taxable income and therefore reduces income taxes. So a company with a tax rate of 40% would report $100 million pretax income which includes a $10 million extraordinary gain this way:

	($ in millions)
Income before tax and extraordinary item ($100 – 10)	$90
Less: Income tax expense	(36)
Income before extraordinary item	54
Extraordinary gain (net of $4 income tax)	6
Net income	$60

> A gain causes an increase in taxes.

If the $100 million pretax income included a $10 million extraordinary loss rather than an extraordinary gain, the loss would be reported net of associated tax savings:

	($ in millions)
Income before tax and extraordinary item ($100 + 10)	$110
Less: Income tax expense	(44)
Income before extraordinary item	66
Extraordinary loss (net of $4 income tax benefit)	(6)
Net income	$ 60

> A loss causes a reduction in taxes.

Additional Consideration

If the extraordinary gain in the earlier example had been of a type taxable at a capital gains tax rate of 30%, it would have been reported net of the specific tax associated with that gain:

Extraordinary gain (net of $3 income tax)   7

> Allocating income taxes within a particular reporting period is intraperiod tax allocation.

Allocating income taxes among financial statement components in this way within a particular reporting period is referred to as *intraperiod tax allocation*. You should recognize the contrast with *inter*period tax allocation—terminology sometimes used to describe allocating income taxes between two or more reporting periods by recognizing deferred tax assets and liabilities. While interperiod tax allocation is challenging and controversial, intraperiod tax allocation is relatively straightforward and substantially free from controversy.

Conceptual Concerns

Some accountants disagree with the FASB's approach to accounting for income taxes. Some of the most persistent objections are outlined below.

Should Deferred Taxes Not Be Recognized? Some feel the income tax expense for a reporting period should be the income tax actually payable currently. Reasons often cited include the contentions that the legal liability for taxes is determined only by the tax return and that taxes are based on aggregate taxable income, not individual components of the aggregate amount. The FASB counters that it is not only possible, but desirable, to separate the tax consequences of individual components of income from the financial reporting of those events. If tax laws permit a company to defer paying tax on a particular event, it is only when, not whether, the tax will be paid that is impacted. Recognizing the tax effect when the event occurs, regardless of when the tax will be paid is consistent with accounting on an accrual basis rather than a cash basis.

Should Deferred Taxes Be Recognized for Only Some Items? Critics sometimes argue that the tax liability for certain recurring events will never be paid and therefore do not represent a liability.[19] An example often cited is the temporary difference due to depreciation. Because the temporary difference recurs frequently (as new assets are acquired), new originating differences more than offset reversing differences causing the balance in the deferred tax liability account to continually get larger. The contention is that no future tax payment will be required, so no liability should be recorded. The FASB's counter argument is that, although the aggregate amount of depreciation differences may get larger, the deferred tax liability for a particular depreciable asset usually does require payment. This is analogous to specific accounts payable requiring payment even though the total balance of accounts payable may grow larger year by year.

Should Deferred Taxes Be Discounted? Some accountants contend that deferred tax assets and liabilities should reflect the time value of money by determining those amounts on a discounted (present value) basis.[20] For some deferred tax amounts such as operating loss carryforwards that might be realized after perhaps 15 years in some cases, the time value might be significant. Practical considerations weighed heavily in the FASB's decision not to permit discounting. Discounting usually would require detailed scheduling of the reversals of all differences reversing in the future, and the selection of appropriate discount rates would pose practical difficulties.

Should Classification Be Based on the Timing of Temporary Difference Reversals? Some feel that deferred tax assets and liabilities should be classified in a balance sheet as current or noncurrent according to the timing of the reversal of the temporary differences that gave rise to them. By this view, those deferred tax assets and liabilities related to temporary differences that will reverse within the coming year should be classified as current, others as noncurrent. Advocates of this view consider it to be consistent with the asset-liability perspective to deferred tax amounts. Again, practical considerations are reflected in the FASB's requirement that a deferred tax asset or deferred tax liability should be classified in a balance sheet as current or noncurrent according to the classification of the asset or liability to which it is related. Classifying a deferred tax liability related to depreciation as noncurrent because the depreciable asset is classified as noncurrent, for example, does not require detailed scheduling of the year-by-year originations and reversals of temporary differences related to depreciation.

Decision-Makers' Perspective

Income taxes represent one of the largest expenditures that many firms incur. When state, local, and foreign taxes are considered along with federal taxes, the total bite can easily consume 40% of income. A key factor, then, in any decision that managers make should be the impact on taxes. Decision makers must constantly be alert to options that minimize or delay taxes. During the course of this chapter, we encountered situations that avoid taxes (for example, interest on municipal bonds) and those that delay taxes (for example, using accelerated depreciation on the tax return). Astute managers make investment decisions that consider the tax effect of available alternatives. Similarly, outside analysts should consider how effectively management has managed its tax exposure and monitor the current and prospective impact of taxes on their interests in the company.

| Investment patterns and other disclosures can indicate potential tax expenditures. |

Consider an example. Large, capital-intensive companies with significant investments in buildings and equipment often have sizable deferred tax liabilities from temporary differences in depreciation. If new investments cause the level of depreciable assets to at least remain the same over time, the deferred tax liability can be effectively delayed indefinitely. Investors and creditors should be watchful for situations that might cause material paydowns of that deferred tax liability, such as impending plant closings or investment patterns that suggest declining levels of depre-

[19]For example, see Paul Chaney and Debra Jeter, "Accounting for Deferred Taxes: Simplicity? Usefulness?" *Accounting Horizons,* June 1989, pp. 7–8.
[20]For example, see Harry Wolk, Dale Martin, and Virginia Nichols, "Statement of Financial Standards No. 96: Some Theoretical Problems," *Accounting Horizons,* June 1989, p. 4.

ciable assets. Unexpected additional tax expenditures can severely diminish an otherwise attractive prospective rate of return.

You also learned in the chapter that deferred tax assets represent future tax benefits. One such deferred tax asset that often reflects sizable future tax deductions is an operating loss carryforward. When a company has a large operating loss carryforward, a large amount of future income can be earned tax free. This tax shelter can be a huge advantage, not to be overlooked by careful analysts.

> Operating loss carryforwards can indicate significant future tax savings.

Managers and outsiders are aware that increasing debt increases risk. Deferred tax liabilities increase reported debt. As discussed and demonstrated in the previous chapter, financial risk often is measured by the debt-to-equity ratio, total liabilities divided by shareholders' equity. Other things being equal, the higher the debt-to-equity ratio, the higher the risk. Should the deferred tax liability be included in the computation of this ratio? Some analysts will argue that it should be excluded, observing that in many cases the deferred tax liability account remains the same or continually grows larger. Their contention is that no future tax payment will be required. Others, though, contend that is no different from the common situation in which long-term borrowings tend to remain the same or continually grow larger. Research supports the notion that deferred tax liabilities are, in fact, viewed by investors as a real liability and they appear to discount it according to the timing and likelihood of the liability's settlement.[21]

> Deferred tax liabilities increase risk as measured by the debt-to- equity ratio.

In short, managers who make decisions based on estimated pretax cash flows and outside investors and creditors who make decisions based on pretax income numbers are perilously ignoring one of the most important aspects of those decisions. Taxes should be a primary consideration in any business decision.

CONCEPT REVIEW EXERCISE

MULTIPLE DIFFERENCES AND OPERATING LOSS

Mid-South Cellular Systems began operations in 1997. That year the company reported taxable income of $25 million. In 1998, its second year of operations, pretax accounting income was $88 million, which included the following amounts:

1. Insurance expense of $14 million, representing one-third of a $42 million, three-year casualty and liability insurance policy that is deducted for tax purposes entirely in 1998.
2. Insurance expense for a $1 million premium on a life insurance policy for the company president. This is not deductible for tax purposes.
3. An asset with a four-year useful life was acquired last year. It is depreciated by the straight-line method on the income statement. MACRS is used on the tax return, causing deductions for depreciation to be more than straight-line depreciation the first two years but less than straight-line depreciation the next two years ($ in millions):

	Income Statement	Tax Return	Difference
1997	$150	$198	$ (48)
1998	150	264	(114)
1999	150	90	60
2000	150	48	102
	$600	$600	0

4. Equipment rental revenue of $80 million, which does not include an additional $20 of advance payment for 1999 rent. $100 million of rental revenue is reported on the 1998 income tax return.

The enacted tax rate is 40%.

Required:
1. Prepare the journal entry to record Mid-South Cellular's income taxes for 1998.
2. What is Mid-South Cellular's 1998 net income?
3. Show how any deferred tax amount(s) should be reported on the 1998 balance sheet. Assume taxable income is expected in 1999 sufficient to absorb any deductible amounts carried forward from 1998.

---

[21]See Dan Givoly and Carla Hayn, "The Valuation of the Deferred Tax Liability: Evidence from the Stock Market," *The Accounting Review*, April 1992, pp. 394–410.

CONCEPT REVIEW EXERCISE

1. Prepare the journal entry to record Mid-South Cellular's income taxes for 1998.

($ in millions)	1997	Current Year 1998	Future Taxable Deductible Amounts 1999	Future Taxable Deductible Amounts 2000	Future Taxable Amounts (total)	Future Deductible Amounts (total)
Accounting income		88				
Permanent difference:						
Life insurance premium		1				
Temporary differences:						
Prepaid insurance		(28)	14	14	28	
Depreciation	(48)	(114)	60	102	162	
Advance rent		20	(20)			(20)
Operating loss		(33)				
Loss carryback	(25)	25				
Loss carryforward		8				(8)
		0			190	(28)
Enacted tax rate	40%	40%			40%	40%
Tax payable (refundable)	(10)	0				
Deferred tax liability					76.0	
Deferred tax asset						(11.2)

Differences in tax reporting and financial reporting of both the prepaid insurance and the depreciation create future taxable amounts.

Both the advance rent and the operating loss carryforward create future deductible amounts.

	Deferred Tax Liability	Deferred Tax Asset
Ending balances:	$76.0	$11.2
Less: Beginning balance ($48* × 40%)	(19.2)	(0.0)
Change in balances	$56.8	$11.2

*1997's only temporary difference

Journal entry at the end of 1998

Income tax expense (to balance)	35.6	
Receivable—income tax refund (determined above)	10.0	
Deferred tax asset (determined above)	11.2	
Deferred tax liability (determined above)		56.8

Income tax expense is composed of three components: (1) the tax deferred until later, reduced by (2) the deferred tax benefit and (3) the refund of 1996 taxes paid.

Note: Adjusting accounting income by the nontemporary difference and the three temporary differences creates a negative taxable income, which is a net operating loss.

2. What is Mid-South Cellular's 1998 net income?

Pretax accounting income	$88.0
Income tax expense	(35.6)
Net income	$52.4

3. Show how any deferred tax amount(s) should be reported on the 1998 balance sheet. Assume taxable income is expected in 1999 sufficient to absorb any deductible amounts carried forward from 1998.

($ in millions)

Related Balance Sheet Account	Classification current—C noncurrent—N	Future Taxable (Deductible) Amounts	Tax Rate	Deferred Tax (Asset) Liability C	N
Prepaid insurance	C	28	× 40%	11.2	
Depreciable assets	N	162	× 40%		64.8
Liability—rent received in advance	C	(20)	× 40%	(8.0)	
Unrelated to any balance sheet account					
Operating loss carryforward	C*	(8)	× 40%	(3.2)	
				0.0	
Net current liability (asset)					
Net noncurrent liability (asset)					64.8

*Deferred tax asset classified entirely as current because 1999 income is expected to be sufficient to realize the benefit of the carryforward

No net current amount

Long-term liabilities:
Deferred tax liability $64.8

Note: These totals [$0.0 + ($64.8) = ($64.8)] sum to the **total** deferred tax liabilities and deferred tax assets from requirement 1 [($76.0) + $11.2 = ($64.8)].

Solution to Financial Reporting Case (at the opening of the chapter)

1. What's the difference? Explain to Laura how differences between financial reporting standards and income tax rules might cause the two tax amounts to differ.

The differences in the rules for computing taxable income and those for financial reporting often cause amounts to be included in taxable income a different year(s) from the year in which they are recognized for financial reporting purposes. Temporary differences result in future taxable or deductible amounts when the temporary differences reverse. As a result, tax payments frequently occur in years different from the years in which the revenues and expenses that cause the taxes are generated.

2. What is the conceptual advantage of determining income tax expense as we do?

Income tax expense is the combination of the current tax effect and the deferred tax consequences of the period. Under the asset-liability approach, the objective of accounting for income taxes is to recognize a deferred tax liability or deferred tax asset for the tax consequences of amounts that will become taxable or deductible in future years as a result of transactions or events that already have occurred. A result is to recognize both the current and the deferred tax consequences of the operations of a reporting period.

3. Are there differences between financial reporting standards and income tax rules that will not contribute to the difference between income tax expense and amount of income taxes paid?

Some differences between accounting income and taxable income are caused by transactions and events that will never affect taxable income or taxes payable. These differences between accounting income and taxable income do not reverse later. These are permanent differences which are disregarded when determining (a) the tax payable currently, (b) the deferred tax effect, and therefore (c) the income tax expense.

The Bottom Line

1. Temporary differences produce future taxable amounts when the taxable income will be increased relative to accounting income in one or more future years. These produce deferred tax liabilities for the taxes to be paid on the future taxable amounts. Income tax expense for the year includes an amount for which payment (or receipt) is deferred in addition to the amount for which payment is due currently. The deferred amount is the change in the tax liability (or asset).

2. When the future tax consequence of a temporary difference will be to decrease taxable income relative to accounting income future deductible amounts are created. These have favorable tax consequences that are recognized as deferred tax assets.

3. Deferred tax assets are recognized for all deductible temporary differences. However, a deferred tax asset is then reduced by a valuation allowance if it is more likely than not that some portion or all of the deferred tax asset will not be realized.

4. Nontemporary differences between the reported amount of an asset or liability in the financial statements and its tax basis are those caused by transactions and events that under existing tax law will never affect taxable income or taxes payable. These are disregarded when determining both the tax payable currently and the deferred tax effect.

5. The deferred tax liability (or asset) for which payment (or receipt) is deferred is based on enacted tax rates and laws applied to the taxable or deductible amounts. If a change in a tax law or rate occurs, the deferred tax liability or asset is adjusted to reflect the change in the amount to be paid or recovered. That effect is reflected in operating income in the year of the enactment of the change in the tax law or rate.

6. When multiple temporary differences exist, the total of the future taxable amounts is multiplied by the future tax rate to determine the appropriate balance for the deferred tax liability, and the total of the future deductible amounts is multiplied by the future tax rate to determine the appropriate balance for the deferred tax asset.

7. Tax laws permit an operating loss to be used to reduce taxable income in other, profitable years by either a carryback of the loss to prior years (3) or a carryforward of the loss to later years (up to 15). The tax benefit of an operating loss carryback or an operating loss carryforward is recognized in the year of the loss.

8. Deferred tax assets and deferred tax liabilities are classified as either current or noncurrent according to how the related assets or liabilities are classified for financial reporting. Disclosure notes should reveal additional relevant information needed for full disclosure pertaining to deferred tax amounts reported on the balance sheet, the components of income tax expense, and available operating loss carryforwards.

9. Through intraperiod tax allocation the total income tax expense for a reporting period is allocated among the financial statement items that gave rise to it; specifically, income (or loss) from continuing operations, discontinued operations, extraordinary items, changes in accounting principle, and prior period adjustments (to the beginning retained earnings balance).

APPENDIX

16 INVESTMENT REVENUE FROM EQUITY METHOD INVESTEES

You should recall from Chapter 12, "Investments," that when an investor accounts for an investment using the equity method, investment revenue is recognized currently on the basis of income earned by the investee, even when that income is not currently distributed as dividends. For example, an investor that owns 25% of the stock of an equity-method investee would report investment revenue equal to 25% of that company's net income whether or not the investor currently receives some or all of that amount as a dividend. The tax code, on the other hand, doesn't include investment revenue until it actually is received.

SFAS 109 requires the presumption that investee earnings not currently distributed as dividends eventually will be distributed. This presumption creates a temporary difference. Investment revenue is reported on the income statement now and on the tax return later—a future taxable amount. It differs, though, from a difference caused by installment income and other similar temporary differences due to a peculiarity in the tax code. Corporations that own stock in other corporations are permitted to exclude from taxation 70% of the dividends they receive. In other words, only 30% of the amounts received as dividends are taxable. Therefore, when a deferred tax liability is recorded for undistributed earnings of an equity-method investee, the liability should be determined by multiplying the tax rate times 30% of the temporary difference. This is shown in Illustration 16A–1.

ILLUSTRATION 16A–1

Undistributed Earnings of Equity-Method Investee

As the investee earns additional net assets, the investment in those net assets increases.

As the investee distributes net assets as dividends, the investment in those net assets declines.

The deferred tax liability is the tax rate times the undistributed earnings times the portion of those earnings that eventually will be taxable.

Hellium Products, Inc., owns 25% of the stock of UNA Corporation, an equity-method investee. UNA reported $240 million net income in 1998 and distributed $40 million in dividends. Hellium's 1998 taxable income is $450 million and its tax rate is 40%. Assuming no other temporary differences, the journal entries to adjust the investment account and record Hellium's 1998 income taxes would be:

	($ in millions)	
Investor's share of net income		
Investment in UNA shares (25% × $240 million)	60	
Investment revenue		60
Investor's share of dividends		
Cash	10	
Investment in UNA shares (25% × $40 million)		10
Income tax expense		
Income tax expense (to balance)	186	
Deferred tax liability (40% × [$60 – 10 million] × 30%)		6
Income tax payable (40% × $450 million)		180

Questions for Review of Key Topics

Question 16–1   A member of the board of directors is concerned that the company's income statement reports income tax expense of $12.3 million, but the income tax obligation to the government for the year is only $7.9 million. How might the corporate controller explain this apparent discrepancy?

Question 16–2   A deferred tax liability (or asset) is described as the tax effect of the temporary difference between the financial statement carrying amount of an asset or liability and its tax basis. Explain this tax effect of the temporary difference. How might it produce a deferred tax liability? A deferred tax asset?

Question 16–3   Sometimes, a temporary difference will produce future deductible amounts. Explain what is meant by future deductible amounts. Describe two general situations that have this effect. How are such situations recognized in the financial statements?

Question 16–4   The benefit of future deductible amounts can be achieved only if future income is sufficient to take advantage of the deferred deductions. For that reason, not all deferred tax assets will ultimately be realized. How is this possibility reflected in the way we recognize deferred tax assets?

Question 16–5   Temporary differences result in future taxable or deductible amounts when the related asset or liability is recovered or settled. Some differences, though, are not temporary. What events create nontemporary or permanent differences? What effect do these have on the determination of income taxes payable? Of deferred income taxes?

Question	16–6	Identify three examples of differences with no deferred tax consequences.
Question	16–7	The income tax rate for Hudson Refinery has been 35% for each of its 12 years of operation. Company forecasters expect a much-debated tax reform bill to be passed by Congress early next year. The new tax measure would increase Hudson's tax rate to 42%. When measuring this year's deferred tax liability, which rate should Hudson use?
Question	16–8	Suppose a tax reform bill is enacted that causes the corporate tax rate to change from 34% to 36%. How would this affect an existing deferred tax liability? How would the change be reflected in income?
Question	16–9	An operating loss occurs when tax-deductible expenses exceed taxable revenues. Tax laws permit the operating loss to be used to reduce taxable income in other, profitable years by either a carryback of the loss to prior years or a carryforward of the loss to later years. How are loss carrybacks and loss carryforwards recognized for financial reporting purposes?
Question	16–10	How are deferred tax assets and deferred tax liabilities reported in a classified balance sheet?
Question	16–11	Additional disclosures are required pertaining to deferred tax amounts reported on the balance sheet. What are the needed disclosures?
Question	16–12	Additional disclosures are required pertaining to the income tax expense reported on the income statement. What are the needed disclosures?
Question	16–13	What is intraperiod tax allocation?
Question	16–14	Some accountants believe that deferred taxes should be recognized only for some temporary differences. What is the conceptual basis for this argument? What is the counter argument that serves as the basis for the FASB's requirement that deferred taxes should be recognized for all temporary differences?
Question 16–15 (Based on Appendix 16)		Lawrence Farm Products reported a deferred tax liability of $360,000 in 1996 relating to investments in equity securities accounted for by the equity method for financial reporting purposes and by the cost method for tax purposes. The financial statement carrying amount of the investment account at the end of 1997 is $3 million and its tax basis is $2 million. Its taxable income is $1.5 million. Lawrence's tax rate is 40%. Determine Lawrence's income tax expense for 1997.

Exercises

Exercise 16–1
Single temporary difference; taxable income given

book income >
tax income = DTL

Alvis Corporation reports *pretax accounting income* of $400,000, but due to a single temporary difference, *taxable income* is only $250,000. At the beginning of the year, no temporary differences existed.

Required:
Assuming a tax rate of 35%, prepare the appropriate journal entry to record Alvis's income taxes.

Exercise 16–2
Single temporary difference; income tax payable given

tax income >
book income = DTA

In 1997, Alworth Corporation collected rent revenue for 1998 tenant occupancy. For income tax reporting, the rent is taxed when collected. For financial statement reporting, the rent is recognized as income in the period earned. The unearned portion of the rent collected in 1997 amounted to $300,000 at December 31, 1997. Alworth had no temporary differences at the beginning of the year.

Required:
Assuming an income tax rate of 40%, and 1997 income tax payable of $950,000, prepare the journal entry to record income taxes for 1997.

Exercise 16–3
Single temporary difference; future deductible amounts; taxable income given

Lance Lawn Services reports bad debt expense using the allowance method. For tax purposes, the expense is deducted when accounts prove uncollectible (the direct write-off method). At December 31, 1997, Lance has accounts receivable and an allowance for uncollectible accounts of $20 million and $1 million, respectively, and taxable income of $75 million. At December 31, 1996, Lance reported a deferred tax asset of $435,000 related to this difference in reporting bad debts, its only temporary difference. The enacted tax rate is 40% each year.

Required:
Prepare the appropriate journal entry to record Lance's income tax provision for 1997.

Exercise 16–4
Deferred tax asset; income tax payable given; valuation allowance

At the end of 1996, Payne Industries had a deferred tax asset account with a balance of $30 million attributable to a temporary book-tax difference of $75 million in a liability for estimated expenses. At the end of 1997, the temporary difference is $70 million. Payne has no other temporary differences and no valuation allowance for the deferred tax asset. Taxable income for 1997 is $180 million and the tax rate is 40%.

Required:

1. Prepare the journal entry(s) to record Payne's income taxes for 1997, assuming it is more likely than not that the deferred tax asset will be realized.

2. Prepare the journal entry(s) to record Payne's income taxes for 1997, assuming it is more likely than not that one-half of the deferred tax asset will not ultimately be realized.

Exercise 16–5
Deferred tax asset; income tax payable given; previous balance in valuation allowance

(This is a variation of the previous exercise, modified to assume a previous balance in the valuation allowance.)

At the end of 1996, Payne Industries had a deferred tax asset account with a balance of $30 million attributable to a temporary book-tax difference of $75 million in a liability for estimated expenses. At the end of 1997, the temporary difference is $70 million. Payne has no other temporary differences. Taxable income for 1997 is $180 million and the tax rate is 40%.

Payne has a valuation allowance of $10 million for the deferred tax asset at the beginning of 1997.

Required:

1. Prepare the journal entry(s) to record Payne's income taxes for 1997, assuming it is more likely than not that the deferred tax asset will be realized.

2. Prepare the journal entry(s) to record Payne's income taxes for 1997, assuming it is more likely than not that one-half of the deferred tax asset will not ultimately be realized.

Exercise 16–6
Single temporary difference; determine taxable income; determine prior year deferred tax amount

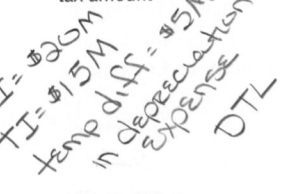

On January 1, 1994, Ameen Company purchased a building for $36 million. ~~Ameen uses straight-line depreciation for financial statement reporting and MACRS for income tax reporting. At December 31, 1996, the carrying value of the building was $30 million and its tax basis was $20 million. At December 31, 1997, the carrying value of the building was $28 million and its tax basis was $13 million. There were no other temporary differences and no nontemporary differences.~~ Pretax accounting income for 1997 was $20 million.

Required:

1. Prepare the appropriate journal entry to record Ameen's 1997 income taxes. Assume an income tax rate of 40%.

2. What is Ameen's 1997 net income?

Exercise 16–7
Multiple choice; determining deferred tax amounts

The following questions dealing with various topics in this chapter are adapted from recent CPA examinations. Determine the response that best completes the statements or questions.

1. Because Jab Co. uses different methods to depreciate equipment for financial statement and income tax purposes, Jab has temporary differences that will reverse during the next year and add to taxable income. Deferred income taxes that are based on these temporary differences should be classified in Jab's balance sheet as a
   a. Contra account to current assets.
   b. Contra account to noncurrent assets.
   c. Current liability.
   d. Noncurrent liability.

Items 2 and 3 are based on the following:

Kent, Inc.'s, reconciliation between financial statement and taxable income for 1997 follows:

Pretax financial income	$150,000
Permanent difference	(12,000)
	138,000
Temporary difference—depreciation	(9,000)
Taxable income	$129,000

Additional information:

	At	
	12/31/96	**12/31/97**
Cumulative temporary differences (future taxable amounts)	$11,000	$20,000

The enacted tax rate was 34% for 1996, and 40% for 1997 and years thereafter.

2. In its December 31, 1997, balance sheet, what amount should Kent report as deferred income tax liability?
   a. $3,600
   b. $6,800
   c. $7,340
   d. $8,000

3. In its 1997 income statement, what amount should Kent report as current portion of income tax expense?
    a. $51,600
    b. $55,200
    c. $55,860
    d. $60,000

4. Mobe Co. reported the following operating income (loss) for its first three years of operations:

1995	$ 300,000
1996	(700,000)
1997	1,200,000

    For each year, there were no deferred income taxes, and Mobe's effective income tax rate was 30%. In its 1996 income tax return, Mobe elected to carry back the maximum amount of loss possible. In its 1997 income statement, what amount should Mobe report as total income tax expense?
    a. $120,000
    b. $150,000
    c. $240,000
    d. $360,000

Exercise 16–8
Single temporary difference; taxable income given; calculate deferred tax liability

Ayres Services acquired an asset for $80 million in 1997. The asset is depreciated for financial reporting purposes over four years on a straight-line basis (no residual value). For tax purposes the asset's cost is deducted (by MACRS). The enacted tax rate is 40%. Amounts for pretax accounting income, depreciation, and taxable income in 1997, 1998, 1999, and 2000 are as follows:

($ in millions)			
	1997	**1998**	**1999**	**2000**
Accounting income	$330	$350	$365	$400
Depreciation on the income statement	20	20	20	20
Depreciation on the tax return	(25)	(33)	(15)	(7)
Taxable income	$325	$337	$370	$413

Required:
For December 31 of each year, determine (a) the temporary book–tax difference for the depreciable asset and (b) the balance to be reported in the deferred tax liability account.

Exercise 16–9
Identifying future taxable amounts and future deductible amounts

Listed below are 10 causes of temporary differences. For each temporary difference, indicate (by letter) whether it will create future deductible amounts (D) or future taxable amounts (T).

Temporary Difference

____ 1. Accrual of loss contingency, tax-deductible when paid.
____ 2. Newspaper subscriptions; taxable when received, recognized for financial reporting when earned.
____ 3. Prepaid rent, tax-deductible when paid.
____ 4. Accrued bond interest expense; tax-deductible when paid.
____ 5. Prepaid insurance, tax-deductible when paid.
____ 6. Unrealized loss from recording investments available for sale at fair market (tax-deductible when investments are sold).
____ 7. Bad debt expense; allowance method for financial reporting; direct write-off for tax purposes.
____ 8. Advance rent receipts on an operating lease (as the lessor), taxable when received.
____ 9. Straight-line depreciation for financial reporting; accelerated depreciation for tax purposes.
____ 10. Accrued expense for employee postretirement benefits; tax-deductible when subsequent payments are made.

Exercise 16–10
Identifying future taxable amounts and future deductible amounts

(This is a variation of the previous exercise, modified to focus on the balance sheet account related to the deferred tax amount.)

Listed below are 10 causes of temporary differences. For each temporary difference indicate the balance sheet account for which the situation creates a temporary difference.

Temporary Difference

1. Accrual of loss contingency, tax-deductible when paid.
2. Newspaper subscriptions; taxable when received, recognized for financial reporting when earned.
3. Prepaid rent, tax-deductible when paid.
4. Accrued bond interest expense; tax-deductible when paid.
5. Prepaid insurance, tax-deductible when paid.
6. Unrealized loss from recording investments available for sale at fair market (tax-deductible when investments are sold).

7.   Bad debt expense; allowance method for financial reporting; direct write-off for tax purposes.
8.   Advance rent receipts on an operating lease (as the lessor), taxable when received.
9.   Straight-line depreciation for financial reporting; accelerated depreciation for tax purposes.
10. Accrued expense for employee postretirement benefits; tax-deductible when subsequent payments are made.

Exercise 16–11

Single temporary difference; nontemporary difference; calculate taxable income

Southern Atlantic Distributors began operations in January 1997 and purchased a delivery truck for $40,000.

Southern Atlantic plans to use straight-line depreciation over a four-year expected useful life for financial reporting purposes. ~~For tax purposes, the deduction is 50% of cost in 1997, 30% in 1998, and 20% in 1999.~~ Pretax accounting income for 1997 was $300,000, which includes interest revenue of $40,000 from municipal bonds. The enacted tax rate is 40%.

Required:

Assuming no differences between accounting income and taxable income other than those described above:

1.   Prepare the journal entry to record income taxes in 1997.
2.   What is Southern Atlantic's 1997 net income?

Exercise 16–12

Single temporary difference; multiple tax rates

Allmond Corporation, organized on January 3, 1997, had pretax accounting income of $14 million and taxable income of $20 million for the year ended December 31, 1997. The 1997 tax rate is 35%. The only difference between financial and taxable income is estimated product warranty costs. Expected payments and scheduled tax rates (based on recent tax legislation) are as follows:

1998	$2 million	30%
1999	1 million	30%
2000	1 million	30%
2001	2 million	25%

Required:

1.   Determine the amounts necessary to record Allmond's income taxes for 1997 and prepare the appropriate journal entry.
2.   What is Allmond's 1997 net income?

Exercise 16–13

Change in tax rates; calculate taxable income

Arnold Industries has pretax accounting income of $33 million for the year ended December 31, 1997. The tax rate is 40%. The only difference between financial and taxable income relates to an operating lease of which Arnold is the lessee. The inception of the lease was December 28, 1997. An $8 million advance rent payment at the inception of the lease is tax-deductible in 1997 but, for financial reporting purposes, represents prepaid rent expense to be recognized equally over the four-year lease term.

Required:

1.   Determine the amounts necessary to record Arnold's income taxes for 1997 and prepare the appropriate journal entry.
2.   Determine the amounts necessary to record Arnold's income taxes for 1998 and prepare the appropriate journal entry. Pretax accounting income was $50 million for the year ended December 31, 1998.
3.   Assume a new tax law is enacted in 1998 that causes the tax rate to change from 40% to 30% beginning in 1999. Determine the amounts necessary to record Arnold's income taxes for 1998 and prepare the appropriate journal entry.
4.   Why is Arnold's 1998 income tax expense different when the tax rate change occurs from what it would be without the change?

Exercise 16–14

Deferred taxes; change in tax rates

Bronson Industries reported a deferred tax liability of $8 million for the year ended December 31, 1996, related to a temporary difference of $20 million. The tax rate was 40%. The temporary difference is expected to reverse in 1998 at which time the deferred tax liability will become payable. There are no other temporary differences in 1996–1998. Assume a new tax law is enacted in 1997 that causes the tax rate to change from 40% to 30% beginning in 1998. (The rate remains 40% for 1997 taxes.) Taxable income in 1997 is $30 million.

Required:

Determine the effect of the change and prepare the appropriate journal entry to record Bronson's income tax expense in 1997. What adjustment, if any, is needed to revise retained earnings as a result of the change?

Exercise 16–15

Multiple temporary differences; record income taxes

The information that follows pertains to Esther Food Products:

a.   At December 31, 1997, temporary differences were associated with the following future taxable (deductible) amounts:

Depreciation	$60,000
Prepaid expenses	17,000
Warranty expenses	(12,000)

b. No temporary differences existed at the beginning of 1997.

c. Pretax accounting income was $80,000 and taxable income was $15,000 for the year ended December 31, 1997.

d. The tax rate is 40%.

Required:

Determine the amounts necessary to record income taxes for 1997 and prepare the appropriate journal entry.

Exercise 16–16
Multiple temporary differences; record income taxes

The information that follows pertains to Richards Refrigeration, Inc.:

a. At December 31, 1997, temporary differences existed between the financial statement carrying amounts and the tax bases of the following:

($ in millions)

	Carrying Amount	Tax Basis	Future Taxable (Deductible) Amount
Buildings and equipment (net of accumulated depreciation)	$120	$90	$30
Prepaid insurance	50	0	50
Liability—loss contingency	25	0	(25)

b. No temporary differences existed at the beginning of 1997.

c. Pretax accounting income was $200 million and taxable income was $145 million for the year ended December 31, 1997. The tax rate is 40%.

Required:

1. Determine the amounts necessary to record income taxes for 1997 and prepare the appropriate journal entry.

2. What is the 1997 net income?

Exercise 16–17
Calculate income tax amounts under various circumstances

Four independent situations are described below. Each involves future deductible amounts and/or future taxable amounts produced by temporary differences:

($ in thousands)

	Situation			
	1	2	3	4
Taxable income	$85	$215	$195	$260
Future deductible amounts	15		20	20
Future taxable amounts		15	15	30
Balance(s) at beginning of the year:				
Deferred tax asset	$ 2		$ 9	$ 4
Deferred tax liability		$ 2	2	

The enacted tax rate is 40%.

Required:

For each situation, determine the:

a. Income tax payable currently.

b. Deferred tax asset—balance.

c. Deferred tax asset—change (dr) cr.

d. Deferred tax liability—balance.

e. Deferred tax liability—change (dr) cr.

f. Income tax expense.

Exercise 16–18
Determine taxable income

Eight independent situations are described below. Each involves future deductible amounts and/or future taxable amounts produced by:

($ in millions)

Temporary Differences Reported First on:

	The Income Statement		The Tax Return	
	Revenue	Expense	Revenue	Expense
1.		$20		
2.	$20			
3.			$20	

	The Income Statement		The Tax Return	
	Revenue	Expense	Revenue	Expense
4.		$20		
5.	$15	$20		
6.		$20	$15	
7.	$15	$20		$10
8.	$15	$20	$ 5	$10

Required:

For each situation, determine taxable income assuming pretax accounting income is $100 million.

Exercise 16–19
Two temporary differences; nontemporary difference

For the year ended December 31, 1997, Fidelity Engineering reported pretax accounting income of $977,000. Selected information for 1997 from Fidelity's records follows:

Interest income on municipal bonds	$32,000
Depreciation claimed on the 1997 tax return in excess of depreciation on the income statement	55,000
Carrying amount of depreciable assets in excess of their tax basis at year-end	85,000
Warranty expense reported on the income statement	26,000
Actual warranty expenditures in 1997	16,000

Fidelity's income tax rate is 40%. At January 1, 1997, Fidelity's records indicated balances of zero and $12,000 in its deferred tax asset and deferred tax liability accounts, respectively.

Required:

1. Determine the amounts necessary to record income taxes for 1997 and prepare the appropriate journal entry.
2. What is Fidelity's 1997 net income?

Exercise 16–20
Operating loss carryforward

No valuation allowance is needed

During 1997, its first year of operations, Baginski Steel Corporation reported an operating loss of $375,000 for financial reporting and tax purposes. The enacted tax rate is 40%.

Required:

1. Prepare the journal entry to recognize the income tax benefit of the operating loss. Assume the weight of available evidence suggests future taxable income sufficient to benefit from future deductible amounts from the operating loss carryforward.
2. Show lower portion of the 1997 income statement that reports the income tax benefit of the operating loss.

Exercise 16–21
Operating loss carryback

Wynn Sheet Metal reported an operating loss of $100,000 for financial reporting and tax purposes in 1997. The enacted tax rate is 40%. Taxable income, tax rates, and income taxes paid in Wynn's first four years of operation were as follows:

	Taxable Income	Tax Rates	Income Taxes Paid
1993	$60,000	30%	$18,000
1994	70,000	30%	21,000
1995	85,000	40%	34,000
1996	75,000	40%	30,000

Required:

1. Prepare the journal entry to recognize the income tax benefit of the operating loss. Wynn elects the carryback option.
2. Show lower portion of the 1997 income statement that reports the income tax benefit of the operating loss.

Exercise 16–22
Operating loss carryback and carryforward

(This exercise is based on the situation described in the previous exercise, modified to include a carryforward in addition to a carryback.)

Wynn Sheet Metal reported an operating loss of $250,000 for financial reporting and tax purposes in 1997. The enacted tax rate is 40%. Taxable income, tax rates, and income taxes paid in Wynn's first four years of operation were as follows:

	Taxable Income	Tax Rates	Income Taxes Paid
1993	$60,000	30%	$18,000
1994	70,000	30%	21,000
1995	85,000	40%	34,000
1996	75,000	40%	30,000

Required:

1. Prepare the journal entry to recognize the income tax benefit of the operating loss. Wynn elects the carryback option.
2. Show lower portion of the 1997 income statement that reports the income tax benefit of the operating loss.

Exercise 16–23
Balance sheet classification

At December 31, 1997, DePaul Corporation had a $16 million balance in its deferred tax asset account and a $68 million balance in its deferred tax liability account. The balances were due to the following cumulative temporary differences:

1. Estimated warranty expense, $15 million: expense recorded in the year of the sale; tax-deductible when paid (one-year warranty).
2. Depreciation expense, $120 million: straight-line on the income statement; MACRS on the tax return.
3. Installment sale income, $50 million: income recorded in the year of the sale; taxable when received equally over the next five years.
4. Bad debt expense, $25 million: allowance method for accounting; direct write-off for tax purposes.

Required:

Show how any deferred tax amounts should be classified and reported on the 1997 balance sheet. The tax rate is 40%.

Exercise 16–24
Single temporary difference; non-temporary difference; multiple tax rates; balance sheet classification

Case Appliances began operations in December 1997. When appliances are sold on an installment basis, Case recognizes installment income for financial reporting purposes in the year of the sale. For tax purposes, installment income is reported by the installment method. 1997 installment income was $600,000 and will be collected over the next three years. Scheduled collections and enacted tax rates for 1998–2000 are as follows:

1998	$150,000	30%
1999	250,000	40%
2000	200,000	40%

Pretax accounting income for 1997 was $810,000, which includes interest revenue of $10,000 from municipal bonds. The enacted tax rate for 1997 is 30 percent.

Required:

1. Assuming no differences between accounting income and taxable income other than those described above, prepare the appropriate journal entry to record Case's 1997 income taxes.
2. What is Case's 1997 net income?
3. How should the deferred tax amount be classified in a classified balance sheet?

Exercise 16–25
Two temporary differences; nontemporary difference; multiple tax rates; balance sheet classification

(This exercise is a variation of the previous exercise, modified to include a second temporary difference.)

Case Appliances began operations in December 1997. When appliances are sold on an installment basis, Case recognizes installment income for financial reporting purposes in the year of the sale. For tax purposes, installment income is reported by the installment method. 1997 installment income was $600,000 and will be collected over the next three years. Scheduled collections and enacted tax rates for 1998-2000 are as follows:

1998	$150,000	30%
1999	250,000	40%
2000	200,000	40%

Case also had product warranty costs of $80,000 expensed for financial reporting purposes in 1997. For tax purposes, only the $20,000 of warranty costs actually paid in 1997 was deducted. The remaining $60,000 will be deducted for tax purposes when paid over the next three years as follows:

1998	$20,000
1999	25,000
2000	15,000

Pretax *accounting* income for 1997 was $810,000, which includes interest revenue of $10,000 from municipal bonds. The enacted tax rate for 1997 is 30 percent.

Required:

1. Assuming no differences between accounting income and taxable income other than those described above, prepare the appropriate journal entry to record Case's 1997 income taxes.

2. What is Case's 1997 net income?

3. How should the deferred tax amounts be classified in a classified balance sheet?

Exercise 16–26
Identifying income tax deferrals

Listed below are ten independent situations. For each situation indicate (by letter) whether it will create a deferred tax asset (A), a deferred tax liability (L), or neither (N).

Situation

____ 1. Advance payments on an operating lease deductible when paid.

____ 2. Estimated warranty costs tax deductible when paid.

____ 3. Rent revenue collected in advance; cash basis for tax purposes.

____ 4. Interest received from investments in municipal bonds.

____ 5. Prepaid expenses tax deductible when paid.

____ 6. Operating loss carryforward.

____ 7. Operating loss carryback.

____ 8. Bad debt expense; allowance method for accounting; direct write-off for tax.

____ 9. Organization costs expensed when incurred; tax deductible over 15 years.

____ 10. Life insurance proceeds received upon the death of the company president.

Exercise 16–27
Concepts; terminology

Listed below are several terms and phrases associated with accounting for income taxes. Pair each item from List A (by letter) with the item from List B that is most appropriately associated with it.

List A	List B
___ 1. No tax consequences.	a. Deferred tax liability.
___ 2. Originates, then reverses.	b. Deferred tax asset.
___ 3. Revise deferred tax amounts.	c. 3 years.
___ 4. Operating loss.	d. Current and deferred tax consequence combined.
___ 5. Future tax effect of prepaid expenses tax-deductible when paid.	e. Temporary difference.
___ 6. Loss carryback.	f. Specific tax rates times amounts reversing each year.
___ 7. Future tax effect of estimated warranty expense.	g. Nontemporary differences.
___ 8. Valuation allowance.	h. When enacted tax rate changes.
___ 9. Phased-in change in rates.	i. Same as related asset or liability.
___ 10. Balance sheet classifications.	j. "More likely than not" test.
___ 11. Individual tax consequences of financial statement components.	k. Intraperiod tax allocation.
___ 12. Income tax expense.	l. Negative taxable income.

Exercise 16–28
Tax effect of change in principle; change in depreciation methods

Clinton Poultry Farms has used the declining balance method of depreciation for conveyor equipment acquired at the beginning of 1995 for financial reporting. At the beginning of 1998, Clinton decides to change to the straight-line method. There is no change in the method used for tax reporting. Clinton's tax rate is 40%.

The effect of this change on depreciation for each year is as follows ($ in 000s):

Year	Straight-Line	Declining Balance	Difference
1995	$ 400	$ 640	$240
1996	400	550	150
1997	400	460	60
	$1,200	$1,650	$450

Required:

1. Prepare the journal entry to record the change in principle. (All tax effects should be reflected in the deferred tax liability account.)

2. Briefly describe any other steps Clinton should take to report this accounting change in the 1997–1998 comparative financial statements.

Exercise 16–29
Intraperiod tax allocation

The following income statement does not reflect intraperiod tax allocation.

Required:

Recast the income statement to reflect intraperiod tax allocation.

INCOME STATEMENT
For the Fiscal Year Ended March 31, 1997

	($ in millions)
Revenues	$830
Cost of goods sold	(350)
Gross profit	480
Operating expenses	(180)
Income tax expense	(86)
Income before extraordinary item and cumulative effect of accounting change	214
Extraordinary casualty loss	(10)
Cumulative effect of change in depreciation methods	(75)
Net income	$129

The company's tax rate is 40%.

Exercise 16–30
Single temporary difference;
future taxable amounts;
taxable income given;
dividends received deduction
[based on Appendix 16]

On January 1, 1997, Marley Services, Inc., a computer software training firm, reported a deferred tax liability of $18,000 relating to a 1995 investment in the common stock of Sealy Electronics. The investment is accounted for by the equity method for financial reporting purposes and as an investment security for tax purposes. The financial statement carrying amount of the investment account at the end of 1997 is $580,000 and its tax basis is $440,000. Marley's 1997 taxable income is $1.2 million and its tax rate is 40%. When undistributed earnings of Sealy are eventually distributed as dividends, 70% of the dividends will be exempt from taxation due to the dividends received deduction.

Required:

Prepare the appropriate journal entry to record Marley's 1997 income taxes.

Problems

Problem 16–1
Determine deferred tax assets
and liabilities

Corning-Howell reported taxable income in 1997 of $120 million. At December 31, 1997, the reported amount of some assets and liabilities in the financial statements differed from their tax bases as indicated below:

	Carrying Amount	Tax Basis
Assets:		
Current		
Accounts receivable (net of allowance)	$ 10 million	$ 12 million
Prepaid insurance	20 million	0
Prepaid rent expense (operating lease)	6 million	0
Noncurrent		
Buildings and equipment (net)	360 million	280 million
Liabilities:		
Current		
Liability—subscriptions received	14 million	0
Long-term		
Liability—postretirement benefits	594 million	0
Shareholders' equity:		
Unrealized gain from recording investments available for sale at fair market*	4 million	0

*Taxable when investments are sold.

The total deferred tax asset and deferred tax liability amounts at January 1, 1997, were $250 million and $40 million, respectively. The enacted tax rate is 40% each year.

Required:

1. Determine the total deferred tax asset and deferred tax liability amounts at December 31, 1997.
2. Determine the increase (decrease) in the deferred tax asset and deferred tax liability accounts at December 31, 1997.
3. Determine the income tax payable currently for the year ended December 31, 1997.
4. Prepare the journal entry to record income taxes for 1997.
5. Show how the deferred tax amounts should be classified and reported on the 1997 balance sheet.

Problem 16–2
Temporary difference;
determine deferred tax
amount for three years;
balance sheet classification

Times-Roman Publishing Company reports the following amounts in its first three years of operation:

($ in thousands)	1997	1998	1999
Pretax accounting income	$250	$240	$230
Taxable income	290	220	260

The difference between pretax accounting income and taxable income is due to subscription revenue for one-year magazine subscriptions being reported for tax purposes in the year received, but reported on the income statement in later years when earned. The income tax rate is 40% each year. Times-Roman anticipates profitable operations in the future.

Required:
1. What is the balance sheet account for which a temporary difference is created by this situation?
2. For each year, indicate the cumulative amount of the temporary difference at year-end.
3. Determine the balance in the related deferred tax account at the end of each year. Is it a deferred tax asset or a deferred tax liability?
4. How should the deferred tax amount be classified and reported on the balance sheet?

Problem 16–3
Change in tax rate; single temporary difference

Dixon Development began operations in December 1997. When lots for industrial development are sold, Dixon recognizes income for financial reporting purposes in the year of the sale. For some lots, Dixon recognizes income for tax purposes when collected. Income recognized for financial reporting purposes in 1997 for lots sold this way was $12 million which will be collected over the next three years. Scheduled collections for 1998–2000 are as follows:

1998	$ 4 million
1999	5 million
2000	3 million
	$12 million

Pretax accounting income for 1997 was $16 million. The enacted tax rate is 40 percent.

Required:
1. Assuming no differences between accounting income and taxable income other than those described above, prepare the journal entry to record income taxes in 1997.
2. Suppose a new tax law, revising the tax rate from 40% to 35%, beginning in 1999, is enacted in 1998, when pretax accounting income was $15 million. Prepare the appropriate journal entry to record income taxes in 1998.
3. If the new tax rate had not been enacted, what would have been the appropriate balance in the deferred tax liability account at the end of 1998? Why?

Problem 16–4
Change in tax rate; record taxes for four years

Zekany Corporation would have had identical income before taxes on both its income tax returns and income statements for the years 1998 through 2000 except for differences in depreciation on an operational asset. The asset cost $120,000 and is depreciated for income tax purposes in the following amounts:

1997	$39,600
1998	52,800
1999	18,000
2000	9,600

The operational asset has a four-year life and no residual value. The straight-line method is used for financial reporting purposes.

Income amounts before depreciation expense and income taxes for each of the four years were as follows.

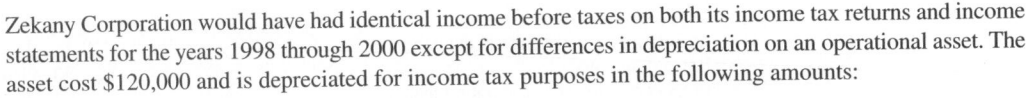

	1997	1998	1999	2000
Accounting income before taxes and depreciation	$60,000	$80,000	$70,000	$70,000

Assume the average and marginal income tax rate for 1997 and 1998 was 30%; however, during 1998 tax legislation was passed to raise the tax rate to 40% beginning in 1999. The 40% rate remained in effect through the years 1999 and 2000. Both the accounting and income tax periods end December 31.

Required:
Prepare the journal entries to record income taxes for the years 1997 through 2000.

Problem 16–5
Change in tax rate; permanent and temporary differences; record taxes for four years

The DeVille Company reported pretax accounting income on its income statement as follows:

1997	$350,000
1998	270,000
1999	340,000
2000	380,000

Included in the income of 1997 was an installment sale in the amount of $50,000. However, for tax purposes, DeVille reported the income in the year cash was collected. Cash collected on the installment sale was $20,000 in 1998, $25,000 in 1999, and $5,000 in 2000.

Included in the 1999 income was $15,000 interest from investments in municipal bonds.

The enacted tax rate for 1997 and 1998 was 30%, but during 1998 new tax legislation was passed reducing the tax rate to 25% for the years 1999 and beyond.

Required:

Prepare the year-end journal entries to record income taxes for the years 1997–2000.

Problem 16–6
Multiple temporary differences; multiple tax rates; classification

The following information relates to Barry Transport Company:

a. Pretax accounting income was $ $41 million and taxable income was $8 million for the year ended December 31, 1997.

b. Temporary differences at December 31, 1997, were related to:

		Future Taxable (Deductible) Amounts
Depreciation	1998	($60 million)
	1999	50 million
	2000	40 million
		$30 million
Prepaid insurance, 1998 coverage		9 million
Loss contingency, to be paid in 1999		(6 million)

c. No temporary differences existed at the beginning of 1997.

d. The tax rate is 40%.

Required:

1. Determine the amounts necessary to record income taxes for 1997 and prepare the appropriate journal entry.
2. How should the deferred tax amounts be classified in a classified balance sheet?
3. Assume the enacted federal income tax law specifies that the tax rate will change from 40% to 35% as of 1999. Determine the amounts necessary to record income taxes for 1997 and prepare the appropriate journal entry.

Problem 16–7
Multiple temporary differences; non-temporary difference; calculate taxable income; balance sheet classification

Sherrod, Inc., reported pretax accounting income of $76 million for 1997. The following information relates to differences between pretax accounting income and taxable income:

a. Income from installment sales included in pretax accounting income in 1997 exceeded that reported for tax purposes by $3 million. The installment receivable account at year-end had a balance of $4 million (representing portions of 1996 and 1997 installment sales), expected to be collected equally in 1998 and 1999.

b. Sherrod was assessed a penalty of $2 million by the Environmental Protection Agency for violation of a federal law in 1997. The fine is to be paid in equal amounts in 1997 and 1998.

c. Sherrod rents its operating facilities but owns one asset acquired in 1996 at a cost of $80 million. Depreciation is reported by the straight-line method assuming a four-year useful life. On the tax return, deductions for depreciation will be more than straight-line depreciation the first two years but less than straight-line depreciation the next two years ($ in millions):

	Income Statement	Tax Return	Difference
1996	$20	$26	$ (6)
1997	20	35	(15)
1998	20	12	8
1999	20	7	13
	$80	$80	0

d. Bad debt expense is reported using the allowance method, $3 million in 1997. For tax purposes, the expense is deducted when accounts prove uncollectible (the direct write-off method), $2 million in 1997. At December 31, 1997, the allowance for uncollectible accounts was $2 million (after adjusting entries). The balance was $1 million at the end of 1996.

e. In 1997, Sherrod accrued an expense and related liability for estimated paid future absences of $7 million relating to the company's new paid vacation program. Future compensation will be deductible on the tax return when actually paid during the next two years ($4 million in 1998; $3 million in 1999).

f. During 1996, accounting income included an estimated loss of $2 million from having accrued a loss contingency. The loss is paid in 1997 at which time it is tax deductible.

Balances in the deferred tax asset and deferred tax liability accounts at January 1, 1997, were $1.2 million and $2.8 million, respectively. The enacted tax rate is 40% each year.

Required:
1. Determine the amounts necessary to record income taxes for 1997 and prepare the appropriate journal entry.
2. What is the 1997 net income?
3. Show how any deferred tax amounts should be classified and reported on the 1997 balance sheet.

Problem 16–8
Multiple temporary differences; nontemporary difference; taxable income given; two years; balance sheet classification

Arndt, Inc,. reported the following for 1997 and 1998 ($ in millions):

	1997	1998
Revenues	$888	$983
Expenses	760	800
Pretax accounting income (income statement)	$128	$183
Taxable income (tax return)	$120	$200
Tax rate: 40%		

a. Expenses each year include $30 million from a two-year casualty insurance policy purchased in 1997 for $60 million. The cost is tax-deductible in 1997.
b. Expenses include $2 million insurance premiums each year for life insurance on key executives.
c. Arndt sells one-year subscriptions to a weekly journal. Subscription sales collected and taxable in 1997 and 1998 were $33 million and $35 million, respectively. Subscriptions included in 1997 and 1998 financial reporting revenues were $25 million ($10 million collected in 1996 but not earned until 1997) and $33 million, respectively. Hint: View this as two temporary differences – one reversing in 1997; one originating in 1997.
d. 1997 expenses included a $17 million unrealized loss from reducing investments (classified as trading securities) to fair value. The investments were sold in 1998.
e. During 1996, accounting income included an estimated loss of $5 million from having accrued a loss contingency. The loss was paid in 1997 at which time it is tax deductible.
f. At January 1, 1997, Arndt had a deferred tax asset of $6 million and no deferred tax liability.

Required:
1. Which of the five differences described are temporary and which are nontemporary differences? Why?
2. Prepare a schedule that (a) reconciles the difference between pretax accounting income and taxable income and (b) determines the amounts necessary to record income taxes for 1997. Prepare the appropriate journal entry.
3. Show how any 1997 deferred tax amounts should be classified and reported on the 1997 balance sheet.
4. Prepare a schedule that (a) reconciles the difference between pretax accounting income and taxable income and (b) determines the amounts necessary to record income taxes for 1998. Prepare the appropriate journal entry.
5. Explain how any 1998 deferred tax amounts should be classified and reported on the 1998 balance sheet.

Problem 16–9
Single temporary difference originates each year for four years

Alsup Consulting sometimes performs services for which it receives payment at the conclusion of the engagement, up to six months after services commence. Alsup recognizes service revenue for financial reporting purposes when the services are performed. For tax purposes, revenue is reported when fees are collected. Service revenue, collections, and pretax accounting income for 1996-1999 are as follows:

	Service Revenue	Collections	Pretax Accounting Income
1996	$650,000	$620,000	$186,000
1997	750,000	770,000	250,000
1998	715,000	700,000	220,000
1999	700,000	720,000	200,000

There are no differences between accounting income and taxable income other than the temporary difference described above. The enacted tax rate for each year is 40 percent.

Required:
1. Prepare the appropriate journal entry to record Alsup's **1997** income taxes.
2. Prepare the appropriate journal entry to record Alsup's **1998** income taxes.
3. Prepare the appropriate journal entry to record Alsup's **1999** income taxes.

(Hint: You may find it helpful to prepare a schedule that shows the balances in service revenue receivable at December 31, 1996–1999.)

Problem 16–10
Operating loss carryback and carryforward; temporary difference; nontemporary difference

Fores Construction Company reported a pretax operating loss of $135 million for financial reporting purposes in 1997. Contributing to the loss were (a) a penalty of $5 million assessed by the Environmental Protection Agency for violation of a federal law and paid in 1997 and (b) an estimated loss of $10 million from accruing a loss contingency. The loss will be tax deductible when paid in 1998.

The enacted tax rate is 40%. There were no temporary differences at the beginning of the year and none originating in 1997 other than those described above. Taxable income in Fores's three previous years of operation was as follows:

1994	$35 million
1995	40 million
1996	30 million

Required:

1. Prepare the journal entry to recognize the income tax benefit of the operating loss in 1997. Fores elects the carryback option.
2. Show the lower portion of the 1997 income statement that reports the income tax benefit of the operating loss.
3. Prepare the journal entry to record income taxes in 1998 assuming pretax accounting income is $60 million. No additional temporary differences originate in 1998.

Problem 16–11
Integrating problem—bonds, leases, taxes

The following is the long-term liabilities section of Tempo Co.'s December 31, 1996, balance sheet:

Long-term liabilities:

Note payable—bank; 15 principal payments of $5,000, plus 10% interest due annually on September 30	$75,000	
Less current portion	5,000	$ 70,000
Capital lease obligation—16 payments of $9,000 due annually on January 1	$76,600	
Less current portion	1,340	75,260
Deferred income tax liability		15,750
Total long-term liabilities		$161,010

a. Tempo's incremental borrowing rate on the date of the lease was 11% and the lessor's implicit rate, which was known by Tempo, was 10%.
b. The only difference between Tempo's taxable income and pretax accounting income is depreciation on a machine acquired on January 1, 1996, for $250,000. The machine's estimated useful life is five years, with no salvage value. Depreciation is computed using the straight-line method for financial reporting purposes and the MACRS method for tax purposes. Depreciation expense for tax and financial reporting purposes for 1997 through 2000 is as follows:

Year	Tax depreciation	Financial depreciation	Tax depreciation over (under) financial depreciation
1997	$80,000	$50,000	$30,000
1998	40,000	50,000	(10,000)
1999	35,000	50,000	(15,000)
2000	30,000	50,000	(20,000)

The enacted federal income tax rates are 30% for 1996 and 1997, and 35% for 1998 through 2000.
c. Included in Tempo's December 1996 balance sheet was a deferred tax asset of $9,000.
d. For the year ended December 31, 1997, Tempo's income before income taxes was $430,000.
e. On July 1, 1997, Tempo received proceeds of $459,725 from a $500,000 bond issuance. The bonds mature in 30 years and interest of 11% is payable each January 1 and July 1. The bonds were issued at a price to yield the investors 12%. Tempo uses the effective interest method to amortize the bond discount.

Required:

1. Prepare a schedule showing Tempo's income before income taxes, current income tax expense, deferred income tax expense, and net income for 1997. Show supporting calculations for current and deferred income tax amounts.
2. Prepare a schedule showing the calculations of Tempo's interest expense for the year ended December 31, 1997.
3. Prepare a long-term liabilities section of Tempo's December 31, 1997, balance sheet. Show supporting calculations.

[AICPA adapted]

Cases

Discussion Case 16–1
Basic concepts

One of the longest debates in accounting history is the issue of deferred taxes. The controversy began in the 1940s and has continued, even after the FASB issued *Statement of Financial Accounting Standards No. 109* in 1992. At issue is the appropriate treatment of tax consequences of economic events that occur in years other than that of the events themselves.

Required:

1. Distinguish between temporary differences and permanent differences. Provide an example of each.
2. Distinguish between intraperiod tax allocation and interperiod tax allocation (deferred tax accounting). Provide an example of each.
3. How are deferred tax assets and deferred tax liabilities classified and reported in the financial statements?

Integrating Case 16–2
Postretirement benefits

Statement of Financial Accounting Standards No. 106 establishes accounting standards for postretirement benefits other than pensions, most notably postretirement health care benefits. Essentially, the standard requires companies to accrue compensation expense each year employees perform services, for the expected cost of providing future postretirement benefits that can be attributed to that service. Typically, companies do not pre-fund these costs for two reasons: (a) unlike pension liabilities, no federal law requires companies to fund nonpension postretirement benefits and (b) funding contributions, again unlike for pension liabilities, are not tax deductible. (The costs aren't tax deductible until paid to, or on behalf of, employees.)

Required:

1. As a result of being required to record the periodic postretirement expense and related liability, most companies now report lower earnings and higher liabilities. How might many companies also report higher assets as a result of *SFAS 106?*
2. One objection to *SFAS 109,* "Accounting for Income Taxes," as cited in the chapter is the omission of requirements to discount deferred tax amounts to their present values. This objection is inappropriate in the context of deferred tax amounts necessitated by accounting for postretirement benefits. Why?

Critical Thought Case 16–3
Intraperiod tax allocation

Russell-James Corporation is a diversified consumer products company. During 1997, Russell-James discontinued its line of cosmetics, which constituted discontinued operations for financial reporting purposes. As vice president of the food products division, you are interested in the effect of the discontinuance on the company's profitability. One item of information you requested was an income statement. The income statement you received (shown below) was labeled *preliminary* and *unaudited:*

Russell-James Corporation
Income Statement
For the Year Ended December 31, 1997

($ in millions, except per share amounts)		
Revenues		$ 300
Cost of goods sold		90
Gross profit		210
Selling and administrative expenses		(60)
Income from continuing operations before income taxes		150
Income taxes		(24)
Income from continuing operations		126
Discontinued operations:		
Loss from operations of cosmetics division	$(100)	
Gain from disposal of cosmetics division	15	(85)
Income before extraordinary item and cumulative effect of accounting change		41
Extraordinary loss from earthquake		(10)
Cumulative effect of change in inventory costing		5
Net income		$ 36
Per share of common stock (100 million shares):		
Income from continuing operations		$1.26
Loss from operations of cosmetics division		(1.00)
Gain from disposal of cosmetics division		.15
Income before extraordinary item and cumulative effect of accounting change		.41
Extraordinary loss from earthquake		(.10)
Cumulative effect of change in inventory costing		.05
Net income		$ .36

You are somewhat surprised at the magnitude of the loss incurred by the cosmetics division prior to its disposal. Another item that draws your attention is the apparently low tax rate indicated by the statement ($24 ÷ $150 = 16%). Upon further investigation you are told the company's tax rate is 40%.

Required:
1. Recast the income statement to reflect intraperiod tax allocation.
2. How would you reconcile the income tax expense shown on the statement above with the amount your recast statement reports?

International Case 16–4
Accounting for income taxes in other countries

The primary objective of the International Accounting Standards Committee (IASC) is to narrow worldwide differences in accounting practices and the presentation of financial information. Although the IASC has worked toward uniformity since 1973, harmonization has by no means been achieved. In the area of accounting for income taxes, significant differences exist from country to country that impact reported earnings and financial position.

Required:
Choose a country other than the United States and:

1. Locate a recent annual report of a non-U.S. company.
2. Determine the way that country accounts for income taxes. Include in your analysis:
   a. The extent of variations between accounting income and taxable income.
   b. Whether these differences create deferred taxes.
   c. Whether tax deferral depends on expectations as to when differences are expected to reverse.
3. Prepare a short report highlighting the similarities and differences between the United States and your chosen country in the way income taxes are accounted for.

Note: You can obtain copies of annual reports from the investor relations department of the corporation, a friendly stockbroker, Public Register's Annual Report Service at www.PRARS.com. or from EDGAR, the Electronic Data Gathering and Retrieval service of the SEC, at www.sec.gov/.

Financial Analysis Case 16–5
Mosinee Paper Corporation

The following disclosure note appeared in the 1993 annual report of the Mosinee Paper Corporation. Mosinee operates in the pulp and paper industry. It produces and sells specialty papers, wax laminated and converted papers, and towel and tissue paper products.

10—Income Taxes (in part)

($ in thousands)	1993	1992
Deferred tax assets:		
Allowances on accounts receivable	$ 638	$ 291
Accrued compensated absences	1,251	1,282
Stock appreciation rights plans	2,007	1,350
Pensions	832	934
Postretirement benefits	5,397	5,411
Reserves	1,020	986
State net operating loss carry forward	3,160	2,178
Alternative minimum tax credit forward	7,271	5,473
Other	245	358
Gross deferred tax assets	21,821	18,263
Less: valuation allowance	(1,081)	(937)
Net deferred tax assets	20,740	17,326
Deferred tax liabilities:		
Property, plant, and equipment	(34,080)	(27,845)
Deferred expenses	(1,200)	(823)
Total gross deferred tax liability	(35,280)	(28,668)
Net deferred tax liability	($14,540)	($11,342)

The total deferred tax liabilities (assets) as presented in the accompanying balance sheets are as follows:

($ in thousands)	1993	1992
Net long-term deferred tax liabilities	$18,081	$13,101
Gross current deferred tax assets	(4,622)	(2,696)
Valuation allowance on deferred tax assets	1,081	937
Net current deferred tax assets	(3,541)	(1,759)
Net deferred tax liability	$14,540	$11,342

A valuation allowance has been recognized for a subsidiary's state tax loss carryforward as cumulative losses create uncertainty about the realization of the tax benefits in future years.

The 1993 income statement reported a provision for income taxes of $7,750,000.

Required:

1. Specifically, which amounts did Mosinee report in its 1993 and 1992 comparative balance sheets related to deferred taxes. Explain how the current and noncurrent classifications are determined.
2. From the information provided by the disclosure note, determine the journal entry recorded by Mosinee to reflect the 1993 income tax expense.
3. Mosinee's debt-to-equity ratio was .68 in 1993, calculated as $171,673 ÷ $252,061. Some analysts argue that long-term deferred tax liabilities should be excluded from liabilities in the computation of the ratio. What is the effect of excluding the gross long-term deferred tax liabilities on Mosinee's debt-to-equity ratio? What is the reasoning behind modifying the ratio this way?

Integrating Case 16–6
Income taxes and investment securities

The following disclosure note appeared in the 1995 annual report of the Wm. Wrigley Jr. Company.

Investments in Debt & Equity Securities
Effective December 31, 1993, the Company adopted *Statement of Financial Accounting Standards (SFAS) No. 115,* "Accounting for Certain Investments in Debt and Equity Securities." The Company's investments in debt securities, which typically mature in one year or less, are held to maturity and valued at the amortized cost, which approximates fair value. The aggregate fair values at December 31, 1995, and December 31, 1994, were, respectively, $82,740,000 and $69,287,000 for municipal securities, and $23,207,000 and $33,392,000 for other debt securities.

The Company's investments in marketable equity securities are held for an indefinite period and have been historically reported at the lower of cost or market. Application of *SFAS No. 115* resulted in unrealized holding gains of $17,544,000 at December 31, 1995, and $12,085,000 at December 31, 1994. The aggregate fair value of the Company's marketable equity securities at December 31, 1995 and 1994 totaled $19,827,000 and $14,687,000 respectively. The unrealized holding gains, net of the related tax effect, added $11,404,000 and $7,855,000 to stockholders' equity at December 31, 1995 and 1994, respectively.

Required:

1. From the information provided by the disclosure note, determine the amount at which Wrigley reported its investment in marketable equity securities in its 1995 balance sheet. Explain how investment securities available for sale are accounted for.
2. What would have been Wrigley's journal entry to reflect the 1995 fair value of the investments?

Writing Case 16–7
Notes, leases, bonds

Chris Green, CPA, is auditing Rayne Co.'s 1997 financial statements. The controller, Dunn, has provided Green with the following information:

a. At December 31, 1996, Rayne had a note payable to Federal Bank with a balance of $90,000. The annual principal payment of $10,000, plus 8% interest on the unpaid balance, was paid when due on March 31, 1997.
b. On January 2, 1997, Rayne leased two automobiles for executive use under a capital lease. Five annual lease payments of $15,000 are due beginning January 3, 1997. Rayne's incremental borrowing rate on the date of the lease was 11% and the lessor's implicit rate, which was known by Rayne, was 10%. The lease was properly recorded at $62,500, before the first payment was made.
c. On July 1, 1997, Rayne received proceeds of $538,000 from a $500,000 bond issuance. The bonds mature in 15 years and interest of 11% is payable semiannually on June 30 and December 31. The bonds were issued at a price to yield investors 10%. Rayne uses the effective interest method to amortize bond premium.
d. For the year ended December 31, 1997, Rayne has adopted *Statement of Financial Accounting Standards No. 109,* "Accounting for Income Taxes." Dunn has prepared a schedule of all differences between financial statement and income tax return income. Dunn believes that as a result of pending legislation, the enacted tax rate at December 31, 1997, will be increased for 1998. Dunn is uncertain which differences to include and which rates to apply in computing deferred taxes under *SFAS 109*. Dunn has requested an overview of *SFAS 109* from Green.

Required:

1. Prepare a schedule of interest expense for the year ended December 31, 1997.
2. Prepare a brief memo to Dunn from Green:
   a. Identifying the objectives of accounting for income taxes.
   b. Defining temporary differences.
   c. Explaining how to measure deferred tax assets and liabilities.
   d. Explaining how to measure deferred income tax expense or benefit.

(AICPA adapted)

Research Case 16–8
Valuation allowance; research an article in *Accounting Horizons*

SFAS 109 requires companies to recognize deferred tax assets for *all* deductible temporary differences and then reduce a deferred tax asset by a valuation allowance if it is more likely than not that some portion or all of the deferred tax asset will not be realized. This is referred to in the *Standard* as the impairment approach. The Board rejected an alternative affirmative approach, under which a firm would start at zero and then adjust the deferred tax asset upward as warranted by positive evidence about realizability, but suggested that either approach would likely lead to the same net deferred tax asset if a more likely than not realization criterion is used. Professors Heiman-Hoffman and Patton, in "An Experimental Investigation of Deferred Tax Asset Judgments under *SFAS 109,*" conducted an empirical test of whether the two approaches lead to the same result.

Required:
1. In your library or from some other source, locate the indicated article in *Accounting Horizons*, March 1994.
2. What is the authors' conclusion as to whether the two approaches lead to the same net deferred tax asset?
3. On what evidence do they base their conclusion?

Integrating Case 16–9
Accounting changes and error correction; six situations; tax effects considered

Williams-Santana, Inc., is a manufacturer of high-tech industrial parts that was started in 1985 by two talented engineers with little business training. In 1997, the company was acquired by one of its major customers. As part of an internal audit, the following facts were discovered. The audit occurred during 1997 before any adjusting entries or closing entries were prepared. The income tax rate is 40% for all years.

a. A five-year casualty insurance policy was purchased at the beginning of 1995 for $35,000. The full amount was debited to insurance expense at the time.
b. On December 31, 1996, merchandise inventory was overstated by $25,000 due to a mistake in the physical inventory count using the periodic inventory system.
c. The company changed inventory cost methods to FIFO from LIFO at the end of 1997 for both financial statement and income tax purposes. The change will cause a $960,000 increase in the beginning inventory at January 1, 1996.
d. At the end of 1996, the company failed to accrue $15,500 of sales commissions earned by employees during 1996. The expense was recorded when the commissions were paid in early 1997.
e. At the beginning of 1995, the company purchased a machine at a cost of $720,000. Its useful life was estimated to be 10 years with no salvage value. The machine has been depreciated by the double-declining-balance method. Its carrying amount on December 31, 1996, was $460,800. On January 1, 1997, the company changed retroactively to the straight-line method.
f. Additional industrial robots were acquired at the beginning of 1994 and added to the company's assembly process. The $1,000,000 cost of the equipment was inadvertently recorded as repair expense. Robots have ten-year useful lives and no material salvage value. This class of equipment is depreciated by the straight-line method.

Required:
For each situation:
1. Identify whether it represents an accounting change or an error. If an accounting change, identify the type of change.
2. Prepare any journal entry necessary as a direct result of the change or error correction as well as any adjusting entry for 1997 related to the situation described. Any tax effects should be adjusted for through the deferred tax liability account.
3. Briefly describe any other steps that should be taken to appropriately report the situation.

Real World Case 16–10
Disclosure issues; balance sheet classifications

The income tax disclosure note accompanying the 1994 financial statements of the Walgreen Company is reproduced below:

Income Taxes
The provision for income taxes consists of the following (*in thousands*):

	1994	1993	1992
Current Provision			
Federal	$145,381	$133,562	$105,551
State	25,458	33,740	15,668
	170,839	167,032	121,219
Deferred provision			
Federal	3,881	(3,903)	6,316
State	1,772	(8,742)	4,842
	5,653	(12,645)	11,158
	$176,492	$154,387	$132,377

The components of the deferred provision were (in thousands):

	1994	1993	1992
Accelerated depreciation	$20,756	$ 17,192	$23,537
Insurance	(2,763)	(14,061)	(278)
Employee benefit plans	(5,767)	(6,518)	(3,430)
Other	(6,573)	(9,258)	(8,671)
	$5,653	$(12,645)	$11,158

The deferred tax assets and liabilities included in the Consolidated Balance Sheet as of August 31, 1994, consists of the following (in thousands):

	Assets	Liabilities	Total
Current			
Insurance	$ 35,886	$ —	$ 35,886
Employee benefit plans	23,898	(12,274)	11,624
Allowances for doubtful accounts	8,841	—	8,841
Inventory	9,938	(22,625)	(12,687)
Other	27,727	(6,689)	21,038
	106,290	(41,588)	64,702
Noncurrent			
Accelerated depreciation	—	(231,738)	(231,738)
Employee benefit plans	13,475	—	13,475
Postretirement	26,039	—	26,039
Other	18,921	(346)	18,575
	58,435	(232,084)	(173,649)
	$164,725	$(273,672)	$(108,947)

   Income taxes paid were $170,146,000, $166,848,000 and $116,417,000 during the fiscal years ended August 31, 1994, 1993 and 1992, respectively. The difference between the statutory income tax rate and the effective tax rate is principally due to state income tax provisions.

Required:

1. How are the deferred taxes classified on Walgreens' 1994 balance sheet?
2. Recreate the journal entry that summarizes the entries Walgreens used to record 1994 income taxes.

International Case 16–11
Comparison of deferred tax accounting in the U.K. and the United States

The British Petroleum Company p.l.c. (BP), based in London, is one of the world's largest petroleum and petrochemical groups. The income tax disclosures accompanying BP's 1993 financial statements are reproduced below:

Accounting Policies (in part)

Deferred Taxation
Deferred taxation is calculated, using the liability method, in respect to timing differences arising primarily from the different accounting and tax treatment of depreciation and petroleum revenue tax. Provision is made or recovery anticipated where timing differences are expected to reverse in the foreseeable future.

Balance sheets (partial)			
at December 31	Note	1993	1992
Total assets less current liabilities		22,660	23,577
Creditors—amounts falling due after one year:			
Finance debt	24	7,144	7,827
Other creditors	25	2,055	2,459
Provision for liabilities and charges:			
Deferred taxation	10	248	226
Other provisions	26	3,365	3,207
Net assets		9,848	9,858

Note 10: Provision for deferred taxation (in part)			£ million	
	Provisions		Gross potential liability	
Analysis of Provision	1993	1992	1993	1992
Depreciation	1,102	1,143	3,321	3,423
Petroleum revenue tax	(500)	(574)	(500)	(574)
Other timing differences	(178)	(159)	(727)	(665)
Advance corporation tax	(176)	(184)	(444)	(640)
	248	226	1,650	1,544

Required:
On the basis of the information the disclosures provide, compare accounting for income taxes in the U.K. with that in the United States.

Internet Case 16–12
Researching the way tax deductions are reported on a corporation tax return; retrieving a tax form from the Internet

The U.S. Treasury maintains an information site on the Internet. As part of this site the Internal Revenue Service provides tax information and services. Among those services is a server for publications and forms which allows a visitor to download a variety of IRS forms and publications.

Required:
1. Access the Treasury site on the Internet. The web address is www.ustreas.gov/. After exploring the information available there, navigate to the IRS server for forms and publications via the IRS home page.
2. Download the corporation tax return, Form 1120.
3. Note the specific deductions listed that are deductible from total income to arrive at taxable income. Are any deductions listed that might not also be included among expenses on the income statement?
4. One of the deductions indicated is "net operating loss deduction." Under what circumstances might a company report an amount for this item?
5. Based on how taxable income is determined, how might temporary differences be created between taxable income and pretax income on the income statement?

Financial Analysis Case 16–13
Reporting deferred taxes

Federal Express Corporation

Refer to the financial statements and related disclosure notes of Federal Express Corporation in the Appendix to Chapter 1. On Federal Express' balance sheet, deferred income taxes are reported as both an asset ($92.6 million in 1996) and a liability ($64 million in 1996).

Required:
1. Explain why deferred income taxes can be reported as both an asset and a liability. Why is the deferred tax asset reported as current and the deferred tax liability as long term?
2. Note 7 in the disclosure notes indicates that deferred tax assets are $443 million in 1996 and deferred tax liabilities are $414 million. How can that be explained in light of the two amounts reported on the balance sheet?
3. Does Federal Express feel the need to record a valuation allowance for its deferred tax assets?

17

PENSIONS

Employee compensation comes in many forms. Salaries and wages, of course, provide direct and current payment for services provided. However, it's commonplace for compensation also to include benefits payable after retirement. We discuss pension benefits in this chapter. Accounting for pension benefits recognizes that they represent deferred compensation for current service. Accordingly, the cost of these benefits is recognized on an accrual basis during the years that employees earn the benefits.

LEARNING OBJECTIVES

After studying this chapter, you should be able to:

1. Explain the fundamental differences between a defined contribution pension plan and a defined benefit pension plan.
2. Distinguish among the accumulated benefit obligation, the vested benefit obligation, and the projected benefit obligation.
3. Describe the five events that might change the balance of the PBO.
4. Explain how plan assets accumulate to provide retiree benefits and understand the role of the trustee in administering the fund.
5. Describe how pension expense is a composite of periodic changes that occur in both the pension obligation and the plan assets.
6. Understand the interrelationships among the elements that constitute a defined benefit pension plan.
7. Describe how pension disclosures fill a reporting gap left by the minimal disclosures in the primary financial statements.

TODAY

DATE_____

THINGS TO DO   FINISHED ✓

#		
1.	Chapter 17 read	
2.	pgs 728-732 (part A)	
3.	732-739 (part B)	
4.		
5.		
6.		
7.		
8.		
9.		
10.		

SPECIAL FOLLOW-UP

#		
1.		
2.		
3.		
4.		
5.		

UNITED DYNAMICS

You read yesterday that many companies in the United States have pension plans that are severely underfunded. This caught your attention in part because you have your office interview tomorrow with United Dynamics. You hadn't really thought that much about the pension plan of your potential future employer, in part because your current employer has a defined contribution 401K plan, for which funding is not a concern. However, United Dynamics is an older firm with a defined benefit plan, for which funding is the employer's responsibility.

To prepare for your interview, you obtained a copy of United Dynamics' financial statements. Unfortunately, the financial statements themselves are of little help. You are unable to find any pension liability on the balance sheet, but the statement does report a relatively small "prepaid pension asset." The income statement reports pension expense for each of the years reported. For help, you search the disclosure notes. In part, the pension disclosure note reads as follows:

Note 7: Pension Plan

United Dynamics has a defined benefit pension plan covering substantially all of its employees. Plan benefits are based on years of service and the employee's compensation during the last three years of employment. The company's funding policy is consistent with the funding requirements of federal law and regulations. The net periodic pension expense for the company included the following components:

The company's pension expense was as follows ($ in millions):

	1997	1996	1995
Current service costs	$ 43	$ 53	$ 42
Interest cost on projected benefit obligation	178	164	152
Return on assets	(213)	(200)	(187)
Net amortization	41	45	26
Net pension costs	$ 49	$ 62	$ 33

The funded status and amounts recognized in the consolidated balance sheets for the Company's defined benefit retirement plan at December 31, 1997 and 1996, were as follows:

($ in millions)	1997	1996
Plan assets at fair value	$2,807	$2,340
Actuarial present value of:		
Vested benefits	$2,116	$1,762
Accumulated benefits	2,455	2,071
Projected benefits	2,628	2,194
Plan assets in excess of projected benefits	$ 180	$ 145
Unamortized prior service cost	164	207
Unamortized net gains	(61)	(66)
Prepaid pension asset recognized in the balance sheet	283	286
Assumptions:		
Discount rate at year-end	7.0%	8.25%
Average rate of increase in compensation	5.5%	5.5 %

"Ouch! I can't believe how much of my accounting I forgot," you complain to yourself. "I'd better get out my old intermediate accounting book."

QUESTIONS

1. Why is underfunding not a concern in your present employment?
2. Were you correct that the pension liability is not reported on the balance sheet? What is the liability?
3. What is the amount of the plan assets available to pay benefits? What are the factors that can cause that amount to change?
4. How is the pension expense influenced by changes in the pension liability and plan assets?
5. Are you interviewing with a company whose pension plan is severely underfunded?

PART A THE NATURE OF PENSION PLANS

Over 80 million American workers are covered by pension plans. The United States' pension funds tripled in size during the previous two decades and now are roughly the size of Japan's gross national product. This powerful investment base now controls about one-fourth of the stock market. At the company level, the enormous size of pension funds is reflected in a periodic pension cost that constitutes one of the largest expenses many companies report. The corporate liability for providing pension benefits, though largely off-balance-sheet, is huge. Obviously, then, the financial reporting responsibility for pensions has important social and economic implications.

Pension plans are designed to provide income to individuals during their retirement years. This is accomplished by setting aside funds during an employee's working years so that at retirement the accumulated funds plus earnings from investing those funds are available to replace wages. Actually, an individual who periodically invests in stocks, bonds, certificates of deposit (CDs), or other investments for the purpose of saving for retirement is establishing a personal pension fund. Often, such individual plans take the form of individual retirement accounts (IRAs) to take advantage of tax breaks offered by that arrangement. In employer plans, some or all of the periodic contributions to the retirement fund often are provided by the employer.

Corporations establish pension plans for a variety of reasons. Sponsorship of pension plans provides employees with a degree of retirement security and fulfills a moral obligation felt by many employers. This security also can induce a degree of job satisfaction and perhaps loyalty that might enhance productivity and reduce turnover. Motivation to sponsor a plan sometimes comes from union demands and often relates to being competitive in the labor market.

> Pension plans often enhance productivity, reduce turnover, satisfy union demands, and allow employers to compete in the labor market.

When established according to tight guidelines, a pension plan gains important tax advantages. Such arrangements are called *qualified plans* because they qualify for favorable tax treatment. In a qualified plan, the employer is permitted an immediate tax deduction for amounts paid into the pension fund (within specified limits). The employees, on the other hand, are not taxed at the time employer contributions are made—only when retirement benefits are received. Moreover, earnings on the funds set aside by the employer are not taxed while in the pension fund, so the earnings accumulate tax free. If you are familiar with the tax advantages of IRAs, you probably recognize the similarity between those individual plans and corporate pension arrangements.

> Qualified pension plans offer important tax benefits.

For a pension plan to be qualified for special tax treatment it must meet the general requirements listed in Graphic 17–1.

GRAPHIC 17–1

Requirements of a Qualified Plan

1. It must cover at least 70% of employees.
2. It cannot discriminate in favor of highly compensated employees.
3. It must be funded in advance of retirement through contributions to an irrevocable trust fund.
4. Benefits must vest after a specified period of service, commonly five years. (We discuss this in more detail later.)
5. It complies with specific restrictions on the timing and amount of contributions and benefits.

Learning objective 1

·Explain the fundamental differences between a defined contribution pension plan and a defined benefit pension plan.

Sometimes, employers agree to annually contribute a specific (defined) amount to a pension fund on behalf of employees but make no commitment regarding benefit amounts at retirement. In other arrangements, employers don't specify the amount of annual contributions but promise to provide determinable (defined) amounts at retirement. These two arrangements describe defined contribution pension plans and defined benefit pension plans, respectively, as shown in Graphic 17–2.

GRAPHIC   17–2

Types of Pension Plans

- **Defined contribution pension plans** promise fixed annual contributions to a pension fund (say, 5% of the employees' pay). The employee chooses (from designated options) where funds are invested—usually stocks or fixed-income securities. Retirement pay depends on the size of the fund at retirement.
- **Defined benefit pension plans** promise fixed retirement benefits defined by a designated formula. Typically, the pension formula bases retirement pay on the employees' (a) years of service, (b) annual compensation (often final pay or an average for the last few years), and sometimes (c) age. Employers are responsible for ensuring that sufficient funds are available to provide promised benefits.

Virtually all new pension plans are defined contribution plans.

Today, about half of workers covered by pension plans are covered by defined contribution plans, half by defined benefit plans. This represents a radical shift from previous years when the traditional defined benefit plan was far more common. However, almost no new pension plans are of the defined benefit variety. In fact, many companies are terminating long-standing defined benefit plans and substituting defined contribution plans. Why the shift? There are two main reasons:

1. Government regulations make defined benefit plans cumbersome and costly to administer.
2. Employers are increasingly unwilling to bear the risk of defined benefit plans; with defined contribution plans, the company's obligation ends when contributions are made.

Both types of plans have a common goal: to provide income to employees during their retirement years. Still, the two types of plans differ regarding who bears the risk—the employer or the employees—for whether the retirement objectives are achieved. The two types of plans also have entirely different implications for accounting and financial reporting. Our discussion of defined contribution plans will be brief. Although these are now the most popular type of corporate pension plan, their relative simplicity permits a rather straightforward accounting treatment that requires little explanation. On the other hand, defined benefit plans require considerably more complex accounting treatment and constitute the primary focus of this chapter.

Defined Contribution Pension Plans

Defined contribution pension plans promise defined periodic contributions to a pension fund, without further commitment regarding benefit amounts at retirement.

Defined contribution pension plans are becoming increasingly popular vehicles for employers to provide retirement income without the paperwork, cost, and risk generated by the more traditional defined benefit plans. Defined contribution plans promise fixed periodic contributions to a pension fund. Retirement income depends on the size of the fund at retirement. No further commitment is made by the employer regarding benefit amounts at retirement.

These plans have several variations. In money purchase plans, employers contribute a fixed percentage of employees' salaries. Thrift plans, savings plans, and 401(k) plans (named after the Tax Code section that specifies the conditions for the favorable tax treatment of these plans) permit voluntary contributions by employees. These contributions typically are matched to a specified extent by employers. Over 21 million employees participate in 401(k) plans. Nearly a trillion dollars is invested in these plans.

When plans link the amount of contributions to company performance, labels include profit-sharing plans, incentive savings plans, 401(k) profit-sharing plans, and similar titles. When employees make contributions to the plan in addition to employer contributions, it's called a *contributory* plan. Sometimes the amount the employer contributes is tied to the amount of the employee contribution.[1] Variations are seemingly endless. Two examples from recent annual reports of Eli Lilly and The Duriron Company are recreated in Graphics 17–3 and 17–4.

---

[1]One popular way for employer companies to provide contributions is with shares of its own common stock. If so, the arrangements usually are designed to comply with government requirements to be designated an employee stock ownership plan (ESOP).

GRAPHIC   17–3

Defined Contribution Plans—
Eli Lilly and Company

Note 9: Retirement Benefits (in Part)

The company has defined contribution savings plans that cover its eligible employees worldwide. The purpose of these defined contribution plans is generally to provide additional financial security during retirement by providing employees with an incentive to make regular savings. Company contributions to the plans are based on employee contributions and the level of company match.

GRAPHIC   17–4

Defined Contribution Plans—
The Duriron Company, Inc.

Note 15: Retirement Benefits (in Part)

The Company also sponsors several defined contribution pension plans. Domestic and Canadian salaried and certain hourly employees . . . may be eligible to participate in thrift and savings plans. Eligible employees may contribute up to 6% of base compensation to these plans and these contributions are matched by the Company. The Company contributes an amount equal to 25% of each employee's contribution and an additional contribution of 5% to 35% if the Company's consolidated return on shareholders' equity exceeds 9%.

OPENING CASE

Question 1

For defined contribution plans, the employer simply records pension expense equal to the cash contribution.

Accounting for these plans is quite easy. Each year, the employer simply records pension expense equal to the amount of the annual contribution. Suppose a plan promises an annual contribution equal to 3% of an employee's salary. If an employee's salary is $110,000 in a particular year, the employer would simply recognize compensation expense in the amount of the contribution:

Pension expense	3,300	
Cash ($110,000 × 3%)		3,300

The employee's retirement benefits are totally dependent upon how well investments perform. Who bears the risk (or reward) of that uncertainty? The employee would bear the risk of uncertain investment returns and, potentially, settle for far less at retirement than at first expected. On the other hand, the employer would be free of any further obligation. Because the actual investments are held by an independent investment firm, the employer is free of that recordkeeping responsibility as well.

Risk is reversed in a defined benefit plan. Because specific benefits are promised at retirement, the employer would be responsible for making up the difference when investment performance is less than expected. We look at defined benefit plans next.

Defined Benefit Pension Plans

Defined benefit plans promise fixed retirement benefits defined by a designated formula.

Uncertainties complicate determining how much to set aside each year to ensure that sufficient funds are available to provide promised benefits.

When setting aside cash to fund a pension plan, the uncertainty surrounding the rate of return on plan assets is but one of several uncertainties inherent in a defined benefit plan. Employee turnover affects the number of employees who ultimately will become eligible for retirement benefits. The age at which employees will choose to retire as well as life expectancies will impact both the length of the retirement period and the amount of the benefits. Inflation, future compensation levels, and interest rates also have obvious influence on eventual benefits.

This is particularly true when pension benefits are defined by a pension formula, as usually is the case. A typical formula might specify that a retiree will receive annual retirement benefits based on the employee's years of service and annual pay at retirement (say, pay level in the final year, highest pay achieved, or average pay in last two or more years). For example, a pension formula might define annual retirement benefits as:

$$1\frac{1}{2}\% \times \text{Years of service} \times \text{Final year's salary}$$

By this formula, the annual benefits to an employee who retires after 30 years of service, with a final salary of $100,000, would be:

$$1^1/_2 \% \times 30 \text{ years} \times \$100,000 = \$45,000$$

Typically, a firm will hire an **actuary,** a professional trained in a particular branch of statistics and mathematics, to assess the various uncertainties (employee turnover, salary levels, mortality, rates of return, etc.) and to estimate the company's obligation to employees in connection with its pension plan. Such estimates are inherently subjective, so regardless of the skill of the actuary, estimates invariably deviate from the actual outcome to one degree or another.[2] For instance, the return on assets can turn out to be more or less than expected. These deviations are referred to as *gains* and *losses* on pension assets. When it's necessary to revise estimates related to the pension obligation because it's determined to be more or less than previously thought, these revisions are referred to as *losses* and *gains,* respectively, on the pension liability. Later, we will discuss the accounting treatment of gains and losses from either source. The point here is that the risk of the pension obligation changing unexpectedly or the pension funds being inadequate to meet the obligation is borne by the employer with a defined benefit pension plan.

The key elements of a defined benefit pension plan are:

1. The *employer's obligation* to pay retirement benefits in the future.
2. The *plan assets* set aside by the employer from which to pay the retirement benefits in the future.
3. The *periodic expense* of having a pension plan.

As you will learn in this chapter, the first two of these elements are not reported directly in the financial statements. This may seem confusing at first because it is inconsistent with the way you're accustomed to treating assets and liabilities. Even though they are not recorded in the formal accounts, it's critical that you understand the composition of both the pension obligation and the plan assets because (a) they affect amounts that actually are reported on the balance sheet, and (b) their balances are reported in disclosure notes. And, importantly, the pension expense reported on the income statement is a direct composite of periodic changes that occur in both the pension obligation and the plan assets.

> In applying accrual accounting to pensions, this *Statement (87)* retains three fundamental aspects of past pension accounting: *delayed recognition* of certain events, reporting *net cost*, and *offsetting* liabilities and assets. Those three features of practice have shaped financial reporting for many years, . . . and they conflict in some respects with accounting principles applied elsewhere.[3]

For this reason, we will devote a considerable portion of our early discussion to understanding the composition of the pension obligation and the plan assets before focusing on the derivation of pension expense and required financial statement disclosures. We will begin with a quick overview of how periodic changes that occur in both the pension obligation and the plan assets affect pension expense. Next we will explore how those changes occur, beginning with changes in the pension obligation followed by changes in plan assets. We'll then return to pension expense for a closer look at how those changes influence its calculation. After that, we will bring together the separate but related parts by using a simple spreadsheet to demonstrate how each element of the pension plan articulates with the other elements.

Pension Expense— An Overview

The annual pension expense reflects changes in both the pension obligation and the plan assets. Graphic 17–5 provides a brief overview of how these changes are included in pension expense. After the overview, we'll look closer at each of the components.

Next we explore each of these pension expense components in the context of its being a part of either (a) the pension obligation or (b) the plan assets. After you learn how the expense components relate to these elements of the pension plan, we'll return to explore further how they are included in the pension expense.

Sidenotes: A pension formula typically defines retirement pay based on the employees' (a) years of service, (b) annual compensation, and sometimes (c) age.

Pension gains and losses occur when the return on plan assets is higher or lower than expected.

Pension gains and losses occur when the pension obligation is lower or higher than expected.

Neither the pension obligation nor the plan assets are reported on the balance sheet.

The pension expense is a direct composite of periodic changes that occur in both the pension obligation and the plan assets.

[2]Changes in estimates regarding actuarial assumptions used in accounting for pension plans are by far the most common type of estimate change. About 45% of surveyed companies reported changes in these estimates (AICPA, *Accounting Trends and Techniques,* 1995). We discuss changes in more detail in Chapter 21.

[3]"Employers' Accounting for Pensions," *Statement of Financial Accounting Standards No. 87,* (Stamford, Conn.: FASB, 1985).

GRAPHIC   17–5

Components of Pension Expense

| Interest and investment return are financing aspects of the pension cost.

| The recognition of some elements of the pension expense is delayed.

Components of Pension Expense

+	**Service cost** ascribed to employee service during the period
+	**Interest** accrued on the pension liability
−	**Return** on the plan assets*
	(Adjusted for: losses or gains)†
	Amortized portion of:
+ or −	**Losses or (gains)** from revisions in the pension liability or from investing plan assets
+	**Prior service cost** attributed to employee service before an amendment to the pension plan‡
=	**Pension Expense**

*Usually decreases pension expense but will increase the expense in periods in which plan assets achieve a negative return.
†The actual return is adjusted for any difference between actual and expected return, resulting in the *expected* return being reflected in pension expense. This loss or gain from investing plan assets is combined with losses and gains from revisions in the pension liability for deferred inclusion in pension expense.
‡The effect of prior service cost could be negative, but only if an amendment reduces benefits and the reduction is applied retroactively, a rare occurrence.

PART

B THE PENSION OBLIGATION AND PLAN ASSETS

The Pension Obligation

OPENING CASE

Question 2

Now we consider more precisely what's meant by the pension obligation. Unfortunately, there's not just one definition, nor is there uniformity concerning which definition is most appropriate for pension accounting. Actually, three different ways to measure the pension obligation have meaning in pension accounting, as shown in Graphic 17–6.

GRAPHIC   17–6

Ways to Measure the Pension Obligation

1. **Accumulated benefit obligation (ABO)** The actuary's estimate of the total retirement benefits (at their discounted present value) earned so far by employees, applying the pension formula using existing compensation levels.
2. **Vested benefit obligation (VBO)** The portion of the accumulated benefit obligation that plan participants are entitled to receive regardless of their continued employment.
3. **Projected benefit obligation (PBO)** The actuary's estimate of the total retirement benefits (at their discounted present value) earned so far by employees, applying the pension formula using estimated future compensation levels. (If the pension formula does not include future compensation levels, the PBO and the ABO are the same.)

Later you will learn that an accumulated benefits approach is used to determine the minimum pension liability that a company must report, a projected benefits approach is used to determine the periodic pension expense, and a vested benefits amount is reported in the disclosure notes together with disclosures of each of the other two amounts. Remember, there is but one obligation; these are three ways to measure it. The relationship among the three is depicted in Graphic 17–7.

Now let's look closer at how the obligation is measured in each of these three ways. Keep in mind, though, that it's not the accountant's responsibility to actually derive the measurement; a professional actuary provides these numbers. However, for the accountant to effectively use the numbers provided, she or he must understand their derivation.

| **Learning objective 2** Distinguish among the accumulated benefit obligation, the vested benefit obligation, and the projected benefit obligation.

Accumulated Benefit Obligation

| The **accumulated benefit obligation** ignores possible pay increases in the future.

The **accumulated benefit obligation (ABO)** is an estimate of the discounted present value of the retirement benefits earned so far by employees, applying the plan's pension formula using existing compensation levels. When we look at a detailed calculation of the projected benefit obligation below, keep in mind that simply substituting the employee's existing compensation in the pension formula for her projected salary at retirement would give us the accumulated benefit obligation.

GRAPHIC   17–7

Alternative Measures of the Pension Obligation

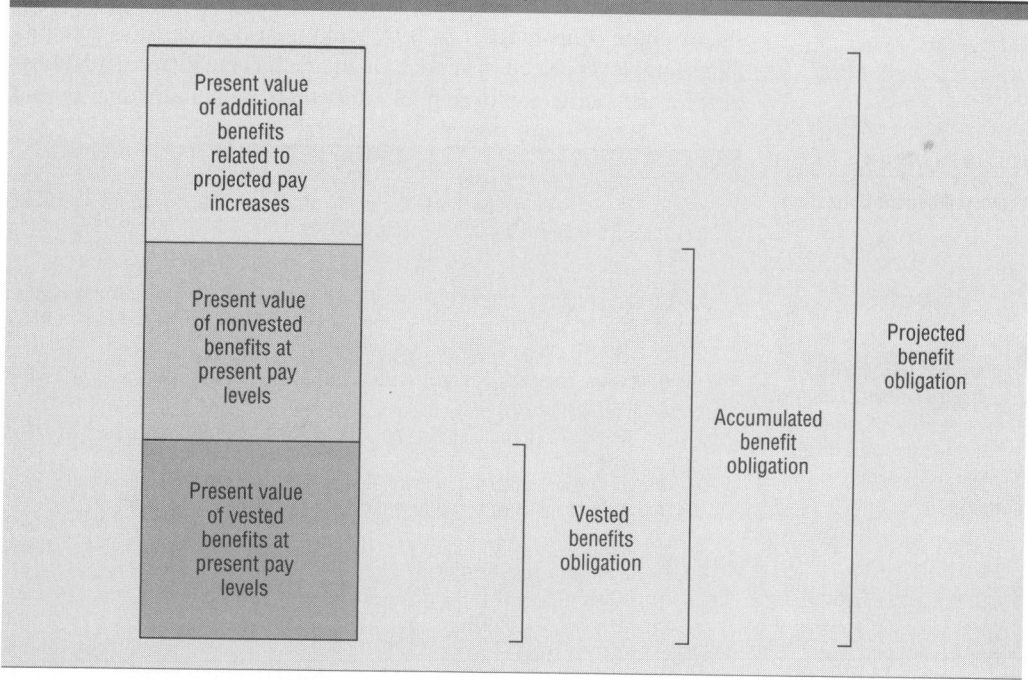

Vested Benefit Obligation

Suppose an employee leaves the company to take another job. Will she still get earned benefits at retirement? The answer depends on whether the benefits are vested under the terms of this particular pension plan. If benefits are fully vested—yes. **Vested benefits** are those that employees have the right to receive even if their employment were to cease today.

Pension plans typically require some minimum period of employment before benefits vest. Before the Employee Retirement Income Security Act (ERISA) was passed in 1974, horror stories relating to lost benefits were commonplace. It was possible, for example, for an employee to be dismissed a week before retirement and be left with no pension benefits. Vesting requirements were tightened drastically to protect employees. These requirements have been changed periodically since then. Beginning in 1989, benefits must vest (a) fully within 5 years or (b) 20% within 3 years with another 20% vesting each subsequent year until fully vested after 7 years. Five-year vesting is most common. ERISA also established the Pension Benefit Guaranty Corporation (PBGC) to impose liens on corporate assets for unfunded pension liabilities in certain instances and to administer terminated pension plans. The PBGC is financed by premiums from employers equal to specified amounts for each covered employee. It makes retirement payments for terminated plans and guarantees basic vested benefits when pension liabilities exceed assets.

> The benefits of most pension plans vest after five years.

Projected Benefit Obligation

As described earlier, when the ABO is estimated, the most recent salary is included in the pension formula to estimate future benefits, even if the pension formula specifies the final year's salary. No attempt is made to forecast what that salary would be the year before retirement. Of course, the most recent salary certainly offers an objective number to measure the obligation, but is it realistic? Since it's unlikely that there will be no salary increases between now and retirement, a more meaningful measurement should include a projection of what the salary might be at retirement.[4] Measured this way, the liability is referred to as the **projected benefit obligation (PBO)**. The PBO measurement may be less reliable than the ABO but is more relevant and representationally faithful.

> **Learning objective 3**
> Describe the five events that might change the balance of the PBO.

> The **PBO** estimates retirement benefits by applying the pension formula using projected future compensation levels.

---

[4]To project future salaries for a group of employees, actuaries usually assume some percentage rate of increase in compensation levels in upcoming years. Recent estimates of the rate of compensation increase have ranged from 4.5% to 7.5%, with 5% being the most commonly reported expectation. (AICPA, *Accounting Trends and Techniques*, 1995.)

To understand the concepts involved, it's helpful to look at a numerical example. We'll simplify the example (Illustration 17–1) by looking at how pension amounts would be determined for a single employee. Keep in mind, though, that in actuality, calculations would be made (by the actuary) for the entire employee pool rather than on an individual-by-individual basis.

ILLUSTRATION 17–1

Projected Benefit Obligation

The projected benefit obligation is the discounted present value of retirement benefits calculated by the projected benefits approach.

The actuary includes projected salaries in the pension formula. The projected benefit obligation is the present value of those benefits.

The lump-sum equivalent at retirement of annuity payments during the retirement period is the present value of those payments.

Jessica Farrow was hired by Global Communications in 1986. The company has a defined benefit pension plan that specifies annual retirement benefits equal to:

1.5% × Service years × Final year's salary

Farrow is expected to retire in 2025 after 40 years service. Her retirement period is expected to be 20 years. At the end of 1995, 10 years after being hired, her salary is $100,000. The interest rate is 6%. The company's actuary projects Farrow's salary to be $400,000 at retirement.*

What is the company's projected benefit obligation with respect to Jessica Farrow?

Steps to calculate the projected benefit obligation:
1. Use the pension formula (including a projection of future salary levels) to determine the retirement benefits earned to date.
2. Find the present value of the retirement benefits as of the retirement date.
3. Find the present value of retirement benefits as of the current date.

3. Present value (n=30, i=6%) of retirement benefits at 1995 is
$688,195 × .17411 =
$119,822 (PBO)

1. Actuary estimates employee has earned (as of 1995) retirement benefits of
1.5% × 10 years × $400,000 =
$60,000 per year

1986   1995   2025   2045
↓
10 years   30 years   20 years
Service period   ↑   **Retirement**

2. Present value (n=20, i=6%) of the retirement annuity at the retirement date is
$60,000 × 11.46992 =
$688,195

*This salary reflects an estimated compound rate of increase of about 5% and should take into account expectations concerning inflation, promotions, productivity gains, and other factors that might influence salary levels.

If the actuary's estimate of the final salary hasn't changed, the PBO a year later at the end of 1996 would be $139,715 as demonstrated in Illustration 17–1a.

ILLUSTRATION 17–1a

PBO in 1996

In 1996 the pension formula includes one more service year.

Also, 1996 is one year closer to the retirement date for the purpose of calculating the present value.

3. Present value (n=29, i=6%) of retirement benefits at 1996 is
$757,015 × .18456 =
$139,715 (PBO)

1. Actuary estimates employee has earned (as of 1996) retirement benefits of 1.5% × 11 years × $400,000 =
$66,000 per year

1986   1996   2025   2045
↓
11 years   29 years   20 years
Service period   ↑   **Retirement**

2. Present value (n=20, i=6%) of the retirement annuity at the retirement date is
$66,000 × 11.46992 =
$757,015

Changes in the PBO. Notice that the PBO increased during 1996 from $119,822 to $139,715 for two reasons:

1. One more service year is included in the pension formula calculation (service cost).
2. The employee is one year closer to retirement, causing the present value of benefits to increase due to the time value of future benefits (interest cost).

These represent two of the events that might possibly cause the balance of the PBO to change. Let's elaborate on these and the three other events that might change the balance of the PBO. The five events are (1) the service cost, (2) the interest cost, (3) prior service cost, (4) gains and losses, and (5) payments to retired employees.

1. Service Cost.   As we just witnessed in the illustration, the PBO increases each year by the amount of that year's **service cost**. This represents the increase in the projected benefit obligation attributable to employee service performed during the period. As we explain later, it also is the primary component of the annual pension expense.

2. Interest Cost.   The second reason the PBO increases is called the **interest cost**. Even though the projected benefit obligation is not formally recognized as a liability in the company's balance sheet, it is a liability nevertheless. And, as with other liabilities, interest accrues on its balance as time passes. The amount can be calculated directly as the assumed discount rate multiplied by the projected benefit obligation at the beginning of the year.[5]

| Each year's service adds to the obligation to pay benefits. |

| Interest accrues on the PBO each year. |

Additional Consideration

We can verify the increase in the PBO as being caused by the service cost and interest cost as follows:

PBO at the beginning of 1996 (end of 1995)			$119,822
Service cost: (1.5% × 1 yr. × $400,000) ×	11.46992 ×	.18456	12,701
Annual retirement benefits from 1996 service	To discount to 2025*	To discount to 1996†	
Interest cost: $119,822 × 6%			7,189
PBO at the end of 1996			$139,712‡

*Present value of an ordinary annuity of $1: $n=20$, $i=6\%$.
†Present value of $1: $n=29$, $i=6\%$.
‡Differs from $139,715 due to rounding.

---

3. Prior Service Cost.   Another reason the PBO might change is when the pension plan itself is *amended* to revise the way benefits are determined. For example, Global Communications in our illustration might choose to revise the pension formula by which benefits are calculated. Let's back up and assume the formula's salary percentage is increased in 1996 from 1.5% to 1.7%:

$$1.7\% \times \text{Service years} \times \text{Final year's salary}$$
(Revised Pension Formula)

Obviously, the annual service cost from this date forward will be higher than it would have been without the amendment. This will cause a more rapid future expansion of the PBO. But it also might cause an immediate increase in the PBO as well. Here's why.

Suppose the amendment becomes effective for future years' service only, without consideration of employee service to date. As you might imagine, the morale and dedication of long-time employees of the company could be expected to suffer. So, for economic as well as ethical reasons, most companies choose to make amendments to pension plans retroactive to prior years. In other words, the more beneficial terms of the revised pension formula are not applied just to future service years, but benefits attributable to all prior service years also are recomputed under the more favorable terms. Obviously, this decision is not without cost to the company. Making the amendment retroactive to prior years adds an extra layer of retirement benefits, increasing the company's benefit obligation. The increase in the PBO attributable to making a plan amendment retroactive is referred to as **prior service cost**.[6] For instance, the following excerpt from a recent annual report of Ecolab, Inc., describes the increase in its PBO as a result of making an amendment retroactive:

| When a pension plan is amended, credit often is given for employee service rendered in prior years. The cost of doing so is called **prior service cost**. |

---

[5]Assumed discount rates should reflect rates used currently in annuity contracts. Discount rates recently reported have ranged from 6.5% to 9.5%, with 8.5% being the most commonly assumed rate. (AICPA, *Accounting Trends and Techniques*, 1995.)

[6]Prior service cost also is created if a defined benefit pension plan is initially adopted by a company that previously did not have one, and the plan itself is made retroactive to give credit for prior years' service. Prior service cost is created by plan amendments far more often than by plan adoptions because most companies already have pension plans, and new pension plans in recent years have predominantly been defined contribution plans.

GRAPHIC   17–8

Prior Service Cost—Ecolab, Inc.

> *Note 1: Retirement Plans (in Part)*
> . . . the company amended its U.S. pension plan to change the formula for pension benefits and to provide a more rapid vesting schedule. The plan amendments resulted in a $6 million increase in the projected benefits obligation.

Let's put prior service cost in the context of our illustration.

At the end of 1995, and therefore the beginning of 1996, the PBO is $119,822. If the plan is amended on January 3, 1996, the PBO could be recomputed as:

PBO without Amendment			PBO with Amendment		
1. 1.5% × 10 yrs. × $400,000 =	$ 60,000		1.7% × 10 yrs..x $400,000 =	$ 68,000	
2. $60,000 × 11.46992 =	$688,195		$68,000 × 11.46992 =	$779,955	
3. $688,195 × .17411 =	$119,822		$779,955 × .17411 =	$135,798	

$15,976
Prior service cost

> **Retroactive benefits from an amendment add additional costs, increasing the company's PBO. This increase is the prior service cost.**

The $15,976 increase in the PBO attributable to applying the more generous terms of the amendment to prior service years is the prior service cost. And, because we assumed the amendment occurred at the beginning of 1996, both the 1996 service cost and the 1996 interest cost would change as a result of the prior service cost. This is how:

PBO at the beginning of 1996 (end of 1995)	$119,822
Prior service cost (determined above)	15,976
PBO including prior service cost at the beginning of 1996	$135,798
Service cost: (1.7% × 1 yr. × $400,000) × 11.46992 × .18456	14,395

Annual retirement benefits from 1996 service   *To discount to 2025**   *To discount to 1996†*

> **Prior service cost increased the PBO at the beginning of the year.**

Interest cost: $135,798‡ × 6%	8,148
PBO at the end of 1996	$158,341

*Present value of an ordinary annuity of $1: n=20, i=6%.
†Present value of $1: n=29, i=6%.
‡Includes the beginning balance plus the prior service cost because the amendment occurred at the beginning of the year.

Additional Consideration

We can verify the PBO balance by calculating it directly:

> **The pension formula reflects the plan amendment.**

3. Present value (n=29, i=6%) of retirement benefits at 1996 is
$857,950 × .18456 =
$158,341* (PBO)

1. Actuary estimates employee has earned (as of 1996) retirement benefits of
1.7% × 11 years × $400,000 =
$74,800 per year

1986	1996		2025	2045

11 years   29 years   20 years
Service period   ↑   **Retirement**

2. Present value (n=20, i=6%) of the retirement annuity at the retirement date is
$74,800 × 11.46992 = **$857,950**

*Adjusted by $2 to compensate for the rounding of present value factors.

The plan amendment would affect not only the year in which it occurs, but also each subsequent year because the revised pension formula determines each year's service cost. Continuing our illustration to 1997 demonstrates this:

PBO at the beginning of 1997 (end of 1996)	$158,341
Service cost: (1.7% × 1 yr. × $400,000) × 11.46992 × .19563	15,258

Annual retirement benefits from 1997 service   *To discount to 2025**   *To discount to 1997†*

> **During 1997, the PBO increased as a result of service cost and interest cost.**

Interest cost: $158,341 × 6%	9,500
PBO at the end of 1997	$183,099

*Present value of an ordinary annuity of $1: n=20, i=6%.
†Present value of $1: n=28, i=6%.

4. Gain or Loss on the PBO.   We mentioned earlier that a number of estimates are necessary to

derive the PBO. When one or more of these estimates requires revision, the estimate of the PBO also will require revision. The resulting decrease or increase in the PBO is referred to as *a gain* or *loss*, respectively. Let's modify our illustration to imitate the effect of revising one of the several possible estimates involved. Suppose, for instance, that new information at the end of 1997 about inflation and compensation trends suggests that the estimate of Farrow's final salary should be increased by 5% to $420,000. This would affect the estimate of the PBO as follows:

PBO without Revised Estimate		PBO with Revised Estimate	
1. 1.7% × 12 yrs. × $400,000 = $ 81,600		1.7% × 12 yrs. × **$420,000** = $ 85,680	
2. $81,600 × 11.46992	= $935,945	**$85,6800** × 11.46992	= $982,743
3. $935,945 × .19563	= $183,099	**$982,743** × .19563	= $192,254

$9,155
Loss on PBO

The difference of $9,155 represents a loss on the PBO because the obligation turned out to be higher than previously expected. Now there would be three elements of the increase in the PBO during 1997:[7]

PBO at the beginning of 1997	$158,341
Service cost (calculated on previous page)	15,258
Interest cost (calculated on previous page)	9,500
Loss on PBO (calculated above)	9,155
PBO at the end of 1997	$192,254

If a revised estimate causes the PBO to be lower than previously expected, a gain would be indicated. Consider how a few of the other possible estimate changes would affect the PBO:

- A change in life expectancies might cause the retirement period to be estimated as 21 years rather than 20 years. Calculation of the present value of the retirement annuity would use *n=21*, rather than *n=20*. The estimate of the PBO would increase.
- The expectation that retirement will occur two years earlier than previously thought would cause the retirement period to be estimated as 22 years rather than 20 years and the service period to be estimated as 28 years rather than 30 years. The new expectation would probably also cause the final salary estimate to change. The net effect on the PBO would depend on the circumstances.
- A change in the assumed discount rate would affect the present value calculations. A lower rate would increase the estimate of the PBO. A higher rate would decrease the estimate of the PBO.

5. Payment of Retirement Benefits.   We've seen how the PBO will change due to the accumulation of service cost from year to year, the accrual of interest as time passes, making plan amendments retroactive to prior years, and periodic adjustments when estimates change. Another change in the PBO occurs when the obligation is reduced as benefits actually are paid to retired employees.

The payment of such benefits is not applicable in our present illustration because we've limited the situation to calculations concerning an individual employee who is several years from retirement. Remember, though, in reality the actuary would make these calculations for the entire pool of employees covered by the pension plan. But the concepts involved would be the same. Graphic 17–9 summarizes the five ways the PBO can change.

Illustration Expanded to Consider the Entire Employee Pool

For our single employee, the PBO at the end of 1997 is $192,254. Let's say now that Global Communications has 2,000 active employees covered by the pension plan and 100 retired employees receiving retirement benefits. Illustration 17–2 expands the numbers to represent all covered employees.

---

[7]The increase in the PBO due to amending the pension formula (prior service cost) occurred in 1996.

The Projected Benefits Obligation Changes as a Result of:

Cause	Effect	Frequency
Service cost	+	Each period
Interest cost	+	Each period (except the first period of the plan, when no obligation exists to accrue interest)
Prior service cost	+*	Only if the plan is amended (or initiated) that period
Loss or gain on PBO	+ or −	Whenever revisions are made in the pension liability estimate
Retiree benefits paid	-	Each period (unless no employees have yet retired under the plan)

*The effect of prior service cost could be negative, but only if an amendment reduces benefits and the reduction is applied retroactively, a rare occurrence.

ILLUSTRATION   17-2

The PBO Expanded to Include
All Employees

The changes in the PBO for Global Communications during 1997 were as follows:

	($ in millions)*
PBO at the beginning of 1997† (amount assumed)	$400
Service cost, 1997 (amount assumed)	41
Interest cost: $400 × 6%	24
Loss (gain) on PBO (amount assumed)	23
Less: Retiree benefits paid (amount assumed)	(38)
PBO at the end of 1997	$450

*Of course, these expanded amounts are not simply the amounts for Jessica Farrow multiplied by 2,000 employees because her years of service, expected retirement date, and salary are not necessarily representative of other employees. Also, the expanded amounts take into account expected employee turnover and current retirees.

†Includes the prior service cost that increased the PBO when the plan was amended in 1996.

> The PBO is not formally recognized on the balance sheet.

We remind you that the PBO is not formally recognized as a liability on the balance sheet. It is, however, actively monitored in the employer's informal pension records because its balance must be reported in disclosure notes to the financial statements. Also, as mentioned earlier and explained later, some of the changes in its balance are included in the calculation of the periodic pension expense.

Pension Plan Assets

> **Learning objective 4**
> Explain how plan assets accumulate to provide retiree benefits and understand the role of the trustee in administering the fund.

> OPENING CASE
>
> Question 3

> A **trustee** manages pension plan assets.

So far our focus has been on the employer's obligation to provide retirement benefits in the future. We turn our attention now to the resources with which the company will satisfy that obligation—the **pension plan assets**. Like the PBO, the pension plan assets are not formally recognized on the balance sheet but are actively monitored in the employer's informal records. Its balance, too, must be reported in disclosure notes to the financial statements, and as explained below, the return on these assets is included in the calculation of the periodic pension expense.

We assumed in the previous section that Global Communications' obligation is $450 million for service performed to date. When employees retire, will there be sufficient funds to provide the anticipated benefits? To ensure sufficient funding, Global will contribute cash each year to a pension fund.

The assets of a pension fund must be held by a **trustee**. A trustee accepts employer contributions, invests the contributions, accumulates the earnings on the investments, and pays benefits from the plan assets to retired employees or their beneficiaries. The trustee can be an individual, a bank, or a trust company. Plan assets are invested in stocks, bonds, and other income-producing assets. The accumulated balance of the annual employer contributions plus the return on the investments (dividends, interest, market price appreciation) must be sufficient to pay benefits as they come due.

When an employer estimates how much it must set aside each year to accumulate sufficient funds to pay retirement benefits as they come due, it's necessary to estimate the return those investments will produce. This is the **expected return on plan assets**. The higher the return, the less the employer must actually contribute. On the other hand, a relatively low return means the difference must be made up by higher contributions. In practice, recent estimates of the rate of return have ranged from 5% to 11.5%, with 9% being the most commonly reported expectation.[8]

In Illustration 17–3 we shift the focus of our numerical illustration to emphasize Global's pension plan assets.

ILLUSTRATION 17–3

How Plan Assets Change

Global Communications funds its defined benefit pension plan by contributing each year the year's service cost plus a portion of the prior service cost. Cash of $48 million was contributed to the pension fund at the end of 1997.

Plan assets at the beginning of 1997 were valued at $300 million. The expected rate of return on the investment of those assets was 9%, but the actual return in 1997 was 10%. Retirement benefits of $38 million were paid at the end of 1997 to retired employees.

What is the value of the company's pension plan assets at the end of 1997?

	($ in millions)
Plan assets at the beginning of 1997	$300
Return on plan assets (10% × $300)	30
Cash contributions	48
Less: Retiree benefits paid	(38)
Plan assets at the end of 1997	$340

A trustee accepts employer contributions, invests the contributions, accumulates the earnings on the investments, and pays benefits from the plan assets.

Recall that Global's PBO at the end of 1997 is $450 million. Because the plan assets are only $340 million, the pension plan is said to be *underfunded*. One reason is that we assumed Global incurred a $60 million prior service cost from amending the pension plan at the beginning of 1996, and that cost is being funded over several years. Another factor is the loss from increasing the PBO due to the estimate revision, since funding has been based on the previous estimate. Later, we'll assume earlier revisions also have increased the PBO. Of course, actual performance of the investments also impacts a plan's funded status.

An *underfunded* pension plan means the PBO exceeds plan assets.

It is typical for pension plans today to be underfunded. Historically, though, that hasn't necessarily been the case. Prior to the Employee Retirement Income Security Act (ERISA) in 1974, many plans were grossly underfunded. The new law established minimum funding standards among other matters designed to protect plan participants. The new standards brought most plans closer to full funding. Then the stock market boom of the 1980s caused the value of plan assets for many pension funds to swell to well over their projected benefit obligations. More than 80% of pension plans were overfunded. As a result, managers explored ways to divert funds to other areas of operations. Today the majority of plans again are underfunded. For the companies with the 50 largest underfunded plans, the Pension Benefit Guaranty Corporation says the difference between the companies' pension liabilities and assets is over $40 billion. Many of these are troubled companies, placing employees at risk. The PBGC guarantees are limited to $2,574 per month, often less than promised pension benefits.

An *overfunded* pension plan means plan assets exceeds the PBO.

We mentioned earlier that the return on plan assets affects not only the value of the plan assets but also the calculation of the amount annually recorded as pension expense. Also, we mentioned earlier that the annual increases in the PBO due to service cost and interest affect the calculation of pension expense, too. Now, let's look at all the ways that changes in the pension liability and the pension plan assets affect pension expense.

PART

C DETERMINING PENSION EXPENSE

The Relationship between Pension Expense and Changes in the PBO and Plan Assets

Like wages, salaries, commissions, and other forms of pay, pension expense is part of a company's compensation for employee services each year. Accordingly, the accounting objective is to achieve a matching of the costs of providing this form of compensation with the benefits of the services performed. However, the fact that this form of

Learning objective 5

Describe how pension expense is a composite of periodic changes that occur in both the pension obligation and the plan assets.

[8]AICPA, *Accounting Trends and Techniques*, 1995.

compensation actually is paid to employees many years after the service is performed means that other elements in addition to the annual service cost will affect the ultimate pension cost. These other elements are related to changes that occur over time in both the pension liability and the pension plan assets. Graphic 17–10 provides a summary of how some of these changes influence pension expense.

GRAPHIC   17–10

Components of the Periodic Pension Expense

OPENING CASE

Question 4

The pension expense reported on the income statement is a composite of periodic changes that occur in both the pension obligation and the plan assets.

How Changes in the Pension Liability and Plan Assets Affect Pension Expense

Changes in the PBO:

Included currently in pension expense:

Service cost—increase in the employer's obligation attributed to employee service during the current period

Interest—interest accrued on the obligation during the current period (balance at the beginning of the period multiplied by the interest rate)

Delayed recognition (recognized in pension expense over time):

Losses or (gains) on the PBO—increases or decreases in the estimate of the PBO from revisions in underlying assumptions

Prior service cost—increase in the employer's obligation due to giving credit to employees for years of service provided before the pension plan is amended (or initiated)

Changes in Plan Assets:

Included currently in pension expense:

Return on the plan assets—increase in the value of plan assets during the period, adjusted for employer contributions and benefits paid to retirees

Adjusted for losses or (gains) on the plan assets ⎯⎯⎯⎯⎯⎯⎯⎯⎯⎯⎯⎯→

Delayed recognition (recognized in pension expense over time): ↓

Losses or (gains) on the plan assets—return on plan assets lower or (higher) than expected

---

We've examined each of the components of pension expense from the viewpoint of its effect on the PBO or on plan assets, using the Global Communications illustration to demonstrate that effect. Now, let's expand the same illustration to see how these changes affect *pension expense*. Illustration 17–4 provides this expanded example.

ILLUSTRATION   17–4

Pension Expense

These are the changes in the PBO and in the plan assets we previously discussed (Illustration 17–2 and Illustration 17–3).

Reports from the actuary and the trustee of plan assets indicate the following changes during 1997 in the PBO and plan assets of Global Communications:

($ in millions)	**PBO**		**Plan Assets**
Beginning of 1997	$400	Beginning of 1997	$300
Service cost	41	Return on plan assets,*	
Interest cost, 6%	24	10% (9% expected)	30
Loss (gain) on PBO	23	Cash contributions	48
Less: Retiree benefits	(38)	Less: Retiree benefits	(38)
End of 1997	$450	End of 1997	$340

*Expected rates of return anticipate the performance of various investments of plan assets. This is not necessarily the same as the discount rate used by the actuary to estimate the pension obligation. Assumed rates of return recently reported have ranged from 5% to 11.5%, with 9% being the most commonly assumed rate. (AICPA, *Accounting Trends and Techniques*, 1995.)

Informal records also indicate a prior service cost incurred at the beginning of the previous year (1996) of $60 million due to a plan amendment increasing the PBO at that time. At the beginning of 1997 Global had an unrecognized net loss of $55 million (previous losses exceeded previous gains). The average remaining service life of the active employee group is 15 years in both 1996 and 1997 (assumed at this point; calculated on page 743).

1997 Pension Expense

Global's 1997 pension expense is determined as follows:		($ in millions)
Service cost (from PBO above)		$41
Interest cost (from PBO above)		24
Actual return on the plan assets (from plan assets above)	($30)	
Adjusted for gain on the plan assets [(10% – 9%) × $300]	3	
Expected return on the plan assets		(27)
Amortization of prior service cost (calculated later)		4
Amortization of the net loss (calculated later)		1
Pension expense		$43

Components of Pension Expense

Illustration 17–4 demonstrates the relationship between some of the changes in the PBO and in plan assets and the components of pension expense: service cost, interest cost, the return on plan assets, prior service cost amortization, and net gain or loss amortization. Let's look at these five components of pension expense one at a time.

1. Service Cost.   The $41 million service cost represents the increase in the projected benefit obligation attributable to employee service performed during 1997 (benefits earned by employees during the year). Each year this is the first component of the pension expense.

2. Interest Cost.   The interest cost is calculated as the interest rate (actuary's discount rate) multiplied by the projected benefit obligation at the beginning of the year. In 1997, this is 6% times $400 million, or $24 million.

> Interest cost is the discount rate times the PBO balance at the beginning of the year.

The PBO is not formally recognized as a liability in the company's balance sheet, but it is a liability nevertheless. The interest expense that accrues on its balance is not separately reported on the income statement but is instead combined with the service cost (and other amounts) as the second component of the annual pension expense.

3. Return on Plan Assets.   Remember, plan assets comprise funds invested in stocks, bonds, and other securities that presumably will generate dividends, interest, and capital gains. Each year these earnings represent the return on plan assets during that year. When accounting for the return, we need to differentiate between its two modes: the *expected* return and the *actual* return.

> The return earned on investment securities increases the plan asset balance.

Actual versus expected return.   We've assumed Global's expected rate of return is 9%, so its expected return on plan assets in 1997 was 9% times $300 million, or $27 million. But, as previously indicated the actual rate of return in 1997 was 10%, producing an actual return on plan assets of 10% times $300 million, or $30 million.

> The interest and return-on-assets components are financial items created only because the compensation is delayed and the obligation is funded currently.

Obviously, investing plan assets in income-producing assets lessens the amounts employers must contribute to the fund. So, the return on plan assets reduces the net cost of having a pension plan. Accordingly, the return on plan assets each year *reduces* the amount recorded as pension expense. Just as the interest expense that accrues on the PBO is included as a component of pension expense rather than being separately reported, the investment revenue on plan assets is not separately reported either. In actuality, both the interest and return-on-assets components of pension expense do not directly represent employee compensation. Instead, they are financial items created only because the compensation is delayed and the obligation is funded currently.

Adjustment for Loss or Gain.   A controversial question is *when* differences between the actual and expected return are recognized in pension expense. It seems logical that since the net cost of having a pension plan is reduced by the actual return on plan assets, the periodic reduction in pension expense should be the actual return on plan assets. However, the FASB concluded that the actual return should first be adjusted by any difference between that return and what the return had been expected to be. That difference is a loss or gain on plan assets and its recognition as part of pension expense is delayed. We will discuss later the circumstances that determine whether and when these amounts are recognized. At this point, note that by adjusting the actual return for any loss or gain, it is actually the *expected* return that is included in the calculation of pension expense. In our illustration, Global's pension expense is reduced by the expected return of $27.

> The return on plan assets reduces the net cost of having a pension plan.

> Any loss or gain is not recognized right away.

4. Amortization of Prior Service Cost.   Recall that the increase in Global's PBO attributable to making its plan amendment retroactive is referred to as the prior service cost. Obviously, prior service cost adds to the cost of having a pension plan. But when should this cost be recognized as pension expense?

Amending a pension plan, and especially choosing to make that amendment retroactive, typically is done with the idea that future operations will benefit from those choices. For that reason, the cost is not recognized as pension expense entirely in the year the plan is amended. Instead, it is recognized as pension expense over the time that the employees who benefited from the retroactive amendment will work for the company in the future. Presumably, this future service period is when the company will receive the benefits of its actions.

> Prior service cost is recognized as pension expense over the future service period of the employees who benefited from the retroactive amendment.

In our illustration, the amendment occurred in 1996, increasing the PBO at that time. For the individual employee, Jessica Farrow, the prior service cost was calculated to be $15,976. Our illustration assumes that translates to $60 million at the beginning of 1996 for all plan participants. The unrecognized prior service cost at the beginning of 1997 is $56 million. The following section explains how this amount was computed.

Straight–Line Method.   One assumption in our illustration is that the average remaining service life of the active employee group is 15 years. To recognize the $60 million prior service cost in equal annual amounts over this period, the amount amortized as an increase in pension expense each year is $4 million:

Amortization of Prior Service Cost

		($ in millions)
Service cost		$41
Interest cost		24
Actual return on the plan assets	(30)	
Adjusted for gain on the plan assets	3	(27)
Amortization of prior service cost ($60 million ÷ 15 years)		**4**
Amortization of net loss		1
Pension expense		$43

By the straight-line method, prior service cost is recognized over the average remaining service life of the active employee group.

Since the amendment occurred at the beginning of 1996, this amount would have been amortized in 1996 as part of the 1996 pension expense. That's why, at the beginning of 1997, the unrecognized prior service cost is $56 million. Another $4 million is included in the 1997 pension expense as well as in the pension expense of each of the next 13 years.

Be sure to note that the prior service cost is not formally recognized as a separate account in the company's records. Its balance is monitored in the informal records, though, to recognize the cost gradually over the 15-year period. Actually, it represents a deferred expense that arose when the cost of making the amendment retroactive increased the employer's obligation to pay retirement benefits (the PBO) but wasn't immediately recognized as an expense.[9] One way to view it is that if we did formally record the prior service cost, we would debit the asset *unrecognized prior service cost* and credit the liability *projected benefit obligation*. In fact, both of these balances are increased, we just don't formally record the increases but informally track those balances instead.

Prior service cost is not formally recognized as a separate account in the company's records.

The informal records would show the balance in the unrecognized prior service cost declining by $4 million each year.

Unamortized Prior Service Cost

	($ in millions)
Unamortized prior service cost at the beginning of 1997	$56
Less: 1997 amortization	(4)
Unamortized prior service cost at the end of 1997	$52

*Note: The balance in this memorandum "account" is not recognized in the financial statements.

Service Method.   Our objective is to match the cost with employee service. The straight-line method described above allocates an equal amount of the prior service cost to each year of the 15-year average service period of affected employees. But consider this: fewer of the affected employees will be working for the company toward the end of that period than at the beginning. Some probably will retire or quit in each year following the amendment.

An allocation approach that reflects the declining service pattern is called the **service method**. This method allocates the prior service cost to each year in proportion to the fraction of the total remaining service years worked in each of those years. To do this, it's necessary to estimate how many of the 2,000 employees working at the beginning of 1996 when the amendment is made will still be employed in each year after the amendment.

Let's suppose, for example, that the actuary estimates that a declining number of these employees still will be employed in each of the next 28 years as indicated in the abbreviated schedule below. The portion of the prior service cost amortized to pension expense each year is $60 million times

---

[9]The FASB proposed recognizing prior service cost as an intangible asset in its Preliminary Views document, but didn't follow this approach in the final document: FASB, "Employers' Accounting for Pension and Other Postemployment Benefits," *Preliminary Views,* November 1982, par. 15b.

a declining fraction. Each year's fraction is that year's service divided by the 28-year total (30,000). This is demonstrated in Graphic 17–11.

GRAPHIC   17–11

Service Method of Amortizing Prior Service Cost

By the service method, prior service cost is recognized each year in proportion to the fraction of the total remaining service years worked that year.

Year	Number of Employees Still Employed (assumed for the illustration)	Fraction of Total Service Years	Prior Service Cost	Amount Amortized
				($ in millions)
1996	2,000	$2,000/30,000$	× $60	= $ 4.0
1997	2,000	$2,000/30,000$	× 60	= 4.0
1998	1,850	$1,850/30,000$	× 60	= 3.7
1999	1,700	$1,700/30,000$	× 60	= 3.4
2000	1,550	$1,550/30,000$	× 60	= 3.1
≈	≈	≈	≈	≈
2021	400	$400/30,000$	× 60	= .8
2022	250	$250/30,000$	× 60	= .5
2023	100	$100/30,000$	× 60	= .2
Totals	30,000	$30,000/30,000$		$60.0
	Total number of service years			Total amount amortized

The service method amortizes an equal amount *per employee* each year.

Conceptually, the service method achieves a better matching of the cost and benefits. In fact, this is the FASB's recommended approach. However, *SFAS 87* permits the consistent use of any method that amortizes the prior service cost at least as quickly.[10] The straight-line method meets this condition and is the approach most often used in practice. In our illustration, the cost is completely amortized over 15 years rather than the 28 years required by the service method. The 15-year average service life is simply the total estimated service years divided by the total number of employees in the group:

$$30,000 \text{ years} \div 2,000 = 15 \text{ years}$$

| Total number of service years | Total number of employees | Average service years |

5. Amortization of Deferred Net Loss or Net Gain.

You learned previously that gains and losses can occur when expectations are revised concerning either the PBO or the return on plan assets. Graphic 17–12 summarizes the possibilities.

GRAPHIC   17–12

Gains and Losses

Gains and losses occur when either the PBO or the return on plan assets turns out to be different than expected.

	Projected Benefits Obligation	Return on Plan Assets
Higher than Expected	Loss	Gain
Lower than Expected	Gain	Loss

We noted earlier that neither a loss (gain) on the PBO nor a loss (gain) on plan assets is immediately recognized in pension expense. There is no conceptual justification for this. After all, these increases and decreases in either the PBO or plan assets immediately impact the net cost of providing a pension plan and, conceptually, should be recognized as they occur. Nevertheless, *SFAS 87* requires that recognition of gains and losses from either source be delayed. Why?— for practical reasons.

---

[10] "Employers' Accounting for Pensions," *Statement of Financial Accounting Standards No. 87,* (Stamford, Conn.: FASB, 1985), par. 26.

Income Smoothing

The FASB acknowledged the conceptual shortcoming of delaying the recognition of a gain or a loss while opting for this more politically acceptable approach. Delayed recognition was favored by a dominant segment of corporate America that was concerned with the effect of allowing gains and losses to immediately impact reported earnings.

The practical justification for delayed recognition is that, over time, gains and losses might cancel one another out. Given this possibility, why create unnecessary fluctuations in reported income by letting temporary gains and losses decrease and increase (respectively) pension expense? Of course, as years pass there may be more gains than losses, or vice versa, preventing their offsetting one another completely. So, if a net gain or a net loss gets "too large," pension expense must be adjusted.

SFAS 87 defines too large rather arbitrarily as being when a net gain or a net loss at the beginning of a year exceeds an amount equal to 10% of the PBO, or 10% of plan assets, whichever is higher.[13] *SFAS 87* refers to this threshold amount as the "corridor." When the corridor is exceeded, the excess is not charged to pension expense all at once. Instead, as a further concession to income smoothing, only a portion of the excess is included in pension expense. The minimum amount that should be included is the excess divided by the average remaining service period of active employees expected to receive benefits under the plan.[14]

In our illustration, we're assuming that at the beginning of 1997 an unrecognized net loss of $55 million is revealed by Global's informal records. Also recall that the PBO and plan assets are $400 million and $300 million, respectively, at that time. The amount amortized to 1997 pension expense is $1 million, calculated as follows:

> The Board believes that it would be conceptually appropriate and preferable to [have] . . . no delay in recognition of gains and losses, or perhaps [to have] . . . gains and losses reported currently in comprehensive income but not in earnings. However, it concluded that those approaches would be too great a change from past practice to be adopted at the present time.[11]

> The Board acknowledges that the delayed recognition included in this Statement results in excluding the most current and most relevant information.[12]

Determining Net Loss Amortization—1997

	($ in millions)
Net loss (previous losses exceeded previous gains)	$55
10% of $400 ($400 is greater than $300): the "corridor"	40
Excess at the beginning of the year	$15
Average remaining service period	÷ 15 years
Amount amortized to 1997 pension expense	**$ 1**

The pension expense is increased because a net loss is being amortized. If a net *gain* were being amortized, the amount would be *deducted* from pension expense because a gain would indicate that the net cost of providing the pension plan had decreased.

Amortization of Net Loss

		($ in millions)
Service cost		$41
Interest cost		24
Actual return on the plan assets	($30)	
Adjusted for gain on the plan assets	3	27
Amortization of prior service cost		4
Amortization of net loss		1
Pension expense		$43

This amortization reduces the unrecognized net loss in 1997 by $1 million. Also recall that (a) Global incurred a 1997 $23 million loss from revising estimates relating to the PBO and (b) a $3 million gain when the 1997 return on plan assets was higher than expected. These three changes affected the unrecognized net loss in 1997 as follows:

---

[11]Ibid., par. 107.

[12]Ibid., par. 88.

[13]For this purpose the FASB specifies the market-related value of plan assets. This can be either the fair market value or a weighted-average fair market value over a period not to exceed five years. We will uniformly assume fair market value in this chapter.

[14]Companies are permitted to amortize the entire unrecognized loss (or gain) rather than just the excess, but few choose that option. (*SFAS 87*, par. 33.)

> The unamortized net loss or gain is not formally recognized as a separate account in the company's records.

Unamortized Net Loss

	($ in millions)
Unamortized net loss at the beginning of 1997	$55
Less: 1997 amortization	(1)
Plus: 1997 loss on PBO	23
Less: 1997 gain on plan assets	(3)
Unamortized net loss at the end of 1997	$74

Note: the balance in this memorandum account is not recognized in the financial statements.

Additional Consideration

This $74 million balance at the end of 1997 would be the beginning balance in 1998. It would be compared with the 1998 beginning balances in the PBO and plan assets to determine whether amortization would be necessary in 1998. If you were to look back to our analyses of the changes in those two balances, you would see the 1998 beginning balances in the PBO and plan assets to be $450 million and $340 million, respectively. The amount amortized to 1998 pension expense will be $1.93 million, calculated as follows:

	($ in millions)
Net loss (previous losses exceeded previous gains)	$74
10% of $450 ($450 is greater than $340)	45
Excess at the beginning of the year	$29
Average remaining service period	÷ 15 years*
Amount amortized to 1998 pension expense	**$ 1.93**

*Assumes the average remaining service period of active employees is still 15 years in 1998 due to new employees joining the firm.

Recording the Periodic Expense and Periodic Funding

By combining its five components in the preceding sections, we determined that Global's pension expense in 1997 is $43 million. Also, recall that Global contributed $48 million cash to the pension fund at the end of 1997. It is not unusual for the cash contribution to differ from that year's pension expense. After all, the determination of the periodic pension expense and the funding of the pension plan are two separate processes. Pension expense is an *accounting* decision. How much to contribute each year is a *financing* decision affected by cash flow and tax considerations, as well as minimum funding requirements of ERISA. Subject to these considerations, cash contributions are actuarially determined with the objective of accumulating (along with investment returns) sufficient funds to provide promised retirement benefits.

The following journal entry would be made by Global in 1997 to record both the annual pension expense and the annual contribution to the pension fund. This is the only journal entry normally required in pension accounting.[15]

To record pension expense and pension funding	($ in millions)	
Pension expense (calculated above)	43	
Prepaid (accrued) pension cost (difference)	5	
Cash (contribution to fund)		48

> A debit balance in prepaid (accrued) pension cost is reported as an asset; a credit balance is reported as a liability.

Notice that in this particular situation, the contribution exceeds the expense. Consistent with other situations when an expense is overpaid, the excess payment represents an asset—prepaid pension cost. Very often, though, the cash payment is less than the expense. In those instances, the underpayment represents a liability. Either way, the difference between the pension expense and the cash contribution is debited or credited, depending on the situation, to a single account: prepaid (accrued) pension cost. When the account has a *debit* balance it represents a cumulative overpayment and is reported as an asset—prepaid pension cost. When it has a *credit* balance it represents a cumulative underpayment and is reported as a liability—accrued pension cost.

---

[15]An exception is when the situation requires an additional liability to be recorded as described in a later section of this chapter.

The pension expense is, of course, reported on the income statement. In addition, the composition of that amount must be reported in disclosure notes. The service cost, interest cost, and return on plan assets should be reported individually, but the effects of other components of pension expense usually are combined in a single net amount. For instance, General Motors Corporation described the composition of its pension expense in the following disclosure note in its 1994 annual report:

GRAPHIC   17–13

Disclosure of Pension Expense—General Motors

The service cost, interest cost, and return on plan assets are reported individually; the effects of other components of pension expense are combined in a single net amount.

Note 13 (in Part): Pensions

1995		U.S. Plans		Non-U.S. Plans
		($ in millions)		
Benefits earned during the year		$ 989.2		$187.0
Interest accrued on benefits earned in prior years		4,916.4		684.0
Return on assets				
Actual return	($12,156.3)		($675.8)	
Less deferred gain	6,624.7	(5,531.6)	213.4	(462.4)
Net amortization		1,054.0		117.7
Net periodic pension cost		$1,428.0		$526.3

GLOBAL PERSPECTIVE

Most large companies in Japan sponsor pension plans that are funded through financial institutions. Contributions to pension funds are tax deductible. Because the taxes levied by the government are reported as income tax expense on the income statement, most Japanese companies report annual pension expense equal to cash contributions to the pension fund.

In other countries, such as Belgium, Finland, India, and New Zealand, pension costs are not covered by accounting standards. In still other countries pension accounting is irrelevant because the occurrence of pension plans is rare (Korea, Argentina, and Brazil, for example).

PART D REPORTING ISSUES

Putting the Pieces Together

Learning objective 6
Understand the interrelationships among the elements that constitute a defined benefit pension plan.

In preceding sections, we've discussed (1) the projected benefit obligation (including changes due to periodic service cost, accrued interest, revised estimates, plan amendments, and the payment of benefits), (2) the plan assets (including changes due to investment returns, employer contributions, and the payment of benefits), (3) the periodic pension expense (comprising components of each of these), and (4) the periodic journal entry. These elements of a pension plan are interrelated. It's helpful to see how each element relates to the others. One way is to bring each part together in a pension spreadsheet. We do this for our 1997 Global illustration in Graphic 17–14.

GRAPHIC   17–14

Pension Spreadsheet

( )s indicate credits; debits otherwise ($ in millions)	PBO	Plan Assets	Prior Service Cost	Net Loss	Pension Expense	Cash	Prepaid (Accrued) Cost
		Informal Records*			Formal Records		
Balance, Jan. 1, 1997	(400)	300	56	55			11
Service cost	(41)				41		
Interest cost, 6%	(24)				24		
Actual return on assets		30			(30)		
Gain on assets†				(3)	3		
Amortization of:							
Prior service cost			(4)		4		
Net loss				(1)	1		
Loss on PBO†	(23)			23			
Contributions to fund		48				(48)	
Retiree benefits paid	38	(38)					
1997 journal entry					43	(48)	5
Balance, Dec. 31, 1997	(450)	340	52	74			16

*Balances in these memorandum accounts are not recognized in the financial statements.
†Deferred for later recognition.

> The debit balance in the prepaid (accrued) pension cost account is increased to $16 million.

You should spend several minutes studying this spreadsheet, focusing on the relationships among the elements that constitute a defined benefit pension plan. Notice that the first numerical column simply repeats the actuary's report of how the PBO changed during the year, as explained previously (Illustration 17–2). Likewise, the second column reproduces the changes in plan assets we discussed earlier (Illustration 17–3). We've also previously noted the changes in the unrecognized prior service cost (page 742) and the unrecognized net loss (page 745) that are duplicated in the third and fourth columns.

The last three columns represent the amounts that are formally recognized in the accounts: (1) the 1997 pension expense determined earlier (page 744), (2) the cash contribution, and (3) the prepaid (accrued) pension cost. These are the three accounts that comprise the journal entry that records the 1997 pension expense and pension funding.

Reconciliation of Funded Status with the Amount Recognized in the Balance Sheet

Another point to notice is that the four off-balance-sheet asset and liability amounts combine to account for the balance in the one pension account that is reported on the balance sheet—the prepaid (accrued) pension cost. This always will be true. The relationship is demonstrated below for both the beginning and ending balances from the spreadsheet:

Reconciliation of Pension Amounts

($ in millions)

	1997 Beginning Balances	1997 Ending Balances
Projected benefit obligation	$(400)	$(450)
Plan assets	300	340
Unamortized prior service cost	56	52
Unamortized net loss	55	74
Prepaid (accrued) pension cost	$ 11	$ 16

> The net total of all the memorandum accounts equals the prepaid (accrued) pension cost balance.

> A pension plan is underfunded when the PBO exceeds the plan assets and overfunded when the opposite is the case.

Here's why this relationship holds. The difference between the employer's obligation (PBO) and the resources available to satisfy that obligation (plan assets) is referred to as the **funded status** of the pension plan. Global's pension plan is underfunded by $100 million at the beginning of 1997 and $110 million at the end of the year. If all the changes in the PBO and plan assets were immediately recognized in pension expense, the balance in the prepaid (accrued) pension cost would report the funded status because that balance is the cumulative difference between what's been expensed and the cash contributions. But remember, not all the changes in the PBO and plan assets are immediately recognized in pension expense. Recognition is delayed for both gains and losses and the prior service cost. So the unrecognized (unamortized) portions of each of these are

> OPENING CASE
>
> **Question 5**

reflected in the funded status but not yet in the prepaid (accrued) pension cost. As a result, the difference between the funded status and the amount recognized in the balance sheet as prepaid (accrued) pension cost can be reconciled by the unrecognized prior service cost and the unrecognized net loss. In fact, this reconciliation must be disclosed in the financial statements.

Minimum Liability

The FASB faced two very controversial decisions in *SFAS 87* concerning the pension liability: (1) should the pension liability be measured as the vested, accumulated, or projected benefit obligation, and (2) should the pension liability (however measured) be reported separately or offset against plan assets? On both issues, the decisions appear to reflect compromises between the Board's conceptual preferences and political considerations.

Measurement

On the measurement issue, disagreement among Board members is evident in the minority opinions of dissenting members as stated in *SFAS 87*. In a 4 to 3 vote for approval, one dissenter based his dissent on the use of the PBO measure in determining the pension expense.[16] Another based his dissent on *not* using the PBO as the reported measure of the pension liability.

> . . . the Board concluded that estimated future compensation levels should be considered in measuring the service cost component and the projected benefit obligation if the plan's benefit formula incorporates them.[17]

As a theoretical preference, however, the majority view appears to favor measurement of the liability as the projected benefit obligation (see the quotation at right). However, while this

> Conceptually, the pension liability is best measured by the projected benefit obligation.

may be the best estimate of an employer's liability related to its pension plan, the PBO is not reported on the balance sheet. The balance sheet reports either an *accrued* pension cost as a liability or a *prepaid* pension cost as an asset, depending on whether the prepaid (accrued) pension cost account has a credit or a debit balance. This balance represents the difference between the PBO and the plan assets when there are no elements of either that haven't yet been recognized in pension expense (unrecognized prior service cost, unrecognized net loss or net gain).[18] However, when elements of delayed recognition exist, the balance is not easily interpreted.

The Board concluded that this reported amount is insufficient when the employer's obligation is underfunded (assets less than liability). In that case, any pension balance on the books should be increased to reflect a minimum liability equal to that underfunded amount. Importantly, though, when measuring the underfunded liability, it is the accumulated benefit obligation (ABO) (rather than the PBO) that is required as the measure of the pension liability. In other words, an employer must report a pension liability at least equal to the amount by which its ABO exceeds its plan assets.

> The minimum pension liability is the excess of the accumulated benefit obligation over the plan assets.

It is not clear why the *SFAS 87* specifies the ABO as the appropriate measurement for this purpose, since the PBO is specified for determining the service cost and interest cost components of the pension expense and since the PBO is apparently the Board's conceptual preference to represent the liability. The motivation appears to be political acceptability—the ABO results in reporting a lower pension liability.

Offsetting

> Offsetting of the pension liability and pension plan assets is inconsistent with the way assets and liabilities in other areas are reported.

Regarding the offsetting of the pension liability and pension plan assets when determining the minimum liability, *SFAS 87* requires offsetting despite an apparent conceptual preference by the Board for recognizing the pension liability and plan assets as separate elements of the balance sheet. The FASB acknowledged that this requirement is made "even though the liability has not been settled, the assets may still be largely controlled, and substantial risks and rewards associated with both of those amounts are clearly borne by the employer."[19] Empirical research supports the

---

[16]It's interesting to note that the FASB now requires 5 "for" votes to promulgate a new standard.

[17]"Employers' Accounting for Pensions," *Statement of Financial Accounting Standards No. 87,* (Stamford, Conn.: FASB, 1985), par. 143.

[18]An unrecognized transition cost described in the next section also would represent an element of the PBO or plan assets that hasn't yet been recognized in pension expense.

[19]"Employers' Accounting for Pensions," *Statement of Financial Accounting Standards No. 87,* (Stamford, Conn.: FASB, 1985), par. 87.

FASB's *conceptual* position, not *SFAS 87*, on this point. A study of stock prices indicates that investors apparently view the pension liability and pension plan assets separately.[20]

Additional Liability

The numerical example in Illustration 17–5 will clarify the implementation of the minimum liability provision.

ILLUSTRATION 17–5

Determining the Minimum Liability

> There is no minimum liability unless the ABO exceeds the fair value of plan assets.

Recall from our earlier illustration that Global Communications informal and formal records revealed the following balances at the end of 1996 (beginning of 1997):

December 31, 1996, balances:

PBO	$(400)
Plan assets	300
Prepaid pension cost—debit	11

Now, let's also assume an accumulated benefit obligation of $330 million:

ABO	330

If the plan assets exceed the ABO, there is no minimum liability the company must report. A minimum liability must be reported only to the extent that the accumulated benefit obligation (ABO) exceeds the fair value of plan assets. So, in this instance, the minimum liability that must be reported is:

ABO	$(330)
Plan assets	300
Minimum liability	$ (30)

The fact that a minimum liability is indicated, as in this situation, doesn't necessarily mean action is required. It might be that the minimum liability requirement already is satisfied by a liability balance already recorded. Remember, though, that the only journal entry recorded in pension accounting (unless the additional liability described next is required) is the following:

Pension expense (calculated each year)	xxx	
Prepaid (accrued) pension cost (difference)		{debit or credit}
Cash (annual contribution)		xxx

As described earlier, this process produces a liability only when the prepaid (accrued) pension cost account has a credit balance. If the account has a debit balance, an asset exists instead.

In our present illustration, is the balance in the prepaid (accrued) pension cost account sufficient to satisfy this minimum liability requirement? No, not in this case.

> Sometimes a credit balance in the prepaid (accrued) pension cost account is sufficient to satisfy the minimum liability requirement.

If the account had a credit balance of more than $30 million, no additional liability would be required. Reporting the accrued pension cost credit balance as a pension liability would be sufficient. If the account had a credit balance of less than $30 million, an additional liability would be required for the difference. The sum of the prepaid (accrued) pension cost and the additional liability would be reported as a single pension liability on the balance sheet.

In our present illustration, the prepaid (accrued) pension cost account has a *debit* balance ($11 million), normally reported as an asset. However, since an underfunded ABO exists, this is unacceptable. An additional liability account must be established to combine with the prepaid (accrued) pension cost account balance to reflect the minimum liability. To progress from a debit balance of $11 million to a credit amount of $30 million, a provision must be made for an additional liability of $41 million.

> Sometimes an additional liability is needed to combine with the prepaid (accrued) pension cost balance to provide the minimum liability.

Minimum liability	$(30)
Less: prepaid pension cost	11
Additional liability	$(41)

We are assuming that there is no balance already in the additional liability account from the previous year. An additional liability must be recorded:

---

[20]Wayne Landsman, "An Empirical Investigation of Pension and Property Rights," *The Accounting Review,* October 1986, pp. 662–92.

Recording an additional liability creates an intangible asset.

	($ in millions)
Intangible pension asset	41
Additional liability	41

The journal entry to record the additional liability includes a debit to an intangible asset. Here's why. Presumably, an employer undertakes a pension obligation with the expectation of future economic benefits. When a portion of the liability is recognized in the accounts, a commensurate amount of the associated asset also is recognized.

Recording the additional liability achieves the objective of providing for a minimum liability of $30 million:

The net total of the prepaid (accrued) pension cost and the additional liability must equal the minimum liability.

Additional liability— credit balance	$(41)
Prepaid (accrued) pension cost—debit balance	11
Pension liability (reported as a single amount on the balance sheet)	$(30)

Additional Consideration

If the intangible asset balance exceeds the unrecognized prior service cost ($56 million in our illustration), the excess should be debited to a shareholders' equity account entitled "unrealized pension cost."* An underfunded pension obligation usually is due primarily to prior service cost not yet funded. Because the unrecognized prior service cost can be thought of as an asset not formally recognized, recording an intangible asset to the extent of this amount is appropriate. However, the portion of an underfunded pension obligation that is due to unrecognized net losses rather than prior service cost is more appropriately represented by a contra equity account.

To illustrate, if prior service cost had been $36 million, rather than $56 million, the journal entry to record the additional liability would have been as follows:

	($ in millions)
Intangible pension asset	36
Unrealized pension cost (contra equity account)	5
Additional liability	41

*If an unrecognized transition liability exists, the upper limit of the intangible asset balance is the sum of that amount and the unrecognized prior service cost. We discuss transition amounts in the next section.

The need for a minimum liability is reevaluated each year.

An additional liability is recorded at year-end only for the purpose of reporting the appropriate minimum liability on the balance sheet. It has no effect whatsoever on pension expense or any other amounts we've discussed to this point. Each year, the necessity of a minimum liability is reassessed, and if necessary, an adjustment is made. For instance, if we move forward a year, taking the December 31, 1997, balances from our earlier example (Graphic 17–14), and assume an accumulated benefit obligation of $350 million on that date, we have the situation depicted in Illustration 17–6.

ILLUSTRATION 17–6

Reassessing the Minimum Liability

December 31, 1997, balances:	
PBO	$(450)
ABO	350
Plan assets	340
Prepaid pension cost (debit)	16
Additional liability (credit)	(41)
Intangible pension asset	41

The minimum liability that must be reported is:	
ABO	$(350)
Plan assets	340
Minimum liability	$ (10)

So, an additional liability balance of only $26 million is needed:	
Minimum liability	$ (10)
Less: prepaid (accrued) pension cost	16
Additional liability	$ (26)

ILLUSTRATION   17–6

continued

The balances in both the additional liability and the intangible pension asset accounts are reduced to $26 million.

Because the additional liability balance already is $41 million from the previous year, the following adjustment is made:

	($ in millions)	
Additional liability ($41 million – 26 million)	15	
Intangible pension asset		15

Transition Cost

When a new accounting standard is enacted, the usual treatment is to apply the new standard retroactively. That is, any liability or asset that would have existed on the transition date if the new standard had been in effect all along usually is recorded on the transition date together with an appropriate offsetting charge to income (expense or revenue).[21] However, this usual treatment was waived for the transition from *APB 8*[22] to *SFAS 87* in 1987.[23] Instead, the FASB adopted a prospective approach that avoids recognizing the transition amount immediately. Delayed recognition of the transition amount is a concession to companies who argued in their response to the exposure draft of the new pension standard that if they were required to report their huge transition liabilities and associated expenses, they would suffer adverse economic consequences.

The transition liability or transition asset is the difference between the funded status of a pension plan under SFAS 87 and the prepaid (accrued) pension cost balance established by the previous standard.

The transition amount as firms adopted *SFAS 87* was the difference between (a) the funded status of their pension plans under the new standard, defined previously as the difference between the PBO and plan assets, and (b) the prepaid (accrued) pension cost existing at that date from following the provisions of the previous standard. This transition liability or transition asset was not recorded. Instead, like prior service cost or unrecognized net gains or net losses, its balance is monitored in the companies' informal records. Subsequently, that balance is periodically amortized to pension expense.

To illustrate, let's assume Global Communications in our continuing illustration adopted *SFAS 87* in 1987 at which time its PBO was calculated to be $200 million and its plan assets were $180 million. Also assume an accrued pension cost balance (that is, a liability) of $5 million produced by applying previous guidelines (*APB Opinion No. 8*). Because the funded status of the plan indicates an underfunded plan of $20 million, but under previous standards Global is reporting only a $5 million liability, a $15 million transition liability is indicated:

Determining the Transition Amount

Balances at transition (1987)	($ in millions)
Projected benefit obligation	$(200)
Plan assets	180
Underfunded PBO	(20)
Accrued pension cost	5
Transition liability	**$ (15)**

The transition amount is amortized to pension expense by the straight-line method over the average remaining service life of employees.

Amortization is by the straight-line method over the average remaining service life of those employed on the transition date. If this period is less than 15 years, the employer can elect to amortize over 15 years. For companies with a transition amount to amortize, the amortized amount constitutes a sixth component of pension expense. Amortizing a transition liability increases pension expense.[24] Amortizing a transition asset decreases pension expense.[25] For instance, if we assume a 15-year amortization period, Global's $15 million transition liability would add $1 million to its pension expense each year for 15 years. In 1997, its pension expense would have included this sixth component in addition to the five we previously discussed:

---

[21]We will discuss accounting changes in Chapter 21.

[22]Accounting Principles Board, "Accounting for the Cost of Pension Plans," *APB Opinion No. 8,* AICPA, 1966.

[23]SFAS 87 was effective for reporting years beginning after December 15, 1986. Early adoption was encouraged, and many firms adopted the standard in their 1986 fiscal years.

[24]A transition liability is sometimes called *transition cost.*

[25]A transition asset is sometimes called a *transition gain.*

1997 Pension Expense, Including Amortization of a Transition Liability

	($ in millions)
Service cost	$41
Interest cost	24
Actual return on the plan assets	(30)
Adjusted for gain on the plan assets	3
Amortization of prior service cost	4
Amortization of net loss	1
Amortization of transition liability ($15 million ÷ 15 yrs)	**1**
Pension expense	$44

Amortizing a transition liability increases pension expense. (Amortizing a transition asset would decrease pension expense.)

It's important to note that the transition amount was a one-time occurrence. Its amount already has been determined by all firms that had pension plans when the new standard was adopted. In fact, in a few years the amount will have been fully amortized by most firms and no longer will appear as a component of these firms' pension expense.

One or more of the other components also might be absent in some situations, as we witnessed earlier in the illustrations. At the very least, though, pension expense will include service cost, interest, and return on plan assets for a funded plan that has existed for more than a year. Graphic 17–15 reexamines the six potential components of pension expense, focusing on their effects on the PBO, plan assets and pension expense.

The transition amount was a one-time occurrence.

GRAPHIC 17–15

Nature of the Components of Pension Expense

Component	Effect on PBO	Effect on Plan Assets	Effect on Pension Expense
Service cost	Increase	None	Increase
Interest cost	Increase	None	Increase
Actual return on plan assets	None	Increase; unless negative	Decrease; unless negative
Prior service cost	Increase	None	Increase (delayed basis)
Losses or gains	Losses increase; gains decrease	Gains increase; losses decrease	Losses increase; gains decrease
Transition amount	Difference between PBO and plan assets from prior periods (adjusted for prepaid/accrued pension cost)		Liability increases; asset decreases

Pension Disclosures— A Compromise

Learning objective 7
Describe how pension disclosures fill a reporting gap left by the minimal disclosures in the primary financial statements.

You learned in the previous sections of this chapter that the pension information actually reported in the financial statements falls short of the conceptual ideal and even shy of the FASB's own preferences. The Board acknowledged that *SFAS 87* represents a political compromise. The "Basis for Conclusions" portion of the *Statement* indicates that its requirements "represent a worthwhile improvement," but that some of the Board's conceptual preferences "would be too great a change from past practice to be adopted at this time."[27]

This Statement requires expanded disclosures intended to provide more complete and more current information than can be practically incorporated in financial statements at this time.[26]

The pension items that are included in the income statement and balance sheet are indicated in Graphic 17–16. Where appropriate for demonstration, amounts from the chapter illustrations (1997) are indicated.

Decision-Makers' Perspective

Although financial statement items are casualties of the political compromises of *SFAS 87*, information provided in the disclosure notes fortunately makes up for some of the deficiencies. Foremost among the useful disclosures are a breakdown of the components of the annual pension

Pension amounts reported in the disclosure notes fill a reporting gap left by the minimal disclosures in the primary financial statements.

---

[26]"Employers' Accounting for Pensions," *Statement of Financial Accounting Standards No. 87,* (Stamford, Conn.: FASB, 1985), par. 88.
[27]Ibid., par. 107.

GRAPHIC   17–16

Financial Statement
Disclosures

Income Statement:	($ in millions)
Pension expense	$43
Balance Sheet:	
Assets:	
Prepaid pension cost	$16
Intangible pension asset	26
Liabilities:	
Pension liability {$16 + (26)}	$(10)
Stockholders' equity:	
Unrealized pension cost	none

expense and an estimate of the projected benefit obligation. Other information also is made available to make it possible for interested analysts to reconstruct the financial statements with pension assets and liabilities included. The items shown in Graphic 17–17 are required to be provided in the disclosure notes (with 1997 amounts from the chapter illustrations where appropriate).

GRAPHIC   17–17

Disclosure Notes

The service cost, interest cost, and return on plan assets should be reported individually, but other components of pension expense can be combined in a single net amount.

The difference between the funded status and the prepaid (accrued) pension cost can be reconciled by the unrecognized prior service cost, net loss or gain, and transition amount.

1. Description of the plan, including:
   ✓ Employee groups covered.
   ✓ Type of benefit formula.
   ✓ Funding policy.
   ✓ Type of assets held and significant nonbenefit liabilities.
   ✓ Nature and effect of significant matters affecting comparability.

2. Composition of pension expense, showing separately the

✓ Service cost.	$ 41
✓ Interest cost.	24
✓ Return on plan assets (actual return, $30, less $3 gain, equals expected return).	(27)
✓ Net total of other components ($4 + $1).	5
	$ 43

3. Reconciliation schedule—relating funded status and balance sheet amounts, including:

✓ Vested benefits.	(amount not assumed)
✓ Accumulated benefit obligation.	$(350)
✓ Projected benefit obligation.	$(450)
✓ Fair value of plan assets.	340
Underfunded amount.	$(110)
✓ Unrecognized prior service cost.	52
✓ Unrecognized net loss (gain).	74
✓ Unrecognized transition cost.	0
✓ Prepaid (accrued) pension cost.	$ 16
✓ Additional liability.	(26)

4. The discount rate (6%), the assumed rate of compensation increase used to measure the PBO (not given), and the expected long-term rate of return on plan assets (9%).

5. Amounts and types of securities included in plan assets, the approximate amount of annual benefits of employees and retirees, the amortization method used, and the existence and nature of any commitments to make future amendments.

Investors and creditors must be cautious of the nontraditional treatment of pension information when developing financial ratios as part of an analysis of financial statements. The various elements of pensions that are not reported separately on the balance sheet (PBO, plan assets, net gains and losses, prior service cost) can be included in ratios such as the debt-to-equity ratio or return on assets, but only by deliberately obtaining those numbers from the disclosure notes and adjusting the computation of the ratios. Similarly, without adjustment, profitability ratios and the times interest earned ratio will be distorted because pension expense includes the financial components of interest on return on assets.

Settlement or Curtailment of Pension Plans

> Companies sometimes terminate defined benefit plans to reduce costs and lessen risk.

> Companies sometimes terminate defined benefit plans to siphon off excess pension fund assets for other purposes.

You learned earlier that many companies are deciding to terminate long-standing defined benefit plans to cut down on cumbersome paperwork and to lessen their exposure to the risk posed by defined benefit plans. Many are substituting defined contribution plans.

Sometimes the motivation to terminate a plan is to take advantage of the excess funding position of many plans that was created by the stock market boom of the 1980s and to divert these assets to another purpose. This trend was given impetus in 1982 when Tengelmann Group took over ailing A&P and used the acquired company's excess pension plan assets to finance its turnaround. Since then, so-called reversion assets have been used, not only in takeovers, but by existing management as well. Exxon, for instance, used $1.6 billion from its $5.6 billion pension fund to bolster operations during a period of depressed oil prices in 1986. Asset reversions are not as common now as in the 1980s, largely because of excise taxes on amounts recovered when plans are terminated and other restrictive legislation taken by Congress to limit terminations.

When a plan is terminated, *SFAS 88* requires a gain or loss to be reported at that time.[28] For instance, Melville Corporation described the termination of its pension plan in the following disclosure note:

GRAPHIC   17–18

Gain on the Termination of a Defined Benefit Plan— Melville Corporation

> ### Retirement Plans (in Part)
>
> . . . As a result of the termination of the defined benefit plans, and after the settlement of the liability to plan participants through the purchase of nonparticipating annuity contracts or lump-sum rollovers into the new 401(k) Profit Sharing Plan, the Company recorded a nonrecurring gain of approximately $4,000,000 which was the amount of plan assets that reverted to the Company. This was accounted for in accordance with *Statement of Financial Accounting Standards No. 88,* "Employers' Accounting for Settlements and Curtailments of Defined Benefit Pension Plans and for Termination Benefits."

CONCEPT REVIEW EXERCISE   PENSION PLANS

Allied Services, Inc., has a noncontributory, defined benefit pension plan. Pension plan assets had a fair market value of $900 million at December 31, 1994.

On January 1, 1995, Allied amended the pension formula to increase benefits for each service year. By making the amendment retroactive to prior years, Allied incurred a prior service cost of $75 million, adding to the previous projected benefit obligation of $875 million. The prior service cost is to be amortized (expensed) over 15 years. The service cost is $31 million for 1995. Both the actuary's discount rate and the expected rate of return on plan assets were 8%. The actual rate of return on plan assets was 10%.

At December 31, $16 million was contributed to the pension fund and $22 million was paid to retired employees. Also, at that time, the actuary revised a previous assumption, increasing the PBO estimate by $10 million. The unrecognized net loss at the beginning of the year was $13 million.

Required:
Determine each of the following amounts as of December 31, 1995, the fiscal year-end for Allied:

1. Projected benefit obligation
2. Plan assets
3. Pension expense

---

[28]"Employers' Accounting for Settlements and Curtailments of Defined Benefit Pension Plans and for Termination Benefits," *Statement of Financial Accounting Standards No. 88,* (Stamford, Conn.: FASB, 1985).

CONCEPT REVIEW EXERCISE

SOLUTION

($ in millions)	Projected Benefit Obligation	Plan Assets	Pension Expense
Balances at Jan. 1	$ 875	$900	$ 0
Prior service cost	75		
Service cost	31		31
Interest cost [($875 + 75)* × 8%]	76		76
Return on plan assets			
Actual ($900 × 10%)		90	
Expected ($900 × 8%)			(72)
Amortization of prior service cost ($75 ÷ 15)			5
Amortization of unrecognized net loss			0†
Loss on PBO	10		
Cash contribution		16	
Retirement payments	(22)	(22)	
Balance at Dec. 31	$1,045	$984	$40

Note: The $18 million gain on plan assets ($90 – 72 million) is not recognized yet; it is carried forward to be combined with previous and future gains and losses, which will be recognized only if the net gain or net loss exceeds 10% of the higher of the PBO or plan assets.

*Since the plan was amended at the beginning of the year, the prior service cost increased the PBO at that time.

†Since the unrecognized net loss ($13) does not exceed 10% of $900 (higher than $875), no amortization is required for 1995.

Solution to Financial Reporting Case (at the opening of the chapter)

1. Why is underfunding not a concern in your present employment?

2. Were you correct that the pension liability is not reported on the balance sheet? What is the liability?

3. What is the amount of the plan assets available to pay benefits? What are the factors that can cause that amount to change?

4. How is the pension expense influenced by changes in the pension liability and plan assets?

5. Are you interviewing with a company whose pension plan is severely underfunded?

In a defined contribution plan, the employer is not obliged to provide benefits beyond the annual contribution to the employees' plan. No liability is created. Unlike retirement benefits paid in a defined benefit plan, the employee's retirement benefits in a defined contribution plan are totally dependent on how well invested assets perform in the marketplace.

Yes. The pension liability is measured (in three ways) and tracked informally, but not reported on the balance sheet. It is disclosed, however, in the notes. For United Dynamics, the PBO in 1997 is $2,628 million, the ABO is $2,455 million, the vested benefit obligation is $2,116 million.

The plan assets at the end of 1997 total $2,807 million. A trustee accepts employer contributions, invests the contributions, accumulates the earnings on the investments, and pays benefits from the plan assets. So the amount is increased each year by employer cash contributions and (hopefully) a return on assets invested. It is decreased by amounts paid out to retired employees.

The pension expense reported on the income statement is a composite of periodic changes that occur in both the pension obligation and the plan assets. For United Dynamics in 1997, the pension expense included the service cost and interest cost, which are changes in the PBO, and the return on plan assets. It also included an amortized portion of prior service costs (a previous change in the PBO) and of net gains (gains and losses result from changes in both the PBO and plan assets)

No. United Dynamics' plan assets exceed the pension obligation, however measured, in each year presented.

The Bottom Line

1.   Pension plans are arrangements designed to provide income to individuals during their retirement years. *Defined contribution* plans promise fixed annual contributions to a pension fund, without further commitment regarding benefit amounts at retirement. *Defined benefit* plans promise fixed retirement benefits defined by a designated formula. The employer sets aside cash each year to provide sufficient funds to pay promised benefits.

2.   The *accumulated benefit obligation* is an estimate of the discounted present value of the retirement benefits earned so far by employees, applying the plan's pension formula to existing compensation levels. The vested benefit obligation is the portion of the accumulated benefit obligation that plan participants are entitled to receive regardless of their continued employment. The projected benefit obligation estimates retirement benefits by applying the pension formula to projected future compensation levels.

3.   The PBO can change due to the accumulation of **service cost** from year to year, the accrual of **interest** as time passes, making plan amendments retroactive to prior years (prior service cost), and periodic adjustments when estimates change (gains and losses). The obligation is reduced as benefits actually are paid to retired employees.

4.   The plan assets consist of the accumulated balance of the annual employer contributions plus the return on the investments (dividends, interest, market price appreciation) less benefits paid to retirees.

5.   The pension expense is a composite of periodic changes in both the pension obligation and the plan assets. Service cost is the increase in the PBO attributable to employee service and is the primary component of pension expense. The interest and return-on-assets components are financial items created only because the compensation is delayed and the obligation is funded currently. Prior service cost is recognized over employees' future service period. Also, neither a loss (gain) on the PBO nor a loss (gain) on plan assets is immediately recognized in pension expense; they are recognized on a delayed basis to achieve income smoothing.

6.   The difference between pension expense and the cash contribution to plan assets is debited or credited to a single account: prepaid (accrued) pension cost. A debit balance in this account is reported as an asset; a credit balance is reported as a liability. This amount equals the net sum of the elements that constitute a defined benefit pension plan that aren't formally recognized in the accounts: the PBO, the plan assets, the unrecognized prior service cost, and the unrecognized net loss (or gain).

7.   Pension amounts reported in the disclosure notes fill a reporting gap left by the minimal disclosures in the primary financial statements. Disclosures include a breakdown of the components of the annual pension expense, an estimate of the projected benefit obligation, and other information to make it possible for interested analysts to reconstruct the financial statements with pension assets and liabilities included.

Questions for Review of Key Topics

Question	17–1	What is a pension plan? What motivates a corporation to offer a pension plan for its employees?
Question	17–2	Qualified pension plans offer important tax benefits. What is the special tax treatment and what qualifies a pension plan for these benefits?
Question	17–3	Lamont Corporation has a pension plan in which the corporation makes all contributions and employees receive benefits at retirement based on the balance in their accumulated pension fund. What type of pension plan does Lamont have?
Question	17–4	What is the vested benefit obligation?
Question	17–5	Differentiate between the accumulated benefit obligation and the projected benefit obligation.
Question	17–6	Name five events that might change the balance of the PBO.
Question	17–7	Name three events that might change the balance of the plan assets.
Question	17–8	What are the components that might be included in the calculation of net pension cost recognized for a period by an employer sponsoring a defined benefit pension plan?
Question	17–9	Define the service cost component of the periodic pension expense.
Question	17–10	Define the interest cost component of the periodic pension expense.
Question	17–11	The return on plan assets is the increase in plan assets (at fair value), adjusted for contributions to the plan and benefits paid during the period. How is the return included in the calculation of the periodic pension expense?
Question	17–12	Define prior service cost. How is it included in pension expense?
Question	17–13	How should gains or losses related to pension plan assets be recognized? How does this treatment compare to that for gains or losses related to the pension obligation?
Question	17–14	Name four pension-related balances that can be described as off-balance-sheet asset and liability amounts.
Question	17–15	Define transition cost.
Question	17–16	What three components of pension expense may be negative (i.e. reduce pension expense)?
Question	17–17	Which are the components of pension expense that involve delayed recognition?
Question	17–18	Evaluate this statement: The excess of the actual return on plan assets over the expected return decreases the employer's pension cost.
Question	17–19	When accounting for pension costs, how should any difference between net periodic pension expense and the payment into the pension fund be reported?
Question	17–20	Compare the way the pension obligation is reported in the balance sheet with the FASB's apparent conceptual preference for reporting that obligation.
Question	17–21	A pension plan is underfunded when the employer's obligation (PBO) exceeds the resources available to satisfy that obligation (plan assets) and overfunded when the opposite is the case. Explain how this funded status can be reconciled with the balance in the prepaid (accrued) pension cost that is reported on the balance sheet.
Question	17–22	Assuming a zero balance in the prepaid (accrued) pension cost account, when must an additional minimum pension liability be recorded? What if the account has a credit balance? A debit balance?

Exercises

Exercise 17–1
Changes in the PBO

Indicate by letter whether each of the events listed below increases (**I**), decreases (**D**), or has no effect (**N**) on an employer's projected benefits obligation.

Events

_____ 1. Interest cost.
_____ 2. Prior service cost is amortized by the straight-line method.
_____ 3. Prior service cost is amortized by the service method.
_____ 4. An increase in the average life expectancy of employees.
_____ 5. A plan amendment that increases benefits is made retroactive to prior years.
_____ 6. An increase in the actuary's assumed discount rate.
_____ 7. Cash contributions to the pension fund by the employer.
_____ 8. Benefits are paid to retired employees.
_____ 9. Service cost.
_____ 10. Return on plan assets during the year lower than expected.
_____ 11. Return on plan assets during the year higher than expected.

Exercise 17–2
Determine the projected benefit obligation

On January 1, 1997, Burleson Corporation's projected benefit obligation was $30 million. During 1997 pension benefits paid by the trustee were $4 million. Service cost for 1997 is $12 million. Pension plan assets (at fair value) increased during 1997 by $6 million as expected. At the end of 1997, there were no unrecognized pension costs. The actuary's discount rate was 10%.

Required:

Determine the amount of the projected benefit obligation at December 31, 1997.

Exercise 17–3
Components of pension expense

Indicate by letter whether each of the events listed below increases (**I**), decreases (**D**), or has no effect (**N**) on an employer's periodic pension expense in the year the event occurs.

Events

_____ 1. Interest cost.
_____ 2. Prior service cost is amortized by the straight-line method.
_____ 3. Prior service cost is amortized by the service method.
_____ 4. Expected return on plan assets.
_____ 5. A plan amendment that increases benefits is made retroactive to prior years.
_____ 6. Actuary's estimate of the PBO is increased.
_____ 7. Cash contributions to the pension fund by the employer.
_____ 8. Benefits are paid to retired employees.
_____ 9. Service cost.
_____ 10. Excess of the actual return on plan assets over the expected return.
_____ 11. Amortization of unrecognized net loss.
_____ 12. Amortization of unrecognized net gain.

Exercise 17–4
Recording pension expense

Harrison Forklift determined its pension expense to be $14 million in 1997.

Required:

Prepare the appropriate general journal entries to record Harrison's pension expense and funding in each of the following independent situations:

1. Harrison contributed $14 million to the pension fund at the end of 1997.
2. Harrison contributed $11 million to the pension fund at the end of 1997.
3. Harrison contributed $16 million to the pension fund at the end of 1997.

Exercise 17–5
Determine pension plan assets

The following data relates to Voltaire Company's defined benefit pension plan during 1997:

	($ in millions)
Plan assets at fair value, January 1	$600
Expected return on plan assets	60
Actual return on plan assets	48
Contributions to the pension fund (end of year)	100
Amortization of unrecognized loss	10
Pension benefits paid (end of year)	11
Pension expense	72

Required:
Determine the amount of pension plan assets at fair value on December 31, 1997.

Exercise 17–6
Changes in the pension obligation; determine service cost

Pension data for Millington Enterprises includes the following:

	($ in millions)
Discount rate, 10%	
Projected benefit obligation, January 1, 1997	$360
Projected benefit obligation, December 31, 1997	465
Accumulated benefit obligation, January 1, 1997	300
Accumulated benefit obligation, December 31, 1997	415
Cash contributions to pension fund, December 31, 1997	150
Benefit payments to retirees, December 31, 1997	54

Required:
Assuming no change in actuarial assumptions and estimates, determine the service cost component of pension expense for 1997.

Exercise 17–7
Changes in plan assets; determine cash contributions

Pension data for Fahy Transportation, Inc., include the following:

	($ in millions)
Discount rate, 7%	
Expected return on plan assets, 10%	
Actual return on plan assets, 11%	
Projected benefit obligation, January 1, 1997	$730
Plan assets (fair market value), January 1, 1997	700
Plan assets (fair market value), December 31, 1997	750
Benefit payments to retirees, December 31, 1997	66

Required:
Assuming cash contributions were made at the end of the year, what was the amount of those contributions for 1997?

Exercise 17–8
Components of pension expense

Pension data for Sterling Properties include the following:

	($ in 000s)
Service cost, 1997	$112
Projected benefit obligation, January 1, 1997	850
Plan assets (fair market value), January 1, 1997	900
Unrecognized prior service cost, (1997 amortization, $8)	80
Unrecognized net loss, (1997 amortization, $1)	101
Unrecognized transition cost	none
Discount rate, 6%	
Expected return on plan assets, 10%	
Actual return on plan assets, 11%	

Required:
Determine pension expense for 1997.

Exercise 17–9
Determine pension expense

Abbott and Abbott has a noncontributory, defined benefit pension plan. At December 31, 1997, Abbott and Abbott received the following information:

Projected Benefit Obligation	($ in millions)
Balance, January 1	$120
Service cost	20
Interest cost	12
Benefits paid	(9)
Balance, December 31	$143

Plan Assets	
Balance, January 1	$ 80
Actual return on plan assets	9
Contributions 1997	20
Benefits paid	(9)
Balance, December 31	$100

The expected long-term rate of return on plan assets was 10%. There was no unrecognized prior service cost, gains and losses, or transition cost on January 1, 1997.

Required:
1. Determine Abbott and Abbott's pension expense for 1997.
2. Prepare the journal entry to record Abbott and Abbott's pension expense and funding for 1997.

Exercise 17–10
Components of pension
expense; journal entry

Pension data for Barry Financial Services, Inc. include the following:

	($ in 000s)
Discount rate, 7%	
Expected return on plan assets, 10%	
Actual return on plan assets, 9%	
Service cost, 1997	$ 310
January 1, 1997:	
Projected benefit obligation	2,300
Accumulated benefit obligation	2,000
Plan assets (fair market value)	2,400
Unrecognized prior service cost, (1997 amortization, $25)	325
Unrecognized net gain, (1997 amortization, $6)	330
Unrecognized transition cost	none
December 31, 1997:	
Cash contributions to pension fund, December 31, 1997	245
Benefit payments to retirees, December 31, 1997	270

Required:
1. Determine pension expense for 1997.
2. Prepare the journal entry to record pension expense and funding for 1997.

Exercise 17–11
PBO calculations; ABO
calculations; present value
concepts

Clark Industries has a defined benefit pension plan that specifies annual retirement benefits equal to:

$$1.2\% \times \text{service years} \times \text{final year's salary}$$

Stanley Mills was hired by Clark at the beginning of 1978. Mills is expected to retire at the end of 2022 after 45 years service. His retirement is expected to span 15 years. At the end of 1997, 20 years after being hired, his salary is $80,000. The company's actuary projects Mills's salary to be $270,000 at retirement. The actuary's discount rate is 7%.

Required:
1. Estimate the amount of Stanley Mills's annual retirement payments for the 15 retirement years earned as of the end of 1997.
2. Suppose Clark's pension plan permits a lump-sum payment at retirement in lieu of annuity payments. Determine the lump-sum equivalent as the present value as of the retirement date of annuity payments during the retirement period.
3. What is the company's projected benefit obligation at the end of 1997 with respect to Stanley Mills?
4. What is the company's accumulated benefit obligation at the end of 1997 with respect to Stanley Mills?
5. If we assume no estimates change in the meantime, what is the company's projected benefit obligation at the end of 1998 with respect to Stanley Mills?
6. What portion of the 1998 increase in the PBO is attributable to 1998 service (the service cost component of pension expense) and to accrued interest (the interest cost component of pension expense)?

Exercise 17–12
Determining the amortization
of unrecognized net gain

Hicks Cable Company has a defined benefit pension plan. Three alternative possibilities for pension-related data at January 1, 1997, are shown below:

	($ in 000s)		
	Case 1	**Case 2**	**Case 3**
Unrecognized net loss (gain), Jan. 1	$ 320	$ (330)	$ 260
1997 loss (gain) on plan assets	(11)	(8)	2
1997 loss (gain) on PBO	(23)	16	(265)
Accumulated benefit obligation, Jan. 1	(2,950)	(2,550)	(1,450)
Projected benefit obligation, Jan. 1	(3,310)	(2,670)	(1,700)
Fair value of plan assets, Jan. 1	2,800	2,700	1,550
Average remaining service period of active employees (years)	12	15	10

Required:
1. For each independent case, calculate any amortization of the net loss or gain that should be included as a component of net pension expense for 1997.
2. Determine the unrecognized net loss or gain as of January 1, 1998.

Exercise 17–13
Pension spreadsheet

A partially completed pension spreadsheet, showing the relationships among the elements that comprise the defined benefit pension plan of Universal Products, is given below. The actuary's discount rate is 5%. At the end of 1995, the pension formula was amended, creating a prior service cost of $120,000. The expected rate of return on assets was 8%, and the average remaining service life of the active employee group is 20 years in the current year as well as the previous two years.

( )s indicate credits; debits otherwise ($ in thousands)	Informal Records				Formal Records		
	PBO	Plan Assets	Prior Service Cost	Net Loss	Pension Expense	Cash	Prepaid (Accrued) Cost
Balance, Jan. 1, 1997	(800)	600	114	80			(6)
Service cost					84		
Interest cost, 5%	(40)						
Actual return on assets					(42)		
Loss on assets				6			
Amortization of:							
Prior service cost							
Net loss							
Gain on PBO				(12)			
Contributions to fund						(48)	
Retiree benefits paid							
1997 journal entry							(34)
Balance, Dec. 31, 1997	(862)		108				

Required:
Copy the incomplete spreadsheet and fill in the missing amounts.

Exercise 17–14
Minimum liability

Willis-Chambers Company has a noncontributory, defined benefit pension plan. On December 31, 1997, the following pension-related data were available:

	($ in millions)
Projected benefit obligation	$25
Accumulated benefit obligation	22
Plan assets (fair value)	20
Accrued pension cost (credit balance)	3

Required:
1. Determine Willis-Chambers' minimum pension liability to be reported on the 1997 balance sheet and prepare any journal entry necessary to achieve that reporting objective.
2. Suppose Willis-Chambers' had a prepaid pension cost of $3 (debit balance), instead of a credit balance. Prepare any journal entry necessary to achieve that reporting objective.

Exercise 17–15
Minimum liability

Norsouth Corporation has a defined benefit pension plan. Norsouth's policy is to fund the plan annually, cash payments being made at the end of each year. Data relating to the pension plan for 1997 are as follows:

	($ in millions)
Prepaid (accrued) pension cost at the beginning of the year—debit balance	$ 8
Net pension expense for 1997	40
Unrecognized prior service cost at year-end	30
Accumulated benefit obligation at year-end	117
Projected benefit obligation at year-end	140
Fair value of plan assets at year-end	105
Payment to trustee at year-end	38

Required:
Determine Norsouth's pension liability to be reported on the 1997 balance sheet and prepare any journal entry necessary to achieve that reporting objective.

Exercise 17–16
Concepts; terminology

Listed below are several terms and phrases associated with pensions. Pair each item from List A (by letter) with the item from List B that is most appropriately associated with it.

List A	List B
_____ 1. Future compensation levels estimated.	a. Additional minimum liability
_____ 2. All funding provided by the employer.	b. Prepaid pension cost
_____ 3. Cumulative employer's contributions in excess of recognized pension.	c. Vested benefit obligation
_____ 4. Retirement benefits specified by formula.	d. Projected benefit obligation
_____ 5. Trade-off between relevance and reliability.	e. Choice between PBO and ABO
_____ 6. Causes a debit to an intangible asset.	f. Noncontributory pension plan
	g. Accumulated benefit obligation

____	7. Current pay levels implicitly assumed.	h. Plan assets
____	8. Created by the passage of time.	i. Interest cost
____	9. Not contingent on future employment.	j. Delayed recognition
____	10. Risk borne by employee.	k. Defined contribution plan
____	11. Increased by employer contributions.	l. Defined benefit plan
____	12. Caused by plan amendment.	m. Prior service cost
____	13. Gain on plan assets.	n. Amortize unrecognized net loss
____	14. Excess over 10% of plan assets or PBO.	

Exercise 17–17
Prior service cost; service method; straight-line method

Frazier Refrigeration amended its defined benefit pension plan on December 31, 1997, to increase retirement benefits earned with each service year. The consulting actuary estimated the prior service cost incurred by making the amendment retroactive to prior years to be $110,000. Frazier's 100 present employees are expected to retire at the rate of approximately 10 each year at the end of each of the next 10 years.

Required:

1. Using the service method, calculate the amount of prior service cost to be amortized to pension expense in each of the next 10 years.
2. Using the straight-line method, calculate the amount of prior service cost to be amortized to pension expense in each of the next 10 years.

Exercise 17–18
Determine pension expense; minimum liability; prior service cost; unrecognized net loss

Beale Management has a noncontributory, defined benefit pension plan. On December 31, 1997 (the end of Beale's fiscal year), the following pension-related data were available:

Projected Benefit Obligation	($ in millions)
Balance, January 1, 1997	$ 480
Service cost	82
Interest cost, discount rate, 10%	24
Gain due to changes in actuarial assumptions in 1997	(10)
Pension benefits paid	(40)
Balance, December 31, 1997	$ 536

Plan Assets	
Balance, January 1, 1997	$500
Actual return on plan assets	40
(Expected return on plan assets, $45)	
Contributions	70
Pension benefits paid	(40)
Balance, December 31, 1997	$ 570

Accumulated Benefits Obligation, Dec. 31, 1997	$ 490

January 1, 1997, balances:	
Prepaid (accrued) pension cost (credit balance)	$ (12)
Unrecognized prior service cost (amortization $8 per year)	48
Unrecognized net gain (any amortization over 15 years)	80
Unrecognized transition cost	none
Intangible pension asset	none

Required:

1. Prepare the 1997 journal entry to record pension expense and funding.
2. Prepare the 1997 journal entry to record any necessary additional pension liability.
3. Suppose that at December 31, 1997, the minimum liability is calculated to be $15 million. Prepare the 1997 journal entry to record any necessary additional pension liability.

Exercise 17–19
Additional minimum liability; multiple years

Goode Corporation established a noncontributory, defined benefit pension plan for its employees at the company's inception in 1981. The plan was amended in 1997. Prior to 1997, Goode had not found it necessary to record an additional minimum pension liability. The following information is available for the reporting years ended December 31:

	($ in 000)		
	1997	**1998**	**1999**
Projected benefit obligation	1,100	1,500	2,000
Accumulated benefit obligation	900	1,050	1,200
Plan assets at fair value	800	975	1,100
(Accrued)/prepaid pension cost	(30)	(25)	5
Unrecognized prior service cost	40		
(to be amortized over five years beginning in 1998)			

Required:

1. Compute the required additional minimum liability for each year, 1997 through 1999.
2. Prepare the journal entry to recognize the additional minimum liability for each year, 1997 through 1999.

Exercise 17–20
Multiple choice

The following questions dealing with pensions are adapted from questions that appeared on recent CPA examinations. Determine the response that best completes the statements or questions.

1. The following information pertains to Lee Corp.'s defined benefit pension plan for 1997:

Service cost	$160,000
Actual and expected return on plan assets	35,000
Unexpected loss on plan assets related to a 1997 disposal of a subsidiary	40,000
Amortization of unrecognized prior service cost	5,000
Annual interest on pension obligation	50,000

   What amount should Lee report as pension expense in its 1997 income statement?
   a. $250,000
   b. $220,000
   c. $210,000
   d. $180,000

2. Interest cost included in the net pension cost recognized by an employer sponsoring a defined benefit pension plan represents the
   a. Amortization of the discount on unrecognized prior service costs.
   b. Increase in the fair value of plan assets due to the passage of time.
   c. Increase in the projected benefit obligation due to the passage of time.
   d. Shortage between the expected and actual returns on plan assets.

3. Webb Co. implemented a defined benefit pension plan for its employees on January 1, 1994. During 1994 and 1995, Webb's contributions fully funded the plan. The following data are provided for 1997 and 1996:

	1997 Estimated	1996 Actual
Projected benefit obligation, December 31	$750,000	$700,000
Accumulated benefit obligation, December 31	520,000	500,000
Plan assets at fair value, December 31	675,000	600,000
Projected benefit obligation in excess of plan assets	75,000	100,000
Pension expense	90,000	75,000
Employer's contribution	?	50,000

   What amount should Webb contribute in order to report an accrued pension liability of $15,000 in its December 31, 1997, balance sheet?
   a. $50,000
   b. $60,000
   c. $75,000
   d. $100,000

4. Payne, Inc., implemented a defined-benefit pension plan for its employees on January 2, 1997. The following data are provided for 1997, as of December 31, 1997:

Accumulated benefit obligation	$103,000
Plan assets at fair value	78,000
Net periodic pension cost	90,000
Employer's contribution	70,000

   What amount should Payne record as additional minimum pension liability at December 31, 1997?
   a. $0
   b. $5,000
   c. $20,000
   d. $45,000

Exercise 17–21
Classifying accounting changes and errors

Indicate with the appropriate letter the nature of each adjustment described below:

Type of Adjustment
   A. Change in principle (general)
   B. Change in principle (exception reported retroactively)
   C. Change in principle (exception reported prospectively)
   D Change in estimate
   E. Correction of an error
   N. Neither an accounting change nor an error

_____ 1. Change from reporting pension benefits according to the provisions of *Accounting Principles Board Opinion 8* to reporting pension benefits according to the provisions of *SFAS 87* in 1987. [*SFAS 87* became generally effective in 1987.]

_____ 2. Change in actuarial assumptions for a defined benefit pension plan.

_____ 3. Determination that the accumulated benefits obligation under a pension plan exceeded the fair value of plan assets at the end of the previous year by $17,000. The only pension-related amount on the balance sheet was prepaid pension costs of $30,000.

_____ 4. Pension plan assets for a defined benefit pension plan achieving a rate of return in excess of the amount anticipated.

_____ 5. Instituting a pension plan for the first time and adopting *Statement of Financial Accounting Standards No. 87,* "Employers' Accounting for Pensions."

Problems

(Problems 1–5 are variations of the same situation, designed to focus on different elements of the pension plan.)

Problem 17–1
ABO calculations; present value concepts

Sachs Brands' defined benefit pension plan specifies annual retirement benefits equal to: 1.6% × service years × final year's salary, payable at the end of each year. Angela Davenport was hired by Sachs at the beginning of 1983 and is expected to retire at the end of 2017 after 35 years service. Her retirement is expected to span 18 years. Davenport's salary is $90,000 at the end of 1997, and the company's actuary projects her salary to be $240,000 at retirement. The actuary's discount rate is 7%.

Required:

1. Draw a time line that depicts Davenport's expected service period, retirement period, and a 1997 measurement date for the pension obligation.
2. Estimate by the accumulated benefits approach the amount of Davenport's annual retirement payments earned as of the end of 1997.
3. What is the company's accumulated benefit obligation at the end of 1997 with respect to Davenport?
4. If no estimates are changed in the meantime, what will be the accumulated benefit obligation at the end of 2000 (three years later) when Davenport's salary is $100,000?

Problem 17–2
PBO calculations; present value concepts

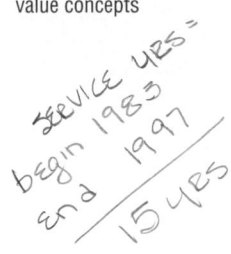

Sachs Brands' defined benefit pension plan specifies annual retirement benefits equal to: 1.6% × service years × final year's salary, payable at the end of each year. Angela Davenport was hired by Sachs at the beginning of 1983 and is expected to retire at the end of 2017 after 35 years service. Her retirement is expected to span 18 years. Davenport's salary is $90,000 at the end of 1997, and the company's actuary projects her salary to be $240,000 at retirement. The actuary's discount rate is 7%.

Required:

1. Draw a time line that depicts Davenport's expected service period, retirement period, and a 1997 measurement date for the pension obligation.
2. Estimate by the projected benefits approach the amount of Davenport's annual retirement payments earned as of the end of 1997.
3. What is the company's projected benefit obligation at the end of 1997 with respect to Davenport?
4. If no estimates are changed in the meantime, what will be the company's projected benefit obligation at the end of 2000 (three years later) with respect to Davenport?

Problem 17–3
Service cost, interest, and PBO calculations; present value concepts

Sachs Brands' defined benefit pension plan specifies annual retirement benefits equal to: 1.6% × service years × final year's salary, payable at the end of each year. Angela Davenport was hired by Sachs at the beginning of 1983 and is expected to retire at the end of 2017 after 35 years service. Her retirement is expected to span 18 years. Davenport's salary is $90,000 at the end of 1997, and the company's actuary projects her salary to be $240,000 at retirement. The actuary's discount rate is 7%.

Required:

1. What is the company's projected benefit obligation at the beginning of 1997 (after 14 years' service) with respect to Davenport?
2. Estimate by the projected benefits approach the portion of Davenport's annual retirement payments attributable to 1997 service.
3. What is the company's service cost for 1997 with respect to Davenport?
4. What is the company's interest cost for 1997 with respect to Davenport?
5. Combine your answers to requirements 1, 3, and 4 to determine the company's projected benefit obligation at the end of 1997 (after 15 years' service) with respect to Davenport.

Problem 17–4
Prior service cost;
components of pension
expense; present value
concepts

Sachs Brands' defined benefit pension plan specifies annual retirement benefits equal to: 1.6% × service years × final year's salary, payable at the end of each year. Angela Davenport was hired by Sachs at the beginning of 1983 and is expected to retire at the end of 2017 after 35 years service. Her retirement is expected to span 18 years. Davenport's salary is $90,000 at the end of 1997, and the company's actuary projects her salary to be $240,000 at retirement. The actuary's discount rate is 7%.

At the beginning of 1998, the pension formula was amended to:

$$1.75\% \times \text{service years} \times \text{final year's salary}$$

The amendment was made retroactive to apply the increased benefits to prior service years.

Required:

1. What is the company's prior service cost at the beginning of 1998 with respect to Davenport after the amendment described above?
2. Since the amendment occurred at the *beginning* of 1998, amortization of the prior service cost begins in 1998. What is the prior service cost amortization that would be included in pension expense?
3. What is the service cost for 1998 with respect to Davenport?
4. What is the interest cost for 1998 with respect to Davenport?
5. Calculate pension expense for 1998 with respect to Davenport, assuming plan assets attributable to her of $150,000 and a rate of return (actual and expected) of 10%.

Problem 17–5
Gain on PBO; present value
concepts

Sachs Brands' defined benefit pension plan specifies annual retirement benefits equal to: 1.6% × service years × final year's salary, payable at the end of each year. Angela Davenport was hired by Sachs at the beginning of 1983 and is expected to retire at the end of 2017 after 35 years service. Her retirement is expected to span 18 years. Davenport's salary is $90,000 at the end of 1997, and the company's actuary projects her salary to be $240,000 at retirement. The actuary's discount rate is 7%.

At the beginning of 1998, changing economic conditions caused the actuary to reassess the applicable discount rate. It was decided that 8% is the appropriate rate.

Required:

Calculate the effect of the change in the assumed discount rate on the PBO at the beginning of 1998 with respect to Davenport.

Problem 17–6
Determine the PBO, plan
assets, pension expense; two
years

Stanley-Morgan Industries adopted a defined benefit pension plan on April 12, 1997. The provisions of the plan were not made retroactive to prior years. A local bank, engaged as trustee for the plan assets, expects plan assets to earn a 10% rate of return. A consulting firm, engaged as actuary, recommends 6% as the appropriate discount rate. The service cost is $150,000 for 1997 and $200,000 for 1998. Year-end funding is $160,000 for 1997 and $170,000 for 1998. No assumptions or estimates were revised during 1997.

Required:

Calculate each of the following amounts as of both December 31, 1997, and December 31, 1998:

1. Projected benefit obligation
2. Plan assets
3. Pension expense
4. Prepaid (accrued) pension cost

Problem 17–7
Determining the amortization
of unrecognized net gain

Herring Wholesale Company has a defined benefit pension plan. On January 1, 1997, the following pension-related data were available:

	($ in 000s)
Unrecognized net gain	$ 170
Accumulated benefit obligation	1,170
Projected benefit obligation	1,400
Fair value of plan assets	1,100
Average remaining service period of active employees	15 years
(expected to remain constant for the next several years)	

The rate of return on plan assets during 1997 was 9%, although it was expected to be 10%. The actuary revised assumptions regarding the PBO at the end of the year, resulting in a $23,000 decrease in the estimate of that obligation.

Required:

1. Calculate any amortization of the net gain that should be included as a component of net pension expense for 1997.
2. Assume the net pension expense for 1997, not including the amortization of the net gain component, is $325,000. What is pension expense for the year?
3. Determine the unrecognized net loss or gain as of January 1, 1998.

Problem 17–8

Pension spreadsheet; journal entry; reconciliation schedule

A partially completed pension spreadsheet showing the relationships among the elements that constitute Winston, Inc.'s, defined benefit pension plan, is given below. At the end of 1994, the pension formula was amended, creating a prior service cost of $30 million. The expected rate of return on assets was 8%, and the average remaining service life of the active employee group is 15 years in the current year as well as the previous three years. The actuary's discount rate is 7%. There is no transition cost.

( )s indicate credits; debits otherwise ($ in millions)	Informal Records				Formal Records		
	PBO	Plan Assets	Prior Service Cost	Net (gain) Loss	Pension Expense	Cash	Prepaid (Accrued) Cost
Balance, Jan. 1, 1997	(600)	800	?	(95)			?
Service cost	?				65		
Interest cost	?				?		
Actual return on assets		?			(72)		
Gain (loss) on assets				?	?		
Amortization of:							
Prior service cost			(2)		?		
Net gain				?	?		
Loss on PBO	(4)			?			
Contributions to fund		?				?	
Retiree benefits paid	?	(52)					
1997 journal entry					?	(30)	?
Balance, Dec. 31, 1997	(659)	850	24	(98)			117

Required:
1. Copy the incomplete spreadsheet and fill in the missing amounts.
2. Prepare the journal entry to record pension expense and funding for 1997.
3. Prepare a schedule that reconciles the funded status of the plan with the amount recorded on the balance sheet at December 31, 1997.

Problem 17–9

Determine pension expense; prepaid (accrued) pension cost; PBO; plan assets

U.S. Metallurgical, Inc., reported the following balances in its financial statements and disclosure notes at December 31, 1996.

Plan assets	$400,000
Projected benefit obligation	(320,000)
Prepaid (accrued) pension cost	$ 80,000

U.S.M.'s actuary determined that 1997 service cost is $60,000. Both the expected and actual rate of return on plan assets are 9%. The interest (discount) rate is 5%. U.S.M. contributed $120,000 to the pension fund at the end of 1997, and retirees were paid $44,000 from plan assets.

Required:
Determine the following amounts at the end of 1997:
1. Pension expense
2. Prepaid (accrued) pension cost
3. Projected benefit obligation
4. Plan assets

Problem 17–10

Determine pension expense, PBO, and plan assets; journal entries; two years

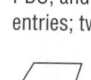

The Kollar Company has a defined benefit pension plan. Pension information concerning the fiscal year 1997 and 1998 are presented below ($ in millions):

Information provided by pension plan actuary:
a. Projected benefit obligation as of December 31, 1996 = $1,800.
b. Prior service cost from plan amendment on January 2, 1997 = $400 (straight-line amortization for 10-year average remaining service period).
c. Service cost for 1997 = $520.
d. Service cost for 1998 = $570.
e. Discount rate used by actuary on projected benefit obligation for 1997 and 1998 = 10%.
f. Payments to retirees in 1997 = $400.
g. Payments to retirees in 1998 = $450.
h. No changes in actuarial assumptions or estimates

Information provided by pension fund trustee:
a. Plan asset balance at fair value on January 1, 1997 = $1,600.
b. 1997 contributions = $540
c. 1998 contributions = $590

d. Expected long-term rate of return on plan assets = 12%.
e. 1997 actual return on plan assets = $180
f. 1998 actual return on plan assets = $210
g. Unrecognized net gain from prior years on January 1, 1997 = $230
h. Unrecognized gains and losses are amortized for 10 years for 1997 and 1998.

Required:
1. Compute pension expense for 1997 and 1998.
2. Prepare the journal entries for 1997 and 1998 pension expense.

Problem 17–11
Determine the PBO, plan assets, pension expense; prior service cost

Lewis Industries adopted a defined benefit pension plan on January 1, 1997. By making the provisions of the plan retroactive to prior years, Lewis incurred a prior service cost of $2 million. The prior service cost was funded immediately by a $2 million cash payment to the fund trustee on January 2, 1997. However, the cost is to be amortized (expensed) over 10 years. The service cost—$250,000 for 1997—is fully funded at the end of each year. Both the actuary's discount rate and the expected rate of return on plan assets were 9%. The actual rate of return on plan assets was 11%. At December 31, the trustee paid $16,000 to an employee who retired during 1997.

Required:
Determine each of the following amounts as of December 31, 1997, the fiscal year-end for Lewis:
1. Projected benefit obligation
2. Plan assets
3. Pension expense

Problem 17–12
Relationship among pension elements

Reconciliation schedules, reconciling the funded status of Hilton Paneling, Inc.'s defined benefit pension plan and the amount recognized in its balance sheet as prepaid (accrued) pension cost, are given below.

($ in 000s)

	1997 Beginning Balances	1997 Ending Balances
Projected benefit obligation	$(2,300)	$(2,501)
Plan assets	2,400	2,591
Funded status	100	90
Unamortized prior service cost	325	300
Unamortized net gain	(330)	(300)
Prepaid (accrued) pension cost	$ 95	$ 90

Retirees were paid $270,000 and the employer contribution to the pension fund was $245,000 at the end of 1997. The expected rate of return on plan assets was 10%, and the actuary's discount rate is 7%. There were no changes in actuarial estimates and assumptions regarding the PBO.

Required:
Determine the following amounts for 1997:
1. Actual return on plan assets
2. Loss or gain on plan assets
3. Service cost
4. Pension expense
5. Average remaining service life of active employees (used to determine amortization of the unrecognized net gain)

Problem 17–13
Determine pension expense; minimum liability; prior service cost; unrecognized net loss

Musseli Transport has a noncontributory, defined benefit pension plan. On December 31, 1997 (the end of the fiscal period), the following pension-related data were available:

Projected Benefit Obligation	($ in 000's)
Balance, January 1, 1997	$ 2,000
Service cost	410
Interest cost, discount rate, 10%	200
Losses (gains) due to changes in actuarial assumptions in 1997	0
Pension benefits paid	(210)
Balance, December 31, 1997	$ 2,400

Plan Assets	
Balance, January 1, 1997	$1,500
Actual return on plan assets (Expected return on plan assets, $135)	150
Contributions	500
Pension benefits paid	(210)
Balance, December 31, 1997	$1,940

Accumulated Benefits Obligation, Dec. 31, 1997	$ 2,100

January 1, 1997, balances:

Prepaid (accrued) pension cost (credit balance)	$ (30)
Unrecognized prior service cost (amortization $40 per year)	240
Unrecognized net loss (any amortization over 15 years)	230
Unrecognized transition cost	none
Intangible pension asset	none

Required:

1. Prepare the 1997 journal entry to record pension expense and funding.
2. Prepare the 1997 journal entry to record any necessary additional pension liability.
3. Suppose that at December 31, 1998, the minimum liability is calculated to be $170,000 and the prepaid (accrued) pension cost has a debit balance of $10,000. Prepare the 1998 journal entry to record any necessary additional pension liability.

Problem 17–14
Comprehensive—pension elements

The following pension-related data pertain to Metro Recreation's noncontributory, defined benefit pension plan for 1997:

	($ in 000s)	
	Jan. 1	**Dec. 31**
Projected benefit obligation	$4,100	$4,380
Accumulated benefits obligation	3,715	3,950
Plan assets (fair value)	4,530	4,975
Interest (discount) rate, 7%		
Expected return on plan assets, 10%		
Unrecognized prior service cost (from Dec. 31, 1996, amendment)	840	
Unrecognized net loss	477	
Unrecognized transition cost (from Jan. 1, 1983, adoption of SFAS 87)	93	
Average remaining service life: 1983—17 years 1997—12 years		
Gain due to changes in actuarial assumptions		44
Contributions to pension fund (end of year)		340
Pension benefits paid (end of year)		295

Required:

Prepare a pension spreadsheet that shows the relationships among the various pension balances, the changes in those balances, and computes pension expense for 1997.

Cases

Writing Case 17–1
Pension concepts

Mark Easterwood is the newly hired assistant controller of Kemp Industries, a regional supplier of hard-wood derivative products. The company sponsors a defined benefit pension plan that covers its 420 employees. On reviewing last year's financial statements, Easterwood was concerned about some items reported in the disclosure notes relating to the pension plan. Portions of the relevant note follow:

Note 8: Pensions

The company has a defined benefit pension plan covering substantially all of its employees. Pension benefits are based on employee service years and the employee's compensation during the last two years of employment. The company' contributes annually the maximum amount permitted by the federal tax code. Plan contributions provide for benefits expected to be earned in the future a well as those earned to date. The following reconciles the plan's funded status and amount recognized in the balance sheet at December 31, 1997 ($ in 000).

Actuarial present value of benefit obligations:

Accumulated benefit obligation (including vested benefits of $318)	$(1,305)
Projected benefit obligation	$(1,800)
Plan assets at fair value	1,575
Projected benefit obligation in excess of plan assets	$ (225)

Kemp's comparative income statements reported net periodic pension expense of $108,000 in 1997 and $86,520 in 1996. Since employment has remained fairly constant in recent years, Easterwood expressed concern over the increase in the pension expense. He expressed his concern to you, a three-year senior accountant at Kemp. "I'm also interested in the differences in these liability measurements," he mentioned.

Required:

Write a memo to Easterwood. In the memo:

1. Explain to Easterwood how the composition of the net periodic pension expense can create the situation he sees. Briefly describe the components of pension expense. The transition amount has been completely amortized, so you need not discuss that element.
2. Briefly explain how pension gains and losses are recognized in earnings.
3. Describe for him the differences and similarities between the accumulated benefit obligation and the projected benefit obligation.
4. Explain the circumstances that would require Kemp to recognize an additional minimum liability.

Critical Thought Case 17–2
Barlow's Wife; relationship among pension elements

LGD Consulting is a medium-sized provider of environmental engineering services. The corporation sponsors a noncontributory, defined benefit pension plan. Alan Barlow, a new employee and participant in the pension plan, obtained a copy of the 1997 financial statements, partly to obtain additional information about his new employer's obligation under the plan. In part, the pension footnote reads as follows:

Note 8: Retirement Benefits

The Company has a defined benefit pension plan covering substantially all of its employees. The benefits are based on years of service and the employee's compensation during the last two years of employment. The company's funding policy is consistent with the funding requirements of federal law and regulations. Generally, pension costs accrued are funded. Plan assets consist primarily of stocks, bonds, commingled trust funds, and cash.

The net periodic pension expense for the company's retirement plan for 1997 included the following components:

		($ in 000s)
Service cost—increase in projected benefit obligation due to benefits earned during the year		$ 85.8
Interest cost on projected benefit obligation		171.4
Return on assets—actual	(183.6)	
Deferred gain (loss)	(17.2)	(200.8)
Net amortization		1.4
Net annual pension cost		$ 57.8

The funded status and amounts recognized in the consolidated balance sheets for the Company's defined benefit retirement plan at December 31, 1997, were as follows:

Plan assets at fair value	$2,631.6
Actuarial present value of benefit obligations	
Vested benefits	1,523.0
Nonvested benefits	124.8
Accumulated benefit obligation	1,647.8
Effect of projected future salary increases	537.0
Projected benefit obligation	2,184.8
Funded status	446.8
Unrecognized net gain	(270.4)
Unrecognized prior service cost	20.4
Prepaid pension cost	$ 196.8

The weighted-average discount rate and rate of increase in future compensation levels assumed in determining the actuarial present value of the projected benefit obligation were 9.3 percent and 7.5 percent, respectively. The weighted-average expected long-term rate of return on plan assets was 10.3 percent.

In attempting to reconcile amounts reported in the footnote with amounts reported in the income statement and balance sheet, Barlow became confused. He was able to find the pension expense on the income statement but was unable to make sense of the balance sheet amounts. Expressing his frustration to his wife, Barlow said, "It appears to me that the company has calculated pension expense as if they have the pension liability and pension assets they include in the footnote, but I can't seem to find those amounts in the balance sheet. In fact, there are several amounts here I can't seem to account for. They also say they've made some assumptions about interest rates, pay increases, and profits on invested assets. I wonder what difference it would make if they assumed other numbers."

Barlow's wife took accounting courses in college and remembers most of what she learned about pension accounting. She attempts to clear up her husband's confusion.

Required:
Assume the role of Barlow's wife. Answer the following questions for your husband.

1. Is Barlow's observation correct that the company has calculated pension expense on the basis of amounts not reported in the balance sheet?
2. What amount would the company report as a pension liability on the balance sheet?
3. What amount would the company report as a pension asset on the balance sheet?
4. Which of the other amounts reported in the disclosure note would the company report on the balance sheet?
5. The disclosure note reports an unrecognized gain as well as a deferred loss. How are these related? What do the amounts mean?
6. One of the components of the pension expense is net amortization. What amounts comprise this component?

Group Interaction Case 17–3
Barlow's Wife; relationship among pension elements

The focus of this case is question 1 in the previous case. Your instructor will divide the class into from two to six groups, depending on the size of the class. The mission of your group is to assess the correctness of Barlow's observation and to suggest the appropriate treatment of the pension obligation. The suggested treatment need not be that required by *SFAS 87*.

Required:

1. Each group member should deliberate the situation independently and draft a tentative argument prior to the class session for which the case is assigned.
2. In class, each group will meet for 10 to 15 minutes in different areas of the classroom. During that meeting, group members will take turns sharing their suggestions for the purpose of arriving at a single group treatment.
3. After the allotted time, a spokesperson for each group (selected during the group meetings) will share the group's solution with the class. The goal of the class is to incorporate the views of each group into a consensus approach to the situation.

Integrating Case 17–4
How was the adoption of *SFAS 87* an exception to the usual method of accounting for changes in accounting principle?

In Chapter 3 you learned that most changes in accounting principle require reporting the cumulative income effect of the change as part of earnings in the year of the change, but that five exceptions require retroactive restatement of prior years' financial statements. Also, a few changes mandated by new FASB accounting standards require neither of those approaches, and instead require or permit prospective application of the new standard. An example of this exception is *SFAS 87*, "Employers' Accounting for Pensions."

Required:
Explain how *SFAS 87* is an exception to the general method of accounting for changes in accounting principle.

Trueblood Accounting Case 17–5
Management's intent differs from the written terms of a deferred compensation plan

The following Robert M. Trueblood case is recommended for use with this chapter. The case provides an excellent opportunity for class discussion, group projects, and writing assignments. The case, along with Professor's Discussion Material, can be obtained from the Deloitte & Touche Foundation.

Case 94-10: *A No Cost Deferred Compensation Arrangement*

This case focuses on management's intent as it relates to a deferred compensation arrangement. Management's intent differs from the written terms of the plan. Decisions are required pertaining to (a) what is the arrangement, (b) how to account for it, and (c) what steps should management take to strengthen the written terms of the arrangement.

International Case 17–6
Accounting for pensions in other countries

Since its inception in 1973, the primary objective of the International Accounting Standards Committee (IASC) has been to narrow differences worldwide in accounting practices and the presentation of financial information. While progress has been made, the goal is far from having been met. Significant differences exist from country to country in the area of accounting for pensions. These differences impact on reported earnings and financial position in countries where these benefits are significant.

Required:
Choose a country other than the United States and:
1. Locate a recent annual report of a non-U.S. company.
2. Determine the way that country accounts for pensions. Include in your analysis:
   a. Whether and how the cost of providing pension benefits is reported in disclosure notes.
   b. Whether the obligation for the pension benefits is accrued in the balance sheet.
   c. The impact on the income statement, if any.

3. Prepare a short report highlighting the similarities and differences between the United States and your chosen country in the way pension benefits are accounted for.

Note: You can obtain copies of annual reports from the investor relations department of the corporation, a friendly stock broker, Public Register's Annual Report Service, at www.PRARS.com., or EDGAR, the Electronic Data Gathering and Retrieval service of the SEC, at www.sec.gov/.

Ethics Case 17–7
401(k) plan contributions

You are in your third year as internal auditor with VXI International, manufacturer of parts and supplies for jet aircraft. VXI began a defined contribution pension plan in 1995. The plan is a so-called 401(k) plan (named after the Tax Code section that specifies the conditions for the favorable tax treatment of these plans) that permits voluntary contributions by employees. Employees' contributions are matched with one dollar of employer contribution for every two dollars of employee contribution. Approximately $500,000 of contributions are deducted from employee paychecks each month for investment in one of three employer-sponsored mutual funds.

While performing some preliminary audit tests you happen to notice that employee contributions to these plans usually do not show up on mutual fund statements for up to two months following the end of pay periods from which the deductions are drawn. On further investigation, you discover that when the plan was first begun, contributions were invested within one week of receipt of the funds. When you question the firm's investment manager about the apparent change in the timing of investments, you are told, "Last year Mr. Maxwell (the CFO) directed me to initially deposit the contributions in the corporate investment account. At the close of each quarter, we add the employer matching contribution and deposit the combined amount in specific employee mutual funds."

Required:
1. What is Mr. Maxwell's apparent motivation for the change in the way contributions are handled?
2. Do you perceive an ethical dilemma?

Internet Case 17–8
Researching pension disclosures; retrieving information from the Internet

EDGAR, the Electronic Data Gathering, Analysis, and Retrieval system, performs automated collection, validation, indexing, acceptance, and forwarding of submissions by companies and others who are required by law to file forms with the U.S. Securities and Exchange Commission (SEC). All publicly traded domestic companies use EDGAR to make the majority of their filings. (Some foreign companies do so voluntarily.) Form 10-K or 10-KSB, including the annual report, is required to be filed on EDGAR. The SEC makes this information available on the Internet.

Required:
1. Access EDGAR on the Internet. The web address is www.sec.gov/.
2. Search for a company with which you are familiar and which you believe is likely to have a pension plan. (Older, established firms are good candidates). Access the company's most recent 10-K filing. Search or scroll to find the financial statements and related notes.
3. From the disclosure notes, determine the type of pension plan(s) the company has.
4. For any defined contribution plans, determine the contributions the company made to the plans on behalf of employees during the most recent three years.
5. For any defined benefit plans, determine the projected benefit obligation for the most recent year. Compare this obligation with the company's total long-term debt. What interest rate was used in estimating the PBO?
6. Repeat steps 2 through 4 for a second firm. Compare and contrast the types of pension plans offered. Are actuarial assumptions the same for defined benefit plans?

Trueblood Accounting Case 17–9
Curtailment of benefit plan; matching principle

The following Robert M. Trueblood case is recommended for use with this chapter. The case provides an excellent opportunity for class discussion, group projects, and writing assignments. The case, along with Professor's Discussion Material, can be obtained from the Deloitte & Touche Foundation.

Case 96-6: *Restructuring Super Timbers*

This case allows students to use their judgment in evaluating plan curtailments relating to early retirement packages, applying the matching principle. Decisions are required pertaining to (a) whether the early retirement packages give rise to curtailment gains or losses, and (b) whether the cost of the COO's annuity contract should be expensed as part of the restructuring charges.

Financial Analysis Case 17–10
Pension disclosures

Refer to the financial statements and related disclosure notes of Federal Express Corporation in the appendix to Chapter 1. Federal Express sponsors pension plans covering substantially all employees. The largest plan covers U.S. domestic employees age 21 and over, with at least one year of service, and provides benefits based on final average earnings and years of service. The plans are described in Note 8.

**Federal Express
Corporation**

Required:

1. Are Federal Express's pension plans overfunded or underfunded?
2. What amounts related to the pension plans are reported by Federal Express on the balance sheets for 1996 and 1995?
3. From the information provided, determine Federal Express's cash contribution to its pension plan assets during 1996.

Real World Case 17–11
Pension amendment

Charles Rubin is a 30-year employee of General Motors. Charles was pleased with recent negotiations between his employer and the United Auto Workers. Among other favorable provisions of the new agreement, the pact also includes a 13% increase in pension payments for workers under 62 with 30 years of service who retire during the agreement. Although the elimination of a cap on outside income earned by retirees has been generally viewed as an incentive for older workers to retire, Charles sees promise for his dream of becoming a part-time engineering consultant after retirement. What has caught Charles's attention is the following excerpt from an article in *The Wall Street Journal*:

DETROIT—**General Motors Corp.** said it will post a $170 million charge in the fourth quarter as a result of increases in retirement benefits for hourly United Auto workers employees.

The charge, related to GM's new tentative national labor contract with the UAW amounts to 22 cents a common and two cents a share of Class H stock, which is tied to the earnings of GM's Hughes Electronics unit, according to a filing with the Securities and Exchange Commission.

GM cautioned that its "unfunded pension obligation and 1997 pension expense are expected to be unfavorably impacted as a result of the recently completed labor negotiations."

Gabriella Stern, "GM to Record a Fourth-Quarter Charge of $170 Million Tied to New UAW Pact," *The Wall Street Journal*, Friday, November 15, 1996

Taking advantage of an employee stock purchase plan, Charles has become an active GM stockholder as well as employee. His stockholder side is moderately concerned by the article's reference to the unfavorable impact of the recently completed labor negotiations.

Required:

1. When a company modifies its pension benefits the way General Motors did, what name do we give the added cost? How is it accounted for?
2. What does GM mean when it says its "unfunded pension obligation and 1997 pension expense are expected to be unfavorably impacted as a result of the recently completed labor negotiations"?

EMPLOYEE BENEFIT PLANS

OVERVIEW

We discussed pension benefits in the previous chapter. Employee benefits also commonly include *postretirement* benefits other than pensions, like retiree health care coverage, as well as a variety of compensation plans provided *during* employment. Accounting for both types of benefits is the *same* in that they are forms of compensation for current service and, therefore, the cost of these benefits is recognized on an accrual basis during the years that employees earn the benefits. Accounting for the two types of benefits is *different* in that postretirement benefits create liabilities while stock-based compensation plans create shareholders' equity in some instances, but liabilities in others. These similarities and dissimilarities cause this to be a transition chapter, an interface between the several liability chapters (13–17) and shareholders' equity (19). Combined, the sequence of Chapters 13–19 represents the right-hand side of a balance sheet—equities.

LEARNING OBJECTIVES   After studying this chapter, you should be able to:

1. Describe the nature of postretirement benefit plans other than pensions and identify the similarities and differences in accounting for those plans and pensions.
2. Explain how the obligation for postretirement benefits is measured and how the obligation changes.
3. Determine the components of postretirement benefit expense.
4. Explain and implement the elective fair value approach for stock compensation plans.
5. Explain and implement the alternate intrinsic value approach to accounting for stock compensation plans.
6. Explain and implement the accounting for stock appreciation rights and differentiate between those that create liabilities and those that create equity.
7. Identify other preretirement compensation plans and the accounting treatment of those plans.

PROPER MOTIVATION?

A recent article in *The Wall Street Journal* discussed the choice by AT&T Corporation of John R. Walter as its president and chief operating officer. The article notes that Mr. Walter's compensation package includes elements beyond salary that are intended to motivate him not only to accept the offer but also to remain with the company and work to increase shareholder value. Excerpts from the article follow:

After months of secrecy and speculation about marquee chief-executive names, AT&T Corp. tapped a little-known executive from the printing industry to succeed chairman Robert E. Allen. John R. Walter, chairman of R.R. Donnelley & Sons Co., will serve for 14 months as AT&T president and chief operating officer before succeeding Mr. Allen as CEO on Jan. 1, 1998. Mr. Walter gets high marks for building a technologically savvy industry leader out of a family-owned printer known mostly for churning out the Good Book and the Big Book—the Bible and the Sears Roebuck catalog.

Mr. Walter is expected to command a far richer compensation package at AT&T: more than $1 million in salary, stock options to buy more than 700,000 shares and a hefty grant of restricted stock, according to individuals close to the situation.

Source: John J. Keller, Joann S. Lublin, James P. Miller and Susan Carey, "Why Did AT&T Choose John Walter?" *The Wall Street Journal,* Thursday, October 24, 1996.

QUESTIONS

1. Besides the compensation mentioned in the article, what other types of compensation do you think Mr. Walter might receive for his services?
2. How can a compensation package such as this serve as an incentive to Mr. Walter?
3. Mr. Walter received a "hefty grant of restricted stock." How should the grant be accounted for by AT&T?
4. Included were stock options to buy more than 700,000 shares. How will the options affect AT&T's compensation expense?

As indicated in the previous chapter, most companies have pension plans that provide for the future payment of retirement benefits to compensate employees for their current services. Many companies also furnish *other postretirement* benefits such as postretirement health care and life insurance benefits. In addition, companies often provide non-salary benefits prior to retirement. These preretirement benefits frequently involve compensation plans in which the amount of compensation is in some way tied to the market value of the employer's common stock. We refer to these as stock-based compensation plans. Still other forms of compensation are tied to performance measures other than stock values.

This chapter is divided into two parts. Postretirement benefit plans other than pensions are described in Part A. Preretirement compensation plans are discussed in Part B.

PART A   POSTRETIREMENT BENEFITS OTHER THAN PENSIONS

Learning objective 1
Describe the nature of postretirement benefit plans other than pensions and identify the similarities and differences in accounting for those plans and pensions.

OPENING CASE

Question 1

Until recently, postretirement benefit costs were accounted for on a pay-as-you-go basis; now they must be accrued.

Postretirement benefits encompass all types of retiree health and welfare benefits other than pensions. These may include medical coverage, dental coverage, life insurance, group legal services, and other benefits. By far the most common is health care benefits. One of every three U.S. workers participates in health care plans that provide for coverage that continues into retirement. The aggregate impact is considerable; the total obligation for all U.S. corporations is about $500 billion.

Prior to 1993, employers accounted for postretirement benefit costs on a pay-as-you-go basis, meaning the expense each year was simply the amount of insurance premiums or medical claims paid, depending on the way the company provides health care benefits. *SFAS 106* requires a completely different approach. The expected future health care costs for retirees now must be recognized as an expense over the years necessary for employees to earn the benefits.[1] This is the accrual basis which also is the basis for pension accounting.

In fact, accounting for postretirement benefits is similar in most respects to accounting for pension benefits. This is because the two forms of benefits are fundamentally similar. Each is a form of deferred compensation earned during the employee's service life and each can be estimated as the present value of the cost of providing the expected future benefits. General Motors described its plan as shown in Graphic 18–1.

GRAPHIC   18–1

Disclosures—General Motors

NOTE 5. Other Postretirement Benefits (in part)

The Corporation and certain of its domestic subsidiaries maintain hourly and salaried benefit plans that provide postretirement medical, dental, vision, and life insurance to retirees and eligible dependents. These benefits are funded as incurred from the general assets of the Corporation. Effective January 1, 1992, the Corporation adopted *SFAS No. 106,* Employers' Accounting for Postretirement Benefits Other Than Pensions. This Statement requires that the cost of such benefits be recognized in the financial statements during the period employees provide service to the Corporation.

Despite the similarities, though, there are a few differences in the characteristics of the benefits that necessitate differences in accounting treatment. Because accounting for the two types of retiree benefits is so nearly the same, our discussion in this chapter will emphasize the differences. This will allow you to use what you learned in the previous chapter regarding pension accounting as a foundation for learning how to account for other postretirement benefits, supplementing that common base only when necessary. Focusing on the differences also will reinforce your understanding of pension accounting.

---

[1]"Employers' Accounting for Postretirement Benefits Other Than Pensions," *Statement of Financial Accounting Standards No. 106,* (Norwalk, Conn.: FASB, 1990). The standard became effective (with some exceptions) in 1993.

What is a Postretirement Benefit Plan?

Before addressing the accounting ramifications, lets look at a typical retiree health care plan.[2] First, it's important to distinguish retiree health care benefits from health care benefits provided during an employee's working years. The annual cost of providing *preretirement* benefits is simply part of the annual compensation expense. However, most companies offer coverage that continues into retirement. It is the deferred aspect of these *postretirement* benefits that creates an accounting issue.

> Eligibility usually is based on age and/or years of service.

Usually a plan promises benefits in exchange for services performed over a designated number of years, or reaching a particular age, or both. For instance, a plan might specify that employees are eligible for postretirement benefits after both working 20 years and reaching age 62 while in service. Eligibility requirements and the nature of benefits usually are specified by a written plan, or sometimes only by company practice.

The Substantive Plan

The basis of accounting is the substantive plan. Usually, this is the written plan. Sometimes, though, a company's consistent practice of providing benefits a certain way is a better indication of the employer's real plan for postretirement benefits. For instance, a consistent practice of increasing or decreasing the retired employee's share of the cost of benefits might not be included in the written plan but better represents the substantive plan and therefore should be the basis for accounting for the plan. Anticipated changes in cost-sharing arrangements are considered when measuring the obligation and expense, before the plan actually is amended, *if* the company (a) can demonstrate the intent and ability to make the change and (b) has communicated the intended change to plan participants.

Postretirement Health Benefits and Pension Benefits Compared

Keep in mind that retiree health benefits differ fundamentally from pension benefits in some important respects:

1. The amount of *pension* benefits generally is based on the number of years an employee works for the company so that the longer the employee works, the higher are the benefits. On the other hand, the amount of *postretirement health care* benefits typically is unrelated to service. It's usually an all-or-nothing plan in which a certain level of coverage is promised on retirement, independent of the length of service beyond that necessary for eligibility.

2. Although coverage might be identical, the cost of providing the coverage might vary significantly from retiree to retiree and from year to year because of differing medical needs.

3. Postretirement health care plans often require the retiree to share in the cost of coverage through monthly contribution payments. For instance, a company might pay 80% of insurance premiums, with the retiree paying 20%. The net cost of providing coverage is reduced by these contributions as well as by any portion of the cost paid by Medicare or other insurance.

4. Coverage often is provided to spouses and eligible dependents.

5. Unlike pension plans, in most postretirement benefit plans, true vesting doesn't exist. An employee who leaves a company after full eligibility but prior to retirement cannot retain rights to benefits. To be eligible for postretirement health care benefits, she or he must retire as an employee of the company.[3]

---

[2] For convenience, our discussion focuses on health care benefits because these are by far the most common type of postretirement benefits other than pensions. But, the concepts we discuss apply equally to other forms of postretirement benefits.

[3] Under COBRA (Consolidated Omnibus B Retirement Act), employers must continue to provide health insurance premiums for 18 months after an employee's employment is terminated (3 years if the employee dies while employed).

Determining the Net Cost of Benefits

To determine the postretirement benefit obligation and the postretirement benefit expense, the company's actuary first must make estimates of what the postretirement benefit costs will be for current employees. Then, contributions to those costs by employees are deducted, as well as Medicare's share of the costs (for retirement years when the retiree will be 65 or more), to determine the estimated net cost of benefits to the employer:

GRAPHIC   18–2

Estimating the Net Cost of Benefits

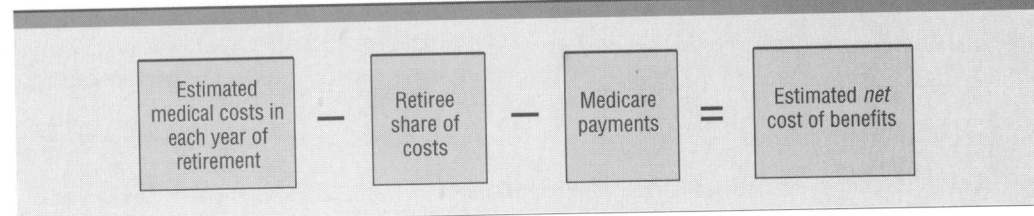

Remember, postretirement health care benefits are anticipated actual costs of providing the promised health care, rather than an amount estimated by a defined benefit formula. This makes these estimates inherently more intricate, particularly because health care costs in general are notoriously difficult to forecast. And, since postretirement health care benefits are partially paid by the retiree and by Medicare, these cost-sharing amounts must be estimated as well.

On the other hand, estimating postretirement benefits costs is similar in many ways to estimating pension costs. Both estimates entail a variety of assumptions to be made by the company's actuary. Many of these assumptions are the same; for instance both require estimates of:

> *Many of the assumptions needed to estimate postretirement health care benefits are the same as those needed to estimate pension benefits.*

1. A discount rate.
2. Expected return on plan assets (if the plan is funded).
3. Employee turnover.
4. Expected retirement age.
5. Expected compensation increases (if the plan is pay-related).
6. Expected age of death.
7. Number and ages of beneficiaries and dependents.

Of course, the relative importance of some estimates is different than for pension plans. Dependency status, turnover, and retirement age, for example, take on much greater significance. Also, additional assumptions become necessary as a result of differences between pension plans and other postretirement benefit plans. Specifically, it's necessary to estimate:

> *Some additional assumptions are needed to estimate postretirement health care benefits besides those needed to estimate pension benefits.*

1. The current cost of providing health care benefits at each age that participants might receive benefits (per capita claims cost).
2. Demographic characteristics of plan participants that might affect the amount and timing of benefits.
3. Benefit coverage provided by Medicare, other insurance, or other sources that will reduce the net cost of employer-provided benefits.
4. The expected health care cost trend rate.

> *The postretirement benefit obligation is the discounted present value of the benefits during retirement.*

Taking these assumptions into account, the company's actuary estimates what the net cost of postretirement benefits will be for current employees in each year of their expected retirement. The discounted present value of those costs is the **postretirement benefit obligation**.

Postretirement Benefit Obligation

There are two related obligation amounts—one measures the total obligation and the other refers to a specific portion of the total:

GRAPHIC   18–3

Two Views of the Obligation for Postretirement Benefits Other Than Pensions

1. **Expected Postretirement Benefit Obligation (EPBO):** The actuary's estimate of the total postretirement benefits (at their discounted present value) expected to be received by plan participants.
2. **Accumulated Postretirement Benefit Obligation (APBO):** The portion of the EPBO attributed to employee service to date.

Learning objective 2
Explain how the obligation
for postretirement benefits
is measured and how the
obligation changes.

Measuring the Obligation

To illustrate, assume the actuary estimates that the net cost of providing health care benefits to a particular employee during her retirement years has a present value of $9,103 as of the end of 1992. This is the EPBO. If the benefits (and therefore the costs) relate to an estimated 35 years of service[4] and seven of those years have been completed, the APBO would be:

$1,821 represents the
portion of the EPBO related
to the first 7 years of the
35-year service period.

$$\underset{\text{EPBO}}{\$9,103} \times \underset{\substack{\text{Fraction attributed} \\ \text{to service to date}}}{^{7}/_{35}} = \underset{\text{APBO}}{\$1,821}$$

If the assumed discount rate is 6%, a year later the EPBO will have grown to $9,649 simply because of a year's interest accruing at that rate ($9,103 × 1.06 = $9,649). Notice that there is no increase in the EPBO for service because, unlike the obligation in most pension plans, the total obligation is not increased by an additional year's service.

The APBO, however, is the portion of the EBPO related to service up to a particular date. Consequently, the APBO will have increased both because of interest and because the service fraction will be higher (service cost):

$2,205 represents the
portion of the EPBO related
to the first 8 years of the
35-year service period.

$$\underset{\text{EPBO}}{\$9,649} \times \underset{\substack{\text{Fraction attributed} \\ \text{to service to date}}}{^{8}/_{35}} = \underset{\text{APBO}}{\$2,205}$$

The two elements of the increase can be separated as follows:

The APBO increases each
year due to (a) interest
accrued on the APBO and
(b) the portion of the EPBO
attributed to that year.

APBO at the beginning of the year	$1,821
Interest cost: $1,821 × 6%	109
Service cost: ($9,649 × ¹/₃₅) portion of EPBO attributed to the year	275
APBO at the end of the year	$2,205

Attribution

Attribution is the process of assigning the cost of benefits to the years during which those benefits are assumed to be earned by employees. The approach required by *SFAS 106* is to assign an equal fraction of the EPBO to each year of service from the employee's date of hire to the employee's full eligibility date.[5] This is the date the employee has performed all the service necessary to have earned all the retiree benefits estimated to be received by that employee.[6] In our earlier example, we assumed the attribution period was 35 years and accordingly accrued $^{1}/_{35}$ of the EPBO each year. The amount accrued each year increases both the APBO and the postretirement benefit expense. In Illustration 18–1 we see how the 35-year attribution (accrual) period was determined.

The cost of benefits are
attributed to the years
during which those benefits
are assumed to be earned
by employees.

Some critics of *SFAS 106* feel there is a fundamental inconsistency between the way we measure the benefits and the way we assign the benefits to specific service periods. The benefits (EPBO) are measured with the concession that the employee may work beyond the full eligibility date; however, the attribution period does not include years of service after that date. The counter argument is the fact that at the full eligibility date the employee will have earned the right to receive the full benefits expected under the plan and the amount of the benefits will not increase with service beyond that date.[7]

The attribution period does
not include years of service
beyond the full eligibility
date even if the employee is
expected to work after that
date.

Postretirement Benefit Expense

Similar to pension expense, there are six potential components of postretirement benefit expense. Graphic 18–4 lists the six components, comparing each with its counterpart in pension accounting.

Learning objective 3
Determine the components
of postretirement benefit
expense.

---

[4] Assigning the costs to particular service years is referred to as the *attribution* of the costs to the years the benefits are assumed earned. We discuss attribution in a later section.

[5] If the plan specifically grants credit only for service from a date after employee's date of hire, the beginning of the attribution period is considered to be the beginning of that credited service period, rather than the employee's date of hire.

[6] Or any beneficiaries and covered dependents.

[7] "Employers' Accounting for Postretirement Benefits Other Than Pensions," *Statement of Financial Accounting Standards No. 106,* (Norwalk, Conn.: FASB, 1990), par. 219–239.

ILLUSTRATION 18–1

Determining the Attribution
Period

The attribution period spans
each year of service from
the employee's date of hire
to the employee's full
eligibility date.

Jessica Farrow was hired by Global Communications at age 22 at the beginning of 1986 and is expected to retire at the end of 2025 at age 61. The retirement period is estimated to be 20 years.*

Global's employees are eligible for postretirement health care benefits after both reaching age 56 while in service and having worked 20 years.

Since Farrow becomes fully eligible at age 56 (the end of 2020), retiree benefits are attributed to the 35-year period from her date of hire through that date. Graphically, the situation can be described as follows:

*You probably recognize this as the situation we used in the previous chapter to illustrate pension accounting.

GRAPHIC   18–4

Comparison of the
Components of
Postretirement Benefit
Expense and of Pension
Expense

The components of
postretirement benefit
expense are quite similar to
the components of pension
expense.

Component	Pension Expense	Postretirement Benefit Expense
Service cost	Portion of the PBO earned in the current period	Portion of the EPBO attributed to the current period
Interest cost	Increase in PBO due to the passage of time	Increase in APBO due to the passage of time
Return on plan assets	Earnings on plan investments	Same, if the postretirement benefit plan is funded
Prior service cost	Amortization of compensation cost from amending the plan	Same, but a negative amendment occurs more often in postretirement benefit plans
Losses or gains	Amortization of unexpected changes in either the obligation or plan assets	Same, and more frequent due to greater difficulty in making health benefit predictions
Transition amount	Amortization of difference between the liability and plan assets at adoption (adjusted for prepaid or accrued pension cost)	Same, and almost always a transition liability because few plans are funded

Recording the Expense

Recording the postretirement benefit expense is similar to recording pension expense. For illustration, assume the components of the expense combine to indicate a postretirement benefit expense of $12 million and that $2 million cash is paid to present retirees. The following journal entry would be appropriate:

	($ in millions)	
Postretirement benefit expense (given)	12	
Accrued postretirement benefit cost (difference)		10
Cash (retiree benefits paid[8])		2
To record postretirement benefit expense and payment of benefits.		

---

[8] Because we're assuming this plan is not funded, retiree benefits are being paid from company funds rather than from plan assets. If the plan were funded, the company's cash payment would have been its contribution to the plan's fund instead of payments to retirees.

The fact that the cash payment is less than the expense is typical. Unlike for pension benefits, the cash paid usually is the amount necessary to pay only the current year's medical costs, rather than an amount to anticipate future years' needs. This is because there are few tax incentives to encourage prefunding of retiree health care benefits like those for pension plans, and these benefits are not subject to the stringent funding requirements relating to pensions under ERISA. As a result, there typically is a cumulative underpayment reported as a liability—accrued postretirement benefit cost.

Components of the Expense

As indicated in Graphic 18–4, the components of the postretirement benefit expense are substantially the same as the components of pension expense. Some differences, though, deserve note.

Service Cost.   It's important to understand that the service cost for pensions reflects additional benefits employees earn from an additional year's service. The service cost for retiree health care plans, on the other hand, is simply an allocation to the current year of a portion of a fixed total cost.

Interest Cost.   As with other liabilities, interest accrues on the accumulated postretirement benefit obligation as time passes. As demonstrated earlier, this amount can be calculated as the assumed discount rate multiplied by the APBO at the beginning of the year. In comparison with pensions, this is analogous to the interest on a pension's projected benefit obligation.

Return on Plan Assets.   Unlike pension plans, many postretirement benefit plans are not funded currently. Those that are funded often are greatly underfunded. However, when these plans are funded, investing plan assets in income-producing assets lessens the amounts employers must eventually contribute to the fund. So, the return on plan assets reduces the net cost of having a postretirement benefit plan. Therefore, similar to pension expense, the return on plan assets each year reduces the amount recorded as postretirement benefit expense. As in the case of pensions, both the interest and return-on-assets components of the postretirement benefit expense do not directly represent employee compensation. Instead, they are financial items created only because the compensation is delayed and the obligation is funded currently.

> Most retiree health plans are not prefunded the way pension plans are.

Amortization of Prior Service Cost.   One difference regarding delayed recognition is that prior service cost is attributed to the service of active employees from the date of the amendment to the full eligibility date, not the expected retirement date.[9] Remember that prior service cost increases or reduces (if a negative plan amendment) the postretirement benefit cost. Since that cost is attributed to service up until the full eligibility date, it's consistent to attribute changes in that amount to a similar period. As with pensions, the pattern of attribution can follow the service method or the straight-line approach.

A negative plan amendment is one that reduces, rather than increases, the accumulated postretirement benefit obligation. This is not a rare occurrence. During the first two years following the adoption of *SFAS 106,* 79% of employers changed retiree medical plans in an effort to control costs. Of those, 78% increased retirees' share of costs; 1% eliminated coverage altogether.[10] The effect of a negative amendment should first be offset against any unrecognized prior service cost and, second, against any unrecognized transition obligation. If an excess remains after offsetting, it is amortized the same way as prior service cost (over the period to full eligibility).

> A negative plan amendment creates negative prior service cost.

Amortization of Deferred Net Losses or Net Gains.   As with pensions, gains and losses can occur when expectations are revised concerning either the obligation (APBO) or the return on plan assets. Graphic 18–5 summarizes the possibilities.

---

[9] If substantially all employees already are fully eligible for benefits when the amendment occurs, prior service cost would be amortized over the life expectancy of eligible employees instead.

[10] Ron Coddington, "USA Snapshots," Hewitt Associates Survey of 992 Large Employers, *USA Today,* November 8, 1994.

Gains and losses occur when either the APBO or the return on plan assets turns out to be different from the expected result.

A net gain or a net loss affects postretirement benefit expense only if it exceeds an amount equal to 10% of the APBO, or 10% of plan assets, whichever is higher.

Since the net gain exceeds an amount equal to the greater of 10% of the APBO or 10% of plan assets, part of the excess is amortized to postretirement benefit expense.

Accounting for losses or gains from revising expectations regarding postretirement benefits is precisely the same as for losses or gains on pensions. That is, neither a loss (gain) on the APBO nor a loss (gain) on plan assets is immediately recognized in postretirement benefit expense. Instead, losses and gains from either source are deferred as a means of smoothing income. The conceptual shortcomings and practical justification are described in more detail in the previous chapter. Here is a brief summary of that process.

Over time, deferred gains and losses tend to cancel one another out. As years pass there may be more gains than losses, or vice versa, preventing their offsetting one another completely. Only if a net gain or a net loss gets too large, must postretirement benefit expense be adjusted. *SFAS 106* defines too large as a net gain or a net loss at the beginning of a year that exceeds an amount equal to 10% of the APBO, or 10% of plan assets, whichever is higher. When this corridor is exceeded, the excess is amortized over the average remaining service period of active employees expected to receive benefits under the plan.

For illustration, assume that at the beginning of 1997, a company has an unrecognized net gain of $110 million. Also assume the APBO and plan assets are $800 million and $120 million, respectively, at that time. The average remaining service period of active employees expected to receive benefits under the plan is 15 years. The amount amortized to 1997 postretirement benefit expense is $2 million, calculated as follows:

Determining Net Gain Amortization—1997

	($ in millions)
Net gain (previous gains exceeded previous losses)	$110
10% of $800 ($800 is greater than $120): the corridor	(80)
Excess at the beginning of the year	30
Average remaining service period	÷ 15 years
Amount amortized to 1997 pension expense	**$ 2**

The amortization of a net gain *reduces* postretirement benefit expense; the amortization of a net loss *increases* postretirement benefit expense. Although losses and gains on other postretirement benefits are accounted for the same as losses and gains on pensions, they actually occur more frequently due to greater difficulty in making health benefit predictions.

Amortization of the Transition Obligation.   The accumulated postretirement benefit obligation existing when *SFAS 106* was adopted (1993 for most companies) is called the *transition obligation*. It, too, is recognized as part of the postretirement benefit expense. Depending on which of the two permitted methods is used, an employer can choose to recognize either:

The transition obligation is the APBO that existed when *SFAS 106* was first implemented.

The transition obligation can be expensed either immediately or over a period of years.

1.   The entire transition obligation immediately.[11]
2.   The transition obligation on a straight-line basis over the plan participants' future service periods (optionally over a 20-year period if that's longer).[12]

You may have noticed that when we first demonstrated the calculation of the APBO on page 777, it was for the seven years of Jessica Farrow's service prior to the adoption of *SFAS 106*. So,

---

[11] If recognized immediately, it is treated as the effect of an accounting change. We discuss the treatment of the adoption of new accounting standards as accounting changes in Chapter 21.

[12] The delayed recognition cannot result in less rapid recognition than accounting for the transition obligation on a pay-as-you-go basis.

the $1,821 APBO existing at that time also was the transition obligation pertaining to this single employee. For the entire employee pool, let's say the transition obligation is $12 million.

If recognized on a delayed basis over 20 years, postretirement benefit expense would include as one of its components $600,000 each year ($12 million ÷ 20) over the 20-year period. Recall that this is precisely the way a transition amount is amortized for pensions as described in the previous chapter. That is, the amortized portion of the transition obligation becomes one of the several components of the annual expense, along with other components including service cost, interest cost, return on plan assets, and amortized portions of unrecognized gains and losses and unrecognized prior service cost.

On the other hand, some companies chose to recognize the entire transition obligation immediately upon adopting *SFAS 106*. Then, the effect was to reduce net income in the year of the change by the total amount by which net income would have been reduced over many years if accrual of the postretirement benefit cost had been required prior to 1993. You should recognize this as the general approach to reporting a change in accounting principle, which the change to *SFAS 106* is. For our previous illustration and assuming a 40% tax rate, the journal entry would be:

		($ in millions)
Cumulative effect of accounting change (net effect)	7.2	
Deferred tax asset ($12 million × 40%)	4.8	
Accrued postretirement benefit cost[13] (EPBO × $^{7}/_{35}$)		12.0
To immediately recognize the transition liability.		

Remember that the cumulative effect of an accounting change is reported on the income statement net of its tax effect. The tax effect in this example requires explanation. First of all, the tax effect is deferred. Although for financial reporting purposes the income is reduced now, only the actual payments for retiree benefits can be deducted for tax purposes. This creates a temporary difference between financial reporting income and taxable income. For most companies, this produces a hefty deferred tax asset. Remember from Chapter 16 that temporary differences that generate future deductible amounts as they reverse give rise to deferred tax assets, representing the future tax benefits from those deductible amounts. In this case, when the postretirement benefit expense (already reported on the income statement) becomes tax deductible when paid in later years, the tax deduction generates lower income taxes. That future tax savings is represented in the meantime by a deferred tax asset.

Although larger for companies that chose to recognize the entire transition obligation when *SFAS 106* was first adopted, a deferred tax asset is created also when companies gradually recognize the obligation in advance of its being paid and deducted for tax purposes.

IBM Corporation chose to recognize the cumulative effect immediately as shown in Graphic 18–6.

GRAPHIC 18–6

Change to New Accounting Standard—IBM Corporation

Nonpension Postretirement Benefits (in part)

The company and its U.S. subsidiaries have defined benefit postretirement plans that provide medical, dental, and life insurance for retirees and eligible dependents. In 1990, the company established plan cost maximums in order to more effectively account for and control future medical costs.

Effective January 1, 1991, the company and its subsidiaries implemented on the immediate recognition basis, *Statement of Financial Accounting Standards (SFAS) 106,* "Employers' Accounting for Postretirement Benefits Other Than Pensions." This statement requires that the cost of these benefits, which are primarily for health care, be recognized in the financial statements during the employee's active working career. The company's previous practice was to accrue these costs principally at retirement.

The transition effect of adopting *SFAS 106* on the immediate recognition basis, as of January 1, 1991, resulted in a charge of $2,263 million to 1991 earnings, net of approximately $350 million of income tax effects.

---

[13] The accrued postretirement benefit cost account is analogous to the prepaid (accrued) pension cost account in the previous chapter which is an asset when it has a debit balance and a liability when it has a credit balance. Since the amount is always a liability when a company recognizes a transition obligation for postretirement benefits, we omit the prepaid portion of the account title.

Actually, the transition amount is measured the same way as it is for pensions: the difference between the APBO and plan assets, adjusted for any existing prepaid or accrued postretirement benefit cost. Theoretically, then, it could be either a transition liability or a transition asset. However, virtually all plans were unfunded in 1993 when most companies began accruing postretirement benefit costs for the first time. As a result, virtually all transition amounts were transition liabilities—quite large ones, in fact.

> So we're talking about hits bigger than the defense budget dragging the net worth of U.S. businesses. The accounting changes don't cost companies cash, but putting their financial portraits in a withering if more realistic light could hurt their ability to raise funds.[14]

The size of the unrecognized liability at transition was a major concern for many employers. For General Electric, the initial liability was $1.8 billion; for IBM it was $2.3 billion. How would shareholders react to recording such a sizable expense and liability all at once?[15] When General Motors announced in 1991 that it would take a one-time charge of $16 billion to $24 billion, the automaker's stock price dropped 4%. Or, if recognized on a delayed basis, what would be the effect of a slow degradation of earnings over a period of years? These concerns caused the decision of how the obligation should be recognized to be among the most controversial issues to face the FASB during its deliberations. Conceptually, the FASB favored requiring immediate recognition of the entire obligation. But, for practical reasons, delayed recognition was permitted as an alternative.[16] Unexpectedly, though, most companies chose to bite the bullet with a one-time charge to earnings. Many firms were experiencing down years in 1993 anyway, and explaining to shareholders a further reduction due to a change in accounting method seemed preferable to having to relive the experience over several years.

If recognized on a delayed basis, the amortization of the transition liability is but one of the six potential components of the postretirement benefit expense listed in Graphic 18–4.

Determining the Expense

Let's return to our earlier, single-employee illustration in which we determined that the APBO increased in 1993 due to (a) the service cost attributed to that year, $275, and (b) interest accrued on the APBO, $109 (see page 777). Let's also assume the plan is unfunded, so there's no return on plan assets. Of course, since this was the first year to recognize the obligation, there would have been no prior service cost or gains and losses as yet. So, the service cost and interest cost would be the only components of the postretirement benefit expense unless the transition cost is being recognized on a delayed basis. If we assume the $1,821 transition liability is amortized over 20 years, the 1993 expense would be $475 million as shown in Graphic 18–7.

GRAPHIC 18–7

Postretirement Benefit Expense

| The situation assumes no plan assets, prior service cost, or net gain or loss. |

Service cost	$275
Interest cost	109
Actual return on the plan assets	(none)
Adjusted for gain or loss on the plan assets	none
Amortization of prior service cost	none
Amortization of net loss	none
Amortization of transition liability ($1,821 ÷ 20 yrs)	91
Postretirement benefit expense	**$475**

Notice that, as for pensions, a single postretirement benefit expense is reported that includes three types of events that might otherwise be reported separately: (1) deferred compensation for employee service ($275), (2) interest created by the passage of time until that compensation is paid ($109), and (3) earnings from the investment of any plan assets (none in this instance).

The transition amount almost always is a transition liability because few plans were funded when *SFAS 106* was adopted.

---

[14] Don Snyder of the General Accounting Office, quoted in Kevin Anderson, "Health-Care Bill," *USA Today,* December 2, 1991.

[15] Some opponents of the requirement to accrue postretirement benefit costs argued that the requirement actually would cause companies to discontinue or reduce benefits offered to employees. Empirical evidence that this did in fact occur was found by Professors Mittelstaedt, Nichols, and Regier in "*SFAS No. 106* and Benefit Reductions in Employer-Sponsored Retiree Health Care Plans," *The Accounting Review,* October, 1995.

[16] "Employers' Accounting for Postretirement Benefits Other Than Pensions," *Statement of Financial Accounting Standards No. 106,* (Norwalk, Conn.: FASB, 1990), par. 252.

Also as for pensions, some changes in the obligation for postretirement benefits are not recognized as they occur. Instead, any prior service cost arising as a result of a plan amendment (or initiation) or gains and losses from changes in either the obligation or the investment of plan assets are recognized systematically over future periods. And the transition amount can be recognized on a delayed basis, too, if the employer elected not to recognize it immediately.

A Comprehensive Illustration

We assumed earlier that the EPBO at the end of 1992 was determined by the actuary to be $9,103. This was the present value on that date of all anticipated future benefits. Then we noted that the EPBO at the end of the next year would have grown by 6% to $9,649. This amount, too, would represent the present value of the same anticipated future benefits, but as of a year later. The APBO, remember, is the portion of the EPBO attributed to service performed to a particular date. So, we determined the APBO at the end of 1993 to be $9,649 × $8/35$, or $2,205. We determined the $275 service cost noted earlier for 1993 as the portion of the EPBO attributed to that year: $9,649 × $1/35$.

Now, let's review our previous discussion of how the EPBO, the APBO, and the postretirement benefit expense are determined by calculating those amounts a year later, at the end of 1994. Before doing so, however, we can anticipate the EPBO to be $9,649 × 1.06, or $10,228, the APBO to be $9/35$ of that amount or $2,630, and the 1994 expense to be $1/35$ of that amount, or $292. In Illustration 18–2 we see if our expectations are borne out by direct calculation.

ILLUSTRATION 18–2 **Determining the Postretirement Benefit Obligation** The EPBO is the discounted present value of the total benefits expected to be earned. The fraction of the EPBO considered to be earned so far is the APBO. The fraction of the EPBO considered to be earned this year is the service cost.	Assume the actuary has estimated the net cost of retiree benefits in each year of Jessica Farrow's 20-year expected retirement period to be the amounts shown in the calculation below. She is fully eligible for benefits at the end of 2020 and is expected to retire at the end of 2025. Calculating the APBO and the postretirement benefit expense at the end of 1994, nine years after being hired, begins with estimating the EPBO as follows. Steps to calculate the expected postretirement benefit obligation at the end of 1994, nine years after being hired: 1. Estimate the cost of retiree benefits in each year of the expected retirement period and deduct anticipated Medicare reimbursements and retiree cost-sharing to derive the net cost to the employer in each year of the expected retirement period. 2. Find the present value of each year's net benefit cost as of the retirement date. 3. Find the present value of the total net benefit cost as of the current date. This is the EPBO. 4. Multiply the EPBO by the attribution fraction, (service to date / total attribution period). This is the APBO. The service cost in any year is simply one year's worth of the EPBO: 5. Multiply the EPBO by $1/\text{total attribution period}$.

The steps are demonstrated in Illustration 18–2a.

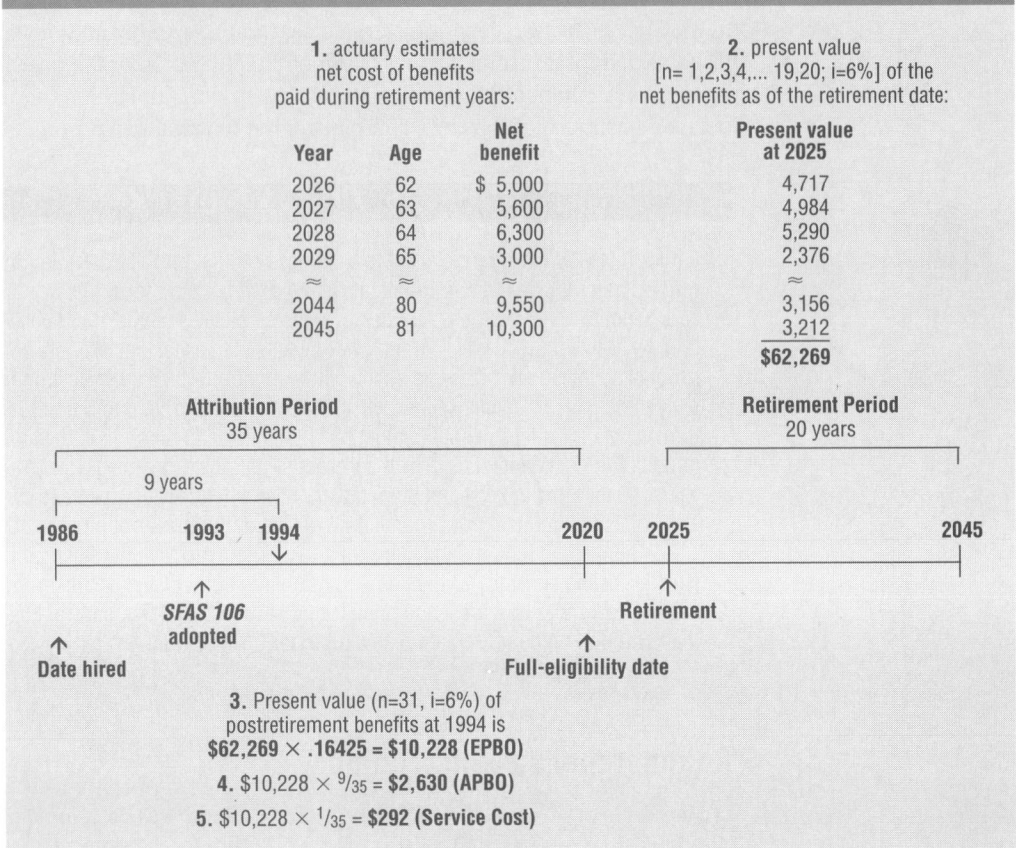

To give you an overall perspective, these numbers are provided for all years of Farrow's employment and retirement years in Appendix 18A.

Disclosures

The disclosures required are very similar to pension disclosures. For instance disclosures provide:

- A description of the plan.
- The net periodic postretirement benefit expense and its components.
- Reconciliation of the funded status of the plan with amounts reported in the balance sheet.
- The weighted-average discount rate, rate of compensation, and expected long-term rate of return used to measure the postretirement benefit obligation.

Some additional disclosures are needed for retiree health benefit plans, specifically:

- The assumed health care cost trend rate used to measure benefit costs for the next year, plus a description of the direction and pattern of change in the assumed trend rates thereafter.
- The effect on various amounts reported of a 1% increase in the health care cost trend rate.

General Motors provided the disclosures shown in Graphic 18–8 in its 1995 annual report.

GRAPHIC 18–8

Postretirement Benefit Disclosures—General Motors

NOTE 12. Postretirement Benefits Other than Pensions (in part)

The components of nonpension postretirement benefit cost are set forth below:

(Dollars in millions)	1995	1994	1993
Benefits earned during the year	$ 617.2	$ 955.4	$ 811.5
Interest accrued on benefits earned in prior years	3,120.0	3,114.2	3,177.5
Termination, curtailment, and settlement benefits	26.4	(233.0)	174.4
Amortization of net actuarial losses	(7.4)	407.4	—
Amortization of prior service cost due to plan changes	(115.9)	(121.7)	—
Total non-pension postretirement benefits cost	$3,640.3	$4,122.3	$4,163.4

The table below displays the components of General Motors' net postretirement benefit obligation, as recognized in the Consolidated Balance Sheet:

(Dollars in millions)	December 31 1995	December 31 1994
Accumulated postretirement benefits obligation (APBO) attributable to		
Current retirees	$23,155.1	$21,562.3
Fully eligible active plan participants	5,295.6	3,984.7
Other active plan participants	12,411.1	11,196.1
APBO	40,861.8	36,743.1
Unamortized prior service cost due to plan changes	795.4	958.3
Unamortized net amount resulting from changes in plan experience and actuarial assumptions	(62.1)	2,316.8
Net obligation recognized in Consolidated Balance Sheet	41,595.1	$40,018.2

The following table summarizes the principal assumptions used in determining the actuarial value of the APBO:

	December 31 1995	December 31 1994
Weighted-average discount rate	7.5%	8.8%
Weighted-average rate of increase in future compensation level related to pay-related life insurance	4.3%	4.2%
Base weighted-average health-care cost trend rate (a)		
1995		8.7%
1996	6.5%	
Ultimate sustained weighted average health care cost trend rate in 2002	5.0%(b)	5.5%

(a) Current year trend rate assumed at beginning of year as adjusted to actual in determining year-end obligations.
(b) Rate remains at 6.5% through 1999, and then decreases on a linear basis through 2002, to the ultimate weighted-average trend rate of 5.0%.

The following decreases would result from a one percentage point increase in the weighted average discount rate:

(Dollars in millions)	1995	1994
APBO	$4,500	$3,800

The following increases would result from one percentage point increase in the weighted-average health-care cost trend rates:

(Dollars in millions)	1995	1994
APBO	$5,000	$3,950
Service and interest components of postretirement expense	$ 470	$ 600

CONCEPT REVIEW EXERCISE   OTHER POSTRETIREMENT BENEFITS

Technology Group, Inc., has an unfunded retiree health care plan. The actuary estimates the net cost of providing health care benefits to a particular employee during his retirement years to have a present value of $24,000 as of the end of 1997 (the EPBO). The benefits and therefore the expected postretirement benefit obligation relate to an estimated 36 years of service and 12 of those years have been completed. The interest rate is 6%.

Required:
Pertaining to the one employee only:

1. What is the accumulated postretirement benefit obligation at the end of *1997?*
2. What is the expected postretirement benefit obligation at the end of *1998?*
3. What is service cost to be included in 1998 postretirement benefit expense?
4. What is interest cost to be included in 1998 postretirement benefit expense?

5. What is the accumulated postretirement benefit obligation at the end of *1998?*
6. Show how the APBO changed during 1998 by reconciling the beginning and ending balances.
7. What is 1998 postretirement benefit expense, assuming no gains or losses, no prior service cost, and no unamortized transition cost?

 CONCEPT REVIEW EXERCISE   SOLUTION

1. What is the accumulated postretirement benefit obligation at the end of *1997?*

    $24,000   × $^{12}/_{36}$ = $8,000
    EPBO   Fraction   APBO
                    earned

2. What is the expected postretirement benefit obligation at the end of *1998?*

    $24,000   ×   1.06   = $25,440
    EPBO   To accrue   EPBO
    1997   interest   1998

3. What is service cost to be included in 1998 postretirement benefit expense?

    $25,440   × $^{1}/_{36}$ = $707
    EPBO   Earned   service
    1998   in 1998   cost

4. What is interest cost to be included in 1998 postretirement benefit expense?

    $8,000 (beginning APBO) × 6% = $480

5. What is the accumulated postretirement benefit obligation at the end of *1998?*

    $25,440   × $^{13}/_{36}$ = $9,187
    EPBO   Fraction   APBO
    1998   earned   1998

6. Show how the APBO changed during 1998 by reconciling the beginning and ending balances.

APBO at the beginning of 1998 (given)	$8,000
Service cost: (from req. 3)	707
Interest cost: (from req. 4)	480
APBO at the end of 1998 (from req. 5)	$9,187

7. What is 1998 postretirement benefit expense, assuming no gains or losses, no prior service cost, and no unamortized transition cost?

Service cost	$ 707
Interest cost	480
Actual return on the plan assets	(not funded)
Adjusted for: gain or loss on the plan assets	(not funded)
Amortization of prior service cost	none
Amortization of net loss	none
Amortization of transition liability	none
Postretirement benefit expense	$1,187

GLOBAL PERSPECTIVE

In the United States, postretirement benefits are accrued in a manner similar to pensions. In Canada, where benefits are commonly provided, three alternatives are permitted: (1) accrual, (2) pay-as-you-go, and (3) accrual only when employees retire. Disclosure of the method used is required. In the United Kingdom, accounting is similar to the United States. In most other countries, little official guidance is offered.

In many countries, postretirement benefits other than pensions are rare. In Japan, for instance, the prevalence of government-sponsored plans has caused most Japanese companies not to provide separate benefits.

PART # B PRERETIREMENT COMPENSATION PLANS

Stock-Based Compensation Plans

Learning objective 4
Explain and implement the elective fair value approach for stock compensation plans.

OPENING CASE

Question 2

The accounting objective is to record compensation expense over the periods in which related services are performed.

Employee compensation plans frequently include stock-based awards. These may be outright awards of shares, stock options, or cash payments tied to the market price of shares. Sometimes only key executives participate in a stock benefit plan. Typically, an executive compensation plan is tied to performance in a strategy that uses compensation to motivate its recipients. Some firms, including Travelers Insurance, pay their directors entirely in shares. Actual compensation depends on the market value of the shares. Obviously, that's quite an incentive to act in the best interests of shareholders.

Although the variations of stock-based compensation plans are seemingly endless, each shares common goals. Whether the plan is a stock award plan, a stock option plan, a stock appreciation rights (SARs) plan, or one of the several similar plans, the goals are to provide compensation to designated employees, while sometimes providing those employees with some sort of performance incentive. Likewise, our goals in accounting for each of these plans are the same for each: (1) to determine the value of the compensation and (2) to expense that compensation over the periods in which participants perform services. The issue is not trivial. The median total compensation of chief executives of the 350 largest U.S. businesses, including salary, bonuses, gains from the exercise of stock options, long-term incentive payouts and the value of restricted stock at the time of grant, was $1,992,490 in 1995.

Stock Award Plans

Usually, restricted shares are subject to forfeiture if the employee doesn't remain with the company.

Executive compensation sometimes includes a grant of shares of stock. Usually, such shares are restricted in such a way as to provide some incentive to the recipient. Typically, restricted stock award plans are tied to continued employment. In a restricted stock plan, shares actually are awarded in the name of the employee, although the company might retain physical possession of the shares. The employee has all rights of a shareholder, subject to certain restrictions or forfeiture. Ordinarily, the shares are subject to forfeiture by the employee if employment is terminated within some specified number of years from the date of grant. The employee usually is not free to sell the shares during the restriction period and a statement to that effect often is inscribed on the stock certificates. These restrictions give the employee incentive to remain with the company until rights to the shares vest. Graphic 18–9 describes the restricted award plan for the Peerless Manufacturing Company.

GRAPHIC   18–9

Restricted Stock Award Plan—Peerless Manufacturing Company

Note F Restricted Stock Plans

The Company has a restricted stock plan whereby the Company can award up to 75,000 shares of common stock to employees. Sale of the stock awarded is restricted for five years from the date of grant. For the year ended June 30, 1995, the Company awarded 12,000 shares of common stock which had a fair value at the date of grant of $135,000. There were no awards for the years ended June 30, 1994 or 1996. Compensation under the plan is charged to earnings over the restriction period and amounted to $63,357, $67,234 and $18,907 in 1996, 1995 and 1994, respectively. At June 30, 1996, 8,750 shares were available for issuance.

OPENING CASE

Question 3

The compensation associated with a share of restricted stock (or nonvested stock) is the market price of an unrestricted share of the same stock. This amount is accrued as compensation expense over the service period for which participants receive the shares, usually from the date of grant to when restrictions are lifted (the vesting date).[17] This is demonstrated in Illustration 18–3.

---

[17] Restricted stock plans usually are designed to comply with Tax Code Section 83 to allow employee compensation to be nontaxable to the employee until the year the shares become substantially vested, which is when the restrictions are lifted. Likewise, the employer gets no tax deduction until the compensation becomes taxable to the employee.

The total compensation is the market value of the shares ($12) times five million shares.

The $60 million is accrued to compensation expense over the four-year service period.

When restrictions are lifted, paid-in capital—restricted stock, is replaced by common stock and paid-in capital—excess of par.

Under its restricted stock award plan, Universal Communications grants five million of its $1 par common shares to certain key executives at January 1, 1997. The shares are subject to forfeiture if employment is terminated within four years. Shares have a current market price of $12 per share.

January 1, 1997

No entry

Calculate total compensation expense:

$12	Fair value per share
x 5 million	Shares awarded
= $60 million	Total compensation

The total compensation is to be allocated to expense over the four-year service (vesting) period: 1997–2000

$60 million ÷ 4 years = $15 million per year

December 31, 1997, 1998, 1999, 2000 ($ in millions)

Compensation expense ($60 million ÷ 4 years)	15	
Paid-in capital—restricted stock		15

December 31, 2000

Paid-in capital—restricted stock (5 million shares at $12)	60	
Common stock (5 million shares at $1 par)		5
Paid-in capital—excess of par (to balance)		55

Once the shares vest and the restrictions are lifted, paid-in capital—restricted stock is replaced by common stock and paid-in capital—excess of par.

Additional Consideration

An alternative way of accomplishing the same result is to debit deferred compensation for the full value of the restricted shares ($60 million in the Illustration) on the date they are granted:

Deferred compensation (5 million shares at $12)	60	
Common stock (5 million shares at $1 par)		5
Paid-in capital—excess of par (to balance)		55

If so, deferred compensation is reported as a reduction in shareholders' equity resulting in a zero net effect on shareholders' equity. Then, deferred compensation is credited when compensation expense is debited over the service period. Just as in Illustration 18–3, the result is an increase in both compensation expense and shareholders' equity each year over the vesting period. If you look at Note 6 in the Federal Express annual report in the appendix to Chapter 1, you'll notice that Federal Express records restricted stock this way.

The amount of the compensation is measured at the date of grant—at the market price on that date. Any market price changes that might occur after that don't affect the total compensation.

If restricted stock is forfeited because, say, the employee quits the company, related entries previously made would simply be reversed. This would result in a decrease in compensation expense in the year of forfeiture. The total compensation, adjusted for the forfeited amount, is then allocated over the remaining service period.

Stock Option Plans

More commonly, employees aren't actually awarded shares, but rather are given the option to buy shares in the future. In fact, options have become an integral part of the total compensation package for key officers of most medium and large companies.[18] As with any compensation plan, the accounting objective is to report compensation expense during the period of service for which the compensation is given.

---

[18] In a recent survey of 600 corporations, 572 companies disclosed the existence of stock option plans. AICPA, *Accounting Trends and Techniques*, 1995.

Expense—The Great Debate.

Stock option plans give employees the option to purchase (a) a specified number of shares of the firm's stock, (b) at a specified price, (c) during a specified period of time. One of the most heated controversies in standard-setting history has been the debate over the amount of compensation to be recognized as expense for stock options. At issue is how the value of stock options is measured, which for most options determines whether any expense at all is recognized.

Conceptually, several ways to measure the compensation are possible. For example, the fair value of the services being compensated seems to be an appealing measure but is difficult to determine objectively. Historically, options have been measured at their intrinsic values—the simple difference between the market price of the shares and the option price at which they can be acquired. For instance, an option that permits an employee to buy $25 stock for $10 has an intrinsic value of $15. However, plans in which the exercise price equals the market value of the underlying stock at the date of grant (which describes most executive stock option plans) have no intrinsic value and therefore result in zero compensation when measured this way, even though the fair value of the options can be quite significant. About half of the chief executives of the largest U.S. companies cashed in stock options in 1995 for a median gain of over $600,000. In 1992, Walt Disney chairman, Michael Eisner, exercised enough stock options to realize a pretax profit of $126.9 million from selling 3.45 million shares. To many, it seems counterintuitive to not recognize compensation expense for plans that routinely provide executives with a substantial part of their total compensation.

This is where the controversy ensues. In 1993, the FASB issued an Exposure Draft of a new standard that would have required companies to measure options at their *fair values* at the time they are granted and to expense that amount over the appropriate service period. To jump straight to the punch line, the FASB bowed to public pressure and agreed to withdraw the requirement before it became a standard. The FASB consented to encourage, rather than require, that fair value compensation be recognized as expense. Companies are permitted to continue accounting under *APB Opinion 25* (the intrinsic value method referred to in the previous paragraph).[20] Companies that choose to ignore the FASB's recommendation to recognize fair value compensation as expense on the income statement are required instead to provide essentially the same information in disclosure notes.[21] Before we move to the details of the two alternative approaches to accounting for fixed stock options, it's important to look back at what led the FASB to first propose fair value accounting and later rescind that proposal.

Although the FASB had included reconsideration of existing stock option accounting on its agenda since 1984, it took intense pressure from the public, the SEC, and Congress to accelerate the project. As the 1990s began, the public was becoming increasingly aware of the enormity of executive compensation in general and compensation in the form of stock options in particular. The lack of accounting for this compensation was apparent, prompting the SEC to encourage the FASB to move forward on their stock option project. Even Congress got into the fray when, in 1992, a bill was introduced that would require firms to report compensation expense based on the fair value of options. Motivated by this encouragement, the FASB issued its exposure draft in 1993. The real disharmony began then. Opposition to the proposed standard was broad and vehement; and that perhaps is an understatement. Critics based their opposition on one or more of three objections:

1. Options with no intrinsic value at issue have zero fair value and should not give rise to expense recognition. This argument carried probably the least weight in the deliberations. The FASB, and even some critics of the proposal, were adamant that options provide valuable compensation at the grant date to recipients.

2. It is impossible to measure the fair value of the compensation on the grant date. The contention of these critics was that employee stock options usually can't be traded in the marketplace and thus don't have readily determinable market prices. The FASB argued

Michael Spindler, chief executive of Apple Computer, reaped hefty profits: Using options, he bought the stock at about $26 and sold it for roughly $46, taking in $2.39 million.[19]

OPENING CASE

Question 4

After lengthy debate, the FASB consented to encourage, rather than require, that the fair value of options be recognized as expense.

There were consistent criticisms of the FASB's requirement to expense option compensation.

---

[19] Diane Abt, "Apple Officials Sell Shares in Computer Firm," *Bloomberb Business News*, September 11, 1995.

[20] "Accounting for Stock Issued to Employees," *Opinions of the Accounting Principles Board No. 25*, (New York: AICPA, 1972).

[21] "Accounting for Stock-Based Compensation," *Statement of Financial Accounting Standards No. 123*, (Stamford Conn.: FASB, 1995).

vigorously that value can be approximated, though, using one of several **option pricing models**. These are statistical models that use computers to incorporate information about a company's stock and the terms of the stock option to estimate the options' fair value. We might say the FASB position is that it's better to be approximately right than precisely wrong.

3. The proposed standard would have unacceptable economic consequences. Essentially, this argument asserted that requiring this popular means of compensation to be expensed would cause companies to discontinue the use of options. Predicted effects ranged from undue penalties on middle-level managers, to stifling the growth of the technology industry and other growth companies, to impeding the recovery of the economy itself.

The opposition included corporate executives, auditors, members of Congress, and the SEC.[22] Ironically, the very groups that provided the most impetus for the rule change initially—the SEC and Congress—were among the most effective detractors in the end. The only group that offered much support at all was the academic community, and that was by-and-large nonvocal support. In reversing its decision, the FASB was not swayed by any of the specific arguments of any opposition group. Dennis Beresford, chair of the FASB, indicated that it was fear of government control of the standard-setting process that prompted the Board to modify its position. The Board remained steadfast that the proposed change was appropriate.

In backing away from its original proposal, the FASB did not completely abandon its position on option accounting. Instead, it decided to encourage, rather than require, expensing of the fair value of option compensation in the income statement. Companies that choose to continue accounting under *APB Opinion 25* must still follow fair value accounting to comply with enhanced disclosure requirements. The disclosures are designed to allow investors and creditors to compare companies that choose the elective accounting approach and those that do not. So, even though the vast majority of companies do not expense option compensation, it's important that we be familiar with the elective approach. The next section describes that approach.

Recognizing the Fair Value of Options (The Elective Fair Value Approach).

> The fair value of a stock option can be determined by employing a recognized option pricing model.

Companies are encouraged, but not required, to estimate the fair value of stock options on the grant date. This requires the use of one of several option pricing models. These statistical models assimilate a variety of information about a company's stock and the terms of the stock option to estimate the options' fair value. The model should take into account the:

> An option pricing model takes into account several variables.

- Exercise price of the option.
- Expected term of the option.
- Current market price of the stock.
- Expected dividends.
- Expected risk-free rate of return during the term of the option.
- Expected volatility of the stock.

Option-pricing theory, on which the pricing models are based, is a topic explored in depth in finance courses and is subject to active empirical investigation and development. A simplified discussion is provided in Appendix 18B.[23]

The total compensation as estimated by the options' fair value is reported as compensation expense over the period of service for which the options are given. The service period is the vesting period in Illustration 18–4.

> Unanticipated forfeitures are treated as a change in estimate, so the effect is a reduction in current and future expense, not previously recorded expense.

Forfeitures.   If previous experience indicates that a material number of the options will be forfeited before they vest (due to employee turnover or violation of other terms of the options), it's permissible, but not required, to adjust the fair value estimate on the grant date to reflect that expectation. For instance, if a forfeiture rate of 4% is expected, the estimated total compensation would be 96% of $80 million.

---

[22] All of the "Big Six" CPA firms lobbied against the proposal. Senator Lieberman of Connecticut introduced a bill in Congress that if passed would have forbidden the FASB from passing a requirement to expense option compensation. One of the SEC's commissioners wrote an editorial in opposition to the proposal: J. Beese, Jr., "A Rule that Stunts Growth," *The Wall Street Journal*, February 8, 1994, p. 18.

[23] An expanded discussion is provided in *SFAS 123*.

ILLUSTRATION   18–4

Stock Option Plan—The Elective Fair Value Approach

At January 1, 1997, Universal Communications grants options that permit key executives to acquire 10 million of the company's $1 par common shares within the next eight years, but not before December 31, 2000 (the vesting date). The exercise price is the market price of the shares on the date of grant, $35 per share. The fair value of the options, estimated by an appropriate option pricing model, is $8 per option.

January 1, 1997

No entry

[handwritten: MV = $35 / EXERCISE PRICE: $35 / Comp. Exp = $0 } APB opinion 25 method]

Calculate total compensation expense:

$ 8	Estimated fair value per option
× 10 million	Options granted
= $80 million	Total compensation

The total compensation is to be allocated to expense over the four-year service (vesting) period: 1997–2000

$80 million ÷ 4 years = $20 million per year

December 31, 1997, 1998, 1999, 2000

	($ in millions)	
Compensation expense ($80 million ÷ 4 years)	20	
Paid-in capital—stock options		20

> Fair value is estimated at the date of grant.

> The value of the award is expensed over the service period for which the compensation is provided.

If no forfeitures had been anticipated, but material forfeitures occur later, amounts previously expensed would not be altered. Instead, paid-in capital—stock options would be reduced by the fair value of options forfeited times the fraction previously expensed. The offsetting credit is to compensation expense, resulting in a decrease in compensation expense in the year of forfeiture. Then, the remaining total compensation, adjusted for the value of forfeited options, would be allocated over the remaining service period.

When Options Are Exercised.   If half the options in Illustration 18–4 (five million shares) are exercised on July 11, 2003, when the market price is $50 per share, the following journal entry is recorded:

> Recording the exercise of options is not affected by the market price on the exercise date.

July 11, 2003	($ in millions)	
Cash ($35 exercise price × 5 million shares)	175	
Paid-in capital—stock options (½ account balance)	40	
Common stock (5 million shares at $1 par per share)		5
Paid-in capital—excess of par (to balance)		210

Notice that the market price at exercise is irrelevant. Changes in the market price of underlying shares do not influence the previously measured fair value of options.

When Unexercised Options Expire.   If options that have vested expire without being exercised, the following journal entry is made (assuming none of the options in our illustration were exercised):

> Paid-in capital—stock options becomes paid-in capital—expiration of stock options, when options expire without being exercised.

	($ in millions)	
Paid-in capital—stock options (account balance)	80	
Paid-in capital—expiration of stock options		80

In effect, we simply rename the paid-in capital attributable to the stock option plan. Compensation expense for the four years' service, as measured on the measurement date, is not affected.

Tax Reasons For How Option Plans Are Structured.   It is common for the option price to be equal to the market price at the date of grant as it is in the preceding illustration. One important reason is the ability to avoid expensing compensation when the elective fair value approach is not chosen. Another reason is that this is one requirement for a plan to qualify as an incentive stock option plan under the Tax Code. There are other requirements, but they are unimportant to our discussion here. Under an **incentive plan**, the recipient pays no tax at the time of the grant or

> Tax treatment favors the executive in an incentive stock option plan.

when the options are exercised. Instead, the tax on the difference between the exercise price and the market price at the exercise date isn't paid until any shares acquired are subsequently sold. On the other hand, the company gets no tax deduction at all. Hewlett Packard provides an example of an incentive plan in Graphic 18–10.

Incentive Compensation Plans (in Part)

The company has three principal stock option plans . . . All plans permit options granted to qualify as "Incentive Stock Options" under the Internal Revenue Code. The exercise price of a stock option is generally equal to the fair market value of the company's common stock on the date the option is granted.

An incentive plan offers favorable tax treatment to the *executive*; but a **nonqualified plan** offers favorable tax treatment to the *employer*. With a nonqualified plan, the employee cannot delay paying tax. The tax that could be deferred until the shares are sold under an incentive plan must be paid at the exercise date under a nonqualified plan. However, the employer is permitted to deduct the difference between the exercise price and the market price at the exercise date. Since tax treatment favors the employer in a nonqualified stock option plan, why are the vast majority of options structured as incentive plans? There are two reasons:

> Tax treatment favors the employer in a nonqualified stock option plan.

> Options usually are structured as incentive plans.

- The favorable tax treatment provided to executives by incentive plans allows companies to use the plans to attract and retain quality management personnel.
- Due to Tax Code requirements, incentive plans typically offer an exercise price equal to the market price on the grant date. The market price usually exceeds the exercise price in a nonqualified plan. This difference allows companies to elect not to report compensation expense for an incentive plan; whereas a nonqualified plan requires earnings to be reduced by compensation expense. We discuss this next.

Additional Consideration

Tax Consequences of Stock-Based Compensation Plans

In Illustration 18–4 we ignored the tax effect. To illustrate the effect on taxes, let's assume Universal Communications' income tax rate is 40%.

Case 1. Recall from our earlier discussion that with an incentive plan, the employer receives no tax deduction at all. If Universal's plan qualifies as an incentive plan, the company will receive no tax deduction upon exercise of the options and thus no tax consequences.

> Because an incentive plan provides no tax deduction, it has no deferred tax consequences.

Case 2. On the other hand, if we assume the plan does not qualify as an incentive plan, Universal will deduct the difference between the exercise price and the market price at the exercise date. Recall from Chapter 16 that this creates a temporary difference between accounting income (for which compensation expense is recorded currently) and taxable income (for which the tax deduction is taken later upon the exercise of the options). Under *SFAS 123*, we assume the temporary difference is the cumulative amount expensed for the options. The following entries would be recorded on the dates shown:

December 31, 1997, 1998, 1999, 2000	($ in millions)	
Compensation expense ($80 million ÷ 4 years)	20	
Paid-in capital—stock options		20
Deferred tax asset (40% × $20 million)	8	
Income tax expense		8

> A deferred tax asset is recognized now for the future tax savings from the tax deduction when the options are exercised.

The after-tax effect on earnings is thus $12 million each year.

If all of the options (ten million shares) are exercised in April, 2002:

Cash ($35 exercise price × 10 million shares)	350	
Paid-in capital—stock options (account balance)	80	
Common stock (10 million shares at $1 par per share)		10
Paid-in capital—excess of par (to balance)		420

If the eventual tax savings exceed the deferred tax asset, the difference is recognized as equity.

a. Options exercised when the tax benefit exceeds the deferred tax asset:
    If the market price is $50 per share:

Income taxes payable [($50 – 35) × 10 million shares × 40%]	60	
Deferred tax asset (4 years × $8 million)		32
Paid-in capital—tax effect of stock options (remainder)*		28

If the eventual tax savings is less than the deferred tax asset, the difference is recognized as a reduction in either tax expense or previously recognized equity from the same source.

b. Options exercised when the tax benefit is less than the deferred tax asset:
    If the market price is $40 per share:

Income taxes payable [($40 – 35) × 10 million shares × 40%]	20	
Income tax expense or Paid-in capital—		
tax effect of stock options† (remainder)	12	
Deferred tax asset (4 years × $8 million)		32

*This treatment is consistent with a provision of *SFAS 109* (par. 36C) that requires the tax effect of an increase or decrease in equity (Paid-in capital—stock options, in this case) be allocated to equity.
†Paid-in capital—tax effect of stock options is debited only if that account has a sufficient credit balance from previous transactions in which the tax benefit exceeded the deferred tax asset.

The tax consequences of all nonqualifying stock options, including those for which companies choose to account for options in accordance with *APB Opinion 25,* as well as restricted stock plans also are accounted for in the manner demonstrated above.

Learning objective 5
Explain and implement the alternate intrinsic value approach to accounting for stock compensation plans.

Recognizing the Intrinsic Value of Options (The Alternate Intrinsic Value Approach).   As pointed out in a previous discussion, most companies are adamantly opposed to expensing the fair value of options. As you might expect, most choose *not* to adopt the elective fair value approach. These companies continue to account for options in accordance with *APB Opinion 25* issued in 1972. By this approach, the value of fixed options is measured at the grant date in an amount equal to their intrinsic values rather than their fair values. Intrinsic value is simply the difference between the market price of the shares and the exercise price at which they can be acquired. In other words, it is the benefit the holder of an option would realize by exercising the option and immediately selling the underlying stock.

An option that permits an employee to buy $25 stock for $10 has an intrinsic value of $15.

An option whose exercise price equals the market price of the underlying stock has zero intrinsic value.

Market Value Equals Exercise Price.   An option whose exercise price equals or exceeds the market price of the underlying stock has zero intrinsic value. This was the situation in Illustration 18–4. Under the *APB Opinion 25* alternate approach, then, no compensation would be recorded for the options described in the illustration. Although the financial statements would be unaffected by the existence of options whose exercise price equals or exceeds the market price, accompanying disclosure notes would report essentially the same information as would have been provided in the financial statements if the elective fair value approach is followed. As a result, companies opting to forgo the elective fair value approach still must make the same fair value calculations (Illustration 18–4) as companies electing that approach. In fact, one required disclosure is pro forma (as if) net income and earnings per share determined as if the elective method had been applied in the financial statements. The objective of the enhanced disclosures is to permit comparability among companies regardless of which method they choose.

Market Value Exceeds Exercise Price.   Suppose the options described in Illustration 18–4 were structured so they did have intrinsic value on the grant date. This would have been the case if Universal's shares had a market value on that date of, say, $37. (Remember, the exercise price was $35.) We make that assumption in Illustration 18–5. Compensation is recorded only to the extent of intrinsic value. However, in addition to their intrinsic value, the fair value of options also includes a time value due to the fact that (a) the holder of an option does not have to pay the exercise price until the option is exercised and (b) the market price of the underlying stock may yet rise and create additional intrinsic value. All options have time value so long as time remains before expiration. The longer the time until expiration, other things being equal, the greater the time value. As a result, all options will be undervalued by not recording their fair values. In fact, as discussed earlier, there usually is no intrinsic value (exercise price equals market price), resulting in no compensation being recorded at all.

good to understand

At January 1, 1997, Universal Communications grants options that permit key executives to acquire 10 million of the company's $1 par common shares within the next eight years, but not before December 31, 2000 (the vesting date). The exercise price is $35 and the market price of the shares $37 per share on the date of grant.

January 1, 1997

No entry

Calculate total compensation expense:

$37	Market value per share
(35)	Exercise price
$ 2	Intrinsic value per option
× 10 million	Options granted
= $20 million	Intrinsic value of award

The total compensation is to be allocated to expense over the four-year service (vesting) period: 1997–2000

$20 million ÷ 4 years = $5 million per year

December 31, 1997, 1998, 1999, 2000 ($ in millions)

Compensation expense ($20 million ÷ 4 years)	5	
Paid-in capital—stock options		5

> Under the alternative intrinsic value approach, compensation is recorded only when an option's market price exceeds its exercise price.

> The intrinsic value of the options is expensed over the service period for which the compensation is provided.

> The terms of performance options vary with some measure of performance to tie rewards to productivity.

> To avoid recording compensation, most options have fixed rather than variable terms.

> Accounting for performance option plans under the alternate approach is similar to accounting for SARs.

Performance Stock Option Plans.   In the restricted stock award plans and stock option plans we discussed in the previous sections, both the number of shares employees can receive and the price they must pay to receive the shares (if any) are known when the awards are granted. For that reason, they often are referred to as *fixed plans.* Sometimes, though, compensation plans are structured in such a way that some of the terms needed to measure the compensation vary in response to some performance measure such as share price, sales, rate of return, or market share. These are known as *variable plans.*

One example of a variable plan is a stock option plan in which the number of shares, the exercise price, or both vary with criteria related to managerial performance. For example, the criteria might be earnings per share, division revenues, rate of return on assets, or some other measure of performance. The number of shares obtainable under the option plan, for instance, might be calculated as some multiple of sales growth over the two years following the grant date. The possibilities are limitless.

To achieve corporate objectives and maximize shareholder wealth, performance option plans are preferable to fixed plans because they directly tie management incentive to firm performance. Unfortunately, the vast majority of option plans have fixed terms. Why? The answer is simple. Unless a company opts for the FASB's elective fair value approach, fixed plans allow the company to avoid reducing earnings with compensation expense (as discussed earlier). On the other hand, in a variable plan, compensation expense usually *is* recorded whether the company chooses the elective fair value approach or not. Here's why:

1. Using the FASB's *elective fair value approach,* the fair value of the options is estimated at the grant date and accrued to expense over the service period. Even when terms vary with future performance, option-pricing models usually are capable of estimating the fair value. In cases when it is not possible to determine fair value, compensation is accrued each year based on the *intrinsic value* of the award, using option terms that would apply if the options were exercised that year.
2. Using the *alternate approach,* the intrinsic value of the options is accrued to expense over the service period. But since the terms are dependent on performance, the measurement date is delayed until compensation can be measured but the expense is estimated and recorded in the meantime. So, as long as performance measures indicate positive compensation under the terms of the options, expense is recorded.

The way we estimate, record, and adjust compensation for revised estimates under the alternate approach is similar to the way we account for stock appreciation rights (SARs), demonstrated in Illustration 18–6 in the next section, except the credit entry to recognize accrued compensation is paid-in capital—stock options, rather than paid-in capital—SAR plan, or liability—SAR plan. Because performance option plans are found much less frequently in practice, we provide a detailed illustration for SARs. Just remember, the approach is the same for performance option plans.

Additional Consideration

Companies that have performance plans or other variable plans may actually choose the elective fair value approach to reduce compensation expense. The amount of estimated compensation under a variable plan is adjusted for changes in the price of the underlying stock after the grant date. This can be avoided if the company opts to determine the total compensation as the fair value of the options on the grant date. The FASB does not permit a mix-and-match approach. If the fair value approach is chosen for performance plans, it must be used for all stock-based plans.

Stock Appreciation Rights

Learning objective 6
Explain and implement the accounting for stock appreciation rights and differentiate between those that create liabilities and those that create equity.

Stock appreciation rights (SARs) overcome a major disadvantage of stock option plans that require employees to actually buy shares when the options are exercised. Even though the options' exercise price may be significantly lower than the market value of the shares, the employee still must come up with enough cash to take advantage of the bargain. This can be quite a burden if the award is sizable. In a nonqualified stock option plan, income taxes also would have to be paid when the options are exercised.[24]

In an SAR plan, the employer pays compensation equal to the increase in share price from a specified level.

SARs offer a solution. Unlike stock options, these awards enable an employee to benefit by the amount that the market price of the company's stock rises without having to buy shares. Instead, the employee is awarded the share appreciation, which is the amount by which the market price on the exercise date exceeds a prespecified price (usually the market price at the date of grant). For instance, if the share price rises from $35 to $50, the employee receives $15 cash for each SAR held. The share appreciation usually is payable in cash or the recipient has the choice between cash and shares. A plan of this type offered by IBM is described in Graphic 18–11.

GRAPHIC   18–11

**Stock Appreciation Rights—
IBM Corporation**

Long-Term Performance Plan (in Part)

SARs offer eligible optionees the alternative of electing not to exercise the related stock option, but to receive payment in cash and/or stock, equivalent to the difference between the option price and the average market price of IBM stock on the date of exercising the right.

If an employer can elect to settle in shares of stock rather than cash, the award is considered to be equity.

If an employee can elect to receive cash, the award is considered to be a liability.

The cash settlement of an equity award is considered the repurchase of an equity instrument.

Is It Debt Or Is It Equity?   In some plans, the employer chooses whether to issue shares or cash at exercise. In other plans, the choice belongs to the employee.[25] Who has the choice determines the way it's accounted for. More specifically, the accounting treatment depends on whether the award is considered an equity instrument or a liability. If the employer can elect to settle in shares of stock rather than cash, the award is considered to be equity. On the other hand, if the employee will receive cash or can elect to receive cash, the award is considered to be a liability.[26]

The distinction between stock-based awards that are considered equity and those that are considered liabilities is based on the definition of liabilities in *SFAC 6*.[27] That statement classifies an instrument as a liability if it obligates the issuer to transfer its assets to the holder. A stock option is an equity instrument if it requires only the issuance of stock. A cash SAR, on the other hand, requires the transfer of assets, and therefore is a liability. This does not mean that a stock option whose issuer may later choose to settle in cash is not an equity instrument. Instead, cash settlement would be considered equivalent to repurchasing an equity instrument for cash.

---

[24] The tax treatment of stock-based plans is discussed in an earlier section.

[25] Many such plans are called tandem plans and award an employee both a cash SAR and an SAR that calls for settlement in an equivalent amount of shares. The exercise of one cancels the other.

[26] The FASB's elective accounting approach mandates the distinction between debt and equity to be whether the employee can choose cash or whether the employer can choose to settle in shares. A company not choosing to follow the elective approach decides which settlement method is most likely. The result usually is the same.

[27] Elements of Financial Statements," *Statement of Financial Accounting Concepts No. 6* (Stamford, Conn.: FASB 1985).

SARs Payable in Shares (Equity).   When an SAR is considered to be equity (because the employer can elect to settle in shares of stock rather than cash), accounting depends on whether or not the company has chosen the elective fair value approach for stock-based compensation plans:

1. Using the *elective fair value approach,* the fair value of the SARs is estimated at the grant date and accrued to expense over the service period. Normally, the fair value of an SAR is the same as the fair value of a stock option with the same terms. The fair value is determined at the grant date and accrued to compensation expense over the service period the same way as for other stock-based compensation plans. The total compensation is not revised for subsequent changes in the price of the underlying stock.

2. Using the *alternative intrinsic value approach,* the intrinsic value of the SARs is accrued to expense over the service period. But since the terms are dependent on future stock price, the eventual compensation is estimated and recorded in the meantime. This is the same method used for performance stock options discussed earlier as well as for cash SARs discussed next.

SARs Payable in Cash (Liability).   When an SAR is considered to be a liability (because the employee can elect to receive cash upon settlement), accounting does *not* depend on whether or not the company has chosen the elective fair value approach for stock-based compensation plans. Instead, consistent with recording other liabilities, the amount of compensation (and related liability) is estimated each period and continually adjusted to reflect changes in the market price of stock until the compensation is finally paid.

> Total compensation expense reported to date is the estimated total compensation multiplied by the fraction of the service period that has expired.

A difficulty in accounting for cash SARs is that the amount of compensation (and eventual liability) are not known for certain until the compensation actually is paid on the date the SAR is exercised. We solve this problem the usual way—by estimating the amounts needed for periodic reporting. The amount of total compensation is estimated at the end of each period as the excess of the current market price of the shares over the prespecified price (usually the market price at the date of grant). A portion of that total compensation is attributed to employee service during each reporting period and is recorded as compensation expense.

The periodic expense (and adjustment to the liability) is the percentage of the total compensation earned to date by recipients of the SARs (based on the elapsed percentage of the service period) reduced by any amounts expensed in prior periods. For example, if the market price at the end of the period is $14 and was $10 at the grant date, the total compensation would be $40 million if 10 million SARs are expected to vest. Let's say two years of a four-year service period have elapsed, and $5 million was expensed the first year. Then, compensation expense the second year would be $15 million, calculated as ($2/4$ of $40 million) minus $5.

An example spanning several years is provided in Illustration 18–6.

ILLUSTRATION   18–6

Stock Appreciation Rights

> When the share price rises above $10, a liability is created.

Universal Communications grants 10 million SARs to key executives at January 1, 1997. Upon exercise, the SARs entitle executives to receive cash or stock equal in value to the excess of the market price at exercise over the share price at the date of grant. The $1 par common shares have a current market price of $10 per share. The SARs vest at the end of 2000 (cannot be exercised until then) and expire at the end of 2004. The year-end share prices following the grant of the SARs are:

1997	$12
1998	$14
1999	$16
2000	$14
2001	$15

January 1, 1997

No entry because the intrinsic value of the SARs is zero: ($10 – $10) × 10 million shares = $0

December 31, 1997   ($ in millions)

Compensation expense*	5	
Liability—SAR plan		5

* Calculation:

($12 – 10) × 10 million × $1/4$ – $0   = $5
Estimated total   Fraction of   Expensed   Current
compensation   service to date   earlier   expense

ILLUSTRATION   18–6

continued

In 1998, both the expense and the liability are adjusted to reflect, not only another year's service but also a revised estimate of total compensation.

The 1999 expense is the revised total compensation to be reported to date ($45 million) less the $20 million expensed previously.

If the share price declines, both the liability and expense are reduced.

December 31, 1998		($ in millions)
Compensation expense*	15	
Liability—SAR plan		15

* Calculation:

($14 – 10) × 10 million	×	$^2/_4$	–	($5 million)	=	$15
Estimated total compensation		Fraction of service to date		Expensed earlier		Current expense

December 31, 1999		
Compensation expense*	25	
Liability—SAR plan		25

* Calculation:

($16 – 10) × 10 million	×	$^3/_4$	–	($5 + $15 million)	=	$25
Estimated total compensation		Fraction of service to date		Expensed earlier		Current expense

December 31, 2000		
Liability—SAR plan	5	
Compensation expense*		5

* Calculation:

($14 – 10) × 10 million	×	$^4/_4$	–	($5 + $15 + 25 million)	=	($5)
Estimated total compensation		Fraction of service to date		Expensed earlier		Current expense

Note that the way we treat changes in compensation estimates entails a catch-up adjustment in the period of change, inconsistent with the usual treatment of a change in estimate. For most changes in estimate, including changes in forfeiture rates and other estimates under the elective fair value approach described earlier, revisions are allocated (to compensation expense in this case) over remaining periods, rather than all at once in the period of change.

We make up for incorrect previous estimates by adjusting expense in the period the estimate is revised.

The liability continues to be adjusted after the service period if the rights haven't been exercised yet.

Compensation expense and the liability continue to be adjusted until the SARs expire or are exercised.

December 31, 2001		($ in millions)
Compensation expense*	10	
Liability—SAR plan		10

*Calculation:

($15 – $10) × 10 million	×	all	–	($5 + $15 + $25 – $5 million)	=	$10
Estimated total compensation		Fraction of service to date		Expensed earlier		Current expense

It's necessary to continue to adjust both compensation expense and the liability until the SARs ultimately either are exercised or lapse.[28] Assume for example that the SARs are exercised on October 11, 2002, when the share price is $14.50, and executives choose to receive the market price appreciation in cash:

Adjustment continues after the service period if the SARs have not yet been exercised.

Any credit to compensation expense may not be more than previous debits to that account.

October 11, 2002		($ in millions)
Liability—SAR plan	5	
Compensation expense*		5
Liability—SAR plan (balance)	45	
Cash		45

*Calculation:

($14.50 – 10) × 10 million	×	all	–	($50 million)	=	$(5)
Actual total compensation		Fraction of service to date		Expensed earlier		Current expense

---

[28] Except that the cumulative compensation expense cannot be negative; that is, the liability cannot be reduced below zero.

Let's look at the changes in the liability—SAR plan account during the 1997–2002 period:

Liability—SAR Plan

				($ in millions)
			5	1997
			15	1998
			25	1999
2000	5			
			10	2001
2002	5			
2002	45			
		0	Balance after exercise	

As discussed earlier, if the employer had retained the choice of settling in shares rather than cash, the award would have been considered an equity instrument at the outset. In that case, unless the company uses the elective fair value approach, paid-in capital—SAR plan would replace the liability account in each of Universal's journal entries above.

Broad-Based (Noncompensatory) Plans

Sometimes long-term stock options are issued to substantially all employees rather than to certain targeted individuals. These so-called broad-based plans typically permit employees to buy shares within some specified number of years, say 10 years, at an exercise price equal to the stock's price on the date the options are granted, or sometimes at a slight discount.

Options of this type traditionally have been referred to as **noncompensatory plans** due to terminology used in the Tax Code. This term also is consistent with the reason most such plans exist. The plans encourage stock ownership among rank and file employees. As stakeholders, employees become more loyal and financially concerned with enhancing the value of common stock. As long as the price discount is no higher than (a) what would be reasonable in a recurring offer to shareholders or others or (b) the share issuance costs avoided by not having to finance a public offering of new stock, no entry is made when options are issued under a broad-based plan. These criteria are considered met if the discount is 5% or less.[29] If and when those options are exercised, the company simply records the sale of new shares.

Graphic 18–12 provides a summary of the effects of each type of stock-based compensation plan on compensation recorded and affected balance sheet categories.

GRAPHIC   18–12

Income Statement and Balance Sheet Impact of Stock-Based Compensation Plans

Type of Plan	Elective Fair Value Approach		Alternative Intrinsic Value Approach	
	Total Compensation	Balance Sheet	Total Compensation	Balance Sheet
Restricted (nonvested) stock award	Fair value Amount fixed at grant date, accrued to service period	Shareholders' equity: Paid-in capital—restricted stock	Same as fair value approach	Same as fair value approach
Fixed stock options	Fair value Amount fixed at grant date, accrued to service period	Shareholders' equity: Paid-in capital—stock options	Intrinsic value Amount fixed at grant date, accrued to service period	Shareholders' equity: Paid-in capital—stock options
Performance (variable) stock options	Fair value Amount fixed at grant date, accrued to service period	Shareholders' equity: Paid-in capital—stock options	Intrinsic value Amount varies until option terms are known; estimates expensed until then	Shareholders' equity: Paid-in capital—stock options

---

[29] A discount of more than 5% without recording compensation expense is permitted by *SFAS 123* if the company can justify it under criteria (a) and (b) above.

GRAPHIC   18 – 12

continued

	Elective Fair Value Approach		Alternative Intrinsic Value Approach	
Type of Plan	**Total Compensation**	**Balance Sheet**	**Total Compensation**	**Balance Sheet**
Stock appreciation rights (share payment choice of employer)	Fair value Amount fixed at grant date, accrued to service period	Shareholders' equity: Paid-in capital—SAR plan	Share price appreciation Amount varies until exercise (or lapse); estimates expensed until then	Shareholders' equity: Paid-in capital—SAR plan
Stock appreciation rights (cash payment choice of employee)	Share price appreciation Amount varies until exercise (or lapse), estimates expensed until then	Liabilities: Liability—SAR plan	Same as fair value approach	Same as fair value approach
Broad-based plans (noncompensatory)	None	Shareholders' equity: (Only when shares are sold)	Same as fair value approach	Same as fair value approach

Various Bonus Plans

In stock-based plans, compensation might be quite generous—if stock prices rise, that is. On the other hand, if stock prices never rise above the prespecified base price, they're worthless. Some executives believe their performance is better measured by other criteria not tied to the unpredictable stock market. This contention has led to the increasing use of several incentive compensation programs not tied to stock prices. Such programs include annual bonuses, performance share plans, long-term cash bonuses, performance unit plans, and phantom stock plans. Regardless of the name and specific form of the plan, the accounting objective once again is to record compensation expense over the appropriate service period.

Annual Bonuses

Sometimes compensation packages include annual bonuses tied to performance objectives designed to provide incentive to executives. The most common performance measures are earnings per share, net income, and operating income, each being used by about a quarter of firms having bonus plans. Nonfinancial performance measures, such as customer satisfaction and product or service quality, also are used by about 13% of these firms.[30] In recent years, **annual bonuses** are gaining in use, not just for executives, but for nonmanagerial personnel as well. Unfortunately for employees, bonuses often take the place of annual raises. This allows a company to increase employee pay without permanently locking the increases in salaries. Bonuses are compensation expense of the period they are earned.

Performance Share Plans and Long-Term Cash Bonuses

Performance share plans offer another way to reward employees on the basis of their productivity.[31] In these arrangements, shares are promised to key personnel, subject to the achievement of specific financial goals. For example, performance shares might represent rights to receive a certain number of shares of common stock provided the company achieves specified income goals over a four-year period.[32] The criteria might be growth in earnings per share, revenue growth or maintenance, rate of return on assets, or some other measure representative of performance. This would give executives additional incentive to see that the company's financial goals are achieved.

---

[30] C. D. Ittner, D. F. Larker, and M. V. Rajan, "The Choice of Performance Measures in Annual Bonus Contracts," Working Paper, The Wharton School, University of Pennsylvania, (August 1995).

[31] These sometimes are called "Restricted Performance Share Plans" (Unisys Corporation), "Stock Performance Plans" (Scott Paper Company), "Stock Incentive Compensation Plans" (Gencorp Inc.), "Incentive Compensation Plans" (Outboard Marine Corporation), and various other titles. Terminology is nonstandard, so the plan's description is more meaningful than the name it's given.

[32] When you study earnings per share in Chapter 20, you will find that "contingently issuable shares" are a factor in their calculation. Be alert when you reach that point that performance shares are an example of contingently issuable shares.

A variation of this plan, **long-term cash bonuses**, pays cash rather than shares. This version is popular among smaller companies, particularly nonpublic companies, in which share prices are not available or issuing additional shares is undesirable.

Many variations exist. **Performance unit plans** pay cash or shares on the basis of the number of performance units employees have earned. Similar to other bonus plans, earning performance units depends on achievement of specific financial goals. The difference is that actual compensation per unit is determined after the fact by a compensation committee. This makes estimating compensation more difficult. **Phantom stock plans** employ a formula to calculate compensation based on changes in one of several possible performance measures (net assets per share, for example) designed to mimic the way stock prices might change. The objective is to approximate share price movements without actually tying compensation to the unpredictable stock market, or in the case of nonpublic companies, nonexistent stock prices.

For any of these plans, compensation expense and a related liability should be accrued annually based on the estimated eventual value of compensation, similar to variable stock-based plans. Sometimes, though, material uncertainties exist concerning how much, or even whether, compensation ultimately will be paid. Consistent with the treatment of contingent liabilities, which many of these plans represent, accrual cannot occur unless it's both probable that payment will be made and the amount can be reasonably estimated.[33] If shares will be issued rather than cash (as in a performance share plan, for instance), a shareholders' equity account is created rather than a liability.

Other Employee Compensation

Stock purchase plans permit employees to buy shares directly from the corporation.

Stock Purchase Plans

Stock purchase plans often permit all employees to buy shares directly from their company at favorable terms. The primary intent of these plans is to encourage employee ownership of the company's shares. These are quite similar to the noncompensatory stock options we discussed earlier. Presumably loyalty is enhanced among employee-shareholders. The employee also benefits because, typically, these plans allow employees to buy shares from their employer without brokerage fees and, perhaps, at a slight discount (often 5%). Some companies even encourage participation by matching or partially matching employee purchases.

As long as (a) substantially all employees can participate, (b) employees have no longer than one month after the price is fixed to decide whether to participate, and (c) the discount is no greater than 5% (or can be justified as reasonable), accounting is straightforward. Simply record the sale of new shares as employees buy shares. Compensation expense replaces the cash debit for any employer-paid portion.

Vacations, Sick Days, and Other Paid Future Absences

Suppose a firm grants two weeks of paid vacation each year to nonsalaried employees. Some take their vacations during the year earned and are compensated then. Some wait. Is the compensation an expense during the year earned for only those who actually are paid that year for their absence? When you recall what you've learned about accrual accounting, you probably conclude otherwise.

An employer should accrue an expense and the related liability for employees' compensation for future absences (such as vacation pay) if the obligation meets four conditions. These conditions, all of which must be met for accrual, are listed in Graphic 18–13.

GRAPHIC   18-13

Conditions for Accrual of Paid Future Absences

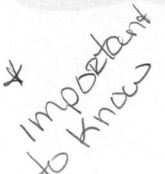
✗ Important to Know

1. The obligation is attributable to employees' services already performed.
2. The paid absence can be taken in a later year—the benefit vests (will be compensated even if employment is terminated) or the benefit can be accumulated over time.
3. Payment is probable.
4. The amount can be reasonably estimated.[34]

---

[33] No pronouncement specifically governs most nonstock-based plans. Because payment is contingent upon a future event, the achievement of performance objectives, the plans usually are best classified as contingent liabilities as covered by "Accounting for Contingencies," *Statement of Financial Accounting Standards No 5*, (Stamford, Conn.: FASB, 1975).

[34] "Accounting for Compensated Absences," *Statement of Financial Accounting Standards No 43*, (Stamford, Conn.: FASB, 1980).

If these conditions look familiar, it's because they are simply the characteristics of a liability we discussed in Chapter 13, adapted to relate to a potential obligation for future absences of employees. Also, be sure to recognize the consistency of these conditions with accruing loss contingencies only when the obligation is both (a) probable and (b) can be reasonably estimated. The situation is demonstrated in Illustration 18–7.

ILLUSTRATION 18–7

Paid Future Absences

Davidson-Getty Chemicals has 8,000 employees. Each employee earns two weeks of paid vacation per year. Vacation time not taken in the year earned can be carried over to subsequent years. During 1997, 2,500 employees took both weeks' vacation, but at the end of the year, 5,500 employees had vacation time carryovers as follows:

Employees	Vacation Weeks Earned But Not Taken	Total Carryover Weeks
2,500	0	0
2,000	1	2,000
3,500	2	7,000
8,000		9,000

During 1997, compensation averaged $600 a week per employee.

When Vacations Were Taken in 1997

Salaries and wages expense		
(2,500 × 2 wks. × $600) + (2,000 × 1 wk. × $600)	4,200,000	
Cash (or wages payable)		4,200,000

December 31, 1997 (adjusting entry)

Salaries and wages expense		
(9,000 carryover weeks × $600)	5,400,000	
Liability—compensated future absences		5,400,000

> When the necessary conditions are met, compensated future absences are accrued in the year the compensation is earned.

The liability for paid absences usually is accrued at the existing wage rate rather than at a rate estimated to be in effect when absences occur.[35] So, if wage rates have risen, the difference between the accrual and the amount paid increases compensation expense that year. For example, let's assume all the carryover vacation time is taken in 1998 and the actual amount paid to employees is $5,700,000:

When 1997 Vacations Are Taken in 1998

Liability—compensated future absences (account balance)	5,400,000	
Salaries and wages expense (difference)	300,000	
Cash (or salaries and wages payable) (given)		5,700,000

> Customary practice should be considered when deciding whether an obligation exists.

Company policy and actual practice should be considered when deciding whether the rights to payment for absences have been earned by services already rendered. Consider an illustrative situation. Suppose scientists in a private laboratory are eligible for paid sabbaticals every seven years. Should a liability be accrued at the end of a scientist's sixth year? No—if sabbatical leave is granted only to perform research beneficial to the employer. Yes—if past practice indicates that sabbatical leave is intended to provide unrestricted compensated absence for past service and other conditions are met.

Custom and practice also influence whether unused rights to paid absences expire or can be carried forward. Obviously, if rights vest (payable even if employment is terminated) they haven't expired. But holiday time, military leave, maternity leave, and jury time typically do not accumulate if unused, so a liability for those benefits usually is not accrued. On the other hand, if it's customary that a particular paid absence, say holiday time, can be carried forward—if employees work on holidays, in this case—a liability is accrued if it's probable that employees will be compensated in a future year.

---

[35] Actually, *SFAS 43* is silent on how the liability should be measured. In practice, most companies choose the current rate because it avoids estimates and usually produces a lower expense and liability.

Interestingly, sick pay quite often meets the conditions for accrual but is specifically excluded by *SFAS 43*, "Accounting for Compensated Absences," from mandatory accrual. Its exclusion is because future absence depends on future illness, which usually is not a certainty. However, similar to other forms of paid absences, the decision of whether to accrue nonvesting sick pay should be based on actual policy and practice. If company policy or custom is that employees are paid sick pay even when their absences are not due to illness, it's appropriate to record a liability for unused sick pay. For example, some companies routinely allow unused sick pay benefits to be accumulated and paid at retirement (or to beneficiaries if death comes before retirement). If each condition is met except that the company finds it impractical to reasonably estimate the amount of compensation for future absences, a disclosure note should describe the situation.

> *Accrual of sick pay is not required, but is permitted.*

Postemployment Benefits

Sometimes employers provide benefits to former or inactive employees after employment but before retirement. These postemployment (rather than postretirement) benefits might include salary continuation, severance benefits, supplemental unemployment benefits, disability-related benefits, job training and counseling, and continuation of benefits such as health care benefits and life insurance coverage.

Often these postemployment benefits resemble other forms of compensated absences like sick pay. If so, the accounting should be the same and employers should recognize the obligation to provide these benefits in accordance with *SFAS 43*. Recall that the liability should be accrued (debit expense; credit liability) if the four conditions of Graphic 18–13 are met. Delta Airlines described its accrual of this expense for 1995 as shown in Graphic 18–14.

> *Sometimes postemployment benefits meet the criteria for accrual as compensated absences.*

GRAPHIC 18–14

Postemployment Benefits—Delta Airlines

Employee Benefit Plans (in part)

The Company provides certain benefits to its former or inactive employees after employment but before retirement. Such benefits primarily include those related to disability and survivorship plans. Effective July 1, 1994, Delta adopted *SFAS 112*, which requires recognition of the liability for postemployment benefits during the period of employment. . . . The Company's postemployment benefit expense for fiscal 1995 was $85 million.

> *Otherwise, postemployment benefits should be treated as loss contingencies.*

If the postemployment benefits don't meet all four conditions, the estimated cost of those benefits should be treated as a contingency and accrued when it is probable that a liability has been incurred and the amount can be reasonably estimated in accordance with *SFAS 5*, "Accounting for Contingencies."[36]

Employee Stock Ownership Plans (ESOPs)

Another common form of deferred compensation is an Employee Stock Ownership Plan (ESOP). An ESOP is a legal entity separate from the sponsoring company and is created by a trust agreement. The sponsoring company contributes to the ESOP shares of stock, or cash which is used to purchase the company's stock. Employees have an ownership interest in the stock but actually receive compensation when they leave the firm, due to retirement or otherwise. The cash that employees receive is raised by the ESOP from selling shares. The sponsoring company gets a tax deduction for the cash or market value of shares contributed to the ESOP, while employees get to defer paying taxes on their compensation until they ultimately receive cash from the ESOP. A benefit to the company is that employees, as owners, have a monetary stake in the well-being of their employer.

As contributions are made to an ESOP, the sponsoring company records compensation expense. For example, if 1 million $1 par shares worth $15 million are contributed, the following entry is recorded:

---

[36] "Employers' Accounting For Postemployment Benefits," *Statement of Financial Accounting Standards No. 112,* (Norwalk, Conn.: FASB, 1992) amends *SFAS No. 5* and *SFAS No. 43*.

	($ in millions)
Compensation expense (fair value of contribution) 15	
Common stock (1 million shares @ $1 par)	1
Paid-in capital—excess of par (difference)	14

Note: If $15 million cash had been contributed instead of shares, cash would substitute for the stock accounts in this entry.

Sometimes, the ESOP borrows cash to buy shares from the employer company. This is called a **leveraged ESOP**. In that case, the sponsoring company records a liability, offset by a contra-equity account. For example, let's say $30 million cash is borrowed by the ESOP and 2 million $1 par shares worth are purchased from the firm with that cash. The following entries are recorded:

	($ in millions)
Deferred compensation—ESOP plan 30	
Liability—ESOP plan (amount borrowed by the ESOP)	30
Cash (received from ESOP) 30	
Common stock (2 million shares @ $1 par)	2
Paid-in capital—excess of par (difference)	28

As the ESOP repays the debt, both the liability and deferred compensation (a contra-equity account) on the employer's books are reduced.[37] Notice that the effect of this accounting treatment is to effectively treat the ESOP's debt as company debt.

CONCEPT REVIEW EXERCISE   PRERETIREMENT COMPENSATION PLANS

Listed below are transactions dealing with various stock benefit plans of Fortune-Time Corporation during the period 1997–1999. The share prices for the $1 par common stock for various dates follow:

January 1, 1997 $45
January 5, 1997 $44
December 31, 1997 $45
December 31, 1998 $46

  a. On January 1, 1997, the company issued 10 million common shares to divisional managers under its restricted stock award plan. The shares are subject to forfeiture if employment is terminated within three years.

  b. On January 1, 1997, the company granted incentive stock options to its senior management exercisable for 1.5 million common shares. The options must be exercised within five years, but not before January 1, 1999. The exercise price of the stock options is equal to the fair market value of the common stock on the date the options are granted. An option pricing model estimates the fair value of the options to be $4 per option. All recipients are expected to remain employed through the vesting date.

  c. On January 5, 1997, the company granted 16 million SARs to its junior managers. The SARs entitle managers to receive their choice of cash or stock equal in value to the excess of the market price at exercise over the share price at the date of grant. The SARs vest at the end of 1998 (cannot be exercised until then) and expire at the end of 2000.

  d. On January 5, 1997, the company granted 3 million performance share rights to key executives. The rights entitle executives to receive 3 million of its $1 par common shares, subject to the achievement of specific financial goals over the next three years. Achievement of the goals is probable at the end of each year.

  e. Recorded compensation expense on December 31, 1997.

[37] "Accounting Practices for Certain Employee Stock Ownership Plans," *Statement of Position No. 76-3* (New York: AICPA, 1976).

f. A divisional manager holding 1 million of the restricted shares left the company to become CEO of a competitor on September 15, 1998, before the required service period ended.

g. Recorded compensation expense on December 31, 1998.

Required:

Prepare the journal entries that Fortune-Time recorded for each of these transactions. Assume the company opts for the elective fair value approach to accounting for stock-based plans. (Ignore any tax effects.)

CONCEPT REVIEW EXERCISE   SOLUTION

January 1, 1997
Restricted Stock Award Plan
No entry.
Total compensation is measured as 10 million shares at $45 = $450 million

Incentive Stock Options

No entry.
Total compensation is measured as 1.5 million shares at $4 = $6 million
(Note: No compensation would be measured unless the elective fair value approach is used.)

SARs

No entry because the SARs have no intrinsic value on the grant date (market price equals reference price).
Performance Share Plan
No entry until compensation is estimated at the end of the reporting period

December 31, 1997		($ in millions)
Restricted stock		
Compensation expense ($450 million ÷ 3 years)	150	
Paid-in capital—restricted stock		150
Incentive options		
Compensation expense ($6 million ÷ 2 years)	3	
Paid-in capital—stock options		3
SARs		
Compensation expense*	8	
Liability—SAR plan		8

* Calculation:

$$(\$45 - 44) \times 16 \text{ million} \times \tfrac{1}{2} - \$0 = \$8$$

Estimated total compensation	Fraction of service to date	Expensed earlier	Current expense

Performance share plan

Compensation expense*	45	
Paid-in capital—performance shares		45

* Calculation:

$$\$45 \times 3 \text{ million} \times \tfrac{1}{3} - \$0 = \$45$$

Estimated total compensation	Fraction of service to date	Expensed earlier	Current expense

September 15, 1998

Restricted stock		
Paid-in capital—restricted stock (10% × $150)	15	
Compensation expense		15

December 31, 1998		
Restricted stock		
Compensation expense [($450 − $150 − $15 million) ÷ 2 years]	142.5	
Deferred compensation expense		142.5
Incentive options		
Compensation expense ($6 million ÷ 2 years)	3	
Deferred compensation expense		3
SARs		
Compensation expense*	24	
Liability—SAR plan		24

* Calculation:

$$(\$46 - \$44) \times \underset{\substack{\text{Estimated total} \\ \text{compensation}}}{16 \text{ million}} \quad \times \quad \underset{\substack{\text{Fraction of} \\ \text{service to date}}}{^2/_2} \quad - \quad \underset{\substack{\text{Expensed} \\ \text{earlier}}}{\$8} \quad = \quad \underset{\substack{\text{Current} \\ \text{expense}}}{\$24}$$

Performance share plan

Compensation expense*	47	
Paid-in capital—performance shares		47

* Calculation:

$$\underset{\substack{\text{Estimated total} \\ \text{compensation}}}{\$46 \times 3 \text{ million}} \quad \times \quad \underset{\substack{\text{Fraction of} \\ \text{service to date}}}{^2/_3} \quad - \quad \underset{\substack{\text{Expensed} \\ \text{earlier}}}{\$45} \quad = \quad \underset{\substack{\text{Current} \\ \text{expense}}}{\$47}$$

Solution to Financial Reporting Case (at the opening of the chapter)

1. Besides the compensation mentioned in the article, what types of compensation do you think Mr. Walter might receive for his services?
2. How can a compensation package such as this serve as an incentive to Mr. Walter?

3. Mr. Walter received a "hefty grant of restricted stock." How should the grant be accounted for by AT&T?
4. Included were stock options to buy more than 700,000 shares. How will the options affect AT&T's compensation expense?

Postretirement benefits might include pension benefits and others that may include medical coverage, dental coverage, life insurance, group legal services, and other benefits. Regardless of whether compensation is received before or after retirement, the cost to AT&T is expensed over the period of service the benefits are earned.

Stock-based plans like the restricted stock and stock options that Mr. Walker is receiving are designed to motivate recipients. If the shares awarded are restricted so that Mr. Walker is not free to sell the shares during the restriction period, he has an incentive to remain with the company until rights to the shares vest. Likewise, stock options can be made exercisable only after a specified period of employment. An additional incentive of stock-based plans is that the recipient has an incentive to take actions that will maximize the value of the shares.

The compensation associated with restricted stock is the market price of unrestricted shares of the same stock. AT&T will accrue this amount as compensation expense over the service period from the date of grant to when restrictions are lifted.

Similar to restricted stock, the value of the options is recorded as compensation over the service period, usually the vesting period. If AT&T elects the FASB's fair value approach, the total compensation will be the fair value of the options at the grant date. Otherwise, it will be the intrinsic value at the grant date, which likely will be zero because the exercise price usually is made equal to the market price at the date of grant. In actuality, AT&T did not elect the FASB's fair value approach.

The Bottom Line

1. Accounting for postretirement benefits is similar in most respects to accounting for pension benefits. Like pensions, other postretirement benefits are a form of deferred compensation. Unlike pensions, their cost is attributed to the years from the employee's date of hire to the full eligibility date.

2. The expected postretirement benefit obligation (EPBO) is the actuary's estimate of the total postretirement benefits (at their discounted present value) expected to be received by plan participants. The accumulated postretirement benefit obligation (APBO) is the portion of the EPBO attributed to employee service to date.

3. The components of postretirement benefit expense are essentially the same as those for pension expense. The transition obligation existing when *SFAS 106* was adopted can be expensed either immediately or over a period of years.

4. By the elective fair value approach, compensation is measured at the grant date using an option-pricing model that considers the exercise price and expected term of the option, the current market price of the underlying stock and its expected volatility, expected dividends, and the expected risk-free rate of return.

5. By the alternate intrinsic value approach to accounting for stock-based compensation plans, compensation is measured as the intrinsic value of the award and expensed over the service period, usually from the date of grant to the vesting date.

6. For stock appreciation rights with variable terms, the award is considered to be equity if the employer can elect to settle in shares of stock rather than cash. If the employee can elect to receive cash, the award is considered to be a liability. In either case, the amount of compensation is continually adjusted to reflect changes in the market price of stock until the compensation is finally paid unless the award is considered equity and the elective fair value approach is used. In that case, fair value is measured at the grant date.

7. Other preretirement compensation plans include annual bonuses, performance share plans, long-term cash bonuses, performance unit plans, and phantom stock plans. Regardless of the name and specific form of the plan, the accounting objective is to record compensation over the appropriate service period.

APPENDIX

18A   RETIREE HEALTH CARE BENEFIT OBLIGATIONS AND EXPENSE—A COMPREHENSIVE ILLUSTRATION

This appendix extends Illustration 18–2 to give you a comprehensive analysis of the retiree benefits and related calculations for all years of the employment and retirement years. Keep in mind, though, that although our illustration includes calculations for an individual employee, in reality the amounts would be determined for the employee group as a whole. The schedule in Illustration 18A–1 indicates (1) the estimated net benefit cost in each of the 20 retirement years; (2) the present value of each of those amounts as of the retirement date; (3) the EPBO each year from the date of hire to retirement; (4) the APBO from the adoption of *SFAS 106* through the retirement years; (5) the service cost each year of the attribution period; (6) the interest cost each year of the attribution period; (7) the transition cost amortization each year of the an assumed 20-year amortization period; and (8) the postretirement benefit expense each year of the attribution period. We assume the plan is not prefunded (no return on plan assets), there are no gains or losses, and no prior service cost.

ILLUSTRATION 18A–1

Schedule of Retiree Health Care Benefit Obligations and Expense

Date of hire →

SFAS 106 adopted →

Attribution period

End of 20-year amortization period for transition obligation →

Full-eligibility date →

Year	Age	Net Benefit[1]	Present Value at 2025[2]	EPBO[3]	Attribution	APBO[4]	Service Cost[5]	Interest Cost (6%)[6]	Trans. Cost[7] (20 yr)	Expense[8]
1986	22			(6,417)						
1987	23			(6,802)						
1988	24			(7,210)						
1989	25			(7,643)						
1990	26			(8,101)						
1991	27			(8,588)						
1992	28			(9,103)	$7/35$				(1,821)	
1993	29			(9,649)	$8/35$	(2,205)	275	109	91	475
1994	30			(10,228)	$9/35$	(2,630)	292	132	91	516
1995	31			(10,842)	$10/35$	(3,098)	310	158	91	559
1996	32			(11,492)	$11/35$	(3,612)	328	186	91	605
1997	33			(12,182)	$12/35$	(4,177)	348	217	91	656
1998	34			(12,913)	$13/35$	(4,796)	369	251	91	711
1999	35			(13,687)	$14/35$	(5,475)	391	288	91	770
2000	36			(14,509)	$15/35$	(6,218)	415	328	91	834
2001	37			(15,379)	$16/35$	(7,030)	439	373	91	904
2002	38			(16,302)	$17/35$	(7,918)	466	422	91	979
2003	39			(17,280)	$18/35$	(8,887)	494	475	91	1,060
2004	40			(18,317)	$19/35$	(9,943)	523	533	91	1,148
2005	41			(19,416)	$20/35$	(11,095)	555	597	91	1,242
2006	42			(20,581)	$21/35$	(12,348)	588	666	91	1,345
2007	43			(21,815)	$22/35$	(13,713)	623	741	91	1,455
2008	44			(23,124)	$23/35$	(15,196)	661	823	91	1,575
2009	45			(24,512)	$24/35$	(16,808)	700	912	91	1,703
2010	46			(25,983)	$25/35$	(18,559)	742	1,008	91	1,842
2011	47			(27,541)	$26/35$	(20,459)	787	1,114	91	1,991
2012	48			(29,194)	$27/35$	(22,521)	834	1,228	91	2,153
2013	49			(30,946)	$28/35$	(24,757)	884	1,351		2,235
2014	50			(32,802)	$29/35$	(27,179)	937	1,485		2,423
2015	51			(34,771)	$30/35$	(29,803)	993	1,631		2,624
2016	52			(36,857)	$31/35$	(32,645)	1,053	1,788		2,841
2017	53			(39,068)	$32/35$	(35,719)	1,116	1,959		3,075
2018	54			(41,412)	$33/35$	(39,046)	1,183	2,143		3,326
2019	55			(43,897)	$34/35$	(42,643)	1,254	2,343		3,597
2020	56			(46,531)	$35/35$	(46,531)	1,329	2,559		3,888

ILLUSTRATION 18A–1
continued

Year	Age	Net Benefit[1]	Present Value at 2025[2]	EPBO[3]	Attribution	APBO[4]	Service Cost[5]	Interest Cost (6%)[6]	Trans. Cost[7] (20 yr)	Expense[8]
2021	57			(49,323)		(49,323)		2,792		2,792
2022	58			(52,282)		(52,282)		2,959		2,959
2023	59			(55,419)		(55,419)		3,137		3,137
2024	60			(58,744)		(58,744)		3,325		3,325
2025	61			(62,269)		(62,269)		3,525		3,525
2026	62	(5,000)	(4,717)			(61,005)		3,736		3,736
2027	63	(5,600)	(4,984)			(59,065)		3,660		3,660
2028	64	(6,300)	(5,290)			(56,309)		3,544		3,544
2029	65	(3,000)	(2,376)			(56,688)		3,379		3,379
2030	66	(3,200)	(2,391)			(56,889)		3,401		3,401
2031	67	(3,500)	(2,467)			(56,802)		3,413		3,413
2032	68	(3,800)	(2,527)			(56,410)		3,408		3,408
2033	69	(4,104)	(2,575)			(55,691)		3,385		3,385
2034	70	(4,432)	(2,623)			(54,600)		3,341		3,341
2035	71	(4,787)	(2,673)			(53,089)		3,276		3,276
2036	72	(5,170)	(2,723)			(51,105)		3,185		3,185
2037	73	(5,583)	(2,775)			(48,587)		3,066		3,066
2038	74	(6,030)	(2,827)			(45,473)		2,915		2,915
2039	75	(6,513)	(2,880)			(41,688)		2,728		2,728
2040	76	(7,034)	(2,935)			(37,156)		2,501		2,501
2041	77	(7,596)	(2,990)			(31,789)		2,229		2,229
2042	78	(8,200)	(3,045)			(25,497)		1,907		1,907
2043	79	(8,850)	(3,101)			(18,176)		1,530		1,530
2044	80	(9,550)	(3,156)			(9,717)		1,091		1,091
2045	81	(10,300)	(3,212)			(0)		583		583
		118,549	(62,269)				18,892	97,836	1,821	118,549
							↘	↓	↙	
								118,549		

[1]Estimated (by actuary) claims each year, less estimated retiree contributions and Medicare reimbursements [amounts assumed in the illustration]
[2]Previous column amount discounted at 6% to the expected retirement date (end of 2025), e.g., n=1 in 2026, n=2 in 2027, . . . , n=20 in 2045
[3]1986 amount is previous column total discounted at 6% to 1986 (n=40); 1987 amount (n=39), etc.; EPBO increases by 6% each year
[4]EPBO times attribution fraction
[5]EPBO times 1/35
[6]Previous year's (beginning of current year's) APBO times 6%; [6% times transition obligation in 1993]
[7]APBO attributed to the 7 years before adoption of SFAS 106: 7/35 × $9,103; amortized over 20 years
[8]Service cost + interest cost + amortization of transition obligation (illustration assumes no return on plan assets, gains or losses, or prior service cost)

Retirement period

APPENDIX

18B

OPTION-PRICING THEORY

Option values have two essential components: (1) intrinsic value and (2) time value.

Intrinsic Value

Intrinsic value is the benefit the holder of an option would realize by exercising the option rather than buying the underlying stock directly. An option that permits an employee to buy $25 stock for $10 has an intrinsic value of $15. An option whose exercise price equals or exceeds the market price of the underlying stock has zero intrinsic value.

Time Value

In addition to their intrinsic value, options also have a time value due to the fact that (a) the holder of an option does not have to pay the exercise price until the option is exercised and (b) the market price of the underlying stock may yet rise and create additional intrinsic value. All options have time value so long as time remains before expiration. The longer the time until expiration, other things being equal, the greater the time value. Time value can be subdivided into two components: (1) the effects of time value of money and (2) volatility value.

Time Value of Money

An option's value is enhanced by the delay in paying cash for the shares.

The time value of money component arises because the holder of an option does not have to pay the exercise price until the option is exercised. Instead, the holder can invest funds elsewhere while waiting to exercise the option. For measurement purposes, the time value of money component is assumed to be the rate of return available on risk-free U.S. Treasury Securities. The higher the time value of money, the higher the value of being able to delay payment of the exercise price.

The time value of money component is the difference between the exercise price and its discounted present value minus the present value of expected dividends.

When the underlying stock pays no dividends, the time value of money component is the difference between the exercise price (a future amount) and its discounted present value. Let's say the exercise price is $30. If the present value (discounted at the risk-free rate) is $24, the time value of money component is $6. On the other hand, if the stock pays a dividend (or is expected to during the life of the option), the time value of money component is lower. The value of being able to delay payment of the exercise price would be partially offset by the cost of foregoing the dividend in the meantime. For instance, if the stock underlying the options just described were expected to pay dividends and the discounted present value of the expected dividends were $2, the time value of money component in that example would be reduced from $6 to $4.

Volatility Value

Volatility enhances the likelihood of stock price appreciation.

The volatility value represents the possibility that the option holder might profit from market price appreciation of the underlying stock while being exposed to the loss of only the value of the option, rather than the full market value of the stock. For example, fair value of an option to buy a share at an exercise price of $30, might be measured as $7. The potential profit from market price appreciation is conceptually unlimited. And yet, the potential loss from the stock's value failing to appreciate is only $7.

A stock's volatility is the amount by which its price has fluctuated previously or is expected to fluctuate in the future. The greater a stock's volatility, the greater the potential profit. It usually is measured as one standard deviation of a statistical distribution. Statistically, if the expected annualized volatility is 25%, the probability is approximately 67% that the stock's year-end price will fall within roughly plus or minus 25% of its beginning-of-year price. Stated differently, the probability is approximately 33% that the year-end stock price will fall outside that range.

Option-pricing models make assumptions about the likelihood of various future stock prices by making assumptions about the statistical distribution of future stock prices that take into account the expected volatility of the stock price. One popular option pricing model, the Black Scholes model, for instance, assumes a log-normal distribution. This assumption posits that the stock price is as likely to fall by half as it is to double and that large price movements are less likely than small price movements. The higher a stock's volatility, the higher the probability of large increases or decreases in market price. Because the cost of large decreases is limited to the option's current value, but the profitability from large increases is unlimited, an option on a highly volatile stock has a higher probability of a large profits than does an option on a less volatile stock.

Summary

In summary, the fair value of an option is (a) its intrinsic value plus (b) its time value of money component plus (c) its volatility component. The variables that affect an option's fair value and the effect of each are indicated in Graphic 18B–1.

GRAPHIC   18B–1

Effect of Variables on an Option's Fair Value

All other factors being equal, if the:	The option value will be:
Exercise price is higher	Lower
Term of the option is longer	Higher
Market price of the stock is higher	Higher
Dividends are higher	Lower
Risk-free rate of return is higher	Higher
Volatility of the stock is higher	Higher

Questions for Review of Key Topics

Question	18–1	The basis of accounting for postretirement benefits other than pensions is the substantive plan. What does this mean? When should anticipated changes be incorporated in the accounting treatment?
Question	18–2	What are the two ways to measure the obligation for postretirement benefits other than pensions? Define these measurement approaches.
Question	18–3	How are the costs of providing postretirement benefits other than pensions expensed?
Question	18–4	The APBO existing when *SFAS 106* was adopted is called the transition obligation. When is it recognized as part of compensation expense?
Question	18–5	The components of postretirement benefit expense are similar to the components of pension expense. In what fundamental way does the service cost component differ between these two expenses?
Question	18–6	The EPBO for Branch Industries at the end of 1997 was determined by the actuary to be $20,000 as it relates to employee Will Lawson. Lawson was hired at the beginning of 1983. He will be fully eligible to retire with health care benefits in 15 years but is expected to retire in 25 years. What is the APBO as it relates to Will Lawson?
Question	18–7	What is restricted stock? Describe how compensation expense is determined and recorded for a restricted stock award plan.
Question	18–8	Stock option plans provide employees the option to purchase (a) a specified number of shares of the firm's stock, (b) at a specified price, (c) during a specified period of time. The most controversial and complex aspect of accounting for stock-based compensation is how the fair value of stock options should be measured. Describe the elective measurement approach suggested by the FASB.
Question	18–9	The Tax Code differentiates between qualified option plans, including incentive plans, and nonqualified plans. What are the major differences in tax treatment between incentive plans and nonqualified plans?
Question	18–10	General Electric Corporation has chosen not to use the elective fair value approach for its stock option plans. Identify the major difference between the elective fair value approach and the alternative intrinsic value approach that GE uses.
Question	18–11	Why are most stock option plans structured as incentive plans?
Question	18–12	The fair value of stock options can be considered to be composed of two main components. What are they?
Question	18–13	LTV Corporation grants SARs to key executives. Upon exercise, the SARs entitle executives to receive either cash or stock equal in value to the excess of the market price at exercise over the share price at the date of grant. How should LTV account for the awards?
Question	18–14	Performance share plans, long-term cash bonuses, performance unit plans, and phantom stock plans, among other variations, promise cash or shares to key personnel, subject to the achievement of specific financial goals. How should an employer account for such plans?
Question	18–15	Under what conditions should an employer accrue an expense and the related liability for employees' compensation for future absences? How do company custom and practice affect the accrual decision?
Question	18–16	Benevolent Corporation provides benefits to former and inactive employees after their employment but before they retire. Included in these postemployment (rather than postretirement) benefits are supplemental unemployment benefits, disability-related benefits, and continuation of health care benefits and life insurance coverage. Should Benevolent accrue a liability to provide these benefits?
Question	18–17	The Gillette Company has an Employee Stock Ownership Plan (ESOP). Its disclosure notes included the following: "The ESOP purchased Series C shares with borrowed funds. The ESOP loan and principal will be repaid on a semiannual basis over a 10-year period by Company contributions to the ESOP and by the dividends paid on the Series C shares." An effect of this is that Gillette has received $100 million cash (from the sale to the ESOP of shares) and now is responsible (indirectly) for the repayment of debt used by the ESOP to acquire the cash. Does this mean the company was able to achieve a sizable amount of off-balance-sheet financing?

Exercises

Exercise 18–1
Postretirement benefits;
determine the APBO and
service cost

Prince Distribution, Inc., has an unfunded postretirement health care benefit plan. Medical care and life insurance benefits are provided to employees who render 10 years service and attain age 55 while in service. At the end of 1997, Jim Lukawitz is 31. He was hired by Prince at age 25 (6 years ago) and is expected to retire at age 62. The expected postretirement benefit obligation for Lukawitz at the end of 1997 is $50,000 and $54,000 at the end of 1998.

Required:

Calculate the accumulated postretirement benefit obligation at the end of 1997 and 1998 and the service cost for 1997 and 1998 as pertaining to Lukawitz.

Exercise 18–2
Postretirement benefits; changes in the APBO

On January 1, 1997, Medical Transport Company's accumulated postretirement benefit obligation was $25 million. At the end of 1997 retiree benefits paid were $3 million. Service cost for 1997 is $7 million. At the end of 1997, there were no unrecognized postretirement benefit costs. Assumptions regarding the trend of future health care costs were revised at the end of 1997, causing the actuary to revise downward the estimate of the APBO by $1 million. The actuary's discount rate is 8%.

Required:

Determine the amount of the accumulated postretirement benefit obligation at December 31, 1997.

Exercise 18–3
Postretirement benefits; determine APBO, EPBO

Classified Electronics has an unfunded retiree health care plan. Each of the company's three employees has been with the firm since its inception at the beginning of 1996. As of the end of 1997, the actuary estimates the total net cost of providing health care benefits to employees during their retirement years to have a present value of $72,000. Each of the employees will become fully eligible for benefits after 28 more years of service but aren't expected to retire for 35 more years. The interest rate is 6%.

Required:

1. What is the expected postretirement benefit obligation at the end of *1997*?
2. What is the accumulated postretirement benefit obligation at the end of *1997*?
3. What is the expected postretirement benefit obligation at the end of *1998*?
4. What is the accumulated postretirement benefit obligation at the end of *1998*?

Exercise 18–4
Postretirement benefits; determine APBO, service cost, interest cost; prepare journal entry

The following data are available pertaining to Household Appliance Company's retiree health care plan for 1997:

Number of employees covered	2
Years employed as of January 1, 1997	3 [each]
Attribution period	25 years
Expected postretirement benefit obligation, Jan. 1	$50,000
Expected postretirement benefit obligation, Dec. 31	$53,000
Interest rate	6%
Funding	none

Required:

1. What is the accumulated postretirement benefit obligation at the beginning of 1997?
2. What is interest cost to be included in 1997 postretirement benefit expense?
3. What is service cost to be included in 1997 postretirement benefit expense?
4. Prepare the journal entry to record the postretirement benefit expense for 1997.

Exercise 18–5
Postretirement benefits; determine EPBO; attribution period

Lorin Management Services has an unfunded postretirement benefit plan. On December 31, 1997, the following data were available concerning changes in the plan's accumulated postretirement benefit obligation with respect to one of Lorin's employees:

APBO at the beginning of 1997		$16,364
Interest cost:	($16,364 × 10%)	1,636
Service cost:	($44,000 × $1/22$)	2,000
	Portion of EPBO attributed to 1997	
APBO at the end of 1997		$20,000

Required:

1. Over how many years is the expected postretirement benefit obligation being expensed (attribution period)?
2. What is the expected postretirement benefit obligation at the *end* of 1997?
3. When was the employee hired by Lorin?
4. What is the expected postretirement benefit obligation at the *beginning* of 1997?

Exercise 18–6
Postretirement benefits; components of postretirement benefit expense

Data pertaining to the postretirement health care benefit plan of Sterling Properties include the following for 1997:

	($ in 000s)
Service cost	$124
Accumulated postretirement benefit obligation, January 1	700
Plan assets (fair market value), January 1	50
Unrecognized prior service cost	none

Unrecognized net gain, (1997 amortization, $1)	91
Unrecognized transition obligation, (1997 amortization, $2)	36
Retiree benefits paid (end of year)	87
Contribution to health care benefit fund (end of year)	185
Discount rate, 7%	
Return on plan assets (actual and expected), 10%	

Required:

1. Determine the postretirement benefit expense for 1997.
2. Prepare the appropriate journal entry to record the postretirement benefit expense and funding for 1997.

Exercise 18–7
Postretirement benefits; amortization of unrecognized net loss

Cahal-Michael Company has a postretirement health care benefit plan. On January 1, 1997, the following plan-related data were available:

	($ in 000s)
Unrecognized net loss	$ 336
Accumulated postretirement benefit obligation	2,800
Fair value of plan assets	500
Average remaining service period to retirement	14 years
Average remaining service period to full eligibility	12 years

The rate of return on plan assets during 1997 was 10%, although it was expected to be 9%. The actuary revised assumptions regarding the APBO at the end of the year, resulting in a $39,000 increase in the estimate of that obligation.

Required:

1. Calculate any amortization of the net loss that should be included as a component of postretirement benefit expense for 1997.
2. Assume the postretirement benefit expense for 1997, not including the amortization of the net loss component, is $212,000. What is the expense for the year?
3. Determine the unrecognized net loss or gain as of December 31, 1997.

Exercise 18–8
Postretirement benefits; amortization of unrecognized transition obligation and prior service cost

Gorky-Park Corporation provides postretirement health care benefits to employees who provide at least 12 years service and reach age 62 while in service. On January 1, 1997, the following plan-related data were available:

	($ in millions)
Unrecognized transition obligation	$ 50
Accumulated postretirement benefit obligation	130
Fair value of plan assets	none
Average remaining service period to retirement	25 years
Average remaining service period to full eligibility	20 years

On January 1, 1997, Gorky-Park amends the plan to provide certain dental benefits in addition to previously provided medical benefits. The actuary determines that the cost of making the amendment retroactive increases the APBO by $20 million. Management chooses to amortize the prior service cost on a straight-line basis. The service cost for 1997 is $34 million. The interest rate is 8%.

Required:

Calculate the postretirement benefit expense for 1997.

Exercise 18–9
Postretirement benefits; negative plan amendment

Southeast Technology provides postretirement health care benefits to employees. On January 1, 1997, the following plan-related data were available:

	($ in 000s)
Unrecognized prior service cost	50
Accumulated postretirement benefit obligation	530
Fair value of plan assets	none
Average remaining service period to retirement	20 years
Average remaining service period to full eligibility	15 years

On January 1, 1997, Southeast amends the plan in response to spiraling health care costs. The amendment establishes an annual maximum of $3,000 for medical benefits that the plan will provide. The actuary determines that the effect of this amendment is to decrease the APBO by $80,000. Management amortizes prior service cost on a straight-line basis. The interest rate is 8%. The service cost for 1997 is $114,000.

Required:

1. Calculate the prior service cost amortization for 1997.
2. Calculate the postretirement benefit expense for 1997.
3. Suppose Southeast had an unrecognized transition obligation of $120,000 at January 1. Calculate the prior service cost amortization for 1997.

Exercise 18–10
Multiple choice

The following question dealing with postretirement benefit plans appeared on a recent CPA examination. Enter the letter corresponding to the response which *best* completes the question.

1. An employer's obligation for postretirement health benefits that are expected to be provided to or for an employee must be fully accrued by the date the
    a. Employee is fully eligible for benefits.
    b. Employee retires.
    c. Benefits are utilized.
    d. Benefits are paid.

Exercise 18–11
Restricted stock award plan

Allied Paper Products, Inc., offers a restricted stock award plan to its vice presidents. On January 1, 1997, the company granted 16 million of its $1 par common shares, subject to forfeiture if employment is terminated within two years. The common shares have a market price of $5 per share on the grant date.

Required:
1. Determine the total compensation cost pertaining to the restricted shares, assuming the company chooses to follow the elective fair value approach for fixed compensation plans.
2. Prepare the appropriate journal entries related to the restricted stock through December 31, 1998.

Exercise 18–12
Restricted stock award plan

On January 1, 1997, VKI Corporation awarded 12 million of its $1 par common shares to key personnel, subject to forfeiture if employment is terminated within three years. On the grant date, the shares have a market price of $2.50 per share.

Required:
1. Determine the total compensation cost pertaining to the restricted shares.
2. Prepare the appropriate journal entry to record the award of restricted shares on January 1, 1997.
3. Prepare the appropriate journal entry to record compensation expense on December 31, 1997.
4. Prepare the appropriate journal entry to record compensation expense on December 31, 1998.
5. Prepare the appropriate journal entry to record compensation expense on December 31, 1999.
6. Prepare the appropriate journal entry to record the lifting of restrictions on the shares at December 31, 1999.

Exercise 18–13
Restricted stock award plan; forfeitures anticipated

Magnetic-Optical Corporation offers a variety of stock-based compensation plans to employees. Under its restricted stock award plan, the company on January 1, 1997, granted 4 million of its $1 par common shares to various division managers. The shares are subject to forfeiture if employment is terminated within three years. The common shares have a market price of $22.50 per share on the grant date.

Required:
1. Determine the total compensation cost pertaining to the restricted shares.
2. Prepare the appropriate journal entry to record the award of restricted shares on January 1, 1997.
3. Prepare the appropriate journal entry to record compensation expense on December 31, 1997.
4. Suppose Magnetic-Optical expected a 10% forfeiture rate on the restricted shares prior to vesting. Determine the total compensation cost, assuming the company chooses to follow the elective fair value approach for fixed compensation plans and chooses to anticipate forfeitures at the grant date.

Exercise 18–14
Stock options; elective fair value approach and alternate intrinsic value approach

American Optical Corporation provides a variety of stock-based compensation plans to its employees. Under its executive stock option plan, the company granted options on January 1, 1997, that permit executives to acquire 4 million of the company's $1 par common shares within the next five years, but not before December 31, 1998 (the vesting date). The exercise price is the market price of the shares on the date of grant, $14 per share. The fair value of the 4 million options, estimated by an appropriate option pricing model, is $3 per option. No forfeitures are anticipated. Ignore taxes.

Required:
1. Determine the total compensation cost pertaining to the options, assuming the company chooses to follow the elective fair value approach for fixed compensation plans.
2. Prepare the appropriate journal entry to record the award of options on January 1, 1997.
3. Prepare the appropriate journal entry to record compensation expense on December 31, 1997.
4. Prepare the appropriate journal entry to record compensation expense on December 31, 1998.
5. Determine the total compensation cost pertaining to the options, assuming the company does not choose to follow the elective fair value approach for fixed compensation plans.

Exercise 18–15
Stock option plan; elective fair value approach; forfeiture of options

On January 1, 1997, Adams-Meneke Corporation granted 25 million incentive stock options to division managers, each permitting holders to purchase one share of the company's $1 par common shares within the next six years, but not before December 31, 1999 (the vesting date). The exercise price is the market price of the shares on the date of grant, currently $10 per share. The fair value of the options, estimated by an appropriate option pricing model, is $3 per option. Adams-Meneke chooses to follow the elective fair value approach for fixed compensation plans.

Required:

1. Determine the total compensation cost pertaining to the options on January 1, 1997.
2. Prepare the appropriate journal entry to record compensation expense on December 31, 1997.
3. Unexpected turnover during 1998 caused the forfeiture of 6% of the stock options. Determine the adjusted compensation cost, and prepare the appropriate journal entry(s) on December 31, 1998.

Exercise 18–16
Stock option plan; elective fair value approach; forfeitures anticipated

Walters Audio Visual, Inc., offers an incentive stock option plan to its regional managers. On January 1, 1997, options were granted for 40 million $1 par common shares. The exercise price is the market price on the grant date—$8 per share. Options cannot be exercised prior to January 1, 1999 and expire December 31, 2003. The fair value of the 40 million options, estimated by an appropriate option pricing model, is $1 per option. Walters chooses to follow the elective fair value approach for fixed compensation plans.

Required:

1. Determine the total compensation cost pertaining to the incentive stock option plan.
2. Prepare the appropriate journal entry to record compensation expense on December 31, 1997.
3. Prepare the appropriate journal entry to record compensation expense on December 31, 1998.
4. Prepare the appropriate journal entry to record the exercise of 75% of the options on March 12, 1999, when the market price is $9 per share.
5. Prepare the appropriate journal entry on December 31, 2003, when the remaining options that have vested expire without being exercised.

(This is a variation of Exercise 18–16, modified to consider nonqualifying stock options.)

Exercise 18–17
Stock option plan; market value exceeds exercise price; alternate intrinsic value approach

Walters Audio Visual, Inc., offers a stock option plan to its regional managers. On January 1, 1997, options were granted for 40 million $1 par common shares. The exercise price is $8 per share. The market price of the shares on the date of grant is $8.50 per share. Options cannot be exercised prior to January 1, 1999, and expire December 31, 2003. Walters chooses not to follow the elective fair value approach for fixed compensation plans.

Required:

1. Determine the total compensation cost pertaining to the stock option plan at January 1, 1997.
2. Prepare the appropriate journal entry to record compensation expense on December 31, 1997.
3. Prepare the appropriate journal entry to record compensation expense on December 31, 1998.
4. Prepare the appropriate journal entry to record the exercise of 75% of the options on March 12, 1999, when the market price is $9 per share.
5. Prepare the appropriate journal entry on December 31, 2003, when the remaining options that have vested expire without being exercised.

Exercise 18–18
Stock option plan; alternate intrinsic value approach

SSG Cycles manufactures and distributes motorcycle parts and supplies. Employees are offered a variety of stock-based compensation plans. Under its nonqualified stock option plan, SSG granted options to key officers on January 1, 1997. The options permit holders to acquire 12 million of the company's $1 par common shares for $11 within the next six years, but not before January 1, 2000 (the vesting date). The market price of the shares on the date of grant is $13 per share. The fair value of the 12 million options, estimated by an appropriate option pricing model, is $3 per option. JBL chooses not to follow the elective fair value approach for fixed compensation plans.

Vesting = 3 yrs

Required:

1. Determine the total compensation cost pertaining to the incentive stock option plan.
2. Prepare the appropriate journal entries to record compensation expense on December 31, 1997, 1998, and 1999.
3. Record the exercise of the options if all of the options are exercised on May 11, 2001, when the market price is $14 per share.

Exercise 18–19
Stock appreciation rights; cash settlement

As part of its stock-based compensation package, International Electronics granted 24 million stock appreciation rights (SARs) to top officers on January 1, 1997. At exercise, holders of the SARs are entitled to receive cash or stock equal in value to the excess of the market price at exercise over the share price at the date of grant. The SARs cannot be exercised until the end of 2000 (vesting date) and expire at the end of 2002. The common shares have a market price of $46 per share on the grant date. All recipients are expected to remain employed through the vesting date. The year-end share prices following the grant of the SARs are:

1997	$50
1998	$49
1999	$50
2000	$51
2001	$50

Required:

1. Prepare the appropriate journal entry to record the award of SARs on January 1, 1997.
2. Prepare the appropriate journal entries pertaining to the SARs on December 31, 1997–2000.
3. The SARs remain unexercised on December 31, 2001. Prepare the appropriate journal entry on that date.
4. The SARs are exercised on June 6, 2002, when the share price is $53, and executives choose to receive the market price appreciation in cash. Prepare the appropriate journal entry(ies) on that date.

Exercise 18–20
Multiple choice

The following questions dealing with stock-based compensation plans appeared on recent CPA examinations. Enter the letter corresponding to the response that *best* completes each of the statements or questions.

1. Wolf Co.'s grant of 30,000 stock appreciation rights enables key employees to receive cash equal to the difference between $20 and the market price of the stock on the date each right is exercised. The service period is 1997 through 1999, and the rights are exercisable in 2000 and 2001. The market price of the stock was $25 and $28 at December 31, 1997 and 1998, respectively. What amount should Wolf report as the liability under the stock appreciation rights plan in its December 31, 1998, balance sheet?
   a. $0
   b. $130,000
   c. $160,000
   d. $240,000

2. On January 2, 1997, Morey Corp. granted Dean, its president, 20,000 stock appreciation rights for past services. Those rights are exercisable immediately and expire on January 1, 2000. On exercise, Dean is entitled to receive cash for the excess of the stock's market price on the exercise date over the market price on the grant date. Dean did not exercise any of the rights during 1997. The market price of Morey's stock was $30 on January 2, 1997, and $45 on December 31, 1997. As a result of the stock appreciation rights, Morey should recognize compensation expense for 1997 of
   a. $0
   b. $100,000
   c. $300,000
   d. $600,000

3. On January 2, 1997, Farm Co., granted an employee an option to purchase 1,000 shares of Farm's stock at $40 per share. The option became exercisable on December 31, 1997 after the employee had completed one year of service, and was exercised on that date. The market prices of Farm's stock were as follows: (Farm chooses not to follow the elective fair value approach.)

January 2, 1997	$50
December 31, 1997	65

   What amount should Farm recognize as compensation expense for 1997?
   a. $0
   b. $10,000
   c. $15,000
   d. $25,000

Exercise 18–21
Paid future absences

JWS Transport Company's employees earn vacation time at the rate of 1 hour per 40-hour work period. The vacation pay vests immediately (that is, an employee is entitled to the pay even if employment terminates). During 1997, total wages paid to employees equaled $404,000, including $4,000 for vacations actually taken in 1997 but not including vacations related to 1997 that will be taken in 1998. All vacations earned before 1997 were taken before January 1, 1997. No accrual entries have been made for the vacations. No overtime premium and no bonuses were paid during the period.

Required:

Prepare the appropriate adjusting entry for vacations earned but not taken in 1997.

Exercise 18–22
Paid future absences

On January 1, 1997, Poplar Fabricators Corporation agreed to grant its employees two weeks vacation each year, with the stipulation that vacations earned each year can be taken the following year. For the year ended December 31, 1997, Poplar Fabricators' employees each earned an average of $900 per week. Seven hundred vacation weeks earned in 1997 were not taken during 1997.

Required:

1. Prepare the appropriate adjusting entry for vacations earned but not taken in 1997.
2. Suppose wage rates for employees have risen by an average of 5 percent by the time vacations actually are taken in 1998. Also, assume wages earned in 1998 (including vacations earned and taken in 1998) were $31,000,000. Prepare a journal entry that summarizes 1998 wages and the payment for 1997 vacations taken in 1998.

Problems

Problem 18–1
Postretirement benefits; EPBO calculations; APBO calculations; transition obligation; present value concepts

Century-Fox Corporation's employees are eligible for postretirement health care benefits after both being employed at the end of the year in which age 60 is attained and having worked for Century-Fox for at least 20 years. Jason Snyder was hired at the beginning of 1981 by Century-Fox at age 34 (he turned 35 during 1981) and is expected to retire at the end of 2008 (age 62). His retirement is expected to span five years (unrealistically short to simplify calculations). The company's actuary has estimated the net cost of retiree benefits in each retirement year as shown below. The discount rate is 6%. The plan is not prefunded.

Year	Age	Expected Net Cost
2009	63	$4,000
2010	64	4,400
2011	65	2,300
2012	66	2,500
2013	67	2,800

Required:

1. Draw a time line that depicts Snyder's attribution period for retiree benefits, expected retirement period, and adoption of *SFAS 106* at the beginning of 1993.
2. Calculate the present value of the net benefits as of the expected retirement date.
3. With respect to Snyder, what is the company's expected postretirement benefit obligation at the beginning of 1993 when *SFAS 106* is adopted?
4. With respect to Snyder, what is the company's accumulated postretirement benefit obligation at the beginning of 1993 when *SFAS 106* is adopted?
5. With respect to Snyder, what is the company's *transition obligation* at the beginning of 1993?
6. What portion of the transition obligation would be included in 1993 postretirement benefit expense if management chooses:
   a. Immediate recognition.
   b. Recognition over future service periods.
   c. Optional recognition over a 20-year period.

(This is a variation of the previous problem, designed to focus on different elements of the postretirement benefit plan.)

Problem 18–2
Postretirement benefits; EPBO calculations; APBO calculations; components of postretirement benefit expense; present value concepts

Century-Fox Corporation's employees are eligible for postretirement health care benefits after both being employed at the end of the year in which age 60 is attained and having worked 20 years. Jason Snyder was hired at the beginning of 1981 by Century-Fox at age 34 (he turned 35 during 1981) and is expected to retire at the end of 2008 (age 62). His retirement is expected to span five years (unrealistically short to simplify calculations). The company's actuary has estimated the net cost of retiree benefits in each retirement year as shown below. The discount rate is 6%. The plan is not prefunded.

Year	Expected Age	Net Cost
2009	63	$4,000
2010	64	4,400
2011	65	2,300
2012	66	2,500
2013	67	2,800

Required:

1. Calculate the present value of the net benefits as of the expected retirement date.
2. With respect to Snyder, what is the company's expected postretirement benefit obligation at the end of 1995?
3. With respect to Snyder, what is the company's accumulated postretirement benefit obligation at the end of 1995?
4. With respect to Snyder, what is the company's accumulated postretirement benefit obligation at the end of 1996?

5. What is the service cost to be included in **1996** postretirement benefit expense?
6. What is the interest cost to be included in **1996** postretirement benefit expense?
7. Show how the APBO changed during 1996 by reconciling the beginning and ending balances.

Problem 18–3
Postretirement benefits;
schedule of postretirement
benefit costs

Stockton Labeling Company has a retiree health care plan. Employees become fully eligible for benefits after working for the company eight years. Stockton hired Misty Newburn on January 1, 1997. As of the end of 1997, the actuary estimates the total net cost of providing health care benefits to Newburn during her retirement years to have a present value of $18,000. The actuary's discount rate is 10%.

Required:
Prepare a schedule that shows the EPBO, the APBO, the service cost, the interest cost, and the postretirement benefit expense for each of the years 1997–2004.

Problem 18–4
Postretirement benefits;
relationship among elements
of postretirement benefit plan

The reconciliation schedules below pertain to the retiree health care plan of Thompson Technologies:

	($ in 000s)	
	1997 Beginning Balances	**1997 Ending Balances**
Accumulated postretirement benefit obligation	$(460)	$(485)
Plan assets	0	75
Funded status	(460)	(410)
Unamortized transition obligation	120	110
Unamortized net gain	(50)	(49)
Accrued postretirement benefit cost	$(390)	$(349)

Thompson began funding the plan in 1997 with a contribution of $127,000 to the pension fund at the end of the year. Retirees were paid $52,000. The actuary's discount rate is 5%. There were no changes in actuarial estimates and assumptions.

Required:
Determine the following amounts for 1997:
1. Service cost
2. Postretirement benefit expense

Problem 18–5
Postretirement benefits;
comprehensive

Eastern Transfer and Storage has a postretirement benefit plan. The company adopted *SFAS 106* for the 1994 fiscal year. The APBO at that date was $375 million and the plan was not funded, resulting in a transition obligation of $375 million at the beginning of the year. The transition obligation is to be amortized over the 15-year average remaining service period of plan participants active at the beginning of the year. Eastern began funding at the end of 1994. The discount rate is 8%, and the expected rate of return on plan assets is 10%.

1994 service cost was $23 million, $60 million was contributed to plan assets at the end of the year, and retiree benefit payments are $20 million. Because of changes in assumptions and estimates at the end of 1994, the APBO is determined to be $92 million higher than anticipated.

Required:
1. Determine the APBO at the end of fiscal year 1994.
2. Determine postretirement benefit expense for fiscal year 1994.
3. Prepare the journal entry to record postretirement benefit expense and funding for fiscal year 1994.
4. Prepare a schedule to reconcile the funded status of the plan with the amount reported on the balance sheet for fiscal year 1994.
5. Eastern's 1995 service cost is $32 million, asset contributions are $90 million, retiree benefit payments are $55 million, and the return on plan assets is $5 million. Determine the APBO and plan assets at December 31, 1995.
6. The average remaining service period of plan participants active at the beginning of the 1995 fiscal year is 14 years. Determine the amortization of the unrecognized net loss for 1995.
7. Determine postretirement benefit expense for fiscal year 1995.
8. Prepare the journal entry to record postretirement benefit expense and funding for fiscal year 1995.
9. Prepare a schedule to reconcile the funded status of the plan with the amount reported on the balance sheet for fiscal year 1995.

Problem 18–6
Stock options; elective fair
value approach and alternate
intrinsic value approach

On October 15, 1996, the board of directors of Ensor Materials Corporation approved a stock option plan for key executives. On January 1, 1997, 20 million stock options were granted, exercisable for 20 million shares of Ensor's $1 par common stock. The options are exercisable between January 1, 1999, and December 31, 2001, at 80% of the quoted market price on January 1, 1997, which was $15. The fair value of the 20 million options, estimated by an appropriate option pricing model, is $7 per option. Two million options were forfeited when an executive resigned in 1998. All other options were exercised on July 12, 2000, when the stock's price jumped unexpectedly to $19 per share.

Required:
1. When is Ensor's stock option measurement date if the company chooses to follow the elective fair value approach for fixed compensation plans? Is it different if they choose the alternative intrinsic value approach?
2. Determine the compensation expense, if any, for the stock option plan in 1997 by each of the two approaches. (Ignore taxes.)
3. What is the effect of forfeiture of the stock options on Ensor's financial statements for 1998 by each approach? Why?

Problem 18–7
Stock option plan; deferred tax effect recognized

Walters Audio Visual, Inc., offers a stock option plan to its regional managers. On January 1, 1997, options were granted for 40 million $1 par common shares. The exercise price is the market price on the grant date, $8 per share. Options cannot be exercised prior to January 1, 1999, and expire December 31, 2003. The fair value of the options, estimated by an appropriate option pricing model, is $2 per option. Because the plan does not qualify as an incentive plan, Walters will receive a tax deduction upon exercise of the options equal to the excess of the market price at exercise over the exercise price. The income tax rate is 40%. Walters chooses to follow the elective fair value approach for fixed compensation plans.

Required:
1. Determine the total compensation cost pertaining to the stock option plan.
2. Prepare the appropriate journal entries to record compensation expense and its tax effect on December 31, 1997.
3. Prepare the appropriate journal entries to record compensation expense and its tax effect on December 31, 1998.
4. Record the exercise of the options and their tax effect if *all* of the options are exercised on March 20, 2002, when the market price is $12 per share.
5. Assume the option plan qualifies as an incentive plan. Prepare the appropriate journal entries to record compensation expense and its tax effect on December 31, 1997.
6. Assuming the option plan qualifies as an incentive plan, record the exercise of the options and their tax effect if *all* of the options are exercised on March 20, 2002, when the market price is $11 per share.

Problem 18–8
Stock option plan; deferred tax effect of a nonqualifying plan; alternate intrinsic value approach

JBL Aircraft manufactures and distributes aircraft parts and supplies. Employees are offered a variety of stock-based compensation plans. Under its nonqualified stock option plan, JBL granted options to key officers on January 1, 1997. The options permit holders to acquire six million of the company's $1 par common shares for $22 within the next six years, but not before January 1, 2000 (the vesting date). The market price of the shares on the date of grant is $26 per share. The fair value of the 6 million options, estimated by an appropriate option pricing model, is $6 per option. JBL chooses not to follow the elective fair value approach for fixed compensation plans. Because the plan does not qualify as an incentive plan, JBL will receive a tax deduction upon exercise of the options equal to the excess of the market price at exercise over the exercise price. The tax rate is 40%.

Required:
1. Determine the total compensation cost pertaining to the incentive stock option plan.
2. Prepare the appropriate journal entries to record compensation expense and its tax effect on December 31, 1997, 1998, and 1999.
3. Record the exercise of the options and their tax effect if *all* of the options are exercised on August 21, 2001, when the market price is $27 per share.

Problem 18–9
Performance share plan

LCI Cable Company grants 1 million performance share rights to key executives at January 1, 1997. The rights entitle executives to receive 1 million of TCI $1 par common shares, subject to the achievement of specific financial goals over the next four years. Attainment of these goals is considered probable initially and throughout the service period. LCI does not employ the elective fair value approach for stock-based compensation plans.

The shares have a current market price of $10 per share. The year-end share prices following the grant of the rights are:

1997	$12
1998	$14
1999	$16
2000	$14

Required:

1. Prepare the appropriate entry when the rights are awarded on January 1, 1997.
2. Prepare the appropriate entries on December 31 of each year 1997–2000.
3. Prepare the appropriate entry when the shares are awarded on January 1, 2001.
4. Suppose the performance objectives aren't met. What action should occur on January 1, 2001.

Problem 18–10
Bonus Compensation

Sometimes compensation packages include bonuses designed to provide performance incentives to employees. The difficulty a bonus can cause accountants is not an accounting problem, but a math problem. The complication is that the bonus formula sometimes specifies that the calculation of the bonus is based in part on the bonus itself. This occurs anytime the bonus is a percentage of income because expenses are components of income, and the bonus is an expense.

Regalia Fashions has an incentive compensation plan through which a division manager receives a bonus equal to 10% of the division's net income. Division income in 1997 before the bonus and income tax was $150,000. The tax rate is 30%.

Required:

1. Express the bonus formula as one or more algebraic equation(s).*
2. Using these formulas calculate the amount of the bonus.
3. Prepare the adjusting entry to record the bonus compensation.
4. Bonus arrangements take many forms. Suppose the bonus specifies that the bonus is 10% of the division's income before tax, but after the bonus itself. Calculate the amount of the bonus.

*Remember when you were studying algebra, and you wondered if you would ever use it?

Cases

Integrating Case 18–1
Postretirement benefits and income taxes

Complying with *SFAS 106*, "Employers' Accounting for Postretirement Benefits Other than Pensions," creates for most companies a temporary difference in connection with income taxation. The difference is due to the fact that the standard requires companies to accrue postretirement benefit expense each year employees perform services, and yet the costs aren't tax-deductible until paid in future years. The following data were available in 1993 when GRE Systems adopted *SFAS 106*:

	($ in millions)
Accumulated postretirement benefit obligation, 1/1/93	$275
Service cost for 1993	43
Interest cost for 1993	32
Benefits paid in 1993 (end of year)	10
Plan assets	0
Average remaining service period	25 years
No unrecognized gains or losses or prior service cost	
No other temporary differences	
Tax rate	40%

Required:

1. Assuming the transition liability is not recognized immediately, what is the postretirement benefit expense for 1993?
2. Indicate the appropriate journal entry to record the 1993 postretirement expense.
3. Assuming taxable income in 1993 is $400 million, indicate the appropriate journal entry to record the 1993 income tax expense.
4. Assuming the transition liability is recognized immediately, indicate the appropriate journal entries to record the 1993 postretirement expense and income tax expense.

Integrating Case 18–2
How was the adoption of *SFAS 106* an exception to the usual method of accounting for changes in accounting principle?

In Chapter 3 you learned that most changes in accounting principle require reporting the cumulative income effect of the change as part of earnings in the year of the change. In Chapter 21, you will discover five exceptions that require retroactive restatement of prior years' financial statements. Also, a few changes mandated by new FASB accounting standards require neither of those approaches and instead require or permit prospective application of the new standard. An example of this exception is *SFAS 106*, "Employers' Accounting for Postretirement Benefits Other Than Pensions."

Required:

Explain how *SFAS 106* is an exception to the general method of accounting for changes in accounting principle.

International Case 18–3
Accounting for postretirement
benefits in other countries

The primary objective of the International Accounting Standards Committee (IASC) is to narrow worldwide differences in accounting practices and the presentation of financial information. Although the IASC has worked toward uniformity since 1973, harmonization has by no means been achieved. In the area of accounting for postretirement benefits, particularly those other than pensions, significant differences exist from country to country. The differences impact on reported earnings and financial position in countries where these benefits are significant.

Required

1. Locate a recent annual report of a non-U.S. company and determine the way that country accounts for postretirement benefits other than pensions. Include in your analysis:
   a. Whether and how the cost of providing benefits is reported in disclosure notes.
   b. Whether the obligation for the benefits is accrued in the balance sheet.
   c. The impact on the income statement, if any.
2. Prepare a short report highlighting the similarities and differences between the United States and your chosen country in the way postretirement benefits are accounted for.

**Trueblood Accounting
Case 18–4**
Stock compensation
arrangements; substance
versus form

The following Robert M. Trueblood case is recommended for use with this chapter. The case provides an excellent opportunity for class discussion, group projects, and writing assignments. The case, along with Professor's Discussion Material, can be obtained from the Deloitte & Touche Foundation.

Case 94-6: *Optional Exercising Equipment*

This case encourages consideration of the substance versus form issue as it relates to accounting for stock compensation arrangements.

Research Case 18–5
Controversial issues in
accounting for stock options;
consult an article in the
Journal of Accountancy

The debate surrounding the creation of accounting standards on accounting for stock options focused on a number of very controversial issues. Professors Ciccotello and Grant, in "Employee Stock Option Accounting," address the comparative impact on small and large firms of recognizing compensation expense for stock options.

Required:

1. In your library or from some other source, locate the indicated article in the *Journal of Accountancy*, January 1995.
2. How would the standard proposed at the time differ from existing standards?
3. According to the authors, how would the new rules impact small companies differently from large companies?
4. In the opinion of the authors, how would the new rules affect the compensation policy of companies affected?

Writing Case 18–6
Stock options; basic
concepts; prepare a memo

You are Assistant Controller of Stamos & Company, a medium-size manufacturer of machine parts. On October 22, 1996, the board of directors approved a stock option plan for key executives. On January 1, 1997, a specific number of stock options were granted. The options were exercisable between January 1, 1999, and December 31, 2001, at 100% of the quoted market price at the grant date. The service period is for 1997 through 1999. The board is considering opting for the elective fair value approach.

   Your boss, the controller, is one of the executives to receive options. Neither he nor you have had occasion to deal with the FASB pronouncement on accounting for stock options. He and you are aware of the traditional approach that can be chosen as an alternative but do not know the newer method. Your boss understands how options might benefit him personally but wants to be aware also of how the options will be reported in the financial statements. He has asked you for a one-page synopsis of accounting for stock options under the elective fair value approach. He instructed you, "I don't care about the effect on taxes or earnings per share—just the basics, please."

Required:
Prepare such a report that includes the following:
1. At what point should the compensation cost be measured? How should it be measured?
2. How should compensation expense be measured for the stock option plan in 1997 and later?
3. If options are forfeited because an executive resigns before vesting, what is the effect of that forfeiture of the stock options on the financial statements?
4. If options are forfeited because they are allowed to lapse after vesting, what is the effect of that forfeiture of the stock options on the financial statements?
5. What is the primary difference between the elective fair value approach and the alternative intrinsic value approach?

Research Case 18–7
Alternative approach to measuring the fair value of stock options; consult an article in *Accounting Horizons*

As described in this chapter, the FASB encourages corporations to measure the fair value of stock options given to employees as part of their compensation package. However, the reliability of fair value estimates is debatable. Employee stock options usually can't be traded in the marketplace and thus don't have a readily determinable market price. This value is approximated using one of several option pricing models. Professor Sunder, in "Economic Incentives as a Substitute for Detailed Accounting Requirements: The Case of Compensation Value of Stock Options," offers an interesting solution to the measurement problem.

Required:

1. In your library or from some other source, locate the indicated article in *Accounting Horizons*, June 1994.
2. What is the alternative described in the article?
3. What is the author's primary argument for the approach?

Research Case 18–8
Controversial issues in accounting for stock options; consult an article in the *Journal of Accountancy*

The debate surrounding the creation of accounting standards on accounting for stock options focused on a number of very controversial issues. Professor Rouse and Mr. Barton, in "Stock Compensation Accounting," outline and discuss the central issues in that debate.

Required:

1. In your library or from some other source, locate the indicated article in the *Journal of Accountancy*, June 1993.
2. Why was the debate controversial?
3. What were the three key questions on which the debate centered?
4. What concerns were outlined by the authors with regard to measurement issues?

Real World Case 18–9
Stock options and income taxes

Proffitt's, Inc., is one of America's fastest growing specialty retailers. The following disclosure note appeared in the company's annual report for the 12 months ending January 28, 1995:

Notes to Consolidated Financial Statements

Note D—Income Taxes (in Part)

During the year ended January 29, 1994, certain incentive and nonqualified stock options (for income tax purposes) were exercised. The difference between the purchase price of the stock established at the date of grant and the fair value at date of exercise was deducted as compensation for income tax purposes without a corresponding expense recorded for financial reporting purposes. The tax benefit of $463,000 relating to such was credited to additional paid-in capital.

Note J—Stock Options (in Part)

Stock option activity was as follows:

	Stock Option Shares (000s)	Price Range	
Balance at February 1, 1992	295	$ 5.250	$ 8.125
Granted	78	12.000	
Exercised	(53)	5.250	12.000
Balance at January 30, 1993	320	5.250	12.000
Granted	199	23.625	28.500
Exercised	(81)	5.25	12.000
Balance at January 29, 1994	438	5.250	28.500
Granted	660	18.250	24.500
Exercised	(70)	5.250	23.625
Canceled	(9)	12.000	23.625
Balance at January 28, 1995	1,019	5.250	28.500

Assume the additional paid-in capital account used for the tax benefit was paid-in capital—tax benefit. Reference to other portions of the annual report reveals the following related information:

Income tax rate	39%
Par value per common share	$.10

Required:

1. Why is there a tax benefit from the options being exercised? How and when is the tax benefit recognized? Why?
2. Assume a $160,000 balance in paid-in capital—stock options pertains to the options exercised in 1994. Was this attributable to incentive options or nonqualifying options? Why?
3. Assume the average market price of the shares when the options were exercised was $26.65. Based on the information provided, prepare the appropriate journal entry to record the exercise of the options for 81,000 shares in the fiscal year ending January 29, 1994. (Hint: Using the information provided concerning the tax benefit, the tax rate, the market price, and the number of shares issued, calculate the average exercise price for the options.)

Critical Thought Case 18–10
Paid future absences

Cates Computing Systems develops and markets commercial software for personal computers and workstations. Three situations involving compensation for possible future absences of Cates' employees are described below.

a. Cates compensates employees at their regular pay rate for time absent for military leave, maternity leave, and jury time. Employees are allowed predetermined absence periods for each type of absence.

b. Members of the new product development team are eligible for three months' paid sabbatical leave every four years. Five members of the team have just completed their fourth year of participation.

c. Company policy permits employees four paid sick days each year. Unused sick days can accumulate and can be carried forward to future years.

Required:
1. What are the conditions that require accrual of an expense and related liability for employees' compensation for future absences?
2. For each of the three situations, indicate the circumstances under which accrual of an expense and related liability is warranted.

Ethics Case 18–11
Stock options

You are in your second year as an auditor with Dantly and Regis, a regional CPA firm. One of the firm's long-time clients is Mayberry-Cleaver Industries, a national company involved in the manufacturing, marketing, and sales of hydrolic devices used in specialized manufacturing applications. Early in this year's audit you discover that Mayberry-Cleaver has changed its method of determining inventory from LIFO to FIFO. Your client's explanation is that FIFO is consistent with the method used by some other companies in the industry. Upon further investigation, you discover an executive stock option plan whose terms call for a significant increase in the shares available to executives if net income this year exceeds $44 million. Some quick calculations convince you that without the change in inventory methods, the target will not be reached; with the change, it will.

Required:
Do you perceive an ethical dilemma? What would be the likely impact of following the controller's suggestions? Who would benefit? Who would be injured?

Group Interaction Case 18–12
Should the present two-category distinction between liabilities and equity be retained?

The current conceptual distinction between liabilities and equity defines liabilities independently of assets and equity, with equity defined as a residual amount. The present proliferation of financial instruments that combine features of both debt and equity and the difficulty of drawing a distinction have led many to conclude that the present two-category distinction between liabilities and equity be eliminated. Two opposing viewpoints are:

View 1: The distinction should be maintained.
View 2: The distinction should be eliminated and financial instruments should instead be reported in accordance with the priority of their claims to enterprise assets.

One type of security that often is mentioned in the debate is mandatorily redeemable preferred stock. Although stock in many ways, such a security also obligates the issuer to transfer assets at a specified price and redemption date. Thus it also has features of debt. In considering this question, focus on conceptual issues regarding the practicable and theoretically appropriate treatment, unconstrained by GAAP.

Required:
1. Which view do you favor? Develop a list of arguments in support of your view prior to the class session for which the case is assigned.
2. In class, your instructor will pair you (and everyone else) with a classmate (who also has independently developed an argument).
    a. You will be given three minutes to argue your view to your partner. Your partner likewise will be given three minutes to argue his or her view to you. During these three-minute presentations, the listening partner is not permitted to speak.
    b. Then after each person has had a turn attempting to convince his or her partner, the two partners will have a three-minute discussion in which they will decide which view is more convincing and arguments will be merged into a single view for each pair.
3. After the allotted time, a spokesperson for each of the two views will be selected by the instructor. Each spokesperson will field arguments from the class in support of that view's position and list the arguments on the board. The class then will discuss the merits of the two lists of arguments and attempt to reach a consensus view, though a consensus is not necessary.

Research Case 18–13
Alternative accounting of stock options; research article in *Accounting Horizons*

The FASB advocates recognizing stock options at fair value. In their article "Extending the Method of Accounting for Stock Appreciation Rights to Employee Stock Options," Professor Steven Balsam suggests as an alternative, the method used to account for SARs.

Required:

1. In your library or from some other source, locate the indicated article in *Accounting Horizons*, December 1994.
2. On what basis does the FASB reject the approach suggested by Professor Balsam?
3. What are the four theoretical reasons Professor Balsam offers for his approach?
4. What is the practical basis Professor Balsam offers for his approach?
5. Do you agree with the author's suggestions?

Internet Case 18–14
Researching the way employee benefits are tested on the CPA Exam; retrieving information from the Internet

The board of examiners of the American Institute of Certified Public Accountants (AICPA) is responsible for preparing the CPA examination. The boards of accountancy of all 50 states, the District of Columbia, Guam, Puerto Rico, and the U.S. Virgin Islands use the examination as the primary way to measure the technical competence of CPA candidates. The content for each examination section is specified by the AICPA and described in outline form.

Required:

1. Access the AICPA web site on the Internet. The web address is www.aicpa.org/.
2. Access the CPA exam section within the site. Locate the content specification portion of the section. Which topics pertaining to employee benefits are specifically listed as testable items on the exam?
3. More than half of the 54 U.S. jurisdictions that license certified public accountants have adopted through legislation or regulation a requirement of 150 semester hours of education as a condition to take the Uniform CPA Examination. Consult the "About the AICPA" section of the site. Determine whether your state has adopted or will adopt the 150-hour requirement and the effective date if applicable.

Trueblood Accounting Case 18–15
Postretirement benefits and contingencies

The following Robert M. Trueblood case is recommended for use with this chapter. The case provides an excellent opportunity for class discussion, group projects, and writing assignments. The case, along with Professor's Discussion Material, can be obtained from the Deloitte & Touche Foundation.

Case 96-2: *Going Back on a Promise*

This case highlights interrelationships between contingencies and postretirement benefits .

Financial Analysis Case 18–16
Reporting postretirement benefits

Federal Express Corporation

Refer to the financial statements and related disclosure notes of Federal Express Corporation in the Appendix to Chapter 1.

Required:

1. What types of postretirement benefits other than pensions does Federal Express provide its retirees? What are the eligibility requirements?
2. When Federal Express adopted *SFAS 106*, did it choose to expense the transition cost immediately or over the average service life of employees?
3. Is the postretirement benefit plan funded? Explain.

SHAREHOLDERS' EQUITY

OVERVIEW

We turn our attention in this chapter from liabilities, which represent the creditors' interests in the assets of a corporation, to the shareholders' residual interest in those assets. The discussions distinguish between the two basic sources of shareholders' equity: (1) *invested* capital and (2) *earned* capital. These two sources are the subjects of Parts B and C of this chapter—paid-in capital and retained earnings. We explore the expansion of corporate capital through the issuance of shares as well as the contraction caused by the retirement of shares or the purchase of treasury shares. Within the context of our discussions of retained earnings, we examine cash dividends, property dividends, stock dividends, and stock splits.

LEARNING OBJECTIVES   After studying this chapter, you should be able to:

1. Describe the components of shareholders' equity and explain how they are reported.
2. Prepare a statement of shareholders' equity and explain its usefulness.
3. Record the issuance of shares when sold for cash, for noncash consideration, and by share purchase contract.
4. Describe what occurs when shares are retired and how the retirement is recorded.
5. Distinguish between the par value method and the cost method of accounting for the purchase and resale of treasury shares.
6. Describe retained earnings and distinguish it from paid-in capital.
7. Explain the basis of corporate dividends, including the similarities and differences between cash and property dividends.
8. Explain stock dividends and stock splits and how they are accounted for.

TODAY

DATE_____

THINGS TO DO — FINISHED ✓

1. Chapter 19
2. pgs- 828-831
3. not covered in class,
4. but are responsible
5. for.
6.
7. Read whole chapter-
8. see page-by-page notes
9.
0.

SPECIAL FOLLOW-UP

1.
2.
3.
4.
5.

TOPS FORM 2151 ®   LITHO IN U.S.A.

... the net. Earlier today you noticed on the ... up almost a dollar a share. You've been ... another all day.

... since the beginning of the year and a cus- ... tomer of its Gap, Banana Republic, and Old Navy ... stores for several years now. The dividends ... not why you bought the stock; you were ... rapidly. That hasn't really happened. There ... for-one split of common stock back in ...

... across the following news article:

... ped Thursday after the retailer said its
... f its common shares.
... rk Stock Exchange.
... et over the next three years. The new pro-
... share buyback.
... id the new program is intended, in part,

... ap's buyback plan? What does ... is intended, in part, to offset future

... buyback?

... cents a share have on Gap's assets? Its

... s assets? Its liabilities? Its shareholders'

PART

A

THE NATURE OF SHAREHOLDERS' EQUITY

Learning objective 1
Describe the components of shareholders' equity and explain how they are reported.

A corporation raises money to fund its business operations by some mix of debt and equity financing. In earlier chapters, we examined debt financing in the form of notes, bonds, leases, and other liabilities. Amounts representing those liabilities denote *creditors' interest* in the company's assets. Now we focus on various forms of equity financing. Specifically, in this chapter we consider transactions that affect shareholders' equity—those accounts that represent the *ownership interests* of shareholders.

In principle, shareholders' equity is a relatively straightforward concept. Shareholders' equity is a residual amount—what's left over after creditor claims have been subtracted from assets (in other words, net assets). You probably recall the residual nature of shareholders' equity from the basic accounting equation:

Net assets equal shareholders' equity.

$$\underbrace{\text{Assets} - \text{Liabilities}}_{\text{Net Assets}} = \text{Shareholders' equity}$$

Ownership interests of shareholders arise primarily from two sources: (1) amounts *invested* by shareholders in the corporation and (2) amounts *earned* by the corporation on behalf of its shareholders. These two sources are reported as (1) paid-in capital and (2) retained earnings.

Shareholders' equity accounts denote the *ownership interests* of shareholders.

Despite being a seemingly clear-cut concept, shareholders' equity and its component accounts often are misunderstood and misinterpreted. As we explore the transactions that affect shareholders' equity and its component accounts, try not to allow yourself to be overwhelmed by unfamiliar terminology or to be overly concerned with precise account titles. Terminology pertaining to shareholders' equity accounts is notoriously diverse. To give you one example—retained earnings is reported variously as *retained income* (NACCO Industries), *reinvested earnings* (Consolidated Papers), *earnings reinvested in the business* (The New York Times Company), *earnings retained for use in the business* (Armada Corporation), *retained earnings reinvested and employed in the business* (L.S. Starret Company), and *accumulated earnings employed in the business* (Outboard Marine). Every shareholders' equity account has several aliases. Indeed, shareholders' equity itself is often referred to as *stockholders' equity, shareowners' equity, shareholders' investment*, and many other similar titles.

GAAP permits many choices in accounting for transactions affecting shareholders' equity.

Complicating matters, transactions that affect shareholders' equity are influenced by corporation laws of individual states in which companies are located. And, as we see later, generally accepted accounting principles provide companies with considerable latitude when choosing accounting methods in this area.

Keeping this perspective in mind while you study the chapter should aid you in understanding the essential concepts. At a very basic level, each transaction we examine can be viewed simply as an increase or decrease in shareholders' equity, per se, without regard to specific shareholders' equity accounts. In fact, for a business organized as a single proprietorship, all capital changes are recorded in a single owner's equity account. The same concepts apply to a corporation. But for corporations, additional considerations make it desirable to separate owners' equity into several separate shareholders' equity accounts. These additional considerations—legal requirements and disclosure objectives—are discussed in following sections of this chapter. So, as you study the separate effects of transactions on retained earnings and specific paid-in capital accounts, you may find it helpful to ask yourself frequently "What is the net effect of this transaction on shareholders' equity?" or, equivalently, "By how much are net assets (assets minus liabilities) affected by this transaction?"

Legal requirements and disclosure objectives make it preferable to separate a corporation's capital into several separate shareholders' equity accounts.

Financial Reporting Overview

Before we examine the events that underlie specific shareholders' equity accounts, let's overview how individual accounts relate to each other. The condensed balance sheet of Exposition Corporation, a hypothetical company, in Graphic 19–1 provides that perspective.

Graphic 19–1 depicts a rather comprehensive situation. It's unlikely that any one company would have shareholders' equity from all of these sources at any one time. Remember that, at this

GRAPHIC   19–1

Detailed Shareholders' Equity Presentation

Assets
minus Liabilities
equals Shareholders' equity

The primary source of paid-in capital is the investment made by shareholders when buying preferred and common stock.

Several other events affect paid-in capital.

Retained earnings represents earned capital.

Exposition Corporation
Balance Sheet ($ in millions)
December 31, 1997

Assets

($3,000)

Liabilities

($1,000)

Shareholders' Equity

Paid-in Capital:	
Capital stock (par):	
Preferred stock, 10%, $10 par, cumulative, nonparticipating	$100
Common stock, $1 par	55
Common stock dividends distributable	5
Additional paid-in capital:	
Paid-in capital – excess of par, common	300
Paid-in capital – excess of par, preferred	50
Receivable from share purchase contract	(40)
Paid-in capital – reacquired shares	8
Paid-in capital – conversion of bonds	7
Paid-in capital – stock options	9
Paid-in capital – stock award plan	5
Paid-in capital – lapse of stock options	1
Total paid-in capital	$ 500
Retained earnings (Note A)	1,070
Accumulated Components of Comprehensive Income:	
Unrealized gains (losses) on investment securities	(85)
Unrealized pension cost	(75)
Foreign currency translation adjustments*	–0–
Treasury Stock (at cost)	(10)
Total shareholders' equity	$1,400

Note A: Assets represented by $300 million of retained earnings are restricted from distribution as dividends in order to facilitate expansion of manufacturing facilities.

*Gains or losses from changes in foreign currency exchange rates. This item is discussed elsewhere in your accounting curriculum. The amount could be an addition to or reduction in shareholders' equity.

point, our objective is only to get a general perspective of the items constituting shareholders' equity. You should, however, note a few aspects of the statement shown in Graphic 19–1.

First, the two primary components of Exposition Corporation's shareholders' equity are paid-in capital and retained earnings. **Paid-in capital** consists primarily of amounts invested by shareholders when they purchase shares of stock from the corporation. In addition, amounts sometimes are invested (or disinvested) by others on behalf of the shareholders. For Exposition Corporation, shareholders invested $470 million ($100 + 55 + 5 + 300 + 50 – 40). An additional $30 million ($8 + 7 + 9 + 5 +1) of paid-in capital arose from financing activities, bringing the total to $500 million. Later in this chapter, we consider in more detail the events and transactions that affect paid-in capital. **Retained earnings** is reported as a single amount, $1,070 million, but a disclosure note provides additional information about a specific restriction on dividends.

The two primary components of shareholders' equity are **paid-in capital** and **retained earnings**.

Second, notice that shareholders' equity of Exposition Corporation is adjusted for three events that are not included in net income and so don't affect retained earnings but are part of "comprehensive income" and therefore are included as separate components of shareholders' equity.[1] You were introduced to two of these transactions in previous chapters—unrealized gains or losses from investments in securities and unrealized pension cost.[2] The other—foreign currency translation adjustments—is covered elsewhere in your accounting curriculum. The final component of shareholders' equity—treasury stock—is discussed later in this chapter.

Some accounts can be viewed as contra-shareholders' equity accounts.

Third, you seldom if ever will see this degree of detail reported in the presentation of paid-in capital. Instead, companies keep track of individual additional paid-in capital accounts in company

---

[1] Comprehensive income is discussed in Chapter 3.

[2] Recall (from Chapter 12), for instance, that changes in the market value of investments classified as available for sale produce unrealized gains (losses) that increase (reduce) shareholders' equity. Remember, too, that reporting an additional minimum pension liability sometimes requires a reduction in shareholders' equity (see Chapter 17).

> Ordinarily, less detail is reported than is kept in company records.

records but ordinarily report these amounts as a single subtotal—additional paid-in capital. Pertinent rights and privileges of various securities outstanding such as dividend and liquidation preferences, call and conversion information, and voting rights are summarized in disclosure notes.[3] The shareholders' equity portion of the balance sheet of Phillips-Van Heusen Corporation, maker of dress shirts and other clothing lines, shown in Graphic 19–2 is a typical presentation format.

GRAPHIC   19–2

Typical Presentation Format—Phillips-Van Heusen Corporation

> Details of each class of stock are reported on the face of the balance sheet or in disclosure notes.

Shareholders' Equity Section of the Balance Sheet Phillips-Van Heusen Corporation		
($ in thousands, except per share amounts)	Jan. 28, 1996	Jan. 29, 1995
Stockholders' Equity		
Preferred stock, par value $100 per share; 150,000 shares authorized; no shares outstanding	—	—
Common stock, par value $1 per share; 100,000,000 shares authorized; shares issued 26,979,352 and 26,610,310	26,979	26,610
Additional paid-in capital	115,977	112,801
Retained earnings	132,336	136,049
Total shareholders' equity	$275,292	$275,460

> **Learning objective 2**
> Prepare a statement of shareholders' equity and explain its usefulness.

The balance sheet reports annual balances of shareholders' equity accounts. However, companies also should disclose the sources of the changes in those accounts.[4] This is the purpose of the **statement of shareholders' equity**. To illustrate, Graphic 19–3 shows how Phillips-Van Heusen Corporation reported the changes in its shareholders' equity balances (shown in Graphic 19–2.)

The changes that Phillips-Van Heusen's statement of shareholders' equity reveal are the exercise of stock options, the years' net income, the declaration of cash dividends, the issuance of treasury shares, the retirement of common shares, the issuance of shares as part of the price of an investment, and the retirement of treasury shares when the company decided to no longer consider shares repurchased as treasury stock.

The Corporate Organization

A company may be organized in any of three ways: (1) a single proprietorship, (2) a partnership, or (3) a corporation. In your introductory accounting course, you studied each form. In this course we focus exclusively on the corporate form of organization.

> Corporations are the dominant form of business organization.

Most well-known companies, such as Exxon, IBM, and General Motors, are corporations. Also, many smaller companies—even one-owner businesses—are corporations. Although fewer in number than proprietorships and partnerships, in terms of business volume, corporations are the predominant form of business organization.

---

[3]"Disclosure of Information about Capital Structure," *Statement of Financial Accounting Standards No. 129,* (Norwalk, Conn.: FASB, 1997).

[4] "Omnibus Opinion," *APB Opinion No. 12,* AICPA, 1967.

GRAPHIC   19–3

Changes in Shareholders'
Equity—Phillips-Van Heusen
Corporation

Phillips-Van Heusen Corporation
Consolidated Statements of Changes in Stockholders' Equity
For the Years Ended Jan. 28, 1996, Jan. 29, 1995, and Jan. 30, 1994
(In thousands, except share data)

	Common Stock Shares	Common Stock $1 par	Additional Paid-in Capital	Retained Earnings	Treasury Stock	Stockholders' Equity
Balance, Jan. 31, 1993	32,704,168	$32,704	$111,422	$241,117	$(173,830)	$211,413
Stock options exercised	486,647	487	6,940	–	–	7,427
Net income	–	–	–	31,858	–	31,858
Cash dividends	–	–	–	(3,920)	–	(3,920)
Issue 150 shares from treasury	–	–	–	–	23	23
Stock repurchased and canceled	(65)	–	(2)	–	–	(2)
Balance, Jan. 30, 1994	33,190,750	33,191	118,360	269,055	(173,807)	246,799
Stock options exercised	148,471	148	2,493	–	–	2,641
Net income	–	–	–	30,015	–	30,015
Cash dividends	–	–	–	(3,984)	–	(3,984)
Retirement of treasury stock	(6,728,576)	(6,729)	(8,041)	(159,037)	173,807	0
Stock repurchased and canceled	(335)	–	(11)	–	–	(11)
Balance, Jan. 29, 1995	26,610,310	26,610	112,801	136,049	0	275,460
Stock options exercised	187,908	188	1,557	–	–	1,745
Net income	–	–	–	294	–	294
Cash dividends	–	–	–	(4,007)	–	(4,007)
Investment in Pyramid Sportswear	181,134	181	1,619	–	–	1,800
Balance, Jan. 28, 1996	26,979,352	$26,979	$115,977	$132,336	$ 0	$275,292

> A **statement of shareholders' equity** reports the transactions that cause changes in its shareholders' equity account balances.

> Accounting for most transactions is the same regardless of the form of business organization.

In most respects, transactions are accounted for in the same way regardless of the form of business organization. Assets and liabilities are unaffected by the way a company is organized. The exception is the method of accounting for capital, the ownership interest in the company. Rather than recording all changes in ownership interests in a single capital account for each owner, as we do for single proprietorships and partnerships, we use the several capital accounts overviewed in the previous section to record those changes for a corporation. Before discussing how we account for specific ownership changes, let's look at the characteristics of a corporation that make this form of organization distinctive and require special accounting treatment.

Limited Liability — biggest advantage for the corp & shareholder

> A corporation is a separate legal entity—separate and distinct from its owners.

The owners are not personally liable for debts of a corporation. Unlike a proprietorship or a partnership, a corporation is a separate legal entity, responsible for its own debts. Shareholders' liability is limited to the amounts they invest in the company when they purchase shares. The limited liability of shareholders is perhaps the single most important advantage of corporate organization. In other forms of business, creditors may look to the personal assets of owners for satisfaction of business debt.

Ease of Raising Capital

> Ownership interest in a corporation is easily transferred.

A corporation is better suited to raising capital than is a proprietorship or a partnership. All companies may raise capital by operating at a profit or by borrowing. However, attracting equity capital is easier for a corporation. Because corporations sell ownership interest in the form of shares of stock, ownership rights are easily transferred. An investor can sell his/her ownership interest at any time and without affecting the corporation or its operations.

> Shareholders do not have a mutual agency relationship.

From the viewpoint of a potential investor, another favorable aspect of investing in a corporation is the lack of mutual agency. Individual partners in a partnership have the power to bind the business to a contract. Therefore, an investor in a partnership must be careful regarding the character and business savvy of fellow co-owners. On the other hand, shareholders' participation in the affairs of a corporation is limited to voting at shareholders' meetings (unless the shareholder also is a manager). Consequently, a shareholder needn't exercise the same degree of care that partners must in selecting co-owners.

Obviously, then, a corporation offers advantages over the other forms of organization, particularly in its ability to raise investment capital. As you might guess, though, these benefits do not come without a price.

Disadvantages

Paperwork! To protect the rights of those who buy a corporation's stock or who loan money to a corporation, the state in which the company is incorporated and the federal government impose expensive reporting requirements. Primarily the required paperwork is intended to ensure adequate disclosure of information needed by investors and creditors.

Corporations are subject to expensive government regulation.

You read earlier that corporations are separate legal entities. As such, they also are separate taxable entities. Often this causes what is referred to as *double taxation*. Corporations first pay income taxes on their earnings. Then, when those earnings are distributed as cash dividends, shareholders pay personal income taxes on the previously taxed earnings. Proprietorships and partnerships are not taxed at the business level; each owner's share of profits is taxed only as personal income.

Corporations are subject to double taxation.

Types of Corporations

When referring to corporations in this text, we are referring to corporations formed by private individuals for the purpose of generating profits. These corporations raise capital by selling stock. There are, however, other types of corporations.

Not-for-profit corporations may be owned:
1. By the public sector.
2. By a governmental unit.

Some corporations such as churches, hospitals, universities, and charities do not sell stock and are not organized for profit. Also, some not-for-profit corporations are government-owned—the Federal Deposit Insurance Corporation (FDIC), for instance. Accounting for not-for-profit corporations is discussed elsewhere in the accounting curriculum.

Corporations organized for profit may be:
1. Publicly held and traded:
*   a. On an exchange.*
*   b. Over-the-counter.*
2. Privately-held.

Corporations organized for profit may be publicly held or privately (or closely) held. The stock of publicly held corporations is available for purchase by the general public. You can buy shares of Trans World Airlines, Ford Motor Company, or Exxon through a stockbroker. These shares are traded on organized national stock exchanges—TWA on the American Stock Exchange, Ford and Exxon on the New York Stock Exchange. Other publicly held stock, like Microsoft Corporation, is not listed on a national exchange but is available over-the-counter from securities dealers, organized through NASDAQ (National Association of Securities Dealers Automated Quotations).

Privately held companies' shares are held by only a few individuals and are not available to the general public.

On the other hand, shares of privately held companies are owned by only a few individuals (perhaps a family) and are not available to the general public. Corporations whose stock is privately held do not need to register those shares with the Securities and Exchange Commission and are spared the voluminous, annual reporting requirements of the SEC. Of course, new sources of equity financing are limited when shares are privately held, as is the market for selling existing shares.

Frequently, companies begin as smaller, privately held corporations. Then as success broadens opportunities for expansion, the corporation goes public. For example, in 1995 upstart Netscape Communications, supplier of Netscape Navigator for the Internet, decided to take public the privately held company. The result was one of the largest initial public offerings ever.

Hybrid Organizations

A corporation can elect to comply with a special set of tax rules and be designated an **S corporation.** S corporations have characteristics of both regular corporations and partnerships. Owners have the limited liability protection of a corporation, but income and expenses are passed through to the owners as in a partnership, avoiding double taxation.

Two relatively recent business structures have evolved in response to liability issues and tax treatment—limited liability companies and limited liability partnerships.

A **limited liability company** offers several advantages. Owners are not liable for the debts of the business, except to the extent of their investment. Unlike a limited partnership, all members of limited liability company can be involved with managing the business without losing liability protection. Like an S corporation, income and expenses are passed through to the owners as in a partnership, avoiding double taxation, but there are no limitations on the number of owners as in an S corporation.

A **limited liability partnership** is similar to a limited liability company, except it doesn't offer all the liability protection available in the limited liability company structure. Partners are liable for their own actions but not entirely liable for the actions of other partners.

The Model Business Corporation Act

The Model Business Corporation Act serves as the model for the corporation statutes of most states.

Corporations are formed in accordance with the corporation laws of individual states. State laws are not uniform, but share many similarities, thanks to the widespread adoption of the **Model Business Corporation Act**.[5] This act is designed to serve as a guide to states in the development of their corporation statutes. It presently serves as the model for the majority of states.

State laws regarding the nature of shares that can be authorized, the issuance and repurchase of those shares, and conditions for distributions to shareholders obviously influence actions of corporations. Naturally, differences among state laws affect how we account for many of the shareholders' equity transactions discussed in this chapter. For that reason, we will focus on the normal case, as described by the Model Business Corporation Act, and note situations where variations in state law might require different accounting. Your goal is not to learn diverse procedures caused by peculiarities of state laws, but to understand the broad concepts of accounting for shareholders' equity that can be applied to any specific circumstance.

Variations among state laws influence GAAP pertaining to shareholders' equity transactions.

The process of incorporating a business is similar in all states. The **articles of incorporation** (sometimes called the *corporate charter*) describe (a) the nature of the firm's business activities, (b) the shares to be issued, and (c) the composition of the initial **board of directors**. The board of directors establishes corporate policies and appoints officers who manage the corporation.

At least some of the shares authorized by the articles of incorporation are sold at the inception of the corporation. Frequently, the initial shareholders include members of the board of directors or officers (who may be one and the same). Ultimately, it is the corporation's shareholders that control the company. Shareholders are the owners of the corporation. By voting their shares, it is they who determine the makeup of the board of directors – who in turn appoint officers, who in turn manage the company.

Shareholders' investment in a corporation ordinarily is referred to as paid-in capital. In the next section, we examine the methods normally used to maintain records of shareholders' investment and to report such paid-in capital in financial statements.

B   PAID-IN CAPITAL

Fundamental Share Rights

In reading the previous paragraphs, you noted that corporations raise equity funds by selling shares of the corporation. Shareholders are the owners of a corporation. If a corporation has only one class of shares, no designation of the shares is necessary, but they typically are labeled *common shares*. Ownership rights held by common shareholders, unless specifically withheld by agreement with the shareholders, are:

a. The right to vote on matters that come before the shareholders, including the election of corporate directors. Each share represents one vote.
b. The right to share in profits when dividends are declared. The percentage of shares owned by a shareholder determines his/her share of dividends distributed.
c. The right to share in the distribution of assets if the company is liquidated. The percentage of shares owned by a shareholder determines his/her share of assets after creditors and preferred shareholders are paid.

For reasons of practicality, the preemptive right usually is excluded.

Another right sometimes given to common shareholders is the right to maintain one's percentage share of ownership when new shares are issued. This is referred to as a *preemptive right*. Each shareholder is offered the opportunity to buy a percentage of any new shares issued equal to the percentage of shares he/she owns at the time. In most states this right must be specifically granted; in others, it is presumed unless contractually excluded.

This right usually is withheld because of the inconvenience it causes corporations when they issue new shares. The exclusion of the preemptive right ordinarily is inconsequential because few shareholders own enough stock to be concerned about their ownership percentage.

---

[5] *Revised Model Business Corporation Act*, the American Bar Association, 1994.

Distinguishing Classes of Shares

It is not uncommon for a firm to have more than one, and perhaps several, classes of shares, each with different rights and limitations. To attract investors, companies have devised quite a variety of ownership securities.

If more than one class of shares is authorized by the articles of incorporation, the specific rights of each (for instance, the right to vote, residual interest in assets, and dividend rights) must be stated. Also, some designation must be given to distinguish each class.

> Terminology varies in the way companies differentiate among share types.

Some of the distinguishing designations often used are:

1. Class A, class B, and so on (NACCO Industries, Inc.).
2. Preferred stock, common stock, and class B stock (Ford Motor Company).
3. Common and preferred (Witco Corporation).
4. Common stock, redeemable preference stock, voting preference stock-first series, voting preference stock-second series, voting preference stock-third series (Pennwalt Corporation).
5. Class A common, Class B common, cumulative prior preference, and serial preferred (New York Times Company).

> It often is difficult to predict the rights and privileges of shares on the basis of whether they are labeled *common* or *preferred*.

In your introductory study of accounting, you probably became most familiar with the common stock, preferred stock distinction. That terminology has deep roots in tradition. Early English corporate charters provided for shares that were preferred over others as to dividends and liquidation rights. These provisions were reflected in early American corporation laws. But as our economy developed, corporations increasingly felt the need for innovative ways of attracting investment capital. The result has been a gradual development of a wide range of share classifications that cannot easily be identified by these historical designations.

To reflect the flexibility that now exists in the creation of equity shares, the Model Business Corporation Act, and thus many state statutes, no longer mention the words common and preferred. But the influence of tradition lingers. Most corporations still designate shares as common or preferred. For consistency with practice, the illustrations you study in this chapter use those designations. As you consider the examples, keep in mind that the same concepts apply regardless of the language used to distinguish shares.

Typical Rights of Preferred Shares

An issue of shares with certain preferences or features that distinguish it from the class of shares customarily called common shares may be assigned any of the several labels mentioned earlier. Very often the distinguishing designation is *preferred shares*. The special rights of preferred shareholders usually include one or both of the following:

Need to know definitions for T/F

a. Preferred shareholders typically have a preference to a specified amount of dividends (stated dollar amount per share or % of par value per share). That is, if the board of directors declares dividends, preferred shareholders will receive the designated dividend before any dividends are paid to common shareholders.
b. Preferred shareholders customarily have a preference (over common shareholders) as to the distribution of assets in the event the corporation is dissolved.

> Shares may be:
> 1. *Convertible* into a specified number of another class of shares.
> 2. *Redeemable* at the option of:
>   a. Shareholders.
>   b. The corporation.

Preferred shareholders sometimes have the **right of conversion** which allows them to exchange shares of preferred stock for common stock at a specified conversion ratio. Alternatively, a **redemption privilege** might allow preferred shareholders the option, under specified conditions, to return their shares for a predetermined redemption price. Similarly, shares may be redeemable at the option of the issuing corporation (sometimes referred to as *callable*).

Preferred shares may be **cumulative** or **noncumulative**. Typically, preferred shares are cumulative, which means that if the specified dividend is not paid in a given year, the unpaid dividends (called *dividends in arrears*) accumulate and must be made up in a later dividend year before any dividends are paid on common shares.

> If preferred shares are not cumulative, dividends not declared in any given year need never be paid.

Preferred shares may be **participating** or **nonparticipating**. A participating feature allows preferred shareholders to receive additional dividends beyond the stated amount. If the preferred shares are fully participating, the distribution of dividends to common and preferred shareholders is a pro rata allocation based on the relative par value amounts of common and preferred stock outstanding. Participating preferred stock, previously quite common, is rare today.

Remember that the designations of common and preferred imply no necessary rights, privileges, or limitations of the shares so designated. Such relative rights must be specified by the contract with shareholders. A corporation can create classes of preferred shares that are indistinguishable from common shares in voting rights and/or the right to participate in assets (distributed as dividends or distributed upon liquidation). Likewise, it is possible to devise classes of common shares that possess preferential rights, superior to those of preferred shares.

You probably also can imagine an issue of preferred shares that is almost indistinguishable from a bond issue. Let's say, for instance, that preferred shares call for annual cash dividends of 10% of the par value, dividends are cumulative, and the shares must be redeemed for cash in 10 years. Although the declaration of dividends rests in the discretion of the board of directors, the contract with preferred shareholders can be worded in such a way that directors are compelled to declare dividends each year the company is profitable. For a profitable company, it would be difficult to draw the line between this issue of preferred shares and a 10%, 10-year bond issue. Even in a more typical situation, preferred shares are somewhat hybrid securities—a cross between equity and debt.

> The line between debt and equity is hard to draw.

The Concept of Par Value

Another prevalent practice (besides labeling shares as common and preferred) that has little significance other than historical is assigning a par value to shares. The concept of par value dates back as far as the concept of owning shares of a business. Par value originally indicated the real value of shares. All shares were issued at that price.

> We have inherited the archaic concept of par value from early corporate law.

During the late 19th and early 20th centuries, many cases of selling shares for less than par value—known as *watered shares*—received a great deal of attention and were the subject of a number of lawsuits. Investors and creditors contended that they relied on the par value as the permanent investment in the corporation and therefore net assets must always be at least that amount. Not only was par value assumed to be the amount invested by shareholders, but it also was defined by early corporation laws as the amount of net assets not available for distribution to shareholders (as dividends or otherwise).

To escape some of the complexities of laws dealing with par value, in 1912 New York enacted corporate law that permitted no par shares. Many other states followed suit. But the utility of the no par option was restricted. One reason was that no par shares usually were given status as an exception to the traditional par value shares, often requiring an arbitrary stated value in place of par value. More importantly, many companies were turning to par value shares with very low par values—often pennies—to escape the watered shares liability of issuing shares below an arbitrary par value and to limit the restrictions on distributions. This practice is common today.

> Shares with nominal par value became common to dodge elaborate statutory rules pertaining to par value shares.

Accountants and attorneys have been aware for decades that laws pertaining to par value and legal capital not only are bewildering but fail in their intent to safeguard creditors from payments to shareholders. A recent action by Bowne & Co., Inc., demonstrates the lack of protection afforded by par value. The company amended its articles of incorporation to reduce the par value of its shares from one dollar to one cent per share.

Actually, to the extent that creditors are led to believe that they are afforded protection, they are misled. Like the designations of common and preferred shares, the concepts of par value and legal capital have been eliminated entirely from the Model Business Corporation Act.[6]

> Most shares continue to bear arbitrarily designated par values.

Many states already have adopted these provisions of the Model Act. But most established corporations issued shares prior to changes in the state statutes. Consequently, most companies have par value shares outstanding and continue to issue previously authorized par value shares. The evolution will be gradual to the simpler, more meaningful provisions of the Model Act.

In the meantime, accountants must be familiar with the outdated concepts of par value and legal capital in order to properly record and report transactions related to par value shares. For that reason, most of the discussion in this chapter centers around par value shares. Largely, this means only that proceeds from shareholders' investment is allocated between stated capital and additional paid-in capital. Be aware, though, that in the absence of archaic laws that prompted the creation of par value shares, there is no theoretical reason to do so.

---

[6] *Revised Model Business Corporation Act*, the American Bar Association, 1994, official comment to Section 6.21.

Accounting for the Issuance of Shares

Shares Sold for Cash

When shares are sold for cash, the capital stock account (usually common or preferred) is credited for the amount representing stated capital. When shares have a designated par value, that amount denotes stated capital and is credited to the stock account. Proceeds in excess of this amount are credited to paid-in capital—excess of par.

ILLUSTRATION   19–1

Shares Sold for Cash

Shareholders' investment is allocated between stated capital and additional paid-in capital.

The total amount received from the sale of no-par shares is credited to the stock account.

Dow Industrial sells 100,000 of its common shares, $1 par per share, for $10 per share:

	($ in 000s)	
Cash (100,000 shares at $10 price per share)	1,000	
Common stock (100,000 shares at $1 par per share)		100
Paid-in capital—excess of par (remainder)		900

The entire proceeds from the sale of no-par stock are deemed stated capital and recorded in the stock account. If the shares are no-par, the entry is as follows:

	($ in 000s)	
Cash (100,000 shares at $10 price per share)	1,000	
Common stock		1,000

Shares Sold on Credit

Preincorporation Subscription Agreements.   In times past, capital to finance new ventures ordinarily was raised by obtaining subscriptions for shares of the impending corporation. These preincorporation subscription agreements typically specified that the subscriber would purchase a certain number of shares if a specified amount of venture capital was obtained.

The classic method of new venture financing by subscription rarely is used today.

A difficult issue was determining what, if any, legal recourse the new company had if a subscriber defaulted. That issue seldom is encountered today. State and federal laws that require elaborate procedures for the registration of new securities make subscription agreements impractical for new ventures. Venture financing by subscription is virtually an activity of the past. Simple contracts to sell shares have replaced preincorporation subscription agreements.

Share Purchase Contracts and Stock Subscriptions.   After incorporation, a subscription agreement is a contract between the subscriber and the corporation. When shares are sold by **share purchase contract**, shares ordinarily are sold in exchange for a promissory note from the subscriber. In essence, the shares are sold on credit. Recording the sale of shares is modified only by including a receivable for the portion of the selling price not yet received.

For illustration, assume the shares described in Illustration 19–1 are sold by share purchase contract, with 60 percent of the selling price to be received after six months.

ILLUSTRATION   19–2

Share Purchase Contracts

A receivable is recorded for the $600,000 not yet received.

Dow Industrial sells and issues 100,000 of its common shares, $1 par per share. The shares are sold by share purchase contract for $10 per share, with **60 percent of the selling price to be received after six months:** Shares have been issued but are restricted from being sold and from voting privileges until paid in full.

	($ in 000s)	
Cash	400	
Receivable from share purchase contract	**600**	
Common stock		100
Paid-in capital—excess of par		900

Reporting the Receivable.   How should the receivable be reported? Your initial response probably is that this account is an *asset*, similar to accounts receivable. Indeed, many accountants hold this view on the basis that receivables for stock fit the definition of assets in *SFAC 6.*[7] This view

---

[7] *Statement of Financial Accounting Concepts No. 6*, "Elements of Financial Statements," FASB, 1985.

Additional Consideration

The receivable can be either stock subscriptions receivable or a note receivable for stock. The distinction is that, if the shares already have been issued, the classification is a note receivable; if the shares have been set aside but won't be issued until the full subscription price is received, the classification is stock subscriptions receivable. When shares have not yet been issued, it's appropriate to report common stock issuable separately from common stock issued. For example, assume the shares in the previous illustration will not be issued until the selling price has been collected in full.

		($ in 000s)
Cash	400	
Stock subscriptions receivable	600	
Common stock issuable		100
Paid-in capital—excess of par		900

---

is supported by the fact that such receivables are legally binding, as discussed earlier, and that the receivable should not be precluded from being an asset merely because it is exchanged for shares rather than assets.

On the other hand, some argue that, although entitled, the company might not pursue collection in case of default, but may instead choose not to issue stock or to cancel restricted stock if already issued. Consequently, they contend that collection is sufficiently uncertain that the receivable is not an asset, but a reduction in paid-in capital. Whether paid-in capital will ultimately increase is not yet determined. Although the FASB is presently reconsidering the question, current practice follows an SEC requirement that a receivable from stock sale be reported as a reduction of paid-in capital rather than an asset.[8] Dow Industrial's paid-in capital, immediately after the stock subscription described in Illustration 19–2, would be reported by this approach as:

> Prevalent practice is to report the receivable as a contra equity account until the selling price is received.

Paid-in Capital:	($ in 000s)
Common stock, 100,000 shares at $1 par	$100
Paid-in capital—excess of par	900
Less: **Receivable from share purchase contract**	(600)
Total paid-in capital	$400

know for exam T/F

Reporting the receivable as a contra equity account results in reporting total paid-in capital only to the extent that unrestricted shares are outstanding. This is the prevalent practice.

Shares Sold for Noncash Consideration

Occasionally, a company might issue its shares for consideration other than cash. It is not uncommon for a new company, yet to establish a reliable cash flow, to pay for promotional and legal services with shares rather than with cash. Similarly, shares might be given in payment for land, or for equipment, or for some other noncash asset.

> Shares should be issued at fair market value.

Even without a receipt of cash to establish the fair market value of the shares at the time of the exchange, the transaction still should be recorded at fair market value. Best evidence of fair market value might be:

a. A quoted market price for the shares.
b. A selling price established in a recent issue of shares for cash.
c. The amount of cash that would have been paid in a cash purchase of the asset or service.
d. An independent appraisal of the value of the asset received.
e. Other available evidence.

Whichever evidence of fair market value seems more clearly evident should be used.[9]

---

[8] SEC Regulation S-X, Rule 5-02.30. The FASB is considering the question as part of its "Financial Instruments" project.

[9] Although stock issuances are not specifically mentioned in *APB Opinion No. 29*, this treatment is consistent with the general rule for accounting for noncash transactions as described in that pronouncement, par. 18 and 25.

ILLUSTRATION 19–3

Shares Sold for Noncash Consideration

> The quoted market price for the shares issued might be the best evidence of fair market value.

DuMont Chemicals issues 1 million of its common shares, $1 par per share, in exchange for a custom-built factory for which no cash price is available. Today's issue of *The Wall Street Journal* lists DuMont's stock at $10 per share:

	($ in millions)	
Property, plant, and equipment (1 million shares at $10 per share)	10	
Common stock (1 million shares at $1 par per share)		1
Paid-in capital – excess of par (remainder)		9

More than One Security Sold for a Single Price

Although uncommon, a company might sell more than one security—perhaps common shares and preferred shares—for a single price. As you might expect, the cash received usually is the sum of the separate market values of the two securities. Of course, each is then recorded at its market value. However, if only one security's value is known, the second security's market value is inferred from the total selling price as demonstrated in Illustration 19–4.

ILLUSTRATION 19–4

More than One Security Sold for a Single Price

> When only one security's value is known ($40 million), the second security's market value ($60 million) is assumed from the total selling price ($100 million).

AP&P issues 4 million of its common shares, $1 par per share, and 4 million of its preferred shares, $10 par, for $100 million. Today's issue of *The Wall Street Journal* lists AP&P's common at $10 per share. There is no established market for the preferred shares:

	($ in millions)	
Cash	100	
Common stock (4 million shares × $1 par)		4
Paid-in capital—excess of par, common		36
Preferred stock (4 million shares × $10 par)		40
Paid-in capital—excess of par, preferred		20

Because the shares sell for a total of $100 million, and the market value of the common shares is known to be $40 million (4 million × $10), the preferred shares are inferred to have a market value of $60 million.

Additional Consideration

In the unlikely event that the total selling price is not equal to the sum of the two market prices (when both market values are known), the total selling price is allocated between the two securities, in proportion to their relative market values. You should note that this is the same approach we use (a) when more than one asset is purchased for a single purchase price to allocate the single price to the various assets acquired, (b) when detachable warrants and bonds are issued for a single price, and (c) any other situation when more than one item is associated with a single purchase price or selling price.

Share Issue Costs

> Share issue costs reduce the net cash proceeds from selling the shares and thus paid-in capital—excess of par.

When a company sells shares, it obtains the legal, promotional, and accounting services necessary to effect the sale. The cost of these services reduces the net proceeds from selling the shares. Since paid-in capital—excess of par is credited for the excess of the proceeds over the par value of the shares sold, the effect of share issue costs is to reduce the amount credited to that account. For example, on completing a public offering of 825,000 shares at a price of $17.75 per share, the Duriron Company, Inc., noted in its financial statements: "The proceeds of the offering, after deducting all associated costs, were $13,491,000 or $16.35 per newly issued share." Duriron's entry to record the sale was:

> The cash proceeds is the net amount received after paying share issue costs.

	($ in millions)	
Cash (825,000 shares at $16.35 net price per share)	13.49	
Common stock (825,000 shares at $1.25 par per share)		1.03
Paid-in capital—excess of par (remainder)		12.46

not Responsible for

Like interest, debt issue costs are an expense of borrowing funds.

You should notice that this treatment differs from how debt issue costs are recorded. In Chapter 14 you learned that the costs associated with a debt issue are recorded in a separate debt issue costs account and amortized to expense over the life of the debt.

It can be argued that share issue costs and debt issue costs are fundamentally different. That view would argue that a debt issue has a fixed maturity and, like interest expense, debt issue costs are part of the expense of borrowing funds for that period of time (even though it's recorded in a separate expense account—debt issue expense). Selling shares, on the other hand, represents a perpetual equity interest. Dividends paid on that capital investment are not an expense; neither are the costs of obtaining that capital investment (share issue costs).

Like dividends, share issue costs are **not** an expense.

Although expensing debt issue costs presently is required by GAAP, the FASB has suggested in *Concept Statement 6* that those costs should be treated the same way as share issue costs. That is, the recorded amount of the debt would be reduced by the debt issue costs instead of recording the costs separately as an asset. Remember, though, that concept statements do not constitute GAAP, so until a new FASB standard is issued to supersede *APB Opinion 21*, the prescribed practice is to record debt issue costs as assets and expense the asset over the maturity of the debt.

 CONCEPT REVIEW EXERCISE   EXPANSION OF CORPORATE CAPITAL

Situation: The shareholders' equity section of the balance sheet of National Foods, Inc., included the following accounts at December 31, 1996:

Shareholders' Equity	($ in millions)
Paid-in capital:	
Common stock, 120 million shares at $1 par,	$ 120
Paid-in capital – excess of par	836
Retained earnings	2,449
Total shareholders' equity	$3,405

Required:
1. During 1997, several transactions affected the stock of National Foods. Prepare the appropriate entries for these events.
   a. On March 11, National Foods sold 10 million of its 9.2% preferred shares, $1 par per share, for $44 per share by share purchase contract. 50% of the selling price was received at the time of sale, a five-year note was received for the remainder. The shares were not issued but held in escrow until the note was paid.
   b. On November 22, 1 million common shares, $1 par per share, were issued in exchange for eight labeling machines. Each machine was built to custom specifications so no cash price was available. National Food's stock was listed at $10 per share.
   c. On November 23, 1 million of the common shares and 1 million preferred shares were sold for $60 million. The preferred shares had not traded since March and their market value was uncertain.
2. Prepare the shareholders' equity sections of comparative balance sheets for National Foods at December 31, 1997 and 1996. Assume that net income for 1997 was $400 million and the only other transaction affecting shareholders' equity was the payment of the 9.2% dividend on the 11 million preferred shares ($1 million).

 CONCEPT REVIEW EXERCISE   SOLUTION

Requirement 1:
   a. On March 11, National Foods sold 10 million of its preferred shares, $1 par per share, for $44 per share by share purchase contract:

$220 million cash (50% × $440 million) was received at the time of sale. The remaining $220 million was to be received later.

		($ in millions)
Cash	220	
Receivable from share purchase contract	220	
Preferred stock (10 million shares × $1 par per share)		10
Paid-in capital—excess of par, preferred		430

b. On November 22, 1 million common shares, $1 par per share, were issued in exchange for 8 labeling machines:

The transaction was recorded at the fair market value of the shares exchanged for the machinery.

Machinery (fair value of shares)	10	
Common stock (1 million shares × $1 par per share)		1
Paid-in capital – excess of par, common (1 million shares × $9)		9

c. On November 23, 1 million of the common shares and 1 million preferred shares were sold for $60 million:

Since the value of only the common stock was known, the preferred stock's market value ($50/share) was inferred from the total selling price.

Cash...	60	
Common stock (1 million shares × $1 par per share)		1
Paid-in capital—excess of par, common		9
Preferred stock (1 million shares × $1 par per share)		1
Paid-in capital—excess of par, preferred (to balance)		49

Requirement 2:

Shareholders' Equity Section of the
BALANCE SHEET
National Foods, Inc.

	1997	1996
	($ in millions)	
Shareholders' Equity		
Preferred stock, 9.2%, $1 par (1997: $10 million + 1 million)	$ 11	$ —
Common stock, $1 par (1997: $120 million + 1 million + 1 million)	122	120
Paid-in capital—excess of par, preferred		
(1997: $430 million + 49 million)	479	—
Paid-in capital—excess of par, common		
(1997: $836 million + 9 million + 9 million)	854	836
Less: Receivable from share purchase contract	(220)	—
Retained earnings (1996: $2,449 million + 400 million - 1 million)	2,848	2,449
Total shareholders' equity	$4,094	$3,405

Reacquired Shares

In the previous section we examined various ways stock might be issued. In this section, we look at situations in which companies reacquire shares previously sold. Most medium- and large-size companies occasionally buy back their own shares. Many have formal share repurchase plans. The motivation often is to support the market price of the shares.

| **Learning objective 4**
Describe what occurs when shares are retired and how the retirement is recorded.

Decreasing the supply of shares in the marketplace supports the price of remaining shares.

OPENING CASE

Question 1

Unlike an investment in another firm's shares, the acquisition of a company's own shares does not create an asset.

Decision-Makers' Perspective

When a company's management feels the market price of its stock is undervalued, it may attempt to support the price by decreasing the supply of stock in the marketplace. A McDonnell Douglas announcement that it planned to buy back nearly 15 percent of its outstanding shares triggered a buying spree that pushed the stock price up over 10% percent.

When announcing plans to repurchase up to 1 million shares of its stock in the open market, World Airways, Inc., President and CEO Charles W. Pollard explained, "We believe a substantial buy-back of shares represents an excellent investment for our shareholders."[10] Although clearly a company may attempt to increase net assets by buying its shares at a low price and selling them back later at a higher price, that investment is not viewed as an asset. Similarly, increases and decreases in net assets from that activity are not reported as gains and losses in the company's income statement. Instead, buying and selling its shares are transactions between the corporation and its owners, analogous to retiring shares and then selling previously unissued shares. You should note the contrast between a company's purchasing of its own shares and its purchasing of shares in another corporation as an investment.

Whether considered an investment or not, the repurchase of shares often is a judicious use of a company's cash. By increasing per share earnings and supporting share price, shareholders

---

[10] "World Airways to Commence 1.0MM Shares Buyback," *PR Newswire*, October 9, 1996.

benefit. In 1995, IBM built up a cash holding of about $11 billion due to a lower cost structure and rising revenues. When the company announced its second $2.5 billion buyback of common stock that same year, Merrill Lynch & Co. called the buyback "a continued good use of cash" that "should increase IBM's per share earnings by about 25 cents next year."[11]

When relatively few shares are needed to complete a transaction, it often is more convenient for a company to reacquire outstanding shares and then transfer them than it is to issue previously unissued shares. For instance, Microsoft recently reported the policy of reacquiring its shares to distribute to employees under its stock option and share repurchase plans as shown in Graphic 19–4. Even if new shares are distributed in such stock-based compensation plans, a buyback of shares around the same time can serve to offset that increase in shares.

Common Stock (in Part)

. . . The Company repurchases its common stock in the open market to provide shares for issuance to employees under stock option and stock repurchase plans. The Company's Board of Directors authorized continuation of this program in 1996. . . .

Similarly, shares might be reacquired to distribute in a stock dividend, a proposed merger, or as a defense against a hostile takeover.[12]

Whatever the reason shares are repurchased, a company has a choice of how to account for the buyback:

1. The shares can be formally retired.
2. The shares can be called *treasury stock* and recorded by either:
   a. The par value method.
   b. The cost method.

Unfortunately, the choice is not dictated by the nature of the buyback, but by practical motivations of the company.

Shares Formally Retired

When a corporation reacquires its own shares, those shares assume the same status as authorized but unissued shares, just the same as if they never had been issued. We saw earlier in the chapter that when shares are sold, both cash (usually) and shareholders' equity are increased; the company becomes larger. Conversely, when cash is paid to retire stock, the effect is to decrease both cash and shareholders' equity; the size of the company literally is reduced.

Shares Viewed as Treasury Stock

In concept, as stated earlier, when a corporation reacquires its own shares, those shares assume the same status as authorized but unissued shares, just as if they never had been issued. Out of tradition and for practical reasons, though, companies usually reacquire shares of previously issued stock without formally retiring them.[13] Shares repurchased and not retired are referred to as **treasury stock**.

Like the concepts of par value and legal capital, the concept of treasury shares no longer is recognized in most state statutes.[14] Some companies, though, are eliminating treasury shares from their financial statements as corporate statutes are modernized.

---

[11] Dan Mandresh, in "IBM Approves Stock Buyback of $2.5 Billion," by Bart Ziegler, *The Wall Street Journal*, July 26, 1995.

[12] A corporate takeover occurs when an individual or group of individuals acquires a majority of a company's outstanding common stock from present shareholders. Corporations that are the object of a hostile takeover attempt—a public bid for control of a company's stock against the company's wishes—often take evasive action involving the reacquisition of shares.

[13] The concept of treasury shares originated long ago when new companies found they could sell shares at an unrealistically low price equal to par value to incorporators, who then donated those shares back to the company. Since these shares already had been issued (though not outstanding), they could be sold at whatever the real market price was without adjusting stated capital.

Because treasury shares are already issued, different rules apply to their purchase and resale than to unissued shares. Companies can:
a. Issue shares without regard to preemptive rights of shareholders.
b. Distribute shares as a dividend to shareholders even without a balance in retained earnings.

[14] The revised Model Business Corporation Act eliminated the concept of treasury shares in 1984 after 1980 revisions had eliminated the concepts of par value and legal capital. Most state laws have since followed suit.

In the next section we consider the two methods available to account for the purchase and subsequent resale of treasury shares: (1) the **par value method** and (2) the **cost method**. By either method, the purchase of treasury shares reduces both cash and shareholders' equity, and any subsequent resale of those shares increases both cash and shareholders' equity. The specific accounts affected depend on the accounting method used. You will notice in the following next two illustrations that the par value method clearly is conceptually superior because it effectively restores the shares to the status of being authorized, but unissued, shares. However, the cost method is easily the most popular in practice because it offers the practical advantages we discussed earlier.

Accounting for Shares Reacquired

Retired Shares.   When shares are formally retired, we should reduce precisely the same accounts that previously were increased when the shares were sold, namely, common (or preferred) stock and paid-in capital—excess of par. The first column of Illustration 19–5 demonstrates this. The paid-in capital—excess of par account shows a balance of $900 million. Thus the 100 million outstanding shares were originally sold for an average of $9 per share above par, or $10 per share. Consequently, when 1 million shares are retired (regardless of the retirement price), American Semiconductor should reduce its common stock account by $1 per share and its paid-in capital—excess of par by $9 per share. Another way to view the reduction is that because 1 percent of the shares are retired, both share account balances (common stock and paid-in capital—excess of par) are reduced by 1 percent.

How we treat the difference between the cash paid to buy the shares and the amount the shares originally sold for (amounts debited to common stock and paid-in capital—excess of par) depends on whether that difference is positive (credit) or negative (debit):

Paid-in capital—share repurchase is debited to the extent of its credit balance before debiting retained earnings.

a.   If a *credit* difference is created (as in Case 1 of Illustration 19–5), we credit paid-in capital—share repurchase.

b.   If a *debit* difference is created (as in Case 2 Illustration 19–5), we debit paid-in capital—share repurchase, but only if that account already has a credit balance. Otherwise, we debit retained earnings. (Reducing the account beyond its previous balance would create a negative balance.)

ILLUSTRATION   19–5

Comparison of Alternatives for Recording Share Buybacks

American Semiconductor's balance sheet included the following:

Shareholders' Equity	($ in millions)
Common stock, 100 million shares at $1 par	$ 100
Paid-in capital—excess of par	900
Paid-in capital—share repurchase	2
Retained earnings	2,000

			Treasury Stock	
	Retirement		Par Value Method	Cost Method
Reacquired 1 million of its common shares				
Case 1: Shares repurchased at $7 per share				
Common stock ($1 par × 1 million shares)	1			
Treasury stock ($1 par × 1 million shares)			1	7
Paid-in capital—excess of par ($9 per share)	9		9	
Paid-in capital—share repurchase (difference)		3	3	
Cash		7	7	7
OR				
Case 2: Shares repurchased at $13 per share				
Common stock ($1 par × 1 million shares)	1			
Treasury stock ($1 par × 1 million shares)			1	13
Paid-in capital—excess of par ($9 per share)	9		9	
Paid-in capital—share repurchase	2*		2*	
Retained earnings (difference)	1		1	
Cash		13	13	13

*Because there is a $2 million credit balance.

Why is paid-in capital credited in Case 1 and retained earnings debited in Case 2? The answer lies in the fact that the payments made by a corporation to repurchase its own shares are a distribution of corporate assets to shareholders.

In Case 1, only $7 million is distributed to shareholders to retire shares that originally provided $10 million of paid-in capital. Thus, some of the original investment ($3 million in this case) remains and is labeled *paid-in capital—share repurchase.*

In Case 2, more cash ($13 million) is distributed to shareholders to retire shares than originally was paid in. The amount paid in comprises the original investment of $10 million for the shares being retired plus $2 million of paid-in capital created by previous repurchase transactions—$12 million total. Thirteen million is returned to shareholders. The additional $1 million paid is viewed as a dividend on the shareholders' investment, and thus a reduction of retained earnings.[15]

> *Payments made by a corporation to retire its own shares are viewed as a distribution of corporate assets to shareholders.*

Treasury Stock

← xtra credit only

> **Learning objective 5**
> Distinguish between the par value method and the cost method of accounting for the purchase and resale of treasury shares.

The par value method.   As you review the entries for treasury stock purchases in the second column of Illustration 19–5, you should note the similarity to how the retirement of shares was recorded in the first column. The reason for the similarity is that using the par value method, we view the purchase of treasury stock as a constructive retirement of the shares. Because the shares are not formally retired, we don't reduce the common stock account itself. We instead reduce common stock indirectly by debiting its valuation account, treasury stock. The two accounts are reported together:

	($ in millions)
Common stock, 100 million shares at $1 par,	$100
Less: Treasury stock, 1 million shares at $1 par	(1)

on exam → *The cost method.*   When the cost method is applied, we view the purchase of treasury stock as a temporary reduction of shareholders' equity, to be reversed later when the treasury stock is resold. The cost of acquiring the shares is "temporarily" debited to the treasury stock account. Recording the effects on specific shareholders' equity accounts is delayed until later when the shares are reissued. In the meantime, the shares assume the fictional status we discussed earlier of being neither unissued nor outstanding. Effectively, we consider the purchase of treasury stock and its subsequent resale to be a "single transaction."

> *When the cost method is used, recording the effects on specific shareholders' equity accounts is delayed until the shares are reissued.*

Reporting Treasury Stock.   Treasury stock accounted for by the par value method is reported on the balance sheet as a reduction in the related stock account (common or preferred). Under the cost method, treasury stock is a reduction in total shareholders' equity, not associated with any specific shareholders' equity account. Using either method total shareholders' equity is the same. Reporting under the two methods is compared in Graphic 19–5 using the situation described above for American Semiconductor after the purchase of treasury stock in Illustration 19–5 (Case 2).

GRAPHIC   19–5

Reporting Treasury Stock on the Balance Sheet

> Under the **par value method** treasury stock is reported as a valuation account.

> Under the **cost method** treasury stock is not associated with any specific shareholders' equity account.

Shareholders' Equity	Par Value Method	Cost Method
	($ in millions)	
Paid-in capital:		
Common stock, 100 million shares at $1 par,	$ 100	$ 100
Less: Treasury stock, 1 million shares (at par)	(1)	
Paid-in capital—excess of par	891	900
Paid-in capital—reacquired shares		2
Retained earnings	1,999	2,000
Treasury stock, 1 million shares (at cost)		(13)
Total shareholders' equity	$2,989	$2,989

yes

---

[15] In the next section of this chapter, you will be reminded that dividends reduce retained earnings. (You first learned this in your introductory accounting course.)

Resale of Shares

After shares are formally retired, any subsequent sale of shares is simply the sale of new, unissued shares and are accounted for accordingly. This is demonstrated in the first column of Illustration 19–6.

When the par value method is used, we view treasury shares as having been constructively retired. So, when the shares later are resold, accounting for the sale is similar to accounting for the sale of previously unissued shares. This is demonstrated in the second column of Illustration 19–6.

ILLUSTRATION   19–6

Comparison of Alternatives for Recording the Sale of Shares after Share Buybacks

American Semiconductor sold 1 million shares after reacquiring shares at $13 per share (Case 2 in Illustration 19–5)

		Treasury Stock	
	Retirement	Par Value Method	Cost Method
Case A: Shares sold at $14 per share			
Cash	14	14	14
Common stock	1		
Treasury stock		1	13
Paid-in capital—excess of par	13	13	
Paid-in capital—share repurchase			1
OR			
Case B: Shares sold at $10 per share			
Cash	10	10	10
Retained earnings			1
Paid-in capital—share repurchase			2*
Common stock	1		
Treasury stock		1	13
Paid-in capital—excess of par	9	9	

*Because there is a $2 million credit balance.

By the cost method, the resale of treasury shares is viewed as the consummation of the single transaction begun when the treasury shares were purchased. The effect of the single transaction of purchasing treasury stock and reselling it for more than cost (Case 2 of Illustration 19–5 and Case A of Illustration 19–6) is to increase both cash and shareholders' equity (by $1 million). The effect of the single transaction of purchasing treasury stock and reselling it for less than cost (Case 2 of Illustration 19–5 and Case B of Illustration 19–6) is to decrease both cash and shareholders' equity (by $3 million).

The cost method is permitted by the profession when a corporation's stock is acquired for purposes other than retirement (formal or constructive), or when ultimate disposition has not yet been decided.[16] Although the par value method is conceptually appealing, the cost method predominates in practice for the practical reasons we noted earlier.

Note that retained earnings may be debited in a treasury stock transaction, but not credited. Also notice that transactions involving treasury stock have no impact on the income statement. This follows the reasoning discussed earlier that a corporation's buying and selling of its own shares are transactions between the corporation and its owners and not part of the earnings process.

Additional Consideration

Treasury Shares Acquired at Different Costs

Note that, when using the cost method, the treasury stock account always is credited for the cost of the reissued shares ($13 million in Illustration 19–6). When shares are reissued, if treasury stock on hand has been purchased at different per share prices, the cost of the shares sold must be determined using a cost flow assumption—FIFO, LIFO, or weighted average—similar to determining the cost of goods sold when inventory items are acquired at different unit costs.

---

[16] "Status of Accounting Research Bulletins," *APB Opinion No. 6*, 1965, par. 12.

CONCEPT REVIEW EXERCISE

TREASURY STOCK

Situation: The shareholders' equity section of the balance sheet of National Foods, Inc. included the following accounts at December 31, 1997:

Shareholders' Equity	($ in millions)
Paid-in capital:	
Preferred stock, 11 million shares at $1 par,	$ 11
Common stock, 122 million shares at $1 par,	122
Paid-in capital—excess of par, preferred	479
Paid-in capital—excess of par, common	854
Less: Receivable from share purchase contract	(220)
Retained earnings	2,848
Total shareholders' equity	$4,094

Required:

1. National Foods reacquired common shares to hold as treasury stock during 1998 and sold shares in two separate transactions later that year. Prepare the entries for both the purchase and subsequent resale of treasury stock during 1998 by both the par value and cost methods.
    a. National Foods purchased 6 million treasury shares at $10 per share.
    b. National Foods sold 2 million treasury shares at $12 per share.
    c. National Foods sold 2 million treasury shares at $7 per share.
2. Prepare the shareholders' equity section of National Foods' balance sheet at December 31, 1998, reporting treasury stock by both the par value and cost methods. Net income for 1998 was $400 million, and preferred shareholders were paid $1 million cash dividends.

CONCEPT REVIEW EXERCISE

SOLUTION

Requirement 1:

a. National Foods **purchased** 6 million shares of treasury stock at **$10** per share:

Par Value Method ($ in millions)			Cost Method ($ in millions)		
Treasury stock (6 million shares × $1) ..	6		Treasury stock		
Paid-in capital—excess of par			(6 million shares × $10)	60	
(6 million shares × $7*)	42		Cash		60
Retained earnings (to balance)	12				
Cash		60			

*$854 million ÷ 120 million shares

b. National Foods **sold** 2 million shares of treasury stock at **$12** per share: ($ in millions)

Cash	24		Cash	24	
Treasury stock			Treasury stock		
(2 million shares × $1)		2	(2 million shares × $10)		20
			Paid-in capital—reacquired shares ...		4
Paid-in capital—excess of par		22			

c. National Foods **sold** 2 million shares of treasury stock at **$7** per share: ($ in millions)

Cash	14		Cash	14	
Treasury stock			Paid-in capital—reacquired shares	4	
(2 million shares × $1 par)		2	Retained earnings (to balance)	2	
Paid-in capital – excess of par		12	Treasury stock		
			(2 million shares × $10)		20

Requirement 2:

Balance Sheet (Shareholders' Equity Section)
NATIONAL FOODS, INC.
At December 31, 1998

	Par Value Method	Cost Method
	($ in millions)	
Shareholders' Equity		
Preferred stock, 11 million shares at $1 par	$ 11	$ 11
Common stock, 122 million shares at $1 par	122	122
Less: Treasury shares, at $1 par, 2 million common shares	(2)	—
Paid-in capital—excess of par, preferred	479	479
Paid-in capital—excess of par, common	846 [1]	854
Less: Receivable from share purchase contract	(220)	(220)
Retained earnings	3,235 [2]	3,245 [3]
Treasury stock, at cost; 2 million common shares	—	(20)
Total shareholders' equity	$4,471	$4,471

[1] $854 - 42 + 22 + 12
[2] $2,848 - 12 + 400 - 1
[3] $2,848 - 2 + 400 - 1

PART C   RETAINED EARNINGS

Characteristics of Retained Earnings

Learning objective 6
Describe retained earnings and distinguish it from paid-in capital.

In the previous section we examined *invested* capital. Now we consider *earned* capital, that is, retained earnings. In general, retained earnings represents a corporation's accumulated, undistributed net income (or net loss). A more descriptive title used by some companies is reinvested earnings. A credit balance in this account indicates a dollar amount of assets previously earned by the firm but not distributed as dividends to shareholders. We refer to a debit balance in retained earnings as a **deficit.**

You saw in the previous section that the buyback of shares (as well as the resale of treasury shares in some cases) can decrease retained earnings. We examine the effect on retained earnings of dividends and stock splits in this section.

Dividends

Learning objective 7
Explain the basis of corporate dividends, including the similarities and differences between cash and property dividends.

Shareholders' initial investments in a corporation are represented by amounts reported as paid-in capital. One way a corporation provides a return to its shareholders on their investments is to pay them a **dividend**, typically cash.[17]

Dividends are distributions of assets the company has earned on behalf of its shareholders. If dividends are paid that exceed the amount of assets earned by the company, then management is, in effect, returning to shareholders a portion of their investments, rather than providing them a return on that investment. So most companies view retained earnings as the amount available for dividends.[18]

Liquidating Dividend

> Any dividend not representing a distribution of earnings should be debited to paid-in capital.

In unusual instances in which a dividend exceeds the balance in retained earnings, the excess is referred to as a **liquidating dividend** because some of the invested capital is being liquidated. This might occur when a corporation is being dissolved and assets (not subject to a superior claim by creditors) are distributed to shareholders. Any portion of a dividend not representing a distribution of earnings should be debited to additional paid-in capital rather than retained earnings.

---

[17] Dividends are not the only return shareholders earn; when market prices of their shares rise, shareholders benefit also. Indeed, many companies have adopted policies of never paying dividends but reinvesting all assets they earn. The motivation is to accommodate more rapid expansion and thus, presumably, increases in the market price of the stock.

[18] Ordinarily, this is not the legal limitation. Most states permit a company to pay dividends so long as, after the dividend, it's assets would not be "less than the sum of its total liabilities plus the amount that would be needed, if the corporation were to be dissolved at the time of the distribution, to satisfy the preferential rights upon dissolution of shareholders whose preferential rights are superior to those receiving the distribution." (Revised Model Business Corporation Act, American Bar Foundation, 1994). Thus, legally, a corporation can distribute amounts equal to total shareholders' equity less dissolution preferences of senior equity securities (usually preferred stock.)

Retained Earnings Restrictions

Sometimes the amount available for dividends purposely is reduced by management. A restriction of retained earnings designates a portion of the balance in retained earnings as being *unavailable for dividends*. A company might restrict retained earnings to indicate management's intention to withhold for some specific purpose the assets represented by that portion of the retained earnings balance. For example, management might anticipate the need for a specific amount of assets in upcoming years to repay a maturing debt, to cover a contingent loss, or to finance expansion of the facilities. Be sure to understand that the restriction itself does not set aside cash for the designated event but merely communicates management's intention not to distribute the stated amount as a dividend.

A restriction of retained earnings normally is indicated by a disclosure note to the financial statements. Although instances are rare, a formal journal entry may be used to reclassify a portion of retained earnings to an "appropriated" retained earnings account.

✓Cash Dividends

You learned in Chapter 14 that paying interest to creditors is a contractual obligation. No such legal obligation exists for paying dividends to shareholders. A liability is not recorded until a company's board of directors votes to declare a dividend. In practice, though, corporations ordinarily try to maintain a stable dividend pattern over time.

When directors declare a cash dividend, we reduce retained earnings and record a liability. Before the payment actually can be made, a listing must be assembled of shareholders entitled to receive the dividend. A specific date is stated as to when the determination will be made of the recipients of the dividend. This date is called the **date of record**. Registered owners of shares of stock on this date are entitled to receive the dividend— even if they sell those shares prior to the actual cash payment. To be a registered owner of shares on the date of record, an investor must purchase the shares before the **ex-dividend date**. This date is four business days before the date of record. Shares purchased on or after that date are purchased ex dividend—without the right to receive the declared dividend. As a result, the market price of a share typically will decline by the amount of the dividend, other things being equal, on the ex-dividend date. Consider Illustration 19–7.

> International Paper Tuesday announced a regular quarterly dividend of 25 cents per common share. The company also declared a regular quarterly dividend of $1 on each preferred share. Both dividends are payable Dec. 16 to holders of record at the close of business on Nov. 22.[19]

On June 1, the board of directors of Craft Industries declares a cash dividend of $2 per share on its 100 million shares, payable to shareholders of record June 15, to be paid July 1:

	($ in millions)	
June 1—declaration date		
Retained earnings	200	
Cash dividends payable (100 million shares at $2/share)		200
June 11—ex-dividend date		
No entry		
June 15—date of record		
No entry		
July 1—payment date		
Cash dividends payable	200	
Cash		200

A sufficient balance in retained earnings permits a dividend to be declared. Remember, though, that retained earnings is a shareholders' equity account representing a dollar claim on assets in general, but not on any specific asset in particular. Sufficient retained earnings does not ensure sufficient cash to make payment. These are two separate accounts having no necessary connection with

---

[19] "Business Briefs," *Memphis Commercial Appeal*, Nov.13, 1996.

one another. When a dividend is "paid from retained earnings," this simply means that sufficient assets previously have been earned to pay the dividend without returning invested assets to shareholders.

Property Dividends *not responsible*

Because cash is the asset most easily divided and distributed to shareholders, most corporate dividends are cash dividends. In concept, though, any asset can be distributed to shareholders as a dividend. When a noncash asset is distributed, it is referred to as a **property dividend** (often called a *dividend in kind*).

In 1994, Litton Industries declared to its shareholders a property dividend in shares of Western Atlas stock that Litton was holding as an investment. Securities held as investments are the assets most often distributed in a property dividend due to the relative ease of dividing these assets among shareholders and determining their fair market values.

> The *fair market value* of the assets to be distributed is the amount recorded for a property dividend.

A property dividend should be recorded at the fair market value of the assets to be distributed. This may require revaluing the asset to fair market value prior to recording the dividend. If so, a gain or loss is recognized for the difference between book value and fair market value. This is demonstrated in Illustration 19–8.

ILLUSTRATION 19–8

Property Dividends

> Before recording the property dividend, the asset first must be written up to fair market value.

On October 1, the board of directors of Craft Industries declares a property dividend of 2 million shares of Beaman Corporation's preferred stock that Craft had purchased in March as an investment (book value: $9 million). The investment shares have a fair market value of $5 per share, $10 million, and are payable to shareholders of record October 15, to be distributed November 1:

		($ in millions)
October 1—declaration date		
Investment in Beaman Corporation preferred stock	1	
Gain on appreciation of investment ($10 – $9)		1
Retained earnings (2 million shares at $5 per share)	10	
Property dividends payable		10
October 15—date of record		
No entry		
November 1—payment date		
Property dividends payable	10	
Investment in Beaman Corporation preferred stock		10

Stock Dividends and Splits

✓ Stock Dividends

> **Learning objective 8**
> Explain stock dividends and stock splits and how they are accounted for.

A **stock dividend** is the distribution of additional shares of stock to current shareholders of the corporation. Be sure to note the contrast between a stock dividend and either a cash or property dividend. A stock dividend affects neither the assets nor the liabilities of the firm. Also, because each shareholder receives the same percentage increase in shares, shareholders' proportional interest in (percentage ownership of) the firm remains unchanged.

The prescribed accounting treatment of a stock dividend requires that shareholders' equity items be reclassified by reducing one or more shareholders' equity accounts and simultaneously increasing one or more paid-in capital accounts. The amount reclassified depends on the *size* of the stock dividend. For a small stock dividend, typically less than 25%, the fair market value of the additional shares distributed is transferred from retained earnings to paid-in capital.[20]

---

[20]The Committee on Accounting Procedure prescribes this accounting treatment in "Restatement and Revision of Accounting Research Bulletins," *Accounting Research Bulletin No. 43*, (New York: AICPA, 1961), chap. 7, sec. B, Pars. 10-14. In this pronouncement, a small stock dividend is defined as one 20 to 25 percent or less. For filings with that agency, the SEC has refined the definition to comprise stock distributions of less than 25%.

ILLUSTRATION 19-9

Stock Dividend

> A small stock dividend requires reclassification to paid-in capital of retained earnings equal to the fair value of the additional shares distributed.

Craft declares and distributes a 10% common stock dividend (10 million shares) when the market value of the $1 par common stock is $12 per share:

	($ in millions)	
Retained earnings (10 million shares at $12 per share)	120	
Common stock (10 million shares at $1 par per share)		10
Paid-in capital—excess of par (remainder)		110

Additional Consideration

The entry above is recorded on the declaration date. Since the additional shares are not yet issued, some accountants would prefer to credit "common stock dividends issuable" at this point, instead of common stock. In that case, when the shares are issued, common stock dividends issuable is debited and common stock credited. The choice really is inconsequential; either way the $10 million amount would be reported as part of paid-in capital on a balance sheet prepared between the declaration and distribution of the shares.

Stock Market Reaction to Stock Distributions.   As a Craft shareholder owning 10 shares at the time of the 10% stock dividend, you would receive an 11th share. Since each is worth $12, would you benefit by $12 when you receive the additional share from Craft? Of course not. If the value of each share were to remain $12 when the 10 million new shares are distributed, the total value of the company would grow by $120 million (10 million shares × $12 per share).

> The market price per share will decline in proportion to the increase in the number of shares distributed in a stock dividend.

A corporation cannot increase its market value simply by distributing additional stock certificates. Because all shareholders receive the same percentage increase in their respective holdings, you, and all other shareholders, still would own the same percentage of the company as before the distribution. Accordingly, the per share value of your shares should decline from $12 to $10.91 so that your 11 shares would be worth $120—precisely what your 10 shares were worth prior to the stock dividend. Any failure of the stock price to actually adjust in proportion to the additional shares issued probably would be due to information other than the distribution reaching shareholders at the same time.

> Early rulemakers felt that per share market prices do not adjust in response to an increase in the number of shares.

Then, what justification is there for capitalizing the market value of the additional shares? In 1941 (and reaffirmed in 1953), accounting rulemakers felt that many shareholders are deceived by small stock dividends, believing they benefit by the market value of their additional shares.[21] Furthermore they erroneously felt that these individual beliefs are collectively reflected in the stock market by per share prices that remain unchanged by stock dividends. Consequently, their prescribed accounting treatment is to reduce retained earnings by the same amount as if cash dividends were paid equal to the market value of the shares issued.

This obsolete reasoning is inconsistent with our earlier conclusion that the market price per share will decline in approximate proportion to the increase in the number of shares distributed. Our intuitive conclusion is supported also by formal research.[22]

> Capitalizing retained earnings for a stock dividend artificially reclassifies earned capital as invested capital.

Besides being based on fallacious reasoning, accounting for stock dividends by artificially reclassifying "earned" capital as "invested" capital conflicts with the reporting objective of reporting shareholders' equity by source. Despite these limitations, this outdated accounting standard still applies.

> Companies sometimes declare a stock dividend in lieu of a real dividend.

Reasons for Stock Dividends.   Since neither the corporation nor its shareholders apparently benefits from stock dividends, why do companies declare them?[23] Occasionally, a company tries to give shareholders the illusion that they are receiving a real dividend.

---

[21] "Restatement and Revision of Accounting Research Bulletins," *Accounting Research Bulletin No. 43,* (New York: AICPA, 1961), chap. 7.

[22] Foster and Vickrey, "The Information Content of Stock Dividend Announcements," *Accounting Review* (April 1978), and Spiceland and Winters, "The Market Reaction to Stock Distributions: The Effect of Market Anticipation and Cash Returns," *Accounting and Business Research* (Summer, 1986).

[23] After hitting a high in the 1940s, the number of stock dividends has declined significantly. Currently, about 3% of companies declare stock dividends in any given year.

Another reason is merely to enable the corporation to take advantage of the accepted accounting practice of capitalizing retained earnings. Specifically, a company might wish to lower an existing balance in retained earnings—otherwise available for *cash* dividends—so it can reinvest the earned assets represented by that balance without carrying a large balance in retained earnings.

✓ Stock Splits

A frequent reason for issuing a stock dividend is actually to induce the per share market price decline that follows. For instance, after a company declares a 100% stock dividend on 100 million shares of common stock, with a per share market price of $12, it then has 200 million shares, each with an approximate market value of $6. The motivation for reducing the per share market price is to increase the stock's *marketability* by making it attractive to a larger number of potential investors.

Additional Consideration

No cash dividends are paid on treasury shares. Usually stock dividends aren't paid on treasury shares either. Treasury shares are essentially equivalent to shares that never have been issued. In some circumstances, though, the intended use of the repurchased shares will give reason for the treasury shares to participate in a stock dividend. For instance, if the treasury shares have been specifically designated for issuance to executives in a stock option plan or stock award plan it would be appropriate to adjust the number of shares by the stock distribution.

A stock distribution of 25% or higher, although often called a "large" stock dividend, is more often referred to as a **stock split**.[24] Thus, a 100% stock dividend could be labeled a 2-for-1 stock split. Conceptually, the proper accounting treatment of a stock dividend or a stock split is to make no journal entry, avoiding the reclassification of earned capital as invested capital . This, in fact, is the prescribed accounting treatment for a stock split.

Since the same common stock account balance (total par) represents twice as many shares, the par value per share should be reduced by one-half. In the previous example, if the par were $1 per share before the stock distribution, then after the 2-for-1 stock split, the par would be $.50 per share.

Microsoft Corp.'s board approved the software company's sixth stock split in 10 years to make the shares more affordable after their rapid rise this year.

The software company said shareholders will receive one additional share on or about Dec. 6 for each share held Nov.22.[25]

Stock Splits Effected in the Form of Stock Dividends (Large Stock Dividends)

If the per share par value of the shares is not changed, the stock distribution is referred to as a *stock split effected in the form of a stock dividend,* or simply a *stock dividend.* In that case, a journal entry increases the common stock account by the par value of the additional shares. To avoid reducing retained earnings in these instances, most companies reduce (debit) paid-in capital—excess of par to offset the credit to common stock:

Craft declares and distributes a 2-for-1 stock split effected in the form of a 100% stock dividend (100 million shares) when the market value of the $1 par common stock is $12 per share:

	($ in millions)	
Paid-in capital—excess of par	100	
Common stock (100 million shares at $1 par per share)		100

---

[24] "Restatement and Revision of Accounting Research Bulletins," *Accounting Research Bulletin No. 43*, (New York: AICPA, 1961), chap. 7, sec. B, par. 11.

[25] *Bloomberg Business News*, Nov. 13, 1996.

Notice that this entry does not reclassify earned capital as invested capital. Some companies, though, choose to debit retained earnings instead.[26]

Some companies capitalize retained earnings when recording a stock split effected in the form of a stock dividend.

	($ in millions)
Retained earnings	100
Common stock (100 million shares at $1 par per share)	100

Briggs & Stratton Corporation described its recent stock split in its 1995 annual report as shown in Graphic 19–6.

GRAPHIC   19–6

**Stock Split Disclosure—
Briggs & Stratton**

(11) Stock Split:

On October 19, 1994, shareholders approved a doubling of the authorized common stock shares to 60,000,000. This allowed the Company to effect a 2-for-1 stock split previously authorized by the Board of Directors. The distribution on November 14, 1994, increased the number of shares outstanding from 14,463,500 to 28,927,000. The amount of $144,000 was transferred from the additional paid-in capital account to the common stock account to record this distribution. All per share amounts in this report have been restated to reflect this stock split.

Additional Consideration

A company choosing to capitalize retained earnings when recording a stock split effected in the form of a stock dividend may elect to capitalize an amount other than par value. Accounting guidelines are vague in this regard, stating only that legal amounts are minimum requirements and do not prevent the capitalization of a larger amount per share.

Source: "Restatement and Revision of Accounting Research Bulletins," *Accounting Research Bulletin No. 43*, (New York: AICPA, 1961), chap. 7, sec. B, Par. 14.

Reverse Stock Split.   A **reverse stock split** occurs when a company decreases, rather than increases, its outstanding shares. After a 1-for-4 reverse stock split, for example, 100 million shares, $1 par per share, would become 25 million shares, $4 par per share. No journal entry is necessary. Of course the market price per share would quadruple, which often is the motivation for declaring a reverse stock split.

Fractional shares.   Typically, a stock dividend or stock split results in some shareholders being entitled to fractions of whole shares. For example, if a company declares a 25% stock dividend, or equivalently a 5-for-4 stock split, a shareholder owning 10 shares would be entitled to $2\,^1/_2$ shares. Another shareholder with 15 shares would be entitled to $3^3/4$ shares.

Cash payments usually are made when shareholders are entitled to fractions of whole shares.

    Cash payments usually are made to shareholders for **fractional shares**. In the situation described above, for instance, if the market price at declaration is $12 per share, the shareholder with 15 shares would receive 3 additional shares and $9 in cash ($12 \times \,^3/4$).

Decision-Makers' Perspective

Profitability is the key to a company's long-run survival. A summary measure of profitability often used by investors and potential investors, particularly common shareholders, is the return on shareholders' equity. This ratio measures the ability of company management to generate net income from the resources that owners provide. The ratio is computed by dividing net income by average shareholders' equity. A variation of this ratio often is used when a company has both preferred and common stock outstanding. The return to com-

The return on shareholders' equity is a popular measure of profitability.

---

[26] The 1995 *Accounting Trends & Techniques* reports that 48 of its 600 sample companies reported a stock split. Of those, 23 debited additional paid-in capital, 9 debited retained earnings, and 16 made no entry. Thus all but 16 were handled as stock splits effected in the form of stock dividends.

mon shareholders' equity is calculated by subtracting dividends to preferred shareholders from the numerator and using average common shareholders' equity as the denominator. The modified ratio focuses on the profits generated on the assets provided by common shareholders.

Although the ratio is useful when evaluating the effectiveness of management in employing resources provided by owners, analysts must be careful not to view it in isolation or without considering how the ratio is derived. Keep in mind that shareholders' equity is a measure of the book value of equity, equivalent to the book value of net assets. Book value measures quickly become out of line with market values. An asset's book value usually equals its market value on the date it's purchased, the two aren't necessarily the same after that. Equivalently, the market value of a share of stock (or of total shareholders' equity) usually is different from its book value. As a result, to supplement the return on shareholders' equity ratio, analysts often relate earnings to the market value of equity, calculating the earnings-price ratio. This ratio is simply the earnings per share divided by the market price per share.

> Book value measures have limited use in financial analysis.

To better understand the differences between the book value ratio and the market value ratio, let's consider the following condensed information reported by Sharp-Novell Industries for 1997 and 1996:

($ in 000s except per share amounts)	1997	1996
Sales	$3,500	$3,100
Net income	125	114
Current assets	$ 750	$ 720
Property, plant, and equipment (net)	900	850
Total assets	$1,650	$1,570
Current liabilities	$ 550	$ 530
Long-term liabilities	540	520
Paid-in capital	210	210
Retained earnings	350	310
Liabilities and shareholders' equity	$1,650	$1,570
Shares outstanding	50,000	50,000
Stock price (average)	$42.50	$42.50

The 1997 return on shareholders' equity is computed by dividing net income by average shareholders' equity:

$$\$125 \div [(\$560 + 520)/2] = \underline{23.1\%}$$

The earnings-price ratio is the earnings per share divided by the market price per share:

$$\text{Earnings per share (1997)} = \$125 \div 50 = \$2.50$$
$$\text{Earnings-price ratio} = \$2.50 \div \$42.50 = \underline{5.9\%}$$

Obviously, the return on the market value of equity is much lower than on the book value of equity. This points out the importance of looking at more than a single ratio when making decisions. While 23.1% may seem like a desirable return, 5.9% is not nearly so attractive. Companies often emphasize the return on shareholders' equity in their annual reports. Alert investors should not accept this measure of achievement at face value. For some companies this is a meaningful measure of performance; but for others, the market-based ratio means more, particularly for a mature firm whose book value and market value are more divergent.

> Share retirement and treasury stock transactions can affect the return to owners.

Decisions managers make with regard to shareholders' equity transactions can significantly impact the return to shareholders. For example, when a company buys back shares of its own stock, the return on shareholders' equity goes up. Net income is divided by a smaller amount of shareholders' equity. On the other hand, the share buyback uses assets, reducing the resources available to earn net income in the future. So, managers as well as outside analysts must carefully consider the decision to reacquire shares in light of the current economic environment, the firm's investment opportunities, and cost of capital to decide whether such a transaction is in the long-term best interests of owners.

> Dividend decisions should be evaluated in light of prevailing circumstances.

The decision to pay dividends requires similar considerations. When earnings are high, are shareholders better off receiving substantial cash dividends or having management reinvest those funds to finance future growth (and future dividends)? The answer, of course, depends on the particular circumstances involved. Dividend decisions should reflect managerial strategy concerning the mix of internal versus external financing, alternative investment opportunities, and industry conditions. High dividends often are found in mature industries and low dividends in growth industries.

ETHICAL DILEMMA

Interworld Distributors has paid quarterly cash dividends since 1975. The dividends have steadily increased from $.25 per share to the latest dividend declaration of $2.00 per share. The board of directors is eager to continue this trend despite the fact that revenues fell significantly during recent months as a result of worsening economic conditions and increased competition. The company founder and member of the board proposes a solution. He suggests a 5% stock dividend in lieu of a cash dividend to be accompanied by the following press announcement:

"In lieu of our regular $2.00 per share cash dividend, Interworld will distribute a 5% stock dividend on its common shares, currently trading at $40 per share. Changing the form of the dividend will permit the Company to direct available cash resources to the modernization of physical facilities in preparation for competing in the 21st century."

What do you think?

CONCEPT REVIEW EXERCISE

CHANGES IN RETAINED EARNINGS

Situation: The shareholders' equity section of the balance sheet of National Foods, Inc., included the following accounts at December 31, 1998:

Shareholders' Equity	($ in millions)
Paid-in capital:	
Preferred stock, 9.09%, 11 million shares at $1 par	$ 11
Common stock, 122 million shares at $1 par	122
Paid-in capital—excess of par, preferred	479
Paid-in capital—excess of par, common	854
Less: Receivable from share purchase contract	(220)
Retained earnings	3,245
Treasury stock, at cost, 2 million common shares	(20)
Total shareholders' equity	$4,471

Required:

1. During 1999, several events and transactions affected the retained earnings of National Foods. Prepare the appropriate entries for these events.

   a. On March 1, the board of directors declared a cash dividend of $1 per share on its 120 million outstanding shares (122 million minus 2 million treasury shares), payable on April 3 to shareholders of record March 11.

   b. On May 5, the board of directors declared a property dividend of 120 million shares of Kroger common stock that National Foods had purchased in February as an investment (book value: $900 million). The investment shares had a fair market value of $8 per share and were distributed May 30 to shareholders of record May 15.

   c. On April 13, a 3-for-2 stock split was declared and distributed. The stock split was effected in the form of a 50% stock dividend. The market value of the $1 par common stock was $20 per share.

   d. On October 13, a 10% common stock dividend was declared and distributed when the market value of the $1 par common stock was $12 per share. Fractional share rights for 1 million equivalent whole shares were paid in cash.

   e. On December 1, the board of directors declared the 9.09% cash dividend on the 11 million preferred shares, payable on December 23 to shareholders of record December 11.

2. Prepare a statement of shareholders' equity for National Foods reporting the changes in shareholders' equity accounts for 1997, 1998, and 1999. Refer to the previous two Concept Reviews in this chapter for the 1997 and 1998 changes. Also, look back to the statement of shareholders' equity in Graphic 19-3 for the format of the statement. Assume that net income for 1999 is $225 million.

CONCEPT REVIEW EXERCISE   SOLUTION

Requirement 1:

a. Cash dividend of $1 per share on its 120 million *outstanding* common shares (122 million minus 2 million treasury shares), payable on April 3 to shareholders of record March 11 (Note: Dividends aren't paid on treasury shares.):

March 1—declaration date		**($ in millions)**
Retained earnings	120	
Cash dividends payable (120 million shares at $1/share)		120
March 11—date of record		
No entry		
April 3—payment date		
Cash dividends payable	120	
Cash		120

The declaration of a dividend reduces retained earnings and creates a liability.

b. Property dividend of 120 million shares of Kroger common stock:

March 5—declaration date		**($ in millions)**
Investment in Kroger common stock	60	
Gain on appreciation of investment ($960 – $900)		60
Retained earnings (fair value of asset to be distributed)	960	
Property dividends payable		960
May 15—date of record		
No entry		
May 30—payment date		
Property dividends payable	960	
Investment in Kroger common stock		960

The investment first must be written up to the $960 million fair market value ($8 × 120 million shares).

The liability is satisfied when the Kroger shares are distributed to shareholders.

c. 3-for-2 stock split effected in the form of a 50% stock dividend:

		($ in millions)
Paid-in capital – excess of par*	60	
Common stock (60 million shares at $1 par per share)		60
*Alternatively, retained earnings may be debited.		

120 million shares times 50% equals 60 million new shares—recorded at par.

d. 10% common stock dividend – fractional share rights for 1 million equivalent whole shares:

		($ in millions)
Retained earnings (18 million shares* at $12 per share)	216	
Common stock (17 million shares at $1 par per share)		17
Paid-in capital—excess of par		
(17 million shares at $11 per share above par)		187
Cash (1 million shares at $12 market price per share)		12
*(120 million + 60 million) × 10% = 18 million shares		

The stock dividend occurs after the 3-for-2 stock split; thus 18 million shares are distributed.

The $12 fair market value of the additional shares is capitalized in this small stock dividend.

e. 9.09% cash dividend on the 11 million preferred shares, payable on December 23 to shareholders of record December 11:

Preferred shareholders annually receive the designated percentage (9.09%) of the preferred's par value ($1 million), if dividends are declared.

December 1-declaration date	($ in millions)	
Retained earnings	1	
Cash dividends payable ($11 million par × 9.09%)		1
December 11—date of record		
No entry		
December 23—payment date		
Cash dividends payable	1	
Cash		1

Requirement 2:

NATIONAL FOODS
Statement of Shareholders' Equity
For the Years Ended Dec. 31, 1998, 1997, and 1996

	Preferred Stock	Common Stock	Additional Paid-in Capital	Receivable from Share Purchase Contract	Retained Earnings	Treasury Stock (at cost)	Total Shareholders' Equity
Balance at Jan. 1, 1996		120	836		2,449		3,405
Sale of preferred shares	10		430	(220)			220
Issuance of common shares		1	9				10
Issuance of common and preferred shares	1	1	58			60	
Net income					400		400
Cash dividends, preferred					(1)		(1)
Balance at Dec. 31, 1996	11	122	1,333	(220)	2,848		4,094
Purchase of treasury shares						(60)	(60)
Sale of treasury shares			4			20	24
Sale of treasury shares			(4)		(2)	20	14
Net income					400		400
Cash dividends, preferred					(1)		(1)
Balance at Dec.31, 1997	11	122	1,333	(220)	3,245	(20)	4,471
Cash dividends, common					(120)		(120)
Property dividends, common					(960)		(960)
3-for-2 split effected in the form of a stock dividend		60	(60)				
10% stock dividend		17	187		(216)		(12)
Preferred dividends					(1)		(1)
Net income					225		225
Balance at Dec.31, 1998	11	199	1,460	(220)	2,173	(20)	3,603

These are the transactions from Concept Review Exercise—Expansion of Corporate Capital.

These are the transactions from Concept Review Exercise—Treasury Stock.

These are the transactions from Concept Review Exercise—Changes in Retained Earnings.

Solution to Financial Reporting Case (at the opening of the chapter)

1. Do you think the stock price increase is related to Gap's buyback plan? What does management mean when it says "the new program is intended, in part, to offset future dilution from stock-based incentive plans" ?
2. What are Gap's choices in accounting for the stock buyback?

3. What effect does the quarterly cash dividend of 7½ cents a share have on Gap's assets? Its liabilities? Its shareholders' equity?

4. What effect did the stock split have on Gap's assets? Its liabilities? Its shareholders' equity?

The stock price increase probably is related to Gap's buyback plan. The marketplace realizes that decreasing the supply of shares supports the price of remaining shares. However, the repurchase of shares is not necessarily the best use of a company's cash. Whether it is in the shareholders' best interests depends on what other opportunities the company has for the cash available.

When new shares are distributed in a stock-based compensation plan, a buyback of shares can serve to offset that increase in shares, offsetting "future dilution from stock-based incentive plans." When a corporation reacquires its own shares, those shares assume the same status as authorized but unissued shares, just as if they never had been issued. However, for exactly the same transaction, companies can choose from among three accounting alternatives: (a) formally retiring them, (b) treasury stock accounted for by the par value method, and (c) treasury stock accounted for by the cost method. In actuality, Gap uses alternative (c).

Each quarter, when directors declare a cash dividend, retained earnings is reduced and a liability is recorded. The liability is paid with cash on the payment date. So, the net effect is an decrease in Gap's assets and its shareholders' equity. The effect on liabilities is temporary.

Conceptually, the proper accounting treatment of a stock split is to make no journal entry. Gap, though, refers to the stock distribution as a "stock split effected in the form of a stock dividend." As a result, a journal entry increases the common stock account by the par value of the additional shares and reduces paid-in capital—excess of par. This merely moves an amount from one part of shareholders' equity to another. Regardless of the accounting method, there is no change in Gap's assets, liabilities, or total shareholders' equity.

The Bottom Line

1. Shareholders' equity is the owners' residual interest in a corporation's assets. It arises primarily from (1) amounts invested by shareholders and (2) amounts earned by the corporation on behalf of its shareholders. These are reported as (1) paid-in capital and (2) retained earnings.

2. A statement of shareholders' equity reports the sources of the changes in individual shareholders' equity accounts.

3. Shares sold by share purchase contract in essence are sold on credit. Shares sold for consideration other than cash (maybe services or a noncash asset) should be recorded at the fair market value of the shares or the noncash consideration, whichever seems more clearly evident.

4. When a corporation retires previously issued shares, those shares assume the same status as authorized but unissued shares—just the same as if they never had been issued. Payments made to retire shares are viewed as a distribution of corporate assets to shareholders.

5. The par value method treats treasury stock as constructively retired. The shares are not formally retired but are accounted for as if the shares were retired. When the cost method is applied, the cost of acquiring the shares is temporarily debited to the treasury stock account. Recording the effects on specific shareholders' equity accounts is delayed until later when the shares are reissued.

6. Retained earnings represents, in general, a corporation's accumulated, undistributed or reinvested net income (or net loss). Distributions of earned assets are dividends.

7. Most corporate dividends are paid in cash. When a noncash asset is distributed, it is referred to as a property dividend. The fair market value of the assets to be distributed is the amount recorded for a property dividend.

8. A stock dividend is the distribution of additional shares of stock to current shareholders. For a small stock dividend (25% or less), the fair value of the additional shares distributed is transferred from retained earnings to paid-in capital. For a stock distribution of 25% or higher, the par value of the additional shares is reclassified within shareholders' equity if referred to as a stock split effected in the form of a stock dividend, but if referred to merely as a stock split, no journal entry is recorded.

APPENDIX

19A

QUASI REORGANIZATIONS

A firm undergoing financial difficulties, but with favorable future prospects, may use a **quasi reorganization** to write down inflated asset values and eliminate an accumulated deficit (debit balance in retained earnings). To effect the reorganization the following procedures are followed:

1. The firm's assets (and perhaps liabilities) are revalued (up or down) to reflect fair market values, with corresponding credits or debits to retained earnings. This process typically increases the deficit.
2. The debit balance in retained earnings (deficit) is eliminated against additional paid-in capital. If additional paid-in capital is not sufficient to absorb the entire deficit, a reduction in capital stock may be necessary (with an appropriate restating of the par amount per share).
3. Retained earnings is dated. That is, disclosure is provided to indicate the date the deficit was eliminated and when the new accumulation of earnings began.

The procedure is demonstrated in Illustration 19A–1. The shareholders approved the quasi reorganization effective January 1, 1997. The plan was to be accomplished by a reduction of inventory by $75 million, a reduction in property, plant, and equipment (net) of $175 million, and appropriate adjustments to shareholders' equity.

ILLUSTRATION 19A–1

Quasi Reorganization

The Emerson-Walsch Corporation has incurred operating losses for several years. A newly elected board of directors voted to implement a quasireorganization, subject to shareholder approval. The balance sheet, on December 31, 1996, immediately prior to the restatement includes the data shown below.

	$ in millions
Cash	$ 75
Receivables	200
Inventory	375
Property, plant, and equipment (net)	400
	$1,050
Liabilities	$ 400
Common stock (800 million shares at $1 par)	800
Additional paid-in capital	150
Retained earnings (deficit)	(300)
	$1,050

When assets are revalued to reflect fair market values, the process often increases the deficit.

	($ in millions)	
To revalue assets:		
Retained earnings	75	
Inventory		75
Retained earnings	175	
Property, plant, and equipment		175
To eliminate a portion of the deficit against available additional paid-in capital:		
Additional paid-in capital	150	
Retained earnings		150
To eliminate the remainder of the deficit against common stock:		
Common stock	400	
Retained earnings		400

The deficit, $550 ($300 + 75 + 175), can be only partially absorbed by the balance of additional paid-in capital.

The remaining deficit, $400 ($300 + 75 + 175 − 150), must be absorbed by reducing the balance in common stock.

The balance sheet immediately after the restatement would include the following:

	($ in millions)
Cash	$ 75
Receivables	200
Inventory	300
Property, plant, and equipment (net)	225
	$800
Liabilities	$400
Common stock (800 million shares at $.50 par)	400
Additional paid-in capital	0
Retained earnings (deficit)	0
	$800

▌ Assets and liabilities reflect current values.

▌ Because a reduced balance represents the same 800 million shares, the par amount per share must be reduced.

▌ The deficit is eliminated.

Note A: Upon the recommendation of the board of directors and approval by shareholders a quasi reorganization was implemented January 1, 1997. The plan was accomplished by a reduction of inventory by $75 million, a reduction in property, plant, and equipment (net) of $175 million, and appropriate adjustments to shareholders' equity. The balance in retained earnings reflects the elimination of a $300 million deficit on that date.

▌ Questions for Review of Key Topics

Question	19–1	Identify and briefly describe the two primary sources of shareholders' equity.
Question	19–2	The balance sheet reports the balances of shareholders' equity accounts. What additional information is provided by the statement of shareholders' equity?
Question	19–3	Identify the three common forms of business organization and the primary difference between the way they are accounted for.

Question	19–4	Corporations offer the advantage of limited liability. Explain what is meant by that statement.
Question	19–5	Distinguish between not-for-profit and for-profit corporations.
Question	19–6	Distinguish between publicly held or privately (or closely) held corporations.
Question	19–7	How does the Model Business Corporation Act affect the way corporations operate?
Question	19–8	The owners of a corporation are its shareholders. If a corporation has only one class of shares, they typically are labeled common shares. Indicate the ownership rights held by common shareholders, unless specifically withheld by agreement.
Question	19–9	What is meant by a shareholder's preemptive right?
Question	19–10	Terminology varies in the way companies differentiate among share types. But many corporations designate shares as common or preferred. What are the two special rights usually given to preferred shareholders?
Question	19–11	Most preferred shares are cumulative. Explain what this means.
Question	19–12	The par value of shares historically indicated the real value of shares and all shares were issued at that price. The concept has changed with time. Describe the meaning of par value as it has evolved to today.
Question	19–13	When shares are sold by share purchase contract, shares ordinarily are issued in exchange for a promissory note from the subscriber and a receivable is recorded for the portion of the selling price not yet received. How is this receivable reported in financial statements?
Question	19–14	At times, companies issue their shares for consideration other than cash. What is the measurement objective in those cases?
Question	19–15	Companies occasionally sell more than one security for a single price. How is the issue price allocated among the separate securities?
Question	19–16	The costs of legal, promotional, and accounting services necessary to effect the sale of shares are referred to as share issue costs. How are these costs recorded? Compare this approach to the way debt issue costs are recorded.
Question	19–17	When a corporation acquires its own shares, those shares assume the same status as authorized but unissued shares, as if they never had been issued. Explain how this is reflected in the accounting records if the shares are formally retired.
Question	19–18	Distinguish between the conceptual basis for the cost method and that for the par value method of accounting for treasury stock.
Question	19–19	The prescribed accounting treatment for stock dividends implicitly assumes that shareholders are fooled by small stock dividends and benefit by the market value of their additional shares. Explain this statement. Is it logical?
Question	19–20	Brandon Components declares a 2-for-1 stock split. What will be the effects of the split, and how should it be recorded?
Question	19–21	What is a reverse stock split? What would be the effect of a reverse stock split on one million $1 par shares? On the accounting records?
Question	19–22	Suppose you own 80 shares of IBM common stock when the company declares a 4% stock dividend. What will you receive as a result?
Question 19–23 (based on Appendix 19A)		A quasi reorganization is sometimes employed by a firm undergoing financial difficulties, but with favorable future prospects. What are two objectives of this procedure? Briefly describe the procedural steps.

Exercises

Exercise 19–1
Issuance of shares; share purchase contract

During its first year of operations, Bekon International, Inc., sold and issued 28 million of its common shares, $1 par per share. During the first year, which ended December 31, 1997, net income was $50 million and no dividends were paid.

Required:

1. Prepare the journal entry to record the sale of the shares for cash at a price of $20 per share.
2. Prepare the journal entry to record the sale of the shares if sold by share purchase contract for $20 per share, with 50% of the selling price to be received after 14 months.
3. Show how shareholders' equity would be reported in Bekon's balance sheet at December 31, 1997, assuming the shares were sold by share purchase contract.
4. Prepare the journal entry to record the collection of the receivable from the share purchase contract during the second year of operations.
5. Show how shareholders' equity would be reported in Bekon's balance sheet at December 31, 1998, assuming no additional changes to shareholders' equity other than 1998 net income of $65 million.

Exercise 19–2
Issuance of shares; noncash consideration

[handwritten: MV of C.S. = $9/share]

During its first year of operations, Eastern Data Links Corporation entered into the following transactions relating to shareholders' equity. The articles of incorporation authorized the issue of 8 million common shares, $1 par per share, and 1 million preferred shares, $50 par per share.

Required:

Prepare the appropriate journal entries to record each transaction:

February   12   Sold 2 million common shares, for $9 per share.
    13   Issued 40,000 common shares to attorneys in exchange for legal services.
    13   Sold 80,000 of its common shares and 4,000 preferred shares for $945,000.
November   15   Issued 380,000 of its common shares in exchange for equipment for which the cash price was known to be $3,688,000. *[handwritten: use FMV of Equipment for stock value]*

Exercise 19–3
Share issue costs; issuance

ICOT Industries issued 15 million of its $1 par common shares for $424 million on April 11, 1997. Legal, promotional, and accounting services necessary to effect the sale cost $2 million.

Required:

1. Prepare the journal entry to record the issuance of the shares.
2. Explain how recording the share issue costs differs from the way debt issue costs are recorded (discussed in Chapter 14).

Exercise 19–4
Effect of cumulative, nonparticipating preferred stock on dividends—3 years

The shareholders' equity of WBL Industries includes the items shown below. The board of directors of WBL declared cash dividends of $8 million, $20 million, and $150 million in its first three years of operation—1997, 1998, and 1999, respectively.

	($ in millions)
Common stock	$100
Paid-in capital—excess of par, common	980
Preferred stock, 8%	200
Paid-in capital—excess of par, preferred	555

Required:

Determine the amount of dividends to be paid to preferred and common stockholders in each of the three years, assuming that the preferred stock is cumulative and nonparticipating.

	Preferred	Common
1997		
1998		
1999		

Exercise 19–5
Retirement of shares

Borner Communications' articles of incorporation authorized the issuance of 130 million common shares. The transactions described below effected changes in Borner's outstanding shares. Prior to the transactions, Borner's shareholders' equity included the following:

Shareholders' Equity	($ in millions)
Common stock, 100 million shares at $1 par,	$100
Paid-in capital – excess of par	300
Retained earnings	210

Required:

Assuming that Borner Communications retires shares it reacquires (restores their status to that of authorized but unissued shares), record the appropriate journal entry for each of the following transactions:

1. On January 7, 1997, Borner reacquired 2 million shares at $5.00 per share.
2. On August 23, 1997, Borner reacquired 4 million shares at $3.50 per share.
3. On July 25, 1998, Borner sold 3 million common shares at $6 per share.

Exercise 19–6
Treasury stock—journal entries—par value method

In 1997, Borland Semiconductors entered into the treasury stock transactions described below. In 1994, Borland had issued 170 million shares of its $1 par common stock at $34 per share.

Required:

Assuming that Borland uses the par value method, record the appropriate journal entry for each of the following transactions:

1. On January 2, 1997, Borland reacquired 10 million shares at $32.50 per share.
2. On March 3, 1997, Borland reacquired 10 million shares at $36 per share.
3. On August 13, 1997, Borland sold 1 million treasury shares at $42 per share.
4. On December 15, 1997, Borland sold 2 million treasury shares at $36 per share.

Exercise 19–7
Treasury Stock: journal
entries—cost method

In 1997, Western Transport Company entered into the treasury stock transactions described below. In 1995, Western Transport had issued 140 million shares of its $1 par common stock at $17 per share.

Required:
Assuming that Western Transport uses the cost method, prepare the appropriate journal entry for each of the following transactions:

1.   On January 23, 1997, Western Transport reacquired 10 million shares at $20 per share.
2.   On September 3, 1997, Western Transport sold 1 million treasury shares at $21 per share.
3.   On November 4, 1997, Western Transport sold 1 million treasury shares at $18 per share.

Exercise 19–8
Treasury stock: cost
method—weighted-average
and FIFO cost

At December 31, 1996, the balance sheet of Meca International included the following shareholders' equity accounts:

Shareholders' Equity	($ in millions)
Common stock, 60 million shares at $1 par	$ 60
Paid-in capital—excess of par	300
Retained earnings	410

Required:
Assuming that Meca International uses the cost method, record the appropriate journal entry for each of the following treasury stock transactions:

1.   On February 12, 1997, Meca reacquired 1 million common shares at $13 per share.
2.   On June 9, 1998, Meca reacquired 2 million common shares at $10 per share.
3.   On May 25, 1999, Meca sold 2 million treasury shares at $15 per share—determine cost as the weighted average cost of treasury shares.
4.   For the previous transaction, assume Meca determines the cost of treasury shares by the FIFO method.

Exercise 19–9
Reporting treasury stock

On two previous occasions, the management of Dennison and Company, Inc., repurchased some of its common shares. Between buyback transactions, the corporation issued common shares under its management incentive plan. Shown below is shareholders' equity following these share transactions, as reported by three different methods of accounting for reacquired shares.

Shareholders' Equity	Method A	Method B	Method C
		(in millions)	
Paid-in capital:			
Preferred stock, $10 par,	$ 150	$ 150	$ 150
Common stock, $1 par,	200	197	200
Less: Treasury stock			(3)
Additional paid-in capital	1,204	1,201	1,201
Retained earnings	2,994	2,979	2,979
Less: Treasury stock	(21)		
Total shareholders' equity	$4,527	$4,527	$4,527

Required:
1.   Infer from the presentation which method of accounting for reacquired shares is represented by each of the three columns.
2.   Explain why presentation formats are different and why some account balances are different for the three methods.

Exercise 19–10
Multiple choice; paid-in capital

The following questions dealing with paid-in capital are adapted from recent CPA examinations. Determine the response that best completes the statements or questions.

1.   East Co. issued 1,000 shares of its $5 par common stock to Howe as compensation for 1,000 hours of legal services performed. Howe usually bills $160 per hour for legal services. On the date of issuance, the stock was trading on a public exchange at $140 per share. By what amount should the additional paid-in capital account increase as a result of this transaction?
     a. $135,000
     b. $140,000
     c. $155,000
     d. $160,000
2.   During 1996, Brad Co. issued 5,000 shares of $100 par convertible preferred stock for $110 per share. One share of preferred stock can be converted into three shares of Brad's $25 par common stock at the option of the preferred shareholder. On December 31, 1997, when the market value of

the common stock was $40 per share, all of the preferred stock was converted. What amount should Brad credit to common stock and to additional paid-in capital—common stock was a result of the conversion?

	Common Stock	Additional Paid-in Capital
a.	$375,000	$175,000
b.	$375,000	$225,000
c.	$500,000	$ 50,000
d.	$600,000	$ 0

3. If a corporation sells some of its treasury stock at a price that exceeds its cost, this excess should be
    a. Reported as a gain in the income statement.
    b. Treated as a reduction in the carrying amount.
    c. Credited to additional paid-in capital.
    d. Credited to retained earnings.

Exercise 19–11
Transactions affecting retained earnings

Shown below in T-account format are the changes affecting the retained earnings of Brenner-Jude Corporation during 1997. At January 1, 1997, the corporation had outstanding 105 million common shares, $1 par per share.

Retained Earnings ($ in millions)

		90	Beginning Balance
Retirement of 5 million common shares for $22 million	2		
		88	Net income for the year
Declaration and payment of a $.33 per share cash dividend	33		
Declaration and distribution of a 4% stock dividend	20		
		123	Ending Balance

Required:

1. From the information provided by the account changes you should be able to recreate the transactions that affected Brenner-Jude's retained earnings during 1997. Prepare the journal entries that Brenner-Jude must have recorded during the year for these transactions.
2. Prepare a statement of retained earnings for Brenner-Jude for the year ended 1997.

Exercise 19–12
Stock dividend

The shareholders' equity of Core Technologies Company on June 30, 1996, included the following:

Common stock, $1 par; authorized, 8 million shares; issued and outstanding, 3 million shares	$ 3,000,000
Paid-in capital—excess of par	12,000,000
Retained earnings	14,000,000

On April 1, 1997, the board of directors of Core Technologies declared a 10% stock dividend on common shares, to be distributed on June 1. The market price of Core Technologies' common stock was $30 on April 1, 1997, and $40 on June 1, 1997.

Required

Prepare the journal entry to record the distribution of the stock dividend on the declaration date.

Exercise 19–13
Stock split

The Cracker Barrel Old Country Store operates stores that provide a combination of restaurant and gift shop services to the motoring public. Its 1995 financial statements included the following:

Stockholders' Equity (Notes 4, 5 and 6):

Common stock - 150,000,000 shares of $.50 par value authorized; shares issued and outstanding:		
1995, 59,992,047; 1994, 59,901,316	29,996,023	29,950,658
Additional paid-in capital	195,420,664	194,073,393
Retained earnings	270,666,211	205,821,866
Total stockholders' equity	496,082,898	429,845,917

5. Common Stock

On January 29, 1993 the Board of Directors declared a three-for-two stock split in the form of a 50% stock dividend distributed to stockholders on March 19, 1993.

At the time of the stock split 39,511,036 shares of common stock were outstanding.

Required:

Prepare the journal entry, if any, that Cracker Barrel recorded at the time of the stock split.

Exercise 19–14
Cash for fractional share rights

Douglas McDonald Company's balance sheet included the following shareholders' equity accounts at December 31, 1997:

Paid-in capital	($ in millions)
Common stock, 900 million shares at $1 par	$ 900
Paid-in capital—excess of par	15,800
Retained earnings	14,888
Total shareholders' equity	$31,588

On March 16, 1998, a 4% common stock dividend was declared and distributed. The market value of the common stock was $21 per share. Fractional share rights represented 2 million equivalent whole shares. Cash was paid in place of the fractional share rights.

Required:

Prepare the appropriate entries for the declaration and distribution of the stock dividend.

Exercise 19–15
Transactions affecting retained earnings

The balance sheet of Consolidated Paper, Inc., included the following shareholders' equity accounts at December 31, 1996:

Paid-in capital	($ in millions)
Preferred stock, 8.8%, 90,000 shares at $1 par	$ 90,000
Common stock, 364,000 shares at $1 par	364,000
Paid-in capital—excess par, preferred	1,437,000
Paid-in capital—excess of par, common	2,574,000
Retained earnings	9,735,000
Treasury stock, at cost; 4,000 common shares	(44,000)
Total shareholders' equity	$14,156,000

During 1997, several events and transactions affected the retained earnings of Consolidated Paper.

Required:

1. Prepare the appropriate entries for these events:
   a. On March 3, the board of directors declared a property dividend of 240,000 shares of Leasco International common stock that Consolidated Paper had been purchased in January as an investment (book value: $700,000). The investment shares had a fair market value of $3 per share and were distributed March 31 to shareholders of record March 15.
   b. On May 3, a 5-for-4 stock split was declared and distributed. The stock split was effected in the form of a 25% stock dividend. The market value of the $1 par common stock was $11 per share.
   c. On July 5, a 2% common stock dividend was declared and distributed. The market value of the common stock was $11 per share.
   d. On December 1, the board of directors declared the 8.8% cash dividend on the 90,000 preferred shares, payable on December 28 to shareholders of record December 20.
   e. On December 1, the board of directors declared a cash dividend of $.50 per share on its common shares, payable on December 28 to shareholders of record December 20.
2. Prepare the shareholders' equity section of the balance sheet for Consolidated Paper, Inc., for the year ended at December 31, 1997. Net income for the year was $810,000.

Exercise 19–16
Change from treasury stock to retired stock

In keeping with a modernization of corporate statutes in its home state, UMC Corporation decided in 1997 to discontinue accounting for reacquired shares as treasury stock. Instead, shares repurchased will be viewed as having been retired, reassuming the status of unissued shares. As part of the change, treasury shares held were reclassified as retired stock. At December 31, 1996, UMC's balance sheet reported the following shareholders' equity:

	($ in millions)
Common stock, $1 par	$ 200
Paid-in capital—excess of par	800
Retained earnings	956
Treasury stock (4 million shares at cost)	(25)
Total shareholders' equity	$1,931

Required:

Identify the type of accounting change this decision represents, and prepare the journal entry to effect the reclassification of treasury shares as retired shares.

Exercise 19–17
Multiple choice; retained earnings

The following questions dealing with retained earnings are adapted from recent CPA examinations. Determine the response that best completes the statements or questions.

1. At December 31, 1996, and 1997, Apex Co. had 3,000 shares of $100 par, 5% cumulative preferred stock outstanding. No dividends were in arrears as of December 31, 1995. Apex did not declare a dividend during 1996. During 1997, Apex paid a cash dividend of $10,000 on its preferred stock. Apex should report dividends in arrears in its 1997 financial statements as a (an)
   a. Accrued liability of $15,000.
   b. Disclosure of $15,000.
   c. Accrued liability of $20,000.
   d. Disclosure of $20,000.

2. On January 2, 1998, Lake Mining Co.'s board of directors declared a cash dividend of $400,000 to stockholders of record on January 18, 1998, payable on February 10, 1998. The dividend is permissible under law in Lake's state of incorporation. Selected data from Lake's December 31, 1997, balance sheet are as follows:

Accumulated depletion	$100,000
Capital stock	500,000
Additional paid-in capital	150,000
Retained earnings	300,000

   The $400,000 dividend includes a liquidating dividend of
   a. $0
   b. $100,000
   c. $150,000
   d. $300,000

3. When a company declares a cash dividend, retained earnings is decreased by the amount of the dividend on the date of
   a. Declaration.
   b. Record.
   c. Payment.
   d. Declaration or record, whichever is earlier.

Exercise 19–18
Profitability ratio

Comparative balance sheets for Softech Canvas Goods for 1997 and 1996 are shown below. Softech pays no dividends, instead reinvesting all earnings for future growth.

Comparative Balance Sheets ($ in 000s)

	December 31	
	1997	**1996**
Assets:		
Cash	$ 50	$ 40
Accounts receivable	100	120
Short-term investments	50	40
Inventory	200	140
Property, plant, and equipment (net)	600	550
	$1,000	$890
Liabilities and Shareholders' Equity:		
Current liabilities	$ 240	$210
Bonds payable	160	160
Paid-in capital	400	400
Retained earnings	200	120
	$1,000	$890

Required:
1. Determine the return on shareholders' equity for 1997.
2. What does the ratio measure?

Exercise 19–19
New stock issues; *Wall Street Journal* announcement

Periodically, *The Wall Street Journal* lists new security issues that include corporate debt issues and stock issues. The following were among the equity offerings reported in the November 14, 1996, issue:

NEW SECURITIES ISSUES

The following were among yesterday's offerings and pricings in the U.S. and non-U.S. capital markets, with terms and syndicate manner, based on information provided by Dow Jones Capital Markets Report.

EQUITY

Amresco Inc. (AMMB)—*7.76 million common shares priced at $21.25 each through underwriters led by Robinson-Humphrey Co.*

Vitesse Semiconductor Corp. (VTSS)—Three million common shares priced at $36 each through underwriters led by Lehman Brothers Inc.

WSJ Nov. 14, 1996

The par amount per share for Amresco's common stock is $.05; for Vitesse Semiconductor it is $.01.

Required:
Prepare the appropriate journal entries to record the sale of both issues to underwriters. Ignore share issue costs.

Exercise 19–20
Stock buyback; *Wall Street Journal* announcement

The following excerpts are from an article that appeared in the November 18, 1996, issue of *The Wall Street Journal.*

"Stock-Repurchase Program Is Doubled to $400 Million"

Wal-Mart Stores Inc., *Bentonville, Ark., said it doubled its common-stock-repurchase program to a total authorization of $400 million. . . . Wal-Mart said the shares will be used for its stock-option and benefit plans. The purchases will be made from time to time on the open market. .... In New York Stock Exchange composite trading Friday, shares of Wal-Mart closed unchanged at $24.50.*

The par amount per share for Wal-Mart common stock is $.10. Paid-in capital—excess of par is $.24 per share on average. Wal-Mart retires the shares it reacquires.

Required:
Suppose Wal-Mart buys back 500,000 of its shares on the open market at the price indicated in the article. Prepare the appropriate journal entry to record the purchase.

Problems

Problem 19–1
Various stock transactions; correction of journal entries

Part A
During its first year of operations, the McCollum Corporation entered into the following transactions relating to shareholders' equity. The corporation was authorized to issue 100 million common shares, $1 par per share.

Required:
Prepare the appropriate journal entries to record each transaction.

| January | 9 | Issued 40 million common shares for $20 per share. |
| March | 11 | Issued 5,000 shares in exchange for custom-made equipment. McCollum's shares have traded recently on the stock exchange at $20 per share. |

Part B
A new staff accountant for the McCollum Corporation recorded the following journal entries during the second year of operations. McCollum retires shares that it reacquires (restores their status to that of authorized but unissued shares).

			(in millions)
Jan. 12	Land	2	
	Paid-in capital – donation of land		2
Sept. 1	Common stock	2	
	Retained earnings	48	
	Cash		50
Dec. 1	Cash	26	
	Common stock		1
	Gain on sale of previously issued shares		25

Required:
Prepare the journal entries that should have been recorded for each of the transactions.

Problem 19–2
Treasury stock—comparison of the cost and par value methods

The shareholders' equity section of the balance sheet of TNL Systems, Inc., included the following accounts at December 31, 1996:

Shareholders' Equity	($ in millions)
Common stock, 240 million shares at $1 par,	$ 240
Paid-in capital—excess of par	1,680
Paid-in capital—reacquired shares	1
Retained earnings	1,100

Required:

1. During 1997, TNL Systems reacquired shares of its common stock to hold as treasury stock and later sold shares in two separate transactions. Prepare the entries for both the purchase and subsequent resale of treasury stock by both the par value and cost methods.

   a. On February 5, 1997, TNL Systems purchased 6 million shares of treasury stock at $10 per share.

   b. On July 9, 1997, the corporation sold 2 million shares of treasury stock at $12 per share.

   c. On November 14, 1999, the corporation sold 2 million shares of treasury stock at $7 per share.

2. Prepare the shareholders' equity section of TNL Systems' balance sheet at December 31, 1999, reporting treasury stock by both the par value and cost methods. Assume all net income earned in 1997–1999 was distributed to shareholders as cash dividends.

Problem 19–3
Reacquired shares—
comparison of retired shares
and treasury shares (cost and
par value methods)

National Supply's shareholders' equity included the following accounts at December 31, 1996:

Shareholders' Equity	
Common stock, 6 million shares at $1 par,	$ 6,000,000
Paid-in capital—excess of par	30,000,000
Retained earnings	86,500,000

Required:

1. National Supply reacquired shares of its common stock in two separate transactions and later sold shares. Prepare the entries for each of the transactions under each of three separate assumptions: the shares are (a) retired, (b) accounted for as treasury stock by the par value method and (c) accounted for as treasury stock by the cost method.

February 15, 1997	Reacquired 300,000 shares at $8 per share.
February 17, 1998	Reacquired 300,000 shares at $5.50 per share.
November 9, 1999	Sold 200,000 shares at $7 per share (assume FIFO cost).

2. Prepare the shareholders' equity section of National Supply's balance sheet at December 31, 1999, assuming the shares are (a) retired, (b) accounted for as treasury stock by the par value method and (c) accounted for as treasury stock by the cost method. Net income was $14 million in 1997, $15 million in 1998, and $16 million in 1999. No dividends were paid during the three year period.

Problem 19–4
Statement of retained
earnings

Comparative Statements of Retained Earnings for Renn-Dever Corporation were reported in its 1997 annual report as follows.

RENN-DEVER CORPORATION
Statements of Retained Earnings

For the years ended December 31,	1997	1996	1995
Balance at beginning of year	$ 6,794,292	$5,464,052	$5,624,552
Net income (loss)	3,308,700	2,240,900	(160,500)
Deductions:			
Stock dividend (34,900 shares)	242,000		
Common shares retired (110,000 shares)		212,660	
Common stock cash dividends	889,950	698,000	0
Balance at end of year	$8,971,042	$6,794,292	$5,464,052

At December 31, 1994, common shares consisted of the following:

Common stock, 1,855,000 shares at $1 par,	$1,855,000
Paid-in capital—excess of par	7,420,000

Required:

Infer from the reports the events and transactions that affected Renn-Dever Corporation's retained earnings during 1995, 1996, and 1997. Prepare the journal entries that reflect those events and transactions.

Problem 19–5
Shareholders' equity
transactions; statement of
shareholders' equity

Listed below are the transactions that affected the shareholders' equity of Branch-Rickie Corporation during the period 1997–1999. At December 31, 1996, the corporation's accounts included:

	($ in 000s)
Common stock, 105 million shares at $1 par,	$105,000
Paid-in capital—excess of par	630,000
Retained earnings	970,000

a. November 1, 1997, the board of directors declared a cash dividend of $.80 per share on its common shares, payable to shareholders of record November 15, to be paid December 1.

b. On March 1, 1998, the board of directors declared a property dividend consisting of corporate bonds of Warner Corporation that Branch-Rickie was holding as an investment. The bonds had a fair market value of $1.6 million, but were purchased two years previously for $1.3 million. Because they were intended to be held to maturity, the bonds had not been previously written up. The property dividend was payable to shareholders of record March 13, to be distributed April 5.

c. On July 12, 1998, the corporation declared and distributed a 5% common stock dividend (when the market value of the common stock was $21 per share). Cash was paid for fractional share rights representing 250,000 equivalent whole shares.

d. On November 1, 1998, the board of directors declared a cash dividend of $.80 per share on its common shares, payable to shareholders of record November 15, to be paid December 1.

e. On January 15, 1999, the board of directors declared and distributed a 3-for-2 stock split effected in the form of a 50% stock dividend when the market value of the common stock was $22 per share.

f. On November 1, 1999, the board of directors declared a cash dividend of $.65 per share on its common shares, payable to shareholders of record November 15, to be paid December 1.

Required:

1. Prepare the journal entries that Branch-Rickie recorded during the three-year period for these transactions.

2. Prepare comparative statements of shareholders' equity for Branch-Rickie for the three-year period ($ in 000s). Net income was $330 million, $395 million, and $455 million for 1997, 1998, and 1999, respectively.

Problem 19–6
Statement of shareholders' equity

Comparative statements of shareholders' equity for Anaconda International Corporation were reported as follows for the fiscal years ending December 31, 1997, 1998, and 1999.

ANACONDA INTERNATIONAL CORPORATION
Statements of Shareholders' Equity
For the Years Ended Dec. 31, 1997, 1998, and 1999 ($ in millions)

	Preferred Stock $10 par	Common Stock $1 par	Additional Paid-in Capital	Receivable from Share Purchase Contract	Retained Earnings	Total Shareholders' Equity
Balance at Jan. 1, 1997		55	495		1,878	2,428
Sale of preferred shares	10		470	(360)		120
Sale of common shares		7	63			70
Cash dividend, preferred					(1)	(1)
Cash dividend, common					(16)	(16)
Net income					290	290
Balance at Dec. 31, 1997	10	62	1028	(360)	2,151	2,891
Received balance from share purchase contract				360		360
Retirement of shares		(3)	(27)		(20)	(50)
Cash dividend, preferred					(1)	(1)
Cash dividend, common					(20)	(20)
3-for-2 split effected in the form of a dividend	5		(5)			
Net income					380	380
Balance at Dec. 31, 1998	15	59	996	0	2,490	3,560
Common stock dividend		6	59		(65)	
Cash dividend, preferred					(1)	(1)
Cash dividend, common					(22)	(22)
Net income					412	412
Balance at Dec. 31, 1999	15	65	1055	0	2,814	3,949

Required:

Infer from the statements the events and transactions that affected Anaconda International Corporation's shareholders' equity during 1997, 1998, and 1999. Prepare the journal entries that reflect those events and transactions.

Problem 19–7
Share issue costs; issuance; dividends; early retirement

During its first year of operations, Cupola Fan Corporation issued 30,000 of $1 par Class B shares for $385,000 on June 30, 1997. Share issue costs were $1,500. One year from the issue date (July 1, 1998), the corporation retired 10% of the shares for $39,500.

Required:

1. Prepare the journal entry to record the issuance of the shares.
2. Prepare the journal entry to record the declaration of a $2 per share dividend on December 1, 1997.
3. Prepare the journal entry to record the payment of the dividend on December 31, 1997.
4. Prepare the journal entry to record the retirement of the shares.

(Note: You may wish to compare your solution to this problem with that of Problem 14–16, which deals with parallel issues of debt issue costs and the retirement of debt.)

Problem 19–8
Effect of preferred stock characteristics on dividends

The shareholders' equity of Kramer Industries includes the data shown below. During 1997, cash dividends of $150 million were declared. Dividends were not declared in 1995 or 1996.

	($ in millions)
Common stock	$200
Paid-in capital—excess of par, common	800
Preferred stock, 10%, nonparticipating	100
Paid-in capital—excess of par, preferred	270

Required:

Determine the amount of dividends payable to preferred shareholders and to common shareholders under each of the following two assumptions regarding the characteristics of the preferred stock.

Assumption A—The preferred stock is noncumulative.
Assumption B—The preferred stock is cumulative.

Problem 19–9
Transactions affecting retained earnings

Indicate by letter whether each of the transactions listed below increases (**I**), decreases (**D**), or has no effect (**N**) on retained earnings. Assume the shareholders' equity of the transacting company includes only common stock, paid-in capital—excess of par, and retained earnings at the time of each transaction.

▌Example

Transactions

N	1. Sale of common stock
___	2. Purchase of treasury stock at a cost *less* than the original issue price (cost method)
___	3. Purchase of treasury stock at a cost *greater* than the original issue price (cost method)
___	4. Declaration of a property dividend
___	5. Purchase of treasury stock at a cost *less* than the original issue price (par value method)
___	6. Purchase of treasury stock at a cost *greater* than the original issue price (par value method)
___	7. Sale of treasury stock for *more* than cost (cost method)
___	8. Sale of treasury stock for *less* than cost (cost method)
___	9. Net income for the year
___	10. Sale of treasury stock for *more* than par and cost (par value method)
___	11. Sale of treasury stock for *less* than par and cost (par value method)
___	12. Declaration of a cash dividend
___	13. Payment of a previously declared cash dividend
___	14. Issuance of convertible bonds for cash
___	15. Declaration and distribution of a 5% stock dividend
___	16. Retirement of common stock at a cost *less* than the original issue price
___	17. Retirement of common stock at a cost *greater* than the original issue price
___	18. A stock split effected in the form of a stock dividend
___	19. A stock split in which the par value per share is reduced (not effected in the form of a stock dividend)
___	20. A net loss for the year

Problem 19–10
Stock dividends received on investments; integrative problem

Ellis Transport Company acquired 1.2 million shares of stock in L&K Corporation at $44 per share. They are classified by Ellis as available for sale. Ellis sold 200,000 shares at $46, received a 10% stock dividend, and then later in the year sold another 100,000 shares at $43.

Hint: There is no entry for the stock dividend, but a new investment per share must be calculated for use later when the shares are sold.

Required:

Prepare journal entries to record these transactions.

Problem 19–11
Various shareholders' equity topics; comprehensive

Part A

In late 1996, the Nicklaus Corporation was formed. The corporate charter authorizes the issuance of 5,000,000 shares of common stock carrying a $1 par value, and 1,000,000 shares of $5 par value, noncumulative, non-participating preferred stock. On January 2, 1997, 3,000,000 shares of the common stock are issued in exchange for cash at an average price of $10 per share. Also on January 2, all 1,000,000 shares of preferred stock are issued at $20 per share.

Required:

1. Prepare journal entries to record these transactions.
2. Prepare the shareholders' equity section of the Nicklaus balance sheet as of March 31, 1997. (Assume net income for the first quarter 1997 was $1,000,000).

Part B

During 1997, the Nicklaus Corporation participated in three treasury stock transactions: (Nicklaus uses the cost method.)

a. On June 30, 1997, the corporation reacquires 200,000 shares for the treasury at a price of $12 per share,
b. On July 31, 1997, 50,000 treasury shares are reissued at $15 per share, and
c. On September 30, 1997, 50,000 treasury shares are reissued at $10 per share.

Required:

1. Prepare journal entries to record these transactions.
2. Prepare the Nicklaus Corporation shareholders' equity section as it would appear in a balance sheet prepared at September 30, 1997. (Assume net income for the second and third quarter was $3,000,000).

Part C

On October 1, 1997, Nicklaus Corporation receives permission to replace its $1 par value common stock (5,000,000 shares authorized, 3,000,000 shares issued, and 2,900,000 shares outstanding) with a new common stock issue having a $.50 par value. Since the new par value is one-half the amount of the old, this represents a 2-for-1 stock split. That is, the shareholders will receive two shares of the $.50 par stock in exchange for each share of the $1 par stock they own. The $1 par stock will be collected and destroyed by the issuing corporation.

On November 1, 1997, the Nicklaus Corporation declares a $.05 per share cash dividend on common stock and a $.25 per share cash dividend on preferred stock. Payment is scheduled for December 1, 1997, to shareholders of record on November 15, 1997.

On December 2, 1997, the Nicklaus Corporation declares a 1% stock dividend payable on December 28, 1997, to shareholders of record on December 14. At the date of declaration, the common stock was selling in the open market at $10 per share. The dividend will result in 58,000 (.01 × 5,800,000) additional shares being issued to shareholders.

Required:

1. Prepare journal entries to record the declaration and payment of these stock and cash dividends.
2. Prepare the December 31, 1997, shareholders' equity section of the balance sheet for the Nicklaus Corporation. (Assume net income for the fourth quarter was $2,500,000).
3. Prepare a statement of shareholders' equity for Nicklaus Corporation for 1997.

Problem 19–12
Quasi reorganization (based on Appendix 19A)

A new CEO was hired to revive the floundering Champion Chemical Corporation. The company had endured operating losses for several years, but confidence was emerging that better times were ahead. The board of directors and shareholders approved a quasireorganization for the corporation. The reorganization included devaluing inventory for obsolescence by $105 million and increasing land by $5 million. Immediately prior to the restatement, at December 31, 1996, Champion Chemical Corporation's balance sheet appeared as follows (in condensed form):

CHAMPION CHEMICAL CORPORATION
Balance Sheet
At December 31, 1996 ($ in millions)

Cash	$ 20
Receivables	40
Inventory	230
Land	40
Buildings and equipment (net)	90
	$420

Liabilities	$240
Common stock (320 million shares at $1 par)	320
Additional paid-in capital	60
Retained earnings (deficit)	(200)
	$420

Required:
1. Prepare the journal entries appropriate to record the quasi reorganization on January 1, 1997.
2. Prepare a balance sheet as it would appear immediately after the restatement.

Cases

Discussion Case 19–1
Treasury stock; stock
dividends; cash dividends

Brady Company has 30,000 shares of $10 par value common stock authorized and 20,000 shares issued and outstanding. On August 15, 1997, Brady purchased 1,000 shares of treasury stock for $12 per share. Brady uses the cost method to account for treasury stock. On September 14, 1997, Brady sold 500 shares of the treasury stock for $14 per share. In October 1997, Brady declared and distributed 2,000 shares as a stock dividend from unissued shares when the market value of the common stock was $16 per share. On December 20, 1997, Brady declared $1 per share cash dividend, payable on January 10, 1998, to shareholders of record on December 31, 1997.

Required:
1. How should Brady account for the purchase and sale of the treasury stock, and how should the treasury stock be presented in Brady's balance sheet at December 31, 1997?
2. How should Brady account for the stock dividend, and how would it affect Brady's shareholders' equity at December 31, 1997? Why?
3. How should Brady account for the cash dividend, and how would it affect Brady's balance sheet at December 31, 1997? Why?

(AICPA adapted)

Integrating Case 19–2
Long-term liabilities and
shareholders' equity

Fay, Inc., finances its capital needs approximately one-third from long-term debt and two-thirds from equity. At December 31, 1996, Fay had the following liability and equity account balances:

11% Debenture bonds payable, face amount	$5,000,000
Premium on bonds payable	352,400
Common stock	8,000,000
Additional paid-in capital	2,295,000
Retained earnings	2,465,000
Treasury stock, at cost	325,000

Transactions during 1997 and other information relating to Fay's liabilities and equity accounts were as follows:

- The debenture bonds were issued on December 31, 1995, for $5,378,000 to yield 10%. The bonds mature on December 31, 2001. Interest is payable annually on December 31. Fay uses the interest method to amortize bond premium.
- Fay's common stock shares are traded on the over-the-counter market. At December 31, 1996, Fay had 2,000,000 authorized shares of $10 par common stock.
- On January 15, 1997, Fay reissued 15,000 of its 25,000 shares of treasury stock for $225,000. The treasury stock had been acquired on February 28, 1996.
- On March 2, 1997, Fay issued a 5% stock dividend on all issued shares. The market price of Fay's common stock at time of issuance was $14 per share.
- On November 1, 1997, Fay borrowed $4,000,000 at 9%, evidenced by an unsecured note payable to United Bank. The note is payable in five equal annual principal installments of $800,000. The first principal and interest payment is due on November 1, 1998.
- On December 31, 1997, Fay owned 10,000 shares of Ryan Corp.'s common stock, which represented a 1% ownership interest. Fay accounts for this marketable equity investment as available for sale. The stock was purchased on May 1, 1996, at $20 per share. The market price was $21 per share on December 31, 1996, and $18 per share on December 31, 1997.
- Fay's net income for 1997 was $2,860,000.

Required:
1. Prepare the long-term liabilities section of Fay's December 31, 1997 balance sheet, including all disclosures applicable to each obligation.
2. Prepare the shareholders' equity section of Fay's December 31, 1997 balance sheet.

3.   Prepare a schedule showing interest expense for the year ended December 31, 1997.

(AICPA adapted)

Group Interaction Case 19–3
Is a receivable for stock issued or to be issued, a recognizable asset, or should it be deducted from equity?

An unsettled question in accounting for stock is: Should a receivable for stock issued or to be issued, such as a note receivable for stock already issued or a stock subscription receivable, be recognized as an asset, or should it be deducted from equity? The prevalent practice is reporting the receivable as a contra equity account. This results in reporting total paid-in capital only to the extent that unrestricted shares are outstanding. However, many accountants believe receivables for stock fit the definition of assets.

Two opposing viewpoints are:

View 1: Receivables for stock should be deducted from equity.
View 2: Receivables for stock should be reported as assets.

In considering this question, focus on conceptual issues regarding the practicable and theoretically appropriate treatment, unconstrained by GAAP.

Required:
1.   Which view do you favor? Develop a list of arguments in support of your view prior to the class session for which the case is assigned.
2.   In class, your instructor will pair you (and everyone else) with a classmate (who also has independently developed an argument).
    a.   You will be given three minutes to argue your view to your partner. Your partner likewise will be given three-minutes to argue his or her view to you. During these three minute presentations, the listening partner is not permitted to speak.
    b.   Then after each person has had a turn attempting to convince his or her partner, the two partners will have a three-minute discussion in which they will decide which view is more convincing and arguments will be merged into a single view for each pair.
3.   After the allotted time, a spokesperson for each of the two views will be selected by the instructor. Each spokesperson will field arguments from the class in support of that view's position and list the arguments on the board. The class then will discuss the merits of the two lists of arguments and attempt to reach a consensus view, though a consensus is not necessary.

Trueblood Accounting Case 19–4
Innovative financing arrangement; what is equity?

The following Robert M. Trueblood case is recommended for use with this chapter. The case provides an excellent opportunity for class discussion, group projects, and writing assignments. The case, along with Professor's Discussion Material, can be obtained from the Deloitte & Touche Foundation.

Case 92-7: *Accounting for an Equity Kicker*

This case considers the issue of whether an "equity kicker" (not in the text but described in the case) given by a borrower to a lender in a financing arrangement should be considered additional interest or whether the borrower has given up an equity interest.

Real World Case 19–5
Initial public offering; Northwest Airlines

In 1994, Northwest Airlines Corporation issued 20 million shares of common stock as an initial public offering. The company had earlier gone private through an acquisition by NWA Corp. in 1989. That company retained a 51% ownership after the 1994 public offering. The Prospectus describing the stock offering included the following information:

Per share data:	
Par value	$ .01
Price to public	13.00
Underwriting discounts and commissions	.65
Estimated expenses payable by the company	$3,850,000

Required:
Prepare a journal entry appropriate to record the sale as described.

Writing Case 19–6
Issuance of shares; share issue costs; prepare a report

You are the newest member of the staff of Brinks & Company, a medium-size investment management firm. You are supervised by Les Kramer, an employee of two years. Les has a reputation as being technically sound but has a noticeable gap in his accounting education. Knowing you are knowledgeable about accounting issues, he requested you provide him with a synopsis of accounting for share issue costs.

"I thought the costs of issuing securities is recorded separately and expensed over time," he stated in a handwritten memo. "But I don't see that for Proffitt's underwriting expenses. What gives?"

He apparently was referring to a disclosure note on a page of Proffitt's annual report, photocopied and attached to his memo. Proffitt's, Inc., is one of America's fastest growing specialty retailers. To raise funds for expansion, the company sold additional shares of its $.10 par common stock. The following disclosure note appeared in the company's annual report for the 12 months ending January 28, 1995:

NOTES TO CONSOLIDATED FINANCIAL STATEMENTS

Note K—Stock Transactions (In Part)

In February and March 1993, the Company sold 2,395,000 shares of Common Stock at $22.25 per share in a public offering. Net proceeds to the Company were approximately $50.2 million after the underwriting discount and offering expenses.

Required:

Write a formal memo to your supervisor. Briefly explain how share issue costs are accounted for and how that accounting differs from that of debt issue costs. To make sure your explanation is understood in context of the footnote, include in your memo the following:

a. At what total amount did the shares sell to the public? How is the difference between this amount and the $50.2 million net proceeds accounted for?
b. The appropriate journal entry to record the sale of the shares.

Critical Thought Case 19–7
Statement of shareholders' equity

The shareholders' equity portion of the balance sheet of Proffitt's, Inc., one of America's fastest growing specialty retailers, is shown below.

PROFFITT'S INC.
Balance Sheet
Shareholders' Equity Section

in thousands, except per share amounts	Jan. 28, 1995	Jan. 29, 1994
Shareholders' Equity		
Preferred stock—$1 par value; 10,000 total shares authorized:		
Series A—600 shares authorized, issued, and outstanding,		
$50 per share liquidation preference	$ 28,850	$ —
Series B—33 shares authorized, no shares outstanding		
Common stock—$.10 par; 100,000 shares authorized, 9,971 and 9,293 shares		
issued and outstanding at January 28, 1995 and January 29, 1994, respectively	997	929
Additional paid-in capital	113,996	100,715
Retained income	36,833	22,399
Total shareholders' equity	**$180,676**	**$124,043**

Disclosures elsewhere in Proffitt's annual report revealed the following changes in shareholders' equity accounts for the years ended Jan. 28, 1995, Jan. 29, 1994, and Jan. 30, 1993:

1995:
1. The only changes in retained earnings during the year ended January 28, 1995, were preferred dividends on preferred stock of $1,694,000 and net income.
2. The Series B preferred stock is convertible. During the year, 3,296 shares were issued. All shares were converted into 160,000 shares of common stock. No gain or loss was recorded on the conversion.
3. Common shares were issued in a public offering and upon the exercise of stock options. On the statement of shareholders' equity, Proffitt reports these two items on a single line entitled: "Issuance of shares."

1994:
1. Net income: $6,063,000.
2. Issuance of common stock: 2,790,000 shares at $56,353,000.

1993:
1. Net income: $6,747,000.
2. Issuance of common stock: 60,000 shares at $413,000.

Required:

From these disclosures, prepare comparative statements of shareholders' equity for the years ended Jan. 28, 1995, Jan. 29, 1994, and Jan. 30, 1993.

Financial Analysis Case 19–8
Analyzing financial statements; price-earnings ratio; dividend payout ratio

IGF Foods Company is a large, primarily domestic, consumer foods company involved in the manufacture, distribution and sale of a variety of food products. Industry averages are derived from Troy's *The Almanac of Business and Industrial Financial Ratios* and Dun and Bradstreet's *Industry Norms and Key Business Ratios.* Following are the 1997 and 1996 comparative income statements and balance sheets for IGF. The market price of IGF's common stock is $47 during 1997. (The financial data we use are from actual financial statements of a well-known corporation, but the company name used in our illustration is fictitious and the numbers and dates have been modified slightly to disguise the company's identity.)

IGF FOODS COMPANY
Years ended December 31, 1997 and 1996

($ in millions)	1997	1996
Comparative Income Statements		
Net sales	$6,440	$5,800
Cost of goods sold	(3,667)	(3,389)
Gross profit	2,773	2,411
Operating expenses	(1,916)	(1,629)
Operating income	857	782
Interest expense	(54)	(53)
Income from operations before tax	803	729
Income taxes	(316)	(287)
Net income	$ 487	$ 442
Net income per share	$2.69	$2.44
Average shares outstanding	181 million	181 million
Comparative Balance Sheets		
Assets		
Current assets		
Cash	$ 48	$ 142
Accounts receivable	347	320
Marketable securities	358	–
Inventories	914	874
Prepaid expenses	212	154
Total current assets	$1,879	$1,490
Property, plant, and equipment (net):	2,592	2,291
Intangibles (net):	800	843
Other assets	74	60
Total assets	$5,345	$4,684
Liabilities And Shareholders' Equity		
Current liabilities		
Accounts payable	$ 254	$ 276
Accrued liabilities	493	496
Notes payable	518	115
Current portion of long-term debt	208	54
Total current liabilities	1,473	941
Long-term debt	534	728
Deferred income taxes	407	344
Total liabilities	2,414	2,013
Shareholders' equity		
Common stock	180	180
Additional paid-in capital	21	63
Retained earnings	2,730	2,428
Total shareholders' equity	2,931	2,671
Total liabilities and shareholders' equity	$5,345	$4,684

Profitability is the key to a company's long-run survival. Profitability measures focus on a company's ability to provide an adequate return relative to resources devoted to company operations.

Required:

1. Calculate the return on shareholders' equity for IGF. The average return for the stocks listed on the New York Stock Exchange in a comparable time period was 18.8%. What information does your calculation provide an investor?
2. Calculate IGF's earnings per share and earnings-price ratio. The average return for the stocks listed on the New York Stock Exchange in a comparable time period was 5.4%. What does your calculation indicate about IGF's earnings?

Research Case 19–9
Preferred stock and the distinction between debt and equity; research an article in *Accounting Horizons*

A continuing debate in accounting circles is whether to maintain, modify, or eliminate the current distinction between debt and equity. For example, is preferred stock debt, or is it equity? Professor Myrtle Clark explores these issues in her article "Entity Theory, Modern Capital Structure Theory, and the Distinction between Debt and Equity." Professor Clark reviews financial economics literature to support her observations.

Required:

1. In your library or from some other source, locate the indicated article in *Accounting Horizons*, September 1993.

2. How is preferred stock classified in traditional financial statements (Exhibit 2)?
3. How is preferred stock classified in Paton's Entity Theory model (Exhibit 3)?
4. How is preferred stock classified in decision-useful financial statements (Exhibit 4)?
5. Which approach does Professor Clark prefer?
6. Does Professor Clark recommend drawing a sharp distinction between debt and equity? Why?
7. Do you agree with the author's conclusions?

International Case 19–10
Accounting for shareholders' equity in other countries

In the United States, shareholders' equity represents a residual amount: assets minus liabilities. It is reported in two primary categories: paid-in (or invested) capital and retained earnings (or earned capital). Worldwide, there is little uniformity in how capital or shareholders' equity is defined or reported on the balance sheet. Significant differences exist from country to country.

Required

1. Choose a country other than the United States and research the way that country accounts for shareholders' equity. Include in your analysis:
    a. How shareholders' equity is defined.
    b. The categories by which it is reported in the financial statements.
    c. What if any requirements exist to separately maintain legal capital.
    d. Restrictions on dividend payments and how dividends are reported.
    e. Whether a statement of shareholders' equity, or equivalent, is reported.
2. Prepare a short report highlighting the similarities and differences between the United States and your chosen country in the way shareholders' equity is accounted for.

Optionally, the report might compare (a) the degree of conservatism in the approaches taken by the two countries or (b) whether cultural differences are likely contributors to the differences observed.

Ethics Case 19–11
The Swiss label maker; value of shares issued for equipment

Bricker Graphics is a privately held company specializing in package labels. Representatives of the firm have just returned from Switzerland, where a Swiss firm is manufacturing a custom-made high speed, color labeling machine. Confidence is high that the new machine will help rescue Bricker from sharply declining profitability. Bricker's chief operating officer, Don Benson, has been under fire for not achieving the company's performance goals of achieving a rate of return on assets of at least 12%.

The afternoon of his return from Switzerland, Benson called Susan Sharp into his office. Susan is Bricker's Controller.

Benson: I wish you had been able to go. We have some accounting issues to consider.
Sharp: I wish I'd been there, too. I understand the food was marvelous. What are the accounting issues?
Benson: They discussed accepting our notes at the going rate for a face amount of $12.5 million. We also discussed financing with stock.
Sharp: I thought we agreed, debt is the way to go for us now.
Benson: Yes, but I've been thinking. We can issue shares for a total of $10 million. The labeler is custom-made and doesn't have a quoted selling price, but the domestic labelers we considered went for around $10 million. It sure would help our rate of return if we keep the asset base as low as possible.

Required:

1. How will Benson's plan affect the return measure? What accounting issue is involved?
2. Is the proposal ethical?
3. Who would be affected if the proposal is implemented?

Internet Case 19–12
Researching the way shareholders' equity transactions are reported; retrieving financial statements from the Internet

EDGAR, the Electronic Data Gathering, Analysis, and Retrieval system, performs automated collection, validation, indexing, acceptance, and forwarding of submissions by companies and others who are required by law to file forms with the U.S. Securities and Exchange Commission (SEC). All publicly traded domestic companies use EDGAR to make the majority of their filings. (Filings by foreign companies are not required to be filed on EDGAR, but some of these companies do so voluntarily.) Form 10-K or 10-KSB, which include the annual report, is required to be filed on EDGAR. The SEC makes this information available on the Internet.

Required:

1. Access EDGAR on the Internet. The web address is www.sec.gov/.
2. Search for a public company with which you are familiar. Access its most recent 10-K filing. Search or scroll to find the statement of shareholders' equity and related note(s). If a statement of shareholders' equity is not provided, try another company.

3. Determine from the statement the transactions that occurred during the most recent three years that affected retained earnings.
4. Determine from the statement the transactions that occurred during the most recent three years that affected common stock. Were any of these transactions identified in requirement 3 also?
5. Cross-reference your findings with amounts reported on the balance sheet. How do these two statements articulate with one another?

Financial Analysis Case 19–13
Reporting shareholders' equity

Federal Express Corporation

Refer to the financial statements of Federal Express Corporation in the appendix to Chapter 1. The market price of the company's common shares ranged from $59 in the first quarter to $82 in the fourth quarter of the fiscal year.

Required:
1. By what method does Federal Express account for treasury stock?
2. What is Federal Express's return on shareholders' equity for 1996? What is its earnings-price ratio? What do these ratios measure?

4

ADDITIONAL TOPICS

EARNINGS PER SHARE

OVERVIEW

Earnings per share is the most commonly cited and reported measure of a company's performance. It is reported in the income statement of all public firms. For a firm with a simple capital structure (no potentially dilutive securities), a single earnings per common share presentation (basic EPS) is sufficient. If a firm's capital structure includes securities that could potentially dilute (reduce) earnings per share (such as convertible securities or stock options), it is classified as a complex capital structure and the company must calculate both basic and diluted earnings per share. The effect of each potentially dilutive security is considered by calculating earnings per share as if the security already had been exercised or converted into additional common shares. In this chapter, we discuss both simple and complex capital structures as well as other issues affecting the determination and presentation of earnings per share.

LEARNING OBJECTIVES   After studying this chapter, you should be able to:

1. Distinguish between a simple and a complex capital structure.
2. Describe what is meant by the weighted-average number of common shares.
3. Differentiate the effect on EPS of the sale of new shares, a stock dividend or stock split, and the reacquisition of shares.
4. Describe how preferred dividends affect the determination of EPS.
5. Describe how options, rights, and warrants are incorporated in the calculation of EPS.
6. Describe how convertible securities are incorporated in the calculation of EPS.
7. Explain the way contingently issuable shares are incorporated in the calculation of EPS.
8. Describe the financial statement presentation of EPS.

REYNOLDS & REYNOLDS

"I guess I'll win that bet!" you announced to no one in particular.

"What bet?" Meg asked. Meg Forsythe was close enough to overhear you.

"When I bought my Reynolds stock last year Larry insisted it was a mistake, that they were going downhill. I bet him a Coke he was wrong. This *Wall Street Journal* article says profits are up 22%," you bragged. Meg was looking over your shoulder now at the article you were pointing at:

Reynolds & Reynolds Co., Dayton, Ohio, reported a 22% jump in fiscal fourth quarter profit, citing growth in sales of business forms and computer systems to auto dealers. In the quarter ended September 30, Reynolds earned $25.1 million, or 29 cents a share, compared with $20.5 million, or 24 cents a share, a year earlier. . . .The year earlier results were restated to reflect a 2-for-1 stock split in September.

Excerpt from: "Profit Jumps 22%, Helped by Sales of Business Forms," *Wall Street Journal,* November 1, 1996.

"Twenty-nine cents a share, huh?" Meg asked. "How many shares do you have? When do you get the check?"

QUESTIONS

1. Meg's questions imply that she thinks you will get cash dividends of 29 cents a share. What does earnings per share really tell you?
2. The article says "the year earlier results were restated to reflect a 2-for-1 stock split in September." What does that mean?
3. You know from statements Reynolds mailed you that company executives hold a number of stock options. If those options are exercised, you know the resulting increase in shares might reduce earnings per share. Is that possibility taken into account when EPS is calculated?

Earnings per share is the single accounting number that receives the most media attention.

OPENING CASE

Question 1

Comparability is a qualitative characteristic of relevant accounting information (*Concept Statement 2*).

A typical corporate annual report contains at least three sets of comparative financial statements, an extensive list of disclosure notes and schedules, and several pages of charts, tables, and textual descriptions. Of this myriad of facts and figures, the single accounting number that is reported most frequently in the media and receives by far the most attention by investors and creditors is **earnings per share**. The reasons for the considerable attention paid to earnings per share certainly include the desire to find a way to summarize the performance of business enterprises into a single number.

> Information . . . gains greatly in usefulness if it can be compared with similar information about other enterprises and with similar information about the same enterprise for other time periods.[1]

Summarizing performance in a way that permits comparisons is difficult because the companies that report the numbers are different from one another. And yet, the desire to condense performance to a single number has created a demand for EPS information. The profession has responded with rules designed to maximize the comparability of EPS numbers by minimizing the inconsistencies in their calculation from one company to the next.[2]

Keep in mind as you study the requirements that a primary goal is comparability. As a result, many of the rules devised to achieve consistency are unavoidably arbitrary, meaning that other choices the FASB might have made in many instances would be equally adequate.

GLOBAL PERSPECTIVE

The International Accounting Standards Committee (IASC) has as a stated objective to narrow worldwide differences in accounting practices and the presentation of financial information. The IASC has worked toward uniformity since 1973, but harmonization has by no means been achieved. The EPS requirements you see in this chapter are a result of cooperation between the FASB and the IASC to develop common requirements for earnings per share. Significant differences still exist among countries that do not choose to follow the international standards in this area.

PART

A   SIMPLE CAPITAL STRUCTURE

Learning objective 1
Distinguish between a simple and a complex capital structure.

A firm has a simple capital structure if it has no **potentially dilutive securities**.

Basic EPS reflects no dilution, only shares now outstanding.

EPS expresses a firm's profitability on a per share basis.

A firm is said to have a **simple capital structure** if it has no outstanding securities that could potentially dilute earnings per share. In this context, to dilute means to *reduce* earnings per share. For instance, if a firm has convertible bonds outstanding and those bonds are converted, the resulting increase in common shares could decrease (or dilute) earnings per share. That is, the new shares represented by the bonds might participate in future earnings. So convertible bonds are referred to as **potentially dilutive securities**. Other potentially dilutive securities are convertible preferred stock and stock options. We will see how the potentially dilutive effects of these securities are included in the calculation of EPS in Part B of this chapter. Now, though, our focus is on the calculation of EPS for a simple capital structure—when no potentially dilutive securities are present. In these cases, the calculation is referred to as **basic EPS**, and is simply earnings available to common shareholders divided by the weighted-average number of common shares outstanding.

In the most elemental setting, earnings per share (or net loss per share) is merely a firm's net income (or net loss) divided by the number of shares of common stock outstanding throughout the year. The calculation becomes more demanding (a) when the number of shares has changed during the reporting period, (b) when the earnings available to common shareholders are diminished by dividends to preferred shareholders, or (c) when we attempt to take into account the impending effect of potentially dilutive securities (which we do in Part B). To illustrate the calculation of EPS in each of its dimensions, we will use only one example in this chapter. We'll start with the most basic situation and then add one new element at a time until we have considered all the principal ways the calculation can be affected. In this way you can see the effect of each component of earnings per share, not just in isolation, but in relation to the effects of other components as well. The basic calculation is shown in Illustration 20–1.

---

[1] "Qualitative Characteristics of Accounting Information," *FASB Statement of Concepts No. 2,* FASB, 1980, par. 111.

[2] "Earnings per Share," *Statement of Financial Accounting Standards No. 128,* Norwalk, Conn.: FASB, 1977.

ILLUSTRATION   20-1

Fundamental Calculation

In the most elemental setting, earnings per share is simply a company's earnings divided by the number of shares outstanding.

Sovran Financial Corporation reported net income of $154 million in 1997 (tax rate 40%). Its capital structure consisted of:

Common stock

January 1   60 million common shares outstanding
(amounts in millions, except per share amount)

Basic EPS:

$$\frac{\text{Net income} \quad \$154}{\underset{\text{Shares outstanding}}{60}} = \$2.57$$

Issuance of New Shares

Because the shares discussed in Illustration 20–1 remained unchanged throughout the year, the denominator of the EPS calculation is simply the number of shares outstanding. But if the number of shares has changed, it's necessary to find the weighted average of the shares outstanding during the period the earnings were generated. For instance, if an additional 12 million shares had been issued on March 1 of the year just ended, we calculate the weighted-average number of shares to be 70 million as demonstrated in Illustration 20-2.

ILLUSTRATION   20-2

Weighted Average

Sovran Financial Corporation reported net income of $154 million for 1997 (tax rate 40%). Its capital structure included:

Common stock

January 1   60 million common shares outstanding
→   **March 1   12 million new shares were sold**
(amounts in millions, except per share amount)

Basic EPS:

$$\frac{\text{Net income} \quad \$154}{\underset{\substack{\text{Shares} \\ \text{at Jan. 1}}}{60} + \underset{\substack{\text{New} \\ \text{shares}}}{12(^{10}/_{12})}} = \frac{\$154}{70} = \$2.20$$

Any new shares issued are time-weighted by the fraction of the period they were outstanding and then added to the number of shares outstanding for the entire period.

Learning objective 2
Describe what is meant by the weighted average number of common shares.

Because the new shares were outstanding only 10 months, or $^{10}/_{12}$ of the year, we increase the 60 million shares already outstanding by the additional shares—weighted by the fraction of the year ($^{10}/_{12}$) they were outstanding. The weighted average is $60 + 12 (^{10}/_{12}) = 60 + 10 = 70$ million shares. The reason for time-weighting the shares issued is that the resources the stock sale provides the company are available for generating income only after the date the shares are sold. So, weighting is necessary to make the shares in the fraction's denominator consistent with the income in its numerator.

Stock Dividends and Stock Splits

OPENING CASE

Question 2

Recall that a stock dividend or a stock split is a distribution of additional shares to existing shareholders. But there's an important and fundamental difference between the increase in shares caused by a stock distribution and an increase from selling new shares. When new shares are sold, both assets and shareholders' equity are increased by an additional investment in the firm by shareholders. On the other hand, a stock dividend or stock split merely increases the number of shares without affecting the firm's assets. In effect, the same pie is divided into more pieces. The result is a larger number of less valuable shares.[3] This fundamental change in the nature of the shares is reflected in a calculation of EPS by simply increasing the number of shares.

---

[3] For a more complete discussion of why the market price per share declines in proportion to the increase in the number of shares see Chapter 19.

In Illustration 20–3, notice that the additional shares created by the stock dividend are *not* weighted for the time period they were outstanding. Instead, the increase is treated as if it occurred at the beginning of the year.

ILLUSTRATION   20–3

Stock Dividends and Stock Splits

Shares outstanding prior to the stock dividend are retroactively restated to reflect the 10% increase in shares—that is, treated as if the distribution occurred at the beginning of the period.

Sovran Financial Corporation reported net income of $154 million in 1997 (tax rate 40%). Its capital structure included:

Common stock

January 1	60 million common shares outstanding
March 1	12 million new shares were sold
→ June 17	**A 10% stock dividend was distributed**
	(amounts in millions, except per share amount)

Basic EPS:

$$\frac{\substack{\text{Net income}\\ \$154}}{\underset{\substack{\text{Shares}\\ \text{at Jan. 1}}}{60} \ \textbf{(1.10)} + \underset{\substack{\text{New}\\ \text{shares}}}{12(^{10}/_{12})} \ \textbf{(1.10)}} = \frac{\$154}{77} = \$2.00$$

Stock dividend adjustment

The number of shares outstanding after a 10% stock dividend is 1.10 times higher than before. This multiple is applied to both the beginning shares and the new shares sold before the stock distribution. If this had been a 25% stock dividend, the multiple would have been 1.25; a 2-for-1 stock split means a multiple of 2; and so on.

Notice that EPS without the 10% stock dividend ($2.20) is 10% more than it is with the stock distribution ($2). This is caused by the increase in the number of shares. But, unlike a sale of new shares, this should not be interpreted as a "dilution" of earnings per share. Shareholders' interests in their company's earnings have not been diluted. Instead, each shareholder's interest is represented by more—though less valuable—shares.

Learning objective 3
Differentiate the effect on EPS of the sale of new shares, a stock dividend or stock split, and the reacquisition of shares.

A simplistic but convenient way to view the effect is to think of the predistribution shares as having been "blue." After the stock dividend, the more valuable "blue" shares are gone, replaced by a larger number of, let's say, "green" shares. From now on, we compute the earnings per "green" share, whereas we previously calculated earnings per "blue" share. We restate the number of shares retroactively to reflect the stock dividend, as if the shares always had been "green." After all, our intent is to let the calculation reflect the fundamental change in the nature of the shares.

Additional Consideration

When last year's EPS is reported again for comparison purposes in the current year's comparative income statements, it too should reflect the increased shares from the stock dividend. For instance, suppose last year's EPS were $2.09: $115 million net income divided by 55 million weighted-average shares. When reported again for comparison purposes in the 1997 comparative income statements, that figure would be restated to reflect the 10% stock dividend [$115 ÷ (55 × 1.10) = $1.90]:

Earnings per Share:	1997	1996
	$2.00	$1.90

The EPS numbers now are comparable—both reflect the stock dividend. Otherwise we would be comparing earnings per "green" share with earnings per "blue" share; this way both are earnings per "green" share.

Reacquired Shares

If shares were reacquired during the period (either retired or as treasury stock), the weighted-average number of shares is reduced. The number of reacquired shares is time-weighted for the *fraction of the year they were not outstanding*, prior to being *subtracted* from the number of shares outstanding during the period. Let's modify our continuing illustration to assume 8 million shares were reacquired on October 1 as treasury stock (Illustration 20–4).

ILLUSTRATION   20–4

Reacquired Shares

Sovran Financial Corporation reported net income of $154 million in 1997 (tax rate 40%). Its capital structure included:

Common stock

January 1	60 million common shares outstanding
March 1	12 million new shares were sold
June 17	A 10% stock dividend was distributed
→ October 1	**8 million shares were reacquired as treasury stock**
	(amounts in millions, except per share amount)

Basic EPS:

$$\frac{\text{Net income} \ \$154}{\underset{\substack{\text{Shares} \\ \text{at Jan. 1}}}{60} \ (1.10) + \underset{\substack{\text{New} \\ \text{shares}}}{12(^{10}/_{12})} \ (1.10) - \underset{\substack{\text{Treasury} \\ \text{shares}}}{8(^{3}/_{12})}} = \frac{\$154}{75} = \$2.05$$

Stock dividend adjustment*

* Not necessary for the treasury shares since they were reacquired after the stock dividend and thus already reflect the adjustment (that is, the shares repurchased are 8 million "new" shares.

The 8 million shares reacquired as treasury stock are weighted by ($^3/_{12}$) to reflect the fact they were not outstanding the last three months of the year.

Compare the adjustment for treasury shares with the adjustment for new shares sold. Each is time-weighted for the fraction of the year the shares were or were not outstanding. But also notice two differences. The new shares are added, while the reacquired shares are subtracted. The second difference is that the reacquired shares are not multiplied by 1.10 to adjust for the 10% stock dividend. The reason is the shares were repurchased after the June 17 stock dividend; the reacquired shares are 8 million of the new post-distribution shares. (To use our earlier representation, these are 8 million "green" shares.) To generalize, when a stock distribution occurred during the reporting period, any sales or purchases of shares that occurred *before* the distribution are increased by the distribution. But the stock distribution does not increase the number of shares sold or purchased, if any, *after* the distribution.

The adjustment for reacquired shares is the same as for new shares sold except the shares are deducted rather than added.

Any sales or purchases of shares that occurred before, but not after, a stock dividend or split are affected by the distribution.

Earnings Available to Common Shareholders

Learning objective 4
Describe how preferred dividends affect the determination of EPS.

Preferred dividends reduce earnings available to common shareholders unless the preferred stock is noncumulative and no dividends were declared that year.

The denominator in an EPS calculation is the weighted-average number of common shares outstanding. Logically, the numerator should similarly represent earnings available to common shareholders. This was automatic in our illustrations to this point because the only shares outstanding were common shares. But when a senior class of shareholders (like preferred stockholders) is entitled to a specified allocation of earnings (like preferred dividends), those amounts are subtracted from earnings before calculating earnings per share.[4] This is demonstrated in Illustration 20–5.

Suppose no dividends were declared for the year. Should we adjust for preferred dividends? Yes, if the preferred stock is cumulative—and most preferred stock is. This means that when dividends are not declared, the unpaid dividends accumulate to be paid in a future year when (if) dividends are subsequently declared. Obviously, the presumption is that, although the year's dividend preference isn't distributed this year, it eventually will be paid.

We have encountered no potentially dilutive securities to this point in our continuing illustration. As a result, we have what is referred to as a simple capital structure. (Although, at this point, you may question this label.) For a simple capital structure, a single presentation of basic earnings per common share is appropriate. We turn our attention now to situations described as complex capital structures. In these situations, two separate presentations are required: basic EPS and diluted EPS.

---

[4] You learned in Chapter 19 that when dividends are declared, preferred shareholders have a preference (over common shareholders) to a specified amount.

ILLUSTRATION   20-5

Preferred Dividends

Sovran Financial Corporation reported net income of $154 million in 1997 (tax rate 40%). Its capital structure included:

Common stock

January 1	60 million common shares outstanding
March 1	12 million new shares were sold
June 17	A 10% stock dividend was distributed
October 1	8 million shares were reacquired as treasury stock

→ **Preferred stock, nonconvertible**

January 1–December 31   5 million 8%, $10 par, shares
(amounts in millions, except per share amount)

Basic EPS:

$$\frac{\text{Net income} \quad \text{Preferred dividends}}{\underset{\substack{\text{Shares} \\ \text{at Jan. 1}}}{60} \quad + \quad \underset{\substack{\text{New} \\ \text{shares}}}{12(^{10}/_{12})\ (1.10)} \quad - \quad \underset{\substack{\text{Treasury} \\ \text{shares}}}{8(^{3}/_{12})}} = \frac{\$150}{75} = \$2.00$$

Stock dividend adjustment

* 8% × $10 par × 5 million shares

> Preferred dividends are subtracted from net income so that "earnings available to common shareholders" is divided by the weighted-average number of common shares.

PART

B   COMPLEX CAPITAL STRUCTURE

Potentially Dilutive Securities

OPENING CASE

Question 3

> In a complex capital structure, a second EPS computation takes into account the assumed effect of potentially dilutive securities.

Imagine a situation in which convertible bonds are outstanding that will significantly increase the number of common shares if bondholders exercise their options to exchange their bonds for shares of common stock. Should these be ignored when earnings per share is calculated? After all, they haven't been converted as yet, so to assume an increase in shares for a conversion that may never occur might mislead investors and creditors. On the other hand, if conversion is imminent, not taking into account the dilutive effect of the share increase might mislead investors and creditors. The profession's solution to the dilemma is to calculate earnings per share twice.

Securities like these convertible bonds, while not being common stock, may become common stock through their exercise or conversion. Therefore, they may dilute (reduce) earnings per share and are called *potentially dilutive securities*. A firm is said to have a complex capital structure if one or more potentially dilutive securities are outstanding. Besides convertible bonds, other potentially dilutive securities are convertible preferred stock, stock options, rights, or warrants, and contingently issuable securities. (We'll discuss each of these shortly.) A firm with a complex capital structure reports two EPS calculations. **Basic EPS** ignores the dilutive effect of such securities, **diluted EPS** incorporates the dilutive effect of all potentially dilutive securities.

Options, Rights, and Warrants

Learning objective 5
Describe how options, rights, and warrants are incorporated in the calculation of EPS.

Stock options, stock rights, and stock warrants are similar. Each gives its holders the right to exercise their option to purchase common stock, usually at a specified exercise price. The dilution that would result from their exercise should be reflected in the calculation of diluted EPS, but not basic EPS.

To include the dilutive effect of a security means to calculate EPS *as if* the potential increase in shares already has occurred (even though it hasn't yet). So, for a stock option (or right, or warrant), we pretend the option has been exercised. In fact, we assume the options were exercised at

ILLUSTRATION   20-6

Stock Options

Sovran Financial Corporation reported net income of $154 million in 1997 (tax rate 40%). Its capital structure included:

Common stock

January 1	60 million common shares outstanding
March 1	12 million new shares were sold
June 17	A 10% stock dividend was distributed
October 1	8 million shares were reacquired as treasury stock

(The average market price of the common shares during 1997 was $25 per share.)

Preferred stock, nonconvertible

January 1–December 31   5 million 8%, $10 par, shares

→ **Executive stock options**

Options granted in 1995, exercisable for 15 million common shares* at an exercise price of $20 per share

*Adjusted for the stock dividend. Prior to the stock dividend, the options were exercisable for $13^7/11$ million of the "old" shares which became 15 million ($13^7/11 \times 1.10$) of the "new" shares after the stock dividend.

(amounts in millions, except per share amounts)

Basic EPS (unchanged)

$$\frac{\underset{\substack{\$154}}{\text{Net income}} \quad - \quad \underset{\substack{\$4}}{\text{Preferred dividends}}}{\underset{\substack{\text{Shares} \\ \text{at Jan. 1}}}{60} \ (1.10) + \underset{\substack{\text{New} \\ \text{shares}}}{12(^{10}/_{12})} \ (1.10) - \underset{\substack{\text{Treasury} \\ \text{shares}}}{8(^3/_{12})}} = \frac{\$150}{75} = \$2$$

Stock dividend adjustment

Diluted EPS

$$\frac{\underset{\substack{\$154}}{\text{Net income}} \quad - \quad \underset{\substack{\$4}}{\text{Preferred dividends}}}{\underset{\substack{\text{Shares} \\ \text{at Jan. 1}}}{60} \ (1.10) + \underset{\substack{\text{New} \\ \text{shares}}}{12(^{10}/_{12})} \ (1.10) - \underset{\substack{\text{Treasury} \\ \text{shares}}}{8(^3/_{12})} + \underset{\substack{\text{Exercise} \\ \text{of options}}}{(\mathbf{15 - 12^a})}} = \frac{\$150}{78} = \$1.92$$

Stock dividend adjustment

^a**Shares Reacquired for Diluted EPS**

15	million shares
× $ 20	(exercise price)
$300	million
÷ $ 25	(average market price)
12	million shares reacquired

Stock options give their holders (company executives in this case) the right to purchase common stock at a specified exercise price ($20 in this case).

The stock options do not affect the calculation of basic EPS.

The calculation of diluted EPS assumes that the shares specified by stock options were issued at the exercise price and that the proceeds were used to buy back (as treasury stock) as many of those shares as can be

Stock options are assumed to have been exercised when calculating EPS.

the beginning of the reporting period, or when the options were issued if that's later. We then assume the cash proceeds from selling the new shares at the exercise price are used to buy back as many shares as possible at the shares' average market price during the year. This is demonstrated in Illustration 20–6.

When we simulate the exercise of the stock options, we calculate EPS as if 15 million shares were sold at the beginning of the year. This obviously increases the number of shares in the denominator by 15 million shares. But it is insufficient to simply add the additional shares without considering the accompanying consequences. Remember, if this hypothetical scenario had occurred, the company would have had $300 million cash proceeds from the exercise of the options (15 million shares × $20 exercise price per share). What would have been the effect on earnings per share? This depends on what the company would have done with the $300 million cash proceeds. Would the proceeds have been used to buy more equipment? Increase the sales force? Expand facilities? Pay dividends?

Obviously, there are literally hundreds of choices, and its unlikely that any two firms would spend the $300 million exactly the same way. But remember, our objective is to create some degree of uniformity in the way firms determine earnings per share so the resulting numbers are comparable. So, standard-setters decided on a single assumption for all firms to provide some degree of comparability.

For diluted EPS, we assume the proceeds from exercise of the options were used to reacquire shares as treasury stock at the average market price of the common stock during the reporting period. Consequently, the weighted-average number of shares is increased by the difference between the shares assumed issued and those assumed reacquired—in our illustration: 15 million shares issued minus 12 million shares reacquired ($300 million ÷ $25 per share) equals 3 million net increase in shares.

The way we take into account the dilutive effect of stock options, rights, and warrants is called the **treasury stock method** because of our assumption that treasury shares are purchased with the cash proceeds of the exercise of the options. In practice, many companies actually do buy back shares in order to reissue those shares when options are exercised.

Additional Consideration

Technically, the number of shares represented by options or warrants should be determined on a quarter by quarter basis. As a result, the net increase in shares is determined for the first quarter for which the market price has been above the exercise price for 11 weeks and for each quarter thereafter (for which the effect is dilutive). Of course, the shares would be appropriately weighted for the time they are assumed outstanding. For example, let's say the $25 average market price in our illustration was the average price for the third and fourth quarters, but the average price for the first two quarters was less than the $20 exercise price. In that case, the share adjustments would have been:

$$+ (15 - 12) \, (^2/_4)$$

Convertible Securities

Sometimes corporations include a conversion feature as part of a bond offering, a note payable, or an issue of preferred stock. Convertible securities can be converted into (exchanged for) shares of stock at the option of the holder of the security. For that reason, convertible securities are potentially dilutive. EPS will be affected if and when such securities are converted and new shares of common stock are issued. In the previous section you learned that the potentially dilutive effect of stock options is reflected in diluted EPS calculations by assuming the options were exercised. Similarly, the potentially dilutive effect of convertible securities is reflected in diluted EPS calculations by assuming they were converted.

By the **if converted method** as it's called, we assume the conversion into common stock occurred at the beginning of the period (or at the time the convertible security is issued, if that's later). We increase the denominator of the EPS fraction by the additional common shares that would have been issued upon conversion. We increase the numerator by the interest (after-tax) on bonds or other debt or preferred dividends that would have been avoided if the convertible securities had not been outstanding due to having been converted.

Convertible Bonds

Now, let's return to our continuing illustration and modify it to include the existence of convertible bonds (Illustration 20–7). We increase the denominator by the 12 million shares that would have been issued if the bonds had been converted. However, if that hypothetical conversion had occurred, the bonds would not have been outstanding during the year. What effect would the absence of the bonds have had on income? Obviously, the bond interest expense (10% × $300 million = $30 million) would have been saved, causing income to be higher. But saving the interest paid would also have meant losing a $30 million tax deduction on the income tax return. With a 40% tax rate that would mean paying $12 million more income taxes. So, to cause earnings to reflect the $18 million after-tax interest that would have been avoided in the event of conversion, we add back the $30 million of interest expense, but deduct 40% × $30 million for the higher tax expense.

ILLUSTRATION   20-7

Convertible Bonds

Sovran Financial Corporation reported net income of $154 million in 1997 (tax rate 40%). Its capital structure included:

Common stock

January 1	60 million common shares outstanding
March 1	12 million new shares were sold
June 17	A 10% stock dividend was distributed
October 1	8 million shares were reacquired as treasury stock

(The average market price of the common shares during 1997 was $25 per share.)

Preferred stock, nonconvertible

January 1–December 31   5 million 8%, $10 par, shares

Executive stock options

Options granted in 1995, exercisable for 15 million common shares* at an exercise price of $20 per share

→ ### Convertible bonds

10%, $300 million face amount issued in 1996, convertible into 12 million common shares*

*Adjusted for the stock dividend. For example, prior to the stock dividend, the bonds were exercisable for $10^1/11$ million of the "old" shares which became 12 million ($10^1/11 \times 1.10$) of the "new" shares after the stock dividend.

(amounts in millions, except per share amounts)

Basic EPS (unchanged)

The convertible bonds do not affect the calculation of basic EPS.

$$\frac{\overset{\text{Net income}}{\$154} \quad \overset{\text{Preferred dividends}}{-4}}{\underset{\substack{\text{Shares} \\ \text{at Jan. 1}}}{60} \ (1.10) + \underset{\substack{\text{New} \\ \text{shares}}}{12(^{10}/_{12})} \ (1.10) - \underset{\substack{\text{Treasury} \\ \text{shares}}}{8(^{3}/_{12})}} = \frac{\$150}{75} = \$2.00$$

Stock dividend adjustment

Diluted EPS

If the bonds had been converted, 12 million more common shares would have been issued, and net income would have been higher by the interest saved (after tax) from not having the bonds outstanding.

$$\frac{\overset{\text{Net income}}{\$154} \ \ \overset{\text{Preferred dividends}}{-4} \ \ \overset{\substack{\textbf{After-Tax} \\ \textbf{Interest Savings}}}{\textbf{+ \$30 - 40\%(30)}}}{\underset{\substack{\text{Shares} \\ \text{at Jan. 1}}}{60} \ (1.10) + \underset{\substack{\text{New} \\ \text{shares}}}{12(^{10}/_{12})} \ (1.10) - \underset{\substack{\text{Treasury} \\ \text{shares}}}{8(^{3}/_{12})} + \underset{\substack{\text{Exercise} \\ \text{of options}}}{(15-12)} \ \underset{\substack{\textbf{Conversion} \\ \textbf{of bonds}}}{\textbf{+ 12}}} = \frac{\$168}{90} = \$1.87$$

Stock dividend adjustment

Additional Consideration

The $300 million of convertible bonds in our illustration were issued at face value. Suppose the bonds had been issued for $282 million. In that case, the adjustment to earnings would be modified to include the amortization of the $18 million bond discount. Assuming straight-line amortization and a 10-year maturity, the adjustment to the diluted EPS calculation would have been

$$\frac{\text{+ [\$30 + (\$18 ÷ 10 years)]} \times \text{(1–40\%)*}}{\text{+ 12}}$$

to reflect the fact that the interest expense would include the $30 million stated interest plus one-tenth of the bond discount.†

*This is an alternative way to represent the after-tax adjustment to interest since subtracting 40% of the interest expense is the same as multiplying interest expense by 60%.
†See Chapter 14 if you need to refresh your memory about bond discount amortization.

Our illustration describes the treatment of convertible bonds. The same treatment pertains to other debt that is convertible into common shares such as convertible notes payable. Remember from our discussion of debt in earlier chapters that all debt is similar whether in the form of bonds, notes, or other configurations.

Additional Consideration

Notice that we assumed the bonds were converted at the beginning of the reporting period since they were outstanding all year. However, if the convertible bonds had been issued during the reporting period, we would assume their conversion occurred on the date of issue. It would be illogical to assume they were converted before they were issued. If the convertible bonds in our illustration had been sold on September 1, for instance, the adjustment to the EPS calculation would have been

$$\frac{+ \; [\$30 - 40\% \; (\$30)] \; (^4/_{12})}{+ \; 12 \; (^4/_{12})}$$

to reflect the fact that the after-tax interest savings and the net increase in shares would have been effective for only four months of the year.

This is our approach not just for convertible bonds, but for any potentially dilutive security. For example, we assumed the options in our illustration were exercised at the beginning of the reporting period so the net increase in shares was not weighted for a fraction of the year outstanding. If the options had been granted to company executives on April 1 the adjustment to the weighted average number of shares would have been

$$+ \; (15 - 12) \; (^9/_{12})$$

to reflect the fact that the net increase in shares would have been effective for only nine months of the year.

We assume convertible securities were converted (or options exercised) at the beginning of the reporting period or at the time the securities are issued, if later.

Convertible Preferred Stock

The potentially dilutive effect of convertible preferred stock is reflected in EPS calculations in much the same way as convertible debt. That is, we calculate EPS as if conversion already had occurred. Specifically, we add shares to the denominator of the EPS fraction and add back to earnings available to common shareholders the preferred dividends that would have been avoided if the preferred stock had been converted. Illustration 20–8 offers an example.

The adjustment for the conversion of the preferred stock should be applied only to diluted EPS computations. However, the existence of another issue of preferred stock also will affect the cal-

ILLUSTRATION   20–8

Convertible Preferred Stock

Sovran Financial Corporation reported net income of $154 million in 1997 (tax rate 40%). Its capital structure included:

Common stock

January 1	60 million common shares outstanding
March 1	12 million new shares were sold
June 17	A 10% stock dividend was distributed
October 1	8 million shares were reacquired as treasury stock

(The average market price of the common shares during 1997 was $25 per share.)

Preferred stock, nonconvertible

January 1–December 31   5 million 8%, $10 par, shares

Executive stock options

Options granted in 1995, exercisable for 15 million common shares* at an exercise price of $20 per share

Convertible bonds

10%, $300 million face amount issued in 1996, convertible into 12 million common shares*

→ **Preferred stock, convertible**

10 million, 8%, cumulative, $10 par, shares issued in 1993, convertible into 5 million shares*

*Adjusted for the stock dividend. For example, prior to the stock dividend, the preferred shares were convertible into $4^5/_{11}$ million of the "old" shares which became 5 million ($4^5/_{11} \times 1.10$) of the "new" shares after the stock dividend.

ILLUSTRATION   20–8

continued

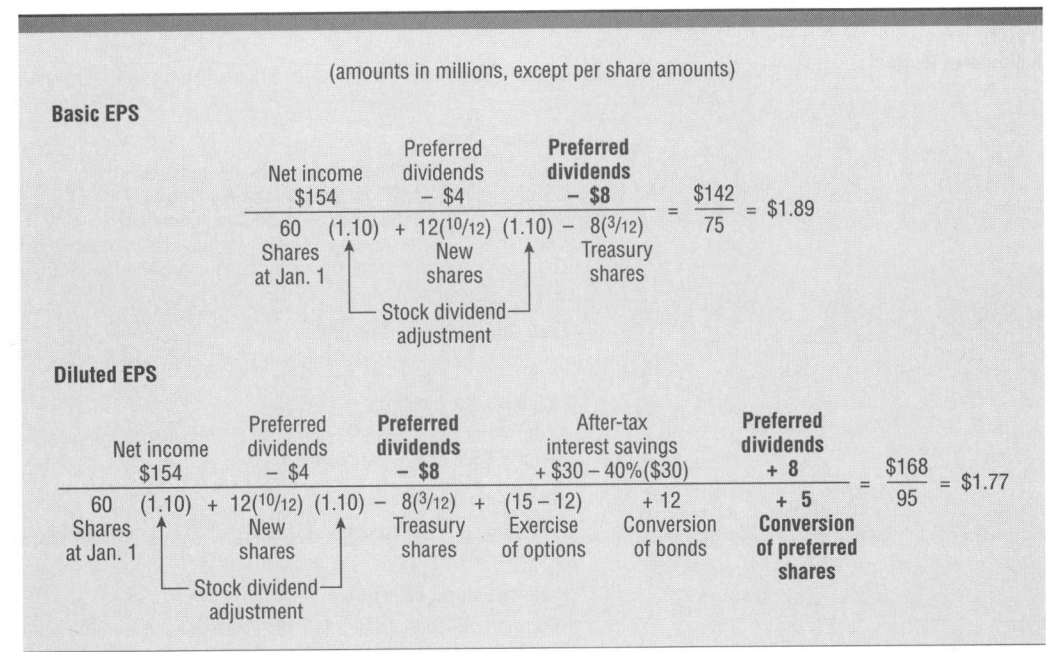

Since diluted EPS is calculated *as if* the preferred shares had been converted, there are no dividends. Earnings available to common shareholders is increased by the dividends that otherwise would have been distributed to preferred shareholders.

culation of basic EPS. The effect on basic EPS is the same as the effect of the first (nonconvertible) issue of preferred stock: the numerator is reduced by the preferred dividends in order to derive earnings available to common shareholders.

This second issue of preferred stock would reduce earnings available to common shareholders by \$8 million (8% × \$100 million par). However, when diluted EPS is calculated, we hypothetically assume the convertible preferred stock was *not* outstanding. Accordingly, no preferred dividends on these shares would have been paid. So we add back the \$8 million preferred dividends in much the same way we added back the interest saved when we assumed convertible bonds were converted. An important difference, though, is that, unlike interest expense, dividends have no tax effect. Dividends are not an expense and no income tax deduction is lost when dividends are not paid. Of course, adding back the preferred dividends that otherwise would have been deducted is equivalent to simply not deducting them in the first place.

Antidilutive Securities

At times, the effect of the conversion or exercise of potentially dilutive securities would be to increase, rather than decrease, EPS. These we refer to as **antidilutive securities**. Such securities are ignored when calculating both basic and diluted EPS.

Options, Warrants, Rights

For illustration, recall the way we treated the stock options in our continuing illustration. In applying the treasury stock method, the number of shares assumed repurchased is fewer than the number of shares assumed sold. This is the case any time the buyback (average market) price is higher than the exercise price. Consequently, there will be a net increase in the number of shares so earnings per share will decline.

On the other hand, when the exercise price is higher than the market price, to assume shares are sold at the exercise price and repurchased at the market price would mean buying back more shares than were sold. This would produce a net decrease in the number of shares. EPS would increase, not decrease, if we were to assume the exercise of stock options, stock warrants, or their equivalent. These would have an antidilutive effect and would not be considered exercised. For that matter, a rational investor would not exercise options at an exercise price higher than the current market price anyway. Let's look at the example provided by Illustration 20–9.

Antidilutive securities are ignored when calculating both basic and diluted EPS.

ILLUSTRATION   20–9

Antidilutive Warrants

Sovran Financial Corporation reported net income of $154 million in 1997 (tax rate 40%). Its capital structure included:

Common stock

January 1   60 million common shares outstanding
March 1   12 million new shares were sold
June 17   A 10% stock dividend was distributed
October 1   8 million shares were reacquired as treasury stock
(The average market price of the common shares during 1997 was $25 per share.)

Preferred stock, nonconvertible

January 1–December 31   5 million 8%, $10 par, shares

Executive stock options

Options granted in 1995, exercisable for 15 million common shares* at an exercise price of $20 per share

Convertible bonds

10%, $300 million face amount issued in 1996, convertible into 12 million common shares*

Preferred stock, convertible

10 million, 8%, cumulative, $10 par, shares issued in 1993, convertible into 5 million shares*

→ **Stock warrants**

Warrants granted in 1996, exercisable for 4 million common shares* at an exercise price of $32.50 per share

*Adjusted for the stock dividend. For example, prior to the stock dividend, the bonds were convertible into $3^7/_{11}$ million of the "old" shares which became 4 million ($3^7/_{11}$ × 1.10) of the "new" shares after the stock dividend.

Calculations:

The calculations of both basic and diluted EPS are unaffected by the warrants because the effect of exercising the warrants would be antidilutive.

> The $32.50 exercise price is higher than the market price, $25, so to assume shares are sold at the exercise price and repurchased at the market price would mean reacquiring more shares than were sold.

To assume 4 million shares were sold at the $32.50 exercise price and repurchased at the lower market price ($25) would mean reacquiring 5.2 million shares—more shares than were assumed sold. Because the effect would be antidilutive, we would simply ignore the warrants in the calculations.

In our continuing illustration, only the stock warrants were antidilutive. Each of the other potentially dilutive securities caused EPS to decline when we considered them exercised or converted. In the case of the executive stock options, it was readily apparent that their effect would be dilutive because the exercise price was less than the market price, indicating that fewer shares could be repurchased (at the average market price) than were assumed issued (at the exercise price). As a result, the denominator increased. When only the denominator of a fraction increases, the fraction itself decreases. On the other hand, in the case of the warrants, it was apparent that their effect would be antidilutive because the exercise price was higher than the market price, which would have decreased the denominator and therefore increased the fraction.

Any potentially dilutive securities not included in dilutive EPS because they are antidilutive should be revealed in the disclosure notes.

Convertible Securities

For convertible securities, though, its not immediately obvious whether the effect of their conversion would be dilutive or antidilutive because the assumed conversion would affect both the numerator and the denominator of the EPS fraction. We discovered each was dilutive only after including the effect in the calculation and observing the result—a decline in EPS. But there's an easier way.

To determine whether convertible securities are dilutive and should be included in a diluted EPS calculation, we can compare the incremental effect of the conversion (expressed as a fraction) with the EPS fraction before the effect of any convertible security is considered. This, of course is our basic EPS. Recall from Illustration 20–8 that basic EPS is $1.89.

For comparison, we determine the "earnings per incremental share" of the two convertible securities:

Conversion of bonds:

> The incremental effect (of conversion) of the bonds is the after-tax interest saved divided by the additional common shares from conversion.

$$\cfrac{\substack{\text{After-tax} \\ \text{interest savings} \\ + \, \$30 - 40\% \, (\$30)}}{\substack{+ \, 12 \\ \text{Conversion} \\ \text{of bonds}}} = \frac{\$18}{12} = \$1.50$$

Conversion of preferred stock:

> The incremental effect (of conversion) of the preferred stock is the dividends that wouldn't be paid divided by the additional common shares from conversion.

$$\cfrac{\substack{\text{Preferred} \\ \text{dividends} \\ + \, \$8}}{\substack{+ \, 5 \\ \text{Conversion of} \\ \text{preferred shares}}} = \$1.60$$

If the incremental effect of a security is higher than basic EPS, it is antidilutive. That's not the case in our illustration.

Order of Entry for Multiple Convertible Securities

A convertible security might seem to be dilutive when looked at individually but, in fact, may be antidilutive when included in combination with other convertible securities. This is because the *order of entry* for including their effects in the EPS calculation determines by how much, or even whether, EPS decreases as a result of their assumed conversion. Because our goal is to reveal the maximum potential dilution that might result, theoretically we should calculate diluted EPS using every possible combination of potentially dilutive securities to find the combination that yields the lowest EPS. But that's not necessary.

We can use the earnings per incremental share we calculated to determine the sequence of including securities' effects in the calculation. We include the securities in reverse order, beginning with the lowest incremental effect (that is, most dilutive), followed by the next lowest, and so on. This is, in fact, the order in which we included the securities in our continuing illustration.

Additional Consideration

Actually, the order of inclusion made no difference in our example, but would in many instances. For example, suppose the preferred stock had been convertible into 4.3 million shares, rather than 5 million shares. The incremental effect of its conversion would have been:

Conversion of Preferred Stock:

$$\cfrac{\substack{\text{Preferred dividends} \\ + \, \$8}}{\substack{+ \, 4.3 \\ \text{Conversion of} \\ \text{preferred shares}}} = \$1.86$$

On the surface, the effect would seem to be dilutive because $1.86 is less than $1.89, basic EPS. In fact, if this were the only convertible security, it would be dilutive. But, after the convertible bonds are assumed converted first, then the assumed conversion of the preferred stock would be *antidilutive:*

With Conversion of Bonds:

> Because the incremental effect of the convertible bonds ($1.50) is lower than the incremental effect of the convertible preferred stock ($1.86), it is included first.

$$\cfrac{\substack{\text{Net income} \\ \$154}\;\substack{\text{Preferred} \\ \text{dividends} \\ -\,\$4}\;\substack{\text{Preferred} \\ \text{dividends} \\ -\,\$8}\;\substack{\text{After-tax} \\ \text{interest savings} \\ +\,\$30-40\%(\$30)}}{\substack{60 \\ \text{Shares} \\ \text{at Jan. 1}}\;\substack{(1.10) + 12(^{10}/_{12})\,(1.10) \\ \text{New} \\ \text{shares}}\;\substack{-\,8(^{3}/_{12}) \\ \text{Treasury} \\ \text{shares}}\;\substack{+\;(15-12) \\ \text{Exercise} \\ \text{of options}}\;\substack{+\;12 \\ \text{Conversion} \\ \text{of bonds}}} = \frac{\$160}{90} = \$1.777$$

Stock dividend adjustment

A convertible security
might seem to be dilutive
when looked at individually
but may be antidilutive
when included in
combination with other
convertible securities.

With Conversion of Preferred Stock:

Although the incremental effect of the convertible preferred stock ($1.86) is lower than basic EPS ($1.89), when included in the calculation after the convertible bonds the effect is antidilutive (EPS increases).

GLOBAL PERSPECTIVE

Earnings per share receives more attention in the United States than in most other countries. In countries that do require EPS disclosures, requirements differ widely. For instance, earnings for the numerator of the EPS calculation are defined in the United States as earnings available for common shareholders, and separate calculations are required for ordinary income and net income when differences exist. In some countries, though, earnings is defined as continuing income from operations only (Norway, e.g.).

In the United States, basic and diluted EPS are reported. Other countries have similar requirements but define the two calculations differently than the United States (that is, the potentially dilutive securities included are different). Some countries require only one of the two calculations. (Japan requires basic only, for example.) Some (Spain, Switzerland, and Germany for instance) require no EPS disclosure at all, but disclosure may be provided anyway.

Some countries require disclosures not provided by U.S. companies. Japan, for instance, also discloses net assets per share.

CONCEPT REVIEW EXERCISE   BASIC AND DILUTED EPS

At December 31, 1997, the financial statements of Clevenger Casting Corporation included the following:

Net income for 1997	$500 million
Common stock, $1 par	
Shares outstanding on January 1	150 million shares
Shares retired for cash on February 1	24 million shares
Shares sold for cash on September 1	18 million shares
2-for-1 split on July 23	
Preferred stock, 10%, $60 par, cumulative, nonconvertible	$70 million
Preferred stock, 8%, $50 par, cumulative, convertible into 4 million	
shares of common stock	$100 million
Common stock warrants outstanding for 4 million shares of common stock;	
the exercise price is $15	
Bonds payable, 12.5%, convertible into 20 million shares of common stock	$200 million

Additional data:

The market price of the common stock averaged $20 during 1997.

The convertible preferred stock and the bonds payable were issued at par in 1995.

The tax rate for the year was 40%.

Required:

Compute basic and diluted earnings per share for the year ended December 31, 1997.

CONCEPT REVIEW EXERCISE   SOLUTION

(amounts in millions, except per share amounts)

Basic EPS

$$\frac{\substack{\text{Net income} \\ \$500}\ \ \ \substack{\text{Preferred} \\ \text{dividends} \\ -\ \$7^a}\ \ \ \substack{\text{Preferred} \\ \text{dividends} \\ -\ \$8^b}}{\underset{\substack{\text{Shares} \\ \text{at Jan. 1}}}{150}\ (2.00)\ -\ \underset{\substack{\text{Retired} \\ \text{shares}}}{24(^{11}/_{12})}\ (2.00)\ +\ \underset{\substack{\text{New} \\ \text{shares}}}{18(^{4}/_{12})}} = \frac{\$485}{262} = \$1.85$$

Stock split adjustment

Diluted EPS

$$\frac{\substack{\text{Net income} \\ \$500}\ \ \substack{\text{Preferred} \\ \text{dividends} \\ -\ \$7^a}\ \ \substack{\text{Preferred}^b \\ \text{dividends} \\ -\ \$8^b}\ \ \substack{\text{After-tax} \\ \text{interest savings} \\ +\ \$25^d -\ 40\%(\$25^d)}}{\underset{\substack{\text{Shares} \\ \text{at Jan. 1}}}{150}\ (2.00)\ -\ \underset{\substack{\text{Retired} \\ \text{shares}}}{24(^{11}/_{12})}\ (2.00)\ +\ \underset{\substack{\text{New} \\ \text{shares}}}{18(^{4}/_{12})}\ +\ \underset{\substack{\text{Exercise} \\ \text{of warrants}}}{(4-3)^c}\ +\ \underset{\substack{\text{Conversion} \\ \text{of bonds}}}{20}} = \frac{\$500}{283} = \$1.77$$

Stock split adjustment

[a]$10\% \times \$70$ million = $7 million
[b]$8\% \times \$100$ million = $8 million

[c]**Exercise of warrants:**

$$\begin{array}{r} 4 \text{ million shares} \\ \times\ \$15 \text{ (exercise price)} \\ \hline \$60 \text{ million} \\ \div\ \$20 \text{ (average market price)} \\ \hline 3 \text{ million shares} \end{array}$$

[d]$12.5\% \times \$200$ million = $25 million

Dilution:

Conversion of 8% Preferred Stock	Conversion of Bonds
$\dfrac{\substack{\text{Preferred} \\ \text{dividends} \\ +\ \$8}}{\substack{+\ 4 \\ \text{Conversion} \\ \text{of preferred} \\ \text{shares}}} = \$2.00^*$	$\dfrac{\substack{\text{After-tax} \\ \text{interest savings} \\ +\ \$25 - 40\%(\$25)}}{\substack{+\ 20 \\ \text{Conversion} \\ \text{of bonds}}} = \$0.75$

*Because the incremental effect of conversion of the preferred stock ($2) is higher than EPS without the conversion of the preferred stock, the conversion would be antidilutive and is not considered in the calculation of diluted EPS.

PART C   ADDITIONAL EPS ISSUES

Contingently Issuable Shares

Sometimes an agreement specifies that additional shares of common stock will be issued, contingent on the occurrence of some future circumstance. For instance, in the disclosure note reproduced in Graphic 20–1, Hunt Manufacturing Co. reported contingent shares in connection with its acquisition of Feeny Manufacturing Company.

At times, contingent shares are issuable to shareholders of an acquired company, certain key executives, or others in the event a certain level of performance is achieved. Contingent performance may be a desired level of income, a target stock price, or some other measurable activity level.

Learning objective 7
Explain the way contingently issuable shares are incorporated in the calculation of EPS.

When calculating EPS, contingently issuable shares are considered to be outstanding in the computation of diluted EPS if the target performance level already is being met (assumed to remain at existing levels until the end of the contingency period). For example, if shares will be issued at

Note 12: (in Part) Acquisitions

... the Company acquired Feeny Manufacturing Company of Muncie, Indiana, for 135,000 shares of restricted common stock with a value of $7.71 per share. Feeny Manufacturing Company is a manufacturer of kitchen storage products. The acquisition was accounted for as a purchase. The purchase agreement calls for the issuance of up to 135,000 additional shares of common stock in fiscal 1992 based on the earnings of Feeny Manufacturing Company. ...

> Contingently issuable shares are considered outstanding in the computation of diluted EPS.

a future date if a certain level of income is achieved and that level of income or more was already earned this year, those additional shares are simply added to the denominator of the diluted EPS fraction.[5]

For clarification, refer to our continuing illustration and assume 3 million additional shares will become issuable to certain executives in the following year (1998) if net income that year is $150 million or more. Recall that net income in 1997 was $154 million, so the additional shares would be considered outstanding in the computation of diluted EPS by simply adding 3 million additional shares to the denominator of the EPS fraction. Obviously, the 1998 condition ($150 million net income or more) has not been met yet since it's only 1997. But because that level of income was achieved in 1997, the presumption is its likely to be earned in 1998 as well.

> If a level of income must be attained before the shares will be issued, and income already is that amount or more, the additional shares are simply added to the denominator.

Assumed issuance of contingently issuable shares (diluted EPS):

$$\frac{\text{No adjustment to the numerator}}{\underset{\text{Additional shares}}{+\ 3}}$$

On the other hand, if the target income next year must be $160 million, the contingent shares would simply be ignored in our calculation.

Summary of the Effect of Potentially Dilutive Securities on Earnings Per Share

You have seen that under certain circumstances, securities that have the potential of reducing earnings per share by becoming common stock are assumed already to have become common stock for the purpose of calculating EPS. The table in Graphic 20–2 summarizes the circumstances under which the dilutive effect of these securities is reflected in the calculation of basic and diluted EPS.

	Is the Dilutive Effect Reflected in the Calculation of EPS?*	
Potentially Dilutive Security	**Basic EPS**	**Diluted EPS**
• Stock options (or warrants, rights)	no	yes
• Convertible securities (bonds, notes, preferred stock)	no	yes
• Contingently issuable shares	no	yes†

*The effect is not included for any security if its effect is antidilutive.
†Unless shares are contingent upon some level of performance not yet achieved.

Graphic 20–3 summarizes the specific effects on the diluted EPS fraction when the dilutive effect of a potentially dilutive security is reflected in the calculation.

Actual Conversions

When calculating EPS in our example, we "pretended" the convertible bonds had been converted at the beginning of the year. What if they actually had been converted, let's say on November 1? Interestingly, diluted EPS would be precisely the same. Here's why:

---

[5] The shares should be included in both basic and diluted EPS if all conditions have actually been met so that there is no circumstance under which those shares would not be issued. In essence, these are no longer contingent shares.

GRAPHIC   20–3

How A Potentially Dilutive
Security is Reflected in a
Diluted EPS Calculation

Potentially Dilutive Security	Modification to the Diluted EPS Fractions:	
	Numerator	**Denominator**
• Stock options (or warrants, rights)	None	Add the shares that would be created by their exercise,* reduced by shares repurchased at the average share price.
• Convertible bonds (or notes)	Add the interest (after-tax) that would have been avoided if the debt had been converted.	Add shares that would be created by the conversion* of the bonds (or notes).
• Convertible preferred stock	Do not deduct the dividends that would have been avoided if the preferred stock had been converted.	Add shares that would have been created by the conversion* of the preferred stock.
• Contingently issuable shares: Issuable upon the mere passage of time. Issuable when specified conditions are met, and those conditions are currently being met	None	Add shares that are issuable.
• Contingently issuable shares: Issuable when specified conditions are met, and those conditions are **not** currently being met	None	None

* At the beginning of the year or when potentially dilutive securities were issued, whichever is later (time-weight the increase in shares if assumed exercised or converted in midyear)

1. The actual conversion would cause an actual increase in shares of 12 million on November 1. These would be time-weighted so the denominator would increase by 12 ($^2/_{12}$). Also, the numerator would be higher because net income actually would be increased by the after-tax interest saved on the bonds for the last two months, [$30 – 40% ($30)] × ($^2/_{12}$). Be sure to note that this would not be an adjustment in the EPS calculation. Instead, net income would actually have been higher by [$30 – 40% ($30)] × ($^2/_{12}$) = $3. That is, reported net income would have been $157 rather than $154.

2. We would assume conversion for the period before November 1 because they were potentially dilutive during that period. The 12 million shares assumed outstanding from January 1 to November 1 would be time-weighted for that 10-month period: 12 ($^{10}/_{12}$). Also, the numerator would be increased by the after-tax interest assumed saved on the bonds for the first 10 months, [$30 – 40% ($30)] × ($^{10}/_{12}$).

Notice that the incremental effect on EPS is the same either way:

Not actually converted:	**Converted on November 1:**	
Assumed after-tax interest savings + $30 – 40%($30)	Actual after-tax interest savings +[$30 – 40%($30)] × ($^2/_{12}$)	Assumed after-tax interest savings + [$30 – 40%($30)] × ($^{10}/_{12}$)
+ 12 Assumed conversion of bonds	+ 12($^2/_{12}$) Actual conversion of bonds	+ 12($^{10}/_{12}$) Assumed conversion of bonds

EPS would be precisely the same whether convertible securities were actually converted or not.

Graphic 20–4 shows the disclosure note Clorox Company reported after the conversion of convertible notes during the year.

GRAPHIC   20–4

Conversion of Notes—
The Clorox Company

1 (in Part): Significant Accounting Policies—Earnings Per Common Share
A $9,000,000 note payable to Henkel Corporation was converted into 1,200,000 shares of common stock on August 1 . . . . Earnings per common share and weighted-average shares outstanding reflect this conversion as if it were effective during all periods presented.

Options or Warrants Outstanding for Only Part of the Period

Options or warrants outstanding for only part of the reporting period are included in the denominator on a time-weighted basis. For example, if options or warrants were issued on April 1, the denominator would include the appropriate incremental shares $\times$ $^9/_{12}$. Likewise, if options or warrants expired on April 1, the weighted-average shares should include the appropriate incremental shares $\times$ $^3/_{12}$.

Similarly, if options or warrants were exercised on April 1, the weighted average shares should include the appropriate incremental shares $\times$ $^3/_{12}$ for the period prior to actual exercise. The weighted average shares should include the appropriate actual shares issued $\times$ $^9/_{12}$ for the period after the exercise.

Financial Statement Presentation of Earnings Per Share Data

Recall from Chapter 3 that the income statement sometimes includes items that require separate presentation within the statement as follows:

Learning objective 8
Describe the financial statement presentation of EPS.

Income from continuing operations

Discontinued operations
Extraordinary items
Cumulative effect of a change in accounting principle

Net income

When the income statement includes one or more of the separately reported items, EPS data (both basic and diluted) must also be reported separately for income from continuing operations and net income. Per share amounts for discontinued operations, extraordinary items, and the cumulative effect of an accounting change would be disclosed either on the face of the income statement or in the notes to financial statements. Presentation of each component of net income on the face of the income statement is illustrated by the partial income statements of Sprint Corporation exhibited in Graphic 20–5.

GRAPHIC   20–5

EPS Disclosure—The Sprint Corporation

Consolidated Statements of Income (partial)

For the Years Ended December 31, (in millions, except per share data)	1995	1994	1993
Income from continuing operations before income taxes	1,480.4	1,387.9	813.1
Income tax provision	(534.3)	(488.7)	(296.0)
Income from Continuing Operations	946.1	899.2	517.1
Discontinued operations, net			
Cellular division	14.5	(15.5)	(38.1)
Other	–	7.0	(12.3)
Extraordinary items, net	(565.3)	—	(29.2)
Cumulative effect of changes in accounting principles net	—	—	(382.6)
Net income	395.3	890.7	54.9
Preferred stock dividends	(2.6)	(2.7)	(2.8)
Earnings applicable to common stock	392.7	888.0	52.1
Earnings per Common Share			
Continuing operations	$ 2.69	$ 2.57	$ 1.50
Discontinued operations	0.04	(0.02)	(0.15)
Extraordinary item	(1.61)	—	(0.08)
Cumulative effect of changes in accounting principles	—	—	(1.12)
Net income	$ 1.12	$ 2.55	$ 0.15
Weighted-average number of common shares	350.1	348.7	343.7

Basic and diluted EPS data should be reported on the face of the income statement for all reporting periods presented in the comparative statements. Businesses without potentially dilutive securities present basic EPS only. Disclosure notes should provide additional disclosures including:

1. A reconciliation of the numerator and denominator used in the basic EPS computations to the numerator and the denominator used in the diluted EPS computations. An example of

---

Additional Consideration

It is possible that a potentially dilutive security would have a dilutive effect on one component of net income but an antidilutive effect on another. When the effect of conversion or exercise has a dilutive effect on one of the required per share amounts but an antidilutive effect on one or more others, the effect should be included in all calculations of diluted EPS.

---

this is presented in Graphic 20–6 using the situation described in Illustration 20–8 of the previous section.

2. Any adjustments to the numerator for preferred dividends.
3. Any potentially dilutive securities that weren't included because they were antidilutive.
4. Any transactions that occurred after the end of the most recent period that would materially affect earnings per share.

GRAPHIC   20–6

Reconciliation of Basic EPS Computations to Diluted EPS Computations.

Earnings per Share Reconciliation:

	Income (Numerator)	Shares (Denominator)	Per Share Amount
Net income	$154		
Preferred dividends	(12)		
Basic earnings per share	$142	75	$1.89
Stock options	None	3*	
Convertible debt	18	12	
Convertible preferred stock	8	5	
Diluted earnings per share	$168	95	$1.77

Note: Stock warrants to purchase an additional 4 million shares at $32.50 per share were outstanding throughout the year but were not included in diluted EPS because the warrants' exercise price is greater than the average market price of the common shares.
*15 million − [(15 million × $20)/$25] = 3 million net additional shares

Decision-Makers' Perspective

The price-earnings ratio measures the quality of a company's earnings.

We noted at the beginning of the chapter that investors and creditors pay a great deal of attention to earnings per share information. One way analysts use the data is in connection with the price-earnings ratio. This ratio is simply the market price per share divided by the earnings per share. It measures the market's perception of the quality of a company's earnings by indicating the price multiple the capital market is willing to pay for the company's earnings. Presumably, this ratio reflects the information provided by all financial information in that the market price reflects analysts' perceptions of the company's growth potential, stability, and relative risk. The price-earnings ratio relates these performance measures with the external judgment of the marketplace concerning the value of the firm.

The ratio measures the quality of earnings in the sense that it represents the market's expectation of future earnings as indicated by current earnings. Caution is called for in comparing price-earnings ratios. For instance, a ratio might be low, not because earnings expectations are low, but because of abnormally elevated current earnings. On the contrary, the ratio might be high, not because earnings expectations are high, but because the company's current earnings are temporarily depressed. Similarly, an analyst should be alert to differences among accounting methods used to measure earnings from company to company when making comparisons.

The dividend payout ratio indicates the percentage of earnings that is distributed to shareholders as dividends.

Another ratio frequently calculated by shareholders and potential shareholders is the dividend payout ratio. This ratio expresses the percentage of earnings that is distributed to shareholders as dividends. The ratio is calculated by dividing dividends per common share by the earnings per share.

This ratio provides an indication of a firm's reinvestment strategy. A low payout ratio suggests that a company is retaining a large portion of earnings for reinvestment for such needs as new facilities and operating needs. Low payouts often are found in growth industries and high payouts in mature industries. Often, though, the ratio is merely a reflection of managerial strategy concerning the mix of internal versus external financing. The ratio also is considered by investors who, for tax or other reasons, prefer current income over market price appreciation, or vice versa.

CONCEPT REVIEW EXERCISE   ADDITIONAL EPS ISSUES

At December 31, 1997, the financial statements of Bahnson General, Inc., included the following:

Net income for 1997 (including a net-of-tax extraordinary loss of $10 million)	$180 million
Common stock, $1 par	
Shares outstanding on January 1	44 million

The share price was $25 and $28 at the beginning and end of the year, respectively.

Additional data:

At January 1, 1997, $200 million of 10% convertible notes were outstanding. The notes were converted on April 1 into 16 million shares of common stock.

An agreement with company executives calls for the issuance of up to 12 million additional shares of common stock in 1998 and 1999 based on the Bahnson's net income in those years. Executives will receive 2 million shares at the end of each of those two years if the company's stock price is at least $26 and another 4 million shares each year if the stock price is at least $29.50.

The tax rate is 40%.

Required:

Compute basic and diluted earnings per share for the year ended December 31, 1997.

CONCEPT REVIEW EXERCISE   SOLUTION

(amounts in millions, except per share amounts)

Basic EPS

$$\frac{\text{Net income}\ \$180}{\underset{\substack{\text{Shares}\\\text{at Jan. 1}}}{44} + \underset{\substack{\text{Actual}\\\text{conversion}\\\text{of notes}}}{16(^9/_{12})}} = \frac{\$180}{56} = \$3.21$$

Diluted EPS.

$$\frac{\underset{}{\text{Net income}}\ \$180 + \overset{\substack{\text{Assumed after-tax}\\\text{interest savings}}}{[\$20 - 40\%(\$20)] \times (^3/_{12})}}{\underset{\substack{\text{Shares}\\\text{at Jan. 1}}}{44} + \underset{\substack{\text{Actual}\\\text{conversion}\\\text{of notes}}}{16(^9/_{12})} + \underset{\substack{\text{Assumed}\\\text{conversion}\\\text{of notes}}}{16(^3/_{12})} + \underset{\substack{\text{Contingent}\\\text{shares}}}{(2 \times 2)}} = \frac{\$183}{64} = \$2.86$$

Convertible Notes: Notice that the effect on diluted EPS would be precisely the same whether the convertible notes were actually converted or not.

Converted on April 1:

$$\frac{\overset{\substack{\text{Net income including}\\\text{actual after-tax}\\\text{interest savings}}}{\$180} + \overset{\substack{\text{Assumed after-tax}\\\text{interest savings}}}{[\$20 - 40\%(\$20)] \times (^3/_{12})}}{\underset{\substack{\text{Shares}\\\text{at Jan. 1}}}{44} + \underset{\substack{\text{Actual}\\\text{conversion}\\\text{of notes}}}{16(^9/_{12})} + \underset{\substack{\text{Assumed}\\\text{conversion}\\\text{of notes}}}{16(^3/_{12})}} = \frac{\$183}{60}$$

Not Actually Converted:

$$\frac{\overset{\substack{\text{Net income without}\\\text{actual after-tax}\\\text{interest savings}}}{\$171^*}}{\underset{\substack{\text{Shares}\\\text{at Jan. 1}}}{44}} + \frac{\overset{\substack{\text{Assumed after-tax}\\\text{interest savings}}}{+\,[\$20-40\%(\$20)]}}{\underset{\substack{\text{Assumed}\\\text{conversion}\\\text{of notes}}}{16}} = \frac{\$183}{60}$$

$^*\$180 - \{[\$20 - 40\%(\$20)] \times (^9/_{12})\} = \$171$

After-tax interest from
April 1 to Dec. 31

Contingently Issuable Shares:

Because the conditions are met for issuing 4 million shares (2 million for each of two years), those shares are simply added to the denominator of diluted EPS. The current share price ($28) is projected to remain the same throughout the contingency period, so the other 8 million shares (4 million for each of two years) are excluded.

Income Statement Presentation:

To determine the per share amounts for income before extraordinary items, we substitute that amount for net income in the numerator (in this case, that means adding back the $10 million extraordinary loss):

Basic: $\dfrac{\$180 + 10}{56} = \$3.39$ Diluted: $\dfrac{\$183 + 10}{64} = \$3.01$

Earnings per share:	Basic*	Diluted
Income before extraordinary items	$3.39	$3.01
Extraordinary loss	(.18)	(.15)
Net income	$3.21	$2.86

*Only diluted EPS is required on the face of the income statement. Basic EPS is reported in the EPS reconciliation shown in the disclosure note (below).

Disclosure Note:
Earnings per Share Reconciliation:

	Income (Numerator)	Shares (Denominator)	Per Share Amount
Basic earnings per share			
Income before extraordinary items	$190	56	$3.39
Extraordinary loss	(10)	56	(.18)
Net income	$180	56	$3.21
Convertible debt	3	4	
Contingently issuable shares	—	4	
Diluted earnings per share			
Income before extraordinary items	$193	64	$3.01
Extraordinary loss	(10)	64	(.15)
Net income	$183	64	$2.86

Solution to Financial Reporting Case (at the opening of the chapter)

1. Meg's questions imply that she thinks you will get cash dividends of 29 cents a share. What does earning per share really tell you?

Earnings per share is a way to summarize the performance of business enterprises into a single number. It is simply earnings expressed on a per share basis. It does not imply anything about cash dividends. Whether some, all, or none of the earnings are distributed depends on the company's reinvestment strategy. A dividend payout ratio expresses the percentage of earnings that is distributed to shareholders as dividends.

2. The article says "the year earlier results were restated to reflect a 2-for-1 stock split in September." What does that mean?

When calculating earnings per share, shares outstanding prior to a stock split (or stock dividend) are retroactively restated to reflect the increase in shares (100% in this instance). That is, it is treated as if the September split occurred at the beginning of the period. When reported again for comparison purposes in the comparative income statements, the year earlier figure also would be restated to reflect the 2-for-1 stock split. Otherwise we would be comparing apples and oranges.

3. You know from statements Reynolds mailed you that company executives hold a number of stock options. If those options are exercised, you know the resulting increase in shares might reduce earnings per share. Is that possibility taken into account when EPS is calculated?

Yes, it is. If we don't take into account the dilutive effect of the share increase we might mislead investors and creditors. So, in addition to basic EPS, we also calculate diluted EPS to include the dilutive effect of options and other potentially dilutive securities. This means to calculate EPS *as if* the potential increase in shares already has occurred (even though it hasn't yet). For Reynolds' stock options, the calculation assumes the options were exercised at the beginning of the reporting period. Then the cash proceeds from selling the new shares are assumed used to buy back as many shares as possible at the shares' average market price during the year.

The Bottom Line

1. A company has a simple capital structure if it has no outstanding securities that could potentially dilute earnings per share. For such a firm, EPS is simply earnings available to common shareholders divided by the weighted average number of common shares outstanding. When potentially dilutive securities are outstanding, the company is said to have a complex capital structure. In that case, two EPS calculations are reported. Basic EPS assumes no dilution. Diluted EPS assumes maximum potential dilution.

2. EPS calculations are based on the weighted-average number of shares outstanding during the period. Any new shares issued during the period are time-weighted by the fraction of the period they were outstanding and then added to the number of shares outstanding for the period.

3. For a stock dividend or stock split, shares outstanding prior to the stock distribution are retroactively restated to reflect the increase in shares. When shares are reacquired, as treasury stock or to be retired, they are time-weighted for the fraction of the period they were not outstanding, prior to being subtracted from the number of shares outstanding during the reporting period.

4. The numerator in the EPS calculation should reflect earnings available to common shareholders. So, any dividends on preferred stock outstanding should be subtracted from reported net income. This adjustment is made for cumulative preferred stock whether or not dividends are declared that period.

5. For diluted EPS, it is assumed that stock options, rights, and warrants are exercised at the beginning of the period (or at the time the options are issued, if later) and the cash proceeds received are used to buy back (as treasury stock) as many of those shares as can be acquired at the average market price during the period.

6. To incorporate convertible securities into the calculation of diluted EPS, the conversion is assumed to have occurred at the beginning of the period (or at the time the convertible security is issued, if later). The denominator of the EPS fraction is adjusted for the additional common shares assumed and the numerator is increased by the interest (after-tax) or preferred dividends that would have been avoided in the event of conversion.

7. Contingently issuable shares are considered outstanding in the computation of diluted EPS when they will later be issued upon the mere passage of time or because of conditions that currently are met.

8. EPS data (both basic and diluted) must be reported separately for income from continuing operations and net income. Per share amounts for discontinued operations, extraordinary items, and an accounting change should be disclosed. Disclosures also should include a reconciliation of the numerator and denominator used in the computations.

Questions for Review of Key Topics

Question	20–1	What is a simple capital structure? How is EPS determined for a company with a simple capital structure?
Question	20–2	When calculating the weighted-average number of common shares, how are stock dividends and stock splits treated? Compare this treatment with that of additional shares sold for cash in midyear.
Question	20–3	Blake Distributors had 100,000 common shares outstanding at the beginning of the year, January 1. On May 13, Blake distributed a 5% stock dividend. On August 1, 1,200 shares were retired. What is the weighted-average number of shares for calculating EPS?
Question	20–4	Why are preferred dividends deducted from net income when calculating EPS? Are there circumstances when this deduction is not made?
Question	20–5	Distinguish between basic and diluted EPS.
Question	20–6	The treasury stock method is used to incorporate the dilutive effect of stock options, stock warrants, and similar securities. Describe this method as it applies to diluted EPS.
Question	20–7	The potentially dilutive effect of convertible securities is reflected in EPS calculations by the if-converted method. Describe this method as it relates to convertible bonds.
Question	20–8	How is the potentially dilutive effect of convertible preferred stock reflected in EPS calculations by the if-converted method? How is this different from the way convertible bonds are considered?
Question	20–9	A convertible security may appear to be dilutive when looked at individually but might be antidilutive when included in combination with other convertible securities. How should the order be determined for inclusion of convertible securities in an EPS calculation to avoid including an antidilutive security?
Question	20–10	Wiseman Electronics has an agreement with certain of its division managers that 50,000 contingently issuable shares will be issued next year in the event operating income exceeds $2.1 million that year. In what way, if any, is the calculation of EPS affected by these contingently issuable shares assuming this year's operating income was $2.2 million? $2.0 million?

Diluted EPS would be precisely the same whether convertible securities were actually converted or not. Why?

When the income statement includes one or more of the separately reported items, such as discontinued operations, extraordinary items, or the cumulative effect of a change in accounting principle, which amounts require per share presentation?

In addition to EPS numbers themselves, what additional disclosures should be provided concerning the EPS information?

Exercises

Exercise 20–1
Shares issued; treasury shares

McDonnell-Myer Corporation reported a $741 million net income in 1997. The company had 544 million common shares outstanding at January 1, 1997, the beginning of its fiscal year. Changes in the number of shares during 1997 are shown below:

February 28   36 million shares were issued as part of the consideration for the purchase of assets from Burrell Corporation.

May   2   As part of an annual share repurchase plan, 6 million shares were reacquired for $47 per share as treasury stock.

Required:
Compute McDonnell-Myer's earnings per share for the year ended December 31, 1997.

Exercise 20–2
Shares issued; stock dividend

For the year ended December 31, 1997, Norstar Industries reported net income of $655,000. At January 1, 1997, the company had 900,000 common shares outstanding. The following changes in the number of shares occurred during 1997:

April   30   Sold 60,000 shares in a public offering.
May   24   Declared and distributed a 5% stock dividend.
June   1   Issued 72,000 shares as part of the consideration for the purchase of assets from a subsidiary.

Required:
Compute Norstar's earnings per share for the year ended December 31, 1997.

Exercise 20–3
Nonconvertible preferred stock

At December 31, 1996 and 1997, Funk & Noble Corporation had outstanding 820 million shares of common stock and 2 million shares of 8%, $100 par value cumulative preferred stock. No dividends were declared on either the preferred or common stock in 1996 or 1997. Net income for 1997 was $426 million. The income tax rate is 40%.

Required:
Compute earnings per share for the year ended December 31, 1997.

Exercise 20–4
Stock dividend; nonconvertible preferred stock

Hardaway Fixtures' balance sheet at December 31, 1996, included the following:

Shares issued and outstanding	
Common Stock, $1 par	$800,000
Nonconvertible preferred stock, $50 par	20,000

On July 21, 1997, Hardaway issued a 25% stock dividend on its common stock. On December 12 it paid $50,000 cash dividends on the preferred stock. Net income for the year ended December 31, 1997, was $2,000,000.

Required:
Compute Hardaway's earnings per share for the year ended December 31, 1997.

Exercise 20–5
Net loss; nonconvertible preferred stock; shares sold

At December 31, 1996, Albrecht Corporation had outstanding 373,000 shares of common stock and 8,000 shares of 9.5%, $100 par value cumulative, nonconvertible preferred stock. On May 31, 1997, Albrecht sold for cash 12,000 shares of its common stock. No cash dividends were declared for 1997. For the year ended December 31, 1997, Ainsworth reported a net loss of $114,000.

Required:
Calculate Albrecht's net loss per share for the year ended December 31, 1997.

Exercise 20–6
Treasury stock; new shares; stock dividends; two years

The Alford Group had 202,000 shares of common stock outstanding at January 1, 1997. The following activities affected common shares during the year: There are no potentially dilutive securities outstanding.

1997
Feb. 28 Purchased 6,000 shares of treasury stock.
Oct. 31 Sold the treasury shares purchased on February 28.
Nov. 30 Issued 24,000 new shares.
Dec. 31 Net income for 1997 is $400,000.

1998
Jan. 15 Declared and issued a 2-for-1 stock split.
Dec. 31 Net income for 1998 is $400,000.

Required:
1. Determine the 1997 EPS.
2. Determine the 1998 EPS.
3. At what amount will the 1997 EPS be presented in the 1998 comparative financial statements?

Exercise 20–7
Stock dividend; nonconvertible preferred stock; treasury shares; shares sold

On December 31, 1996, Berclair, Inc. had 200 million shares of common stock and 3 million shares of 9%, $100 par value cumulative preferred stock issued and outstanding. On March 1, 1997, Berclair purchased 24 million shares of its common stock as treasury stock. Berclair issued a 5% common stock dividend on July 1, 1997. Four million treasury shares were sold on October 1. Net income for the year ended December 31, 1997, was $150 million.

Required:
Compute Berclair's earnings per share for the year ended December 31, 1997.

(Note: This is a variation of the previous exercise, modified to include stock options.)

Exercise 20–8
Stock dividend; nonconvertible preferred stock; treasury shares; shares sold; stock options

On December 31, 1996, Berclair, Inc., had 200 million shares of common stock and 3 million shares of 9%, $100 par value cumulative preferred stock issued and outstanding. Berclair issued a 5% common stock dividend on July 1, 1997. On March 1, 1997, Berclair purchased 24 million shares of its common stock as treasury stock. Four million treasury shares were sold on October 1. Net income for the year ended December 31, 1997, was $150 million.

Also outstanding at December 31, 1997, were stock options granted to key executives on September 13, 1996. The options are exercisable for 30 million common shares at an exercise price of $56 per share. During 1997, the market price of the common shares averaged $70 per share peaking at $80 on December 31.

Required:
Compute Berclair's basic and diluted earnings per share for the year ended December 31, 1997.

(Note: This is a variation of the previous exercise, modified to include the exercise of stock options.)

Exercise 20–9
Stock dividend; nonconvertible preferred stock; treasury shares; shares sold; stock options exercised

On December 31, 1996, Berclair, Inc., had 200 million shares of common stock and 3 million shares of 9%, $100 par value cumulative preferred stock issued and outstanding. Berclair issued a 5% common stock dividend on July 1, 1997. On March 1, 1997, Berclair purchased 24 million shares of its common stock as treasury stock. Four million treasury shares were sold on October 1. Net income for the year ended December 31, 1997, was $150 million.

Also outstanding at December 31, 1997, were stock options granted to key executives on September 13, 1996. The options are exercisable for 30 million common shares at an exercise price of $56 per share. During 1997, the market price of the common shares averaged $70 per share peaking at $80 on December 31.

The options were exercised on September 1, 1997.

Required:
Compute Berclair's basic and diluted earnings per share for the year ended December 31, 1997.

(Note: This is a variation of Exercise 20–8, modified to include convertible bonds.)

Exercise 20–10
Stock dividend; nonconvertible preferred stock; treasury shares; shares sold; stock options; convertible bonds

On December 31, 1996, Berclair, Inc., had 200 million shares of common stock and 3 million shares of 9%, $100 par value cumulative preferred stock issued and outstanding. Berclair issued a 5% common stock dividend on July 1, 1997. On March 1, 1997, Berclair purchased 24 million shares of its common stock as treasury stock. Four million treasury shares were sold on October 1. Net income for the year ended December 31, 1997, was $150 million. The income tax rate is 40%.

Also outstanding at December 31 were stock options granted to key executives on September 13, 1996. The options are exercisable for 30 million common shares at an exercise price of $56 per share. During 1997, the market price of the common shares averaged $70 per share peaking at $80 on December 31.

$62.5 million of 8% bonds, convertible into 6 million common shares, were issued at face value in 1993.

Required:
Compute Berclair's basic and diluted earnings per share for the year ended December 31, 1997.

Exercise 20–11
Stock options

Stock options exercisable at $50 per share to obtain 24,000 shares of common stock were outstanding during a period when the average market price of the common stock was $60 and the ending market price was $55.

Required:
By how many shares will the assumed exercise of these options increase the weighted-average number of shares outstanding when calculating diluted earnings per share?

Exercise 20–12
Convertible preferred stock

Ahnberg Corporation had 800,000 shares of common stock issued and outstanding at December 31, 1996. No common shares were issued during 1997. On January 1, 1997, Ahnberg issued 100,000 shares of convertible preferred stock. The preferred shares are convertible into 200,000 shares of common stock. During 1997 Ahnberg paid $60,000 cash dividends on the preferred stock. Net income for the year ended December 31, 1997, was $1,500,000.

Required:
Compute Ahnberg's basic and diluted earnings per share for the year ended December 31, 1997.

Exercise 20–13
Convertible preferred stock;
convertible bonds

Information from the financial statements of the Ames Fabricators, Inc., included the following:

	December 31	
	1997	**1996**
Common shares	100,000	100,000
Convertible preferred shares (convertible into 32,000 shares of common)	12,000	12,000
10% convertible bonds (convertible into 30,000 shares of common)	$1,000,000	$1,000,000

Ames' net income for the year ended December 31, 1997, is $500,000. The income tax rate is 40%. Ames paid dividends of $5 per share on its preferred stock during 1997.

Required:
Compute basic and diluted earnings per share for the year ended December 31, 1997.

Exercise 20–14
Shares sold; convertible
bonds

Wagnell's, Inc., had 50 million shares of common stock outstanding at January 1, 1997. On October 1, 1997, an additional 12 million shares of common stock were issued for cash. Wagnell's also had $400 million of 10% convertible bonds outstanding at December 31, 1997. The bonds are convertible into 10 million shares of common stock. Wagnell's net income for the year ended December 31, 1997, is $250 million. The income tax rate is 40%.

Required:
Compute basic and diluted earnings per share for the year ended December 31, 1997.

Exercise 20–15
Shares issued; stock options

For the year ended December 31, 1997, Croft Industries reported net income of $900 million. During the year, the market price of Croft's common stock averaged $12, ending 1997 at $12.25 per share. At January 1, 1997, Croft had 191 million common shares outstanding. On May 1 Croft sold 9 million shares in a public offering. Stock options exercisable for 48 million shares at an exercise price of $11 were outstanding throughout the year. Croft's only debt consisted of $83 million of 10% short-term bank notes. The company's income tax rate is 40%.

Required:
Compute Croft's basic and diluted earnings per share for the year ended December 31, 1997.

Exercise 20–16
Shares issued; stock options

Stanley Department Stores reported net income of $720,000 for the year ended December 31, 1997.

Additional information:

Common shares outstanding at Jan. 1, 1997	80,000
Stock warrants outstanding throughout 1997	24,000

(Each warrant is exercisable for one common share at an exercise price of $37.50)
During the year, the market price of Stanley's common stock averaged $45, ending 1997 at $50 per share.
On Aug. 30 Stanley sold 15,000 common shares.
Stanley's only debt consisted of $50,000 of 10% short-term bank notes.
The company's income tax rate is 40%.

Required:

Compute Stanley's basic and diluted earnings per share for the year ended December 31, 1997.

Exercise 20–17
Contingently issuable shares

During its first year of operations, McCollum Tool Works entered into the following transactions relating to shareholders' equity. The corporation was authorized to issue 100 million common shares, $1 par per share.

Jan.   2   Issued 35 million common shares for cash.
       3   Entered an agreement with the company president to issue up to 2 million additional shares of common stock in 1998 based on the earnings of McCollum in 1998. If net income exceeds $140 million, the president will receive 1 million shares; 2 million shares if net income exceeds $150 million.
Mar. 31   Issued 4 million shares in exchange for plant facilities.

Net income for 1997 was $148 million.

Required:

Compute basic and diluted earnings per share for the year ended December 31, 1997.

Exercise 20–18
New shares; contingent agreements

Anderson Steel Company began 1997 with 600,000 shares of common stock outstanding. On March 31, 1997, 100,000 new shares were sold at a price of $45 per share. The market price has risen steadily since that time to a high of $50 per share at December 31. No other changes in shares occurred during 1997, and no securities are outstanding that can become common stock. However, there are two agreements with officers of the company for future issuance of common stock. Both agreements relate to compensation arrangements reached in 1996. The first agreement grants to the company president a right to 10,000 shares of stock each year the closing market price is at least $48. The agreement begins in 1998 and expires in 2001. The second agreement grants to the controller a right to 15,000 shares of stock if she is still with the firm at the end of 2005. Net income for 1997 was $2,000,000.

Required:

Compute Anderson Steel Company's basic and diluted EPS for the year ended December 31, 1997.

Exercise 20–19
Concepts; terminology

Listed below are several terms and phrases associated with earnings per share. Pair each item from List A (by letter) with the item from List B that is most appropriately associated with it.

<table>
<tr><td colspan="2" align="center">**List A**</td><td colspan="2">**List B**</td></tr>
<tr><td>____</td><td>1. Subtract preferred dividends.</td><td>a.</td><td>Options exercised.</td></tr>
<tr><td>____</td><td>2. Time-weighted by $^5/_{12}$.</td><td>b.</td><td>Simple capital structure.</td></tr>
<tr><td>____</td><td>3. Time-weighted shares assumed issued plus time-weighted actual shares.</td><td>c.</td><td>Basic EPS.</td></tr>
<tr><td>____</td><td>4. Midyear event treated as if it occurred at the beginning of the reporting period.</td><td>d.</td><td>Convertible preferred stock.</td></tr>
<tr><td></td><td></td><td>e.</td><td>Earnings available to common shareholders.</td></tr>
<tr><td>____</td><td>5. Preferred dividends do not reduce earnings.</td><td>f.</td><td>Antidilutive.</td></tr>
<tr><td>____</td><td>6. Single EPS presentation.</td><td>g.</td><td>Increased marketability.</td></tr>
<tr><td>____</td><td>7. Stock split.</td><td>h.</td><td>Extraordinary items.</td></tr>
<tr><td>____</td><td>8. Potentially dilutive security.</td><td>i.</td><td>Stock dividend.</td></tr>
<tr><td>____</td><td>9. Exercise price exceeds market price.</td><td>j.</td><td>Add after-tax interest to numerator.</td></tr>
<tr><td>____</td><td>10. No dilution assumed.</td><td>k.</td><td>Diluted EPS.</td></tr>
<tr><td>____</td><td>11. Convertible bonds.</td><td>l.</td><td>Noncumulative, undeclared preferred dividends.</td></tr>
<tr><td>____</td><td>12. Contingently issuable shares.</td><td></td><td></td></tr>
<tr><td>____</td><td>13. Maximum potential dilution.</td><td>m.</td><td>Common shares retired in August.</td></tr>
<tr><td>____</td><td>14. Per share amounts for net income and for income from continuing operations.</td><td>n.</td><td>Include in diluted EPS when conditions for issuance are met.</td></tr>
</table>

Problems

Problem 20–1
Net loss; stock dividend; nonconvertible preferred stock; treasury shares; shares sold; extraordinary loss

On December 31, 1996, Ainsworth, Inc., had 600 million shares of common stock outstanding. Twenty million shares of 8%, $100 par value cumulative, nonconvertible preferred stock were sold on January 2, 1997. On April 30, 1997, Ainsworth purchased 30 million shares of its common stock as treasury stock. Twelve million treasury shares were sold on August 31. Ainsworth issued a 5% common stock dividend on June 12, 1997. No cash dividends were declared in 1997. For the year ended December 31, 1997, Ainsworth reported a net loss of $140 million, including an after-tax extraordinary loss of $400 million from a litigation settlement.

Required:

1. Determine Ainsworth's net loss per share for the year ended December 31, 1997.
2. Determine the per share amount of income or loss from continuing operations for the year ended December 31, 1997.
3. Prepare an EPS presentation that would be appropriate to appear on Ainsworth's 1997 and 1996 comparative income statements. Assume EPS were reported in 1996 as $.75, based on net income (no extraordinary items) of $450 million and a weighted-average number of common shares of 600 million.

(Note: This problem is based on the same situation described in Problem 19–4 in Chapter 19, modified to focus on EPS rather than recording the events that affected retained earnings.)

Problem 20–2
EPS from statement of retained earnings

Comparative Statements of Retained Earnings for Renn-Dever Corporation were reported as follows for the fiscal years ending December 31, 1997, 1998, and 1999.

RENN-DEVER CORPORATION
Statements of Retained Earnings

For the years ended December 31,	1999	1998	1997
Balance at beginning of year	$6,794,292	$5,464,052	$5,624,552
Net income (loss)	3,308,700	2,240,900	(160,500)
Deductions:			
Stock dividend (34,900 shares)	242,000		
Common shares retired, September 30 (110,000 shares)		212,660	
Common stock cash dividends	889,950	698,000	0
Balance at end of year	$8,971,042	$6,794,292	$5,464,052

At December 31, 1996, paid-in capital consisted of the following:

Common stock, 1,855,000 shares at $1 par,	$1,855,000
Paid-in capital–excess of par	7,420,000

No preferred stock or potentially dilutive securities were outstanding during any of the periods shown.

Required:

Compute Renn-Dever's earnings per share as it would have appeared on income statements for the years ended December 31, 1997, 1998, and 1999.

Problem 20–3
EPS from statement of shareholders' equity

Comparative Statements of Shareholders' Equity for Locke Intertechnology Corporation were reported as follows for the fiscal years ending December 31, 1995, 1996, and 1997.

LOCKE INTERTECHNOLOGY CORPORATION
Statements of Shareholders' Equity
For the Years Ended Dec. 31, 1995, 1996, and 1997 ($ in millions)

	Preferred Stock, $10 par	Common Stock, $1 par	Additional Paid-in Paid-in Capital	Retained Earnings	Total Shareholders' Equity
Balance at Jan. 1, 1995		55	495	1,878	2,428
Sale of preferred shares	10		470		480
Sale of common shares, 7/1		9	81		90
Cash dividend, preferred				(1)	(1)
Cash dividend, common				(16)	(16)
Net income				290	290
Balance at Dec. 31, 1995	10	64	1,046	2,151	3,271
Retirement of common shares, 4/1		(4)	(36)	(20)	(60)
Cash dividend, preferred				(1)	(1)
Cash dividend, common				(20)	(20)
3 for 2 split effected in the form of a common stock dividend, 8/12		30	(30)		
Net income				380	380
Balance at Dec. 31, 1996	10	90	980	2,490	3,570
10% common stock dividend, 5/1		9	90	(99)	
Sale of common shares, 9/1		3	31		34
Cash dividend, preferred				(2)	(2)
Cash dividend, common				(22)	(22)
Net income				412	412
Balance at Dec. 31, 1997	10	102	1,101	2,779	3,992

Required:

Infer from the statements the events and transactions that affected Locke Intertechnology Corporation's shareholders' equity and compute earnings per share as it would have appeared on the income statements for the years ended December 31, 1995, 1996, and 1997. No potentially dilutive securities were outstanding during any of the periods shown.

Problem 20–4
Nonconvertible preferred stock; treasury shares; shares sold; stock dividend

On December 31, 1996, Dow Steel Corporation had 600,000 shares of common stock and 3 million shares of 8%, noncumulative, nonconvertible preferred stock issued and outstanding. Dow issued a 4% common stock dividend on May 15 and paid cash dividends of $400,000 and $75,000 to common and preferred shareholders, respectively, on December 15, 1997.

On February 28, 1997, Dow sold 60,000 common shares. In keeping with its long-term share repurchase plan, 2,000 shares were retired on July 1. Dow's net income for the year ended December 31, 1997, was $2,100,000. The income tax rate is 40%.

Required:
Compute Dow's earnings per share for the year ended December 31, 1997.

(Note: Problem 20–5 is a variation of Problem 20–4, modified to include stock options.)

Problem 20–5
Nonconvertible preferred stock; treasury shares; shares sold; stock dividend; options

On December 31, 1996, Dow Steel Corporation had 600,000 shares of common stock and 3 million shares of 8%, noncumulative, nonconvertible preferred stock issued and outstanding. Dow issued a 4% common stock dividend on May 15 and paid cash dividends of $400,000 and $75,000 to common and preferred shareholders, respectively, on December 15, 1997.

On February 28, 1997, Dow sold 60,000 common shares. In keeping with its long-term share repurchase plan, 2,000 shares were retired on July 1. Dow's net income for the year ended December 31, 1997, was $2,100,000. The income tax rate is 40%.

As part of an incentive compensation plan, Dow granted stock options to division managers at December 31 of the current and each of the previous two years. Each option permits its holder to buy one share of common stock at an exercise price equal to market value at the date of grant. Information concerning the number of options granted and common share prices follows:

Date granted	Options Granted	Share Price
	(adjusted for the stock dividend)	
December 31, 1995	3,000	$33
December 31, 1996	8,000	$24
December 31, 1997	6,500	$31

The market price of the common stock averaged $32 per share during 1997.

Required:
Compute Dow's earnings per share for the year ended December 31, 1997.

(Note: Problem 20–6 is a variation of Problem 20–5, modified to include convertible bonds and contingently issuable shares.)

Problem 20–6
Nonconvertible preferred stock; treasury shares; shares sold; stock dividend; options; convertible bonds; contingently issuable shares

On December 31, 1996, Dow Steel Corporation had 600,000 shares of common stock and 3 million shares of 8%, noncumulative, nonconvertible preferred stock issued and outstanding. Dow issued a 4% common stock dividend on May 15 and paid cash dividends of $400,000 and $75,000 to common and preferred shareholders, respectively, on December 15, 1997.

On February 28, 1997, Dow sold 60,000 common shares. Also, as part of a 1996 agreement for the acquisition of Merrill Cable Company, another 23,000 shares (already adjusted for the stock dividend) are to be issued to former Merrill shareholders on December 31, 1998, if Merrill's 1998 net income is at least $500,000. In 1997, Merrill's net income was $630,000.

In keeping with its long-term share repurchase plan, 2,000 shares were retired on July 1. Dow's net income for the year ended December 31, 1997, was $2,100,000. The income tax rate is 40%.

As part of an incentive compensation plan, Dow granted stock options to division managers at December 31 of the current and each of the previous two years. Each option permits its holder to buy one share of common stock at an exercise price equal to market value at the date of grant. Information concerning the number of options granted and common share prices follows:

Date granted	Options Granted	Share Price
	(adjusted for the stock dividend)	
December 31, 1995	3,000	$33
December 31, 1996	8,000	$24
December 31, 1997	6,500	$31

The market price of the common stock averaged $32 per share during 1997.

On July 12, 1995, Dow issued $800,000 of convertible 10% debentures at face value. Each $1,000 bond is convertible into 30 common shares (adjusted for the stock dividend).

Required:

Compute Dow's basic and diluted earnings per share for the year ended December 31, 1997.

Problem 20–7
Antidilution

Alciatore Company earned a 1997 net income of $150,000. The weighted-average number of common shares outstanding for 1997 was 40,000. The average stock price for 1997 was $33. Assume an income tax rate of 40 percent.

Required:

For each of the following independent situations, indicate whether the security is antidilutive for diluted EPS.

1. 10,000 shares of 7.7% of $100 par convertible, cumulative preferred stock. Each share may be converted into two common shares.
2. 8% convertible 10-year, $500,000 of bonds, issued at face value. The bonds are convertible to 5,000 shares of common stock.
3. Stock options exercisable at $30 per share after January 1, 1999.
4. Warrants for 1,000 common shares with an exercise price of $35 per share.
5. A contingent agreement to issue 5,000 shares of stock to the company president if net income is at least $125,000 in 1998.

Problem 20–8
Convertible bonds; treasury shares

At December 31, 1997, the financial statements of Hollingsworth Industries included the following:

Net income for 1997	$560 million
Bonds payable, 10%, convertible into 36 million shares of common stock	$300 million
Common stock	
Shares outstanding on January 1	400 million
Treasury shares purchased for cash on September 1	30 million

Additional data:

The bonds payable were issued at par in 1995. The tax rate for 1997 year was 40%.

Required:

Compute basic and diluted EPS for the year ended December 31, 1997.

Problem 20–9
Options; convertible preferred; additional shares

On January 1, 1997, Tonge Industries had outstanding 440,000 common shares (par $1) that originally sold for $20 per share, and 4,000 shares of 10% cumulative preferred stock (par $100), convertible into 40,000 common shares.

On October 1, 1997, Tonge sold and issued an additional 16,000 shares of common stock at $33. At December 31, 1997, there were common stock options outstanding, issued in 1996, and exercisable for 20,000 shares of common stock at an exercise price of $30. The market price of the common stock at year-end was $48. During the year the price of the common shares had averaged $40.

Net income was $650,000. The tax rate for the year was 40%.

Required:

Compute basic and diluted EPS for the year ended December 31, 1997.

Problem 20–10
Stock options; warrants; nonconvertible preferred; convertible bonds; shares sold

Mason Corporation's capital structure is as follows:

	December 31	
	1997	**1996**
Outstanding shares of:		
Common stock	336,000	300,000
Nonconvertible preferred stock	10,000	10,000
8% convertible bonds	$1,000,000	$1,000,000

The following additional information is available:

- On September 1, 1997, Mason sold 36,000 additional shares of common stock.
- Net income for the year ended December 31, 1997, was $750,000.
- During 1997 Mason paid dividends of $3.00 per share on its nonconvertible preferred stock.
- The 8% convertible bonds are convertible into 40 shares of common stock for each $1,000 bond.
- Unexercised stock options to purchase 30,000 shares of common stock at $22.50 per share were outstanding at the beginning and end of 1997. The average market price of Mason's common stock was $36 per share during 1997. The market price was $33 per share at December 31, 1997.
- Warrants to purchase 20,000 shares to common stock at $38 per share were attached to the preferred stock at the time of issuance. The warrants, which expire on December 31, 2002, were outstanding at December 31, 1997.
- Mason's effective income tax rate was 40% for 1996 and 1997.

Required:

1. Compute the number of shares that should be used for the computation of basic earnings per common share for the year ended December 31, 1997.
2. Compute the basic earnings per common share for the year ended December 31, 1997.
3. Compute the number of shares that should be used for the computation of diluted earnings per common share for the year ended December 31, 1997.
4. Compute the diluted earnings per common share for the year ended December 31, 1997.

(AICPA adapted)

Cases

Critical Thought Case 20–1
Where are the profits?

Sugarbaker Construction Company has experienced generally steady growth since its inception in 1950. Management is proud of its record of having maintained or increased its earnings per share in each year of its existence.

Recessionary pressures in the construction industry have led to disturbing dips in revenues the past two years. Despite concerted cost-cutting efforts, profits have actually declined in each of the two previous years. Net income in 1995, 1996, and 1997 was as follows:

1995	$145 million
1996	$134 million
1997	$ 95 million

A major shareholder has hired you to provide advice on whether to continue her present investment position or to curtail that position. Of particular concern is the declining profitability, despite the fact that earnings per share have continued a pattern of growth:

	Basic	Diluted
1995	$2.15	$1.91
1996	$2.44	$2.12
1997	$2.50	$2.50

She specifically asks you to explain this apparent paradox. During the course of your investigation you discover the following events:

- For the decade ending December 31, 1994, Sugarbaker had 60 million common shares and 20 million shares of 8%, $10 par nonconvertible preferred stock outstanding. Cash dividends have been paid quarterly on both.
- On July 1, 1996, half the preferred shares were retired in the open market. The remaining shares were retired on December 30, 1996.
- $55 million of 8% nonconvertible bonds were issued at the beginning of 1997 and a portion of the proceeds were used to call and retire $50 million of 10% debentures (outstanding since 1992) that were convertible into 9 million common shares.
- In 1995, management announced a share repurchase plan by which up to 24 million common shares would be retired. 12 million shares were retired on March 1 of both 1996 and 1997.
- Sugarbaker's income tax rate is 40% and has been for the last several years.

Required:

Explain the apparent paradox to which your client refers. Include calculations that demonstrate your explanation.

Writing Case 20–2
Dilution

"I thought I understood earnings per share," lamented Brad Dawson, "but you're telling me we need to pretend our convertible bonds have been converted! Or maybe not?"

Dawson, your boss, is the new manger of the Fabricating division of BVT Corporation. His background is engineering and he has only a basic understanding of earnings per share. Knowing you are an accounting graduate, he asks you to explain the questions he has about the calculation of the company's EPS. His reaction is to your explanation that the company's convertible bonds might be included in this year's calculation.

"Put it in a memo!" he grumbled as he left your office.

Required:

Write a memo to Dawson. Explain the effect on earnings per share of each of the following:

1. Convertible securities.
2. Antidilutive securities.

Discussion Case 20–3
EPS concepts

Raun Company had the following account titles on its December 31, 1997, trial balance:

> 6% cumulative convertible preferred stock, $100 par value
> Paid-in capital in excess of par—preferred stock
> Common stock, $1 stated value
> Paid-in capital in excess of stated value—common stock
> Retained earnings

The following additional information about the Raun Company was available for the year ended December 31, 1997:

- There were 2,000,000 shares of preferred stock authorized of which 1,000,000 were outstanding. All 1,000,000 shares outstanding were issued in January 2, 1995, for $120 a share. The preferred stock is convertible into common stock on a one-for-one basis until December 31, 2003; thereafter the preferred stock ceases to be convertible and is callable at par value by the company. No preferred stock has been converted into common stock, and there were no dividends in arrears at December 31, 1997.
- The common stock has been issued at amounts above stated value per share since incorporation in 1979. Of the 5,000,000 shares authorized, there were 3,500,000 shares outstanding at January 1, 1997. The market price of the outstanding common stock has increased slowly, but consistently, for the last five years.
- The company has an employee stock option plan where certain key employees and officers may purchase shares of common stock at 100% of the market price at the date of the option grant. All options are exercisable in installments of one-third each year, commencing one year after the date of the grant, and expire if not exercised within four years of the grant date. On January 1, 1997, options for 70,000 shares were outstanding at prices ranging from $47.00 to $83.00 a share. Options for 20,000 shares were exercised at $47.00 to $79.00 a share during 1997. No options expired during 1997 and additional options for 15,000 shares were granted at $86.00 a share during the year. The 65,000 options outstanding at December 31, 1997, were exercisable at $54.00 to $86.00 a share: of these, 30,000 were exercisable at that date at prices ranging from $54.00 to $79.00 a share.
- The company also has an employee stock purchase plan where the company pays one-half and the employee pays one-half of the market price of the stock at the date of the subscription. During 1997, employees subscribed to 60,000 shares at an average price of $87.00 a share. All 60,000 shares were paid for and issued late in September 1997.

On December 31, 1997, there was a total of 355,000 shares of common stock set aside for the granting of future stock options and for future purchases under the employee stock purchase plan. The only changes in the stockholders' equity for 1997 were those described above, 1997 net income, and cash dividends paid.

Required:
Explain how the amount of the denominator should be determined to compute diluted earnings per share for presentation in the financial statements. Be specific as to the handling of each item. If additional information is needed to determine whether an item should be included or excluded or the extent to which an item should be included, identify the information needed and how the item would be handled if the information were known. Assume Raun Company had substantial net income for the year ended December 3l, 1997.

(AICPA adapted)

International Case 20–4
Reporting earnings per share
in other countries

A key objective of the International Accounting Standards Committee (IASC) is to narrow worldwide differences in accounting practices and the presentation of financial information. Although the IASC has worked toward uniformity since 1973, harmonization has by no means been achieved. Toward this end, the United States has cooperated with the IASC in developing common requirements for earnings per share. Still significant differences exist from country to country that do not choose to follow the international standards in this area.

Required:
1. Choose a country other than the United States and obtain an annual report for a company based in that country. Research the way that country reports earnings per share. Include in your analysis:
   a. The extent of variations in the definition of earnings for the numerator of the EPS calculation.
   b. Whether both basic and diluted EPS are reported in the financial statements of the non-U.S. firm.
   c. Whether additional related disclosures are provided.
2. Prepare a short report highlighting the similarities and differences between the United States and your chosen country in the way earnings per share and related amounts are reported.

Note: You can obtain copies of annual reports from the investor relations department of the corporation, from a friendly stockbroker, from Public Register's Annual Report Service, on the Internet at www.PRARS.com. or from EDGAR, the Electronic Data Gathering and Retrieval service of the SEC, at www.sec.gov/.

Financial Analysis Case 20–5
Analyzing financial statements; price-earnings ratio; dividend payout ratio

IGF Foods Company is a large, primarily domestic, consumer foods company involved in the manufacture, distribution and sale of a variety of food products. Industry averages are derived from Troy's *The Almanac of Business and Industrial Financial Ratios* and Dun and Bradstreet's *Industry Norms and Key Business Ratios*. Following are the 1997 and 1996 comparative income statements and balance sheets for IGF. The market price of IGF's common stock is $47 during 1997. (The financial data we use are from actual financial statements of a well-known corporation, but the company name used in our illustration is fictitious and the numbers and dates have been modified slightly to disguise the company's identity.)

IGF FOODS COMPANY
Years Ended December 31, 1997 and 1996

($ in millions)	1997	1996
Comparative Income Statements		
Net sales	$6,440	$5,800
Cost of goods sold	(3,667)	(3,389)
Gross profit	2,773	2,411
Operating expenses	(1,916)	(1,629)
Operating income	857	782
Interest expense	(54)	(53)
Income from operations before tax	803	729
Income taxes	(316)	(287)
Net income	$ 487	$ 442
Net income per share	$2.69	$2.44
Average shares outstanding	181 million	181 million
Comparative Balance Sheets		
Assets		
Total current assets	$1,879	$1,490
Property, plant, and equipment (net):	2,592	2,291
Intangibles (net):	800	843
Other assets	74	60
Total assets	$5,345	$4,684
Liabilities And Shareholders' Equity		
Total current liabilities	$1,473	$ 941
Long-term debt	534	728
Deferred income taxes	407	344
Total liabilities	2,414	2,013
Shareholders' equity:		
Common stock	180	180
Additional paid-in capital	21	63
Retained earnings	2,730	2,428
Total shareholders' equity	2,931	2,671
Total liabilities and shareholders' equity	$5,345	$4,684

Some ratios express income, dividends, and market prices on a per share basis. As such, these ratios appeal primarily to common shareholders, particularly when weighing investment possibilities. These ratios focus less on the fundamental soundness of a company and more on its investment characteristics.

Required:
1. Earnings per share expresses a firm's profitability on a per share basis. Calculate earnings per share for IGF.
2. Calculate IGF's price-earnings ratio. The average price-earnings ratio for the stocks listed on the New York Stock Exchange in a comparable time period was 18.5. What does your calculation indicate about IGF's earnings?
3. Calculate IGF's dividend payout ratio. What information does the calculation provide an investor?

Ethics Case 20–6
International Network Solutions

International Network Solutions provides products and services related to remote access networking. The company has grown rapidly during its first 10 years of operations. As its segment of the industry has begun to mature, though, the fast growth of previous years has begun to slow. In fact, this year revenues and profits are roughly the same as last year.

One morning, nine weeks before the close of the fiscal year, Rob Mashburn, CFO, and Jessica Lane, controller, were sharing coffee and ideas in Lane's office.

Lane: About the Board meeting Thursday. You may be right. This may be the time to suggest a share buy-back program.

Mashburn: To begin this year, you mean?

Lane: Right! I know Barber will be lobbying to use the funds for our European expansion. She's probably right about the best use of our funds, but we can always issue more notes next year. Right now, we need a quick fix for our EPS numbers.

Mashburn: Our shareholders are accustomed to increases every year.

Required:
1. How will a buyback of shares provide a "quick fix" for EPS?
2. Is the proposal ethical?
3. Who would be affected if the proposal is implemented?

Integrating Case 20–7
Executive stock options and EPS

Cisco Systems, Inc., headquartered in San Jose, California, is the world's leading supplier of internetworking of geographically dispersed computer networks. Cisco's 1996 annual report included the following disclosure note:

---

11. Stock Option Plans

The Company established a Stock Option Plan in 1987 under which it has reserved a total of 221.3 million shares of common stock for issuance to employees, officers, directors, consultants, and independent contractors. Both incentive and nonqualified stock options have been granted at prices not less than fair market value at the date of grant as determined by the Board of Directors. Although the Board has the authority to set other terms, the options are generally 25% exercisable one year from the date of grant and then ratably over the following 36 months.

At July 28, 1996, approximately 21,700,000 outstanding options were exercisable.

The financial statement also reported 649,284,000 shares of common stock outstanding at the end of the year and the shares used in EPS calculations were 666,586,000.

Required:
1. How might the employee stock options described in footnote 11 affect earnings per share?
2. If we assume the actual number of common shares and number of options did not change during the year, how could we reconcile the shares outstanding, the shares used in EPS calculations, and the number of options outstanding?

Internet Case 20–8
Determining and comparing price-earnings ratios; retrieving stock prices and earnings per share numbers from the Internet

A number of sites on the Internet allow the retrieval of current stock price information. Among those sites are USA Today (web.usatoday.com/) and Money Online (pathfinder.com/). EDGAR, the Electronic Data Gathering, Analysis, and Retrieval system, (www.sec.gov/) performs automated collection, validation, indexing, acceptance, and forwarding of submissions by companies and others who are required by law to file forms with the U.S. Securities and Exchange Commission (SEC). Form 10-K or 10-KSB, which include the annual report, is required to be filed on EDGAR. The SEC makes this information available on the Internet.

Required:
1. Access any site on the Internet that permits you to get a current stock quote. Determine the current price of Microsoft Corporation's common stock (MSFT) and that of Intel Corporation (INTC).
2. Access EDGAR on the Internet. Search for Microsoft and access its most recent 10-K or 10-Q filing. Search or scroll to find the income statement and related note(s). Determine the most recent earnings per share. Repeat this step for Intel.
3. Calculate the price-earnings ratio for each company.
4. Compare the PE ratios of Microsoft and Intel. What information might be gleaned from your comparison?

Real World Case 20–9
Kellogg's EPS; PE ratio; news article

While eating his Kellogg's Frosted Flakes one October morning, Fred Sparring noticed the following article in his local paper:

KELLOGG COMPANY MAKES EARNINGS PER SHARE PROJECTION
Battle Creek, Mich. Oct. 25—Kellogg Company (NYSE: K) today announced third quarter earnings per share, excluding nonrecurring charges, of $.85 compared to $1.05 a year ago. The result is consistent with a projection made by the company on September 4.
Third quarter net earnings, excluding nonrecurring charges, were $180.8 million compared to $230 million in 1995, with sales of $1.68 billion compared to $1.84 billion. Global volume increased by 1 percent to

a record level with strength in ready-to-eat cereal volume outside the United States and convenience foods volume more than offsetting continued softness in U.S. cereal volume.

"As previously forecast, our third quarter performance was influenced significantly by competitive conditions in the U.S. cereal category," said Arnold G. Langbo, Kellogg Company chairman of the board and chief executive officer. "We continue to believe our strategy of lower prices combined with efficient promotion spending is the right strategy to deliver long-term growth.

"We are encouraged by many favorable business developments from the third quarter," Langbo said, "including the successful launch of Kellogg's Honey Crunch Corn Flakes(TM) cereal in the U.S., record cereal volume performances in our high-potential Latin American and Asia-Pacific divisions, double-digit volume growth from our fast-developing convenience foods business, and continued progress in reducing costs as part of our ongoing programs to increase consumer value worldwide."

The company recorded pretax nonrecurring charges of $24.8 million ($21.3 million after tax, or $.10 per share), including a $15 million provision to possibly settle certain unexplained litigation in Europe, during the third quarter of 1996. Including these charges, earnings per share were $.75 and net earnings were $159.5 million.

Shares of the world's leading cereal maker fell $1.125 to $64.375 in composite New York Stock Exchange trading.

PRNewswire

Consulting sources on the internet, Fred was able to determine that EPS the previous three quarters totaled $1.01.

Required:

1. What does the article mean by "earnings per share, excluding nonrecurring charges"? Is that the way EPS is calculated?
2. Using the numbers provided, determine the price/earnings ratio for Kellogg Company. What information does this ratio impart?

ACCOUNTING CHANGES AND ERROR CORRECTIONS

OVERVIEW

Chapter 3 provided an overview of accounting changes and error correction. Later, we discussed changes encountered in connection with specific assets and liabilities as we dealt with those topics in subsequent chapters.

Now, in this chapter, we revisit accounting changes and error correction with the intent to synthesize the way these are handled in a variety of situations that might be encountered in practice. We see that most changes in accounting principles are recorded and reported using the current approach, changes in estimates are accounted for prospectively, and both changes in reporting entities and the correction of errors are handled retroactively.

LEARNING OBJECTIVES   After studying this chapter, you should be able to:

1. Differentiate among the three types of accounting changes and distinguish among the retroactive, current, and prospective approaches to accounting for and reporting accounting changes.
2. Determine the cumulative effect of an accounting change and describe how changes in accounting principle typically are reported.
3. Explain how and why some changes in accounting principle are reported retroactively or prospectively.
4. Explain how and why changes in estimates are reported prospectively.
5. Describe the situations that constitute a change in reporting entity.
6. Understand and apply the four-step process of correcting and reporting errors, regardless of the type of error or the timing of its discovery.

MARTIN'S PEPSI

"How can an accounting change cost a company $55 million?" Martin asked as he handed you the 1996 annual report for PepsiCo, Inc. He had circled a section on the 1996, 1995, 1994 comparative income statements that showed a reduction in 1994 income. The circled section was:

Cumulative Effect of Accounting Changes:
Postemployment benefits (net of income tax benefit of $29)   (55)

"I was comparing profits over the three years shown when I came across this," he continued. "When I bought Pepsi shares last month, I promised myself I would monitor things pretty closely, but it's not as easy as I thought it would be."

As an accounting graduate, you can understand Martin's confusion and proceed to answer his question.

QUESTIONS

1. How would you respond to Martin's question?
2. Are all changes in accounting method reported this way? Are there other accounting changes that are reported differently?

You learned early in your study of accounting that two of the qualitative characteristics of accounting information that contribute to its relevance and reliability are *consistency* and *comparability*. Though we strive to achieve and maintain these financial reporting attributes, we cannot ignore the forces of change. Ours is a dynamic business environment. The economy is increasingly a global one. Technological advances constantly transform both day-to-day operations and the flow of information about those operations. The accounting profession's response to the fluid environment often means issuing new standards that require companies to change accounting methods. Often, developments within an industry or the economy will prompt a company to voluntarily switch methods of accounting or to revise estimates or expectations. In short, change is inevitable. The question then becomes a matter of how best to address change when reporting financial information from year to year.

In the first part of this chapter, we differentiate among the various types of accounting changes that businesses face, with a focus on the most meaningful and least disruptive ways to report those changes. Then, in the second part of the chapter, we direct our attention to a closely related circumstance—the correction of errors.

PART A   ACCOUNTING CHANGES

Accounting changes fall into one of three categories listed in Graphic 21–1.[1]

GRAPHIC   21–1

Types of Accounting Changes

Type of Change	Description	Examples
Change in accounting principle	Change from one generally accepted accounting principle to another.	• Change depreciation methods. • Adopt a new FASB standard. • Change methods of inventory costing. • Change from cost method to equity method, or vice versa. • Change from completed contract to percentage-of-completion, or vice versa.
Change in accounting estimate	Revision of an estimate because of new information or new experience.	• Change estimate of useful life of depreciable asset. • Change estimate of residual value of depreciable asset. • Change estimate of bad debt percentage. • Change estimate of periods benefited by intangible assets. • Change actuarial estimates pertaining to a pension plan.
Change in reporting entity	Change from reporting as one type of entity to another type of entity.	• Consolidate a subsidiary not previously included in consolidated financial statements. • Report consolidated financial statements in place of individual statements.

The correction of an error is another adjustment sometimes made to financial statements that is not actually an accounting change but is accounted for similarly. Errors occur when transactions are either recorded incorrectly or not recorded at all as shown in Graphic 21–2.

GRAPHIC   21–2

Correction of Errors

Type	Description	Examples
Error correction	Correction of an error caused by a transaction being recorded incorrectly or not at all.	• Mathematical mistakes. • Inaccurate physical count of inventory. • Change from the cash basis of accounting to the accrual basis. • Failure to record an adjusting entry. • Recording an asset as an expense, or vice versa. • Fraud or gross negligence.

[1] "Accounting Changes," *Accounting Principles Board Opinion No. 20*, (New York: AICPA, 1971).

Learning objective 1
Differentiate among the three types of accounting changes and distinguish among the retroactive, current, and prospective approaches to accounting for and reporting accounting changes.

Three approaches to reporting accounting changes and error corrections are used, depending on the situation.

1. Using the **retroactive approach,** financial statements issued in previous years are restated to reflect the impact of the change whenever those statements are presented again for comparative purposes. An advantage of this approach is that it achieves comparability among financial statements. All financial statements presented are prepared on the same basis. However, some argue that public confidence in the integrity of financial data suffers when numbers previously reported as correct are later superseded. On the other hand, proponents argue the opposite—that it's impossible to maintain public confidence unless the financial statements are comparable.

    The balance in retained earnings at the beginning of the year is adjusted by the cumulative effect of the change on prior years' income, not only in the company records but also on the face of the statement of shareholders' equity (or statement of retained earnings). Any balances other than retained earnings that would be different after the change also are adjusted as part of the same journal entry.

> The **retroactive approach** offers *consistency* and *comparability*, perhaps at the expense of public confidence.

2. Under the **current approach**, prior years' statements are not restated. Instead, the cumulative effect of the change on prior years' income is determined and is included as a separate component of income in the year of the change. Be sure to notice that this increases or decreases retained earnings for the effect on prior years by way of the current income statement rather than by actually restating income in those prior years as in the retroactive approach.

    Certain key numbers from prior years' statements, however, are restated to reflect the impact of the change and are reported on a pro forma (as-if) basis. The amounts recast this way are income before extraordinary items, net income, and related per share amounts. The pro forma disclosure is intended to mitigate the potential confusion caused by having comparative financial statements not being prepared on the basis of the same accounting methods. Another reporting practice that helps in this regard is that the auditor's report accompanying the financial statements of the change year directs attention to the change by specifically indicating that it has occurred.

    Since prior years' financial statements are not restated under this approach, some argue that financial statement integrity is better maintained. Others argue the opposite—that the lack of consistency and comparability reduces user confidence.

> The cumulative effect on prior years' income is included as a separate component of income under the **current approach**.

> Key income numbers from prior years' statements are reported on a pro forma basis.

3. The **prospective approach** requires neither a restatement of prior years' financial statements nor a current recognition of the past effect of the change. Instead, the change is merely implemented and its effects are reflected in the financial statements of the current and future years only.

> The effects of a change are reflected in the financial statements of only the current and future years under the **prospective approach**.

Now, let's look at each type of accounting change, one at a time, focusing on the selective application of these approaches.

Change in Accounting Principle

Accounting is not an exact science. Professional judgment is required to apply a set of principles, concepts, and objectives to specific sets of circumstances. This means choices must be made. In your study of accounting to date, you've encountered many areas where choices are necessary. For example, management must choose whether to use accelerated or straight-line depreciation. Is FIFO, LIFO, or average cost most appropriate to measure inventories? Would the completed contract or percentage-of-completion method best reflect the performance of our construction operations? Should we adopt a new FASB standard early or wait until it's mandatory? These are but a few of the accounting choices management makes.

Learning objective 2
Determine the cumulative effect of an accounting change and describe how changes in accounting principle typically are reported.

You also probably recall that consistency and comparability are two fundamental qualitative characteristics of accounting information. To achieve these attributes of information, accounting choices, once made, should be consistently followed from year to year. This doesn't mean, though, that methods can never be changed. Changing circumstances might make a new method more appropriate. A change in economic conditions, for instance, might prompt a company to change accounting methods. The most extensive voluntary accounting change ever—a switch by hundreds of companies from FIFO to LIFO in the mid-1970s, for example—was a result of height-

> Although consistency and comparability are desirable, changing to a new method sometimes is appropriate.

ened inflation. Changes within a specific industry, too, can lead a company to switch methods, often to adapt to new technology or to be consistent with others in the industry. And, of course, a change might be mandated. This happens when the FASB issues a new accounting standard. In 1993, all firms were required to switch from accounting for income taxes according to *APB 11*[2] to the method prescribed by *SFAS 109*. For these reasons, it's not uncommon for a company to switch from one accounting method to another. This is called a **change in accounting principle**.

Motivation for Accounting Choices: Decision-Makers' Perspective

It would be nice to think that all accounting choices are made by management in the best interest of fair and consistent financial reporting. Unfortunately, other motives influence the choices among accounting methods and whether to change methods. It has been suggested that the effect of choices on management compensation, on existing debt agreements, and on union negotiations each can affect management's selection of accounting methods.[3] For instance, research has suggested that managers of companies with bonus plans are more likely to choose accounting methods that maximize their bonuses (often those that increase net income).[4] Other research has indicated that the existence and nature of debt agreements and other aspects of a firm's capital structure can influence accounting choices.[5] Whether a company is forbidden from paying dividends if retained earnings fall below a certain level, for example, can affect the choice of accounting methods.

A financial analyst must be aware that different accounting methods used by different firms and by the same firm in different years complicate comparisons. Financial ratios, for example, will differ when different accounting methods are used, even when there are no differences in attributes being compared.

Investors and creditors also should be alert to instances in which companies change accounting methods. They must consider not only the effect on comparability but also possible hidden motivations for making the changes. Are managers trying to compensate for a downturn in actual performance with a switch to methods that artificially inflate reported earnings? Is the firm in danger of violating debt covenants or other contractual agreements regarding financial position? Are executive compensation plans tied to reported performance measures? Fortunately, the nature and effect of changes are reported in the financial statements. Although a justification for a change is provided by management, analysts should be wary of accepting the reported justification at face value without considering a possible hidden agenda.

Choices are not always those that tend to increase income. As you learned in Chapter 8, many companies use the LIFO inventory method because it reduces income and therefore reduces the amount of income taxes that must be paid currently. Also, some very large and visible companies might be reluctant to report high income that might render them vulnerable to union demands, government regulations, or higher taxes.[6]

Let's turn our attention now to situations involving changes in methods and how we account for those changes.

The Current Approach: Most Changes in Accounting Principle

The cumulative effect of a change in accounting principle should be reflected in the financial statements of the change year. Previous financial statements included for comparative purposes should be presented as previously reported. Recall from our earlier discussion that this is the current approach to accounting for a change.

---

[2] *SFAS 96* for those companies that voluntarily adopted that interim standard.

[3] R.L. Watts and J.L. Zimmerman, "Towards a Positive Theory of the Determination of Accounting Standards," *The Accounting Review*, January, 1978, and "Positive Accounting Theory: A Ten Year Perspective," *The Accounting Review*, January, 1990.

[4] For example, see P.M. Healy, "The Effect of Bonus Schemes on Accounting Decisions," *Journal of Accounting and Economics*, April, 1985, and Dhaliwal, D., G. Salamon, and E. Smith, "The Effect of Owner versus Management Control on the Choice of Accounting Methods," *Journal of Accounting and Economics*, July, 1982.

[5] R.M. Bowen., E.W. Noreen, and J.M. Lacy, "Determinants of the Corporate Decision to Capitalize Interest," *Journal of Accounting and Economics*," August, 1981.

[6] This political cost motive is suggested by R.L. Watts and J.L. Zimmerman, "Positive Accounting Theory: A Ten Year Perspective," *The Accounting Review*, January, 1990, and M. Zmijewski and R. Hagerman, "An Income Strategy Approach to the Positive Theory of Accounting Standard Setting/Choice," *Journal of Accounting and Economics*, August, 1981.

Determining the Effect of the Change.   The cumulative effect of a change in accounting principle is the cumulative effect on the income of previous years from having used the previous method rather than the new method. Stated differently, it's the difference between the balance in retained earnings at the beginning of the period of the change and what that balance would have been if the new method had been applied all along.

Here's an example:

ILLUSTRATION   21-1

Change in Accounting Principle

The current approach avoids changing accounting data reported previously.

Universal Semiconductors switched from the SYD depreciation method to straight-line depreciation in 1997. The change affects its precision equipment purchased at the beginning of 1995 at a cost of $60 million. The machinery has an expected useful life of five years and no estimated salvage value.

Cumulative effect of the change:	($ in millions)	
	SYD	**Straight Line**
1995 depreciation	$20 ($60 × $^5/_{15}$)	$12 ($60 ÷ 5)
1996 depreciation	16 ($60 × $^4/_{15}$)	12 ($60 ÷ 5)
Accumulated depreciation and 1995–96 reduction in income	$36	$24

Difference
$12

1. Reporting the Cumulative Income Effect.

The cumulative income effect is reported on the income statement as a separate item of income, between extraordinary items and net income. It should be reported net of the tax effect of the change. In other words, it should be increased or decreased by the difference between income tax expense as reported in previous years and what it would have been if the new accounting method had been used in those years.[7]

If Universal's tax rate is 40%, the cumulative tax effect of the depreciation change would be $4.8 million ($12 million × 40%). This is because, under straight-line depreciation, the reduction of income for depreciation would be $12 million less, causing tax expense to be higher by that amount times the tax rate.[8] The higher tax expense partially offsets the lower depreciation expense when determining the net, after-tax, cumulative effect of the change. Reporting of the cumulative effect is shown here:

The cumulative after-tax effect on prior years' income is a separate item of income between extraordinary items and net income.

Reported as a separate component of income:	($ in millions)	
	1997	**1996**
Income before extraordinary items and accounting change	$xxx	$xxx
Extraordinary gain (loss), net of tax	xx	xx
Cumulative effect of accounting change (net of $4.8 tax)	7.2	
Net income	$xxx	$xxx

7.2
+4.8
12M

Promus Companies reported a change in accounting principle in its 1994 annual report. Notice in Graphic 21–3 that (a) the cumulative effect on prior years is reported in 1994, both in the determination of net income and in the EPS presentation, and (b) the cumulative effect is shown after both discontinued operations and extraordinary items.

---

[7] You should notice that reporting this income amount net of its tax effect is consistent with the way we report other special items on the income statement net of tax. Remember, extraordinary gains and losses are reported separately on the income statement, net of their tax impact, as are discontinued operations.

[8] It actually is the deferred portion of the tax expense that increases rather than the current portion. Because the change is not made for tax purposes, neither taxable income nor the currently payable tax would change. The increase in accounting income, though, would have increased the temporary difference between accounting income and taxable income. Thus, the deferred tax liability (and therefore the deferred portion of income tax expense) would have been higher.

GRAPHIC   21–3

Income Statement Presentation of an Accounting Change—Promus Companies

($ in 000s, except per share amounts)	1994	1993	1992
Income from continuing operations	49,984	74,867	49,577
Earnings from discontinued hotel operations, net of tax provisions of $26,798, $13,869 and $1,401 (Note 2)	36,319	16,926	1,841
Income before extraordinary items and cumulative effect of change in accounting policy	86,303	91,793	51,418
Extraordinary items, net of tax benefit (provision) of $3,415 and $(753) and (Note 7)	—	(5,447)	1,074
Cumulative affect of change in accounting policy, net of tax benefit of $4,317 (Note 4)	(7,932)	—	—
Net Income	$ 78,371	$ 86,346	$ 52,492
Earnings (loss) per share			
Continuing operations	$0.49	$0.73	$0.49
Discontinued operations, net	0.35	0.16	0.02
Extraordinary items, net	—	(0.05)	0.01
Cumulative effect of change in accounting policy, net	(0.08)	—	—
Net income	$0.76	$0.84	$0.52
Average common shares outstanding	102,810	102,562	101,116

Note 4: Change in Accounting Policy

Effective January 1, 1994, Promus changed its accounting policy relating to preopening costs incurred during development of new casino entertainment and hotel projects. Promus's new policy is to defer preopening costs as incurred prior to opening and to expense them upon opening of each project. Previously, Promus had capitalized such costs and amortized them to expense over 36 months from the date of opening. As a result of this change, operating results for the year ended December 31, 1994, reflect the cumulative charge against earnings, net of income taxes, of $7.9 million, or $0.08 per share, to write off the unamortized preopening costs related to projects opened in prior years. Operating results for 1994 also include preopening costs charged to expense of $15.3 million, primarily related to projects opened during 1994.

2. Account Adjustment for the Change.   Besides income, other financial statement amounts usually would have been different if a new method had been applied in previous years. In our illustration, accumulated depreciation would have been less if straight-line rather than SYD depreciation had been used. The balance in this account should be adjusted to reflect the new method:

	($ in millions)
Accumulated depreciation (cumulative effect determined above)	12.0
Deferred tax liability ($12 × 40%)	4.8
Cumulative effect of accounting change (net effect)	7.2

Accumulated depreciation would have been $12 million less and net income $7.2 million more if straight-line rather than SYD depreciation had been used.

The reason for the credit to deferred tax liability requires some explanation. Remember from Chapter 16 that when taxable income is less than pretax accounting income because of a temporary difference, a deferred tax liability is recorded. This liability reflects the tax that eventually will be paid when the difference later reverses and taxable income is higher than pretax accounting income. In our illustration, tax depreciation would have been more than SYD depreciation during the two previous years, but the temporary difference would have been greater still if accounting income had been based on straight-line depreciation.[9] So, we need to increase the deferred tax liability from what it is now to what it would have been if straight-line depreciation had been used the two previous years. It's not necessary to know what the old or new balance is, only that the new balance should be $4.8 million higher.

---

[9] Presently, the accelerated depreciation method prescribed by the tax code is the Modified Accelerated Cost Recovery System (MACRS). The method is described in Chapter 11. For our purposes now, recall that this method produces tax deductions higher in the first years of an asset's useful life than does straight-line (and usually SYD) depreciation. The opposite is true in the later years of the asset's useful life.

Additional Consideration

If the switch had been from straight-line to SYD depreciation, rather than from SYD to straight-line, the effects would have been reversed and the journal entry to record the effects would be:

	($ in millions)	
Cumulative effect of accounting change (net effect)	7.2	
Deferred tax liability ($12 × 40%)	4.8	
Accumulated depreciation (cumulative effect determined above)		12.0

> The effect of the change on certain key income numbers is reported for the current period and on a pro forma (as-if) basis for all prior periods included.

3. Pro Forma Disclosure of Key Income Items.   Remember, prior years' financial statements are *not* restated under the current approach. However, the effect of the change on certain key income numbers should be disclosed for the current period and on a "pro forma" (as if) basis for the financial statements of all prior periods that are included for comparison with the current financial statements. Specifically, income statements should include pro forma restatement of (a) income before extraordinary items, (b) net income, and (c) earnings per share. In other words, these specific items, calculated as if the new method had been in effect in those prior years, are reported as supplemental information.

4. Disclosure Note.   A description of the change, justification for the change, and the effect of the change on the current period's income should be provided in the disclosure notes to the financial statements. When the Quaker Oats Company adopted the LIFO cost flow assumption for valuing the majority of its grocery products inventory, the change was justified as follows:

GRAPHIC   21–4

Disclosure of a Change to LIFO— The Quaker Oats Company

Note 1: Summary of Significant Accounting Policies (in part)
. . . The Company believes that the use of the LIFO method better matches current costs with current revenues. . . .

Frequently, when a company changes depreciation methods, the change will be effective only for assets placed in service after that date. Of course, that means there would be no cumulative effect on prior years' earnings because the change doesn't affect assets depreciated in prior periods.

GRAPHIC   21–5

Change in Depreciation Method for Newly Acquired Assets— Rohm and Haas Company

Note 12: Land, Buildings, and Equipment, Net (in part)
. . . the company changed its method of depreciation for newly acquired buildings and equipment to the straight-line method. The change had no cumulative effect on prior years' earnings but did increase (current year) net earnings by $9 million, or $.14 per share. . . .

Additional Consideration

Companies subject to the reporting requirements of the Securities and Exchange Commission (most public companies) must prepare quarterly financial statements in addition to their annual reports. For interim reporting, the cumulative effect of an accounting change should be reported in the *first* quarter of the fiscal year in which the change is made, even if the change actually is made in a later quarter. The reported amount is the cumulative effect on the income of previous years from using the previous method rather than the new method as of the beginning of that fiscal year. If the change occurs in an interim period other than the first, financial statement information for prechange interim periods are restated to reflect the new accounting method when those prior statements are presented again.[*]

[*]"Reporting Accounting Changes in Interim Financial Statements," *Statement of Financial Accounting Standards No. 3*, (Stamford, Conn.: FASB, 1974).

The Retroactive Approach: Certain Specified Changes in Accounting Principle

Learning objective 3
Explain how and why some changes in accounting principle are reported retroactively or prospectively.

Because of their unique nature, some changes in accounting principle are more appropriately accounted for by the retroactive approach rather than the current approach. For these exceptions to the general manner of treating changes in accounting principle, prior years' financial statements are restated to reflect the use of the new accounting method. Restatement is required for the changes indicated in Graphic 21–6.

GRAPHIC   21–6

Changes in Accounting Principle Requiring Retroactive Restatement

OPENING CASE

Question 2

Prior years' statements are restated under the **retroactive approach**.

1. A retroactive change required by a specific accounting standard
   a. Some FASB statements require retroactive application for the initial transition to the new standards. (Prior years were restated to reflect the loss contingency provisions of *SFAS 11*. The FASB requires restatement of all prior period earnings per share data upon the adoption of the EPS provisions described in the previous chapter. *SFAS 109* states a preference for the restatement of prior years to reflect the liability method of accounting of income taxes but also permits reporting the cumulative effect instead.*
   b. Some FASB statements and other authoritative pronouncements require retroactive application for specific changes in accounting methods. (For a change from the cost method to the equity method of accounting for long-term investments, *APB 18* requires the retroactive application of the equity method.)
2. A change from the LIFO method to another inventory valuation method.
3. A change from the percentage of completion to the completed contract method (or vice versa) in accounting for long-term construction contracts.
4. A change to or from the full cost method in the oil and gas and other extractive industries.†
5. Changes made when a closely held corporation first issues financial statements to obtain equity financing, for registering securities, or for effecting a business combination.

*"Accounting for Contingencies – Transition Method," *Statement of Financial Accounting Standards No. 11*, (Stamford, Conn.: FASB, 1975); "Earnings per Share," *Statement of Financial Accounting Standards No. 128*, (Norwalk, Conn.: FASB, 1997); "Accounting for Income Taxes," *Statement of Financial Accounting Standards No. 109*, (Norwalk, Conn.: FASB, 1992). Pro forma amounts are not required when a company chooses to report the cumulative effect due to complexity and cost of doing so—the same reason restatement is not mandatory.
†Extensive discussion of accounting by extractive industries is beyond the scope of this text.

Beginning retained earnings of the earliest year reported is adjusted for any portion of the cumulative income effect attributable to years prior to those reported.

These exceptions receive special treatment—restating prior years for the income effect of the change, rather than reporting that effect as part of income in the year the change occurs. The predominant reason is that the effect of these changes usually is quite large. Not only would net income be distorted in the year of the change if the total effect is recognized currently, but prior statements would be rendered meaningless if not restated.

Financial statements are restated for each year reported for comparative purposes, and the income effect for years prior to those reported is accounted for as an adjustment to beginning retained earnings of the earliest year reported.

ILLUSTRATION   21–2

Changes in Principle Requiring Retroactive Restatement

Account balances are adjusted to what they would have been if the new method had been used in previous years.

Traci Wright Fashions had used the LIFO method of costing inventories but at the beginning of 1998 decided to change to the FIFO method. The inventory as reported at the end of 1997 using LIFO would have been $20 million higher using FIFO.

Retained earnings had been reported at the end of 1996 and 1997 as $240 million and $260 million, respectively (reflecting the LIFO method). Those amounts reflecting the FIFO method would have been $250 million and $272 million, respectively. 1997 net income had been reported at the end of 1997 as $28 million (LIFO method) but would have been $30 million using FIFO. After changing to FIFO, 1998 net income was $36 million. Dividends of $8 million were paid each year. The tax rate is 40%.

The journal entry to record the change in principle at the beginning of 1998 would be:

	($ in millions)	
Inventory (additional inventory if FIFO had been used)	20	
Retained earnings (additional net income if FIFO had been used)		12
Deferred tax liability (40% × $20 million)		8

Retained earnings is increased by $12 million because the net income in years prior to 1998 would have been higher by that amount, and net income increases retained earnings. Changing inventory methods for financial reporting requires the same change for tax purposes. The Internal Revenue Code requires that taxes saved previously from having used another inventory method ($8 million in this case) must now be repaid (over no longer than 6 years). In the meantime, there is temporary book-tax difference for the inventory account, reflected in the deferred tax liability.

Net income, which was reported in 1997 as $28 million would be restated to $30 million in the 1998–1997 comparative income statements. The comparative income statements and balance sheets also would be restated to reflect the following items as if the FIFO method had been used in 1997:

> Earnings per share
> Inventory (and total assets)
> Retained earnings (and total shareholders' equity)

Because the switch to FIFO occurred at the beginning of 1998, after the journal entry above, the 1998 numbers already reflect the new method.

The change would be reflected in the 1998–1997 comparative statements of shareholders' equity by adjusting the beginning balance of retained earnings for any portion of the cumulative income effect attributable to years prior to 1997. The adjusted balance is then followed by any increases or decreases to retained earnings during the year (net income, dividends, etc.).

Prior years' financial statements are restated to reflect the use of the new accounting method.

TRACI WRIGHT FASHIONS
Statement of Shareholders' Equity
For the Years Ended Dec. 31, 1998 and 1997

($ in millions)

	Common Stock	Additional Paid-in Capital	Retained Earnings	Total Shareholders' Equity
Balance at Jan. 1, 1997			240	
Adjustment due to change from the LIFO to the FIFO method of accounting for inventories			10*	
Balance at Jan. 1 as adjusted			250	
Net income (restated to FIFO)			30†	
Cash dividends			(8)	
Balance at Dec. 31, 1997			272	
Net income (using FIFO)			36	
Cash dividends			(8)	
Balance at Dec. 31, 1998			300	

* Difference in net income before 1997: $250 million – $240 million
† (given)

Because it's the earliest year reported, 1997's beginning retained earnings is adjusted for the portion of the cumulative income effect attributable to years prior to those reported.

Similarly, if three-year comparative statements were provided, it would be the balance in retained earnings at the beginning of *1996* that would be adjusted for any portion of the cumulative income effect attributable to years prior to 1996. Retained earnings is adjusted for the earliest year reported in the comparative statements.

A disclosure note from an annual report of SPS Technologies, Inc., is shown in Graphic 21–7 that illustrates the footnote description of a change from the LIFO method to another inventory valuation method.

GRAPHIC   21–7

Change in Accounting Principle: Retroactive Approach—SPS Technologies, Inc.

A change from the LIFO method to another method of costing inventory is a change in principle requiring retroactive restatement.

Note 2: Change in Accounting Principle

During the first quarter of 1990, the Company changed its basis of valuing inventories in the United States from the last-in, first-out (LIFO) method to the average cost method. In 1989 and prior years, the cost of substantially all inventories in the United States, except tools, was determined using the LIFO method. The change to the average cost method will conform all inventories of the Company to the same method of valuation. The Company believes that the average cost method of inventory valuation provides a more meaningful presentation of the financial position of the Company since it reflects more recent costs in the balance sheet. Under the current economic environment of low inflation and an expected reduction in inventories and lower production costs, the Company believes that the average cost method also results in a better matching of current costs with current revenues.

The effect of the change in accounting principle was to reduce the net loss reported for 1990 by $318,000, or $.06 per share. The change has been applied to prior years by retroactively restating the financial statements as required by generally accepted accounting principles. The effect of this restatement was to increase retained earnings as of January 1, 1988, by $9,579,000. The restatement decreased 1989 net earnings by $1,871,000, or $37 per share and increased 1988 net earnings by $2,234,000, or $45 per share.

The Prospective Approach: Certain Specified Changes in Accounting Principle

Question 2

It usually is impractical for a company changing to LIFO to report the cumulative income effect.

A Change to the LIFO Method.   When a company changes to the LIFO inventory method from another inventory method, accounting records of prior years usually are inadequate to determine the cumulative income effect of the change or to determine pro forma disclosures for prior years. It would be necessary, for instance, to make assumptions as to when specific LIFO inventory layers were created in years prior to the change. Because of the impracticality of doing so, a company changing to LIFO does not report the cumulative income effect in current income nor revise the balance in retained earnings. Instead, the base year inventory for all future LIFO calculations is the beginning inventory in the year the LIFO method is adopted. The only disclosure required is a footnote to the financial statements describing the nature of and justification for the change, the effect of the change on current period earnings, and an explanation as to why the cumulative income effect was omitted. When the Penn Central Corporation adopted the LIFO cost flow assumption for valuing its communications wire and cable inventories, the change was reported as follows:

GRAPHIC   21–8

Disclosure of a Change to LIFO—The Penn Central Corporation

> ### Note 6: Inventories (in part)
> Effective January 1, 1990, the Company changed its method of valuing a significant component of its communications wire and cable inventories from the FIFO to the LIFO method. Management believes the LIFO method results in a better matching of current costs with current revenues.
>
> The effect of the change in 1990 was to decrease net income by $16 million, or $.03 per share. The cumulative effect of this accounting change and the pro forma effects on prior years' earnings have not been included because such effects are not reasonably determinable.

A related situation occurred when Kmart changed price indexes used in determining LIFO inventories:

GRAPHIC   21–9

Disclosure of a Change in Method of Determining Inventories—Kmart Corporation

> ### Note F: Merchandise Inventories (in part)
> During 1990, the company changed its method of accounting for LIFO inventories in U.S. Kmart stores. Prior to 1990, the company used the U.S. Department of Labor's Department Store Price Index to measure inflation in retail prices. In 1990, the company developed and used internal price indices to measure inflation in the retail prices of its merchandise inventories. The company believes the use of internal indices results in a more accurate measurement of the impact of inflation in the prices of merchandise sold in its stores. This change reduced the LIFO charge in 1990 by $105 million net of tax, or $52 per share. The company was not able to determine the cumulative effect of this change nor the impact on any individual year prior to 1990.

Some new accounting standards require or permit prospective application of the new standard.

Mandated by New Accounting Standards.   A few changes mandated by new accounting standards require or permit prospective application of the new standard. Examples are *SFAS 87*, "Employers' Accounting for Pensions,"[10] and *SFAS 106*, "Employers' Accounting for Postretirement Benefits Other than Pensions," in which the transition amount due to changing from the old standard must (*SFAS 87*) or may (*SFAS 106*) be amortized to expense on a prospective basis over the average remaining service life of those employed on the transition date.[11]

Regardless of whether a change is accounted for currently, retroactively, or prospectively, the most important responsibility is to communicate to users of the financial statements that a change has occurred as well as the nature and effect of the change.

---

[10] "Employers' Accounting for Pensions," *Statement of Financial Accounting Standards No. 87*, (Stamford, Conn.: FASB, 1985).

[11] The transition amounts for the two standards are discussed in Chapter 17 and Chapter 18.

Change in Accounting Estimate

You've encountered many instances during your study of accounting in which it's necessary to make estimates of uncertain future events. Depreciation, for example, entails estimates not only of the useful lives of depreciable assets, but their anticipated salvage values as well. Anticipating uncollectible accounts receivable, predicting warranty expenses, amortizing intangible assets, and making actuarial assumptions for pension benefits are but a few of the accounting tasks that require estimates.

Learning objective 4
Explain how and why changes in estimates are reported prospectively.

Accordingly, estimates are an inherent aspect of accounting. Unfortunately, though, estimates routinely turn out to be wrong. No matter how carefully known facts are considered and forecasts are prepared, new information and experience frequently force the revision of estimates.[12] Of course, if the original estimate was based on erroneous information or calculations or was not made in good faith, the revision of that estimate constitutes the correction of an error.

Revisions are viewed as a natural consequence of making estimates.

Changes in estimates are accounted for prospectively. When a company revises a previous estimate, prior financial statements are *not* restated, nor is a cumulative effect of the change included in current income. Instead, the company merely incorporates the new estimate in any related accounting determinations from then on. So, it usually will affect some aspects of both the balance sheet and the income statement in the current period and future periods. A disclosure note should describe the effect of a change in estimate on income before extraordinary items, net income, and related per-share amounts for the current period.

OPENING CASE

Question 2

A change in estimate is reflected in the financial statements of the current period and future periods.

When Owens-Corning Fiberglass revised estimates of the useful lives of some of its depreciable assets, the change was disclosed in its annual report as shown in Graphic 21–10.

GRAPHIC   21–10

Change in Estimate—Owens-Corning Fiberglass Corporation

Note 6: Depreciation of Plant and Equipment

During 1993, the Company completed a review of its fixed asset lives. The Company determined that as a result of actions taken to increase its preventative maintenance and programs initiated with its equipment suppliers to increase the quality of their products, actual lives for certain asset categories were generally longer than the useful lives for depreciation purposes. Therefore, the Company extended the estimated useful lives of certain categories of plant and equipment, effective April 1, 1993. The effect of this change in estimate reduced depreciation expense for the year ended December 31, 1993, by $14 million and increased income before cumulative effect of accounting change by $8 million ($.19 per

Here's an example of another change in estimate.

ILLUSTRATION   21–3

Change in Accounting Estimate

Universal Semiconductors estimates bad debt expense as 2% of credit sales. After a review during 1997, Universal determined that 3% of credit sales is a more realistic estimate of its collection experience. Credit sales in 1997 are $300 million. The effective income tax rate is 40%.

Neither bad debt expense nor the allowance for uncollectible accounts reported in prior years is restated. No account balances are adjusted. The cumulative effect of the estimate change is not reported in current income. Rather, in 1997 and later years, the adjusting entry to record bad debt expense simply will reflect the new percentage. In 1997, the entry would be:

($ in millions)

Bad debt expense (3% × $300 million)	9	
Allowance for uncollectible accounts		9

---

[12] By far the most common estimate change is a revision of estimates regarding actuarial assumptions used in accounting for pension plans. Over the past several years an average of about 35% of surveyed companies reported changes in these estimates. A distant second are changes in depreciable lives. AICPA, *Accounting Trends and Techniques,* 1995.

The after-tax effect of the change in estimate is $1.8 million [$300 million $\times$ (3% − 2%) = $3 million, less 40% of $3 million]. Assuming 100 million outstanding shares of common stock, the effect is described in a disclosure note to the financial statements as follows:

Note A: Accounts Receivable

In 1997, the company revised the percentage used to estimate bad debts. The change provides a better indication of collection experience. The effect of the change was to decrease 1997 net income by $1.8 million, or $.018 per share.

Sometimes, it's not easy to distinguish between a change in principle and a change in estimate. For example, if a company begins to capitalize rather than expense the cost of tools because their benefits beyond one year become apparent, the change could be construed as either a change in principle or a change in the estimated life of the asset. When the distinction is not possible, the change should be treated as a change in estimate.

> When it's not possible to distinguish between a change in principle and a change in estimate, the change should be treated as a change in estimate.

ETHICAL DILEMMA

The net income of Union Carbide increased in 1980 by over $200 million, due almost entirely to three changes in accounting principle: (a) the depreciation method was changed, resulting in lower expense, (b) interest costs during construction were capitalized rather than expensed, and (c) the method for recognizing investment tax credits (not available under current tax law) was changed to a method that reduced expenses.
 What ethical question does this situation suggest?

Change in Reporting Entity

A reporting entity can be a single company, or it can be a group of companies that reports a single set of financial statements. For example, the consolidated financial statements of Philip Morris Cos., Inc., report the financial position and results of operations not only for the parent tobacco company but also for its subsidiaries which include Kraft General Foods. Sometimes, changes occur that cause the financial statements to be those of a different reporting entity. The issuance of *SFAS 94*, "Consolidation of All Majority-Owned Subsidiaries," resulted in hundreds of reporting entities being altered to include previously unconsolidated finance subsidiaries. For instance, General Motors' consolidated financial statements now include its finance subsidiary, GMAC, as part of the reporting entity. A **change in reporting entity** occurs as a result of (1) presenting consolidated financial statements in place of statements of individual companies, (2) changing specific companies that constitute the group for which consolidated or combined statements are prepared, or (3) a business combination accounted for as a pooling of interests.[13]

A change in reporting entity is reported by restating all previous periods' financial statements as if the new reporting entity existed in those periods.[14] In the first set of financial statements after the change, a disclosure note should describe the nature of the change and the reason it occurred. Also, the effect of the change on net income, income before extraordinary items, and related per share amounts should be indicated for all periods presented. These disclosures aren't necessary in subsequent financial statements. Hewlett-Packard Company changed the composition of its reporting entity in response to *SFAS 94* and described it this way:

> **Learning objective 5**
> Describe the situations that constitute a change in reporting entity.

> The issuance of *SFAS 94* resulted in many companies consolidating previously unconsolidated subsidiaries.

> A change in reporting entity requires that financial statements of prior periods be retroactively restated to report the financial information for the new reporting entity in all periods.

GRAPHIC   21−11

Change in Reporting Entity— Hewlett-Packard Company

Note 12: Accounting and Reporting Changes (in part)

The Company implemented *Statement of Financial Accounting Standards No. 94 (SFAS 94),* Consolidation of All Majority-Owned Subsidiaries," in fiscal 1989. With the adoption of *SFAS 94,* the company consolidated the accounts of Hewlett-Packard Finance Company (HPFC), a wholly-owned subsidiary previously accounted for under the equity method, with those of the company. The change resulted in an increase in consolidated assets and liabilities but did not have a material effect on the company's financial position. Since HPFC was previously accounted for under the equity method, the change did not affect net earnings. Prior years' consolidated financial information has been restated to reflect this change for comparative purposes.

---

[13] A pooling of interests is a method of accounting used when two or more companies combine to operate essentially as a single company. This and other accounting issues pertaining to business combinations are discussed in advanced accounting or consolidations courses.

[14] When those statements are presented again for comparative purposes.

Error Correction

The correction of an error is not actually an accounting change but is accounted for similarly. In fact, it's accounted for retroactively like a change in reporting entity and like some changes in accounting principle.

More specifically, previous years' financial statements that were incorrect as a result of the error are retroactively restated to reflect the correction. And, of course, any account balances that are incorrect as a result of the error are corrected by a journal entry. If retained earnings is one of the incorrect accounts, the correction is reported as a prior period adjustment to the beginning balance in a statement of shareholders' equity (or statement of retained earnings if that's presented instead).[15] And, as for accounting changes, a disclosure note is needed to describe the nature of the error and the impact of its correction on operations. We discuss the correction of errors in more detail in Part B of this chapter. But first, let's compare the three approaches for reporting accounting changes and error corrections:

> Previous years' financial statements are retroactively restated to reflect the correction of an error.

GRAPHIC   21–12

Approaches to Reporting Accounting Changes and Error Corrections

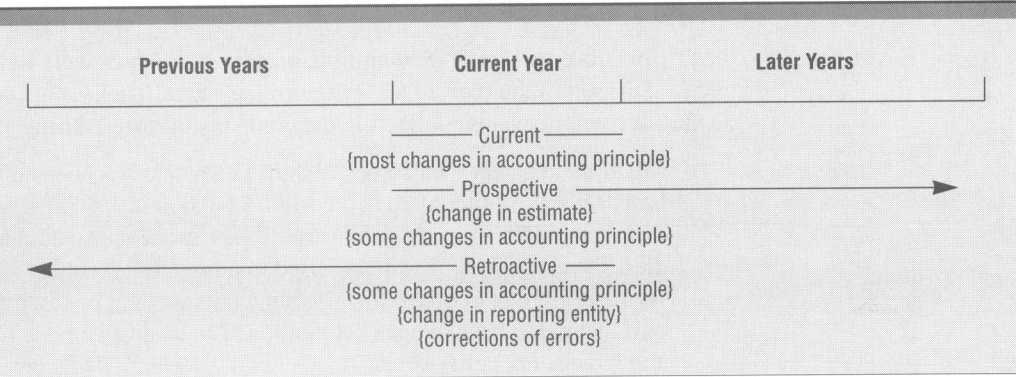

A comparison of accounting treatments is provided by Graphic 21–13.

GRAPHIC   21–13

Accounting Changes and Errors: A Summary

	Change in Accounting Principle			Change in Estimate	Change in Reporting Entity	Error
	Most Changes	**Retroactive Exceptions[1]**	**Prospective Exceptions[2]**			
Method of accounting	Current	Retroactive	Prospective	Prospective	Retroactive	Retroactive
Restate prior years' statements?	No	Yes	No	No	Yes	Yes
Pro forma disclosures of income and EPS ?	Yes	No	No	No	No	No
Cumulative effect on prior years' income reported:	On income statement between E.O. items and net income.	As adjustment to retained earnings of earliest year reported.[3]	Not reported.[4]	Not reported.	Not reported.	As adjustment to retained earnings of earliest year reported.[3]
Journal entry	To record cumulative income effect and adjust affected balances to new method.	To adjust retained earnings and any other affected balances to the new method.	None, but subsequent accounting is affected by the change.	None, but subsequent accounting is affected by the new estimate.	Involves consolidated financial statements discussed in other courses.	To correct any balances that are incorrect as a result of the error.
Disclosure note?	Yes	Yes	Yes	Yes	Yes	Yes

[1] See Graphic 21–6, page 918.
[2] Change to LIFO and certain mandated changes.
[3] On the statement of shareholders' equity or statement of retained earnings.
[4] Transition amount disclosed for some new standards.

---

[15] "Prior Period Adjustments," *Statement of Financial Accounting Standards No. 16*, (Stamford, Conn.: FASB, 1977).

Modern Business Machines began operations in 1992. The 1997 financial statements reported net income as follows:

($ in millions, except per share amount)	
Revenues	$500
Cost of goods sold	(180)
Gross profit	320
Operating expenses	(175)
Income before taxes	145
Income tax expense	(58)
Net income	$ 87
Earnings per common share: (100 million shares)	$ 0.87

In 1998, revenues were $590 million, operating expenses were $190 million, and the company realized a $10 million (before tax) extraordinary gain. The tax rate is 40% for all years. The following accounting changes affecting the company occurred during 1998:

1. MBM has a patent on a copier design. The patent has been amortized on a straight-line basis since it was acquired at a cost of $340,000 in 1995. During 1998, it was decided that the benefits from the patent would be experienced over a total of 10 years rather than the 17-year legal life now being used to amortize its cost.
2. At the beginning of 1998, MBM changed its method of valuing inventory from the FIFO cost method to the average cost method. The change is made for both financial reporting and income tax purposes. At December 31, 1997, MBM's inventories were $205 million on a FIFO cost basis. Inventories would have totaled $170 million at December 31, 1997, if determined on an average cost basis. The difference was reflected in cost of goods sold as follows:

Cost of Goods Sold ($ in millions)			
	FIFO	Average Cost	Difference
1992–1996	$600	$625	$25
1997	180	190	10
1998	230	240	10
			$45

Required:

Prepare all journal entries needed in 1998 related to each change. Also, briefly describe any other measures MBM would take in connection with reporting the changes. Prepare comparative income statements for 1998 and 1997.

1. Change in estimate

	($ in 000s)
Patent amortization expense (determined below)	40
Patent	40

Calculation of annual amortization after the estimate change:

	$340,000	Cost
$20,000		Old annual amortization ($340,000 ÷ 17 years)
× 3 years	(60,000)	Amortization to date (1995, 1996, 1997)
	280,000	Unamortized cost
	÷ 7	Estimated remaining life (10 years − 3 years)
	$ 40,000	New annual amortization

A disclosure note should describe the effect of a change in estimate on income before extraordinary items, net income, and related per-share amounts for the current period.

2. Change in principle

	($ in millions)
Cumulative effect of accounting change (net effect)	21
Income tax payable ($35 million × 40%)	14
Inventory ($205 million – 170 million)	35

The cumulative income effect is reported on the income statement as a separate item of income between extraordinary items and net income. It should be reported net of the $14 million tax effect of the change.

Income statements should include pro forma restatement of (a) income before extraordinary items, (b) net income, and (c) earnings per share for both income amounts. In other words, these specific items, calculated as if the new method had been in effect in those prior years, are reported as supplemental information. Also, the nature of and justification for the change should be described in the disclosure notes to the financial statements.

Comparative Income Statements

($ in millions, except per share amounts)	**1998**	**1997**
Revenues	$590	$500
Cost of goods sold	(240)	(180)
Gross profit	350	320
Operating expenses	(190)	(175)
Income before taxes	160	145
Income tax expense	(64)	(58)
Income before extraordinary item and accounting change	96	87
Extraordinary gain (net of $4 tax)	6	
Cumulative effect of accounting change (net of $14 tax benefit)	(21)	
Net income	$ 81	$ 87
Earnings per share:		
Before extraordinary item and accounting change	$ .96	$ .87
Extraordinary gain	.06	
Cumulative effect of accounting change	(.21)	
Earnings per share	$ .81	$ .87
Pro forma amounts assuming the change is applied retroactively:		
Income before extraordinary items	$ 96	$ 81*
Per common share	$0.96	$0.81
Net income	$ 102†	$ 81†
Earnings per common share	$1.02	$0.81

*$87 million – ([$190 million – $180 million] less tax)
 $87 million – ($10 million less 40% of $10 million)
  $87 million – $6 million
†$96 million + $6 million extraordinary gain

PART
B

CORRECTION OF ACCOUNTING ERRORS

Nobody's perfect. People make mistakes, even accountants. When errors are discovered, they should be corrected.[16] The following graphic describes the steps to be taken to correct an error, if the effect of the error is material.[17]

Learning objective 6
Understand and apply the four-step process of correcting and reporting errors, regardless of the type of error or the timing of its discovery.

[16] Interestingly, it appears that not all accounting errors are unintentional. Research has shown that firms with errors that overstate income are more likely "to have diffuse ownership, lower growth in earnings and fewer income-increasing GAAP alternatives available, and are less likely to have audit committees," suggesting that "overstatement errors are the result of managers responding to economic incentives." M. L. DeFond. and J. Jiambalvo., "Incidence and Circumstances of Accounting Errors," *The Accounting Review*, July, 1991.

[17] In practice, the vast majority of errors are not material with respect to their effect on the financial statements and are, therefore, simply corrected in the year discovered (step 1 only).

GRAPHIC   21–14

Steps to Correct an Error

The retroactive approach is used for the correction of errors.

The correction of an error is treated as a prior period adjustment.

1. A journal entry is made to correct any account balances that are incorrect as a result of the error.
2. Previous years' financial statements that were incorrect as a result of the error are retroactively restated to reflect the correction (for all years reported again for comparative purposes).
3. If retained earnings is one of the accounts incorrect as a result of the error, the correction is reported as a prior period adjustment to the beginning balance in a statement of shareholders' equity (or Statement of retained earnings if that's presented instead).
4. A disclosure note should describe the nature of the error and the impact of its correction on net income.

Prior Period Adjustments

Before we see these steps applied to the correction of an error, one of the steps requires elaboration. As discussed in Chapter 3, the correction of errors is the more common of only two situations that are considered to be prior period adjustments.[18] A prior period adjustment refers to an addition to or reduction in the beginning retained earnings balance in a statement of shareholders' equity (or statement of retained earnings if that's presented instead).

In an earlier chapter we saw that a statement of shareholders' equity is the most commonly used way to report the events that cause components of shareholders' equity to change during a particular reporting period. Some companies, though, choose to report the changes that occur in the balance of retained earnings separately in a statement of retained earnings. When it's discovered that the ending balance of retained earnings in the period prior to the discovery of an error was incorrect as a result of that error, the balance must be corrected when it appears as the beginning balance the following year. However, simply reporting a corrected amount might cause misunderstanding for someone familiar with the previously reported amount. Explicitly reporting a prior period adjustment on the statement itself avoids this confusion. Assume, for example, the following comparative statements of retained earnings:

A statement of retained earnings reports the events that cause changes in retained earnings.

Statement of Retained Earnings
For the Years Ended December 31, 1999 and 1998

	1999	1998
Balance at beginning of year	$600,000	$450,000
Net income	400,000	350,000
Less: Dividends	(200,000)	(200,000)
Balance at end of year	$800,000	$600,000

Now suppose that in 2000 it's discovered that an error in 1998 caused that year's net income to be overstated by $20,000 (it should have been $330,000). This means retained earnings both years were overstated. Comparative statements the following year, when the error is discovered, would include a prior period adjustment as shown below:

Statement of Retained Earnings
For the Years Ended December 31, 2000 and 1999

	2000	1999
Balance at beginning of year	$ 780,000	$600,000
Prior period adjustment		(20,000)
Corrected balance		$580,000
Net income	500,000	400,000
Less: Dividends	(200,000)	*(200,000)
Balance at end of year	$1,080,000	$780,000

The incorrect balance as previously reported is corrected by the prior period adjustment.

At least two years' (as in our example) and often three years' statements are reported in comparative financial statements. The prior period adjustment is applied to beginning retained earnings for the year following the error, or for the earliest year being reported in the comparative financial statements when the error occurs prior to the earliest year presented.[19]

---

[18] The other is an adjustment that results from the realization of income tax benefits of preacquisition operating loss carryforwards of purchased subsidiaries. See "Prior Period Adjustments," *Statement of Financial Accounting Standards No. 16* (Stamford, Conn: FASB, 1977). This situation arises in connection with consolidations which is covered in many advanced accounting courses.

[19] The retained earnings balances in years after the first year also are adjusted to what those balances would be if the error had not occurred, but a company may choose not to explicitly report those adjustments as separate line items.

Error Correction Illustrated

Now let's discuss these procedures to correct errors in the context of a variety of the most common types of errors. Since there are literally thousands of possibilities, it's not practical to describe every error in every stage of its discovery. However, by applying the process to the situations described below, you should become sufficiently comfortable with the *process* that you could apply it to whatever situation you might encounter.

> You shouldn't try to memorize how specific errors are corrected; you should learn the *process* needed to analyze whatever errors you might encounter.

As you study these examples, be sure to notice that it's significantly more complicated to deal with an error if (a) it affected net income in the reporting period in which it occurred and (b) it is not discovered until a later period.

Error Discovered in the Same Reporting Period that It Occurred

If an accounting error is made and discovered in the same accounting period, the original erroneous entry should simply be reversed and the appropriate entry recorded. The possibilities are limitless. Let's look at the one in Illustration 21–4.

ILLUSTRATION   21–4

Error Discovered in the Same Reporting Period that It Occurred

G.H. Little, Inc., paid $3 million for replacement computers and recorded the expenditure as maintenance expense. The error was discovered a week later.

To reverse erroneous entry	($ in millions)	
Cash	3	
Maintenance expense		3
To record correct entry		
Equipment	3	
Cash		3

Note: These entries can, of course, be combined.

Error Affecting Previous Financial Statements, but Not Net Income

If an error did *not* affect net income in the year it occurred, it's relatively easy to correct. Examples are incorrectly recording salaries payable as accounts payable, recording a loss as an expense, or classifying a cash flow as an investing activity rather than a financing activity on the statement of cash flows.

ILLUSTRATION   21–5

Error Affecting Previous Financial Statements, but Not Net Income

Step 1

Step 2

Step 3

Step 4

MDS Transportation incorrectly recorded a $2 million note receivable as accounts receivable. The error was discovered a year later.

To correct incorrect accounts	($ in millions)	
Note receivable	2	
Accounts receivable		2

When reported for comparative purposes in the current year's annual report, last year's balance sheet would be restated to report the note as it should have been reported last year. Since last year's net income was not affected by the error, the balance in retained earnings was not incorrect. So no prior period adjustment to that account is necessary. A disclosure note would describe the nature of the error, but there would be no impact on net income, income before extraordinary items, and earnings per share to report.

Error Affecting a Prior Year's Net Income

Most errors affect net income in some way. When they do, they affect the balance sheet as well. Both statements must be retroactively restated; the statement of cash flows sometimes is affected, too. As with any error, all incorrect account balances must be corrected. Because these errors affect income, one of the balances that will require correcting is retained earnings. Complicating matters, income taxes often are affected by income errors. In those cases, amended tax returns are prepared either to pay additional taxes or to claim a tax refund for taxes overpaid.

In the illustrations that follow (except as indicated), we ignore the tax effects of the errors and their correction to allow us to focus on the errors themselves rather than their tax aspects.

In 1997, internal auditors discovered that Seidman Distribution, Inc. had debited an expense account for the $7 million cost of sorting equipment purchased at the beginning of 1995. The equipment's useful life was expected to be five years with no residual value. Straight-line depreciation is used by Seidman.

Analysis:

($ in millions)

	Correct (Should have been recorded)			Incorrect (As recorded)		
1995	Equipment	7.0		Expense	7.0	
	Cash		7.0	Cash		7.0
1995	Expense	1.4		Depreciation entry omitted		
	Accum. deprec.		1.4			
1996	Expense	1.4		Depreciation entry omitted		
	Accum. deprec.		1.4			

During the two-year period, depreciation expense was understated by $2.8 million, but other expenses were overstated by $7 million, so net income during the period was understated by $4.2 million. This means retained earnings is currently understated by that amount.
Accumulated depreciation is understated by $2.8 million.

To correct incorrect accounts   ($ in millions)

Equipment	7.0	
Accumulated depreciation		2.8
Retained earnings		4.2

The 1995 and 1996 financial statements that were incorrect as a result of the error are retroactively restated to report the equipment acquired and to reflect the correct amount of depreciation expense and accumulated depreciation, assuming both statements are reported again for comparative purposes in the 1997 annual report.

Because retained earnings is one of the accounts that are incorrect as a result of the error, a correction to that account of $4.2 million is reported as a prior period adjustment to the 1997 beginning retained earnings balance in Seidman's comparative statements of shareholders' equity. A correction would be made also to the 1996 beginning retained earnings balance. That prior period adjustment, though, would be for the pre-1996 difference: $7 million − 1.4 million = $5.6 million. If 1995 statements also are included in the comparative report, no adjustment would be necessary for that period because the error didn't occur until after the beginning of 1995.

Also, a disclosure note accompanying Seidman's 1997 financial statements should describe the nature of the error and the impact of its correction on each year's net income (understated by $5.6 million in 1995 and overstated by $1.4 million in 1996), income before extraordinary items (same as net income), and earnings per share.

The effect of most errors is different, depending on **when** the error is discovered. For example, if the error in Illustration 21–6 is not discovered until 1998, rather than 1997, accumulated depreciation would be understated by another $1.4 million, or a total of $4.2 million. If not discovered until 2001 or after, no correcting entry at all would be needed. By then, the sum of the omitted depreciation amounts ($1.4 million × 5 years) would equal the expense incorrectly recorded in 1995 ($7 million), so the retained earnings balance would be the same as if the error never had occurred. Also, the asset would have been disposed of—if the useful life estimate was correct—so neither the equipment nor accumulated depreciation would need to be recorded. Of course, any statements of prior years that were affected and are reported again in comparative statements still would be restated, and a footnote would describe the error.

Most errors, in fact, eventually self-correct. An example of an uncommon instance in which an error never self-corrects would be an expense account debited for the cost of land. Because land doesn't depreciate, the error would continue indefinitely, unless the land is sold.

Some errors correct themselves the following year. For instance, if a company's ending inventory is incorrectly counted or otherwise misstated, the income statement would be in error for the year of the error and the following year, but the balance sheet would be incorrect only for the year the error occurs. After that, all account balances will be correct. This is demonstrated in Illustration 21–7.

Additional Consideration

We ignored the tax impact of the error and its correction in our previous example (Illustration 21–6). To consider taxes, we need to know whether depreciation was also omitted from the tax return and the depreciation methods used for tax reporting. Let's say that depreciation was omitted from the tax return also, and that straight-line depreciation is used by Seidman for both tax and financial reporting. The tax rate is 40%.

Total operating expenses (nontax) still would have been overstated by $4.2 million over the two-year period. But that would have caused taxable income to be understated and the tax liability and income tax expense to be understated by 40% of $4.2 million, or $1.68 million. So net income and retained earnings would have been understated by only $2.52 million:

Operating expenses *overstated*	$4.20 million
Income tax expense *understated*	(1.68) million
Net income (and retained earnings) *understated*	$2.52 million

To correct incorrect accounts: ($ in millions)

Equipment	7.00	
Accumulated depreciation		2.80
Income tax payable (40% × $4.2 million)		1.68
Retained earnings		2.52

If depreciation had been omitted from the income statement but not from the tax return, or if accelerated depreciation was used for tax reporting but straight-line depreciation for financial reporting, the credit to income tax payable in the correcting entry would be replaced by a credit to deferred tax liability.

ILLUSTRATION   21–7

Error Affecting Net Income: Inventory Misstated

When analyzing inventory errors or other errors that affect cost of goods sold, you may find it helpful to visualize the determination of cost of goods sold, net income, and retained earnings.

In early 1997, Overseas Wholesale Supply discovered that $1 million of inventory had been inadvertently excluded from its 1995 ending inventory count.

Analysis:

U = Understated   O = Overstated

1995		1996	
Beginning inventory		Beginning inventory	U
Plus: Net purchases		Plus: Net purchases	
Less: Ending inventory	U	Less: Ending inventory	
Cost of goods sold	O	Cost of goods sold	U
Revenues		Revenues	
Less: Cost of goods sold	O	Less: Cost of goods sold	U
Less: Other expenses		Less: Other expenses	
Net income	U	Net income	O
Retained earnings	U	Retained earnings	*corrected*

If error discovered in 1996 (before closing):   ($ in millions)

Inventory	1	
Retained earnings		1

If error discovered in 1997 or later:

No correcting entry needed

If the error is discovered in 1996, the 1995 financial statements that were incorrect as a result of the error are retroactively restated to reflect the correct inventory amounts, cost of goods sold, and retained earnings when those statements are reported again for comparative purposes in the 1996 annual report. If the error is discovered in 1997, the 1996 financial statements also are retroactively restated to reflect the correct inventory amounts and cost of goods sold (retained earnings would not require adjustment), even though no correcting entry would be needed at that point.

Because retained earnings is one of the accounts incorrect if the error is discovered in 1996, the correction to that account is reported as a prior period adjustment to the 1996 beginning retained earnings balance in Overseas' statement of shareholders' equity. Of course, no prior period adjustment is needed if the error isn't discovered until 1997 or later.

Also, a disclosure note in Overseas' annual report should describe the nature of the error and the impact of its correction on each year's net income (understated by $1 million in 1995; overstated by $1 million in 1996), income before extraordinary items (same as net income), and earnings per share.

Step 1

Step 2

Step 3

Step 4

Other error corrections that benefit from a similar analysis are the overstatement of ending inventory, the overstatement or understatement of beginning inventory, and errors in recording merchandise purchases (or returns).

Here's how Erly Industries, Inc., reported in its 1991 financial statements the correction of an inventory error:

GRAPHIC   21–15

Disclosure of Error Correction— Erly Industries, Inc.

Note 3 (in Part): Correction of Errors

. . . In connection with the year-end accounting closing for the fiscal year ended March 31, 1991, it was discovered that inventory accounts were overstated and included capitalized operating losses generated from inefficiencies in rice milling and other production expenses which should have been charged to operations in the year incurred. Subsequent investigation revealed that previously reported results of operations were overstated as follows: 1988—$219,000; 1989—$1,047,000; stockholders' equity was overstated as follows: 1988—$219,000; 1989—$1,266,000; 1990—$3,051,000; 1991—$3,372,000. Accordingly, the previously reported financial results for the fiscal years ended March 31, 1990, 1989; and 1988 and the first three quarters of fiscal year 1991 have been restated for the effects of the errors.

The correction is reported as a prior period adjustment to beginning retained earnings balance in Erly's statement of shareholders' equity. The adjustment is made to the 1988 balance since that's the earliest year included in the comparative statements. The retained earnings balances in years after 1988 also are adjusted to what those balances would be if the error had not occurred, but Erly chose not to report those adjustments separately.

GRAPHIC   21–16

Prior Period Adjustment— Erly Industries, Inc.

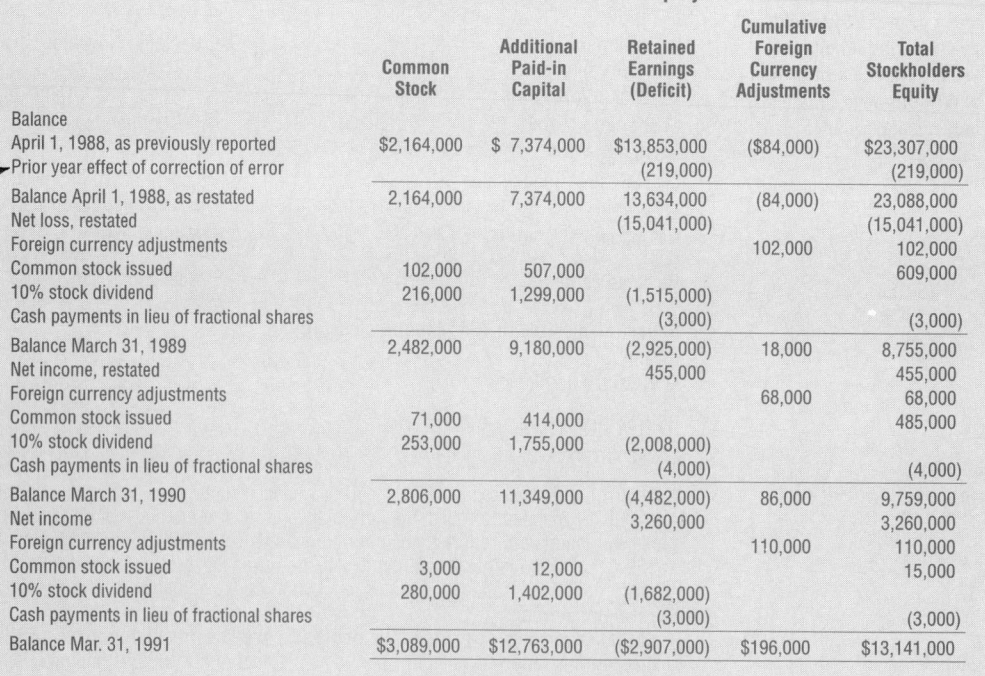

ERLY INDUSTRIES, INC.
Consolidated Statements of Stockholders' Equity

	Common Stock	Additional Paid-in Capital	Retained Earnings (Deficit)	Cumulative Foreign Currency Adjustments	Total Stockholders Equity
Balance					
April 1, 1988, as previously reported	$2,164,000	$ 7,374,000	$13,853,000	($84,000)	$23,307,000
Prior year effect of correction of error			(219,000)		(219,000)
Balance April 1, 1988, as restated	2,164,000	7,374,000	13,634,000	(84,000)	23,088,000
Net loss, restated			(15,041,000)		(15,041,000)
Foreign currency adjustments				102,000	102,000
Common stock issued	102,000	507,000			609,000
10% stock dividend	216,000	1,299,000	(1,515,000)		
Cash payments in lieu of fractional shares			(3,000)		(3,000)
Balance March 31, 1989	2,482,000	9,180,000	(2,925,000)	18,000	8,755,000
Net income, restated			455,000		455,000
Foreign currency adjustments				68,000	68,000
Common stock issued	71,000	414,000			485,000
10% stock dividend	253,000	1,755,000	(2,008,000)		
Cash payments in lieu of fractional shares			(4,000)		(4,000)
Balance March 31, 1990	2,806,000	11,349,000	(4,482,000)	86,000	9,759,000
Net income			3,260,000		3,260,000
Foreign currency adjustments				110,000	110,000
Common stock issued	3,000	12,000			15,000
10% stock dividend	280,000	1,402,000	(1,682,000)		
Cash payments in lieu of fractional shares			(3,000)		(3,000)
Balance Mar. 31, 1991	$3,089,000	$12,763,000	($2,907,000)	$196,000	$13,141,000

An error also would occur if a revenue or an expense is recorded in the wrong accounting period. Illustration 21–8 offers an example.

ILLUSTRATION 21–8

**Error Affecting Net Income:
Failure to Record Sales
Revenue**

In 1997, General Paper Company discovered that $3,000 of merchandise (credit) sales the last week of 1996 were not recorded until the first week of 1997. The merchandise sold was appropriately excluded from 1996 ending inventory.

Analysis:

($ in 000s)

	Correct (Should have been recorded)			**Incorrect** (As recorded)	
1996	Accounts receivable	3		No entry	
	Sales revenue		3		
1997	No entry			Accounts receivable	3
				Sales revenue		3

1996 sales revenue was incorrectly recorded in 1997, so 1996 net income was understated. Retained earnings is currently understated in 1997. 1997 sales revenue is overstated.

 Step 1

To correct incorrect accounts	($ in 000s)
Sales revenue	3
Retained earnings	3

Note: If the sales revenue had not been recorded at all, the correcting entry would include a debit to accounts receivable rather than sales revenue.

 Step 2

 Step 3

     The 1996 financial statements that were incorrect as a result of the error are retroactively restated to reflect the correct amount of sales revenue and accounts receivable when those statements are reported again for comparative purposes in the 1997 annual report.

     Because retained earnings is one of the accounts incorrect as a result of the error, the correction to that account is reported as a prior period adjustment to the 1996 beginning retained earnings balance in General Paper's comparative statements of shareholders' equity.

 Step 4

     Also, a disclosure note in General Paper's 1997 annual report should describe the nature of the error and the impact of its correction on each year's net income ($3,000 in 1996), income before extraordinary items ($3,000 in 1996), and earnings per share.

As mentioned at the outset, we've made no attempt to demonstrate the correction process for every kind of error in every stage of its discovery. However, after seeing the process applied to the few situations described, you should feel comfortable that the process is the same regardless of the specific situation you might encounter.

ETHICAL DILEMMA

As a second-year accountant for McCormack Chemical Company, you were excited to be named assistant manager of the Agricultural Chemicals Division. After two weeks in your new position, you were supervising the year-end inventory count when the senior manager mentioned that two carloads of herbicides were omitted from the count and should be added. Upon checking, you confirm your understanding that the inventory in question had been deemed to be unsaleable. "Yes," your manager agreed, "but we'll write that off next year when our bottom line won't be so critical to the continued existence of the Agricultural Chemicals Division. Jobs and families depend on our division showing well this year."

CONCEPT REVIEW EXERCISE   CORRECTION OF ERRORS

In 1998, the following errors were discovered by the internal auditors of Development Technologies, Inc.

1. 1997 accrued wages of $2 million were not recognized until they were paid in 1998.
2. A $3 million purchase of merchandise in 1998 was recorded in 1997 instead. The physical inventory count at the end of 1997 was correct.

Required:
Prepare the journal entries needed in 1998 to correct each error. Also, briefly describe any other measures Development Technologies would take in connection with correcting the errors. (Ignore income taxes.)

CONCEPT REVIEW EXERCISE   SOLUTION

Step 1:

1. To reduce 1998 wages expense and reduce retained earnings to what it would have been if the expense had reduced net income in 1997.

	($ in millions)	
Retained earnings	2	
Wages expense		2

2. To include the $3 million in 1998 purchases and increase retained earnings to what it would have been if 1997 cost of goods sold had not included the $3 million purchases.

Analysis:

U = Understated   O = Overstated

1997		**1998**	
Beginning inventory		Beginning inventory	
Purchases	O	Purchases	U
Less: Ending inventory			
Cost of goods sold	O		
Revenues			
Less: Cost of goods sold	O		
Less: Other expenses			
Net income	U		
↓			
Retained earnings	U		

	($ in millions)	
Purchases	3	
Retained earnings		3

Step 2:

The 1997 financial statements that were incorrect as a result of the errors would be retroactively restated to reflect the correct wages expense, cost of goods sold, (income tax expense if taxes are considered), net income, and retained earnings when those statements are reported again for comparative purposes in the 1998 annual report.

Step 3:

Because retained earnings is one of the accounts incorrect, the correction to that account is reported as a *"prior period adjustment"* to the 1997 beginning retained earnings balance in the comparative Statements of Shareholders' Equity.

Step 4:

Also, a *disclosure note* should describe the nature of the error and the impact of its correction on each year's net income, income before extraordinary items, and earnings per share.

Solution to Financial Reporting Case (at the opening of the chapter)

1. How would you respond to Martin's question?

The accounting change did not really cost Pepsi $55 million. Like the amount reported for most changes in accounting principle, this is the cumulative income effect from years prior to the change to the new accounting method. In this instance, it is the cumulative effect on the income of previous years from not having accrued postretirement benefits in the way that became mandatory in 1994. It is reported, net of tax, on the income statement as a separate item of income between extraordinary items and net income.

2. Are all changes in accounting method reported this way? Are there other accounting changes that are reported differently?

Most, but not all. There are five exceptions that are reported by retroactively adjusting prior financial statements to reflect the new method. A few allow or permit prospective application only. Besides a change in accounting principle, the two other accounting changes are changes in estimate, which are reported prospectively, and changes in reporting entity, which are reported retroactively.

The Bottom Line

1. Accounting changes are categorized as:

a. Changes in *principle*

b. Changes in *estimates*

c. Changes in *reporting entity*.

Accounting changes can be accounted for: retroactively (prior years restated); currently (cumulative effect reported currently); or prospectively (only current and future years affected).

2. Most changes in accounting principles are recorded and reported by the "current approach." The cumulative income effect (net of the tax effect) is reported as a separate item of income between extraordinary items and net income. The effect of the change on certain key income numbers should be reported for the current period and on a pro forma (as-if) basis for the financial statements of all prior periods included, and the nature of and justification for the change, as well as the effect on current earnings, should be described in the disclosure notes.

3. Because of their unique nature, prior years' financial statements are restated to reflect some changes in accounting principle. Also, a change to LIFO and a few changes mandated by new accounting standards are accounted for prospectively.

4. Changes in estimates are accounted for prospectively. When a company revises a previous estimate, prior financial statements are not restated, nor is a cumulative effect of the change included in current income. Instead, the company merely incorporates the new estimate in any related accounting determinations from then on.

5. A change in reporting entity requires that financial statements of prior periods be retroactively restated to report the financial information for the new reporting entity in all periods.

6. When errors are discovered, they should be corrected and accounted for retroactively. Previous years' financial statements that were incorrect as a result of an error are retroactively restated, and any account balances that are incorrect are corrected by a journal entry. If retained earnings is one of the accounts incorrect, the correction is reported as a prior period adjustment to the beginning balance in a statement of shareholders' equity. And, a disclosure note should describe the nature of the error and the impact of its correction on operations.

Questions for Review of Key Topics

Question   21–1   For accounting purposes, we classify accounting changes into three categories. What are they? Provide a short description of each.

Question   21–2   There are three accounting approaches to reporting accounting changes. What are they?

Question   21–3   How we account for changes in accounting principle depends on the type of change. However, most changes in accounting principle are accounted for by the current approach. Describe this general way of recording and reporting changes in accounting principle.

Question   21–4   Lynch Corporation changes from the sum-of-the-years'-digits method of depreciation for existing assets to the straight-line method. How should the cumulative effect be reported of the change on the amount of retained earnings at the beginning of the period of the change?

Question   21–5   Sugarbaker Designs, Inc., changed from the FIFO inventory costing method to the average cost method during 1998. Which items from the 1997 financial statements should be restated on the basis of the average cost method when reported in the 1998 comparative financial statements?

Question   21–6   Most accounting principles are recorded and reported by the "current approach." But, because of their unique nature, some changes in accounting principle are more appropriately reported by the *retroactive approach* instead. For these exceptions to the general way of accounting for changes in accounting principle, prior years' financial statements are restated to reflect the use of the new accounting method. What are the exceptions for which restatement is required?

Question   21–7   Southeast Steel, Inc., changed from the FIFO inventory costing method to the LIFO method during 1997. How would this change likely be reported in the 1998 comparative financial statements?

Question	**21–8**	Direct Assurance Company revised the estimates of the useful life of a trademark it had acquired three years earlier. How should the change be accounted for?
Question	**21–9**	It's not easy sometimes to distinguish between a change in principle and a change in estimate. In these cases, how should the change be accounted for?
Question	**21–10**	For financial reporting, a reporting entity can be a single company, or it can be a group of companies that reports a single set of financial statements. When changes occur that cause the financial statements to be those of a different reporting entity, we account for the situation as a change in reporting entity. What are the situations deemed to constitute a change in reporting entity?
Question	**21–11**	The issuance of *SFAS 94,* "Consolidation of All Majority-Owned Subsidiaries," required Ford Motors to include a previously unconsolidated finance subsidiary as part of the reporting entity. How did Ford report the change?
Question	**21–12**	Describe the process of correcting an error when it's discovered in a subsequent reporting period.
Question	**21–13**	If merchandise inventory is understated at the end of 1997, and the error is not discovered, how will net income be affected in 1998?
Question	**21–14**	If it is discovered that an extraordinary repair in the previous year was incorrectly debited to repair expense, how will retained earnings be reported in the current year's statement of shareholders' equity?
Question	**21–15**	What action is required when it is discovered that a five-year insurance premium payment of $50,000 two years ago was debited to insurance expense? (Ignore taxes.)
Question	**21–16**	Suppose the error described in the previous question is not discovered until six years later. What action will the discovery of this error require?

Exercises

Exercise 21–1
Change in principle; change in depreciation methods

Clinton Poultry Farms has used for financial reporting the declining balance method of depreciation for conveyor equipment acquired at the beginning of 1995. At the beginning of 1998, Clinton decides to change to the straight - line method. There is no change in the method used for tax reporting. Clinton's tax rate is 40%. The effect of this change on depreciation for each year is as follows ($ in 000s):

Year	Straight Line	Declining Balance	Difference
1995	$ 400	$ 640	$240
1996	400	550	150
1997	400	460	60
	$1,200	$1,650	$450

Required:
1. Prepare the journal entry to record the change in principle. (All tax effects should be reflected in the deferred tax liability account.)
2. Briefly describe any other steps Clinton should take to report this accounting change in the 1997-1998 comparative financial statements.

Exercise 21–2
Change in accounting principle; change in depreciation methods

Deere Company constructed a machine at a total cost of $35 million in 1994. The machine was being depreciated over a 10-year life using the sum-of-the-years'-digits method. The residual value is expected to be $2 million. At the beginning of 1997 Deere decided to change to the straight-line method.

Required:
Prepare all appropriate journal entry(s) relating to the machine for 1997. (Ignore income tax effects.)

Exercise 21–3
Change in principle; change to the percentage-of-completion method

The Long Island Construction Company has used the completed - contract method of accounting for construction contracts. At the beginning of 1998, the company decides to change to the percentage-of-completion method for financial reporting purposes, but will continue to use the completed-contract method for tax reporting. The following table presents information concerning the change. The income tax rate for all years is 40%.

	Income before Income Tax		
	Percentage of Completion Method	Completed Contract Method	Difference
Before 1997	$15 million	$8 million	$7 million
1997	8 million	5 million	3 million
1998	10 million	9 million	1 million

Required:

1. Prepare the journal entry to record the change in principle. (All tax effects should be reflected in the deferred tax liability account.)
2. Determine the net income to be reported in the 1998–1997 comparative income statements.
3. Which other 1997 amounts would be reported differently in the 1998–1997 comparative income statements and 1998–1997 comparative balance sheets than they were reported the previous year?
4. How would the change be reflected in the 1998–1997 comparative statements of shareholders' equity? Cash dividends were $1 million each year.

Exercise 21–4
Change in principle; change to the equity method

Exercise 12–13 deals with investments and change to the equity method.

Exercise 21–5
Classifying accounting changes

Indicate with the appropriate letter the nature of each situation described below:

Type of Change

PC   Change in principle reported currently
~~PR   Change in principle reported retroactively~~
~~PP   Change in principle reported prospectively~~
E   Change in estimate
R   Change in reporting entity
N   Not an accounting change

_____ 1. Change from declining balance depreciation to straight-line.
_____ 2. Change in the estimated useful life of office equipment.
_____ 3. Technological advance that renders worthless a patent with an unamortized cost of $45,000.
_____ 4. Change from determining lower of cost or market for inventories by the individual item approach to the aggregate approach.
_____ 5. Change from LIFO inventory costing to weighted-average inventory costing.
_____ 6. Settling a lawsuit for less than the amount accrued previously as a loss contingency.
_____ 7. Including in the consolidated financial statements a subsidiary acquired several years earlier that was appropriately not included in previous years.
_____ 8. Change by a retail store from reporting bad debt expense on a pay-as-you-go basis to the allowance method.
_____ 9. A shift of certain manufacturing overhead costs to inventory that previously were expensed as incurred to more accurately measure cost of goods sold. (Either method is generally acceptable.)
_____ 10. Pension plan assets for a defined benefit pension plan achieving a rate of return in excess of the amount anticipated.

[handwritten note in margin: Change from non-GAAP to GAAP is an error correction]

Exercise 21–6
Change in inventory costing methods

In 1998, the Quayle Company changed its method of valuing inventory from the FIFO method to the average cost method. At December 31, 1997, Quayle's inventories were $32 million (FIFO). Quayle's records indicated that the inventories would have totaled $23.8 million at December 31, 1997, if determined on an average cost basis.

Required:

1. Prepare the journal entry to record the adjustment. (Ignore income taxes.)
2. Briefly describe other steps Quayle should take to report the change.

Exercise 21–7
Change from the treasury stock method to retired stock

Exercise 19–16 deals with treasury stock and a change to considering reacquired stock to be retired.

Exercise 21–8
Multiple choice; accounting changes

The following questions dealing with accounting changes are adapted from questions that appeared on recent CPA examinations. Determine the response that best completes the statements or questions.

1. When a company changes from the straight-line method of depreciation for previously recorded assets to the double-declining balance method, which of the following should be reported?

	Cumulative Effects of Change in Accounting Principle	Pro Forma Effects of Retroactive Application
a.	No	No
b.	No	Yes
c.	Yes	Yes
d.	Yes	No

2. On January 1, 1997, Roem Corp. changed its inventory method to FIFO from LIFO for both financial and income tax reporting purposes. The change resulted in a $500,000 increase in the January 1, 1997, inventory. Assume that the income tax rate for all years is 30%. The cumulative effect of the accounting change should be reported by Roem in its 1997.
   a. Retained earnings statement as a $350,000 addition to the beginning balance.
   b. Income statement as a $350,000 cumulative effect of accounting change.
   c. Retained earnings statement as a $500,000 addition to the beginning balance.
   d. Income statement as a $500,000 cumulative effect of accounting change.
3. A company has included in its consolidated financial statements this year a subsidiary acquired several years ago that was appropriately excluded from consolidation last year. This results in:
   a. An accounting change that should be reported prospectively.
   b. An accounting change that should be reported by restating the financial statements of all prior periods presented.
   c. A correction of an error.
   d. Neither an accounting change nor a correction of an error.

Exercise 21–9
Deferred taxes; change in tax rates

Exercise 16–14 deals with deferred taxes and a change in tax rates.

Exercise 21–10
Book royalties

Dreighton Engineering Group receives royalties on a technical manual written by two of its engineers and sold to William B. Irving Publishing, Inc. Royalties are 10% of net sales, receivable on October 1 for sales in January through June and on April 1 for sales in July through December of the prior year. Sales of the manual began in July 1996, and Dreighton accrued royalty revenue of $31,000 at December 31, 1996, as follows:

Receivable—royalty revenue	31,000	
Royalty revenue		31,000

Dreighton received royalties of $36,000 on April 1, 1997, and $40,000 on October 1, 1997. Irving indicated to Dreighton on December 31 that book sales subject to royalties for the second half of 1997 are expected to be $500,000.

Required:
1. Prepare any journal entries Dreighton should record during 1997 related to the royalty revenue.
2. What adjustments, if any, should be made to retained earnings or to the 1996 financial statements? Explain.

Exercise 21–11
Loss contingency

Exercise 13–16 deals with a change in the estimated amount of a loss contingency.

Exercise 21–12
Warranty expense

Woodmier Lawn Products introduced a new line of commercial sprinklers in 1997 that carry a one-year warranty against manufacturer's defects. Because this was the first product for which the company offered a warranty, trade publications were consulted to determine the experience of others in the industry. Based on that experience, warranty costs were expected to approximate 2% of sales. Sales of the sprinklers in 1997 were $2,500,000. Accordingly, the following entries relating to the contingency for warranty costs were recorded during the first year of selling the product:

Accrued liability and expense		
Warranty expense (2% × $2,500,000)	50,000	
Estimated warranty liability		50,000
Actual expenditures (summary entry)		
Estimated warranty liability	23,000	
Cash, wages payable, parts and supplies, etc.		23,000

In late 1998, the company's claims experience was evaluated and it was determined that claims were far more than expected—3% of sales rather than 2%.

Required:

1. Assuming sales of the sprinklers in 1998 were $3,600,000 and warranty expenditures in 1998 totaled $88,000, prepare any journal entries related to the warranty.
2. Assuming sales of the sprinklers were discontinued after 1997, prepare any journal entry(s) in 1998 related to the warranty.

Exercise 21–13
Change in estimate; useful life of patent

Exercise 11–13 deals with a change in the estimated life of a patent.

Exercise 21–14
Change in inventory costing methods

Exercise 9–19 deals with a change in inventory costing methods.

Exercise 21–15
Accounting change involving machinery

Exercise 3–8 deals with an accounting change involving machinery.

Exercise 21–16
Accounting change involving machinery

Exercise 3–9 deals with an accounting change involving machinery.

Exercise 21–17
Change in estimate; equipment

Exercise 11–14 deals with changes in estimates involving equipment.

Exercise 21–18
Accounting change; depreciation

Exercise 11–16 deals with a change in depreciation methods.

Exercise 21–19
Error correction; inventory error

During 1997, WMC Corporation discovered that its ending inventories reported on its financial statements were misstated by the following amounts:

1995	understated by	$120,000
1996	overstated by	150,000

WMC uses the periodic inventory system and the FIFO cost method.

Required:

1. Determine the effect of these errors on retained earnings at January 1, 1997, before any adjustments. Explain your answer. (Ignore income taxes.)
2. Prepare a journal entry to correct the error.
3. What other step(s) would be taken in connection with the error?

Exercise 21–20
Error correction

DeSoto Water Works purchased a machine at the end of 1996 at a cost of $65,000 and recorded the following journal entry:

Buildings	65,000	
Cash		65,000

The error was discovered in 1997.

Required:

1. Prepare a journal entry to correct the error.
2. What other step(s) would be taken in connection with the error?

Exercise 21–21
Error correction; operational asset

Exercise 11–17 deals with an error related to recording an operational asset.

Exercise 21–22
Error corrections; investment

On December 12, 1997, an investment costing $80,000 was sold for $100,000. The total of the sale proceeds was credited to the investment account.

Required:

1. Prepare the journal entry to correct the error assuming it is discovered before the books are adjusted or closed in 1997. (Ignore income taxes.)
2. Prepare the journal entry to correct the error assuming it is not discovered until early 1998. (Ignore income taxes.)

Exercise 21–23
Error in amortization schedule

Wilkins Food Products, Inc., acquired a packaging machine from Lawrence Specialists Corporation. Lawrence completed construction of the machine on January 1, 1995. In payment for the machine Wilkins issued a three-year installment note to be paid in three equal payments at the end of each year. The payments include interest at the rate of 10%.

Lawrence made a conceptual error in preparing the amortization schedule which Wilkens failed to discover until 1997. The error had caused Wilkens to understate interest expense by $45,000 in 1995 and $40,000 in 1996.

Required:

1. Determine which accounts are incorrect as a result of these errors at January 1, 1997, before any adjustments. Explain your answer. (Ignore income taxes.)
2. Prepare a journal entry to correct the error.
3. What other step(s) would be taken in connection with the error?

Exercise 21–24
Multiple choice; errors

The following questions dealing with errors are adapted from questions that appeared on recent CPA examinations. Determine the response that best completes the statements or questions.

1. During 1998, Paul company discovered that the ending inventories reported on its financial statements were incorrect by the following amounts:

1996	$60,000 understated
1997	75,000 overstated

   Paul uses the periodic inventory system to ascertain year-end quantities that are converted to dollar amounts using the FIFO cost method. Prior to any adjustments for these errors and ignoring income taxes, Paul's retained earnings at January 1, 1998, would be
   a. Correct
   b. $15,000 overstated.
   c. $75,000 overstated.
   d. $135,000 overstated.

2. Terry, Inc., is a calendar-year corporation whose financial statements for 1996 and 1997 included errors as follows:

Year	Ending Inventory	Depreciation Expense
1996	$15,000 overstated	$12,500 overstated
1997	5,000 understated	4,000 understated

   Assume that purchases were recorded correctly and that no correcting entries were made at December 31, 1996 or at December 31, 1997. Ignoring income taxes, by how much should Terry's retained earnings be retroactively adjusted at January 1, 1998?
   a. $13,500 increase.
   b. $3,500 decrease.
   c. $1,500 decrease.
   d. $1,000 decrease.

3. After the issuance of its 1997 financial statements Terry, Inc. discovered a computational error of $150,000 in the calculation of its December 31, 1997 inventory. The error resulted in a $150,000 overstatement in the cost of goods sold for the year ended December 31, 1997. In October 1998, Terry paid $500,000 in settlement of litigation instituted against it during 1997. Ignore income taxes. In the 1998 financial statements the December 31, 1997, retained earnings balance, as previously reported, should be adjusted by a:
   a. $150,000 credit.
   b. $350,000 debit.
   c. $500,000 debit.
   d. $650,000 credit.

Exercise 21–25
Error correction; accrued interest on bonds

Exercise 14–23 deals with the correction of an error in accrued interest on bonds.

Exercise 21–26
Error correction; three errors

Below are three independent and unrelated errors.

a. On December 31, 1996, Wolfe-Bache Corporation failed to accrue office supplies expense of $1,800. In January 1997, when it received the bill from its supplier, Wolfe-Bache made the following entry:

Office supplies expense	1,800	
Cash		1,800

b. On the last day of 1996, Midwest Importers received a $90,000 prepayment from a tenant for 1997 rent of a building. Midwest recorded the receipt as rent revenue.

c. At the end of 1996, Dinkins-Lowery Corporation failed to accrue interest of $8,000 on a note receivable. At the beginning of 1997, when the company received the cash, it was recorded as interest revenue.

Required:
For each error:

1. What would be the effect of each error on the income statement and the balance sheet in the 1996 financial statements?
2. Prepare any journal entries each company should record in 1997 to correct the errors.

Exercise 21–27
Inventory errors

Exercise 9–21 deals with inventory errors.

Exercise 21–28
Inventory error

Exercise 9–22 deals with an inventory error.

Exercise 21–29
Classifying accounting changes and errors

Indicate with the appropriate letter the nature of each adjustment described below:

Type of Adjustment
A. Change in principle (general)
B. Change in principle (exception reported retroactively)
C. Change in principle (exception reported prospectively)
D. Change in estimate
E. Change in reporting entity
F. Correction of an error

needs to be capitalized ↳*this is an error correction*

_____ 1. Change from expensing <u>extraordinary</u> repairs to capitalizing the expenditures.
_____ 2. Change in the residual value of machinery.
_____ 3. Change from FIFO inventory costing to LIFO inventory costing.
_____ 4. Change in the percentage used to determine bad debts.
_____ 5. Change from LIFO inventory costing to FIFO inventory costing.
_____ 6. Change from reporting pension benefits according to the provisions of *Accounting Principles Board Opinion 8* to reporting pension benefits according to the provisions of *SFAS 87* in 1987. (*SFAS 87* became generally effective in 1987.)
_____ 7. Change in the composition of a group of firms reporting on a consolidated basis.
_____ 8. Change from sum-of-the-years'-digits depreciation to straightline.
_____ 9. Change from the percentage-of-completion method by a company in the long-term construction industry.
_____ 10. Change in actuarial assumptions for a defined benefit pension plan.

Problems

Problem 21–1
Change in principle; change in depreciation methods

During 1996 and 1997, Faulkner Manufacturing used the sum-of-the-years'-digits (SYD) method of depreciation for its operational assets, for both financial reporting and tax purposes. At the beginning of 1998, Faulkner decided to change to the straight - line method for both financial reporting and tax purposes. A tax rate of 40% is in effect for all years.

The effect of this change on net income for each year is as follows ($ in 000s):

Year	Straight Line	SYD	Difference	Taxes	Net Change in Income
1996	$2,000	$3,200	$1,200	$480	$ 720
1997	2,000	2,800	800	320	480
	$4,000	$6,000	$2,000	$800	$1,200

Income from continuing operations (before income tax) for 1998 and 1997 were $6 million and $5 million, respectively. There were no extraordinary items. There were 1 million common shares outstanding each year.

Required:
1. Prepare the journal entry to record the change in principle. (All tax effects should be reflected in the deferred tax liability account.)
2. Prepare the 1998–1997 comparative income statements beginning with income from continuing operations. Include per share amounts and any necessary pro forma disclosures.

Problem 21–2
Change in inventory costing methods; comparative income statements

Shown below are net income amounts as they would be determined by Weihrich Steel Company by each of three different inventory costing methods. ($ in 000s)

	FIFO	Average Cost	LIFO
pre-1996	$2,800	$2,540	$2,280
1996	750	600	540
	$3,550	$3,140	$2,820

Required:
1. Assume that Weihrich used FIFO before 1997, and then in 1997 decided to switch to average cost. Prepare the journal entry to record the change in principle and briefly describe any other steps Weihrich should take to appropriately report the situation. (Ignore income tax effects.)
2. Assume that Weihrich used LIFO before 1997, and then in 1997 decided to switch to average cost. Prepare the journal entry to record the change in principle and briefly describe any other steps Weihrich should take to appropriately report the situation. (Ignore income tax effects.)
3. Assume that Weihrich used FIFO before 1997, and then in 1997 decided to switch to LIFO. Prepare the journal entry to record the change in principle and briefly describe any other steps Weihrich should take to appropriately report the situation. (Ignore income tax effects.)

Problem 21–3
Change in inventory costing methods; comparative income statements

The Cecil-Booker Vending Company changed its method of valuing inventory from the weighted-average cost method to the FIFO cost method at the beginning of 1998. At December 31, 1997, inventories were $120,000 (average cost basis) and were $124,000 a year earlier. Cecil-Booker's accountants determined that the inventories would have totaled $155,000 at December 31, 1997, and $160,000 at December 31, 1996, if determined on a FIFO basis. A tax rate of 40% is in effect for all years.

One hundred thousand common shares were outstanding each year. Income from continuing operations was $400,000 in 1997 and $525,000 in 1998. There were no extraordinary items either year.

Required:
1. Prepare the journal entry to record the change in principle. (All tax effects should be reflected in the deferred tax liability account.)
2. Prepare the 1998–1997 comparative income statements beginning with income from continuing operations. Include per share amounts and any necessary pro forma disclosures.

Problem 21–4
Change in principle; change in method of accounting for long-term construction

The Pyramid Construction Company has used the completed-contract method of accounting for construction contracts during its first two years of operation, 1996 and 1997. At the beginning of 1998, Pyramid decides to change to the percentage-of-completion method for both tax and financial reporting purposes. The following table presents information concerning the change for 1996–1998. The income tax rate for all years is 40%.

	Income before Income Tax				
	Percentage of Completion Method	Completed Contract Method	Difference	Income Tax Effect	Difference after Tax
1996	$ 90,000	$60,000	$30,000	$12,000	$18,000
1997	45,000	36,000	9,000	3,600	5,400
Total	$135,000	$96,000	$39,000	$15,600	$23,400
1998	$ 51,000	$46,000	$ 5,000	$ 2,000	$ 3,000

Pyramid issued 50,000 $1 par, common shares for $230,000 when the business began, and there have been no changes in paid-in capital since then. Dividends were not paid the first year, but $10,000 cash dividends were paid in both 1997 and 1998.

Required:

1. Prepare the journal entry to record the change in principle. (All tax effects should be reflected in the deferred tax liability account.)
2. Prepare the 1998–1997 comparative income statements beginning with income before income taxes.
3. Prepare the 1998–1997 comparative statements of shareholders' equity. (Hint: The 1996 statements reported retained earnings of $36,000. This is $60,000 − [$60,000 × 40%]).

Problem 21–5
Accounting changes; six situations

Described below are six independent and unrelated situations involving accounting changes. Each change occurs during 1997 before any adjusting entries or closing entries were prepared. Assume the tax rate for each company is 40% in all years. Any tax effects should be adjusted through the deferred tax liability account.

a. Fleming Home Products introduced a new line of commercial awnings in 1996 that carry a one-year warranty against manufacturer's defects. Based on industry experience, warranty costs were expected to approximate 3% of sales. Sales of the awnings in 1996 were $3,500,000. Accordingly, warranty expense and a warranty liability of $105,000 were recorded in 1996. In late 1997, the company's claims experience was evaluated and it was determined that claims were far fewer than expected: 2% of sales rather than 3%. Sales of the awnings in 1997 were $4,000,000 and warranty expenditures in 1997 totaled $91,000.

b. On December 30, 1993, Rival Industries acquired its office building at a cost of $1,000,000. It has been depreciated on a straight-line basis assuming a useful life of 40 years and no salvage value. However, plans were finalized in 1997 to relocate the company headquarters at the end of 2004. The vacated office building will have a salvage value at that time of $700,000.

c. Hobbs-Barto Merchandising, Inc., changed inventory cost methods to LIFO from FIFO at the end of 1997 for both financial statement and income tax purposes. Under FIFO, the inventory at January 1, 1998, is $690,000.

d. At the beginning of 1993, the Hoffman Group purchased office equipment at a cost of $330,000. Its useful life was estimated to be 10 years with no salvage value. The equipment has been depreciated by the sum-of-the-years'-digits method. On January 1, 1997, the company changed to the straight-line method.

e. In November, 1995, the State of Minnesota filed suit against Huggins Manufacturing Company, seeking penalties for violations of clean air laws. When the financial statements were issued in 1996, Huggins had not reached a settlement with state authorities, but legal counsel advised Huggins that it was probable the company would have to pay $200,000 in penalties. Accordingly, the following entry was recorded:

Loss – litigation	200,000	
Liability – litigation		200,000

Late in 1997, a settlement was reached with state authorities to pay a total of $350,000 in penalties.

f. At the beginning of 1997, Jantzen Specialties, which uses the sum-of-the-years'-digits method changed to the straight-line method for newly acquired buildings and equipment. The change increased current year net earnings by $445,000.

Required:

For each situation:
1. Identify the type of change.
2. Prepare any journal entry necessary as a direct result of the change as well as any adjusting entry for 1997 related to the situation described.
3. Briefly describe any other steps that should be taken to appropriately report the situation.

Problem 21–6
Accounting changes; ten situations

On January 2, 1999, Quo, Inc., hired Reed to be its controller. During the year, Reed, working closely with Quo's president and outside accountants, made changes in accounting policies, corrected several errors dating from 1998 and before, and instituted new accounting policies. Quo's 1999 financial statements will be presented in comparative form with its 1998 financial statements.

Required:

Items 1 through 10 represent Quo's transactions. **List A** represents possible classifications of these transactions as: a change in accounting principle, a change in accounting estimate, a correction of an error in previously presented financial statements, or neither an accounting change nor an accounting error.

List B represents the general accounting treatment required for these transactions. These treatments are:

Cumulative effect approach   Include the cumulative effect of the adjustment resulting from the accounting change or error correction in the 1999 financial statements, and do not restate the 1998 financial statements.

Retroactive restatement approach   Restate the 1998 financial statements and adjust 1998 beginning retained earnings if the error or change affects a period prior to 1998.

Prospective approach   Report 1999 and future financial statements on the new basis, but do not restate 1998 financial statements.

Number a sheet of paper from 1 to 10. For each item, select one from List A and one from List B and indicate the best answer to each of the 10 items.

List A (Select one)	List B (Select one)
A. Change in accounting principles	X. Cumulative effect approach
B. Change in accounting estimate	Y. Retroactive restatement approach
C. Correction of an error in previously presented financial statements	Z. Prospective approach
D. Neither an accounting change nor an accounting error.	

Items to Be Answered:

1. Quo manufactures heavy equipment to customer specifications on a contract basis. On the basis that it is preferable, accounting for these long-term contracts was switched from the completed-contract method to the percentage-of-completion method.
2. As a result of a production breakthrough, Quo determined that manufacturing equipment previously depreciated over 15 years should be depreciated over 20 years.
3. The equipment that Quo manufactures is sold with a five-year warranty. Because of a production breakthrough, Quo reduced its computation of warranty costs from 3% of sales to 1% of sales.
4. Quo changed from LIFO to FIFO to account for its finished goods inventory.
5. Quo changed from FIFO to average cost to account for its raw materials and work in process inventories.
6. Quo sells extended service contracts on its products. Because related services are performed over several years, in 1999 Quo changed from the cash method to the accrual method of recognizing income from these service contracts.
7. During 1999, Quo determined that an insurance premium paid and entirely expensed in 1998 was for the period January 1, 1998, through January 1, 2000.
8. Quo changed its method of depreciating office equipment from an accelerated method to the straight-line method to more closely reflect costs in later years.
9. Quo instituted a pension plan for all employees in 1999 and adopted *Statement of Financial Accounting Standards No. 87,* Employers' Accounting for Pensions. Quo had not previously had a pension plan.
10. During 1999, Quo increased its investment in Worth, Inc., from a 10% interest, purchased in 1998 to 30% and acquired a seat on Worth's board of directors. As a result of its increased investment, Quo changed its method of accounting for investment in subsidiary from the cost method to the equity method.

(AICPA adapted)

Problem 21–7
Error; a change in principle; operational assets

Problem 11–11 deals with the correction of an error related to recording an operational asset and a change in depreciation methods.

Problem 21–8
Change in inventory costing methods

Problem 9–11 deals with a change in inventory costing methods.

Problem 21–9
Depreciation methods; change in methods

Problem 11–1 deals with a change in depreciation methods.

Problem 21–10
Depletion; change in estimate

Problem 11–7 deals with a change in an estimate involving a natural resource.

Problem 21–11
Straight–line depreciation; change in useful life and residual value

Problem 11–9 deals with changes in the useful life and residual value of machinery.

Problem 21–12
Accounting changes and error correction; eight situations; tax effects ignored

Williams-Santana, Inc., is a manufacturer of high-tech industrial parts that was started in 1985 by two talented engineers with little business training. In 1997, the company was acquired by one of its major customers. As part of an internal audit, the following facts were discovered. The audit occurred during 1997 before any adjusting entries or closing entries were prepared.

- a. A five-year casualty insurance policy was purchased at the beginning of 1995 for $35,000. The full amount was debited to insurance expense at the time.
- b. Effective January 1, 1997, the company changed the salvage value used in calculating depreciation for its office building. The building cost $600,000 on December 29, 1986, and has been depreciated on a straight-line basis assuming a useful life of 40 years and a salvage value of $100,000. Declining real estate values in the area indicate that the salvage value will be no more than $25,000.
- c. On December 31, 1996, merchandise inventory was overstated by $25,000 due to a mistake in the physical inventory count using the periodic inventory system.
- d. The company changed inventory cost methods to FIFO from LIFO at the end of 1997 for both financial statement and income tax purposes. The change will cause a $960,000 increase in the beginning inventory at January 1, 1998.
- e. At the end of 1996, the company failed to accrue $15,500 of sales commissions earned by employees during 1996. The expense was recorded when the commissions were paid in early 1997.
- f. At the beginning of 1995, the company purchased a machine at a cost of $720,000. Its useful life was estimated to be 10 years with no salvage value. The machine has been depreciated by the double declining balance method. Its carrying amount on December 31, 1996, was $460,800. On January 1, 1997, the company changed retroactively to the straight-line method.
- g. Bad debt expense is determined each year as 1% of credit sales. Actual collection experience of recent years indicates that 0.75% is a better indication of uncollectible accounts. Management effects the change in 1997. Credit sales for 1997 are $4,000,000; in 1996 they were $3,700,000.
- h. Additional industrial robots were acquired at the beginning of 1994 and added to the company's assembly process. The $1,000,000 cost of the equipment was inadvertently recorded as repair expense. Robots have ten-year useful lives and no material salvage value. This class of equipment is depreciated by the straight-line method.

Required:

For each situation:
1. Identify whether it represents an accounting change or an error. If an accounting change, identify the type of change.
2. Prepare any journal entry necessary as a direct result of the change or error correction as well as any adjusting entry for 1997 related to the situation described. (Ignore tax effects.)
3. Briefly describe any other steps that should be taken to appropriately report the situation.

(This problem is a variation of the previous problem, modified to consider income tax effects.)

Problem 21–13
Accounting changes and error correction; eight situations; tax effects considered

Williams-Santana, Inc., is a manufacturer of high-tech industrial parts that was started in 1985 by two talented engineers with little business training. In 1997, the company was acquired by one of its major customers. As part of an internal audit, the following facts were discovered. The audit occurred during 1997 before any adjusting entries or closing entries were prepared. The income tax rate is 40% for all years.

- a. A five-year casualty insurance policy was purchased at the beginning of 1995 for $35,000. The full amount was debited to insurance expense at the time.
- b. Effective January 1, 1997, the company changed the salvage values used in calculating depreciation for its office building. The building cost $600,000 on December 29, 1986, and has been depreciated on a straight-line basis assuming a useful life of 40 years and a salvage value of $100,000. Declining real estate values in the area indicate that the salvage value will be no more than $25,000.
- c. On December 31, 1996, merchandise inventory was overstated by $25,000 due to a mistake in the physical inventory count using the periodic inventory system.
- d. The company changed inventory cost methods to FIFO from LIFO at the end of 1997 for both financial statement and income tax purposes. The change will cause a $960,000 increase in the beginning inventory at January 1, 1998.
- e. At the end of 1996, the company failed to accrue $15,500 of sales commissions earned by employees during 1996. The expense was recorded when the commissions were paid in early 1997.

f. At the beginning of 1995, the company purchased a machine at a cost of $720,000. Its useful life was estimated to be ten years with no salvage value. The machine has been depreciated by the double declining balance method. Its carrying amount on December 31, 1996, was $460,800. On January 1, 1997, the company changed retroactively to the straight-line method.

g. Bad debt expense is determined each year as 1% of credit sales. Actual collection experience of recent years indicates that 0.75% is a better indication of uncollectible accounts. Management effects the change in 1997. Credit sales for 1997 are $4,000,000; in 1996 they were $3,700,000.

h. Additional industrial robots were acquired at the beginning of 1994 and added to the company's assembly process. The $1,000,000 cost of the equipment was inadvertently recorded as repair expense. Robots have 10-year useful lives and no material salvage value. This class of equipment is depreciated by the straight-line method.

Required:

For each situation:

1. Identify whether it represents an accounting change or an error. If an accounting change, identify the type of change.
2. Prepare any journal entry necessary as a direct result of the change or error correction as well as any adjusting entry for 1997 related to the situation described. Any tax effects should be adjusted for through the deferred tax liability account.
3. Briefly describe any other steps that should be taken to appropriately report the situation.

Problem 21–14
Errors; change in estimate; change in principle; restatement of previous financial statements

Whaley Distributors is a wholesale distributor of electronic components. Financial statements for the year ended December 31, 1996, reported the following amounts and subtotals ($ in millions):

	Assets	Liabilities	Shareholders' Equity	Net Income	Expenses
1995	$740	$330	$410	$210	$150
1996	$820	$400	$420	$230	$175

In 1997 the following situations occurred or came to light:

a. Internal auditors discovered that ending inventories reported on the financial statements the two previous years were misstated due to faulty internal controls. The errors were in the following amounts:

| 1995 inventory | overstated by $12 million |
| 1996 inventory | understated by 10 million |

b. A liability was accrued in 1995 for a probable payment of $7 million in connection with a lawsuit ultimately settled in December 1997 for $4 million.

c. A patent costing $18 million at the beginning of 1995, expected to benefit operations for a total of six years, has not been amortized since acquired.

d. Whaley's conveyer equipment has been depreciated by the sum-of-the-years'-digits (SYD) basis since constructed at the beginning of 1995 at a cost of $30 million. It has an expected useful life of five years and no expected residual value. At the beginning of 1997, Whaley decided to switch to straight-line depreciation.

Required:

For each situation:

1. Prepare any journal entry necessary as a direct result of the change or error correction as well as any adjusting entry for 1997 related to the situation described. (Ignore tax effects.)
2. Determine the amounts to be reported for each of the five items shown above from the 1995 and 1996 financial statements when those amounts are reported again in the 1997, 1996, 1995 comparative financial statements.

Problem 21–15
Correction of errors; eight situations

Cord Corp., a nonpublic enterprise, requires audited financial statements for credit purposes. After making normal adjusting entries, but before closing the accounting records for the year ended December 31, 1997, Cord's controller prepared the following financial statements for 1997:

CORD CORP.
Balance Sheet
December 31, 1997

Assets

Cash	$1,225,000
Marketable equity securities, at cost	125,000
Accounts receivable	460,000

Allowance for doubtful accounts	(55,000)
Inventories	530,000
Property and equipment	620,000
Accumulated depreciation	(280,000)
Total assets	$2,625,000

Liabilities and Stockholders' Equity

Accounts payable and accrued liabilities	1,685,000
Income tax payable	110,000
Common stock, $20 par	300,000
Additional paid-in capital	75,000
Retained earnings	455,000
Total liabilities and stockholders' equity	$2,625,000

CORD CORP.
Income Statement
For the Year Ended December 31, 1997

Net sales	$1,700,000
Operating expenses:	
Cost of sales	570,000
Selling and administrative	448,000
Depreciation	42,000
Total operating expenses	1,060,000
Income before income tax	640,000
Income tax expense	192,000
Net income	$ 448,000

Cord's tax rate for all income items was 30% for all affected years, and it made estimated tax payments when due. During the course of the audit, the following additional information (not considered when the above statements were prepared) was obtained:

a. The investment portfolio consists of short-term investments for which total market value exceeded cost at December 31, 1996. On February 2, 1997, Cord sold one investment costing $100,000 for $130,000. The total of the sale proceeds was credited to the investment account.

b. At December 31, 1997, the market value of the remaining securities in the portfolio was $142,000.

c. The $530,000 inventory total, which was based on a physical count at December 31, 1997, was priced at cost. Subsequently, it was determined that the inventory cost was overstated by $66,000. At December 31, 1997, the inventory's market value approximated the adjusted cost.

d. Pollution control devices costing $48,000, which is high in relation to the cost of the original equipment, were installed on December 29, 1996, and were charged to repairs in 1996.

e. The original equipment referred to in Item 4, which had a remaining useful life of six years on December 20, 1996, is being depreciated by the straight-line method for both financial and tax reporting.

f. A lawsuit was filed against Cord in October 1997 claiming damages of $250,000. Cord's legal counsel believes that an unfavorable outcome is probable, and a reasonable estimate of the court's award to the plaintiff is $60,000, which will be paid in 1999 if the case is settled.

g. Cord determined that its accumulated benefits obligation under the pension plan exceeded the fair value of plan assets by $40,000 at December 31, 1997. Cord has unrecognized prior service cost of $50,000 at December 31, 1997. Cord funds the total pension expense each year.

Required:
Prepare journal entries, without explanations, to record the effects of the foregoing data on Cord's accounting records at December 31, 1997. Do **not** prepare corrected financial statements for 1997. The journal entries should be numbered to correspond with the numbers in the additional information. Include as the last entry any necessary adjustments to the 1997 income tax expense, and support your computations for this entry.

(AICPA adapted)

Problem 21–16 Accounting changes; three situations	Problem 11–10 deals with three unrelated situations involving accounting changes related to operational assets.
Problem 21–17 Inventory errors	Problem 9–12 deals with inventory errors.

Problem 21–18
Correction of errors; six errors

Conrad Wholesale Supply underwent a restructuring in 1997. The company conducted a thorough internal audit, during which the following facts were discovered. The audit occurred during 1997 before any adjusting entries or closing entries are prepared.

    a.   Additional computers were acquired at the beginning of 1995 and added to the company's office network. The $45,000 cost of the computers was inadvertently recorded as maintenance expense. Computers have five-year useful lives and no material salvage value. This class of equipment is depreciated by the straight-line method.

    b.   Two weeks prior to the audit, the company paid $17,000 for assembly tools and recorded the expenditure as office supplies. The error was discovered a week later.

    c.   On December 31, 1996, merchandise inventory was understated by $78,000 due to a mistake in the physical inventory count. The company uses the periodic inventory system.

    d.   Two years earlier, the company recorded a 4% stock dividend (2,000 common shares, $1 par) as follows:

Retained earnings	2,000	
Common stock		2,000

        The shares had a market price at the time of $12 per share.

    e.   At the end of 1996, the company failed to accrue $104,000 of interest expense that accrued during the last four months of 1996 on bonds payable. The bonds which were issued at face value mature in 2001. The following entry was recorded on March 1, 1997, when the semiannual interest was paid:

Interest expense	156,000	
Cash		156,000

    f.   A three-year liability insurance policy was purchased at the beginning of 1996 for $72,000. The full premium was debited to insurance expense at the time.

Required:

For each error, prepare any journal entry necessary to correct the error as well as any year-end adjusting entry for 1997 related to the situation described. (Ignore income taxes.)

Cases

Discussion Case 21–1
Accounting changes; independent situations

Situation I

Situation II

Situation III

Sometimes a business entity will change its method of accounting for certain items. The change may be classified as a change in accounting principle, a change in accounting estimate, or a change in reporting entity.

    Listed below are three independent, unrelated sets of facts relating to accounting changes.

    A company determined that the depreciable lives of its fixed assets are presently too long to fairly match the cost of the fixed assets with the revenue produced. The company decided at the beginning of the current year to reduce the depreciable lives of all of its existing fixed assets by five years.

    On December 31, 1998, Gary Company owned 51 percent of Allen Company, at which time Gary reported its investment on a nonconsolidated basis due to political uncertainties in the country in which Allen was located. On January 2, 1999, the management of Gary Company was satisfied that the political uncertainties were resolved and the assets of the company were in no danger of nationalization. Accordingly, Gary will prepare consolidated financial statements for Gary and Allen for the year ended December 31, 1999.

    A company decides in January 1999 to adopt the straight-line method of depreciation for plant equipment. The straight-line method will be used for new acquisitions as well as for previously acquired plant equipment for which depreciation had been provided on an accelerated basis.

Required:

For each of the situations described above, provide the information indicated below. Complete your discussion of each situation before going on to the next situation.

    1.   Type of accounting change.

    2.   Manner of reporting the change under current generally accepted accounting principles including a discussion, where applicable, of how amounts are computed.

    3.   Effect of the change on the balance sheet and income statement.

    4.   Footnote disclosures that would be necessary.

Discussion Case 21–2
Various changes

Boulder Company appropriately changed its depreciation method for its production machinery from the double-declining-balance method to the production method effective January 1, 1997.

In addition, effective January 1, 1997, Boulder appropriately changed the salvage values used in computing depreciation for its office equipment.

On December 31, 1997, Boulder appropriately changed the specific subsidiaries constituting the group of companies for which consolidated financial statements are presented.

Required:
1. Identify any accounting changes in the three situations described above. For each accounting change identified, indicate whether Boulder should show:
    a. The cumulative effect of a change in accounting principle in net income of the period of change.
    b. Pro forma effects of retroactive application for all prior periods currently.
    c. Restatement of the financial statements of all prior periods presented currently.
2. a. Why are accounting principles, once adopted, normally continued?
    b. What is the rationale for disclosure of a change from one generally accepted accounting principle to another generally accepted accounting principle?

(AICPA adapted)

Discussion Case 21–3
Various changes

On January 1, 1997, Windsor Corp. made the following changes in its accounting policies:

*   Changed from the LIFO inventory method to the FIFO inventory method.
*   Adopted the straight-line depreciation method for all future machinery acquisitions, but continued to use sum-of-the-years' digits depreciation method for all machinery purchased before 1997.
*   Changed from the cash to the accrual basis of accounting for accumulated vacation pay.
*   Windsor prepares two-year comparative financial statements.

Required:
1. What type of accounting change is the change from the LIFO to the FIFO inventory costing method? How should Windsor report this change in its 1997 comparative financial statements?
2. What type of accounting change is Windsor's change from the sum-of-the-years' digits to the straight-line depreciation method for all machinery purchased after 1997? How should Windsor report this change?
3. What type of change occurs when recognition of vacation pay expense changed from the cash basis to the accrual basis? How should Windsor report this change?

(AICPA adapted)

Integrating Case 21–4
Change to dollar-value LIFO

Webster Products, Inc. adopted the dollar-value LIFO method of determining inventory costs for financial and income tax reporting on January 1, 1997. Webster continues to use the FIFO method for internal decision-making purposes. Webster's FIFO inventories at December 31, 1997, 1998, and 1999, were $300,000, $412,500, and $585,000, respectively. Internally generated cost indices are used to convert FIFO inventory amounts to dollar-value LIFO amounts. Webster estimated these indices as follows:

1997	1.00
1998	1.25
1999	1.50

Required:
1. Determine Webster's dollar-value LIFO inventory at December 31, 1998 and 1999.
2. Describe how the change should have been reported in Webster's 1997 financial statements.

Discussion Case 21–5
Concepts

Berkeley Company, a manufacturer of many different products, changed its depreciation method for its production machinery from the double-declining-balance method to the straight-line method effective January 1, 1999. The straight-line method was determined to be preferable.

In addition, Berkeley changed the salvage values used in computing depreciation for its office equipment. This change was made on January 1, 1999, because additional information was obtained.

On December 31, 1999, Berkeley changed the specific subsidiaries comprising the group of companies for which consolidated financial statements are presented.

Required:
1. What kind of accounting change is each of the three situations described above? For each situation indicate whether or not each should show:
    The cumulative effect of a change in accounting principle in net income of the period of change.
    Pro forma effects of retroactive application.
    Restatement of the financial statements of all prior periods.

2. Why does a change in accounting principle have to be disclosed by the company?

(AICPA adapted)

Writing Case 21–6
Change in loss contingency;
write a memo

Late in 1998, you and two other officers of Curbo Fabrications Corporation just returned from a meeting with officials of The City of Jackson. The meeting was unexpectedly favorable even though it culminated in a settlement with city authorities that your company pay a total of $475,000 to cover the cost of violations of city construction codes. Jackson had filed suit in November 1996 against Curbo Fabrications Corporation, seeking civil penalties and injunctive relief for violations of city construction codes regulating earthquake damage standards. Alleged violations involved several construction projects completed during the previous three years. When the financial statements were issued in 1997, Curbo had not reached a settlement with state authorities, but legal counsel had advised the Company that it was probable the ultimate settlement would be $750,000 in penalties. The following entry had been recorded:

Loss—litigation	750,000	
Liability—litigation		750,000

The final settlement, therefore, was a pleasant surprise. While returning from the meeting conversation turned to reporting the settlement in the 1998 financial statements. You drew the short straw and were selected to write a memo to Janet Zeno, the Financial Vice President, advising the proper course of action.

Required:
Write the memo. Include descriptions of any journal entries related to the change in amounts. Briefly describe other steps Curbo should take to report the settlement.

Critical Thought Case 21–7
Two wrongs make a right?

Early one Wednesday afternoon, Ken and Larry studied in the dormitory room they shared at Fogelman College. Ken, an accounting major, was advising Larry, a management major, regarding a project for Larry's Business Policy class. One aspect of the project involved analyzing the 1992 annual report of Scott Paper Company. Though not central to his business policy case, a footnote had caught Larry's attention.

Depreciation and Cost of Timber Harvested (in part)

(Millions)	1992	1991	1990
Depreciation of buildings, machinery and equipment	$260.9	$329.8	$322.5
Cost of timber harvested and amortization of logging roads	4.9	4.9	4.9
	$265.8	$334.7	$327.4

Beginning in 1992, the Company revised the estimated average useful lives used to compute depreciation for most of its pulp and paper mill equipment from 16 years to 20 years and for most of its finishing and converting equipment from 12 years to 15 years. These revisions were made to more properly reflect the true economic lives of the assets and to better align the Company's depreciable lives with the predominant practice in the industry. The change had the effect of increasing net income by approximately $55 million.

"If I understand this right, Ken, the company is not going back and recalculating a lower depreciation for earlier years. Instead they seem to be leaving depreciation overstated in earlier years and making up for that by understating it in current and future years," Larry mused. "Is that the way it is in accounting? Two wrongs make a right?"

Required:
What are the two wrongs to which Larry refers? Is he right?

Ethics Case 21–8
Softening the blow

Late one Thursday afternoon, Joy Martin, a veteran audit manager with a regional CPA firm, was reviewing documents for a long-time client of the firm, AMT Transport. The year-end audit was scheduled to begin Monday.

For three months, the economy had been in a down cycle and the transportation industry was particularly hard hit. As a result, Joy expected AMT's financial results would not be pleasant news to shareholders. However, what Joy saw in the preliminary statements made her sigh aloud. Results were much worse than she feared.

"Larry (the company president) already is in the doghouse with shareholders," Joy thought to herself. "When they see these numbers, they'll hang him out to dry."

"I wonder if he's considered some strategic accounting changes," she thought, after reflecting on the situation. "The bad news could be softened quite a bit by changing inventory methods from LIFO to FIFO or reconsidering some of the estimates used in other areas."

Required:

1. How would the actions contemplated contribute toward "softening" the bad news?
2. Do you perceive an ethical dilemma? What would be the likely impact of following up on Joy's thoughts? Who would benefit? Who would be injured?

Integrating Case 21–9
Error; a change in principle; change in estimate; operational assets; inventories

Case 11–8 deals with the correction of an error, a change in principle, and a change in estimate related to operational assets and inventories.

Discussion Case 21–10
Change in inventory costing methods

Case 9–6 deals with a change in inventory costing methods.

Real World Case 21–11
Change in inventory costing methods

Case 9–7 deals with a change in inventory costing methods.

Internet Case 21–12
Change in inventory costing methods

Case 9–8 deals with a change in inventory costing methods.

Discussion Case 21–13
Inventory errors

Case 9–9 deals with inventory errors.

Ethics Case 21–14
Inventory errors

Case 9–10 deals with an ethical dilemma involving inventory errors.

Ethics Case 21–15
Asset impairment

Case 11–11 deals with an ethical dilemma involving changes related to equipment.

Internet Case 21–16
Researching the way changes in pension estimates are reported; retrieving disclosures from the Internet

It's financial statements preparation time at Center Industries where you have been assistant controller for two months. Ben Huddler, the controller, seems to be pleasant but unpredictable. Today, though your schedule is filled with meetings with internal and outside auditors and two members of the board of directors, Ben made a request. "As you know, we're increasing the discount rate on our pension plan. I'd like to know how others have reported similar changes. Can you find me an example?" he asked. "I'd bet you could get one off that Internet thing you're always using." As a matter of fact, you often use EDGAR, the Electronic Data Gathering, Analysis, and Retrieval system, (www.sec.gov/) to access financial statements filed with the U.S. Securities and Exchange Commission (SEC).

Required:

1. Access EDGAR on the Internet. Access a recent 10-K filing of a firm you think might have a pension plan. About a third of 10-Ks report such changes. You may need to look up several companies before you find what you're looking for. Older, established companies are most likely to have defined benefit plans.

    (Note: You may be able to focus your search by searching with key words and phrases in one of the several "search engines" available on the Internet. Some, including Pathfinder Search (pathfinder.com/) focus their search on business publications.)
2. Copy the portion of the pension disclosures that report the actuarial assumptions and changes.
3. What information is provided about the effect of the change on the company's estimated pension obligation?

22

THE STATEMENT OF CASH FLOWS REVISITED

OVERVIEW

The objective of financial reporting is to provide investors and creditors with useful information, primarily in the form of financial statements. The balance sheet and the income statement—the focus of your study in earlier chapters—do not provide all the information needed by these decision makers. In this chapter, you will learn how the statement of cash flows, prescribed by *SFAS 95*, fills the information gap left by the other financial statements.

The statement lists all cash inflows and cash outflows during each reporting period and classifies them as cash flows from (a) operating, (b) investing, or (c) financing activities. Investing and financing activities that do not directly affect cash also are reported.

LEARNING OBJECTIVES   After studying this chapter, you should be able to:

1. Explain the usefulness of cash flow information.
2. Describe the purpose of the statement of cash flows.
3. Relate the statement of cash flows to its historical evolution.
4. Define cash equivalents.
5. Distinguish among operating activities, investing activities, and financing activities.
6. Identify transactions that represent noncash investing and financing activities.
7. Prepare a statement of cash flows with the aid of a spreadsheet.
8. Reconcile net income to net cash flows from operating activities (the indirect method).

WHERE'S THE CASH?

"What do you mean you can't afford a wage increase?" union negotiator Vince Barr almost shouted. "We've all seen your income statement. You had record earnings this year."

This is the first day of negotiations with the company's union representatives. As company controller, you know it's going to be up to you to explain the company's position on the financial aspects of the negotiations. In fact, you've known for some time that a critical point of contention would be the moderate increase in this year's profits after three years of level or slightly declining earnings. Not helping the situation is that the company has always used accelerated depreciation on its equipment which it began replacing this year at considerably higher prices than it cost several years back.

QUESTIONS

1. What are the cash flow aspects of the situation that Mr. Barr may be overlooking in making his case for a wage increase? How can a company's operations generate a healthy profit and yet produce meager or even negative cash flows?
2. What information can a statement of cash flows provide about a company's investing activities that can be useful in decisions such as this?
3. What information can a statement of cash flows provide about a company's financing activities that can be useful in decisions such as this?

Decision-Makers' Perspective: Usefulness of Cash Flow Information

Learning objective 1
Explain the usefulness of cash flow information.

A fund manager of a major insurance company, considering investing $8,000,000 in the common stock of Apple Computer, asks herself: "What are the prospects of future dividends and market-price appreciation? Will we get a return commensurate with the cost and risk of our investment?" A bank officer, examining an application for a business loan, asks himself: "If I approve this loan, what is the likelihood of the borrower making interest payments on time and repaying the loan when due?" Investors and creditors continually face these and similar decisions that require projections of the relative ability of a business to generate future cash flows and of the risk associated with those forecasts.

Investors and creditors require cash flows from the corporation.

Cash flows to investors and creditors depend on the corporation generating cash flows to itself.

To make these projections, decision makers rely heavily on the information reported in periodic financial statements. In the final analysis, cash flows into and out of a business enterprise are the most fundamental events on which investors and creditors base their decisions. Naturally, these decisions focus on the prospects of the decision makers receiving cash returns from their dealings with the firm. However, it is the ability of the firm to generate cash flows to itself that ultimately determines the potential for cash flows from the firm to investors and creditors.

The financial statements that have been the focus of your study in earlier chapters—the income statement and the balance sheet—offer information helpful in forecasting future cash-generating ability. Some important questions, however, are not easily answered from the information these statements provide. For example, meaningful projections of a company's future profitability and risk depend on answers to such questions as:

- In what types of activities is the company investing?
- Are these activities being financed with debt? with equity? by cash generated from operations?
- Are facilities being acquired to accommodate future expansion?
- How does the amount of cash generated from operations compare with net income over time?
- Why isn't the increase in retained earnings reflected as an increase in dividends?
- What happens to the cash received from the sale of assets?
- By what means is debt being retired?

Many decisions benefit from information about the company's underlying cash flow process.

The information needed to answer these and similar questions is found in the continuous series of cash flows that the income statement and the balance sheet describe only indirectly. This underlying cash flow process is considered next.

Cash Inflows and Outflows

Cash continuously flows into and out of an active business. Businesses disburse cash to acquire operational assets to maintain or expand productive capacity. When no longer needed, these assets may be sold for cash. Cash is paid to produce or purchase inventory for resale, as well as to pay for the expenses of selling these goods. The ultimate outcome of these selling activities is an inflow of cash. Cash might be invested in securities of other firms. These investments provide cash inflows during the investment period in the form of dividends or interest and at the end of the investment period when the securities are sold. To raise cash to finance their operations, firms sell stock and/or acquire debt. Cash payments are made as dividends to shareholders and interest to creditors. When debt is repaid or stock repurchased, cash flows out of the firm. To help you visualize the continuous process of cash receipts and cash payments, that process is diagrammed in Graphic 22–1. The diagram also previews the way we will later classify the cash flows on a statement of cash flows.

Embodied in this assortment of cash flows is a wealth of information that investors and creditors require to make educated decisions. Much of the value of the underlying information provided by the cash flows is lost when reported only indirectly by the balance sheet and the income statement. Each cash flow eventually impacts decision makers by affecting the balances of various accounts on the balance sheet. Also, many of the cash flows—those related to income-producing activities—are represented on the income statement. However, they are not necessarily reported in the period the cash flows occur because the income statement measures activities on an accrual basis. The statement of cash flows fills the information gap by reporting the cash flows directly.

GRAPHIC   22-1

Cash Inflows and Cash
Outflows

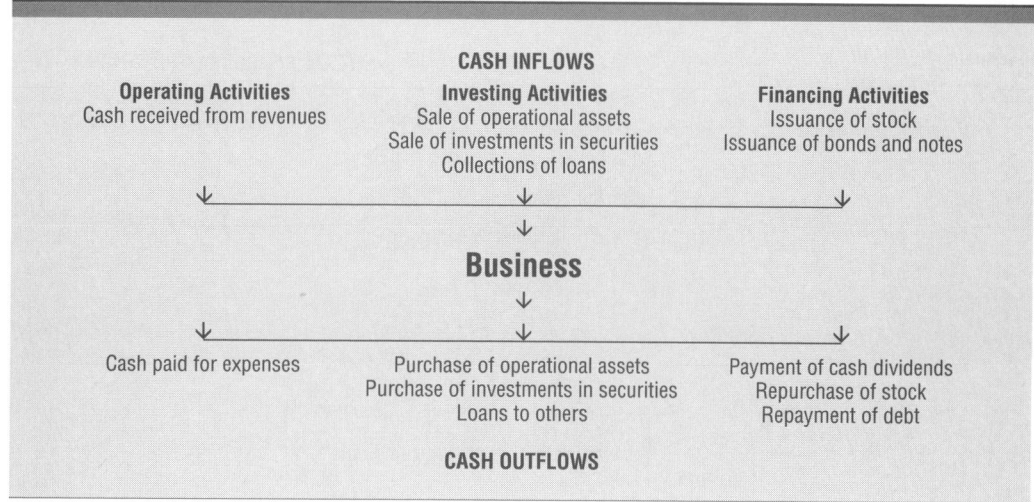

Role of the Statement of Cash Flows

Learning objective 2
Describe the purpose of the
statement of cash flows.

The statement of cash flows
provides information about
cash flows that is lost when
reported only indirectly by
the balance sheet and the
income statement.

A typical statement of cash flows is shown in Graphic 22–2. The statement lists all cash inflows and cash outflows during the reporting period. To enhance the informational value of the presentation, the cash flows are classified according to the nature of the activities that bring about the cash flows. The three primary categories of cash flows are (1) cash flows from operating activities, (2) cash flows from investing activities, and (3) cash flows from financing activities. Classifying each cash flow by source (operating, investing, or financing activities) is more informative than simply listing the various cash flows. Notice, too, that the noncash investing and financing activities—investing and financing activities that do not directly increase or decrease cash—also are reported. *FASB Statement 95*, requiring the statement of cash flows, was issued in direct response to *FASB Concept Statement 1*, which states that the primary objective of financial reporting is to "provide information to help investors and creditors, and others assess the amounts, timing, and uncertainty of prospective net cash inflows to the related enterprise."[1]

Many companies have experienced bankruptcy because they were unable to generate sufficient cash to satisfy their obligations. Doubtless, many investors in the stock of these firms would have been spared substantial losses if the financial statements had been designed to foresee the cash flow problems the companies were experiencing. A prominent illustration is the demise of W.T. Grant during the 1970s. Grant's statement of changes in financial position (the predecessor of the statement of cash flows) reported working capital from operations of $46 million in 1972. Yet, if presented, a statement of cash flows would have reported cash flows from operating activities of negative $10 million. In fact, the unreported cash flow deficiency grew to $114 million in 1973, while working capital from operations was reported as having increased by $1 million. That year, without the benefit of cash flow information, investors were buying Grant's stock at prices that represented up to 20 times its earnings.[2]

The statement of cash flows for National Brands Corporation (NBC), shown in Graphic 22–2, is intended at this point in the discussion to illustrate the basic structure and composition of the statement. Later we will see how the statement of cash flows for NBC is prepared from the information typically available for this purpose. We will refer to NBC's statement of cash flows frequently throughout the chapter as the discussion becomes more specific regarding the criteria for classifying cash flows in the three primary categories and as we identify the specific cash flows to be reported on the statement. We will examine the content of the statement in more detail following a look at how this relatively recent financial statement has evolved to its present form over the course of the last several decades.

---

[1] "Objectives of Financial Reporting by Business Enterprises," *FASB Statement of Financial Accounting Concepts No. 1*, par. 37.

NATIONAL BRANDS CORPORATION
Statement of Cash Flows
For Year Ended December 31, 1997 ($ in millions)

Cash flows from operating activities:

Cash inflows:

From customers	$98	
From investment revenue	3	
Cash outflows:		
To suppliers of goods	(50)	
To employees	(11)	
For interest	(3)	
For insurance	(4)	
For income taxes	(11)	
Net cash flows from operating activities		$22

Cash flows from investing activities:

Purchase of land	(30)	
Purchase of short-term investment	(12)	
Sale of land	18	
Sale of equipment	5	
Net cash flows from investing activities		(19)

Cash flows from financing activities:

Sale of common shares	26	
Retirement of bonds payable	(15)	
Payment of cash dividends	(5)	
Net cash flows from financing activities		6
Net increase in cash		9
Cash balance, January 1		20
Cash balance, December 31		$29

Noncash investing and financing activities:

Acquired $20 million of equipment by issuing a 12%, 5-year note.	$20

Evolution of the Statement of Cash Flows

Learning objective 3
Relate the statement of cash flows to its historical evolution.

Early efforts to instill the standard of accrual accounting intentionally suppressed the widespread practice of cash flow reporting.

Responding to the need for some type of funds flow reporting, funds statements flourished, typically defining funds as working capital.

In light of the obvious value of cash flow information, it's interesting to note that the statement of cash flows has been a required financial statement only since 1988. The relatively recent requirement completes a full-cycle movement of accounting thought back to cash flow reporting, which, in different form, was common practice several decades ago.

During the early part of this century and continuing into the mid-1930s, the preparation of financial statements on a cash basis was a widely used means of financial reporting, particularly by small and medium-sized companies. It is important to realize, however, that the cash flow reporting requirements of today are quite different from the cash flow reporting practiced during that earlier era, when emphasis was placed on cash-based income determination. The accounting profession was fully aware that accrual accounting (recognizing revenues when earned, expenses when incurred) provides a far better measure of a company's profitability. However, without official standards to ensure the general use of accrual accounting, cash-based reporting flourished. Motivated by the desire to instill the standard of accrual accounting, a concerted effort was exerted to suppress cash-based methods.

As cash-flow reporting abated, the need for some type of funds-flow reporting became apparent and a funds statement began to appear in the annual reports of many companies. Because the statement was not required and there was no officially prescribed format, the definition and presentation of funds varied widely among firms that issued the statement. The mounting bias against cash-based reporting certainly influenced many firms to choose alternate definitions of funds.

---

2 Cheryl A. Zega, "The New Statement of Cash Flows," *Management Accounting*, September 1988.

Prompted by increasing concerns over the lack of uniformity in the reporting of funds flow, the AICPA sponsored a 1961 research study by Perry Mason (the accountant, not the lawyer) entitled "Cash Flow Analysis and the Funds Statement." The study recommended that a funds statement be required.[3] Two years later, *APB Opinion 3* officially recommended, but did not require, a "Statement of Source and Application of Funds."[4] The noncash bias was evident in this opinion. It cautioned against the use of terms such as cash flow and cash earnings and defined funds generally as working capital (current assets minus current liabilities).

The first official requirement that a funds statement be included as an integral part of a complete set of financial statements was issued in 1971. *APB Opinion 19* required a statement of changes in financial position that reported funds flows classified as either sources (increases) or applications (decreases) of funds, as well as any significant nonfund investing and financing activities. Funds could be defined as either cash or working capital.[5] Although defining funds as cash was permitted, a working capital definition predominated practice until the early 1980s. This preference was influenced by the historical bias, described earlier, against cash flow reporting.

The Financial Executives Institute recommended that its members report on a cash basis after being persuaded by many accounting professors and practitioners that a cash-based definition of funds is more meaningful than a working capital definition.[6] This recommendation provided the impetus for a dramatic increase in the number of firms choosing to define funds as cash in their statements of changes in financial position.[7]

The increasingly widespread acceptance of cash-flow reporting, coupled with a recommendation in 1984 of FASB *Concept Statement 5* that a full set of financial statements show cash flows during the period, virtually assured the eventual requirement of a statement of cash flows.[8] In November, 1987, the FASB prescribed *SFAS 95* (to supersede *APB Opinion 19*), described in this chapter.

> **Early official recommendations confessed a noncash bias.**

> **The statement of changes in financial position was the predecessor to the statement of cash flows.**

GLOBAL PERSPECTIVE

A statement of cash flows (or funds flow statement some places) is optional in many countries. France, Germany and some other West European countries are examples. In some countries, like the United Kingdom, it's required only for large firms.

Cash and Cash Equivalents

> **Learning objective 4**
> Define cash equivalents.

> **There is no differentiation between amounts held as cash and amounts held in cash equivalent investments.**

Skilled cash managers will invest temporarily idle cash in short-term investments to earn interest on those funds, rather than maintain an unnecessarily large checking account. The FASB views short-term, highly liquid investments that can be readily converted to cash, with little risk of loss, as cash equivalents. Amounts held as investments of this type are essentially equivalent to cash because they are quickly available for use as cash. Therefore, on the statement of cash flows there is no differentiation between amounts held as cash (e.g., currency and checking accounts) and amounts held in cash equivalent investments. So, when we refer in this chapter to cash, we are referring to the total of cash and cash equivalents.

> **Each firm's policy regarding which short-term, highly liquid investments it classifies as cash equivalents should be disclosed in the notes to the financial statements.**

Examples of cash equivalents are money market funds, treasury bills, and commercial paper. To be classified as cash equivalents, these investments must have a maturity date not longer than three months from the date of purchase. Flexibility is permitted in designating cash equivalents. Each company must establish a policy regarding which short-term, highly liquid investments it classifies as cash equivalents. The policy should be consistent with the company's customary motivation for acquiring various investments and should be disclosed in the notes to the statement.[9] A recent annual report of Exxon Corporation provides this description of its cash equivalents:

---

[3] Perry Mason, " Cash Flow Analysis and the Funds Statement," *Accounting Research Study No. 2,* 1961.

[4] "The Statement of Source and Application of Funds," *Opinions of the Accounting Principles Board No. 3,* 1963, par. 8.

[5] "Reporting Changes in Financial Position," *Opinions of the Accounting Principles Board No. 19,* 1971.

[6] See, for example, Lloyd C. Heath, "Let's Scrap the Funds Statement," *The Journal of Accountancy,* October 1978, and Edward Swanson and Richard Vandermeersch, "Statement of Financing and Investing Activities," *The CPA Journal,* November 1981.

[7] Allen H. Seed, III, *The Funds Statement—Structure and Use,* Financial Executives Research Foundation, 1984.

[8] "Recognition and Measurement in Financial Statements of Business Enterprises," *FASB Statement of Financial Accounting Concepts No. 5,* par. 13.

[9] A change in that policy is treated as a change in accounting principle.

GRAPHIC   22-3

Disclosure of Cash
Equivalents—Exxon
Corporation

Note 4: Cash Flow Information (in part)

The consolidated statement of cash flows provides information about changes in cash and cash equivalents. All short-term marketable securities, generally with original maturities of three months or less, that are readily convertible to known amounts of cash and are so near maturity that they present insignificant risk of changes in value because of changes in interest rates, are classified as cash equivalents.

Transactions that involve merely transfers from cash to cash equivalents (such as the purchase of a three-month treasury bill), or from cash equivalents to cash (such as the sale of a treasury bill), should not be reported on the statement of cash flows. The total of cash and cash equivalents is not altered by such transactions.[10] The cash balance reported on the balance sheet also represents the total of cash and cash equivalents, which allows us to compare the change in that balance with the net increase or decrease in the cash flows reported on the statement of cash flows.

Primary Elements of the Statement of Cash Flows

This section describes the three primary activity classifications: (1) operating activities, (2) investing activities, and (3) financing activities; and two other requirements of the statement of cash flows: (4) the reconciliation of the net increase or decrease in cash with the change in the balance of the cash account and (5) noncash investing and financing activities.

Cash Flows from Operating Activities.   The income statement reports the success of a business in generating a profit from its operations. Net income (or loss) is the result of combining the revenues earned during the reporting period, regardless of when cash is received, and the expenses incurred in generating those revenues, regardless of when cash is paid. This is the accrual concept of accounting that has been emphasized throughout your study of accounting. Information about net income and its components, measured by the accrual concept, generally provides a better indication of current operating performance than does information about current cash receipts and payments.[11] Nevertheless, as indicated earlier, the cash effects of earning activities also provide useful information that is not directly accessible from the income statement. The first cash flow classification in the statement of cash flows reports that information.

Cash flows from operating activities are both inflows and outflows of cash that result from activities reported on the income statement. In other words, this classification of cash flows includes the elements of net income, but reported on a cash basis. The components of this section of the statement of cash flows, and their relationship with the elements of the income statement, are illustrated in Graphic 22–4.

Income Statement	Cash Flows from Operating Activities
Revenues:	Cash inflows:
Sales and service revenue	Cash received from customers
Investment revenue	Cash revenue received (e.g., dividends, interest)
Noncash revenues and gains	
(e.g., gain on sale of assets)	(Not reported)
Less: Expenses:	Less: Cash outflows:
Cost of goods sold	Cash paid to suppliers of inventory
Salaries expense	Cash paid to employees
Noncash expenses and losses (e.g., depreciation,	
amortization, bad debts, loss on sale of assets)	(Not reported)
Interest expense	Cash paid to creditors
Other operating expenses	Cash paid to insurance companies and others
Income tax expense	Cash paid to the government
Net income	*Net cash flows from operating activities*

---

[10] An exception is the sale of a cash equivalent at a gain or loss. This exception is described in more detail later in the chapter.

[11] *FASB Statement of Financial Accounting Concepts No. 1*, par. 44.

To see the concept applied, let's look again at the cash flows from operating activities reported by National Brands Corporation. That section of the statement of cash flows is extracted from Graphic 22–2 and reproduced in Graphic 22–5.

GRAPHIC   22–5

Cash Flows from Operating Activities

Cash flows from operating activities are the elements of net income, but reported on a cash basis.

Cash flows from operating activities:		
Cash inflows:		
From customers	$98	
From investment revenue	3	
Cash outflows:		
To suppliers of goods	(50)	
To employees	(11)	
For interest	(3)	
For insurance	(4)	
For income taxes	(11)	
Net cash flows from operating activities		$22

Cash inflows from operating activities exceeded cash outflows for expenses by $22 million. We'll see later (in Illustration 22–1) that NBC's net income from the same operating activities was only $12 million. Why did operating activities produce net cash inflows greater than net income? The reason will become apparent when we determine, in a later section, the specific amounts of these cash flows.

You also should be aware that the generalization stated earlier that cash flows from operating activities include the elements of net income reported on a cash basis is not strictly true for all elements of the income statement. Notice in Graphic 22–5 that no cash effects are reported for depreciation and amortization of operational assets, nor for gains and losses from the sale of those assets. Cash outflows occur when operational assets are acquired, and cash inflows occur when the assets are sold. However, as described later, the acquisition and subsequent resale of operational assets are classified as investing activities, rather than as operating activities.

Quite the opposite, the purchase and the sale of inventory are considered operating activities. The cash effects of these transactions—namely, (1) cash payments to suppliers and (2) cash receipts from customers—are included in the determination of cash flows from operating activities. Why are inventories and operational assets treated differently when classifying their cash effects if both are acquired for the purpose of producing revenues? The essential difference is that inventory typically is purchased for the purpose of being sold as part of the firm's current operations, while an operational asset is purchased as an investment to benefit the business over a relatively long period of time.

OPENING CASE

Question 2

Cash outflows and cash inflows due to the acquisition and disposition of assets (other than inventory and assets classified as cash equivalents) are reported as cash flows from investing activities.

Cash flows from Investing Activities.   Companies periodically invest cash to replace or expand productive facilities such as property, plant, and equipment. Investments might also be made in other assets, such as securities of other firms, with the expectation of a return on those investments. Information concerning these investing activities can provide valuable insight to decision makers regarding the nature and magnitude of operational assets being acquired for future use, as well as provide clues concerning the company's ambitions for the future.

Cash flows from investing activities are both outflows and inflows of cash caused by the acquisition and disposition of assets other than (a) inventory and (b) assets classified as cash equivalents. Included in this classification are cash payments to acquire (1) property, plant, and equipment and other productive assets (except inventories), (2) investments in securities (except cash equivalents), and (3) nontrade receivables. When these assets later are liquidated, any cash receipts from their disposition also are classified as investing activities. For instance, cash received from the sale of assets or from the collection of a note receivable (principal amount only) represents cash inflows from investing activities.

For illustration, notice the cash flows reported as investing activities by NBC. That section of the statement of cash flows is extracted from Graphic 22–2 and reproduced in Graphic 22–6.

NBC reports as investing activities the cash paid to purchase both land and a short-term investment. The other two investing activities reported are cash receipts for the sale of assets—equip-

GRAPHIC 22–6

Cash Flows from Investing Activities

Cash flows from investing activities include investments in assets and their subsequent sale.

Cash flows from investing activities:		
Purchase of land	(30)	
Purchase of short-term investment	(12)	
Sale of land	18	
Sale of equipment	5	
Net cash flows from investing activities		(19)

ment and land—that were acquired in earlier years. The specific transactions creating these cash flows are described in a later section of this chapter.

The purchase and sale of inventories are not considered investing activities. Inventories are purchased for the purpose of being sold as part of the firm's primary operations, so their purchase and sale are classified as operating activities.

Also, the purchase and sale of assets classified as cash equivalents are not reported as investing activities. In fact, these activities usually are not reported on the statement of cash flows. For example, when temporarily idle cash is invested in a money market fund, considered to be a cash equivalent, the total of cash and cash equivalents does not change. Likewise, when the cash is later withdrawn from the money market fund, the total remains unchanged. The exception is when cash equivalents are sold at a gain or a loss. In that case, the total of cash and cash equivalents actually increases or decreases in the process of transferring from one cash equivalent account to another cash equivalent account. As a result, the change in cash would be reported as a cash flow from operating activities. This is illustrated later in the chapter.

OPENING CASE

Question 3

Cash inflows and cash outflows due to the external financing of a business are reported as Cash flows from financing activities.

Cash Flows from Financing Activities. Not only is it important for investors and creditors to be informed about how a company is investing its funds, but also how its investing activities are being financed. Hopefully, the primary operations of the firm provide a source of internal financing. Information revealed in the cash flows from operating activities section of the statement of cash flows lets statement users know the extent of available internal financing. However, a major portion of financing for many companies is provided by external sources, specifically by shareholders and creditors.

Cash flows from financing activities are both inflows and outflows of cash resulting from the external financing of a business. We include in this classification cash inflows from (a) the sale of common and preferred stock and (b) the issuance of bonds and other debt securities. Subsequent transactions related to these financing transactions, such as (a) the repurchase of common or preferred stock (to retire the stock or as treasury stock), (b) the repayment of debt, and (c) the payment of cash dividends to shareholders, are also classified as financing activities.

For illustration, refer to the following excerpt from Graphic 22–2.

GRAPHIC 22–7

Cash Flows from Financing Activities

Cash flows from financing activities include the sale or repurchase of shares, the issuance or repayment of debt securities, and the payment of cash dividends.

Cash flows from financing activities:		
Sale of common shares	26	
Retirement of bonds payable	(15)	
Payment of cash dividends	(5)	
Net cash flows from financing activities		6

The cash received from the sale of common stock is reported as a financing activity. Since the sale of common stock is a financing activity, providing a cash return (dividend) to common shareholders also is a financing activity. Similarly, when the bonds being retired were sold in a prior year, that cash inflow was reported as a financing activity. In the current year, when the bonds are retired, the resulting cash outflow is likewise classified as a financing activity.

At first glance, it may appear inconsistent to classify the payment of cash dividends to shareholders as a financing activity when, as stated earlier, paying interest to creditors is classified as an operating activity. But remember, cash flows from operating activities should reflect the cash effects of items that enter into the determination of net income. Interest expense is a deter-

Interest, unlike dividends, is a determinant of net income and therefore an operating activity.

minant of net income. A dividend, on the other hand, is a distribution of net income and not an expense.[12]

Reconciliation with Change in Cash Balance.
One of the first items you may have noticed about NBC's statement of cash flows is that there is a net change in cash of $9 million. Is this a significant item of information provided by the statement? The primary objective of the statement of cash flows is not to tell us that cash increased by $9 million. We can readily see the increase or decrease in cash by comparing the beginning and ending balances in the cash account in comparative balance sheets. Instead, the purpose of the statement of cash flows is to explain why cash increased by $9 million.

To reinforce the fact that the net amount of cash inflows and outflows explains the change in the cash balance, the statement of cash flows includes a reconciliation of the net increase (or decrease) in cash with the company's beginning and ending cash balances. Notice, for instance, that on NBC's statement of cash flows, the reconciliation appears as:

Net increase in cash	$ 9
Cash balance, January 1	20
Cash balance, December 31	$29

> The net amount of cash inflows and outflows reconciles the change in the company's beginning and ending cash balances.

Noncash Investing and Financing Activities.
Suppose NBC were to borrow $20 million cash from a bank, issuing a long-term note payable for that amount. This transaction would be reported on a statement of cash flows as a financing activity. Now suppose NBC used that $20 million cash to purchase new equipment. This second transaction would be reported as an investing activity.

Instead of two separate transactions, as indicated by Graphic 22–2, NBC acquired $20 million of new equipment by issuing a $20 million long-term note payable in a single transaction. Undertaking a significant investing activity and a significant financing activity as two parts of a single transaction does not diminish the value of reporting these activities. For that reason, transactions that do not increase or decrease cash, but which result in significant investing and financing activities, must be reported in related disclosures.

> **Learning objective 6**
> Identify transactions that represent noncash investing and financing activities.

These noncash investing and financing activities, such as NBC's acquiring equipment (an investing activity) by issuing a long-term note payable (a financing activity), are reported in a separate disclosure schedule or note. NBC reported this transaction in the following manner:

> **Noncash investing and financing activities:**
> Acquired $20 million of equipment by issuing a 12%, 5-year note.

> Noncash investing and financing activities are reported also.

It's convenient to report noncash investing and financing activities on the same page as the statement of cash flows as did NBC only if there are few such transactions. Otherwise, precisely the same information would be reported in disclosure notes to the financial statements.[13]

Examples of noncash transactions that would be reported in this manner are:

1. Acquiring an asset by incurring a debt payable to the seller.
2. Acquiring an asset by entering into a capital lease.
3. Converting debt into common stock or other equity securities.
4. Exchanging noncash assets or liabilities for other noncash assets or liabilities.

Noncash transactions that do not affect a company's assets or liabilities, such as the distribution of stock dividends, are not considered investing or financing activities and are not reported. Recall from Chapter 19 that stock dividends merely increase the number of shares of stock owned by existing shareholders. From an accounting standpoint, the stock dividend causes a dollar amount to be transferred from one part of shareholders' equity (retained earnings) to another part of shareholders' equity (paid-in capital). Neither assets nor liabilities are affected; therefore, no investing or financing activity has occurred.

---

[12] Not all accountants are satisfied with the FASB's distinctions among operating, investing, and financing activities. See for example, Hugo Nurnberg, "Inconsistencies and Ambiguities in Cash Flow Statements under FASB Statement No. 95," *Accounting Horizons*, June 1993.

[13] "Statement of Cash Flows," *Statement of Financial Accounting Standards No. 95*, (Stamford, Conn.: FASB, 1987), par. 74.

Additional Consideration

A transaction involving an investing and financing activity may be part cash and part noncash. For example, a company might pay cash for a part of the purchase price of new equipment and issue a long-term note for the remaining amount. In our previous illustration NBC issued a note payable for the $20 million cost of the equipment it acquired. Suppose the equipment were purchased in the following manner:

Equipment	20	
Cash		6
Note payable		14

In that case, $6 million would be reported under the caption "Cash flows from investing activities," and the noncash portion of the transaction – issuing a $14 million note payable for $14 million of equipment – would be reported as a "noncash investing and financing activity." NBC's statement of cash flows, if modified by the assumption of a part cash / part noncash transaction, would report these two elements of the transaction as follows:

Cash flows from investing activities:		
Purchase of land	$(30)	
Purchase of short-term investments	(12)	
Sale of land	18	
Sale of equipment	5	
Purchase of equipment	**(6)**	
Net cash flows from investing activities		(25)
Noncash investing and financing activities:		
Acquired $20 million of equipment by paying cash and issuing a 12%, 5-year note as follows:		
Cost of equipment	$20 million	
Cash paid	6 million	
Note issued	$14 million	

Preparation of the Statement of Cash Flows

Learning objective 7
Prepare a statement of cash flows with the aid of a spreadsheet.

The objective in preparing the statement of cash flows is to identify all transactions and events that represent operating, investing, or financing activities and to list and classify those activities in proper statement format. Typically, the information available to assist the statement preparer includes an income statement for the year and balance sheets for both the current and preceding years (comparative statements). The accounting records also can provide additional information about transactions that caused changes in account balances during the year.

The typical year-end data is provided for NBC in Illustration 22–1.

We have referred frequently to the statement of cash flows of NBC to illustrate the nature of the activities the statement reports. Now we will see how that statement is developed from the data provided in Illustration 22–1.

In situations involving relatively few transactions, it is possible to prepare the statement of cash flows by merely inspecting the available data and logically determining the reportable activities. Few real-life situations are sufficiently simple to be solved this way. Usually, it is more practical to use some systematic method of analyzing the available data to ensure that all operating, investing, and financing activities are detected. A common approach is to use either a manual or electronic spreadsheet to organize and analyze the information used to prepare the statement.[14]

Reconstructing the events and transactions that occurred during the period helps identify the operating, investing, and financing activities to be reported.

Whether the statement of cash flows is prepared by an unaided inspection and analysis or with the aid of a systematic technique such as spreadsheet analysis, the analytical process is the same. To identify the activities to be reported on the statement, we use available data to reconstruct the events and transactions that involved operating, investing, and financing activities during the year. It is helpful to reproduce the journal entries that were recorded at the time of the transaction. Examining reconstructed journal entries makes it easier to visualize whether a reportable activity is involved and how that activity is to be classified.

---

[14] The T–account method is a second systematic approach to the preparation of the statement of cash flows. This method is identical in concept and similar in application to the spreadsheet method. The T-account method is used to prepare the statement of cash flows for NBC in Appendix 22B.

ILLUSTRATION   22–1

Comparative Balance Sheets and Income Statement

NATIONAL BRANDS CORPORATION
Comparative Balance Sheets
December 31, 1997 and 1996 ($ in millions)

Assets:	1997	1996
Cash	$ 29	$ 20
Accounts receivable	32	30
Short-term investments	12	0
Inventory	46	50
Prepaid insurance	3	6
Land	80	60
Buildings and equipment	81	75
Less: Accumulated depreciation	(16)	(20)
	$267	$221
Liabilities:		
Accounts payable	$ 26	$ 20
Salaries payable	3	1
Income tax payable	6	8
Notes payable	20	0
Bonds payable	35	50
Less: Discount on bonds	(1)	(3)
Shareholders' Equity:		
Common stock	130	100
Paid-in capital–excess of par	29	20
Retained earnings	19	25
	$267	$221

National Brands Corporation
Income Statement
For the Year Ended December 31, 1997 ($ in millions)

Revenues:		
Sales revenue	$100	
Investment revenue	3	
Gain on sale of land	8	$111
Expenses:		
Cost of goods sold	60	
Salaries expense	13	
Depreciation expense	3	
Bond interest expense	5	
Insurance expense	7	
Loss on sale of equipment	2	
Income tax expense	9	99
Net income		$ 12

Additional information from the accounting records:

a. A portion of company land, purchased in a previous year for $10 million, was sold for $18 million.
b. Equipment that originally cost $14 million, and which was one-half depreciated, was sold for $5 million cash.
c. The common shares of Mazuma Corporation were purchased for $12 million as a short-term investment.
d. Property was purchased for $30 million cash for use as a parking lot.
e. On December 30, 1997, new equipment was acquired by issuing a 12%, five-year, $20 million note payable to the seller.
f. On January 1, 1997, $15 million of bonds were retired at maturity.
g. The increase in the common stock account is attributable to the issuance of a 10% stock dividend (1 million shares) and the subsequent sale of 2 million shares of common stock. The market price of the $10 par value common stock was $13 per share on the dates of both transactions.
h. Cash dividends of $5 million were paid to shareholders.

Preparing a Spreadsheet

> There can be no cash inflow or cash outflow without a corresponding change in a noncash account.

An important advantage gained by using a spreadsheet is that it ensures that no reportable activities are inadvertently overlooked. Spreadsheet analysis relies on the fact that, in order for cash to increase or decrease, there must be a corresponding change in a noncash account. Therefore, if we can identify the events and transactions that caused the change in each noncash account during the year, we will have identified all the operating, investing, and financing activities that are to be included in the statement of cash flows.

The beginning and ending balances of each account are entered on the spreadsheet. Then, as journal entries are reconstructed in our analysis of the data, those entries are recorded on the spreadsheet so that the debits and credits of the spreadsheet entries explain the changes in the account balances. Only after spreadsheet entries have explained the changes in all account balances, can we feel confident that all operating, investing, and financing activities have been identified. The spreadsheet is designed in such a way that, as we record spreadsheet entries that explain account balance changes, we are simultaneously identifying and classifying the activities to be reported on the statement of cash flows.

We begin by transferring the comparative balance sheets and income statement to a blank spreadsheet. For illustration, refer to the 1997 and 1996 balances in the completed spreadsheet for NBC, shown in Illustration 22–1a. Notice that the amounts for elements of the income statement are ending balances resulting from accumulations during the year. Beginning balances in each of these accounts are always zero.

Following the balance sheets and income statement, we allocate space on the spreadsheet for the statement of cash flows. Although at this point we have not yet identified the specific cash flow activities shown in the completed spreadsheet, we can include headings for the major cate-

ILLUSTRATION 22–1a

Spreadsheet

NATIONAL BRANDS CORPORATION
Spreadsheet for the Statement of Cash Flows

	Dec. 31 1996	Changes Debits		Changes Credits		Dec. 31 1997
Balance Sheet						
Assets:						
Cash	20	(19)	9			29
Accounts receivable	30	(1)	2			32
Short-term investments	0	(12)	12			12
Inventory	50			(4)	4	46
Prepaid insurance	6			(8)	3	3
Land	60	(13)	30	(3)	10	80
Buildings and equipment	75	(14)	20 **X**	(9)	14	81
Less: Accumulated depreciation	(20)	(9)	7	(6)	3	(16)
	221					267
Liabilities:						
Accounts payable	20			(4)	6	26
Salaries payable	1			(5)	2	3
Income tax payable	8	(10)	2			6
Notes payable	0			(14)	20	20
Bonds payable	50	(15)	15			35
Less: Discount on bonds	(3)			(7)	2	(1)
Shareholders' Equity:						
Common stock	100			(16)	10	
				(17)	20 **X**	130
Paid-in capital—excess of par	20			(16)	3	
				(17)	6	29
Retained earnings	25	(16)	13			
		(18)	5	(11)	12	19
	221					267
Income Statement						
Revenues:						
Sales revenue				(1)	100	100
Investment revenue				(2)	3	3
Gain on sale of land				(3)	8	8
Expenses:						
Cost of goods sold		(4)	60			(60)
Salaries expense		(5)	13			(13)
Depreciation expense		(6)	3			(3)
Bond interest expense		(7)	5			(5)
Insurance expense		(8)	7			(7)
Loss on sale of equipment		(9)	2			(2)
Income tax expense		(10)	9			(9)
Net income		(11)	**12**			**12**

ILLUSTRATION   22–1

concluded

| | Changes | | |
	Debits	Credits	Net
Statement of Cash Flows			
Operating activities:			
Cash inflows:			
From customers	(1) 98		
From investment revenue	(2) 3		
Cash outflows:			
To suppliers of goods		(4) 50	
To employees		(5) 11	
To bondholders		(7) 3	
For insurance expense		(8) 4	
For income taxes		(10) 11	
Net cash flows			22
Investing activities:			
Sale of land	(3) 18		
Sale of equipment	(9) 5		
Purchase of S-T investment		(12) 12	
Purchase of land		(13) 30	
Net cash flows			(19)
Financing activities:			
Retirement of bonds payable		(15) 15	
Sale of common shares	(17) 26		
Payment of cash dividends		(18) 5	
Net cash flows			6
Net increase in cash		(19) 9	9
Totals	376	376	

gories of activities: cash flows from operating activities, cash flows from investing activities, and cash flows from financing activities. Leaving several lines between headings allows adequate space to include the specific cash flows identified in subsequent analysis.

The spreadsheet entries shown in the two changes columns, which separate the beginning and ending balances, explain the increase or decrease in each account balance. You will see in the next section how these entries were reconstructed. Although spreadsheet entries are in the form of debits and credits like journal entries, they are entered on the spreadsheet only. They are not recorded in the formal accounting records. In effect, these entries duplicate, frequently in summary form, the actual journal entries used to record the transactions as they occurred during the year.

To reconstruct the journal entries, we analyze each account, one at a time, deciding at each step what transaction or event caused the change in that account. Often, the reason for the change in an account balance is readily apparent from viewing the change in conjunction with that of a related account elsewhere in the financial statements. Sometimes it is necessary to consult the accounting records for additional information to help explain the transaction that resulted in the change.

You may find it helpful to diagram in T-account format the relationship between accounts to better visualize certain changes, particularly in your initial study of the chapter. The analysis that follows is occasionally supplemented with such diagrams to emphasize *why*, rather than merely *how*, specific cash flow amounts emerge from the analysis.

Although there is no mandatory order in which to analyze the accounts, it is convenient to begin with the income statement accounts, followed by the balance sheet accounts. We analyze the accounts of NBC in that order below. Although our analysis of each account culminates in a spreadsheet entry, keep in mind that the analysis described also is appropriate to identify reportable activities when a spreadsheet is not used.[15]

> Spreadsheet entries duplicate the actual journal entries used to record the transactions as they occurred during the year.

---

[15] The spreadsheet entries also are used to record the same transactions when the T-account method is used. We refer again to these entries when that method is described in Appendix 22B.

Income Statement Accounts

As described in an earlier section, cash flows from operating activities are inflows and outflows of cash that result from activities reported on the income statement. Thus, to identify those cash inflows and outflows, we begin by analyzing the components of the income statement. It is important to keep in mind that the amounts reported on the income statement usually do not represent the cash effects of the items reported. For example, NBC reports sales revenue of $100 million. This does not mean, however, that it collected $100 million cash from customers during the year. In fact, by referring to the beginning and ending balances in accounts receivable, we see that cash received from customers could not have been $100 million. Since accounts receivable increased during the year, some of the sales revenue earned must not yet have been collected. This is explained further in the next section.

The cash effects of other income statement elements can be similarly discerned by referring to changes in the balances of the balance sheet accounts that are directly related to those elements. So, to identify cash flows from operating activities we examine, one at a time, the elements of the income statement in conjunction with any balance sheet accounts affected by each element.

1. Sales Revenue. Accounts receivable is the balance sheet account that is affected by sales revenue. Specifically, accounts receivable is increased by credit sales and is decreased as cash is received from customers. We can compare sales and the change in accounts receivable during the year to determine the amount of cash received from customers. This relationship can be viewed in T–account format as follows:

Accounts Receivable

Beginning balance	30		
Credit sales	100	?	Cash received
(*increases A/R*)			(*decreases A/R*)
Ending balance	32		

We see from this analysis that cash received from customers must have been **$98** million. Note that even if some of the year's sales were cash sales, say $40 million cash sales and $60 million credit sales, the result is the same:

Accounts Receivable

Beginning balance	30		Cash sales	$40
Credit sales	60	58	Received on account	58
Ending balance	32		Cash received	$98

Thus, cash flows from operating activities should include cash received from customers of $98 million. The net effect of sales revenue activity during the year can be summarized in the following entry.

		($ in millions)
Entry (1) Cash (received from customers)		98
Accounts receivable (given)		2
Sales revenue ($100 – 0)		100

The entry above appears as entry (1) in the completed spreadsheet for NBC, shown in Illustration 22-1a. The entry explains the changes in two account balances—accounts receivable and sales revenue. Since the entry affects cash, it also identifies a cash flow to be reported on the statement of cash flows. The $98 million debit to cash is therefore entered in the statement of cash flows section of the spreadsheet under the heading of cash flows from operating activities.

Notice that we enter the cash portion of the entry as one of several cash flows on the statement of cash flows rather than as a debit to the cash account. Only after all cash inflows and outflows have been identified will the net change in cash be entered as a debit to the cash account. In fact, the entry to reconcile the $9 million increase in the cash account and the $9 million net increase in cash on the statement of cash flows will serve as a final check of the accuracy of our spreadsheet analysis.

Additional Consideration

Notice that bad debt expense does not appear on the income statement and allowance for uncollectible accounts does not appear on the balance sheet. We have assumed that bad debts are immaterial for NBC. When this is not the case, it's necessary to consider the write-off of bad debts as we determine cash received from customers. Here's why.

When using the allowance method to account for bad debts, a company estimates the dollar amount of customer accounts that will ultimately prove uncollectible and records both bad debt expense and allowance for uncollectible accounts for that estimate.

Bad debts expense	xxx	
Allowance for uncollectible accounts		xxx

Then, when accounts actually prove uncollectible, accounts receivable and the allowance are reduced.

Allowance for uncollectible accounts	xxx	
Accounts receivable		xxx

In our illustration, we concluded that NBC received $2 million less cash ($98 million) than sales for the year ($100 million) because accounts receivable increased by that amount. However, if a portion of the change in accounts receivable had been due to write-offs of bad debts, that conclusion would be incorrect. Let's say, for instance, that NBC had bad debt expense of $2 million and its allowance for uncollectible accounts had increased by $1 million. Because the allowance for uncollectible accounts would be credited by $2 million in the adjusting entry for bad debts expense, necessarily there also would have been a $1 million debit to the account in order for there to have been a net increase (credit) in its balance of only $1 million. That debit would occur due to write-offs of bad debts totaling $1 million.

		($ in millions)
Allowance for uncollectible accounts	1	
Accounts receivable		1

This would indicate that a portion ($1 million credit) of the total change in accounts receivable ($2 million debit) would have been due to write-offs of bad debts, and the remaining change ($3 million debit) would have been due to cash collections being less than sales revenue. Cash received from customers would have been only $97 million in that case. We can view this in the framework of our T-account analysis as follows:

Accounts Receivable

Beginning balance	30		
Credit sales	100	97	Cash received
		1	Bad debt write-offs
Ending balance	32		

The effect of write-offs of bad debts can be explicitly considered by combining all the accounts related to sales and collection activities into a single summary spreadsheet entry:

			($ in millions)
Entry (1)	Cash (received from customers)	97	
	Accounts receivable ($32 – 30)	2	
	Bad debts expense (from income statement)	2	
	Allowance for uncollectible accounts ($3 – 2)		1
	Sales revenue ($100 – 0)		100

This single entry summarizes all transactions related to sales, bad debts expense, write-offs of accounts receivable, and cash collections from sales.

The remaining spreadsheet entries are described in subsections 2 through 19. When including the entries on the spreadsheet, it is helpful to number the entries sequentially to provide a means of retracing the steps taken in the analysis if the need arises.

2. Investment Revenue.

The income statement reports investment revenue of $3 million. Before concluding that this amount was received in cash, we first refer to the balance sheets to see whether a change in an account there indicates otherwise. A change in either of two balance sheet accounts, (a) investment revenue receivable or (b) long-term investments, might indicate that cash received from investment revenue differs from the amount reported on the income statement.

a. If we observe either an increase or a decrease in an *investment revenue receivable* account (e.g., interest receivable, dividends receivable), we would conclude that the amount of cash received during the year was less than (if an increase) or more than (if a decrease) the amount of revenue reported. The analysis would be identical to that of sales revenue and accounts receivable.

b. Also, an unexplained increase in a *long-term investment* account might indicate that a portion of investment revenue has not yet been received in cash. Recall from Chapter 12 that when using the equity method to account for investments in the stock of another corporation, investment revenue is recognized as the investor's percentage share of the investee's income, whether or not the revenue is received currently as cash dividends. For example, assume the investor owns 25% of the common stock of a corporation that reports net income of $12 million and pays dividends of $4 million. This situation would have produced a $2 million increase in long-term investments, which can be demonstrated by reconstructing the journal entries for the recognition of investment revenue and the receipt of cash dividends:

Note (margin): Changes in related accounts might indicate that investment revenue reported on the income statement is a different amount from cash received from the investment.

	($ in millions)	
Long-term investments	3	
Investment revenue ($12 × 25%)		3
Cash ($4 × 25%)	1	
Long-term investments		1

A combined entry would produce the same results:

	($ in millions)	
Long-term investments	2	
Cash ($4 × 25%)	1	
Investment revenue ($12 × 25%)		3

The $2 million net increase in long-term investments would represent the investment revenue not received in cash. This would also explain why there is a $3 million increase (credit) in investment revenue. If these events had occurred, we would prepare a spreadsheet entry identical to the combined entry above. The spreadsheet entry would (a) explain the $2 million increase in long-term investments, (b) explain the $3 million increase in investment revenue, and (c) identify a $1 million cash inflow from operating activities.

However, because neither an investment revenue receivable account nor a long-term investment account appears on the comparative balance sheets, we can conclude that $3 million of investment revenue was collected in cash. Entry (2) on the spreadsheet is:

Note (margin): Because no other transactions are apparent that would have caused a change in investment revenue, we can conclude that $3 million of investment revenue was collected in cash.

	($ in millions)	
Entry (2) Cash (received from investment revenue)	3	
Investment revenue ($3 – 0)		3

3. Gain on Sale of Land.

The third item reported on the income statement is an $8 million gain on the sale of land. Recall that our objective in analyzing each element of the statement is to determine the cash effect of that element. To do so, we need additional information about the transaction that caused this gain. The accounting records—item (a) in Illustration 22–1—indicate that land that originally cost $10 million was sold for $18 million. The entry recorded in the journal when the land was sold also serves as our spreadsheet entry:

A gain (or loss) is simply the difference between cash received in the sale of an asset and the book value of the asset—not a cash flow.

		($ in millions)
Entry (3)	Cash (received from sale of land)	18
	Land (given)	10
	Gain on sale of land ($8 – 0)	8

The cash effect of this transaction is a cash increase of $18 million. We therefore include the debit as a cash inflow in the statement of cash flows section of the spreadsheet. However, unlike the cash effect of the previous two spreadsheet entries, it is not reported as an operating activity. The sale of land is an investing activity, so this cash inflow is listed under that heading of the spreadsheet. The entry also accounts for the $8 million gain on sale of land. The $10 million credit to land does not, by itself, explain the $20 million increase in that account. As we will later discover, another transaction also affected the land account.

It is important to understand that the gain is simply the difference between cash received in the sale of land (reported as an investing activity) and the book value of the land. To report the $8 million gain as a cash flow from operating activities, in addition to reporting $18 million as a cash flow from investing activities, would be to report the $8 million twice.

4. Cost of Goods Sold.   During the year NBC sold goods that had cost $60 million. This does not necessarily indicate that $60 million cash was paid to suppliers of those goods. To determine the amount of cash paid to suppliers, we look to the two current accounts affected by merchandise purchases—inventory and accounts payable. The analysis can be viewed as a two-step process.

First, we compare cost of goods sold with the change in inventory to determine the cost of goods *purchased* (not necessarily cash paid) during the year. To facilitate our analysis, we can examine the relationship in T-account format:

Inventory

Beginning balance	50		
Cost of goods **purchased**	?	60	Cost of goods **sold**
(increases inventory)			*(decreases inventory)*
Ending balance	46		

From this analysis, we see that **$56** million of goods were *purchased* during the year. It is not necessarily true, though, that $56 million cash was paid to suppliers of these goods. By looking at the change in accounts payable, we can determine the cash paid to suppliers:

Accounts Payable

		20	Beginning balance
Cash paid to suppliers	?	56	Cost of goods *purchased*
(decreases A/P)			*(increases A/P)*
		26	Ending Balance

Determining the amount of cash paid to suppliers means looking at not only the cost of goods sold, but also the changes in both inventory and accounts payable.

We now see that cash paid to suppliers was **$50** million. The spreadsheet entry that summarizes merchandise acquisitions is:

Although $60 million of goods were sold during the year, only $50 million cash was paid to suppliers of these goods.

		($ in millions)
Entry (4)	Cost of goods sold ($60 – 0)	60
	Inventory ($46 – 50)	4
	Accounts payable ($26 – 20)	6
	Cash (paid to suppliers of goods)	50

5. Salaries Expense.   The balance sheet account affected by salaries expense is salaries payable. By analyzing salaries expense in relation to the change in salaries payable, we can determine the amount of cash paid to employees:

Salaries Payable

Cash paid to employees *(decreases salaries payable)*	**?**	1	Beginning balance
		13	Salaries expense *(increases salaries payable)*
		3	Ending Balance

This analysis indicates that only **$11** million cash was paid to employees; the remaining $2 million of salaries expense is reflected as an increase in salaries payable.

Viewing the relationship in journal entry format provides the same conclusion and also gives us the entry used in our spreadsheet analysis:

Although salaries expense was $13 million, only $11 million cash was paid to employees.

		($ in millions)	
Entry (5)	Salaries expense ($13 – 0)	13	
	Salaries payable ($3 – 1)		2
	Cash (paid to employees)		11

6. Depreciation Expense.   The income statement reports depreciation expense of $3 million. The entry used to record depreciation, which also serves as our spreadsheet entry, is:

Depreciation expense does not require a current cash expenditure.

		($ in millions)	
Entry (6)	Depreciation expense ($3 – 0)	3	
	Accumulated depreciation		3

Depreciation is a noncash expense. It is merely an allocation in the current period of a prior cash expenditure (for the depreciable asset). Therefore, unlike the other entries to this point, the depreciation entry has no effect on the statement of cash flows. However, it does explain the change in the depreciation account and a portion of the change in accumulated depreciation.

7. Interest Expense.   Recall from Chapter 14 that bond interest expense differs from the amount of cash paid to bondholders when bonds are issued at either a premium or a discount. The difference between the two amounts is the reduction of the premium or discount. By referring to the balance sheet, we see that NBC's bonds were issued at a discount. Since we know that bond interest expense is $5 million and that $2 million of the discount was reduced in 1997, we can determine that $3 million cash was paid to bondholders by recreating the entry that summarizes the recording of bond interest expense.

Bond interest expense is not the same as the amount of cash paid to bondholders when bonds are issued at either a premium or a discount.

		($ in millions)	
Entry (7)	Bond interest expense ($5 – 0)	5	
	Discount on bonds payable ($1 – 3)		2
	Cash (paid to bondholders)		3

Recording this entry on the spreadsheet explains the change in both the bond interest expense and discount on bonds payable accounts. It also provides us with another cash outflow from operating activities. Of course, if a premium were being reduced, rather than a discount, the cash outflow would be greater than the expense.

Additional Consideration

If the balance sheet had revealed an increase or decrease in an accrued bond interest payable account, the entry calculating cash paid to bondholders would require modification. For example, if NBC had a bond interest payable account, and that account had increased (a credit) by $1 million, the entry would have been:

		($ in millions)
Entry (7)	Bond interest expense	5
(revised)	Discount on bonds payable	2
	Bond interest payable	1
	Cash (paid to bondholders)	2

If the amount owed to bondholders increased by $1 million, they obviously were paid $1 million less cash than if there had been no change in the amount owed them. Similarly, if bond interest payable decreased by $1 million, the opposite would be true; that is, cash paid them would have been $1 million more.

8. Insurance Expense.   A decrease of $3 million in the prepaid insurance account indicates that cash paid for insurance coverage was $3 million less than the $7 million insurance expense for the year. Viewing prepaid insurance in T-account format clarifies this point.

Prepaid Insurance

Beginning balance	6		
Cash paid for insurance	?	7	Insurance expense
(increases prepaid insurance)			*(decreases prepaid insurance)*
Ending balance	3		

From this analysis, we can conclude that $4 million was paid for insurance. We reach the same conclusion by preparing the following spreadsheet entry:

Since $3 million of prepaid insurance was allocated to insurance expense, only $4 million of the expense was paid in cash during the period.

		($ in millions)
Entry (8)	Insurance expense ($7 – 0)	7
	Prepaid insurance ($3 – 6)	3
	Cash (paid for insurance)	4

The entry accounts for the change in both the insurance expense and prepaid insurance accounts and also identifies a cash outflow from operating activities.

9. Loss on Sale of Equipment.   A $2 million loss on the sale of equipment is the next item reported on the income statement. To determine the cash effect of the sale of equipment, we need additional information about the transaction. The information we need is provided in item (b) of Illustration 22–1. Recreating the journal entry for the transaction described, gives us the following spreadsheet entry:

Recreating the journal entry for the sale of equipment reveals a $5 million cash inflow from investing activities.

		($ in millions)
Entry (9)	Cash (from the sale of equipment)	5
	Loss on sale of equipment ($2 – 0)	2
	Accumulated depreciation ($14 × 50%)	7
	Buildings and equipment (given)	14

The $5 million cash inflow is entered in the statement of cash flows section of the spreadsheet as an investing activity. The $2 million debit to the loss on sale of equipment explains the change in that account balance. Referring to the spreadsheet, we see that a portion of the change in accumulated depreciation was accounted for in entry (6). The debit to accumulated depreciation in the entry above completes the explanation for the change in that account. However, the credit to buildings and equipment only partially justifies the change in that account. We must assume that the analysis of a subsequent transaction will account for the unexplained portion of the change.

Recognize too that the loss, like the gain in entry (3), has no cash effect in the current period. Therefore, it is not reported on the statement of cash flows.

10. Income Tax Expense.   The final expense reported on the income statement is income tax expense. Since income taxes payable is the balance sheet account affected by this expense, we look to the change in that account to help determine the cash paid for income taxes. A T-account analysis can be used to find the cash effect as follows:

Income Tax Payable

Cash paid for income tax *(decreases the liability)*	**?**	8	Beginning balance
		9	Income tax expense
		6	Ending balance

This analysis reveals that **$11** million cash was paid for income taxes, $2 million more than the year's expense. The overpayment explains why the liability for income taxes decreased by $2 million.

The same conclusion can be reached from the following spreadsheet entry, which represents the net effect of income taxes on NBC's accounts.

		($ in millions)	
Entry (10)	Income tax expense ($9 – 0)	9	
	Income tax payable ($6 – 8)	2	
	Cash (paid for income taxes)		11

Additional Consideration

Entry (10) would require modification in either of the two independent situations described below.

1. Note that NBC does not have a deferred income tax account. Recall from Chapter 16 that temporary differences between taxable income and pretax accounting income give rise to deferred taxes. If temporary differences had been present, which would be evidenced by a change in a deferred income taxes account, the calculation of cash paid for income taxes would require modification. Assume, for example, that a deferred income tax liability account had experienced a credit change of $1 million for the year. In that case, the previous spreadsheet entry would be revised as follows:

		($ in millions)	
Entry (10)	Income tax expense	9	
(revised)	Income tax payable	2	
	Deferred income liability		1
	Cash (paid for income taxes)		10

   As the revised entry indicates, only $10 million cash would have been paid in this situation, rather than $11 million. The $1 million difference represents the portion of the income tax expense whose payment is deferred to a later year.

2. The spreadsheet entry also would be affected if the income statement includes either an extraordinary gain or an extraordinary loss. Recall from Chapter 3 and Chapter 16 that the income tax effect of an extraordinary item is not reflected in income tax expense, but instead is separately reported as a reduction in the extraordinary item. For example, if NBC's loss on the sale of equipment had been due to an extraordinary event, the tax savings from that loss would be reported as a reduction in the extraordinary loss rather than as a reduction in income tax expense. (Since the loss reduces taxable income by $2 million, assuming a marginal tax rate of 50%, taxes would be reduced by $1 million.) The lower portion of the income statement would have appeared as shown below, in comparison with the presentation in Illustration 22–1:

Ordinary Loss		**Extraordinary Loss**		
(from Illustration 22-1)		Income tax expense		**(10)**
		Income before extraordinary items		**$13**
Loss on sale of equipment	(2)	E.O. loss – sale of equip.	$2	
Income tax expense	**(9)**	Less: Tax savings	**(1)**	(1)
Net income	**$12**	Net income		**$12**

Without the tax savings produced by the loss, income tax expense would have been $10 million, rather than $9 million. But the tax savings still reduces the amount of cash paid for income taxes, even though it is reported separately from the income tax expense. Therefore, whether the loss is extraordinary or not, the amount of cash paid for income taxes is the same. If the loss is extraordinary, entry (10) would be modified as follows:

		($ in millions)	
Entry (10)	Income tax expense (on ordinary income)	10	
(revised)	Income tax payable	2	
	Income tax expense (savings from extraordinary loss)		1
	Cash (paid for income taxes)		11

Entry (9) would be unaffected. Whether or not the loss is extraordinary, it is not reported on the statement of cash flows, and the cash inflow from the sale is reported as an investing activity.

11. Net Income.   The balance in the retained earnings account at the end of the year includes an increase due to net income. If we are to account for all changes in each of the accounts, we must include the following spreadsheet entry, which represents the closing of net income to retained earnings.

This entry partially explains the change in the retained earnings account.

		($ in millions)	
Entry (11)	Net income	12	
	Retained earnings		12

This entry does not affect amounts reported on the statement of cash flows. We include the entry in the spreadsheet analysis only to help explain account balance changes.

Balance Sheet Accounts

To identify all the operating, investing, and financing activities when using a spreadsheet, we must account for the changes in each account on both the income statement and the balance sheet. Thus far, we have explained the change in each income statement account. Since the transactions that gave rise to some of those changes involved balance sheet accounts as well, some changes in balance sheet accounts have already been explained. We now reconstruct the transactions that caused changes in the remaining balances.

With the exception of the cash account, the accounts are analyzed in the order of their presentation on the statement of cash flows. As noted earlier, we save the entry that reconciles the change in the cash account with the net change in cash from the statement of cash flows as a final check on the accuracy of the spreadsheet.

12. Short-Term Investments.   Since the change in accounts receivable was explained previously [in entry(1)], we proceed to the next asset on the balance sheet. The balance in short-term investments increased from zero to $12 million. In the absence of evidence to the contrary, we could assume that the increase is due to the purchase of short-term investments during the year. This assumption is confirmed by item (c) of Illustration 22–1.

The entry to record the investment and our spreadsheet entry is:

The $12 million increase in the short-term investments account is due to the purchase of short-term investments during the year.

		($ in millions)	
Entry (12)	Short-term investment ($12 – 0)	12	
	Cash (purchase of short-term investment)		12

The $12 million cash outflow is entered in the statement of cash flows section of the spreadsheet as an investing activity.

Additional Consideration

Recall that some highly liquid, short-term investments such as money market funds, treasury bills, or commercial paper might be classified as cash equivalents. If the short-term investment above were classified as a cash equivalent, its purchase would have no effect on the total of cash and cash equivalents. In other words, since cash would include this investment, its purchase would constitute both a debit and a credit to cash. We would neither prepare a spreadsheet entry nor report the transaction on the statement of cash flows.

Likewise, a sale of a cash equivalent would not affect the total of cash and cash equivalents and would not be reported.

An exception would be if the cash equivalent investment were sold for either more or less than its acquisition cost. For example, assume a treasury bill classified as a cash equivalent were sold for $1 million more than its $2 million cost. The sale would constitute both a $3 million increase and a $2 million decrease in cash. We see the effect more clearly if we reconstruct the transaction in journal entry format:

		($ in millions)
Cash	3	
Gain on sale of cash equivalent		1
Cash (cash equivalent investment)		2

The spreadsheet entry to reflect the net increase in cash would be:

			($ in millions)
Entry (X)	Cash (from sale of cash equivalents)	1	
	Gain on sale of cash equivalent		1

The $1 million net increase in cash and cash equivalents would be reported as a cash inflow from **operating** activities.

13. Land. The changes in the balances of both inventory and prepaid insurance were accounted for in previous spreadsheet entries: (4) and (8). Land is the next account whose change has yet to be fully explained. We discovered in a previous transaction that a sale of land caused a $10 million reduction in the account. Yet, the account shows a net increase of $20 million. It would be logical to assume that the unexplained increase of $30 million was due to a purchase of land. The transaction described in item (d) of Illustration 22–1 supports that assumption and is portrayed in the following spreadsheet entry:

A $30 million purchase of land accounts for the portion of the $20 million increase in the account that was not previously explained by the sale of land.

			($ in millions)
Entry (13)	Land (given)	30	
	Cash (purchase of land)		30

The $30 million payment is reported as a cash outflow from investing activities.

14. Buildings and Equipment. When examining a previous transaction [entry (9)], we determined that the buildings and equipment account was reduced by $14 million from the sale of used equipment. And yet the account shows a net increase of $6 million for the year. The accounting records [item (e) of Illustration 22-1] reveal the remaining unexplained cause of the net increase. New equipment costing $20 million was purchased by issuing a $20 million note payable. Recall from the discussion in a previous section of this chapter that, although this is a noncash transaction, it represents both a significant investing activity (investing in new equipment) and a significant financing activity (financing the acquisition with long-term debt).

The journal entry used to record the transaction when the equipment was acquired also serves as our spreadsheet entry:

Investing in new equipment is a significant investing activity and financing the acquisition with long-term debt is a significant financing activity.

			($ in millions)
Entry (14)	Buildings and equipment (given)	20	
	Note payable (given)		20

Distinguishing (*X*) the spreadsheet entry reminds us to include a noncash investing and financing activity when we prepare the statement of cash flows.

Remember that the statement of cash flows section of the spreadsheet will serve as the basis for our preparation of the formal statement. But the noncash entry above will not affect the cash flows section of the spreadsheet. Because we want to report this noncash investing and financing activity when we prepare the statement of cash flows, it is helpful to "mark" the spreadsheet entry as a reminder not to overlook this transaction when the statement is prepared. Crosses (*X*) serve this purpose on the spreadsheet in Illustration 22–1a.

Additional Consideration

When a debt, such as the note payable above, is paid, the payment is reported on a statement of cash flows as a financing activity. However, any interest paid on the debt is reported as a cash outflow from operating activities. The reason is that interest expense is a component of net income, and the cash effects of income statement elements are reported as cash flows from operating activities.

---

15. Bonds Payable.   The balance in the bonds payable account decreased during the year by $15 million. Illustration 22–1, item (f), reveals the cause. Cash was paid to retire $15 million face value of bonds. The spreadsheet entry that duplicates the journal entry that was recorded when the bonds were retired is:

		($ in millions)	
Entry (15)	Bonds payable ($35 – 50)	15	
	Cash (retirement of bonds payable)		15

The cash outflow is reported as a financing activity.

Additional Consideration

The description of the transaction stipulated that $15 million of bonds were retired at their maturity on the first day of the year. Thus, any discount or premium on the bonds would have been completely amortized before the start of the year. If bonds are retired prior to their scheduled maturity, any unamortized discount or premium would be removed from the accounts at that time. For instance, assume that the bonds above were callable at $16 million and that $1 million of unamortized discount remained when they were retired by a call at that price. The spreadsheet entry would be revised as follows:

		($ in millions)	
Entry (15)	Bonds payable	15	
(revised)	Extraordinary loss on early extinguishment of bonds	2	
	Discount on bonds payable		1
	Cash (retirement of bonds payable)		16

The loss, of course, would not be reported on the statement of cash flows. The amortization of the discount, however, would affect a previous spreadsheet entry. In entry (7) we concluded that the decrease in discount on bonds payable was due to the amortization of $2 million of the discount when recording bond interest expense. However, if the early retirement assumed above had occurred, that transaction would have accounted for $1 million of the $2 million decrease in the discount. Entry (7) would be modified as follows:

		($ in millions)	
Entry (7)	Bond interest expense	5	
(revised)	Discount on bonds payable		1
	Cash (paid to bondholders)		4

Remember, too, that the tax savings from the loss would be reported on the income statement as a reduction of the extraordinary loss, rather than as a reduction of the income tax expense. Therefore, the spreadsheet entry that determines the amount of cash paid for income taxes would require the modification described in subsection 10 (Additional Consideration) above.

16–17. Common Stock. The comparative balance sheets indicate that the common stock account balance increased by $30 million. We look to the accounting records—Illustration 22–1, item (g)—for an explanation. Two transactions, a stock dividend and a sale of new shares of common stock, combined to cause the increase. To create the spreadsheet entries for our analysis, we replicate the journal entries for the two transactions as described below.

Remember from Chapter 19 that to record a small stock dividend, we capitalize retained earnings for the market value of the shares distributed—in this case, 1 million shares times $13 per share, or $13 million. The entry is:

	($ in millions)	
Entry (16) Retained earnings (1 million shares × $13)	13	
Common stock (1 million shares × $10 par)		10
Paid-in capital—excess of par (difference)		3

> Although, this transaction does not identify a cash flow, nor does it represent an investing and financing activity, we include the spreadsheet entry to help explain changes in the three account balances affected.

Also recall from the discussion of noncash investing and financing activities earlier in the chapter, that stock dividends do not represent a significant investing nor financing activity. Therefore, this transaction is not reported on the statement of cash flows. We include the entry in our spreadsheet analysis only to help explain changes in the account balances affected.

The sale of 2 million shares of common stock at $13 per share is represented by the following spreadsheet entry:

	($ in millions)	
Entry (17) Cash (from sale of common stock)	26	
Common stock ([$130 – 100] – $10)		20
Paid-in capital—excess of par ([$29 – 20] – $3)		6

> The sale of common shares explains the remaining increase in the common stock account and the remaining increase in paid-in capital – excess of par.

The cash inflow is reported on the statement of cash flows as a financing activity.

Additional Consideration

If cash is paid to retire outstanding shares of stock or to purchase those shares as treasury stock, the cash outflow would be reported on a statement of cash flows as a financing activity.

Together, the two entries above account for both the $30 million increase in the common stock account and the $9 million increase in paid-in capital—excess of par.

18. Retained Earnings. The stock dividend entry above includes a $13 million reduction of retained earnings. Previously, we saw in entry (11) that net income increased retained earnings by $12 million. The net reduction of $1 million accounted for by these two entries leaves $5 million of the $6 million net decrease in the account unexplained. Without additional information about the $5 million decrease in retained earnings, we might assume it was due to a $5 million cash dividend. This assumption is unnecessary, though, because the cash dividend is described in Illustration 22–1, item (h). The spreadsheet entry is:

> The cash dividend accounts for the previously unexplained change in retained earnings.

	($ in millions)	
Entry (18) Retained earnings	5	
Cash (payment of cash dividends)		5

The cash outflow is reported as a financing activity.

19. Completing the Spreadsheet.   In preparing the spreadsheet to this point, we have analyzed each noncash account on both the income statement and the balance sheet. Our purpose was to identify the transactions that, during the year, had affected each account. By recreating each transaction in the form of a spreadsheet entry—in effect, duplicating the journal entry that had been used to record the transaction—we were able to explain the change in the balance of each account. That is, the debits and credits in the changes columns of the spreadsheet account for the increase or decrease in each noncash account. When a transaction being entered on the spreadsheet included an operating, investing, or financing activity, we entered that portion of the entry under the corresponding heading of the statement of cash flows section of the spreadsheet. Since, as noted earlier, there can be no operating, investing, or financing activity without a corresponding change in one or more of the noncash accounts, we should feel confident at this point that we have identified all of the activities that should be reported on the statement of cash flows.

To check the accuracy of the analysis, we compare the change in the balance of the cash account with the net change in cash flows produced by the activities listed in the statement of cash flows section of the spreadsheet. The net increase or decrease in cash flows from each of the statement of cash flows categories is extended to the extreme right column of the spreadsheet. By reference to Illustration 22–1a, we see that net cash flows from operating, investing, and financing activities are: $22 million; ($19 million); and $6 million, respectively. Together these activities provide a net increase in cash of $9 million. This amount corresponds to the increase in the balance of the cash account from $20 million to $29 million. To complete the spreadsheet, we include the final spreadsheet entry:

		($ in millions)	
Entry (19)	Cash	9	
	Net increase in cash		
	(from statement of cash flows activities)		9

As a final check of accuracy, we can confirm that the total of the debits is equal to the total of the credits in the changes columns of the spreadsheet.[16]

> The cash flows section of the spreadsheet provides the information to be reported in the statement of cash flows.

The spreadsheet is now complete. The statement of cash flows can now be prepared directly from the spreadsheet simply by presenting the items included in the statement of cash flows section of the spreadsheet in the appropriate format of the statement.

ETHICAL DILEMMA

"We must get it," Courtney Lowell, president of Industrial Fasteners, roared. "Without it we're in big trouble." The "it" Mr. Lowell referred to is the renewal of a $14 million loan with Community First Bank. The big trouble he fears is the lack of funds necessary to repay the existing debt and few, if any, prospects for raising the funds elsewhere.

Mr. Lowell had just hung up the phone after a conversation with a bank vice-president in which it was made clear that this year's statement of cash flows must look better than last year's. Mr. Lowell knows that improvements are not on course to happen. In fact, cash flow projections were dismal.

Later that day, Tim Cratchet, assistant controller, was summoned to Mr. Lowell's office. "Cratchet," Lowell barked, "I've looked at our accounts receivable. I think we can generate quite a bit of cash by selling or factoring most of those receivables. I know it will cost us more than if we collect them ourselves, but it sure will make our cash flow picture look better."

Is there an ethical question facing Cratchet?

---

[16] The mechanical and computational aspects of the spreadsheet analysis are simplified greatly when performed on an electronic spreadsheet such as Lotus 123 or Microsoft Excel.

The comparative balance sheets for 1997 and 1996 and the income statement for 1997 are given below for Beneficial Drill Company. Additional information from Beneficial Drill's accounting records are provided also.

Required:

Prepare the statement of cash flows of Beneficial Drill Company for the year ended December 31, 1997. Present cash flows from operating activities by the direct method and use a spreadsheet to assist in your analysis.

Beneficial Drill Company
Comparative Balance Sheets
December 31, 1997 and 1996 ($ in millions)

Assets:	1997	1996
Cash	$ 20	$ 40
Accounts receivable	99	100
Less: Allowance for uncollectible accounts	(5)	(4)
Investment revenue receivable	3	2
Inventory	115	110
Prepaid insurance	2	3
Long-term investments	77	60
Land	110	80
Buildings and equipment	220	240
Less: Accumulated depreciation	(35)	(60)
Patent	15	16
	$621	$587

Liabilities:		
Accounts payable	$ 23	$ 30
Salaries payable	2	5
Bond interest payable	4	2
Income tax payable	6	7
Deferred income tax liability	5	4
Notes payable	15	0
Bonds payable	150	130
Less: Discount on bonds	(9)	(10)

Shareholders' Equity:		
Common stock	210	200
Paid-in capital—excess of par	44	40
Retained earnings	178	179
Less: Treasury stock (at cost)	(7)	0
	$621	$587

Beneficial Drill Company
Income Statement
For Year Ended December 31, 1997 ($ in millions)

Revenues:		
Sales revenue	$200	
Investment revenue	6	
Investment revenue – sale of treasury bills	1	$207
Expenses:		
Cost of goods sold	110	
Salaries expense	30	
Depreciation expense	5	
Patent amortization expense	1	
Bad debts expense	4	
Insurance expense	3	
Bond interest expense	14	
Extraordinary loss on destruction of equipment	$10	
Less: Tax savings	(5)	5
Income tax expense	12	(184)
Net income		$ 23

Additional information from the accounting records:

a. During 1997, $3 million of customer accounts were written off as uncollectible.

b. Investment revenue includes Beneficial Drill Company's $3 million share of the net income of Hammer Company, an equity method investee.

c. Treasury bills were sold during 1997 at a gain of $1 million. Beneficial Drill Company classifies its investments in treasury bills as cash equivalents.

d. A machine that originally cost $60 million and was one-half depreciated, was rendered unusable by a freak bolt of lightning. Most major components of the machine were unharmed and were sold for $20 million.

e. Temporary differences between pretax accounting income and taxable income caused the deferred income tax liability to increase by $1 million.

f. The common stock of Wrench Corporation was purchased for $14 million as a long-term investment.

g. Land costing $30 million was acquired by paying $15 million cash and issuing a 13%, seven-year, $15 million note payable to the seller.

h. New equipment was purchased for $40 million cash.

i. $20 million of bonds were sold at face value.

j. On January 19, Drill issued a 5% stock dividend (1 million shares). The market price of the $10 par value common stock was $14 per share at that time.

k. Cash dividends of $10 million were paid to shareholders.

l. In November, 500,000 common shares were repurchased as treasury stock at a cost of $7 million. Drill uses the cost method to account for treasury stock.

 CONCEPT REVIEW EXERCISE

SOLUTION

Page references indicate the location within the chapter of discussions pertaining to the referenced items.

BENEFICIAL DRILL COMPANY
Spreadsheet for the Statement of Cash Flows

	Dec. 31 1996	Changes Debits		Changes Credits		Dec. 31 1997	page ref.
Balance Sheet							
Assets:							
Cash	40			(20)	20	20	975
Accounts receivable	100			(1)	1	99	964
Less: Allowance for uncollectible accounts	(4)			(1)	1	(5)	965
Investment revenue receivable	2	(2)	1			3	966
Inventory	110	(4)	5			115	967
Prepaid insurance	3			(8)	1	2	969
Long-term investments	60	(2)	3				966
		(13)	14			77	971
Land	80	(14)	30			110	972
Buildings and equipment	240	(15)	40	(10)	60	220	969, 972
Less: Accumulated depreciation	(60)	(10)	30 X	(6)	5	(35)	968–69
Patent	16			(7)	1	15	968
	587					621	
Liabilities:							
Accounts payable	30	(4)	7			23	967
Salaries payable	5	(5)	3			2	968
Bond interest payable	2			(9)	2	4	968
Income tax payable	7	(11)	1			6	970
Deferred tax liability	4			(11)	1	5	970
Notes payable	0			(14)	15 X	15	972
Bonds payable	130			(16)	20	150	973
Less: Discount	(10)			(9)	1	(9)	968
Shareholders' Equity:							
Common stock	200			(17)	10	210	959
Paid-in capital—excess of par	40			(17)	4	44	959
Retained earnings	179	(17)	14				959, 974
		(18)	10	(12)	23	178	971
Less: Treasury stock	0	(19)	7			(7)	974
	587					621	

	Dec. 31 1996	Changes Debits	Changes Credits	Dec. 31 1997	page ref.
Income Statement					
Revenues:					
Sales revenue			(1) 200	200	964
Investment revenue			(2) 6	6	966
Investment revenue—					
sale of treasury bills			(3) 1	1	972
Expenses:					
Cost of goods sold		(4) 110		(110)	967
Salaries expense		(5) 30		(30)	968
Depreciation expense		(6) 5		(5)	968
Patent amortization expense		(7) 1		(1)	968
Bad debts expense		(1) 4		(4)	965
Insurance expense		(8) 3		(3)	969
Bond interest expense		(9) 14		(14)	968
Extraordinary loss		(10) 10		(10)	969
Less: Tax savings			(11) 5	5	970
Income tax expense		(11) 12		(12)	970
Net income		(12) 23		23	971
Statement of Cash Flows				**Net**	
Operating activities:					956
Cash inflows:					
From customers		(1) 198			964
From investment revenue		(2) 2			966
From sale of treasury bills		(3) 1			972
Cash outflows:					
To suppliers of goods			(4) 122		967
To employees			(5) 33		968
For insurance expense			(8) 2		969
For bond interest expense			(9) 11		968
For income taxes			(11) 7		970
Net cash flows				26	
Investing activities:					957
Sale of equipment		(10) 20			969
Purchase of LT investments			(13) 14		971
Purchase of land			(14) 15		972
Purchase of equipment			(15) 40		972
Net cash flows				(49)	
Financing activities:					958
Sale of bonds payable		(16) 20			973
Payment of cash dividends			(18) 10		974
Purchase of treasury stock			(19) 7		974
Net cash flows				3	
Net decrease in cash		(20) 20		(20)	975
Totals		638	638		975

BENEFICIAL DRILL COMPANY
Statement of Cash Flows ($ in millions)
For Year Ended December 31, 1997

Cash flows from operating activities:

Cash inflows:		
From customers	$198	
From investment revenue	2	
From sale of treasury bills	1	
Cash outflows:		
To suppliers of goods	(122)	
To employees	(33)	
For insurance expense	(2)	
For bond interest expense	(11)	
For income taxes	(7)	
Net cash flows from operating activities		$26

Cash flows from investing activities:

Sale of equipment	$ 20	
Purchase of long-term investments	(14)	
Purchase of land	(15)	
Purchase of equipment	(40)	
Net cash flows from investing activities		(49)

Cash flows from financing activities:

Sale of bonds payable	$20	
Payment of cash dividends	(10)	
Purchase of treasury stock	(7)	
Net cash flows from financing activities		3
Net decrease in cash		($20)
Cash balance, January 1		40
Cash balance, December 31		$20

Noncash investing and financing activities:
Acquired $30 million of land by paying cash and issuing a 13%, 7-year note as follows:

Cost of land	$30
Cash paid	15
Note issued	$15

Alternative Presentation of Cash Flows From Operating Activities – Indirect Method

The presentation of cash flows from operating activities illustrated to this point in the chapter is referred to as the **direct method**. By this method, the cash effect of each operating activity (i.e., income statement item) is reported directly on the statement of cash flows. For instance, cash received from customers is reported as the cash effect of sales activities: cash paid to suppliers is reported as the cash effect of cost of goods sold; etc. Income statement items that have *no* cash effect, such as depreciation expense, bad debt expense, gains, and losses, are simply not reported.

Learning objective 8
Reconcile net income to net cash flows from operating activities (the indirect method).

A permissible alternative is the **indirect method**, by which the net cash increase or decrease from operating activities is derived indirectly by starting with reported net income and working backwards to convert that amount to a cash basis. The derivation by the indirect method of net cash flows from operating activities for NBC is illustrated in Illustration 22–1b.

ILLUSTRATION 22–1b

Indirect Method

The indirect method derives the net cash increase or decrease from operating activities indirectly, by starting with reported net income and "working backwards" to convert that amount to a cash basis.

Cash Flows from Operating Activities—Indirect Method *and* Reconciliation of Net Income to Net Cash Flows from Operating Activities	
Net income	$12
Adjustments for noncash effects:	
Increase in accounts receivable	(2)
Gain on sale of land	(8)
Decrease in inventory	4
Increase in accounts payable	6
Increase in salaries payable	2
Depreciation expense	3
Discount on bonds payable	2
Decrease in prepaid insurance	3
Loss on sale of equipment	2
Decrease in income tax payable	(2)
Net cash flows from operating activities	$22

Notice that the indirect method yields the same $22 million net cash flows from operating activities as did the direct method described earlier. This is understandable when you consider that the indirect method simply reverses the differences between the accrual-based income statement and cash flows from operating activities as follows:

Components of net income that do *not* increase or decrease cash:

- Amounts that were subtracted in determining net income but did not reduce cash are added back to net income to reverse the effect of their having been subtracted. For example, depreciation expense and the loss on sale of equipment are added back to net income.
- Similarly, amounts that were added in determining net income but did not increase cash are subtracted from net income to reverse the effect of their having been added. For example, the gain on sale of land is deducted from net income.

Components of net income that *do* increase or decrease cash:

- For components of net income that increase or decrease cash, but by an amount different from that reported on the income statement, net income is adjusted for changes in the balances of related balance sheet accounts to convert the effects of those items to a cash basis. For example, sales of $100 million are included on the income statement as a component of net income, and yet, as we determined earlier, only $98 million cash was collected from customers during the reporting period. Sales are converted to a cash basis by subtracting the $2 million increase in accounts receivable. Following our previous analysis of the cash effects of the remaining components of net income, those items are similarly converted to a cash basis by adjusting net income for increases and decreases in related accounts.
- For components of net income that increase or decrease cash by an amount exactly the same as that reported on the income statement, no adjustment of net income is required. For example, investment revenue of $3 million is included in the $11 million net income amount. As we determined earlier [subsection (2)], $3 million also is the amount of cash received from that activity. Therefore, this element of net income already represents its cash effect and needs no adjustment.

The indirect method is compared with the direct method in Graphic 22–8, using the data of NBC. To better illustrate the relationship between the two methods, the adjustments to net income using the indirect method are presented parallel to the related cash inflows and cash outflows of the direct method. The income statement is included in the graphic to demonstrate that the indirect method also serves to reconcile differences between the elements of that statement and the cash flows reported by the direct method.

GRAPHIC   22–8

Comparison of the Indirect Method and the Direct Method of Determining Cash Flows from Operating Activities

Income Statement		Cash Flows from Operating Activities			
		Indirect Method		Direct Method	
		Net income	$12		
		Adjustments:			
Sales	$100	Increase in accounts receivable	(2)	Cash received from customers	$98
Investment revenue	3	(No adjustment—no investment revenue receivable or long-term investments)		Cash received from investments	3
Gain on sale of land	8	Gain on sale of land	(8)	(Not reported—no cash effect)	
Cost of goods sold	(60)	Decrease in inventory	4	Cash paid to suppliers	
		Increase in accounts payable	6		(50)
Salaries expense	(13)	Increase in salaries payable	2	Cash paid to employees	(11)
Depreciation expense	(3)	Depreciation expense	3	(Not reported—no cash effect)	
Interest expense	(5)	Decrease in bond discount	2	Cash paid for interest	(3)
Insurance expense	(7)	Decrease in prepaid insurance	3	Cash paid for insurance	(4)
Loss on sale of equipment	(2)	Loss on sale of equipment	2	(Not reported – no cash effect)	
Income tax expense	(9)	Decrease in income tax payable	(2)	Cash paid for income taxes	(11)
Net Income	**$ 12**	**Net cash flows from operating activities**	**$22**	**Net cash flows from operating activities**	**$22**

The direct method is more informative, but the indirect method is permissible.

Although either the direct method or the indirect method is permitted, the FASB strongly encourages companies to report cash flows from operating activities by the direct method. The obvious appeal of this approach is that it reports specific operating cash receipts and operating cash payments, which is consistent with the primary objective of the statement of cash flows. Investors and creditors gain additional insight into the specific sources of cash receipts and payments from operating activities revealed by this reporting method. Also, statement users can more readily interpret and understand the information presented because the direct method avoids the confusion caused by reporting noncash items and other reconciling adjustments under the caption *cash flows from operating activities.*

Whether cash flows from operating activities are reported by the direct method or by the indirect method, the financial statements must report a reconciliation of net income to net cash flows from operating activities. When the direct method is used, the reconciliation is presented in a separate schedule and is identical to the presentation of net cash flows from operating activities by the indirect method. In other words, Illustration 22–1b also serves as the reconciliation schedule to accompany a statement of cash flows using the direct method. Obviously, a separate reconciliation schedule is not required when using the indirect method because the cash flows from operating activities section of the statement of cash flows *is* a reconciliation of net income to net cash flows from operating activities.[17]

Notice that the direct and indirect methods are alternative approaches to deriving net cash flows from **operating** activities only. The choice of which method is used for that purpose does not affect the way cash flows from **investing** and **financing** activities are identified and reported.

The statements of cash flows from an annual report of Hughes Supply, Inc. are shown in Graphic 22-9.

GRAPHIC   22-9

Statement of Cash Flows—
Hughes Supply

CONSOLIDATED STATEMENTS OF CASH FLOWS
(in thousands)

	Fiscal Years Ended		
	January 26, 1996	January 27, 1995	January 28, 1994
Increase (Decrease) in Cash and Cash Equivalents:			
Cash flows from operating activities:			
Cash received from customers	$1,073,951	$861,732	$718,603
Cash paid to suppliers and employees	(1,034,589)	(846,357)	(712,125)
Interest received	3,454	2,323	2,001
Interest paid	(7,273)	(4,825)	(5,134)
Income taxes paid	(15,230)	(9,181)	(5,544)
Net cash provided by (used in) operating activities	20,313	3,692	(2,199)
Cash flows from investing activities:			
Capital expenditures	(11,853)	(11,915)	(8,885)
Proceeds from sale of property and equipment	1,228	743	709
Business acquisitions, net of cash	(10,009)	(11,099)	(3,934)
Net cash used in investing activities	(20,634)	(22,271)	(12,110)
Cash flows from financing activities:			
Net borrowings (payments) under short-term debt arrangements	6,245	23,832	16,733
Proceeds from issuance of long-term debt	–	–	580
Principal payments on:			
Long-term notes	(4,150)	(1,266)	(2,918)
Capital lease obligations	(844)	(725)	(660)
Proceeds from issuance of common shares under stock option plans	1,273	546	77
Purchase of common shares	(520)	(213)	(49)
Dividends paid	(1,736)	(1,188)	(629)
Net cash provided by (used in) financing activities	268	20,986	13,134
Net increase (decrease) in cash and cash equivalents	(53)	2,407	(1,175)
Cash and cash equivalents, beginning of year	3,485	1,078	2,253
Cash and cash equivalents, end of year	$ 3,432	$ 3,485	$ 1,078

The reconciliation schedule was reported in the disclosure note reproduced in Graphic 22–10 shown at the top of the following page.

For most companies, expenditures for interest and for taxes are significant. Cash payments for interest and for taxes usually are specifically indicated when the direct method is employed as is the case for Hughes Supply. When the indirect method is used, those amounts aren't readily apparent and should be separately reported either on the face of the statement or in an accompanying disclosure note.

Decision-Makers' Perspective: Cash Flow Ratios

We have emphasized the analysis of financial statements from a decision-maker's perspective throughout this text. Often that analysis included the development and comparison of financial ratios. Ratios based on income statement and balance sheet amounts enjoy a long tradition of

---

[17] It is permissible to present the reconciliation in a separate schedule and to report the net cash flows from operating activities as a single line item on the statement of cash flows.

GRAPHIC   22–10

Supplemental Disclosure—
Hughes Supply

Note 10-Supplemental Cash Flows Information:

The following is a reconciliation of net income (loss) to net cash provided by (used in) operating activities (in thousands):

	Fiscal Years Ended		
	January 26, 1996	January 27, 1995	January 28, 1994
Net income (loss)	$16,050	$11,485	$ 6,524
Adjustments to reconcile net income (loss) to net cash provided by (used in) operating activities			
Depreciation	8,669	8,217	7,038
Amortization	1,916	839	762
Provision for doubtful accounts	1,849	1,381	1,938
Gain on sale of property and equipment	(621)	(294)	(270)
Undistributed (earnings) losses of affiliate	115	(139)	(171)
Treasury shares contributed to employee benefit plan	–	500	–
Changes in assets and liabilities net of effects of business acquisitions:			
(Increase) decrease in:			
Accounts receivable	(8,872)	(13,819)	(16,894)
Inventories	1,129	(16,539)	(4,688)
Other current assets	(1,119)	(835)	(81)
Other assets	(1,063)	(262)	178
Increase (decrease) in:			
Accounts payable and accrued expenses	6,095	13,770	4,399
Accrued interest and income taxes	(2,249)	2,840	(487)
Other noncurrent liabilities	225	397	178
Increase in deferred income taxes	(1,811)	(3,849)	(625)
Net cash provided by (used in) operating activities	$ 20,313	$ 3,692	$ (2,199)

acceptance from which several standard ratios, including those described in earlier chapters, have evolved. To gain another viewpoint, some analysts supplement their investigation with cash flow ratios. Some cash flow ratios are derived by simply substituting cash flow from operations (CFFO) from the statement of cash flows in place of net income in many ratios, not to replace those ratios but to complement them. For example, the times interest earned ratio can be modified to reflect the number of times the cash outflow for interest is provided by cash inflow from operations and any of the profitability ratios can be modified to determine the cash generated from assets, shareholders' equity, sales, etc. Graphic 22–11 summarizes the calculation and usefulness of several representative cash flow ratios.

GRAPHIC   22–11

Cash Flow Ratios

	Calculation	Measures
Performance Ratios		
Cash flow to sales	$\dfrac{\text{CFFO}}{\text{Net sales}}$	Cash generated by each sales dollar
Cash return on assets	$\dfrac{\text{CFFO}}{\text{Average total assets}}$	Cash generated from all resources
Cash return on shareholders' equity	$\dfrac{\text{CFFO}}{\text{Average shareholders' equity}}$	Cash generated from owner-provided resources
Cash to income	$\dfrac{\text{CFFO}}{\text{Income from continuing operations}}$	Cash-generating ability of continuing operations
Cash flow per share	$\dfrac{\text{CFFO} - \text{preferred dividends}}{\text{Weighted-average shares}}$	Operating cash flow on a per share basis
Sufficiency Ratios		
Debt coverage	$\dfrac{\text{Total liabilities}}{\text{CFFO}}$	Financial risk and financial leverage
Interest coverage	$\dfrac{\text{CFFO} + \text{interest} + \text{taxes}}{\text{Interest}}$	Ability to satisfy its fixed obligations

GRAPHIC   22–11
continued

Reinvestment	$\dfrac{\text{CFFO}}{\text{Cash outflow for noncurrent assets}}$	Ability to acquire assets with operating cash flows
Debt payment	$\dfrac{\text{CFFO}}{\text{Cash outflow for LT debt repayment}}$	Ability to pay debts with operating cash flows
Dividend payment	$\dfrac{\text{CFFO}}{\text{Cash outflow for dividends}}$	Ability to pay dividends with operating cash flows
Investing and financing activity	$\dfrac{\text{CFFO}}{\text{Cash outflows for investing and financing activities}}$	Ability to acquire assets, pay debts, and make distributions to owners

Cash flow ratios have received limited acceptance to date due, in large part, to the long tradition of accrual-based ratios coupled with the relatively brief time that all companies have published statements of cash flows. A lack of consensus on cash flow ratios by which to make comparisons also has slowed their acceptance. Nevertheless, cash flow ratios offer insight in the evaluation of a company's profitability and financial strength.[18]

Solution to Financial Reporting Case (at the opening of the chapter)

1. What are the cash flow aspects of the situation that Mr. Barr may be overlooking in making his case for a wage increase? How can a company's operations generate a healthy profit and yet produce meager or even negative cash flows?

Positive net income does not necessarily indicate a healthy cash position. A statement of cash flows provides information about cash flows not seen when looking only at the balance sheet and the income statement. Although cash flows from operating activities result from the same activities that are reported on the income statement, the income statement reports the activities on an accrual basis. That is, revenues reported are those earned during the reporting period, regardless of when cash is received, and the expenses incurred in generating those revenues, regardless of when cash is paid. Thus, the very same operations can generate a healthy profit and yet produce meager or even negative cash flows.

2. What information can a statement of cash flows provide about a company's investing activities that can be useful in decisions such as this?

Cash flows from investing activities result from the acquisition and disposition of assets. Information about investing activities is useful to decision makers regarding the nature and magnitude of productive assets being acquired for future use. In the union negotiations, for instance, Mr. Barr may not be aware of the substantial investments underway to replace and update equipment and the cash requirements of those investments. Relatedly, the relatively low depreciation charges accelerated depreciation provides in the later years of assets' lives may cause profits to seem artificially high given the necessity to replace those assets at higher prices.

3. What information can a statement of cash flows provide about a company's financing activities that can be useful in decisions such as this?

Information about financing activities provides insights into sources of a company's external financing. Recent debt issues, for instance, might indicate a need for higher cash flows to maintain higher interest charges. Similarly, recent external financing activity may suggest that a company might be near its practical limits from external sources and, therefore, a greater reliance on internal financing through operations.

The Bottom Line

1.   Decision makers focus on the prospects of receiving a cash return from their dealings with a firm. But it is the ability of the firm to generate cash flows to itself that ultimately determines the potential for cash flows to investors and creditors.

2.   The statement of cash flows fills an information gap left by the balance sheet and the income statement by presenting information about cash flows that the other statements either do not provide or provide only indirectly.

3.   The stipulation that companies present the statement of cash flows is a relatively recent requirement. *SFAS 95* completed a full-cycle movement of accounting thought back to cash flow reporting, which, in different form, was common practice several decades ago.

---

[18] Proposals for informative sets of cash flow ratios are offered by Charles Carslaw and John Mills, "Developing Ratios for Effective Cash Flow Analysis," *Journal of Accountancy*, November 1991, and Don Giacomino and David Mielke, "Cash Flows: Another Approach to Ratio Analysis," *Journal of Accountancy*, March 1993.

4. Cash includes cash equivalents. These are short-term, highly liquid investments that can readily be converted to cash with little risk of loss.

5. Cash flows from operating activities are both inflows and outflows of cash that result from activities reported on the income statement. Cash flows from investing activities are related to the acquisition and disposition of assets, other than inventory and assets classified as cash equivalents. Cash flows from financing activities result from the external financing of a business.

6. Noncash investing and financing activities, such as acquiring equipment (an investing activity) by issuing a long-term note payable (a financing activity), are reported in a related disclosure schedule or note.

7. A spreadsheet provides a systematic method of preparing a statement of cash flows by analyzing available data to insure that all operating, investing, and financing activities are detected. Recording spreadsheet entries that explain account balance changes simultaneously identifies and classifies the activities to be reported on the statement of cash flows.

8. Either the direct or the indirect method can be used to calculate and present the net cash increase or decrease from operating activities. Unlike the direct method, which directly lists cash inflows and outflows, the indirect method derives cash flows indirectly, by starting with reported net income and working backwards to convert that amount to a cash basis.

APPENDIX

22A

SPREADSHEET FOR THE INDIRECT METHOD

A spreadsheet is equally useful in preparing a statement of cash flows whether we use the direct or the indirect method of determining cash flows from operating activities. The format of the spreadsheet differs only with respect to operating activities. The analysis of transactions for the purpose of identifying cash flows to be reported is the same. To illustrate, Illustration 22A–1 provides a spreadsheet analysis of the data for NBC.

Two differences should be noted between the spreadsheet in Illustration 22A–1 and the spreadsheet we used earlier for the direct method. First, in the statement of cash flows section of the spreadsheet, under the heading of "cash flows from operating activities," specific cash inflows and cash outflows are replaced by net income and the required adjustments for noncash effects. Second, we do not include an income statement section. This section is unnecessary because, using the indirect method, we are not interested in identifying specific operating activities that cause increases and decreases in cash. Instead, we need from the income statement only the amount of net income, which is converted to a cash basis by adjusting for any noncash amounts included in net income. The spreadsheet entries in journal entry form for the indirect method are illustrated in Illustration 22A–2.

Remember that there is no mandatory order in which the account changes must be analyzed. However, since we determine net cash flows from operating activities by working backwards from net income when using the indirect method, it is convenient to start with the spreadsheet entry that represents the credit to retained earnings due to net income. This entry corresponds to spreadsheet entry (11) of the direct method. By entering the debit portion of the entry as the first item under the cash flows from operating activities (CFOA), we establish net income as the initial amount of cash flows from operating activities, which is then adjusted to a cash basis by subsequent entries. Entries (2)–(4) duplicate the transactions that involve noncash components of net income. Changes in current assets and current liabilities that represent differences between revenues and expenses and the cash effects of those revenues and expenses are accounted for by entries (5)–(11). Spreadsheet entries (12)–(19) explain the changes in the balance sheet not already accounted for by previous entries, and are identical to entries (12)–(19) recorded using the direct method.

ILLUSTRATION 22A–1

Indirect Method

NATIONAL BRANDS CORPORATION
Spreadsheet for the Statement of Cash Flows

	Dec. 31 1996	Changes Debits		Credits		Dec. 31 1997
Balance Sheet						
Assets:						
Cash	20	(19)	9			29
Accounts receivable	30	(5)	2			32
Short-term investments	0	(12)	12			12
Inventory	50			(6)	4	46
Prepaid insurance	6			(8)	3	3
Land	60	(13)	30	(2)	10	80
Buildings and equipment	75	(14)	20X	(3)	14	81
Less: Accumulated depreciation	(20)	(3)	7	(4)	3	(16)
	221					267
Liabilities:						
Accounts payable	20			(7)	6	26
Salaries payable	1			(9)	2	3
Income tax payable	8	(11)	2			6
Notes payable	0			(14)	20X	20
Bonds payable	50	(15)	15			35
Less: Discount on bonds	(3)			(10)	2	(1)
Shareholders' Equity:						
Common stock	100			(16)	10	
				(17)	20	130
Paid-in capital–excess of par	20			(16)	3	
				(17)	6	29
Retained earnings	25	(16)	13			
		(18)	5	(1)	12	19
	221					267
Statement of Cash Flows						
Operating activities:						
Net income		(1)	12			
Adjustments for noncash effects:						
Gain on sale of land				(2)	8	
Depreciation expense		(4)	3			
Loss on sale of equipment		(3)	2			
Increase in accounts receivable				(5)	2	
Decrease in inventory		(6)	4			
Increase in accounts payable		(7)	6			
Decrease in prepaid insurance		(8)	3			
Increase in salaries payable		(9)	2			
Amortization of discount		(10)	2			
Decrease in income tax payable				(11)	2	
Net cash flows						22
Investing activities:						
Purchase of land				(13)	30	
Purchase of S-T investment				(12)	12	
Sale of land		(2)	18			
Sale of equipment		(3)	5			
Net cash flows						(19)
Financing activities:						
Sale of common shares		(17)	26			
Retirement of bonds payable				(15)	15	
Payment of cash dividends				(18)	5	
Net cash flows						6
Net increase in cash				(19)	9	9
Totals			198		198	

ILLUSTRATION 22A–2

Spreadsheet Entries for the Indirect Method

Entry (1) Net income—CFOA   12
    Retained earnings   12
Establishes net income as the initial amount of cash flows from operating activities, to be adjusted to a cash basis by subsequent entries.

Entry (2) Cash (received from sale of land)   18
    Land   10
    Gain on sale of land—CFOA   8
Deducts the noncash gain added in determining net income, explains a portion of the change in land, and identifies a cash inflow from investing activities.

Entry (3) Cash (received from sale of equipment)   5
    Loss on sale of equipment—CFOA   2
    Accumulated depreciation   7
    Buildings and equipment   14
Adds back the noncash loss subtracted in determining net income, explains portions of the changes in accumulated depreciation and buildings and equipment, and identifies a cash inflow from investing activities.

Entry (4) Depreciation expense—CFOA   3
    Accumulated depreciation   3
Adds back the noncash expense subtracted in determining net income.

Entry (5) Accounts receivable   2
    Increase in accounts receivable—CFOA   2
Reduces net income to reflect $98 million cash received from customers rather than $100 million sales.

Entry (6) Decrease in inventory—CFOA   4
    Inventory   4
Increases net income to reflect a deduction of $56 million cost of goods purchased rather than $60 million cost of goods sold.

Entry (7) Increase in accounts payable—CFOA   6
    Accounts payable   6
Increases net income to reflect a deduction of $50 million cash paid to suppliers rather than $56 million cost of goods purchased

Entry (8) Decrease in prepaid insurance—CFOA   3
    Prepaid insurance   3
Increases net income to reflect a deduction of $10 million cash paid for insurance rather than $13 million insurance expense.

Entry (9) Increase in salaries payable—CFOA   2
    Salaries payable   2
Increases net income to reflect a deduction of $11 million cash paid to employees rather than $13 million salaries expense.

Entry (10) Amortization of discount on bonds—CFOA   2
    Discount on bonds   2
Increases net income to reflect a deduction of $3 million cash paid for bond interest rather than $5 million bond interest expense.

Entry (11) Income taxes payable   2
    Decrease in income taxes payable—CFOA   2
Reduces net income to reflect a deduction of $11 million cash paid for income taxes rather than $9 million income tax expense.

Entry (12) Short-term investment   12
    Cash (purchase of short-term investment)   12
Explains the increase in the short-term investment account and identifies a cash outflow from investing activities.

Entry (13) Land   30
    Cash (purchase of land)   30
Explains a portion of the change in the land account and identifies a cash outflow from investing activities.

Entry (14) Buildings and equipment   20
    Note payable   20
Partially explains the changes in the buildings and equipment and notes payable accounts and identifies a noncash investing and financing activity.

Entry (15) Bonds payable   15
    Cash (retirement of bonds payable)   15
Explains the decrease in the bonds payable account and identifies a cash outflow from financing activities.

Entry (16)	Retained earnings	13	
	Common stock		10
	Paid-in capital—excess of par		3
	Partially explains the changes in the retained earnings, common stock, and paid-in capital in excess of par accounts.		
Entry (17)	Cash (from sale of common stock)	26	
	Common stock		20
	Paid-in capital—excess of par		6
	Partially explains the changes in the common stock and paid-in capital— excess of par accounts and identifies a cash inflow from financing activities.		
Entry (18)	Retained earnings	5	
	Cash (payment of cash dividends)		5
	Partially explains the change in the retained earnings account and identifies a cash outflow from financing activities.		
Entry (19)	Cash	9	
	Net increase in cash (from statement of cash flows activities)		9
	Reconciles the net increase in cash from operating, investing, and financing activities to the increase in the cash balance.		

The statement of cash flows presenting net cash flows from operating activities by the indirect method is illustrated in Illustration 22A–3.

ILLUSTRATION 22A-3

Statement of Cash Flows— Indirect Method

All parts of the statement of cash flows except operating activities are precisely the same as in the direct method.

NATIONAL BRANDS CORPORATION
Statement of Cash Flows ($ in millions)
For Year Ended December 31, 1997

Cash flows from operating activities:		
Net income	$12	
Adjustments for noncash effects:		
Depreciation expense	3	
Loss on sale of equipment	2	
Gain on sale of land	(8)	
Increase in accounts receivable	(2)	
Decrease in inventory	4	
Increase in accounts payable	6	
Decrease in prepaid insurance	3	
Increase in salaries payable	2	
Amortization of discount on bonds	2	
Decrease in income tax payable	(2)	
Net cash flows from operating activities		$22
Cash flows from investing activities:		
Purchase of land	($30)	
Purchase of short-term investment	(12)	
Sale of land	18	
Sale of equipment	5	
Net cash flows from investing activities		(19)
Cash flows from financing activities:		
Sale of common shares	$26	
Retirement of bonds payable	(15)	
Payment of cash dividends	(5)	
Net cash flows from financing activities		6
Net increase in cash		$ 9
Cash balance, January 1		20
Cash balance, December 31		$29
Noncash investing and financing activities:		
Acquired $20 million of equipment by issuing a 12%, 5-year note.	$20	

22B

THE T-ACCOUNT METHOD OF PREPARING THE STATEMENT OF CASH FLOWS

> The T–account method serves the same purpose as a spreadsheet in assisting in the preparation of a statement of cash flows.

This chapter demonstrates the use of a spreadsheet to prepare the statement of cash flows. A second systematic approach to the preparation of the statement is referred to as the T–account method. The two methods are identical in concept. Both approaches reconstruct the transactions that caused changes in each account balance during the year, simultaneously identifying the operating, investing, and financing activities to be reported on the statement of cash flows. The form of the two methods differs only by whether the entries for those transactions are recorded on a spreadsheet or in T–accounts. In both cases, entries are recorded until the net change in each account balance has been explained.

Some accountants feel that the T–account method is less time-consuming than preparing a spreadsheet but accomplishes precisely the same goal. Since both methods are simply analytical techniques to assist in statement preparation, the choice is a matter of personal preference.

The following five steps outline the T–account method:

1. Draw T–accounts for each income statement and balance sheet account.
2. The T–account for cash should be drawn considerably larger than other T–accounts because more space is required to accommodate the numerous debits and credits to cash. Also, the cash T-account will serve the same purpose as the statement of cash flows section of the spreadsheet in that the formal statement of cash flows is developed from the cash flows reported there. Therefore, it is convenient to partition the cash T–account with headings for "Operating Activities," "Investing Activities," and "Financing Activities" before entries are recorded.
3. Enter each account's net change on the appropriate side (debit or credit) of the uppermost portion of each T–account. These changes will serve as individual check figures for determining whether the increase or decrease in each account balance has been explained. These first three steps establish the basic work form for the T–account method.
4. Reconstruct the transactions that caused changes in each account balance during the year and record the entries for those transactions directly in the T–accounts. Again using NBC as an example, the entries we record in the T–accounts are exactly the same as the spreadsheet entries we created in the chapter when using the spreadsheet method. The analysis we used in creating those spreadsheet entries is equally applicable to the T–account method. For that reason, that analysis is not repeated here. The completed T–account work form for NBC is presented below. Account balance changes are provided by Illustration 22–1.

BALANCE SHEET ACCOUNTS
Cash (statement of cash flows)

		9			
Operating Activities:					
From customers	(1)	98	50	(4)	To suppliers of goods
From investment revenue	(2)	3	11	(5)	To employees
			3	(7)	For interest
			4	(8)	For insurance
			11	(10)	For income taxes
Investing Activities:					
Sale of land	(3)	18	12	(12)	Purchase of short-term investment
Sale of equipment	(9)	5	30	(13)	Purchase of land
Financing Activities:					
Sale of common stock	(17)	26	15	(15)	Retirement of bonds payable
			5	(18)	Payment of cash dividends

Accounts Receivable		Short-term Investments	
2		12	
(1) 2		(12) 12	

Inventory		Prepaid Insurance		Land	
4		3		20	
4 (4)		3 (8)		(13) 30 | 10 (3)	

Buildings and Equipment		Accumulated Depreciation		Accounts Payable	
6			4		6
X(14) 20 | 14 (9)		(9) 7 | 3 (6)			6 (4)

Salaries Payable		Income Tax payable		Notes Payable	
	2		2		20
	2 (5)	(10) 2			20 (14)X

Bonds Payable		Discount on Bonds		Common Stock	
	15	2			30
(15) 15			2 (7)		10 (16)
					20 (17)

Paid-in Capital— excess of par		Retained Earnings	
	9		6
	3 (16)	(16) 13	
	6 (17)	(18) 5 | 12 (11)	

X Noncash Investing and Financing Activity

INCOME STATEMENT ACCOUNTS

Sales Revenue		Investment Revenue		Gain on Sale of Land	
	100		3		8
	100 (1)		3 (2)		8 (3)

Cost of Goods Sold		Salaries Expense		Depreciation Expense	
60		13		3	
(4) 60		(5) 13		(6) 3	

Interest Expense		Insurance Expense		Loss on Sale of Equipment	
5		7		2	
(7) 5		(8) 7		(9) 2	

Income Tax Expense		Net Income (Income Summary)	
9		12	
(10) 9		(11) 12	

5. After all account balances have been explained by T-account entries, prepare the statement of cash flows from the cash T–account, being careful also to report noncash investing and financing activities. The statement of cash flows for NBC appears in Graphic 22–2.

Questions for Review of Key Topics

Question   22–1   Effects of all cash flows affect the balances of various accounts reported on the balance sheet. Also, the activities that cause some of these cash flows are reported on the income statement. What, then, is the need for an additional financial statement that reports cash flows?

Question   22–2   The statement of cash flows has been a required financial statement only since 1988. Is cash flow reporting a totally new concept? Explain.

Question   22–3   Is an investment in treasury bills always classified as a cash equivalent? Explain.

Question	22–4	Transactions that involve merely purchases or sales of cash equivalents generally are not reported on a statement of cash flows. Describe an exception to this generalization. What is the essential characteristic of the transaction that qualifies as an exception?
Question	22–5	What are the differences between cash flows from operating activities and the elements of an income statement?
Question	22–6	Do cash flows from operating activities report all the elements of the income statement on a cash basis? Explain.
Question	22–7	Investing activities include the acquisition and disposition of assets. Provide four specific examples. Identify two exceptions.
Question	22–8	The sale of stock and the sale of bonds are reported as financing activities. Are payments of dividends to shareholders and payments of interest to bondholders also reported as financing activities? Explain.
Question	22–9	Does the statement of cash flows report only transactions that cause an increase or a decrease in cash? Explain.
Question	22–10	How would the acquisition of a building be reported on a statement of cash flows if purchased by issuing a mortgage note payable in addition to a significant cash down payment?
Question	22–11	Perhaps the most noteworthy item reported on an income statement is net income—the amount by which revenues exceed expenses. The most noteworthy item reported on a statement of cash flows is **not** the amount of net cash flows. Explain.
Question	22–12	What is the purpose of the changes columns of a spreadsheet to prepare a statement of cash flows?
Question	22–13	Given sales revenue of $200,000, how can it be determined whether or not $200,000 cash was received from customers?
Question	22–14	When an asset is sold at a gain, why is the gain not reported as a cash inflow from operating activities?
Question	22–15	Are ordinary losses and extraordinary losses treated alike in preparing a statement of cash flows? Explain.
Question	22–16	When determining the amount of cash paid for income taxes, what would be indicated by an increase in the deferred income tax liability account?
Question	22–17	When using the indirect method of determining net cash flows from operating activities, how is bad debt expense reported? Why? What other expenses are reported in a like manner?
Question	22–18	When using the direct method of determining net cash flows from operating activities, how are revenues and expenses reported on the statement of cash flows if their cash effects are identical to the amounts reported on the income statement?
Question	22–19	Why does the FASB recommend the direct method over the indirect method?
Question	22–20	Compare the manner in which investing activities are reported on a statement of cash flows prepared by the direct method and by the indirect method.

Exercises

Exercise 22–1
Classification of cash flows

Listed below are several transactions that typically produce either an increase or a decrease in cash. Indicate by letter whether the cash effect of each transaction is reported on a statement of cash flows as an operating (**O**), investing (**I**) or financing (**F**) activity.

Transactions

Example	_F_	1. Sale of common stock
	____	2. Sale of land
	____	3. Purchase of treasury stock
	____	4. Merchandise sales
	____	5. Issuance of a long-term note payable
	____	6. Purchase of merchandise
	____	7. Repayment of note payable
	____	8. Employee salaries
	____	9. Sale of equipment at a gain
	____	10. Issuance of bonds
	____	11. Acquisition of bonds of another corporation
	____	12. Payment of semiannual interest on bonds payable
	____	13. Payment of a cash dividend
	____	14. Purchase of building
	____	15. Collection of nontrade note receivable (principal amount)
	____	16. Loan to another firm
	____	17. Retirement of common stock
	____	18. Income taxes
	____	19. Issuance of a short-term note payable
	____	20. Sale of a copyright

Exercise 22–2
Determine cash paid to suppliers of merchandise

Shown below in T-account format are the beginning and ending balances ($ in millions) of both inventory and accounts payable.

Inventory

Beginning balance	90
Ending balance	93

Accounts Payable

	14 Beginning balance
	16 Ending Balance

Required:
1. Use a T-account analysis to determine the amount of cash paid to suppliers of merchandise during the reporting period if cost of goods sold was $300 million.
2. Prepare the spreadsheet entry that represents the net effect of merchandise purchases during the reporting period.

Exercise 22–3
Determine cash received from customers

Determine the amount of cash received from customers for each of the six independent situations below. All dollars are in millions.

Situation	Sales Revenue	Accounts Receivable Increase (Decrease)	Bad Debt Expense	Allowance for Uncollectible Accounts Increase (Decrease)	Cash Received from Customers
1	100	-0-	-0-	-0-	?
2	100	5	-0-	-0-	?
3	100	(5)	-0-	-0-	?
4	100	5	2	2	?
5	100	(5)	2	1	?
6	100	5	2	(1)	?

Exercise 22–4
Spreadsheet entries for cash received from customers

For each of the four independent situations below, prepare the spreadsheet entries necessary to determine the amount of cash received from customers and to explain the change in each account shown. All dollars are in millions.

Situation	Sales Revenue	Accounts Receivable Increase (Decrease)	Bad Debt Expense	Allowance for Uncollectible Accounts Increase (Decrease)	Cash Received from Customers
1	200	-0-	-0-	-0-	?
2	200	10	-0-	-0-	?
3	200	10	4	4	?
4	200	10	4	(2)	?

Exercise 22–5
Determine cash paid to suppliers of merchandise

Determine the amount of cash paid to suppliers of merchandise for each of the nine independent situations below. All dollars are in millions.

Situation	Cost of Goods Sold	Inventory Increase (Decrease)	Accounts Payable Increase (Decrease)	Cash Paid to Suppliers
1	100	0	0	?
2	100	3	0	?
3	100	(3)	0	?
4	100	0	7	?
5	100	0	(7)	?
6	100	3	7	?
7	100	3	(7)	?
8	100	(3)	(7)	?
9	100	(3)	7	?

Exercise 22–6
Spreadsheet entries for cash paid to suppliers of merchandise

For each of the five independent situations below, prepare the spreadsheet entry that determines the amount of cash paid to suppliers and explains the change in each account shown. All dollars are in millions.

Situation	Cost of Goods Sold	Inventory Increase (Decrease)	Accounts Payable Increase (Decrease)	Cash Paid to Suppliers
1	200	0	0	?
2	200	6	0	?
3	200	0	14	?
4	200	6	14	?
5	200	(6)	(14)	?

Exercise 22–7
Determine cash paid for bond interest

Determine the amount of cash paid to bondholders for bond interest for each of the six independent situations below. All dollars are in millions.

Situation	Bond Interest Expense	Bond Interest Payable Increase (Decrease)	Unamortized Discount Increase (Decrease)	Cash Paid for Interest
1	10	0	0	?
2	10	2	0	?
3	10	(2)	0	?
4	10	0	(3)	?
5	10	2	(3)	?
6	10	(2)	(3)	?

Exercise 22–8
Determine cash paid for bond interest

For each of the four independent situations below, prepare a single spreadsheet entry that determines the amount of cash paid for bond interest and explains the change (if any) in each of the accounts shown. All dollars are in millions.

Situation	Bond Interest Expense	Bond Interest Payable Increase (Decrease)	Unamortized Discount Increase (Decrease)	Cash Paid for Interest
1	20	0	0	?
2	20	4	0	?
3	20	0	(6)	?
4	20	(4)	(6)	?

Exercise 22–9
Determine cash paid for income taxes

Determine the amount of cash paid for income taxes in each of the nine independent situations below. All dollars are in millions.

Situation	Income Tax Expense	Income Tax Payable Increase (Decrease)	Deferred Tax Liability Increase (Decrease)	Cash Paid for Taxes
1	10	0	0	?
2	10	3	0	?
3	10	(3)	0	?
4	10	0	2	?
5	10	0	(2)	?
6	10	3	2	?
7	10	3	(2)	?
8	10	(3)	(2)	?
9	10	(3)	2	?

Exercise 22–10
Spreadsheet entries for cash paid for income taxes

For each of the five independent situations below, prepare a single spreadsheet entry that determines the amount of cash paid for income taxes and explains the change (if any) in each of the accounts shown. All dollars are in millions.

Situation	Income Tax Expense	Income Tax Payable Increase (Decrease)	Deferred Tax Liability Increase (Decrease)	Cash Paid for Taxes
1	10	0	0	?
2	10	3	0	?
3	10	0	(2)	?
4	10	3	2	?
5	10	(3)	(2)	?

Exercise 22–11
Indirect method; reconciliation of net income to net cash flows from operating activities

The accounting records of EZ Company provided to data below. Prepare a reconciliation of net income to net cash flows from operating activities.

Net income	$50,000
Depreciation expense	$7,000
Increase in inventory	$1,500
Decrease in salaries payable	$800
Decrease in accounts receivable	$2,000
Amortization of goodwill	$500
Amortization of premium on bonds	$1,000
Increase in accounts payable	$4,000
Cash dividends	$12,000

Exercise 22–12
Spreadsheet entries from statement of retained earnings

The statement of retained earnings of Gary Larson Publishers is presented below.

GARY LARSON PUBLISHERS
Statement of Retained Earnings
For the Year Ended December 31, 1996 ($ in millions)

Retained earnings, January 1		$200
Add:	Net income	75
Deduct:	Cash dividend	(25)
	Stock dividend (1 million shares of $1 par common stock)	(16)
	Property dividend (Garfield Company preferred stock held	
	as a short-term investment)	(12)
	Sale of treasury stock (cost $53 million)	(10)
Retained earnings, December 31		**$212**

Required:

For the transactions that affected Larson's retained earnings, reconstruct the journal entries that can be used as spreadsheet entries in the preparation of a statement of cash flows. Also indicate any investing and financing activities you identify from this analysis that should be reported on the statement of cash flows.

Exercise 22–13

Relationship among the income statement, cash flows from operating activities (direct method and indirect method)

The following schedule relates the income statement with cash flows from operating activities, derived by both the direct and indirect methods, in the format illustrated by Graphic 22–8 in the chapter. The amounts for income statement elements are missing.

Cash flows From Operating Activities

INCOME STATEMENT		INDIRECT METHOD		DIRECT METHOD	
		Net income	$?		
		Adjustments :			
Sales	$?	Decrease in accounts receivable	12	Cash received from customers	$612
Cost of goods sold	?	Increase in inventory	(24)		
		Decrease in accounts payable	(36)	Cash paid to suppliers	(420)
Salaries expense	?	Increase in salaries payable	12	Cash paid to employees	(66)
Depreciation expense	?	Depreciation expense	18	(Not reported—no cash effect)	
Insurance expense	?	Decrease in prepaid insurance	18	Cash paid for insurance	(24)
Loss on sale of land	?	Loss on sale of land	12	(Not reported—no cash effect)	
Income tax expense	?	Increase in income tax payable	12	Cash paid for income taxes	(42)
Net Income	**$?**	**Net cash flows from operating activities**	**$60**	**Net cash flows from operating activities**	**$60**

Required:
Deduce the missing amounts and prepare the income statement.

Exercise 22–14

Reconciliation of net cash flows from operating activities to net income

The income statement and the cash flows from operating activities section of the statement of cash flows are provided below for Far Side Company. The merchandise inventory account balance neither increased nor decreased during the reporting period. Far Side had no liability for either insurance, deferred income taxes, or interest at any time during the period.

FAR SIDE COMPANY
Income Statement
For the Year Ended December 31, 1996 ($ in 000s)

Sales		$312
Cost of goods sold		(188)
Gross margin		$124
Salaries expense	$41	
Insurance expense	22	
Depreciation expense	11	
Depletion expense	5	
Bond interest expense	10	(89)
Gains and losses:		
Gain on sale of equipment		25
Loss on sale of land		(8)
Income before tax		$ 52
Income tax expense		(26)
Net Income		**$ 26**

Cash flows From Operating Activities:

Cash received from customers	$258
Cash paid to suppliers	(175)
Cash paid to employees	(37)
Cash paid for interest	(9)
Cash paid for insurance	(16)
Cash paid for income taxes	(14)
Net cash flows from operating activities	**$ 7**

Required:
Prepare a schedule to reconcile net income to net cash flows from operating activities.

Exercise 22–15
Cash flows from operating activities (direct method) derived from an income statement and cash flows from operating activities (indirect method)

The income statement and a schedule reconciling cash flows from operating activities to net income are provided below ($ in 000) for Peach Computers.

PEACH COMPUTERS Income Statement For the Year Ended December 31, 1997		
Sales		$305
Cost of goods sold		(185)
Gross margin		$120
Salaries expense	$41	
Insurance expense	19	
Depreciation expense	11	
Loss on sale of land	5	76
Income before tax		$ 44
Income tax expense		(22)
Net Income		$ 22

Reconciliation of Net Income to Net Cash Flows from Operating Activities	
Net income	$22
Adjustments for noncash effects:	
Depreciation expense	11
Loss on sale of land	5
Decrease in accounts receivable	6
Increase in inventory	(13)
Decrease in accounts payable	(8)
Increase in salaries payable	5
Decrease in prepaid insurance	9
Increase in income tax payable	20
Net cash flows from operating activities	$57

Required:
1. Calculate each of the following amounts for Peach Computers:
   a. Cash received from customers during the reporting period.
   b. Cash paid to suppliers of goods during the reporting period.
   c. Cash paid to employees during the reporting period.
   d. Cash paid for insurance during the reporting period.
   e. Cash paid for income taxes during the reporting period.
2. Prepare the cash flows from operating activities section of the statement of cash flows (direct method).

Exercise 22–16
Indirect method; reconciliation of net income to net cash flows from operating activities

The accounting records of EZ Company provided the data below. Prepare a reconciliation of net income to net cash flows from operating activities.

Net loss	$5,000
Depreciation expense	6,000
Increase in salaries payable	500
Decrease in accounts receivable	2,000
Increase in inventory	2,300
Amortization of patent	300
Reduction in discount on bonds	200

Exercise 22–17
Cash flows from operating activities (direct method)—includes loss on sale of cash equivalents and extraordinary loss

Portions of the financial statements for Trapper John Company are provided below.

TRAPPER JOHN COMPANY Income Statement For the Year Ended December 31, 1997 ($ in millions)		
Sales		$660
Cost of goods sold		(250)
Gross margin		410
Salaries expense	$110	
Depreciation expense	90	
Patent amortization expense	5	
Interest expense	20	
Loss on sale of cash equivalents	3	(228)
Income before taxes and extraordinary loss		182
Income tax expense		(91)
Income before extraordinary loss		91
Extraordinary loss (earthquake)	10	
Less: Tax savings	(5)	(5)
Net Income		$ 86

TRAPPER JOHN COMPANY
Selected Accounts from Comparative Balance Sheets
December 31, 1997 and 1996 ($ in millions)

	Year		
	1997	**1996**	**Change**
Cash	$102	$100	$ 2
Accounts receivable	220	232	(12)
Inventory	440	450	(10)
Accounts payable	140	134	6
Salaries payable	80	86	(6)
Interest payable	25	20	5
Income taxes payable	15	10	5

Required:
Prepare the cash flows from operating activities section of the statement of cash flows for Trapper John Company using the *direct method.*

Exercise 22–18
Cash flows from operating activities (indirect method) includes loss on sale of cash equivalents and extraordinary loss

Refer to the data provided in the previous exercise for Trapper John Company.

Required:
Prepare the cash flows from operating activities section of the statement of cash flows for Trapper John Company using the *indirect method.*

Exercise 22–19
Cash flows from operating activities (direct method)— includes loss on sale of cash equivalents and extraordinary gain

Portions of the financial statements for Radar Company are provided below.

RADAR COMPANY
Income Statement
For the Year Ended December 31, 1997 ($ in 000)

Sales		$1,320
Cost of goods sold		(500)
Gross margin		820
Salaries expense	$220	
Depreciation expense	180	
Goodwill amortization expense	10	
Interest expense	40	
Loss on sale of cash equivalents	6	(456)
Income before taxes and extraordinary gain		364
Income tax expense		(182)
Income before extraordinary gain		182
Extraordinary gain (early extinguishment of debt)	20	
Less: Tax on gain	(10)	10
Net Income		$ 192

RADAR COMPANY
Selected Accounts from Comparative Balance Sheets
December 31, 1997 and 1996 ($ in 000)

	Year		
	1997	**1996**	**Change**
Cash	$102	$100	$ 2
Accounts receivable	220	232	(12)
Inventory	440	450	(10)
Accounts payable	140	134	6
Salaries payable	80	86	(6)
Interest payable	25	20	5
Income taxes payable	15	10	5

Required:
Prepare the cash flows from operating activities section of the statement of cash flows for Radar Company using the *direct method.*

Exercise 22–20
Cash flows from operating activities (indirect method)— includes loss on sale of cash equivalents and extraordinary gain

Refer to the data provided in the previous exercise for Radar Company.

Required:
Prepare the cash flows from operating activities section of the statement of cash flows for Radar Company using the *indirect method.*

Exercise 22–21
Statement of cash flows;
direct method

Comparative balance sheets for 1997 and 1996, a statement of income for 1997, and additional information from the accounting records of Whoops, Inc., are provided below ($ in millions).

WHOOPS, INC.
Comparative Balance Sheets
December 31, 1997 and 1996 ($ in millions)

	1997	1996
Assets:		
Cash	$ 24	$110
Accounts receivable	178	132
Prepaid insurance	7	3
Inventory	285	175
Buildings and equipment	400	350
Less: Accumulated depreciation	(119)	(240)
	$775	$530
Liabilities:		
Accounts payable	$ 87	$100
Accrued expenses payable	6	11
Notes payable	50	0
Bonds payable	160	0
Shareholders Equity:		
Common stock	400	400
Retained earnings	72	19
	$775	$530

WHOOPS, INC.
Statement of Income
For Year Ended December 31, 1997 ($ in millions)

Revenues:		
Sales revenue		$2,000
Expenses:		
Cost of goods sold	$1,400	
Depreciation expense	50	
Operating expenses	447	1,897
Net income		$ 103

Additional information from the accounting records:

a. During 1997 $230 million of equipment was purchased to replace $180 million of equipment (95% depreciated) sold at book value.

b. In order to maintain the usual policy of paying cash dividends of $50 million, it was necessary for Whoops to borrow $50 million from its bank.

Required:
Prepare the statement of cash flows of Whoops, Inc., for the year ended December 31, 1997. Present cash flows from operating activities by the direct method and (unless your instructor directs you otherwise) use a spreadsheet to assist in your analysis. (You may omit the schedule to reconcile net income with cash flows from operating activities.)

Exercise 22–22
Pension plan funding

Mayer Corporation has a defined benefit pension plan. Mayer's policy is to fund the plan annually, cash payments being made at the end of each year. Data relating to the pension plan for 1997 are as follows:

	($ in millions) December 31	
	1997	**1996**
Prepaid (accrued) pension cost	$ 5	$ (1)
Net pension expense for 1997:		
Service cost	$112	
Interest cost (6% × $850)	51	
Actual return on the plan assets (11% × $900 = $99)		
Adjusted for: $9 gain on the plan assets*	(90)	
Amortization of prior service cost	8	
Amortization of net loss	1	
	$ 82	

*(11% × $900) – (10% × $900)

Required:
Recreate the journal entry used to record Mayer's 1997 pension expense in order to determine the cash paid to the pension trustee as reported on the statement of cash flows.

Exercise 22–23
Multiple choice

The following questions dealing with cash flows are adapted from questions that appeared in the "Financial Accounting & Reporting—Business Enterprises" section of recent CPA examinations. Determine the response that best completes the statements or questions.

1. The primary purpose of a statement of cash flows is to provide relevant information about
    a. Difference between net income and associated cash receipts and disbursements.
    b. An enterprise's ability to generate future positive net cash flows.
    c. The cash receipts and cash disbursements of an enterprise during a period.
    d. An enterprise's ability to meet cash operating needs.

Items 2 and 3 are based on the following:

In preparing its cash flow statement for the year ended December 31, 1997, Reve Co. collected the following data:

Gain on sale of equipment	$ (6,000)
Proceeds from sale of equipment	10,000
Purchase of A.S., Inc. bonds (par value $200,000)	(180,000)
Amortization of bond discount	2,000
Dividends declared	(45,000)
Dividends paid	(38,000)
Proceeds from sales of treasury stock (carrying amount $65,000)	75,000

In its December 31, 1997, statement of cash flows,

2. What amount should Reve report as net cash used in investing activities?
    a. $170,000
    b. $176,000
    c. $188,000
    d. $194,000
3. What amount should Reve report as net cash provided by financing activities?
    a. $20,000
    b. $27,000
    c. $30,000
    d. $37,000

Exercise 22–24
Statement of cash flows;
indirect method
(based on Appendix 22A)

Refer to the data provided in Exercise 22–21 for Whoops, Inc.

Required:
Prepare the statement of cash flows for Whoops, Inc. using the indirect method to report operating activities.

Exercise 22–25
Statement of cash flows;
T–account method
(based on Appendix 22B)

Refer to the data provided in Exercise 22–21 for Whoops, Inc.

Required:
Prepare the statement of cash flows (direct method) for Whoops, Inc. Use the T-account method to assist in your analysis.

Problems

Problem 22–1
Classifications of cash flows
from investing and financing
activities

Listed below are transactions that might be reported as investing and/or financing activities on a statement of cash flows. Possible reporting classifications of those transactions are provided also.

Required:
Indicate the reporting classification of each transaction by entering the appropriate classification code.

Classifications:
+ I Investing activity (cash inflow)
− I Investing activity (cash outflow)
+ F Financing activity (cash inflow)
− F Financing activity (cash outflow)
  N Noncash investing and financing activity
  X Not reported as an investing and/or a financing activity

Transactions

Example	$+$ I 1. Sale of land.
	_____ 2. Issuance of common stock for cash.
	_____ 3. Purchase of treasury stock.
	_____ 4. Conversion of bonds payable to common stock.
	_____ 5. Lease of equipment by capital lease.
	_____ 6. Sale of patent.
	_____ 7. Acquisition of building for cash.
	_____ 8. Issuance of common stock for land.
	_____ 9. Collection of note receivable (principal amount).
	_____ 10. Issuance of bonds.
	_____ 11. Issuance of stock dividend.
	_____ 12. Payment of property dividend.
	_____ 13. Payment of cash dividends.
	_____ 14. Issuance of short-term note payable for cash.
	_____ 15. Issuance of long-term note payable for cash.
	_____ 16. Purchase of marketable securities (not cash equivalent).
	_____ 17. Payment of note payable.
	_____ 18. Cash payment for 5-year insurance policy.
	_____ 19. Sale of equipment.
	_____ 20. Issuance of note payable for equipment.
	_____ 21. Acquisition of common stock of another corporation.
	_____ 22. Repayment of long-term debt by issuing common stock.
	_____ 23. Appropriation of retained earnings for plant expansion.
	_____ 24. Payment of semiannual interest on bonds payable.
	_____ 25. Retirement of preferred stock.
	_____ 26. Loan to another firm.
	_____ 27. Sale of inventory to customers.
	_____ 28. Purchase of marketable securities (cash equivalents).

Problem 22–2
Statement of cash flows;
direct method; spreadsheet

The comparative balance sheets for 1997 and 1996 and the statement of income for 1997 are given below for U.B. Wright Company. Additional information from Wright's accounting records is provided also.

U.B. WRIGHT COMPANY
Comparative Balance Sheets
December 31, 1997 and 1996 ($ in 000s)

	1997	1996
Assets:		
Cash	$ 42	$ 30
Accounts receivable	73	75
Short-term investment	40	15
Inventory	75	70
Land	50	60
Buildings and equipment	550	400
Less: Accumulated depreciation	(115)	(75)
	$715	$575
Liabilities:		
Accounts payable	$ 28	$ 35
Salaries payable	2	5
Interest payable	5	3
Income tax payable	9	12
Notes payable	0	30
Bonds payable	160	100
Shareholders' Equity:		
Common stock	250	200
Paid-in capital—excess of par	126	100
Retained earnings	135	90
	$715	$575

U.B. WRIGHT COMPANY
Income Statement
For Year Ended December 31, 1997 ($ in 000)

Revenues:		
Sales revenue		$380
Expenses:		
Cost of goods sold	$130	
Salaries expense	45	
Depreciation expense	40	
Interest expense	12	
Loss on sale of land	3	
Income tax expense	70	300
Net income		$ 80

Additional information from the accounting records:

a. Land that originally cost $10,000 was sold for $7,000.
b. The common stock of I.B Wrong Corporation was purchased for $25,000 as a short-term investment not classified as a cash equivalent.
c. New equipment was purchased for $150,000 cash.
d. A $30,000 note was paid at maturity on January 1.
e. On January 1, 1997, $60,000 of bonds were sold at face value.
f. Common stock ($50,000 par) was sold for $76,000.
g. Net income was $80,000 and cash dividends of $35,000 were paid to shareholders.

Required:

Prepare the statement of cash flows of U.B. Wright Company for the year ended December 31, 1997. Present cash flows from operating activities by the direct method and (unless your instructor directs you otherwise) use a spreadsheet to assist in your analysis. (You may omit the schedule to reconcile net income with cash flows from operating activities.)

Problem 22–3
Statement of cash flows;
direct method; spreadsheet

The comparative balance sheets for 1997 and 1996 and the statement of income for 1997 are given below for National Intercable Company. Additional information from NIC's accounting records is provided also.

NATIONAL INTERCABLE COMPANY
Comparative Balance Sheets
December 31, 1997 and 1996 ($ in millions)

	1997	1996
Assets:		
Cash	$ 72	$ 55
Accounts receivable	181	170
Less: Allowance for uncollectible accounts	(8)	(6)
Prepaid insurance	7	12
Inventory	170	165
Long-term investment	66	90
Land	150	150
Buildings and equipment	290	270
Less: Accumulated depreciation	(85)	(75)
Trademark	24	25
	$867	$856
Liabilities:		
Accounts payable	$ 30	$ 45
Salaries payable	3	8
Deferred income tax liability	18	15
Lease liability	80	0
Bonds payable	145	275
Less: Discount on bonds	(22)	(25)
Shareholders' Equity:		
Common stock	310	290
Paid-in capital—excess of par	95	85
Preferred stock	50	0
Retained earnings	158	163
	$867	$856

NATIONAL INTERCABLE COMPANY
Income Statement
For Year Ended December 31, 1997 (in millions)

Revenues:

Sales revenue	$320	
Investment revenue	15	
Gain on sale of investments	5	$340
Expenses:		
Cost of goods sold	$125	
Salaries expense	55	
Depreciation expense	25	
Trademark amortization expense	1	
Bad debts expense	7	
Insurance expense	13	
Bond interest expense	30	(256)
Income before tax and extraordinary items		$ 84
Income tax expense		(38)
Income before extraordinary items		$ 46
Extraordinary loss (tornado)	$ 42	
Less: Tax savings	(21)	(21)
Net income		**$ 25**

Additional information from the accounting records:

a. During 1997 $5 million of customer accounts were written off as uncollectible.

b. Investment revenue includes National Intercable Company's $6 million share of the net income of Central Fiber Optics Corporation, an equity method investee.

c. A long-term investment in bonds, originally purchased for $30 million, was sold for $35 million.

d. Pretax accounting income exceeded taxable income causing the deferred income tax liability to increase by $3 million.

e. A building that originally cost $60 million, and which was one-fourth depreciated, was destroyed by a tornado. Some undamaged parts were sold for $3 million.

f. A building was acquired by a seven-year capital lease; present value of lease payments, $80 million.

g. $130 million of bonds were retired at maturity.

h. $20 million par value of common stock was sold for $30 million, and $50 million of preferred stock was sold at par.

i. Shareholders were paid cash dividends of $30 million.

Required:

1. Prepare a spreadsheet for preparation of the statement of cash flows (direct method) of National Intercable Company for the year ended December 31, 1997.

2. Prepare the statement of cash flows. (A reconciliation schedule is not required.)

Problem 22–4
Statement of cash flows;
direct method; use
spreadsheet

The comparative balance sheets for 1997 and 1996 and the statement of income for 1997 are given below for Dux Company ($ in $000). Additional information from Dux's accounting records is provided also.

DUX COMPANY
Comparative Balance Sheets
December 31, 1997 and 1996 ($ in 000)

	1997	1996
Assets:		
Cash	$ 33	$ 20
Accounts receivable	48	50
Less: Allowance for uncollectible accounts	(4)	(3)
Inventory	55	50
Dividends receivable	3	2
Long-term investment	15	10
Land	70	40
Buildings and equipment	225	250
Less: Accumulated depreciation	(25)	(50)
	$420	$369
Liabilities:		
Accounts payable	$ 13	$ 20
Salaries payable	2	5
Interest payable	4	2
Income tax payable	7	8

Notes payable	30	0
Bonds payable	95	70
Less: Discount on bonds	(2)	(3)
Shareholders' Equity:		
Common stock	210	200
Paid-in capital—excess of par	24	20
Retained earnings	45	47
Less: Treasury stock (at cost)	(8)	0
	$420	$369

DUX COMPANY
Income Statement
For Year Ended December 31, 1997 ($ in 000)

Revenues:		
Sales revenue	$200	
Dividend revenue	3	$203
Expenses:		
Cost of goods sold	$120	
Salaries expense	25	
Depreciation expense	5	
Bad debts expense	1	
Interest expense	8	
Loss on sale of building	3	
Income tax expense	16	178
Net income		$ 25

Additional information from the accounting records:

a. A building that originally cost $40,000, and which was three-fourths depreciated, was sold for $7,000.

b. The common stock of Byrd Corporation was purchased for $5,000 as a long-term investment.

c. Property was acquired by issuing a 13%, seven-year, $30,000 note payable to the seller.

d. New equipment was purchased for $15,000 cash.

e. On January 1, 1997, $25,000 of bonds were sold at face value.

f. On January 19, Dux issued a 5% stock dividend (1,000 shares). The market price of the $10 par value common stock was $14 per share at that time.

g. Cash dividends of $13,000 were paid to shareholders.

h. On November 12, 500 shares of common stock were repurchased as treasury stock at a cost of $8,000. Dux uses the cost method to account for treasury stock.

Required:

Prepare the statement of cash flows of Dux Company for the year ended December 31, 1997. Present cash flows from operating activities by the direct method and (unless your instructor directs you otherwise) use a spreadsheet to assist in your analysis. (You may omit the schedule to reconcile net income with cash flows from operating activities.)

Problem 22–5
Statement of cash flows;
direct method; use
spreadsheet

Comparative balance sheets for 1997 and 1996 and a statement of income for 1997 are given below for Metagrobolize Industries. Additional information from the accounting records of Metagrobolize also is provided.

METAGROBOLIZE INDUSTRIES
Comparative Balance Sheets
December 31, 1997 and 1996 ($ in 000)

	1997	1996
Assets:		
Cash	$ 600	$ 375
Accounts receivable	600	450
Inventory	900	525
Land	675	600
Building	900	900
Less: Accumulated depreciation	(300)	(270)
Equipment	2,850	2,250
Less: Accumulated depreciation	(525)	(480)
Goodwill	1,200	1,500
	$6,900	$5,850

Liabilities:

Accounts payable	$ 750	$ 450
Accrued expenses payable	300	225
Lease liability—land	150	0

Shareholders' Equity:

Common stock	3,150	3,000
Paid-in capital—excess of par	750	675
Retained earnings	1,800	1,500
	$6,900	$5,850

METAGROBOLIZE INDUSTRIES
Income Statement
For Year Ended December 31, 1997 ($ in 000)

Revenues:

Sales revenue	$2,654	
Gain on sale of land	90	$2,735

Expenses:

Cost of goods sold	$ 600	
Depreciation expense-building	30	
Depreciation expense-equipment	315	
Loss on sale of equipment	15	
Amortization of goodwill	300	
Operating expenses	500	1,760
Net income		**$ 975**

Additional information from the accounting records:

a. During 1997, equipment with a cost of $300,000 (90% depreciated) was sold.
b. The statement of retained earnings reveals reductions of $225,000 and $450,000 for stock dividends and cash dividends, respectively.

Required:

Prepare the statement of cash flows of Metagrobolize for the year ended December 31, 1997. Present cash flows from operating activities by the direct method and (unless your instructor directs you otherwise) use a spreadsheet to assist in your analysis. (You may omit the schedule to reconcile net income with cash flows from operating activities.)

Problem 22–6
Cash flows from operating activities (direct method) derived from an income statement and cash flows from operating activities (indirect method)

The income statement and a schedule reconciling cash flows from operating activities to net income are provided below ($ in millions) for Mike Roe Computers.

MIKE ROE COMPUTERS
Income Statement
For the Year Ended December 31, 1997

Sales		$150
Cost of goods sold		(90)
Gross margin		60
Salaries expense	$20	
Insurance expense	10	
Depreciation expense	5	
Bad debt expense	2	
Interest expense	6	(43)
Gains and losses:		
Gain on sale of equipment		12
Loss on sale of land		(3)
Income before tax		26
Income tax expense		(13)
Net Income		**$ 13**

Reconciliation of Net Income to Net Cash Flows from Operating Activities

Net income	$13
Adjustments for noncash effects:	
Decrease in accounts receivable	3
Gain on sale of equipment	(12)
Increase in inventory	(6)
Increase in accounts payable	9
Increase in salaries payable	3
Depreciation expense	5
Increase in allowance for uncoll.	2
Decrease in bond discount	3
Decrease in prepaid insurance	2
Loss on sale of land	3
Increase in income tax payable	6
Net cash flows from operating activities	**$31**

Required:

1. Calculate each of the following amounts for Mike Roe Computers:
    a. Cash received from customers during the reporting period.
    b. Cash paid to suppliers of goods during the reporting period.
    c. Cash paid to employees during the reporting period.
    d. Cash paid for interest during the reporting period.
    e. Cash paid for insurance during the reporting period.
    f. Cash paid for income taxes during the reporting period.

2. Prepare the cash flows from operating activities section of the statement of cash flows (direct method).

Problem 22–7
Cash flows from operating activities (direct method) derived from an income statement and cash flows from operating activities (indirect method)

The income statement and a schedule reconciling cash flows from operating activities to net income are provided below ($ in millions) for Macrosoft Corporation.

MACROSOFT CORPORATION
Income Statement
For the Year Ended December 31, 1997
($ in millions)

Sales		$310
Cost of goods sold		(120)
Gross margin		$190
Salaries expense	$ 40	
Insurance expense	20	
Depreciation expense	10	
Patent amortization expense	4	
Interest expense	12	(86)
Loss on sale of land		(6)
Gain on sale of cash equivalents		2
Income before taxes and extraordinary gain		100
Income tax expense		(50)
Income before extraordinary gain		50
Extraordinary gain		
(extinguishment of debt)	24	
Less: Tax on gain	(12)	12
Net Income		**$ 62**

Reconciliation of Net Income
to Net Cash Flows from
Operating Activities

Net income	$ 62
Adjustments for noncash effects:	
Depreciation expense	10
Patent amortization expense	4
Loss on sale of land	6
Extraordinary gain (extinguishment of debt)	(24)
Decrease in accounts receivable	6
Increase in inventory	(12)
Increase in accounts payable	18
Decrease in bond discount	1
Increase in salaries payable	6
Decrease in prepaid insurance	4
Increase in income tax payable	10
Net cash flows from operating activities	**$ 91**

Required:
Prepare the cash flows from operating activities section of the statement of cash flows (direct method).

Problem 22–8
Cash flows from operating activities (direct method and indirect method)—deferred income tax liability and amortization of bond discount

Portions of the financial statements for Bellow Company are provided below.

BELLOW COMPANY
Income Statement ($ in 000)
For the Year Ended December 31, 1997

Sales		$800
Cost of goods sold		(300)
Gross margin		500
Salaries expense	$120	
Insurance expense	40	
Depreciation expense	123	
Interest expense	50	(333)
Gains and losses:		
Gain on sale of buildings		11
Loss on sale of machinery		(12)
Income before tax		166
Income tax expense		(78)
Net Income		**$ 88**

BELLOW COMPANY
Selected Accounts from Comparative Balance Sheets ($ in 000)
December 31, 1997 and 1996

	Year		
	1997	**1996**	**Change**
Cash	$134	$100	$ 34
Accounts receivable	324	216	108
Inventory	321	425	(104)
Prepaid insurance	66	88	(22)
Accounts payable	210	117	93
Salaries payable	102	93	9
Deferred income tax liability	60	52	8
Bond discount	190	200	(10)

Required:
1. Prepare the cash flows from operating activities section of the statement of cash flows for Bellow Company using the direct method.
2. Prepare the cash flows from operating activities section of the statement of cash flows for Bellow Company using the indirect method.

Problem 22–9
Cash flows from operating activities (direct method and indirect method)—gain on sale of cash equivalents and extraordinary loss

Portions of the financial statements for Hawkeye Company are provided below.

HAWKEYE COMPANY
Income Statement
For the Year Ended December 31, 1997

Sales		$900
Cost of goods sold		(350)
Gross margin		$550
Salaries expense	$220	
Depreciation expense	190	
Bad debt expense	12	
Interest expense	40	
Gain on sale of cash equivalents	(4)	(458)
Income before taxes and extraordinary loss		$ 92
Income tax expense		(46)
Income before extraordinary loss		$ 46
Extraordinary loss (flood damage)	$ 12	
Less: Tax savings	(6)	(6)
Net Income		$ 40

HAWKEYE COMPANY
Selected Accounts from Comparative Balance Sheets
December 31, 1997 and 1996

	Year		
	1997	1996	Change
Cash	$212	$200	$ 12
Accounts receivable	418	432	(14)
Allowance for uncollectibles	23	11	12
Inventory	860	850	10
Accounts payable	210	234	(24)
Salaries payable	180	188	(8)
Interest payable	55	50	5
Income taxes payable	90	104	(14)

Required:
1. Prepare the cash flows from operating activities section of the statement of cash flows for Hawkeye Company using the direct method.
2. Prepare the cash flows from operating activities section of the statement of cash flows for Hawkeye Company using the indirect method.

Problem 22–10
Relationship among the income statement, cash flows from operating activities (direct method and indirect method)

The following schedule relates the income statement with cash flows from operating activities, derived by both the direct and indirect methods, in the format illustrated by Graphic 22–8 in the chapter. Some elements necessary to complete the schedule are missing.

Cash Flows from Operating Activities

Income Statement		Indirect Method		Direct Method	
		Net income	$?		
		Adjustments :			
Sales	$300	Decrease in accounts receivable	6	Cash received from customers	$?
Gain on sale of equipment	24	Gain on sale of equipment	(24)	(Not reported—no cash effect)	
Cost of goods sold	(?)	Increase in inventory	(12)		
		Increase in accounts payable	18	Cash paid to suppliers	(174)
Salaries expense	(39)	? in salaries payable	6	Cash paid to employees	(33)
Depreciation expense	(9)	Depreciation expense	9	Cash paid for depreciation	?
Bad debt expense	(3)	Bad debt expense	3	(Not reported—no cash effect)	
Interest expense	(?)	Decrease in bond discount	3	Cash paid for interest	(9)
Insurance expense	(21)	Decrease in prepaid insurance	9	Cash paid for insurance	(?)
Loss on sale of land	(6)	Loss on sale of land	6	(Not reported—no cash effect)	
Income tax expense	(27)	Increase in income tax payable	?	Cash paid for income taxes	(21)
Net Income	$?	Net cash flows from operating activities	$57	Net cash flows from operating activities	$57

Required:
Complete the schedule by determining each of the following missing elements:
1. Cash received from customers
2. Cost of goods sold
3. ? in salaries payable (Increase? or decrease?)
4. Cash paid for depreciation
5. Interest expense

6. Cash paid for insurance
7. Increase in income tax payable
8. Net income

Problem 22–11
Prepare a statement of cash flows; direct method

The comparative balance sheets for 1997 and 1996 and the income statement for 1997 are given below for Arduous Company. Additional information from Arduous's accounting records is provided also.

ARDUOUS COMPANY
Comparative Balance Sheets
December 31, 1997 and 1996 ($ in millions)

	1997	1996
Assets:		
Cash	$ 116	$ 81
Accounts receivable	200	202
Less: Allowance for uncollectible accounts	(10)	(8)
Investment revenue receivable	6	4
Inventory	205	200
Prepaid insurance	4	8
Long-term investment	156	125
Land	196	150
Buildings and equipment	412	400
Less: Accumulated depreciation	(97)	(120)
Patent	30	32
	$1,218	$1,074
Liabilities:		
Accounts payable	$ 50	$ 65
Salaries payable	6	11
Bond interest payable	8	4
Income tax payable	12	14
Deferred income tax liability	11	8
Notes payable	23	0
Lease liability	82	0
Bonds payable	215	275
Less: Discount on bonds	(22)	(25)
Shareholders' Equity:		
Common stock	430	410
Paid-in capital—excess of par	95	85
Preferred stock	75	0
Retained earnings	242	227
Less: Treasury stock (at cost)	(9)	0
	$1,218	$1,074

ARDUOUS COMPANY
Income Statement
For Year Ended December 31, 1997 (in millions)

Revenues:			
Sales revenue		$410	
Investment revenue		11	
Gain on sale of treasury bills		2	$423
Expenses:			
Cost of goods sold		180	
Salaries expense		65	
Depreciation expense		12	
Patent amortization expense		2	
Bad debts expense		8	
Insurance expense		7	
Bond interest expense		28	
Extraordinary loss (flood)	$18		
Less: Tax savings	(9)	9	
Income tax expense		45	356
Net income			$ 67

Additional information from the accounting records:

a. During 1997, $6 million of customer accounts were written off as uncollectible.
b. Investment revenue includes Arduous Company's $6 million share of the net income of Demur Company, an equity method investee.
c. Treasury bills were sold during 1997 at a gain of $2 million. Arduous Company classifies its investments in treasury bills as cash equivalents.

d.   A machine that originally cost $70 million which was one-half depreciated was rendered unusable by a rare flood. Most major components of the machine were unharmed and were sold for $17 million.

e.   Temporary differences between pretax accounting income and taxable income caused the deferred income tax liability to increase by $3 million.

f.   The preferred stock of Tory Corporation was purchased for $25 million as a long-term investment.

g.   Land costing $46 million was acquired by issuing $23 million cash and a 15%, four-year, $23 million note payable to the seller.

h.   A building was acquired by a 15-year capital lease; present value of lease payments, $82 million.

i. $60 million of bonds were retired at maturity.

j.   In February, Arduous issued a 4% stock dividend (4 million shares). The market price of the $5 par value common stock was $7.50 per share at that time.

k.   In April, 1 million shares of common stock were repurchased as treasury stock at a cost of $9 million. Arduous uses the cost method to account for treasury stock.

Required:

Prepare the statement of cash flows of Arduous Company for the year ended December 31, 1997. Present cash flows from operating activities by the direct method and (unless your instructor directs you otherwise) use a spreadsheet to assist in your analysis. (A reconciliation schedule is not required.)

Problem 22–12
Transactions affecting
retained earnings

Shown below in T-account format are the changes affecting the retained earnings of Brenner-Jude Corporation during 1997. At January 1, 1997, the corporation had outstanding 105 million common shares, $1 par per share.

Retained Earnings ($ in millions)

		90	Beginning balance
Retirement of 5 million common shares for $22 million	2		
		88	Net income for the year
Declaration and payment of a $.33 per share cash dividend	33		
Declaration and distribution of a 4% stock dividend	20		
		123	Ending balance

Required:

1.   From the information provided by the account changes you should be able to recreate the transactions that affected Brenner-Jude's retained earnings during 1997. Reconstruct the journal entries which can be used as spreadsheet entries in the preparation of a statement of cash flows. Also indicate any investing and financing activities you identify from this analysis that should be reported on the statement of cash flows.

2.   Prepare a statement of retained earnings for Brenner-Jude for the year ended 1997.

   (You may wish to compare your solution to this problem with the parallel situation described in Exercise 19–10.)

Problem 22–13
Various cash flows

Following are selected balance sheet accounts of Zach Corp. at December 31, 1997 and 1996, and the increases or decreases in each account from 1996 to 1997. Also presented is selected income statement information for the year ended December 31, 1997, and additional information.

Selected balance sheet accounts	1997	1996	Increase (Decrease)
Assets:			
Accounts receivable	$ 34,000	$ 24,000	$10,000
Property, plant, and equipment	277,000	247,000	30,000
Accumulated depreciation	(178,000)	(167,000)	(11,000)
Liabilities and stockholders' equity:			
Bonds payable	49,000	46,000	3,000
Dividends payable	8,000	5,000	3,000
Common stock, $1 par	22,000	19,000	3,000
Additional paid-in capital	9,000	3,000	6,000
Retained earnings	104,000	91,000	13,000

Selected income statement information for the year ended December 31, 1997

Sales revenue	$155,000
Depreciation	33,000
Gain on sale of equipment	13,000
Net income	28,000

Additional information

a. Accounts receivable relate to sales of merchandise.

b. During 1997, equipment costing $40,000 was sold for cash.

c. During 1997, $20,000 of bonds payable were issued in exchange for property, plant, and equipment. There was no amortization of bond discount or premium.

Required:

Items 1 through 5 represent activities that will be reported in Zach's statement of cash flows for the year ended December 31, 1997. The following two responses are required for each item:

- Determine the amount that should be reported in Zach's 1997 statement of cash flows.
- Using the list below, determine the category in which the amount should be reported in the statement of cash flows
  - O. Operating activity
  - I. Investing activity
  - F. Financing activity

	Amount	Category
1. Cash collections from customers (direct method).	_____	_____
2. Payments for purchase of property, plant, and equipment.	_____	_____
3. Proceeds from sale of equipment.	_____	_____
4. Cash dividends paid.	_____	_____
5. Redemption of bonds payable.	_____	_____

(AICPA adapted)

Problem 22–14
Statement of cash flows; indirect method; limited information

The comparative balance sheets for 1997 and 1996 are given below for Surmise Company. Net income for 1997 was $50 million.

SURMISE COMPANY
Comparative Balance Sheets
December 31, 1997 and 1996 ($ in millions)

	1997	1996
Assets:		
Cash	$ 45	$ 40
Accounts receivable	92	96
Less: Allowance for uncollectible accounts	(12)	(4)
Prepaid expenses	8	5
Inventory	145	130
Long-term investment	80	40
Land	100	100
Buildings and equipment	411	300
Less: Accumulated depreciation	(142)	(120)
Patent	16	17
	$743	$604
Liabilities:		
Accounts payable	$ 17	$ 32
Accrued liabilities	(2)	10
Notes payable	35	0
Lease liability	111	0
Bonds payable	65	125
Shareholders' Equity:		
Common stock	60	50
Paid-in capital—excess of par	245	205
Retained earnings	212	182
	$743	$604

Required:

Prepare the statement of cash flows of Surmise Company for the year ended December 31, 1997. Use the indirect method to present cash flows from operating activities because you do not have sufficient information to use the direct method. You will need to make reasonable assumptions concerning the reasons for changes in some account balances. A spreadsheet or T-account analysis will be helpful.

The following problems use the technique learned in Appendix 22A:

Problem 22–15
Statement of cash flows; indirect method

Refer to the data provided in the Problem 22–4 for Dux Company.

Required:

Prepare the statement of cash flows for Dux Company using the *indirect method*.

Problem 22–16
Statement of cash flows;
indirect method

Refer to the data provided in Problem 22–5 for Metagrobolize Industries.

Required:
Prepare the statement of cash flows for Metagrobolize Industries using the *indirect method*.

Problem 22–17
Statement of cash flows;
indirect method

Refer to the data provided in Problem 22–11 for Arduous Company.

Required:
Prepare the statement of cash flows for Arduous Company using the *indirect method*.

The following problems use the technique learned in Appendix 22B:

Problem 22–18
Statement of cash flows;
T-account method

Refer to the data provided in the Problem 22–4 for Dux Company.

Required:
Prepare the statement of cash flows for Dux Company. Use the T-account method to assist in your analysis.

Problem 22–19
Statement of cash flows;
T-account method

Refer to the data provided in Problem 22–5 for Metagrobolize Industries.

Required:
Prepare the statement of cash flows for Metagrobolize Industries. Use the T-account method to assist in your analysis.

Problem 22–20
Statement of cash flows;
T-account method

Refer to the data provided in Problem 22–11 for Arduous Company.

Required:
Prepare the statement of cash flows for Arduous Company. Use the T-account method to assist in your analysis.

Cases

Critical Thought Case 22–1
Distinguish income and cash
flows

"Why can't we pay our shareholders a dividend?" shouted your new boss. "This income statement you prepared for me says we earned $5 million in our first half-year!"

You were hired last month as the chief accountant for Enigma Corporation which was organized on July 1 of the year just ended. You recently prepared the financial statements below:

ENIGMA CORPORATION
Income Statement
For the Six Months Ended Dec. 31, 1997 ($ in millions)

Sales revenue	$75
Cost of goods sold	(30)
Depreciation expense	(5)
Remaining expenses	(35)
Net income	$ 5

ENIGMA CORPORATION
Balance Sheet
December 31, 1997 ($ in millions)

Cash	$ 1
Accounts receivable (net)	20
Merchandise inventory	15
Machinery (net)	44
Total	$80
Accounts payable	$ 2
Accrued expenses payable	7
Notes payable	36
Common stock	30
Retained earnings	5
Total	$80

You have just explained to your boss, Robert James, that although net income was $5 million, operating activities produced a net decrease in cash. Unable to understand your verbal explanation, he has asked you to prepare a written report.

Required:
Prepare a report explaining the apparent discrepancy between Enigma's profitability and its cash flows. To increase the chances of your boss's understanding the situation, include in your report a determination of net cash flows from operating activities by both the direct and indirect methods. Your report should also include a narrative explanation of how it is possible for operating activities to simultaneously produce a positive net income and negative net cash flows.

Critical Thought Case 22–2
Distinguish income and cash flows

You are a loan officer for First Benevolent Bank. You have an uneasy feeling as you examine a loan application from Daring Corporation. The application included the following financial statements.

DARING COMPANY
Income Statement
For the Year Ended December 31, 1997

Sales revenue	$100,000
Cost of goods sold	(50,000)
Depreciation expense	(5,000)
Remaining expenses	(25,000)
Net income	$ 20,000

DARING COMPANY
Balance Sheet
December 31, 1997

Cash	$ 5,000
Accounts receivable	25,000
Inventory	20,000
Operational assets	55,000
Accumulated depreciation	(5,000)
Total	$100,000
Accounts payable	$ 10,000
Interest payable	5,000
Note payable	45,000
Common stock	20,000
Retained earnings	20,000
Total	$100,000

It is not Daring's profitability that worries you. The income statement submitted with the application shows net income of $20,000 in Daring's first year of operations. By referring to the balance sheet, you see that this net income represents a 20% rate of return on assets of $100,000. Your concern stems from the recollection that the note payable reported on Daring's balance sheet is a two-year loan you approved earlier in the year.

You also recall the promising new company that, just last year, defaulted on another of your bank's loans when it failed due to its inability to generate sufficient cash flows to meet its obligations. Before requesting additional information from Daring, you decide to test your memory of the intermediate accounting class you took in night school by attempting to prepare a statement of cash flows from the information available in the loan application.

Required:
Prepare a statement of cash flows using the direct method. Are your concerns justified?

Discussion Case 22–3
Objectives

The statement of cash flows normally is a required basic financial statement for each period for which an income statement is presented.

Required:
1. What are the objectives of the statement of cash flows?
2. What are two types of transactions that would be disclosed in a separate schedule in the statement of cash flows although they don't affect cash during the report period?
3. What effect, if any, would each of the following seven items have on the preparation of a statement of cash flows assuming the direct method is used to present cash flows from operating activities?
   a. Accounts receivable—trade.
   b. Inventory.
   c. Depreciation.
   d. Deferred tax liability.
   e. Issuance of long-term debt in payment for a building.
   f. Payoff of the current portion of debt.
   g. Sale of a fixed asset resulting in a loss.

(AICPA adapted)

Trueblood Accounting Case 22–4
SFAS 95 requirements; substance over form

The following Robert M. Trueblood case is recommended for use with this chapter. The case provides an excellent opportunity for class discussion, group projects, and writing assignments. The case, along with Professor's Discussion Material, can be obtained from the Deloitte & Touche Foundation.

Case 90–4: *Reporting Cash Flows*

The objective of this case is to work with the application of *SFAS 95* in the context of the repayment of a loan and the acquisition of a company. An opportunity also is provided to deal with the issue of substance over form in applying *SFAS 95* requirements.

Integrative Case 22–5
Postretirement benefits and accounting for income taxes

The operating activities section of the comparative statements of cash flows from a recent Walgreen annual report is reproduced below:

WALGREEN CO. AND SUBSIDIARIES
Consolidated Statements of Cash Flows
For the Years Ended August 31, 1993, 1992, and 1991
(Dollars in Thousands)

	1993	1992	1991
Cash flows from operating activities			
Net Earnings	$221,666	$220,628	$194,965
Adjustments to reconcile net earnings to net cash provided by operating activities—			
Cumulative effect of accounting changes—			
Postretirement benefits other than pensions	35,813	—	—
Income taxes	(13,190)		
Depreciation and amortization	104,660	92,109	84,346
Deferred income taxes	(12,645)	11,158	3,259
Loss on closing distribution center	—	—	4,118
Other	(1,772)	(719)	(2,745)
Changes in current assets and liabilities—			
Inventories	(99,867)	(82,173)	(83,998)
Accrued expenses and other liabilities	70,767	52,737	30,857
Trade accounts payable	15,502	46,143	17,014
Other current assets	(7,814)	(3,095)	(2,281)
Accounts receivable, net	(7,427)	(3,079)	(24,813)
Income taxes	184	4,802	(2,374)
Net cash provided by operating activities	305,877	338,511	218,348

Required:

Why are the two adjustments for accounting changes included on the statement of cash flows? Why is one added and the other subtracted?

International Case 22–6
Comparison of deferred tax accounting in Australia and the United States.

Foster's Brewing Group Limited, based in Australia, is an international brewer and marketer of beer. Brands include Foster's Lager, Molson, and Carlton. The consolidated statements of cash flows from Foster's 1994 annual report are reproduced below:

FOSTER'S BREWING GROUP LIMITED
Consolidated Statements of Cash Flows (in part)
For the Years Ended 30 June, 1994 and 1993
(in millions of Australian dollars)

Operating activities	1994	1993
Receipts from customers	6,822.7	9,401.7
Payments to suppliers, employees, principals	(6,407.2)	(9,075.0)
Dividends received	5.0	1.8
Interest received	48.0	117.8
Interest paid	(209.9)	(376.2)
Income tax (paid)/refunded	(59.7)	4.4
Funds withdrawn from Molson Breweries Partnership	75.1	95.1
Net cash flows from operating activities	274.0	169.6
Investing and other activities		
Payments to acquire controlled entities		
(net of cash balances acquired)	(18.5)	(123.9)
Payments to acquire outside equity interest in controlled entities	(21.2)	—
Payments for property, plant and equipment	(161.1)	(145.4)
Payments for acquisition of investments and other assets	(48.3)	(11.6)
Loans made	(212.5)	(298.9)
Proceeds from repayment of loans	239.3	354.1
Proceeds from sale of controlled entities	85.8	13.2
Proceeds from sale of property, plant and equipment	34.4	45.7

Proceeds from sale of partnership interest	—	192.5
Proceeds from sale of other investments and other assets	**427.6**	281.5
Proceeds from issue of shares (net)	—	1,008.7
Dividends paid	**(134.1)**	(40.6)
Repayment of Rural Loan funding	**(150.0)**	—
Redemption of preference shares	—	(7.5)
Net cash flows on behalf of controlled entities		
Other	—	9.2
Net cash flows from investing and other activities	**41.4**	1,277.0
Total cash flows from activities	**315.4**	1,446.6
Cash at the beginning of the financial year	**114.8**	159.2
Gross additional borrowings	**125.3**	3,279.2
Gross repayment of borrowings	**(462.7)**	(4,788.0)
Effect of exchange rate changes on foreign currency cash		
flows and cash balances	**(0.6)**	18.1
Cash at the end of the financial year	**92.2**	115.1

Note: Supplemental disclosure notes reconciling payments to acquire controlled entities and cash proceeds from sale of controlled entities are provided in the annual report but not reproduced here.

Required:
On the basis of the information the disclosures provide, compare cash flow reporting in Australia with that in the U.S.A.

Ethics Case 22–7
Where's the cash?

After graduating near the top of his class, Ben Naegle was hired by the local office of a Big 6 CPA firm in his hometown. Two years later, impressed with his technical skills and experience, Park Electronics, a large regional consumer elections chain, hired Ben as assistant controller. This was last week. Now Ben's initial excitement has turned to distress.

The cause of Ben's distress is the set of financial statements he's stared at for the last four hours. For some time prior to his recruitment, he had been aware of the long trend of moderate profitability of his new employer. The reports on his desk confirm the slight, but steady, improvements in net income in recent years. The trend he was just now becoming aware of, though, was the decline in cash flow from operations.

Ben had sketched out the following comparison ($ in millions):

	1997	1996	1995	1994
Income from operations	$140.0	$132.0	$127.5	$127.0
Net income	38.5	35.0	34.5	29.5
Cash flow from operations	1.6	17.0	12.0	15.5

Profits? Yes. Increasing profits? Yes. The cause of his distress? The ominous trend in cash flow which is consistently lower than net income.

Upon closer review, Ben noticed three events in the last two years that, unfortunately, seemed related:

a. Park's credit policy had been loosened; credit terms were relaxed and payment periods were lengthened,
b. Accounts receivable balances had increased dramatically,
c. Several of the company's compensation arrangements, including that of the controller and the company president, were based on reported net income.

Required:
1. What is so ominous about the combination of events Ben sees?
2. What course of action, if any, should Ben take?

Research Case 22–8
Cash flow ratio analysis; research article in the *Journal of Accountancy*

The FASB requirement to prepare a statement of cash flows is a relatively recent development in the evolution of financial reporting. Partially as a result, widespread use of cash flow ratios has been slow to develop. Professors Giacomino and Mielke, in "Cash Flows: Another Approach to Ratio Analysis," propose a complete set of cash flow ratios to complement accrual-based ratios in financial statement analysis.

Required:
1. In your library or from some other source, locate the indicated article in the *Journal of Accountancy*, March 1993.
2. What are the two categories of ratios proposed by the authors? What do the ratios in each category purport to measure?
3. Based on the survey described in the study, what conclusions do the authors draw concerning appropriateness of inter-industry comparisons of ratios?

Research Case 22–9
Statement of cash flows; classifying interest on borrowed funds; research article in the *Accounting Horizons*

The statement of cash flows classifies interest as an operating activity and the receipt and payment of borrowed funds as financing activities. Implementing this classification requirement has produced several methods of classifying the cash flows related to long-term debt. Professors Vent, Cowling, and Sevalstad, in "Cash Flow Comparability: Accounting for Long-Term Debt under *SFAS 95*," identify and illustrate four such methods and point out problems posed by the variation in methods used.

Required:

1. In your library or from some other source, locate the indicated article in the *Accounting Horizons*, December 1995.
2. What are four methods of classifying long-term debt identified by the authors? Are readers of financial statements usually aware of the method used?
3. What conclusions do the authors draw concerning the effect of financial statements usefulness? What solution do they propose?

Internet Case 22–10
Researching the way cash flows are reported; retrieving information from the Internet

EDGAR, the Electronic Data Gathering, Analysis, and Retrieval system, performs automated collection, validation, indexing, acceptance, and forwarding of submissions by companies and others who are required by law to file forms with the U.S. Securities and Exchange Commission (SEC). All publicly traded domestic companies use EDGAR to make the majority of their filings. (Filings by foreign companies are not required to be filed on EDGAR, but some of these companies do so voluntarily.) Form 10-K or 10-KSB, which include the annual report, is required to be filed on EDGAR. The SEC makes this information available on the Internet.

Required:

1. Access EDGAR on the Internet. The web address is www.sec.gov/.
2. Search for a public company with which you are familiar. Access its most recent 10-K filing. Search or scroll to find the statement of cash flows and related note(s).
3. Is the direct or indirect method used to report operating activities? What is the largest adjustment to net income in reconciling net income and cash flows from operations in the most recent year?
4. What are the cash payments for interest and for taxes?
5. What has been the most significant investing activity for the company in the most recent three years?
6. What has been the most significant financing activity for the company in the most recent three years?
7. Repeat requirements 2–6 for another company.

Financial Analysis Case 22–11
Information from cash flow activities

Federal Express Corporation

Refer to the financial statements and related disclosure notes of Federal Express Corporation in the appendix to Chapter 1. Notice that financing activities created a sizable net reduction in cash in each of the three years reported. Investing activities have required large and increasing amounts of cash over the same period.

Required:

1. From the information provided on the statement of cash flows, explain what allows Federal Express to expand its business as evidenced by the investing activities, while at the same time not raising (in fact, decreasing) cash through financing activities.
2. Describe the four activities listed under financing activities for the 1996 fiscal year. [Hint: Federal Express's Statement of Changes in Common Stockholders' Investment (statement of shareholders' equity) will help you determine the nature of the "Other, net" activity.] What is the most notable financing activity reported?
3. What are the cash payments Federal Express made for interest and for income taxes in each of the three years reported? (Hint: See the disclosure notes.)

INDEX

A

ABO; *see* Accumulated benefit obligation
Abt, Diane, 789 n
Accelerated cost recovery system, 462
Accelerated methods, 449 450
Accounting
   accrual concept, 954
   for defined benefit plans, 731
   for defined contribution plans, 730
   for issuance of shares, 834–835
   for shares reacquired, 840–841
   for treasury stock, 841
   usefulness of cash flow information, 952
Accounting changes, 913
   interim reporting of, 172
   types of, 912
Accounting equation, 56–57, 85
Accounting errors
   affecting prior year's net income, 927–931
   affecting statement but not income, 927
   correcting, 923, 925–932
      illustration of, 927–931
      prior period adjustments, 926
   discovered in same reporting period, 927
Accounting model
   accounting equation, 56–57
   account relationships, 58–59
   economic events, 56
Accounting principles; *see also* Change in
      accounting principle
   cumulative effect of change in, 116–119
   full-disclosure, 27
   historical cost, 25
   matching, 26
   realization, 25–26, 144, 169
Accounting Principles Board, 11
   Opinion No. 3, 955
   Opinion No. 7, 842 n
   Opinion No. 8, 751
   Opinion No. 11, 676
   Opinion No. 12, 828 n
   Opinion No. 17, 456
   Opinion No. 19, 955
   Opinion No. 21, 280, 837
   Opinion No. 25, 789, 790, 793
   Opinion No. 29, 411 n, 835 n
   Opinions, 9
Accounting processing cycle steps
   adjusted trial balance, 74–75
   adjusting entries, 69–75
   closing, 80–81
   obtaining source documents, 59–60
   post-closing trial balance, 81
   posting, 60, 65–66
   preparing financial statements, 77–80
   preparing unadjusted trial balance, 66–67
   recording to journal, 59–65
   transaction analysis, 60–61
Accounting Research Bulletins, 9
   No. 43, 358, 360, 448, 846 n, 847 n,
      848n, 849
Accounting standards; *see* Standards
Accounts, 58–59
   permanent, 59
   temporary, 59
Accounts payable
   balance sheet reporting, 197
   as current liabilities, 531–532
Accounts receivable
   assigning of, 291–293
   balance sheet reporting, 194
   definition of, 279
   factoring, 293–295, 534
   initial valuation of, 279–281
   pledging, 291, 534
   and sales revenue, 964–965
   subsequent valuation of, 281–286
   uncollectible, 283–286
Accounts receivable aging schedule, 284
Accrual accounting, 8, 21, 69
   conversion from cash basis, 83–84
Accrual concept, 956
Accruals, 72–73
   and gain contingencies, 547–548
   and loss contingencies, 546–547
Accrued interest, 572, 630–631
Accrued liabilities, 72–73, 197, 535–536
Accrued receivables, 73
Accumulated benefit obligation, 732
   and pension liability, 748–749
Accumulated depreciation, 71
Accumulated postretirement benefit obligation,
      776–777
Acid-test ratio, 208, 550
Acquisition by exchange
   dissimilar assets, 411–412
   similar assets, 412–415
Acquisition costs, 403
ACRS; *see* Activity-based depreciation
      methods
Activity-based depreciation methods, 448–451
Activity ratios, 165–166
Actual return on pension assets, 741
Actuary, 731
Additional markup, 366
Additional pension plan liability, 749–751
Additions, 465–466
Adjusted trial balance, 74–75
Adjusting entries
   accruals, 72–73
   estimates, 74
   prepayments, 70–72
   purpose of, 69–75
Advanced Micro Devices, Inc., 184
Advance payments on leases, 626–627
Advances from customers, 537
Adverse opinion, 205
Aging schedule, 284
AIA; *see* American Institute of Accountants
Allen, Robert E., 773
Allocation base, 447–448
Allocation method, 447–448
Allowance for doubtful accounts, 18, 283
Allowance for uncollectible accounts, 74
Allowance method, 20
   bad debt, 283
Alternate intrinsic value approach, 793–794
Alt Microsystems, Inc., 529–530, 550–551
Amdahl Corporation, 161
American Airlines, 671
American Institute of Accountants, 9
American Institute of Certified Public
      Accountants, 9, 11, 28
   on cash flow analysis, 955
American Semiconductor, 841, 842
American Ship Building Company, 151
American Stock Exchange, 830
Amortization
   of additional depreciation, 502
   calculation of, 456–457
   of deferred net gains or losses, 779–780
   explanation of, 446
   of net loss/gain, 743
   prior service cost, 779
   of prior service cost, 741–742
   of purchased goodwill, 500–501
   service method, 742–743
   straight-line method, 742
   of transition liability, 751–752
   of transition obligation, 780–782
Amortization schedule, 577–578
Anderson, Kevin, 782 n
Anheuser-Busch Companies, Inc., 613

Annual bonuses, 799
Annuities
   accounting applications of present value
      techniques, 252–254
   deferred, 247–249
   definition of, 243
   future value of, 244–245
   ordinary, 243
   present value of, 245–249
   solving for unknown values in, 249–251
Annuity due, 243–244
Antidilutive securities
   convertible securities, 886–887
   options, warrants, and rights, 885–886
   order entry for multiple convertibles
      securities, 887–888
APBO; *see* Accumulated postretirement
    benefit obligation
Apple Computer, 116, 506, 789, 952
A&P stores, 754
ARB; *see Accounting Research Bulletins*
Armada Corporation, 826
Arthur Anderson LLP, 15
Arthur D. Little, Inc., 12
Articles of incorporation, 831
Assets; *see also* Operational assets
   current, 79, 193–195
   deferred tax, 682–685
   definition of, 21, 192
   exchange of dissimilar, 411–412
   exchange of similar, 412–415
   intangible, 196
   monetary, 242
   noncurrent, 195–196
   other, 196, 278
Asset turnover ratio, 166
Assigning of accounts receivable, 291–293
Assumptions underlying GAAP, 24–25
AT&T, 12, 156, 773, 805
Attribution, 777
Attribution period, 777–778
Auditors, 14–15
Auditors' report, 203–205
Available for sale, 492–493
Average accumulated expenditures, 419
Average collection period, 165–166, 298
Average cost method, 325–326
Average days in inventory, 166, 337

B

Bad debt expense, 74, 283
Balance sheet, 78–79
   accounts on statement of cash flows,
      971–975
   bonds payable, 973
   buildings and equipment, 972–973
   classifications
      assets, 193–196
      liabilities, 196–198
      shareholder's equity, 198
   common stock, 974
   definition, 191
   definition of, 212
   elements of, 192
   impact of leasing on, 653–654
   land account, 972
   reporting deferred tax on, 696–697
   reporting investment securities on, 497–498
   retained earnings, 974
   short-term investments, 971–972
   usefulness and limitations, 191–192
Balance sheet approach, 284–285, 678–679
Banana Republic, 825
Bank reconciliation, 275–277
Bankruptcy, 191–192
Bargain purchase option, 623–624, 639–641

Bargain renewal options, 623
Basic earnings per share, 876
   and potentially dilutive securities, 880
Beaman Corporation, 846
Bearer bonds, 573
Beese, J., Jr., 790 n
Beresford, Dennis, 790
Billings on construction contract account,
   149–150
Black and Decker Corporation, 533
Black Clawson Company, 12
Board of directors, 831
Boeing Company, 620
Boise Cascade Corporation, 400, 445
Bond indenture, 573
Bonds
   convertible, 584–586
   debt issue costs, 582–583
   with detachable warrants, 586–587
   determining interest on
      effective interest method for, 576–579
      straight line method for, 579–581
   at a discount, 575, 580–581
   explanation of, 572–581
   induced conversion, 585–586
   recording buying and selling of, 574–576
   sold at a premium, 575, 580–581
   zero-coupon, 583–584
Bonds payable, 973
Bonus plans, 535–536
   annual bonuses, 799
   long-term cash bonuses, 799–800
   performance share plans, 799–800
Book value, 850
Bowen, R. M., 914 n
Bowne & Company, 833
BPO; *see* Bargain purchase option
Briggs and Stratton, 849
Bristol-Myers Squibb Company, 566–567
British Airways, 229
British Petroleum, 670, 724
Brown, Robert Moren, 331 n
Brown & Sharpe Manufacturing Company, 459
Buildings, cost of, 403
Buildings and equipment account, 972–973
Businessland, 653–654

C

Cadbury Schweppes, 140
Callable shares, 832
Campbell Soup Company, 533, 547
   fiscal year, 24
Canada, 786
Capital
   invested versus earned, 824
   paid-in, 827, 831–844
   raised by corporations, 829–830
Capital budgeting decisions, 416–417
Capitalization
   of new cost, 466
   of operational assets, 401–407, 418–422
   of research and development costs, 425
Capital leases, 620
   definition, 622
   and installment notes, 621–622
   sale-leaseback, 648–650
Capital market, 5
Carey, Susan, 773
Carslaw, Charles, 923 n
Carter Hawley Hale Stores, Inc., 191
Cash, 955–956
   balance sheet reporting, 194
   bank reconciliation, 275–277
   internal control of, 274–275
   petty, 277–278

   restricted, and compensating balances,
      278–279
   stock appreciation rights payable in, 796–798
Cash balance, reconciling changes in, 959
Cash basis accounting, 7–8
   conversion from, to accrual basis, 83–84
Cash disbursements
   internal control procedures, 275
   journal, 88
Cash discounts, 290–281, 321–323
Cash dividends, 845–846
Cash equivalents, 201, 274, 955–956; *see
   also* Cash
   balance sheet reporting, 194
"Cash Flow Analysis and the Funds Statement"
   (Mason), 955
Cash flow information, 952
Cash flow ratios, 981–983
Cash flows
   cash versus accrual accounting and, 7–8
   direct presentation method, 979
   from financing activities, 126
   from financing activities, 958–959
   indirect presentation method, 979
   inflows and outflows, 952–953
   from investing activities, 125–126, 957–598
   negative, 7 n
   and noncash investing and financing
      activities, 126
   from operating activities, 124–125,
      956–957, 979–983
   perspective on, 6–7
   retail inventory method, 368–369
   valuing single amount, 237–243
Cash inflows, 952–953
Cash outflows, 952–953
Cash receipts
   internal control procedures, 275
   journal, 90
Cash surrender value, 512–513
Caterpillar, 299
CBS Records, 14
Celgene Corporation, 205
Certificates of deposit, 728
Certified Public Accountant, 15
Champion International, 394–395, 783
Chaney, Paul, 702 n
Change in accounting estimate, 912, 921–922
Change in accounting principle, 118–119
   and changing circumstances, 913–914
   current approach, 914–917
   motivation for accounting choices, 914
   prospective approach, 920
   retroactive approach, 918–919
Change in reporting entity, 922
Chapter Opening Cases (Financial Reporting
   Cases)
   A Question of Interest, 399, 426–427
   Cracker Barrel Old Country Store, 487, 507
   Does It Count, 357, 378
   Eli Lily, 103, 127–128
   Engineering Profits, 57, 84–85
   Inventory Measurement at General Motors,
      315, 340
   It's a Hit, 619, 654
   John Smiley's Settlement, 235, 254
   Martin's Pepsi, 911, 932–933
   Misguided Marketing Major, 3, 29
   Proper Motivation?, 773, 805
   Reynolds & Reynolds, 875, 895
   Service Leader, Inc., 571, 601
   The Gap, 825, 853
   United Dynamics, 727–728, 755
   Wentworth's Wife, 529–530, 550–551
   What's In a Name?, 445, 468
   What's It Worth?, 189–190, 211

What's the Difference?, 675, 705
Where's the Cash?, 951, 983
You Don't Have to be a Rocket
  Scientist, 143, 169
You Give the Lecture, 273, 299–300
Checks outstanding, 276
Chess King, 351
Chicago Mercantile Exchange, 526
Chock Full O'Nuts Corporation, 293
Chrysler Corporation, 295
Cisco Systems, 492–493
Citicorp, 631
Clark, Myrtle, 870–871
Clean opinion, 15
Clorox Company, 24, 109–112, 891
Closely held corporations, 830
Closing process, 80–81
Coastal Corporation, 455–456
COBRA (Consolidated Omnibus B Retirement
  Act), 775 n
Coca-Cola Company, 14, 404, 405, 599–600
Coddington, Ron, 12 n, 779n
Colgate-Palmolive Company, 14, 274
Collections for third parties, 537
Collins Industries, Inc., 534
Commercial paper, 535
Commissions, 535–536
Committee on Accounting Procedure, 9, 11
Common shares
  on balance sheet, 974
  compared to preferred shares, 832–833
  definition, 831
  earnings per share, 879–880
Comparability, 19
Comparative financial statements, 164
Compensating balance, 278–279, 533
Compensation, disclosure of, 205–206
Competitive disadvantage costs, 19
Completed contract method, 145–146
Completed performance method, 156
Complex capital structure, 880–888
Composite depreciation method, 453–454
Compound interest, 236
Comprehensive income, 122–124
  definition of, 23
Conceptual framework
  constraints on, 19–20
  elements of financial statements, 21–23
  ethics in accounting, 27–28
  objectives of financial reporting, 16–17
  purpose of, 15
  qualitative characteristics of
    information, 17–19
  recognition and measurement
    concepts, 23–27
Conservatism, 20
Consignment, 320–321
Consistency, 19
Consolidated financial statements, 201, 498–499
Consolidation, 498–499
Constraint
  conservatism as, 20
  cost effectiveness as, 19
  materiality as, 20
Construction in progress account, 146
Contingencies, 540–548; see also Gain
  contingencies; Loss contingencies
Contingently issuable securities, 889–890
Contingent rentals, 633–645
Contracts
  long-term
    completed contract method, 145–146
    losses on, 151–152
    percentage-of-completion method, 146–147
  purchase commitment, 379–381
  warranty, 542–544

Contributing pension plans, 729
Control accounts, 88
Conventional retail method, 367–368
Convertible bonds, 573, 584–586, 882–884
Convertible preferred stock, 884–885
Convertible securities
  actual conversions and EPS, 890–891
  antidilutive securities, 886–887
  bonds, 882–884
  multiple, 887–888
  preferred stock, 884–885
Copyrights, 405, 456
Corporate charter, 831
Corporate takeover, 839 n
Corporations
  complex capital structure, 880–888
  creditor's interest, 826
  disadvantages of, 830
  ease of raising capital, 829–830
  explanation of, 5–6
  hybrid organization, 830
  limited liability, 829
  Model Business Corporation Act, 831
  multinational, 14
  organization of, 828–829
  ownership interest, 826
  profitability ratio, 849–850
  quasi reorganization, 854–855
  reacquired shares, 838–842
  reasons for pension plans, 728
  retained earnings, 844–852
  simple capital structure, 876–880
  types of, 830
Cost accounting method, 840–841
Cost allocation
  amortization, 456
  for change in depreciation method, 460
  for changes in estimates, 459
  comparison with MACRS, 462
  depletion, 454–456
  error corrections, 461–462
  and impairment of value, 462–464
  measuring, 447–451
  overview of, 446–447
  partial period, 457–459
Cost allocation depreciation; see Depreciation
Cost effectiveness, 19
Cost flows
  and inventories, 323–333
  retail inventory methods
    approximating average cost, 367
    conventional retail method, 367–368
Cost indexes, 338–339
Cost method, 490
Cost of goods sold, 316, 967
Cost recovery method, 159
Costs of share issuance, 836–837
Cost-to-cost method, 147
Cost-to-retail percentage, 365
Coupon bonds, 573
Coupons, 545
CPA; see Certified Public Accountant
Cracker Barrel Old Country Store, 487, 507
Craft Industries, 845–846, 847
Credit balance, 844
Credit differences, 840
Credit lines, 533
Creditors' interest, 572, 826
Critical event, 25
Cumulative effect of a change in accounting
  principle
  accounting for, 116–119
  change in accounting estimate, 118–119
  change in reporting entity, 119
Cumulative preferred shares, 832
Current approach

to change in accounting principle, 914–917
to error correction, 913
Current assets, 193–195; see also Assets
Current liabilities, 197; see also Liabilities
  accounts payable, 531–532
  explanation of, 531
  liquidity of, 549–550
  short-term notes payable, 532–534
  trade notes payable, 532
Current liabilities commercial paper, 535
Current maturities of long-term debt, 197
Current ratio, 207–208, 550

D

Date of record, 845
Davidson-Getty Chemicals, 801
Dayton Hudson, 365
DDB; see Double-declining balance method
Dean Foods Company, 546–547
Debenture bond, 573
Debt; see also Bonds; Liabilities; Notes;
    Troubled debt
    restructuring
  agreement restrictions, 621
  callable, 538, 573
  long-term
    current maturities of, 197, 538
    financial statement disclosures of, 598–601
  retirement of, 592–593
  variations in instruments of, 583–587
Debt coverage ratio, 982
Debt financing, 826
Debt issue costs, 582–583
Debt payment ratio, 983
Debt to equity ratio, 209–210
DeChow, Patricia, 8 n
Decision usefulness of information, 19
Default risk, 207
Deferrals; see Prepayments
Deferred annuity, 247–249
Deferred gross profit, 158
Deferred net gains or losses, amortization,
    779–780
Deferred payments, 408–410
Deferred tax; see also Income tax
  and changes in tax laws, 690–692
  concept of, 676
  concerns with, 701–702
  financial statement presentation, 696–698
  and operating losses, 694–696
  valuation allowance, 685–687
Deferred tax assets, 682–685
Deferred tax liabilities
  balance sheet approach to, 678–679
  multiple temporary differences, 692–694
  nontemporary differences, 687–688
  rate considerations, 689–692
  reporting, 675–676
  temporary differences, 677–682
Deficit, 844
Defined benefit pension plans
  definition, 729
  description, 731–732
  reporting issues, 746–754
Defined contribution pension plans, 729–730
DeFond, M. L., 925 n
Dell Computer, 26
Deloitte & Touche, 770
Delta Airlines, 802
Dennison and Company, Inc., 858
Department of Labor's Department Store Price
    Index, 920
Department Store Price Index, 920
Depletion
  calculation of, 454–456
  explanation of, 446

Deposits
  outstanding, 276
  refundable, 536
Depreciation, 201, 921
  activity-based methods of, 450–451
  amortization of additional, 502
  change in method of, 460
  explanation of, 446
  group and composite methods of, 453–454
  on leases assets, 629–630
  retirement and replacement methods of, 469–470
  selecting method for, 451–452
  time-based methods of, 448–450
Depreciation expense, 71, 968
Derivatives
  accounting for, 511
  definition of, 508
  disclosures, 511–512
  financial instruments, 509–511
Detachable stock purchase warrants, 586–587
Development costs, 403–404
Development stage enterprise, 406
Dhaliwad, D., 331 n, 914 n
Diluted earnings per share, 880
Direct-financing leases, 620
Direct method of reporting cash flow, 125, 979
Direct write-off method, 20, 286
Disclaimer, 205
Disclosure notes, 27, 917; see also Financial disclosures
  minimum interim reporting requirements, 172
  noteworthy events and transactions, 201–203
  on pension plans, 753
  reporting deferred tax in, 697–698
  subsequent events, 201
  summary of significant accounting policies, 200–201
Disclosures
  General Motors, 774
  Microsoft share repurchase, 839
  postretirement benefit disclosures, 784–785
Discontinued operation
  disposal in same year as measurement date, 110–112
  disposal in year after measurement date, 112–113
  explanation of, 109–110
  and interim reporting, 171
Discounting, 291
Discounting notes receivable, 295–297
Disposal date, 111
Dissaggregated information reporting, 212–214
Distribution to owners, 22
Dividend in kind, 846
Dividend payment ratio, 983
Dividend payout ratio, 893–894
Dividends, 844–849
  cash dividends, 845–846
  decisions on, 849–851
  liquidating dividend, 844
  property dividends, 846
  retained earnings restrictions, 845
  stock dividends, 846–848
  stock splits, 848–849
Dividends in arrears, 832
Dollar-value LIFO, 338–339, 371–373
Dollar-value LIFO retail, 371–373
Donated assets, 410–411
Double-declining-balance method, 449–450
Double-entry system, 58–59
Double taxation, 830
Du Pont, 376
Du Pont analysis, 167 n
Duracell International, Inc., 401, 456

Duriron Company, Inc., 730
DVL; see Dollar-value LIFO

E
Early extinguishment of debt, 592–593
Earned capital, 824
  retained earnings, 844–852
Earnings per share, 13, 14, 120–121, 171
  and actual conversions, 890–891
  antidilutive securities, 885–888
  for common shares, 879–880
  in complex capital structure, 880–888
  and contingently issuable securities, 889–890
  and convertible securities, 882–885
  decisions about, 893–894
  effect of potentially dilutive securities, 890
  on financial statement, 892–893
  global perspective, 876, 888
  and issuance of new shares, 877
  measure of performance, 874
  options, rights, and warrants, 880–882
  outstanding options and warrants, 892
  and potentially dilutive securities, 880
  and reacquired shares, 878–879
  in simple capital structure, 876–880
  and stock dividends, 877–878
  and stock splits, 877–878
Earnings-price ratio, 850
Eastman Kodak, 376
Ecolab, Inc., 506, 736
Economic entity assumption, 24
Economic environment
  cash flow, 6–7
  corporations in, 5–6
Economic events, 56
Economic life, 624
Effective interest method, 576–579
Effective rate, 236
Effective yield, 237
Eisner, Michael, 789
EITF Issues, 10, 118, 411 n
Elective fair value approach, 790–791
Electrolux, 184
Electronic Data Gathering, Analysis, and Retrieval System, 770
Eli Lilly, 103, 127–128, 730
Embassy Suites, 121
Emerging Issues Task Force, 10; see also EITF Issues
Emhart Corporation, 573
Employee Retirement Income Security Act, 733, 739, 745
Employee stock option plans, 729 n
Employee stock ownership plans, 802–803
Entries, reversing, 87–88
Environmental Protection Agency, 541–542
EPBO; see Expected postretirement benefit obligation
EPS; see Earnings per share
Equipment costs, 401–402
Equity
  definition of, 21, 192
  return on shareholders' equity, 169, 210
  shareholder's, 21, 59, 192, 198–199
  stock appreciation rights payable in, 796
  stockholder's, 21, 59, 192, 198–199
Equity method
  and consolidated financial statements, 498–499
  further adjustments, 500–502
  investment revenue from, 706
  joint ventures, 506
  reporting for, 502–504
  significant influence, 499–500
Equity securities, 410

Error correction, 120, 923, 925–932
  reporting methods, 913
Errors
  in bank reconciliation, 276
  disclosure of, 202
  income tax, 699–700
  inventory, 376–378
  involving operational assets, 461–462
Estimates, 74
  changes in, 459
Estimation, dollar-value LIFO, 339
Ethics
  analytical model for, 28
  bad debt expense, 285
  Champion International, 783
  current ratio dilemma, 208
  dilemmas in, 28
  of inventory valuation, 360
  of land asset valuation, 408
  and leasing, 641
  and professionalism, 27–28
  of recording contingencies, 546
Ex-dividend date, 845
Executory costs, 641–642
Exercise of options, 791
Exercise price, 793
Expected postretirement benefit obligation, 776–777
Expected return on pension assets, 738–739, 741
Expenses
  bad debt, 74
  definition of, 8, 22, 104–105
  income tax, 105
  in interim reporting, 171
  prepaid, 70–71, 195
  relation ship to revenue, 26
Exploration costs, 403
Extended warranty contracts, 543–544
External events, 56
External users, 4
Extraordinary items, 113–116
  and interim reporting, 171
Exxon, 828, 830, 955–956

F
Factoring, 291
  of accounts receivable, 293–295, 534
Fair value, 835
  adjusting investments to, 491–492
  determining, 490
  selling securities adjusted to, 493
  of stock options, 789–791
FASAC; see Financial Accounting Standards Advisory Council
Federal Deposit Insurance Corporation, 830
Federal Express
  acid-test ratio, 208
  allowance for doubtful accounts, 18, 283–284
  asset reporting, 193–197
  audit report, 15, 44
  current ratio, 207
  debt to equity ratio, 209
  earnings per share, 120
  financial analysis case, 313, 355, 770–771
  financial case analysis, 872
  financial statements, 30–44
  fiscal year, 24
  history, 4
  liability reporting, 196–198
  net income, 23
  operating and nonoperating activities, 105–106
  shareholder's equity reporting, 199

statement of cash flows, 1012
times interest earned ratio, 210–211
Federal Paper Company, Inc., 329
Feedback value, 17
Feeny Manufacturing Company, 890
Fieldcrest Cannon, Inc., 115
FIFO costing method, 326–327, 913–914, 918–920
Financial accounting environment
  development of financial accounting and reporting standards
    and GAAP, 8
    global marketplace, 14
    historical perspective, 9–11
    political aspect, 11–13
    role of auditor, 14–15
  economic environment and financial reporting
    capital market, 5–6
    cash versus accrual accounting, 7–8
    investment-credit decision in, 6–7
  focus of, 4
Financial Accounting Foundation, 10
Financial Accounting Standards Advisory Council, 10 n
Financial Accounting Standards Board, 743; see also Conceptual framework
  and cash flow information, 6
  Emerging Issues Task Force, 10
  on executive stock options, 13
  Financial Accounting Standards Advisory Council, 10 n
  on income smoothing, 744
  Interpretation No. 35, 497
  on liquid investments, 955
  on oil and gas exploration, 11–12
  organization, 9–10
  on pension liability, 748
  Preliminary Views, 742 n
  on reporting receivables, 835
  on retiree health care expense, 12–13
  on return on pension assets, 741
  standard-setting process, 13
  on stock option plans, 789–790, 794
  on transition obligation, 782
Financial disclosure; *see also* Disclosure notes
  auditors' report, 203–205
  director and executive compensation, 205–206
  of lease arrangements, 651–652
  of long-term debt, 598–601
  management discussion and analysis, 203
  management responsibilities, 203
Financial Executives Institute, 955
Financial flexibility, 192
Financial futures contract, 509–510
Financial instruments, 201, 508
Financial intermediaries, 4
Financial leverage, 209
Financial reporting
  cash versus accrual method, 7–8
  change in entity, 922
  changes in, 912
  definition, 5
  objectives of, 16–17
  by operating segment, 212–214
  for pension plans, 746–754
    minimum liability, 748–749
    pension disclosures, 752–753
    reconciling funded status with amount recognized, 747–748
    settlement or curtailment, 754
    transition costs, 751–752
  of receivables, 834–835
  of shareholders' equity, 826–828
  for treasury stock, 841
Financial Reporting Releases, 9

Financial statements
  balance sheet, 78–79
  common types of, 4
  comparative, 164
  consolidated, 498–499
  earnings per share on, 892–893
  elements of, 21–23
  in equity method, 500
  error correction, 912–913, 923, 925–932
  of Federal Express, 30–44
  income statement, 77–78
  interim, 144 n, 170–172
  statement of cash flows, 79
  statement of shareholders' equity, 80
Financing activities, 79, 126, 981
  cash flows from, 958–959
  noncash, 959–960
Financing activities ratio, 983
Financing ratios, 208–211
Financing with receivables, 291–297
Finished goods, 316
Firestone Tire & Rubber, 14, 376
First Boston Corporation, 12, 582
First-in, first out method; *see* FIFO costing method
Fiscal year, 24
Fixed assets, 398 n
Fixed-asset turnover ratio, 417
Fixed stock option plans, 795
Florida Steel, 376
F.O.B. (free on board) destination, 320
F.O.B. (free on board) shipping point, 320
Ford Motor Company, 354, 447, 541–542, 545, 830, 832
Foreign Corrupt Practices Act, 202
Foreign currency futures, 511
Forfeitures, 790–791
Forsythe, Meg, 875
Forward contract, 511
Foster's Brewing Group Limited, 1010–1011
401(k) plans, 729
Fractional shares, 849
Franchisee, 162
Franchisor, 162
Franchises, 405, 456
Franchise sales, 162–163
Freight-in on purchases, 321
FRRs; *see* Financial Reporting Releases, 9
Full-cost approach, 11–12, 418
Full-cost method, 428
Full-disclosure principle, 27
Fundamental share rights, 831
Funded status of pension plans, 747–748
Future deductible amounts, 682
Future value
  of annuity due, 244–245
  of ordinary annuity, 244
  of single amount, 237–238
  tables, 256–261
FV; *see* Future value

G

GAAP; *see* Generally accepted accounting principles
Gain contingencies, 547–548
Gain/loss on disposal, 111–112
Gain on sale of land, 966–967
Gains, 22, 105
Gap, Inc., 825, 853
GASB; *see* Government Accounting Standards Board
General Electric, 782
General journal, 65
General ledger, 58–59, 85
  posting to, 65–66
Generally accepted accounting principles, 837

assumptions underlying, 24–25
historical perspective and standards, 9–11
role of, 8
sources of, 8–11
General Mills, 531–533, 538
General Motors, 315, 340, 354, 400, 782, 828
  case, 771
  postretirement benefits, 774
  postretirement benefit disclosures, 784–785
Gernon, Helen, 14 n
Giacomino, Don, 983 n, 1011
Gibson Greetings, 509
Gillette, 14
Global financial market, 535
Global marketplace, accounting standards in, 14
Global perspective
  on bad debts, 287
  on balance sheets, 199
  on capitalization of research and development costs, 425
  on debt disclosure, 600
  on depreciation, 452
  on disaggregated disclosures, 214
  on disclosure practices, 205–206
  on earnings per share, 876, 888
  on financial versus tax accounting, 688
  on goodwill valuation, 407
  on income statements, 123
  on interest capitalization, 423
  on inventory measurement, 330, 331
  on inventory valuation, 359
  on investment reporting, 507
  on nonoperating leases, 634
  on operational asset valuation, 464
  pension plans, 746
  on pension plans, 746
  postretirement plans, 786
  on profit recognition, 150
  on revenue recognition, 160
  shareholders' equity, 828
  shareholder's equity, 828
  statement of cash flows, 955
  on statement of cash flows, 125
GMAC, 922
Going concern assumption, 24
Going concern explanation, 205
Goods in transit, 320
Goods on consignment, 320–321
Goodwill, 406–407
  amortization of purchased, 500–501
Government Accounting Standards Board, 10
Gross investment in the lease, 636
Gross margin, 336
Gross margin method, 363–365
Gross method
  for recording cash discounts, 280–281, 321–322
  for recording leases, 628
  for recording notes payable, 588–589
Gross profit, 336
Gross profit method, 363–365
Gross profit ratio, 336
Group depreciation method, 453–454
Guarantees, 542–544

H

Hagerman, R., 914 n
Half-year convention, 459
Hamel, Sally, 354
Harrah's, 121
Hasbro, Inc., 545
Healy, P. M., 331 n, 914 n
Heath, Lloyd C., 955 n
Hedging, 509–512
Held to maturity, 489–490

Hershey Foods Corporation, 204, 299, 439
Hewlett-Packard, 52–53, 299, 922
Historical cost principle, 25
Horizontal analysis, 164
Hunt Manufacturing Company, 889
Hybrid organization, 830

I

IASC; *see* International Accounting Standards
    Committee
IBM, 14, 194, 195, 201–202, 227–228, 299,
    316, 358, 410, 425–426, 456, 483–484,
    506, 619, 620, 651–652, 828, 839
    postretirement benefits, 781–782
IBM Credit Corporation, 631
If converted method, 882
Illegal acts, disclosure of, 202
IMA; *see* Institute of Management
    Accountants
Impaired receivables, 289
Impairment of value, 462–464, 494, 513–514
Implicit rate of interest, 410, 588, 642–644
Improvements, 466
Incentive plan, 791–792
Income
    comprehensive, 122–124
    other comprehensive, 123
    taxable, 105
Income from continuing operations, 104–107
Income/loss from operations, 111
Income smoothing, 119, 744–745
Income statement, 77–78
    accounts on statement of cash flows,
      964–971
    comprehensive income, 122–124
    correction of accounting errors, 120
    cost of goods sold, 967
    depreciation expense, 968
    earnings per share disclosure, 120–121
    gain on sale of land, 966–967
    global perspective on, 123
    impact of leasing on, 653–654
    income from continuing operations,
      104–107
    income from continuing sources
      income tax expense, 105
      multiple-step format, 107
      operating versus nonoperating
        activities, 105
      single-step format, 106
    income tax expense, 970
    insurance expense, 969
    interest income, 968
    investment revenue, 966
    loss on sale of equipment, 969
    net income, 971
    pension plan reporting, 746
    presentation of accounting change, 916
    purpose of, 102
    salaries expense, 967–968
    sales revenue, 964–965
    separately reported items
      cumulative effect of accounting principle
        change, 116–119
      discontinued operations, 109–113
      events requiring, 107–108
      extraordinary items, 113–116
      intraperiod tax allocation, 108–109
Income statement approach, 283–284
Income summary, 80–81
Income tax; *see also* Deferred tax; Tax
    treatment
    and change in accounting principle, 698–699
    error correction, 699–700
    intraperiod allocation of, 700–701
    and inventory, 330–331, 365–366

on investment revenue, 504
    management of, 702–703
Income tax expense, 105, 698, 970
Incremental borrowing, 642 n
Indirect method of reporting cash flow, 125,
    979
    spreadsheet, 984–987
Individual retirement accounts, 728
Induced conversion, 585–586
Inflation, 373
Initial direct costs, 644
Initial markup, 366
Installment notes, 590–591
    and capital leases, 621–622
Installment sales, 156–159
Installment sales method, 157–158
Institute of Internal Auditors, 28
Institute of Management Accountants, 28
Insurance expense, 83–84, 969
Intangible assets, 196, 201
    amortization of, 456–457
    definition of, 400–401
    valuation of, 404–407
Intangible rights, 467
Intel Corporation, 161
Interest
    accrued, 535
    and calculating future value, 237
    capitalization for self-constructed
      assets, 418–422
    creditor's, 572
    on notes, 286–287, 287–288, 533–534
    rates on leases, 642–644
    simple versus compound, 236–237
Interest-bearing notes, 288–289
Interest cost
    in pension expense, 741
    of pension plans, 735
    of postretirement benefits, 779
Interest coverage ratio, 982
Interest income, 968
Interest rate swaps, 510–511
Interim financial statements, 144 n
Interim reporting, 170–172
Internal control, 274
Internal events, 56, 69, 85
Internal Revenue Service, 551
International Accounting Standards, 14
International Accounting Standards
    Committee, 14, 819, 876
International Paper, 452, 845
Interworld Distributors, 851
Intraperiod tax allocation, 108–109, 700–701
    versus interperiod tax allocation, 110 n
Intrinsic value, 807
Inventory
    average days in, 337
    balance sheet reporting, 195
    cost flow
      average cost, 325–326
      choice of method for, 330–333
      comparison of methods for, 329
      FIFO method, 326–327
      LIFO method, 327–329
      specific identification, 324–325
    expenditures included in, 21–323
    financial analysis, 335–337
    gross profit method, 363–365
    method changes
      from LIFO method, 376
      to LIFO method, 375–376
      not involving LIFO, 374–375
    physical quantities included in, 320–321
    pools, 337–338
    reporting
      adjusting cost to market, 361

applying lower of cost or
    market, 360–361
    determining market value for, 358–361
    systems
      periodic, 317–319
      perpetual, 317–320
      perpetual versus periodic, 319–320
    turnover ratio, 336–337
    types of
      manufacturing, 316–317
      merchandising, 316
    valuation, 201
Inventory errors, 376–378
Inventory estimation techniques; *see* Retail
    inventory method
Inventory systems, perpetual, 63
Inventory turnover ratio, 166, 336–337
Invested capital, 824
    shareholders' equity, 826–842
Investing activities, 79, 125–126, 981
    cash flows from, 957–958
    noncash, 959–960
Investing activities ratio, 983
Investment revenue, 966
Investment revenue receivable account, 966
Investments; *see also* Equity method;
    Investment securities
    in derivatives, 508–512
    impairment of, 513–514
    in life insurance policies, 512–513
    reporting categories for, 488
    reporting of short-term, 194
    special purpose fund, 512
Investments and funds, 195
Investments by owners, 22
Investment securities
    financial statement reporting of, 495–498
    held for unspecified time
      available for sale, 492–493
      recording of, 490–492
      trading, 494–495
    held to maturity, 489–490
    transfers between reporting categories, 495
Investments of funds, 278
Irregularities, disclosure of, 202
Ittner, C. D., 799 n

J

Japan, 786
Jeter, Debra, 702 n
Jiambalvo, J., 925 n
Johnson & Johnson, 114, 168–169, 299
Journal, 60
    general, 65
    special, 60, 88–89
Journal entry, 60–65

K

Keller, John J., 773
Kellogg's, case, 907–908
Kimberly-Clark Corp., 488
Kirk, Donald J., 18
Kmart, 24, 138–139, 279, 357, 365, 378, 464,
    644–645, 920
Kraft General Foods, 488, 922

L

L. S. Starret Company, 826
Lacy, J. M., 914 n
Land, cost of, 401
Land account, 972
Land improvements, 403
Landsman, Wayne, 749 n
Langenderfer, Harold Q., 28 n
Large stock dividends, 848–849

Larker, D. F., 799 n
Last-in, first-out method; *see* LIFO costing method
LCM; *see* Lower-of-cost-or-market rule
Leasehold improvements, 627
Leases
    advantages of, 620–621
    bargain purchase options, 639–641
    capital, 648–650
    capital, versus installment notes, 621–622
    classification, 621–625
    classification of, 620
    and contingent rentals, 644–645
    disclosure requirements, 651–652
    discount rate on, 642–644
    executory costs, 641–642
    financial statement impact of, 652–654
    lessor's initial direct cost of, 644
    leveraged, 651
    nonoperating, 627–631
    operating, 625–627, 650
    real estate, 650–651
    and residual value, 634–639
    sale-leaseback arrangement, 648–650
    sales-type, 632–633
    summary of, 645–646
    valuation of long-term, 252–253
Ledger
    general, 58–59, 65–66
    subsidiary, 59, 88
Lehman Brothers, 116
Leisenring, James, 509
Lessee, 620
Lessor, 620
Lester, Jim, 352
Lev, B., 299, 337
Leveraged employee stock ownership plan, 803
Leveraged leases, 651
Liabilities
    accrued, 72–73, 197
    from advance collections, 536–537
    characteristics of, 530–531
    versus contingencies, 540
    current, 79, 197
    current versus noncurrent, 538–539
    deferred tax, 677–682
    definition of, 21, 192
    long-term, 197
    monetary, 242
    payroll-related, 551–552
Life insurance policies, 512–513
LIFO costing method, 327–329, 913–914, 918–920
    change from, 376
    change to, 375–376
    conformity rule, 331
    dollar-value, 338–339
    dollar-value retail, 371–373
    inventory pools, 337–338
    liquidation, 331–332
    retail method, 368–369
    specific goods, 337
    unit, 337
Limited liability, 829
Limited liability company, 830
Limited liability partnership, 830
Line of credit, 533
Liquidating dividend, 844
Liquidity, 192
    analyzing, 207–211
    measurement of, 549–550
Liquidity ratios, 207–208, 550
Litigation claims, 545–546
Litton Industries, 846
Long-term cash bonuses, 799–800

Long-term debt, 572
Long-term liabilities, 198; *see also* Bonds
Long-term notes
    exchanged for assets or services, 588–589
    installment, 590–591, 621–622
    issued for cash, 587
Long-term solvency, 192
Loss carryback, 695–696
Loss carryforward, 694–695, 698
Loss contingencies
    accrual of, 546–547
    explanation of, 541
    litigation claims, 545–546
    premiums, 544–545
    product warranties and guarantees, 542–544
    reporting of, 541–542
    unasserted claims and assessments, 547
Losses
    definition of, 22, 105
    operating, 694–696
Loss on sale of equipment, 969
Lotus, 425
Lotus 1-2-3, 975 n
Lower-of-cost-or-market rule, 358–361, 380–381
Lublin, Joann S., 773
Lump-sum purchases, 407–408

M

MACRS; *see* Modified accelerated cost recovery system
Management discussion and analysis (MDA), 203
Management responsibilities, 203
Managerial accounting, 4
Mandresh, Dan, 839 n
Manufacturing inventories, 316–317
Marathon Oil, 376
Markdown, 366
Markdown cancellation, 366
Market value
    of bonds, 578
    equals exercise price, 793
    exceeds exercise price, 793
    of inventory, 358–361
Markup cancellation, 366
Markup on cost, 366
Martin, Dale, 702 n
Mason, Perry, 955
Matching principle, 26, 69, 104, 142
Materiality, 19, 20
Maxi Corporation, 354
May Department Stores, 365
Maytag Corporation, 299, 417, 593
McCormack Chemical Company, 931
McCullen, Kay, 563
McDonald's Corporation, 162, 405
McDonnell Douglas, 143, 838
MDA; *see* Management and discussion analysis
Measurement, 23
    of minimum pension liability, 748
    of postretirement benefit obligation, 777
Measurement date, 111
Medicare, 776
Meek, Gary, 14 n
Melville Corporation, 754
Merchandising inventory, 316
Merck & Co., Inc., 168–169, 452
Merrill Lynch, 582, 839
Merry-Go-Round Enterprises, 351–352
Messing, Richard F., 12 n
Microsoft Corporation, 204, 209, 400, 425, 506, 830, 839
Microsoft Excel, 975 n
Midland Financial Group, Inc., 489–490

Mielke, David, 983 n, 1011
Miller, James P., 773
Miller, Paul L., 12 n
Mills, John, 923 n
Minimum lease payments, 624, 628
Minimum pension liability
    and additional liability, 749–751
    measurement, 748
    offsetting, 748–749
Model Business Corporation Act, 831
Modified accelerated cost recovery system, 462, 916 n
Modified half-year convention, 459 n
Modifying comments, 27
Moncrief Company, 352–353
Monetary assets, 242
Monetary liabilities, 242
Monetary unit assumption, 24–25
Money, time value of, 236–237
Moody's Investors Service, Inc., 575
Mortgage bond, 573
Mosinee Paper Corporation, 721–722
Motorola Corporation, 161, 541–542
Mueller, Gerhard G., 14 n
Multiple convertible securities, 887–888
Multiple-step income statement format, 107

N

NACCO Industries, 826, 832
NASDAQ, 830
National Brands Corporation, 953–954, 957–962
National Semiconductor Corporation, 441
Natural resources
    definition of, 400
    depletion of, 454–456
    valuation of, 403–404
Negative equity, 191
Net assets; *see* Equity
Net cash flows
    from financing activities, 126
    from investing activities, 126
    from operating activities, 125
Net costs of postretirement benefit obligation, 776
Net earnings, 22 n
Net gain, amortization of, 743
Net income, 22
    components that increase or decrease cash, 979–981
    definition of, 8
    errors affecting, 927–931
    on income statement, 971
    and inventory, 330–331
Net loss, 22
    amortization of, 743
Net markdown, 366
Net markup, 366
Net method
    for recording cash discounts, 280–281, 321–323
    for recording leases, 628
    for recording notes payable, 589
Net operating cash flow, 7
Net realizable value, 25, 358–359
Net realizable value less a normal profit margin, 358–359
Netscape Communications, 830
Netscape Navigator, 830
Neutrality, 18
New York Stock Exchange, 830
New York Times Company, 537, 826, 832
Nichols, Virginia, 702 n
Noncash acquisitions
    acquisition by exchange, 411–415
    deferred payments, 408–410

donated assets, 410–411
    issuance of equity securities, 410
Noncash considerations, 835
Noncash financing activities, 126, 959–960
Noncash investing activities, 126, 959–960
Noncompensatory plans, 798
Noncumulative preferred shares, 832
Noncurrent assets, 195–196
Noncurrent liabilities; *see* Liabilities
Noninterest-bearing notes, 289–290, 534
Nonoperating activities, 105
Nonoperating leases, 627–631
Nonparticipating preferred shares, 832
Nonqualified stock option plan, 792
Nontemporary differences, 687–688
Nontrade receivables, 279
    balance sheet reporting, 194
Noreen, E. W., 914 n
Northwest Airlines Corporation, 566
Notes payable
    balance sheet reporting, 197
    long-term, 587–592
    short-term, 532–534
Notes receivable
    balance sheet reporting, 194
    discounting, 295–297
    interest bearing, 288–289
    noninterest-bearing, 289–290
    subsequent valuation of, 290–291
Not-for-profit corporations, 830
Nova Nordisk A/S, 354
NRV; *see* Net realizable value
Nurnberg, Hugo, 685 n, 959 n

O

Offsetting, 748–749
Oil and gas accounting, 427–428
Old Navy Clothing stores, 825
Open accounts, 531–535
Operating activities, 79, 105, 124–125,
    956–957
    cash flow from, 979–983
Operating cycle, 193
Operating leases, 620, 625–627, 650
Operating loss carryback, 694, 695–696
Operating loss carryforward, 694–695, 698
Operating segment, 212–214
Operational assets, 195; *see also* Assets;
        Noncash acquisitions
    definition of, 400
    disposition of, 467
    expenditures after acquisition
        additions, 465–466
        costs of defending intangible rights, 467
        improvements, 466
        rearrangements, 466–467
        repairs and maintenance, 465
    research and development, 422–426
    self-constructed, 417–422
    types of, 400–401
    valuation at acquisition
        costs to be capitalized, 401–407
        lump-sum purchases, 407–408
Operational assets depreciation; *see*
        Depreciation
Operational risk, 207
Option pricing models, 790
    intrinsic value, 807
    time value, 808
    volatility value, 808
Options, 511
Orange County, California, 509
Ordinary annuity, 243
Organization costs, 405–406, 457
Original transaction value, 25
Other comprehensive income, 123

Outboard Marine, 826
Overhead allocation for self-constructed
    assets, 418
Overhead costs, 316
Overnight Success (Trimble), 4 n
Owens-Corning Fiberglass Corporation, 119,
    503, 921
Ownership interest, 826

P

Paid absences, 800–802
Paid-in capital, 21, 57, 198, 827, 831–844
    share repurchase, 841
Parenthetical comments, 27
Partial periods, 457–459
Participating preferred shares, 832
Partnerships, 105 n
Par value, 833
Par value accounting method, 840–841
Patents, 405, 456
Payroll deductions, 551–552
PBO; *see* Pension benefit obligation
Peerless Manufacturing Company, 787
Pension Benefit Guaranty Corporation,
    733, 739
Pension benefit obligation
    changes in, 734–737
    and funded status, 747–748
    gains and losses on, 737
    illustration of, 737–738
    payment of benefits, 737
    pension expense and changes in, 739–745
Pension disclosures, 752–753
Pension expense
    and changes in PBO and plan assets,
        739–741
    components, 731–732, 741–743
    determining, 739–746
    income smoothing, 744–745
    recording periodic expense/funding,
        745–746
Pension formula, 731
Pension gains and losses, 731
    adjustment for, 741
Pension liability, 731
    and additional liability, 749–751
    measurement, 748
    offsetting, 748–749
Pension obligation, 732–738
    accumulated benefit obligation, 732
    projected benefit obligation, 733–738
    valuation of, 253–254
    vested benefit obligation, 733
Pension plan assets, 738–739
    employer's pension obligation, 731
    pension expense and changes in, 737–741
    periodic expense, 731
    return on, 741
Pension plans
    compared to postretirement benefits, 775
    determining pension expense, 739–746
    expected return, 738–739
    financial reporting for, 746–754
    gains and losses on, 737
    global perspective, 746
    interest cost, 735
    nature of, 728–732
        defined benefit plans, 729, 730–731
        defined contribution plans, 729–730
        pension expense, 731–732
    pension obligation, 732–738
    prior service cost, 735–736
    service costs, 735
    settlement or curtailment, 754
    trustee, 738

    underfunded, 739
    United Dynamics, 727–728
Pension spreadsheet, 747
Pentair, Inc., 506
Penwalt Corporation, 832
PepsiCo, Inc., 583, 599–600, 911, 932
Percentage depletion, 456
Percentage-of-completion method, 146–147
Performance ratios, 982
Performance share plans, 799–800
Performance stock option plans, 794–795
Performance unit plans, 800
Periodic average cost, 325
Periodic FIFO, 326–327
Periodic inventory systems, 317–319
Periodicity assumption, 24
Periodic LIFO, 328
Periodic pension expense, 745–746
Periodic pension funding, 745–746
Permanent accounts, 59
Permanent difference, 687
Perpetual average cost, 325–326
Perpetual FIFO, 327
Perpetual inventory system, 63, 317–320
Perpetual LIFO, 328–329
Petty cash, 277–278
Phantom stock plans, 800
Phaseout period, 111
Philip Morris, 462–463, 922
Phillips-Van Heusen, 828–829
Physical flow, and inventory, 330
Piper Jaffray, 509
Plant assets, 400
Pledging of accounts receivable, 293, 534
Point-of-sale, 25
Polaroid Corporation, 358, 360, 381
Politics of setting accounting standards, 9–11
Pollard, Charles W., 838
Pooling of interest method, 922
Positive equity, 191
Post-closing trial balance, 81
Postemployment benefits, 802
Posting, 60–65
Postretirement benefit expense, 777–785
    components, 779–782
    determining, 782–784
    recording, 778–779
Postretirement benefit obligation,
    776–777
Postretirement benefits, 772; *see also*
        Pension plans
    compared to pension plans, 775
    determining net costs, 776
    global perspective, 786
    health benefits, 775
    health care obligations and expense,
        806–807
    at IBM, 781
    nature of, 775–777
    other than pensions, 774–786
    scope of, 774
    substantive plan, 775
Potentially dilutive securities, 876
    definition, 880
    effect on earnings per share, 890
Predictive value, 17
Preemptive right, 831
Preferred shares, 832–833
    convertible, 884–885
Preincorporation subscription agreements, 834
Premiums, 544–545
Prepaid expenses, 70–71
    balance sheet reporting, 195
Prepaid pension cost, 748
Prepayments
    alternative recording method, 72

prepaid expenses, 70–72
unearned revenues, 71
Preretirement compensation plans
bonus plans, 799–800
employee stock ownership plans, 802–803
paid absences, 800–802
post-employment benefits, 802
sick days, 800–802
stock-based, 787–789
stock purchase plan, 800
vacation days, 800–802
Present value
of annuity due, 246–247
of bonds, 578
of deferred annuity, 247–249
of ordinary annuity, 245–246
of receivables and payables, 242–243
of single amount, 238–239
solving for unknown values in, 249–251
tables, 256–261
Primary market, 6
Principles; see Accounting principles
Prior period adjustments, 120, 926
Prior service cost
amortization, 779
amortization of, 741–742
of pension plans, 735–736
unrecognized, 742
Privately held corporations, 830
Procter & Gamble Co., 488, 509
Production basis of recognizing revenue, 361
Professionalism, 27–28
Profitability analysis
illustration of, 168–169
using financial statement information for, 164–169
Profitability ratios, 166–167, 849–850
Profit margin on sales, 167
Pro forma disclosure, 917
Progress to date, 146–147
Projected benefit obligation, 733–738
Promus Companies, 120–121
Property, plant, and equipment, 195–196
definition of, 400
valuation of, 401–404
Property dividends, 846
Proportional performance method, 156
Prospective approach
to change in accounting principle, 920
to error correction, 913
Provision for income taxes; see Income
tax expense
Proxy statement, 206
Publicly held corporations, 830
Purchase commitments, 379–381
Purchase discounts; see Cash discounts
Purchase returns, 321
Purchases journal, 88
PV; see Present value
PVA; see Present value of ordinary annuity
PVAD; see Present value of annuity due

Q
Quaker Oats Company, 917
Qualified opinion, 205
Qualified pension plans, 728
Qualitative characteristics
constraints to, 19–20
primary, 17–18
secondary, 18, 19
Quasi reorganization, 854–855
Quick ratio, 208, 550

R
R. R. Donnelley and Sons Company, 773
Rajan, M. V., 799 n

Ralston Purina Company, 118, 201
Rate of return, 6
Ratio analysis, 982–983
activity ratios, 165–166
importance of, 164–165
profitability ratios, 166–167
Raw materials, 316
R&D; see Research and development
Reacquired shares, 878–879
Readers Digest Association, Inc., 537
Read-Rite Corporation, 312
Real estate leases, 650–651
Real estate sales, 160
Realization principle, 25–26, 69, 144
Rearrangements, 466–467
Receivables, 834–835
accrued, 73
current
accounts receivable, 279–286
financing with, 291–297
notes receivable, 288–291
definition of, 279
Receivables turnover ratio, 165–166, 298
Recognition, 23; see also Revenue
recognition
Recourse, factoring with or without, 294–295
Redemption privilege, 832
Reduction of accumulated depreciation, 466
Refinancing of short-term obligations, 538–539
Refundable deposits, 536
Registered bond, 573
Reinvestment ratio, 983
Related-party transactions, 202
Relevance, 17
Reliability, 17–18
Rent abatement, 627
Repairs and maintenance, 465
Replacement cost, 358–359
Replacement depreciation method, 469–470
Representational faithfulness, 18
Research and development, 422–426
Residual value, 447–448
and bargain purchase option, 640
guaranteed, 635–637
not guaranteed, 637–639
Residual value and title retention, 634–635
Restricted cash, 278–279
Restricted stock award plan, 787–788
Restructuring costs, 115–116
Retail inventory method
cost flow methods in, 365–367
explanation of, 365–366
other issues in, 369–370
retail terminology for, 366–367
Retail land sales, 160
Retained earnings, 21, 57, 198, 826
on balance sheet, 974
definition, 827
restrictions, 845
Retiree health care obligations and
expense, 806–807
Retirement benefits, 737
Retirement depreciation method, 469
Retroactive approach
to change in accounting principle, 918–919
to error correction, 913
Return, 4 n
Return on assets, 167
Return on plan assets, 741
of postretirement benefits, 779
Return on shareholders' equity, 167, 210
Returns; see Sales returns
Revenue
definition of, 8, 22, 104–105
in interim reporting, 171

relationship to expense, 26
unearned, 71
Revenue recognition
after delivery
installment sales, 156–159
real estate sales, 160
right of return, 161–162
before delivery
on long-term contracts, 145–153
on service sales, 155–156
and franchise sales, 162–163
global perspective on, 150
at point of delivery, 144–145
and realization principle, 144–145
timing of, 25–26
Reverse stock split, 849
Reversing entries, 87–88
Revised Model Business Corporation Act, 84 n
Reynolds & Reynolds Company, 875
Ricks, William E., 331 n
Right of conversion, 832
Right of return, 161–162
Risk, 4 n
disclosure of, 598
in investment decisions, 6
Risk analysis
financing ratios, 208–211
liquidity ratios, 207–208
RJR Nabisco, 488
ROA; see Return on assets
Robert M. Trueblood cases, 185, 438–440,
481, 523–525, 563–564, 613–614
Rockness, Joanne W., 28 n
Rohm and Haas Company, 460

S
Safeway, Inc., 353, 671
Salamon, G., 331 n, 914 n
Salaries, 535–536
Salaries expense, 967–968
Sale-leaseback transaction, 648–650
Sales allowance, 281
Sales discounts account, 281
Sales journal, 89
Sales returns, 281–283
Sales revenue, 964–965
Sales-type leases, 620, 632–633
Salomon Brothers, 582
Sara Lee Corporation, 299, 313, 316–317, 331,
336–337
SCF; see Statement of cash flows
S corporations, 830
Scott Paper Co., 488
Secondary market, 5–6
Secured loans, 534
Securities and Exchange Commission, 9, 11,
353, 770, 830
accrued restructuring costs concern, 116
on reporting receivables, 835
on stock distribution, 846 n
on stock option plans, 789–790
web address, 49–50
Seed, Allen H., Jr., 955 n
Self-constructed assets, 417–422
Separation of duties, 274–275
Serial bonds, 573
Service, sale of, 155–156
Service cost
in pension expense, 741
of pension plans, 735
of postretirement benefits, 779
Service life, 447
Service method of amortization, 742–743
SFAC; see Statements of Financial Accounting
Concepts

SFAS; *see* Statements of Financial Accounting Standards
Shareholders' dividends, 844–849
Shareholders' equity, 21, 57, 192, 198–199, 826–831
  book value, 850
  in corporate organizations, 828–831
  definition and sources, 826
  financial reporting, 826–828
  global perspective, 828
Shareholders' rights
  classes of shares, 832–833
  fundamental share rights, 831
  paid-in capital, 831–844
  with preferred shares, 832–833
Share purchase contracts, 834
Shares
  accounting for reacquisition of, 840–841
  classes of, 832–833
  contingently issuable, 889–890
  formally retired, 839
  fractional, 849
  issuance of
    and earnings per share, 877
    issue costs, 836–837
    for single price, 834
    sold for cash, 834
    sold for noncash considerations, 835–836
    sold on credit, 834–835
  par value concept, 833
  reacquired, 838–842
  resale of, 842
  treasury stock, 839–840
Sharp-Novell Industries, 850
Shell Oil, 332
Short-term investments, 971–972
Sick days, 800–802
Significant influence, 499–500
Silicon Graphics Inc., 189–190
Simple capital structure, 876–880
Simple interest, 236
Single-step income statement format, 106
Sinking fund, 573
Smith, E., 331 n, 914 n
Smith, Fred, 4
Snyder, Don, 782 n
Software development costs, 425–426
Solectron Corporation, 268
Solvency
  analyzing, 207–211
  long-term, 192
Source documents, 59–50
Special journals, 60, 88–89
  cash disbursements journal, 88
  cash receipts journal, 90
  purchases journal, 88
  sales journal, 89
Specific goods LIFO, 337
Specific identification method, 324–325
Specific interest method, 421
Specific performance method, 156
Spindler, Michael, 789
Spreadsheet, 961–963, 975
  for indirect cash flow presentation, 984–987
  steps for using, 87–88
Sprint Corporation, 523, 555, 892
SPS Technologies, Inc., 919
Standard Oil of Ohio, 376
Standard & Poor's Corporation, 575
Standards
  current organization for setting, 9–11
  history of, 9–11
  mandated new, 920
  process of setting, 13
State Farm Insurance, 104
Statement of cash flows, 79

cash and cash equivalents, 955–956
cash flows from operating activities, 979–983
classifying cash flow on, 124–127
evolution of, 954–960
global perspective, 955
impact of leasing on, 654
preparation of, 960–975
  balance sheet accounts, 971–975
  income statement accounts, 964–971
  spreadsheet, 961–963
primary elements
  cash flows from financing activities, 958–959
  cash flows from investing activities, 957–958
  cash flows from operating activities, 956–957
  noncash investing/financing, 959–960
  reconciliation with change in cash balance, 959
purpose of, 102
reporting investment securities on, 497–498
role of, 953–954
T-account method, 959 n, 963–964, 988–989
usefulness of, 124
Statement of cash flows; *see also* Cash flows
Statements of Financial Accounting Concepts
  No. 1, 16–17, 21, 953, 956 n
  No. 2, 17, 876 n
  No. 3, 15
  No. 4, 15
  No. 5, 23, 955
  No. 6, 15, 21–23, 536 n, 547, 795, 834–835, 837
  purpose of, 10
Statements of Financial Accounting Standards
  No. 2, 422–423
  No. 3, 917
  No. 5, 800 n, 802
  No. 7, 406
  No. 11, 918
  No. 13, 635
  No. 14, 213
  No. 16, 923 n, 926 n
  No. 19, 11–12, 428
  No. 34, 418
  No. 43, 800 n, 801 n, 802
  No. 45, 162
  No. 66, 160
  No. 86, 425
  No. 87, 731, 743–744, 748, 751–752, 920
  No. 88, 754
  No. 94, 119 n, 922
  No. 95, 125, 950, 953, 955, 959 n, 1012
  No. 96, 676, 914 n
  No. 106, 13, 118, 720, 772, 777, 779, 780–781, 782 n, 818, 920
  No. 109, 676, 706, 720, 914, 918
  No. 112, 802
  No. 115, 485, 493
  No. 116, 410
  No. 121, 463, 468
  No. 123, 789 n, 790 n
  No. 128, 876 n
  No. 129, 828 n
  origin of, 10
Statement of financial position; *see* Balance sheet
Statement of shareholders' equity, 80, 828
Stock appreciation rights
  debt versus equity, 795–798
  definition, 795
Stock award plans, 787–788
Stock-based compensation plans
  noncompensatory plans, 798

purpose, 787
  stock award plans, 787–788
  tax consequences, 792
Stock dividends, 846–848
  and earnings per share, 877–878
  reasons for, 847–848
  stock splits in form of, 848–849
Stock market, 847
Stock option plans, 788–795
  alternate intrinsic value approach, 793–794
  expense issues, 789–790
  fair value recognition, 789–791
  incentive plan, 791–792
  nonqualified, 792
  option pricing theory, 807–808
  stock appreciation rights, 795–798
Stock options
  antidilutive securities, 885–886
  and earnings per share, 880–882
  outstanding, 892
Stock purchase plan, 800
Stock rights
  antidilutive securities, 885–886
  and earnings per share, 880–882
Stock splits, 848–849
  and earnings per share, 877–878
  effected in form of stock dividends, 848–849
Stock subscriptions, 834
Stock warrants
  antidilutive securities, 885–886
  and earnings per share, 880–882
  outstanding, 892
Stokely Van Camp, 376
Straight-line amortization, 742
Straight-line method, 448–450, 579–581
Subordinated debenture, 573
Subsequent events, 201, 202
Subsidiary ledger, 88
Subsidiary ledgers, 59
Substantial performance concept, 162
Substitution, 466
Successful efforts method, 11–12, 427–428
Sufficiency ratios, 982–983
Summary of significant accounting policies, 200–201
Sum-of-the-years' digits method, 449
Supplemental financial statements, 27
Swanson, Edward, 955 n
SYD method; *see* Sum-of-the-years' digits method

T
T-account method, 960 n, 988–989
T-accounts, 58
Taxable income, 105
Tax basis, 678
Tax law changes, 690–692
Tax rates, 689–692
Tax treatment
  of corporations, 830
  employees' withholding, 551
  employers' payroll, 552
  qualified pension plans, 728
  stock-based compensation plans, 792
  of stock options, 791–793
Technological feasibility, 425–426
Teledyne, 648–649
Temporary accounts, 59
Temporary differences, 677
  multiple, 692–694
  types of, 678–682
Tengelmann Group, 754
Texaco, Inc., 428
Thiagarajan, S. R., 299, 337
Time-based depreciation methods, 448–450
Timeliness, 17

and periodicity assumption, 24
Times interest earned ratio, 210–211
Times-Lehrer Industries, 675
Time value, 793, 808
Time value of money, 808; *see also* Annuities;
    Future value; Present value
  concept of, 236
  determining unknowns in, 239–241
  valuing single cash amount, 237–241
Timing differences in bank reconciliation, 275
Title transfer and revenue recognition, 144
Trade discounts, 280
Trademarks, 405
Tradename, 405
Trade notes payable, 532
Trade receivables, 279
  balance sheet reporting, 194
Trading securities, 494–495
Transaction analysis, 60–61
Transactions, 56–57
Transition amount
  amortization of, 780–782
  of pension plans, 751–752
Transportation-in on purchases, 321
Trans World Airlines, 595, 830
Treasury stock, 839–840
  accounting for, 841
Treasury stock method, 882
Trial balance
  adjusted, 74–75
  unadjusted, 66–67
Trimble, Vance, 4 n
Tropicana Products, 14
Troubled debt restructuring
  debt continued with modified terms in,
    595–598
  debt settled in, 594–598
  investment impairment due to, 513–514

Trueblood, Robert M.
  Cases, 141, 185, 438, 440, 481, 524, 563,
    565, 613–614, 769–770, 819, 822, 868,
    1,010
Trustees, of pension plans, 738
Tyson Foods, Inc., 202, 313, 336–337,
    400, 422

U
Unadjusted trial balance, 66–67
Uncertainty; *see* Risk
Uncollectible accounts, 285–286
Underfunded pension plans, 739
Unearned revenues, 71
Union Carbide, 922
United Charities, 675
United Dynamics, case, 727–728
United Kingdom, 786
United Parcel Service, 209, 211
Unit LIFO, 337
Units-of-production method, 450–451
Universal Communications, 788, 791, 796
Unocal Corporation, 293–294
Unqualified opinion, 205
Unrealized holding gains and losses, 491–492
Unrecognized prior service cost, 742
Useful life, 447

V
Vacation days, 800–802
Valuation
  of accounts receivable, 279–286
  of notes receivable, 288–291
Valuation allowance, 685–687
Value; *see* Future value; Present value
Vandermeersch, Richard, 955 n
Variable stock option plans, 795
Verifiability, 17

Vertical analysis, 164
Vested benefits, 733
Volatility value, 808

W
W. T. Grant Company, 953
Walgreen Company, 723–724, 1010
Wall Street Journal, 773, 875
Wal-Mart Stores, 24, 104, 652–654
Walt Disney Company, 203, 399, 426–427
Walter, John R., 773, 805
Warranties, 542–544
Wasting assets, 403
Watered shares, 833
Watts, R. L., 914 n
Weighted-average method, 421
Weinglass, Leonard "Boogie," 352
Wells Fargo & Company, 291
Western Atlas, 846
Whirlpool, 299, 417
Willens, Robert, 116
Witco Corporation, 832
Wm. Wrigley Jr. Company, 722
Wolk, Harry, 702 n
Working capital, 207
Work-in-process, 316
World Airways, Inc., 838
Worthy, Ford S., 119 n

Y-Z
Yield, 237, 238
Zega, Cheryl, 954 n
Zero-coupon bonds, 583–584
Zimmerman, J. L., 914 n
Zmijewski, M., 914 n
Zoo Doo Compost Company, 562–563